Fodor's 2001

California

Fodor's Travel Publications • New York, Toronto, London, Sydney, Auckland
www.fodors.com

CONTENTS

MAPS

Circled letters in text correspond to letters on the photographs. For more information on the sights pictured, turn to the indicated page number Ⓐ〉 on each photograph.

DESTINATION CALIFORNIA

California is too big, too diverse, too full of charming surprises to be a single state. You do not visit just one California. You choose a particular California. If you are looking for natural beauty, the Big Sur coastline isn't a bad place to start, but it's only one gem on a long, long list. If you favor worldly pleasures, San Francisco and the Wine Country beckon. Sybarites needing a fix are well advised to head to Palm Springs. Aficionados of the edgy love L.A. Wherever you go in the Golden State, there's plenty to fall in love with: very few visitors go home unsmitten.

THE NORTH COAST

Ⓑ 53

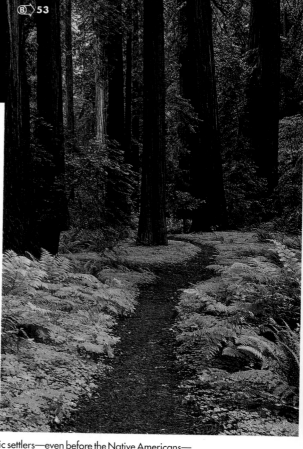

The shore running north from San Francisco to Oregon is a place for retreat—for restoring the soul. But although its pleasures are low-key, they are hardly unrefined. Elegant country inns, cozy Victorian B&Bs, and rustic lodges provide comfortable bases for touring. Many are destinations in themselves. Architecture hints at the area's history, as in Ⓐ**Mendocino** and other towns that dot the coast, which have a New England flavor. Some of their founders built out of nostalgia, bringing classic Americana to the continent's edge as a tonic for homesickness. But before them, before the missionaries and the Hispanic settlers—even before the Native Americans—there was the land and its beauty. Sample it at Ⓑ**Humboldt Redwoods State Park,** whose majestic trees inspire awe, even reverence, and at Stinson Beach and Ⓒ**Point Reyes National Seashore.** All that beautiful coastline makes for excellent whale-watching, as well. If no Gold Rush had built San Francisco, if Los Angeles were still a bunch of orange groves in search of a freeway, this glory would still be worth the trip.

The earth's molten inner cauldron shaped this region, whose landscape is defined by reminders of ancient volcanic activity. Most notable is Ⓑ**Mount Shasta,** a dormant volcano that tops 14,000 feet. Eerie folklore surrounds the peak, mythology about its special powers. But its size and beauty are fantastical enough.

THE FAR NORTH

Tramping up it in summer and schussing down it in winter are two of the joys of being here. Anglers and boaters flock to Ⓐ**Lake Shasta** for its many watery diversions. Houseboating is popular. At Lassen Volcanic National Park, steam is the theme, especially along Ⓒ**Bumpass Hell Trail,** a paradise of hot springs, steam vents, and mud pots waiting to be discovered by hikers with a sense of wonder. Note that Mount Lassen is still active—it last went off in 1914—but if the Far North is your kind of place, you're probably not the kind of person to worry about a little magma under your feet.

THE WINE COUNTRY

America's answer to Tuscany, California's Wine Country—Napa and Sonoma counties—looks and feels like its Italian counterpart, with its rolling hills and soft Mediterranean climate. Wines made here have long won awards and have made the area a force in the industry and a vibrant destination for food-and-wine lovers. Don't think you need a cultivated palate to enjoy yourself here, however. Local wine makers such as Ⓐ**Sebastiani Vineyards** happily educate the uninitiated during tours and in their tasting rooms. If you're lucky you might arrive in time to see the grape harvest at Ⓓ**Domaine Chandon** or elsewhere. Whenever you visit, you will be greeted by row upon row of vines and wonderful food in scores of superb restaurants. No wonder the West Coast headquarters of the Ⓔ**Culinary Institute of America** is located in St. Helena. You may not want to take its courses, but you can *order* a few courses at the institute's Wine Spectator Greystone Restaurant. The good life is also a hallmark of local inns and spas, including Rutherford's Ⓒ**Auberge du Soleil**

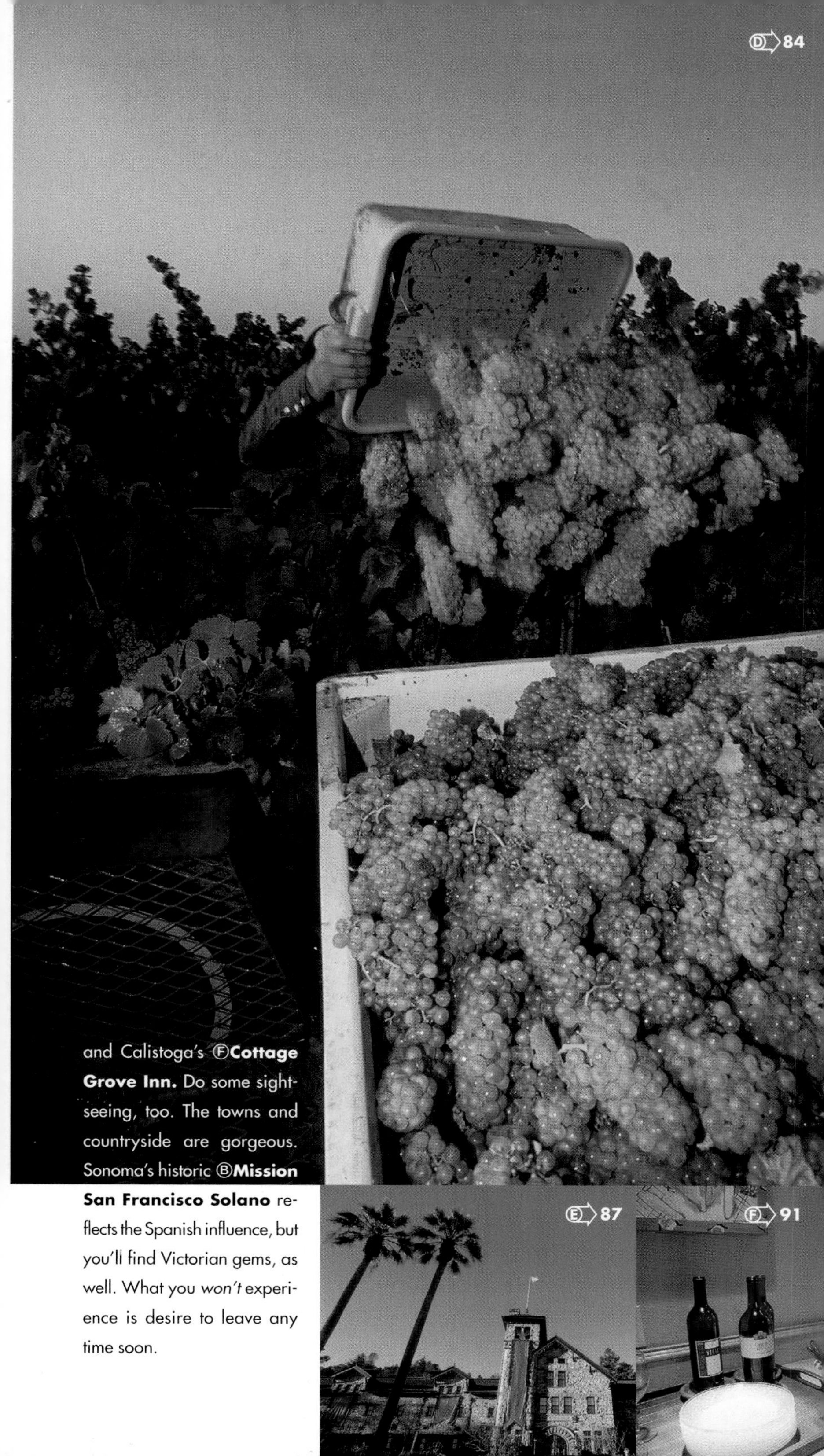
D 84
E 87
F 91

and Calistoga's Ⓕ**Cottage Grove Inn.** Do some sightseeing, too. The towns and countryside are gorgeous. Sonoma's historic Ⓑ**Mission San Francisco Solano** reflects the Spanish influence, but you'll find Victorian gems, as well. What you *won't* experience is desire to leave any time soon.

SAN FRANCISCO

Ⓐ 104

This is simply the most beautiful city in the United States, and one of the most beautiful in the world. It is to the urban landscape what Yosemite is to the natural one. As a visitor you can rub elbows with its lucky citizens in the Ⓐ**cable cars** that negotiate hilly Hyde Street with aplomb, and admire the rosy rococo Ⓑ**Palace of Fine Arts.** In sun or fog, drive or walk across the landmark Ⓒ**Golden Gate Bridge** and take in sweeping views of the city from atop Coit Tower. Just strolling

Ⓑ 132

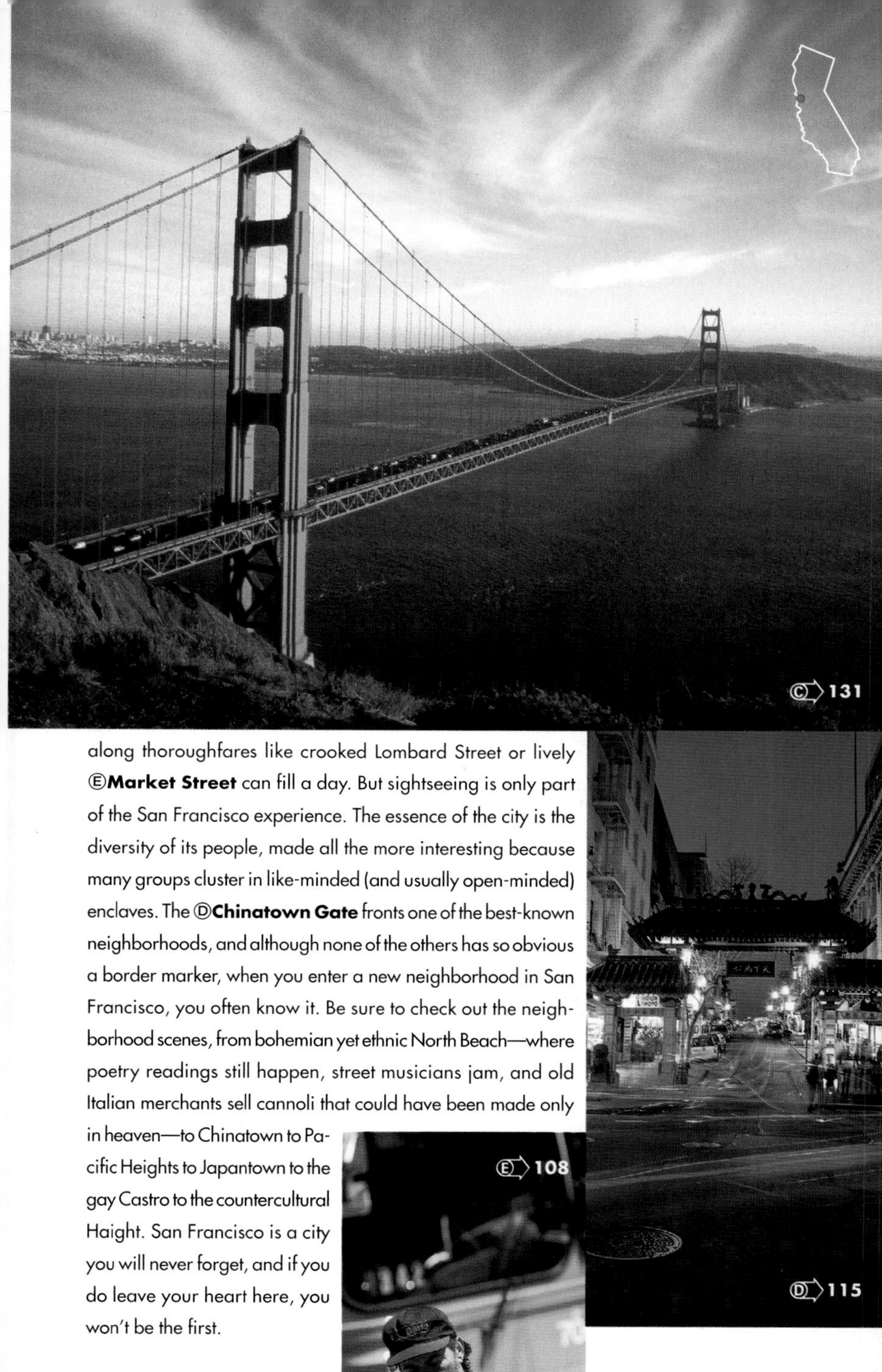

along thoroughfares like crooked Lombard Street or lively Ⓔ**Market Street** can fill a day. But sightseeing is only part of the San Francisco experience. The essence of the city is the diversity of its people, made all the more interesting because many groups cluster in like-minded (and usually open-minded) enclaves. The Ⓓ**Chinatown Gate** fronts one of the best-known neighborhoods, and although none of the others has so obvious a border marker, when you enter a new neighborhood in San Francisco, you often know it. Be sure to check out the neighborhood scenes, from bohemian yet ethnic North Beach—where poetry readings still happen, street musicians jam, and old Italian merchants sell cannoli that could have been made only in heaven—to Chinatown to Pacific Heights to Japantown to the gay Castro to the countercultural Haight. San Francisco is a city you will never forget, and if you do leave your heart here, you won't be the first.

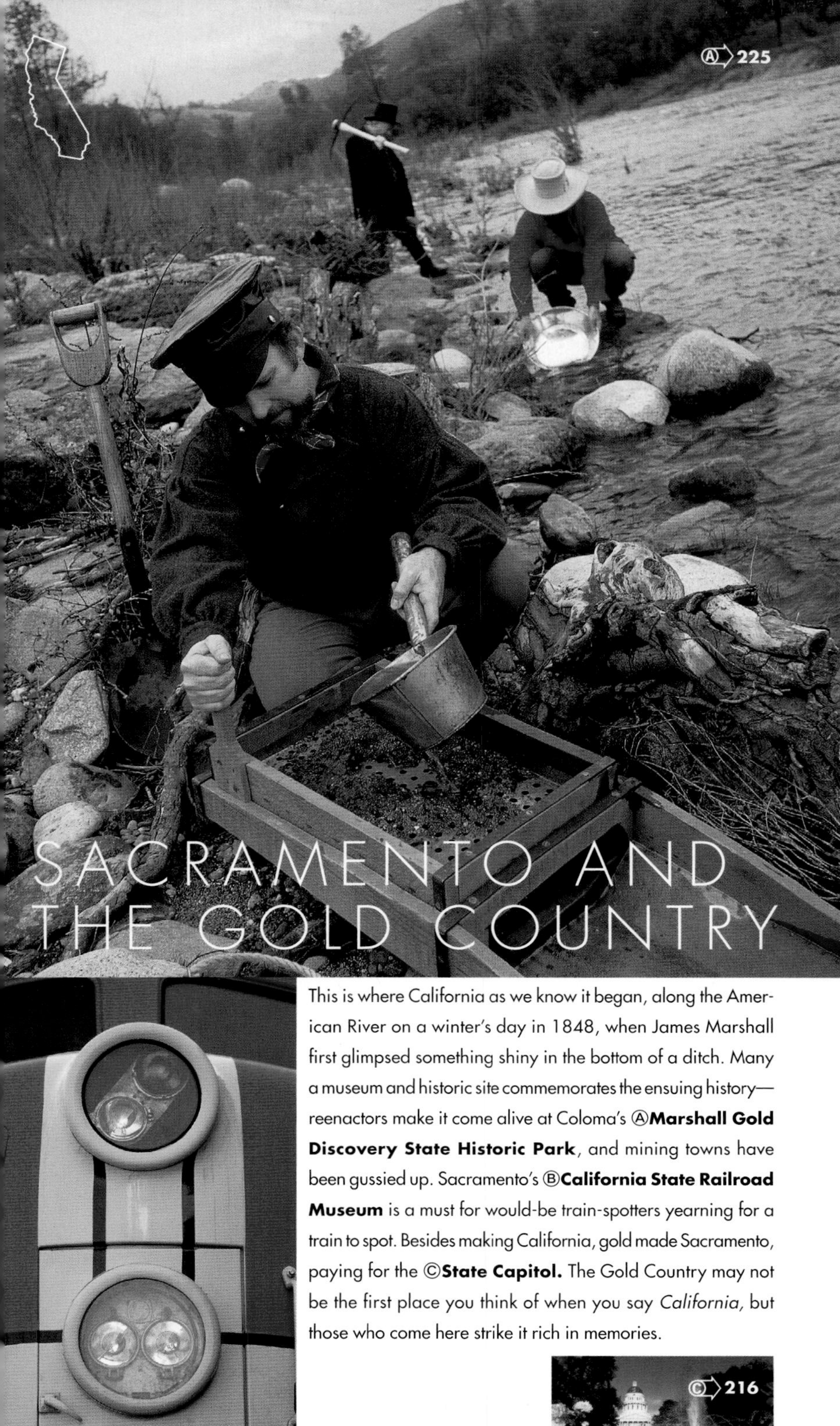

Ⓐ 225

SACRAMENTO AND THE GOLD COUNTRY

This is where California as we know it began, along the American River on a winter's day in 1848, when James Marshall first glimpsed something shiny in the bottom of a ditch. Many a museum and historic site commemorates the ensuing history—reenactors make it come alive at Coloma's Ⓐ**Marshall Gold Discovery State Historic Park**, and mining towns have been gussied up. Sacramento's Ⓑ**California State Railroad Museum** is a must for would-be train-spotters yearning for a train to spot. Besides making California, gold made Sacramento, paying for the Ⓒ**State Capitol.** The Gold Country may not be the first place you think of when you say *California*, but those who come here strike it rich in memories.

Ⓑ 216

Ⓒ 216

LAKE TAHOE

Ⓐ 246

Deep, clear, intensely blue-green, and surrounded by forests, this lake straddling the California–Nevada border is one of North America's prettiest alpine lakes. That strict environmental controls have kept it pristine is no small feat, considering its popularity. If you're staying on the California side you can golf, fish, hike or ski at Ⓒ**Squaw Valley, USA,** or pop in to see Ⓐ**Vikingsholm,** an authentic replica of a 1,200-year-old Viking castle, built in 1929 on the shore of jewel-like Ⓑ**Emerald Bay** by a woman of means. On the Nevada side, gambling is king and casinos abound, but once you leave the bright lights of the gaming tables, natural wonders surround you again.

THE SIERRA NATIONAL PARKS

At Yosemite, Kings Canyon, and Sequoia national parks, nature has outdone itself, carving magnificent glacial valleys out of a landscape sized for titans. To appreciate the scale of Ⓐ**Yosemite Valley,** consider El Capitan, rising 3,593 feet above the valley, the cliff-sided giant known as Half Dome, and Yosemite Falls, North America's tallest cascade. Even the trees are Bunyanesque—every park has a sequoia grove. Not far from Yosemite are the ghost town of Bodie, Mammoth Mountain ski area, and Ⓑ**Mono Lake,** where tufa formations, resembling giants' fingers, seem borrowed from some other planet.

Ⓑ 271

THE SAN JOAQUIN VALLEY

Don't race through the San Joaquin Valley on your way to the national parks. California's farm country is a face of the state worth knowing, with attractions ranging from Victorian houses to rafting on the Ⓐ**Kern River.** Parts of the river test experts; others are forgiving enough for children to enjoy. To stoke up for the white water, munch on fresh strawberries and other fruit, sold up and down the Valley at roadside stands in Ⓑ**Bakersfield,** Fresno, and beyond. What you find in the produce aisles back home probably comes from here—asparagus, apples, grapes, oranges. The vast agricultural tracts of the Valley can be beautiful, and markets and festivals celebrating their bounty are numerous. Stop and linger, and you may well want to return.

For many the coast between Carmel and Santa Cruz presents California at its best. The many things that make the state so wonderful to visit converge here—from history, on view at the Ⓐ**Carmel Mission,** to natural splendor, unforgettable on 17-Mile Drive as it meanders along the Pacific past wind-bent cypress trees, to Ⓓ**Pebble Beach,** where golfing pilgrims come to perform their devotions. The coastal towns will charm you with great looks, great food, and occasional quirkiness. If the monarch butterflies clustered on the pine and eucalyptus trees in Ⓑ**Pacific Grove** every winter don't entice you, nothing will. John Steinbeck immortalized

MONTEREY BAY

Monterey's Cannery Row in his 1945 novel of the same name. Today the sardine canneries are gone, and the fantastic Ⓒ**Monterey Bay Aquarium,** re-creating the local marine habitat, stands on a street that Steinbeck would hardly recognize.

Ⓑ 326

Ⓒ 321

Ⓓ 330

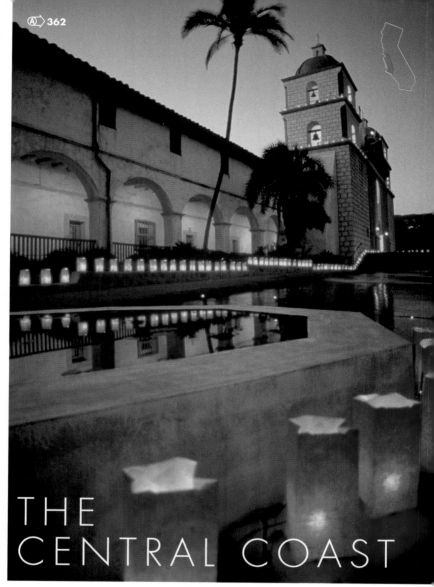

Ⓐ 362

THE CENTRAL COAST

Between Santa Barbara and wildly beautiful Big Sur is the staggeringly scenic Highway 1. The velvety Coastal Range rises from the pavement on the east; to the west the Pacific drops precipitously, spreading as far as the eye can see in stupendous vistas. Santa Barbara manages to blend sophistication and tranquillity, stimulation and repose, in perfect doses. Ⓐ**Mission Santa Barbara** is just one of the graceful sights, and newspaper baron William Randolph Hearst's Ⓑ**Hearst Castle** wows one and all.

Ⓑ 349

LOS ANGELES

Ⓐ 384

Ⓑ 401

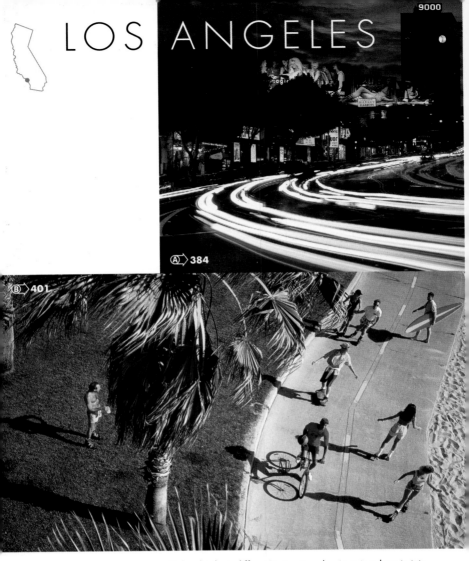

It's hard to be indifferent to Los Angeles. Love it or hate it, it is a city unlike any other. Start forming your own impressions along Ⓐ**Sunset Boulevard.** It'll take you through Hollywood all the way to the sea, through the city's multiple layers, including wealthy Bel-Air and Beverly Hills. The sheer length of the drive underscores the city's sprawl. When you get to the ocean you can experience the beach culture that's so integral to life here. Check out Ⓑ**Venice Boardwalk,** where Angelenos surf, skate, bodybuild, and stage some of the wackiest street theater in the galaxy. Most of it is fun and none of it is buttoned-down. Also pure L.A. are theme parks like

Ⓒ**Universal Studios Hollywood,** where you can "live the movies," from *Jurassic Park* to *Back to the Future*, and Ⓓ **Mann's Chinese Theatre,** where celebrities press their hands and other body parts into cement for posterity. When you're ready for shopping (high-class or funky), nightlife (from alternative to swing), or dining (from *taquerías* to Asian-fusion innovators), you'll find it in L.A. Amid the freeways and smog, the city's numerous beauty spots sometimes come as a surprise—at the Richard Meier–designed Ⓔ**Getty Center,** or at sunset, when a cinematic glow bathes Ⓕ**Griffith Park Observatory** and ribbons of violet serve as backdrop for the twinkling town. Be here then, and you may think you're surveying a city of angels.

ORANGE COUNTY

©Disney Enterprises, Inc.

If Orange County issued its own license plates, they would have to read: "Quintessential Southern California." The glitz of L.A. drops off here, and what remains is an uncomplicated lifestyle with a serious focus on fun in the sun. The biggest draw for most visitors is Ⓑ**Disneyland,** the only one of Disney's magic kingdoms built while Walt was still alive. With its diminutive, idyllic Main Street and moss-hung New Orleans Square, it has an ineffable charm, a certain softness that you don't find in other Disney realms. For thrill rides, head for another vintage theme park nearby, Knott's Berry Farm, whose founder also created the boysenberry. Meanwhile, the Pacific exerts an irresistible pull. Some neighborhoods in Orange County's beach towns could be sisters to Beverly Hills and are well worth a gawk. Here and elsewhere on the coast, between Ⓒ**Laguna Beach** and Ⓐ**Huntington Beach,** beach life is thrilling. It's the perfect opportunity to work on your tan or learn to surf among masters.

SAN DIEGO

Ⓐ 561

California's beautiful southernmost city is also its most laid-back, rendered deliciously mellow, almost like a small town, by near-perfect weather. The sun shines perpetually on lush Balboa Park, on Shamu's Sea World home, on Pacific-pounded strands like Ⓐ**Mission Beach** and pretty La Jolla's Black's Beach. Residents of the San Diego Zoo, one of the world's greats, love the weather, too. So do denizens of the zoo's Ⓑ**Wild Animal Park,** in nearby Escondido. Sunshine also blessed early California; historic sites such as Old Town and the Ⓒ**Mission San Diego de Alcalá,** Father Junípero Serra's first California outpost (1769), recall the days.

Ⓒ 530

Ⓑ 574

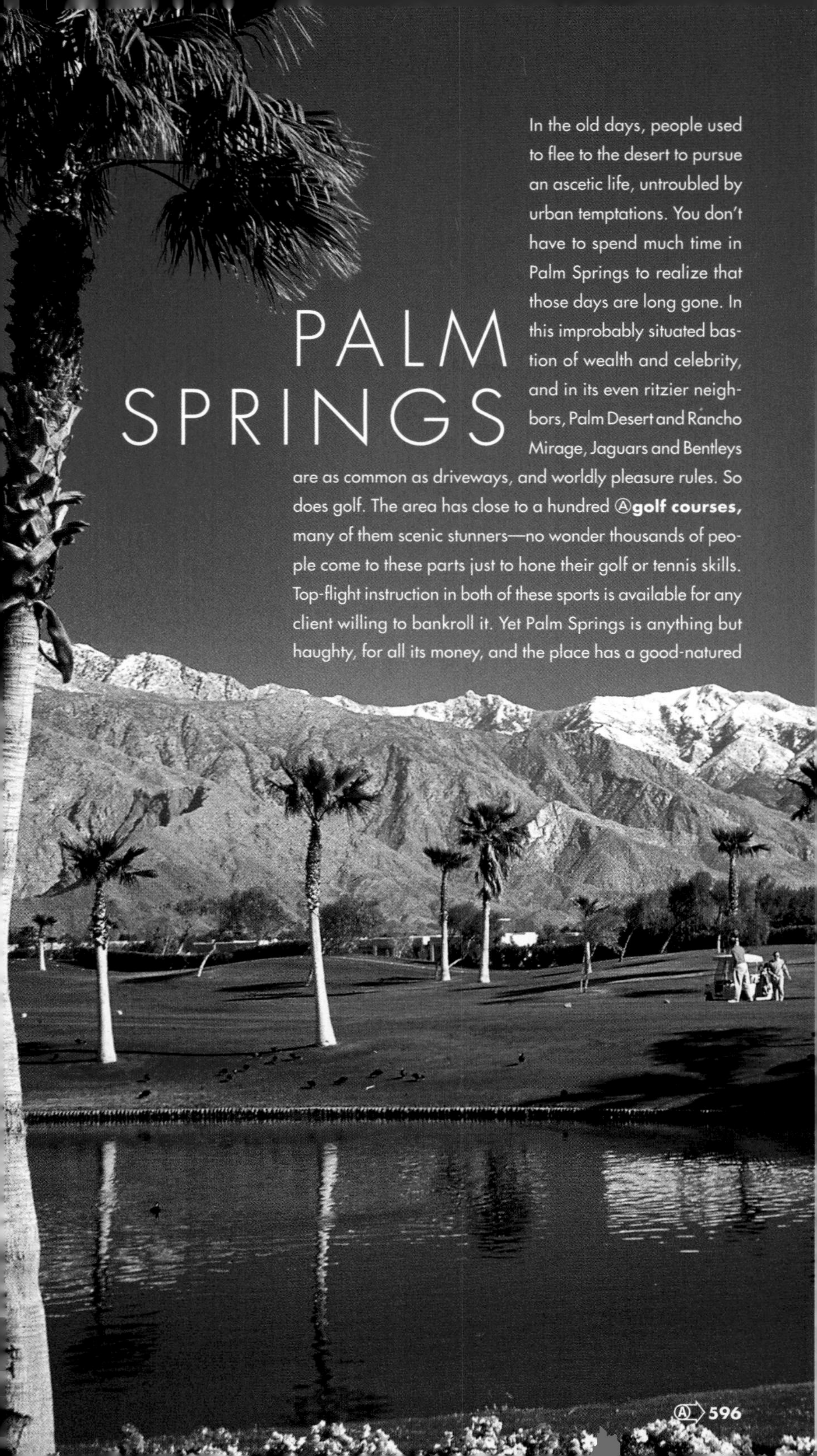

PALM SPRINGS

In the old days, people used to flee to the desert to pursue an ascetic life, untroubled by urban temptations. You don't have to spend much time in Palm Springs to realize that those days are long gone. In this improbably situated bastion of wealth and celebrity, and in its even ritzier neighbors, Palm Desert and Rancho Mirage, Jaguars and Bentleys are as common as driveways, and worldly pleasure rules. So does golf. The area has close to a hundred Ⓐ**golf courses,** many of them scenic stunners—no wonder thousands of people come to these parts just to hone their golf or tennis skills. Top-flight instruction in both of these sports is available for any client willing to bankroll it. Yet Palm Springs is anything but haughty, for all its money, and the place has a good-natured

Ⓐ⇨ 596

spirit that you'll sense at venues like the Ⓓ**Fabulous Palm Springs Follies,** a revue starring retired showgirls, singers, and other entertainers. Life here, or just vacation, can also be downright sybaritic, especially if you're staying at one of the many luxury resorts, where you can guiltlessly abandon yourself to total pampering. (If you don't, what's the point?) Understand that the pampering has a serious ob-

jective: to restore you physically, emotionally, and, yes, even spiritually. At Ⓒ**La Quinta,** for instance, you can receive sacred stone therapy, which uses techniques practiced originally by Native Americans. Connecting with the desert's wild beauty at Ⓑ**Joshua Tree National Park** can be restorative as well. The slanting late-afternoon or early morning light casts a tint (some say a spell) on the boulders and on the strange, towering trees that give the park its name, lending an otherworldly (some say supernatural) texture to the moment. Decide for yourself.

THE MOJAVE DESERT AND DEATH VALLEY

Ⓐ 612

A trip to Ⓐ**Death Valley** and the Mojave Desert may sound like the stuff of comedy routines, but discerning travelers who have experienced the great empty spaces of this stirring wilderness and heard the lore of the hardy late-19th-century mule teams at Furnace Creek know better. If you decide to join them, follow a few cardinal rules: Start at a visitor center and collect all the pamphlets. Read what they say and *follow the instructions*. Always have a full tank of gas. Bring water and keep drinking, even when you're not thirsty. Wear a hat. Don't expect to move too fast at mid-

Ⓒ 614

Ⓑ 617

day. The desert, which so amply rewards the wise, can have serious consequences for the foolish. After your return to civilization, if you thirst for culture, visit Marta Becket, proprietress and performer at Ⓑ**Marta Becket's Amargosa Opera House** in Death Valley Junction. But do make reservations; she fills the house before she brings it down. Becket's oasis of the arts is no less improbable (which is to say, *extremely*) than

Ⓓ 614

Ⓔ 620

Ⓒ**Scotty's Castle,** a Moorish mansion built in 1924. See Ⓔ**Calico Ghost Town,** once a wealthy silver mining center. If it's vast scenery you're looking for, check out the sand dunes near Ⓓ**Stovepipe Wells Village,** or the Trona Pinnacles, the brilliantly colored Artists Palette, the magnificently panoramic Dante's View, or archetypal Red Rock Canyon State Park. To really get away from it all, take in the desolate salt flats at Ⓕ**Badwater,** 282 feet below sea level. On land in the Western Hemisphere, at least, you can't sink any lower than this. And, if you visit in the summer, you can't get much hotter.

Ⓕ 615

GREAT ITINERARIES

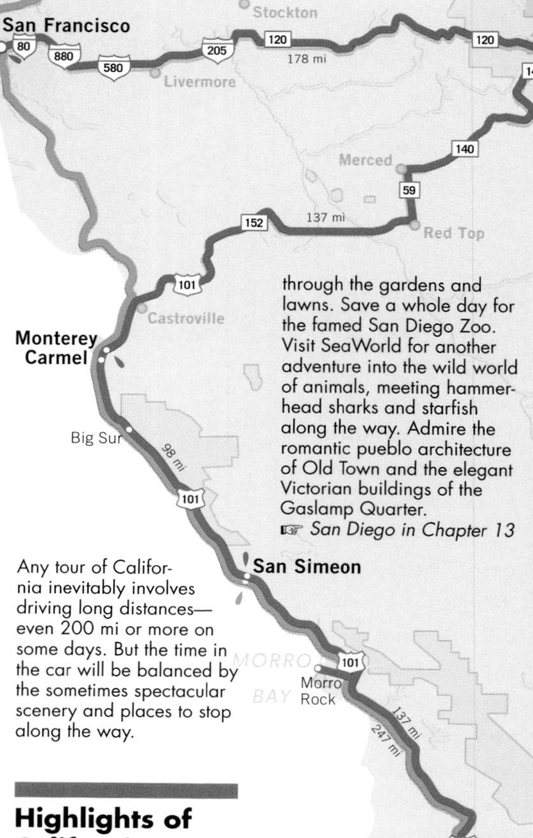

Any tour of California inevitably involves driving long distances—even 200 mi or more on some days. But the time in the car will be balanced by the sometimes spectacular scenery and places to stop along the way.

Highlights of California

11 days

California comprises so many different lands and people that to visit only one area would be to see only a single color in a rainbow. There is something tantalizing about life here that has as much to do with the silence of Yosemite as with the glitz of Hollywood. Tour some of the treasures of California, and you will soon understand why this is the Golden State.

SAN DIEGO

2 days. Start in Balboa Park, where you can visit more than a dozen museums and art galleries while strolling through the gardens and lawns. Save a whole day for the famed San Diego Zoo. Visit SeaWorld for another adventure into the wild world of animals, meeting hammerhead sharks and starfish along the way. Admire the romantic pueblo architecture of Old Town and the elegant Victorian buildings of the Gaslamp Quarter.

☞ *San Diego in Chapter 13*

ORANGE COUNTY

1 day. There is no place in the world quite like Disneyland. Step into Walt's fantasia for a day and experience the lightness of pure fun. As you continue to drive to Santa Barbara, you'll pass through Los Angeles.

☞ *Chapter 12*

SANTA BARBARA

2 days. Framed by ocher mountains and a lapis ocean, Santa Barbara is a pleasant place to shop, eat, and wander along the beach. As you drive the Pacific Coast Highway northward you'll wind through grassy inland hills to the cool breezes of Morro Bay. Ancient and volcanic Morro Rock dominates the horizon here.

☞ *Santa Barbara in Chapter 10*

SAN SIMEON

1 day. Hearst Castle is nothing short of a fantasy. The main Casa Grande and its decadently named "cottages" (mansions in their own right) are decorated with museum-worthy art. Formal gardens, crystalline pools, and splendid terraces complete the grandeur.

☞ *San Simeon in Chapter 10*

MONTEREY AND CARMEL

3 days. As you drive the Pacific Coast Highway through Ⓐ Big Sur, delight in delicate waterfalls, dense redwood groves, and breathtaking coastal cliffs. This earthly beauty is a way of life in Carmel and Monterey, where the crashing ocean and twisted splendor of cypresses provide a backdrop for shops and restaurants. The 17-Mile Drive gives you a glimpse of the mansions and golf courses of Pebble Beach. Be prepared for the long drive from the coast to Yosemite.

☞ *Chapter 9*

YOSEMITE
2 days. The incomparable majesty of marvels like Half Dome and the sublime smell of sweet meadow air make Yosemite a world unto itself. Yosemite Valley is home to the park's most picturesque creations: gushing Yosemite Falls, proud and mighty El Capitan, and untamed Bridalveil Falls. The Mariposa Grove of Big Trees is both humbling and inspiring. Sunrise and starlight from atop Glacier Point are sensational. From here, drive to San Francisco to end your trip.
☞ *Yosemite National Park in Chapter 7*

Beaches and Deserts

6 to 10 days

Southern California's beaches and deserts somehow produce a miracle of color and life. Black hills are striped with a rainbow of eroded earth; white sand is forever speckled with neon bikinis; and every spring, muted slopes of sage and shale give birth to a flurry of fuchsia and yellow flowers. Amid the kaleidoscope swirls a vibrant blend of surfers and starlets, jackrabbits and Joshua trees, and a nightly spectacle of city lights and starry skies. The horizon provides the most spectacular vision of all: Technicolor sunsets not even a postcard can capture. You may want to begin this tour in San Diego or end in Los Angeles.

PALM SPRINGS
2 or 3 days. Once a hideaway for Tinseltown stars, this oasis of green golf courses and extravagant homes stands alone in the midst of a subtle and delicate land. The view from the Tramway's 8,516-ft peak illuminates the startling contrast between ⒷPalm Springs and the slopes of the San Jacinto Mountains. Named after the biblical character for their prayer-like stances, the trees of Joshua Tree National Park are strikingly silhouetted against the open skies of this vast area.
☞ *Chapter 14*

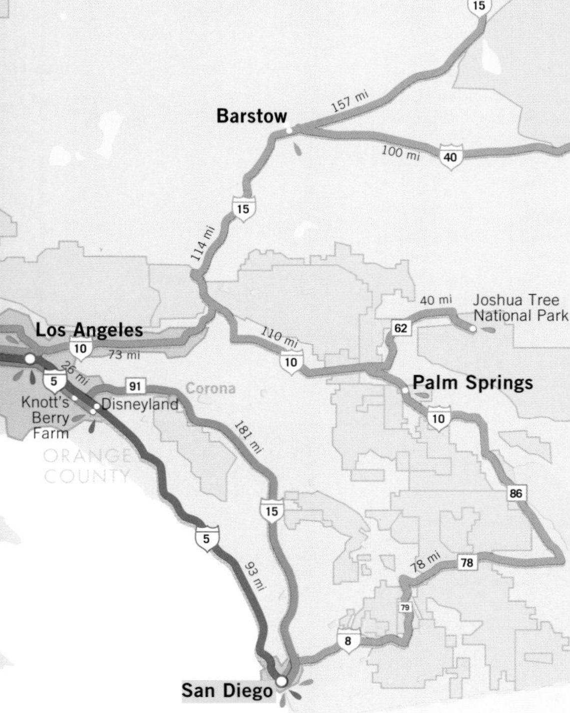

BARSTOW
2 or 3 days. The Mojave Desert can look bleak from the road, but its subtle charms are entrancing. Go for a hike along one of the many trails to experience the musky smell of sage and mesquite and the tenacity of wildflowers rooted in crumbling soil. Death Valley National Park is the final frontier in unconventional beauty. Enjoy the area in the soft light of dawn or late afternoon to avoid intense temperatures. Consider spending a night at one of the campgrounds or hotels within the park; it's a fairly long drive back to Barstow.
☞ *Mojave Desert and Death Valley in Chapter 15*

SANTA MONICA
1 or 2 days. The drive to Santa Monica Bay propels you out of the intensity of the desert toward the bright blue water. Sunbathe and swim on the white sands of Malibu. The boardwalk along Venice Beach is known for its daily parade of chain-saw jugglers and tattooed sun worshipers. Well-oiled bodybuilders pump iron at Venice's Muscle Beach, an open-air gym with Plexiglas walls that provide passersby a full view.
☞ *Santa Monica in Chapter 11*

SANTA BARBARA
1 or 2 days. Santa Barbara County offers a variety of coastal areas, the most popular and accessible of which is East Beach. The region's most captivating shorelines are within Channel Islands National Park and Marine Sanctuary, an expansive and undeveloped home to creatures including blue whales and endangered brown pelicans. For a day trip, take a cruise to Anacapa Island to admire lava tubes and sea caves and to watch seals basking at the base of 100-ft cliffs.
☞ *Santa Barbara in Chapter 10*

The Great Outdoors
9 to 12 days

If you've come to California looking for sun, sand, and surf, Northern California comes as a surprise. Towns here are remote and woodsy, colors are deep and intense rather than sun-washed. Residents of the northern coast and mountains have never disputed the image of California as a set of sunny beaches. They're happy to keep their emerald trees and sapphire seas a secret. San Francisco is the best city in which to begin and end this tour.

INVERNESS
2 days. Throughout Marin County, the California coast shows one of its most dramatic incarnations. Cliffs drop into secret coves. Waves spill over the horizon. Pelicans migrate from one volcanic sea stack to another. Stinson Beach is a placid stretch of white sand amid the chaos. Inland, the shade of Muir Woods National Monument offers ample room for contemplation. Point Reyes National Seashore is the undisputed jewel in the crown that is the Pacific Coast. Don't miss the black, white, and red sand beaches and beckoning lighthouse.
☞ *Southern Coastal Marin County in Chapter 1*

MENDOCINO
1 or 2 days. North into Mendocino County, the coast is tamer but no less striking. Year-round blooms and Victorian buildings filled with shops, restaurants, and bed-and-breakfasts make Mendocino feel uniquely refined. If the weather is divine (which it can be at any time of year), take advantage of the local state parks' rugged and uncrowded shorelines.
☞ *Sonoma and Mendocino in Chapter 1*

NAPA
2 days. The hills of Napa and Sonoma counties offer wineries as varied and colorful as the vintages they produce. French castles and farmhouses mingle with long rows of grapevines. Vineyards offer distinctive wines in beautiful and friendly settings. Fine dining is a way of life.
☞ *The Napa Valley in Chapter 3*

SOUTH LAKE TAHOE
2 or 3 days. Although deep powdery snow is rightly the Lake Tahoe area's most famous commodity, outdoor adventure abounds year-round. From Crystal Bay you can bicycle, rock climb, and water-ski—or spend the day golfing. On the lake's southern shore, hike the steep trail down to Vikingsholm for a tour of this elaborately decorated neo-Nordic mansion, then cool off in tropical-looking Emerald Bay. Even if you spend more time at the blackjack tables than outdoors, be sure to ride the Heavenly Tram for a panoramic view of the area, which is, well, heavenly.
☞ *South Lake Tahoe in Chapter 6*

YOSEMITE
2 or 3 days. Yosemite Valley offers the classic views immortalized by photographer Ansel Adams: Half Dome's glossy face, the stately grandeur of El Capitan, and Bridalveil and ©Yosemite Falls, whose only rivals for perfection are each other.
☞ *Yosemite National Park in Chapter 7*

California with Kids

12 to 15 days

As a real-world land of make-believe, California seems to have been created just for children. Fantasy comes to life in castles, museums, and exotic animals. New fairy tales are created daily in the studios and streets of Hollywood. Check local newspapers for seasonal children's events.

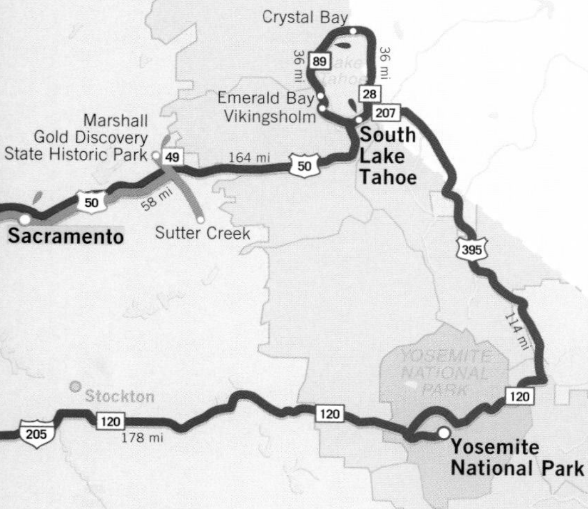

SACRAMENTO

2 days. You won't strike it rich in the Gold Country, but you can catch the spirit of the Mother Lode at Marshall Gold Discovery State Historic Park. Along historic Highway 49, towns such as Sutter Creek maintain the charm of the area's colorful past. Save an afternoon to wander the streets of Old Sacramento. Ride a tugboat taxi and marvel at old locomotives in the California State Railroad Museum.

☞ *Chapter 5*

SAN FRANCISCO

2 or 3 days. Seeing the city from a cable car is sure to thrill, and Coit Tower offers a scenic panorama. But high above the bay, the Golden Gate Bridge wins for best photo opportunity. Along the water, sample the chocolates that made Ghirardelli Square

famous and bark back at the sea lions lounging at Pier 39. Ride a ferry to ⒹAlcatraz to see the island prison. Golden Gate Park's green pastures, woods, and water can offer a whole day of entertainment. If the weather doesn't cooperate, head inside to the Exploratorium or California Academy of Sciences for outrageous hands-on exhibits.

☞ *Chapter 4*

SAN SIMEON

2 or 3 days. Allow plenty of time to enjoy the Pacific Coast Highway's curves through temperate rain forests and salty seascapes as you drive south from San Francisco. While picnicking atop the craggy cliffs of Big Sur, keep your eyes peeled for otters, seals, and sea lions surfing the waves below. Spend at least one afternoon daydreaming at Hearst Castle, a hilltop estate of unrivaled luxury. The drive to Los Angeles is long, so allow ample time.

☞ *San Simeon in Chapter 10*

LOS ANGELES

2 or 3 days. No visit is complete without a trip to Universal Studios for a behind-the-scenes look at the glamorous world of the movies. Night or day, stargaze for famous names along the Hollywood Walk of Fame. Haven't had your fill of celebrities yet? Seek out the rich and famous in Beverly Hills. Head to the Page Museum at La Brea Tar Pits and visit the onetime digs of woolly mammoths.

☞ *Chapter 11*

ORANGE COUNTY

2 days. Disneyland fulfills every kid's dreams. Knott's Berry Farm also offers diversion for the imagination, complete with international cuisine and lively shows recreating California history.

☞ *Chapter 12*

SAN DIEGO

2 days. In ⒺSan Diego the first stop should be the San Diego Zoo. Wander the landscaped grounds and you're sure to find something you've never seen before, perhaps a two-headed corn snake or an East African bongo. Spend the next day at SeaWorld to see Shamu the killer whale and the world's largest collection of sharks.

☞ *Chapter 13*

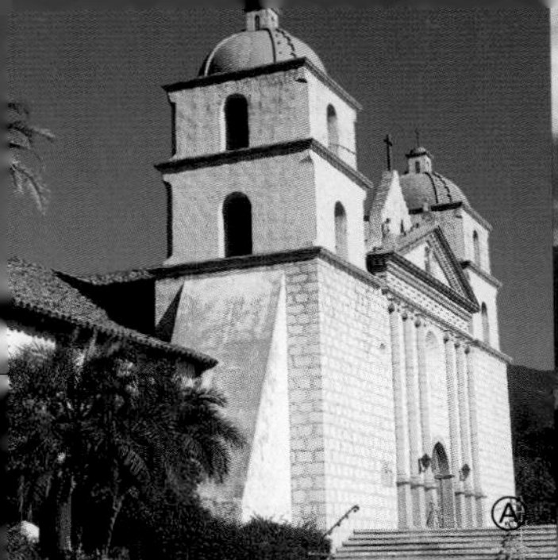

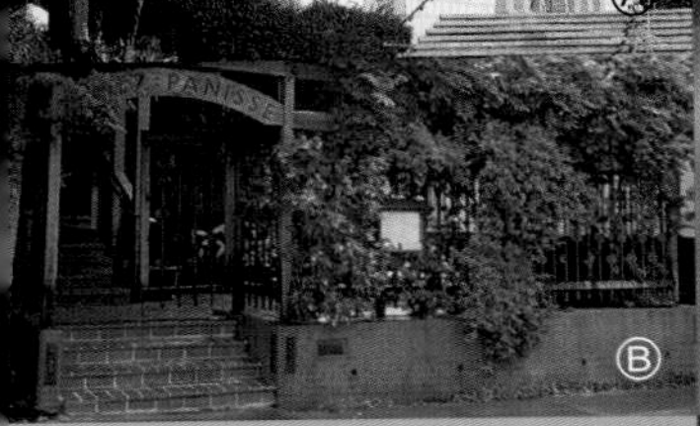

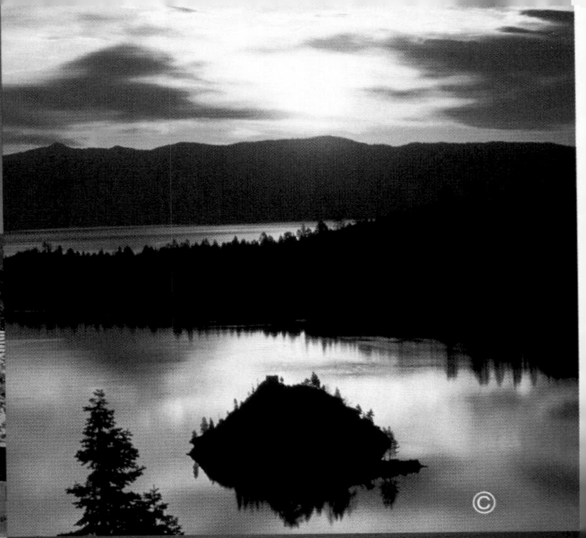

FODOR'S CHOICE

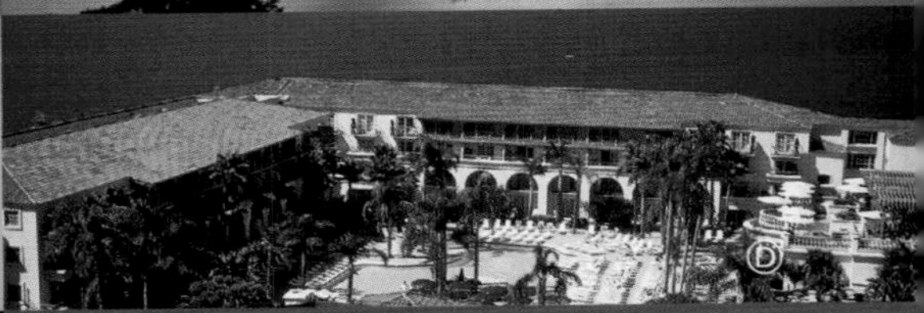

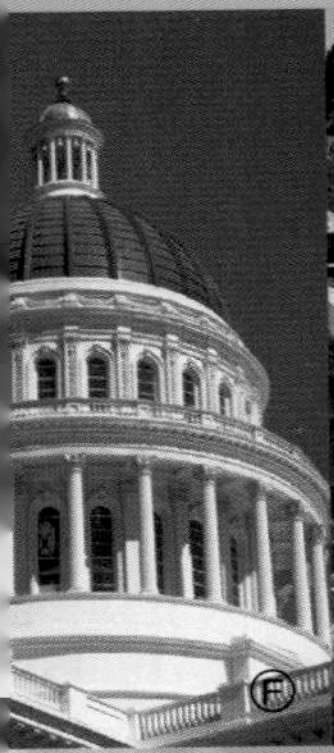

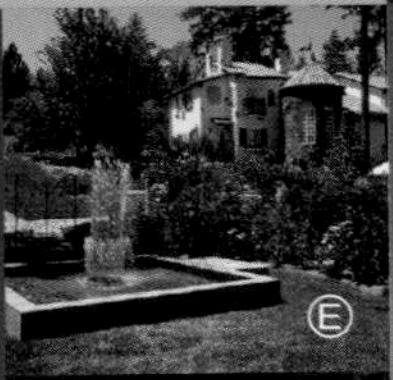

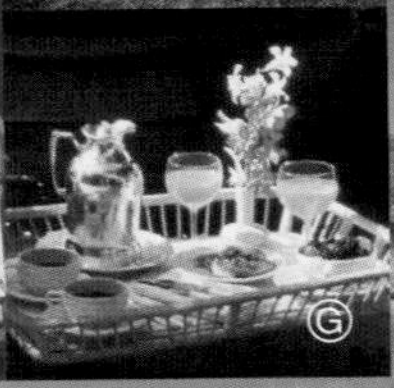

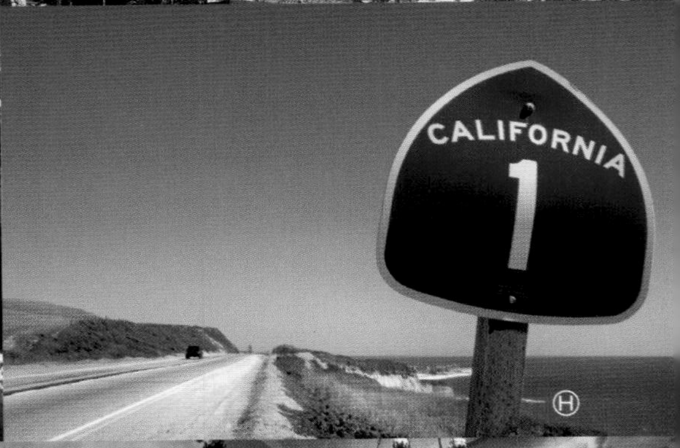

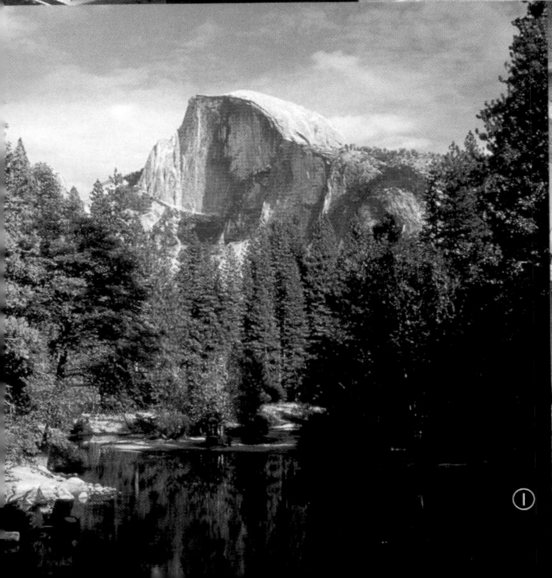

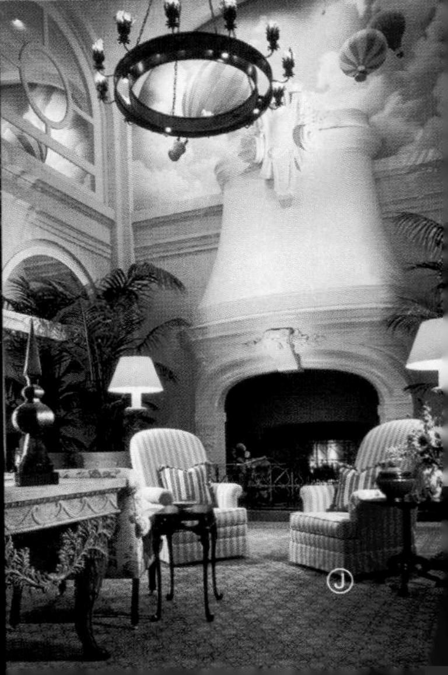

Even with so many special places in California, Fodor's writer's and editors have their favorites. Here are a few that stand out.

BREATHTAKING SIGHTS

Ⓘ **El Capitan and Half Dome, Yosemite.** El Capitan, the world's largest exposed granite monolith, and Half Dome, rising 4,733 ft above the valley floor with a 2,000-ft cliff on its fractured west side, are nothing short of mesmerizing. ☞ p. 266

Golden Gate Bridge Vista Point, Marin County. On a clear day San Francisco glistens from this vantage point at the bridge's north end. ☞ p. 131

Ⓗ **Highway 1, Big Sur to San Simeon.** This stretch of twisting coastal highway affords amazing ocean vistas. ☞ p. 347

Kings Canyon Highway. From late spring to early fall the stretch of Highway 180 in Kings Canyon National Park from Grant Grove to Cedar Grove is spectacular. Peer into the nation's deepest gorge and up to the High Sierra's gorgeous canyons. ☞ p. 281

La Jolla Cove at sunset. Always beautiful, it's never more splendid than when the setting sun gilds the cove and backlights the towering palms. ☞ p. 526

Mulholland Drive, Los Angeles. One of L.A.'s most famous thoroughfares winds through the Hollywood Hills, across the spine of the Santa Monica Mountains, almost to the Pacific. It's slow going, but the grand homes and the city and San Fernando Valley views are sensational. ☞ p. 401

17-Mile Drive, Pebble Beach. The wonders are both man-made and natural along this road between Pacific Grove and Carmel. Robert Louis Stevenson described the gnarled and twisted Monterey cypress en route as "ghosts fleeing before the wind." ☞ p. 330

Ⓒ **View from Emerald Bay Lookout, Lake Tahoe.** Massive glaciers carved this fjordlike bay millions of years ago. Famed for its jewel-like shape and colors, it surrounds Fannette, Tahoe's only island. Survey the glorious scene from the lookout. ☞ p. 246

HISTORIC BUILDINGS

Griffith Observatory and Planetarium, Los Angeles. One of the world's largest telescopes is open to the public for viewing every clear night. *Rebel Without a Cause* immortalized its planetarium. ☞ p. 386

Hearst Castle, San Simeon. This stunning pleasure palace towers over 127 acres at the heart of newspaper magnate William Randolph Hearst's 250,000-acre ranch. ☞ p. 349

Mann's Chinese Theatre, Hollywood. The former Grauman's Chinese is a fantasy of pagodas and temples. Check out the celebrity hand- and footprints in the courtyard pavement. ☞ p. 388

Ⓐ **Mission Santa Barbara.** Twin bell towers and Greco-Roman columns and statuary embellish the queen of the California missions. Established in 1786, it's still an active church. ☞ p. 362

Ⓕ **State Capitol, Sacramento.** With its lacy plasterwork, the rotunda of this 1869 structure is like a Fabergé egg. The 40-acre Capitol Park outside is one of the state's oldest gardens. ☞ p. 216

FLAVORS

Patina, Hollywood. Here, in one of L.A.'s best restaurants, the spare, elegant setting is as beguiling as Joachim Splichal's contemporary cuisine. *$$$$* ☞ p. 417

Café Beaujolais, Mendocino. Peaceful, backwoods Mendocino charm pervades this cottage, and the cooking is great, to boot. The cross-cultural menu may include corn crepes filled with barbecued rock shrimp and served with avocado and blood-orange *pico de gallo*. *$$$* ☞ p. 49

Ⓑ **Chez Panisse, Berkeley.** The legendary Alice Waters still masterminds the culinary wizardry here. The prix-fixe menu in the formal restaurant changes daily; fare in the informal café is simpler and less expensive but no less exciting. *$$$–$$$$* ☞ p. 197

George's at the Cove, La Jolla. Come for the splendid cove view in the elegant main dining room and for the wonderful fresh seafood. *$$$–$$$$* ☞ p. 541

Jardinière, San Francisco. One of the city's most talked-about restaurants is also the hot ticket before symphony, opera, and theater events. Chef Traci Des Jardins provides the creative touch. *$$$–$$$$* ☞ p. 150

RETREATS

Ⓔ **Château du Sureau, Oakhurst.** This fairy-tale castle is also home to Erna's Elderberry House restaurant, one of California's best. You may find it hard to tear yourself away to visit nearby Yosemite National Park. *$$$$* ☞ p. 274

Ⓖ **Hotel Bel-Air, Bel-Air**. This ultra-luxurious escape in a secluded wooded canyon feels like a grand country home. To splurge, request a room with its own hot tub on the patio. *$$$$* ☞ p. 440

Post Ranch Inn, Big Sur. In this indulgent hideaway, each room has its own hot tub, stereo, private deck, and massage table—in addition to dizzying Pacific or mountain views. *$$$$* ☞ p. 348

Ⓓ **Ritz-Carlton, Laguna Niguel**. Hallmark Ritz-Carlton service and an unrivaled setting on the edge of the Pacific have made a star of this grand hotel with the feel of a Mediterranean country villa. *$$$$* ☞ p. 499

Ⓙ **Hotel Monaco, San Francisco.** The whimsical postmodern Monaco stands out for its snappy public areas, comfortable rooms, and devotion to pampering its guests. *$$$* ☞ p. 170

1 THE NORTH COAST

FROM MUIR BEACH TO CRESCENT CITY

Migrating whales and other sea mammals swim past the dramatic bluffs that make the 400 mi of shoreline north of San Francisco to the Oregon state line among the most photographed landscapes in the country. Along cypress- and redwood-studded Highway 1 you will find many small inns, uncrowded state beaches and parks, art galleries, and restaurants serving imaginative dishes that showcase locally produced ingredients.

By Marty Olmstead

BETWEEN SAN FRANCISCO BAY and the Oregon state line lies the aptly named Redwood Empire, where national, state, and local parks welcome visitors year-round. The shoreline's natural attributes are self-evident, but the area is also rich in human history, having been the successive domain of Native American Miwoks and Pomos, Russian fur traders, Hispanic settlers, and more contemporary fishing folk and loggers. All have left visible legacies. Only a handful of towns in this sparsely populated region have more than 1,000 inhabitants.

Pleasures and Pastimes

Beaches

The waters of the Pacific Ocean along the North Coast are fine for seals, but most humans find the temperatures downright arctic. When it comes to spectacular cliffs and seascapes, though, the North Coast beaches are second to none. Explore tidal pools, watch for sea life, or dive for abalone. Don't worry about crowds: on many of these beaches you will have the sands largely to yourself.

Dining

Despite its small population, the North Coast lays claim to several well-regarded restaurants. Seafood is abundant, as are locally grown vegetables and herbs. In general, dining options are more varied near the coast than inland. Dress is usually informal, though dressy casual is the norm at some of the pricier establishments listed below.

CATEGORY	COST*
$$$$	over $50
$$$	$30–$50
$$	$20–$30
$	under $20

**per person for a three-course meal, excluding drinks, service, and 7¼% tax*

Fishing

Depending on the season, you can fish for rockfish, salmon, and steelhead in the rivers. Charters leave from Fort Bragg, Eureka, and elsewhere for ocean fishing. There's particularly good abalone diving around Jenner, Fort Ross, Point Arena, Westport, and Trinidad.

Lodging

Restored Victorians, rustic lodges, country inns, and chic new hotels are among the accommodations available along the North Coast. In several towns there are only one or two places to spend the night; some of these lodgings are destinations in themselves. Make summer and weekend B&B reservations as far ahead as possible—rooms at the best inns often sell out months in advance.

CATEGORY	COST*
$$$$	over $175
$$$	$120–$175
$$	$80–$120
$	under $80

**All prices are for a standard double room, excluding 8%–10% tax.*

[symbol] following the text of a review is your signal that the property has a Web site, where you will find details and, usually, images; for a link, visit www.fodors.com/urls.

Whale-Watching

From any number of excellent observation points along the coast, you can watch gray whales during their annual winter migration season or, in the summer and fall, blue or humpback whales. Another option is a whale-watching cruise (☞ Contacts and Resources *in* the North Coast A to Z, *below*).

Exploring the North Coast

Exploring the northern California coast is easiest by car. Highway 1 is a beautiful, if sometimes slow and nerve-racking, drive. You'll want to stop frequently to appreciate the views, and there are many portions of the highway along which you won't drive faster than 20–40 mph. You can still have a fine trip even if you don't have much time, but be realistic and don't plan to drive too far in one day. The itineraries below proceed north from San Francisco.

Numbers in the text correspond to numbers in the margin and on the North Coast maps.

Great Itineraries

IF YOU HAVE 3 DAYS

Some of the finest redwoods in California are found less than 20 mi north of San Francisco in **Muir Woods National Monument** ①. After walking through the woods, stop for an early lunch in **Inverness** (on Sir Francis Drake Boulevard, northwest from Highway 1) or continue on Highway 1 to **Fort Ross State Historic Park** ⑦. Catch the sunset and stay the night in 🏨 **Gualala.** On day two, drive to 🏨 **Mendocino** ⑨. Spend the next day and a half browsing the many galleries, shops, historic sites, beaches, and parks of this cliffside enclave. Return to San Francisco via Highway 1, or the quicker (3½ hours, versus up to 5) and less winding route of Highway 128 east (off Highway 1 at the Navarro River, 10 mi south of Mendocino) to U.S. 101 south.

IF YOU HAVE 7 DAYS

Early on your first day, walk through **Muir Woods National Monument** ①. Then visit **Stinson Beach** ② for a walk on the shore and lunch. In springtime and early summer head north on Highway 1 to Bolinas Lagoon, where you can see bird nestings at **Audubon Canyon Ranch** ③. At other times of the year (or after you've visited the ranch) continue north on Highway 1. One-third of a mile beyond **Olema,** look for a sign marking the turnoff for the **Bear Valley Visitor Center** ⑤, the gateway to the **Point Reyes National Seashore.** Tour the reconstructed Miwok village near the visitor center. Spend the night in nearby 🏨 **Inverness** or one of the other coastal Marin towns. The next day, stop at Goat Rock State Beach and **Fort Ross State Historic Park** ⑦ on the way to 🏨 **Mendocino** ⑨. On your third morning, head to **Fort Bragg** for a visit to the **Mendocino Coast Botanical Gardens.** If you're in the mood to splurge, drive inland on Highway 1 to U.S. 101 north and spend the night at the Benbow Inn in 🏨 **Garberville.** Otherwise, linger in the Mendocino area and drive inland the next morning. On day four continue north through parts of **Humboldt Redwoods State Park** ⑪, including the Avenue of the Giants. Stop for the night in the Victorian village of 🏨 **Ferndale** ⑫ and visit the cemetery and the Ferndale Museum. On day five drive to 🏨 **Eureka** ⑬. Have lunch in Old Town, visit the shops, and get a feel for local marine life on a Humboldt Bay cruise. Begin day six by driving to **Patrick's Point State Park** ⑮ to enjoy stunning views of the Pacific from a point high above the surf. Have a late lunch overlooking the harbor in **Trinidad** before returning to Eureka for the night. Return to San Francisco on day seven. The drive back takes six hours on U.S. 101; it's nearly twice as long if you take Highway 1.

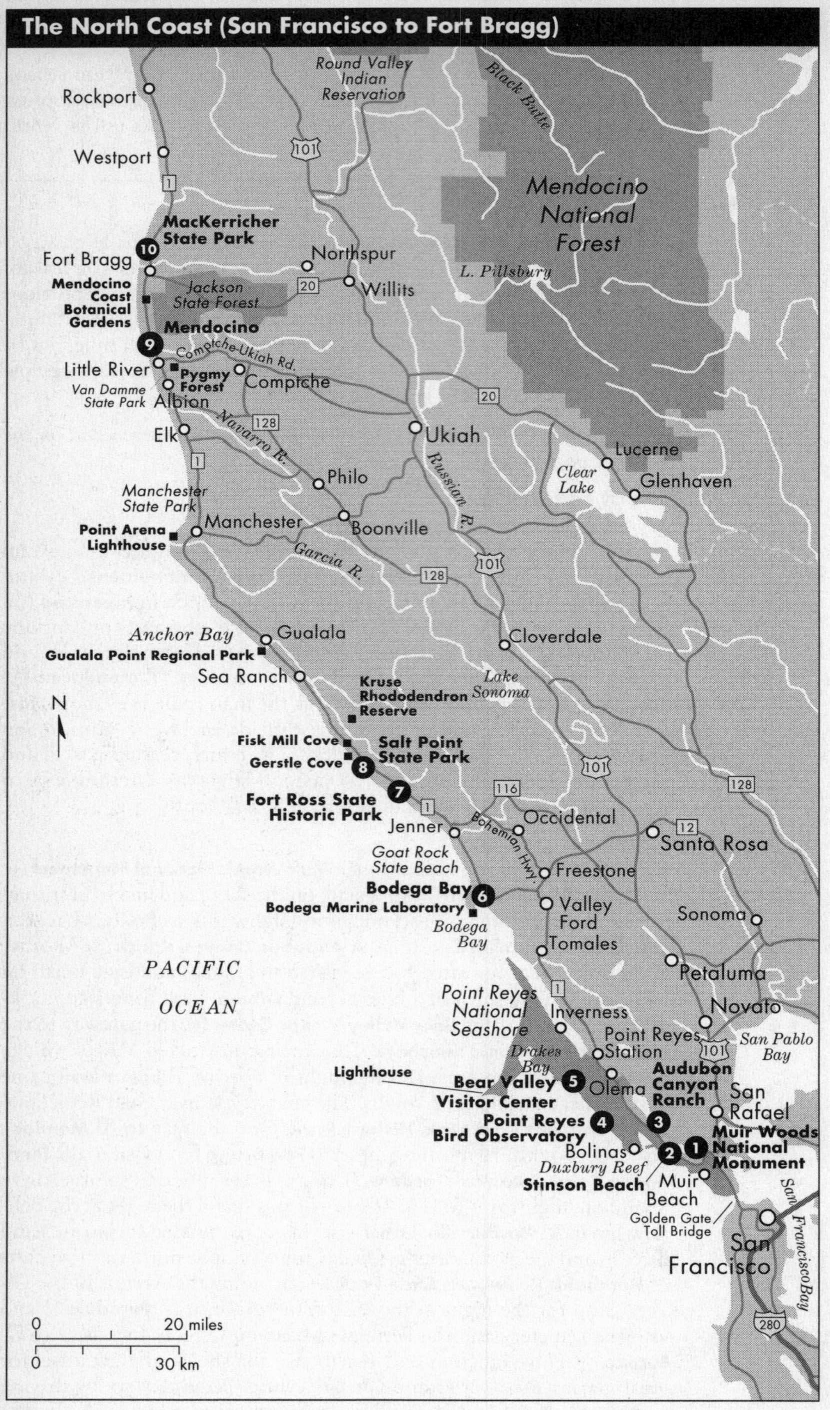

The North Coast (San Francisco to Fort Bragg)
Round Valley Indian Reservation
Black Butte
Mendocino National Forest
L. Pillsbury
Rockport
Westport
MacKerricher State Park
Fort Bragg
Northspur
Willits
Mendocino Coast Botanical Gardens
Jackson State Forest
Mendocino
Comptche-Ukiah Rd.
Little River
Pygmy Forest
Comptche
Van Damme State Park
Albion
Navarro R.
Elk
Ukiah
Russian R.
Lucerne
Clear Lake
Glenhaven
Philo
Manchester State Park
Boonville
Point Arena Lighthouse
Manchester
Garcia R.
Anchor Bay
Gualala
Gualala Point Regional Park
Sea Ranch
Cloverdale
Lake Sonoma
Kruse Rhododendron Reserve
Fisk Mill Cove
Salt Point State Park
Gerstle Cove
Fort Ross State Historic Park
Jenner
Bohemian Hwy.
Occidental
Santa Rosa
Goat Rock State Beach
Freestone
Bodega Bay
Bodega Marine Laboratory
Valley Ford
Sonoma
Bodega Bay
Tomales
Petaluma
PACIFIC OCEAN
Point Reyes National Seashore
Inverness
Novato
Point Reyes Station
San Pablo Bay
Drakes Bay
Lighthouse
Audubon Canyon Ranch
Bear Valley Visitor Center
Olema
San Rafael
Point Reyes Bird Observatory
Muir Woods National Monument
Bolinas
Duxbury Reef
Stinson Beach
Muir Beach
Golden Gate Toll Bridge
San Francisco
San Francisco Bay
0 20 miles
0 30 km

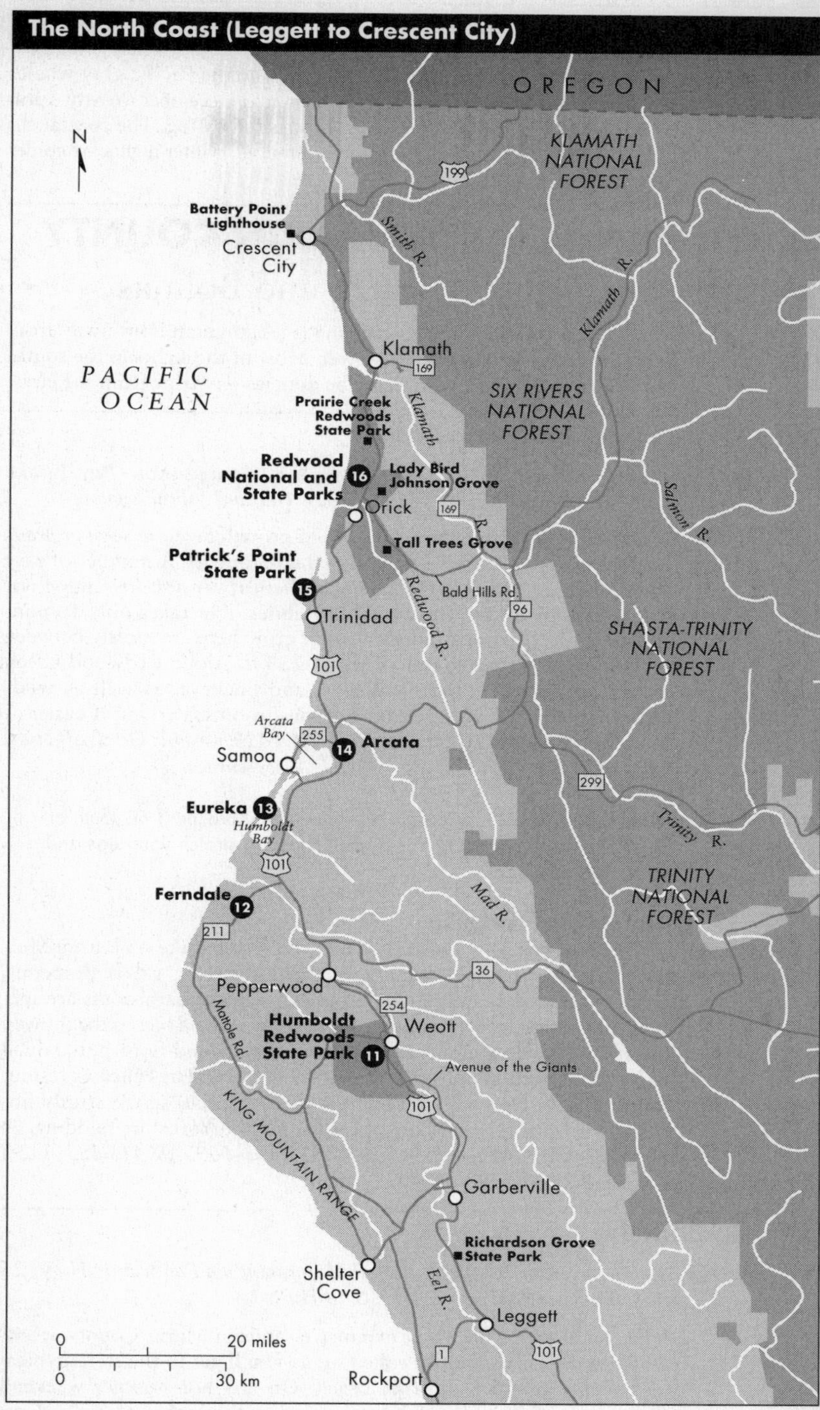
The North Coast (Leggett to Crescent City)
OREGON
KLAMATH NATIONAL FOREST
199
Battery Point Lighthouse
Crescent City
Smith R.
Klamath R.
Klamath
169
PACIFIC OCEAN
Prairie Creek Redwoods State Park
Klamath
SIX RIVERS NATIONAL FOREST
Redwood National and State Parks
16
Lady Bird Johnson Grove
Orick
169
Salmon R.
Tall Trees Grove
Patrick's Point State Park
15
Bald Hills Rd.
96
Trinidad
Redwood R.
SHASTA-TRINITY NATIONAL FOREST
101
Arcata Bay
255
14
Arcata
Samoa
299
Eureka
13
Humboldt Bay
Trinity R.
101
TRINITY NATIONAL FOREST
Mad R.
Ferndale
12
211
36
Pepperwood
254
Mattole Rd.
Humboldt Redwoods State Park
Weott
11
Avenue of the Giants
101
KING MOUNTAIN RANGE
Garberville
Richardson Grove State Park
Shelter Cove
Eel R.
Leggett
0
20 miles
0
30 km
1
101
Rockport

When to Tour the North Coast

The North Coast is a year-round destination, though when you go determines what you will see. The migration of the Pacific gray whales is a wintertime phenomenon, roughly from mid-December to early April. In July and August, views are often obstructed by fog. The coastal climate is quite similar to San Francisco's, although winter nights are colder than in the city.

SOUTHERN COASTAL MARIN COUNTY

Muir Woods, Stinson Beach, and Bolinas

Much of the Marin County coastline is less than an hour away from San Francisco, but the pace is slower. Most of the sights in the southern coastal Marin area can easily be done as day trips from the city.

Muir Woods National Monument

★ ❶ *17 mi from San Francisco, north on U.S. 101 and west on Hwy. 1 (take Mill Valley/Stinson Beach exit off U.S. 101 and follow signs).*

The world's most popular grove of old-growth *Sequoia sempervirens* was one of the country's first national monuments. A number of easy hikes can be accomplished in an hour. There's even a short valley-floor trek, accessible to travelers with disabilities, that takes only 10 minutes to walk. The coast redwoods that grow here are mostly between 500 and 800 years old and as tall as 236 ft. Along Redwood Creek are other trees—live oak, madrone, and buckeye, as well as wildflowers (even in winter), ferns, and mushrooms. Parking is easier at Muir Woods before 10 AM and after 4 PM. ✉ *Panoramic Hwy., off Hwy. 1,* ☎ *415/388–2595.* *$2.* *Daily 8 AM–sunset.*

OFF THE BEATEN PATH — **MUIR BEACH** – Small but scenic, this patch of shoreline 3 mi south of Muir Woods off Highway 1 is a good place to stretch your legs and gaze out at the Pacific.

Dining and Lodging

$$$–$$$$ ★ **Pelican Inn.** This Tudor-style B&B is a five-minute walk from Muir Beach. Rooms have Oriental rugs, English prints, velvet draperies, hanging tapestries, and half-tester beds. Even the bathrooms are special, with Victorian-style hardware and hand-painted tiles in the shower. Locals and tourists compete at darts in the ground-floor pub, which has a wide selection of brews, sherries, and ports. The Pelican's restaurant ($$–$$$; closed on Monday January–March) serves sturdy English fare, from fish-and-chips to prime rib and Yorkshire pudding. ✉ *10 Pacific Way, at Hwy. 1, 94965,* ☎ *415/383–6000,* FAX *415/383–3424. 7 rooms. Restaurant, pub. MC, V. BP.*

Stinson Beach

❷ *8 mi from Muir Woods National Monument via Panoramic Hwy.; 25 mi from San Francisco, U.S. 101 to Hwy. 1.*

Stinson Beach has the most expansive sands in Marin County. It's as close (when the fog hasn't rolled in) as you'll get to the stereotypical feel of a southern California beach. On any hot summer weekend every road to Stinson Beach is jam-packed, so factor this into your plans.

Dining and Lodging

$–$$ **Sand Dollar.** This friendly, modest pub serves hamburgers and other sandwiches for lunch and decent seafood for dinner; there's an outdoor dining deck. ✉ *3458 Hwy. 1,* ☎ *415/868–0434. AE, D, MC, V.*

$–$$ ✕ **Stinson Beach Grill.** A great selection of beer and wine, art on the walls, and outdoor seating on a heated deck are among the draws here. The food is good, too. Seafood, including several types of oysters, is served at lunch and dinner. Pasta, lamb, chicken, and Southwestern specialties are on the evening menu. ✉ *3465 Hwy. 1,* ☏ *415/868–2002. AE, DC, MC, V.*

$$$–$$$$ **Casa del Mar.** A rambling garden and white stucco walls gives this—one of Stinson's few inns—a decidedly Mediterranean ambience. Throughout the inn, the owner exhibits his extensive collection of works by local artists. Accommodations are on the small side, but light colors and the many windows create a feeling of spaciousness. ✉ *37 Belvedere Ave., 94970,* ☏ *415/868–2124 or 800/552–2124. 6 rooms. AE, MC, V.*

Bolinas

3 The **Audubon Canyon Ranch,** a 1,000-acre wildlife sanctuary along the Bolinas Lagoon, is open to the public during nesting season. Among the 60 species of birds that can be spotted here with the aid of telescopes and hidden observations posts are great blue herons and egrets. There are many miles of hiking trails through the preserve that offer tremendous views of the Bolinas Lagoon and Stinson Beach. A small museum surveys the geology and natural history of the region. ✉ *4900 Hwy. 1, along Bolinas Lagoon,* ☏ *415/868–9244.* *$10 donation requested.* *Mid-Mar.–mid-July, weekends 10–4.*

An unmarked road running west from Highway 1 about 2 mi beyond Audubon Canyon Ranch leads to the sleepy town of **Bolinas.** Don't expect a warm welcome: some residents of Bolinas are so wary of tourism that whenever the state tries to post road signs, they take them down.

Nightlife

Smiley's Schooner Saloon (✉ 41 Wharf Rd., ☏ 415/868–1311) hosts live music on Friday and Saturday.

POINT REYES NATIONAL SEASHORE

Duxbury Reef, Olema, and Inverness

The Point Reyes National Seashore, which borders the northern reaches of the Golden Gate National Recreation Area (☞ Chapter 4), is a great place for hiking to secluded beaches, viewing wildlife, and driving through rugged, rolling grasslands. Highlights include the ½-mi Earthquake Trail, which passes by what is believed to be the epicenter of the 1906 quake that destroyed much of San Francisco, and the late-19th-century Point Reyes Lighthouse, a good spot to watch for whales. Horses and mountain bikes are permitted on some trails. The towns of Olema, Point Reyes Station, and Inverness, all in or near the national seashore area, have dining, lodging, and recreational facilities.

Duxbury Reef Area

2 mi northwest of Bolinas off Mesa Rd.

4 Birders love the **Point Reyes Bird Observatory,** a sanctuary and research center within the Point Reyes National Seashore but more easily accessible from Bolinas. The area harbors nearly 225 bird species. As you hike the trails, you're likely to see biologists banding the birds to aid in studying their life cycles. Trails pass waterfalls and a lake and lead to the national seashore. ✉ *West on Mesa Rd. off Olema–Bolinas Rd.,* ☏ *415/868–0655.* *Free.* *Visitor center daily sunrise–sunset.*

Mile-long **Duxbury Reef,** a nature preserve, is the largest shale intertidal reef in North America. Check a tide table if you plan to explore the reef, which is accessible only at low tide. Look for starfish, barnacles, sea anemones, purple urchins, limpets, sea mussels, and the occasional red and black abalone. ✉ *From Bolinas, take Mesa Rd. off Olema–Bolinas Rd.; turn left on Overlook Dr. and right on Elm Ave. to beach parking lot.*

Olema

9 mi north of Bolinas on Hwy. 1.

★ ❺ The Point Reyes National Seashore's **Bear Valley Visitor Center** has exhibits of park wildlife. The rangers here dispense advice about beaches, the Point Reyes Lighthouse, whale-watching, hiking trails, and camping. A reconstructed Miwok village, a short walk from the visitor center, provides insight into the daily lives of the region's first human inhabitants. ✉ *Bear Valley Rd. west of Hwy. 1,* ☎ *415/663–1092.* *Free.* ⏲ *Weekdays 9–5, weekends 8–5.*

Outdoor Activities and Sports

Many of the beaches in Point Reyes National Seashore are accessible off Bear Valley Road. **Limantour Beach** (✉ end of Limantour Beach Rd.) is one of the most beautiful of Point Reyes sands; trails lead to other beaches north and south of here. **Five Brooks Stables** (✉ 8001 Hwy. 1, ☎ 415/663–1570) rents horses and equipment. Trails from the stables wind through the Point Reyes woods and along the beaches.

Point Reyes Station

2 mi north of Olema on Hwy. 1.

The best place to find out what's going on in Point Reyes Station, a stop on the North Pacific Coast Narrow-Gauge Railroad until 1933, is Toby's Feed Barn. Toby's sells offbeat gifts (many festooned with cows) to tourists and locals and feed and grain to local farmers. There's a market on Main Street for picking up picnic supplies.

Lodging

$ **Point Reyes Hostel.** These dorm-style lodgings in an old clapboard ranch house are a good deal for budget travelers. A family room is limited to those with children five and under and must be reserved well in advance. ✉ *Off Limantour Rd., Box 247, 94956,* ☎ *415/663–8811. MC, V.*

Shopping

Gallery Route One (✉ 11101 Hwy. 1, ☎ 415/663–1347), a nonprofit cooperative, shows the works of area artists.

Inverness

4 mi from Point Reyes Station on Sir Francis Drake Blvd., northwest from Hwy. 1.

Inverness boomed after the 1906 earthquake when wealthy San Franciscans built summer homes in its hills. Today many of the structures serve as full-time residences or small inns. A deli, a grocery store, restaurants, and shops are along Sir Francis Drake Boulevard.

★ The **Point Reyes Lighthouse Visitors Center** is a 45-minute drive from Inverness, across rolling hills that resemble Scottish heath. Parking near the lighthouse is difficult on weekends during summer. The view alone persuades most people to make the effort of walking down—and then back up—the hundreds of steps from the cliff tops to the lighthouse below. ✉ *Western end of Sir Francis Drake Blvd.,* ☎ *415/669–1534.* ⏲ *Thurs.–Sun. 10–5 (steps close at 4:30).*

Dining and Lodging

$ ✕ **Grey Whale.** This casual place is a good stop for pizza, sandwiches, salad, pastries, and espresso. ✉ *12781 Sir Francis Drake Blvd.,* ☎ *415/669–1244. MC, V.*

$$$–$$$$ ★ ✕ **Manka's.** Rustic wood-paneled dining rooms glowing with candlelight provide the setting for creative American cuisine. Specialties include line-caught fish, grilled caribou and pheasant, and homemade desserts. Two of the four smallish guest rooms above the restaurant have private decks overlooking Tomales Bay. Rooms in the redwood annex and two cabins are also available. The restaurant, open for dinner only, is closed on Tuesday and Wednesday year-round and from Sunday through Thursday January–March. ✉ *30 Calendar Way, 94937,* ☎ *415/669–1034. 14 rooms. Restaurant. MC, V. BP.*

$$$–$$$$ **Blackthorne Inn.** There's no other inn quite like the Blackthorne, a combination of whimsy and sophistication in a wooded setting. This imaginative structure has as its centerpiece a 3,500-square-ft deck. The solarium was made with timbers from San Francisco wharves; the outer walls are salvaged doors from a railway station. A glass-sheathed octagonal tower called the Eagle's Nest crowns the inn. ✉ *266 Vallejo Ave., Box 712, Inverness Park 94937,* ☎ *415/663–8621. 5 rooms, 2 with shared bath. Hot tub. MC, V. BP.*

$$$–$$$$ **Ten Inverness Way.** This is the kind of place where guests sit around after breakfast and share tips for hiking the nearby Point Reyes National Seashore. The living room of this low-key inn has a stone fireplace and a player piano. The rooms contain such homespun touches as patchwork quilts, well-worn antiques, and dormer ceilings with skylights. ✉ *Inverness Way, Box 63, 94937,* ☎ *415/669–1648,* FAX *415/669–7403. 5 rooms. Hot tub. MC, V. BP.*

Shopping

Shaker Shops West (✉ 5 Inverness Way, ☎ 415/669–7256) carries fine reproduction Shaker furniture and gift items.

Valley Ford

23 mi north of Point Reyes Station on Hwy. 1.

Bird-watching is a favorite pastime in Valley Ford, where blue herons, egrets, hawks, and owls nest.

Lodging

$–$$ **Inn at Valley Ford.** The rooms at this B&B, a Victorian farmhouse built in the late 1860s, are named after literary figures, characters, or periods. Books commemorating each chamber's theme grace the inn's bookshelves. The breakfast comes with old-fashioned cream scones. ✉ *14395 Hwy. 1, Box 439, 94972,* ☎ *707/876–3182. 4 rooms with shared baths. DC, MC, V. BP.*

SONOMA AND MENDOCINO

Occidental and Bodega Bay to Fort Bragg

The gently rolling countryside of coastal Marin gives way to more dramatic scenery north of Bodega Bay. Cattle cling for their lives (or so it seems) to steep inclines alongside the increasingly curvy highway, now traveling right along the coast. The stunning vistas make this one of the most attractive stretches of coastline north of San Francisco.

Occidental

10 mi from Valley Ford, north on Hwy. 1, east on Hwy. 12 (Bodega Hwy.), and north on Bohemian Hwy.

A village in a clearing that's surrounded by the redwood forests, orchards, and vineyards of western Sonoma County, Occidental is so small that you might drive right through the town and barely take notice. A 19th-century logging hub with a present-day bohemian feel, Occidental has a top-notch B&B, good eats, and a handful of art galleries and crafts and clothing boutiques, all of which make the town an ideal base for day trips to Sonoma Coast beaches, Bodega Bay, Armstrong Redwoods Reserve, and Point Reyes National Seashore.

Dining and Lodging

$–$$ ✕ **Bohemian Café.** The name says it all. This is California free-to-be-you-and-me at its best. Colorful murals hang on the walls, and the crowd is mostly young and clad in tie-dyed togs. The main lunch and dinner staple is pizza with a decidedly unconventional twist: the Mediterranean has rock shrimp, spinach, roasted peppers, and apricots; the Bustelo is an even more outré combination of tomato, bell pepper, onion, chorizo, cumin, pineapple, hot sauce, honey, and Parmesan cheese. Rounding out the menu are unusual salads (one with strawberries, spinach, and walnuts), plus some more mainstream pastas and entrées. Breakfast is served daily except Monday and Tuesday. ✉ *3688 Bohemian Hwy.,* ☎ *707/874–3931. Reservations not accepted. MC, V.*

$$$–$$$$ ★ **The Inn at Occidental.** Jack Bullard had to open an inn to have a place to show off his collections. Every room here showcases a collection of one sort or another. Antique English and Irish cut-glass jars decorate the Cut Glass room, which has its own sunny garden and outdoor whirlpool tub. A fireplace, fine Asian rugs, and antique clocks create a cozy but dignified mood in the ground-floor living room. Antiques, quilts, and original artwork fill the guest rooms in the main house. Bullard must have needed more exhibition space, because in late 1999 he added a new wing with eight more rooms. Homemade granola and fresh-squeezed orange juice are served for breakfast, along with entrées such as eggs Florentine or orange pancakes with Vermont maple syrup. ✉ *3657 Church St., Box 857, 95465,* ☎ *707/874–1047 or 800/522–6324,* FAX *707/874–1078. 16 rooms. AE, D, MC, V. BP.*

OFF THE BEATEN PATH — **OSMOSIS ENZYME BATHS** – The tiny town of Freestone, 3 mi south of Occidental and 7½ mi east of Bodega Bay off Highway 12 (Bodega Highway), is famous regionally as the home of the unique Osmosis Enzyme Baths. This spa, in a two-story clapboard house on extensive grounds, specializes in several treatments, including a detoxifying "dry" bath in a blend of enzymes and fragrant wood shavings. After 20 minutes in the tub, opt for a 75-minute massage in one of the freestanding Japanese-style pagodas near the creek that runs through the property. ✉ *209 Bohemian Hwy., Freestone,* ☎ *707/823–8231.*

Bodega Bay

❻ *8 mi from Valley Ford on Hwy. 1; 65 mi north of San Francisco via U.S. 101 and Hwy. 1.*

Bodega Bay (where Alfred Hitchcock's film *The Birds* takes place) is one of the busiest harbors on the Sonoma County coast. Commercial boats pursue fish as well as the famed Dungeness crabs. T-shirt shops and galleries line both sides of Highway 1; a short drive around the harbor leads to the Pacific. This is the last stop, town-wise, before Gualala, and a good spot for stretching your legs and taking in the salt air. For a closer look, visit the **Bodega Marine Laboratory** (☎ 707/875–2211 for directions), on a 326-acre reserve on nearby Bodega Head. The lab gives free one-hour tours and peeks at intertidal invertebrates, such as sea stars and sea anemones, on Friday from 2 to 3:45.

Dining and Lodging

$$$–$$$$ **Inn at the Tides.** The condominium-style buildings at this complex have spacious rooms with high ceilings and an uncluttered decor. All rooms have views of the harbor, and some have fireplaces. The inn's two restaurants ($$–$$$) serve both old-style and more adventurous seafood dishes. In season you can buy a slab of salmon or live or cooked crab at a seafood market across the highway and have the kitchen prepare it for you. ✉ *800 Hwy. 1, Box 640, 94923,* ☎ *707/875–2751 or 800/541–7788,* FAX *707/875–2669. 86 rooms. 2 restaurants, bar, refrigerators, room service, pool, hot tub, sauna, coin laundry. AE, MC, V. CP.*

$$$$ **Sonoma Coast Villa.** In this secluded spot in the coastal hills between Valley Ford and Bodega Bay sits a most unusual inn. Founded as an Arabian horse ranch in 1976, the 60-acre property has a single-story row of accommodations beside a swimming pool. Red-tile roofs, a stucco exterior, Mediterranean-style landscaping, and two courtyards create a European ambience. Rooms have slate floors, French doors, beam ceilings, and wood-burning fireplaces. The small restaurant serves full breakfasts and late-night weekend buffets to guests but is closed to the public. ✉ *16702 Hwy. 1, Bodega 94922,* ☎ *707/876–9818 or 888/404–2255,* FAX *707/876–9856. 12 rooms. Restaurant, pool, hot tub, spa. AE, MC, V.*

Outdoor Activities and Sports

Bodega Bay Sportfishing (✉ Bay Flat Rd., ☎ 707/875–3344) charters ocean-fishing boats and rents equipment. The operators of the 700-acre **Chanslor Guest Ranch** (✉ 2660 Hwy. 1, ☎ 707/875–2721) lead guided horseback rides.

Shopping

The **Ren Brown Gallery** (✉ 1781 Hwy. 1, ☎ 707/875–2922) in the north end of town is renowned for its selection of Asian arts, crafts, furnishings, and design books. This two-floor gallery also represents a number of local artists worth checking out.

Jenner

10 mi north of Bodega Bay on Hwy. 1.

The Russian River empties into the Pacific Ocean at Jenner. The town has a couple of good restaurants and some shops. South of the river is windy **Goat Rock State Beach,** where a colony of sea lions (walk north from the parking lot) resides most of the year. The beach is open daily from 8 AM to sunset; there's no day-use fee.

Dining

$$–$$$ ★ **River's End.** At the right time of year, diners at this rustic restaurant can view sea lions lazing on the beach below. The creative fare is eclectic with seafood, venison, and duck dishes ranging in style from Continental to Indonesian. ✉ *Hwy. 1, north end of Jenner,* ☎ *707/865–2484. MC, V. Closed weekdays Jan.–Feb. and Tues.–Wed. Mar.–June.*

Fort Ross State Historic Park

7 *9 mi north of Jenner on Hwy. 1.*

Fort Ross, completed in 1821, became Russia's major fur-trading outpost in California. The Russians brought Aleut hunters down from Alaska. By 1841 the area was depleted of seals and otters, and the Russians sold their post to John Sutter, later of gold-rush fame. After a local Anglo rebellion against the Mexicans, the land fell under U.S. domain, becoming part of California in 1850. The state park service has reconstructed Fort Ross, including its Russian Orthodox chapel, a redwood stockade, the officers' barracks, and a blockhouse. The excellent museum here documents the history of the fort and some of the North Coast. ✉ *Hwy. 1,* ☎ *707/847–3286.* 🎫 *$3 per vehicle (day use).* ⏲ *Daily 10–4:30. No dogs allowed past the parking lot.*

Lodging

$–$$$$ 🏨 **Fort Ross Lodge.** Conveniently located about 1½ mi north of the historic site, this lodge has a wind-bitten feel to it. Some of the rooms have views of the shoreline; others have private hot tubs. Six hill units have saunas, hot tubs, and fireplaces. ✉ *20705 Hwy. 1, 95450,* ☎ *707/847–3333,* FAX *707/847–3330. 22 rooms. Refrigerators. AE, MC, V.*

Salt Point State Park

❽ *11 mi north of Jenner on Hwy. 1.*

Salt Point State Park yields a glimpse of nature virtually untouched by humans. At the 6,000-acre park's **Gerstle Cove** you'll probably catch sight of seals sunning themselves on the beach and deer roaming in the meadow. Don't miss the unusual caverns in the sandstone, caused by centuries of erosion by wind and rain, called tafonis. A very short drive leads to Fisk Mill Cove. A five-minute walk uphill brings you to a dramatic overview of Sentinel Rock and the pounding surf below. ✉ *Hwy. 1,* ☎ *707/847–3221; 800/444–7275 for camping information.* 🎫 *$2 per vehicle (day use). Camping $12.* ⏲ *Daily sunrise–sunset.*

Kruse Rhododendron Reserve, a peaceful, 317-acre forested park, has thousands of rhododendrons that bloom in light shade in the late spring. ✉ *Hwy. 1, north of Fisk Mill Cove.* 🎫 *Free.*

Lodging

$–$$ 🏨 **Stillwater Cove Ranch.** Seventeen miles north of Jenner, this former boys' school that overlooks Stillwater Cove has been transformed into a pleasant, if spartan, place to lodge. ✉ *22555 Hwy. 1, 95450,* ☎ *707/847–3227. 6 rooms. No credit cards.*

Sea Ranch

18 mi northwest of Fort Ross on Hwy. 1.

Sea Ranch is a dramatically positioned development of stylish homes on 5,000 acres overlooking the Pacific. To appease critics the developers provided public beach–access trails off Highway 1 south of Gualala. Even some militant environmentalists deem the structures designed by William Turnbull and Charles Moore to be reasonably congruent with the surroundings; some folks find the weathered wood buildings beautiful.

Dining and Lodging

$$$$ ✕🏨 **Sea Ranch Lodge.** High on a bluff with ocean views, the lodge is close to beaches, trails, and golf. Some rooms have fireplaces, while others have hot tubs. Handcrafted wood furnishings and quilts create an earthy, contemporary look. The restaurant ($$–$$$), which overlooks the Pacific, serves good seafood and homemade desserts. ✉ *60 Sea Walk Dr., Box 44, 95497,* ☎ *707/785–2371 or 800/732–7262,* FAX *707/785–2243. 20 rooms, 2 suites. Restaurant. AE, MC, V. BP.*

$$–$$$$ 🏨 **Sea Ranch Escape.** The Sea Ranch houses, sparsely scattered on a grass meadow fronting a stretch of ocean, are a striking sight from Highway 1. Groups or families can rent fully furnished homes for two nights

or more. Linen, housekeeping, and catering services are available for a fee. You can dine at superb nearby restaurants or stock up on provisions from one of the markets in Gualala and make use of the full kitchens. All homes have TVs and VCRs, some have hot tubs, and some allow pets. The rates are most expensive for accommodations next to the surf. ✉ *60 Sea Walk Dr., Box 238, 95497,* ☎ *707/785–2426 or 800/732–7262,* FAX *707/785–2124. 55 houses. In-room VCRs. MC, V.*

Gualala

11 mi north of Sea Ranch on Hwy. 1

This former lumber port remains a sleepy drive-through except for the several ocean-view motels that serve as headquarters for visitors exploring the coast. The town lies north of the Gualala River—a good place for fishing. On the river's Sonoma side, **Gualala Point Regional Park** (✉ Hwy. 1, ☎ 707/785–2377), open daily from 8 AM until sunset, is an excellent whale-watching spot. The park has picnicking ($3 day-use fee) and camping ($15 per night). Campsites, available on a first-come, first-served basis, have fire rings, flush toilets, showers, and water but no hookups.

Dining and Lodging

$–$$$$ ✕ **St. Orres.** Two onion-dome towers evoke the area's Russian heritage at one of the North Coast's most eye-catching inns. The main house is further accented by balconies, stained-glass windows, and wood-inlaid towers. Two rooms overlook the sea, and the other six have views of the garden or a stand of pines. The tranquil woods behind the house hold 12 cottages; eight have woodstoves or fireplaces. The inn's restaurant (closed on Tuesday and Wednesday in winter) serves dinner only, a fixed-price meal ($$$–$$$$) with a choice of five entrées (meat or fish) plus soup and salad. ✉ *Hwy. 1, 2 mi north of Gualala, Box 523, 95445,* ☎ *707/884–3303,* FAX *707/884–3903. 8 rooms with shared baths, 12 cottages. Restaurant, hot tub, sauna, beach. MC, V. BP.*

$$$–$$$$ **Whale Watch Inn.** The largest accommodations at this inn are in the main house, but all have their merits. Most rooms do indeed have views (through cypress trees) down the coast, where whales often come close to shore on their northern migration in early spring. Year-round, the scent of pine and salt-sea air fills the rooms, all of which have fireplaces and small decks. Some rooms have whirlpool baths or kitchens. A 132-step stairway leads down to a small, virtually private beach. Set amid 2½ acres, the inn maintains well-kept gardens that bloom even in winter. Breakfast is served in your room. ✉ *35100 Hwy. 1, 95445,* ☎ *707/884–3667 or 800/942–5342,* FAX *707/884–4815. 18 rooms. AE, MC, V. BP.*

$$–$$$$ ★ **Old Milano Hotel.** Fronted by a greensward that sweeps down to the ocean cliffs, the Old Milano, a 1905 mansion on the National Register of Historic Places, is one of California's premier B&Bs. Exceptional antiques decorate the rooms. Five of the upstairs rooms have ocean views; all the upstairs rooms share bathrooms. The downstairs master suite has a private sitting room and a picture window framing the sea. Those in search of something different might consider one of the new cottages that have fireplaces or whirlpool baths or the caboose (yes, an authentic train car) with a wood-burning stove and brakeman's seats perfect for enjoying the sunset. Dinner, not included in the rates, is served on weekends and most weeknights. ✉ *38300 Hwy. 1, 95445,* ☎ *707/884–3256,* FAX *707/884–4249. 13 rooms. Hot tub. MC, V. BP.*

$ **Gualala Hotel.** Gualala's oldest hotel, which once housed timber-mill workers, has small, no-nonsense rooms furnished with well-worn antiques. Most rooms share baths. Rooms in the front have ocean views (and some street noise). The intensely atmospheric first-floor saloon was an old Jack London haunt. ✉ *39301 Hwy. 1,* ☎ *707/884–3441,* FAX *707/884–3908. 19 rooms, 5 with private bath. Restaurant, bar. AE, D, MC, V.*

En Route For a dramatic view of the surf and, in winter, migrating whales, take the marked road off Highway 1 north of the fishing village of Point Arena to the **Point Arena Lighthouse** (☎ 707/882–2777). First constructed in 1870, the lighthouse was destroyed by the 1906 earthquake that also devastated San Francisco. Rebuilt in 1907, it towers 115 ft from its base 50 ft above the sea. The lighthouse is open for tours daily from 11 until 3:30, from 10 in summer; admission is $2.50. As you continue north on Highway 1 toward Mendocino there are several beaches, most notably the one at **Manchester State Park,** 3 mi north of Point Arena. If you're driving directly to Mendocino from points south and want to grab a quick lunch or a good cup of coffee, visit the café at the **Greenwood Pier Inn** (✉ 5928 Hwy. 1, ☎ 707/877–9997) in Elk.

Elk

39 mi north of Gualala on Hwy. 1.

Dining and Lodging

$$$$ ✕🏨 **Harbor House.** Constructed in 1916 by a timber company, this redwood ranch-style house has a dining room with a view of the Pacific. Five of the six rooms in the main house have fireplaces, and some are furnished with antiques original to the house. There are also four smallish cottages with fireplaces and decks. The room rates include breakfast and dinner. The restaurant ($$; reservations essential), which serves California cuisine on a prix fixe menu, is highly recommended; there's limited seating for those not spending the night. ✉ *5600 S. Hwy. 1, 95432,* ☎ *707/877–3203 or 800/720–7474. 10 rooms. Restaurant. No credit cards. MAP.*

$$–$$$$ ★ ✕🏨 **Elk Cove Inn.** Innkeeper Elaine Bryant loves the look of surprise on guests' faces when they see the rooms perched on a bluff above the surf that pounds on a virtually private beach. The plushest suites are in a stone and cedar shingle Arts and Crafts–style building separate from the main house. All rooms have wet bars, refrigerators, stereos, and fireplaces; some have wood-burning stoves. The older accommodations range from a viewless but smartly furnished small room to a huge ocean-view suite with a whirlpool tub. The breakfast is a massive buffet. The dining room ($–$$), open Tuesday and Wednesday, serves California cuisine ranging from roast chicken to Thai shrimp. The full bar is open daily. Ask about off-season discount packages. ✉ *6300 S. Hwy. 1, Box 367, 95432,* ☎ *707/877–3321 or 800/275–2967,* FAX *707/877–1808. 10 rooms, 4 suites. Restaurant, bar, beach. AE, MC, V. BP.*

Albion

4 mi north of Elk on Hwy. 1.

Dining and Lodging

$$–$$$ ✕ **Ledford House.** There's nothing between this bluff-top restaurant and the Pacific Ocean but a great view. Entrées at this wood-and-glass structure are divided into hearty bistro dishes, mainly stews and pastas, and equally large-portioned examples of California cuisine—ahi tuna, grilled meats, and the like. ✉ *3000 N. Hwy. 1,* ☎ *707/937–0282. AE, MC, V. Closed Mon. in summer, Mon.–Tues. in winter. No lunch.*

$$$$ ✕🏨 **Albion River Inn.** Contemporary New England–style cottages at this inn overlook the dramatic bridge and seascape where the Albion

River empties into the Pacific. All but two have decks facing the ocean. Six have hot tubs with ocean views. The decor ranges from antique furnishings to wide-back willow chairs. In the glassed-in dining room ($$$), which serves grilled dishes and fresh seafood, the views are as captivating as the food. ✉ *3790 N. Hwy. 1, Box 100, 95410,* ☎ *707/937–1919; 800/479–7944 from northern CA;* FAX *707/937–2604. 20 rooms. Restaurant. AE, D, DC, MC, V. BP.*

Little River

3 mi north of Albion on Hwy. 1.

Van Damme State Park is one of the coast's best spots for abalone diving. The visitor center here has interesting displays on ocean life and Native American history. ✉ *Hwy. 1,* ☎ *707/937–5804 for park; 707/937–4016 for visitor center.*

The nearby **Pygmy Forest** contains wizened trees, some more than a century old, that stand only 3–4 ft tall. Highly acidic soil and poor drainage combine to stunt their growth. To reach the forest by car, turn east on Little River Airport Road, ½ mi south of Van Damme State Park, and continue 3½ mi to the clearly marked parking area.

Dining and Lodging

$$–$$$ ✕ **Little River Inn Restaurant.** There are fewer than a dozen entrées on the inn's menu, but they're varied: loin of lamb, petrale sole, grilled polenta with vegetables. Main courses come with soup or salad. Less expensive appetizers, salads, and sandwiches are served in the ocean-view Ole's Whale Watch Bar. ✉ *7551 N. Hwy. 1,* ☎ *707/937–5942. AE, MC, V.*

$$$–$$$$ ✕ **Heritage House.** The cottages at this resort have stunning ocean views. All the rooms contain plush furnishings and period antiques, and many have private decks, fireplaces, and whirlpool tubs. The dining room ($$$), also with a Pacific panorama, serves breakfast, brunch, and dinner. Salmon, quail, sirloin, and elegant desserts are the standouts on the evening menu. ✉ *Hwy. 1, 95456,* ☎ *707/937–5885 or 800/235–5885,* FAX *707/937–0318. 66 rooms. Restaurant. MC, V. Closed Jan.–mid-Feb. and most of Dec.*

$$–$$$$ ★ **Glendeven Inn.** The New England–style main house of this tranquil inn has five rooms, all with private baths, three with fireplaces. A converted barn holds an art gallery and a two-bedroom suite with a kitchen. The 1986 Stevenscroft building, whose four rooms have fireplaces, has a high gable roof and weathered barnlike siding. ✉ *8221 N. Hwy. 1, 95456,* ☎ *707/937–0083 or 800/822–4536,* FAX *707/937–6108. 9 rooms, 1 suite. AE, MC, V. BP.*

Mendocino

★ 9 *2 mi north of Little River on Hwy. 1; 153 mi from San Francisco, north on U.S. 101, west on Hwy. 128, and north on Hwy. 1.*

Logging created the first boom in the windswept town of Mendocino, which flourished for most of the second half of the 19th century. As the timber industry declined during the early 20th century many residents left, but the town's setting was too beautiful for it to remain neglected for long. Artists and craftspeople began flocking here in the 1950s, and in their wake came entrepreneurial types who opened restaurants, cafés, and inns. By the 1970s a full-scale revival was under way. A bit of the old town can be seen in such dives as Dick's Place, a bar near the Mendocino Hotel, but the rest of the small downtown area is devoted almost exclusively to contemporary restaurants and shops.

Mendocino may look familiar to fans of *Murder, She Wrote;* the town played the role of Cabot Cove, Maine, in the television show. The subterfuge worked because so many of the original settlers had come here from the Northeast and built houses in the New England style. The Blair House at 45110 Little Lake Street was the home of Jessica Fletcher (Angela Lansbury's character) in the series. Mendocino has also played the part of a California town, most notably in the Elia Kazan film of John Steinbeck's novel *East of Eden.* The building on Main Street (at Kasten Street) that houses the astronomy-oriented Out of This World store was the Bay City Bank in the 1955 movie, which starred James Dean.

An 1861 structure holds the **Kelley House Museum,** whose artifacts include antique cameras, Victorian-era clothing, furniture, and historical photographs of Mendocino's logging days. ✉ *45007 Albion St.,* ☎ *707/937–5791.* 🎫 *$1.* ⏲ *June–Sept., daily 1–4; Oct.–May, Fri.–Mon. 1–4.*

The **Mendocino Art Center** (✉ 45200 Little Lake St., ☎ 707/937–5818), which hosts exhibits and art classes and contains a gallery and a theater, is the nexus of Mendocino's flourishing art scene. The tiny green and red **Temple of Kwan Tai** (✉ Albion St., west of Kasten St., ☎ 707/937–5123), the oldest Chinese temple on the North Coast, dates from 1852. It's open only by appointment, but you can peer in the window and see everything there is to see.

The restored **Ford House,** built in 1854, serves as the visitor center for Mendocino Headlands State Park. The house has a scale model of Mendocino as it looked in 1890, when the town had 34 water towers and a 12-seat outhouse. History walks leave from Ford House on Saturday afternoon at 1. The park itself consists of the cliffs that border the town; access is free. ✉ *Main St., west of Lansing St.,* ☎ *707/937–5397.* 🎫 *Free.* ⏲ *Daily 11–4, with possible midweek closings in winter.*

★ The **Mendocino Coast Botanical Gardens** offer something for nature lovers every season. Even in winter, heather and Japanese tulips bloom. Along 2 mi of coastal trails, with ocean views and observation points for whale-watching, is a splendid array of flowers. The rhododendrons are at their peak from April through June, and fuchsias and azaleas are resplendent. You can have lunch or dinner at the on-site Gardens Grill. ✉ *18220 N. Hwy. 1, between Mendocino and Fort Bragg,* ☎ *707/964–4352.* 🎫 *$5.* ⏲ *Mar.–Oct., daily 9–5; Nov.–Feb., daily 9–4.*

Side Trip to the Anderson Valley

Mendocino's ocean breezes might seem too cool for grape growing, but summer days can be quite warm just over the hills in the Anderson Valley, where the cool nights permit a longer ripening period. Chardonnays and pinot noirs find the valley's climate particularly hospitable. Tasting here is a decidedly more laid-back affair than in the Napa and Sonoma valleys. Most tasting rooms are open from 11 to 5 daily and charge a nominal fee (usually deducted if you purchase any wines) to sample a few vintages. To get to the Anderson Valley from Mendocino take Highway 1 south to Highway 128 east.

Husch (✉ 4400 Hwy. 128, Philo, ☎ 707/895–3216), one of the valley's oldest wineries, sells award-winning chardonnays and a superb gewürztraminer. At the elegant tasting room at **Roederer Estate** (✉ 4501 Hwy. 128, Philo, ☎ 707/895–2288), you can taste (for $3) sparkling wines produced by the American affiliate of the famous French champagne maker. **Pacific Echo** (✉ 8501 Hwy. 128, Philo, ☎ 800/824–7754) was the first Anderson Valley winery to produce award-winning sparkling wines. If you're not up for a trip to the valley, **Fet-**

zer Vineyards (✉ Main St. between Lansing and Kasten Sts., Mendocino, ☎ 707/937–6191) has a tasting room next to the Mendocino Hotel.

Dining and Lodging

$$$ ★ ✕ **Cafe Beaujolais.** This famous restaurant is housed in a charming cottage that makes it all the more appealing. The ever-evolving menu is cross-cultural and includes such delicacies as Yucatecan Thai crab cakes and a barbecued rock-shrimp-filled corn crepe with avocado and blood-orange pico de gallo. Owner Margaret Fox runs the mail-order Cafe Beaujolais bakery—be sure to take home a package or two of her irresistible *panforte,* a dense cake made with almonds, hazelnuts, or macadamia nuts. ✉ *961 Ukiah St.,* ☎ *707/937–5614. MC, V.*

$$–$$$ ✕ **955 Ukiah.** The interior of this smart restaurant is woodsy and the California cuisine creative. Specialties include fresh fish, duck cannelloni, peppercorn New York steak, and pastas topped with the house sauce. ✉ *955 Ukiah St.,* ☎ *707/937–1955. MC, V. Closed Mon.–Tues. July–Nov., Mon.–Wed. Dec.–June. No lunch.*

$$$$ ★ ✕🏨 **Stanford Inn by the Sea.** This warm, family-run property is spread among several buildings set back from the highway. The older rooms have wood-paneling; the newer ones are quite chic, and suites have ocean-view decks, four-poster or sleigh beds, fireplaces or woodstoves, and paintings by local artists. The inn is the only one on the North Coast with an organic garden *and* resident llamas. The inn's dining room ($$–$$$) serves pizzas, salads, soups, pastas, and, for dinner only, gourmet vegetarian entrées. ✉ *South of Mendocino, east on Comptche–Ukiah Rd. (off Hwy. 1), Box 487, 95460,* ☎ *707/937–5615 or 800/331–8884,* FAX *707/937–0305. 23 rooms, 10 suites. Refrigerators, indoor pool, hot tub, sauna, bicycles. AE, D, DC, MC, V. BP.* 🚭

$$–$$$$ ✕🏨 **MacCallum House.** With the most meticulously restored Victorian exterior in Mendocino, this 1882 inn, complete with gingerbread trim, transports patrons back to another era. Comfortable furnishings and antiques enhance the period feel. In addition to the main house, there are individual cottages and barn suites around a garden with a gazebo. The menu at the redwood-paneled restaurant ($$–$$$; reservations essential) changes quarterly. The focus is on local seafood and organic and free-range meats. ✉ *45020 Albion St., Box 206, 95460,* ☎ *707/937–0289 or 800/609–0492. 20 rooms. Restaurant, bar. MC, V.*

$$–$$$$ ✕🏨 **Mendocino Hotel & Garden Suites.** From the street, this hotel looks like something out of the Wild West, with a period facade and balcony that overhangs the raised sidewalk. Stained-glass lamps, polished wood, and Persian carpets lend the hotel a swank 19th-century appeal. All but 14 of the rooms have private baths. Deluxe garden rooms have fireplaces and TVs. The wood-paneled dining room ($$–$$$), fronted by a glassed-in solarium, serves fine fish entrées and the best deep-dish ollalieberry pies in California. ✉ *45080 Main St., Box 587, 95460,* ☎ *707/937–0511 or 800/548–0513,* FAX *707/937–0513. 51 rooms. Restaurant, bar, room service. AE, MC, V.* 🚭

$$–$$$$ 🏨 **Agate Cove Inn.** Facing the Mendocino Headlands across a rocky cove, this inn is ideally situated for watching whales during the winter. Adirondack chairs are set on a small deck for just that purpose; borrow the inn's binoculars for a closer look. Each blue-and-white cottage unit is individually decorated, mostly in quilts, floral wallpaper, and canopy or four-poster beds. There are four single and four duplex cottages; two more rooms are in the 1860s farmhouse, where country breakfasts are prepared on an antique woodstove in a kitchen with a full view of the Pacific. ✉ *11201 N. Lansing St., 95460,* ☎ *707/937–0551,* FAX *707/937–0550. 10 rooms. MC, V. BP.* 🚭

$$–$$$$ 🏨 **C. O. Packard House.** One of four landmark homes on "Executive Row," this Carpenter's Gothic Victorian was opened in 1998 by a hus-

band-and-wife team of interior decorators. Four oddly shaped rooms are dazzlingly sophisticated with custom wall finishings, jet massage baths, and a mix of French and English antiques. A garden cottage is large enough to accommodate four but is less elegant than the rooms in the main house. ✉ *45170 Little Lake St., 95460,* ☎ *707/937–2677 or 888/453–2677,* FAX *707/937–1323. 4 rooms and 1 cottage. D, DC, MC, V. BP.*

$$–$$$$ **Joshua Grindle Inn.** The original farmhouse of this B&B on a 2-acre hilltop has five guest rooms, a parlor, and a dining room. Two other buildings, the Watertower (an upper room has windows on all four sides) and the Cottage, hold five additional rooms. Furnishings throughout are simple but comfortable American antiques: Salem rockers, wing chairs, steamer-trunk tables, painted pine beds. ✉ *44800 Little Lake Rd., 95460,* ☎ *707/937–4143. 10 rooms. MC, V. Full breakfast.*

$–$$$$ **Blackberry Inn.** Each single-story unit here has a false front, creating the image of a frontier town. There's a bank, a saloon, Belle's Place (of hospitality), and "offices" for doctors and sheriffs, as well as other themed accommodations. The rooms are cheery and spacious. Most have wood-burning stoves or fireplaces and at least partial ocean views. The inn is a short drive east of town down a quiet side street. Two rooms have kitchenettes. ✉ *44951 Larkin Rd., 95460,* ☎ *707/937–5281 or 800/950–7806,* FAX *707/937–3136. 16 rooms. MC, V. CB.*

$–$$$$ ★ **Whitegate Inn.** With a white picket fence, a latticework gazebo, and a romantic garden, the Whitegate is a picture-book Victorian. High ceilings, floral fabrics, and pastel walls define the public spaces and the luxurious rooms, some of which have fireplaces. Best of all, you can watch the ocean breakers from the deck out back. ✉ *499 Howard St., 95460,* ☎ *707/937–4892 or 800/531–7282,* FAX *707/937–1131. 6 rooms. AE, D, DC, MC, V. BP.*

Nightlife and the Arts

Mendocino Theatre Company (✉ Mendocino Art Center, 42500 Little Lake St., ☎ 707/937–4477) has been around for more than two decades. The community theater's repertoire ranges from such classics as *Uncle Vanya* to more recent plays such as *Other People's Money.*

Patterson's Pub (✉ 10485 Lansing St., ☎ 707/937–4782), an Irish-style watering hole, is a friendly gathering place day or night, though it does become boisterous as the evening wears on. Bands entertain on Friday night.

Outdoor Activities and Sports

Catch-a-Canoe and Bicycles Too (✉ Stanford Inn by the Sea, Mendocino, ☎ 707/937–0273) rents regular and outrigger canoes as well as mountain and suspension bicycles.

Shopping

Many artists exhibit their wares in Mendocino, and the streets of this compact town are so easily walkable that you're sure to find a gallery with something that strikes your fancy. You might start at the **Mendocino Art Center** (☞ *above*). **Old Gold** (✉ 6 Albion St., ☎ 707/937–5005) is a good place to look for locally crafted jewelry.

Fort Bragg

10 mi north of Mendocino on Hwy. 1.

Fort Bragg has changed more than any other coastal town in the past few years. The decline in what was the top industry, timber, is being offset in part by a boom in charter-boat excursions and other tourist pursuits. The city is also attracting many artists, some lured from Mendocino, where the cost of living is higher. This basically blue-collar town is the commercial center of Mendocino County.

The **Skunk Train,** a remnant of the region's logging days, dates from 1885 and travels a route—through redwood forests inaccessible to automobiles—from Fort Bragg to the town of Willits, 40 mi inland. A fume-spewing self-propelled train car that shuttled passengers along the railroad earned the nickname Skunk Train, and the entire line has been called that ever since. Excursions are now given on historic trains and replicas of the Skunk Train motorcar that smell less foul than the original. In summer you can go partway, to Northspur, a three-hour round-trip, or make the full seven-hour journey to Willits and back. ✉ *Foot of Laurel St., Fort Bragg,* ☎ *707/964–6371 or 800/777–5865.* 🎫 *$35 for Fort Bragg–Willits, $27 for Fort Bragg–Northspur.* ⏲ *Fort Bragg–Northspur: departs early June–late Sept., daily 9:20 AM and 1:40 PM; Fort Bragg–Willits: late Sept.–mid-June, daily 10 AM and 2 PM.*

★ ❿ **MacKerricher State Park** includes 10 mi of sandy beach and several square miles of dunes. Fishing (at two freshwater lakes, one stocked with trout), canoeing, hiking, jogging, bicycling, camping (☞ *below*), and harbor-seal watching at Laguna Point are among the popular activities, many of which are accessible to travelers with disabilities. Whales can often be spotted from December to mid-April from the nearby headland. Rangers lead nature hikes throughout the year. ✉ *Hwy. 1, 3 mi north of Fort Bragg,* ☎ *707/937–5804.* 🎫 *Free.*

Dining, Lodging, and Camping

$–$$$ ✕ **Sharon's by the Sea.** The views of Noyo Harbor are up close and scenic at this one-story restaurant at the end of the pier. Seafood is the other reason to visit this unpretentious establishment, which replaced another restaurant at this site. ✉ *32096 No. Harbor Dr., at the south end of Fort Bragg,* ☎ *707/962–0680. AE, MC, V.*

$$ ✕ **The Restaurant.** The name may be generic, but this place isn't. California cuisine is served in a dining room that doubles as an art gallery. A jazz brunch takes place on Sunday. ✉ *418 N. Main St.,* ☎ *707/964–9800. MC, V. Closed Wed. No lunch Mon., Tues., Wed.*

$–$$ ✕ **Samraat Restaurant.** Soothing pastels and sitar music set the mood for good, inexpensive Indian dishes. Tandoori, curry, and seafood are specialties. ✉ *546 S. Main St.,* ☎ *707/964–0386. MC, V.*

$ ✕ **Headlands Coffee House.** The coffeehouse acts as a cultural center and local gathering place. Musicians perform most nights. ✉ *120 E. Laurel St.,* ☎ *707/964–1987. No credit cards.*

$$–$$$ 🏨 **Weller House Inn.** This 1886 mansion was transformed into an inn in 1998. Guest accommodations on the first and second floors are decorated with Victorian-style wallpaper and furnishings; the baths have hand-painted tiles. The third floor features a 900-square-ft ballroom (now the breakfast room) paneled in rare California redwood. ✉ *524 Stewart St., 95437,* ☎ *707/964–4415 or 800/877–8935,* FAX *707/964–4198. 8 rooms. Breakfast room. AE, D, DC, MC, V. BP.*

$–$$$ 🏨 **Surf and Sand Lodge.** You have to go north of Fort Bragg to find lodgings with unimpeded ocean views, and they're just what you'll get at this souped-up motel. As its name implies, it's practically on the beach. Right out the door are pathways down to the rock-strewn shore. The six cheaper rooms don't have views, but all the bright and fresh accommodations come with enough amenities (including coffeemakers, hair dryers, and binoculars) to make you feel that you're staying somewhere grander than a motel. The fancier of the second-story rooms have hot tubs and fireplaces. ✉ *1131 N. Main St., 95437,* ☎ *707/964–9383 or 800/964–0184,* FAX *707/964–0314. 30 rooms. Refrigerators, in-room VCRs. AE, D, MC, V.*

MacKerricher State Park. The campsites at MacKerricher (☞ *above*) are in woodsy settings ¼ mi or so from the ocean. Reservations on summer weekends should be made as early as possible, although each day 25 sites are available on a first-come, first-served basis. ✉ *Hwy. 1, 3 mi north of Fort Bragg,* ☎ *707/937–5804 for park; 800/444–7275 for campsite reservations taken Apr.–mid-Oct.* *$12 per campsite. 143 sites.*

Nightlife

Caspar Inn & Blues Cafe (✉ 14957 Caspar Rd., ☎ 707/964–5565) presents blues, rock, and alternative rock Thursday through Saturday.

Outdoor Activities and Sports

Ricochet Ridge Ranch (✉ 24201 N. Hwy. 1, ☎ 707/964–7669) guides groups on horseback to the Mendocino–Fort Bragg beaches. **Matlick's *Tally Ho II*** (✉ 11845 N. Main St., ☎ 707/964–2079) operates whale-watching trips from December through mid-April, as well as fishing excursions all year.

En Route North on Highway 1 from Fort Bragg past the mill town of Westport, the road cuts inland around the **King Range,** a stretch of mountain so rugged that it was impossible to build the intended major highway through it. Highway 1 joins U.S. 101 at the town of Leggett. **Richardson Grove State Park,** north of Leggett along U.S. 101, marks your first encounter with the truly giant redwoods, but there are even more magnificent stands farther north in Humboldt and Del Norte counties.

REDWOOD COUNTRY

Garberville to Crescent City

The majestic redwoods that grace California's coast become more plentiful as you head north. Their towering ancient presence defines the landscape.

Garberville

70 mi from Fort Bragg, north and east on Hwy. 1 and north on U.S. 101; 197 mi north of San Francisco on U.S. 101.

Although it's the largest town in the vicinity of Humboldt Redwoods State Park, Garberville hasn't changed a whole lot since timber was king. The town is a pleasant place to stop for lunch, pick up picnic provisions, or poke through arts-and-crafts stores. A few miles below Garberville is an elegant Tudor resort, the **Benbow Inn** (☞ *below*). Even if you are not staying there, stop in for a drink or a meal and take a look at the architecture and gardens.

Dining and Lodging

$ ✕ **Woodrose Cafe.** This unpretentious eatery serves basic breakfast items on the weekends and healthy lunches every day. Dishes include chicken, pasta, and vegetarian specials. ✉ *911 Redwood Dr.,* ☎ *707/923–3191. No credit cards. No dinner.*

$$$–$$$$ ★ ✕ **Benbow Inn.** South of Garberville alongside the Eel River, this three-story Tudor-style manor resort is the equal of any in the region. The most luxurious of the antiques-filled rooms are on the terrace, with fine river views; some rooms have fireplaces, and 18 have TVs with VCRs. Guests have canoeing, tennis, golf, and pool privileges at an adjacent property. The wood-panel dining room ($$–$$$) serves American cuisine, with the focus on fresh salmon and trout. ✉ *445 Lake Benbow Dr., 95542,* ☎ *707/923–2124 or 800/355–3301. 55 rooms, 1 cottage. Restaurant, lobby lounge, refrigerators, lake. AE, D, MC, V. Closed early Jan.–early Apr.*

Humboldt Redwoods State Park

11 *15 mi north of Garberville on U.S. 101.*

The **Avenue of the Giants** (Highway 254) begins about 7 mi north of Garberville and winds north, more or less parallel to U.S. 101, toward Pepperwood. Some of the tallest trees on the planet tower over this stretch of two-lane blacktop. The Avenue follows the south fork of the Eel River and cuts through part of the more than 53,000-acre Humboldt Redwoods State Park.

At the **Humboldt Redwoods State Park Visitor Center** you can pick up information about the redwoods, waterways, and recreational opportunities. Brochures are available for a self-guided auto tour of the park. Stops on the auto tour include short and long hikes into redwood groves. ✉ *Avenue of the Giants, 2 mi south of Weott,* ☎ *707/946–2409 for park; 707/946–2263 for visitor center.* *Free; $2 day-use fee for parking and facilities in Williams Grove and Women's Federation Grove.* ⏲ *Park open 24 hrs year-round. Visitor center Mar.–Oct., daily 9–5; Nov.–Feb., Thurs.–Sun. 10–4.*

Four miles north of the visitor center on the Avenue of the Giants is **Founders Grove,** reached via a ½-mi trail. One of the most impressive trees here—the 362-ft-long Dyerville Giant—fell to the ground in 1991; its root base points skyward 35 ft. Six miles north of the Visitor Center on Mattole Road is **Rockefeller Forest.** The largest remaining coast redwood forest, it contains 40 of the 100 tallest trees in the world.

Ferndale

12 *30 mi from Weott, north on U.S. 101 to Hwy. 211 west.*

The residents of the stately town of Ferndale maintain some of the most sumptuous Victorian homes in California, many of them built by 19th-century Scandinavian, Swiss, and Portuguese dairy farmers who were drawn to the mild climate. The queen of them all is the **Gingerbread Mansion** (☞ Lodging, *below*). A beautiful sloped graveyard sits on Ocean Avenue west of Main Street. Many shops carry a map with self-guided tours of this lovingly preserved town.

The main building of the **Ferndale Museum** hosts changing exhibitions of Victoriana and has an old-style barbershop and a display of Wiyot Indian baskets. In the annex are a horse-drawn buggy, a re-created blacksmith's shop, and antique farming, fishing, and dairy equipment. ✉ *515 Shaw Ave.,* ☎ *707/786–4466.* *$1.* ⏲ *June–Sept., Tues.–Sat. 11–4, Sun. 1–4; Oct.–Dec. and Feb.–May, Wed.–Sat. 11–4, Sun. 1–4.*

Lodging

$$$–$$$$ **Gingerbread Mansion.** This photogenic Victorian B&B rivals San Francisco's "painted ladies" for dazzle. The mansion's carved friezes set off its gables, and turrets delight the eye. The comfortable parlors and spacious bedrooms are laid out in flowery Victorian splendor. Some rooms have views of the mansion's English garden, and one has side-by-side bathtubs. The newer of the two spectacular suites is the Veneto, which features handpainted scenes of Venice on the walls and ceiling as well as marble floors. Ask about off-season discounts. ✉ *400 Berding St., off Brown St., Box 40, 95536,* ☎ *707/786–4000 or 800/952–4136. 10 rooms, 2 suites. AE, MC, V. Full breakfast.*

Outdoor Activities and Sports

Eel River Delta Tours (✉ 285 Morgan Slough Rd., ☎ 707/786–4187) conducts a two-hour boat trip that emphasizes the wildlife and history of the Eel River's estuary and salt marsh.

Shopping

Ferndale's shops are lined up along Main Street. **Golden Gait Mercantile** (✉ 421 Main St., ☎ 707/786–4891) seems to be lost in a time warp, what with Burma Shave products and old-fashioned long johns as well as penny candy. For gifts, you can't do better than **The Cottage at Withywindle** (✉ 358 Main St., ☎ 707/786–4763), which specializes in home accessories from rugs to clocks and antiques, and carries a selection of gourmet products.

Eureka

13 *10 mi north of Ferndale and 269 mi north of San Francisco on U.S. 101.*

Eureka, population 28,500, is the North Coast's largest city. It has gone through cycles of boom and bust, first with mining and later with timber and fishing. There are nearly 100 Victorian buildings here, many of them well preserved. The most splendid is the **Carson Mansion** (✉ M and 2nd Sts.), built in 1885 for timber baron William Carson. A private men's club occupies the house. Across the street is another extravaganza popularly known as the **Pink Lady.**

For proof that contemporary architects have the skills to design lovely Victoriana, take a look at the **Carter House** (✉ 3rd and L Sts.) B&B and keep in mind that it was built in the 1980s, not the 1880s.

At the **Chamber of Commerce** you can pick up maps with self-guided driving tours of Eureka's architecture, and find out about organized tours. ✉ *2112 Broadway,* ☎ *707/442–3738 or 800/356–6381.* ⏲ *Weekdays 9–5.*

The **Clarke Memorial Museum** contains extraordinary northwestern California Native American basketry and artifacts of Eureka's Victorian, logging, and maritime eras. ✉ *240 E St.,* ☎ *707/443–1947.* 🎫 *Donations accepted.* ⏲ *Feb.–Dec., Tues.–Sat. noon–4.*

The structure that gave **Fort Humboldt State Historic Park** its name once protected white settlers from the Native Americans. Ulysses S. Grant was posted here in 1854. The old fort is no longer around, but on its grounds are a museum, some ancient steam engines (operators rev them up on the third Saturday of the month), and a logger's cabin. The park is a good place for a picnic. ✉ *3431 Fort Ave.,* ☎ *707/445–6567.* 🎫 *Free.* ⏲ *Daily 9–5.*

To explore the waters around Eureka, take a **Humboldt Bay Harbor Cruise.** You can observe some of the region's bird life while sailing past fishing boats and decaying timber mills during a 75-minute narrated cruise. ✉ *Pier at C St.,* ☎ *707/445–1910 or 707/444–9440.* 🎫 *$9.50; cocktail-cruise fare $6.50.* ⏲ *Departs May–Oct., daily 1, 2:30, and 4 (no 4 o'clock cruise on Sun.). Cocktail cruise departs Tues.–Sat. at 5:30.*

Dining and Lodging

$$–$$$ ✕ **Restaurant 301.** Mark and Christi Carter, owners of Eureka's fanciest hotels, also run the town's best restaurant. Most of the vegetables and herbs used here are grown at the hotel's greenhouse and nearby ranch. Try the sea scallops, roasted pork chop, spring rack of lamb, or local petrale sole, and don't skip the appetizers—especially if the vegetable ragouts or gnocchi are on the menu. The wine list is one of the finest in the country. ✉ *301 L St.,* ☎ *707/444–8062. AE, D, DC, MC, V. No lunch.*

$$ ✕ **Chemin de Fer.** The prix fixe menu changes daily but often includes the likes of grilled duck, prawns with curry and pears, pork tenderloin, sea scallops with mango, and nearly a dozen first courses. The

dessert list is even longer. ✉ *518 F St.,* ☎ *707/441–9292. AE, MC, V. Closed Mon. No lunch weekends.*

$–$$ ✕ **Cafe Waterfront.** This small eatery across from the marina has a long bar with a TV. Sandwiches and affordable seafood dishes are the menu mainstays. ✉ *102 F St.,* ☎ *707/443–9190. MC, V.*

$–$$ ✕ **Celestino's in Old Town.** Pastas and made-to-order pizzas dominate the menu of this large restaurant, which serves grilled meats and several vegetarian choices (as well as vegan dishes on request). The tasty appetizers include grilled eggplant rolls and fried calamari. ✉ *421 3rd St.,* ☎ *707/444–8995. AE, MC, V. Closed Mon. No lunch Sat.*

$ ✕ **Ramone's.** A casual bakery café, Ramone's serves light sandwiches. ✉ *2223 Harrison Ave.,* ☎ *707/442–6082. MC, V. No dinner.*

$ ★ ✕ **Samoa Cookhouse.** The recommendation here is more for atmosphere, of which there is plenty: this is a longtime loggers' hangout. The Samoa's cooks serve three substantial set meals family style at long wooden tables. Meat dishes predominate. Save room (if possible) for dessert. ✉ *Cookhouse Rd. (from U.S. 101, cross Samoa Bridge, turn left onto Samoa Rd., then left 1 block later onto Cookhouse Rd.),* ☎ *707/442–1659. AE, D, MC, V.*

$$$–$$$$ ★ **Carter House.** Whether you like small inns, country hotels, or the charm of a cottage, the Carter family has something to offer. The Carter House, built in 1982 following the floor plan of a San Francisco mansion, has large rooms with heirloom furniture. Two doors down, the three-room Victorian Bell Cottage is decorated in contemporary Southwestern style. The three-story Hotel Carter, catercorner to the Carter House, has an elegant lobby and suites. Breakfast is served in the hotel's sunny corner dining room. ✉ *301 L St., 95501,* ☎ *707/444–8062,* FAX *707/445–8067. 35 rooms, 8 suites. AE, D, DC, MC, V. BP.*

$$–$$$$ ★ **An Elegant Victorian Mansion.** This meticulously restored Eastlake mansion in a residential neighborhood east of the Old Town lives up to its name. Each room is completely decked out in period furnishings and wall coverings, down to the carved-wood beds, fringed lamp shades, and pull-chain commodes. The innkeepers may even greet you in vintage clothing and entertain you with silent movies on tape, old records played on the windup Victrola, croquet on the rose-encircled lawn, and guided tours of local Victoriana in their antique automobile. ✉ *1406 C St., 95501,* ☎ *707/444–3144,* FAX *707/442–5594. 4 rooms. Sauna, croquet, bicycles, laundry service. MC, V. BP.*

Nightlife

Lost Coast Brewery & Cafe (✉ 617 4th St., ☎ 707/445–4480), a bustling microbrewery, is the best place in town to relax with a pint of ale or porter. Soups, salads, and light meals are served for lunch and dinner.

Outdoor Activities and Sports

Hum-Boats (✉ 2 F St., ☎ 707/443–5157) provides sailing rides, sailboat rentals, guided kayak tours, and sea kayak rentals and lessons (year round; by appointment only in winter). The company also runs a water-taxi service on Humboldt Bay.

Shopping

Eureka has several art galleries in the district running from C to I streets between 2nd and 3rd streets. Specialty shops in Old Town include the original **Restoration Hardware** (✉ 417 2nd St., ☎ 707/443–3152), a good place to find stylish yet functional home and garden accessories and clever polishing and cleaning products. The **Irish Shop** (✉ 334 2nd St., ☎ 707/443–8343) carries imports from the Emerald Isle, mostly fine woolens.

Arcata

14 *9 mi north of Eureka on U.S. 101.*

The home of Humboldt State University is one of the few California burgs to retain a town square. A farmers' market takes place in the square on Saturday morning from May through November. For a self-guided tour of Arcata that includes some of its restored Victorian buildings, pick up a map from the **Chamber of Commerce** (✉ 1062 G St., ☎ 707/822–3619), open weekdays from 10 to 4.

Dining and Lodging

$–$$ ✕ **Abruzzi.** Salads and hefty pasta dishes take up most of the menu at this upscale Italian restaurant in the lower level of Jacoby's Storehouse, off the town square. One specialty is linguine *pescara,* with a spicy seafood-and-tomato sauce. ✉ *H and 8th Sts.,* ☎ *707/826–2345. AE, D, MC, V. No lunch.*

$ ✕ **Crosswinds.** This restaurant serves Continental cuisine in a sunny Victorian setting, at prices that attract students from Humboldt State University. ✉ *10th and I Sts.,* ☎ *707/826–2133. MC, V. Closed Mon. No dinner.*

$–$$$ 🏨 **Hotel Arcata.** Rooms are clean and modest, but flowered bedspreads and claw-foot bathtubs lend a bit of character to this historic landmark overlooking the town square. ✉ *708 9th St., 95521,* ☎ *707/826–0217 or 800/344–1221,* FAX *707/826–1737. 32 rooms. Restaurant. AE, D, DC, MC, V. CP.*

Shopping

For its size, Arcata has an impressive selection of book, housewares, clothing, fabric, and other shops, especially near its town square. **Plaza Design** (✉ 808 G St., ☎ 707/822–7732) specializes in gifts, papers, and innovative furnishings.

Trinidad

14 mi north of Arcata on U.S. 101.

Trinidad got its name from the Spanish mariners who entered the bay on Trinity Sunday, June 9, 1775. The town became a principal trading post for the mining camps along the Klamath and Trinity rivers. As mining, and then whaling, faded, so did the luster of this former boomtown. Development has overlooked this scenic spot for now, making it one of the quietest towns that still has inns and dining spots. Picturesque Trinidad Bay's harbor cove and rock formations look both raw and tranquil.

Dining and Lodging

$–$$ ★ ✕ **Larrupin' Cafe.** Considered by many locals to be one of the best places to eat on the North Coast, this restaurant has earned widespread fame for its mesquite-grilled ribs and fresh fish dishes, served in a bright-yellow two-story house on a quiet country road 2 mi north of Trinidad. ✉ *1658 Patrick's Point Dr.,* ☎ *707/677–0230. Reservations essential. No credit cards. Closed Mon.–Tues. in winter, Tues. in summer. No lunch.*

$–$$ ✕ **Merryman's Restaurant.** Fresh fish and a romantic oceanfront setting make this a perfect spot for hungry romance lovers. ✉ *100 Moonstone Beach,* ☎ *707/677–3111. No credit cards. Closed weekdays Oct.–early Apr. No lunch.*

$ ✕ **Seascape.** With its glassed-in main room and deck for outdoor dining, this casual spot is an ideal place to take in the scenery of Trinidad Bay. The breakfasts are great, the lunches are substantial, and the dinners showcase local seafood. ✉ *At pier,* ☎ *707/677–3762. MC, V.*

$$$ **Trinidad Bay Bed & Breakfast.** This Cape Cod–style shingle house overlooks the harbor and the coastline to the south. The innkeepers provide a wealth of information about the nearby wilderness, beach, and fishing habitats. A crackling fire warms the living room in chilly weather. *560 Edwards St., Box 849, 95570, 707/677–0840, FAX 707/677–9245. 2 rooms and 2 suites (1 with fireplace). MC, V. BP. Closed Dec.–Jan.*

$$–$$$ **Turtle Rocks Oceanfront Inn.** Unobstructed ocean views from most of the rooms make this inn a desirable choice for nature lovers. Named for some of the enormous formations within view offshore, this B&B has a two-tier "Whale Watch" deck where you can sit on rocking chairs or chaise longues and take catnaps or scan the horizon. Contemporary and antique furnishings decorate the spacious rooms, all but one of which have decks. *3392 Patrick's Point Dr., 95570, 707/677–3707. 6 rooms, 1 suite. MC, V. BP.*

Patrick's Point State Park

15 *5 mi north of Trinidad and 25 mi north of Eureka on U.S. 101.*

Patrick's Point is the ultimate California coastal park. On a forested plateau almost 200 ft above the surf, it has stunning views of the Pacific, great whale- and sea-lion-watching in season, picnic areas, bike paths, and hiking trails through old-growth forest. There are tidal pools at Agate Beach and a small museum with natural-history exhibits. The park's campsites have fire rings, flush toilets, showers, and water. *707/677–3570. $2 per vehicle (day use); Camping $12 per vehicle.*

Redwood National and State Parks

16 *22 mi north (Orick entrance) of Trinidad on U.S. 101.*

After 115 years of intensive logging, this 106,000-acre parcel of tall trees came under government protection in 1968, marking the California environmentalists' greatest victory over the timber industry. Redwood National and State Parks encompasses three state parks (Prairie Creek Redwoods, Del Norte Coast Redwoods, and Jedediah Smith Redwoods) and is more than 40 mi long. There is no admission fee to the national or state parks, but the state parks charge $2 to use facilities such as the beach or picnic areas. *Park Headquarters, 1111 2nd St., Crescent City, 707/464–6101 ext. 5064.*

At the **Redwood Information Center** you can get brochures, advice, and a free permit to drive up the steep, 17-mi road (the last 6 mi are gravel) to reach the **Tall Trees Grove,** where a 3-mi round-trip hiking trail leads to the world's first-, third-, and fifth-tallest redwoods. Whale-watchers will find the deck of the visitor center an excellent observation point, and birders will enjoy the nearby Freshwater Lagoon, a popular layover for migrating waterfowl. *Off U.S. 101, Orick, 707/464–6101 ext. 5265.*

Within **Lady Bird Johnson Grove,** off Bald Hills Road, is a short circular trail to resplendent redwoods. This section of the park was dedicated by, and named for, the former first lady. For additional views, take Davison Road to Fern Canyon. This gravel road winds through 4 mi of second-growth redwoods, then hugs a bluff 100 ft above the pounding Pacific surf for another 4 mi.

To reach the entrance to **Prairie Creek Redwoods State Park** (707/464–6101 ext. 5300) take the Prairie Parkway exit off the U.S. 101 bypass. Extra space has been paved alongside the parklands, providing fine vantage points from which to observe an imposing herd of Roosevelt elk grazing in the adjoining meadow. Revelation Trail in Prairie Creek is fully accessible to visitors with disabilities.

Lodging and Camping

$ **Hostelling International—Redwood National Park.** This century-old inn is a stone's throw from the ocean; hiking begins just beyond its doors. Lodging is dormitory style. *14480 U.S. 101, at Wilson Creek Rd. (20 mi north of Orick), Klamath, 95548, ☎ FAX 707/482–8265. No credit cards.*

Freshwater Lagoon. A strip of sand between the ocean and Freshwater Lagoon holds an unofficial, primitive campground with no water or hookups—but great views. *West side of U.S. 101, 1½ mi south of Orick (¼ mi south of Redwood Information Center), ☎ 707/464–6101 ext. 5265. $5 donation.*

Crescent City

40 mi north of Orick on U.S. 101.

Del Norte County's largest town (population just under 5,000) is named for the shape of its harbor; during the 1800s this was an important steamship stop. At the bottom of B Street at **Popeye's Landing** you can rent a crab pot, buy some bait, and try your luck at crabbing. At low tide from April through September, you can walk from the pier across the ocean floor to the oldest lighthouse on the North Coast, **Battery Point Lighthouse** (☎ 707/464–3089). Tours ($2) of the 1856 structure are given from May through October, Wednesday through Sunday between 10 and 4 and by appointment the rest of the year.

Dining and Lodging

$–$$ **Harbor View Grotto.** This glassed-in dining hall overlooking the Pacific prides itself on its fresh fish entrées. The white two-story building is marked only by a neon sign that reads "Restaurant." *155 Starcross Way, ☎ 707/464–3815. D, MC, V.*

$ **Curly Redwood Lodge.** A single redwood tree produced the 57,000 board ft of lumber used to build this lodge. The room decor makes the most of that tree, with paneling, platform beds, and dressers built into the walls. *701 U.S. 101 S, 95531, ☎ 707/464–2137, FAX 707/464–1655. 36 rooms. AE, DC, MC, V.*

En Route Travelers continuing north to the Smith River near the Oregon state line will find fine trout and salmon fishing as well as a profusion of flowers. Ninety percent of America's lily bulbs are grown in this area.

THE NORTH COAST A TO Z

Arriving and Departing

By Bus

Greyhound buses (☎ 800/231–2222) travel along U.S. 101 from San Francisco to Seattle, with regular stops in Eureka and Crescent City. Bus drivers will stop in other towns along the route if you specify your destination when you board.

By Car

Highway 1 and U.S. 101 are the main north–south coastal routes. Highway 1 is often curvy and difficult all along the coast. Driving directly to Mendocino from San Francisco is quicker if instead of driving up the coast on Highway 1 you take U.S. 101 north to Highway 128 west (from Cloverdale) to Highway 1 north. Once it gets into Humboldt County, U.S. 101 itself becomes as twisting as Highway 1 as it continues on to the northernmost corner of the state. **Hertz** (☎ 800/654–3131) rents cars at the Arcata/Eureka Airport (☞ *below*).

By Plane

Arcata/Eureka Airport (✉ off U.S. 101, McKinleyville, ☎ 707/839–5401) receives United Express (☎ 800/241–6522) flights from San Francisco to Arcata/Eureka.

Getting Around

By Bus

Humboldt Transit Authority (☎ 707/443–0826) connects Eureka, Arcata, Scotia, Fortuna, and Trinidad.

By Car

Although there are excellent services along Highway 1 and U.S. 101, the main routes through the North Coast, gas stations and mechanics are few and far between on the smaller roads. If you're running low on fuel and see a gas station, stop for a refill.

Contacts and Resources

Emergencies

Ambulance (☎ 911). **Fire** (☎ 911). **Police** (☎ 911).

Guided Tours

New Sea Angler and Jaws (✉ Bodega Bay, ☎ 707/875–3495) runs cruises and fishing charters daily weather permitting. **Oceanic Society Expeditions** (☎ 415/474–3385) conducts whale-watching and other nature cruises north and west of San Francisco throughout much of the year.

Visitor Information

Eureka/Humboldt County Convention and Visitors Bureau (✉ 1034 2nd St., Eureka 95501, ☎ 703/443–5097 or 800/346–3482). **Fort Bragg–Mendocino Coast Chamber of Commerce** (✉ Box 1141, Fort Bragg 95437, ☎ 707/961–6300 or 800/726–2780). **Redwood Empire Association** (✉ Cannery, 2801 Leavenworth St., San Francisco 94133, ☎ 415/543–8334). **Sonoma County Tourism Program** (✉ 2300 County Center Dr., Room B260, Santa Rosa 95405, ☎ 707/565–5383). **West Marin Chamber of Commerce** (✉ Box 1045, Point Reyes Station 94956, ☎ 415/663–9232).

2 THE FAR NORTH

INCLUDING MOUNT SHASTA, LAKE SHASTA, AND LASSEN VOLCANIC NATIONAL PARK

Soaring mountain peaks, wild rivers brimming with fish, and almost unlimited recreational possibilities make the Far North a sports-lover's paradise. You won't find many hot nightspots and cultural enclaves, but you will find some of the best hiking, fishing, and hunting in the state. The region offers a glimpse of old California—natural, awesome, and inspiring.

By Marty Olmstead

Updated by Gordon Young

FOR MORE THAN A FEW CALIFORNIANS, the state stops a few miles north of the San Francisco Bay Area. Their loss. The Far North offers natural beauty that is relatively unmarred by development, congestion and traffic. Instead, the landscape owes its wondrous qualities to volcanic activity. Lassen Volcanic National Park at the southern end of the Cascade Range is dominated by 10,457-ft Mount Lassen and is home to 50 wilderness lakes, sulfur vents, and bubbling mud pots. But the enduring image of the region has to be Mount Shasta: At 14,162-ft, its snow-capped peak is visible for miles, beckoning outdoor adventurers of all kinds.

Pleasures and Pastimes

Dining

Redding, the urban center of the Far North, has the greatest selection of restaurants. In the smaller towns, cafés and simple restaurants are the rule, though trendy, innovative restaurants have been opening. Dress is always informal in the Far North.

CATEGORY	COST*
$$$$	over $50
$$$	$30–$50
$$	$20–$30
$	under $20

**per person for a three-course meal, excluding drinks, service, and 8¼% tax*

Lodging

Aside from the large chain hotels and motels in the Redding area, most accommodations in the Far North blend rusticity, simplicity, and coziness. Many visitors to rural areas spend much of their time in the outdoors and prefer informal campsites and motels. Wilderness resorts close in fall and reopen after the snow season ends in May.

CATEGORY	COST*
$$$$	over $175
$$$	$120–$175
$$	$80–$120
$	under $80

**All prices are for a standard double room, excluding 8% tax.*

following the text of a review is your signal that the property has a Web site, where you will find details and, usually, images; for a link, visit www.fodors.com/urls.

Outdoor Activities and Sports

In the Far North almost all of the attractions are found outdoors. Cascading rivers, mammoth lakes, and bountiful streams draw sportfishers. Hikers, backpackers, hunters, skiers, and other outdoor enthusiasts flock to Castle Crags State Park and Lassen Volcanic National Park. In winter the uncrowded slopes of Mount Shasta tempt skiers. For information about campgrounds, contact Lassen Volcanic National Park or the Shasta Cascade Wonderland Association (☞ Contacts and Resources *in* The Far North A to Z, *below*).

Exploring the Far North

The Far North encompasses three vast counties—Tehama, Shasta, and Trinity—and part of Butte County. The area stretches from the valleys east of the Coast Range to the Nevada border and from the almond and olive orchards north of Sacramento to the Oregon border.

Numbers in the text correspond to numbers in the margin and on the Far North map.

Great Itineraries

IF YOU HAVE 3 DAYS

From I–5 north of Redding, head northeast on Highways 299 and 89 to **McArthur-Burney Falls Memorial State Park** ⑥. To appreciate the falls, take a short stroll to the overlook or hike down for a closer view. Continue north on Highway 89. Long before you arrive in the town of **Mount Shasta** ⑦ you will spy the conical peak for which it is named. The central Mount Shasta exit east leads out of town along the **Everett Memorial Highway.** Take this scenic drive, which climbs to almost 8,000 ft. The views of the mountain and the valley below are extraordinary. Stay overnight in town. On the second day, head south on I–5 toward the **Lake Shasta Caverns** ⑧ and the **Shasta Dam** ⑨. **Lake Shasta** is visible on both sides of the highway as it crosses the water near the dam, which is on the west side of I–5. Spend the night either in **Weaverville** ⑩, on Highway 299, or in **Redding** ⑪, on I–5. Near Redding, Highway 299 leads west toward the **Whiskeytown-Shasta-Trinity National Recreation Area.** Wherever you stay, take in Weaverville—don't miss its **Weaverville Joss House**—on your third day.

IF YOU HAVE 5 OR 6 DAYS

Get a glimpse of the Far North's heritage in **Red Bluff** ② before heading north on I–5 to the town of **Mount Shasta.** ⑦ On day two drop by the Forest Service Ranger Station to check on trail conditions on **Mount Shasta** and pick up maps. Pack a picnic lunch before taking the **Everett Memorial Highway** up the mountain. After exploring the mountain, head south on I–5 and spend the night in **Dunsmuir** at the **Railroad Car Resort,** where all the accommodations are old cabooses. On your third day, take an early morning hike in nearby **Castle Crags State Park.** Continue south on I–5 and tour **Shasta Dam** ⑨. Spend the night camping in the area or in **Redding** ⑪. On your fourth morning, head west on Highway 299 and visit the town of **Shasta.** Continue west on 299 to **Weaverville** ⑩ and stay the night there or back in Redding. If you will be leaving the area on your fifth day but have a little time, zip north and visit **Lake Shasta Caverns** ⑧. If you're staying and it's between late May and early October, spend the next day and a half exploring **Lassen Volcanic National Park.** Highway 44 heads east from Redding into the park.

When to Tour the Far North

This region attracts the greatest number of tourists during the summer, which can be dry and scorching. The valley around Redding is mild in the winter, but cooler temperatures prevail at the higher elevations to the east and north. In winter Mount Shasta is a good downhill ski area. The remainder of the Far North is too cold for outdoor pleasures, and snow closes the roads to the region's most awesome sights, including much of Lassen Volcanic National Park, from October until late May. Many restaurants and museums here have limited hours and sometimes close for stretches of the off season.

FROM CHICO TO MOUNT SHASTA

The Far North's most spectacular scenery lies along the two-lane roads that crisscross the region, which is bisected by I–5. East of I–5 are dramatic mountain peaks. To the west you'll find heavily forested areas and interesting small towns.

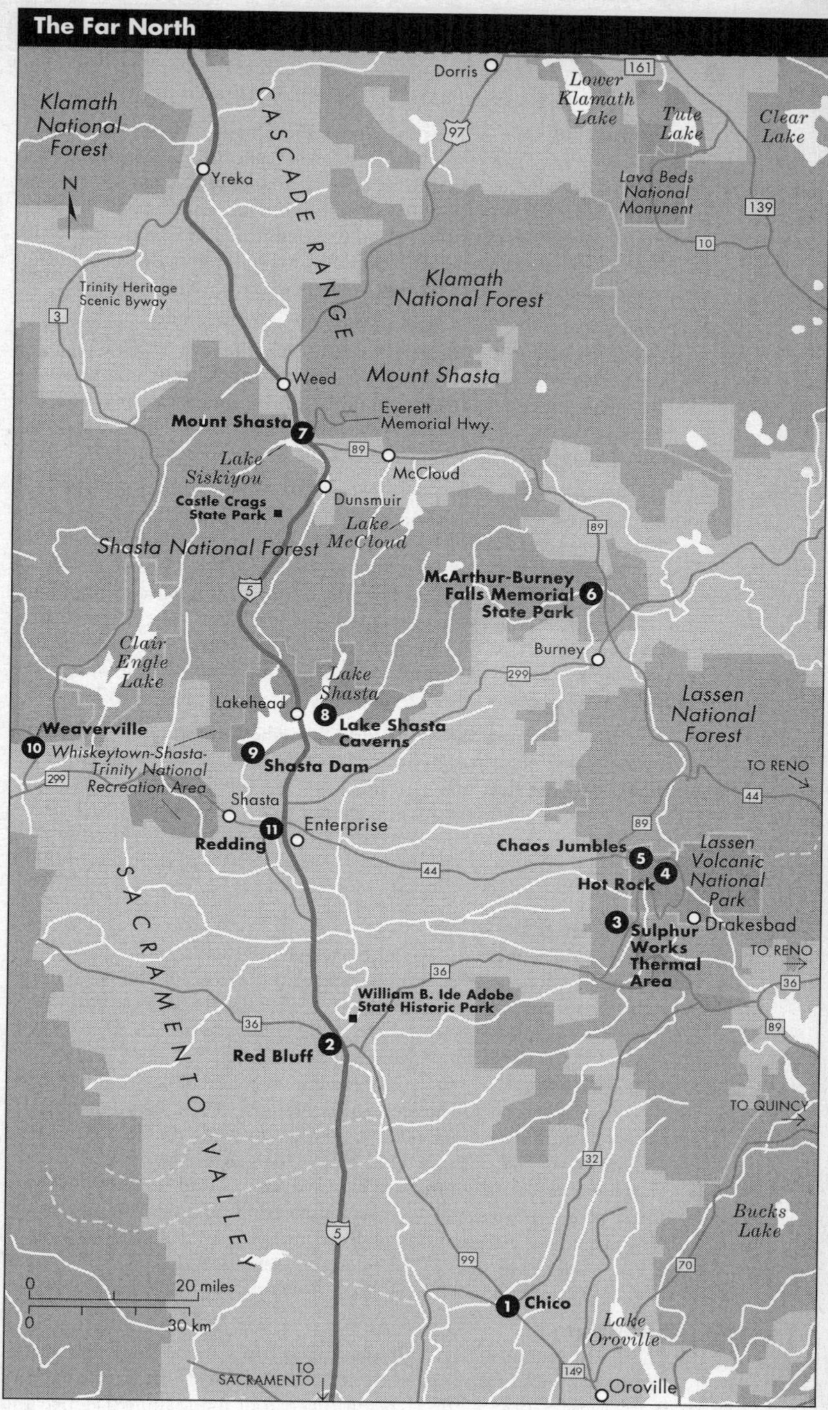
The Far North
Dorris
161
Lower Klamath Lake
Tule Lake
Clear Lake
Klamath National Forest
N
Yreka
CASCADE RANGE
97
Lava Beds National Monument
139
10
Klamath National Forest
Trinity Heritage Scenic Byway
3
Weed
Mount Shasta
Everett Memorial Hwy.
Mount Shasta
7
89
McCloud
Lake Siskiyou
Dunsmuir
Castle Crags State Park
Lake McCloud
Shasta National Forest
89
5
McArthur-Burney Falls Memorial State Park
6
Clair Engle Lake
Burney
299
Lake Shasta
Lakehead
8
Lake Shasta Caverns
Lassen National Forest
Weaverville
10
Whiskeytown-Shasta-Trinity National Recreation Area
9
Shasta Dam
TO RENO
299
44
Shasta
11
Enterprise
Redding
89
Chaos Jumbles
5
4
Hot Rock
Lassen Volcanic National Park
44
3
Sulphur Works Thermal Area
Drakesbad
TO RENO
SACRAMENTO VALLEY
36
36
William B. Ide Adobe State Historic Park
36
89
2
Red Bluff
TO QUINCY
32
5
Bucks Lake
99
70
0
20 miles
0
30 km
1
Chico
Lake Oroville
TO SACRAMENTO
149
Oroville

Chico

❶ *180 mi from San Francisco, east on I–80, north on I–505 to I–5, and east on Hwy. 32; 86 mi north of Sacramento on Hwy. 99.*

Chico sits just west of Paradise in the Sacramento Valley and offers a welcome break from the monotony of I–5. Home to California State University at Chico, scores of local artisans, and acres of almond orchards in the surrounding area, the town of 53,000 boasts an interesting mix of academics, the arts, and agriculture. But Chico's true claim to fame is the popular Sierra Nevada Brewery, keeping locals and Californians across the state happy with its distinctive microbrews.

★ The sprawling, 3,670-acre **Bidwell Park** (☎ 530/895–4972), where scenes from *Gone with the Wind* were filmed, straddles Big Chico Creek and gives the region a recreational oasis of playgrounds; a golf course; swimming areas; and paved biking, hiking, and in-line skating trails. The second-largest city-run park in the country starts as a slender strip downtown and expands eastward toward the Sierra foothills.

Bidwell Mansion, now painted a distinctive salmon with grey trim, was built between 1865 and 1868 by General John Bidwell, the founder of Chico. He and his wife settled into this 26-room Italianate mansion designed by Henry W. Cleaveland, architect of San Francisco's original Palace Hotel. The one-hour tour takes in the dining room, parlor, library, and a half-dozen bedrooms, whose guests included President Rutherford B. Hayes, naturalist John Muir, and General William T. Sherman. ✉ *Bidwell Mansion State Historic Park, 525 The Esplanade,* ☎ *530/895–6144.* 🎫 *$1.* ⏲ *Weekdays noon–5, weekends 10–5; last tour daily at 4.*

★ The award-winning **Sierra Nevada Brewing Company,** one of the pioneers of the microbrewery movement, still has a hands-on approach to beer-making that makes touring its sparkling brewery a pleasure. You can enjoy a hearty lunch or dinner in the brew pub, which serves standard pub fare and interesting entrées. ✉ *1075 E. 20th St.,* ☎ *530/345–2739.* 🎫 *Free.* ⏲ *Tours Tues.–Fri. at 2:30, Sat. noon–3 on the ½-hr. Closed Mon.*

Dining and Lodging

$$–$$$ ✕ **Red Tavern.** With its warm, butter-yellow walls and mellow lighting, this is Chico's most refined restaurant. Look for the lamb chops with lemon-pine nut crust or the stuffed Atlantic Salmon with Swiss chard, bacon, and sage butter. ✉ *1250 Esplanade, 95926,* ☎ *530/894–3463. AE, MC, V. Closed Sun. and Mon.*

$–$$ ✕ **Kramore Inn.** Crepes—from ham and avocado to crab cannelloni—are the inn's specialty. The menu also includes salads, Asian dishes, and several pastas. Brunch is available on the weekends. ✉ *1903 Park Ave.,* ☎ *530/343–3701. AE, D, MC, V.* ⏲ *Open Tues.–Sun.*

$$–$$$ 🏨 **Johnson's Country Inn.** Nestled near an almond orchard five minutes from downtown, this Victorian-style farmhouse with a wraparound veranda is a welcome change from motel row. Johnson's, built in 1992, is full of antiques and modern conveniences. ✉ *3935 Morehead Ave., 95928,* ☎ FAX *530/345–7829. 4 rooms. AE, MC, V. BP.* 🚭

Shopping

There are numerous art galleries to visit in Chico. Shop and watch demonstrations of glass blowing at the **Satava Art Glass Studio** (✉ 819 Wall St., ☎ 530/345–7985). Beautiful custom-made stained etched and beveled glass is created at **Needham Studios** (✉ 237 Broadway, ☎ 530/345–4718). **Made in Chico** (✉ 232 Main St., ☎ 530/894–7009) carries locally made goods, including handwoven scarves, beautiful pottery, salad dressings, and mustards.

Close-Up

BREWING UP SUCCESS

IT DIDN'T TAKE Ken Grossman long to recognize the limitations of the chemistry set he played with while growing up near Los Angeles in the 1960s. So at the tender age of 14, Grossman brewed up his first batch of homemade beer in his bedroom.

"Kenny always had projects going," his mother remembers. "Chemistry sets, all sorts of things. So when he brought home some new jars and plastic tubes, I didn't think much of it. He didn't say anything about beer, but when I found out, I was not pleased."

Today, Grossman's beer is getting a far better reception. Sierra Nevada Brewing Company (☞ Chico, *above*), founded in 1981 by Grossman and business partner Paul Camusi, is revered by the locals and legendary among beer lovers across the country. Beer expert Michael Jackson—not to be confused with the pop singer—calls it "the Château Latour of American micros." *The Malt Advocate,* a respected magazine devoted to libations of all sorts, named Sierra Nevada "Brewery of the Year" in 1998. And Sierra Nevada has won a slew of gold medals over the years at the annual Great American Beer Festival.

Sales have kept pace with all the accolades. In 1986, Sierra Nevada was producing about 5,000 barrels a year. By 1997, the brewery had reached maximum capacity—300,000 barrels. That spurred an ambitious expansion that will allow Sierra Nevada to eventually brew 500,000 barrels.

The best way to experience Sierra Nevada, now the 11th largest brewery in the United States, is to pay a visit to the brewery on East 20th Street in Chico. Although Sierra's brewing methods are very traditional, the brewery itself is a state-of-the-art facility. Four large copper brewing vessels are visible through huge windows open to the outside. Informative, behind-the-scenes tours (conducted daily at 2:30 and continuously from noon to 3 on Saturday) offer insight into the brewing process from the malt mill to the bottle shop.

The comfortable taproom and restaurant is the logical place to visit after the tour. The food is simple, hearty, and delicious. The fish-and-chips are a local favorite, but the barbecued chicken marinated in Sierra Nevada's special Malt Glaze is also a great choice.

Although not as well known, Sierra Nevada produces a line of spicy mustards that are available at the brewery. The Stoneground Stout is a traditional beer-hall hot mustard in the German style. Pale Ale Honey Spice is a blend of sweetness and heat, and Spicy Brown Porter is a Dijon style mustard that uses Sierra Nevada Porter rather than white wine.

But the beer is the real attraction here. The Pale Ale, with its deep amber color and full-bodied taste, put Sierra Nevada on the map and shouldn't be missed. The hearty Stout is dark and rich with a pronounced roasted flavor. The adventuresome should try Bigfoot Ale, a powerful barley wine–style offering with an intense maltiness and bittersweet taste. (Be careful, though, because this type of beer has a much higher alcohol content.) Sierra Nevada also brews a variety of other styles, including porters, bocks, wheat beers, and brown ales. The Celebration Ale, which the *San Francisco Chronicle* once called the "best beer ever made in America," is available for a short time around the holiday season. The release of this seasonal favorite is a sure sign that winter has arrived.

— Gordon Young

Red Bluff

❷ *179 mi north of San Francisco, I–80 to I–505 to I–5.*

Unlike many California towns, Red Bluff is not yet obsessed with attracting tourists, and that's its charm. Established in the mid-19th century as a shipping center and named for the color of its soil, Red Bluff is home to dozens of restored Victorians and a downtown that still resembles a stage set for a western movie. It's a great home base for outdoor adventures in the area. The **Red Bluff-Tehama County Chamber of Commerce** (☞ Contacts and Resources *in* the Far North A to Z, *below*) is an ideal source of information.

The **Kelly-Griggs House Museum,** a beautifully restored 1880s home, holds an impressive collection of antique furniture, housewares, and clothing arranged as though a refined Victorian-era family were still in residence. An engraved silver tea server waits at the end table; a "Self Instructor in Penmanship" sits on a desk; and in the upstairs parlor costumed mannequins seem eerily frozen in time. (Yes, this could be the set of a horror film.) The museum's collection includes carved china cabinets and Native American basketry. *Persephone,* the painting over the fireplace, is by Sarah Brown, daughter of abolitionist John Brown, whose family settled in Red Bluff. ✉ *311 Washington St.,* ☎ *530/527–1129.* 🎫 *Donation suggested.* ⏲ *Thurs.–Sun. 1–4.*

The **William B. Ide Adobe State Historic Park** is a memorial to the first and only president of the short-lived California Republic of 1846. The Bear Flag Party proclaimed California a sovereign nation, no longer under the dominion of Mexico, and the republic existed for 25 days before it was occupied by the United States. The flag concocted for the republic has survived, with only minor refinements, as California's state flag. This adobe was built in the 1850s and comes complete with period furnishings. ✉ *21659 Adobe Rd.,* ☎ *530/529–8599.* 🎫 *$1 per vehicle.* ⏲ *Park and picnic facilities 8 AM–sunset year-round; home 11–4 in summer (in winter, look for ranger to unlock house).*

Dining and Lodging

$$ ✕ **Crystal Steak & Seafood Co.** As in many restaurants that offer steak and seafood, it's best to stick with the beef here. The meat is tender, flavorful, and cooked to perfection. ✉ *243 S. Main St.,* ☎ *530/527–0880. AE, D, DC, MC, V.* ⏲ *Lunch weekdays 11–2; Dinner Sun.–Sat. 5–9:30.*

$ ✕ **Snack Box.** Unabashedly corny pictures and knickknacks, many depicting cattle and sheep, decorate the renovated Victorian cottage that holds the Snack Box. The food need make no apologies, however. Soups, omelets, country-fried steaks, and even simple items such as grilled-cheese sandwiches are perfectly crafted. ✉ *257 Main St., 1 block from Kelly-Griggs House Museum,* ☎ *530/529–0227. MC, V. No dinner.*

$ 🏨 **Lamplighter Lodge.** Simple rooms, some with refrigerators, are available. The pool area is a great place to relax on sweltering summer days. ✉ *210 S. Main St., 96080,* ☎ *530/527–1150. 48 rooms, 2 suites. Pool. AE, D, DC, MC, V.*

Lassen Volcanic National Park

45 mi east of Redding on Hwy. 44; 48 mi east of Red Bluff on Hwy. 36.

Lassen Volcanic National Park provides a look at three sides of the world's largest plug volcano. Except for the Nordic ski area, the park is largely inaccessible from late October to late May because of heavy snow. The Lassen Park Road (the continuation of Highway 89 within the park) is closed to cars in winter but open to intrepid cross-country skiers, conditions permitting. Even in the best of weather, services are sparse. In the southwest corner of the park, a café and a gift shop are open during the summer. The *Lassen Park Guide,* available for a nominal fee at the visitor center and park entrance, details these and other facilities. ✉ *Visitor center: 38050 Hwy. 36 E, Mineral 96063,* ☎ *530/595–4444.* 🎫 *$10 per vehicle, $5 on foot or bicycle; $8–$14 for campsites (reservations not accepted).* ⊙ *Visitor center weekdays 8–4:30 year-round, summer weekends 8–4:30; hrs sometimes vary.*

In 1914 the 10,457-ft Mount Lassen began a series of 300 eruptions that continued for seven years. Molten rock overflowed the crater, and the mountain emitted clouds of smoke and hailstorms of rocks and volcanic cinders. Proof of the volcano's volatility becomes evident shortly
3 after you enter the park at the **Sulphur Works Thermal Area.** Boardwalks take you over bubbling mud and hot springs and through sulfur-emitting steam vents. ✉ *Lassen Park Rd., south end of park.*

The **Lassen Peak Hike** winds 2½ mi to the mountaintop. It's a tough climb—2,000 ft uphill on a steady, steep grade—but the reward is a spectacular view. At the peak you can take a peek into the rim and view the entire park (and much of the Far North). Bring sunscreen and water. ✉ *Off Lassen Park Rd. at Mile Marker 22.*

Along **Bumpass Hell Trail,** a scenic 3-mi round-trip hike to the park's most interesting thermal-spring area, you can view hot and boiling springs, steam vents, and mud pots up close. There is a gradual climb of 500 ft during the first mile before a 250-ft descent to the springs. Stay on trails and boardwalks near the thermal areas. What appears to be firm ground may be only a thin crust over scalding mud. ✉ *Off Lassen Park Rd., 5 mi north of Sulphur Works Thermal Area.*

4 **Hot Rock,** a 400-ton boulder, tumbled down from the summit during the volcano's active period and was still hot to the touch when locals discovered it nearly two days later. Although cool now, it's still an impressive sight. ✉ *Lassen Park Rd., north end of park.*

5 **Chaos Jumbles** was created 300 years ago when an avalanche from the Chaos Crags lava domes spread hundreds of thousands of rocks, many of them 2 ft–3 ft in diameter, over a couple of square miles. ✉ *Lassen Park Rd., north end of park.*

Dining, Lodging, and Camping

$$$$ ✕🏨 **Drakesbad Guest Ranch.** This century-old guest ranch, at elevation 5,700 ft near Lassen Volcanic National Park's southern border, is isolated from most of the rest of the park, which is one reason it is so popular. Rooms in the lodge, bungalows, and cabins don't have electricity; they're lighted by kerosene lamps. But the spartan accommodations are clean and comfortable and have furnace heat and either a half or full bath. All meals are included in the room rate. Breakfast and lunch are simple affairs, but evening meals are rather elegant. Reservations should be made well ahead, as the waiting list can be up to two years long. ✉ *Chester–Warner Valley Rd., north from Hwy. 36 (booking office: 2150 N. Main St., Suite 5, Red Bluff 96080),* ☎ *530/529–1512,* FAX *530/529–4511. 19 rooms. Dining room, pool, badminton, horseback riding, horseshoes, Ping-Pong, volleyball, fishing. D, MC, V.* ⊙ *Early June.–early Oct. FAP.*

$ ✕🏨 **Lassen Mineral Lodge.** Reserve rooms at this motel-style property, located at 5,000 ft, as far ahead as possible. You can rent cross-country skis, snowshoes, and snowboards at the lodge's ski shop. There's also a general store. ✉ *Hwy. 36, Mineral 96063,* ☎ *530/595–4422. 20 rooms. Restaurant, bar. AE, D, MC, V.*

Manzanita Lake Campground. The largest of Lassen Volcanic National Park's seven campgrounds (reservations are not accepted at any of them) is near the northern entrance. A trail near the campground leads to Chaos Crags Lake. *Off Lassen Park Rd. 2 mi east of junction of Hwys. 44 and 89, 530/595–4444. 179 sites. $14. Mid-May–mid-Oct.*

McArthur-Burney Falls Memorial State Park

6 *30 mi north of Lassen Volcanic National Park on Hwy. 89.*

Just inside the southern boundary of this state park, Burney Creek wells up from the ground and divides into two cascades that fall over a 129-ft cliff and into a pool below. While not the highest or largest waterfall in the state, it is possibly the most beautiful. Countless ribbonlike falls stream from hidden moss-covered crevices—an ethereal backdrop to the main cascades. Each day 100 million gallons of water rush over these falls; Theodore Roosevelt proclaimed them "the eighth wonder of the world." A self-guided nature trail descends to the foot of the falls. There is a lake and beach for swimming. A campground, picnic sites, and other facilities are available. The camp store is open from Memorial Day to Labor Day. *24898 Hwy. 89, Burney 96013, 530/335–2777; 800/444–7275 for campground reservations (necessary in summer). $2 per vehicle (day use); $12 for campsites.*

Mount Shasta

7 *52 mi from McArthur-Burney Falls Memorial State Park on Hwy. 89; 61 mi north of Redding on I–5.*

Mount Shasta—the mountain and the town—made headlines in 1987 when participants in the worldwide Harmonic Convergence descended on the region, believing the mountain held special powers. They weren't the first. Legends of eerie phenomena and mythical animals have been part of the mountain's folklore for decades.

The crown jewel of the 2.5-million-acre Shasta–Trinity National Forest, Mount Shasta is popular with day hikers, especially in spring, when such flowers as the fragrant Shasta lily adorn the rocky slopes. But few people make it to the perennially ice-packed summit of this 16-million-year-old dormant volcano. A paved road travels only as high as the timberline, and the final 6,000 ft are a tough climb of rubble, ice, and snow.

The town of Mount Shasta isn't exactly a tourist destination, but it has real character and some fine restaurants. Outdoor lovers and backcountry skiers abound, and they are more than willing to offer advice on the most beautiful spots in the region.

Dining and Lodging

$–$$$ **Lily's.** This restaurant in a white clapboard home—complete with picket fence—serves everything from steaks and pastas to Mexican and vegetarian dishes. Among the unusual salads are a spicy shrimp-and-chicken dish and the Jalisco—steak and greens with tomatoes. The huevos rancheros are a delicious choice for brunch. *1013 S. Mt. Shasta Blvd., 530/926–3372. AE, D, MC, V.*

$$ **Trinity Café.** This cozy little restaurant has gained popularity in the area with California cuisine that changes weekly. Offerings range from game dishes such as roast duck breast with seared foie gras to grilled ahi on a bed of chard with a red wine vinaigrette. *622 N. Mt. Shasta Blvd., 530/926–6200. MC, V. Wed.–Sun.*

$–$$ **Michael's Restaurant.** Wood paneling, candlelight, and wildlife prints by local artists create an unpretentious setting for such favorites as prime rib and Italian specialties such as stuffed calamari, filet mignon scallopini, and linguine pesto. ✉ *313 N. Mt. Shasta Blvd.,* ☎ *530/926–5288. AE, D, MC, V.* ⏲ *Tues.–Sat.*

$ ✕ **Has Beans.** This coffee shop is a favorite gathering spot for locals. Fliers posted inside offer loads of insider information on life in Mount Shasta. Enjoy the pastries made fresh daily. ✉ *1101 Mt. Shasta Blvd.,* ☎ *530/926–3602. No credit cards.*

$–$$ **Best Western Tree House Motor Inn.** The clean, standard rooms at this motel less than a mile from downtown Mount Shasta are decorated with natural-wood furnishings. Some rooms have vaulted ceilings and mountain views. ✉ *111 Morgan Way, at I–5 and Lake St., 96067,* ☎ *530/926–3101 or 800/528–1234,* FAX *530/926–3542. 94 rooms, 4 suites. Restaurant, refrigerators, indoor pool, hot tub. AE, D, DC, MC, V.*

Outdoor Activities and Sports

HIKING

The **Forest Service Ranger Station** (☎ 530/926–4511) keep tabs on trail conditions and offers avalanche reports (☎ 530/926–9613).

MOUNTAIN CLIMBING

Fifth Season Mountaineering Shop (✉ 300 N. Mt. Shasta Blvd., ☎ 530/926–3606) rents skiing and climbing equipment and operates a recorded 24-hour climber-skier report (☎ 530/926–5555). **Shasta Mountain Guides** (☎ 530/926–3117) leads hiking, climbing, and ski-touring groups to the summit of Mount Shasta.

SKIING

Mt. Shasta Board & Ski Park. On the southeast flank of Mount Shasta are three lifts on 425 skiable acres. It's a great place for novices, since three-quarters of the trails are for beginning or intermediate skiers. There are not many challenges for advanced skiers, however. The area's vertical drop is 1,390 ft, with a top elevation of 6,600 ft. The longest run is 1¼ mi. You can ski until 10 PM from Wednesday through Saturday. A package for beginners, available through the ski school, includes a lift ticket, ski rental, and a lesson. The school also runs the SKIwee program for children ages four–seven. Within the base lodge are food and beverage facilities, a ski shop, and a ski-rental shop. ✉ *Hwy. 89 exit east from I–5, south of Mt. Shasta,* ☎ *530/926–8686 or 800/754–7427.*

OFF THE BEATEN PATH

LAVA BEDS NATIONAL MONUMENT –Volcanic activity created the rugged landscape of this intriguing monument. It is distinguished by cinder cones, lava flows, spatter cones, pit craters and more than 300 underground lava tube caves. During the Modoc War (1872–1873), the Modoc Indians under the leadership of Captain Jack took refuge in a natural lava fortress now known as "Captain Jack's Stronghold." They managed to hold off U.S. Army forces numbering up to 20 times their strength for five months. When exploring, wear hard-sole boots, and pick up the necessary equipment (lights, "bump" hats, etc.) at the Indian Well Visitor Center, at the park's south end. Guided walks and cave tours, which take place between Memorial Day and Labor Day, depart from the visitor center. Campfire programs—the topic is determined by the ranger—are offered nightly in summer months. ✉ *94 mi from the town of Mt. Shasta; head north on I–5, northeast on U.S. 97 at Weed, east on Hwy. 161 (3 mi north of Dorris), and south on Hill Rd. (from town of Burney head east on Hwy. 299 and north on Hwy. 139),* ☎ *530/667–2282. $4 per vehicle; $2 per visitor on foot or bicycle; $10 camping in summer and $6 in winter.* ⏲ *Park 24 hrs. Visitor center daily 8–5.*

Dunsmuir

10 mi south of Mt. Shasta on I–5.

Castle Crags State Park surrounds the town of Dunsmuir, which was named for a 19th-century Scottish coal baron who offered to build a fountain if the town was renamed in his honor. The town's other major attraction is the **Railroad Park Resort** (☞ *below*), where guests spend the night in restored railcars.

Named for its 6,000-ft glacier-polished crags which tower over the Sacramento River, **Castle Crags State Park** offers swimming and fishing, hiking in the backcountry, and a view of Mount Shasta. The 4,350-acre park features 28 mi of hiking trails, including a 2.7 mi access trail to **Castle Wilderness,** part of the **Shasta–Trinity National Forest.** There are excellent trails at lower altitudes, along with picnic areas, rest rooms, showers, and plenty of campsites. ✉ *Off I–5, 6 mi south of Dunsmuir,* ☎ *530/235–2684.* 🎟 *$2 per vehicle (day use); $12 (campsites).*

Lodging

$ **Dunsmuir Inn Bed & Breakfast.** It's not fancy, but this homey inn—a good deal considering that rates include a made-to-order country breakfast—is comfortable and within easy walking distance of the historic downtown area. All rooms have clawfoot tubs with bubble bath within easy reach. ✉ *5423 Dunsmuir Ave., 96025,* ☎ *530/235–4543 or 888/386–7684. 5 rooms. AE, D, MC, V. BP.*

$ **Railroad Park Resort.** The antique cabooses here were collected over more than three decades and have been converted into cozy, wood-panel motel rooms in honor of Dunsmuir's railroad legacy. The resort has a vaguely *Orient Express*–style dining room and a lounge fashioned from vintage railcars. The landscaped grounds contain a huge steam engine and a restored water tower. There's also an RV park. ✉ *100 Railroad Park Rd., 96025,* ☎ *530/235–4440 or 800/974–7245,* FAX *530/235–4470. 23 cabooses, 4 cabins. Restaurant, pool, hot tub, camping. AE, D, MC, V.*

Lake Shasta Area

34 mi south of Mt. Shasta (to town of Lakehead) on I–5; 12 mi north of Redding on I–5.

There are many versions of "Shasta" to enjoy—the mountain, lake, river, town, dam, and forest—all named after the Native Americans known as the Shatasla or Sastise who inhabited the region.

8 Stalagmites, stalactites, odd flowstone deposits, and crystals entice visitors of all ages to the **Lake Shasta Caverns.** A two-hour tour includes a catamaran ride across the McCloud arm of Lake Shasta and a bus ride up Grey Rock Mountain to the cavern entrance. The caverns are 58°F year-round, making them an enticingly cool retreat on a hot summer day. The high point is the awe-inspiring cathedral room. The guides are friendly, enthusiastic, and knowledgeable. ✉ *Shasta Caverns Rd. exit from I–5,* ☎ *530/238–2341 or 800/795–2283.* 🎟 *$15.* ⏲ *Daily 9–4; tours Memorial Day–Labor Day on the ½ hr, Sept., Apr., and May on the hr, Oct.–Mar. at 10, noon, and 2.*

★ Twenty-one varieties of fish—from rainbow trout to salmon—inhabit **Lake Shasta.** The lake region is also home to the largest nesting population of bald eagles in California. You can rent fishing boats, ski boats, sailboats, canoes, paddleboats, Jet Skis, and windsurfing boards at one of the many marinas and resorts along the 370-mi shoreline. Lake Shasta is known as the houseboat capital of the world (☞ Outdoor Activities and Sports, *below*)

★ 9 **Shasta Dam** is the second-largest concrete dam in the United States (Grand Coulee in Washington is the largest). At dusk the sight is magical, with Mount Shasta gleaming above the not-quite-dark water and deer frolicking on the nearby hillside. The dam is lit after dark, but there is no access from 10 PM to 6 AM. The visitor center has computerized photographic tours of the dam construction, video presentations, fact sheets, and historic displays. The friendly staff is very knowledgable about the area. ✉ *16349 Shasta Dam Blvd.,* ☎ *530/275–4463.* ⏲ *Dam 6 AM–10 PM; visitor center 8:30–4:30; tours Memorial Day–Sept., daily 9–4 on the hr; Oct.–Memorial Day, weekdays 10, 11, 1, and 3, and weekends 9–4 on the hr.*

Dining

$$–$$$ ✕ **Tail o' the Whale.** This restaurant overlooking Lake Shasta is distinguished by its nautical decor. Seafood, pasta, prime rib, and poultry are the specialties. ✉ *10300 Bridge Bay Rd., Bridge Bay exit from I–5,* ☎ *530/275–3021. D, MC, V.*

Outdoor Activities and Sports

FISHING

The Fishin' Hole (✉ 3844 Shasta Dam Blvd., Central Valley, ☎ 530/275–4123) carries supplies and provides information about conditions, licenses, and fishing packages.

HOUSEBOATING

Houseboats come in all sizes except small. As a rule these moving homes come with cooking utensils, dishes, and most of the equipment you'll need. You supply food and linens. Renters are given a short course in how to maneuver the boats before they set out on cruises. It's not difficult, as the houseboats are slow moving. You can fish, swim, sunbathe on the flat roof, or sit on the deck and watch the world go by. The shoreline of Lake Shasta is beautifully ragged, with countless inlets; it's not hard to find privacy. Expect to spend a minimum of $200 a day for a craft that sleeps six. There is usually a three-night minimum in peak season. **Shasta Cascade Wonderland Association** (☞ Contacts and Resources *in* the Far North A to Z, *below*) has more information.

Weaverville

10 *46 mi west of Redding on Hwy. 299 (called Main St. in town).*

Weaverville is an enjoyable mixture of gold rush history and tourist kitsch. Named after John Weaver, who was one of three men who built the first cabin here in 1850, the town has an impressive downtown historic district. It's a popular headquarters for family vacations and biking, hiking, fishing, hunting, and gold-panning excursions.

★ Weaverville's real attraction is the **Weaverville Joss House,** a Taoist temple built in 1874 and called Won Lim Miao, "The Temple of the Forest Beneath the Clouds," by Chinese miners. The oldest continuously used Chinese temple in California, it attracts worshipers from around the world. With its golden altar, carved wooden canopies, and intriguing artifacts, the Joss House is a piece of California history that can best be appreciated in the company of a guide ($2 for a 40-min. tour). The original temple building and many of its furnishings—some of which had come from China—were burned in 1873, but members of the local Chinese community soon rebuilt it. ✉ *Oregon and Main Sts.,* ☎ *530/623–5284.* 🎫 *Free for museum; $2 for guided tour.* ⏲ *Memorial Day–Labor Day, daily 10–5; rest of yr Wed.–Sun. 10–5.*

The **Trinity County Courthouse** (✉ Court and Main Sts.), built in 1857 as a store, office building, and hotel, was converted to county use in 1865. The Apollo Saloon in the basement became the county jail.

Trinity County Historical Park is home to the Jake Jackson Memorial Museum, which has a blacksmith shop, a replica stamp mill, and the original jail cells of the Trinity County Courthouse. ✉ *408 Main St.,* ☎ *530/623–5211.* ⏲ *May–Oct., daily 10–5; Nov.–Apr., Tues. and Sat. noon–4.*

Dining and Lodging

$–$$ ✕ **La Grange Café.** This eatery is one of the few places in Weaverville open for lunch and dinner six days a week. Stick to such basics as chicken and pasta, as the kitchen is not as dependable when it comes to dishes such as trout. On the plus side, La Grange serves plenty of vegetables and sells beer and wine. ✉ *315 N. Main St.,* ☎ *530/623–5325. AE, D, MC, V. Closed Sun.*

$ ✕ **La Casita.** Here you'll find the traditional selection—all the quesadillas (including one with roasted chili peppers), tostadas, enchiladas, tacos, and tamales you could want, many of them available in a vegetarian version. This casual spot is open from late morning through early evening, so it's great for a mid-afternoon snack. ✉ *254 Main St.,* ☎ *530/623–5797. No credit cards.*

$ 🏨 **Red Hill Motel.** This is the best choice among Weaverville motels. One cozy cabin that has a full kitchen is popular with families. ✉ *Red Hill Rd., Box 234, 96093,* ☎ *530/623–4331. 4 rooms, 10 cabins. AE, D, MC, V.*

OFF THE BEATEN PATH

TRINITY HERITAGE SCENIC BYWAY – This road, shown on many maps as Highway 3, runs north from Weaverville for 120 mi up to its intersection with I–5, south of Yreka. The Trinity Alps and Lewiston Lake, formed by the Trinity Dam, are visible all along this beautiful, forest-lined road, which is often closed during the winter months. A major portion of the route follows the path established by early miners and settlers as it climbs from 2,000 ft to 6,500 ft.

Outdoor Activities and Sports

Below the Lewiston Dam, east of Weaverville on Highway 299, is the **Fly Stretch** of the Trinity River, a world-class fly-fishing area. The **Pine Cove Boat Ramp** provides quality fishing access for visitors with disabilities—decks here are built over prime trout-fishing water. Contact the **Weaverville Ranger Station** (☎ 530/623–2121) for maps and information about hiking trails in the Trinity Alps Wilderness.

Shopping

Hays Bookstore (✉ 106 Main St., ☎ 530/623–2516) carries books on the natural history, attractions, and sights of the Far North.

Redding

⓫ *218 mi from San Francisco on I–80 to I–505 to I–5 north; 12 mi south of Lake Shasta on I–5.*

As the largest city in the Far North, Redding is an ideal headquarters for exploring the surrounding countryside.

Dining and Lodging

$–$$$ ✕ **Hatch Cover.** This establishment's dark-wood paneling and views of the adjacent Sacramento River give diners a shipboard feel, especially on the outside deck. The menu emphasizes seafood, but you can also get steaks and combination plates. The appetizer menu is extensive. ✉ *202 Hemsted Dr. (from Cypress Ave. exit off I–5, turn left,* *then right on Hemsted Dr.), ☎ 530/223–5606. AE, D, MC, V. No lunch weekends.*

$–$$ ✕ **Jack's Grill.** Although it's hard to tell from the outside, this steak house and bar is immensely popular for its 16-ounce steaks. Be prepared to eat meat; it's your only choice here. The place is usually jam-packed and noisy. ✉ *1743 California St., ☎ 530/241–9705. AE, D, MC, V. Closed Sun. No lunch.*

$–$$$ ✕🏨 **The Red Lion.** Landscaped grounds and a large patio area with outdoor food service are the highlights here. Rooms are spacious and comfortable. Waters, the lobby's fancy restaurant ($$–$$$), is a popular place for locals. Pets are allowed with advance notice. ✉ *1830 Hilltop Dr. (Hwy. 44/299 exit east from I–5), 96002, ☎ 530/221–8700, FAX 530/221–0324. 192 rooms, 2 suites. Restaurant, bar, coffee shop, room service, pool, wading pool, hot tub, exercise room. AE, D, DC, MC, V.*

$$$–$$$$ 🏨 **Brigadoon Castle Bed & Breakfast.** Fifteen winding miles from I–5 is an 83-acre estate crowned with an Elizabethan-style castle that opened as a B&B in 1996. Marble baths, antiques, and luxurious fabrics make the Brigadoon an elegant retreat. A separate cottage has a kitchen and a hot tub. From Friday through Sunday the rates include dinner. ✉ *9036 Zogg Mine Rd., Igo 96047, ☎ 530/396–2785 or 888/343–2836, FAX 530/396–2784. 4 rooms, 1 cottage. Hot tub. AE, D, MC, V. BP.*

$ 🏨 **Howard Johnson Express.** Here's a budget option—doubles with queen-size beds go for around $50—off I–5's Cypress exit. ✉ *2731 Bechelli La., ☎ 530/223–1935 or 800/354–5222, FAX 530/223–1176. 75 rooms, 2 suites. Pool. AE, D, DC, MC, V.*

Outdoor Activities and Sports

The **Fly Shop** (✉ 4140 Churn Creek Rd., ☎ 530/222–3555) sells fishing licenses and has information about guides, conditions, and fishing packages. **Park Marina Watersports** (✉ 2210 Twin View Blvd., ☎ 530/246–8388) rents rafts and canoes from May through September.

THE FAR NORTH A TO Z

Arriving and Departing

By Bus

Greyhound (☎ 800/231–2222) buses travel I–5, serving Chico, Red Bluff, Redding, Dunsmuir, and Mount Shasta. **Amtrak** (☎ 800/872–7245) runs connecting buses through Redding, Red Bluff, and Chico.

By Car

Interstate 5, an excellent four-lane divided highway, runs up the center of California through Red Bluff and Redding and continues north to Oregon. Chico is east of I–5 on Highway 32. Lassen Park can be reached by Highway 36 from Red Bluff or (except in winter) Highway 44 from Redding. Highway 299 leads from Redding to McArthur-Burney Falls Memorial State Park. Highways 36 and 299 are good two-lane roads that are kept open year-round. If you are traveling through this area in winter, however, always carry snow chains in your car.

By Plane

Chico Municipal Airport (✉ 150 Airpark Blvd., off Cohasset Rd., ☎ 530/898–2359) and **Redding Municipal Airport** (✉ Airport Rd., ☎ 530/224–4320) are served by **United Express** (☎ 800/241–6522). **Horizon Air** (☎ 800/547–9308) also uses the airport in Redding.

By Train

Amtrak (☎ 800/872–7245) has stations in Chico (✉ W. 5th and Orange Sts.), Redding (✉ 1620 Yuba St.), and Dunsmuir (✉ 5750 Sacramento Ave.).

Getting Around

By Bus

Butte County Transit (☎ 530/342–0221 or 800/822–8145) serves Chico, Oroville, and elsewhere. **Chico Area Transit System** (CATS; ☎ 530/342–0221) provides bus service within Chico. The vehicles of the **Redding Area Bus Authority** (☎ 530/241–2877) operate daily except Sunday. **STAGE** (☎ 530/842–8295) buses travel from Montague to Dunsmuir, stopping in Mount Shasta and other towns, and provide service in Scott Valley.

By Car

An automobile is virtually essential to tour the Far North unless you arrive by bus, plane, or train and plan to stay put in one town or resort.

Contacts and Resources

Car Rental

Avis (✉ Redding Municipal Airport, ☎ 530/221–2855 or 800/331–1212). **Enterprise** (✉ 357 E. Cypress Ave., Redding, ☎ 530/223–0700 or 800/325–8007). **Enterprise** (✉ 570 Antelope Blvd., Red Bluff, ☎ 530/529–0177 or 800/325–8007). **Hertz** (✉ Redding Municipal Airport, ☎ 530/221–4620 or 800/654–3131).

Emergencies

Ambulance (☎ 911). **Fire** (☎ 911). **Police** (☎ 911).

Visitor Information

Chico Chamber of Commerce (✉ 300 Salem St., 95928, ☎ 530/891–5556 or 800/852–8570). **Shasta Cascade Wonderland Association** (✉ 1699 Hwy. 273, Anderson 96007, ☎ 530/365–7500 or 800/326–6944). **Red Bluff-Tehama County Chamber of Commerce** (✉ 100 Main St., Red Bluff, 96080, ☎ 530/527–6220 or 800/655–6225).

3 THE WINE COUNTRY

You don't have to be a wine enthusiast to appreciate the mellow beauty of Napa and Sonoma counties, whose rolling hills and verdant vineyards resemble those of Tuscany and Provence. Here, among state-of-the-art wineries, fabulous restaurants, and luxury hotels where aromatherapy and massage are daily rituals, you just might discover that life need have no nobler purpose than enjoying the fruits of the earth.

Updated by Marty Olmstead

IN 1862, AFTER AN EXTENSIVE TOUR of the wine-producing areas of Europe, Count Agoston Haraszthy de Mokcsa reported a promising prognosis about his adopted California: "Of all the countries through which I passed, not one possessed the same advantages that are to be found in California . . . California can produce as noble and generous a wine as any in Europe; more in quantity to the acre, and without repeated failures through frosts, summer rains, hailstorms, or other causes."

The "dormant resources" that the father of California's viticulture saw in the balmy days and cool nights of the temperate Napa and Sonoma valleys are in full fruition today. The wines produced here are praised and savored by connoisseurs throughout the world. The area also continues to be a proving ground for the latest techniques of grape growing and wine making.

In 1975 Napa Valley had no more than 20 wineries; today there are more than 240. In Sonoma County, where the web of vineyards is looser, there are well over 150 wineries, and development is now claiming the cool Carneros region, at the head of the San Francisco Bay, deemed ideal for growing the chardonnay grape. Within these combined regions of the Wine Country, at least 120 wineries have opened in the last seven years alone. Nowadays many individual grape growers produce their own wines instead of selling their grapes to larger wineries. As a result, smaller "boutique" wineries harvest excellent, reasonably priced wines that have caught the attention of connoisseurs and critics, while the larger wineries consolidate land and expand their varietals.

Pleasures and Pastimes

Dining

Many star chefs from urban areas throughout the United States have migrated to the Wine Country, drawn by the area's renowned produce and world-class wines—the products of fertile soil and near-perpetual sun during the growing season. As a result of this marriage of imported talent and indigenous bounty, food now rivals wine as the principal attraction of the region.

With few exceptions (which are noted in individual restaurant listings), dress is informal. Where reservations are indicated as essential, you may need to reserve a week or more ahead. During the summer and early fall harvest seasons you may need to book several months ahead.

CATEGORY	COST*
$$$$	over $50
$$$	$30–$50
$$	$20–$30
$	under $20

**per person for a three-course meal, excluding drinks, service, and 10% tax*

Hot-Air Ballooning

Day after day, colorful balloons fill the morning sky high above the Wine Country's valleys. Balloon flights take place soon after sunrise, when the calmest, coolest conditions offer maximum lift and soft landings. Prices depend on the duration of the flight, number of passengers, and services. Some companies provide such extras as pickup at your lodging or champagne brunch after the flight. Expect to spend at least $175 per person.

Lodging

In a region where first-class restaurants and wineries attract connoisseurs from afar, it's no surprise that elegant lodgings have sprung up. Most local bed-and-breakfasts have historic Victorian and Spanish architecture and serve a full breakfast highlighting local produce. The newer hotels and spas are often state-of-the-art buildings offering such comforts as massage treatments or spring water–fed pools.

Not surprisingly, a stay in the Wine Country is expensive. Since Santa Rosa is the largest population center in the area, it has the widest selection of moderately priced rooms. Try there if you've failed to reserve in advance or have a limited budget. Many B&Bs are fully booked long in advance of the summer and fall seasons, and small children are often discouraged as guests. For all accommodations in the area, rates are lower on weeknights and about 20% less in the winter.

CATEGORY	COST*
$$$$	over $175
$$$	$120–$175
$$	$80–$120
$	under $80

**All prices are for a standard double room, excluding 10% tax.*

following the text of a review is your signal that the property has a Web site, where you will find details and, usually, images; for a link, visit www.fodors.com/urls.

Spas and Mud Baths

Mineral water soaks, mud baths, and massage are rejuvenating local traditions. Calistoga is famous for its warm, spring water–fed mineral tubs and mud baths full of volcanic ash. Sonoma, St. Helena, and other towns also have full-service spas.

Wine Tasting

For those new to the wine tasting game, Robert Mondavi (☞ Oakville, *below*) and Korbel Champagne Cellars (☞ Healdsburg, *below*) give general tours geared toward teaching novices the basics on how wine and champagne are made and what to look for when tasting. Unless otherwise noted, the wineries in this chapter are open daily year-round and charge no fee for admission, tours, or tastings.

Exploring the Wine Country

Numbers in the text correspond to numbers in the margin and on the Wine Country map.

Great Itineraries

The Wine Country is comprised of two main areas: the Napa Valley and the Sonoma Valley. Five major paths cut through both valleys: U.S. 101 and Highways 12 and 121 through Sonoma County, and Highway 29 north from Napa. The 25-mi Silverado Trail, which runs parallel to Highway 29 north from Napa to Calistoga, is a more scenic, less crowded route with a number of distinguished wineries. Because the Wine Country is expansive, it's best to plan smaller, separate trips over the course of several days.

IF YOU HAVE 2 DAYS

Start at the circa-1857 **Buena Vista Carneros Winery** ㉙. From there, take Highway 12 north to the Oakville Grade to historic **St. Helena,** taking time to admire the views of Sonoma and Napa valleys from the Mayacamas Mountains. After lunch in St. Helena, take the 30-minute tour of **Beringer Vineyards** ㉑. The next day drive to **Calistoga** for an

Arrowood Vineyards 32
Artesa 5
Beaulieu Vineyard . . 18
Benziger Family Winery 31
Beringer Vineyards 21
Buena Vista Carneros Winery . . . 29
Caymus Vineyards 16
Charles Krug Winery 22
Château Montelena 27
Château Potelle 7
Clos du Val 8
Clos Pegase 26
Cuvaison 25
Domaine Carneros . . . 4
Domaine Chandon 11
Dry Creek Vineyard 37
Ferrari-Carano Winery 39
Freemark Abbey Winery 23
Frog's Leap 17
Gloria Ferrer Champagne Caves 2
Hess Collection Winery and Vineyards 6
Kenwood Vineyards 33
Landmark Vineyards 34
Matanzas Creek Winery 35
Mumm Napa Valley 14
Niebaum-Coppola Estate 19
Opus One 13
Pine Ridge 9
Quivira 38
Ravenswood 30
RMS Brandy Distillery 3
Robert Mondavi 12
Rochioli Vineyards and Winery 36
Rutherford Hill Winery 15
St. Supery 20
Sebastiani Vineyards 28
Simi Winery 40
Stag's Leap Wine Cellars 10
Sterling Vineyards 24
Viansa 1

The Wine Country

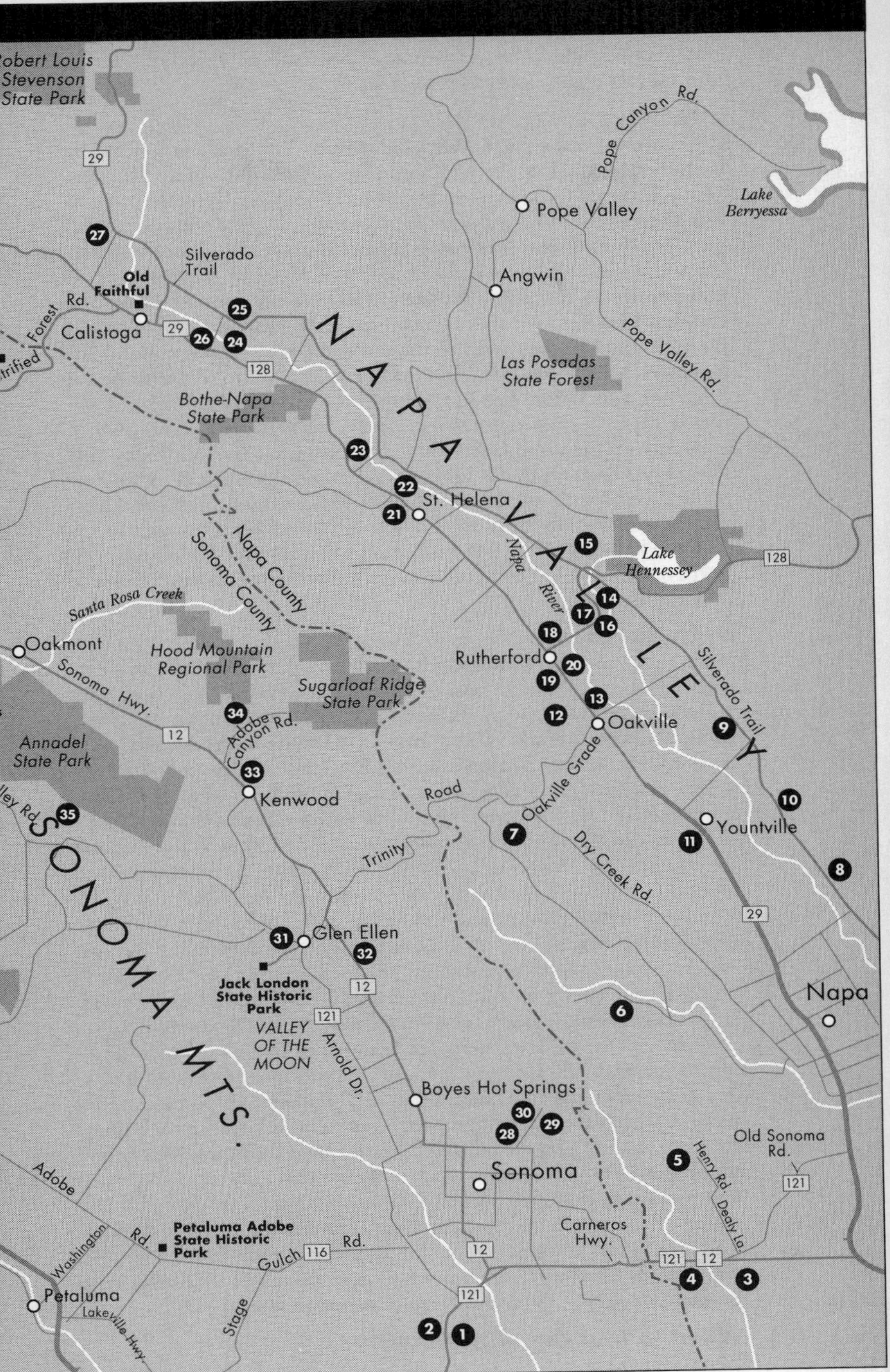

Robert Louis Stevenson State Park
29
Silverado Trail
Old Faithful
Forest Rd.
Calistoga
Petrified
27
25
26
24
128
Bothe-Napa State Park
NAPA VALLEY
Pope Canyon Rd.
Pope Valley
Lake Berryessa
Angwin
Pope Valley Rd.
Las Posadas State Forest
23
22
21
St. Helena
Napa River
15
Lake Hennessey
128
Napa County
Sonoma County
Santa Rosa Creek
14
17
16
18
Oakmont
Hood Mountain Regional Park
Sonoma Hwy.
Sugarloaf Ridge State Park
Rutherford
20
19
13
12
Oakville
Silverado Trail
9
34
Adobe Canyon Rd.
12
Annadel State Park
33
Kenwood
Road
Oakville Grade
10
35
Valley Rd.
7
Yountville
11
Dry Creek Rd.
8
Trinity
29
SONOMA MTS.
31
Glen Ellen
32
Jack London State Historic Park
12
121
VALLEY OF THE MOON
Arnold Dr.
Napa
6
Boyes Hot Springs
30
28
29
Old Sonoma Rd.
5
Henry Rd.
Sonoma
121
Dealy La.
Adobe Rd.
Washington
Petaluma Adobe State Historic Park
Gulch
116
Rd.
Carneros Hwy.
12
121
12
4
3
Petaluma
Lakeville Hwy.
121
Stage
2
1

early-morning balloon ride, an afternoon trip to the mud baths, and a visit to **Clos Pegase** ㉖ before heading back to St. Helena for dinner at Greystone—the Culinary Institute of America's beautiful West Coast campus and highly acclaimed restaurant.

IF YOU HAVE 4 DAYS

Concentrate on the Napa Valley, starting at Yountville and traveling north to Calistoga. Make your first stop in **Oakville,** where the circa-1880s Oakville Grocery—once a Wells Fargo Pony Express stop—is indisputably the most popular place for picnic supplies. Enjoy the picnic grounds at **Robert Mondavi** ⑫ before touring the winery and tasting the wine. If time permits, spend the night in the town of **Rutherford** and visit either **Rutherford Hill Winery** ⑮ or the **Niebaum-Coppola Estate** ⑲, or continue north to **St. Helena.** Take a look at the Silverado Museum and visit the shopping complex surrounding the **Freemark Abbey Winery** ㉓. On the third day drive to **Calistoga** for a balloon ride before heading north to Old Faithful Geyser of California, then continue on to Robert Louis Stevenson State Park, which encompasses the summit of Mount St. Helena. On the fourth day take Highway 29 just north of Calistoga proper, head west on Petrified Forest Road and then south on Calistoga Road, which runs into Highway 12. Follow Highway 12 southeast to **Glen Ellen** for a taste of the Sonoma Valley. Visit Jack London State Historic Park, then loop back north on Bennett Valley Road to beautiful **Matanzas Creek Winery** ㉟ in Santa Rosa.

IF YOU HAVE 7 DAYS

Begin in the town of **Sonoma,** whose colorful plaza and mission evoke early California's Spanish past. Afterward, head north to **Glen Ellen** and the Valley of the Moon. Picnic and explore the grounds at Jack London State Historic Park. Next morning visit **Kenwood Vineyards** ㉝ before heading north to **Healdsburg** in Dry Creek Valley via Santa Rosa and U.S. 101. In this less-trafficked haven of northern Sonoma County, a host of "hidden" wineries—including **Ferrari-Carano Winery** ㊴—lie nestled in the woods along the roads. Spend the night in **Healdsburg.** On the third day cross over into Napa Valley—take Mark Springs Road east off U.S. 101's River Road exit and follow the signs on Porter Creek Road to Petrified Forest Road to Highway 29. Spend the day (and the night) in the quaint town of **Calistoga,** noted for its mud baths and mineral springs. Wake up early on the fourth day for a balloon ride. If you're feeling energetic, take to the Silverado Trail for a bike ride with stops at **Cuvaison** ㉕, **Stag's Leap Wine Cellars** ⑩, and **Clos du Val** ⑧. On day five, visit the galleries, shops, and eateries of St. Helena before heading to the Oakville Grocery, a must-see (and must-taste) landmark. Spend the night and visit the wineries in **Rutherford.** On day six, explore nearby **Yountville,** stopping for lunch at one of its many acclaimed restaurants before heading up the hill to the **Hess Collection Winery and Vineyards** ⑥, on Mt. Veeder, where a brilliant art collection and excellent wines may keep you occupied for hours. Splurge on dinner at Domaine Chandon. On your last day return to the town of Sonoma via the Carneros Highway, stopping for a look at how brandies are made at the **RMS Brandy Distillery** ③, then moving on to the landmark **Buena Vista Carneros Winery** ㉙, or **Gloria Ferrer Champagne Caves** ②.

When to Tour the Wine Country

From September until December the entire Wine Country celebrates its bounty with street fairs and festivals. The Napa Valley Wine Festival takes place the first weekend in November. The Sonoma County Harvest Fair, with its famous grape stomp, is held the first weekend in October.

In season (April–October), Napa Valley draws crowds of tourists, and traffic along Highway 29 from St. Helena to Calistoga is often backed up on weekends. The Sonoma Valley, Santa Rosa, and Healdsburg are less crowded. In season and over holiday weekends it's best to book lodging, restaurant, and winery reservations well in advance. Many wineries give tours at specified times and require appointments.

To avoid crowds, visit the Wine Country during the week and get an early start (most wineries open around 10). Pack a sun hat, since summer is usually hot and dry, and autumn can be even hotter.

CARNEROS REGION

One of the most important viticultural areas in the Wine Country straddles southern Sonoma and Napa counties. The Carneros region has a long, cool growing season tempered by maritime breezes and lingering fogs off the San Pablo Bay—optimum slow-growing conditions for pinot noir and chardonnay grapes.

Southern Sonoma County

36 mi from San Francisco, north on U.S. 101, east on Hwy. 37, and north on Hwy. 121.

1 Sam Sebastiani, of the famous Sebastiani family, decided to strike out on his own and with his wife, Vicki, opened **Viansa.** Reminiscent of a Tuscan villa, the winery's ocher-color building is surrounded by olive trees and overlooks the valley. The varietals produced here depart from the traditionally Californian and include muscat canelli and nebbiolo. ✉ *25200 Arnold Dr., Sonoma County,* ☎ *707/935–4700.* ⏲ *Daily 10–5. Tours by appointment.*

2 The array of sparkling and still wines at **Gloria Ferrer Champagne Caves** originated with a 700-year-old stock of Ferrer grapes. The method here is to age the wines in a "cava," or cellar, where several feet of earth maintain a constant temperature. ✉ *23555 Carneros (Hwy. 121),* ☎ *707/996–7256.* 🎫 *Tasting fees vary.* ⏲ *Daily 10:30–5:30. Tours hourly 11–4.*

Southern Napa County

7 mi east of Hwy. 121/Hwy. 116 junction on Hwy. 121/12.

3 Learn the history and folklore of rare alembic brandy at the **RMS Brandy Distillery.** Tours include an explanation of the double-distillation; a view of the French-built alembic distillation pots that resemble Aladdin's lamp; a trip to the atmospheric oak barrel house; and a sensory evaluation of vintage brandies. ✉ *1250 Cuttings Wharf Rd., Napa (from Domaine Carneros, head 1 mi east on Carneros Hwy.),* ☎ *707/253–9055,* FAX *707/253–0116.* ⏲ *Apr.–Oct., daily 10–5; Nov.–Mar., daily 10:30–4:30. Tours on the hr.*

4 **Domaine Carneros** occupies a 138-acre estate dominated by a classic château inspired by Champagne Taittinger's historic Château de la Marquetterie in France. Carved into the hillside beneath the winery, Domaine Carneros's cellars produce sparkling wines reminiscent of the Taittinger style and using only Carneros grapes. ✉ *1240 Duhig Rd., Napa,* ☎ *707/257–0101,* FAX *707/257–3020.* 🎫 *Tasting fees vary.* ⏲ *Daily 10:30–6. Tours Mon.–Thurs. at 11, 1, and 3; Fri.–Sun. hourly 11–4.*

THE NAPA VALLEY

The Napa Valley is the undisputed capital of American wine production, with more than 240 wineries. Famed for its unrivaled climate and neat rows of vineyards, the area is made up of small, quirky towns whose Victorian Gothic architecture—narrow, gingerbread facades and pointed arches—is reminiscent of a distant world. Calistoga feels like an Old West frontier town, with wooden-plank storefronts and people in cowboy hats. St. Helena is posh, with tony shops and elegant restaurants. Yountville is compact and redolent of American history, yet fast becoming an up-to-the-minute culinary hub.

Napa

46 mi from San Francisco, east and north on I–80 to Hwy. 37 west to Hwy. 29 north.

The oldest town in the Napa Valley—established in 1848—it also claims an advantageous location. Most destinations in both the Napa and Sonoma valleys are easily accessible from here. For those seeking an affordable alternative to the hotels and B&Bs in the heart of the Wine Country, Napa is a good option.

❺ Bunkered into a scenic Carneros hilltop, **Artesa** has replaced Codorniu Napa, not only in name but in focus. The Spanish owners are producing primarily still wines under the talented wine maker Don Van Staaveren (formerly of Chateau St. Jean). ✉ *1345 Henry Rd., north off Old Sonoma Rd. and Dealy La.,* ☎ *707/224–1668,* FAX *707/224–1672.* ⏲ *Daily 10–5. Tours daily; times vary.*

★ ❻ The **Hess Collection Winery and Vineyards** is a delightful discovery on a hilltop 9 mi northwest of Napa (don't give up; the road leading to the winery is long and winding). Within the simple, rustic limestone structure, circa 1903, you'll find Swiss owner Donald Hess's personal art collection. Cabernet sauvignon is the real strength here, though Hess also produces some fine chardonnays. ✉ *4411 Redwood Rd., west off Hwy. 29,* ☎ *707/255–1144,* FAX *707/253–1682.* ⏲ *Daily 10–4.*

❼ **Chateau Potelle,** on the slopes of Mt. Veeder, produces acclaimed estate zinfandel, chardonnay, and cabernet sauvignon, which thrive in the poor soil at nearly 2,000 ft above the valley floor. It's a quiet, out-of-the-way spot for a picnic. ✉ *3875 Mt. Veeder Rd. (5 mi west of Hwy. 29 off the Oakville Grade),* ☎ *707/255–9440.* ⏲ *Thurs.–Mon. 11–5 (winter hrs vary).*

❽ **Clos du Val,** founded by French owner Bernard Portet, produces a celebrated reserve cabernet. It also makes zinfandel, pinot noir, merlot, sangiovese, and chardonnay. ✉ *5330 Silverado Trail,* ☎ *707/259–2200.* 🎟 *Tasting fee $5.* ⏲ *Daily 10–5. Tours by appointment.*

❾ Small **Pine Ridge** makes estate-bottled wines, including chardonnay, cabernet, and merlot. Tours include barrel tastings in the winery's caves. ✉ *5901 Silverado Trail,* ☎ *707/253–7500,* FAX *707/253–1493.* ⏲ *Daily 11–5. Tours by appointment at 10:15, 1, and 3.*

Dining and Lodging

$$$ ✕ **Silverado Country Club.** There are two restaurants and a bar and grill at this large, famous resort. The elegant Vintner's Court, with California–Pacific Rim cuisine, serves dinner only; there is a seafood buffet on Friday night and a champagne brunch on Sunday. Royal Oak serves steak and seafood nightly. The bar and grill is open for and lunch year-round. In the summer lunch offerings include an outdoor barbecue with chicken and hamburgers. ✉ *1600 Atlas Peak Rd. (follow signs* *to Lake Berryessa), ☎ 707/257–0200 or 800/532–0500. Reservations essential. AE, D, DC, MC, V. Vintner's Court closed Mon.–Thurs. No dinner Sun.*

$–$$$ ✕ **Foothill Café.** On the less glamorous side of Highway 29, this low-key restaurant is a big favorite with locals who may or may not know that the chef is an alumnus of Masa's in San Francisco. ✉ *2766 Old Sonoma Rd., ☎ 707/252–6178. MC, V. Closed Mon.–Tues.*

$–$$ ✕ **Bistro Don Giovanni.** Even in winter, the valley views from the covered patio here are extraordinary. The wine list is as locally representative as the menu is eclectic. Don't miss the individual pizzas cooked in a wood-burning oven, the handmade pastas or the focaccia sandwiches concealing grilled vegetables. ✉ *4110 St. Helena Hwy. (Hwy. 29), ☎ 707/224–3300. AE, D, MC, V.*

$–$$ ✕ **Celadon.** Dishes such as flash-fried calamari with a chipotle chili and ginger glaze and small tasting plates such as a large crab cake laced with whole-seed mustard sauce make this an ideal place to sample contemporary cuisine accompanied by any of a dozen wines available by the glass. ✉ *1040 Main St., ☎ 707/254–9690. AE, MC, V. Closed Sun.*

$$$–$$$$ **Silverado Country Club and Resort.** This luxurious if somewhat staid 1,200-acre property in the hills east of Napa has cottages, kitchen apartments, and one- to three-bedroom efficiencies, many with fireplaces. With two golf courses, nine pools, and 23 tennis courts, it's a place for serious sports enthusiasts and anyone who enjoys the conveniences of a full-scale resort. ✉ *1600 Atlas Peak Rd. (6 mi east of Napa via Hwy. 121), 94558, ☎ 707/257–0200 or 800/532–0500, FAX 707/257–2867. 277 condo units. 3 restaurants, bar, 9 pools, 2 18-hole golf courses, 23 tennis courts, bicycles. AE, D, DC, MC, V.*

$$ **Chateau Hotel.** Despite the name, this is a pretty simple motel with only the barest nod to France. Clean rooms, a great location, Continental breakfast, facilities for travelers with disabilities, and discounts for senior citizens make up for its lack of charm. ✉ *4195 Solano Ave. (west of Hwy. 29, exit at Trower Ave.), 94558, ☎ 707/253–9300; 800/253–6272 in CA, FAX 707/253–0906. 115 rooms. Refrigerators, pool, hot tub. AE, D, DC, MC, V. CP.*

Outdoor Activities and Sports

BICYCLING

For rentals try **Napa Valley Bike Tours and Rentals** (✉ 4080 Byway E, Napa, ☎ 707/255–3377, FAX 707/255–3380).

FISHING

You can fish from the banks of the Napa River at **John F. Kennedy Park** (✉ 2291 Streblow Dr., ☎ 707/257–9529). Call ahead for river conditions.

GOLF

The 18-hole **Chardonnay Club** (✉ 2555 Jameson Canyon Rd., ☎ 707/257–8950) course is a favorite among Bay Area golfers. The greens fee, $70 weekdays and $90 weekends, includes a cart. Within the vicinity of the Silverado Trail, the **Silverado Country Club** (✉ 1600 Atlas Peak Rd., ☎ 707/257–0200) has two challenging 18-hole courses with a beautiful view at every hole. The greens fee is $145, including a cart; you must be a guest (of the hotel, a member, or another club) to play.

Yountville

13 mi north of the town of Napa on Hwy. 29.

Yountville has become the valley's boomtown. No other small town in the entire Wine Country has as many inns, restaurants, or shops—and new ones seem to open every few months. A popular attraction is

Vintage 1870 (⊠ 6525 Washington St., ☎ 707/944–2451), a 26-acre complex of boutiques, restaurants, and gourmet stores. The vine-covered brick buildings were built in 1870 and housed a winery, livery stable, and distillery. The original mansion of the property is now the popular Mexican-style **Compadres Bar and Grill.** Nearby is the **Pacific Blues Café,** housed in the train depot Samuel Brannan built in 1868 for his privately owned Napa Valley Railroad. At **Yountville Park** there's a picnic area with tables, barbecue pits, and a view of grapevines.

At the intersection of Madison and Washington streets is Yountville's quaint and historic **Washington Square.** The town's original main square is now a complex of boutiques and family-style restaurants. **Pioneer Cemetery,** the final resting place of the town's founder, George Yount, is across the street from Washington Square.

10 In 1995, the World Wine Championships gave **Stag's Leap Wine Cellars** a platinum award for its 1990 reserve chardonnay, designating it the highest-ranked premium chardonnay in the world. ⊠ *5766 Silverado Trail,* ☎ *707/944–2020.* 🎫 *Tasting fee $3.* ⊙ *Daily 10–4. Tours by appointment.*

11 French-owned **Domaine Chandon** claims one of Yountville's prime pieces of real estate, on a knoll west of downtown. Tours of the sleek, modern facilities on the beautifully maintained property include sample flutes of the sparkling wine. ⊠ *California Dr., west of Hwy. 29,* ☎ *707/944–2280.* ⊙ *Jan.–Mar., Wed.–Sun. 11–6; Apr.–Dec., 10–7. Tours on the hr.*

Dining and Lodging

$$$$ ★ ✕ **French Laundry.** Napa Valley's most acclaimed restaurant can be found inside an old converted brick building on a residential street corner. The prix fixe menus, which include four or five courses, always include two or three additional surprises—little bitefuls—to start, such as a tiny ice cream cone filled with salmon tartare or a quail egg sandwiched between a crown of caviar and a base of brioche. A full three hours will likely pass before you reach dessert. Reservations are hard won and not accepted more than two months in advance, but lunch is a little easier to come by. ⊠ *6640 Washington St.,* ☎ *707/944–2380. Reservations essential. AE, MC, V. Closed 1st 2 wks in Jan.; lunch hrs and days vary with the season.*

$$$ ✕ **Brix.** Overlooking vineyards and the Mayacamas Mountains, the spacious yellow-and-green dining room invites you to sit back and enjoy the East–West menu. Scallops are served with a Thai lime-butter sauce, and salmon is flavored with a light soy glaze. A wood-burning oven is used for cooking pizzas. ⊠ *7377 St. Helena Hwy.,* ☎ *707/944–2749. AE, D, DC, MC, V.*

$$–$$$ ✕ **Bistro Jeanty.** In 1998 Philippe Jeanty opened his own restaurant with a menu inspired by the cooking of his French childhood. His traditional cassoulet will warm those nostalgic for bistro cooking, while classic coq au vin rises above the ordinary with the infusion of a spicy red wine sauce. The scene here is Gallic through and through with a small bar and a handful of tables in a crowded room. ⊠ *6510 Washington St.,* ☎ *707/944–0103. MC, V. Closed last wk of Jan.–1st wk of Feb.*

$$–$$$ ✕ **Bouchon.** Thomas and Joseph Keller, flush with the success of their French Laundry (*above*), opened a second restaurant in the fall of 1998. Late-night diners (and restaurant employees who work until the wee hours) are pleased it's open until 2 AM. French country fare—*steak frites,* leg of lamb, and sole meunière—are served amid elegant antique chandeliers and a snazzy zinc bar. ⊠ *6534 Washington St.,* ☎ *707/944–8037. AE, MC, V.*

$$–$$$ ★ ✕ **Livefire.** Opened in 1998 on Yountville's expanding restaurant row, this is a cozy spot warmed with such earthy colors as mustard and terra-cotta. Fish, ribs, and poultry come piping hot out of a French rotisserie or a Chinese smoker. Service is top-notch. ✉ *5518 Washington St., 1 mi north of Yountville,* ☎ *707/944–1500. AE, D, DC, MC, V.*

$$ ★ ✕ **Mustards Grill.** Everyone's favorite Napa Valley restaurant attracts wine makers and other locals as well as hungry tourists. Grilled fish, steak, local fresh produce, and an impressive wine list are the trademarks of this boisterous bistro with a black-and-white marble floor and upbeat artwork. The thin, crisp, golden onion rings are addictive. ✉ *7399 St. Helena Hwy., 1 mi north of Yountville,* ☎ *707/944–2424 or 800/901–8098. Reservations essential. D, DC, MC, V.*

$ ✕ **The Diner.** An unpretentious classic, this breakfast-oriented eatery serves local sausages and house potatoes that are not to be missed. ✉ *6476 Washington St.,* ☎ *707/944–2626. MC, V. Closed Mon.*

$$$$ **La Residence.** Even though it's within feet of the St. Helena Highway, "La Res," as it's known, is secluded and romantic enough to make you feel as if you've flown to France. The hotel is housed in two buildings: the Mansion, a renovated 1870s Gothic Revival manor house built by a riverboat captain from New Orleans; and Cabernet Hall, a French-style barn. Both buildings overlook a pool, a manicured garden, and towering oaks that bathe the entire property in shade. ✉ *4066 St. Helena Hwy. (Hwy. 29), 4 mi south of Yountville,* ☎ *707/253–0337,* FAX *707/253–0382. 20 rooms. Dining room, pool, hot tub, business services. AE, DC, MC, V. BP.*

$$$$ **Napa Valley Lodge.** Balconies, covered walkways, and a red-tile roof imbue this inn with the ambience of a hacienda. The large pool area is landscaped with lots of greenery. Many spacious second-floor rooms have vineyard views. Fresh brewed coffee and the morning paper are complimentary. ✉ *2230 Madison St., at Hwy. 29,* ☎ *707/944–2468 or 800/368–2468,* FAX *707/944–9362. 55 rooms. Refrigerators, pool, hot tub, sauna, exercise room. AE, D, DC, MC, V. CP.*

$$$$ **Vintage Inn.** Accommodations in this luxurious inn are arranged in two-story villas throughout the 3½-acre property. All the spacious rooms have fireplaces, whirlpool baths, refrigerators, private patios, hand-painted bedspreads, window seats, and shuttered windows. ✉ *6541 Washington St., 94599,* ☎ *707/944–1112 or 800/351–1133,* FAX *707/944–1617. 80 rooms. Refrigerators, pool, hot tub, tennis court, bicycles. AE, D, DC, MC, V. CP.*

$$$ **Petit Logis.** Murals and 11-ft ceilings infuse each unique room with a European elegance. Breakfast, included in the room rate, is offered at one of two nearby restaurants. ✉ *6527 Yount St., 94599,* ☎ *707/944–2332. 5 rooms. MC, V. BP.*

Hot-Air Ballooning

Balloons Above the Valley (✉ Box 3838, Napa 94558, ☎ 707/253–2222; 800/464–6824 in CA) is a reliable organization; rides are $175 per person. Also try **Napa Valley Balloons** (✉ Box 2860, Yountville 94599, ☎ 707/944–0228; 800/253–2224 in CA), which charges $185 per person.

Oakville

2 mi west of Yountville on Hwy. 29.

There are three reasons to visit the town of Oakville: its grocery store, its scenic mountain grade, and its magnificent, highly exclusive winery. The **Oakville Grocery** (✉ 7856 St. Helena Hwy.), built in the late 1880s to serve as a grocery store and Wells Fargo Pony Express stop, carries gourmet foods and difficult-to-find wines. Custom-packed picnic baskets are a specialty. Along the mountain range that divides Napa and Sonoma, the **Oakville Grade** is a twisting half-hour route with breathtaking views of both valleys.

12 At **Robert Mondavi,** the most famous winery in the nation, visitors are encouraged to take the 60-minute production tour with complimentary tasting, before trying the reserve reds ($1–$5 per glass). In-depth three- to four-hour tours and gourmet lunch tours are also popular. ✉ *7801 St. Helena Hwy.,* ☎ *707/259–9463.* ⏲ *Daily 9–5. Tours by appointment.*

13 **Opus One,** the combined venture of famed California wine maker Robert Mondavi and French baron Philippe Rothschild, is famed for its vast semicircular cellar modeled on the Château Mouton Rothschild winery in France. The state-of-the-art facilities produce about 20,000 cases of ultrapremium Bordeaux-style red wine. ✉ *7900 St. Helena Hwy.,* ☎ *707/963–1979,* FAX *707/944–1753.* 🎫 *Tasting fee $25.* ⏲ *Daily 10–3:30. Tours by appointment.*

Rutherford

1 mi northwest of Oakville on Hwy. 29.

From a fast-moving car, Rutherford is a quick blur of dark forest, a rustic barn or two, and maybe a country store. But don't speed by this tiny hamlet. With its singular microclimate and soil, this is an important viticultural center.

14 **Mumm Napa Valley** is considered one of California's premier sparkling-wine producers. Its Napa Brut Prestige and ultrapremium Vintage Reserve are the best known. The excellent tour and comfortable tasting room are two more good reasons to visit. ✉ *8445 Silverado Trail,* ☎ *707/942–3434.* 🎫 *Tasting fees vary.* ⏲ *May–Oct., daily 10:30–6; Nov.–Apr., daily 10–5. Tours daily 11–4.*

15 The wine at **Rutherford Hill Winery** is aged in French oak barrels stacked in more than 30,000 square ft of caves—one of the largest such facilities in the nation. Tours of the caves can be followed by a picnic in oak, olive, or madrone orchards. ✉ *200 Rutherford Hill Rd., off the Silverado Trail,* ☎ *707/963–7194.* 🎫 *Tasting fees vary.* ⏲ *Daily 10–5. Tour times vary seasonally; call ahead.*

A 100% cabernet sauvignon special selection is the claim to fame for
16 **Caymus Vineyards.** Caymus also turns out a superior white, the Conundrum Proprietary, made of an unusual blend of grapes—sauvignon blanc, semillon, chardonnay, muscat canelli, and viognier. ✉ *8700 Conn Creek Rd.,* ☎ *707/963–4204.* ⏲ *Daily 10–4:30. No tours.*

17 **Frog's Leap** is the perfect place for wine novices to begin their education. Owners John and Julie Williams maintain a sense of humor and a humble attitude that translates into an informative and satisfying experience. They also happen to produce some of the finest zinfandel, cabernet sauvignon, and sauvignon blanc in the Wine Country. ✉ *8815 Conn Creek Rd.,* ☎ *707/963–4704.* ⏲ *Tours by appointment.*

18 **Beaulieu Vineyard** utilizes the same wine-making process, from crush to bottle, as it did the day it opened in 1900. The winery's cabernet is a benchmark of the Napa Valley. The Georges du Latour Private Reserve consistently garners high marks from major wine publications. ✉ *1960 St. Helena Hwy. (Hwy. 29),* ☎ *707/963–2411.* 🎫 *Tasting fee $18 in Reserve Room.* ⏲ *Daily 10–5. Tours daily 11–4.*

In the 1970s, filmmaker Francis Ford Coppola bought the old Niebaum estate, a part of the world-famous Inglenook estate. He resurrected an early Inglenook-like quality red with his first bottle of Rubicon, released

19 in 1985. Since then, **Niebaum-Coppola Estate** has consistently received high ratings. When you're through touring the winery, take a look at the Coppola movie memorabilia, which includes Don Corleone's desk and chair from *The Godfather.* ✉ *1991 St. Helena Hwy. (Hwy. 29),* ☎ *707/963–9099.* 🎫 *Tasting fee $7.50.* ⏲ *Daily 10–5. Tours daily; times vary.*

20 **St. Supery** makes such excellent sauvignon blanc that it often sells out, but you can usually sample that variety as well as chardonnay, several red wines, and two kosher wines in the tasting room. This winery's unique discovery center allows visitors to inhale distinct wine aromas and match them with actual scents of black pepper, cherry, citrus, and the like. ✉ *8440 St. Helena Hwy. S (Hwy. 29),* ☎ *707/963–4507.* 🎫 *Tasting fee $5 (lifetime).* ⏲ *Daily 9:30–5.*

Dining and Lodging

$$$$ ★ ✕ **La Toque.** This understated restaurant, housed in the Rancho Caymus Inn, specializes in intense flavors such as braised chanterelles, ravioli with chestnuts and rabbit, and cannellini-cranberry ragout. The cheese courses and dessert menu are worth saving some room for. ✉ *1140 Rutherford Rd.,* ☎ *707/963–9770. Reservations essential. AE, MC, V. Closed Mon. and Tues. No dinner Sun.*

$$$$ ★ ✕🏨 **Auberge du Soleil.** This stunning property, terraced on a hill studded by olive trees, offers some of the valley's best views. The hotel's renowned restaurant has a frequently changing menu that emphasizes local produce and also includes such unusual specialties as roasted lobster sausage. Slow-roasted garlic with homemade pretzels and pan-seared salmon sandwiches are standouts on the moderately priced bar menu. Guest rooms are decorated with a nod to the spare side of Southwestern style. ✉ *180 Rutherford Hill Rd. (off Silverado Trail just north of Rte. 128), 94573,* ☎ *707/963–1211 or 800/348–5406,* FAX *707/963–8764. 50 rooms. Restaurant, pool, hot tub, massage, steam room, 3 tennis courts, exercise room. AE, D, DC, MC, V.*

$$$–$$$$ 🏨 **Rancho Caymus Inn.** California-Spanish in style, this cozy inn has well-maintained gardens and large suites with kitchens and whirlpool baths. Well-chosen details include beehive fireplaces, tile murals, stoneware basins, and llama-hair blankets. ✉ *1140 Rutherford Rd. (junction of Hwys. 29 and 128), 94573,* ☎ *707/963–1777 or 800/845–1777,* FAX *707/963–5387. 26 rooms. Restaurant. DC, MC, V. 2-night minimum Apr.–Nov.*

St. Helena

2 mi northwest of Oakville on Hwy. 29.

By the time Charles Krug planted grapes in St. Helena around 1860, quite a few vineyards already existed. Today the town greets visitors with its abundant selection of wineries—many of which lie along the route from Yountville to St. Helena—and restaurants, including Greystone on the West Coast campus of the Culinary Institute of America.

Arguably the most beautiful winery in the Napa Valley, the 1876
21 **Beringer Vineyards** is also the oldest continuously operating one. In 1883 the Beringer brothers, Frederick and Jacob, built the mansion where tastings are now held. Tours, given every 30 minutes, include a visit to underground wine tunnels made of volcanic ash that were dug by Chinese laborers during the 19th century. ✉ *2000 Main St.,* ☎ *707/963–4812.* ⏲ *Daily 9:30–4; summer hrs sometimes extend to 5. Tours daily.*

22 **Charles Krug Winery** opened in 1861 when Count Haraszthy loaned Krug a small cider press. Today, it is run by the Peter Mondavi fam-

ily. The gift shop stocks everything from gourmet food baskets with grape-shape pasta to books about the region and its wines. The joint tasting and tour fee is $3. ✉ *2800 N. Main St.,* ☎ *707/963–5057.* ⏲ *Daily 10:30–5:30. Tours 11:30, 1:30, and 3:30.*

23 **Freemark Abbey Winery,** was originally called the Tychson Winery after Josephine Tychson, the first woman to establish a winery in California. It has long been known for its cabernets, whose grapes come from the fertile Rutherford Bench. ✉ *3022 St. Helena Hwy. N,* ☎ *707/963–9694.* ⏲ *Daily 10–4:30. Tour daily at 2.*

Grape-seed mud wraps and Ayurvedic-inspired massages performed by two attendants are among the trademarks of the upscale **Health Spa Napa Valley** (✉ 1030 Main St., ☎ 707/967–8800), which has a pool and a health club. Should your treatments leave you too limp to operate your car, you can walk to Tra Vigne (*below*) and other St. Helena restaurants.

Dining and Lodging

$$$–$$$$ ✕ **Terra.** A romantic restaurant housed in a 100-year-old stone foundry, Terra is especially known for its exquisite Mediterranean-inspired dishes, many with Asian touches. The sweetbreads ragout, rock shrimp salad, and osso buco are memorable. ✉ *1345 Railroad Ave.,* ☎ *707/963–8931. Reservations essential. DC, MC, V. Closed Tues. No lunch.*

$$–$$$ ✕ **Brava Terrace.** Vegetables plucked straight from the restaurant's own garden enliven chef Fred Halpert's trademark New American cuisine. Brava has a comfortably casual ambience with a full bar, a large stone fireplace, a romantic outdoor terrace overlooking a shady brook, and a heated deck with views of the valley floor and Howell Mountain. ✉ *3010 St. Helena Hwy. (Hwy. 29), ½ mi north of downtown St. Helena,* ☎ *707/963–9300. Reservations essential. AE, D, DC, MC, V. Closed Wed. Nov.–Apr. and last 2 wks of Jan.*

$$–$$$ ✕ **Wine Spectator Greystone Restaurant.** This restaurant, housed in the handsome old Christian Brothers' winery, is run by the Culinary Institute of America. Century-old stone walls house a large and bustling restaurant, with cooking, baking, and grilling stations in full view. The menu has a Mediterranean spirit and emphasizes such small plates as bruschetta topped with wild mushrooms and *muhammara,* a spread of roasted red peppers and walnuts. ✉ *2555 Main St.,* ☎ *707/967–1010. AE, DC, MC, V.*

$–$$$ ✕ **Showley's.** This local favorite is well worth a little detour from the beaten path. Try such starters as the chili *en nogada,* made with pork, pine nuts, and chutney and served with a walnut–crème fraîche sauce. ✉ *1327 Railroad Ave.,* ☎ *707/963–1200. AE, MC, V. Closed Mon.*

$–$$ ★ ✕ **Tra Vigne.** This fieldstone building has been transformed into a striking trattoria with a huge wood bar, high ceilings, and plush banquettes. Homemade mozzarella, olive oil and vinegar, and house-cured pancetta and prosciutto contribute to a mouthwatering tour of Tuscan cuisine. The outdoor courtyard in summer and fall is a sun-splashed Mediterranean vision of striped umbrellas and awnings, crowded café tables, and rustic pots overflowing with flowers. ✉ *1050 Charter Oak Ave., off Hwy. 29,* ☎ *707/963–4444. Reservations essential. D, DC, MC, V.*

$$$$ ✕🏨 **Meadowood Resort.** Secluded at the end of a semi-private road, this 256-acre resort has accommodations in a rambling country lodge and several bungalows. The elegant dining room specializes in California Wine Country cooking, either à la carte or as part of a prix-fixe menu. The Grill, a less formal, less expensive restaurant, serves a lighter menu of pizzas and spa food for breakfast and lunch (and early dinners on Friday and Saturday). ✉ *900 Meadowood La., 94574,* ☎ *707/963–3646 or 800/458–8080,* FAX *707/963–5863. 40 rooms, 45 suites.*

2 restaurants (reservations essential), bar, room service, 2 pools, hot tub, massage, sauna, steam room, 9-hole golf course, 7 tennis courts, croquet, health club. AE, D, DC, MC, V.

$$$$ ★ **Wine Country Inn.** Surrounded by a pastoral landscape of hills, old barns, and stone bridges, this is a peaceful New England–style retreat. Rural antiques fill all the rooms, most of which overlook the vineyards with either a balcony, patio, or deck. Most rooms have fireplaces, and some have private hot tubs. A hearty country breakfast is served buffet style in the sun-splashed common room. ✉ *1152 Lodi La. (off Hwy. 29), 94574,* ☎ *707/963–7077,* FAX *707/963–9018. 24 rooms. Pool, hot tubs. MC, V. BP.*

$$$–$$$$ **Harvest Inn.** The larger-than-average rooms at this Tudor-esque inn are on the dark side, but the lushly landscaped grounds are lovely. Most rooms have wet bars, refrigerators, antique furnishings, and fireplaces. Complimentary breakfast is served on the patio overlooking the vineyards. ✉ *1 Main St., 94574,* ☎ *707/963–9463 or 800/950–8466,* FAX *707/963–4402. 55 rooms. Refrigerators, 2 pools, hot tub. AE, D, DC, MC, V. CP.*

$$–$$$ **El Bonita Motel.** A cute motel with such pleasant touches as window boxes and landscaped grounds, the conveniently located El Bonita has relatively elegant furnishings. ✉ *195 Main St. (Hwy. 29), 94574,* ☎ *707/963–3216 or 800/541–3284,* FAX *707/963–8838. 41 rooms. Pool. AE, MC, V.*

Shopping

Handcrafted candles made on the premises are for sale at the **Hurd Beeswax Candle Factory** (✉ 3020 St. Helena Hwy. N, ☎ 707/963–7211). **On the Vine** (✉ 1234 Main St., ☎ 707/963–2209) presents wearable art and unique jewelry inspired by food and wine themes. At **I. Wolk Gallery** (✉ 1235 Main St., ☎ 707/963–8800) you'll find everything from abstract and contemporary realist paintings to high-quality works on paper and sculpture. The **Art on Main** (✉ 1359 Main St., ☎ 707/963–3350) features oils, watercolors, ceramics, and etchings by northern California artists.

Calistoga

3 mi northwest of St. Helena on Hwy. 29.

In addition to its wineries, Calistoga is noted for its mineral water, hot mineral springs, mud baths, steam baths, and massages. The Calistoga Hot Springs Resort was founded in 1859 by maverick entrepreneur Sam Brannan, whose ambition was to found "the Saratoga of California." He tripped up the pronunciation of the phrase at a formal banquet—it came out "Calistoga"—and the name stuck.

The **Sharpsteen Museum** has a magnificent diorama of the Calistoga Hot Springs Resort in its heyday. Other exhibits document Robert Louis Stevenson's time in the area and the career of museum founder Ben Sharpsteen, an animator at the Walt Disney studio. ✉ *1311 Washington St.,* ☎ *707/942–5911.* *Free.* *May–Oct., daily 10–4; Nov.–Apr., daily noon–4.*

Indian Springs, an old-time spa, has been pumping out 212°F water from its three geysers for more than a century. The place offers some of the best bargains on mud bathing and short massages, and has a large mineral-water pool for guests. ✉ *1712 Lincoln Ave.,* ☎ *707/942–4913.* *Daily 9–7. Reservations recommended for spa treatments.*

24 **Sterling Vineyards** sits on a hilltop to the east of Calistoga, its pristine white Mediterranean-style buildings reached by an aerial tramway

from the valley floor. ✉ *1111 Dunaweal La.,* ☎ *707/942–3300.* 🎟 *Tram $6.* ⏲ *Daily 10:30–4:30.*

25 **Cuvaison** specializes in chardonnay, merlot, and cabernet sauvignon for the export market. Two small picnic areas on the grounds look out over Napa Valley. ✉ *4550 Silverado Trail,* ☎ *707/942–6266.* 🎟 *Tasting fees vary.* ⏲ *Daily 10–5. Tours by appointment.*

★ 26 Designed by postmodern architect Michael Graves, **Clos Pegase** is a one-of-a-kind structure packed with unusual art objects from the collection of art book publisher and owner Jan Shrem. ✉ *1060 Dunaweal La.,* ☎ *707/942–4981.* ⏲ *Daily 10:30–5. Tours at 11 and 2.*

27 **Château Montelena** is a vine-covered stone French château constructed circa 1882 and set amid Chinese-inspired gardens, complete with an artificial lake with gliding swans and islands crowned by Chinese pavilions. ✉ *1429 Tubbs La.,* ☎ *707/942–5105; 800/222–7288 outside the Bay Area.* 🎟 *Tasting fees vary.* ⏲ *Daily 10–4. Tours by appointment at 11 and 2.*

Many families bring children to Calistoga to see **Old Faithful Geyser of California** blast its 60-ft tower of steam and vapor about every 40 minutes. One of just three regularly erupting geysers in the world, it is fed by an underground river that heats to 350°F. ✉ *1299 Tubbs La., 1 mi north of Calistoga,* ☎ *707/942–6463.* 🎟 *$6.* ⏲ *Apr.–Sept., daily 9–6; Oct.–Mar., daily 9–5.*

The **Petrified Forest** contains the remains of the volcanic eruptions of Mount Saint Helens 3.4 million years ago. The force of the explosion uprooted the gigantic redwoods, covered them with volcanic ash, and infiltrated the trees with silica and minerals, causing petrifaction. ✉ *4100 Petrified Forest Rd., 5 mi west of Calistoga,* ☎ *707/942–6667.* 🎟 *$4.* ⏲ *Daily 10–5 (until 6 in summer).*

Robert Louis Stevenson State Park, on Highway 29, 3 mi northeast of Calistoga, encompasses the summit of Mount St. Helena. It was here, in the summer of 1880, in an abandoned bunkhouse of the Silverado Mine, that Stevenson and his bride, Fanny Osbourne, spent their honeymoon. The stay inspired Stevenson's "The Silverado Squatters." The park's 3,000 acres are mostly undeveloped.

Dining and Lodging

$$–$$$ ★ ✕ **Catahoula Restaurant and Saloon.** This sleek restaurant, named after Louisiana's state dog, is the brainchild of chef Jan Birnbaum, whose credentials include stints at the Quilted Giraffe in New York and Campton Place in San Francisco. Using a large wood-burning oven, Birnbaum turns out such dishes as spicy gumbo with andouille sausage cooked over a wood fire. ✉ *Mount View Hotel, 1457 Lincoln Ave.,* ☎ *707/942–2275. Reservations essential. MC, V. Closed Tues. and Jan.*

$$–$$$ ✕ **Wappo Bar Bistro.** This colorful restaurant is an adventure in international dining with a menu ranging from Asian noodles and Thai shrimp curry to chile rellenos. ✉ *1226 S. Washington St.,* ☎ *707/942–4712. AE, MC, V. Closed Tues.*

$–$$$ ✕ **All Seasons Café.** Bistro cuisine takes a California spin in this sun-filled setting with marble tables and a black-and-white checkerboard floor. The seasonal menu includes organic greens, wild mushrooms, local game birds, and house-smoked beef. The café shares space with a well-stocked wineshop. ✉ *1400 Lincoln Ave.,* ☎ *707/942–9111. MC, V. No lunch Wed.*

$$ ✕ **Calistoga Inn.** Grilled meat and fish for dinner and soups, salads, and sandwiches for lunch are prepared with flair at this microbrew-

ery with a tree-shaded outdoor patio. ✉ *1250 Lincoln Ave.,* ☎ *707/942–4101. AE, MC, V.*

$–$$ ✕ **Pacifico.** Technicolor ceramics and subtropical plants adorn this Mexican restaurant that serves Oaxacan and other fare. Fajitas and moles are among the specialties. ✉ *1237 Lincoln Ave.,* ☎ *707/942–4400. MC, V.*

$$$$ **Cottage Grove Inn.** These 16 elegant and contemporary cottages are shaded by elm trees. Rooms have skylights and plush furnishings. Fireplaces, CD players, VCRs, two-person hot tubs, and porches with wicker rocking chairs add to the coziness. Spas and restaurants are within walking distance. Rates include Continental breakfast and afternoon wine and cheese. ✉ *1711 Lincoln Ave., 94515,* ☎ *707/942–8400 or 800/799–2284,* FAX *707/942–2653. 16 rooms. Breakfast room, refrigerators. AE, D, DC, MC, V. CP.*

$$$$ **Meadowlark Country House.** The ambience is decidedly laid-back and sophisticated at this inn surrounded by 20 hillside acres just north of downtown Calistoga. The main house, built in 1886, and a newer building down a gravel path hold unfussy but country-stylish rooms. ✉ *601 Petrified Forest Rd., 94515,* ☎ *707/942–5651 or 800/942–5651,* FAX *707/942–5023. 7 rooms. Breakfast room, pool, hot tub, sauna. AE, MC, V. BP.*

$$$–$$$$ **Mount View Hotel.** The Mount View is one of the valley's most historic resorts. A full-service European spa offers state-of-the-art pampering, and three cottages are each equipped with a private redwood deck, Jacuzzi, and wet bar. ✉ *1457 Lincoln Ave., 94515,* ☎ *707/942–6877,* FAX *707/942–6904. 33 rooms. Restaurant, pool, spa. AE, MC, V.*

$$$ **Brannan Cottage Inn.** This pristine Victorian cottage with lacy white fretwork, large windows, and a shady porch is the only one of Sam Brannan's 1860 resort cottages still standing on its original site. Rooms have private entrances, and elegant stenciled friezes of stylized wildflowers cover the walls. ✉ *109 Wapoo Ave., 94515,* ☎ *707/942–4200. 6 rooms. Breakfast room. MC, V. BP.*

$$ **Calistoga Spa Hot Springs.** The spa's no-nonsense motel-style rooms have kitchenettes stocked with utensils and coffeemakers, which makes them popular with families and travelers on a budget. The on-premises spa includes mineral baths, mud baths, swimming pools, and a hot tub. ✉ *1006 Washington St., 94515,* ☎ *707/942–6269,* FAX *707/942–4214. 57 rooms. Snack bar, kitchenettes, 2 pools, wading pool, hot tub, spa, meeting room. MC, V.*

Outdoor Activities and Sports

BIKING

Getaway Adventures and Bike Shop (✉ 1117 Lincoln Ave., ☎ 707/942–0332 or 800/499–2453) rents bikes and conducts winery and other bike tours.

GLIDING, HOT-AIR BALLOONING

The **Calistoga Balloon Adventures** (☎ 707/944–2822) charters early morning flights (exact times vary) out of Calistoga or, depending on weather conditions, St. Helena, Oakville, or Rutherford. The company's deluxe balloon flight ($165 per person) includes a catered brunch finale at the Marriott in Napa or the Cafe Sarifornia in Calistoga.

Shopping

For connoisseurs seeking extraordinary values, the **All Seasons Café Wine Shop** (✉ 1400 Lincoln Ave., ☎ 707/942–6828) is a true find. A wineshop inside the **Calistoga Wine Stop** (✉ 1458 Lincoln Ave., ☎ 707/942–5556) carries 500 vintages.

THE SONOMA VALLEY

While the Napa Valley is upscale and elegant, Sonoma Valley is rustic and unpretentious. Its name is Miwok for *many moons*. Here, family-run wineries treat visitors like friends, and tastings are usually free. The more than 145 wineries in Sonoma boast that they win more awards than their neighbors in Napa. They credit the rocky soil that forces the vines to root deeper, producing intensely flavored grapes that translate into especially complex reds.

Sonoma

14 mi west of Napa on Hwy. 12; 45 mi from San Francisco, north on U.S. 101, east on Hwy. 37, and north on Hwy. 121/12.

Sonoma is the oldest town in the Wine Country. Its historic town plaza is the site of the last and the northernmost of the 21 missions established by the Franciscan order of Father Junípero Serra. The **Mission San Francisco Solano,** whose chapel and school were used to bring Christianity to the Native Americans, is now a museum with a fine collection of 19th-century watercolors. ✉ *114 Spain St. E,* ☎ *707/938–1519.* 🎟 *$2, includes the Sonoma Barracks on the central plaza and General Vallejo's home, Lachryma Montis (*☞ *below).* ⏲ *Daily 10–5.*

28 Originally planted by Franciscans of the Sonoma Mission in 1825, the **Sebastiani Vineyards** were bought by Samuele Sebastiani in 1904. Red wines are king here. ✉ *483 4th St. E,* ☎ *707/938–5532.* ⏲ *Daily 10–5. Tours 10:30–4.*

29 **Buena Vista Carneros Winery** (follow signs from the plaza) is the oldest continually operating winery in California. It was here, in 1857, that Count Agoston Haraszthy de Mokcsa laid the basis for modern California wine making, bucking the conventional wisdom that vines should be planted on well-watered ground by instead planting on well-drained hillsides. ✉ *18000 Old Winery Rd., off Napa Rd.,* ☎ *707/938–1266.* ⏲ *Daily 10:30–4:30. Tour daily at 2.*

30 **Ravenswood,** literally dug into the mountains like a bunker, is famous for its zinfandel. The merlot should be tasted as well. From late May through Labor Day the winery serves barbecued chicken and ribs ($7–$10). ✉ *18701 Gehricke Rd., off E. Spain St.,* ☎ *707/938–1960.* ⏲ *Daily 10–4:30. Tours by appointment at 10:30.*

A tree-lined driveway leads to **Lachryma Montis,** which General Mariano G. Vallejo, the last Mexican governor of California, built for his large family in 1851. The Victorian Gothic house is secluded in the midst of beautiful gardens. ✉ *W. Spain St. near 3rd St. E,* ☎ *707/938–1519.* 🎟 *$3.* ⏲ *Daily 10–5. Tours by appointment.*

Dining and Lodging

$$–$$$ ✕ **Cafe La Haye.** In a postage-stamp size kitchen, skillful chefs turn out a half-dozen main courses that star on a small but worthwhile menu. This offbeat café serves up some of the best food in the Wine Country. ✉ *140 E. Napa St.,* ☎ *707/935–5994. MC, V. Closed Sun.–Mon. No lunch Tues.–Fri.*

$$–$$$ ✕ **Heirloom.** Opened in late 1998 on the ground floor of the historic Sonoma Hotel, this comfortable restaurant offers seating in a back room and on the patio, but the liveliest tables are in the large bar area. Typical dishes are Argentine rib eye with cardoon and potato gratin and a popular roasted quail appetizer. ✉ *110 W. Spain St.,* ☎ *707/939–6955. AE, D, DC, MC, V.*

$-$$$ ✕ **La Salette.** Chef-owner Manny Azevedo, born in the Azores and raised in Sonoma, found culinary inspiration in his wide-ranging travels. The flavors of his dishes, such as Mozambique prawns with tomatoes and grilled plantains and salt cod baked with white onions, stand strong while complementing each other. ✉ *18625 Hwy. 12,* ☎ *707/938–1927. MC, V.*

$-$$ ✕ **The Café.** Overstuffed booths, ceiling fans, and an open kitchen give this corner bistro an informal feel. Country breakfasts, pizza from the wood-burning oven, and tasty Californian renditions of northern Italian cuisine are the specialties. The limited menu includes several spa cuisine options. ✉ *Sonoma Mission Inn, 18140 Sonoma Hwy., 2 mi north of Sonoma on Hwy. 12 at Boyes Blvd.,* ☎ *707/938–9000. AE, DC, MC, V.*

$-$$ ✕ **Ristorante Piatti.** A beautiful room opens onto one of the finest patios in the valley at this, the first in a minichain of California trattorias. Pizza from the wood-burning oven and northern Italian specials (spit-roasted chicken, ravioli with lemon cream) are served in a rustic setting with an open kitchen and bright wall murals, or on the terrace. ✉ *El Dorado Hotel, 405 1st St. W,* ☎ *707/996–2351. AE, MC, V.*

$ ✕ **La Casa.** Whitewashed stucco and red tiles evoke Old Mexico at this restaurant just around the corner from Sonoma's plaza. Locals love the casual atmosphere and the margaritas. ✉ *121 E. Spain St.,* ☎ *707/996–3406. AE, DC, MC, V.*

$$$$ ✕🏨 **Sonoma Mission Inn & Spa.** A $21-million upgrade transformed the cramped spa at this turn-of-the-20th-century resort into a world-class venue. The beautifully landscaped Mission-style property also features a separate Olympic-size pool supplied, as are most local facilities, by warm mineral water pumped up from wells beneath the property. Gourmet and classic spa food is served at the Grille and at the less formal Café (☞ *above*). ✉ *18140 Hwy. 12 (2 mi north of Sonoma at Boyes Blvd.), Box 1447, 95476,* ☎ *707/938–9000 or 800/358–9022; 800/862–4945 in CA;* FAX *707/996–5358. 198 rooms, 30 suites. 2 restaurants, 2 bars, coffee shop, 2 pools, hot tub, spa. AE, DC, MC, V.*

$$$-$$$$ 🏨 **Thistle Dew Inn.** The public rooms of this turn-of-the-20th-century Victorian home a half block from Sonoma Plaza are filled with collector's-quality Arts and Crafts furnishings. Four of the six rooms have private entrances and decks, and all have queen-size beds with antique quilts, private baths, and air-conditioning. ✉ *171 W. Spain St., 95476,* ☎ *707/938–2909; 800/382–7895 in CA. 6 rooms. Breakfast room, bicycles. AE, MC, V. BP.*

$$ 🏨 **Vineyard Inn.** Built as a roadside motor court in 1941, this inn with red-tile roofs brings a touch of Mexican village charm to an otherwise lackluster and somewhat noisy location at the junction of two main highways. ✉ *23000 Arnold Dr. (at junction of Hwys. 116 and 121), 95476,* ☎ *707/938–2350 or 800/359–4667,* FAX *707/938–2353. 9 rooms, 4 suites. Breakfast room. AE, MC, V. CP.*

Shopping

Several shops in the four-block **Sonoma Plaza** attract food lovers from miles around. **The Sonoma Cheese Factory** (✉ Sonoma Plaza, 2 Spain St., ☎ 707/996–1000), run by the same family for four generations, makes Sonoma Jack cheese and the tangy Sonoma Teleme.

Glen Ellen

7 mi north of Sonoma on Hwy. 12.

Jack London lived in the Sonoma Valley for many years. The craggy, quirky, and creek-bisected town of Glen Ellen commemorates him with place-names and nostalgic establishments. **Jack London Village**

(✉ 14301 Arnold Dr., ☎ 707/935–1240) has many interesting shops such as The Ranch Store (☎ 707/935–2311), which carries garden art, local farm foods, handmade quilts, and rustic furnishings. The **Jack London Bookstore** (✉ 14300 Arnold Dr., ☎ 707/996–2888), across the street from Jack London Village, carries many of London's books.

In the hills above Glen Ellen—known as the Valley of the Moon—lies **Jack London State Historic Park.** London's collection of South Seas and other artifacts are on view at the House of Happy Walls, a museum of London's effects. ✉ *2400 London Ranch Rd.,* ☎ *707/938–5216.* *Parking $6.* ⏲ *Park, daily 9:30–5; museum, daily 10–5.*

31 One of the best-known local wineries is **Benziger Family Winery,** which specializes in premium estate and Sonoma County wines. Benziger's Imagery Series is a low-volume release of unusual red and white wines distributed in bottles with labels designed by well-known artists from all over the world. ✉ *1883 London Ranch Rd.,* ☎ *707/935–3000.* *Tasting fees vary.* ⏲ *Daily 10–4:30. Tours every ½ hr, Mar.–Sept., 9:30–5; Oct.–Feb., 9:30–4.*

32 **Arrowood Vineyards** is neither as old nor as famous as some of its neighbors, but wine makers and critics are quite familiar with the excellent handcrafted wines produced here. The winery's harmonious architecture overlooking the Valley of the Moon earned it an award from the Sonoma Historic Preservation League. ✉ *14347 Sonoma Hwy.,* ☎ *707/938–5170.* ⏲ *Daily 10–4:30. Tours by appointment.*

Dining and Lodging

$$–$$$ ✕ **The Girl & the Fig.** Mustard-yellow walls, mismatched yellow chairs, and changing art exhibits set a bohemian tone here. The food, which may include apricot-glazed poussin, is almost overshadowed by a unique wine list focusing largely on regional Rhône-style varietals. ✉ *13690 Arnold Dr.,* ☎ *707/938–3634. AE, MC, V.*

$$$$ **Gaige House Inn.** Built in the 19th century as a personal residence, the Gaige House was bought in 1996 by owners who have added chic, contemporary rooms to the mix of older, more traditional accommodations on the two main floors. A large pool surrounded by a green lawn, striped awnings, white umbrellas, and magnolias conjure a manicured Hamptons-like glamour. ✉ *13540 Arnold Dr., 95442,* ☎ *707/935–0237 or 800/935–0237,* FAX *707/935–6411. 13 rooms. Breakfast room, pool, outdoor hot tub. AE, D, MC, V. BP.*

$$$–$$$$ **Beltane Ranch.** On a slope of the Mayacamas range on the eastern side of the Sonoma Valley lies this 100-year-old house built by a retired San Francisco madam. Beltane Ranch, surrounded by miles of trails through oak-studded hills, is part of a working cattle and grape-growing ranch. The rooms, all with private baths and antique furniture, open onto the building's wraparound porch. ✉ *11775 Sonoma Hwy. (Hwy. 12), 95442,* ☎ *707/996–6501. 5 rooms. Tennis court, hiking, horseshoes. No credit cards.*

$$–$$$ **Glenelly Inn.** Just outside the hamlet of Glen Ellen, this sunny little establishment, built as an inn in 1916, offers all the comforts of home—plus a hot tub in the garden. Innkeeper Kristi Hallamore serves breakfast in front of the common room's cobblestone fireplace and provides local delicacies in the afternoon. ✉ *5131 Warm Springs Rd., 95442,* ☎ *707/996–6720,* FAX *707/996–5227. 8 rooms. Breakfast room, outdoor hot tub. MC, V. CP.*

Kenwood

3 mi north of Glen Ellen on Hwy. 12.

Kenwood has a historic train depot and several restaurants and shops that specialize in locally produced goods. Its inns, restaurants, and winding roads nestle in soothing bucolic landscapes.

33 The beautifully rustic grounds at **Kenwood Vineyards** complement the attractive tasting room and artistic bottle labels. The winery is best known for its Jack London Vineyard reds—pinot noir, zinfandel, merlot, and a unique Artist Series cabernet. ✉ *9592 Sonoma Hwy.,* ☎ *707/833–5891.* ⏲ *Daily 10–4:30. No tours.*

34 **Landmark Vineyards.** The landscaping and design of this boutique winery, established by the heirs of John Deere, are as classical as its winemaking methods. Landmark's Damaris Reserve and Overlook chardonnays have been particularly well received, as has the winery's Grand Detour pinot noir. ✉ *101 Adobe Canyon Rd., off Sonoma Hwy.,* ☎ *707/833–1144 or 800/452–6365.* ⏲ *Daily 10–4:30. No tours.*

Dining

$$–$$$ ✕ **Kenwood Restaurant & Bar.** One of the enduring favorites in an area known for fine dining, this is where Napa and Sonoma chefs eat on their nights off. Indulge in California country cuisine in the sunny, South of France–style dining room or head through the French doors to the patio for a memorable view of the vineyards. ✉ *9900 Hwy. 12,* ☎ *707/833–6326. MC, V. Closed Mon.*

$ ✕ **Café Citti.** The aroma of garlic envelops the neighborhood whenever the Italian chef-owner is roasting chickens at this homey roadside café. ✉ *9049 Hwy. 12,* ☎ *707/833–2690. MC, V.*

ELSEWHERE IN SONOMA COUNTY

At nearly 1,598 square mi, Sonoma is far too large a county to cover in one or two days. The land mass extends from San Pablo Bay south to Mendocino County and from the Mayacamas Mountains on the Napa side west to the Pacific Ocean. Wineries can be found from the cool flatlands of the south to the hot interior valleys to the foggy coastal regions. Sonoma, though less famous than Napa, in fact is home to more award-winning wines.

Santa Rosa

8 mi northwest of Kenwood on Hwy. 12.

Santa Rosa is the Wine Country's largest city and a good bet for moderately priced hotel rooms, especially for those who have not reserved in advance.

★ 35 **Matanzas Creek Winery** specializes in three varietals—sauvignon blanc, merlot, and chardonnay. All three have won glowing reviews from various magazines. Huge windows in the recently expanded visitor center overlook a field of 3,100 tiered and fragrant lavender plants. Acres and acres of gardens planted with unusual grasses and plants from all over the world have caught the attention of horticulturists. ✉ *6097 Bennett Valley Rd.,* ☎ *707/528–6464.* ⏲ *Daily 10–4:30. Tours by appointment.*

Dining and Lodging

$$–$$$ ✕ **Café Lolo.** This casual but sophisticated spot is the territory of chef and co-owner Michael Quigley, who has single-handedly made downtown Santa Rosa a culinary destination. Don't pass up the chocolate kiss, an individual cake with a wonderfully soft, rich center. ✉ *620 5th St.,* ☎ *707/576–7822. AE, MC, V. Closed Sun. No lunch Sat.*

$$–$$$ ✕ **John Ash & Co.** The first Wine Country restaurant to tout locally grown ingredients in the 1980s, John Ash has maintained its status despite the departure of its namesake chef in 1991. With patio seating outside and a cozy fireplace indoors, the slightly formal restaurant looks like a Spanish villa. ✉ *4330 Barnes Rd. (River Rd. exit west from U.S. 101),* ☎ *707/527–7687. Weekend reservations essential. AE, DC, MC, V. No lunch Mon.*

$–$$$ ✕ **Mistral.** As Mediterranean as the wind for which it's named, this warm and gracious restaurant tries to make everybody happy. The extensive menu ranges from braised mahimahi to grilled pork tenderloin and offers a wide-ranging wine list to match. ✉ *1229 N. Dutton Ave.,* ☎ *707/578–4511. AE, D, DC, MC, V. No lunch weekends.*

$ ✕ **Mixx.** Great service and an eclectic mix of dishes define this small restaurant with large windows, high ceilings, and Italian blown-glass chandeliers. House-made ravioli, grilled Cajun prawns, and lamb curry are among the favorites of the many regulars. ✉ *135 4th St., at Davis (behind the mall on Railroad Sq.),* ☎ *707/573–1344. AE, D, MC, V. Closed Sun. No lunch Sat.*

$$$$ **Vintner's Inn.** Set on 50 acres of vineyards, this French provincial inn has large rooms, many with wood-burning fireplaces, and a trellised sundeck. Discount passes to an affiliated health club are available, and VCRs can be rented for a small fee. ✉ *4350 Barnes Rd. (River Rd. exit west from U.S. 101), 95403,* ☎ *707/575–7350 or 800/421–2584,* FAX *707/575–1426. 44 rooms. Restaurant, hot tub. AE, DC, MC, V. CP.*

$$$–$$$$ ★ **Fountaingrove Inn.** A redwood sculpture and a wall of cascading water distinguish the lobby at this elegant, comfortable inn. A buffet breakfast is complimentary, and there's also an elegant restaurant with piano music and a stellar menu. Guests have access to a nearby 18-hole golf course, a tennis court, and a health club, all for an additional fee. ✉ *101 Fountaingrove Pkwy. (near U.S. 101), 95403,* ☎ *707/578–6101 or 800/222–6101,* FAX *707/544–3126. 126 rooms. Restaurant, in-room data ports, room service, pool, hot tub, meeting rooms. AE, D, DC, MC, V. CP.*

$$–$$$ **Los Robles Lodge.** This pleasant, relaxed motel overlooks a pool that's set into a grassy landscape. Some rooms have whirlpools. ✉ *1985 Cleveland Ave. (Steele La. exit west from U.S. 101), 95401,* ☎ *707/545–6330 or 800/255–6330,* FAX *707/575–5826. 100 rooms. Restaurant, coffee shop, lounge, pool, outdoor hot tub, coin laundry. AE, DC, MC, V.*

Outdoor Activities and Sports

GOLF

The **Fountaingrove Country Club** (✉ 1525 Fountaingrove Pkwy., ☎ 707/579–4653) has an 18-hole course. The greens fee runs $55–$75. **Oakmont Golf Club** (✉ west course: 7025 Oakmont Dr., ☎ 707/539–0415; east course: 565 Oak Vista Ct., ☎ 707/538–2454) has two 18-hole courses. The greens fee is $25–$33.

HOT-AIR BALLOONING

For views of the ocean coast, the Russian River, and San Francisco on a clear day, **Above the Wine Country Balloons and Tours** (☎ 707/538–7359 or 800/759–5638) operates out of Santa Rosa. The cost is $195 per person, including a champagne brunch at the Kendall-Jackson Wine Center.

Healdsburg

17 mi north of Santa Rosa on U.S. 101.

The countryside around Dry Creek Valley and Healdsburg is a fantasy of pastoral bliss, beautifully overgrown and in constant repose. Alongside the relatively untrafficked roads, country stores offer just-plucked fruits and vine-ripened tomatoes.

Healdsburg itself is centered around a fragrant plaza surrounded by shady trees, appealing antiques shops, and restaurants. A whitewashed bandstand is the venue for free summer concerts, where the music ranges from jazz to bluegrass.

36 **Rochioli Vineyards and Winery** claims one of the prettiest picnic sites in the area, with tables overlooking vineyards. The winery makes one of the county's best chardonnays. ✉ *6192 Westside Rd.,* ☎ *707/433–2305.* ⏲ *Daily 10–5.*

37 **Dry Creek Vineyard,** whose fumé blanc is an industry benchmark, is also earning notice for its reds, especially zinfandels and cabernets. ✉ *3770 Lambert Bridge Rd.,* ☎ *707/433–1000.* ⏲ *Daily 10:30–4:30. Tours by appointment.*

38 An unassuming winery in a wood and cinder-block barn, **Quivira** produces some of the most interesting wines in Dry Creek Valley. Though it is known for its exquisitely balanced and fruity zinfandel, it also makes a superb blend of red varietals called Dry Creek Cuvée. ✉ *4900 W. Dry Creek Rd.,* ☎ *707/431–8333.* ⏲ *Daily 10–4:30. Tours by appointment.*

39 Noted for its beautiful Italian villa–style winery and visitor center, **Ferrari-Carano Winery** produces chardonnays, fumé blancs, and merlots. Tours take you between the rows of grapevines right into the vineyards themselves. ✉ *8761 Dry Creek Rd.,* ☎ *707/433–6700.* ⏲ *Daily 10–5. Tours by appointment.*

40 **Simi Winery.** Giuseppe and Pietro Simi, two brothers from Italy, began growing grapes in Sonoma in 1876. Though their winery's operations are strictly high-tech these days, its tree-studded entrance area and stone buildings recall a more genteel era. ✉ *16275 Healdsburg Ave. (take Dry Creek Rd. exit off U.S. 101),* ☎ *707/433–6981.* ⏲ *Daily 10–4:30. Tours at 11, 1, and 3.*

OFF THE BEATEN PATH

KORBEL CHAMPAGNE CELLARS – In order to be called champagne, a wine must be made in the French region of Champagne or it's just sparkling wine. But despite the objections of the French, champagne has entered the lexicon of California wine makers, and many refer to their sparkling wines as champagne. Whatever you call it, Korbel produces a tasty, reasonably priced wine. The winery's 19th-century buildings and gorgeous rose gardens are a delight in their own right. ✉ *13250 River Rd., Guerneville,* ☎ *707/824–7000.* ⏲ *Oct.–Apr., daily 9–4:30; May–Sept., daily 9–5. Tours on the hr 10–3.*

Dining and Lodging

$$ ✕ **Bistro Ralph.** In a town where good restaurants rarely seem to last, Ralph Tingle has sustained success with his California home-style cuisine, serving up a small menu that changes weekly. The stark industrial setting includes a stunning wine rack of graceful curves fashioned in metal and wood. ✉ *109 Plaza St., off Healdsburg Ave.,* ☎ *707/433–1380. Reservations essential. MC, V. No lunch weekends.*

$$$$ ★ **Applewood Inn.** On a knoll in the shelter of towering redwoods, this hybrid inn has two distinct types of accommodations. Those in the original Belden House are comfortable but modest in scale. Most of the 10 accommodations in the newer buildings, both salmon-pink stucco, are larger and airier, particularly the second-floor rooms. ✉ *13555 Hwy. 116, Guerneville 95421,* ☎ *707/869–9093,* FAX *707/869–9170. 15 cottages. Dining room, pool, outdoor hot tub. AE, MC, V. BP.*

$$$–$$$$ **Healdsburg Inn on the Plaza.** This 1900 brick building on the town plaza has a bright solarium and a roof garden. The rooms, most with fireplaces, are spacious, with quilts and pillows piled high on antique beds. In the bathrooms claw-foot tubs are outfitted with rubber ducks. Full breakfast, afternoon coffee and cookies, and early evening wine and popcorn are included. ✉ *110 Matheson St., Box 1196, 95448,* ☎ *707/433–6991. 10 rooms. Breakfast room. MC, V. BP.*

$$$–$$$$ **The Honor Mansion.** This photogenic 1883 Italianate Victorian opened in 1994 to rave reviews for its interior decor. Antiques, feather beds, and fancy water bottles add a luxurious ambience to the rooms in the main house. A separate cottage is available in the rear. ✉ *14891 Grove St., 95448,* ☎ *707/433–4277 or 800/554–4667,* FAX *707/431–7173. 8 rooms. Breakfast room, pool, hot tub. D, MC, V. BP.*

$$$–$$$$ **Madrona Manor.** The oldest continuously operating inn in the area, this 1881 Victorian mansion, surrounded by 8 acres of wooded and landscaped grounds, provides a storybook setting. Sleep either in the splendid three-story mansion, the carriage house, or one of two separate cottages. ✉ *1001 Westside Rd. (take central Healdsburg exit from U.S. 101, turn left on Mill St.), Box 818, 95448,* ☎ *707/433–4231 or 800/258–4003,* FAX *707/433–0703. 21 rooms. Restaurant, pool. MC, V. BP.*

$–$$ **Best Western Dry Creek Inn.** Continental breakfast and a bottle of wine are complimentary at this three-story Spanish Mission–style motel; there's also a coffee shop next door. Midweek discounts are available, and direct bus service from San Francisco's airport can be arranged. ✉ *198 Dry Creek Rd., 95448,* ☎ *707/433–0300 or 800/222–5784;* FAX *707/433–1129. 102 rooms. Pool, hot tub, coin laundry. AE, D, DC, MC, V. CP.*

Shopping

Oakville Grocery (✉ 124 Matheson St., ☎ 707/433–3200) has a bustling Healdsburg branch filled with wine, produce, and deli items. Head to **Salami Tree** (✉ 304 Center St., ☎ no phone) for picnic supplies. Every Saturday morning from early May to October, Healdsburg locals gather at the open-air **Farmers' Market** (✉ North Plaza parking lot, North and Vine Sts., ☎ 707/431–1956) to pick up supplies from local producers of vegetables, fruits, flowers, cheeses, and olive oils.

THE WINE COUNTRY A TO Z

Arriving and Departing

By Bus

Greyhound (☎ 800/231–2222) runs buses from the Transbay Terminal at 1st and Mission streets in San Francisco to Sonoma and Santa Rosa.

By Car

From San Francisco, cross the Golden Gate Bridge, go north on U.S. 101, east on Highway 37, and north and east on Highway 121. For Sonoma wineries, head north at Highway 12; for Napa, turn left (to the northwest) when Highway 121 runs into Highway 29.

From Berkeley and other East Bay towns, take I–80 north to Highway 37 west to Highway 29 north. From points north of the Wine Country, take U.S. 101 south to Geyserville and follow Highway 128 southeast into the Napa Valley.

Getting Around

By Bus

Sonoma County Area Transit (☎ 707/585–7516) and **Napa Valley Transit** (☎ 707/255–7631) both provide transportation between towns in their respective Wine Country counties.

By Car

Although traffic on the two-lane country roads can be heavy, the best way to get around the sprawling Wine Country is by private car. Rentals are available at the airports and in San Francisco, Oakland, Sonoma, Santa Rosa, and Napa.

Contacts and Resources

B&B Reservation Agencies

Bed & Breakfast Exchange (✉ 1407 Main St., Suite 102, St. Helena, ☎ 707/942–5900). The **Bed & Breakfast Association of Sonoma** (✉ 3250 Trinity Rd., Glen Ellen, ☎ 800/969–4667). **The Wine Country Inns of Sonoma County** (☎ 707/433–4667; 800/354–4743 for brochure). **Wine Country Reservations** (☎ 707/257–7757).

Emergencies

Ambulance (☎ 911). **Police** (☎ 911).

Guided Tours

Full-day guided tours of the Wine Country usually include lunch and cost about $60 per person. The guides, some of whom are winery owners themselves, know the area well and may show you some lesser-known cellars. Reservations are usually required.

Gray Line (✉ 350 8th St., San Francisco 94103, ☎ 415/558–9400) has bright red double-decker buses that tour the Wine Country. **Great Pacific Tour Co.** (✉ 518 Octavia St., San Francisco 94102, ☎ 415/626–4499) operates full-day tours of Napa and Sonoma, including a summer picnic lunch and a winter restaurant lunch, in passenger vans that seat 14. **HMS Travel Group** (✉ 707 4th St., Santa Rosa 95404, ☎ 707/526–2922 or 800/367–5348) offers customized tours of the Wine Country for six or more people, by appointment only. The **Napa Valley Wine Train** (✉ 1275 McKinstry St., Napa 94559, ☎ 707/253–2111 or 800/427–4124) allows you to enjoy lunch, dinner, or weekend brunch on one of several restored 1915 Pullman railroad cars that run between Napa and St. Helena. Dinner costs $75, lunch $68.50, brunch $59.50; per-person prices include train fare, meals, tax, and service. On weekend brunch trips and weekday lunch trips you can ride a special "Deli" car for $27.50. In winter service is sometimes limited to Thursday through Sunday; call ahead.

Visitor Information

Napa Valley Conference and Visitors Bureau (✉ 1310 Napa Town Center, Napa 94559, ☎ 707/226–7459). The **North Coast Visitors Bureau** (✉ The Cannery, 2801 Leavenworth St., 2nd floor, San Francisco 94133, ☎ 415/543–8334). **Sonoma County Tourism Program** (✉ 2300 County Center Dr., Room B260, Santa Rosa 95403, ☎ 707/565–5383). **Sonoma Valley Visitors Bureau** (✉ 453 First St. E, Sonoma 95476, ☎ 707/996–1090).

4 SAN FRANCISCO

WITH SIDE TRIPS TO MARIN COUNTY, THE EAST BAY, THE INLAND PENINSULA, AND THE SOUTH BAY

Brace yourself for the brilliant colors of ornately painted, bay-window Victorians; the sounds of foghorns and cable car lines; and the crisp, salty smell of the bay. San Francisco's world-famous landmarks—the Golden Gate Bridge, Alcatraz, the Transamerica Pyramid—provide an unforgettable backdrop for its eclectic neighborhoods, from bustling Chinatown and bacchanalian North Beach to the left-of-center Castro district and the city's new cultural and new-media center, SoMa.

IN ITS FIRST LIFE, SAN FRANCISCO was little more than a small, well-situated settlement. Founded by Spaniards in 1776, it was prized for its natural harbor, so commodious that "all the navies of the world might fit inside it," as one visitor wrote. Around 1849 the discovery of gold at John Sutter's sawmill in the nearby Sierra foothills transformed the sleepy little settlement into a city of 30,000. As millions of dollars' worth of gold was panned and blasted out of the hills, a "western Wall Street" sprang up. Just when gold production began to taper off, prospectors turned up a rich vein of silver in Virginia City, Nevada. San Francisco, the nearest financial center, saw its population soar to 342,000. But it was the 1869 completion of the transcontinental railway, linking the once-isolated western capital to the rest of the nation, that turned San Francisco into a major city.

Loose, tolerant, and even licentious are words that are used to describe San Francisco. Bohemian communities thrive here. As early as the 1860s the Barbary Coast—a collection of taverns, whorehouses, and gambling joints along Pacific Avenue close to the waterfront—was famous, or infamous. North Beach, the city's Little Italy, became the home of the Beat movement in the 1950s (Herb Caen, the city's best-known columnist, coined the term "beatnik"). City Lights, a bookstore and publishing house that still stands on Columbus Avenue, brought out, among other titles, Allen Ginsberg's *Howl* and *Kaddish*. In the '60s, the Haight-Ashbury district became synonymous with hippiedom, giving rise to such legendary bands as Jefferson Airplane and the Grateful Dead. The Free Speech Movement began across the Bay at the University of California at Berkeley, and Stanford University's David Harris, who went to prison for defying the draft, numbered among the nation's most famous student leaders. The '70s saw lesbians and gay men from around the country descend on the Castro, turning the one-time Irish neighborhood into the country's best-known gay enclave.

Technically speaking, San Francisco is only California's fourth-largest city, behind Los Angeles, San Diego, and nearby San Jose. But that statistic is misleading: the Bay Area, extending from the bedroom communities north of Oakland and Berkeley south through the peninsula and the San Jose area, is really one continuous megacity, with San Francisco as its heart.

EXPLORING SAN FRANCISCO

Revised by Denise M. Leto

San Francisco is a relatively small city. About 750,000 residents live on a 46.6-square-mi tip of land between San Francisco Bay and the Pacific Ocean. San Franciscans cherish the city's colorful past; many older buildings have been spared from demolition and nostalgically converted into modern offices and shops. Longtime locals rue the sites that got away—railroad and mining boom–era residences lost in the 1906 earthquake, the baroque Fox Theater, and Playland at the Beach. Despite acts of God, the indifference of developers, and the mixed record of the city's planning commission, much of the architectural and historical interest remains. Bernard Maybeck, Julia Morgan, Willis Polk, and Arthur Brown Jr. are among the noteworthy architects whose designs can still be seen.

Union Square Area

Much of San Francisco may feel like a collection of small towns strung together, but the Union Square area bristles with big-city bravado. The city's finest department stores do business here, along with exclusive

Exploring San Francisco (*Boxes Refer to Detail Maps*)

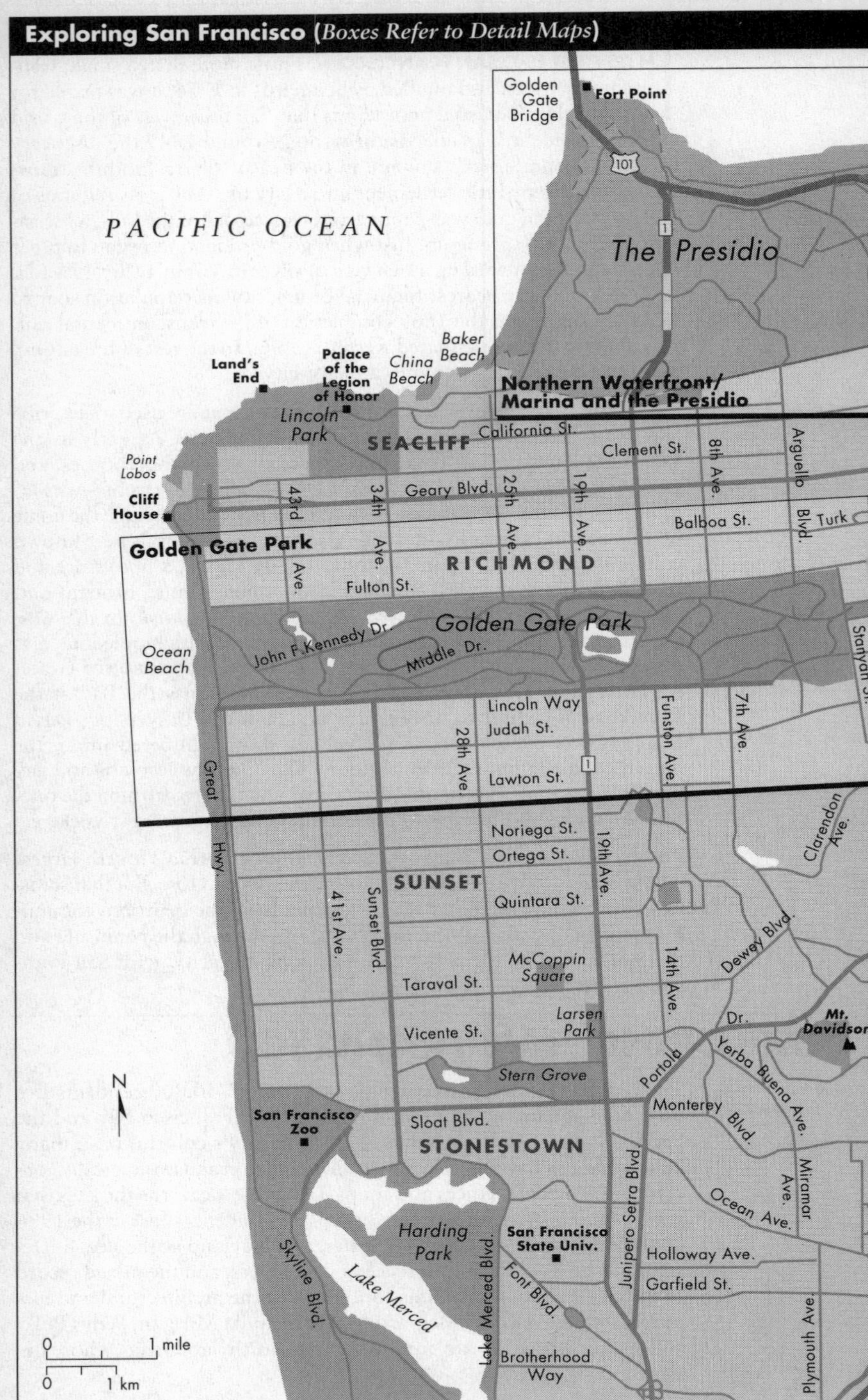

Golden Gate Bridge
Fort Point
101
1
PACIFIC OCEAN
The Presidio
Baker Beach
China Beach
Palace of the Legion of Honor
Land's End
Northern Waterfront/ Marina and the Presidio
Lincoln Park
SEACLIFF
California St.
Clement St.
8th Ave.
Arguello Blvd.
Point Lobos
Cliff House
43rd Ave.
34th Ave.
Geary Blvd.
25th Ave.
19th Ave.
Balboa St.
Turk
Golden Gate Park
RICHMOND
Fulton St.
Golden Gate Park
John F. Kennedy Dr.
Middle Dr.
Stanyan St.
Ocean Beach
Lincoln Way
Judah St.
Funston Ave.
7th Ave.
28th Ave.
Lawton St.
Great Hwy.
Noriega St.
Ortega St.
19th Ave.
Clarendon Ave.
SUNSET
Quintara St.
41st Ave.
Sunset Blvd.
McCoppin Square
14th Ave.
Dewey Blvd.
Taraval St.
Larsen Park
Dr.
Mt. Davidson
Vicente St.
Portola
Yerba Buena Ave.
Stern Grove
N
San Francisco Zoo
Sloat Blvd.
Monterey Blvd.
STONESTOWN
Miramar Ave.
Ocean Ave.
Junipero Serra Blvd.
Harding Park
San Francisco State Univ.
Holloway Ave.
Garfield St.
Skyline Blvd.
Lake Merced
Lake Merced Blvd.
Font Blvd.
Brotherhood Way
Plymouth Ave.
0
1 mile
0
1 km

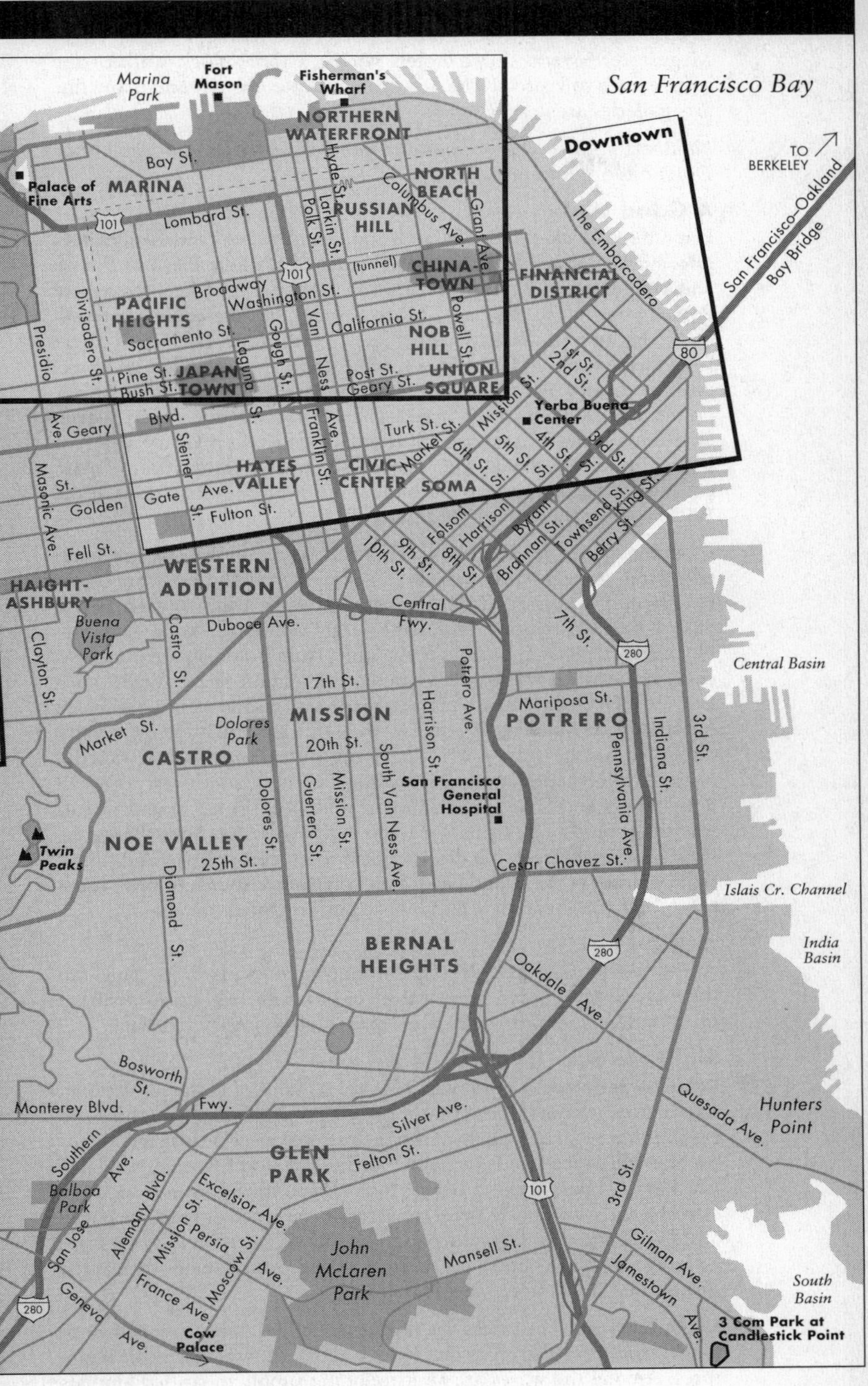
San Francisco Bay
Downtown
TO BERKELEY
San Francisco–Oakland Bay Bridge
Marina Park
Fort Mason
Fisherman's Wharf
NORTHERN WATERFRONT
NORTH BEACH
RUSSIAN HILL
CHINA-TOWN
FINANCIAL DISTRICT
PACIFIC HEIGHTS
NOB HILL
UNION SQUARE
JAPAN TOWN
Palace of Fine Arts
MARINA
Bay St.
Lombard St.
Broadway
Washington St.
California St.
Sacramento St.
Pine St.
Bush St.
Post St.
Geary St.
Geary Blvd.
Turk St.
Market St.
Mission St.
The Embarcadero
Columbus Ave.
Grant Ave.
Powell St.
Hyde St.
Larkin St.
Polk St.
Van Ness Ave.
Gough St.
Laguna St.
Divisadero St.
Presidio Ave.
(tunnel)
1st St.
2nd St.
3rd St.
4th St.
5th St.
6th St.
Yerba Buena Center
HAYES VALLEY
CIVIC CENTER
SOMA
Franklin St.
Steiner St.
Golden Gate Ave.
Fulton St.
Masonic Ave.
Fell St.
HAIGHT-ASHBURY
WESTERN ADDITION
Buena Vista Park
Clayton St.
Castro St.
Duboce Ave.
Central Fwy.
10th St.
9th St.
8th St.
7th St.
Folsom
Harrison
Bryant
Brannan St.
Townsend St.
King St.
Berry St.
Central Basin
17th St.
MISSION
Mariposa St.
POTRERO
Potrero Ave.
Harrison St.
Dolores Park
20th St.
CASTRO
Market St.
South Van Ness Ave.
Mission St.
Guerrero St.
Dolores St.
San Francisco General Hospital
Pennsylvania Ave.
Indiana St.
3rd St.
Twin Peaks
NOE VALLEY
25th St.
Diamond St.
Cesar Chavez St.
Islais Cr. Channel
India Basin
BERNAL HEIGHTS
Oakdale Ave.
Bosworth St.
Monterey Blvd.
Fwy.
Quesada Ave.
Hunters Point
Silver Ave.
GLEN PARK
Felton St.
Southern
Balboa Park
San Jose Ave.
Alemany Blvd.
Excelsior Ave.
Mission St.
Persia Ave.
Moscow St.
France Ave.
Geneva Ave.
John McLaren Park
Mansell St.
Gilman Ave.
Jamestown Ave.
South Basin
Cow Palace
3 Com Park at Candlestick Point
101
80
280

emporiums such as Tiffany & Co. and big-name franchises such as Niketown, Planet Hollywood, Borders Books and Music, and the Virgin Megastore. Several dozen hotels within a three-block walk of the square cater to visitors. The downtown theater district and many fine arts galleries are nearby.

Numbers in the text correspond to numbers in the margin and on the Downtown San Francisco map.

A Good Walk

Begin three blocks south of Union Square at the **San Francisco Visitors Information Center** ①, on the lower level of Hallidie Plaza at Powell and Market streets. Up the escalators on the east side of the plaza, where Powell Street dead-ends into Market Street, lies the **cable car terminus** ② for two of the city's three lines. Head north on Powell Street from the terminus to Geary Street, make a left, and walk west 1½ blocks into the theater district for a peek at the **Geary Theater** ③. Backtrack on the north side of Geary Street, where the sturdy and stately **Westin St. Francis Hotel** ④ dominates Powell Street between Geary and Post streets. **Union Square** ⑤ is across Powell Street from the hotel's main entrance. You can pick up discount and full-price event tickets at the **TIX Bay Area** ⑥ booth in the square.

From the square head south on Stockton Street to O'Farrell Street and take a spin through **F.A.O. Schwarz** ⑦ (also on Stockton Street are Planet Hollywood and the Virgin Megastore). Walk back toward Union Square past Geary Street and make a right on **Maiden Lane** ⑧, a two-block alley directly across Stockton Street from Union Square that runs east parallel to Geary Street. When the lane ends at Kearny Street, turn left, walk 1½ blocks to Sutter Street, make a right, and walk a half block to the **Hallidie Building** ⑨. After viewing this historic building, reverse direction and head west 1½ blocks up Sutter Street to the fanciful beaux-arts–style **Hammersmith Building** ⑩, on the southwest corner of Sutter Street and Grant Avenue. In the middle of the next block of Sutter Street stands a glorious Art Deco building at **450 Sutter Street** ⑪. From here, backtrack a half block east to Stockton Street and take a right. In front of the Grand Hyatt hotel sits **Ruth Asawa's Fantasy Fountain** ⑫. Union Square is a half block south on Stockton Street.

TIMING

Allow two hours to see everything around Union Square. Stepping into the massive Macy's department store or browsing in boutiques can eat up countless hours. If you're a shopper, give yourself extra time.

Sights to See

2 **Cable car terminus.** San Francisco's cable cars were declared National Landmarks (the only ones that move) in 1964. Two of the three operating lines begin and end their runs here. The Powell–Mason line climbs up Nob Hill, then winds through North Beach to Fisherman's Wharf. The Powell–Hyde line also crosses Nob Hill but then continues up Russian Hill and down Hyde Street to Victorian Park, across from the Buena Vista Café and near Ghirardelli Square. Buy your ticket ($2 one-way) on board, at nearby hotels, or at the police/information booth near the turnaround. ✉ *Powell and Market Sts.*

7 **F.A.O. Schwarz.** The prices are not Toys "R" Us, but it's worth stopping by this three-floor playland to look at the elaborate fairy-tale sculptures. Among the wares are an astounding supply of stuffed animals (the priciest is a whopping $15,000) and just about every other toy imaginable. ✉ *48 Stockton St.,* ☎ *415/394–8700.* ⏲ *Mon.–Sat. 10–7, Sun. noon–6.*

11 **450 Sutter Street.** Handsome Maya-inspired designs adorn the exterior and interior surfaces of this 1928 Art Deco skyscraper, a masterpiece of terra-cotta and other detailing. ✉ *Between Stockton and Powell Sts.*

3 **Geary Theater.** Built in 1910, the Geary has a serious neoclassic design lightened by colorful carved terra-cotta columns depicting a cornucopia of fruits. Damaged heavily in the 1989 earthquake, the Geary has been completely restored to highlight its historic, gilded splendor. The American Conservatory Theater, one of North America's leading repertory companies, uses the 1,035-seat Geary as its main venue. ✉ *415 Geary St. (box office at 405 Geary St.),* ☎ *415/749–2228.*

9 **Hallidie Building.** Named for cable car inventor Andrew S. Hallidie, this 1918 structure is best viewed from across the street. Willis Polk's revolutionary glass-curtain wall—believed to be the world's first such facade—hangs a foot beyond the reinforced concrete of the frame. The reflecting glass, decorative exterior fire escapes that appear to be metal balconies, and Venetian Gothic cornice are worth noting. Ornamental bands of birds at feeders stretch across the building on several stories. ✉ *130 Sutter St., between Kearny and Montgomery Sts.*

10 **Hammersmith Building.** Glass walls and a colorful design distinguish this four-story beaux-arts–style structure, built in 1907. The building, once described as a "commercial jewel box," was originally designed for use as a jewelry store. ✉ *301 Sutter St., at Grant Ave.*

8 **Maiden Lane.** This former red-light district reported at least one murder a week during the late 19th century. After the 1906 fire destroyed the brothels, the street emerged as Maiden Lane, and it has since become a semi-chic pedestrian mall stretching two blocks, between Stockton and Kearny streets. Traffic is prohibited most days between 11 and 5, when the lane becomes a patchwork of umbrella-shaded tables. Masses of daffodils and balloons lend a carnival mood during the annual spring festival, when throngs of street musicians, arts-and-crafts vendors, and spectators emerge.

With its circular interior ramp and skylights, the handsome brick 1948 structure at **140 Maiden Lane**, the only Frank Lloyd Wright building in San Francisco, is said to have been his model for the Guggenheim Museum in New York. It now holds several small art galleries. ✉ *Between Stockton and Kearny Sts.*

12 **Ruth Asawa's Fantasy Fountain.** Local artist Ruth Asawa's sculpture, a wonderland of real and mythical creatures, honors the city's hills, bridges, and architecture. Children and friends helped Asawa shape the hundreds of tiny figures from baker's clay; these were assembled on 41 large panels from which molds were made for the bronze casting. ✉ *In front of Grand Hyatt at 345 Stockton St.*

1 **San Francisco Visitors Information Center.** A multilingual staff operates this facility below the cable car terminus. You can pick up discount coupons—the savings can be significant, especially for families—as well as maps and pamphlets here. ✉ *Hallidie Plaza, lower level, Powell and Market Sts.,* ☎ *415/391–2000.* ⏲ *Weekdays 9–5, weekends 9–3.*

6 **TIX Bay Area.** This excellent service provides half-price day-of-performance tickets (cash or traveler's checks only) to all types of performing arts events, as well as regular full-price box office services for concerts, clubs, and sporting events (credit cards accepted). Half-price tickets for Sunday and Monday events are sold on Saturday. Also sold at the booth is the **Golden Gate Park Explorer Pass** ($14; good for discount admission to the main attractions in Golden Gate Park), Muni Pass-

Downtown San Francisco

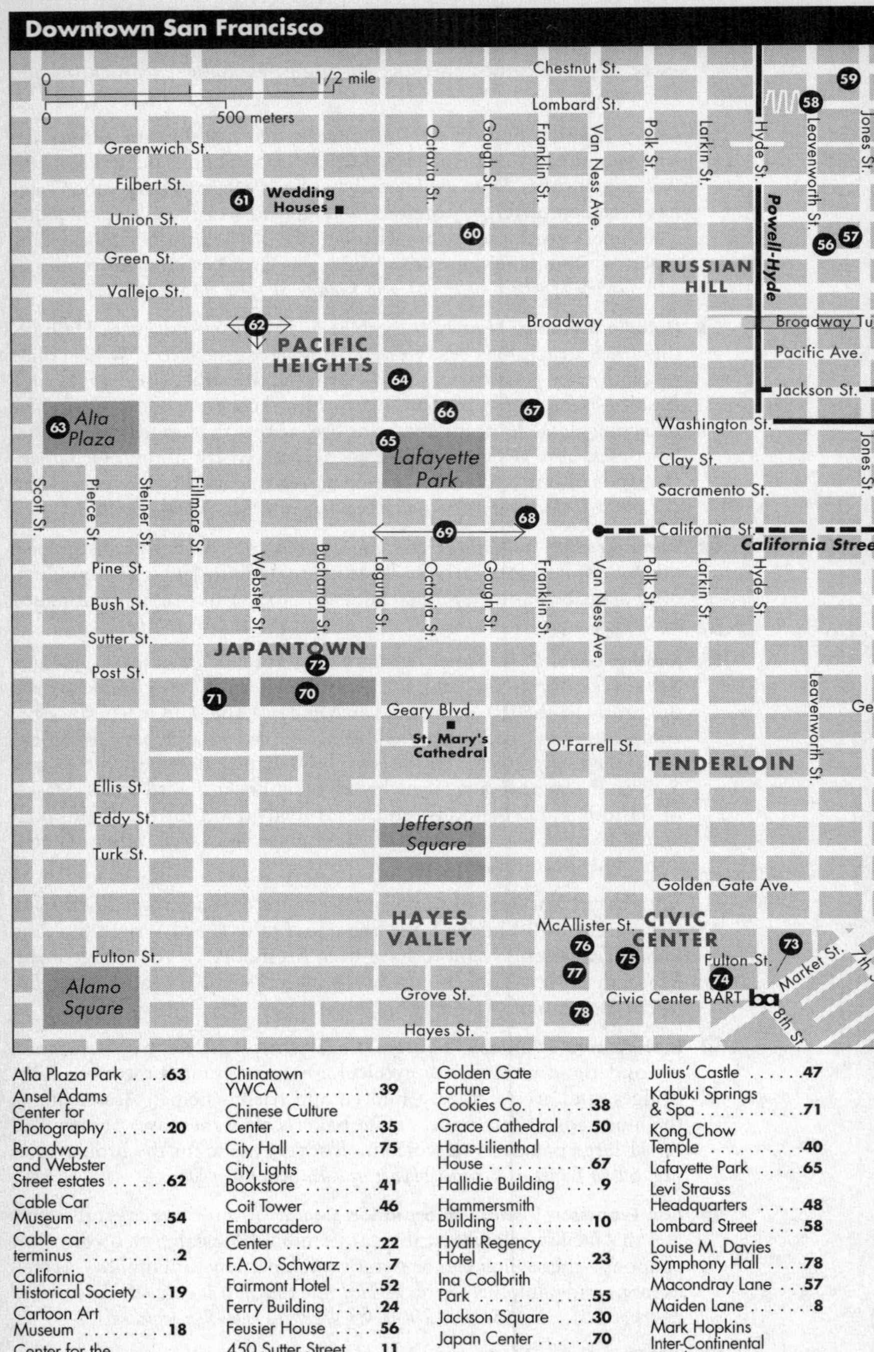

Alta Plaza Park 63
Ansel Adams Center for Photography 20
Broadway and Webster Street estates 62
Cable Car Museum 54
Cable car terminus 2
California Historical Society . . . 19
Cartoon Art Museum 18
Center for the Arts 14
Chinatown Gate . . . 32
Chinatown YWCA 39
Chinese Culture Center 35
City Hall 75
City Lights Bookstore 41
Coit Tower 46
Embarcadero Center 22
F.A.O. Schwarz 7
Fairmont Hotel 52
Ferry Building 24
Feusier House 56
450 Sutter Street . . . 11
Franklin Street buildings 68
Geary Theater 3
Golden Gate Fortune Cookies Co. 38
Grace Cathedral . . . 50
Haas-Lilienthal House 67
Hallidie Building 9
Hammersmith Building 10
Hyatt Regency Hotel 23
Ina Coolbrith Park 55
Jackson Square 30
Japan Center 70
Japan Center Mall 72
Jewish Museum 26
Julius' Castle 47
Kabuki Springs & Spa 71
Kong Chow Temple 40
Lafayette Park 65
Levi Strauss Headquarters 48
Lombard Street 58
Louise M. Davies Symphony Hall 78
Macondray Lane . . . 57
Maiden Lane 8
Mark Hopkins Inter-Continental Hotel 53
Masonic Auditorium 49

San Francisco Bay
TO FISHERMAN'S WHARF
Chestnut St.
Lombard St.
Greenwich St.
Filbert St.
Union St.
Green St.
Vallejo St.
Powell-Mason
Columbus Ave.
NORTH BEACH
TELEGRAPH HILL
Pier 23
Pier 19
Pier 17
Pier 15
Pier 9
Pier 7
Pier 5
Pier 3
Pier 1
The Embarcadero
Front St.
Davis St.
Mason St.
Powell St.
Grant Ave.
Montgomery St.
Hotaling Pl.
Sansome St.
Battery St.
Taylor St.
Stockton St.
Washington St.
Drumm St.
Justin Herman Plaza
NOB HILL
Waverly Pl.
Clay St.
FINANCIAL DISTRICT
CHINATOWN
Halleck St.
Steuart St.
Audiffred Building
Spear St.
Main St.
Pine St.
Bush St.
Sutter St.
Post St.
O'Farrell St.
Ellis St.
Eddy St.
Turk St.
Kearny St.
Embarcadero BART
Beale St.
Fremont St.
1st St.
UNION SQUARE
Montgomery St. BART
Maiden Ln.
Lotta's Fountain
New Montgomery St.
2nd St.
Howard St.
Folsom St.
Market St.
Harrison St.
80
Bryant St.
3rd St.
Hawthorne St.
Mission St.
YERBA BUENA GARDENS
Powell St. BART
5th St.
6th St.
4th St.
Folsom St.
Brannan St.
Townsend St.
Howard St.
SOMA
Sea Change
Pier 24
Pier 26
Pier 28
Pier 30
Pier 32
Pier 34
Pier 36
Pier 38
Pier 40
N

ports, and adult Fast Passes for use on the transit system. ✉ *Stockton St. between Geary and Post Sts., Union Square,* ☎ *415/433–7827.* ⏲ *Tues.–Thurs. 11–6, Fri.–Sat. 11–7.*

5 **Union Square.** The heart of San Francisco's downtown since 1850, the 2.6-acre square takes its name from the violent pro-union demonstrations staged here prior to the Civil War. At center stage, the *Victory Monument,* by Robert Ingersoll Aitken, commemorates Commodore George Dewey's victory over the Spanish fleet at Manila in 1898. The 97-ft Corinthian column, topped by a bronze figure symbolizing naval conquest, was dedicated by Theodore Roosevelt in 1903 and withstood the 1906 earthquake. The square fills daily with a familiar kaleidoscope of characters: office workers sunning and brown-bagging, street musicians, the occasional preacher, and a fair share of homeless people. It often hosts public events such as fashion shows, free noontime concerts, and noisy demonstrations. ✉ *Between Powell, Stockton, Post, and Geary Sts.*

4 **Westin St. Francis Hotel.** The second-oldest hotel in the city, established in 1904, was conceived by railroad baron and financier Charles Crocker and his associates as a hostelry for their millionaire friends. Swift service and sumptuous surroundings—glass chandeliers, a gilt ceiling, and marble columns—have always been hallmarks of the property. After the hotel was ravaged by the 1906 fire, a larger, more luxurious Italian Renaissance–style residence was opened in 1907 to attract loyal clients from among the world's rich and powerful. The hotel's checkered past includes the ill-fated 1921 bash thrown by silent-film comedian Fatty Arbuckle at which a woman became ill and later died. In 1975 Sara Jane Moore, standing among a crowd outside the hotel, attempted to shoot then-president Gerald R. Ford. As might be imagined, no plaques commemorate these events in the lobby. The ever-helpful staff will, however, direct you to tea (daily from 3 to 5) or champagne and caviar in the **Compass Rose** (☎ 415/774–0167) lounge. Elaborate Chinese screens, secluded seating alcoves, and soothing background music make this an ideal rest stop after frantic shopping or sightseeing. ✉ *335 Powell St., at Geary St.,* ☎ *415/397–7000.*

South of Market (SoMa) and the Embarcadero

South of Market was once known as South of the Slot, in reference to the cable car slot that ran up Market Street. Ever since gold rush miners set up their tents in 1848, SoMa has played a major role in housing immigrants to the city. Except for a brief flowering of elegance during the mid-19th century, these streets were reserved for newcomers who couldn't yet afford to move to another neighborhood. Industry took over most of the area when the 1906 earthquake collapsed most of the homes into their quicksand bases.

Key players in San Francisco's arts scene migrated to SoMa in the 1990s. At the heart of the action are the San Francisco Museum of Modern Art and the Center for the Arts at Yerba Buena Gardens. But the neighborhood is changing again. The gentrifying South Park area is where the cybercrowd from *Wired* magazine and other new-media companies tank up on lattes and toasted baguettes. Even with the influx of money, the neighborhood still has an edge that keeps it interesting.

Numbers in the text correspond to numbers in the margin and on the Downtown San Francisco map.

A Good Walk

The **San Francisco Museum of Modern Art** ⑬ dominates a half block of 3rd Street between Howard and Mission streets. Use the crosswalk near SFMOMA's entrance to head across 3rd Street into Yerba Buena

Gardens. To your right after you've walked a few steps, a sidewalk leads to the main entrance of the **Center for the Arts** ⑭. Straight ahead is the East Garden of Yerba Buena Gardens and beyond that, on the 4th Street side of the block, is the **Metreon** ⑮ entertainment, retail, and restaurant complex. A second-level walkway in the southern portion of the East Garden, above the Martin Luther King Jr. waterfall, arches over Howard Street, leading to the main (south) entrance to **Moscone Convention Center** ⑯ and the **Rooftop@Yerba Buena Gardens** ⑰ facilities. Exit the rooftop near Folsom Street, cross 4th Street, turn right, and head back past Howard Street to Mission Street; a half block west on Mission Street is the **Cartoon Art Museum** ⑱. From here backtrack east on Mission Street (toward SFMOMA) past the monolithic San Francisco Marriott, also known as the "jukebox" Marriott because of its exterior design. East of the Marriott is dour-looking St. Patrick's Catholic Church, which hosts a notable chamber-music series. Cross 3rd Street and continue a third of a block to the headquarters of the **California Historical Society** ⑲. Across Mission Street is the **Ansel Adams Center for Photography** ⑳.

Backtrack a few steps on Mission Street to 3rd Street, where you can walk north and cross over Market Street to where 3rd, Market, Kearny, and Geary streets converge. In the traffic triangle here stands historic Lotta's Fountain. Walk back to the south side of Market Street from the fountain and head east (left, toward the waterfront) to the **Palace Hotel** ㉑. Enter via the Market Street entrance, checking out the Pied Piper Bar, Garden Court restaurant, and main lobby. Exit via the lobby onto New Montgomery Street and make a left, which will bring you back up to Market Street. Turn right and you'll see several unusual Market Street buildings as you walk to the waterfront. Toward the end of Market Street a three-tier pedestrian mall connects the five buildings of the **Embarcadero Center** ㉒ office-retail complex. Embarcadero 5, at the very end of Market Street, houses the **Hyatt Regency Hotel** ㉓. On the waterfront side of the hotel is Justin Herman Plaza, home in summer to the city's more upscale farmers' market.

Across the busy Embarcadero roadway from the plaza stands the port's trademark, the **Ferry Building** ㉔. Near here slithers a portion of the 5-ft-wide, 2½-mi-long glass-and-concrete Promenade Ribbon, which spans the waterfront from the base of Telegraph Hill past the Ferry Building to the South Beach area.

The ornate Audiffred Building, on the southwest corner of the Embarcadero and Mission Street, houses Boulevard restaurant on the ground floor of the 1889 structure. Head west on Mission Street along the side of Boulevard and cross Steuart Street. In the middle of the block is the entrance to the historic sections of **Rincon Center** ㉕, worth seeing for the famous murals and the old Rincon Annex Post Office. Continue south within the center to its newer portions and make a left as you exit through the doors near Chalkers Billiards. Across Steuart Street you'll see the Jewish Community Federation Building, which houses **The Jewish Museum** ㉖.

TIMING

The walk above takes a good two hours, more if you visit the museums and galleries. SFMOMA merits about two hours; the Center for the Arts, the Cartoon Art Museum, and the Ansel Adams Center 45 minutes each.

Sights to See

⑳ **Ansel Adams Center for Photography.** Ansel Adams created this center in Carmel in 1967, and some of his work is always on display. Recent exhibits have included works by contemporary Native American photographers and images of a World War II–era Japanese internment camp shot by Adams, Dorothea Lange, and Toyo Miyataki. ⊠ *655 Mission St.,* ☎ *415/495–7000.* 🎫 *$5.* ⏲ *Daily 11–5, 1st Thurs. of month 11–8.*

19 **California Historical Society.** The society, founded in 1871, administers a vast repository of Californiana—500,000 photographs, 150,000 manuscripts, and thousands of books, periodicals, and paintings. ⊠ *678 Mission St.,* ☎ *415/357–1848.* 🎫 *$2, free 1st Tues. of month.* ⏲ *Tues.–Sat. 11–5 (galleries close between exhibitions).*

18 **Cartoon Art Museum.** Krazy Kat, Zippy the Pinhead, Batman, and other colorful cartoon icons greet you as you walk in the door to the Cartoon Art Museum. In addition to a 12,000-piece permanent collection, a 3,000-volume library, and a CD-ROM gallery, changing exhibits examine everything from the impact of underground comics to the output of women and African-American cartoonists. ⊠ *814 Mission St., 2nd floor,* ☎ *415/227–8666.* 🎫 *$5 (pay what you wish 1st Wed. of month).* ⏲ *Tues.–Fri. 11–5, Sat. 10–5, Sun. 1–5.*

14 **Center for the Arts.** The dance, music, theater, visual arts, films, and videos presented at this facility in Yerba Buena Gardens range from the community-based to the international. ⊠ *701 Mission St.,* ☎ *415/978–2787.* 🎫 *Galleries $5, free 1st Thurs. of month 5 PM–8 PM.* ⏲ *Galleries and box office: Tues.–Sun. 11–6 (until 8 PM Thurs. and Fri.).*

22 **Embarcadero Center.** John Portman designed this five-block complex built during the 1970s and early 1980s. Shops and restaurants abound on the first three levels; there's ample office space on the floors above. Louise Nevelson's 54-ft-high black-steel sculpture, *Sky Tree,* stands guard over Building 3 and is among 20-plus artworks throughout the center. The indoor-outdoor **SkyDeck** atop Embarcadero 1 (buy tickets on the ground floor and take the mezzanine-level elevator) provides an enticing 360-degree view of the city and interactive multimedia presentations about San Francisco history and culture. Tickets ($7) to the deck, which is open daily 9:30–9, sometimes sell out days in advance for certain hours; call the hot line for information. ⊠ *Clay St. between Battery St. (Embarcadero 1) and the Embarcadero (Embarcadero 5),* ☎ *415/772–0734 for Embarcadero Center information, 888/737–5933 for SkyDeck hot line, 415/772–0590 for SkyDeck ticket booth.*

24 **Ferry Building.** The beacon of the port area, erected in 1896, has a 230-ft clock tower modeled after the campanile of the cathedral in Seville, Spain. On April 18, 1906, the four great clock faces on the tower, powered by the swinging of a 14-ft pendulum, stopped at 5:17—the moment the great earthquake struck—and stayed still for 12 months. A waterfront promenade that extends from the piers on the north side of the Ferry Building south to the Bay Bridge is great for jogging, inline skating, watching sailboats on the bay, or enjoying a picnic. Ferries behind the building sail to Sausalito, Larkspur, Tiburon, and the East Bay. ⊠ *The Embarcadero at the foot of Market St.*

23 **Hyatt Regency Hotel.** John Portman designed this hotel noted for its 17-story hanging garden. Christmas is the best time to see it, when strands of tiny white lights hang down above the lobby starting at the 12th floor. The four glass elevators facing the lobby are fun to ride, unless you suffer from vertigo. The Hyatt played a starring role in the 1970s disaster movie *The Towering Inferno.* ⊠ *Embarcadero 5,* ☎ *415/788–1234.*

26 **The Jewish Museum.** The exhibits at this small museum survey Jewish art, history, and culture. Call ahead before visiting; the museum some-

times closes between exhibits. ✉ *121 Steuart St.,* ☎ *415/788–9990.* 🎟 *$5, free 1st Mon. of month.* ⊙ *Sun.–Wed. 11–5, Thurs. 11–8. Hrs may vary.*

15 **Metreon.** Kid-play meets the 21st century at this Sony entertainment center with interactive play areas based on such books as Maurice Sendak's *Where the Wild Things Are* and a three-screen, three-dimensional installation that illustrates principles discussed in architect David Macauley's *The Way Things Work.* There's also a 15-screen multiplex, an IMAX theater, retail shops, and restaurants. ✉ *4th St. between Mission and Howard Sts.,* ☎ *800/638–7366.*

16 **Moscone Convention Center.** The site of the 1984 Democratic convention, Moscone is distinguished by a contemporary glass-and-girder lobby at street level (all convention exhibit space is underground) and a column-free interior. ✉ *Howard St. between 3rd and 4th Sts.*

21 **Palace Hotel.** The city's oldest hotel opened in 1875. Fire destroyed the original Palace following the 1906 earthquake despite the hotel's 28,000-gallon reservoir fed by four artesian wells; the current building dates from 1909. President Warren Harding died at the Palace while still in office in 1923, and the body of King Kalakaua of Hawaii spent a night here after he died in San Francisco in 1891. The managers play up this ghoulish past with talk of a haunted guest room. Free **guided tours** (☎ 415/557–4266) of the hotel's grand interior take in the glass-dome Garden Court restaurant, mosaic-tile floors in Oriental-rug designs, and Maxfield Parrish's wall-size painting *The Pied Piper,* the centerpiece of the Pied Piper Bar. ✉ *2 New Montgomery St.,* ☎ *415/512–1111.* ⊙ *Tours Tues. and Sat. 10:30 AM, Thurs. 2 PM.*

25 **Rincon Center.** A sheer five-story column of water resembling a mini-rainstorm stands out as the centerpiece of the indoor arcade at this mostly modern office-retail complex. The lobby of the Streamline Moderne–style former post office on the Mission Street side contains a Works Project Administration **mural by Anton Refregier.** The 27 panels depict California life from the days when Native Americans were the state's sole inhabitants through World War I. A permanent exhibit below the murals contains photographs and artifacts of life in the Rincon area during the 1800s. ✉ *Between Steuart, Spear, Mission, and Howard Sts.*

★ 17 **Rooftop@Yerba Buena Gardens.** Fun is the order of the day among these brightly colored concrete and corrugated-metal buildings atop Moscone Convention Center South. A historic **Looff carousel** ($1 per ride) twirls from Wednesday to Sunday between noon and 6. South of the carousel is **Zeum** (☎ 415/777–2800, 🌐), a high-tech interactive arts and technology center ($7 adults, $5 children ages 5–18) geared to children ages 8 and over. Zeum is open in summer Wednesday to Sunday between 11 and 5, and in winter on weekends and school holidays from 11 to 5. Also part of the rooftop complex are gardens, an ice-skating rink, and a bowling alley. ✉ *4th St. between Howard and Folsom Sts.*

★ 13 **San Francisco Museum of Modern Art (SFMOMA).** Mario Botta designed the striking SFMOMA facility, completed in early 1995, which consists of a sienna brick facade and a central tower of alternating bands of black and white stone. Inside, natural light from the tower floods the central atrium and some of the museum's galleries. A black-and-gray stone staircase leads from the atrium to four floors of galleries. Works by Matisse, Picasso, O'Keeffe, Kahlo, Pollock, and Warhol form the heart of the diverse permanent collection. The adventurous programming includes traveling exhibits and multimedia installations. The café, accessible from the street, provides a comfortable, reasonably priced refuge for drinks and light meals. ✉ *151 3rd St.,* ☎ *415/*

357–4000. $9, free 1st Tues. of each month, ½-price entry Thurs. 6–9. Memorial Day–Labor Day, Fri.–Tues. 10–6, Thurs. 10–9; Labor Day–Memorial Day, Fri.–Tues. 11–6, Thurs. 11–9.

★ **Yerba Buena Gardens.** The centerpiece of the SoMa redevelopment area is the two blocks that encompass the Center for the Arts, Metreon, Moscone Center, and the Rooftop@Yerba Buena Gardens (☞ *above*). A circular walkway lined with benches and sculptures surrounds the East Garden, a large patch of green amid this visually stunning complex. The waterfall memorial to Martin Luther King Jr. is the focal point of the East Garden. Powerful streams of water surge over large, jagged stone columns, mirroring the enduring force of King's words that are carved on the stone walls. ✉ *Between 3rd, 4th, Mission, and Folsom Sts.* *Sunrise–10 PM.*

The Heart of the Barbary Coast

The gold rush brought streams of people to San Francisco, transforming the onetime frontier town into a cosmopolitan city almost overnight. The population of San Francisco jumped from a mere 800 in 1848 to more than 25,000 in 1850, and to nearly 150,000 in 1870. Along with the prospectors came many other fortune seekers. Saloon keepers, gamblers, and prostitutes all flocked to the so-called Barbary Coast. Along with the money came crime. In 1852 the city suffered an average of two murders each day. Hardly a day would pass without bloodshed in the city's estimated 500 bars and 1,000 gambling dens.

By 1917 the excesses of the Barbary Coast had fallen victim to the Red-Light Abatement Act and the ire of church leaders—the wild era was over, and the young city was forced to grow up. Since then the red-light establishments have edged upward to the Broadway strip of North Beach, and Jackson Square evolved into a sedate district of refurbished brick buildings decades ago. Only one remnant of the era remains. Below Montgomery Street between California Street and Broadway, underlying many building foundations along the former waterfront area (long since filled in), lay at least 100 ships abandoned by frantic crews and passengers caught up in gold fever.

Numbers in the text correspond to numbers in the margin and on the Downtown San Francisco map.

A Good Walk

Bronze sidewalk plaques mark the street corners along the 50-site, 3.8-mi-long Barbary Coast Trail. The trail begins at the Old Mint, at 5th and Mission streets, and runs north through downtown, Chinatown, Jackson Square, North Beach, and Fisherman's Wharf, ending at Aquatic Park. For information about the sites on the trail, pick up a brochure at the San Francisco Visitors Information Center (☞ Union Square Area, *above*).

To catch the highlights of the Barbary Coast Trail and a glimpse of a few important Financial District structures, start at Montgomery and Market streets (above the Montgomery BART/Muni station). Walk east on Market Street toward the Ferry Building to Sansome Street and turn left. At 155 Sansome Street is the Stock Exchange Tower. Around the corner (to the left) on Pine Street is the **Pacific Stock Exchange** ㉗ building. Continue north on Sansome. Turn left on California and right on Montgomery Street. Between California and Sacramento streets is the **Wells Fargo Bank History Museum** ㉘.

Two blocks north on Montgomery from the Wells Fargo museum stands the **Transamerica Pyramid** ㉙, between Clay and Washington streets. A tranquil redwood grove graces the east side of the pyramid. Walk through it, and you'll exit on Washington Street, across which you can see Hotaling Place to your left. Walk west (left) to the corner, cross Washington Street, and walk back to Hotaling Place. This historic alley is your entrance to **Jackson Square** ㉚, the heart of the Barbary Coast. Of particular note here are the former A. P. Hotaling whiskey distillery, on the corner of Hotaling Place, and the 1850s structures around the corner in the 700 block of Montgomery Street. To see these buildings, walk west on Jackson from the distillery and make a left on Montgomery Street. Continue south on Montgomery Street to Washington Street, make a right, and cross Columbus Avenue. Head north (to the right) up Columbus Avenue to the **San Francisco Brewing Company** ㉛, the last standing saloon of the Barbary Coast era and a place overflowing with freshly brewed beers and history.

TIMING

Two hours should be enough time to see everything on this tour—unless you plan on trying all the homemade beers at the San Francisco Brewing Company. The Wells Fargo Museum (open only on weekdays) deserves a half hour. Evenings and weekends are peaceful times to admire the area's distinctive architecture. If you want to see activity, go on a weekday around lunchtime.

Sights to See

30 **Jackson Square.** Here was the heart of the Barbary Coast of the Gay '90s. Though most of the red-light district was destroyed in the 1906 fire, old redbrick buildings and narrow alleys recall the romance and rowdiness of the early days. Some of the city's earliest business buildings, survivors of the 1906 quake, still stand in Jackson Square, between Montgomery and Sansome streets.

27 **Pacific Stock Exchange.** Ralph Stackpole's monumental 1930 granite sculptural groups, *Earth's Fruitfulness* and *Man's Inventive Genius,* flank this imposing structure, which dates from 1915. The Stock Exchange Tower, around the corner at 155 Sansome Street, is a 1930 modern classic by architects Miller and Pfleuger, with an Art Deco gold ceiling and a black marble wall entry. ✉ *301 Pine St. (tower around corner at 155 Sansome St.).*

31 **San Francisco Brewing Company.** Built in 1907, this pub looks like a museum piece from the Barbary Coast days. An old upright piano sits in the corner under the original stained-glass windows. Take a seat at the mahogany bar and look down at the white-tile spittoon. In an adjacent room look for the handmade copper brewing kettle used to produce a dozen beers—with such names as Pony Express—by means of old-fashioned gravity-flow methods. ✉ *155 Columbus Ave.,* ☎ *415/434–3344.*

29 **Transamerica Pyramid.** The city's most photographed high-rise is the 853-ft Transamerica Pyramid. Designed by William Pereira and Associates in 1972, the initially controversial icon has become more acceptable to most locals over time. A fragrant redwood grove along the east side of the building, replete with benches and a cheerful fountain, is a placid patch in which to unwind. ✉ *600 Montgomery St.*

28 **Wells Fargo Bank History Museum.** There were no formal banks in San Francisco during the early years of the gold rush, and miners often entrusted their gold dust to saloon keepers. In 1852 Wells Fargo opened its first bank in the city, and the company established banking offices in the mother-lode camps, using stagecoaches and pony express riders to service the burgeoning state. The museum displays samples of nuggets and gold dust from mines, a mural-size map of the Mother Lode,

original art by Western artists Charles M. Russell and Maynard Dixon, mementos of the poet bandit Black Bart, and an old telegraph machine on which you can practice sending codes. The showpiece is the red Concord stagecoach, the likes of which carried passengers from St. Joseph, Missouri, to San Francisco in three weeks during the 1850s. ✉ *420 Montgomery St.,* ☎ *415/396–2619.* *Free.* ⏲ *Weekdays 9–5.*

Chinatown

Prepare to have your senses assaulted in Chinatown. Pungent smells waft out of restaurants, fish markets, and produce stands. Good-luck banners of crimson and gold hang beside dragon-entwined lampposts, pagoda roofs, and street signs with Chinese calligraphy. Honking cars chime in with shoppers bargaining loudly in Cantonese or Mandarin. Add to this the visual assault of millions of Chinese-theme goods spilling out of the shops along Grant Avenue, and you get an idea of what Chinatown is all about.

Numbers in the text correspond to numbers in the margin and on the Downtown San Francisco map.

A Good Walk

While wandering through Chinatown's streets and alleys, don't forget to look up. Above street level, many older structures—mostly brick buildings that replaced rickety wooden ones destroyed during the 1906 earthquake—have ornate balconies and cornices. The architecture in the 900 block of Grant Avenue (at Washington Street) and Waverly Place (west of and parallel to Grant Avenue between Sacramento and Washington streets) is particularly noteworthy, though some locals decry it and similar examples as inauthentic adornment meant to make their neighborhood seem "more Chinese."

Visitors usually enter Chinatown through the green-tile **Chinatown Gate** ㉜, on Grant Avenue at Bush Street. Shops selling souvenirs, jewelry, and home furnishings line Grant north past the gate. A veritable museum, the store sells centuries-old antiques rather than six-month-old goods made in Taiwan. **Old St. Mary's Cathedral** ㉝ towers over the corner of Grant Avenue and California Street. Continue on Grant Avenue to Clay Street and turn right. A half block down on your left is **Portsmouth Square** ㉞. A walkway on the eastern edge of the park leads over Kearny Street to the third floor of the Holiday Inn, where you'll find the **Chinese Culture Center** ㉟.

Backtrack on the walkway to Portsmouth Square and head west up Washington Street a half block to the **Old Chinese Telephone Exchange** ㊱ (now the Bank of Canton), and then continue west on Washington Street. Cross Grant Avenue and look for Waverly Place a half block up on the left. One of the best examples of this alley's traditional architecture is the **Tin How Temple** ㊲. After visiting Waverly Place and Tin How, walk back to Washington Street. Several herb shops do business in this area. Two worth checking out are Superior Trading Company at Number 837 and the Great China Herb Co. at Number 857. These Chinese pharmacies carry everything from tree roots and bark to over-the-counter treatments for impotence.

Across Washington Street from Superior is Ross Alley. Head north on Ross Alley toward Jackson Street, stopping along the way to watch the bakers at the **Golden Gate Fortune Cookies Co.** ㊳. Turn right on Jackson Street. When you get to Grant Avenue, don't cross it. If you'd like to sample some aromatic teas, turn right on Grant Avenue and visit the Ten Ren Tea Co., a few doors away at Number 949. For some of

Chinatown's best pastries, turn left and stop by Number 1029, the Golden Gate Bakery, where the moon cakes are delicious.

Head west (up the hill) on Pacific Avenue to Stockton Street, turn left, and walk south past Stockton Street's markets. At Clay Street make a right and head halfway up the hill to the **Chinatown YWCA** ㊴. Return to Stockton Street and make a right; a few doors down is the **Kong Chow Temple** ㊵, and next door is the elaborate Chinese Six Companies building.

TIMING

Allow at least two hours to see Chinatown. Brief stops will suffice at the cultural center and temples. The restaurants don't invite lingering, so if you're lunching, a half hour should be adequate unless you choose one of the higher-end places.

Sights to See

32 **Chinatown Gate.** Stone lions flank the base of this pagoda-top gate, the official entrance to Chinatown and a symbolic and literal transition from the generic downtown atmosphere to what sometimes seems like another country altogether. The lions and the glazed clay dragons atop the largest of the gate's three pagodas symbolize, among other things, wealth and prosperity. The fish whose mouths wrap tightly around the crest of this pagoda symbolize prosperity. The four Chinese characters immediately beneath the pagoda represent the philosophy of Sun Yat-sen (1866–1925), the leader who unified China in the early 20th century. The vertical characters under the left pagoda read "peace" and "trust," the ones under the right pagoda "respect" and "love." ✉ *Grant Ave. at Bush St.*

39 **Chinatown YWCA.** Julia Morgan, the architect known for the famous Hearst Castle and the first woman in California to be licensed as an architect, designed this handsome redbrick building, which originally served as a meeting place and residence for Chinese women in need of social services. ✉ *965 Clay St.*

35 **Chinese Culture Center.** Inside the center are the works of Chinese and Chinese-American artists as well as traveling exhibits relating to Chinese culture. Walking tours ($15; make reservations one week ahead) of historic points in Chinatown take place on most days at 10:30 AM. ✉ *Holiday Inn, 750 Kearny St., 3rd floor,* ☎ *415/986–1822.* 🎫 *Free.* 🕓 *Tues.–Sun. 10–4.*

38 **Golden Gate Fortune Cookies Co.** The workers at this small factory sit at circular motorized griddles. A dollop of batter drops onto a tiny metal plate, which rotates into an oven. A few moments later out comes a cookie that's pliable and ready for folding. A bagful of cookies costs $2 or $3. ✉ *56 Ross Alley (west of and parallel to Grant Ave. between Washington and Jackson Sts.),* ☎ *415/781–3956.* 🕓 *Daily 10–7.*

40 **Kong Chow Temple.** The god to whom the members of this temple pray represents honesty and trust. Take the elevator up to the fourth floor, where incense fills the air. Amid the statuary, flowers, orange offerings, and richly colored altars (red wards off evil spirits and signifies virility, green symbolizes longevity, and gold majesty) are a couple of plaques announcing that MRS. HARRY S. TRUMAN CAME TO THIS TEMPLE IN JUNE 1948 FOR A PREDICTION ON THE OUTCOME OF THE ELECTION . . . THIS FORTUNE CAME TRUE. ✉ *855 Stockton St.,* ☎ *415/434–2513.* 🎫 *Free.* 🕓 *Mon.–Sat. 9–4.*

36 **Old Chinese Telephone Exchange.** Most of Chinatown burned down after the 1906 earthquake, and this 1909 building set the style for the new Chinatown. The exchange's operators were renowned for their

prodigious memories, about which the San Francisco Chamber of Commerce boasted in 1914: "These girls respond all day with hardly a mistake to calls that are given (in English or one of five Chinese dialects) by the name of the subscriber instead of by his number—a mental feat that would be practically impossible to most high-schooled American misses." ✉ *Bank of Canton, 743 Washington St.*

33 **Old St. Mary's Cathedral.** This building, whose structure includes granite quarried in China, was dedicated in 1854 and served as the city's Catholic cathedral until 1891. Across California Street in **St. Mary's Park** the late local sculptor Beniamino Bufano's 12-ft-tall stainless-steel and rose-color granite statue of Sun Yat-sen towers over the site of the Chinese leader's favorite reading spot during his years in San Francisco. ✉ *Grant Ave. and California St.*

34 **Portsmouth Square.** Captain John B. Montgomery raised the American flag here in 1846, claiming the area from Mexico. The square—a former potato patch—was the plaza for Yerba Buena, the Mexican settlement that was renamed San Francisco. Robert Louis Stevenson, the author of *Treasure Island,* lived on the edge of Chinatown in the late 19th century and often visited this site, chatting with the sailors who hung out here. Some of the information he gleaned about life at sea found its way into his fiction. With its pagoda-shape structures, Portsmouth Square is a favorite spot for morning tai chi. By noon dozens of men huddle around Chinese chess tables, engaged in not-always-legal competition. Undercover police occasionally rush in to break things up, but this ritual, like tai chi, is an established way of life. ✉ *Bordered by Walter Lum Pl. and Kearny, Washington, and Clay Sts.*

★ 37 **Tin How Temple.** Day Ju, one of the first three Chinese to arrive in San Francisco, dedicated this temple to the Queen of the Heavens and the Goddess of the Seven Seas in 1852. Climb three flights of stairs—on the second floor is a mah-jongg parlor whose patrons hope the spirits above will favor them. In the temple's entryway, elderly ladies can often be seen preparing "money" to be burned as offerings to various Buddhist gods or as funds for ancestors to use in the afterlife. Red-and-gold lanterns adorn the ceiling—the larger the lamp the larger its donor's contribution to the temple—and the smell of incense is usually thick. Oranges and other offerings rest on altars to various gods. ✉ *125 Waverly Pl.,* ☎ *no phone.* 🎫 *Free (donations accepted).* ⏲ *Daily 10–4.*

North Beach and Telegraph Hill

Novelist and resident Herbert Gold calls North Beach "the longest-running, most glorious American bohemian operetta outside Greenwich Village." Indeed, to anyone who's spent some time in its eccentric old bars and cafés or wandered the neighborhood, North Beach evokes everything from the Barbary Coast days to the no-less-rowdy beatnik era. Italian bakeries appear frozen in time, homages to Jack Kerouac and Allen Ginsberg pop up everywhere, and the modern equivalent of the Barbary Coast's "houses of ill repute," strip joints, do business on Broadway.

More than 125,000 Italian-American residents once lived in North Beach, but now only about 2,000, most of them elderly, do. Now the neighborhood is largely Chinese, and as neighborhood real-estate prices have escalated, a number of young professionals have moved in as well. But walk down narrow Romolo Place (off Broadway east of Columbus Avenue) or Genoa Place (off Union Streetwest of Kearny Street) or Medau Place (off Filbert Street west of Grant Avenue) and you can feel the immigrant Italian roots of this neighborhood.

Numbers in the text correspond to numbers in the margin and on the Downtown San Francisco map.

A Good Walk

Stand on the northwest corner of Broadway and Columbus Avenue to get your bearings. To the southwest is Chinatown. The Financial District skyscrapers loom overhead to the south of the intersection of Columbus Avenue and Broadway, though one of the earliest and shortest examples, the triangular Sentinel Building, where Kearny Street and Columbus Avenue meet at an angle, grabs the eye with its unusual shape and mellow green patina. East across Columbus Avenue is the Condor, where in 1964 local celeb Carol Doda became the nation's first dancer at a nightclub to go topless. (These days Doda runs a lingerie shop at 1850 Union Street and the Condor is a sports bar.) Around the same time, North Beach was a nexus of comedy. Bill Cosby, Phyllis Diller, Dick Gregory, the Smothers Brothers, and other talents cut their teeth at clubs such as the hungry i and the Purple Onion. To the north of Broadway and Columbus Avenue is the heart of Italian North Beach.

Walk southeast across Columbus Avenue to **City Lights Bookstore** ㊶, where you can pick up a book by one of the beat writers or just soak up the ambience. Head up the east side of Columbus Avenue (the same side as the Condor) past Grant Avenue. On the northeast corner of Columbus Avenue and Vallejo Street is the Victorian-era **St. Francis of Assisi Church** ㊷. Go east on Vallejo Street to Grant Avenue and make another left. Check out the the eclectic shops and old-time bars and cafés between Vallejo and Union streets.

Turn left at Union Street and head west to **Washington Square** ㊸, an oasis of green amid the tightly packed streets of North Beach. At Union and Stockton streets is San Francisco's oldest Italian restaurant, Fior d'Italia, which opened in 1886. After the 1906 earthquake and fire, the restaurant operated out of a tent until its new quarters were ready. On the north side, on Filbert Street, stands the double-turreted **Saints Peter and Paul Catholic Church** ㊹. After you've had your fill of North Beach, head up **Telegraph Hill** ㊺ from Washington Square. Atop the hill is **Coit Tower** ㊻. People in poor health will not want to attempt the walk up the steep hill; Coit Tower can be reached by car (though parking is very tight) or public transportation—board Muni Bus 39-Coit at Washington Square. To walk, head east up Filbert Street at the park; turn left at Grant Avenue and go one block north, then right at Greenwich Street and ascend the steps on your right. Cross the street at the top of the first set of stairs and continue up the curving stone steps to Coit Tower.

On the other side of Coit Tower, the Greenwich Street steps take you down the east side of Telegraph Hill, with stunning views of the bay en route. At Montgomery Street, perched on the side of the hill, is **Julius' Castle** ㊼ restaurant. A block to the right at 1360 Montgomery Street, where the Filbert steps intersect, is a brilliant Art Deco apartment building. Descend the Filbert steps amid roses, fuchsias, irises, and trumpet flowers—courtesy of Grace Marchant, who labored for nearly 30 years to transform a dump into one of San Francisco's hidden treasures in the 1900s. At the foot of the hill is the serene **Levi Strauss headquarters** ㊽.

TIMING

It takes a little more than an hour to walk the tour, but the point in both North Beach and Telegraph Hill is to linger—set aside at least a few hours.

Sights to See

★ 41 **City Lights Bookstore.** The hangout of Beat-era writers—Allen Ginsberg and Lawrence Ferlinghetti among them—remains a vital part of San Francisco's literary scene. Still leftist at heart, in 1999 the store unveiled a replica of a revolutionary mural destroyed in Chiapas, Mexico, by military forces. ✉ *261 Columbus Ave.,* ☎ *415/362–8193.*

★ 46 **Coit Tower.** Among San Francisco's most distinctive skyline sights, the 210-ft-tall Coit Tower stands as a monument to the city's volunteer firefighters. During the gold rush, Lillie Hitchcock Coit (known as Miss Lil) was said to have deserted a wedding party and chased down the street after her favorite engine, Knickerbocker Number 5, while clad in her bridesmaid finery. She was soon made an honorary member of the Knickerbocker Company, and after that always signed her name as "Lillie Coit 5" in honor of her favorite fire engine. Lillie died in 1929 at the age of 86, leaving the city $125,000 to "expend in an appropriate manner . . . to the beauty of San Francisco." ✉ *Telegraph Hill Blvd., at Greenwich St. or Lombard St.,* ☎ *415/362–0808.* *$3.75.* *Daily 10–6:30.*

47 **Julius' Castle.** Every bit as romantic as its name implies, this contemporary Italian restaurant commands a regal view of the bay from its perch high up Telegraph Hill. An official historic landmark, whose founder, Julius Roz, had his craftsmen use materials left over from the 1915 Panama–Pacific International Exposition, the restaurant has a dark-paneled Victorian interior that befits the elegant setting. ✉ *1541 Montgomery St.,* ☎ *415/392–2222.* *Daily 5 PM–10 PM.*

48 **Levi Strauss headquarters.** This carefully landscaped complex appears so collegiate it is affectionately known as Levi Strauss University. ✉ *Levi's Plaza, 1155 Battery St.*

42 **St. Francis of Assisi Church.** This 1860 building stands on the site of the frame parish church that served the Catholic community during the gold rush. Its solid terra-cotta facade complements the many brightly colored restaurants and cafés nearby. ✉ *610 Vallejo St.,* ☎ *415/983–0405.* *Daily 11–5.*

44 **Saints Peter and Paul Catholic Church.** Camera-toting tourists focus their lenses on the Romanesque splendor of what's often called the Italian Cathedral. Completed in 1924, the cathedral has Disney-esque stone-white towers that are local landmarks. On the first Sunday of October a mass followed by a parade to Fisherman's Wharf celebrates the Blessing of the Fleet. ✉ *666 Filbert St., at Washington Square.*

45 **Telegraph Hill.** Telegraph Hill got its name from one of its earliest functions—in 1853 it became the location of the first Morse Code Signal Station. Hill residents command some of the best views in the city, as well as the most difficult ascents to their aeries (the flower-lined steps flanking the hill make the climb more than tolerable for visitors, though). The Hill rises from the east end of Lombard Street to a height of 284 ft and is capped by Coit Tower (☞ *above*). ✉ *Between Lombard, Filbert, Kearny, and Sansome Sts.*

43 **Washington Square.** Once the daytime social heart of Little Italy, this grassy patch has changed character numerous times over the years. The Beats hung out in the 1950s, hippies camped out (sometimes literally) in the 1960s and early 1970s, and nowadays you're just as likely to see children of Southeast Asian descent tossing a Frisbee as Italian men or women chatting about their children and the old country. In the morning elderly Asians perform the motions of tai chi, but by mid-morning groups of conservatively dressed Italian men in their 70s and 80s

begin to arrive. ✉ *Bordered by Columbus Ave. and Stockton, Filbert, and Union Sts.*

Nob Hill and Russian Hill

Once called the Hill of Golden Promise, this area was officially dubbed Nob Hill during the 1870s when "the Big Four"—Charles Crocker, Leland Stanford, Mark Hopkins, and Collis Huntington, who were involved in the construction of the transcontinental railroad—built their hilltop estates. The lingo is thick from this era: Those on the hilltop were referred to as "swells" and the hill itself was called Snob Hill, a term that survives to this day. By 1882 so many estates had sprung up on Nob Hill that Robert Louis Stevenson called it "the hill of palaces." But the 1906 earthquake and fire destroyed all the palatial mansions.

Just nine blocks or so from downtown and a few blocks north of Nob Hill, Russian Hill has long been home to old San Francisco families, who were joined during the 1890s by bohemian artists and writers that included Charles Norris, George Sterling, and Maynard Dixon. Several stories explain the origin of Russian Hill's name, though none is known to be true. One legend has it that during San Francisco's early days, the steep hill (294 ft) was the site of a cemetery for unknown Russians; another version attributes the name to a Russian sailor of prodigious drinking habits who drowned when he fell into a well on the hill. The bay views here are some of the city's best.

Numbers in the text correspond to numbers in the margin and on the Downtown San Francisco map.

A Good Walk

The Van Ness–California cable car line runs up to Nob Hill. If you're not up for a strenuous walk, this is the best way to get here from the Financial District or the Embarcadero. Begin on California and Taylor streets at the **Masonic Auditorium** ㊾. Across California Street is the majestic **Grace Cathedral** ㊿. From the cathedral walk east (toward Mason Street and downtown) on California Street to the **Pacific Union Club** 51. Across Mason Street from the Pacific Union Club is the lush **Fairmont Hotel** 52. Directly across California Street from the Fairmont is the **Mark Hopkins Inter-Continental Hotel** 53, famed for panoramic views from its Top of the Mark lounge. Head east down the hill one block to Powell Street to the Renaissance Stanford Court Hotel. From here walk north on Powell Street three blocks to Washington Street and then west one block to Mason Street to the **Cable Car Museum** 54.

From the Cable Car Museum continue four blocks north on Mason Street to Vallejo Street, turn west, and start climbing the steps that lead to the multilevel **Ina Coolbrith Park** 55. At the top, you can see the Vallejo steps area across Taylor Street from the park. The Flag House, one of several brown-shingle prequake buildings in this area, is to your left at Taylor Street. Cross Taylor Street and ascend the Vallejo steps; the view east takes in downtown and the Bay Bridge. Continue west from the top of the Vallejo steps to two secluded Russian Hill alleys. Down and to your left is Florence Place, an enclave of 1920s stucco homes, and down a bit farther on your right is Russian Hill Place, with a row of 1915 Mediterranean town houses designed by Willis Polk. After reemerging on Vallejo Street from the alleys, walk north (right) on Jones Street one short block to Green Street. Head west (left) halfway down the block to the octagonal **Feusier House** 56. Backtrack to Jones Street, and head north to **Macondray Lane** 57. Walk west (to the left) on Macondray Lane and follow it to Leavenworth Street. Head north (to the right) on Leavenworth Street to the bottom of **Lombard Street** 58, the "crookedest street in the world." Continue north one block on Leavenworth Street and then east one block on Chestnut Street to the **San Francisco Art Institute** (59).

TIMING

The tour above covers a lot of ground, much of it steep. If you're in reasonably good shape you can complete this walk in 3½–4 hours, including 30-minute stops at Grace Cathedral and the Cable Car Museum.

Sights to See

★ 54 **Cable Car Museum.** San Francisco once had more than a dozen cable car barns and powerhouses. The only survivor, this 1907 redbrick structure, an engaging stopover between Russian Hill and Nob Hill, contains photographs, old cable cars, signposts, ticketing machines, and other memorabilia dating from 1873. The massive powerhouse wheels that move the entire cable car system steal the show. The design is so simple it seems almost unreal. You can also go downstairs to the sheave room and check out the innards of the system. ✉ *1201 Mason St., at Washington St.,* ☎ *415/474–1887.* *Free.* ⏲ *Oct.–Mar., daily 10–5; Apr.–Sept., daily 10–6.*

52 **Fairmont Hotel.** The Fairmont's dazzling opening was delayed a year by the 1906 quake, but since then the marble palace has hosted presidents, royalty, and movie stars. Things have changed since its early days, however: On the eve of World War I you could get a room for as low as $2.50 per night, meals included. Nowadays, prices go as high as $8,000, which buys a night in the eight-room, Persian art–filled penthouse suite that was showcased regularly in the TV series *Hotel.* On Friday and Saturday from 3 to 6 and on Sunday from 1 to 6, afternoon tea is served in the plush lobby, all done up in flamboyant rose-floral carpeting, lush red-velvet chairs, gold faux-marble columns, and gilt ceilings. Don't miss an evening cocktail (the ambience demands you order a mai tai) in the kitschy **Tonga Room,** complete with tiki huts, a sporadic tropical rainstorm, and a floating (literally) bandstand. ✉ *950 Mason St.,* ☎ *415/772–5000.*

56 **Feusier House.** Octagonal houses were once thought to make the best use of space and enhance the physical and mental well-being of their occupants. A brief mid-19th-century craze inspired the construction of several in San Francisco. Only the Feusier House, built in 1857 and now a private residence surrounded by lush gardens, and the Octagon House (☞ Pacific Heights, *below*), remain standing.

50 **Grace Cathedral.** The seat of the Episcopal Church in San Francisco, this soaring Gothic structure, erected on the site of Charles Crocker's mansion, took 53 years to build. The gilded bronze doors at the east entrance were taken from casts of Ghiberti's Gates of Paradise, which are on the baptistery in Florence, Italy. A black-and-bronze stone sculpture of St. Francis by Beniamino Bufano greets visitors as they enter.

The 35-ft-wide Labyrinth, a large, purplish rug, is a replica of the 13th-century stone labyrinth on the floor of the Chartres Cathedral. All are encouraged to walk the ¼-mi-long labyrinth, a ritual based on the tradition of meditative walking. The AIDS Interfaith Chapel, to the right as you enter Grace, contains a sculpture by the late artist Keith Haring and panels from the AIDS Memorial Quilt. ✉ *1100 California St., at Taylor St.,* ☎ *415/749–6300.* ⏲ *Sun.–Fri. 7–6, Sat. 8–5.*

55 **Ina Coolbrith Park.** This attractive park is unusual because it's vertical—that is, rather than one open space, it's composed of a series of terraces up a very steep hill. A poet, Coolbrith entertained literary greats in her

Macondray Lane home near the park. In 1915 she was named poet laureate of California. ⊠ *Vallejo St. between Mason and Taylor Sts.*

★ 58 **Lombard Street.** The block-long "Crookedest Street in the World" makes eight switchbacks down the east face of Russian Hill between Hyde and Leavenworth streets. Join the line of cars waiting to drive down the steep hill, or walk down the steps on either side of Lombard. You'll take in super views of North Beach and Coit Tower whether you walk or drive. ⊠ *Lombard St. between Hyde and Leavenworth Sts.*

57 **Macondray Lane.** Enter this "secret garden" under a lovely wooden trellis and walk down a quiet cobbled pedestrian street lined with Edwardian cottages and flowering plants and trees. A flight of steep wooden stairs at the end of the lane leads down to Taylor Street—on the way down you can't miss the bay views. If you've read any of Armistead Maupin's *Tales of the City* books, you may find the lane vaguely familiar. ⊠ *Jones St. between Union and Green Sts.*

53 **Mark Hopkins Inter-Continental Hotel.** Built on the ashes of railroad tycoon Mark Hopkins's grand estate, this 19-story hotel went up in 1926. A combination of French château and Spanish Renaissance architecture, with noteworthy terra-cotta detailing, it has hosted statesmen, royalty, and Hollywood celebrities. The **Top of the Mark** is remembered fondly by thousands of World War II veterans who jammed the lounge before leaving for overseas duty. Wives and sweethearts watching the ships depart gave the room's northwest nook its name—Weepers' Corner. With its 360-degree views, the lounge is a wonderful spot for a nighttime drink. ⊠ *1 Nob Hill, at California and Mason Sts.,* ☎ *415/392–3434.*

49 **Masonic Auditorium.** Formally called the California Masonic Memorial Temple, this building was erected by Freemasons in 1957. The impressive lobby mosaic, done mainly in rich greens and yellows, depicts the Masonic fraternity's role in California history and industry. There's also an intricate model of King Solomon's Temple in the lobby. ⊠ *1111 California St.,* ☎ *415/776–4917.* ⊙ *Lobby weekdays 8–5.*

51 **Pacific Union Club.** The former home of silver baron James Flood cost a whopping $1.5 million in 1886, when even a stylish Victorian like the Haas-Lilienthal House cost less than $20,000. All that cash did buy some structural stability. The Flood residence (to be precise, its shell) was the only Nob Hill mansion to survive the 1906 earthquake and fire. The Pacific Union Club, a bastion of the wealthy and powerful, purchased the house in 1907 and commissioned Willis Polk to redesign it. ⊠ *1000 California St.*

59 **San Francisco Art Institute.** A Moorish-tile fountain in a tree-shaded courtyard immediately draws the eye as you enter the institute. The highlight of a visit is Mexican master Diego Rivera's *The Making of a Fresco Showing the Building of a City* (1931), in the student gallery to your immediate left once inside the entrance. Rivera himself is in the fresco—his back is to the viewer—and he's surrounded by his assistants.

The older portions of the Art Institute were erected in 1926. Ansel Adams created the school's fine-arts photography department in 1946, and school directors established the country's first fine-arts film program. Notable faculty and alumni have included painter Richard Diebenkorn and photographers Dorothea Lange, Edward Weston, and Annie Leibovitz. **Walter/McBean Gallery** (⊠ ☎ 415/749–4564) exhibits the often provocative works of established artists. ⊠ *800 Chestnut St.,* ☎ *415/771–7020.* 🎟 *Galleries free.* ⊙ *Walter/McBean Gallery Mon.–Sat. 11–6; student gallery daily 9–9.*

Pacific Heights

Some of the city's most expensive and dramatic real estate—including mansions and town houses priced at $2 million and up—is in Pacific Heights. Grand Victorians line the streets, and from almost any point in this neighborhood you get a magnificent view.

Numbers in the text correspond to numbers in the margin and on the Downtown San Francisco map.

A Good Walk

Pacific Heights lies on an east–west ridge along the city's northern flank from Van Ness Avenue to the Presidio and from California Street to the bay. The first stop is the **Octagon House** (60), at the corner of Gough (rhymes with "cough") and Union streets. Stroll west through the upscale shopping district of Union Street. The modest **Wedding Houses** sit on the north side of Union Street just before Buchanan Street. Continue one block farther to Webster Street and then one block north to Filbert Street. You can't miss the elaborate, schizophrenically styled **Vedanta Society** (61), on the southwest corner of Filbert and Webster streets.

Prepare for a steep climb as you head south up Webster Street. At the crest of the hill, four notable **Broadway and Webster Street estates** (62) stand within a block of each other. Two are on the north side of Broadway to the west of the intersection, one is on the same side to the east, and the last is south a half block on Webster Street. After viewing the estates, continue south on Webster Street to Pacific Avenue and turn right (west). You'll pass some apartment buildings in the first block and a half, then single-family homes. The Italianate gem at 2475 Pacific Avenue sat on a 25-acre farm in the 1850s. Several Queen Anne homes stand tall on the south side of the 2500 block (between Steiner and Pierce streets); a three-story circular glass-walled staircase distinguishes the more modern home at Number 2510, on the north side. Continue west on Pacific Avenue to Scott Street, and walk south into **Alta Plaza Park** (63).

Catch your breath at the park, and then walk east on Jackson Street several blocks to the **Whittier Mansion** (64), on the corner of Jackson and Laguna streets. Make a right on Laguna Street and a left at the next block, Washington Street. The patch of green that spreads southeast from here is **Lafayette Park** (65). Walk on Washington Street along the edge of Lafayette Park past the formal French **Spreckels Mansion** (66), at the corner of Octavia Street, and continue east two more blocks to Franklin Street. Turn left (north); halfway down the block stands the handsome **Haas-Lilienthal House** (67). Head back south on Franklin Street, stopping to view several **Franklin Street buildings** (68). At California Street, turn right (west) to see more **noteworthy Victorians** (69) on that street and Laguna Street.

TIMING

Set aside about two hours to see the sights mentioned here, not including the tours of the Haas-Lilienthal House and the Octagon House. Unless you're in great shape, it'll be a slow walk up extremely steep Webster Street from the Union Street sights, and although most of the attractions are walk-bys, you'll be covering a good bit of pavement.

Sights to See

63 **Alta Plaza Park.** Landscape architect John McLaren, who also created Golden Gate Park, designed Alta Plaza in 1910, modeling its terracing on the Grand Casino in Monte Carlo, Monaco. From the top you can see Marin to the north, downtown to the east, Twin Peaks to the south, and Golden Gate Park to the west. ⊠ *Between Clay, Steiner, Jackson, and Scott Sts.*

62 **Broadway and Webster Street estates.** Broadway uptown, unlike its garish North Beach stretch, is home to some prestigious addresses. At **2222 Broadway** is a three-story palace with an intricately filigreed doorway built by Comstock silver mine heir James Flood and later donated to a religious order. The Convent of the Sacred Heart purchased the Grant House at **2220 Broadway.** These two buildings, along with a Flood property at **2120 Broadway,** are all used as school quarters. A gold mine heir, William Bourn II, commissioned Willis Polk to build the nearby mansion at **2550 Webster St.**

68 **Franklin Street buildings.** Don't be fooled by the **Golden Gate Church** (⊠ 1901 Franklin St.)—what at first looks like a stone facade is actually redwood painted white. A Georgian-style residence built in the early 1900s for a coffee merchant sits at **1735 Franklin.** On the northeast corner of Franklin and California streets is a **Christian Science church;** built in the Tuscan Revival style, it's noteworthy for its terra-cotta detailing. The **Coleman House** (⊠ 1701 Franklin St.) is an impressive twin-turreted Queen Anne mansion built for a gold rush mining and lumber baron. Don't miss the large stained-glass window on the house's north side. ⊠ *Franklin St. between Washington and California Sts.*

67 **Haas-Lilienthal House.** A small display of photographs on the bottom floor of this elaborate 1886 Queen Anne house, which cost a mere $18,500 to build, makes clear that it was modest compared with some of the giants that fell victim to the 1906 earthquake and fire. The carefully kept rooms provide an intriguing glimpse into late 19th-century life. Volunteers conduct one-hour house tours two days a week and an informative two-hour tour of the eastern portion of Pacific Heights on Sunday afternoon. ⊠ *2007 Franklin St., between Washington and Jackson Sts.,* ☎ *415/441–3004.* 🎫 *$5.* ⏲ *Wed. noon–4 (last tour at 3), Sun. 11–5 (last tour at 4). Pacific Heights tours ($5) leave the house Sun. at 12:30.*

65 **Lafayette Park.** Clusters of trees dot this four-block-square oasis for sunbathers and dog-and-Frisbee teams. ⊠ *Between Laguna, Gough, Sacramento, and Washington Sts.*

69 **Noteworthy Victorians.** Two **Italianate Victorians** (⊠ 1818 and 1834 California St.) stand out on the 1800 block of California. A block farther is the Victorian-era **Atherton House** (⊠ 1990 California St.), whose mildly daffy design incorporates Queen Anne, Stick-Eastlake, and other architectural elements. The oft-photographed **Laguna Street Victorians,** on the west side of the 1800 block of Laguna Street, cost between $2,000 and $2,600 when they were built in the 1870s. ⊠ *California St. between Franklin and Octavia Sts.*

60 **Octagon House.** This eight-sided home sits across the street from its original site on Gough Street. It's full of antique American furniture, decorative arts (paintings, silver, rugs), and documents from the 18th and 19th centuries. White quoins accent each of the eight corners of the pretty blue-gray exterior. An award-winning Colonial-style garden completes the picture. ⊠ *2645 Gough St.,* ☎ *415/441–7512.* 🎫 *Free (donations encouraged).* ⏲ *Feb.–Dec., 2nd Sun. and 2nd and 4th Thurs. of each month, noon–3; group tours weekdays by appointment.*

66 **Spreckels Mansion.** This estate was built for sugar heir Adolph Spreckels and his wife, Alma. Mrs. Spreckels was so pleased with her house that she commissioned George Applegarth to design another building in a similar vein: the California Palace of the Legion of Honor (☞ Lincoln Park and the Western Shoreline, *below*). ⊠ *2080 Washington St., at Octavia St.*

61 **Vedanta Society.** A pastiche of Colonial, Queen Anne, Moorish, and Hindu opulence, with turrets battling onion domes and Victorian detailing everywhere, this 1905 structure was the first Hindu temple in the West. ✉ *2963 Webster St.,* ☎ *415/922–2323.*

Wedding Houses. These identical white double-peak homes (joined in the middle) were erected in the late 1870s or early 1880s by dairy rancher James Cudworth as wedding gifts for his two daughters. ✉ *1980 Union St.*

64 **Whittier Mansion.** This was one of the most elegant 19th-century houses in the state, with a Spanish-tile roof and scrolled bay windows on all four sides. An anomaly in a town that lost most of its grand mansions to the 1906 quake, the Whittier Mansion was built so solidly that only a chimney toppled over during the disaster. ✉ *2090 Jackson St.*

Japantown

Around 1860 a wave of Japanese immigrants arrived in San Francisco, which they called Soko. After the 1906 earthquake and fire, many of these newcomers settled in the Western Addition. By the 1930s they had opened shops, markets, meeting halls, and restaurants and established Shinto and Buddhist temples. Known as Japantown, this area was virtually deserted during World War II when many of its residents, including second- and third-generation Americans, were forced into so-called relocation camps. Today Japantown, or "Nihonmachi," is centered on the southern slope of Pacific Heights, north of Geary Boulevard between Fillmore and Laguna streets. The Nihonmachi Cherry Blossom Festival is celebrated on two weekends in April.

Numbers in the text correspond to numbers in the margin and on the Downtown San Francisco map.

A Good Walk

Several key components of San Francisco's history intersect at Geary Boulevard and Fillmore Street. The three-block **Japan Center** (70) sits on a portion of the area settled by Japanese and Japanese-Americans in the early 20th century. The stretch of Fillmore on either side of Geary Boulevard was a center of African-American culture during the mid-20th century.

Near the southwest corner of Geary Boulevard and Fillmore Street is the entrance to the legendary Fillmore Auditorium, where such 1960s bands as Jefferson Airplane and the Grateful Dead performed. Two doors west of the Fillmore Street was the People's Temple (since demolished), the headquarters of the cult run by the Reverend Jim Jones, whose flock participated in a mass suicide in Guyana in November 1978.

Kabuki Springs & Spa (71) is on the northeast corner of Geary Boulevard and Fillmore Street. Head north on Fillmore Street to Post Street and make a right. Pass the entrance to the eight-screen AMC Kabuki theater and enter the Japan Center mid-block, in the Kinokuniya Building. A second-level bridge spans Webster Street, connecting the Kinokuniya and Kintetsu buildings. After exiting the Kintetsu Building, pop across Post Street to the open-air **Japan Center Mall** (72), a short block of shoji-screened buildings on Buchanan Street between Post and Sutter streets.

TIMING

The distance covered in the tour is extremely short, and apart from the worthwhile Kabuki Springs & Spa there isn't much to see here. Not including a visit to the Kabuki Springs, an hour will probably suffice.

Sights to See

(70) **Japan Center.** The noted American architect Minoru Yamasaki created this 5-acre complex that opened in 1968. The development includes a hotel (the Radisson Miyako, at Laguna and Post streets); shops selling Japanese furnishings, clothing, cameras, tapes and records, porcelain, pearls, and paintings; an excellent spa; and a multiplex cinema.

(72) **Japan Center Mall.** The buildings lining this open-air mall are of the shoji school of architecture. Seating in this area can be found on local artist Ruth Asawa's twin origami-style fountains, which sit in the middle of the mall; they're squat circular structures made of fieldstone. ⊠ *Buchanan St. between Post and Sutter Sts.*

★ (71) **Kabuki Springs & Spa.** Japantown's house of tranquility got a complete makeover in 1999. The feel is less Japanese than before. Balinese urns decorate the communal bath area, and you're just as likely to hear soothing flute or classical music as you are Kitaro. The massage palette has also expanded well beyond the traditional shiatsu technique. The experience is no less relaxing, however, and the treatment regimen now includes facials, salt scrubs, and mud and seaweed wraps. You can take your massage in a private room with a bath or in a curtained-off area. The communal baths ($12 before 5 PM, $16 after 5 and all weekend) contain hot and cold tubs, a large Japanese-style bath, a sauna, a steam room, and showers. The baths are open for men only on Monday, Thursday, and Saturday, and for women only on Wednesday, Friday, and Sunday. A 90-minute massage-and-bath package with a private room costs $90. A package that includes an hour-long massage and the use of the communal baths costs $75. ⊠ *1750 Geary Blvd.,* ☎ *415/922–6000.* ⊙ *Daily 10–10.*

Civic Center

The Civic Center—the beaux-arts complex between McAllister and Grove streets and Franklin and Hyde streets that includes City Hall, the War Memorial Opera House, the Veterans Building, and the old Public Library —is a product of the "City Beautiful" movement of the early 20th century. City Hall, completed in 1915 and renovated in 1999, is the centerpiece.

Numbers in the text correspond to numbers in the margin and on the Downtown San Francisco map.

A Good Walk

Start at **United Nations Plaza** (73), set on an angle between Hyde and Market streets. Walk west across the plaza toward Fulton Street, which dead-ends at Hyde Street, and cross Hyde Street. Towering over the block of Fulton Street between Hyde and Larkin streets is the Pioneers Monument. The new main branch of the **San Francisco Public Library** (74) is south of the monument. North of it is the old library. The patch of green west of the library is Civic Center Plaza, and beyond that is **City Hall** (75). Beyond it you'll see three grand edifices, each of which takes up most of its block. On the southwestern corner of McAllister Street and Van Ness Avenue is the **Veterans Building** (76). A horseshoe-shape carriage entrance on its south side separates the building from the **War Memorial Opera House** (77). In the next block of Van Ness Avenue, across Grove Street from the opera house, is **Louise M. Davies Symphony Hall** (78).

TIMING

Walking around the Civic Center shouldn't take more than about 45 minutes. Another half hour or more can be spent browsing the shops along Hayes Street. On Wednesday or Sunday allot some extra time to take in the farmers market in United Nations Plaza.

Sights to See

75 **City Hall.** This masterpiece of granite and marble was modeled after St. Peter's cathedral in Rome. City Hall's bronze and gold-leaf dome, which is even higher than the U.S. Capitol's version, dominates the area. Some noteworthy events that have taken place here include the marriage of Marilyn Monroe and Joe DiMaggio (1954), the hosing—down the central staircase—of civil rights and freedom of speech protesters (1960), the murders of Mayor George Moscone and openly gay Supervisor Harvey Milk (1978), the torching of the lobby by angry members of the gay community in response to the light sentence given to the former supervisor who killed them (1979), and the weddings of scores of gay couples in celebration of the passage of San Francisco's Domestic Partners Act (1991). The palatial interior, full of grand arches and with a sweeping central staircase, is impressive. Free tours are also available weekdays at 10, noon, 12:30, and 2; and weekends at 12:30 and 2. Across Polk Street is **Civic Center Plaza,** with lawns, walkways, seasonal flower beds, and a playground. ✉ *Between Van Ness Ave. and Polk, Grove, and McAllister Sts.,* ☎ *415/554–6023.*

78 **Louise M. Davies Symphony Hall.** Fascinating and still futuristic looking after two decades, this 2,750-seat hall is the home of the San Francisco Symphony. The glass wraparound lobby and pop-out balcony high on the southeast corner are visible from the outside. Henry Moore created the bronze sculpture that sits on the sidewalk at Van Ness Avenue and Grove Street. The hall's 59 adjustable Plexiglas acoustical disks cascade from the ceiling like hanging windshields. Scheduled tours (75 minutes), which meet at the Grove Street entrance, take in Davies and the nearby opera house and Herbst Theatre. ✉ *201 Van Ness Ave.,* ☎ *415/552–8338.* 🎫 *Tours $5.* ⊙ *Tours Mon. (except holidays) hourly 10–2.*

74 **San Francisco Public Library.** The main library, which opened in 1996, is a modernized version of the old beaux-arts library that sits just across Fulton Street. The several specialty rooms include centers for the hearing and visually impaired, a gay and lesbian history center, and African-American and Asian centers. At the library's core is a five-story atrium with a skylight, a grand staircase, and murals painted by local artists. Tours of the library are conducted Wednesday, Friday, and Saturday at 2:30 PM. ✉ *100 Larkin St., between Grove and Fulton Sts.,* ☎ *415/557–4400.* ⊙ *Mon. 10–6, Tues.–Thurs. 9–8, Fri. 11–5, Sat. 9–5, Sun. noon–5.*

73 **United Nations Plaza.** This monument is inscribed with the goals and philosophy of the United Nations charter, which was signed at the War Memorial Opera House in 1945. On Wednesday and Sunday a farmers market fills the space with homegrown produce and plants. ✉ *Fulton St. between Hyde and Market Sts.*

76 **Veterans Building.** Performing and visual arts organizations occupy much of this 1930s structure. **Herbst Theatre** (☎ 415/392–4400) hosts lectures, music, and dance performances. The street-level **San Francisco Arts Commission Gallery** (☎ 415/554–6080), open from Wednesday to Saturday between noon and 5:30, displays the works of local artists. The **San Francisco Performing Arts Library and Museum** (☎ 415/255–4800) on the fourth floor functions mainly as a research center, collecting the San Francisco Bay Area's rich performing arts legacy. The gallery is open during the afternoon from Wednesday through Saturday. ✉ *401 Van Ness Ave.*

77 **War Memorial Opera House.** During San Francisco's Barbary Coast days, operagoers smoked cigars, didn't check their revolvers, and ex-

pressed their appreciation with "shrill whistles and savage yells," as one observer put it. The old opera houses were destroyed in the quake, but lusty support for opera lives on in this edifice. Modeled after its European counterparts, the building has a vaulted and coffered ceiling, marble foyer, two balconies, and a huge silver Art Deco chandelier that resembles a sunburst. ✉ *301 Van Ness Ave.,* ☏ *415/621–6600.*

The Northern Waterfront

For the sights, sounds, and smells of the sea, hop the Powell–Hyde cable car from Union Square and take it to the end of the line. The views as you descend Hyde Street down to the bay are breathtaking—tiny sailboats bob in the whitecaps, Alcatraz hovers ominously in the distance, and the Marin Headlands form a rugged backdrop to the Golden Gate Bridge. Once you reach sea level at the cable car turnaround, Aquatic Park and the National Maritime Museum are immediately to the west, and the commercial attractions of the Fisherman's Wharf area are to the east. Bring good walking shoes and a jacket or sweater for mid-afternoon breezes or foggy mists.

Numbers in the text correspond to numbers in the margin and on the Northern Waterfront/Marina and the Presidio map.

A Good Walk

Begin at Polk and Beach streets at the **National Maritime Museum** ①. (Walk west from the cable car turnaround; Bus 19 stops at Polk and Beach streets, and Bus 47-Van Ness stops one block west at Van Ness Avenue and Beach Street.) Across Beach Street from the museum is **Ghirardelli Square** ②, a complex of shops, cafés, and galleries in an old chocolate factory. Continue east on Beach Street to Hyde Street and make a left. At the end of Hyde Street is the **Hyde Street Pier** ③. South on Hyde Street a block and a half is the former Del Monte **Cannery** ④, which holds more shops, cafés, and restaurants. Walk east from the Cannery on Jefferson Street to **Fisherman's Wharf** ⑤. A few blocks farther east is **Pier 39** ⑥.

TIMING

For the entire Northern Waterfront circuit, set aside three or four hours, not including boat tours, which will take from one to three hours or more. All the attractions here are open daily.

Sights to See

★ **Alcatraz Island.** The boat ride to the island is brief (15 minutes) but affords beautiful views of the city, Marin County, and the East Bay. The audio tour, highly recommended, includes observations of guards and prisoners about life in one of America's most notorious penal colonies. Plan your schedule to allow at least three hours for the visit and boat rides combined. Reservations, even in the off-season, are recommended. ✉ *Pier 41,* ☏ *415/773–1188 for boat schedules and information; 415/705–5555 or 800/426–8687 for credit-card ticket orders; 415/705–1042 for park information.* 🎟 *$12.25 or $9 without audio ($19.75 for evening tours, including audio); add $2.25 per ticket to charge by phone.* ⏲ *Ferry departures Sept.–May 23, daily 9:30–2:15 (4:20 for evening tour); May 24–Aug., daily 9:30–4:15 (6:30 and 7:30 for evening tour).*

❹ **Cannery.** This three-story structure was built in 1894 to house what became the Del Monte Fruit and Vegetable Cannery. Today the Cannery is home to shops, art galleries, and some unusual restaurants. The **Museum of the City of San Francisco** (☏ 415/928–0289), on the third floor, displays historical items, maps, and photographs, as well as the 500-pound head of the Goddess of Progress statue, which crowned the

Northern Waterfront/Marina and the Presidio

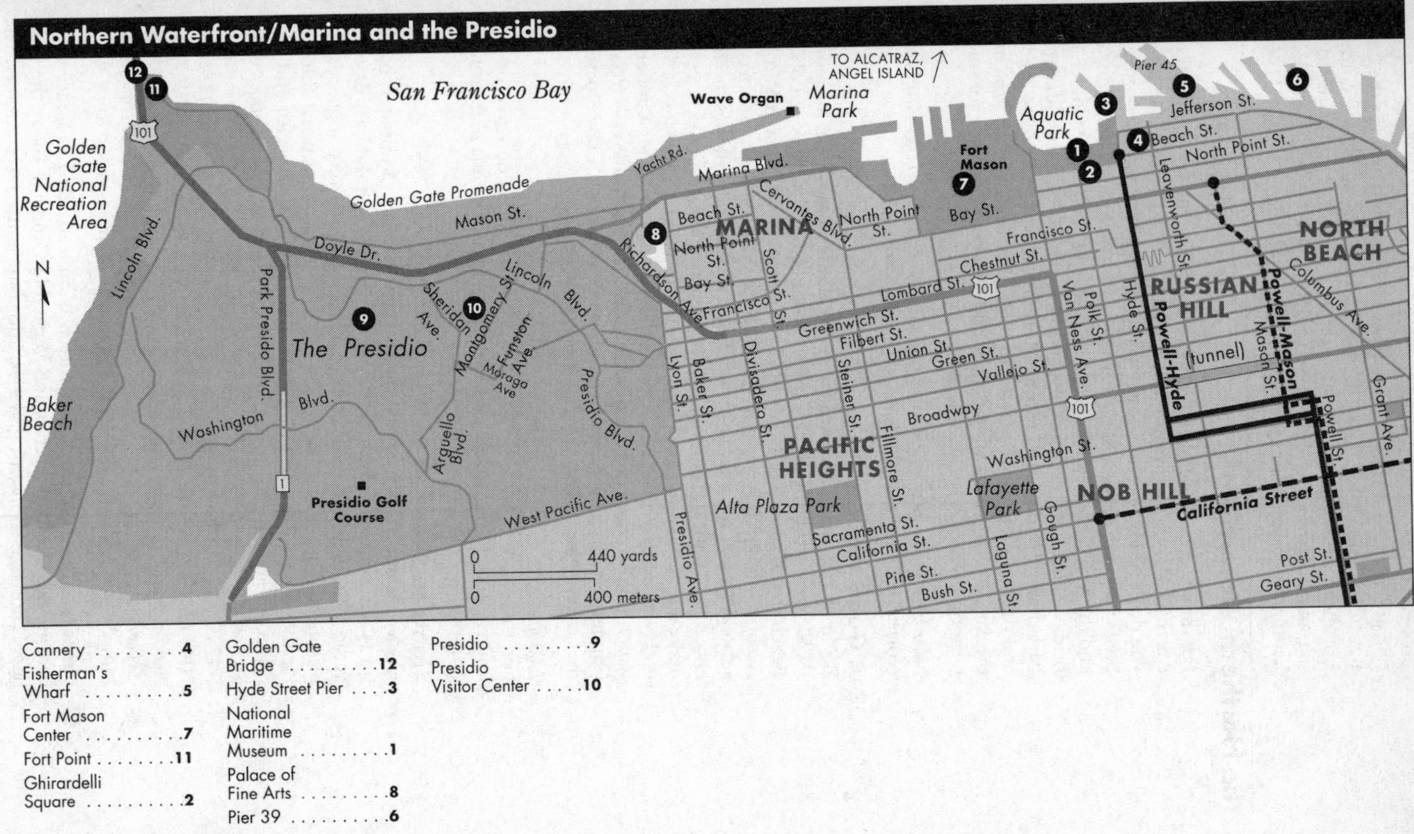

Cannery 4
Fisherman's Wharf 5
Fort Mason Center 7
Fort Point 11
Ghirardelli Square 2
Golden Gate Bridge 12
Hyde Street Pier 3
National Maritime Museum 1
Palace of Fine Arts 8
Pier 39 6
Presidio 9
Presidio Visitor Center 10

City Hall building that crumbled during the 1906 earthquake. Admission to the museum is free. ✉ *2801 Leavenworth St.,* ☎ *415/771–3112.*

5 **Fisherman's Wharf.** Ships creak at their moorings; seagulls cry out for a handout. By mid-afternoon the fishing fleet is back to port. The chaotic streets of the wharf are home to numerous seafood restaurants, among them sidewalk stands where shrimp and crab cocktails are sold in disposable containers. T-shirts and sweats, gold chains galore, redwood furniture, acres of artwork (precious little of it original) also beckon visitors. Everything's overpriced, especially the so-called novelty museums, which can provide a diversion if you're touring with antsy children. The best of the lot, though mostly for its kitsch value, is **Ripley's Believe It or Not** (✉ 175 Jefferson St., ☎ 415/771–6188). For an intriguing if mildly claustrophobic glimpse into life on a submarine during World War II, drop by the **USS *Pampanito*** (✉ Pier 45, ☎ 415/775–1943). The sub, open daily from 9 to 6 (until 8 between Memorial Day and Labor Day), sank six Japanese warships and damaged four others. Admission is $6. ✉ *Jefferson St. between Leavenworth St. and Pier 39.*

2 **Ghirardelli Square.** Most of the redbrick buildings in this early 20th-century complex were part of the Ghirardelli chocolate factory. Now they house name-brand emporiums, restaurants, and galleries that sell everything from crafts and knickknacks to sports memorabilia. Placards throughout the square describe the factory's history. ✉ *900 N. Point St.,* ☎ *415/775–5500.*

3 **Hyde Street Pier.** The pier, one of the wharf area's best bargains, always crackles with activity. The highlight of the pier is its collection of historic vessels, all of which can be boarded: the *Balclutha,* an 1886 full-rigged three-mast sailing vessel that sailed around Cape Horn 17 times; the *Eureka,* a side-wheel ferry; the *C. A. Thayer,* a three-mast schooner; and the *Hercules,* a steam-powered tugboat. ✉ *Hyde and Jefferson Sts.,* ☎ *415/556–3002 or 415/556–0859.* 🎫 *$5.* ⏲ *Labor Day–Memorial Day, daily 9:30–5; Memorial Day–Labor Day, daily 9:30–5:30.*

1 **National Maritime Museum.** You'll feel as if you're out to sea when you step inside this sturdy, rounded structure. Part of the San Francisco Maritime National Historical Park, which includes Hyde Street Pier, the museum exhibits ship models, maps, and other artifacts chronicling the development of San Francisco and the West Coast through maritime history. ✉ *Aquatic Park at the foot of Polk St.,* ☎ *415/556–3002.* 🎫 *Donation suggested.* ⏲ *Daily 10–5.*

6 **Pier 39.** This is the most popular—and commercial—of San Francisco's waterfront attractions, drawing millions of visitors each year to browse through its dozens of shops. Check out the **Marine Mammal Store & Interpretive Center** (☎ 415/289–7373), a quality gift shop and education center whose proceeds benefit Sausalito's Marine Mammal Center, and the **National Park Store** (☎ 415/433–7221), with books, maps, and collectibles sold to support the National Park Service. Brilliant colors enliven the double-decker **Venetian Carousel,** often awhirl with happily howling children ($2 a ride). The din on the northwest side of the pier comes courtesy of the hundreds of sea lions that bask and play on the docks. At **Underwater World** (☎ 415/623–5300 or 888/732–3483), moving walkways transport visitors through a space surrounded on three sides by water filled with indigenous San Francisco Bay marine life, from fish and plankton to sharks. ✉ *Beach St. at the Embarcadero.*

The Marina and the Presidio

The Marina district was a coveted place to live until the 1989 earthquake, when the area's homes suffered the worst damage in the city—largely because the Marina is built on landfill. Many home owners and renters fled in search of more solid ground, but young professionals quickly replaced them, changing the tenor of this formerly low-key neighborhood. The number of upscale coffee emporiums skyrocketed. A bank became a Williams-Sonoma and the local grocer gave way to a Pottery Barn.

West of the Marina is the sprawling Presidio, a former military base. The Presidio has superb views and the best hiking and biking areas in San Francisco; a drive through the area can also be rewarding.

Numbers in the text correspond to numbers in the margin and on the Northern Waterfront/Marina and the Presidio map.

A Good Drive

Though you can visit the sights below using public transportation, this is the place to use your car if you have one. You might even consider renting one for a day to cover the area, as well as Lincoln Park, Golden Gate Park, and the western shoreline.

Start at **Fort Mason Center** ⑦, whose entrance for automobiles is off Marina Boulevard at Buchanan Street. If you're coming by bus, take Bus 30-Stockton heading north (and later west); get off at Chestnut and Laguna streets and walk north three blocks to the pedestrian entrance at Marina Boulevard and Laguna Street. To get from Fort Mason to the **Palace of Fine Arts** ⑧ by car, make a right on Marina Boulevard. The road curves past a small marina and the Marina Green. Turn left at Divisadero Street, right on North Point Street, left on Baker Street, and right on Bay Street, which passes the Palace's lagoon and dead-ends at the Lyon Street parking lot. Part of the Palace complex is the **Exploratorium,** a hands-on science museum. (If you're walking from Fort Mason to the Palace, the directions are easier: Follow Marina Boulevard to Scott Street. Cross to the south side of the street—away from the water—and continue past Divisadero Street to Baker Street, and turn left; you'll see the Palace's lagoon on your right. To take Muni, walk back to Chestnut and Laguna streets and take Bus 30-Stockton continuing west; get off at North Point and Broderick streets and walk west on North Point.)

The least confusing way to drive to the **Presidio** ⑨ from the Palace is to exit from the south end of the Lyon Street parking lot and head east (left) on Bay Street. Turn right (south) onto Baker Street, and right (west) on Francisco Street, taking it across Richardson Avenue to Lyon Street. Turn south (left) on Lyon Street and right (west) on Lombard Street, and go through the main gate to Presidio Boulevard. Turn right on Presidio Boulevard, which becomes Lincoln Boulevard. Make a left at Montgomery Street; a half block up on the right is the **Presidio Visitor Center** ⑩. (To take the bus to the Presidio, walk north from the Palace of Fine Arts to Lombard Street and catch Bus 28 heading west; it stops on Lincoln near the visitor center.)

From the visitor center head north a half block to Sheridan Avenue, make a right, and make a left when Sheridan runs into Lincoln Boulevard. Lincoln Boulevard winds through the Presidio past a large cemetery and some vista points. After a couple of miles you'll see a parking lot marked FORT POINT on the right. Park and follow the signs leading to **Fort Point** ⑪, walking downhill through a lightly wooded area. To walk the short distance to the **Golden Gate Bridge** ⑫, follow the signs from the Fort Point parking lot; to drive across the bridge, continue on Lincoln Boulevard a bit and watch for the turnoff on the right. Bus 28 serves stops fairly near these last two attractions.

TIMING

The time it takes to see this area will vary greatly depending on whether you'll be taking public transportation or driving. If you drive, plan to spend at least three hours, not including a walk across the Golden Gate Bridge or hikes along the shoreline. A great way to see the area is on bicycle; the folks at the Presidio Visitor Center (☞ *below*) will help you find the closest rental outfit.

Sights to See

★ **Exploratorium.** The curious of all ages flock to this fascinating "museum of science, art, and human perception" within the Palace of Fine Arts. The more than 650 exhibits focus on sea and insect life, computers, electricity, patterns and light, language, the weather, and much more. Reservations are required to crawl through the pitch-black, touchy-feely **Tactile Dome,** an adventure of 15 minutes. The object is to crawl and climb through the space relying solely on the sense of touch. ✉ *3601 Lyon St., at Marina Blvd.,* ☎ *415/561–0360 for general information; 415/561–0362 for Tactile Dome reservations.* *$9, free 1st Wed. of month; Tactile Dome admission $3 extra.* ⏲ *Memorial Day–Labor Day, daily 10–6 (Wed. until 9); Labor Day–Memorial Day, Tues., Thurs.–Sun., and most Mon. holidays 10–5, Wed. 10–9.*

7 **Fort Mason Center.** Originally a depot for the shipment of supplies to the Pacific during World War II, Fort Mason was converted into a cultural center in 1977. It houses several worthwhile museums. The **Museo Italo-Americano** (☎ 415/673–2200) mounts impressive exhibits of the works of Italian and Italian-American artists. The exhibits at the **San Francisco African-American Historical and Cultural Society** (☎ 415/441–0640) document past and contemporary black arts and culture. The **San Francisco Craft and Folk Art Museum** (☎ 415/775–0990) is an airy space with exhibits of American folk art, tribal art, and contemporary crafts. Next door is the **SFMOMA Rental Gallery** (☎ 415/441–4777), where the art is available for sale or rent. Most of the museums and shops at Fort Mason close by 6 or 7. The museum admission fees range from pay-what-you-wish to $4. ✉ *Buchanan St. and Marina Blvd.,* ☎ *415/979–3010 for event information.*

11 **Fort Point.** Designed to mount 126 cannons with a range of up to 2 mi, Fort Point was constructed between 1853 and 1861 to protect San Francisco from sea attack during the Civil War—but it was never used for that purpose. It was, however, used as a coastal defense fortification post during World War II, when soldiers stood watch here. This National Historic Site is a museum filled with military memorabilia. The building has a gloomy air and is suitably atmospheric. On days when Fort Point is staffed, guided group tours and cannon drills take place. ✉ *Marine Dr. off Lincoln Blvd.,* ☎ *415/556–1693.* *Free.* ⏲ *Daily 10–5.*

★ 12 **Golden Gate Bridge.** The suspension bridge that connects San Francisco with Marin County has long wowed sightseers with its rust-color beauty, 750-ft towers, and simple but powerful Art Deco design. At nearly 2 mi, the Golden Gate, completed in 1937 after four years of construction, was built to withstand winds of more than 100 mph. The east walkway yields a glimpse of the San Francisco skyline as well as the islands of the bay. The view west takes in the wild hills of the Marin Headlands, the curving coast south to Land's End, and the majestic Pacific Ocean. A vista point on the Marin side affords a spectacular view of the city. On sunny days sailboats dot the water, and brave windsurfers test the often-treacherous tides beneath the bridge. Muni Buses 28 and 29 make stops at the Golden Gate Bridge toll plaza, on the San Francisco side. ✉ *Lincoln Blvd. near Doyle Dr. and Fort Point,* ☎ *415/921–5858.* ⏲ *Daily, 24 hrs for cars and bikes, 5 AM–9 PM for pedestrians.*

★ 8 **Palace of Fine Arts.** San Francisco's rosy rococo Palace of Fine Arts is at the western end of the Marina. The palace is the sole survivor of the many tinted plaster buildings (a temporary classical city of sorts) built for the 1915 Panama-Pacific International Exposition, the world's fair that celebrated San Francisco's recovery from the 1906 earthquake and fire. The expo lasted for 288 days and the buildings extended about a mile along the shore. Bernard Maybeck designed this faux Roman Classic beauty, which was reconstructed in concrete and reopened in 1967. ✉ *Baker and Beach Sts.,* ☎ *415/561–0364 for palace tours.*

9 **Presidio.** Part of the Golden Gate National Recreation Area, the Presidio was a military post for more than 200 years. Don Juan Bautista de Anza and a band of Spanish settlers first claimed the area in 1776. It became a Mexican garrison in 1822 when Mexico gained its independence from Spain; U.S. troops forcibly occupied the Presidio in 1846. The U.S. Sixth Army was stationed here until October 1994, when the coveted space was transferred into civilian hands. The more than 1,400 acres of rolling hills, majestic woods, and redbrick army barracks present an air of serenity on the edge of the city. There are two beaches, a golf course, a visitor center (☞ *below*), and picnic sites, and the views of the bay, the Golden Gate Bridge, and Marin County are sublime. ✉ *Between the Marina and Lincoln Park.*

10 **Presidio Visitor Center.** National Park Service employees at what's officially the William P. Mott Jr. Visitor Center dispense maps, brochures, and schedules for guided walking and bicycle tours, along with information about the Presidio's past, present, and future. The building also houses the **Presidio Museum**, which focuses on the role played by the military in San Francisco's development. ✉ *Montgomery St. between Lincoln Blvd. and Sheridan Ave.,* ☎ *415/561–4323.* *Free.* ⏲ *Daily 9–5.*

Golden Gate Park

William Hammond Hall conceived one of the nation's great city parks and began in 1870 to put into action his plan for a natural reserve with no reminders of urban life. Hammond began work in the Panhandle and eastern portions of Golden Gate Park, but it took John McLaren the length of his tenure as park superintendent, from 1890 to 1943, to complete the transformation of 1,000 desolate brush- and sand-covered acres into a rolling, landscaped oasis. On Sunday John F. Kennedy Drive is closed to cars and comes alive with joggers, cyclists, and in-line skaters. In addition to cultural and other attractions there are public tennis courts, baseball diamonds, soccer fields, and trails for horseback riding. The fog can sweep into the park with amazing speed; always bring a sweatshirt or jacket.

Because the park is so large, a car will come in handy if you're going to tour it from one end to the other. Muni also serves the park. Buses 5-Fulton and 21-Hayes stop along its northern edge, and the N-Judah light-rail car stops a block south of the park between Stanyan Street and 9th Avenue, then two blocks south and the rest of the way west.

Numbers in the text correspond to numbers in the margin and on the Golden Gate Park map.

A Good Walk

Begin on the park's north side at Fulton Street and 6th Avenue, where the Bus 5-Fulton and Bus 21-Hayes from downtown stop. Walk south into the park at 6th Avenue. The road you'll come to is John F. Kennedy Drive. Turn left on the blacktop sidewalk and head east. Across the drive on your right is the Rhododendron Dell. Past the first stop sign you'll see the exterior gardens of the **Conservatory of Flowers** ① on your left. Explore the gardens, then walk south (back toward Kennedy Drive) from the conservatory entrance. Continue east on Kennedy Drive a short way to the three-way intersection and turn right (south) at Middle Drive East.

Less than a block away at the intersection of Middle and Bowling Green drives you'll see a sign for the National AIDS Memorial Grove. Before you enter the grove, follow the curve of Bowling Green Drive to the left, past the **Bowling Green** ② to the **Children's Playground** ③. Reverse direction on Bowling Green Drive and enter the **National AIDS Memorial Grove** ④, a sunken meadow that stretches west along Middle Drive East. At the end of the wheelchair-access ramp make a left to view the Circle of Friends, then continue west along the graded paths to another circle with a poem by Thom Gunn. Exit north from this circle. As you're standing in the circle looking at the poem, the staircase to take is on your left. At the top of the staircase make a left and continue west on Middle Drive East. You'll come to the back entrance of the **California Academy of Sciences** ⑤.

At the end of Middle Drive East, turn right and follow the signs leading to the **Shakespeare Garden** ⑥. After touring the garden, exit via the path on which you entered and turn left (to the south). A hundred feet shy of the Ninth Avenue and Lincoln Way entrance to Golden Gate Park is the main entrance to **Strybing Arboretum & Botanical Gardens** ⑦.

Backtrack from the gardens to the path you started on and make a right. As the path continues to wind north and west, you'll see a large fountain off to the left. Just before you get to the fountain, make a right and head toward the duck pond. A wooden footbridge on the pond's left side crosses the water. Signs on the other side identify the mallards, geese, American coots, mews, and other fowl in the pond. Stay to the right on the path, heading toward the exit gate. Just before the gate, continue to the right to the Primitive Garden. Take the looped boardwalk past ferns, gingko, cycads, conifers, moss, and other plants. At the end of the loop, make a left and then a right, exiting via the Eugene L. Friend gate. Go straight ahead on the crosswalk to the blacktop path on the other side. Make a right, walk about 100 ft, and make a left on Tea Garden Drive. A few hundred feet east of here is the entrance to the **Japanese Tea Garden** ⑧.

Tour the Japanese Tea Garden, exiting near the gate you entered. Make a left, and you'll soon pass the **Asian Art Museum** ⑨ and **M. H. de Young Memorial Museum** ⑩. Near the main entrance to the de Young is a crosswalk that leads south to the Music Concourse, with its gnarled trees, century-old fountains and sculptures, and the Golden Gate Bandshell. Turn left at the closest of the fountains and head east toward the bronze sculpture of Francis Scott Key.

Turn left at the statue and proceed north through two underpasses. At the end of the second underpass, you'll have traveled about 2 mi. If you're ready to leave the park, take the short staircase to the left of the blue and green playground equipment. At the top of the staircase is the 10th Avenue and Fulton Street stop for the Bus 5-Fulton heading back downtown. If you're game for walking ½ mi more, make an immediate left as you exit the second underpass, cross 10th Avenue, and make a right on John F. Kennedy Drive. After 2/10 mi you'll see the Rose Garden on your right. Continue west to the first stop sign. To the left is a sign for **Stow Lake** ⑪. Follow the road past the log cabin to the boathouse.

From Stow Lake it's the equivalent of 30 long blocks on John F. Kennedy Drive to the western end of the park and the ocean. By foot or vehicle, your goal is the **Dutch Windmill** ⑫ and adjoining garden. A block to the south is the **Beach Chalet** ⑬.

TIMING

You can easily spend a whole day in Golden Gate Park, especially if you walk the whole distance. Set aside at least an hour each for the Academy of Sciences, the Asian Art Museum, and the de Young Museum. Even if you plan to explore just the eastern end of the park (up to Stow Lake), allot at least four hours.

Sights to See

★ ❾ **Asian Art Museum.** The museum's collection includes more than 12,000 sculptures, paintings, and ceramics from 40 countries, illustrating major periods of Asian art. On the first floor are special exhibitions as well as galleries dedicated to works from Korea and China. On the second floor are treasures from Iran, Turkey, Syria, India, Tibet, Nepal, Pakistan, India, Japan, Afghanistan, and Southeast Asia. ⊠ *Tea Garden Dr. off John F. Kennedy Dr., near 10th Ave. and Fulton St.,* ☎ *415/668–8921 or 415/379–8801.* *$7 ($2 off with Muni transfer), good also for same-day admission to the M. H. de Young Museum and the Legion of Honor Museum in Lincoln Park; free 1st Wed. of month.* ⊙ *Tues.–Sun. 9:30–4:45, 1st Wed. of month until 8:45.*

⓭ **Beach Chalet.** This Spanish Colonial–style structure, architect Willis Polk's last design, was built in 1925 after his death. A wraparound mural by Lucien Labaudt depicts San Francisco in the 1930s; the labels describing the various panels add up to a minihistory of Depression-era life in the city. A three-dimensional model of Golden Gate Park, artifacts from the 1894 Mid-Winter Exposition and other park events, a visitor center, and a gift shop that sells street signs and other city paraphernalia are on the first floor as well. On a clear day, the brewpub-restaurant upstairs has views past Ocean Beach to the Farallon Islands, about 30 mi offshore. ⊠ *1000 Great Hwy., at west end of John F. Kennedy Dr.*

OFF THE BEATEN PATH

BUFFALO PADDOCK – The original denizens of the paddock arrived at the park in 1894 for the Mid-Winter Exposition. The present herd, from Wyoming, was acquired in 1984. ⊠ *John F. Kennedy Dr. west of Spreckels Lake.*

★ ❺ **California Academy of Sciences.** A three-in-one attraction, the nationally renowned academy houses an aquarium, numerous science and natural-history exhibits, and a planetarium. Leopard sharks, silver salmon, sea bass, and other fish loop around the mesmerizing Fish Roundabout, the big draw at **Steinhart Aquarium.** Feeding time is 2 PM. At the Touch Tide Pool, you can cozy up to starfish, hermit crabs, and other critters. Elsewhere at Steinhart swim dolphins, sea turtles, piranhas, manatees, and other sea life. The multimedia earthquake exhibit in the Earth and Space Hall at the **Natural History Museum** simulates quakes, complete with special effects. Videos and displays in the Wild California Hall describe the state's wildlife, and there's a re-creation of the environment of the rocky Farallon Islands. There is an additional $2.50 charge for **Morrison Planetarium** shows (☎ 415/750–

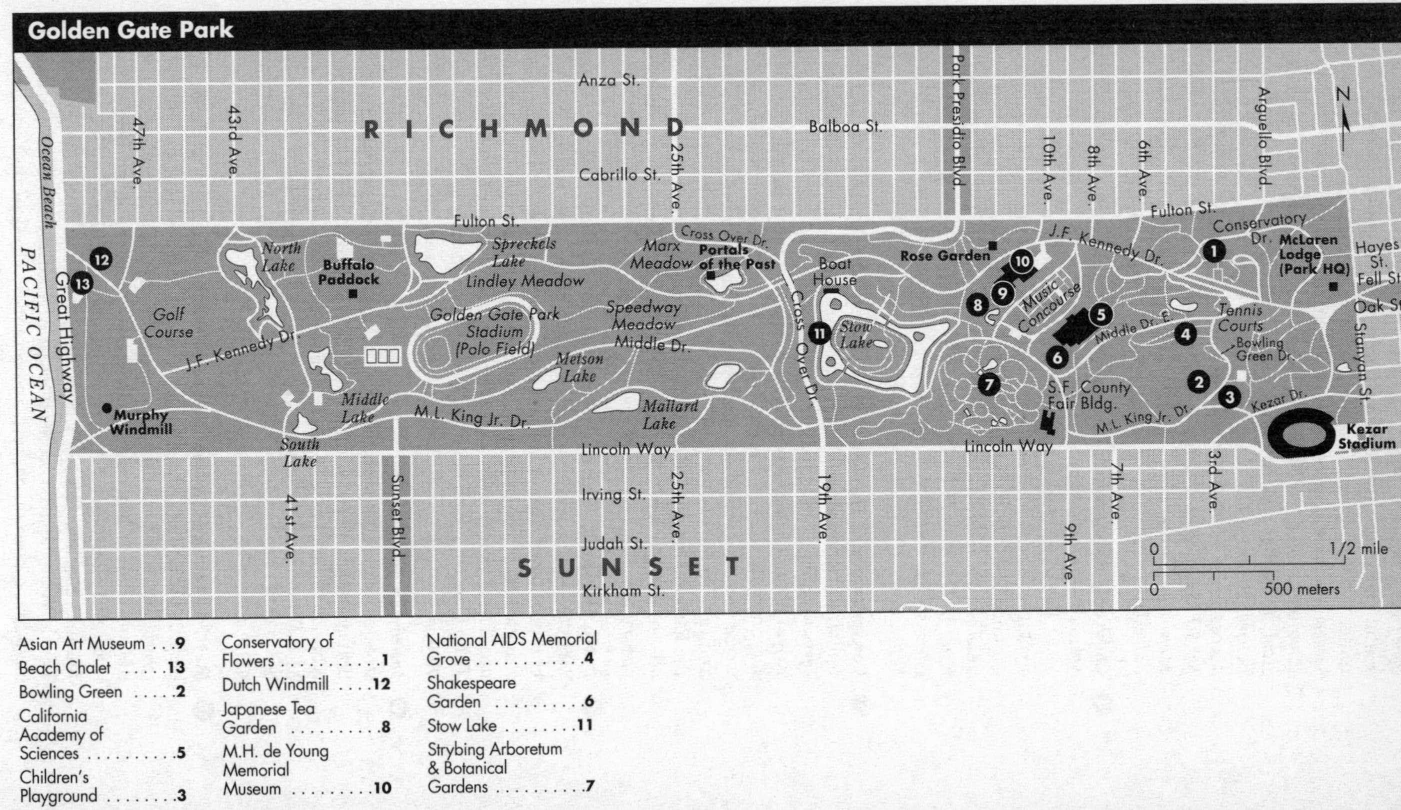

Asian Art Museum . . . **9**	Conservatory of Flowers **1**	National AIDS Memorial Grove **4**
Beach Chalet **13**	Dutch Windmill **12**	Shakespeare Garden **6**
Bowling Green **2**	Japanese Tea Garden **8**	Stow Lake **11**
California Academy of Sciences **5**	M.H. de Young Memorial Museum **10**	Strybing Arboretum & Botanical Gardens **7**
Children's Playground **3**		

7141 for schedule), which you enter through the Natural History Museum. Daily multimedia shows present the night sky through the ages under a 55-ft dome, complete with special effects and music. The **Laserium** presents evening laser-light shows (☎ 415/750–7138 for schedule and fees) at Morrison Planetarium, accompanied by rock, classical, and other types of music. A cafeteria is open daily until one hour before the museum closes. ✉ *Music Concourse Dr. off South Dr., across from Asian Art and de Young museums,* ☎ *415/750–7145.* 🎫 *$8.50 ($1 discount with Muni transfer), free 1st Wed. of month.* ⏲ *Memorial Day–Labor Day, daily 9–6; Labor Day–Memorial Day, daily 10–5; 1st Wed. of month closes at 8:45* PM.

❸ **Children's Playground.** A menagerie of handcrafted horses and other animals—among them cats, frogs, roosters, and a tiger—twirl on the 1912 Herschell-Spillman Carousel, inside a many-windowed circular structure. The Romanesque-style Sharon Building looms over the playground. The 1887 structure has been rebuilt twice, following the earthquake of 1906 and a 1980 fire. ✉ *Bowling Green Dr., off Martin Luther King Jr. Dr.,* ☎ *415/753–5210 or 415/831–2700.* 🎫 *Playground free, carousel $1.* ⏲ *Playground open daily dawn–midnight; carousel June–Sept., daily 10–5; Oct.–May, Fri.–Sun. 10–4:30.*

❶ **Conservatory of Flowers.** The oldest building in the park and the last remaining wood-frame Victorian conservatory in the country, the Conservatory, which was built in the late 1870s, is a copy of the one in the Royal Botanical Gardens in Kew, England. On the east side of the Conservatory (to the right as you face the building), cypress, pine, and redwood trees surround the **Fuchsia Garden,** which blooms in summer and fall. To the west several hundred feet on John F. Kennedy Drive is the **Rhododendron Dell.** The dell contains the most varieties—850 in all—of any garden in the country. ✉ *John F. Kennedy Dr. at Conservatory Dr.*

⓬ **Dutch Windmill.** The restored 1902 Dutch Windmill once pumped 20,000 gallons of well water per hour to the reservoir on Strawberry Hill (☞ Stow Lake, *below*). With its heavy cement bottom and wood-shingled arms and upper section the windmill cuts quite the sturdy figure. The structure overlooks the equally photogenic **Queen Wilhelmina Tulip Garden,** which bursts into full bloom in early spring and late summer. ✉ *Between 47th Ave. and the Great Hwy.*

★ ❽ **Japanese Tea Garden.** A serene 4-acre landscape of small ponds, streams, waterfalls, stone bridges, Japanese sculptures, *mumsai* (planted bonsai) trees, perfect miniature pagodas, and some nearly vertical wooden "humpback" bridges, the tea garden was created for the 1894 Mid-Winter Exposition. ✉ *Tea Garden Dr. off John F. Kennedy Dr.,* ☎ *415/752–4227 or 415/752–1171.* 🎫 *$3.50.* ⏲ *Mar.–Sept., daily 9–6:30; Oct.–Feb., daily 8:30–5:30.*

❿ **M. H. de Young Memorial Museum.** Works on display at the de Young include American paintings, sculpture, textiles, and decorative arts from Colonial times through the present day. The John D. Rockefeller III Collection of American Paintings is especially noteworthy, with more than 200 paintings of American masters like John Singleton Copley, Thomas Eakins, George Caleb Bingham, and John Singer Sargent. The de Young also has collections of African and Native American art, including sculpture, baskets, and ceramics. The **Café de Young** has outdoor seating in the lovely Oakes Garden. ✉ *Tea Garden Dr. off John F. Kennedy Dr., near 10th Ave. and Fulton St.,* ☎ *415/863–3330.* 🎫 *$7 ($2 off with Muni transfer), good also for same-day admission to the Asian Art Museum and the Legion of Honor Museum in Lincoln*

Park; free 1st Wed. of month. ⏲ *Tues.–Sun. 9:30–5, 1st Wed. of month until 8:45.*

4 **National AIDS Memorial Grove.** This 15-acre grove, started in the early 1990s by people with AIDS and their families and friends, was conceived as a living memorial to those the disease has claimed. Hundreds of volunteers toiled long and hard raising funds and clearing this patch of green. A 1996 poem by San Franciscan Thom Gunn in the tan fieldstone circle at the west end of the grove reads: WALKER WITHIN THIS CIRCLE PAUSE/ALTHOUGH THEY DIED OF ONE CAUSE/REMEMBER HOW THEIR LIVES WERE DENSE/WITH FINE COMPACTED DIFFERENCE. ⊠ *Middle Dr. E, west of tennis courts.*

6 **Shakespeare Garden.** Two hundred flowers and herbs mentioned in the Bard's plays grow here. Bronze-engraved passages contain relevant floral quotations. ⊠ *Middle Dr. E at southwest corner of California Academy of Sciences.*

11 **Stow Lake.** One of the most picturesque spots in Golden Gate Park, this placid body of water surrounds Strawberry Hill. A couple of bridges allow you to cross over and ascend the hill. Down below, rent a boat, surrey, or bicycle or stroll around the perimeter. ⊠ *Off John F. Kennedy Dr. ½ mi west of 10th Ave.,* ☎ *415/752–0347.*

7 **Strybing Arboretum & Botanical Gardens.** The 55-acre arboretum specializes in plants from areas with climates similar to that of the Bay Area, such as the west coast of Australia, South Africa, and the Mediterranean; more than 8,000 plant and tree varieties bloom in gardens throughout the grounds. Among the highlights are the biblical, fragrance, California native plants, succulents, and primitive gardens, the new and old world cloud forests, and the duck pond. ⊠ *9th Ave. at Lincoln Way,* ☎ *415/661–1316.* 🎟 *Free.* ⏲ *Weekdays 8–4:30, weekends and holidays 10–5. Tours leave the bookstore daily at 1:30 and weekends at 10:30.*

Lincoln Park and the Western Shoreline

From Land's End in Lincoln Park you'll have some of the best views of the Golden Gate (the name was originally given to the opening of San Francisco Bay long before the bridge was built) and the Marin Headlands. From the historic Cliff House south to the sprawling San Francisco Zoo, the Great Highway and Ocean Beach run along the western edge of the city. The wind is often strong along the shoreline, summer fog can blanket the ocean beaches, and the water is cold and usually too rough for swimming. Carry a jacket and bring binoculars.

Numbers in the text correspond to numbers in the margin and on the Lincoln Park and the Western Shoreline map.

A Good Drive

A car is useful out here. There are plenty of hiking trails, and buses travel to all the sights mentioned, but the sights are far apart. Start at **Lincoln Park** ①. The park entrance is at 34th Avenue and Clement Street. Those without a car can take Bus 38-Geary—get off at 33rd Avenue and walk north (to the right) one block on 34th Avenue to the entrance. At the end of 34th Avenue (labeled on some maps as Legion of Honor Drive within Lincoln Park) is the **California Palace of the Legion of Honor** ②. From the museum, head back out to Clement Street and follow it west. At 45th Avenue Clement turns into Seal Rock Drive. When Seal Rock dead-ends at 48th Avenue, turn left on El Camino del Mar and right on Point Lobos Avenue. After a few hundred yards, you'll see parking lots for **Sutro Heights Park** ③ and the **Cliff House** ④. (To get from the Legion of Honor to Point Lobos Avenue by public transit, take Bus 18 from the Legion of Honor parking lot west to the corner of 48th and Point Lobos avenues.) Two large concrete lions near the southeast corner of 48th and Point Lobos guard the entrance to Sutro Heights Park. After taking a quick spin through the park, exit past the lions, cross Point Lobos, make a left, and walk down to the Cliff House. From the Cliff House it's a short walk farther downhill to **Ocean Beach** ⑤. From here the **San Francisco Zoo** ⑥ is a couple of miles south, at the intersection of the Great Highway and Sloat Boulevard.

TIMING

Set aside at least three hours for this tour—more if you don't have a car. An hour can easily be spent in the Palace of the Legion of Honor and 1½ hours at the zoo.

Sights to See

★ ❷ **California Palace of the Legion of Honor.** Spectacularly situated on cliffs overlooking the ocean, the Golden Gate Bridge, and the Marin Headlands, this landmark building is a fine repository of European art. A pyramidal glass skylight in the entrance court illuminates the lower-level galleries, which exhibit prints and drawings; English and European porcelain; and ancient Assyrian, Greek, Roman, and Egyptian art. The 20-plus galleries on the upper level are devoted to the permanent collection of European art from the 14th century to the present day. The noteworthy Rodin collection includes two galleries devoted to the master and a third with works by Rodin and other 19th-century sculptors. An original cast of Rodin's *The Thinker* welcomes you as you walk through the courtyard. The **Legion Café,** on the lower level, has a garden terrace and a view of the Golden Gate Bridge. North of the museum (across Camino del Mar) is George Segal's *The Holocaust,* a sculpture that evokes life in concentration camps during World War II. ✉ *34th Ave. at Clement St.,* ☎ *415/863–3330 for 24-hr information.* 🎫 *$8 ($2 off with Muni transfer), good also for same-day admission to Asian Art and M. H. de Young museums; free 2nd Wed. of month.* ⏲ *Tues.–Sun. 9:30–5.*

❹ **Cliff House.** Three buildings have occupied this site since 1863. The original Cliff House hosted several U.S. presidents and wealthy locals who would drive their carriages out to Ocean Beach; it was destroyed by fire on Christmas Day 1894. The second Cliff House, the most beloved and resplendent of the three, was built in 1896; it rose eight stories with an observation tower 200 ft above sea level. The current building dates from 1909. The complex, which includes restaurants, a pub, and a gift shop, will remain open while undergoing a gradual renovation to restore its early 20th-century look. The dining areas overlook Seal Rock (the barking marine mammals sunning themselves are actually sea lions).

Below the Cliff House is the splendid **Musée Mécanique** (☎ 415/386–1170), a time-warped arcade with antique mechanical contrivances, including peep shows and nickelodeons. Some favorites are the giant, rather creepy "Laughing Sal," an arm-wrestling machine, and mechanical fortune-telling figures who speak from their curtained boxes. The museum opens daily from Memorial Day to Labor Day between 10 and 8 and the rest of the year on weekdays between 11 and 7 and on weekends between 10 and 7. Admission is free, but you may want to bring change to play the games.

The Musée Mécanique looks out on a fine observation deck and the **Golden Gate National Recreation Area Visitors' Center** (☎ 415/556–8642), which contains fascinating historical photographs of the Cliff

California Palace of the Legion of Honor 2
Cliff House 4
Lincoln Park . . . 1
Ocean Beach 5
San Francisco Zoo 6
Sutro Heights Park 3

Lincoln Park and the Western Shoreline

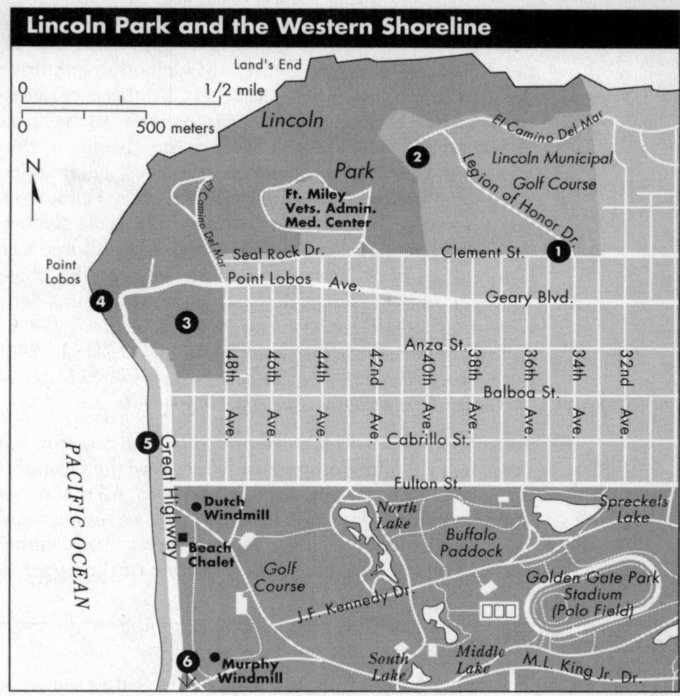

House and the glass-roof Sutro Baths. The Sutro complex, which comprised six enormous baths, 500 dressing rooms, and several restaurants, covered 3 acres north of the Cliff House. The baths burned down in 1966. You can explore the ruins on your own or take ranger-led walks on weekends. ✉ *1090 Point Lobos Ave.,* ☎ *415/386–3330.* ⏲ *Weekdays 8 AM–10:30 PM, weekends 8 AM–11 PM; cocktails served nightly until 2 AM.*

❶ **Lincoln Park.** At one time most of the city's cemeteries were here, segregated by nationality. In 1900, the Board of Supervisors voted to ban burials within city limits. Large Monterey cypresses line the fairways at Lincoln Park's 18-hole golf course. There are scenic walks throughout the 275-acre park, with postcard-perfect views from many spots. The trail out to **Land's End** starts outside the Palace of the Legion of Honor, at the end of El Camino del Mar. Be careful if you hike here; landslides are frequent. ✉ *Entrance at 34th Ave. at Clement St.*

❺ **Ocean Beach.** Stretching 3 mi along the western side of the city, this is a good beach for walking, running, or lying in the sun—but not for swimming. Surfers here wear wet suits year-round as the water is extremely cold. Riptides are also very dangerous here. Paths on both sides of the Great Highway lead from Lincoln Way to Sloat Boulevard (near the zoo). ✉ *Along the Great Hwy. from the Cliff House to Sloat Blvd. and beyond.*

❻ **San Francisco Zoo.** More than 1,000 birds and animals—220 species altogether—reside at the zoo. Among the more than 130 endangered species are the snow leopard, Sumatran tiger, jaguar, and Asian elephant. A favorite attraction is the greater one-horned rhinoceros, next to the African elephants. Another popular resident is Prince Charles, a rare white tiger and the first of its kind to be exhibited in the West. **Gorilla World** is one of the largest and most natural gorilla habitats of any zoo in the world. Fifteen species of rare monkeys—including colobus monkeys, white ruffed lemurs, and macaques—live and play at the two-tier **Primate Discovery Center**. Magellanic penguins waddle about **Penguin Island,**. Feeding time is 3 PM. Koalas peer out from among the trees in **Koala Crossing,** and kangaroos and wallabies headline the **Walkabout** exhibit. The 7-acre **Puente al Sur** (Bridge to the South) re-creates habitats on that continent, replete with a giant anteater, tapir, and a capybaras (the world's largest rodents). The **Feline Conservation Center,** is a natural setting for rare cats. Don't miss the big-cat feeding at the **Lion House** Tuesday–Sunday at 2. The **children's zoo** has a population of about 300 mammals, birds, and reptiles, plus an insect zoo, a baby-animal nursery, a deer park, a nature trail, a nature theater, and a restored 1921 Dentzel carousel. ✉ *Sloat Blvd. and 45th Ave. (Muni L-Taraval streetcar from downtown),* ☎ *415/753–7080.* 🎫 *$9 ($1 off with Muni transfer), free 1st Wed. of month.* ⏲ *Daily 10–5; children's zoo weekdays 11–4, weekends 10:30–4:30.*

❸ **Sutro Heights Park.** Crows and other large birds battle the heady breezes at this cliff-top park on what were the grounds of the home of former San Francisco mayor Adolph Sutro. All that remains of the main house is its foundation. Climb up for a sweeping view of the Pacific Ocean and the Cliff House below, and try to imagine what the perspective might have been like from one of the upper floors. ✉ *Point Lobos and 48th Aves.*

Mission District

The sunny Mission district wins out in San Francisco's system of microclimates—it's always the last to succumb to fog. Home to Italian and Irish communities in the early 20th century, the Mission has been heavily Latino since the late 1960s, when immigrants from Mexico and Central America began arriving. Despite its distinctive Latino flavor, the Mission has in recent years seen an influx of Chinese, Vietnamese, Arabic, and other immigrants, along with a young bohemian crowd enticed by cheaper rents and the burgeoning arts and entertainment scene. The Mission, still a bit scruffy in patches, lacks some of the glamour of other neighborhoods, but a walk through it provides the opportunity to mix with a heady cross section of San Franciscans.

Numbers in the text correspond to numbers in the margin and on the Mission District/Noe Valley map.

A Good Walk

The spiritual heart of the old Mission lies within the thick, white adobe walls of **Mission Dolores** ①, where Dolores Street intersects with 16th Street. From the mission, cross Dolores Street and head east on 16th Street. Tattooed and pierced hipsters abound a block from Mission Dolores, but the eclectic area still has room for a place like **Creativity Explored** ②, where people with developmental disabilities work on art and other projects. Take a right onto 18th Street, where you can view the mural adorning the **Women's Building** ③.

Head south on ValenciaStreet and make a right on 24th Street. The atmosphere becomes distinctly Latin American. Record stores sell the latest Spanish-language hits, family groceries sell Latin-American delicacies, and restaurants serve authentic dishes from several nations. A half block east of Folsom Street, mural-lined **Balmy Alley** ④ runs south from 24th Street to 25th Street. View the murals then head back up Balmy Alley to 24th and continue east a few steps to the **Precita Eyes Mural Arts and Visitors Center** ⑤. From the center continue east past St. Peter's Church, where Isías Mata's mural, *500 Years of Resistance,* on the exterior of the rectory, reflects on the struggles and survival of Latin-American cultures. At 24th and Bryant streets is the **Galería de la Raza/Studio 24** ⑥ art space.

TIMING

The above walk takes about two hours, including brief stops at the various sights listed. If you plan to go on a mural walk with Precita Eyes, add at least another hour.

Sights to See

❹ **Balmy Alley.** Mission District artists have transformed the walls of their neighborhood with paintings. Balmy Alley is one of the best-executed examples. The entire one-block alley is filled with murals. Local children working with adults started the project in 1971. ✉ *24th St. between and parallel to Harrison and Treat Sts. (alley runs south to 25th St.).*

❷ **Creativity Explored.** An atmosphere of joyous, if chaotic, creativity pervades the workshops of Creativity Explored, an art education center and gallery for developmentally disabled adults. On weekdays, you can drop by and see the artists at work. ✉ *3245 16th St.,* ☎ *415/863–2108.* 🎫 *Free.* ⏲ *Weekdays 8:30–3:30.*

❻ **Galería de la Raza/Studio 24.** San Francisco's premiere showcase for Latino art, the gallery exhibits the works of local and international artists. Next door is the nonprofit Studio 24, which sells prints and paintings by Chicano artists, as well as folk art, mainly from Mexico. ✉ *2857 24th St., at Bryant St.,* ☎ *415/826–8009.* ⏲ *Wed.–Sun. noon–6.*

❶ **Mission Dolores.** Mission Dolores encompasses two churches standing side by side. Completed in 1791, the small adobe building known as Mission San Francisco de Asís is the oldest standing structure in San Francisco and the sixth of the 21 California missions founded by Father Junípero Serra in the 18th and early 19th centuries. There is a small museum, and the pretty little mission cemetery (made famous by a scene in Alfred Hitchcock's *Vertigo*) maintains the graves of mid-19th-century European immigrants. Services are held in both the Mission San Francisco de Asís and next door in the handsome multidome basilica. ✉ *Dolores and 16th Sts.,* ☎ *415/621–8203.* 🎫 *$2, audio tour $5.* ⏲ *Daily 9–4.*

❺ **Precita Eyes Mural Arts and Visitors Center.** This nonprofit arts organization sponsors guided walks of the Mission District's murals. The bike and walking trips, which take between one and three hours, pass by several dozen murals. Bike tours depart from the **Precita Eyes Mural Center** (✉ 348 Precita Ave.); 11 AM walking tours meet at Cafe Venice at 24th and Mission streets. ✉ *2981 24th St.,* ☎ *415/285–2287.* 🎫 *Free to center, $5–$10 for tours.* ⏲ *Center weekdays 10–5, weekends 10–4; walks weekends at 11 and 1:30 or by appointment; bike tours 2nd Sun. of month at 11.*

❸ **Women's Building.** The cornerstone of the female-owned and -run businesses in the neighborhood is the Women's Building, which since 1979 has held workshops and conferences of particular interest to women. The building's two-sided exterior mural depicts women's peacekeeping efforts over the centuries. ✉ *3543 18th St.,* ☎ *415/431–1180.* ⏲ *Weekdays 9–5.*

Noe Valley

Noe Valley and adjacent Twin Peaks were once known as Rancho San Miguel, a parcel of land given to the last Mexican mayor of San Francisco (then known as Yerba Buena) in 1845. Mayor Don José de Jesús Noe built his ranch house at 22nd and Eureka streets, and the area con-

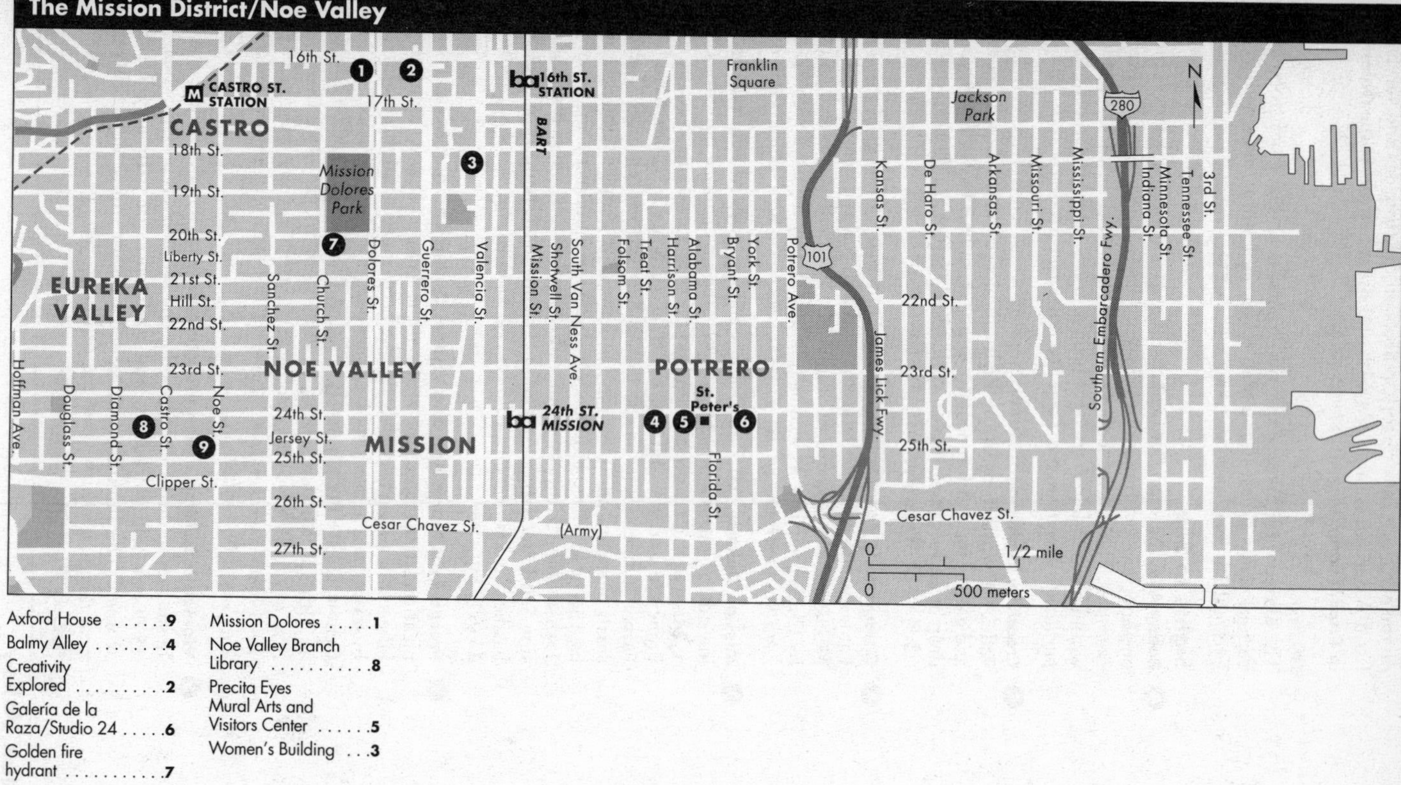

Axford House 9
Balmy Alley 4
Creativity Explored 2
Galería de la Raza/Studio 24 6
Golden fire hydrant 7
Mission Dolores 1
Noe Valley Branch Library 8
Precita Eyes Mural Arts and Visitors Center 5
Women's Building . . . 3

tinued as a bucolic farming community until 1906. Because Noe Valley was so little affected by the quake, many of the displaced headed here and decided to stay. It was predominantly working class and largely Irish until the 1970s, when it saw an influx of well-heeled liberals.

Numbers in the text correspond to numbers in the margin and on the Mission District/Noe Valley map.

A Good Walk

Start at Church and 24th streets (the J-Church streetcar from downtown stops here). Walk north to the southeast corner of 20th and Church streets, where a **golden fire hydrant** ⑦ figured in the 1906 earthquake and fire.

Proceed west on 20th Street past Victorian houses of various vintages and make a left at Sanchez Street. As you make the turn, you'll see the meticulously maintained Spanish Mission–style residence at 701 Sanchez Street. Continue south on Sanchez Street one block to Liberty Street. Across Sanchez Street at this intersection a staircase leads to the upper level of Liberty Street. Walk up it, enjoy the views of Pacific Heights north from the top, then look south across Liberty Street, where you'll see another set of stairs. Take them (from the landing on a sunny day you'll have views of the Bay Bridge and Oakland) and continue south.

It isn't hard to figure out how Hill Street, parallel to and between 21st and 22nd streets, got its name. The street was once known as Nanny Goat Hill for the goats that grazed there. Proceed downhill on Sanchez Street. Make a right at 22nd Street, where Victorian houses line both sides of the street. Make a left at Noe Street, walk south to 24th Street, and make a right. Continue west on 24th Street to Castro Street and turn left. Walk the short block to Jersey Street and head west (right). Halfway down the block is the **Noe Valley Branch Library** ⑧. From the library, backtrack east on Jersey Street, make a right at Noe Street, walk a half block to 25th Street, and make a left. As you walk down 25th Street you'll see the side of the Art Deco James Lick Middle School. On the northwest corner of 25th and Noe streets is the **Axford House** ⑨, a private home.

TIMING

This loop through Noe Valley takes about an hour, not counting stops to shop or sip tea or coffee.

Sights to See

9 **Axford House.** This mauve house was built in 1877, when the Mission was still a rural area, as evidenced by the hayloft in the gable of the adjacent carriage house. The house is perched a few feet above the sidewalk. Several types of roses grow in the well-maintained garden that surrounds the house. ✉ *1190 Noe St., at 25th St.*

7 **Golden fire hydrant.** When all the other fire hydrants went dry during the fire that followed the 1906 earthquake, this one kept pumping. Noe Valley and the Mission District were thus spared the devastation wrought elsewhere in the city, which explains the goodly number of prequake homes here. ✉ *Church and 20th Sts., southeast corner, across from Mission Dolores Park.*

8 **Noe Valley Branch Library.** In the early 20th century philanthropist Andrew Carnegie told Americans he would build them elegant libraries if they would fill them with books. A community garden flanks part of the yellow-brick library Carnegie financed, and there's a deck where you can relax and admire Carnegie's inspired structure. ✉ *451 Jersey St.,* ☎ *415/695–5095.* ⏲ *Tues. 10–9, Wed. 1–9, Thurs. 10–6, Fri. 1–6, Sat. noon–6.*

The Castro

The Castro district is one of the liveliest and most welcoming neighborhoods in the city, especially on weekends. Come Saturday and Sunday, the streets teem with folks out shopping, pushing political causes, heading to art films, and lingering in bars and cafés. Cutting-edge clothing stores and gift shops predominate, and pretty young pairs of all genders and sexual persuasions (even heterosexual) hold hands.

Numbers in the text correspond to numbers in the margin and on the Castro and the Haight map.

A Good Walk

Begin at **Harvey Milk Plaza** ① on the southwest corner of 17th and Market streets. Across Castro Street from the plaza is the neighborhood's landmark, the **Castro Theatre** ②. Many shops line Castro Street between 17th and 19th streets, 18th Street between Sanchez and Eureka streets, and Market Street heading east toward downtown. After exploring the shops on 18th and Castro streets, head west up 19th Street to Douglass Street and turn right. On the corner of Douglass and Caselli streets sprawls **Clarke's Mansion** ③. Continue north on Douglass Street to 18th Street and make a right. Cross Castro Street and make a left on Noe Street. At the intersection of 16th, Market, and Noe streets, cross Market Street and turn left on the north side of the Market. At Number 2362 is the **Names Project** ④, the birthplace and continuing workshop for the AIDS Memorial Quilt.

For an unforgettable vista, continue west on Market Street. Make a right at Castro Street, walk one block to 16th Street, turn left, and head up the steep hill to Flint Street. Turn right on Flint Street and follow the trail on the left (just past the tennis courts) up the hill. The beige buildings on the left contain the **Randall Museum** ⑤ for children. Turn right up the dirt path, which soon loops back up Corona Heights. At the top you'll be treated to an all-encompassing view of the city.

TIMING

Allot an hour to an hour and a half to visit the Castro district. Set aside an extra hour to hike Corona Heights and visit the Randall Museum.

Sights to See

★ ❷ **Castro Theatre.** The neon marquee is the neighborhood's great landmark, and the 1,500-seat theater, which opened in 1922, is the grandest of San Francisco's few remaining movie palaces. Before many shows the theater's pipe organ rises from the orchestra pit and an organist plays pop and movie tunes, usually ending with the Jeanette McDonald standard "San Francisco" (go ahead, sing along). ✉ *429 Castro St.,* ☎ *415/621–6120.*

❸ **Clarke's Mansion.** Built for attorney Alfred "Nobby" Clarke, this off-white baroque Queen Anne home completed in 1892 was dubbed Clarke's Folly when his wife refused to inhabit it because it was in an unfashionable part of town—at the time, everyone who was anyone lived on Nob Hill. ✉ *250 Douglass St., between 18th and 19th Sts.*

❶ **Harvey Milk Plaza.** An 18-ft-long rainbow flag, a gay icon, flies above this plaza named for the man who electrified the city in 1977 by being elected to its Board of Supervisors as an openly gay candidate. The liberal Milk hadn't served a full year of his term before he and Mayor George Moscone, also a liberal, were shot in November 1978 at City Hall. The gay community became enraged when the famous "Twinkie defense"—that junk food had led to diminished mental capacity—resulted in a manslaughter verdict for the killer. During the so-called White Night Riot of May 21, 1979, gays and their sympathizers stormed City

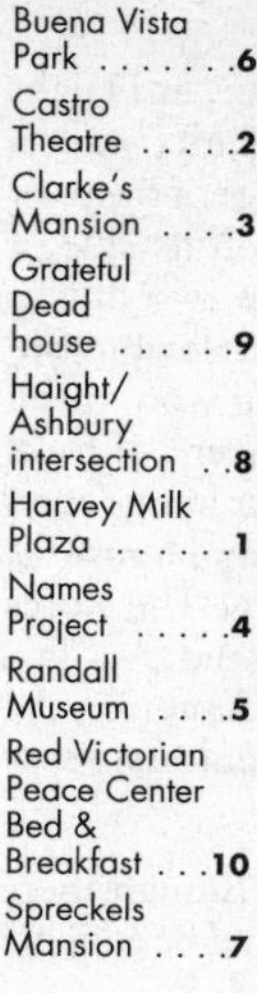

Buena Vista Park 6
Castro Theatre 2
Clarke's Mansion 3
Grateful Dead house 9
Haight/ Ashbury intersection . .8
Harvey Milk Plaza 1
Names Project 4
Randall Museum 5
Red Victorian Peace Center Bed & Breakfast . . .10
Spreckels Mansion 7

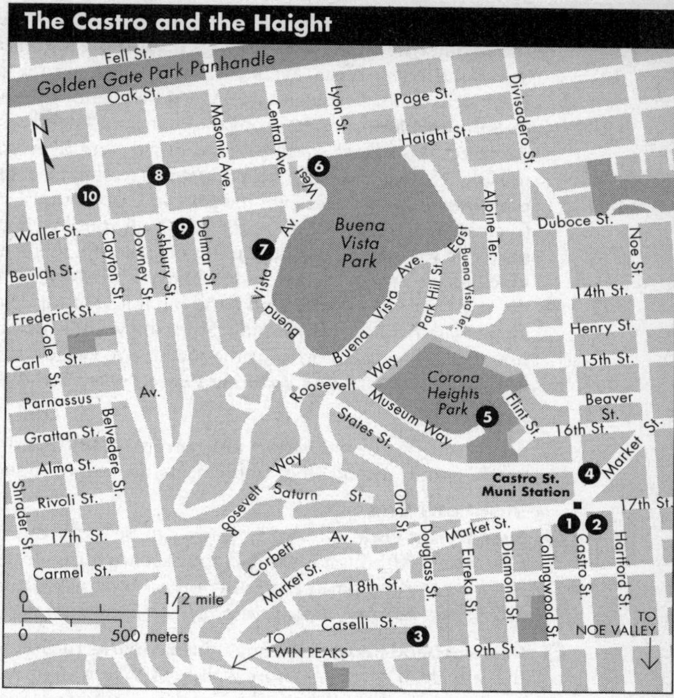

Hall, torching its lobby and several police cars. ✉ *Southwest corner of Castro and Market Sts.*

❹ **Names Project.** Open to anyone who wishes to work on a panel or view the work of those who have, the Names Project has created a gigantic quilt made of more than 42,000 hand-sewn and -decorated panels, pieced together by loved ones to serve as a memorial to those who have died of AIDS. ✉ *2362 Market St.,* ☎ *415/863–1966.* ⏲ *Mon.–Sat. noon–7, Sun. noon–6; quilting bee Wed. 7* PM*–10* PM *and 2nd Sat. of month 1–5.*

❺ **Randall Museum.** The highlight of this facility is the educational animal room, popular with children, where you can observe birds, lizards, snakes, spiders, and other creatures that cannot be released to the wild because of injury or other problems. ✉ *199 Museum Way, off Roosevelt Way,* ☎ *415/554–9600.* *Free.* ⏲ *Tues.–Sat. 10–5.*

The Haight

Once an enclave of large middle-class families of European immigrants, the Haight began to change during the late 1950s and early 1960s. Families were fleeing to the suburbs, and the big old Victorians were deteriorating or being chopped up into cheap housing. Young people found the neighborhood an affordable spot in which they could live according to new precepts. By 1966 the Haight had become a hot spot for rock bands such as the Grateful Dead—whose members moved into a big Victorian near the corner of Haight and Ashbury streets—and Jefferson Airplane, whose grand mansion was north of the district at 2400 Fulton Street.

Numbers in the text correspond to numbers in the margin and on the Castro and the Haight map.

A Good Walk

Start your visit on the western edge of **Buena Vista Park** ⑥, at Haight Street and Buena Vista Avenue West. If you're up for a climb, walk a few blocks south on Buena Vista Avenue West along the edge of the park to **Spreckels Mansion** ⑦. From the mansion, backtrack on its side of the street to Central Avenue. Head down Central Avenue two blocks to Haight Street, and make a left. Continue west to the fabled **Haight/Ashbury intersection** ⑧. Despite the franchise operations, you won't need to close your eyes to conjure the 1960s. A motley contingent of folks attired in retro fashions and often sporting hippie-long hair hangs here. One block south of Haight and Ashbury is the **Grateful Dead house** ⑨, the pad that Jerry Garcia and band inhabited in the 1960s. The stores along Haight Street up to Shrader Street are worth checking out. At Clayton Street, you can stop in at the meditative Peace Arts Center on the ground floor of the **Red Victorian Peace Center Bed & Breakfast** ⑩.

TIMING

The distance covered here is only several blocks, and although there are shops aplenty and other amusements, an hour or so should be enough.

Sights to See

6 **Buena Vista Park.** Great city views can be had from this eucalyptus-filled park. Although it's not exactly sedate (drug deals are common), it's a very pretty park, especially on a sunny day. Don't wander here after dark. ✉ *Haight St. between Lyon St. and Buena Vista Ave. W.*

9 **Grateful Dead house.** Nothing unusual marks the house of legend. On the outside, it's just one more well-kept Victorian on a street that's full of them—but true fans of the Dead may find some inspiration here. ✉ *710 Ashbury St., just past Waller St.*

8 **Haight/Ashbury intersection.** On October 6, 1967, hippies took over the intersection of Haight and Ashbury streets to proclaim the "Death of Hip." If they thought hip was dead then, they'd find absolute confirmation of it today, what with the Gap holding court on one quadrant of the famed corner. Among the folks who hung out in or near the Haight during the late 1960s were writers Richard Brautigan, Allen Ginsberg, Ken Kesey, and Gary Snyder; anarchist Abbie Hoffman; rock performers Marty Balin, Jerry Garcia, Janis Joplin, and Grace Slick; LSD champion Timothy Leary; and filmmaker Kenneth Anger.

10 **Red Victorian Peace Center Bed & Breakfast.** In 1977 Sami Sunchild acquired the Red Vic, built as a hotel in 1904, with the aim of preserving the best of 1960s ideals. She decorated her rooms with 1960s themes—one chamber is called the Flower Child Room—and on the ground floor opened the Peace Art Center. Here you can buy her paintings, T-shirts, and "meditative art." ✉ *1665 Haight St.,* ☎ *415/864–1978.*

7 **Spreckels Mansion.** Not to be confused with the Spreckels Mansion of Pacific Heights, this house was built for sugar baron Richard Spreckels in 1887. Later tenants included Jack London and Ambrose Bierce. ✉ *737 Buena Vista Ave. W.*

DINING

By Sharon Silva

San Francisco has more restaurants per capita than any other city in the United States, and nearly every ethnic cuisine is represented, from Afghan to Indian to Vietnamese. Diversity is the key to the city's culinary richness, and it has absolutely spoiled the locals. Whether it's the best tapas this side of Barcelona or the silkiest seared foie gras this side of Paris, San Francisco has it all—most often within convenient walking distance.

CATEGORY	COST*
$$$$	over $50
$$$	$30–$50
$$	$20–$30
$	under $20

**per person for a three-course meal, excluding drinks, service, and 8.5% sales tax*

🖱 *following the text of a review is your signal that the property has a Web site, where you will find details and, usually, images; for a link, visit www.fodors.com/urls.*

The Castro

Contemporary

$$$ ✕ **Mecca.** This sleek bar and restaurant on the edge of the Castro is a mecca for both local Armani-clad cocktailers and Bay Area foodies. If clubbing is not your thing, reserve a seat in the dining area, away from the always-crowded, velvet-curtained circular bar that anchors the cavernous space. The American menu comes with an Asian accent. Choices include an iced shellfish platter, curried potato samosas with pineapple salsa, shrimp dumplings with a spicy tahini sauce, roast chicken, and lemon-mascarpone cheesecake. ✉ *2029 Market St.,* ☎ *415/621–7000. AE, DC, MC, V. No lunch.*

$$–$$$ ✕ **2223.** Opened in the mid-1990s, when the Castro was a dining-out wasteland, the smart, sophisticated 2223—the address became the name when the principals couldn't come up with a better one—was an instant success and has continued to attract a loyal clientele. That means you'll need a strong pair of lungs, however, as the restaurant's popularity and absence of sound buffers make conversation difficult. Thin-crust pizzas, a huge warm spinach salad, coconut tiger prawns on a Thai-inspired noodle salad, and super-thick pork chops with yams and red cabbage are among the kitchen's best dishes. ✉ *2223 Market St.,* ☎ *415/431–0692. AE, DC, MC, V. No lunch weekdays.*

Chinatown

Chinese

$–$$ ✕ **Great Eastern.** Cantonese chefs are known for their expertise with seafood, and the kitchen at Great Eastern lives up to that venerable tradition. In the busy dining room, large tanks are filled with Dungeness crabs, black bass, abalone, catfish, shrimp, rock cod, and other creatures of the sea, and a wall-hung menu in both Chinese and English specifies the cost of selecting what can be pricey indulgences. Sea conch stir-fried with yellow chives, crab with vermicelli in a clay pot, and steamed fresh scallops with garlic sauce are among the chef's many specialties. In the wee hours Chinese night owls often drop in for a plate of noodles or a bowl of *congee* (rice gruel). ✉ *649 Jackson St.,* ☎ *415/986–2550. AE, MC, V.*

$–$$ ✕ **R&G Lounge.** The name conjures up an image of a dark bar with a cigarette-smoking piano player, but the restaurant, on two floors, is actually as bright as a new penny. Downstairs (entrance on Kearny Street) is a no-tablecloth dining room that is always packed at lunch and dinner. The classier upstairs space (entrance on Commercial Street), complete with shoji-lined private rooms, is a favorite stop for Chinese businessmen on expense accounts and anyone seeking exceptional Cantonese banquet fare. A menu with photographs helps diners decide among the many wonderful dishes, from pea shoots stir-fried with garlic to soy sauce chicken to deep-fried salt-and-pepper Dungeness crab. ✉ *631 Kearny St.,* ☎ *415/982–7877 or 415/982–3811. AE, DC, MC, V.*

Absinthe 77
Acquerello 96
Antica Trattoria 17
Aqua 42
B44 48
Beach Chalet 81
Betelnut 14
Bistro Aix 9
Bix 34
Bizou 61
Black Cat 31
Boulevard 46
Café Claude 50
Café Marimba 7
Campton Place Restaurant 54
Capp's Corner 26
Carta 78
Cassis Bistro 11
Cypress Club 35
Enrico's Sidewalk Cafe 28
Farallon 69
Fifth Floor 65
Fleur de Lys 71
Florio 94
Fog City Diner 19
Fringale 62
Garden Court 56
Gary Danko 4
Gaylord's 3
Grand Café 66
Great Eastern 30
Greens 1
Harbor Village 44
Harris' 15
Hawthorne Lane 58
Hayes Street Grill 76
Helmand 29
Il Fornaio 20
Izzy's Steak & Chop House 8
Jardinière 75
Kabuto Sushi 89
Katia's 84
Kokkari 33
Kyo-ya 57
La Folie 16
La Vie 91
Laghi 93
Le Central 51
Le Colonial 70
Le Soleil 88
L'Osteria del Forno 22
LuLu 64
MacArthur Park 32
Masa's 52
Maykadeh 24
McCormick & Kuleto's 2
Mifune 85

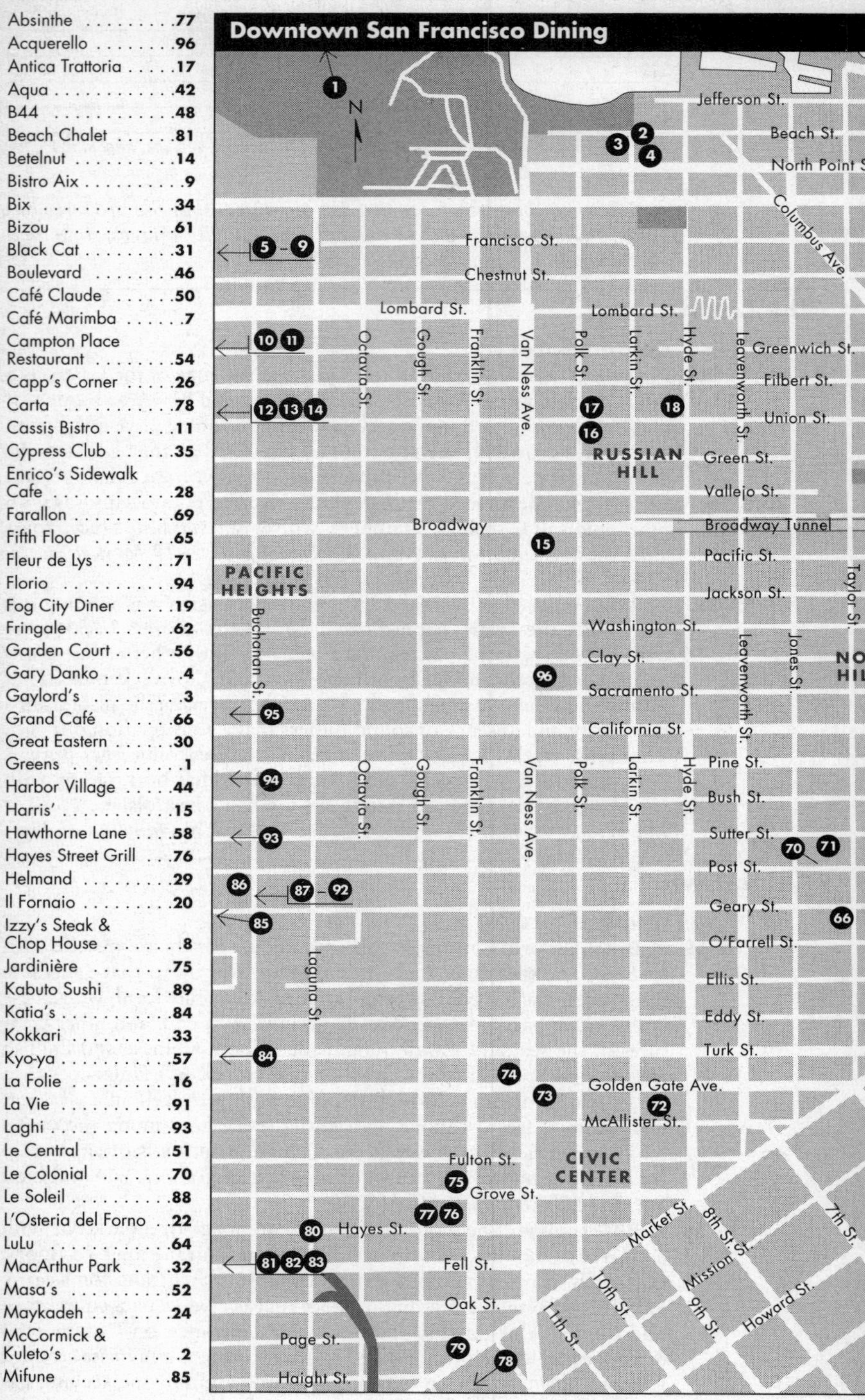

Millennium 72
Mo's Grill 63
Momo's 60
Moose's 21
One Market 45
Oritalia 53
Palio d'Asti 40
Pane e Vino 12
Parc Hong Kong Restaurant 90
Park Chow 82
Pastis 25
Plouf 49
PlumpJack Café 10
Postrio 67
R&G Lounge 39
Ristorante Ideale 27
Ritz-Carlton Dining Room and Terrace . . .38
Rose Pistola 23
Rose's Cafe 13
Rubicon 36
San Tung No. 2 83
Sanppo 86
Scala's Bistro 68
South Park Café 59
Splendido 43
Stars 73
Straits Café 87
Suppenkuche 80
Ton Kiang 92
Vivande Porta Via . . .95
Vivande Ristorante . .74
World Wrapps 5
Yank Sing . . .37, 47, 55
Zarzuela 18
Zinzino 6
Zuni Café & Grill . . .79

Civic Center

Contemporary

$$$–$$$$ ★ ✕ **Jardinière.** One of the city's most talked-about restaurants since its opening in the late 1990s, Jardinière continues to be *the* place to dine before a performance at the nearby Opera House and Davies Symphony Hall or any time you have something to celebrate. The chef-owner is Traci Des Jardins, who made her name at the Financial District's clubby Rubicon. The sophisticated interior, with its eye-catching oval atrium and curving staircase, is the work of designer Pat Kuleto. First courses of sweetbreads, duck confit, and foie gras are pricey but memorable ways to launch any repast. A temperature-controlled cheese room lets you trade in a wedge of chocolate torte for a more European finish. ✉ *300 Grove St.,* ☎ *415/861–5555. Reservations essential. AE, DC, MC, V. No lunch.*

$$ ✕ **Carta.** The defining idea here is a difficult one to carry off: a different menu from a different country or region every two months. Yet Carta makes it work beautifully. The talented chefs, alums of some of the city's toniest spots, travel to an assortment of destinations: Oaxaca, Turkey, the Dordogne, Morocco, and New England, to name just a few. There are usually about 10 small plates, three main courses, and three desserts. Carta has expanded into the space next door to create a warm, lavish dining room and comfy bar. A lounge menu is in effect daily from mid-afternoon. ✉ *1772 Market St.,* ☎ *415/863–3516. AE, DC, MC, V. No lunch Sat.*

Italian

$$$ ✕ **Vivande Ristorante.** Owner-chef Carlo Middione, a highly regarded authority on the food of southern Italy, has long run a smart take-out shop and casual dining room in Lower Pacific Heights. His larger *ristorante,* within walking distance of the Opera House and Symphony Hall, features the same rustic fare found at the original location, like risotto laced with seafood, pasta tossed with a tangle of mushrooms, and a hearty osso buco. ✉ *670 Golden Gate Ave.,* ☎ *415/673–9245. AE, MC, V.*

Mediterranean

$$$ ★ ✕ **Zuni Café & Grill.** Zuni's Italian-Mediterranean menu and unpretentious atmosphere pack in an eclectic crowd from early morning to late evening. A spacious, window-filled balcony dining area overlooks the large zinc bar, where shellfish, one of the best oyster selections in town, and drinks are dispensed. A whole roast chicken and Tuscan bread salad for two is a popular order here, but don't overlook the smooth, lemony asparagus soup, the lamb's tongue salad, or the grilled rabbit. Even the hamburgers have an Italian accent—they're topped with Gorgonzola and served on herbed focaccia. The kitchen's shoestring potatoes are addictive, and the coffee granita swirled with cream is pure heaven. ✉ *1658 Market St.,* ☎ *415/552–2522. Reservations essential. AE, MC, V. Closed Mon.*

Seafood

$$–$$$ ✕ **Hayes Street Grill.** More than a dozen different kinds of seafood are chalked on the blackboard each night at this bustling restaurant. The fish is simply grilled, with a choice of sauces ranging from tomato salsa to a spicy Sichuan peanut concoction to beurre blanc. Fresh crab slaw and superb crab cakes are regular appetizers, and for dessert, the crème brûlée is legendary. ✉ *320 Hayes St.,* ☎ *415/863–5545. Reservations essential. AE, D, DC, MC, V. No lunch weekends.*

Vegetarian

$$ ✕ **Millennium.** Tucked into the former carriage house of the venerable Abigail Hotel, Millennium offers what it describes as "organic cui-

sine." That label translates to a menu of low-fat, dairy-free dishes made with organic ingredients that keep vegans and their carnivore friends equally satisfied. The kitchen looks to the Mediterranean, with pastas and polenta among its most successful dishes. For true believers, there are organic wines and beers. ✉ *246 McAllister St.,* ☎ *415/487–9800. MC, V. No lunch.*

Cow Hollow/Marina

French

$–$$ ✕ **Bistro Aix.** This lively bistro is a comfortable space composed of light wood banquettes, paper-top tablecloths, and a heated patio. The friendly service and attractive prices draw diners from the surrounding neighborhood and beyond. On weekdays, an early-bird two-course prix-fixe dinner is available for not much more than the price of a movie ticket. Addictive cracker crust pizzas, superb steamed mussels, and crisp-skinned roast chicken are additional draws. ✉ *3340 Steiner St.,* ☎ *415/202–0100. MC, V. No lunch.*

$–$$ ✕ **Cassis Bistro.** Take a seat at the tiny bar and enjoy a glass of wine while you wait for a free table in this sunny yellow, postage stamp–size operation that recalls the small bistros tucked away on side streets in French seaside towns. The servers have solid Gallic accents; the food—onion tart, veal ragout, braised rabbit, tarte Tatin—is comfortingly home style; and the prices are geared toward the penurious. Bare hardwood floors make conversations a challenge on busy nights. ✉ *2120 Greenwich St.,* ☎ *415/292–0770. No credit cards. Closed Sun. and Mon. No lunch.*

Italian

$$–$$$ ✕ **Pane e Vino.** A long table topped with prosciutto, a wheel of Parmigiano-Reggiano, and various antipasti seduces everyone who enters this highly popular trattoria. Polenta with mushrooms, grilled bass, and house-made sausages are among the dishes regulars can't resist. The Italian-born owner-chef concentrates on specialties from Tuscany and the north, dishing them up in a charming room decorated with rustic wooden furniture and colorful pottery. ✉ *3011 Steiner St.,* ☎ *415/346–2111. MC, V. No lunch Sun.*

$$–$$$ ✕ **Zinzino.** The long, narrow dining space—a study in industrial-chic—at this animated *ristorante* ends in a heated patio that fills up on all but the chilliest nights. The menu is irresistible. Thin pizzas are topped with prosciutto and arugula, eggplant and bread crumbs, or fennel sausage and caramelized onions. A stuffed double-cut pork chop arrives with maple-glazed potatoes, and a wood-fired half chicken is paired with polenta. ✉ *2355 Chestnut St.,* ☎ *415/346–6623. MC, V. No lunch.*

Mediterranean

$$$ ✕ **PlumpJack Café.** This clubby dining room, with its smartly attired clientele of bankers and brokers, socialites and society scions, takes its name from an opera composed by famed oil tycoon and music lover Gordon Getty, whose sons are two of the partners here. The regularly changing menu spans the Mediterranean, with bruschetta topped with ham and a rich, creamy cheese, skate with brown butter and capers, pasta with lamb and broccoli rabe, and hazelnut soufflé among the possibilities. The wine cellar includes some of the most reasonably priced vintages in town. ✉ *3127 Fillmore St.,* ☎ *415/463–4755. AE, MC, V. Closed Sun. No lunch Sat.*

Mexican

$–$$ ✕ **Café Marimba.** Fanciful folk art adorns the walls of this colorful Mexican café, where an open kitchen turns out contemporary renditions of regional specialties: silken *mole negro* (sauce of chilies and chocolate) from Oaxaca, served in tamales and other dishes; shrimp prepared with roasted onions and tomatoes in the style of Zihuatanejo; and chicken with a marinade from Yucatán stuffed into an excellent taco. Although the food is treated to many innovative touches, authenticity plays a strong role—even the guacamole is made to order in a *molcajete,* the three-legged lava-rock version of a mortar. Fresh fruit drinks and tangy margaritas are good thirst quenchers. ✉ *2317 Chestnut St.,* ☎ *415/776–1506. AE, MC, V. No lunch Mon.*

Pan-Asian

$$ ✕ **Betelnut.** A pan-Asian menu and an adventurous drinks list—with everything from house-brewed rice beer to martinis—draw a steady stream of hip diners to this Union Street landmark. Richly lacquered walls, bamboo ceiling fans, and hand-painted posters create a comfortably exotic mood in keeping with the unusual but accessible food. A new chef arrived with the millennium and delivered some minor changes to the original menu, punching up some Western influences. Don't pass up a plate of the tasty stir-fried dried anchovies, chilies, peanuts, garlic, and green onions. ✉ *2030 Union St.,* ☎ *415/929–8855. D, DC, MC, V.*

Steak

$$–$$$ ✕ **Izzy's Steak & Chop House.** Izzy Gomez was a legendary San Francisco saloon keeper, and his namesake eatery carries on the tradition. Here, in this old-fashioned, clamorous spot, you'll find terrific steaks, chops, and seafood plus all the trimmings, from cheesy scalloped potatoes to creamed spinach. A collection of Izzy memorabilia and antique advertising art covers almost every inch of wall space. ✉ *3345 Steiner St.,* ☎ *415/563–0487. AE, DC, MC, V. No lunch.*

Vegetarian

$$–$$$ ✕ **Greens.** Long popular with vegetarians and carnivores alike, this beautiful restaurant with expansive bay views is owned and operated by the Green Gulch Zen Buddhist Center of Marin County. The dining room offers a wide, eclectic, and creative spectrum of meatless cooking—corn fritters, black bean soup, thin-crust pizzas, Southwestern-inspired savory tarts, a grilled tofu sandwich on potato bread, and house-made pasta tossed with wild mushrooms. Dinners are à la carte on weeknights, but only a five-course prix fixe dinner is served on Saturday. Sunday brunch is a good time to watch local sailboat owners take out their crafts. ✉ *Bldg. A, Fort Mason (enter across Marina Blvd. from Safeway),* ☎ *415/771–6222. MC, V. No lunch Mon., no dinner Sun.*

Embarcadero North

American

$$ ✕ **Fog City Diner.** The diner is an American institution, and Fog City Diner is arguably among the sleekest examples of that beloved national tradition. The long, narrow dining room emulates a luxurious railroad car, with dark wood paneling, huge windows, shiny chrome fixtures, and comfortable booths. The menu is both classic and contemporary, from burgers and fries, chili dogs and hot fudge sundaes to crab cakes and salads of baby lettuce with candied walnuts. The shareable "small plates" are a fun way to go. ✉ *1300 Battery St.,* ☎ *415/982–2000. D, DC, MC, V.*

$$ ✕ **MacArthur Park.** At happy hour, a sea of suits fills this handsomely renovated pre-earthquake brick warehouse. Much of the crowd stays on for the legendary baby back ribs, but the oak-wood smoker and mesquite grill also turn out a wide variety of other all-American dishes, from steaks to hamburgers to seafood. Coleslaw aficionados will appreciate the horseradish-spiked dressing that coats their favorite salad, and enthusiasts of the skinny french fry will fill up on what is served here. ✉ *607 Front St.,* ☎ *415/398–5700. AE, DC, MC, V. No lunch weekends.*

Chinese

$$–$$$ ✕ **Harbor Village.** At lunchtime, businesspeople looking to impress their clients fill the dining room of this outpost of upmarket Cantonese cooking, all of them enjoying the extraordinary array of dim sum. At dinnertime, fresh seafood from the restaurant's own tanks, crisp Peking duck, and various exotica—bird's nest in supreme broth, shark fin, and crab roe—are among the most popular requests from the loyal customers who regularly fill this 400-seat branch of a Hong Kong establishment. The setting is opulent, with Chinese antiques and teak furnishings; a gallery of private rooms harbors large banquet tables perfect for celebrating any special occasion. ✉ *4 Embarcadero Center,* ☎ *415/781–8833. AE, DC, MC, V.*

French

$$$$ ★ ✕ **Gary Danko.** At his late-'90s eponymous restaurant, Chef Gary Danko delivers the same fine-food restaurant that won him a 1995 James Beard award as best chef in California during his stint at the city's Ritz-Carlton. He has borrowed the hotel's pricing system, too, pegging the cost of a dinner at the number of courses, from three to six. The plates run the gamut from featherlight scallop mousse to roast lobster on mashed potatoes with wild mushrooms to a truly decadent chocolate soufflé. The look of the wood-paneled, banquette-lined room and the smooth gait of the staff are as high class as the food is. ✉ *800 N. Point St.,* ☎ *415/749–2060. Reservations essential. AE, DC, MC, V. No lunch.*

$$–$$$ ✕ **Pastis.** At lunchtime the sunny cement bar and sleek wooden banquettes in this exposed brick dining room are crowded with workers from nearby offices; they come to fuel up on steamed salmon with celery root or grilled prawns marinated in pastis (anise-flavor liqueur). The evening menu may include a dreamy seared foie gras with *verjuice* (sour grape juice), buttery boned oxtail with *ravigote* sauce (with capers, onions, and herbs), and a thick, juicy veal chop with shallot sauce. Pastis, with its French and Basque plates, is chef-owner Gerald Hirigoyen's popular successor to his SoMa bistro Fringale (☞ South of Market, *below*). ✉ *1015 Battery St.,* ☎ *415/391–2555. AE, MC, V. Closed Sun. No lunch Sat.*

Greek

$$$ ✕ **Kokkari.** Sophistication is written all over this large and handsome taverna. In its warm and inviting interior, complete with an outsized fireplace, displays of rustic cookware and pottery, and a lively bar, folks sit down to a full menu of sunny Aegean plates. Most savvy diners start off with a trio of dips—eggplant, yogurt and cucumber, *taramasalata* (fish roe pureed with olive oil, lemon, and bread crumbs)—served with freshly baked pita and then move on to such Athenian standards as moussaka, roast octopus salad, and braised lamb shank. For a true island experience, cap off your meal with a cup of thick Greek coffee. ✉ *200 Jackson St.,* ☎ *415/981–0983. AE, DC, MC, V. Closed Sun. No lunch Sat.*

Italian

$$–$$$ ✕ **Splendido.** The stunning view of the Ferry Building and the bay, the spectacular lighting, the limestone pillars, and the open kitchen combine to make this restaurant a southern European oasis on the Embarcadero. In the past, the food has been a mix of Mediterranean cuisines. But the menu has moved more firmly into the Italian camp with silky spinach and ricotta ravioli with brown butter and sage, gnocchi with seafood and peas in a light tomato sauce, thin, crisp pizzas, and grilled meats and fish. ✉ *Embarcadero 4,* ☎ *415/986–3222. AE, DC, MC, V. No lunch weekends.*

Embarcadero South

Contemporary

$$$ ✕ **Boulevard.** Two of San Francisco's top restaurant talents—chef Nancy Oakes and designer Pat Kuleto—are responsible for this highly successful eatery in one of the city's most magnificent buildings. The setting is the 1889 Audiffred Building, a Parisian look-alike that was one of the few downtown buildings to survive the 1906 earthquake and fire. Oakes's menu is seasonally in flux, but you can always count on her signature juxtaposition of delicacies such as foie gras with homey comfort foods such as spit-roasted pork loin and roasted chicken. For those who can't find or afford a table during regular hours, Boulevard offers a less formal weekday afternoon bistro service. ✉ *1 Mission St.,* ☏ *415/543–6084. Reservations essential. AE, D, DC, MC, V. No lunch weekends.*

$$$ ✕ **One Market.** A giant among American chefs, Bradley Ogden gained fame at Campton Place and later at his Lark Creek Inn in Marin County. This huge, bustling brasserie across from the Ferry Building is his popular San Francisco outpost. The handsome two-tier dining room, done in mustard tones, seats 170, and a spacious bar-café serves snacks, including addictive wire-thin onion rings and oysters on the half shell, beginning at noon. The kitchen has had its ups and downs, however, due to a serious spate of executive chef turnover, although the turn of the millennium seems to have settled the staff down. ✉ *1 Market St.,* ☏ *415/777–5577. Reservations essential. AE, DC, MC, V. Closed Sun. No lunch Sat.*

Financial District

Chinese

$ ✕ **Yank Sing.** The city's oldest teahouse, Yank Sing began in Chinatown in the late 1950s but moved to the Financial District more than a decade ago. The kitchen prepares 100 varieties of dim sum on a rotating basis, serving some 60 varieties daily. The Battery Street location seats 300, while the older Stevenson Street site is far smaller, a cozy refuge for neighborhood office workers who fuel up on steamed buns and parchment chicken at lunchtime. The latest site is a large space in Rincon Center, on the Embarcadero. ✉ *427 Battery St.,* ☏ *415/362–1640; 49 Stevenson St., at Market St.,* ☏ *415/541–4949; One Rincon Center, 101 Spear St.,* ☏ *415/957–9300. AE, DC, MC, V. Stevenson branch closed Sun.; Rincon branch closed weekends. No dinner.*

Contemporary

$$$ ✕ **Cypress Club.** Although restaurateur John Cunin calls his fashionable spot a "San Francisco brasserie," the term is more descriptive of the food—which pleases the contemporary American palate—than the classy but far-out decor. It could be interpreted as anything from a parody of an ancient temple to a futuristic space bar, with stone mosaic floors, hammered copper arches, wall murals depicting scenes of northern California, yards of curved wood, imposing pillars, and overstuffed velvet upholstery. ✉ *500 Jackson St.,* ☏ *415/296–8555. AE, DC, MC, V. No lunch.*

$$$ ✕ **Rubicon.** With such investors as Robin Williams, Robert De Niro, and Francis Ford Coppola, this sleek, cherrywood-lined restaurant was destined to be famous. Set in a stately stone building dating from 1908, Rubicon has the dignified air of a men's club in the downstairs dining room and a somewhat less appealing atmosphere in the more ascetic upstairs space. The excellent fare, primarily sophisticated renditions of seafood, meats, and poultry, is served on both floors to Hollywood big shots, suits from nearby office towers, and San Francisco's glamorous set. ✉ *558 Sacramento St.,* ☎ *415/434–4100. AE, DC, MC, V. Closed Sun. No lunch Sat.*

French

$$–$$$ ✕ **Plouf.** This sleek spot, handsomely turned out in chrome and the color of the sea, is a gold mine for mussel lovers, with eight generously portioned, reasonably priced preparations from which to choose. Among them are *marinière* (garlic and parsley), apple cider, leeks and cream, and crayfish and tomato. Order a side of fries and that's all most appetites will need. Other main courses run the gamut from steak frites to sautéed grouper with saffron-citrus sauce. Plouf is French for "splash," and the appetizers maintain the seaside theme, with plenty of raw oysters on the half shell and a seafood salad of rock shrimp, mussels, and octopus among the offerings. ✉ *40 Belden Pl.,* ☎ *415/986–6491. MC, V. Closed Sun. No lunch Sat.*

$ ✕ **Café Claude.** This standout French bistro is in an alley near the Notre Dame des Victoires Catholic church and the French consulate. The interior design is comfortably French, with a zinc bar, old-fashioned banquettes, and cinema posters that once actually outfitted a bar in the City of Light's 11th arrondissement. Order a salade niçoise or simple daube from the French-speaking staff, and you might forget what country you're in. On Friday and Saturday nights, the boisterous crowds regularly spill out into the alleyway. ✉ *7 Claude La.,* ☎ *415/392–3505. AE, DC, MC, V. Closed Sun.*

Japanese

$$–$$$$ ✕ **Kyo-ya.** Rarely replicated outside Japan, the refined experience of dining in a fine Japanese restaurant has been introduced with extraordinary authenticity at this showplace within the Palace Hotel. In Japan a "kyo-ya" is a nonspecialized restaurant that serves a wide range of food. Here, the range is spectacular, encompassing tempuras, one-pot dishes, deep-fried and grilled meats, and three dozen sushi selections. The lunch menu is more limited than dinner but does include a *shokado,* a sampler of four dishes encased in a lacquered box. ✉ *Palace Hotel, 2 New Montgomery St., at Market St.,* ☎ *415/546–5000. AE, D, DC, MC, V. Closed Sun. No lunch Mon. and Sat.*

Seafood

$$$–$$$$ ★ ✕ **Aqua.** This quietly elegant and ultrafashionable spot is among the city's most lauded seafood restaurants—and among the most expensive. Chef-owner Michael Mina creates contemporary versions of French, Italian, and American classics. Mussel, crab, or lobster soufflé; chunks of lobster alongside lobster-stuffed ravioli; and the signature ultrarare ahi tuna paired with foie gras are especially good. Desserts are miniature museum pieces—try the warm chocolate tart—and the wine list is superb. ✉ *252 California St.,* ☎ *415/956–9662. Reservations essential. Jacket and tie. AE, DC, MC, V. Closed Sun. No lunch Sat.*

Spanish

$$–$$$ ★ ✕ **B44.** Tiny Belden Place is a restaurant gold mine, with a cluster of wonderful European eateries. This Spanish addition, with its spare, modern decor, abstract poster art, and open kitchen, draws locals who love the menu of authentic Catalan tapas and paellas. Among the superb small plates are white anchovies with pears and Idiazábal cheese; sherry-scented fish cheeks with garlic, parsley, and chili; warm octopus with tiny potatoes; and blood sausage with white beans and *aioli.* The paellas bring together such inviting combinations as chicken, rabbit, and mushrooms or monkfish, squid, shrimp, mussels, and clams. ✉ *44 Belden Pl.,* ☎ *415/986–6287. AE, MC, V. Closed Sun. No lunch Sat.*

The Haight

Contemporary

$$$ ✕ **Eos Restaurant & Wine Bar.** The culinary marriage of California cuisine and the Asian pantry is the specialty of chef-owner Arnold Wong, who serves an impressive East-West menu at this popular spot. Grilled skirt steak is marinated in a Thai red curry and served with mashed potatoes and bok choy; rock shrimp cakes arrive with a gingery mayonnaise; and pan-roasted lemongrass-scented sea bass is paired with wasabi mashed potatoes. Sometimes diners may find the competing flavors dizzying, but Wong's faithful following keeps his innovative kitchen in motion. ✉ *901 Cole St.,* ☎ *415/566–3063. Reservations essential. AE, MC, V. No lunch.*

Indian

$$–$$$ ✕ **Indian Oven.** This handsome, cozy Victorian storefront never lacks for customers. Many of these lovers of subcontinental food come here to order the tandoori specialties—chicken, lamb, breads—but the *sag paneer* (spinach with Indian cheese) and *aloo gobhi* (potatoes and cauliflower with black mustard seeds and other spices) are also excellent. You can start your meal with crisp vegetable *pakoras* (fritters), served with a sprightly tamarind chutney, chased with an Indian beer or a tall, cool glass of fresh lemonade. A complete meal, called a *thali* for the metal plate on which it is served, includes a choice of entrée, plus soup, a curried vegetable, cardamom-scented basmati rice, nan, and chutney. ✉ *223 Fillmore St.,* ☎ *415/626–1628. AE, D, DC, MC, V. No lunch.*

Thai

$–$$ ★ ✕ **Thep Phanom.** The fine Thai food and the lovely interior at this Lower Haight institution keep local food critics and restaurant goers singing its praises. Duck is deliciously prepared in a variety of ways—in a fragrant curry, minced for salad, resting atop a bed of spinach. Other specialties are seafood in various guises, stuffed chicken wings, and fried quail. A number of daily specials supplement the regular menu, and a wonderful mango sorbet is sometimes offered for dessert. ✉ *400 Waller St.,* ☎ *415/431–2526. AE, D, DC, MC, V. No lunch.*

Japantown

Japanese

$–$$ ✕ **Sanppo.** This modestly priced, casual spot has an enormous selection of almost every type of Japanese food: yakis, nabemono dishes, donburi, udon, and soba, not to mention featherlight tempura and sushi. Grilled eel on rice in a lacquered box and a tempting array of small dishes for snacking make Sanppo a favorite of locals and visitors alike. Ask for validated parking at the Japan Center garage. ✉ *1702 Post St.,* ☎ *415/346–3486. Reservations not accepted. MC, V.*

$ ✕ **Mifune.** Thin, brown soba and thick, white udon are the specialties at this North American outpost of an Osaka-based noodle empire. A line often snakes out the door, but the house-made noodles, served both hot and cold and with more than a score of toppings, are worth the wait. Seating is at rustic wooden tables, where diners can be heard slurping down big bowls of such traditional Japanese combinations as fish cake–crowned udon and *tenzaru* (cold noodles and hot tempura with a gingery dipping sauce) served on lacquered trays. ✉ *Japan Center, Kintetsu Bldg., 1737 Post St.,* ☎ *415/922–0337. Reservations not accepted. AE, D, DC, MC, V.*

Lower Pacific Heights

French

$$–$$$ ✕ **Florio.** San Franciscans are always ready to fall in love with little French bistros, and this has made Florio a hit. It has all the elements: simple decor reminiscent of a Paris address, excellent roasted chicken and *pommes frites,* and some reasonably priced French wines. Of course, there are also bouillabaisse, steamed mussels, and duck confit. Forgo the pastas, but don't pass up the crème caramel. The room can get noisy, so don't come here hoping for a quiet tête-à-tête. ✉ *1915 Fillmore St.,* ☎ *415/775–4300. MC, V. No lunch.*

Italian

$$–$$$ ✕ **Laghi.** For many years, Laghi was a much-loved trattoria in the Richmond District, where it was housed in a small storefront with little available parking. In late 1998, chef-owner Gino Laghi moved his estimable operation to this much larger space, complete with open kitchen, big banquettes, and a sleek wine bar. Old customers and new fans quickly flocked here to enjoy the pastas, including pumpkin-filled ravioli with butter and sage; creamy risottos with everything from fiddlehead ferns to porcini mushrooms to truffles; and roasted rabbit and other game. The wine list of Italian labels is reasonably priced. ✉ *2101 Sutter St.,* ☎ *415/931–3774. AE, DC, MC, V. No lunch weekends.*

The Mission District

Cambodian

$ ✕ **Angkor Borei.** This Cambodian restaurant deep in the Mission is a modest yet handsome space decorated with lovely Khmer objects. The menu offers a wonderful array of curries, plump spring rolls, and delicate crepes stuffed with vegetables and a smattering of meat and seafood. Chicken threaded onto skewers, grilled, and served with mildly pickled vegetables is a house specialty. Aromatic Thai basil, lemongrass, and softly sizzling chilies lace many of the dishes at this true neighborhood restaurant. ✉ *3471 Mission St.,* ☎ *415/550–8417. AE, D, MC, V. No lunch Sun.*

Contemporary

$$$ ✕ **42 Degrees.** This industrial-style space, with its curving metal staircase and seductive view of the bay, has been a draw since the mid-'90s. The name refers to the latitude on which Provence, Tuscany, and northern Spain lie. The opening chef left in mid-1999, and the kitchen suffered. But the California menu, infused with Mediterranean touches, is back on track. The choices change regularly and range from creamy bone marrow on toast to curried cauliflower fritters to crisp flat bread with Champagne grapes, onion, and thyme to veal cheeks with an herbed mustard crust. ✉ *235 16th St.,* ☎ *415/777–5558. MC, V. Closed Mon. and Tues. No lunch.*

French

$$–$$$ ✕ **Foreign Cinema.** The San Francisco Bay Area is known as home to many of the country's most respected independent filmmakers, making this innovative dining spot a surefire hit with local cinemaphiles. Not only can folks who enter the hip, loftlike space sit down to orders of pan-seared foie gras, herb-crusted chicken breast with garlic mashed potatoes, and rib-eye steak with *pommes frites* and red wine butter, but they can also watch such foreign classics as Fellini's *La Dolce Vita* and Bergman's *The Seventh Seal,* plus a passel of current indie features, projected in the large courtyard. ✉ *2534 Mission St.,* ☎ *415/648–7600. MC, V. Closed Mon. No lunch.*

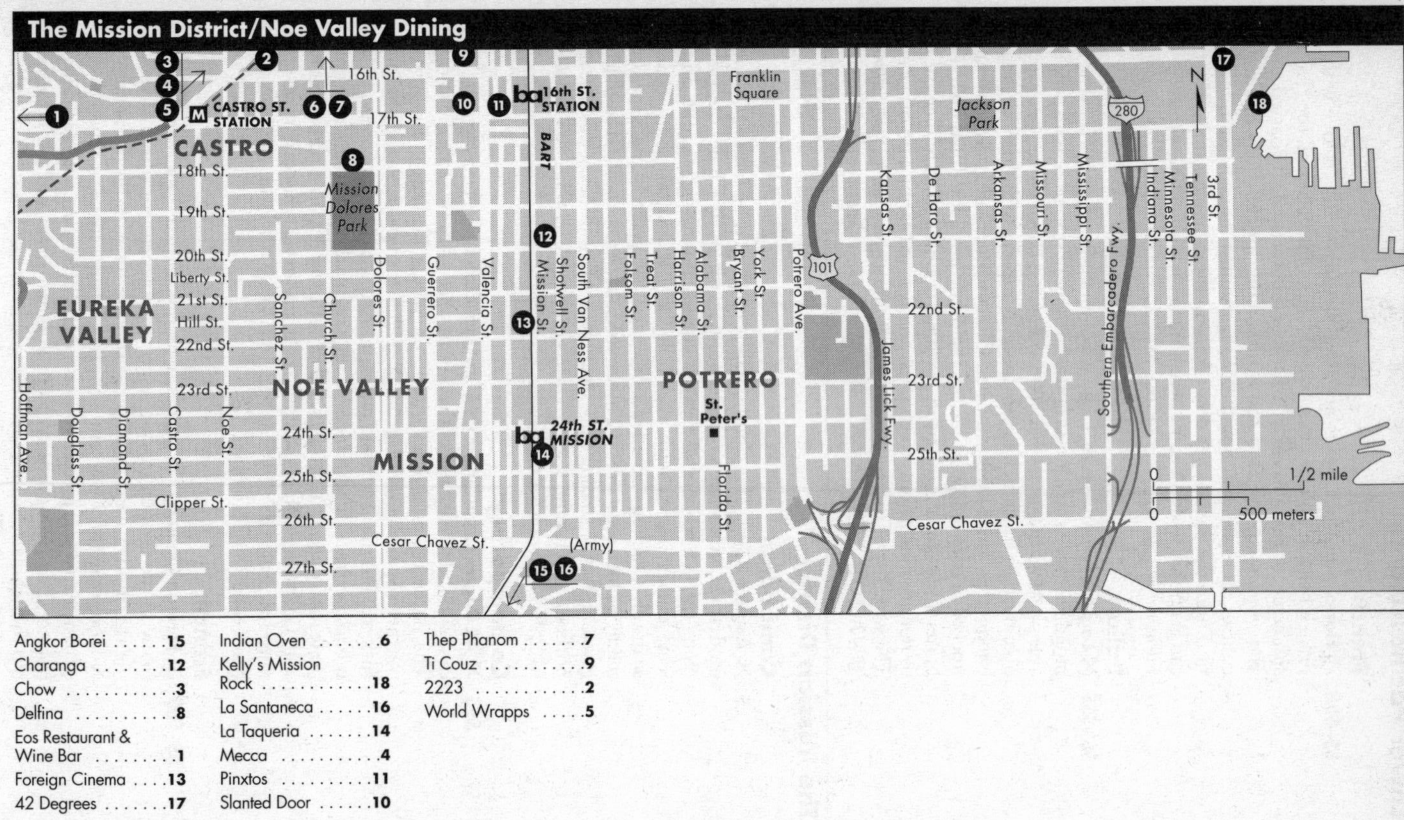
The Mission District/Noe Valley Dining
16th St.
CASTRO ST. STATION
17th St.
16th ST. STATION
Franklin Square
Jackson Park
280
N
CASTRO
18th St.
Mission Dolores Park
BART
3rd St.
Tennessee St.
Minnesota St.
Indiana St.
Mississippi St.
Missouri St.
Arkansas St.
De Haro St.
Kansas St.
19th St.
20th St.
Liberty St.
21st St.
Hill St.
22nd St.
EUREKA VALLEY
Sanchez St.
Church St.
Dolores St.
Guerrero St.
Valencia St.
Mission St.
Shotwell St.
South Van Ness Ave.
Folsom St.
Treat St.
Harrison St.
Alabama St.
Bryant St.
York St.
Potrero Ave.
101
22nd St.
Southern Embarcadero Fwy.
23rd St.
NOE VALLEY
POTRERO
St. Peter's
23rd St.
James Lick Fwy.
Hoffman Ave.
Douglass St.
Diamond St.
Castro St.
Noe St.
24th St.
24th ST. MISSION
MISSION
25th St.
25th St.
Florida St.
0
1/2 mile
0
500 meters
Clipper St.
26th St.
Cesar Chavez St.
(Army)
Cesar Chavez St.
27th St.
Angkor Borei 15
Charanga 12
Chow 3
Delfina 8
Eos Restaurant &
Wine Bar 1
Foreign Cinema 13
42 Degrees 17
Indian Oven 6
Kelly's Mission
Rock 18
La Santaneca 16
La Taqueria 14
Mecca 4
Pinxtos 11
Slanted Door 10
Thep Phanom 7
Ti Couz 9
2223 2
World Wrapps 5

$–$$ ✕ **Ti Couz.** Big, thin buckwheat crepes just like you find in Brittany are the specialty here, filled with everything from savory ham and Gruyère cheese to bittersweet chocolate. Despite its doubling in size in 1999, the blue-and-white dining room is always crowded. With the expansion came the introduction of two bars, one serving raw seafood and one serving mixed drinks. Still, the best beverage to sip in this Gallic spot is French hard cider served in classic pottery bowls. ✉ *3108 16th St.,* ☎ *415/252–7373. MC, V.*

Italian

$$–$$$ ★ ✕ **Delfina.** Although noisy and outfitted with benches and chairs that ensure neighborhood chiropractors a sure supply of new clients, Delfina is always hopping. Indeed, within several months of opening in 1999, success forced chef-owner Craig Stoll to take over a neighboring storefront to accommodate the throngs. The loyal crowd comes for the simple, yet exquisite Italian fare: grilled sardines, bitter greens tossed with walnuts and pancetta, halibut riding atop olives and braised fennel, and a wonderful tart made with puckery but sweet Meyer lemons. ✉ *3621 18th St.,* ☎ *415/552–4055. MC, V. No lunch.*

Latin

$–$$ ✕ **Charanga.** Cozy and lively, this neighborhood tapas restaurant, named for a Cuban salsa style that relies on flute and violins, serves an eclectic mix of small plates, from mushrooms cooked with garlic and sherry to *patatas bravas* (twice-fried potatoes with a roasted-tomato sauce), to ceviche. Asian influences show up on this Latin table as well, in such dishes as shrimp and calamari with coconut rice and ginger sauce. The small dining room, with its walls of exposed brick and soothing green, is a friendly, fun place to eat and socialize. Order a pitcher of sangria and enjoy yourself. ✉ *2351 Mission St.,* ☎ *415/282–1813. Reservations not accepted. MC, V. Closed Sun. and Mon. No lunch.*

Mexican

$ ✕ **La Taqueria.** Although there are a number of taquerias in the Mission, this attractive spot, with its arched exterior and modest interior, is one of the oldest and finest. The tacos are superb: a pair of warm corn tortillas topped with your choice of meat—*carne asada* (grilled steak) and *carnitas* (slowly cooked pork) are favorites—and a spoonful of perfectly fresh salsa. Big appetites may want to try one of the burritos, a large flour tortilla wrapped around hearty spoonfuls of meat, rice, beans, and salsa. Chase your chili-laced meal with a cooling *agua fresca* (fresh fruit cooler) of watermelon or pineapple. ✉ *2889 Mission St.,* ☎ *415/285–7117. No credit cards.*

Spanish

$$ ✕ **Pintxos.** A big exhibition kitchen, distressed tabletops, blue and yellow halogen lights, sea-blue tiles, wooden floors, and a chef from Barcelona set the tone here, as do small plates of seafood-stuffed red peppers in a pool of squid ink, roasted peppers and eggplant with anchovies and olives, and sweetbreads in sherry. Among the big plates are escabèche of rabbit and pork loin with apples. ✉ *557 Valencia St.,* ☎ *415/565–0207. MC, V. Closed Sun. No lunch Sat.*

Vietnamese

$$ ✕ **Slanted Door.** Behind the canted facade of this trendy north Mission restaurant, you'll find what owner Charles Phan describes as "real Vietnamese home cooking." There are fresh spring rolls packed with rice noodles, pork, shrimp, and pungent mint leaves, and fried vegetarian imperial rolls concealing bean thread noodles, cabbage, and taro. Five-spice chicken, green papaya salad, and a special of

steamed sea bass fillet are among the best dishes. ✉ *584 Valencia St.,* ☎ *415/861-8032. MC, V. Closed Mon.*

Nob Hill

French

$$$$ ★ ✕ **Ritz-Carlton Dining Room and Terrace.** There are two distinctly different places to eat in this neoclassic Nob Hill showplace. The Dining Room is formal and elegant and has a harpist playing. It serves only three- to five-course dinners, priced by the course, not by the item. The Terrace, a cheerful, informal spot with a large garden patio for outdoor dining, serves breakfast, lunch, and dinner. In the Dining Room executive chef Sylvain Portay, who was previously chef de cuisine at New York's Le Cirque, turns out an urbane seasonal French menu—squab with foie gras, lobster salad with caviar cream, rabbit stuffed with herbs, and a dreamy chocolate soufflé. ✉ *600 Stockton St.,* ☎ *415/296-7465. AE, D, DC, MC, V. Closed Sun. No lunch.*

North Beach

American

$$$ ✕ **Bix.** In a historic building that was an assay office in gold rush days, this old-fashioned supper club was the brainchild of the owners of Fog City Diner. Bix is reminiscent of a theater, with a bustling bar—memorable martinis and generous gin fizzes—and dining tables downstairs and banquettes on the balcony. The menu offers contemporary renditions of classic American fare, from Waldorf salad to bananas Foster. There's live music in the evening. ✉ *56 Gold St.,* ☎ *415/433-6300. AE, D, DC, MC, V. No lunch weekends.*

Contemporary

$$-$$$ ✕ **Black Cat.** The menu at this combination restaurant and jazz lounge, the latter called the Blue Bar, is made up of dishes that reflect the city's ethnic diversity. You'll find the Wharf's shellfish soups and sand dabs with tartar sauce, North Beach's pastas, Chinatown's roast duck and chow mein, and the Barbary Coast's chops and grills here. The name is taken from a famous San Francisco café-bar, a bohemian hangout for everyone from artists to trade unionists from the 1930s to the 1960s. The ambience is a spirited one, with live jazz and a tempting bar menu—salt-and-pepper mixed fried seafood, *fritto misto* of artichokes and mushrooms—served up until the wee hours in the seriously blue lounge. ✉ *501 Broadway,* ☎ *415/981-2233. AE, DC, MC, V.*

$$ ✕ **Enrico's Sidewalk Café.** For years this historic North Beach hangout was more a drinking spot than a dining destination, but a reliable kitchen has changed all that. Diners regularly tuck into the Caesar salad, thin-crust pizzas, steamed mussels, thick, juicy hamburgers, and nicely tossed pastas and grilled fish, while gently swaying to first-rate live music. Grazers will be happy to find a slew of eclectic tapas, from smoked salmon bruschetta to fried oysters. ✉ *504 Broadway,* ☎ *415/982-6223. AE, DC, MC, V.*

Italian

$$-$$$ ★ ✕ **Rose Pistola.** Chef-owner Reed Hearon's popular 130-seat spot draws huge crowds. The name honors one of North Beach's most revered barkeeps, and the food celebrates the neighborhood's Ligurian roots. A wide assortment of small cold and hot antipasti—roasted peppers, house-cured fish, fava beans and pecorino cheese, crostini topped with cheese, arugula, and figs—and pizzas from the wood-burning oven are favorites, as is the classic San Francisco seafood stew called cioppino. A large and inviting bar area opens onto the sidewalk, and an immense exhibition kitchen lets customers keep an eye on their or-

ders. ✉ *532 Columbus Ave.,* ☎ *415/399–0499. Reservations essential. AE, MC, V.*

$ ✕ **L'Osteria del Forno.** An Italian-speaking staff, a small, unpretentious dining area, and irresistible aromas drifting from the open kitchen make customers who pass through the door of this modest storefront operation feel as if they've just stumbled into Italy. The kitchen produces small plates of simply cooked vegetables, a few baked pastas, a roast of the day, creamy polenta, and wonderful thin-crust pizzas—including a memorable "white" pie topped with porcini mushrooms and mozzarella. ✉ *519 Columbus Ave.,* ☎ *415/982–1124. Reservations not accepted. No credit cards. Closed Tues.*

Mediterranean

$$$ ✕ **Moose's.** Restaurateur Ed Moose is well known in San Francisco, having run another popular North Beach spot before he opened this high-traffic dining room a decade ago. Politicians and media types followed him from his former digs, making celebrity sightings a regular sport here. In 1997, Brian Whitmer, who has done stints at Montrachet in New York and Montrio in Carmel, joined Moose's as executive chef and managing partner, introducing a Mediterranean menu with heavy French, Italian, and Californian accents. Among his popular creations are risotto with wild mushrooms and sturgeon wrapped in pancetta. The surroundings are classic and comfortable, with views of Washington Square and Russian Hill. ✉ *1652 Stockton St.,* ☎ *415/989–7800. Reservations essential. AE, DC, MC, V. No lunch Mon.–Wed.*

Middle Eastern

$$ ✕ **Maykadeh.** Although it sits in the middle of a decidedly Italian neighborhood, this authentic Persian restaurant serves a large following of faithful customers. Lamb dishes with rice are the specialties, served in a setting so elegant that the modest check comes as a surprise. The chicken, lamb, and beef kabobs and the *chelo* (Persian pilaf) are popular choices. Anyone looking for a hearty, traditional plate should order *ghorme sabzee,* lamb shank braised with onions, garlic, leeks, red beans, and a bouquet of Middle Eastern spices. ✉ *470 Green St.,* ☎ *415/362–8286. MC, V.*

Northern Waterfront

Seafood

$$ ✕ **McCormick & Kuleto's.** This seafood emporium in Ghirardelli Square is a visitor's dream come true: a fabulous view of the bay from every seat in the house; an Old San Francisco atmosphere; and dozens of varieties of fish and shellfish prepared in scores of globe-circling ways, from tacos, pot stickers, and fish cakes to grills, pastas, and stew. The food has its ups and downs—stick with the simplest preparations, such as oysters on the half shell and grilled fish—but even on foggy days you can count on the view. ✉ *Ghirardelli Sq. at Beach and Larkin Sts.,* ☎ *415/929–1730. AE, D, DC, MC, V.*

Richmond District

Chinese

$$–$$$ ✕ **Parc Hong Kong Restaurant.** The name has changed and so has the owner, but this upmarket Cantonese restaurant has the same chef and staff that made it a Richmond District legend known for serving such classy plates as smoked black cod and Peking duck. The kitchen is celebrated for its seafood, which is plucked straight from tanks; in the cool months, Dungeness crab and Maine lobster are sometimes priced to sell. Chefs here keep up with whatever is hot in Hong Kong eateries, so check with the generally genial waiters to find out what's new on the menu. ✉ *5322 Geary Blvd.,* ☎ *415/668–8998. AE, D, DC, MC, V.*

$–$$ ★ ✕ **Ton Kiang.** The lightly seasoned Hakka cuisine of southern China, rarely found in this country, was introduced to San Francisco at this restaurant, with such regional specialties as salt-baked chicken, braised stuffed bean curd, delicate fish and beef balls, and casseroles of meat and seafood cooked in clay pots. Don't overlook the seafood offerings here—salt-and-pepper squid or shrimp, braised catfish, or stir-fried crab, for example. The dim sum is arguably the finest in the city; especially noteworthy are the dumplings stuffed with shark's fin. ✉ *5821 Geary Blvd.,* ☎ *415/387–8273. MC, V.*

Japanese

$$–$$$ ✕ **Kabuto Sushi.** For one of the most spectacular acts in town, head down Geary Boulevard past Japantown to tiny Kabuto. Here, behind the sushi counter, master chef Sachio Kojima has been flashing his knives for nearly two decades, serving up everything from buttery yellow fin tuna to perfectly fresh raw shrimp to golden sea urchin on pads of pearly rice. In addition to exceptional sushi and sashimi, traditional Japanese dinners are served in the adjoining dining room. For an authentic experience, request tatami seating in the shoji-screened area. Be sure to consider the excellent selection of sakes. ✉ *5116 Geary Blvd.,* ☎ *415/752–5652. MC, V. Closed Mon. No lunch.*

Russian

$–$$ ✕ **Katia's.** This bright Richmond District gem offers Russian food with considerable flair at remarkably reasonable prices. Try the borscht, a dollop of sour cream topping a mélange of beets, cabbage, and other vegetables. Small plates of smoked salmon and blini, marinated mushrooms, and meat- or vegetable-filled piroshki are also wonderful ways to start a meal, and light chicken or potato cutlets or delicate *pelmeni* (small meat-filled dumplings in broth) are fine main courses. Save room for a meringue drizzled with berry sauce or a flaky napoleon. ✉ *600 5th Ave.,* ☎ *415/668–9292. AE, DC, MC, V. Closed Mon.*

Singaporean

$–$$ ✕ **Straits Café.** This highly popular restaurant serves the unique fare of Singapore, a cuisine that combines the culinary traditions of China, India, and the Malay archipelago. That exotic mix translates into complex curries, stir-fried seafood, chewy Indian breads, fragrant satays, and seafood noodle soups. The handsome dining room includes one wall that re-creates the old shop-house fronts of Singapore. ✉ *3300 Geary Blvd.,* ☎ *415/668–1783. AE, MC, V.*

Vietnamese

$–$$ ✕ **Le Soleil.** The food of Vietnam is the specialty of this pastel, light-filled restaurant in the heart of Inner Richmond. An eye-catching painting of Saigon hangs on one wall, and a large aquarium of tropical fish adds to the tranquil mood. The kitchen prepares traditional dishes from every part of the country. Try the excellent raw-beef salad; crisp, flavorful spring rolls; a simple stir-fry of chicken and aromatic fresh basil leaves; or large prawns simmered in a clay pot. ✉ *133 Clement St.,* ☎ *415/668–4848. MC, V.*

Russian Hill

French

$$$$ ★ ✕ **La Folie.** Long a favorite of dedicated Francophiles, this small, terribly Parisian establishment is a gem. The surroundings are truly lovely, but the food is the true star here, especially the five-course discovery menu that allows a sample of such rarified mouthfuls as lobster salad

with a mango vinaigrette and quail with white truffles. Much of the food is edible art—whimsical presentations in the form of savory terrines, *galettes* (flat, round cakes), and napoleons—or such elegant accompaniments as bone-marrow flan. The exquisite fare and professional service come at a hefty price, so save this special place for a very special occasion. ✉ *2316 Polk St.,* ☎ *415/776–5577. Reservations essential. AE, D, DC, MC, V. Closed Sun. No lunch.*

Italian

$$$ ✕ **Acquerello.** This elegant restaurant—white tablecloths, fresh flowers, exquisite china—is one of the most romantic spots in town. Both the service and the food are exemplary, and the menu covers the full range of Italian cuisine. The gnocchi and tortellini are memorable, as are the fish dishes. Chef Suzette Gresham's fine creations include a first course of squab paired with greens and pine nuts, and a main of beef fillet stuffed with prosciutto and Parmesan cheese. ✉ *1722 Sacramento St.,* ☎ *415/567–5432. AE, D, DC, MC, V. Closed Sun. and Mon. No lunch.*

Spanish

$$ ✕ **Zarzuela.** Until the mid-'90s San Francisco lacked a great tapas restaurant—but Spanish-born chef Lucas Gasco changed all that when he and partner Andy Debanne opened their charming Zarzuela. The small, crowded storefront serves nearly 40 different hot and cold tapas plus some dozen main courses. There is a tapa to suit every palate, from poached octopus atop new potatoes and hot garlic-flecked shrimp to slabs of manchego cheese with paper-thin slices of serrano ham. Hop a cable car to get here, as parking is nightmarish. ✉ *2000 Hyde St.,* ☎ *415/346–0800. Reservations not accepted. D, MC, V. Closed Sun.*

Steak

$$$ ★ ✕ **Harris'.** Ann Harris knows her beef. She grew up on a Texas cattle ranch and was married to the late Jack Harris of Harris Ranch fame. In her own large, New York–style restaurant she serves some of the best dry-aged steaks in town, but don't overlook the starter of spinach salad or the entrée of calves' liver with onions and bacon. Be sure to include a side of the fine creamed spinach. If you're a martini drinker, take this opportunity to enjoy an artful example of the cocktail. ✉ *2100 Van Ness Ave.,* ☎ *415/673–1888. AE, D, DC, MC, V. No lunch.*

South of Market

American

$ ✕ **Mo's Grill.** The term "burger" takes on new meaning at Mo's. Located in the top level of the Yerba Buena Gardens art complex, this eatery is devoted to what is arguably America's favorite food, and it dresses it up in a variety of ways: with Monterey Jack and avocado, with apple-smoked bacon, with sautéed mushrooms, with cheese and chilies, and more. But beef burgers—freshly ground daily and hand-formed—are not the only story here. Salmon, venison, buffalo, lamb, and turkey burgers are also cooked over the volcanic-rock grill, and sides of fries or onion rings fill out the plates deliciously. ✉ *772 Folsom St.,* ☎ *415/957–3779. MC, V.*

Contemporary

$$$$ ★ ✕ **Fifth Floor.** San Franciscans began fighting for tables at this topflight hotel dining room within days of its opening in 1999. And chef George Morrone's elegant, sophisticated, visually stunning plates are the reason why. The 75-seat room is done in dark wood and zebra-striped carpeting, and such exquisite dishes as seared tuna with foie gras and medallions of beef and lamb in a pastry crust with a trio of vegetables purees are served. There's even ice cream made to order—yes, the ma-

chine churns out a creamy, cool, rich serving for one. ✉ *Palomar Hotel, 12 Fourth St.,* ☏ *415/348–1555. Reservations essential. AE, DC, MC, V. Closed Sun. No lunch.*

$$$ ★ ✕ **Hawthorne Lane.** In 1995 Anne and David Gingrass, of Postrio fame (☞ Union Square, *below*), joined the booming bevy of SoMa eateries with this instantly popular establishment on a quiet alley a block or so from the Moscone Center and the Museum of Modern Art. At the tables in the large, high-ceiling bar, you can order a selection of irresistible small plates—Thai-style squid, skewers of grilled chicken, and tempura-battered green beans with mustard sauce, plus anything on the full menu. Patrons in the somewhat formal, light-flooded dining room engage in more serious eating, from perfectly seared foie gras to grilled quail on scalloped potatoes, all turned out with Mediterranean and Asian touches. ✉ *22 Hawthorne St.,* ☏ *415/777–9779. Reservations essential. D, DC, MC, V. No lunch weekends.*

French

$$–$$$ ✕ **Bizou.** Chef Loretta Keller serves a distinctive French country menu at this comfortable corner bistro, the name of which translates as "kiss." Partisans of her rustic cooking cite the thin, crisp pizza topped with caramelized onions, fried snap beans with aioli or fig sauce, and skate panfried in brown butter as evidence of her talents. The space itself is small and unpretentious. Outsized windows mean it's also sunny and bright. ✉ *598 4th St.,* ☏ *415/543–2222. AE, MC, V. Closed Sun. No lunch Sat.*

$$–$$$ ★ ✕ **Fringale.** The bright yellow paint on this small, dazzling bistro stands out like a beacon on an otherwise bleak industrial street, attracting a well-dressed clientele. They come for the reasonably priced French-Basque–inspired creations of Biarritz-born chef Gerald Hirigoyen, whose classic *frisées aux lardons* (curly salad greens with crisp bacon cubes and a poached egg), steak frites, duck confit with tiny French lentils, and flaky apple tart are hallmarks of the regularly changing menu. ✉ *570 4th St.,* ☏ *415/543–0573. Reservations essential. AE, MC, V. Closed Sun. No lunch Sat.*

$$ ✕ **South Park Café.** This utterly Parisian spot is open from early morning for your caffe latte to late at night for a wedge of fruit tart or a flute of champagne. No place in the City of Light itself serves a more authentic steak frites than this warm, sometimes clamorous spot overlooking a grassy square. A notable first-course is the salad greens with baked goat cheese. For an entrée try the *boudin noir* (black sausage) with sautéed apples or roast chicken with thin, crisp fries. ✉ *108 South Park, at Bryant St.,* ☏ *415/495–7275. MC, V. Closed Sun. No lunch Sat.*

Mediterranean

$$–$$$ ★ ✕ **LuLu.** Since its opening day in 1993, a seat at this boisterous restaurant has been one of the hottest tickets in town. The food, under the watchful eye of executive chef Jody Denton, is satisfyingly uncomplicated and delectable. Under the high barrel-vaulted ceiling, beside a large open kitchen, diners feast on sizzling mussels roasted in an iron skillet, plus pizzas, pastas, and wood-roasted poultry, meats, and shellfish. Sharing dishes is the custom here. The café that adjoins the restaurant on one side serves food until late at night. ✉ *816 Folsom St.,* ☏ *415/495–5775. Reservations essential. AE, DC, MC, V.*

Union Square

Contemporary

$$$–$$$$ ✕ **Postrio.** There's always a chance to catch a glimpse of some celebrity here, including Postrio's owner, superchef Wolfgang Puck, who periodically commutes from Los Angeles to make an appearance in the restau-

rant's open kitchen. A stunning three-level bar and dining area is highlighted by palm trees and museum-quality contemporary paintings. Attire is formal. The food is Puckish Californian with Mediterranean and Asian overtones—Chinese roast duck with mango sauce, house-cured salmon on a giant blini—and the desserts, such as chocolate soufflé cake with white chocolate ice cream, are irresistible. Substantial breakfast and bar menus (with great pizza) can be found here as well. ✉ *545 Post St.,* ☎ *415/776–7825. Reservations essential. AE, D, DC, MC, V.*

$$$ ✕ **Oritalia.** For many years, Oritalia—the name is a blend of the Orient and Italy—was a small, highly regarded restaurant in Lower Pacific Heights. In the late '90s it moved downtown, to a much larger space in the Juliana Hotel. The burnt orange dining room, with silk-clad chandeliers, ample booths, and carefully chosen Asian artifacts, is a handsome site for the menu of unusual dishes. For example, roast chicken with Asian greens is served with polenta-stuffed ravioli, while seared ahi tuna arrives with a lemony risotto. Steamed mussels in coconut sauce and veal carpaccio with ginger-tomato confit are two of the intriguing starters. Desserts are especially imaginative, with such luscious concoctions as a caramel and chocolate tower built from chocolate ganache and caramel cream. ✉ *586 Bush St.,* ☎ *415/782–8122. AE, DC, MC, V. No lunch.*

$$–$$$ ✕ **Grand Café.** In the heart of the theater district, this inviting combination dining room and bar is a magnet for folks seeking everything from an early morning breakfast to a late-night snack. The Californian-French menu served in the dining room includes such crowd pleasers as duck confit and slow-braised lamb shanks, while the bar serves hearty sandwiches and thin-crust pizzas. The dramatic and somewhat imposing dining room, formerly a hotel ballroom, is decorated with fanciful sculptures of stylized human figures, chandeliers, and eight murals that evoke such early 20th-century styles as expressionism and fauvism. ✉ *Hotel Monaco, 501 Geary St.,* ☎ *415/292–0101. AE, D, DC, MC, V.*

French

$$$$ ✕ **Fleur de Lys.** The creative cooking of French chef-partner Hubert Keller has brought every conceivable culinary award to this romantic spot, which some consider the best French restaurant in town. The menu changes constantly, but such dishes as seared foie gras, truffled vichyssoise, and venison medallions with tender braised greens are Keller hallmarks. Perfectly smooth service adds to the overall enjoyment of eating here. The elaborately canopied dining room is reminiscent of a sheikh's tent. ✉ *777 Sutter St.,* ☎ *415/673–7779. Reservations essential. Jacket required. AE, DC, MC, V. Closed Sun. No lunch.*

$$$$ ✕ **Masa's.** Julian Serrano headed up the kitchen at this pretty, flower-filled dining spot in the Vintage Court hotel for more than a dozen years, carrying on the tradition of the restaurant's late founder, Masa Kobayashi. In 1998, the torch was passed to Chad Callahan, who had served as the number two chef for several years. Most regulars agree that Callahan has made this celebrated food temple his own, in a style, although somewhat lightened, that they have come to expect. Dinners are prix fixe, with two menus offered, a four-course menu du jour and a five-course menu, both laced with truffles and foie gras and both priced at a king's ransom. ✉ *648 Bush St.,* ☎ *415/989–7154. Reservations essential. Jacket and tie. AE, D, DC, MC, V. Closed Sun. and Mon. No lunch.*

Italian

$$–$$$ ✕ **Scala's Bistro.** Smart leather-and-wood booths, an extravagant mural along one wall, and an appealing menu of Italian plates make this one of downtown's most attractive destinations. A large open kitchen stands at the rear of the fashionable dining room, where regulars and out-of-town visitors alike sit down to breakfast, lunch, and dinner. Grilled Portobello mushrooms and a tower of fried calamari or zucchini are among the favorite antipasti, and the pastas and grilled meats are satisfying. ✉ *432 Powell St.,* ☎ *415/395–8555. AE, D, DC, MC, V.*

Seafood

$$$ ★ ✕ **Farallon.** Outfitted with sculpted purple-and-pink jellyfish lamps, kelp-covered columns, sea urchin chandeliers, and seashell covered walls, this swanky Pat Kuleto–designed restaurant is loaded with style *and* customers. Chef Mark Franz, who gained his fame at Stars, cooks up exquisite seafood that draws serious diners from coast to coast. Such showy concoctions as spot prawns, scallops, and lobster suspended in a pyramid of aspic, and corn ravioli with truffles and foie gras appear on the regularly shifting menu. ✉ *450 Post St.,* ☎ *415/956–6969. AE, DC, MC, V. No lunch Sun.*

Vietnamese

$$–$$$ ✕ **Le Colonial.** Until the mid-'90s, Trader Vic's, a well-known Polynesian-inspired haunt of the city's social elite, occupied this restaurant. In 1998, Le Colonial refurbished the space—stamped tin ceiling, period photographs, slow-moving fans, tropical plants—creating a 1920s French colonial setting in which to serve its upscale Vietnamese food. The space still draws the local blue bloods, this time for its spring rolls, creamy coconut soup, steamed sea bass, coconut curry prawns, and sticky rice in a lotus leaf. Upstairs, a suave lounge with couches is the ideal place to sip a cocktail before dinner. ✉ *20 Cosmo Pl.,* ☎ *415/931–3600. AE, MC, V. Closed Sun. No lunch Sat.*

LODGING

Revised by Andy Moore

Few cities in the United States can rival San Francisco's variety in lodging. There are plush hotels ranked among the finest in the world, renovated older buildings with a European flair, and the popular chain hotels found in most American cities. One of the brightest spots in the lodging picture is the proliferation of small bed-and-breakfasts housed in elegant Victorian edifices, where evening hors d'oeuvres and wine service are common practice. Another trend is the growing number of ultradeluxe modern hotels, such as the Radisson Miyako, Hotel Nikko, and the Mandarin Oriental, which specialize in attentive Asian-style hospitality.

San Francisco hotel prices may come as a not-so-pleasant surprise. Weekend rates for double rooms start at about $75 but average about $165 per night citywide. The good news is that discounts are not hard to come by. The **San Francisco Convention and Visitors Bureau** (☎ 415/391–2000) publishes a free lodging guide with a map and listings of San Francisco and Bay Area hotels. **San Francisco Reservations** (☎ 800/677–1500) handles advance reservations at more than 220 Bay Area hotels.

CATEGORY	COST*
$$$$	over $300
$$$	$200–$300
$$	$100–$200
$	under $100

**All prices are for a standard double room, excluding 14% tax.*

Union Square/Downtown

$$$$ ★ 🏨 **Campton Place.** Behind a simple brownstone facade with a white awning, in the heart of busy Union Square, quiet reigns. Highly attentive personal service—from unpacking assistance to nightly turndown—

begins the moment uniformed doormen greet guests outside the marble-floor lobby. Rooms, though a little smaller than those at other luxury hotels, are supremely elegant, with pear-wood-accented walls and maple armoires and desks. Room windows, some with window seats, overlook an atrium, which lends a cozy, residential feel. ✉ *340 Stockton St., 94108,* ☎ *415/781–5555 or 800/235–4300,* FAX *415/955–5536. 101 rooms, 9 suites. Restaurant, bar, in-room safes, minibars, no-smoking rooms, room service, dry cleaning, laundry service, concierge, business services, meeting rooms, parking (fee). AE, DC, MC, V.*

$$$$ **Hotel Nikko.** In every Nikko lobby on five continents is a fountain, intended as a gathering place where guests can relax and socialize. The rooms, some of the most handsome in the city, feature inlaid cherrywood furniture with clean, elegant lines; gold drapes; wheat-color wall coverings; and ingenious window shades, which screen the sun while allowing views of the city. Service throughout the hotel is attentive and sincere, and the staff is multilingual. Don't miss the excellent fifth-floor fitness facility ($6 fee), which has traditional *ofuros* (Japanese soaking tubs), a *kamaburo* (Japanese sauna), and a glass-enclosed swimming pool and whirlpool. Shiatsu massages are also available. ✉ *222 Mason St., 94102,* ☎ *415/394–1111 or 800/645–5687,* FAX *415/421–0455. 502 rooms, 22 suites. Restaurant, bar, sushi bar, in-room data ports, minibars, room service, indoor pool, beauty salon, Japanese baths, massage, sauna, exercise room, dry cleaning, laundry service, concierge, business services, meeting rooms, car rental, parking (fee). AE, D, DC, MC, V.*

$$$$ **Pan Pacific Hotel.** Exotic flower arrangements and elegant Asian touches set this business-oriented hotel apart from others. A graceful bronze sculpture Elbert Weinberg created for the hotel in 1988, *Joie de Danse,* encircles the fountain in the 21-story lobby atrium. Guest rooms, which have soft green and beige color schemes and black-and-gold quilted bedspreads with Asian block-print designs, feature elegant bathrooms lined with terra-cotta Portuguese marble. Complimentary personal valet service, a "flying pantry" (a room-service kitchen in an elevator), and a fleet of luxury cars that drop guests at nearby destinations free of charge add up to a pampering experience. ✉ *500 Post St., 94102,* ☎ *415/771–8600 or 800/327–8585,* FAX *415/398–0267. 311 rooms, 19 suites. Restaurant, bar, lobby lounge, in-room data ports, in-room safes, minibars, no-smoking floors, refrigerators, room service, exercise room, piano, dry cleaning, laundry service, concierge, business services, meeting rooms, parking (fee). AE, D, DC, MC, V.*

$$$–$$$$ **The Clift.** Towering over San Francisco's theater district is the venerable Clift. Its crisp, forest-green awnings and formal door service provide subtle hints of the elegance within. In the lobby, dark paneling and enormous chandeliers lend a note of grandeur. Rooms—some rich with dark woods and burgundies, others refreshingly pastel—all have large writing desks. The Art Deco Redwood Room, paneled with wood from a single 2,000-year-old tree, is popular for power breakfasts and, at the end of the working day, draws an upscale crowd for cocktails and dinner. ✉ *495 Geary St., 94102,* ☎ *415/775–4700 or 800/652–5438,* FAX *415/441–4621. 218 rooms, 108 suites. Restaurant, bar, in-room data ports, minibars, no-smoking floor, room service, exercise room, dry cleaning, laundry service, concierge, meeting rooms, parking (fee). AE, DC, MC, V.*

$$$–$$$$ **Westin St. Francis.** Guests as illustrious as Emperor Hirohito, Queen Elizabeth II, and many presidents, as well as countless convention and tour groups, have stayed here since it opened in 1904. No wonder; with an imposing facade, black-marble lobby, and gold-top columns, the St. Francis looks more like a great public building than a hotel. The effect is softened by the columns and exquisite woodwork of the Com-

Downtown San Francisco Lodging

The Abigail **21**
Adelaide Inn **48**
The Andrews **17**
The Archbishop's Mansion **19**
The Argent **69**
Bed and Breakfast Inn . . **10**
Bel-Aire Travelodge . . **2**
Bijou **65**
Campton Place **53**
Chancellor Hotel . . . **51**
The Clarion **76**
Clarion Bedford Hotel . . . **18**
The Clift **56**
Commodore International **43**
Coventry Motor Inn . . **5**
Cow Hollow Motor Inn and Suites **3**
El Drisco Hotel **13**
Embassy Suites San Francisco Airport—Burlingame **71**
The Fairmont Hotel . . **29**
Galleria Park **54**
Golden Gate Hotel **47**
Grant Plaza Hotel . . **41**
Harbor Court **38**
Hotel Bohème **28**
Hotel Del Sol **4**
Hotel Diva **57**
Hotel Majestic **15**
Hotel Milano **66**
Hotel Monaco **63**
Hotel Nikko **64**
Hotel Palomar **67**
Hotel Rex **46**
Hotel Sofitel–San Francisco Bay **72**
Hotel Triton **42**
The Huntington **30**
Hyatt at Fisherman's Wharf **24**
Hyatt Regency **37**
Hyatt Regency San Francisco Airport . . . **73**
Inn at the Opera . . . **22**

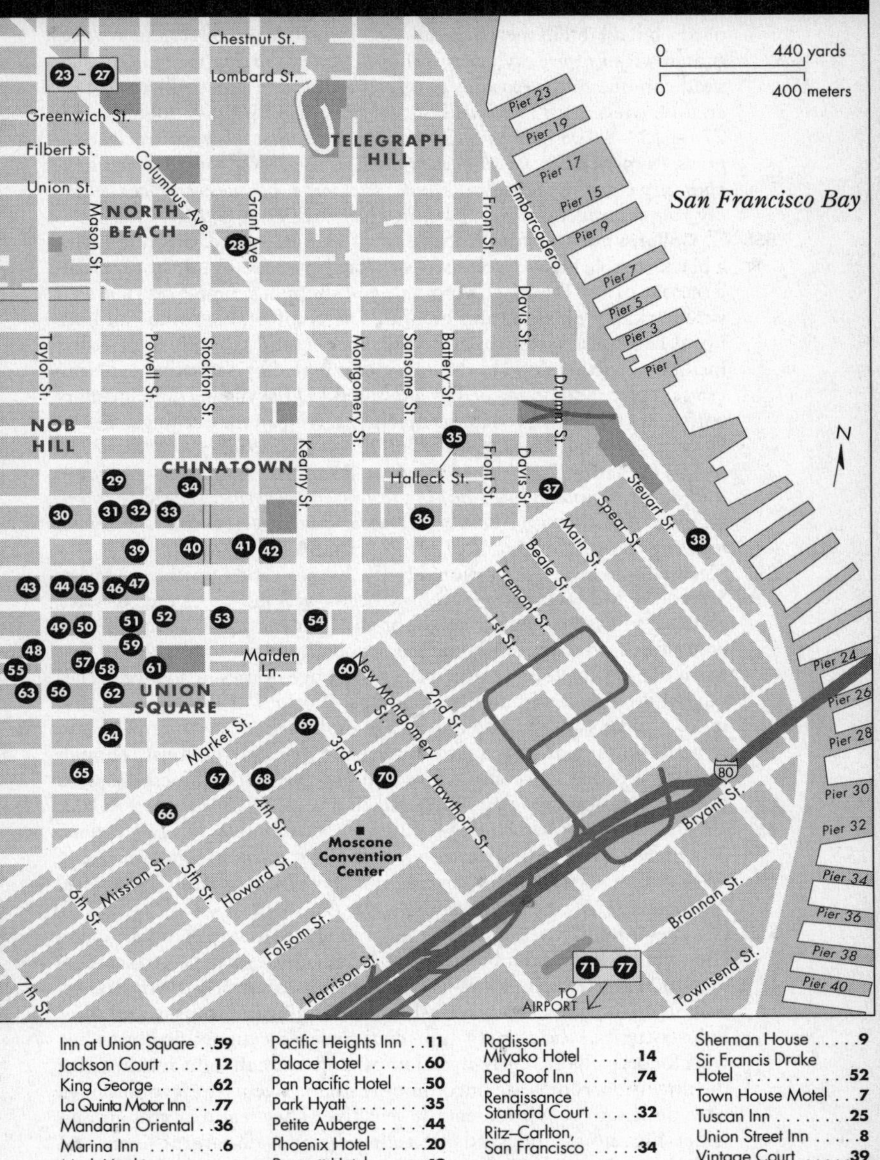

Inn at Union Square . . 59
Jackson Court 12
King George 62
La Quinta Motor Inn . . 77
Mandarin Oriental . . 36
Marina Inn 6
Mark Hopkins Inter-Continental . . . 31
Marriott at Fisherman's Wharf . 23
The Maxwell 58
Nob Hill Lambourne . . 40
Pacific Heights Inn . . 11
Palace Hotel 60
Pan Pacific Hotel . . . 50
Park Hyatt 35
Petite Auberge 44
Phoenix Hotel 20
Prescott Hotel 49
Presidio Travelodge . . 1
Radisson Hotel at Fisherman's Wharf 26
Radisson Miyako Hotel 14
Red Roof Inn 74
Renaissance Stanford Court 32
Ritz-Carlton, San Francisco 34
San Francisco Marriott 68
San Francisco Residence Club 33
San Remo 27
Shannon Court Hotel . 55
Sherman House 9
Sir Francis Drake Hotel 52
Town House Motel . . . 7
Tuscan Inn 25
Union Street Inn 8
Vintage Court 39
W San Francisco . . . 70
The Westin 75
Westin St. Francis . . 61
White Swan Inn . . . 45
York Hotel 16

pass Rose bar and restaurant, a romantic retreat from the bustle of Union Square. Many rooms in the original building are small by modern standards, but all retain their original Victorian-style moldings and are decorated with Empire-style furnishings. Even if you don't stay here, take a ride on one of the exterior glass elevators for a real thrill and an incredible view. ✉ *335 Powell St., 94102,* ☎ *415/397–7000,* FAX *415/774–0124. 1,108 rooms, 84 suites. 3 restaurants, 2 bars, in-room data ports, in-room safes, no-smoking floors, room service, health club, nightclub, dry cleaning, laundry service, concierge, business services, meeting rooms, travel services, parking (fee). AE, D, DC, MC, V.*

$$$ ★ **Galleria Park.** A few blocks east of Union Square, this hotel with a black-marble facade is close to the Chinatown Gate and Crocker Galleria, one of San Francisco's most elegant shopping complexes. The staff is remarkably pleasant and helpful. The comfortable rooms all have floral bedspreads, stylish striped wallpaper, and white furniture that includes a writing desk. In the lobby, dominated by a massive Art Nouveau fireplace and brightened by a restored 1911 skylight, complimentary coffee and tea are served in the mornings, wine in the evenings. ✉ *191 Sutter St., 94104,* ☎ *415/781–3060 or 800/792–9639; 800/792–9855 in CA,* FAX *415/433–4409. 169 rooms, 8 suites. 2 restaurants, in-room data ports, minibars, no-smoking floors, room service, exercise room, jogging, dry cleaning, laundry service, concierge, business services, meeting rooms, parking (fee). AE, D, DC, MC, V.*

$$$ ★ **Hotel Monaco.** Unquestionably the hippest hotel north of Market Street, the Monaco, with its yellow beaux-arts facade, stands in stark contrast to its more stately neighbor, the Clift (☞ *above*). The contrast continues inside, where a French inglenook fireplace climbs almost two stories above the lobby toward the three huge domes of a vaulted ceiling hand-painted with hot-air balloons, World War I–era planes, and miles of blue sky. The hotel hosts a complimentary evening wine and appetizer hour featuring a tarot reader and massage therapist. Though small, the rooms are comfortable and inviting, with Chinese-inspired armoires and high-back upholstered chairs. ✉ *501 Geary St., 94102,* ☎ *415/292–0100 or 800/214–4220,* FAX *415/292–0111. 181 rooms, 20 suites. Restaurant, bar, in-room data ports, in-room safes, minibars, no-smoking rooms, room service, spa, dry cleaning, laundry service, business services, parking (fee). AE, D, DC, MC, V.*

$$$ **Hotel Triton.** This just may be the zaniest place to stay in town. Guests enter via a whimsical lobby of three-leg furniture, star-pattern carpeting, and inverted gilt pillars—stylized spoofs of upside-down Roman columns. The hotel caters to fashion, entertainment, music, and film-industry types, who seem to appreciate the iridescent multicolor rooms with S-curve chairs, curly-neck lamps, and oddball light fixtures. On the downside, rooms are uncommonly small. Twenty-four rooms have been designated environmentally sensitive. They feature extra air and water filtration, biodegradable toiletries, and all-natural linens. ✉ *342 Grant Ave., 94108,* ☎ *415/394–0500 or 888/364–2622,* FAX *415/394–0555. 133 rooms, 7 suites. In-room data ports, minibars, no-smoking floors, exercise room, dry cleaning, laundry service, business services, meeting rooms, parking (fee). AE, D, MC, V.*

$$$ **Inn at Union Square.** With its tiny but captivating lobby with trompe l'oeil bookshelves painted on the walls, this small hotel feels like someone's home. The comfortable rooms, some decorated in old-world Georgian style with fireplaces, some in a lighter, more contemporary style, all include nice touches such as goose-down pillows, fresh flowers, and morning newspapers. Bathrooms have attractive granite vanities and massaging showerheads. Brass lion's-head door knockers are a unique detail. You're likely to see your fellow guests lounging by the wood-burning fireplaces found in each floor's tiny sitting area, where evening

wine and hors d'oeuvres are served. ✉ *440 Post St., 94102,* ☎ *415/397–3510 or 800/288–4346,* FAX *415/989–0529. 20 rooms, 10 suites. In-room data ports, parking (fee). AE, DC, MC, V.*

$$$ ★ **Prescott Hotel.** A gourmet's delight might be the best way to describe this plush hotel, thanks to its partnership with Wolfgang Puck's Postrio, one of San Francisco's best restaurants. Cuisine-conscious guests can order room service from the restaurant or dine at tables reserved for hotel guests—no small perk considering it can otherwise take months to get a reservation at Postrio. The Prescott's rooms, which vary only in size and shape, are traditional in style and decorated with striped wallpaper in shades of brown and blue; bathrooms have marble-top sinks and gold fixtures. There's a brick-and-wood fireplace in the hunting lodge–style living room. ✉ *545 Post St., 94102,* ☎ *415/563–0303 or 800/283–7322,* FAX *415/563–6831. 155 rooms, 9 suites. Restaurant, bar, lobby lounge, in-room data ports, minibars, no-smoking floors, room service, exercise room, concierge, business services, meeting rooms, parking (fee). AE, D, DC, MC, V.*

$$$ **Sir Francis Drake Hotel.** Beefeater-costumed doormen welcome you into the regal lobby of this 1928 landmark property, which has wrought-iron balustrades, chandeliers, and Italian marble. The guest rooms look neoclassical, with boldly striped fabrics and mahogany and cherrywood furniture. The hotel's surprisingly affordable restaurant, Scala's Bistro, serves excellent food in its dramatic though somewhat noisy bi-level dining room. ✉ *450 Powell St., 94102,* ☎ *415/392–7755 or 800/227–5480,* FAX *415/391–8719. 412 rooms, 5 suites. 2 restaurants, in-room data ports, minibars, no-smoking rooms, exercise room, nightclub, dry cleaning, laundry service, concierge, business services, meeting rooms, parking (fee). AE, D, DC, MC, V.*

$$–$$$ ★ **Hotel Rex.** Literary and artistic creativity are celebrated at the stylish Hotel Rex, where thousands of books, largely antiquarian, line the 1920s-style lobby. Original artwork adorns the walls, and the proprietors even host book readings and round-table discussions in the common areas, which are decorated in warm, rich tones. Upstairs, quotations from works by California writers are painted on the terra-cotta–color walls near the elevator landings. Good-size rooms have writing desks and lamps with whimsically hand-painted shades. Restored period furnishings upholstered in deep, rich hues evoke the spirit of 1920s salon society, but rooms also have modern amenities such as voice mail and CD players. ✉ *562 Sutter St., 94102,* ☎ *415/433–4434 or 800/433–4434,* FAX *415/433–3695. 92 rooms, 2 suites. Bar, lobby lounge, in-room data ports, minibars, no-smoking rooms, room service, dry cleaning, laundry service, concierge, parking (fee). AE, D, DC, MC, V.*

$$–$$$ **The Maxwell.** Behind dramatic black-and-red curtains, the Maxwell's lobby makes an impression with boldly patterned furniture in rich velvets and brocades. The hotel is handsome, stylish, and just a block from Union Square. Rooms have a clubby, retro feel and deep jewel tones, with classic Edward Hopper prints on the walls. Baths also sport a retro 1930s look with pedestal sinks with white porcelain faucet handles, but high-tech tools such as in-room computers make the Maxwell right up-to-date. ✉ *386 Geary St., 94102,* ☎ *415/986–2000 or 888/734–6299,* FAX *415/397–2447. 150 rooms, 3 suites. Restaurant, bar, in-room data ports, no-smoking rooms, room service, laundry service, concierge, parking (fee). AE, D, DC, MC, V.*

$$–$$$ **York Hotel.** Hitchcock fans may recognize the exterior of this reasonably priced, family-owned hotel four blocks west of Union Square. It's the building where Kim Novak stayed in *Vertigo*. Inside, the peach-stone facade and ornate, high-ceiling lobby give the hotel a touch of elegance. The moderate-size rooms—all with huge closets—are a tasteful mix of Mediterranean styles, with a terra-cotta, burgundy, and forest-green

color scheme. The Plush Room cabaret, where well-known entertainers perform four to five times a week, is the York's drawing card. This is perhaps the most gay-friendly of San Francisco's high-end hotels. ✉ *940 Sutter St., 94109,* ☎ *415/885–6800 or 800/808–9675,* FAX *415/885–2115. 91 rooms, 5 suites. Bar, in-room data ports, in-room safes, minibars, no-smoking floors, exercise room, nightclub, laundry service, concierge, business services, parking (fee). AE, D, DC, MC, V.*

$$ **The Andrews.** Two blocks west of Union Square, this Queen Anne–style abode with a gold-and-buff facade began its life in 1905 as the Sultan Turkish Baths. Today Victorian antique reproductions, old-fashioned flower curtains with lace sheers, iron bedsteads, and large closets more than make up for the diminutive size of guest rooms (the scrupulously clean bathrooms are even smaller). The buffet-style Continental breakfast, served on each floor, is complimentary. ✉ *624 Post St., 94109,* ☎ *415/563–6877 or 800/926–3739,* FAX *415/928–6919. 48 rooms. Restaurant, no-smoking floors, concierge, parking (fee). AE, DC, MC, V.*

$$ **Bijou.** With plush velvet upholstery and rich detailing, this hotel is a nostalgic tribute to 1930s cinema. The lobby's tiny theater, Le Petit Theatre Bijou, treats guests to screenings from the hotel's collection of 65 San Francisco–theme films from *The Maltese Falcon* to *What's Up Doc?* The smallish but cheerful rooms are decorated with black-and-white movie stills. For those who want to be in pictures, the handcrafted chrome ticket booth in the lobby offers a hot line with information on current San Francisco film shoots seeking extras. ✉ *111 Mason St., at Eddy St., 94102,* ☎ *415/771–1200 or 800/771–1022,* FAX *415/346–3196. 65 rooms. No-smoking rooms, laundry service, concierge, parking (fee). AE, D, DC, MC, V.*

$$ **Chancellor Hotel.** Built for the 1915 Panama Pacific International Exposition, the Chancellor was the tallest building in San Francisco when it opened. Although not as grand now as some of its neighbors, this busy hotel is one of the best buys on Union Square for visitors wanting comfort without extravagance. Floor-to-ceiling windows in the modest lobby overlook cable cars on Powell Street en route to nearby Union Square or Fisherman's Wharf. The moderate-size Edwardian-style rooms have high ceilings and blue, cream, and rose color schemes; deep bathtubs are a treat. Connecting rooms are available for families, and the Chancellor Café is a handy place for meals. ✉ *433 Powell St., 94102,* ☎ *415/362–2004 or 800/428–4748,* FAX *415/362–1403. 135 rooms, 2 suites. Restaurant, bar, in-room safes, no-smoking floors, room service, laundry service, concierge, car rental, parking (fee). AE, D, DC, MC, V.*

$$ **Clarion Bedford Hotel.** Guests pass under Art Nouveau arches carved with grapevines and birds to enter the bright yellow lobby of this handsome 1929 building. Avant-garde film posters from 1920s Russia adorn the walls. The light and airy rooms are decorated in yellow and peach with white furniture, canopied beds, and vibrant floral bedspreads. Most rooms in this 17-story property (it's the tallest on the block) have gorgeous bay and city views, but the baths are small. Business-class guest rooms feature special desk lighting and an ergonomic chair. ✉ *761 Post St., 94109,* ☎ *415/673–6040 or 800/227–5642,* FAX *415/563–6739. 137 rooms, 7 suites. Restaurant, bar, lobby lounge, in-room data ports, minibars, room service, dry cleaning, laundry service, parking (fee). AE, D, DC, MC, V.*

$$ **Commodore International.** Entering the lobby is like stepping onto the main deck of an ocean liner of yore: Neodeco chairs look like the backdrop for a film about transatlantic crossings; and steps away is the Titanic Café, where goldfish bowls and bathysphere-inspired lights add to the sea-cruise mood. The fairly large rooms with monster closets are painted in soft yellows and golds and decorated with photographs of San Francisco landmarks. If red is your color, you may find yourself glued to a seat in the hotel's Red Room, a startlingly scarlet cocktail lounge filled with well-dressed hipsters. ✉ *825 Sutter St., 94109,* ☎ *415/923–6800 or 800/338–6848,* FAX *415/923–6804. 112 rooms, 1 suite. Restaurant, in-room data ports, no-smoking rooms, nightclub, dry cleaning, laundry service, concierge, parking (fee). AE, D, MC, V.*

$$ **Hotel Diva.** A striking black-granite and layered green-glass facade beckons guests into the Diva's lobby, where a stylized 1920s ocean liner motif takes over. Nautical touches in the rooms include cobalt-blue carpets and brushed-steel headboards echoing the shape of ocean waves. Although the Diva's proximity to the Curran Theater attracts actors, musicians, and others of an artistic bent, the hotel is also popular with business travelers, who have free access to the compact business center, and families, who entertain themselves with the in-room Nintendo and VCRs. ✉ *440 Geary St., 94102,* ☎ *415/885–0200 or 800/553–1900,* FAX *415/346–6613. 88 rooms, 23 suites. Restaurant, in-room data ports, in-room safes, minibars, no-smoking floors, room service, in-room VCRs, exercise room, dry cleaning, laundry service, concierge, business services, meeting room, parking (fee). AE, D, DC, MC, V.*

$$ **King George.** The staff at the King George has prided itself on service and hospitality since the hotel's opening in 1914, when guest rooms started at $1 a night. Prices have remained relatively low compared to other hotels in the neighborhood. The front desk and concierge staff are adept at catering to their guests' every whim: they'll book anything from a Fisherman's Wharf tour to a dinner reservation. Rooms are compact but nicely furnished in classic English style, with walnut furniture and a royal-red and green color scheme. High tea at the Windsor Tearoom is an authentic English treat. ✉ *334 Mason St., 94102,* ☎ *415/781–5050 or 800/288–6005,* FAX *415/391–6976. 141 rooms, 1 suite. Tea shop, in-room data ports, in-room safes, no-smoking floors, dry cleaning, laundry service, concierge, business services, meeting rooms, parking (fee). AE, D, DC, MC, V.*

$$ **Petite Auberge.** The dozens of teddy bears in the reception area may seem a bit precious, but the rooms in this re-creation of a French country inn never stray past the mark. Rooms are small, each has a teddy bear, bright flowered wallpaper, an old-fashioned writing desk, and a much-needed armoire—there's little or no closet space. Most rooms have working fireplaces; the suite has a whirlpool tub. Afternoon tea, wine, and hors d'oeuvres are served in the lobby by the fire, and a full breakfast is included. The entire inn is no-smoking. ✉ *863 Bush St., 94108,* ☎ *415/928–6000 or 800/365–3004,* FAX *415/775–5717. 25 rooms, 1 suite. Breakfast room, parking (fee). AE, DC, MC, V.*

$$ **Shannon Court Hotel.** Passing through the elaborate wrought-iron and glass entrance into the marble-tile lobby of the Shannon Court evokes the old-world charm of turn-of-the-20th-century San Francisco. This hotel has some of the most spacious standard rooms in the Union Square area; many have sofa beds for families. Two of the luxury suites on the 16th floor have rooftop terraces with lofty city views. Complimentary morning coffee and afternoon tea and cookies are served in the lobby area. ✉ *550 Geary St., 94102,* ☎ *415/775–5000 or 800/228–8830,* FAX *415/928–6813. 168 rooms, 4 suites. Restaurant, bar, lobby lounge, no-smoking floor, refrigerators, dry cleaning, laundry service, concierge, parking (fee). AE, D, DC, MC, V.*

$$ **Vintage Court.** This bit of the Napa Valley just off Union Square has inviting rooms—some with sunny window seats, all with large writing desks—decorated with jade-and-rose floral fabrics. The Wine Country theme extends to the complimentary wine served nightly in front of the lobby fireplace, and a low-cost deluxe Continental break-

fast also adds to the congenial atmosphere. ✉ *650 Bush St., 94108,* ☎ *415/392–4666 or 800/654–1100,* FAX *415/433–4065. 107 rooms, 1 suite. Restaurant, bar, minibars, no-smoking floors, refrigerators, exercise room, parking (fee). AE, D, DC, MC, V.*

$$ **White Swan Inn.** A library with book-lined walls and a crackling fire is the heartbeat of the White Swan, and home-baked snacks and afternoon tea are served in the lounge, where comfortable chairs and sofas also invite lingering. Each of the good-size rooms in this wonderfully warm and inviting inn has a fireplace (there are 26 guest rooms and 30 fireplaces on the property), private bath, refrigerator, and reproduction Edwardian furniture. The breakfasts (included in the room rate) here are famous, and guests can purchase the inn's cookbook to try to duplicate their crab-and-cheese soufflé toasts, chocolate scones, or artichoke pesto puffs at home. ✉ *845 Bush St., 94108,* ☎ *415/775–1755 or 800/999–9570,* FAX *415/775–5717. 23 rooms, 3 suites. Breakfast room, in-room data ports, no-smoking floors, concierge, meeting rooms, parking (fee). AE, MC, V.*

$–$$ **Golden Gate Hotel.** Captain Nemo, a 25-pound black-and-white cat who must live very well indeed, serves as the unofficial doorman for this homey, family-run B&B three blocks northwest of Union Square. Built in 1913 as a hotel, the four-story Edwardian has a yellow-and-cream facade with black trim, and bay windows front and back. The original "birdcage" elevator lifts guests to hallways lined with historical photographs and guest rooms individually decorated with antiques, wicker pieces, and Laura Ashley bedding and curtains. ✉ *775 Bush St., 94108,* ☎ *415/392–3702 or 800/835–1118,* FAX *415/392–6202. 25 rooms, 14 with bath. Lobby lounge, no-smoking floor, parking (fee). AE, DC, MC, V.*

$ **Adelaide Inn.** The bedspreads at this quiet retreat may not match the drapes or carpets, and the floors may creak, but the rooms are sunny, clean, and remarkably cheap. Tucked away in an alley, the funky European-style pension hosts many guests from Germany, France, and Italy, making it fun to chat over complimentary coffee and rolls downstairs in the mornings. There are sinks in every room, but all baths (down the hall) are shared. ✉ *5 Isadora Duncan Ct., at Taylor St. between Geary and Post Sts., 94102,* ☎ *415/441–2474 or 415/441–2261,* FAX *415/441–0161. 18 rooms with shared bath. Breakfast room, in-room data ports. AE, MC, V.*

$ ★ **Grant Plaza Hotel.** One block in from the Chinatown Gate guarded by its famous stone lions, this hotel may seem worlds away from Union Square, yet it and the Financial District are only a stone's throw away. Amazingly low room rates for this part of town make the Grant Plaza a find for budget travelers wanting to look out their window at the exotic architecture and fascinating street life of Chinatown. The smallish rooms, all with private baths, are very clean and modern. Rooms on the top floor are newer, slightly brighter, and a bit more expensive; for a quieter stay ask for one in the back. All rooms have electronic locks, voice mail, and satellite TV. ✉ *465 Grant Ave., 94108,* ☎ *415/434–3883 or 800/472–6899,* FAX *415/434–3886. 71 rooms, 1 suite. Concierge, parking (fee). AE, DC, MC, V.*

Financial District

$$$$ ★ **Mandarin Oriental.** Since the Mandarin comprises the top 11 floors (38 to 48) of San Francisco's third-tallest building—the California Center—all rooms provide sweeping panoramic vistas of the city and beyond. The glass-enclosed sky bridges that connect the front and back towers of the hotel are almost as striking as the views. Rooms are decorated in light creamy yellow with black accents; those facing west fill

up quickly because of their dramatic views of the Golden Gate Bridge and the Pacific Ocean. And because the windows actually open, unlike in many modern buildings, you can hear the "ding ding" of the California Street cable cars down below as you peer miles into the scenic distance (they even provide binoculars). The Mandarin Rooms in each tower have extra-deep bathtubs right next to picture windows; enjoy a decadent bathing experience above the city with loofah sponges, plush robes, and silk slippers. ✉ *222 Sansome St., 94104,* ☎ *415/276–9888 or 800/622–0404,* FAX *415/433–0289. 154 rooms, 4 suites. Lobby lounge, in-room data ports, in-room safes, minibars, no-smoking floors, room service, exercise room, dry cleaning, laundry service, concierge, business services, meeting rooms, parking (fee). AE, D, DC, MC, V.*

$$$$ **Palace Hotel.** This landmark hotel—with a guest list that has included Thomas Edison, Amelia Earhart, Bing Crosby, and 10 American presidents—was the world's largest and most luxurious hotel when it opened in 1875. Totally rebuilt after the earthquake and fire of 1906 (which sent Italian opera star Enrico Caruso into the street wearing nothing but a towel and vowing never to return to San Francisco), today its historic splendor is best seen in the stunning entryway and the fabulous Belle Epoque Garden Court restaurant (☞ Financial District *in* Dining), with its graceful chandeliers and lead-glass ceiling. Rooms, with twice-daily maid service and nightly turndown, feature high ceilings, antique reproduction furnishings, and marble bathrooms with luxury bath products. The hotel's 20-yard indoor lap pool is the longest hotel pool in the city. ✉ *2 New Montgomery St., 94105,* ☎ *415/512–1111,* FAX *415/543–0671. 517 rooms, 33 suites. 3 restaurants, bar, room service, health club, laundry service, parking (fee). AE, D, DC, MC, V.*

$$$$ **Park Hyatt.** Contemporary in design but with a touch of old-world style, the Park Hyatt is a well-managed property across Battery Street from the Embarcadero Center. Convenient to the waterfront, downtown, and the South of Market area, the hotel's public areas feature large floral displays and fine artworks on the walls. The good-size rooms are decorated with Australian lacewood, polished granite, stylish furniture, and fresh flowers. Amenities include voice mail and Neutrogena toiletries. Fitness and TV buffs can watch the four TVs in the fitness center, wearing headphones receiving the four different audio channels. ✉ *333 Battery St., 94111,* ☎ *415/392–1234 or 800/492–8822,* FAX *415/421–2433. 323 rooms, 37 suites. Restaurant, 2 bars, in-room data ports, minibars, room service, exercise room, dry cleaning, laundry service, business services, parking (fee). AE, D, DC, MC, V.*

$$$–$$$$ ★ **Hyatt Regency.** The gray bunkerlike exterior of the Hyatt Regency, at the foot of Market Street, is an unlikely introduction to the spectacular 17-story atrium lobby within, with its full-size trees, running stream, and huge fountain. In addition to a plethora of meeting spaces, it has the Embarcadero Center, with more than 100 shops and restaurants, as its neighbor. Rooms, some with bay-view balconies and all with city or bay views, are decorated in deep gold, blue, and russet with blond wood furniture. ✉ *5 Embarcadero Center, 94111,* ☎ *415/788–1234 or 800/233–1234,* FAX *415/398–2567. 760 rooms, 45 suites. 2 restaurants, bar, lobby lounge, no-smoking floors, room service, exercise room, concierge, parking (fee). AE, D, DC, MC, V.*

$$$ ★ **Harbor Court.** Within shouting distance of the Bay Bridge and the hot South of Market area with its plentiful nightclubs and restaurants, this cozy hotel, formerly an Army/Navy YMCA, is noted for the exemplary service of its warm, friendly staff. Some guest rooms, with double sets of soundproof windows, overlook the bay; others face a dressed-up rooftop. Rooms are smallish but fancily decorated with partially canopied, plushly upholstered beds, tastefully faux-textured walls, and fine reproductions of late 19th-century nautical and nature prints. In the

evening complimentary wine is served in the cozy lounge, sometimes accompanied by live guitar. ✉ *165 Steuart St., 94105,* ☎ *415/882–1300 or 800/346–0555,* FAX *415/882–1313. 130 rooms, 1 suite. In-room data ports, minibars, no-smoking floors, room service, dry cleaning, laundry service, business services, parking (fee). AE, D, DC, MC, V.*

South of Market (SoMa)

$$$$ ★ **Hotel Palomar.** Famous "boutique hotel" trailblazer Bill Kimpton (Hotel Monaco) transformed the top five floors of the green-tiled and turreted 1908 Pacific Place Building into an urbane and luxurious oasis above the busiest part of the city. Guests enter under a glass-and-steel fan-shape canopy into a spare, modern lobby with a harlequin-pattern wooden floor and stylish gunmetal and brass registration desk. Rooms have muted leopard-pattern carpeting, walls covered in raffia weave, and bold navy and cream striped drapes. The look is from the '40s, but the cordless phones, CD players, and all-in-one faxing/copying/printing machines are definitely modern. Aveda products are provided in the sparkling baths, where a "tub menu" (consisting of items from aromatherapy infusions to cigars and brandy) tempts adventurous bathers. ✉ *12 Fourth St., 94103,* ☎ *415/348–1111 or 877/294–9711,* FAX *415/348–0302. 182 rooms, 16 suites. Restaurant, bar, lobby lounge, in-room data ports, minibars, no-smoking floor, room service, exercise room, dry cleaning, laundry service, concierge, business services, meeting rooms, parking (fee). AE, D, DC, MC, V.*

$$$$ **San Francisco Marriott.** When this huge 40-story hotel opened in 1989, critics alternately raved about and condemned its distinctive design—modern Art Deco, with large fanlike windows across the top (it's called the "jukebox Marriott" by locals). The glitzy lobby features a mirrored ceiling and a 50-ft beaded crystal chandelier. An adjacent five-story glass-topped atrium encloses the dining court (two restaurants and a lounge) lush with tropical plants. An impressive collection of original paintings and sculptures graces the public areas. The functional though bland standard rooms have chain-type decor, but some have excellent views. Some of the more interesting suites are split-level with spiral staircases. Conventioneers often stay here, and it's a good choice for art buffs hoping to visit the nearby San Francisco Museum of Modern Art and the Yerba Buena Center. ✉ *55 Fourth St., 94103,* ☎ *415/896–1600 or 800/228–9290,* FAX *415/896–6177. 1,366 rooms, 134 suites. 3 restaurants, bar, 2 piano bars, sports bar, in-room data ports, minibars, room service, indoor pool, hot tub, sauna, exercise room, dry cleaning, laundry service, concierge, business services, convention center, meeting rooms, car rental, parking (fee). AE, D, DC, MC, V.*

$$$$ **W San Francisco.** Epitomizing cool modernity and urban chic both in its decor and in the crowd it attracts, the 31-story W San Francisco has become *the* place to drink, dine, and stay in the new center of San Francisco. Contributing to its success, of course, has been its prime location next to SFMOMA. Stone, corrugated metal, frosted glass, and other industrial elements in the public spaces are offset by accents of polished mahogany and broad-striped carpeting. Dimly lit hallways lead to smallish guest rooms, each with either a cozy corner sitting area or an upholstered window seat. The luxurious beds have pillow-top mattresses and goose-down comforters and pillows. Cordless phones, Aveda bath products, and stereos with CD players are added bonuses. ✉ *181 Third St., 94103,* ☎ *415/777–5300 or 877/946–8357,* FAX *415/817–7823. 418 rooms, 5 suites. Restaurant, bar, café, in-room data ports, in-room safes, in-room VCRs, minibars, no-smoking floor, refrigerators, room service, indoor pool, hot tub, massage, exercise*

room, dry cleaning, laundry service, concierge, business services, meeting rooms, parking (fee). AE, D, DC, MC, V.

$$$ **The Argent.** Rising 36 stories over one of the busiest intersections in the city, the Argent has a luxuriously appointed lobby and handsome, clublike lounge with live music every evening but Sunday. The bar and adjacent restaurant overlook a sunny outdoor garden. Guest rooms, comfortably furnished in mild tones, all feature floor-to-ceiling picture windows, with dramatic views of the city from the higher floors. About half of the larger-than-average rooms face south and are especially sunny, overlooking Yerba Buena Gardens and the city, bay, and hills beyond. The equally scenic rooms on the north side afford a glimpse of of the Golden Gate Bridge, the Bay, and Alcatraz. ✉ *50 Third St., 94103,* ☎ *415/974–6400 or 877/222–6699,* FAX *415/543–8268. 641 rooms, 26 suites. Restaurant, bar, lobby lounge, in-room data ports, in-room safes, minibars, no-smoking floor, refrigerators, room service, massage, exercise room, piano, dry cleaning, laundry service, concierge, business services, meeting rooms, parking (fee). AE, D, DC, MC, V.*

$$$ **Hotel Milano.** The Milano is a shopper's and culture-maven's delight—adjacent to the San Francisco Shopping Centre and Nordstrom and a stone's throw from all the museums and attractions south of Market Street. The eight-story hotel's stately 1913 neoclassical facade gives way to a warm and stylish lobby with a large Alexander Calder–style mobile over the lounge area. Guest rooms are spacious and handsomely decorated in warm earth tones with contemporary Italian furnishings. Weary shoppers and museum goers can soak, steam, or bake away fatigue in the split-level fitness center on the seventh and eighth floors. ✉ *55 Fifth St., 94103,* ☎ *415/543–8555 or 800/398–7555,* FAX *415/543–5885. 108 rooms. Restaurant, bar, sushi bar, in-room data ports, in-room safes, minibars, no-smoking floor, room service, hot tub, sauna, steam room, exercise room, dry cleaning, laundry service, concierge, business services, meeting rooms, parking (fee). AE, D, DC, MC, V.*

Nob Hill

$$$$ **Mark Hopkins Inter-Continental.** A circular drive leads up to this regal Nob Hill landmark with elaborate Spanish Renaissance terra-cotta ornaments atop the central tower and two stately wings. The lobby (commencing restorations at press time) has floor-to-ceiling mirrors and marble floors. The dramatic, neoclassically furnished rooms glow with warm earth tones, and bathrooms are lined with Italian marble. Rooms on the upper floors have views of either the Golden Gate Bridge or the downtown cityscape. Prince Phillip, Liz Taylor, and Elvis Presley have all boogied here. ✉ *999 California St., 94108,* ☎ *415/392–3434 or 800/662–4455,* FAX *415/421–3302. 342 rooms, 38 suites. Restaurant, 2 bars, room service, exercise room, dry cleaning, laundry service, concierge, business services, meeting rooms, car rental, parking (fee). AE, D, DC, MC, V.*

$$$$ ★ **Ritz-Carlton, San Francisco.** Consistently rated one of the top hotels in the world by *Condé Nast Traveler,* The Ritz-Carlton is a stunning tribute to beauty, splendor, and warm, sincere service. Beyond the neoclassical facade with its 17 Ionic columns (the building was originally Met Life's headquarters in 1909), crystal chandeliers illuminate an opulent lobby adorned with Georgian antiques and a collection of museum-quality 18th- and 19th-century paintings. The hotel's fitness center is a destination in its own right, with an indoor swimming pool, steam baths, saunas, and a whirlpool; you can even get an in-room massage. Rooms are luxuriously appointed with feather beds with 300-count Egyptian cotton sheets and down comforters. Afternoon tea in the Lobby Lounge—which overlooks the hotel's beautifully landscaped

garden courtyard—is a San Francisco institution. ✉ *600 Stockton St., at California St., 94108,* ☏ *415/296–7465 or 800/241–3333,* FAX *415/986–1268. 332 rooms, 44 suites. 2 restaurants, bar, lobby lounge, in-room data ports, health club, dry cleaning, laundry service, concierge, business services, meeting rooms, parking (fee). AE, D, DC, MC, V.*

$$$–$$$$ ★ **The Fairmont.** Commanding the top of Nob Hill like a European palace, the Fairmont, which served as the model for the St. Gregory in the TV series *Hotel,* has experienced plenty of real-life drama: It served as city headquarters during the 1906 earthquake and hosted dignitaries who penned the charter for the United Nations in 1945 (the 40 flags out front represent the nations signing the charter). In 1999–2000, the hotel restored architect Julia Morgan's original, elegant 1907 interiors. Guest rooms, in either buttery yellow, pale cantaloupe, or light-blue color schemes, all have high ceilings and feature fine dark wood furniture and colorful Asian touches such as Chinese porcelain lamps. Don't forget happy hour at the Tonga Room, complete with tiki huts, a live band floating in a tropical lagoon, and a famous thunderstorm every half hour. ✉ *950 Mason St., 94108,* ☏ *415/772–5000 or 800/527–4727,* FAX *415/837–0587. 531 rooms, 65 suites. 4 restaurants, 4 bars, in-room data ports, minibars, no-smoking rooms, room service, barbershop, beauty salon, health club, shops, nightclub, baby-sitting, dry cleaning, laundry service, concierge, business services, meeting rooms, car rental, parking (fee). AE, D, DC, MC, V.*

$$$–$$$$ **The Huntington.** The family-owned, ivy-covered redbrick Huntington Hotel provides an oasis of gracious personal service in an atmosphere of understated luxury. The privacy of the hotel's many celebrated guests, from Bogart and Bacall to Picasso and Pavarotti, has always been impeccably preserved. Rooms and suites, many of which have great views of Grace Cathedral, the bay, or the city skyline, are large because they used to be residential apartments. Most rooms have wet bars, all have large antique desks, and some suites have kitchens. ✉ *1075 California St., 94108,* ☏ *415/474–5400 or 800/227–4683,* FAX *415/474–6227. 100 rooms, 40 suites. Restaurant, bar, in-room data ports, in-room safes, no-smoking rooms, room service, dry cleaning, laundry service, concierge, meeting rooms, parking (fee). AE, D, DC, MC, V.*

$$$ **Nob Hill Lambourne.** This urban retreat, designed with the traveling executive in mind, takes pride in pampering business travelers with personal computers, fax machines, and personalized voice mail; a small on-site spa with massages, body scrubs, manicures, and pedicures helps them relax. If that's not enough, videos on such topics as stress reduction and yoga are available on request, rooms come with white-noise machines and rice-hull pillows, and vitamins and chamomile tea arrive with turndown service. Rooms have queen-size beds with hand-sewn mattresses, silk-damask bedding, and contemporary furnishings in muted colors. ✉ *725 Pine St., at Stockton St., 94108,* ☏ *415/433–2287 or 800/274–8466,* FAX *415/433–0975. 14 rooms, 6 suites. Lobby lounge, in-room data ports, in-room VCRs, no-smoking floors, spa, business services, parking (fee). AE, D, DC, MC, V.*

Fisherman's Wharf/North Beach

$$$ **Marriott at Fisherman's Wharf.** Behind an unremarkable sand-color facade, the Marriott strikes a grand note with its lavish, low-ceiling lobby with marble floors, a double fireplace, and English club–style furniture. Rooms, all with forest-green, burgundy, and cream color schemes, were renovated in 1998 and have either a king-size bed or two double beds. Restaurant Spada serves breakfast and dinner only, while lunch is served in the lobby lounge. ✉ *1250 Columbus Ave., 94133,* ☏ *415/775–7555 or 800/228–9290,* FAX *415/474–2099. 269* *rooms, 16 suites. Restaurant, bar, no-smoking floors, health club, piano, meeting rooms, parking (fee). AE, D, DC, MC, V.*

$$–$$$ ★ **Radisson Hotel at Fisherman's Wharf.** Occupying an entire city block, and part of a complex including 25 shops and restaurants, this is the only bayfront hotel at Fisherman's Wharf and the nearest to Pier 39 and the bay cruise docks. The medium-size lobby has plenty of comfortable couches and chairs. Eighty percent of the rooms have views of the bay and overlook a landscaped courtyard and pool. Rooms are simple and bright. ✉ *250 Beach St., 94133,* ☎ *415/392–6700 or 800/578–7878,* FAX *415/986–7853. 355 rooms. 3 restaurants, in-room data ports, no-smoking rooms, pool, exercise room, concierge, parking (fee). AE, D, DC, MC, V.*

$$ **Hotel Bohème.** In the middle of historic North Beach, the Bohème gives guests a taste of the past with coral-color walls, bistro tables, and memorabilia recalling the beat generation. Allen Ginsberg, who stayed here many times, could in his later years be seen sitting in a window tapping away on his laptop computer. Screenwriters from Francis Coppola's nearby American Zoetrope studio stay here often, as do poets and other artists. Beds feature unnecessary but fun mosquito netting. Enjoy complimentary sherry in the lobby while you deliberate over the many nearby Italian restaurants. ✉ *444 Columbus Ave., 94133,* ☎ *415/433–9111,* FAX *415/362–6292. 15 rooms. In-room data ports, no-smoking floors. AE, D, MC, V.*

$ ★ **San Remo.** This three-story, blue-and-white 1906 Italianate Victorian just a few blocks from Fisherman's Wharf in an older, more authentic section of North Beach) was once home to longshoremen and Beats. A narrow stairway from the street leads to the front desk, and labyrinthine hallways to the small but charming rooms with lace curtains, forest-green wooden floors, brass beds, and other antique furnishings. All rooms eschew phones and TVs. The upper floors are brighter, being closer to the skylights that provide sunshine to the many potted plants in the brass-banistered hallways. About a third of the rooms contain sinks; all rooms share scrupulously clean black-and-white tile shower and toilet facilities with pull-chain toilets. ✉ *2237 Mason St., 94133,* ☎ *415/776–8688 or 800/352–7366,* FAX *415/776–2811. 61 rooms with shared bath, 1 suite. No-smoking rooms, coin laundry, parking (fee). AE, DC, MC, V.*

Pacific Heights, Cow Hollow, and the Marina

$$$$ ★ **Sherman House.** This magnificent Italianate mansion at the foot of residential Pacific Heights is San Francisco's most luxurious small hotel. Rooms are individually decorated with Biedermeier, English Jacobean, or French Second Empire antiques. The decadent mood is enhanced by tapestrylike canopies over four-poster feather beds; wood-burning fireplaces with marble mantels; and sumptuous bathrooms, some with whirlpool baths. The six romantic suites attract honeymooners from around the world. Room rates include evening wine and hors d'oeuvres in an upstairs sitting room. ✉ *2160 Green St., 94123,* ☎ *415/563–3600 or 800/424–5777,* FAX *415/563–1882. 8 rooms, 6 suites. Dining room, in-room VCRs, room service, piano, concierge. AE, DC, MC, V.*

$$$ **El Drisco Hotel.** In one of the wealthiest and most beautiful residential neighborhoods in San Francisco, the understatedly elegant El Drisco is a quiet haven for anyone overwhelmed by the busier parts of the city. Understandably, the hotel serves as a celebrity hideaway from time to time; Val Kilmer and Linda Ronstadt were recent guests. Some of the 1903 Edwardian rooms, pale yellow and white and outfitted with genteel furnishings and luxury amenities (you can take the plush little

slippers home), face the Golden Gate Bridge; others have a commanding view of the eastern or southern parts of the city. Each night at turndown, the staff leaves an oatmeal cookie and the next day's weather forecast. Continental breakfast (included in the room rate) is served in the sunny breakfast room on a lower floor, and there is a lovely sitting room off the lobby. ✉ *2901 Pacific Ave., 94115,* ☎ *415/346–2880 or 800/634–7277,* FAX *415/567–5537. 24 rooms, 19 suites. Breakfast room, in-room data ports, in-room VCRs, minibars, no-smoking rooms, refrigerators, exercise room, dry cleaning, laundry service, concierge. AE, D, DC, MC, V.*

$$–$$$ ★ **Union Street Inn.** Innkeeper David Coyle was a chef for the Duke and Duchess of Bedford, England, and his partner Jane Bertorelli has been innkeeping for 15 years. With the help of her many family heirlooms, they've made this ivy-draped 1902 Edwardian a delightful B&B inn filled with antiques and unique artwork. Equipped with candles, fresh flowers, and wineglasses, rooms are very popular with honeymooners. The private Carriage House, which has its own whirlpool tub and shower under a skylight, is separated from the main house by an old-fashioned English garden complete with lemon trees. An elaborate complimentary breakfast is served to guests in the parlor, in the garden, or in their rooms. ✉ *2229 Union St., 94123,* ☎ *415/346–0424,* FAX *415/922–8046. 6 rooms. Breakfast room, no-smoking rooms, parking (fee). AE, MC, V. BP.*

$$ **Bed and Breakfast Inn.** Hidden in an alley off Union Street between Buchanan and Laguna, this ivy-covered Victorian (San Francisco's first B&B) contains English country–style rooms full of antiques, plants, and floral paintings. Though the rooms with shared baths are quite small, the other rooms and two suites have ample space. The Mayfair, a private apartment above the main house, comes complete with a living room, kitchenette, and spiral staircase leading to a sleeping loft. ✉ *4 Charlton Ct., at Union St., 94123,* ☎ *415/921–9784,* FAX *415/921–0544. 9 rooms, 5 with bath; 2 apartments. Breakfast room, parking (fee). MC, V. CP.*

$$ ★ **Hotel Del Sol.** Once a typical '50s-style motor court, the Hotel Del Sol has been converted into an anything-but-typical artistic statement playfully celebrating California's vibrant (some might say wacky) culture. The sunny courtyard and yellow-and-blue three-story building are candy for the eyes. Rooms face boldly striped patios, citrus trees, and a hammock and heated swimming pool under towering palm trees. Even the carports have striped dividing drapes. Rooms evoke a beach house feeling with plantation shutters, tropical-stripe bedspreads, and rattan chairs. Some rooms have brick fireplaces, and suites for families with small children are outfitted with bunk beds, child-friendly furnishings, a kitchenette, and games. There are even free kites for kids. ✉ *3100 Webster St., 94123,* ☎ *415/921–5520 or 877/433–5765,* FAX *415/931–4137. 47 rooms, 10 suites. In-room data ports, in-room safes, no-smoking rooms, pool, sauna, laundry service, concierge, free parking. AE, D, DC, MC, V.*

$–$$ **Pacific Heights Inn.** One of the most genteel-looking motels in town, this two-story motor court near the busy intersection of Union Street and Van Ness Avenue is dressed up with wrought-iron railings and benches, hanging plants, and pebble exterior walkways facing onto the parking lot. Rooms are on the small side, with floral bedspreads and brass beds. Most of the units are suites, some with kitchens, some with extra bedrooms. Morning pastries and coffee are served in the lobby. ✉ *1555 Union St., 94123,* ☎ *415/776–3310 or 800/523–1801,* FAX *415/776–8176. 15 rooms, 25 suites. Kitchenettes, no-smoking rooms, free parking. AE, DC, MC, V.*

$ **Cow Hollow Motor Inn and Suites.** Solidly built by the same family that runs it, this large, modern hotel has interior corridors and rooms that are more spacious than average, with sitting/dining areas. Decorated with blue carpeting and bedspreads and floral wallpaper, the rooms have dark wood traditional furniture of good quality. Some rooms have views of the Golden Gate Bridge. The large suites here ($195–$245) seem very much like typical San Francisco apartments with their hardwood floors, Oriental carpets, antique furnishings, fireplaces, and fully equipped kitchens. ✉ *2190 Lombard St., 94123,* ☎ *415/921–5800,* FAX *415/922–8515. 117 rooms, 12 suites. Restaurant, no-smoking floor, meeting room, free parking. AE, DC, MC, V.*

Civic Center/Van Ness

$$$ **Radisson Miyako Hotel.** Near the Japantown complex and not far from Fillmore Street and Pacific Heights, this pagoda-style hotel is popular with business travelers. Some guest rooms are in the tower building; others are in the garden wing, which has a traditional Japanese garden with a waterfall. Japanese-style rooms have futon beds with tatami mats, while Western rooms have traditional beds with mattresses—but all feature gorgeous Asian furniture and original artwork. Most have their own soaking rooms with a bucket and stool and a Japanese tub (1 ft deeper than Western tubs), and in-room shiatsu massages are available. ✉ *1625 Post St., at Laguna St., 94115,* ☎ *415/922–3200 or 800/533–4567,* FAX *415/921–0417. 205 rooms, 15 suites. Restaurant, bar, in-room data ports, minibars, exercise room, dry cleaning, laundry service, business services. AE, D, DC, MC, V.*

$$–$$$ ★ **The Archbishop's Mansion.** Everything here is extravagantly romantic, starting with the cavernous common areas, where a chandelier used in the movie *Gone With the Wind* hangs above a 1904 Bechstein grand piano once owned by Noel Coward. The 15 guest rooms, each named for a famous opera, are individually decorated with intricately carved antiques; many have whirlpool tubs or fireplaces (there are 16 fireplaces in the mansion). Though not within easy walking distance of many restaurants or attractions, its perch on the corner of Alamo Square near the Painted Ladies—San Francisco's famous Victorian homes—makes for a scenic, relaxed stay. ✉ *1000 Fulton St., 94117,* ☎ *415/563–7872 or 800/543–5820,* FAX *415/885–3193. 10 rooms, 5 suites. Breakfast room, lobby lounge, in-room data ports, in-room VCRs, no-smoking rooms, piano, meeting room, limited free parking. AE, MC, V.*

$$–$$$ ★ **Inn at the Opera.** This seven-story hotel a block or so from city hall, Davies Hall, and the War Memorial Opera House has hosted the likes of Pavarotti and Baryshnikov, as well as lesser lights of the music, dance, and opera worlds. Behind the marble-floor lobby are rooms of various sizes, decorated with creamy pastels and dark wood furnishings. The bureau drawers are lined with sheet music, and every room is outfitted with terry robes, a microwave oven, a minibar, and a basket of apples. A major attraction is the sumptuous, dimly lighted Ovation restaurant. Stars congregate in its mahogany-and green-velvet interior before and after performances. ✉ *333 Fulton St., 94102,* ☎ *415/863–8400 or 800/325–2708; 800/423–9610 in CA,* FAX *415/861–0821. 30 rooms. Restaurant, lobby lounge, room service, concierge, parking (fee). AE, DC, MC, V.*

$$ **Hotel Majestic.** One of San Francisco's original grand hotels, and once the decade-long residence of screen stars Joan Fontaine and Olivia de Havilland, this five-story white 1902 Edwardian surrounds you with elegance. Most of the romantic guest rooms have gas fireplaces; a mix of French and English antiques; and either a large, hand-painted, four-poster canopied bed or two-poster bonnet twin beds. Some have original claw-foot bathtubs. Afternoons bring complimentary sherry and homemade biscotti to the exquisite lobby, replete with black-marble stairs, antique chandeliers, plush Victorian chairs, and a white-marble fireplace. The hotel's Café Majestic has a turn-of-the-20th-century San Francisco mood and an innovative menu of California cuisine with an Asian touch. ✉ *1500 Sutter St., 94109,* ☎ *415/441–1100 or 800/869–8966,* FAX *415/673–7331. 48 rooms, 9 suites. Restaurant, bar, dry cleaning, laundry service, parking (fee). AE, DC, MC, V.*

$$ **Phoenix Hotel.** From the piped-in, poolside jungle music to the aquatic-theme ultrahip Backflip restaurant and lounge immersed in shimmering hues of blue and green, the Phoenix evokes the tropics—or at least a fun, kitschy version of it. Although probably not the place for a traveling executive seeking peace and quiet—or anyone put off by its location on the fringes of the seedy Tenderloin District—the Phoenix does boast a list of celebrity guests, including such big-name bands as R.E.M. and Pearl Jam. Rooms are simple, with handmade bamboo furniture, tropical-print bedspreads, and original art by local artists. All rooms face the courtyard pool (with a mural by Francis Forlenza on its bottom) and sculpture garden. ✉ *601 Eddy St., 94109,* ☎ *415/776–1380 or 800/248–9466,* FAX *415/885–3109. 41 rooms, 3 suites. Restaurant, bar, room service, pool, massage, nightclub, laundry service, free parking. AE, D, DC, MC, V.*

The Airport

$$$$ ★ **Hotel Sofitel–San Francisco Bay.** Parisian boulevard lampposts, a Métro sign, and a kiosk covered with posters bring an unexpected bit of Paris to this bay-side hotel. The French-theme public spaces—the Gigi Brasserie, La Fougasse Restaurant, and La Terrasse Bar—have a light, open, airy feeling that extends to the rooms, each of which has a minibar and writing desk. ✉ *223 Twin Dolphin Dr., Redwood City 94065,* ☎ *650/598–9000 or 800/763–4835,* FAX *650/598–0459. 379 rooms, 42 suites. 2 restaurants, bar, lobby lounge, minibars, health club, laundry service, concierge, meeting rooms, free parking. AE, DC, MC, V.*

$$–$$$ ★ **Embassy Suites San Francisco Airport–Burlingame.** With excellent service and facilities, this California mission–style hostelry is one of the most lavish in the airport area. Set on the bay with up-close views of planes taking off and landing, it consists entirely of suites that open onto a nine-story atrium and tropical garden replete with ducks, parrots, fish, and a waterfall. Living rooms all have a work area, sleeper sofa, wet bar, television, microwave, and refrigerator. ✉ *150 Anza Blvd., Burlingame 94010,* ☎ *650/342–4600 or 800/362–2779,* FAX *650/343–8137. 340 suites. Restaurant, bar, no-smoking rooms, refrigerators, room service, indoor pool, sauna, exercise room, concierge, business services, free parking. AE, DC, MC, V.*

$$–$$$ **Hyatt Regency San Francisco Airport.** The spectacular 29,000-square-ft, eight-story lobby atrium of this dramatic Hyatt Regency 2 mi south of the airport encloses a world of water, light, and air. You'll feel like you're outdoors and the weather is always perfect. This is the largest airport convention hotel in northern California, boasting a high level of personal service for business and leisure travelers alike. Almost every service and amenity one could think of is here, including several dining options, athletic facilities, and entertainment options. Rooms are modern and well equipped. ✉ *1333 Bayshore Hwy., Burlingame 94010,* ☎ *650/347–1234,* FAX *650/696–2669. 767 rooms, 26 suites. Restaurant, café, deli, lobby lounge, piano bar, sports bar, in-room data ports, no-smoking floor, room service, pool, outdoor hot tub, exercise room, jogging, dry cleaning, laundry service, concierge, business services, convention center, meeting rooms, airport shuttle, car rental, free parking. AE, D, DC, MC, V.*

NIGHTLIFE AND THE ARTS

Updated by Sharron S. Wood

San Francisco has a tremendous variety of evening entertainment, from ultrasophisticated piano bars to come-as-you-are dives that reflect the city's gold rush past. Although it's a compact city with the prevailing influences of some neighborhoods spilling into others, the following generalizations should help you find the kind of entertainment you're looking for. **Nob Hill** is noted for its plush piano bars and panoramic skyline lounges. **North Beach,** infamous for its nude "dance clubs," has cleaned up its image considerably and yet still maintains a sense of its beatnik past in atmospheric bars and coffeehouses. **Fisherman's Wharf,** although touristy, is great for people-watching. Tony **Union Street** is home away from home for singles in search of company. South of Market—**SoMa,** for short—has become a hub of nightlife, with a bevy of popular dance clubs, bars, and supper clubs in renovated warehouses and auto shops. The gay and lesbian scenes center around the **Castro District** and the clubs and bars along **Polk Street.** Twentysomethings and alternative types should check out the ever-funky **Mission District** and **Haight Street** scenes.

Nightlife

Bars generally close between midnight and 2 AM. Bands and other performers usually begin between 8 PM and 11 PM. The cover charge at smaller clubs ranges from $3 to $10. At the larger venues the cover may go up to $30, and tickets can often be purchased through **BASS** (☎ 415/776–1999 or 510/762–2277).

For information on who is performing where, check out the *San Francisco Chronicle*'s pink "Datebook" insert—or consult the *San Francisco Bay Guardian,* free and available in racks around the city, listing neighborhood, avant-garde, and budget-priced events. The *S.F. Weekly* is also free and packed with information on arts events around town. Another handy reference is the weekly magazine *Key,* offered free in most major hotel lobbies.

Cabarets

asiaSF (✉ 201 9th St., at Howard St., ☎ 415/255–2742) is the hottest place in town for saucy, sexy fun. The entertainment, as well as gracious food service, is provided by "gender illusionists." **Club Fugazi** (✉ 678 Green St., at Powell St., ☎ 415/421–4222) is famous for *Beach Blanket Babylon,* a wacky musical revue that has run since 1974. Although the choreography is colorful, the singers brassy, and the songs witty, the real stars are the comically exotic costumes and famous ceiling-high "hats"—worth the price of admission in themselves. Order tickets as far in advance as possible.

The Marsh (✉ 1062 Valencia St., near 22nd St., ☎ 415/826–5750), in the Mission District, books an eclectic mix of alternative and avant-garde theater, performance art, comedy, and the occasional musical act, with an emphasis on solo performances and seldom-staged plays. **Plush Room** (✉ 940 Sutter St., between Leavenworth and Hyde Sts., ☎ 415/885–2800), in the York Hotel, is an intimate cabaret space that began in the 1920s as a speakeasy. The luster may have faded a bit, but the 120-seat room still books some excellent talent.

Dance Clubs

El Rio (✉ 3158 Mission St., between Cesar Chavez and Valencia Sts., ☎ 415/282–3325) is a casual Mission District spot with salsa dancing on Sunday (from 4 PM), Arab dance on Thursday, a global dance party on Friday, and live rock starting at 9 PM on weekends. **Hi-Ball**

Lounge (✉ 473 Broadway, between Kearny and Montgomery Sts., ☎ 415/397–9464), is a small, unpretentious North Beach club. Patrons sip swanky cocktails and swing until they sweat every night. **Metronome Ballroom** (✉ 1830 17th St., at De Haro St., ☎ 415/252–9000), where lessons in all sorts of ballroom dance are given every day, is at its most lively on weekend nights, when ballroom, Latin, and swing dancers come for lessons and revelry.

Roccapulco (✉ 3140 Mission St., between Precita and Cesar Chavez Sts., ☎ 415/648–6611), formerly Cesar's Latin Palace, got a face-lift and a spit-shine and is once again bringing in crowds. This cavernous Mission District dance hall and restaurant features salsa lessons on Wednesday, live salsa music on Friday and Saturday, and belly dancing on Sunday. **330 Ritch Street** (✉ 330 Ritch St., between 3rd and 4th Sts., ☎ 415/541–9574), a popular SoMa nightclub, blends stylish modern decor with swing, lounge, and ambient sounds.

Jazz

Blue Bar (✉ 501 Broadway, at Columbus Ave., ☎ 415/981–2233), tucked beneath the retro beat-generation restaurant Black Cat, finds thirty- and fortysomethings lounging in funky aqua armchairs around Formica tables. **Cafe du Nord** (✉ 2170 Market St., between Church and Sanchez Sts., ☎ 415/861–5016) hosts some of the coolest jazz, blues, and alternative sounds in town. The atmosphere in this basement bar could be called "speakeasy hip." **Elbo Room** (✉ 647 Valencia St., between 17th and 18th Sts., ☎ 415/552–7788) is a convivial spot to hear up-and-coming jazz acts upstairs, or to relax in the dark, moody bar downstairs. **Enrico's** (✉ 504 Broadway, at Kearny St., ☎ 415/982–6223) was the city's hippest North Beach hangout after its 1958 opening. Today it's hip once again, with an indoor/outdoor café, a fine menu, and mellow nightly jazz combos.

Jazz at Pearl's (✉ 256 Columbus Ave., near Broadway, ☎ 415/291–8255) is one of the few reminders of North Beach's heady beatnik days. With mostly straight-ahead jazz acts and dim lighting, this club has a mellow feel. **Kimball's East** (✉ 5800 Shellmound St., Emeryville, ☎ 510/658–2555), in an East Bay shopping complex, hosts such jazz, blues, and R&B talents as Jeffrey Osborne, Tito Puente, and Mose Allison. **Moose's** (✉ 1652 Stockton St., near Union St., ☎ 415/989–7800), one of North Beach's most popular restaurants, also features great sounds in its small but stylish bar area.

Storyville (✉ 1751 Fulton St., between Central and Masonic Sts., ☎ 415/441–1751) is a dressy, classic jazz club featuring such performers as Elvin Jones, James Moody, and local favorite John Handy. **Yoshi's** (✉ 510 Embarcadero St., between Washington and Clay Sts., Oakland, ☎ 510/238–9200) is one of the area's best jazz venues. J. J. Johnson, Betty Carter, local favorite Kenny Burrell, Joshua Redman, and Cecil Taylor have played here.

Piano Bars

Grand Views (✉ 345 Stockton St., at Sutter St., ☎ 415/398–1234), on the top floor of the Grand Hyatt, offers piano music and a view of North Beach and the bay. **Ovation** (✉ 333 Fulton St., near Franklin St., ☎ 415/553–8100), in the Inn at the Opera, is a popular spot for a romantic rendezvous. **Redwood Room** (✉ 495 Geary St., near Taylor St., ☎ 415/775–4700), in the Clift Hotel, is an Art Deco lounge with a low-key but sensuous ambience.

The **Ritz-Carlton Hotel** (✉ 600 Stockton St., at Pine St., ☎ 415/296–7465) has a tastefully appointed lobby lounge where a harpist plays during high tea (weekdays 2:30–5, weekends 1–5). At 5:30, the lounge shifts to piano, and a jazz trio comes on at 8 PM Tuesday–Saturday. **Washington Square Bar and Grill** (✉ 1707 Powell St., near Union St., ☎ 415/982–8123), affectionately known as the "Washbag" by locals, hosts pianists performing jazz and popular standards.

Rock, Pop, Folk, and Blues

Bimbo's 365 Club (✉ 1025 Columbus Ave., at Chestnut St., ☎ 415/474–0365) has a plush main room and an adjacent lounge that retain a retro ambience perfect for the "Cocktail Nation" programming that keeps the crowds hopping. **Bottom of the Hill** (✉ 1233 17th St., at Texas St., ☎ 415/621–4455), in Potrero Hill, showcases some of the city's best local alternative rock. The atmosphere is ultra low-key, although the occasional blockbuster act—Alanis Morissette, Pearl Jam—has been known to hop on stage. **The Fillmore** (✉ 1805 Geary Blvd., at Fillmore St., ☎ 415/346–6000), San Francisco's most famous rock music hall, serves up a varied menu of national and local acts: rock, reggae, grunge, jazz, folk, acid house, and more.

Freight and Salvage Coffee House (✉ 1111 Addison St., Berkeley, ☎ 510/548–1761), one of the finest folk houses in the country, hosts some of the most talented practitioners of folk, blues, Cajun, and bluegrass music. **Great American Music Hall** (✉ 859 O'Farrell St., between Polk and Larkin Sts., ☎ 415/885–0750) is a great eclectic nightclub. Acts run the gamut from the best in blues, folk, and jazz to alternative rock. **John Lee Hooker's Boom Boom Room** (✉ 1601 Fillmore St., at Geary Blvd., ☎ 415/673–8000) attracts old-timers and hipsters alike with top-notch blues acts and, occasionally, a show by the man himself.

Justice League (✉ 628 Divisadero St., near Hayes St., ☎ 415/289–2038) offers live jazz, hip-hop, and world grooves, as well as DJ-driven dance nights. **Last Day Saloon** (✉ 406 Clement St., between 5th and 6th Aves., ☎ 415/387–6343) hosts major entertainers and rising local bands with a varied schedule of blues, funk, country, and jazz. **Lou's Pier 47** (✉ 300 Jefferson St., at Jones St., Fisherman's Wharf, ☎ 415/771–0377) is the place for jazz, blues, and seafood. Bands typically start playing in the late afternoon and continue until midnight.

Paradise Lounge (✉ 1501 Folsom St., at 11th St., ☎ 415/861–6906), a quirky lounge with three stages for eclectic live music, DJ events, and dancing, also has beyond-the-fringe performances at the adjoining Transmission Theatre. **Pier 23** (✉ Pier 23, at the Embarcadero, ☎ 415/362–5125), a waterfront restaurant by day, turns into a packed club by night, with a musical spectrum ranging from Caribbean and salsa to Motown and reggae. **Red Devil Lounge** (✉ 1695 Polk St., at Clay St., ☎ 415/921–1695) is a plush, trendy supper club featuring local and up-and-coming live funk, rock, and jazz acts.

The Saloon (✉ 1232 Grant Ave., near Columbus Ave., ☎ 415/989–7666) is a favorite blues and rock spot among North Beach locals in the know. **Slim's** (✉ 333 11th St., between Harrison and Folsom Sts., ☎ 415/522–0333), one of SoMa's most popular nightclubs, specializes in national touring acts—mostly classic rock, blues, jazz, and world music. Co-owner Boz Scaggs helps bring in the crowds and famous headliners. **The Warfield** (✉ 982 Market St., at 6th St., ☎ 415/775–7722), once a movie palace, is one of the city's largest rock-and-roll venues. Performers range from Porno for Pyros to Suzanne Vega to Harry Connick Jr.

Skyline Bars

Carnelian Room (✉ 555 California St., at Kearny St., ☎ 415/433–7500), on the 52nd floor of the Bank of America Building, has what is perhaps the loftiest view of San Francisco's magnificent skyline. Enjoy dinner or cocktails at 779 ft above the ground. **Cityscape** (✉ 333 O'Farrell St., at Mason St., ☎ 415/771–1400), in the tower of the Hilton Hotel, offers dancing until 12:30 or 1 AM. **Crown Room** (✉ 950 Mason St., at California St., ☎ 415/772–5131), on the 23rd floor of the Fairmont Hotel, is one of the most luxurious of the city's skyline bars. Riding the glass-enclosed elevator is an experience in itself.

Equinox (✉ 5 Embarcadero Center, ☎ 415/788–1234), on the 22nd floor of the Hyatt Regency, is known for its revolving 360-degree views of the city. **Harry Denton's Starlight Room** (✉ 450 Powell St., between Post and Sutter Sts., ☎ 415/395–8595), on the 21st floor of the Sir Francis Drake Hotel, recreates the 1950s high life with rose-velvet booths, romantic lighting, and staff clad in tuxes or full-length gowns. **Phineas T. Barnacle** (✉ 1090 Point Lobos Ave., at the western end of Geary Blvd., ☎ 415/666–4016), inside the Cliff House, provides a unique panorama of Seal Rock and the Pacific Ocean.

Top of the Mark (✉ 999 California St., at Mason St., ☎ 415/392–3434), in the Mark Hopkins Inter-Continental, was immortalized by a famous magazine photograph as a hot spot for World War II servicemen on leave or about to ship out. **View Lounge** (✉ 55 4th St., between Mission and Market Sts., ☎ 415/896–1600), on the 39th floor of the San Francisco Marriott, features superb views though Art Deco windows.

San Francisco's Favorite Bars

Backflip (✉ 601 Eddy St., at Larkin St., ☎ 415/771–3547), in the hipster Phoenix Hotel, is a clubhouse for a space-age rat pack—a combination of aqua-tiled retro and Jetsons-attired waitresses and bartenders. **Bix** (✉ 56 Gold St., off Montgomery St., ☎ 415/433–6300), a North Beach institution, is occasionally credited with the invention of the martini. **Blondies' Bar and No Grill** (✉ 540 Valencia St., near 16th St., ☎ 415/864–2419) features an enclosed "smoking lounge" in the back, which makes it a favorite of those who like to light up.

Buena Vista Café (✉ 2765 Hyde St., at Beach St., ☎ 415/474–5044), the wharf area's most popular bar, introduced Irish coffee to the New World—or so they say. **Cypress Club** (✉ 500 Jackson St., at Columbus Ave., ☎ 415/296–8555) is an eccentric restaurant-bar where sensual, '20s-style opulence clashes with Fellini/Dalí frivolity. **Edinburgh Castle** (✉ 950 Geary St., between Larkin and Polk Sts., ☎ 415/885–4074), pours out happy and sometimes baleful Scottish folk tunes.

House of Shields (✉ 39 New Montgomery St., at Market St., ☎ 415/392–7732), a saloon-style bar with a large wine cellar, attracts an older, Financial District crowd after work. **Specs'** (✉ 12 Saroyan Pl., off Columbus Ave., ☎ 415/421–4112), a hidden hangout for artists and poets, is an old-fashioned watering hole reminiscent of the North Beach of days gone by. **The Tonga Room** (✉ 950 Mason St., at California St., ☎ 415/772–5278), on the Fairmont Hotel's terrace level, features fake palm trees, grass huts, and faux monsoons—courtesy of sprinkler-system rain and simulated thunder and lightning.

Tosca Café (✉ 242 Columbus Ave., near Broadway, ☎ 415/391–1244) has an Italian flavor, with opera on the jukebox and an antique espresso machine that's nothing less than a work of art. **Vesuvio Café** (✉ 255 Columbus Ave., at Broadway, ☎ 415/362–3370) is little altered since its 1960s heyday. The second-floor balcony is a fine vantage point for watching the colorful Broadway-Columbus intersection.

Gay and Lesbian Nightlife

Gay Male Bars

THE CASTRO

The Café (✉ 2367 Market St., at 17th St., ☎ 415/861–3846) is often crowded with locals and visitors alike. **Café Flore** (✉ 2298 Market St., at Noe St., ☎ 415/621–8579) attracts a mixed crowd including poets, punks, and poseurs. **The Metro** (✉ 3600 16th St., at Market St., ☎ 415/703–9750) is a semi-upscale bar with a balcony overlooking the intersection of Noe, 16th, and Market streets. **Midnight Sun** (✉ 4067 18th St., at Castro St., ☎ 415/861–4186), one of the Castro's longest-standing and most popular bars, has riotously programmed giant video screens. Don't expect to be able to hear yourself think.

POLK STREET AREA

The Cinch (✉ 1723 Polk St., between Washington and Clay Sts., ☎ 415/776–4162) is a Wild West–theme neighborhood bar with pinball machines and pool tables. **Divas** (✉ 1002 Post St., at Larkin St., ☎ 415/928–6006), in the rough-and-tumble Tenderloin, is *the* place for transvestites, transsexuals, and their admirers. **Kimo's** (✉ 1351 Polk St., at Pine St., ☎ 415/885–4535), a laid-back club, has floor-to-ceiling windows that provide a great view of hectic Polk Street. **N Touch** (✉ 1548 Polk St., at Sacramento St., ☎ 415/441–8413), a tiny dance bar, has long been popular with Asian–Pacific Islander gay men. **The Swallow** (✉ 1750 Polk St., between Washington and Clay Sts., ☎ 415/775–4152) is a quiet, posh bar that caters to an older gay male clientele.

SOMA

Rawhide II (✉ 280 7th St., between Howard and Folsom Sts., ☎ 415/621–1197) is a rare thing—a San Francisco bar where you can put on your boots and two-step the night away. **SF-Eagle** (✉ 398 12th St., at Harrison St., ☎ 415/626–0880) hosts innumerable contests, such as those for finding Mr. Heart Throb or Mr. SF Leather, which are mostly AIDS benefits. **The Stud** (✉ 399 9th St., at Harrison St., ☎ 415/252–7883) is still going strong after more than 30 years. Its DJs mix up-to-the-minute music with carefully chosen highlights from the glory days of gay disco.

OTHER PARTS OF TOWN

Esta Noche (✉ 3079 16th St., near Valencia St., ☎ 415/861–5757), a longtime Mission District establishment, draws a steady crowd of Latino gays, including some of the city's wildest drag queens. **Lion Pub** (✉ 2062 Divisadero St., at Sacramento St., ☎ 415/567–6565), one of the community's more established enterprises, is a cozy neighborhood bar with an ever-changing array of antiques. **Martuni's** (✉ 4 Valencia St., at Market St., ☎ 415/241–0205), an elegant, low-key bar at the intersection of the Castro, the Mission, and Hayes Valley, draws a mixed crowd that enjoys cocktails in a refined environment.

Lesbian Bars

Club Q (✉ 177 Townsend St., at 3rd St., ☎ 415/647–8258), a monthly (first Friday of every month) dance party, is geared to "women and their friends." **CoCo Club** (✉ 139 8th St., entrance on Minna St., ☎ 415/626–2337) offers a variety of theme nights, including a drag cabaret, a coed erotic cabaret, and a woman's speakeasy. **G Spot** (✉ 401 6th St., at Harrison St., ☎ 415/337–4962), at SoMa's End Up club, features house, hip-hop, and R&B every Saturday from 9 PM.

Hollywood Billiards (✉ 61 Golden Gate Ave., near Taylor St., ☎ 415/252–9643), a macho pool hall six nights a week, has become the unlikely host of a smoldering lesbian scene every Wednesday. **The Lex-**

ington Club (✉ 3464 19th St., at Lexington St., ☎ 415/863–2052) is where, according to the slogan, "Every night is ladies' night." **Wild Side West** (✉ 424 Cortland Ave., between Mission and Bayshore Sts., ☎ 415/647–3099), though a bit out of the way in Bernal Heights, is a mellow neighborhood hangout where there's always a friendly pool game going on.

The Arts

Half-price, same-day tickets to many local and touring stage shows go on sale (cash only) at 11 AM from Tuesday to Saturday at the **TIX Bay Area** (☎ 415/433–7827) booth, on the Stockton Street side of Union Square, between Geary and Post streets. The city's charge-by-phone ticket service is **BASS** (☎ 415/776–1999 or 510/762–2277), with one of its centers in the TIX booth (☞ *above*) and another at Tower Records (✉ Bay St. at Columbus Ave., ☎ 415/885–0500), near Fisherman's Wharf. **City Box Office** (✉ 153 Kearny St., Suite 401, at Sutter St., ☎ 415/392–4400) has a charge-by-phone service for many concerts and lectures.

Dance

The **San Francisco Ballet** (✉ 301 Van Ness Ave., ☎ 415/865–2000) has regained much of its luster under artistic director Helgi Tomasson, and both classical and contemporary works have won admiring reviews. Tickets and information are available at the Opera House (✉ 301 Van Ness Ave., ☎ 415/865–2000).

The **Margaret Jenkins Dance Company** (☎ 415/826–8399) is a nationally acclaimed modern troupe. **Smuin Ballets/SF** (☎ 415/665–2222) is renowned for integrating pop music into its performances. **ODC/San Francisco** (☎ 415/863–6606) mounts an annual Yuletide version of *The Velveteen Rabbit* at the Center for the Arts. **Joe Goode Performance Group** (☎ 415/648–4848) is known for its physicality and high-flying style. The **Dancers Group/Footwork** (☎ 415/824–5044) is a small but significant local company.

Film

The **Castro Theatre** (✉ 429 Castro St., near Market St., ☎ 415/621–6120), designed by Art Deco master Timothy Pfleuger, is worth visiting for its decor alone; it also offers revivals as well as foreign and independent engagements. Across the bay, the spectacular Art Deco **Paramount Theatre** (✉ 2025 Broadway, near 19th St. BART station, Oakland, ☎ 510/465–6400) alternates between vintage flicks and live performances.

The **Roxie Cinema** (✉ 3117 16th St., between Valencia and Guerrero Sts., ☎ 415/863–1087) specializes in film noir and new foreign and indie features. The avant-garde **Red Vic Movie House** (✉ 1727 Haight St., between Cole and Shrader Sts., ☎ 415/668–3994) screens an adventurous lineup of contemporary and classic American and foreign titles in a funky setting. The **Cinematheque** (☎ 415/558–8129) splits its experimental film and video schedule between the San Francisco Art Institute (✉ 800 Chestnut St., at Jones St., ☎ 415/558–8129) and the Yerba Buena Center for the Arts (✉ 701 Mission St., at 3rd St., ☎ 415/978–2787).

Music

San Francisco Opera. Founded in 1923, this world-renowned company has resided in the Civic Center's War Memorial Opera House since it was built in 1932. Over its season, the opera presents approximately 70 performances of 10 operas from September to January and June to July. The box office is at 199 Grove Street, at Van Ness Avenue. ✉ *301 Van Ness Ave., at Grove St.,* ☎ *415/864–3330.*

San Francisco Symphony. The symphony performs from September to May, with additional summer performances of light classical musical and show tunes. Michael Tilson Thomas, who is known for his innovative programming of 20th-century American works, is the musical director, and he and his orchestra often perform with soloists of the caliber of Andre Watts, Midori, and Bay Area resident Frederica von Stade. Tickets run $12–$100. ✉ *Davies Symphony Hall, 201 Van Ness Ave., at Grove St.,* ☏ *415/864–6000.*

Theater

The most venerable commercial theater is the **Curran** (✉ 445 Geary St., at Mason St., ☏ 415/551–2000). The **Golden Gate** (✉ Golden Gate Ave. at Taylor St., ☏ 415/551–2000) is a stylishly refurbished movie theater, now primarily a musical house. The gorgeously restored 2,500-seat **Orpheum** (✉ 1192 Market St., at Hyde St., ☏ 415/551–2000) is used for the biggest touring shows. The **American Conservatory Theater** is one of the nation's leading regional theaters. The ACT ticket office (☏ 415/749–2228) is at 405 Geary Street. Next door to ACT is its home, the **Geary Theater.**

The leading producer of new plays is the **Magic Theatre** (✉ Bldg. D, Fort Mason Center, Laguna St. at Marina Blvd., ☏ 415/441–8822). **Marines Memorial Theatre** (✉ 609 Sutter St., at Mason St., ☏ 415/771–6900) offers touring shows plus some local performances. **Theatre on the Square** (✉ 450 Post St., between Mason and Powell Sts., ☏ 415/433–9500) is a popular smaller venue. For commercial and popular success, nothing beats *Beach Blanket Babylon,* the zany revue that has been running since 1974 at North Beach's **Club Fugazi** (☞ Cabarets *in* Nightlife, *above*).

OUTDOOR ACTIVITIES AND SPORTS

Beaches

Updated by Lisa Alcalay Klug

Nestled in a quiet cove between the lush hills adjoining Fort Mason, Ghirardelli Square, and the crowds at Fisherman's Wharf, **Aquatic Park** has a tiny, ¼-mi-long sandy beach with gentle water. Keep an eye out for members of the Dolphin Club (☏ 415/441–9329), who come every morning for a dip in these ice-cold waters.

Baker Beach is a local favorite, with gorgeous views of the Golden Gate Bridge and the Marin Headlands. Its bold waves make swimming a dangerous prospect, but the mile-long shoreline is ideal for fishing, building sand castles, or watching sea lions play in the surf. On warm days, the entire beach is packed with bodies, including nudists, tanning in the sun.

One of the city's safest swimming beaches, **China Beach** was named for the poor Chinese fishermen who once camped here. This 600-ft strip of sand, just south of the Presidio, offers swimmers gentle waters as well as changing rooms, rest rooms, and showers.

South of the Cliff House, **Ocean Beach** is certainly not the city's cleanest shore, but its wide, sandy expanse stretches for miles, making it ideal for long walks and runs. You may spot sea lions sunning themselves atop the stony offshore islands. Because of extremely dangerous currents, swimming is not recommended. After the sun sets in summer, bonfires typically form a string of lights along the beach.

Participant Sports

Because of its natural beauty, physical fitness and outdoor activities are a way of life in the Bay Area. For a listing of running races, tennis tournaments, bicycle races, and other participant sports, check the monthly issues of *City Sports* magazine, available free at sporting goods stores, tennis centers, and other recreational sites.

Bicycling

San Francisco has a number of scenic routes of varied terrain. With its legendary hills, the city offers countless cycling challenges—but also plenty of level ground. To avoid the former, look for a copy of the *San Francisco Biking/Walking Guide* ($2.50) in bookstores.

The Embarcadero gives you a clear view of open waters and the Bay Bridge on the pier side and sleek high-rises on the other. Rent a bike ($5–$7 per hour) at Start to Finish (✉ 599 2nd St., ☎ 415/243–8812). **Golden Gate Park** is a beautiful maze of roads and hidden bike paths, with rose gardens, lakes, waterfalls, museums, horse stables, bison, and ultimately, a spectacular view of the Pacific Ocean. Rent a bike for about $25 per day at Park Cyclery (✉ 1749 Waller St., ☎ 415/751–7368). **The Marina Green** is a picturesque lawn stretching along Marina Boulevard, adjacent to Fort Mason. Rent a bike ($5–$7 per hour) at the Lombard branch of Start to Finish (✉ 2530 Lombard St., at Divisadero St., ☎ 415/202–9830).

Boating and Sailing

San Francisco Bay offers year-round sailing, but tricky currents and strong winds make the bay hazardous for inexperienced navigators.

A Day on the Bay (☎ 415/922–0227) is ideally located in San Francisco's small craft marina, just minutes from the Golden Gate Bridge and open waters. **Cass' Marina** (✉ 1702 Bridgeway, at Napa St., ☎ 415/332–6789), in Sausalito, will rent you any of a variety of 22- to 35-ft sailboats, as long as there's a qualified sailor in your group. **Stow Lake** (☎ 415/752–0347), in Golden Gate Park, has rowboat, pedal boat, and electric boat rentals.

Fishing

San Franciscans cast lines from the Municipal Pier, Fisherman's Wharf, Baker Beach, or Aquatic Park. **Lovely Martha's Sportfishing** (✉ Fisherman's Wharf, Berth 3, ☎ 650/871–1691) offers salmon-fishing excursions as well as bay cruises. **Wacky Jacky** (✉ Fisherman's Wharf, Pier 45, ☎ 415/586–9800) will take you salmon fishing in a sleek, fast, and comfortable 50-ft boat. At San Francisco's Lake Merced, you can rent rods and boats, purchase permits and licenses (up to $4 for a permit and $10 for a two-day license) and buy bait at the **Lake Merced Boating & Fishing Company** (✉ 1 Harding Rd., ☎ 415/681–3310).

Golf

Golfers can putt to their hearts' content in San Francisco. Call the **golf information line** (☎ 415/750–4653) to get detailed directions to the city's public golf courses or to reserve a tee time ($1 reservation fee per player) up to seven days in advance. **Glen Eagles Golf Course** (✉ 2100 Sunnydale Ave., ☎ 415/587–2425) is a challenging nine-hole, par-36 course in McLaren Park. **Golden Gate** (✉ 47th Ave. between Fulton St. and John F. Kennedy Dr., ☎ 415/751–8987) is a nine-hole, par-27 course in Golden Gate Park just above Ocean Beach. **Harding Park Golf Course** (✉ Harding Rd. and Skyline Blvd., ☎ 415/664–4690) has an 18-hole, par-72 course. **Lincoln Park** (✉ 34th Ave. and Clement St., ☎ 415/221–9911) has an 18-hole, par-68 course. The **Presidio Golf Course** (✉ 300 Finley Rd. at Arguello Blvd., ☎ 415/561–4661) is an 18-hole, par-72 course.

Tennis

The San Francisco Recreation and Parks Department maintains 132 public tennis courts throughout the city. The six courts at **Mission Dolores Park** (✉ 18th and Dolores Sts.) are available on a first-come, first-served basis. The 21 courts in **Golden Gate Park** (☎ 415/753–7001) are the only public ones for which you can make advance reservations. Fees range from $5 to $10. For gorgeous views, head up to the steeply sloped **Buena Vista Park** (✉ Buena Vista Ave. and Haight St., ☎ 415/831–2700). Popular with Marina locals, the four lighted courts at the **Moscone Recreation Center** (✉ 1800 Chestnut St., at Buchanan St., The Marina, ☎ 415/292–2006) are free but sometimes require a wait. In the southeast corner of the beautiful Presidio, **Julius Kahn Playground** (✉ W. Pacific Ave. between Spruce and Locust Sts., ☎ 415/753–7001) has four free courts.

Spectator Sports

For a local perspective on Bay Area sports, look in sports bars and sporting goods stores for the *Bay Sports Review,* which lists game schedules and features interviews with sports luminaries.

Baseball

The **San Francisco Giants** have moved from their former home, 3Com Park, to a new downtown bay-front stadium, Pacific Bell Park (✉ 24 Willie Mays Plaza, between 2nd and 3rd Sts., ☎ 415/467–8000 or 800/734–4268). To avoid traffic jams, take one of the city buses or Muni lines that run nearby; call **Muni** (☎ 415/673–6864) for the stop nearest you.

The **Oakland A's** play at the Oakland Coliseum (✉ 7000 Coliseum Way, off I–880, north of Hegenberger Rd., Oakland, ☎ 510/638–0500). Same-day tickets can usually be purchased at the stadium. To reach the Oakland Coliseum, take a BART train to the Coliseum stop.

Basketball

The **Golden State Warriors** play NBA basketball at the Arena in Oakland (✉ 7000 Coliseum Way, off I–880, north of Hegenberger Rd., Oakland, ☎ 510/986–2200) from November to April.

Football

The NFC West's **San Francisco 49ers** play at 3Com Park (✉ 3Com Park at Candlestick Point, Jamestown Ave. and Harney Way, San Francisco, ☎ 415/656–4900). Tickets are almost always sold out far in advance. The AFC West's **Oakland Raiders** play at the Oakland Coliseum (✉ 7000 Coliseum Way, off I–880, north of Hegenberger Rd., Oakland).

Hockey

Tickets for the NHL's **San Jose Sharks** are available from BASS (☎ 510/762–2277). Games are held at the San Jose Arena.

Soccer

The **San Jose Earthquakes** (✉ 1257 S. 10th St., at Alma Dr., San Jose, ☎ 408/985–4625) play major-league soccer at Spartan Stadium.

SHOPPING

Updated by Sharron S. Wood

From fringe fashions in the Haight to leather chaps in the Castro, San Francisco's many distinctive neighborhoods offer consumers a bit of everything. There are ginseng health potions in Chinatown, fine antiques and art in Jackson Square, handmade kites and kimonos in Japantown, and bookstores throughout the city, specializing in everything from Beat poetry to ecology. For those who prefer the mainstream, there are high-end boutiques on Union Street and fine department stores in Union Square.

Major Shopping Districts

The Castro/Noe Valley

The Castro, often called the gay capital of the world, is also a major shopping destination for nongay travelers. The Castro is filled with men's clothing boutiques, home accessory stores, and various specialty stores. Especially notable is **A Different Light,** one of the country's premier gay and lesbian bookstores. **Under One Roof** (✉ 549 Castro St., between 18th and 19th Sts., ☎ 415/252–9430) donates the profits from its home and garden items, gourmet foods, bath products, books, frames, and cards to northern California AIDS organizations.

Just south of the Castro on 24th Street, largely residential Noe Valley is an enclave of gourmet food stores, used-CD shops, clothing boutiques, and specialty gift stores. At **Panetti's** (✉ 3927 24th St., between Noe and Sanchez Sts., ☎ 415/648–2414) you'll find offbeat novelty items, whimsical picture frames, journals, and more.

Chinatown

The intersection of Grant Avenue and Bush Street marks the gateway to Chinatown. Here, hordes of shoppers and tourists are introduced to 24 blocks of shops, restaurants, and markets—a nonstop tide of activity. The **Great China Herb Co.** (✉ 857 Washington St., between Grant Ave. and Stockton St., ☎ 415/982–2195), where they add up the bill on an abacus, is one of the biggest herb stores around.

Embarcadero Center

Five modern towers of shops, restaurants, offices, and a popular movie theater—plus the Hyatt Regency Hotel—make up the Embarcadero Center, downtown at the end of Market Street.

Fisherman's Wharf

A constant throng of sightseers crowds Fisherman's Wharf, and with good reason: Pier 39, the Anchorage, Ghirardelli Square, and the Cannery are all here, each with shops and restaurants, as well as outdoor entertainment—musicians, mimes, and magicians.

The Haight

Haight Street is a perennial attraction for visitors, if only to see the sign at Haight and Ashbury streets—the geographic center of the Flower Power movement during the 1960s. These days chain stores such as The Gap and Ben and Jerry's have taken over large storefronts near the famous intersection, but it's still possible to find high-quality vintage clothing, funky jewelry, folk art from around the world, and used records and CDs galore in this always-busy neighborhood.

Hayes Valley

Hayes Valley, just west of the Civic Center, is packed with art galleries and such unusual stores as **Worldware** (✉ 336 Hayes St., between Gough and Franklin Sts., ☎ 415/487–9030), where everything from clothing to furniture to candles is made of organic materials.

Jackson Square

Elegant Jackson Square is home to a dozen or so of San Francisco's finest retail antiques dealers, many of which occupy Victorian-era buildings.

Japantown

The **Japan Center** (✉ between Laguna and Fillmore Sts. and Geary Blvd. and Post St.) is five acres of shopping under one roof. The three-block complex includes an 800-car public garage and three shop-filled buildings. Especially worthwhile are the Kintetsu and Kinokuniya buildings, where shops and showrooms sell cameras, tapes and records, jewelry, antique kimonos, *tansu* chests, paintings, and more.

The Marina District

Chestnut Street, one block north of Lombard Street and stretching from Fillmore to Broderick streets, caters to the shopping whims of Marina District residents, many of whom go for clingy designer clothing and quality housewares.

The Mission

The diverse Mission District, home to a large Latino population, plus young artists and musicians of all nations, draws bargain hunters with its many used clothing, vintage furniture, and alternative book stores. Shoppers can unwind with a cup of *café con leche* at one of dozens of cafés.

North Beach

Sometimes compared to New York City's Greenwich Village, North Beach is only a fraction of the size, clustered tightly around Washington Square and Columbus Avenue. Most of its businesses are small eateries, cafés, and shops selling clothing, antiques, and vintage wares. Once the center of the Beat movement, North Beach still has a bohemian spirit that's especially apparent at rambling **City Lights Bookstore** (⊠ 261 Columbus Ave., at Broadway, ☎ 415/362–8193), where the Beat poets live on.

Pacific Heights

Pacific Heights residents seeking fine items for their luxurious homes head straight for Fillmore Street between Post Street and Pacific Avenue, and Sacramento Street between Lyon and Maple streets, where private residences alternate with good bookstores, fine clothing and gift shops, housewares stores, and art galleries. A local favorite is the **Sue Fisher King Company** (⊠ 3067 Sacramento St., between Baker and Broderick Sts., ☎ 415/922–7276), whose quality home accessories fit right into this upscale neighborhood.

South of Market

The gritty warehouse and semi-industrial zone south of Market, called SoMa, is home to dozens of discount outlets, most open daily, which have sprung up along the streets and alleyways bordered by 2nd, Townsend, Howard, and 10th streets. At the other end of the spectrum are the high-class gift shops of the **San Francisco Museum of Modern Art** (⊠ 151 3rd St., between Mission and Howard Sts., ☎ 415/357–4035) and the **Center for the Arts Gift Shop** (⊠ 701 Mission St., at 3rd St., ☎ 415/978–2710, ext. 168). Both sell handmade jewelry and other great gift items.

Union Square

Serious shoppers head straight to Union Square, San Francisco's main shopping area and the site of most department stores, including **Macy's** (⊠ Stockton and O'Farrell Sts., ☎ 415/397–3333), **Neiman Marcus** (⊠ 150 Stockton St., at Geary Blvd., ☎ 415/362–3900), and **Saks Fifth Avenue** (⊠ 384 Post St., at Powell St., ☎ 415/986–4300). The **San Francisco Shopping Centre** (⊠ 865 Market St., between 4th and 5th Sts., ☎ 415/495–5656), across from the cable car turnaround at Powell and Market streets, is distinguished by spiral escalators that wind up through the sunlit atrium. Inside are more than 35 retailers. At Post and Kearny streets, the **Crocker Galleria** (⊠ 50 Post St., ☎ 415/393–1505) is a complex of 40 or so mostly upscale shops and restaurants that sit underneath a glass dome.

Union Street

Out-of-towners sometimes confuse Union Street—a popular stretch of shops and restaurants five blocks south of the Golden Gate National Recreation Area—with downtown's Union Square. Nestled at the foot of a hill between Pacific Heights and the Marina District, the street is lined with high-end clothing, antiques, and jewelry shops. **Union Street Goldsmith** (✉ 1909 Union St., at Laguna St., ☎ 415/776–8048), a local favorite since 1976, prides itself on its wide selection of such rare gemstones as golden sapphires and violet tanzanite.

SIDE TRIPS FROM SAN FRANCISCO

One of San Francisco's best assets is its surroundings. To the north is idyllic Marin County, home to Mediterranean-style waterfronts, redwood-shaded communities, and vast parklands. To the east are Berkeley and Oakland—one a colorful university town and the other a multifaceted port. South of the city are Silicon Valley and the peninsula, where cattle ranches and California mission architecture coexist with modern industry. Point your car in any direction and you're bound to discover what makes the Bay Area such a coveted place to live.

Sausalito

Updated by Marty Olmstead

Like much of San Francisco, Sausalito had a raffish reputation before it went upscale. Discovered in 1775 by Spanish explorers, the town served as a port for whaling ships during the 19th century. By the mid-1800s wealthy San Franciscans were making Sausalito their getaway across the bay. They built lavish Victorian summer homes in the hills, many of which still stand today. Sausalito developed its bohemian flair in the 1950s and '60s, when a group of artists, led by a charismatic Greek portraitist named Varda, established an artists' colony and a houseboat community here. Since then Sausalito has also become a major yachting center, and restaurants attract visitors for fresh seafood as well as spectacular views. The town remains friendly and casual, although summer traffic jams can fray nerves. If possible, visit on a weekday—and take the ferry.

The U.S. Army Corps of Engineers uses the **Bay Model,** a 400-square-ft replica of the entire San Francisco Bay and the San Joaquin–Sacramento River delta, to reproduce the rise and fall of tides, the flow of currents, and the other physical forces at work on the bay. At the same site is the ***Wapama,*** a hulking World War I–era steam freighter being restored by volunteers. ✉ *2100 Bridgeway, at Marinship Way,* ☎ *415/332–3871.* 🎫 *Free.* ⏲ *Labor Day–Memorial Day, Tues.–Sat. 9–4; Memorial Day–Labor Day, Tues.–Fri. 9–4 and weekends 10–6.*

Some of the more than 450 **houseboats** that make up Sausalito's floating homes community line the shore of Richardson Bay. The sight of these colorful, quirky abodes is one of Marin County's most famous views. For a view of the houseboats, head north on Bridgeway from downtown, turn right on Gate 6 Road, and park where it dead-ends at the public shore.

The **Bay Area Discovery Museum** fills five former military buildings with entertaining and enlightening hands-on exhibits. From San Francisco take the Alexander Avenue exit from U.S. 101 and follow signs to East Fort Baker. ✉ *557 McReynolds Rd., at E. Fort Baker,* ☎ *415/487–4398.* 🎫 *$7.* ⏲ *Summer, Tues.–Sun. 10–5; fall–spring, Tues.–Thurs. 9–4 and Fri.–Sun. 10–5.*

The Bay Area

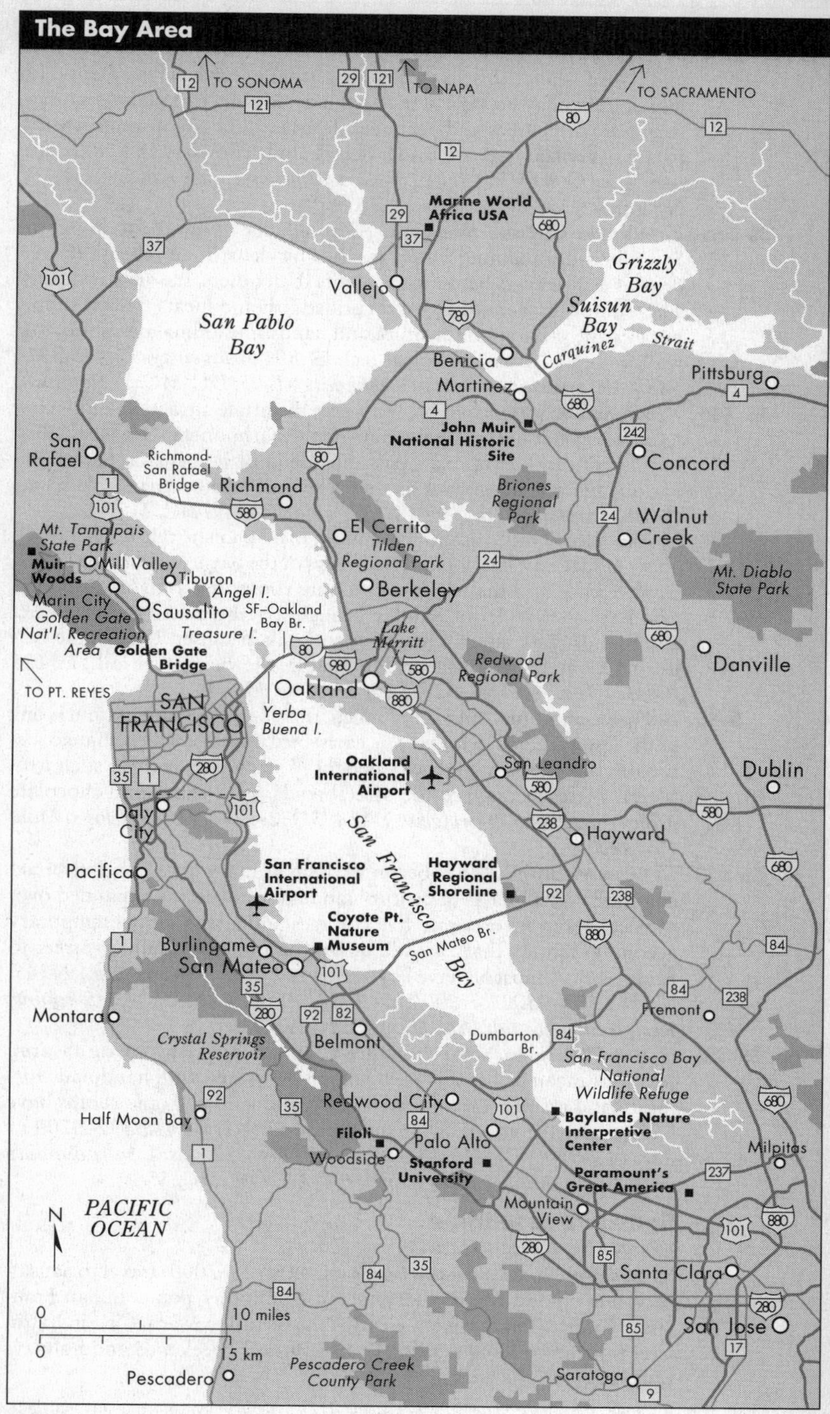
TO SONOMA
TO NAPA
TO SACRAMENTO
Marine World Africa USA
Grizzly Bay
Suisun Bay
San Pablo Bay
Vallejo
Benicia
Carquinez Strait
Pittsburg
Martinez
John Muir National Historic Site
Concord
San Rafael
Richmond-San Rafael Bridge
Richmond
Briones Regional Park
Walnut Creek
Mt. Tamalpais State Park
Muir Woods
Mill Valley
Tiburon
El Cerrito
Tilden Regional Park
Mt. Diablo State Park
Marin City
Golden Gate Nat'l. Recreation Area
Sausalito
Angel I.
Berkeley
SF–Oakland Bay Br.
Treasure I.
Lake Merritt
Golden Gate Bridge
Danville
Redwood Regional Park
TO PT. REYES
SAN FRANCISCO
Oakland
Yerba Buena I.
Oakland International Airport
San Leandro
Dublin
Daly City
San Francisco Bay
Hayward
Pacifica
San Francisco International Airport
Hayward Regional Shoreline
Coyote Pt. Nature Museum
San Mateo Br.
Burlingame
San Mateo
Montara
Fremont
Crystal Springs Reservoir
Belmont
Dumbarton Br.
San Francisco Bay National Wildlife Refuge
Redwood City
Half Moon Bay
Baylands Nature Interpretive Center
Filoli
Palo Alto
Woodside
Stanford University
Milpitas
Paramount's Great America
Mountain View
PACIFIC OCEAN
N
Santa Clara
San Jose
0
10 miles
0
15 km
Pescadero
Pescadero Creek County Park
Saratoga

Dining and Lodging

$$$–$$$$ ✕ **Ondine.** Jutting out into the bay with clear views of San Francisco and Angel Island, this second-story setting is extremely romantic for dinner or Sunday brunch. Star dishes include kung pao seafood sausage stir-fried with chilies and peanuts, foie gras with langoustines, swordfish with saffron spaetzle, and a rich abalone chowder. ✉ *558 Bridgeway Ave.,* ☎ *415/331–1133. Reservations essential. AE, DC, MC, V. No lunch.*

$$–$$$ ✕ **Mikayla at Casa Madrona.** Although the food at this longtime Sausalito hilltop dining room (reached by elevator and then a flower-decked walkway) is better some nights than others, the view is superb. The California menu is based on grilled fish and meats treated simply but elegantly. Bamboo furniture and handsome animal designs on the walls give the space a tropical feel. ✉ *801 Bridgeway,* ☎ *415/331–5888. Reservations essential weekends. AE, D, DC, MC, V. No lunch.*

$$–$$$ ✕ **Spinnaker.** Spectacular bay views are the prime attraction in this contemporary building on a point beyond the harbor near the yacht club—but diners can fuel up on a passable menu of homemade pastas and various seafood specialties as they gaze out at the remarkable scene. ✉ *100 Spinnaker Dr.,* ☎ *415/332–1500. AE, D, DC, MC, V.*

$$ ✕ **Alta Mira.** This Sausalito landmark, in a Spanish-style hotel a block above Bridgeway, has unparalleled views of the bay from both the heated front terrace and the windowed dining room. It's a favored destination Bay Area–wide for Sunday brunch (try the famed eggs Benedict and Ramos Fizz), alfresco lunch, or cocktails at sunset. Though the California-Continental cuisine is forgettable, the view never fails. ✉ *125 Bulkley Ave.,* ☎ *415/332–1350. AE, DC, MC, V.*

$–$$ ✕ **Christophe.** Small and very French, this charming dining room is one of the few bargains in town. The early-bird dinners, which change seasonally, are a penny-pincher's delight. The choices include such irresistible plates as duck confit, sweetbreads, pork roast, and chocolate profiteroles. ✉ *1919 Bridgeway,* ☎ *415/332–9244. MC, V. Closed Mon. No lunch.*

$$–$$$ 🏨 **Casa Madrone.** What began as a small inn with a handful of accommodations in a 19th-century landmark house has expanded over the decades to incorporate five cottages and a bevy of contemporary accommodations that cascade down the hill from Bulkley Street to Bridgeway. Almost all have bay views. ✉ *801 Bridgeway Ave., 94965,* ☎ *415/332–0502 or 800/567–9524,* FAX *415/332–2537. 35 rooms. Restaurant, hot tub. AE, D, DC, MC, V.*

$$–$$$ 🏨 **Hotel Sausalito.** Soft yellow, green, and orange tones create a warm, Mediterranean feel at this well-run inn decorated with handmade furniture and tasteful original art and reproductions. Some rooms have harbor or park views. ✉ *16 El Portal, 94965,* ☎ *415/332–0700 or 888/442–0700,* FAX *415/332–8788. 14 rooms, 2 suites. In-room data ports, no-smoking rooms, concierge. AE, DC, MC, V.*

Sausalito Essentials

ARRIVING AND DEPARTING

By Bus: Golden Gate Transit buses (☎ 415/923–2000) travel to Sausalito from 1st and Mission streets and from other points in San Francisco. For Mt. Tamalpais State Park, take Bus 20 to Marin City; in Marin City transfer to Golden Gate Transit Bus 63 (weekends and holidays only) to reach the park.

By Car: Take U.S. 101 north across the Golden Gate Bridge. For Sausalito, take the first exit, Alexander Avenue, just past Vista Point; follow signs to Sausalito and then go north on Bridgeway to the municipal parking lot near the center of town.

By ferry: Golden Gate Ferry (☎ 415/923–2000) crosses the bay to Sausalito from the south wing of the Ferry Building at Market Street and the Embarcadero; the trip takes 30 minutes. **Blue and Gold Fleet** ferries (☎ 415/705–5555,) depart daily for Sausalito from Pier 41 at Fisherman's Wharf.

VISITOR INFORMATION

Sausalito Visitor Center (✉ 777 Bridgeway, 94965, ☎ 415/332–0505).

The East Bay

In the last 10 years, especially, growth in the Silicon Valley has blurred the lines between "South Bay" and "East Bay," as towns in both areas have become bedroom communities for workers in the high-tech industry. When San Franciscans refer to the East Bay, they mean Berkeley and Oakland.

Berkeley

Although the University of California dominates Berkeley's history and contemporary life, the university and the town are not synonymous. The city of 100,000 facing San Francisco across the bay has other interesting attributes. Berkeley is culturally diverse and politically adventurous, a breeding ground for social trends, a continuing bastion of the counterculture, and an important center for Bay Area writers, artists, and musicians.

Numbers in the text correspond to numbers in the margin and on the Berkeley map.

1 The **U.C. Berkeley Art Museum** houses a surprisingly interesting collection of works spanning five centuries, with an emphasis on contemporary art. Changing exhibits line the spiral ramps and balcony galleries. On the ground floor, the **Pacific Film Archive** offers programs of historic and contemporary films. ✉ *2626 Bancroft Way,* ☎ *510/642–0808; 510/642–1124 for film-program information.* *$6.* ⏲ *Wed. and Fri.–Sun. 11–5, Thurs. 11–9.*

More than 13,500 species of plants from all over the world flourish
2 in the 34-acre **U.C. Botanical Garden**—thanks to Berkeley's temperate climate. Informative tours of the garden are given weekends at 1:30. ✉ *Centennial Dr.,* ☎ *510/642–3343.* *$3.* ⏲ *Daily 9–4:45.*

3 The fortresslike **Lawrence Hall of Science,** a dazzling hands-on science center, lets children look at insects under microscopes, solve crimes using chemical forensics, and explore the physics of baseball. ✉ *Centennial Dr.,* ☎ *510/642–5132.* *$6.* ⏲ *Daily 10–5.*

4 **Tilden Park** (☎ 510/562–7275), an oasis in the midst of the city, has a botanical garden, an 18-hole golf course, and an environmental education center. You'll find paths and picnic sites on its 2,000 acres. Both kids and kids at heart will love the park's miniature steam trains, pony rides, and the vintage menagerie-style carousel.

Dining and Lodging

$$$–$$$$ ★ ✕ **Chez Panisse Café & Restaurant.** The famed Alice Waters remains the mastermind behind the culinary wizardry at this legendary eatery. In the downstairs restaurant, formality and personal service create the ambience of a private club. Upstairs in the café the atmosphere is informal. Try the Parmigiano-Reggiano cheese and arugula. ✉ *1517 Shattuck Ave., north of University Ave.,* ☎ *510/548–5525 for restaurant; 510/548–5049 for café. Reservations essential for restaurant. AE, D, DC, MC, V. Closed Sun.*

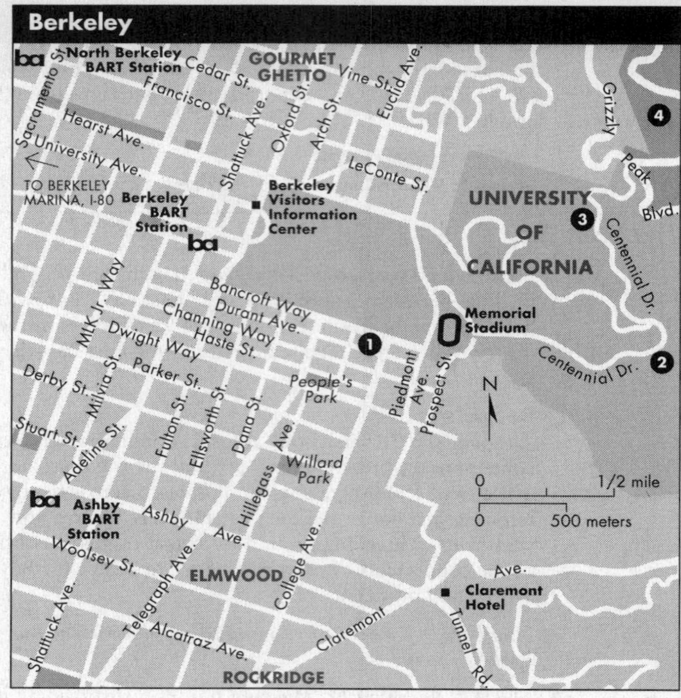

$$ ✕ **Café Rouge.** After you've finished shopping, take a seat in this spacious two-story bistro, complete with zinc bar, skylights, and festive lanterns. The short, seasonal menu runs the gamut from the sophisticated—grilled steelhead trout with chicory, white beans, and black truffle vinaigrette—to the everyday—a hamburger topped with cheddar. ✉ *1782 4th St.,* ☎ *510/525–1440. AE, MC, V. No dinner Mon.*

$$ ✕ **Lalime's.** The Mediterranean food served in this charming, flower-covered house is a favorite of Berkeleyites. The dining room, on two levels, is done in light colors, creating a cheerful mood that makes this the perfect spot for any special occasion. ✉ *1329 Gilman St.,* ☎ *510/527–9838. Reservations essential. AE, DC, MC, V. No lunch.*

$$ **Hotel Durant.** Long the mainstay of parents visiting their children at U.C. Berkeley, the Hotel Durant is a good option for those who want to be a short walk from campus and from the restaurants and shops of Telegraph Avenue. ✉ *2600 Durant Ave., 94704,* ☎ *510/845–8981,* FAX *510/486–8336. 140 rooms. Restaurant, bar, no-smoking rooms, room service, dry cleaning, laundry service, business services, meeting rooms, parking (fee). AE, D, DC, MC, V.*

$$ **Rose Garden Inn.** The two landmark homes that make up the Rose Garden Inn were built in the early 1900s by James and John Marshall, concrete tycoons responsible for laying Berkeley's original sidewalks. Though the inn has added modern touches to each room (cable television and telephones), the exquisite feel of a bygone era lingers. ✉ *2740 Telegraph Ave., 94705,* ☎ *510/549–2145,* FAX *510/549–1085. 40 rooms. No-smoking rooms, free parking. AE, D, DC, MC, V.*

Oakland

Once a bedroom community for San Francisco, the city became a hub of shipbuilding and industry almost overnight when the United States entered World War II. In the '60s and '70s an intense community pride gave rise to such militant groups as the Black Panther Party and the

Symbionese Liberation Army but was little match for the economic hardships and racial tensions that plagued Oakland. In many neighborhoods the reality was widespread poverty and gang violence—subjects that dominated the songs of such Oakland-bred rappers as the late Tupac Shakur.

Today a renovated downtown area and the thriving Jack London Square have injected new life into the city. Some areas, such as Piedmont and Rockridge, are perfect places for browsing, eating, or just relaxing between sightseeing trips to Oakland's architectural gems, rejuvenated waterfront, and numerous green spaces.

Numbers in the text correspond to numbers in the margin and on the Oakland map.

★ ❶ One of Oakland's top attractions, the **Oakland Museum of California** is an inviting series of landscaped buildings that display the state's art, history, and natural wonders. The museum is the best possible introduction to a tour of California, and its detailed exhibits can help fill the gaps on a brief visit. ✉ *1000 Oak St., at 10th St.,* ☎ *510/238–2200 or 800/625–6873.* 🎫 *$6.* ⏲ *Wed.–Sat. 10–5, Sun. noon–5.*

A proud reminder of the days when Oakland was a wealthy bedroom
❷ community, the **Camron-Stanford House** exudes dignity from its foundation up to its ornate widow's walk. Built in 1876, the Victorian boasts six painstakingly redecorated period rooms. ✉ *1418 Lakeside Dr.,* ☎ *510/836–1976.* 🎫 *$4.* ⏲ *Wed. 11–4 and Sun. 1–5.*

❸ **Lake Merritt** is a 155-acre oasis surrounded by parks, with several outdoor attractions on its north side.

❹ On the north shore of Lake Merritt, the **Rotary Nature Center and Waterfowl Refuge** is the nesting site of herons, egrets, geese, and ducks in the spring and summer. ✉ *Perkins St. at Bellevue Ave.,* ☎ *510/238–3739.* ⏲ *Daily 10–5.*

★ ❺ The **Paramount Theatre** (✉ 2025 Broadway, ☎ 510/465–6400) is perhaps the most glorious example of Art Deco architecture in the Bay Area. When classic films are screened here, the theater recaptures the thrill of moviegoing in the good old days.

❻ **Preservation Park** is a surprisingly idyllic little business community made up of 14 restored Victorians with tidy, bright green lawns.

When the author Jack London lived in Oakland, he spent many a day
❼ boozing and brawling in the waterfront area now called **Jack London Square** (✉ Embarcadero at Broadway, ☎ 510/814–6000). Home to shops, restaurants, small museums, and historic sites, the square contains a bronze bust of London, author of *The Call of the Wild, The Sea Wolf, Martin Eden,* and other books. The tiny, wonderful **Heinold's First and Last Chance Saloon** (✉ 56 Jack London Sq., ☎ 510/839–6761), one of London's old haunts, is still serving after 119 years, although it's a little worse for the wear since the 1906 earthquake.

East Bay Essentials

ARRIVING AND DEPARTING

By car: Take I–80 east across the Bay Bridge. For Berkeley, take the University Avenue exit through downtown Berkeley to the campus or take the Ashby Avenue exit and turn left on Telegraph Avenue to the traditional campus entrance; there is a parking garage on Channing Way. For Oakland, take I–580 off the Bay Bridge to the Grand Avenue exit for Lake Merritt. To reach downtown and the waterfront, take I–980 from I–580 and exit at 12th Street.

Camron-Stanford House 2
Jack London Square 7
Lake Merritt . . .3
Oakland Museum of California 1
Paramount Theatre 5
Preservation Park 6
Rotary Nature Center and Waterfowl Refuge 4

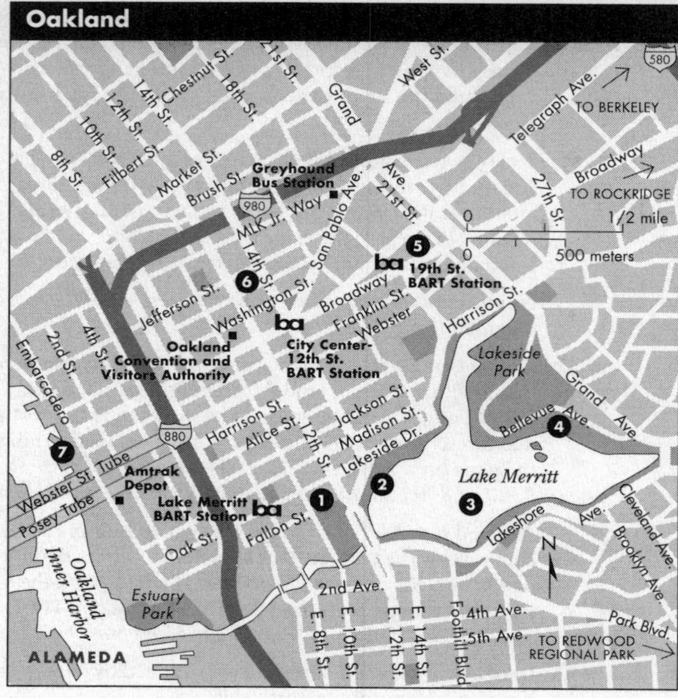

By ferry: The **Alameda–Oakland Ferry** (☎ 510/522–3300) runs several times daily between San Francisco's Ferry Building, Alameda, and the Clay Street dock near Jack London Square. Purchase tickets on board.

By train: BART trains (☎ 415/992–2278) make stops in downtown Berkeley and in several parts of Oakland.

VISITOR INFORMATION

Berkeley Convention and Visitors Bureau (✉ 2015 Center St., 94704, ☎ 510/549–8710). **Oakland Convention and Visitors Bureau** (✉ 550 10th St., Suite 214, 94607, ☎ 510/839–9000).

The Inland Peninsula

Less glamorous than so-called "marvelous Marin" and the colorful East Bay, the Inland Peninsula is often passed over by visitors to the Bay Area. But the peninsula also has lovely rolling hills, redwood forests, and historic mansions.

Palo Alto

Stanford University, 30 mi south of San Francisco, has its roots among the peninsula's estates. Originally the property was former California governor Leland Stanford's farm for breeding horses. For all its stature as one of the nation's leading universities, Stanford is still known as "The Farm." Free one-hour **walking tours** leave daily at 11 and 3:15 from the Visitor Information Center (☎ 650/723–2560 or 650/723–2053) in front of Memorial Hall on Serra Street, opposite Hoover Tower.

★ After a 10-year closure for structural repairs necessitated by the 1989 earthquake, the Stanford Museum, now named the **Iris and B. Gerald Cantor Center for Visual Arts,** is bigger and better than ever. Works span the centuries as well as the globe, from pre-Columbian to modern, including the world's largest collection of Rodin sculptures outside Paris.

✉ Lomita Dr. and Museum Way, off Palm Dr. at Stanford University, ☎ 650/723–4177. Free. Wed.–Sun. 11–5 (Thurs. until 8). Rodin Sculpture Garden tours Sat. 11, Sun. 3.

For a look at some less-traditional art, seek out the inconspicuous **Papua New Guinea Sculpture Garden,** tucked into a small, heavily wooded plot of land. The garden is filled with tall, ornately carved wooden poles, drums, and carved stones—all created on location by 10 artists from Papua New Guinea who spent six months here in 1994. *✉ Santa Teresa St. and Lomita Dr. Free.*

Dining and Lodging

$$$–$$$$ ✕ **Spago.** Silicon Valley's best and brightest have made a hit out of Wolfgang Puck's splashy, dashing Spago. The fare is inventive Californian, the service flawless. Dinner might include barbecued free-range squab with herbed risotto and caramelized fennel or tamarind-glazed rack of lamb. *✉ 265 Lytton Ave., ☎ 650/833–1000. Reservations essential. AE, D, DC, MC, V. No lunch weekends.*

$$$ ★ ✕ **Zibibbo.** This lively restaurant's eclectic menu includes selections from an oak-fired oven, rotisserie, grill, and oyster bar. Service is family-style, with large platters placed in the center of the table—all the better to taste just a bite of the skillet-roasted mussels, Swiss chard tart with goat cheese and currants, leg of lamb with chickpea-tomato tagine, and more. *✉ 430 Kipling St., ☎ 650/328–6722. AE, MC, V.*

$$–$$$ ★ ✕ **Evvia.** An innovative Greek menu and a stunning interior ensure that Evvia always packs in a crowd. Though the menu is written out in Greek (with English translations), there's an unmistakable California influence in such dishes as *lahanika pilafi* (risotto with butternut squash, mint, and leeks). *✉ 420 Emerson St., ☎ 650/326–0983. Reservations essential. AE, DC, MC, V. No lunch weekends.*

$$$ ★ **Garden Court Hotel.** This stylish boutique hotel has a European flair. From the outside it looks like an Italian villa, complete with columns and arches, a dormer roof, and balconies dressed up with bougainvillea. Every room has a private terrace looking out on a beautiful central courtyard filled with potted plants. *✉ 520 Cowper St., 94301, ☎ 650/322–9000 or 800/824–9028, FAX 650/324–3609. 62 rooms. Restaurant, bar, in-room data ports, in-room VCRs, room service, exercise room, laundry service, concierge, business services. AE, D, DC, MC, V.*

$–$$ ★ **Cowper Inn.** In a quiet, residential neighborhood five minutes from downtown Palo Alto, this former Victorian home is one of the least expensive lodging options in the area, and it's charming to boot. Each of the 14 rooms is unique, but all have handmade quilts. The cozy parlor has a brick fireplace, piano, and a big window looking out on tree-lined Cowper Street. Guests are invited to help themselves to almonds and sherry throughout the day. *✉ 705 Cowper St., 94301, ☎ 650/327–4475, FAX 650/329–1703. 14 rooms. Breakfast room, piano. AE, MC, V. CP.*

Inland Peninsula Essentials

ARRIVING AND DEPARTING

By car: The most pleasant direct route down the peninsula is I–280, the Junipero Serra Freeway, which passes along Crystal Springs Reservoir. For Stanford University, exit at Sand Hill Road and drive east. Turn right on Arboretum Drive, then right again on Palm Drive, which leads to the center of campus.

By train: CalTrain (☎ 800/660–4287) runs from 4th and Townsend streets to Palo Alto ($4 each way); from there take the free **Marguerite shuttle bus** (☎ 650/723–9362) to the Stanford campus and the Palo Alto area. Buses run about every 15 minutes 6 AM–7:45 PM and are timed to connect with trains and public transit buses.

VISITOR INFORMATION

Palo Alto Chamber of Commerce (✉ 325 Forest Ave., 94301, ☎ 650/324–3121).

The South Bay

The South Bay contains old-fashioned neighborhoods, abundant green hills, and the prestigious corporate corridors of Silicon Valley—all within minutes of each other. To the surprise of many visitors, the world's high-tech capital is wonderfully multifaceted, with some of the Bay Area's finest restaurants and shops.

San Jose

Updated by Victoria Schlesinger

In the last few years the downtown has become a major destination for entertainment, arts, nightlife, and sports at the San Jose Sports Arena.

Numbers in the text correspond to numbers in the margin and on the San Jose map.

55 mi south of San Francisco on U.S. 101 or I–280.

4 **Cathedral Basilica of St. Joseph.** The Renaissance-style cathedral, built in 1877, is completely restored and has extraordinary stained-glass windows and murals. The multidome cathedral occupies the site where a small adobe church served the first residents of the Pueblo of San Jose in 1803. ✉ *90 S. Market St.,* ☎ *408/283–8100.*

1 **Children's Discovery Museum.** An angular purple building across the creek from the convention center at the rear of the Discovery Meadow park, the museum exhibits interactive installations on science, the humanities, and the arts. ✉ *180 Woz Way, at Auzerais St.,* ☎ *408/298–5437.* *$6.* *Tues.–Sat. 10–5, Sun. noon–5.*

★ **Egyptian Museum and Planetarium.** The museum exhibits the West Coast's largest collection of Egyptian and Babylonian antiquities, including mummies and an underground replica of a rock tomb. The planetarium offers such programs as the popular "Celestial Nile," which describes the significant role astrology played in ancient Egyptian myths and religions. ✉ *1342 Naglee Ave., at Park Ave.,* ☎ *408/947–3636.* *$7 museum, $4 planetarium.* *Daily 10–5, planetarium weekdays only.*

6 **Fallon House.** San Jose's seventh mayor, Thomas Fallon, built this Victorian mansion in 1855. The house's period-decorated rooms can be viewed on a 90-minute tour that includes the Peralta Adobe (☞ *below*). ✉ *175 W. St. John St.,* ☎ *408/993–8182.* *$6.* *Guided tours Tues.–Sun. noon–5.*

2 **Guadalupe River Park.** This downtown park includes a carousel, children's playground, and artwork honoring five champion figure skaters from the area. ✉ *345 W. Santa Clara St.,* ☎ *408/277–5904.* *Free.*

7 **Peralta Adobe.** California pepper trees shade the circa-1797 last remaining structure from the pueblo that was once San Jose. The whitewashed two-room home has been furnished to illustrate life during the Mexican rancho era. ✉ *184 W. St. John St.,* ☎ *408/993–8182.* *$6 (includes admission to Fallon House).* *Guided tours Tues.–Sun. noon–5.*

3 **San Jose Museum of Art.** Housed in a former post office building, the museum has a permanent collection that includes paintings, large-scale multimedia installations, photographs, and sculptures by local and nationally known artists. ✉ *110 S. Market St.,* ☎ *408/294–2787.* *$7, free 1st Thurs. of month.* *Tues.–Wed. and Fri.–Sun. 10–5, Thurs. 10–8.*

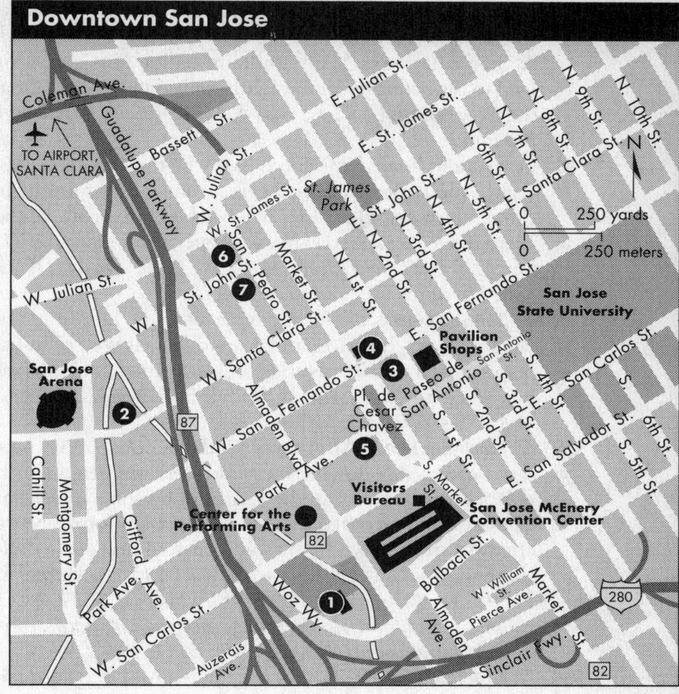

★ ♘ **5** **Tech Museum of Innovation.** San Jose's nationally recognized museum of technology has high-tech and hands-on exhibits that allow visitors to discover and demystify such disciplines as multimedia, communications, biotechnology, robotics, and space exploration. ✉ *201 S. Market St., at Park Ave.,* ☎ *408/294–8324.* 🎫 *$9 for museum, $12 for IMAX, $19.95 for both.* ⏲ *Daily 10–5.*

Winchester Mystery House. Convinced that spirits would harm her if construction ever stopped, firearms heiress and house owner Sarah Winchester constantly added to her house. For 38 years, beginning in 1884, she kept hundreds of carpenters working around the clock, creating a bizarre 160-room Victorian labyrinth with stairs going nowhere and doors that open into walls. The brightly painted house is a favorite family attraction. Explore the house on the 65-minute daytime tours, or come on a Friday the 13th for an evening flashlight tour. ✉ *525 S. Winchester Blvd., between Stevens Creek Blvd. and I–280,* ☎ *408/247–2101.* 🎫 *Estate tour $14.95.* ⏲ *Daily 9–5:30 (last admission at 5).*

Dining and Lodging

$$$–$$$$ ★ ✕ **Emile's.** Swiss chef and owner Emile Mooser's menu is a blend of classical European and contemporary Californian influences. Specialties include house-cured gravlax, rack of lamb, fresh game, and Grand Marnier soufflé. The interior is distinguished by romantic lighting, stunning floral displays, and an unusual leaf sculpture on the ceiling. ✉ *545 S. 2nd St.,* ☎ *408/289–1960. AE, D, DC, MC, V. Closed Sun.–Mon. No lunch Tues.–Thurs. and Sat.*

$$–$$$ ✕ **Bella Mia.** Locals love this restaurant for such fresh pastas dishes as salmon ravioli in tomato dill sauce and pasta carbonara. Trailing vines, a bubbling fountain, and outdoor heating make the outdoor patio a pleasant place to eat year-round. ✉ *58 S. 1st St.,* ☎ *408/280–1993. AE, D, DC, MC, V.*

$$ ✕ **Menara Moroccan Restaurant.** The delicious cumin- and coriander-spiced food is only part of the reason to come here for a leisurely meal. Arched entryways, lazily spinning ceiling fans, and a tile fountain all lend to the exotic decor. A nightly belly dancing performance completes the experience. ✉ *41 E. Gish Rd.,* ☎ *408/453–1983. AE, D, MC, V. No lunch.*

$$ ★ ✕ **71 Saint Peter.** This could easily be the best restaurant in San Jose. Each dish is prepared with care, from the seafood linguine, a mix of clams, shrimp, and scallops in a basil tomato broth, to the roasted duck prepared in a raspberry–black pepper demi-glace. ✉ *71 N. San Pedro St.,* ☎ *408/971–8523,* FAX *408/938–3440. AE, D, DC, MC, V. Closed Sun. No lunch Sat.*

$ ✕ **Señora Emma's.** This taqueria serves up large and tasty portions of nachos, tacos, burritos, and quesadillas, as well as full meals. You can help yourself to several kinds of salsas, limes, and jalapeños at the salsa bar and get a margarita at the full bar. ✉ *177 N. Santa Clara St.,* ☎ *408/279–3662. AE, MC, V.*

$$$ ★ **Fairmont Hotel.** Affiliated with the famous San Francisco hotel of the same name, this downtown gem offers the utmost in luxury and sophistication. Get lost in the lavish lobby sofas under dazzling chandeliers or dip your feet in the fourth-floor pool. Rooms have every imaginable comfort, from down pillows and custom-designed comforters to oversize bath towels changed twice a day. ✉ *170 S. Market St., at Fairmont Pl., 95113,* ☎ *408/998–1900 or 800/866–5577,* FAX *408/287–1648. 541 rooms. 3 restaurants, lobby lounge, no-smoking floors, room service, pool, health club, business services. AE, D, DC, MC, V.*

$$$ **Hotel De Anza.** This lushly appointed Art Deco hotel has hand-painted ceilings, a warm coral-and-green color scheme, and an enclosed terrace with towering palms and dramatic fountains. ✉ *233 W. Santa Clara St., 95113,* ☎ *408/286–1000 or 800/843–3700,* FAX *408/286–0500. 91 rooms, 9 suites. Restaurant, bar, in-room data ports, in-room VCRs, minibars, exercise room. AE, D, DC, MC, V.*

$$ **The Briar Rose Bed & Breakfast Inn.** This charming bed-and-breakfast is set on nearly half an acre of gardens in a restored 1875 Victorian farmhouse. There are plenty of thoughtful touches in the rooms, such as antique furniture and feather mattresses, and a lovely front parlor with a marble fireplace. ✉ *897 E. Jackson St., 95112,* ☎ *408/279–5999,* FAX *408/279–4534. 5 rooms, 1 cottage. Breakfast room, in-room data ports, in-room VCRs. AE, D, DC, MC, V. BP.*

South Bay Essentials

ARRIVING AND DEPARTING

By car: The quickest route to San Jose from San Francisco is I–280. From there take the Guadalupe Parkway (also known as Highway 87) north, then the Santa Clara Street exit east for the most direct route to downtown San Jose.

By plane: San Jose International Airport (✉ 1661 Airport Blvd. off Hwy. 87, ☎ 408/277–4759) is served by most major airlines.

By train: CalTrain (☎ 800/660–4287) runs from 4th and Townsend streets in San Francisco to Santa Clara's Railroad and Franklin streets stop near the university ($4.75 one-way) and to San Jose's Rod Diridon station ($5.25 one-way).

VISITOR INFORMATION

San Jose Convention and Visitors Bureau information hot line (☎ 408/295–2265).

SAN FRANCISCO A TO Z

Arriving and Departing

By Bus

Greyhound (☏ 800/231–2222) serves San Francisco from the Transbay Terminal at 1st and Mission streets.

By Car

Interstate 80 finishes its westward journey from New York's George Washington Bridge at the San Francisco–Oakland Bay Bridge. U.S. 101 enters the city from the north at the Golden Gate Bridge and continues south down the peninsula, along the west side of the San Francisco Bay.

By Plane

San Francisco International Airport (✉ U.S. 101, south of San Francisco, ☏ 650/761–0800) is the major gateway to San Francisco. **Oakland Airport** (✉ 1 Airport Dr., off I–880, ☏ 510/577–4000) is across the bay. **San Jose International Airport** (☏ 408/277–4759) is 3 mi from downtown San Jose (☞ South Bay A to Z, *above*).

Carriers serving San Francisco include Alaska, America West, American, Continental, Delta, Midwest Express, Northwest, Reno Air, Southwest, TWA, United, and US Airways. Carriers flying into Oakland include America West, American, Delta, Southwest, and United. Carriers serving San Jose include Alaska, America West, American Continental, Delta, Northwest, TWA, and United. *See* Air Travel *in* Smart Travel Tips A to Z for airline phone numbers.

BETWEEN THE AIRPORT AND DOWNTOWN

From SFO: A taxi ride from SFO to downtown costs about $30.The **SFO Airporter** (☏ 415/495–8404) picks up passengers outside baggage claim (lower level) and stops at selected downtown hotels ($10). **SuperShuttle** (☏ 415/558–8500) stops at the upper-level traffic islands. The cost ranges from $10 to $13 depending on your destination within San Francisco. **Bayporter Express** (☏ 415/467–1800) shuttles to the East Bay (about $20) also depart from SFO's upper-level traffic islands. The cheapest way to get from the airport to San Francisco is via **SamTrans** (☏ 800/660–4287). Bus 7B (55 minutes; $2.20) and 7F (35 minutes; $3; only one small carry-on bag permitted) head to San Francisco; Bus 3X stops at the Colma BART station (☞ BART, Getting Around, *below*), where you can board a train headed downtown. Board the SamTrans buses on the upper (departures) level. If you have questions about the taxis, buses, and trains that serve the airport, you can talk to one of the staff members of the **Ground Transportation Hotline** (☏ 800/736–2008).

To drive to downtown San Francisco from the airport, take U.S. 101 north to the Civic Center (Ninth Street), Seventh Street, or Fourth Street exit. If you're headed to the Embarcadero or Fisherman's Wharf, take U.S. 101 north to just past 3Com Park and exit onto I–280 north, which you'll follow to the Fourth Street/King Street exit. King Street becomes the Embarcadero a few blocks east of the exit. The Embarcadero winds around the waterfront to Fisherman's Wharf.

From Oakland International: A taxi from Oakland's airport to downtown San Francisco costs between $30 and $35. **America's Shuttle** (☏ 515/841–0272 or 415/515–0273), Bayporter Express (☞ *above*), and other shuttles serve major hotels and provide door-to-door service to the East Bay and San Francisco; Bayporter Express also serves the Peninsula and the South Bay. The best way to get to San Francisco via public transit is to take the AIR BART bus ($2) to the Coliseum/Oakland International Airport BART station (BART fares vary depending on where you're going; the ride to San Francisco costs $2.75).

If you're driving to San Francisco from Oakland International Airport, take Hegenberger Road east to I–880 north and follow signs to I–80 west (eventually the San Francisco–Oakland Bay Bridge).

By Train

Amtrak (☎ 800/872–7245) trains—the *Zephyr,* from Chicago via Denver, and the *Coast Starlight,* traveling between Los Angeles and Seattle—stop in Emeryville (✉ 5885 Landregan St.) and Oakland (✉ 245 2nd St., in Jack London Sq.). Shuttle buses connect the Emeryville station and San Francisco's Ferry Building (✉ 30 Embarcadero, at the foot of Market St.).

Getting Around

By Bus and Light Rail

San Francisco Municipal Railway System, or Muni (☎ 415/673–6864), includes buses, light-rail vehicles, and antique trolleys. There is 24-hour service; the fare is $1. The exact fare is always required; dollar bills or change are accepted. Transfers are issued free upon request at the time the fare is paid. They are valid for 90 minutes to two hours for two boardings of a bus or streetcar in any direction.

A $6 pass good for unlimited travel all day on all routes can be purchased from ticket machines at cable-car terminals and at the Visitor Information Center in Hallidie Plaza.

You can use **Bay Area Rapid Transit (BART)** (☎ 650/992–2278) trains to reach Oakland, Berkeley, Concord, Richmond, Fremont, Colma, and Martinez. Trains also travel south from San Francisco as far as Daly City. Fares run from $1.10 to $4.70, and a $3 excursion ticket buys a three-county tour.

By Cable Cars

Cable cars are popular, crowded, and an experience to ride: move toward one quickly as it pauses, wedge yourself into any available space, and hold on! The fare (for one direction) is $2. Exact change is preferred, but operators will make change up to $20. There are self-service ticket machines (which do make change) at a few major stops and at all the terminals. The one exception is the busy cable car terminal at Powell and Market streets; purchase tickets at the kiosk there.

The Powell-Mason line (No. 59) and the Powell-Hyde line (No. 60) begin at Powell and Market streets near Union Square and terminate at Fisherman's Wharf. The California Street line (No. 61), often less crowded than the other two, runs east and west from Market Street near the Embarcadero to Van Ness Avenue.

By Car

Driving in San Francisco can be a challenge because of the hills, the one-way streets, and the traffic. Curb your wheels when parking on hills, and use public transportation whenever possible. This is a great city for walking and a so-so city for parking. On certain streets, parking is forbidden during rush hours. Look for the warning signs. Illegally parked cars are towed.

The commercial parking lots downtown are often full and always expensive. The city-owned **Ellis-O'Farrell Garage** (✉ 123 O'Farrell St., at Stockton St., ☎ 415/986–4800), **5th and Mission Garage** (✉ 833 Mission St., at 5th St., ☎ 415/982–8522), and **Sutter-Stockton Garage** (✉ 444 Stockton St., at Sutter St., ☎ 415/982–7275) have the most reasonable rates in the downtown area. If you're going to North Beach and Chinatown, try the **766 Vallejo Garage** (✉ 766 Vallejo St., at Powell St., ☎ 415/989–4490) in North Beach. A few blocks south in Chinatown is the convenient, if expensive, **Portsmouth Square Garage** (✉ 733 Kearny St., at Clay St., ☎ 415/982–6353). The **Pier 39 Garage** (✉ 2550 Powell St., at the Embarcadero, ☎ 415/705–5418) and the **Wharf Garage** (✉ Fisherman's Wharf, 350 Beach St., at Taylor St., ☎ 415/921–0226) are two large garages along the Northern Waterfront.

Contacts and Resources

Doctors

Two hospitals with 24-hour emergency rooms are **San Francisco General Hospital** (✉ 1001 Potrero Ave., ☎ 415/206–8000) and the **Medical Center at the University of California, San Francisco** (✉ 500 Parnassus Ave., ☎ 415/476–1000). **Physician Access Medical Center** (✉ 26 California St., ☎ 415/397–2881) is a drop-in clinic in the Financial District, open weekdays 7:30 AM–4:30 PM.

Emergencies

Ambulance (☎ 911). **Fire** (☎ 911). **Police** (☎ 911).

Guided Tours

ORIENTATION TOURS

In addition to bus and van tours of the city, most tour companies run excursions to various Bay Area and northern California destinations such as Marin County and the Wine Country, as well as farther flung areas such as Monterey and Yosemite. City tours generally last 3½ hours and cost between $25 and $30. It's wise to reserve space on tours at least a day ahead. Tour companies include **Golden Gate Tours** (☎ 415/788–5775), **Gray Line Tours** (☎ 415/558–9400), **Great Pacific Tour** (☎ 415/626–4499), and **Tower Tours** (☎ 415/434–8687).

WALKING TOURS

Trevor Hailey's 3¾-hour **Cruising the Castro** (☎ 415/550–8110) tour focuses on the history and development of the city's gay and lesbian community. The cost is $35, which includes brunch. Reservations are required. The **Chinatown with the "Wok Wiz"** (☎ 415/981–8989) tour by cookbook author Shirley Fong-Torres and her staff is a 3½-hour spin through Chinese markets, other businesses, and a fortune-cookie factory. The $37 fee includes lunch; the cost is $25 without lunch. Shorter group tours start at $15 per person. **Chinese Cultural Heritage Foundation** (☎ 415/986–1822) conducts two walking tours of Chinatown. The Heritage Walk leaves on Saturday at 2 PM and lasts about two hours; the cost is $15. The Culinary Walk, a three-hour stroll through the markets and food shops, plus a dim sum lunch, is given from Tuesday through Friday at 10:30 AM; the fee is $30. **City Guides** (☎ 415/557–4266), a free service sponsored by the Friends of the Library, tours Chinatown, North Beach, Coit Tower, Pacific Heights mansions, Japantown, the Haight-Ashbury, historic Market Street, the Palace Hotel, and downtown roof gardens and atriums. Schedules are available at the San Francisco Visitors Center at Powell and Market streets and at library branches.

Late-Night Pharmacies

Several Walgreens Drug Stores have 24-hour pharmacies (✉ 498 Castro, at 18th St., ☎ 415/861–3136; 25 Point Lobos, near 42nd Ave. and Geary St., ☎ 415/386–0736; and 3201 Divisadero St., at Lombard St., ☎ 415/931–6417). The downtown Walgreens pharmacy (✉ 135 Powell St., near Market St., ☎ 415/391–7222) is open weekdays 8–8, Saturday 9–5, and Sunday 10–6.

Visitor Information

North Coast Visitors Bureau (✉ The Cannery, 2801 Leavenworth St., 2nd floor, 94133, ☎ 415/394–5991). **San Francisco Convention and Visitors Bureau** (✉ 900 Market St., at Powell St., 94102, ☎ 415/391–2000).

5 SACRAMENTO AND THE GOLD COUNTRY

INCLUDING HIGHWAY 49 FROM NEVADA CITY TO MARIPOSA

The gold-mining region of the Sierra Nevada foothills is a less expensive, if less sophisticated, region of California but not without its pleasures, natural and man-made. Spring brings wildflowers, and in fall the hills are colored by bright-red berries and changing leaves. The hills are golden in the summer—and hot. The Gold Country has a mix of indoor and outdoor activities, one of the many reasons it's a great place to take the kids.

Updated by Andy Moore

JAMES MARSHALL TURNED UP a gold nugget in the tailrace of a sawmill he was constructing along the American River and ushered in a whole new era for California. Before January 24, 1848, what would become the Golden State was a beautiful but sparsely populated land over which Mexico and the United States were still wrestling for ownership. With Marshall's discovery and its subsequent confirmation by President James Polk in his State of the Union speech on December 5, 1848, prospectors came to seek their fortunes in the Mother Lode.

As gold fever seized the nation, California's population of 15,000 swelled to 265,000 within three years—44,000 newcomers arrived by ship in San Francisco in the first 10 months alone, the majority of them men under 40, either unattached or with families back east. Most spent about two years in California before returning home, usually with empty pockets or having barely broken even. The consequences of the gold rush were more than monetary: '49ers—the term used to describe those who arrived in search of gold—who remained in California contributed to a freer culture that eschewed many of the constricting conventions of the eastern states.

The boom brought on by the gold rush lasted scarcely 20 years, but it changed California forever. It produced 546 mining towns, of which fewer than 250 remain. The hills were alive, not only with prospecting and mining but also with business, the arts, gambling, and a fair share of crime. Opera houses went up alongside brothels, and the California State Capitol in Sacramento was built with the gold dug out of the hills. Some of the nation's most treasured writers—Mark Twain and Bret Harte among them—began their careers writing about the mining camps. Gold-rush lore immortalized notorious bandits: when the law finally caught up with the debonair Black Bart, who targeted Wells Fargo stagecoaches and left behind poems (signed "Black Bart—PO-8") at his crime scenes, he turned out to be a well-known San Franciscan. Legend has it that Joaquin Murieta's crime spree—he robbed miners, then partied at local saloons—followed an assault on him and his family by Yankee prospectors.

Mexican miners weren't the only victims of the Yankee juggernaut. California's leaders in the mid-19th century engaged in a systematic plan to exterminate the local Native American population. Bounties were paid and private militias were hired to wipe out the Native Americans or sell them into slavery. A law in force from 1850 to 1863 prohibited nonwhites from appearing as witnesses in civil cases. Not surprisingly, verdicts and damage awards favored white plaintiffs and defendants.

The northern California cities of Sacramento, San Francisco, and Stockton grew quickly to meet the needs of the surrounding goldfields. Saloon keepers and canny merchants recognized that the real gold was to be made from the '49ers. Potatoes and onions sold for as much as $1 each, making entrepreneurs such as storekeeper Samuel Brannan millionaires. Much important history was made in Sacramento, the key center of commerce during this period. Pony Express riders ended their nearly 2,000-mi journeys in the city in the 1860s. The transcontinental railroad, conceived here by the Big Four (Leland Stanford, Mark Hopkins, Collis P. Huntington, and Charles Crocker), was completed in 1869.

By the 1960s the scars mining had inflicted on the landscape had largely healed. To promote tourism, townspeople began restoring vintage structures, historians developed museums, and the state established parks and recreation areas to preserve this extraordinary episode in American history. Today visitors flock to Nevada City, Auburn, Coloma,

Sutter Creek, and Columbia, not only to relive the past but also to explore museums and art galleries and to stay at inns.

Pleasures and Pastimes

Adventuring

Scenic and challenging Gold Country rivers, particularly the American and Tuolumne, lure white-water enthusiasts each spring and summer. Early morning hot-air balloon excursions float above treetops in deep canyons of the American River. Throughout the region weekend prospectors pan for gold, turning up nuggets frequently enough to inspire others to participate.

Dining

American, Italian, and Mexican fare are common in the Gold Country, but chefs also prepare ambitious Continental, French, and California cuisine. It's not difficult to find the makings for a good picnic in most towns.

CATEGORY	COST*
$$$$	over $50
$$$	$30–$50
$$	$20–$30
$	under $20

**per person for a three-course meal, excluding drinks, service, and 7¼% tax*

Lodging

Full-service hotels, budget motels, small inns, and even a fine hostel can all be found in Sacramento. The main accommodations in the larger towns along Highway 49—among them Placerville, Nevada City, Auburn, and Mariposa—are chain motels and inns. Many Gold Country B&Bs occupy former mansions, miners' cabins, and other historic buildings.

For information about area B&Bs, contact: **Amador County Innkeepers Association** (☎ 209/267–1710 or 800/726–4667); **Gold Country Inns of Tuolumne County** (☎ 209/533–1845); or **Historic Bed & Breakfast Inns of Grass Valley & Nevada City** (☎ 530/477–6634 or 800/250–5808).

CATEGORY	COST*
$$$$	over $175
$$$	$120–$175
$$	$80–$120
$	under $80

**All prices are for a standard double room, excluding 7¼% tax (12% in Sacramento).*

✎ following the text of a review is your signal that the property has a Web site, where you will find details and, usually, images; for a link, visit www.fodors.com/urls.

Shopping

Shoppers visit the Gold Country in search of antiques, collectibles, art, quilts, toys, tools, decorative items, and furnishings. Handmade quilts and crafts can be found in Sutter Creek, Jackson, and Amador City. Auburn and Nevada City support many gift boutiques.

Exploring Sacramento and the Gold Country

Visiting Old Sacramento's museums is a good way to steep yourself in history, but the Gold Country's heart lies along Highway 49, which winds the 325-mi north–south length of the historic mining area. The highway, often a twisting, hilly, two-lane road, begs for a convertible with the top down.

Numbers in the text correspond to numbers in the margin and on the Gold Country and Sacramento maps.

Great Itineraries

IF YOU HAVE 1 DAY

Drive east from Sacramento on I–80 to **Auburn** ⑰ for a tour of the **Placer County Courthouse** and its museum. Travel south on Highway 49 to the **Marshall Gold Discovery State Historic Park** ⑱ at Coloma. Head back to Sacramento for a drink at the bar on the *Delta King* and an evening stroll and dinner along the waterfront in **Old Sacramento** ①–⑧. The historical attractions will be closed, but you'll still get a feel for life here during the last half of the 19th century.

IF YOU HAVE 3 DAYS

Begin your tour on Highway 49 north of I–80. Walk deep into the recesses of the **Empire Mine** ⑯ near **Grass Valley,** and then drive 4 mi north on Highway 49 for a visit to the **Miners Foundry** in **Nevada City** ⑮. After lunch, travel south to **Auburn** ⑰, where you can take in the **Placer County Courthouse** and museum, have dinner, and spend the night. Early the next morning head south to tour **Marshall Gold Discovery State Historic Park** ⑱ in Coloma. Continue south to **Sutter Creek** ⑳ and spend the afternoon exploring the boutiques and antiques stores. If exploring a good vintage is more your game, take a detour to the **Shenandoah Valley,** southeast of **Placerville,** and taste some wine. Either way, spend the night in Sutter Creek. Return early the next day to **Sacramento** to visit the **California State Railroad Museum** ① and **Sutter's Fort** ⑬.

IF YOU HAVE 5 DAYS

Visit the **Empire Mine** ⑯, **Nevada City** ⑮, and **Auburn** ⑰ on day one. See Coloma's **Marshall Gold Discovery State Historic Park** ⑱ on the second day, and then continue on to **Sutter Creek** ⑳. On your third morning, visit the **Amador County Museum** in **Jackson** ㉑ before heading south on Highway 49 and east on Highway 4 for lunch in **Murphys** ㉓. Back on Highway 49 still southward is **Columbia State Historic Park** ㉔. You can relive the 1800s by dining and spending the night at the City Hotel. If you've been itching to pan for gold, do that in the morning in the state park, and then head back to **Sacramento** (Highway 49 north to Highway 16 west) for a riverboat cruise. Visit the **California State Railroad Museum** ① and **Sutter's Fort** ⑬ on day five.

When to Tour the Gold Country

The Gold Country is the most pleasant in the spring, when the wildflowers are in bloom, and in the fall. Summers are beautiful but hot: temperatures near or above 100°F are common. Sacramento winters tend to be cold and foggy. Throughout the year Gold Country towns stage community and ethnic celebrations. In December many towns deck themselves out for Christmas. Sacramento hosts the annual Jazz Jubilee in May and the California State Fair in August. Flowers bloom on Daffodil Hill in March.

SACRAMENTO

The gateway to the Gold Country, the seat of state government, and an agricultural hub, the city of Sacramento plays many important contemporary roles. Nearly 2 million people live in the metropolitan area, and the continuing influx of newcomers seeking opportunity, sunshine, and lower housing costs than in coastal California have made

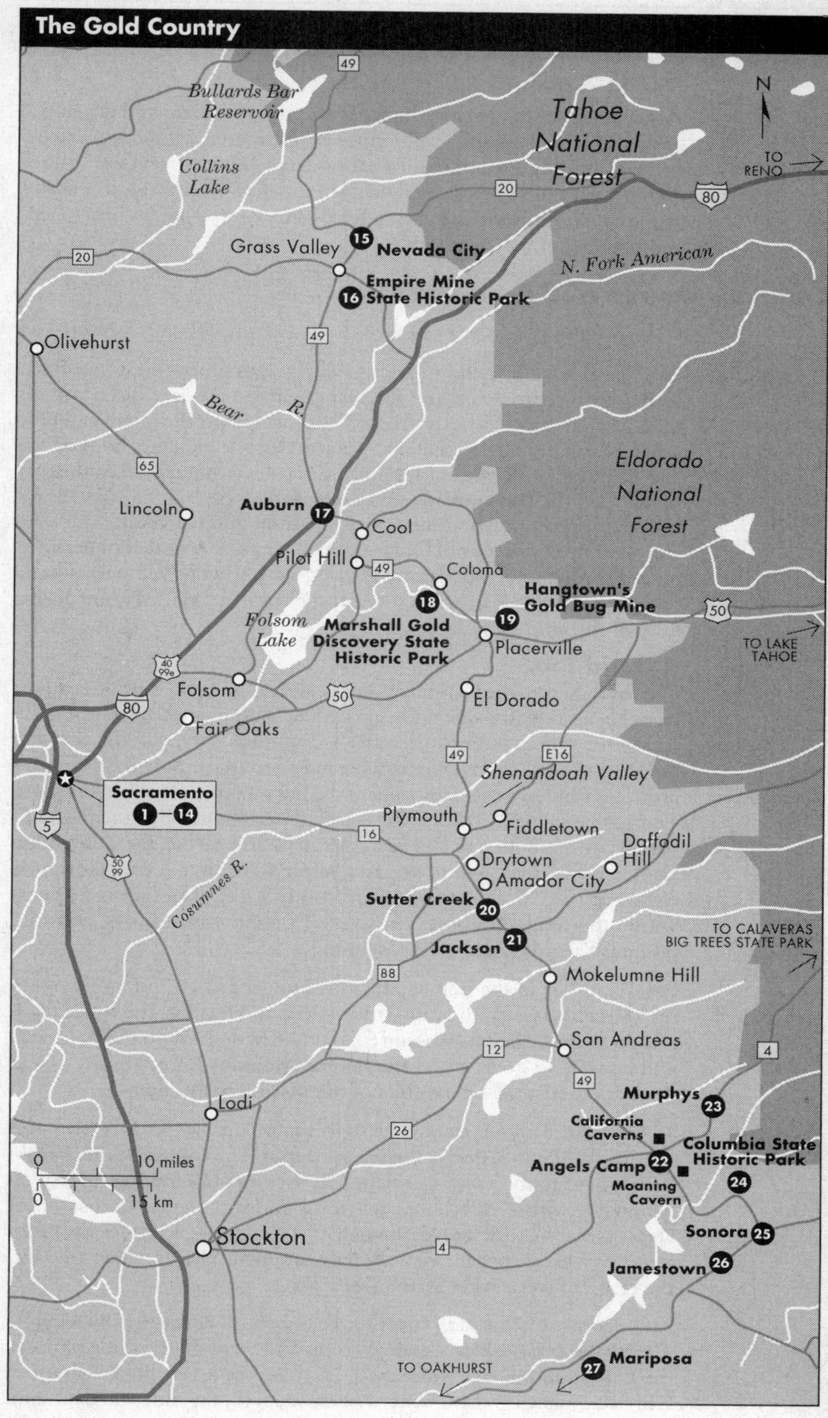
The Gold Country
Bullards Bar Reservoir
Collins Lake
Tahoe National Forest
N
TO RENO
20
80
49
Grass Valley
15 Nevada City
N. Fork American
Empire Mine
16 State Historic Park
Olivehurst
Bear R.
65
Eldorado National Forest
Lincoln
Auburn 17
Cool
Pilot Hill
Coloma
18
Hangtown's Gold Bug Mine 19
50
Folsom Lake
Marshall Gold Discovery State Historic Park
Placerville
TO LAKE TAHOE
40 99e
Folsom
El Dorado
Fair Oaks
E16
Shenandoah Valley
Sacramento
1—14
5
Plymouth
Fiddletown
16
Daffodil Hill
Drytown
Amador City
Cosumnes R.
Sutter Creek 20
Jackson 21
TO CALAVERAS BIG TREES STATE PARK
88
Mokelumne Hill
San Andreas
12
4
Murphys 23
California Caverns
Lodi
26
Columbia State Historic Park
Angels Camp 22
24
Moaning Cavern
0 10 miles
0 15 km
Sonora 25
Stockton
Jamestown 26
Mariposa 27
TO OAKHURST

it one of the nation's fastest-growing regions. Midtown's many new cafés and downtown's revived K Street Mall are testaments to Sacramento's growing sophistication.

Sacramento contains more than 2,000 acres of natural and developed parkland. This "city of a million trees" is planted with grand old evergreens, deciduous and fruit-bearing trees (some streets are littered with oranges in springtime), and even giant palms, giving it a shady, lush quality. Genteel Victorian edifices sit side-by-side with Art Deco and postmodern skyscrapers.

Old Sacramento and Downtown

87 mi northeast of San Francisco, I–80 to Hwy. 99 or I–5 North.

Wooden sidewalks and horse-drawn carriages on cobblestone streets lend a 19th-century feel to Old Sacramento, a 28-acre district along the Sacramento River waterfront. The museums at the north end hold artifacts of state and national significance. Historic buildings house shops and restaurants. River cruises and train rides bring gold-rush history to life. Call the **Old Sacramento Events Hotline** (☎ 916/558–3912) for information about living-history re-creations and merchant hours. An entertaining audio tour of Old Sacramento can be found at nine kiosks placed throughout the historic district, which, when fed with special tokens or 50 cents in quarters, activate the voice of "Mark Twain" telling tales of the gold-rush days.

A Good Tour

Old Sacramento, the Capitol and park surrounding it, and Sutter's Fort lie on an east–west axis that begins at the Sacramento River. The walk from Old Sacramento to the state's Capitol is easy, passing through the Downtown Plaza shopping mall and pedestrians-only K Street. This area takes on a festive atmosphere during an outdoor market held on Thursday evening. A DASH (Downtown Area Shuttle) bus and the number 30 city bus both link Old Sacramento, K Street Mall, the Convention Center, downtown, midtown, and Sutter's Fort in a loop that travels eastward on J Street and westward on L Street. The fare is 50 cents within this area, and buses run every 15 minutes weekdays, every 20 minutes Saturday, and every 30 minutes Sunday.

Park your car in the municipal garage under I–5 at 2nd Street (enter on I Street between 2nd and 3rd streets), and head to the superb **California State Railroad Museum** ①, then browse through the hardware and household items at the **Huntington, Hopkins & Co. Store** ②. Next door are the hands-on exhibits of the **Discovery Museum** ③.

To learn more about Sacramento's role in rail history walk a few paces south to the **Central Pacific Passenger Depot.** The **Central Pacific Freight Depot,** next to the passenger depot, houses a **Public Market** (closed on Monday), whose merchants sell food and gift items. Across Front Street is the historic **Eagle Theater** ④. The foot of K Street (at Front Street) is a great spot for viewing the Sacramento River wharf area and the restored stern-wheeler the *Delta King.*

At the corner of 2nd and J streets is the historic **B. F. Hastings Building** ⑤. The **Visitor Information Center** ⑥ is on 2nd Street in the same block as the **California Military Museum** ⑦. A must-see a few blocks south of Old Sacramento is the **Crocker Art Museum** ⑧, the oldest art museum in the American West. From here walk south on Front Street to the **Towe Auto Museum** ⑨. If you'd rather skip the automotive museum, walk up 3rd Street to the Capitol Mall, which leads to the **Capitol** ⑩. If you're still going strong, explore the **Golden State Museum** ⑪ at O

Sacramento

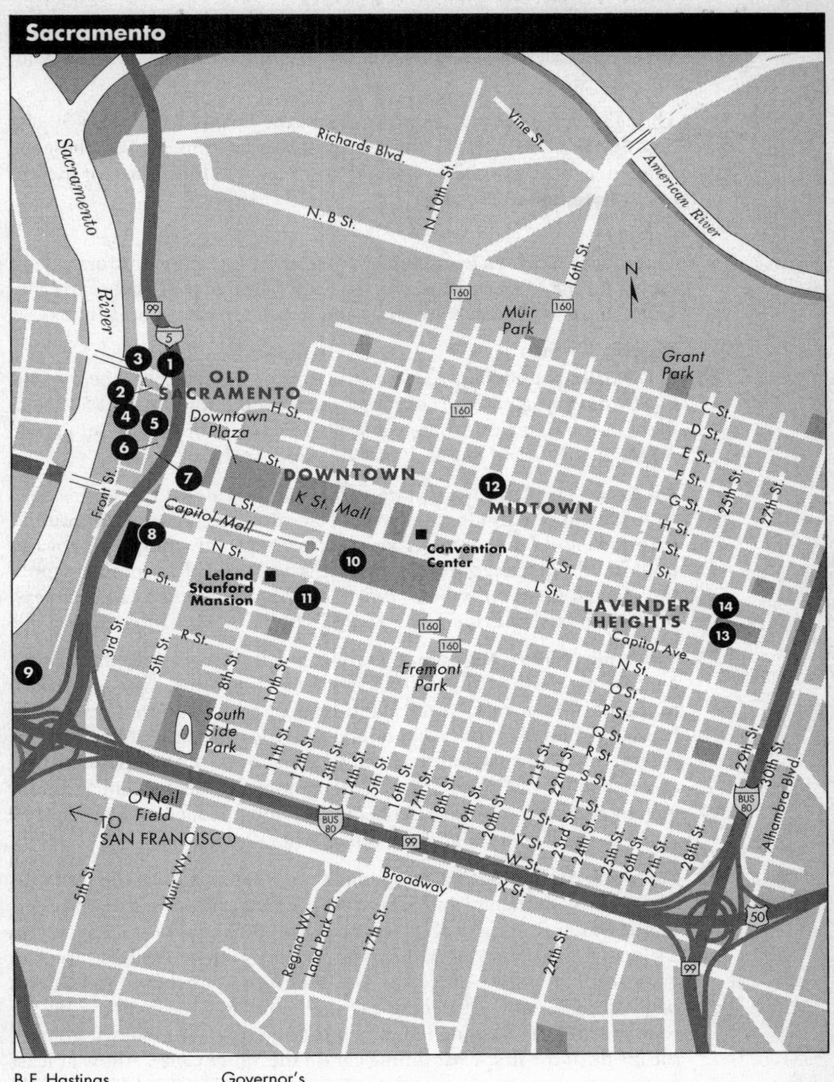

B.F. Hastings Building 5
California Military Museum 7
California State Railroad Museum . . . 1
Capitol. 10
Crocker Art Museum 8
Discovery Museum 3
Eagle Theater 4
Golden State Museum 11
Governor's Mansion. 12
Huntington, Hopkins & Co. Store 2
State Indian Museum 14
Sutter's Fort 13
Towe Auto Museum 9
Visitor Information Center 6

and 10th streets, one block south of the Capitol, or walk north to H Street then east to **Governor's Mansion** ⑫. Otherwise, walk back to your car via J Street.

Though it requires a drive or a ride on the DASH or number 30 city bus, **Sutter's Fort** ⑬ is worth the trip. It was Sacramento's earliest settlement; evocative exhibits bring that era back to life. North of the fort is the **State Indian Museum** ⑭.

TIMING

This tour makes for a leisurely day. Most of the attractions are open daily, except for the Military Museum, the Eagle Theater, the Crocker Art Museum, and the Golden State Museum, which are closed on Monday.

Sights to See

❺ **B. F. Hastings Building.** A reconstruction of the first chambers of the California Supreme Court occupies the second floor of this 1853 building. On the first floor there's a Wells Fargo History Museum and an ATM. ✉ *1000 2nd St.,* ☎ *916/440–4263.* ⏲ *Daily 10–5.*

Cal Expo. The California State Fair, a celebration of the state's agricultural and other industries, takes place at the Cal Expo fairgrounds. Livestock and other animals are always on display, competing for ribbons in untold categories. Other events are also held here throughout the year. ✉ *Exposition Blvd. (north of downtown, take Cal Expo exit off I–80 Business Loop),* ☎ *916/263–3247.* ⏲ *Mid-Aug.–Sept.*

❼ **California Military Museum.** A storefront entrance leads to three floors containing more than 30,000 artifacts—uniforms, weapons, photographs, documents, medals, and flags of all kinds—that trace Californians' roles in military and militia activities throughout U.S. history. An interesting display outlines military life for African-Americans; another includes Civil War–era medical equipment. More recent additions include exhibits on women in the military and prisoners of war. ✉ *1119 2nd St.,* ☎ *916/442–2883.* 🎫 *$3.* ⏲ *Tues.–Sun. 10–4.*

★ 🐤 ❶ **California State Railroad Museum.** Near what was once the terminus of the transcontinental and Sacramento Valley railroads (the actual terminus was at Front and K streets), this 100,000-square-ft museum has 21 locomotives and railroad cars on display and 46 exhibits. You can walk through a post-office car and peer into cubbyholes and canvas bags of mail, enter a sleeping car that simulates the swaying on the roadbed and the flashing lights of a passing town at night, or glimpse the inside of the first-class dining car on the *Super Chief.* Allow at least two hours to enjoy the museum. ✉ *125 I St.,* ☎ *916/445–6645.* 🎫 *$3.* ⏲ *Daily 10–5.*

★ ❿ **Capitol.** The Golden State's Capitol was built in 1869. The lacy plasterwork of the 120-ft-high rotunda has the complexity and color of a Fabergé egg. Underneath the gilded dome are marble floors, glittering chandeliers, monumental staircases, original artwork, replicas of 19th-century state offices, and legislative chambers decorated in the style of the 1890s. Guides conduct tours of the building and the 40-acre Capitol Park, which contains a rose garden, an impressive display of camellias (Sacramento's city flower), and the California Vietnam Veterans Memorial. ✉ *Capitol Mall and 10th St.,* ☎ *916/324–0333.* 🎫 *Free.* ⏲ *Daily 9–5; tours hourly 9–4.*

🐤 **Central Pacific Passenger Depot.** At this reconstructed 1876 station there's rolling stock to admire, a typical waiting room, and a small restaurant. Rides on a steam-powered train depart from the freight depot, south of the passenger depot. The train makes a 40-minute loop along the Sacramento riverfront. ✉ *930 Front St.,* ☎ *916/445–6645.* 🎫 *$3* *(free with same-day ticket from California State Railroad Museum); train ride $5 additional. Depot daily 10–5. Train operates every weekend Apr.–Sept., 1st weekend of month Oct.–Dec.*

★ 8 **Crocker Art Museum.** The oldest art museum in the American West has a collection of art from Europe, Asia, and California, including *Sunday Morning in the Mines* (1872), a large canvas by Charles Christian Nahl depicting the mining industry of the 1850s, and the magnificent *The Great Canyon of the Sierra, Yosemite* (1871) by Thomas Hill. The museum's lobby and ballroom retain the original 1870s woodwork, plaster moldings, and imported English tiles. *216 O St., 916/264–5423. $5.50. Tues.–Wed. and Fri.–Sun. 10–5, Thurs. 10–9.*

3 **Discovery Museum.** The building that holds this child-oriented museum is a replica of the 1854 City Hall and Waterworks. The emphasis is on interactive exhibits that combine history, science, and technology to examine the evolution of everyday life in the Sacramento area. You can sift for gold, examine a Native American thatch hut, or experience the goings-on in the print shop of the old *Sacramento Bee* newspaper. The Gold Gallery displays nuggets and veins. *101 I St., 916/264–7057. $5. June–Aug., daily 10–5; Sept.–May, Tues.–Sun. 10–5.*

4 **Eagle Theater.** When the Eagle opened in 1849, audiences paid between $3 and $5 in gold coin or dust to sit on rough boards and watch professional actors. This replica was constructed with the tentlike canvas and ship's-timber walls of olden times, though now there's insulation and the bench seats are cushioned. The theater hosts programs that range from a 13-minute slide show called *City of the Plains,* to puppet shows and juggling acts. *925 Front St., 916/323–6343. Fees vary depending on the program. Tues.–Fri. 10–4.*

★ 11 **Golden State Museum.** Drawing from the vast collections of the California State Archives, this state-of-the-art museum vividly portrays the story of California's land, people, and politics. Exhibits utilize modern technology, but there are also scores of archival drawers that visitors can pull out to see the real artifacts of history and culture—from the California State Constitution to surfing magazines. Board a 1949 cross-country bus to view a video on immigration, visit a Chinese herb shop inhabited by a holographic proprietor, or stand on a gubernatorial balcony overlooking a sea of cameras and banners. Admission includes the use of an innovative personal audio guide—choose an adult or children's program and the level of detail you desire for each exhibit. There's also a café where you can take a break from the fun. *1020 O St., at 10th St., 916/653–7524. $6.50. Tues.–Sat. 10–5, Sun. noon–5.*

12 **Governor's Mansion.** This 15-room house was built in 1877 and used by the state's chief executives from the early 1900s until 1967, when Ronald Reagan vacated it in favor of a newly built home in the more upscale suburbs. Many of the Italianate mansion's interior decorative details were ordered from the Huntington, Hopkins & Co. hardware store, one of whose partners, Albert Gallatin, was the original occupant. Each of the seven marble fireplaces has a petticoat mirror that ladies strolled past to see if their slips were showing. The mansion is said to have been one of the first homes in California to have an indoor bathroom. *1526 H St., 916/323–3047. $3. Daily 10–4; tours hourly.*

2 **Huntington, Hopkins & Co. Store.** This museum is a replica of the 1855 hardware store opened by Collis Huntington and Mark Hopkins, two of the Big Four businessmen who established the Central Pacific Railroad. Picks, shovels, gold pans, and other paraphernalia miners used

during the gold rush are on display, along with typical household hardware and appliances from the 1880s. Some items, such as blue enamelware, wooden toys, and oil lamps, are for sale. ✉ *113 I St.,* ☎ *916/323–7234.* ⏲ *Hours vary.*

Leland Stanford Mansion. The home of Leland Stanford, a railroad baron, California governor, and U.S. senator, was built in 1856, with additions in 1862 and the early 1870s. This once-grand edifice is currently undergoing major renovations. Some of the floors of the mansion, which will operate as a museum and a site for official state receptions, may be open to the public by late 2001, but meanwhile it is interesting to view the exterior transformation as it progresses. ✉ *802 N St.,* ☎ *916/324–0575.*

★ 14 **State Indian Museum.** Among the interesting displays at this well-organized museum is one devoted to Ishi, the last Yahi Indian to emerge from the mountains, in 1911. Ishi provided scientists insight into the traditions and culture of this group of Native Americans. Arts-and-crafts exhibits, a demonstration village, and an evocative 10-minute video bring to life the multifaceted past and present of California's native peoples. ✉ *2618 K St.,* ☎ *916/324–0971,* *$3.* ⏲ *Daily 10–5.*

★ 13 **Sutter's Fort.** Sacramento's earliest settlement was founded by German-born Swiss immigrant John Augustus Sutter in 1839. Audio speakers at each stop along a self-guided tour explain exhibits that include a blacksmith's shop, a bakery, a prison, living quarters, and livestock areas. Costumed docents sometimes reenact fort life, demonstrating crafts, food preparation, and firearms maintenance. ✉ *2701 L St.,* ☎ *916/445–4422.* *$3.* ⏲ *Daily 10–5.*

9 **Towe Auto Museum.** With more than 150 vintage automobiles on display, and exhibits ranging from the Hall of Technology to Dreams of Speed and Dreams of Cool, this museum explores automotive history and car culture. Docents provide information about specific models, including a 1931 Chrysler, a 1960 Lotus, and a luxurious and sleek 1927 Hispano-Suiza. A 1920s roadside café and garage exhibit re-creates the early days of motoring. A gift shop sells vintage-car magazines, model kits, and other car-related items. ✉ *2200 Front St., 1 block off Broadway,* ☎ *916/442–6802.* *$6.* ⏲ *Daily 10–6.*

6 **Visitor Information Center.** Obtain brochures about nearby attractions, arrange lodgings, check local restaurant menus, and get advice from the helpful staff here. ✉ *1101 2nd St., at K St.,* ☎ *916/442–7644.* ⏲ *Wed.–Sun. 9–5.*

Dining

$$–$$$ ★ ✕ **Biba.** Owner Biba Caggiano is an authority on Italian cuisine, author of several cookbooks, and the star of a national TV show on cooking. The Capitol crowd flocks here for homemade ravioli, osso buco, grilled pork loin, and a variety of veal and rabbit specials. ✉ *2801 Capitol Ave.,* ☎ *916/455–2422. AE, DC, MC, V. Closed Sun. No lunch Sat.*

$$–$$$ ★ ✕ **City Treasure.** A curved wall of windows shows off the warm interior of this restaurant to its fashionable midtown neighbors. Burnished copper tables and lamps, grapevine-pattern booths and banquettes, and locally produced artwork create a delightful setting. The eclectic menu changes seasonally. Smoked salmon croutons, jambalaya, grilled salmon, and braised lamb shanks are among the past offerings. The triple-layer chocolate cake is a must for dessert. From the list of more than 200 California wines, you can choose one of almost 50 by the glass, or have a trio—a sampler of three 3-ounce pours. ✉ *1730 L St.,* ☎ *916/447–7380. AE, D, DC, MC, V. No lunch Sat.*

$$–$$$ ✕ **Frank Fat's.** A longtime favorite of lawmakers and lobbyists, Frank Fat's is renowned more for its watering-hole atmosphere than its so-so Chinese food. The menu emphasizes Cantonese cuisine, but there are items from other regions as well. Signature dishes include brandy-fried chicken, honey-glazed walnut prawns, plus a couple of American items: New York steak and banana cream pie. ✉ *806 L St.,* ☎ *916/442–7092. AE, MC, V. No lunch weekends.*

$$–$$$ ✕ **Moxie.** Despite its simple decor and banklike schedule—the place is closed all holidays—Moxie has earned a reputation as one of the best restaurants in Sacramento. Start with the pork short ribs glazed with red wine and basil or grilled eggplant with feta and capers, and then move on to such entrées as spicy jambalaya, roasted duck in espresso–red wine sauce, or prawns carbonara. ✉ *2028 H St.,* ☎ *916/443–7585. AE, D, DC, MC, V. Closed Sun.–Mon. and Aug.*

$$–$$$ ✕ **Rio City Café.** Eclectic lunch and dinner menus and huge floor-to-ceiling windows with views of an Old Sacramento wharf are the dual attractions of this bright restaurant. Rio City serves both light and hearty fare: calamari salad, New York steak with wild mushroom demi-glaze, mesquite grilled salmon on garlic mashed potatoes, and duck breast with ginger apple marmalade over couscous. ✉ *1110 Front St.,* ☎ *916/442–8226. AE, D, DC, MC, V.*

$$–$$$ ✕ **Twenty Eight.** An intimate space with smoked mirrors, a golden crushed satin ceiling, richly upholstered furniture, and artful lighting, Twenty Eight further charms with genteel and attentive service. The food—appetizers such as roasted butternut squash soup and main courses that include sesame-crusted ahi tuna with crispy noodles and Colorado lamb chops with artichoke risotto and black olive sauce—is as refined as the decor. ✉ *2730 N St.,* ☎ *916/456–2800. AE, D, DC, MC, V. Closed Sun. No lunch.*

$–$$$ ✕ **California Fats.** The menu at this Old Sacramento spot combines intriguing flavors. Among the dishes are wok-fried seafood in a spicy bean sauce, herb-roasted chicken from the wood-fired oven, and ginger-roasted salmon with wild rice and potato cakes. ✉ *1015 Front St.,* ☎ *916/441–7966. AE, MC, V. No lunch weekends.*

$–$$$ ✕ **Paragary's Bar and Oven.** Pastas and brick-oven pizzas are the specialties of this casual spot. You won't go hungry here—portions are enormous. A waterfall flows near the back patio, which holds hundreds of plants. ✉ *1401 28th St.,* ☎ *916/457–5737. AE, D, DC, MC, V. No lunch weekends.*

$–$$ ✕ **Centro.** The motorcycle with a skeleton rider in the front window denotes the vibrant wackiness that spices up this popular midtown Mexican eatery. Bright yellow booths and salsa music contribute to the ambience, but the tasty food—well outside the taco-burrito realm—is the real attraction. Dishes include citrus-marinated rotisserie chicken with plantains and pork slow-roasted in banana leaves. The bar carries more than 60 Mexican tequilas, but it's easy to lose count after the first two. ✉ *2730 J St.,* ☎ *916/442–2552. AE, DC, MC, V. No lunch weekends.*

Lodging

$$$$ 🏨 **The Sterling Hotel.** This gleaming white Victorian mansion just three blocks from the Capitol has been transformed into a small luxury hotel. The marble-floor lobby and breakfast room have colorful Chinese rugs and comfy fireside lounging areas. Rose-hue guest rooms feature handsome furniture including four-poster or canopy beds. The bathrooms are tiled in Italian marble and have Jacuzzi tubs. Cookies or pastries baked on the premises are delivered to guest's rooms each evening, and an expanded Continental breakfast buffet is included in the room rate. Restaurant Chanterelle ($$–$$$) serves contemporary

Continental cuisine in it's candlelit dining room and pleasant patio area. ✉ *1300 H St., 95814,* ☎ *916/448–1300 or 800/365–7660,* FAX *916/448–8066. 14 rooms, 2 suites. Restaurant, bar, breakfast room, in-room data ports, no-smoking rooms, room service, dry cleaning, business services, meeting rooms, parking (fee). AE, D, DC, MC, V.*

$$$–$$$$ ★ **Amber House Bed & Breakfast Inn.** Three separate homes compose this B&B near the Capitol. The original house, the Poet's Refuge, is a Craftsman-style home with five bedrooms named for famous writers. Next door the 1913 Mediterranean-style Artist's Retreat has a French Impressionist motif. The third, an 1897 Dutch Colonial Revival home named Musician's Manor, has gardens where weddings occasionally take place. All rooms have private baths tiled with Italian marble. Several rooms have fireplaces and bathrooms with skylights and two-person hot tubs. ✉ *1315 22nd St., 95816,* ☎ *916/444–8085 or 800/755–6526,* FAX *916/552–6529. 14 rooms. No-smoking rooms, bicycles. AE, D, DC, MC, V. BP.*

$$$–$$$$ **Hartley House.** Innkeeper Randy Hartley's great-grandfather built Hartley House in 1906. The quiet midtown inn prides itself on having the feel of a small European hotel. All the antiques-filled rooms, which are named after British cities, have stereos and satellite TV. Breakfast is cooked to order. Guests have access to a secluded courtyard hot tub. ✉ *700 22nd St., 95816,* ☎ *916/447–7829 or 800/831–5806,* FAX *916/447–1820. 5 rooms. In-room data ports, hot tub. AE, D, DC, MC, V. BP.*

$$–$$$$ **Delta King.** This grand old riverboat, now permanently moored on Old Sacramento's waterfront, once transported passengers between Sacramento and San Francisco. Among many design elements of note are its main staircase, mahogany paneling, and brass fittings. The best of the 44 staterooms are on the river side toward the back of the boat. ✉ *1000 Front St., 95814,* ☎ *916/444–5464 or 800/825–5464,* FAX *916/447–5959. 44 rooms. Restaurant, bar, meeting rooms, parking (fee). AE, D, DC, MC, V. CP.*

$$–$$$$ ★ **Hyatt Regency at Capitol Park.** With a marble-and-glass lobby and luxurious rooms, this hotel across from the Capitol and adjacent to the convention center is arguably Sacramento's finest. The best rooms have Capitol Park views. The service and attention to detail are outstanding. ✉ *1209 L St., 95814,* ☎ *916/443–1234,* FAX *916/321–6699. 500 rooms, 24 suites. 2 restaurants, bar, pool, hot tub, exercise room, dry cleaning, laundry service, concierge, business services, meeting rooms, car rental, parking (fee). AE, D, DC, MC, V.*

$$$ **Best Western Sutter House.** Many of the pleasant, modern rooms in this downtown hotel open onto a courtyard surrounding a pool. The stylish restaurant, Grape's, serves contemporary cuisine. ✉ *1100 H St., 95814,* ☎ *916/441–1314, 800/830–1314 in CA,* FAX *916/441–5961. 97 rooms, 1 suite. Restaurant, lounge, no-smoking floor, pool, laundry service, free parking. AE, D, DC, MC, V. CP.*

$$$ **Holiday Inn Capitol Plaza.** Despite its decided lack of charm, this hotel has modern rooms and the best location for visiting Old Sacramento and the Downtown Plaza. It's also within walking distance of the Capitol. ✉ *300 J St., 95814,* ☎ *916/446–0100,* FAX *916/446–0117. 358 rooms, 6 suites. Restaurant, bar, pool, convention center. AE, DC, MC, V.*

$$$ **Radisson Hotel Sacramento.** Mediterranean-style two-story buildings clustered around a large artificial lake on an 18-acre landscaped site contain good-size rooms, with Art Deco appointments and furnishings. Many have patios or balconies. More of a resort than other Sacramento-area hotels, the Radisson presents summer jazz concerts in a lakeside amphitheater and holds barbecues on warm evenings. ✉

500 Leisure La., 95815, ☎ 916/922–2020, FAX 916/649–9463. 292 rooms, 22 suites. 2 restaurants, bar, room service, pool, outdoor hot tub, exercise room, jogging, boating, bicycles, meeting rooms. AE, D, DC, MC, V.

$ **Sacramento International Hostel.** This landmark 1885 Victorian mansion has a grand mahogany staircase, a stained-glass atrium, frescoed ceilings, and carved and tiled fireplaces. Dormitory rooms and bedrooms suitable for singles, couples, and families are available, as is a shared kitchen. ✉ *900 H St., 95814,* ☎ *916/443–1691 or 800/909–4776 ext. 40,* FAX *916/443–4763. 70 beds. MC, V.*

Nightlife and the Arts

Downtown Events Line (☎ 916/442–2500) has recorded information about seasonal events in the downtown area.

The **Blue Cue** (✉ 1004 28th St., ☎ 916/442–7208), upstairs from Centro restaurant, is an eclectic billiard lounge that features a very large selection of single-malt Scotch whiskeys. The **Fox and Goose** (✉ 1001 R St., ☎ 916/443–8825), a casual pub with live music (including open-mike Monday), has been rated the "best breakfast spot" by the *Sacramento Bee*. Traditional pub food (fish and chips, Cornish pasties) is served on weekday evenings from 5:30 to 9:30. **Harlow's** (✉ 2708 J St., ☎ 916/441–4693) draws a young crowd to its Art Deco bar–nightclub for live music after 9.

Sacramento Community Center Theater (✉ 13th and L Sts., ☎ 916/264–5181) hosts concerts, opera, and ballet. The **Sacramento Light Opera Association** (✉ 1419 H St., ☎ 916/557–1999) presents Broadway shows at the Sacramento Community Center Theater and in the huge Music Circus tent during summer. If you want the really BIG picture, the historic **Esquire Theater** at 13th Street on the K Street Mall screens IMAX movies.

Outdoor Activities and Sports

The basement-level **California Family Health & Fitness** (✉ 428 J St., at 5th St., ☎ 916/442–9090) has a workout area, weight machines, and a sauna. The fee for nonmembers is $10. **Jedediah Smith Memorial Bicycle Trail** runs for 23 mi from Old Sacramento to Beals Point in Folsom, mostly along the American River. The **Sacramento Kings** of the National Basketball Association play at the Arco Arena (✉ 1 Sports Pkwy., ☎ 916/928–6900).

Shopping

Among the many T-shirt and frozen-yogurt emporiums in Old Sacramento are some interesting art galleries and bookstores. Top local artists and craftspeople exhibit their works at **Artists' Collaborative Gallery** (✉ 1007 2nd St., ☎ 916/444–3764). **Gallery of the American West** (✉ 121 K St., ☎ 916/446–6662) has a large selection of Native American arts and crafts. The **Elder Craftsman** (✉ 130 J St., ☎ 916/264–7762) specializes in items made by local senior citizens.

Arden Fair Mall, northeast of downtown off I–80 in the North Area, is Sacramento's largest shopping center. **Downtown Plaza,** comprising the K Street Mall along with many neighboring shops and restaurants, has shopping and entertainment. There's a Thursday-night market, and an outdoor ice-skating rink in winter. **Pavilions Mall** (✉ Fair Oaks Blvd. and Howe Ave.) has many boutiques.

THE GOLD COUNTRY

Highway 49 from Nevada City to Mariposa

Highway 49 winds the length of the gold-mining area, linking the towns of Nevada City, Grass Valley, Auburn, Placerville, Sutter Creek, Sonora, and Mariposa. Most are gentrified versions of once-rowdy mining camps, vestiges of which remain in roadside museums, old mining structures, and historic inns.

Nevada City

15 *62 mi north of Sacramento, I–80 to Hwy. 49.*

Nevada City, once known as the Queen City of the Northern Mines, is the most appealing of the northern Mother Lode towns. The iron-shutter brick buildings that line the narrow downtown streets contain antiques shops, galleries, bookstores, boutiques, B&Bs, restaurants, and a winery. Horse-drawn carriage tours add to the romance, as do gas street lamps. At one point in the 1850s Nevada City had a population of nearly 10,000, enough to support much cultural activity. The **Nevada City Chamber of Commerce** (✉ 132 Main St., ☎ 530/265–2692) has books about the area and a free walking-tour map.

With its gingerbread-trim bell tower, **Firehouse No. 1** is one of the Gold Country's most photographed buildings. A museum, it houses relics of the fateful Donner Party (would-be settlers who fell victim to a severe Sierra Nevada snowstorm), gold-rush artifacts, and a Chinese joss house (temple). ✉ *214 Main St.,* ☎ *530/265–5468.* ⏲ *Apr.–Nov., daily 11–4; Dec.–Mar., weekends 11–4.*

The redbrick **Nevada Theatre,** constructed in 1865, is California's oldest theater building in continuous use. Mark Twain, Emma Nevada, and many other notable persons of bygone times appeared on its stage. The Nevada, home of the **Foothill Theater Company** (☎ 530/265–8587 or 888/730–8587), screens films and hosts theatrical and musical events. ✉ *401 Broad St.,* ☎ *530/265–6161; film showtimes 520/274–3456.*

The **Miners Foundry,** erected in 1856, produced machines for gold mining and logging. The Pelton Water Wheel, a source of power for the mines (the wheel also jump-started the hydroelectric power industry), was invented here. A cavernous building, the foundry hosts plays, concerts, an antiques show, and other events. ✉ *325 Spring St.,* ☎ *530/265–5040. Closed Mon.*

You can watch while you sip at the **Nevada City Winery,** where the tasting room overlooks the production area. ✉ *Miners Foundry Garage, 321 Spring St.,* ☎ *530/265–9463.* ⏲ *Tastings daily noon–5.*

Dining and Lodging

$$–$$$ ✕ **Country Rose Café.** The lengthy country-French menu at this antiques-laden café includes seafood, beef, lamb, chicken, and ratatouille. If you crave seafood try the swordfish Oscar, topped with crab, shrimp, and bernaise sauce. In the summer there is outdoor service on a verdant patio. ✉ *300 Commercial St.,* ☎ *530/265–6248. AE, D, DC, MC, V.*

$$–$$$ ✕ **Friar Tuck's.** A guitar player performs (and patrons sing along) at this vaguely 1960s-retro gathering spot that feels like a wine cellar. Rack of lamb, roast duck, fondue, Iowa beef, and Hawaiian fish specials are on the menu. There's an extensive wine and beer list as well as a full bar. ✉ *111 N. Pine St.,* ☎ *530/265–9093. AE, MC, V. No lunch.*

$$–$$$ ✕ **Kirby's Creekside Restaurant & Bar.** This two-level restaurant/bar complex perches over the quieter side of Deer Creek. You can dine on the large outdoor deck in warm weather or sit by the fireplace on chilly days. Among the inventive Continental preparations is the pork loin stuffed with roasted peppers. In the Chef's Culinary Adventure, the chef designs a meal (of three–six courses) for you based on your food preferences. ✉ *101 Broad St.,* ☎ *530/265–3445. AE, D, MC, V.*

$–$$ ✕ **Cirino's.** American-Italian dishes—seafood, pasta, and veal—are served at this informal bar and grill. The restaurant's handsome Brunswick bar is of gold-rush vintage. ✉ *309 Broad St.,* ☎ *530/265–2246. AE, D, MC, V.*

$$–$$$ **Deer Creek Inn.** The main veranda of this 1860 Queen Anne Victorian overlooks a huge lawn that rolls past a rose-covered arbor to the creek below. You can play croquet on the lawn or pan for gold in the creek. All rooms have king or queen beds. Some rooms have two-person tubs. ✉ *116 Nevada St., 95959,* ☎ *530/265–0363 or 800/655–0363,* FAX *530/265–0980. 5 rooms. AE, MC, V. BP.*

$$–$$$ **Flume's End.** This charming inn was built at the end of a large flume that once brought water into Nevada City's mines. The gurgling sounds of water now help to lull guests into relaxation. Lovely hardwood floors and antiques add an air of elegance. Two guest rooms have hot tubs and most, including a small cottage, have creek views. ✉ *317 S. Pine St., 95959,* ☎ *530/265–9665 or 800/991–8118. 6 rooms. MC, V. BP.*

$$–$$$ ★ **Red Castle Historic Lodgings.** A state landmark, this 1857 Gothic Revival mansion stands on a forested hillside overlooking Nevada City. Its brick exterior is trimmed with white icicle woodwork. A steep private pathway leads down through the terraced gardens into town. Handsome antique furnishings and Oriental rugs decorate the rooms. Home-cooked recipes are featured at the opulent afternoon tea service and morning breakfast buffet. ✉ *109 Prospect St., 95959,* ☎ *530/265–5135 or 800/761–4766. 4 rooms, 3 suites. MC, V. BP.*

$ **Northern Queen Inn.** Most of the accommodations at this bright creekside inn are typical motel units, but there are eight two-story chalets and eight rustic cottages with efficiency kitchens and gas log fireplaces in a secluded, wooded area. Guests ride free on the hotel's narrow-gauge railroad, which offers excursions through Maidu Indian homelands and a Chinese cemetery from gold-rush days. ✉ *400 Railroad Ave. (Sacramento St. exit off Hwy. 49), 95959,* ☎ *530/265–5824 or 800/226–3090,* FAX *530/265–3720. 70 rooms, 16 suites. Restaurant, refrigerators, pool, hot tub, convention center. AE, D, DC, MC, V.*

Grass Valley

4 mi south of Nevada City on Hwy. 49.

More than half of California's total gold production was extracted from mines around Grass Valley. Unlike in neighboring Nevada City, urban sprawl surrounds Grass Valley's historic downtown. The Empire Mine and the North Star Power House and Pelton Wheel Exhibit are among the Gold Country's most fascinating exhibits.

A great source of local information, the **Grass Valley/Nevada County Chamber of Commerce** is in a reproduction of the home on this site that was owned by the notorious dancer Lola Montez. Lola, who arrived in Grass Valley in the early 1850s, was no great talent—her popularity among miners derived from her suggestive spider dance—but her loves, who reportedly included composer Franz Liszt, were legendary. According to one account, she arrived in California after having been "permanently retired from her job as Bavarian king Ludwig's mistress," literary muse, and political adviser. She seems to have pushed too hard for democracy, which contributed to his overthrow and her banishment as a witch—or so the story went. The memory of licentious Lola lingers in Grass Valley, as does her bathtub (on the front porch of the house). ✉ *248 Mill St.,* ☎ *530/273–4667.*

The landmark **Holbrooke Hotel,** built in 1851, hosted Lola Montez, Mark Twain, Ulysses S. Grant, and a stream of other U.S. presidents. Its restaurant/saloon is one of the oldest still operating west of the Mississippi. ✉ *212 W. Main St.,* ☎ *530/273–1353 or 800/933–7077.*

★ 16 The hard-rock gold mine at **Empire Mine State Historic Park** was one of California's richest. An estimated 5.8 million ounces were extracted from its 367 mi of underground passages between 1850 and 1956. On the 50-minute tours you can walk into a mine shaft, peer into the mine's deeper recesses, and view the owner's "cottage," which features exquisite woodwork. The visitor center has mining exhibits, and a picnic area is nearby. ✉ *10791 E. Empire St. (exit south from Hwy. 49),* ☎ *530/273–8522.* *$3.* *May–Aug., daily 9–6; Sept.–Apr., daily 10–5. Tours in summer on the hr 11–4; winter weekends only at 1 (cottage only) and 2 (mine yard only), weather permitting.*

The **North Star Power House and Pelton Wheel Exhibit** stars a 32-ft-high enclosed waterwheel (invented by Lester Allen Pelton) said to be the largest ever built. It was used to power mining operations and was a forerunner of the modern turbines that generate hydroelectricity. Hands-on displays are geared to children. There's a picnic area nearby. ✉ *Empire and McCourtney Sts. (Empire St. exit north from Hwy. 49),* ☎ *530/273–4255.* *Donation requested.* *May–mid-Oct., daily 10–5.*

Lodging

$$–$$$ **Murphy's Inn.** A gold baron built the main inn here as a wedding present for his bride. Both the 1866 inn, which revels in its Victorian opulence, and the historic Donation Day House across the street contain antiques, lace curtains, and floral print wallpaper. Half the guest rooms have their own fireplaces. ✉ *318 Neal St., 95945,* ☎ *530/273–6873 or 800/895–2488. 5 rooms, 3 suites. AE, MC, V. BP.*

Auburn

17 *24 mi south of Grass Valley on Hwy. 49; 34 mi northeast of Sacramento on I–80.*

Auburn is the Gold Country town most accessible to travelers on the interstate. An important transportation center during the gold rush, Auburn has a small old-town district with narrow climbing streets, cobblestone lanes, wooden sidewalks, and many original buildings. A $1 trolley operated by the **Placer County Visitor Information Center** (☎ 530/887–2111 or 800/427–6463) loops through downtown and Old Town, with stops at some hotels and inns. Fresh produce, flowers, baked goods, and gifts are for sale at the **farmers' market** held each Saturday morning.

Auburn's standout structure is the **Placer County Courthouse.** The classic gold-dome building houses the Placer County Museum, which documents the area's history—Native American, railroad, agricultural, and mining—from the early 1700s to 1900. ✉ *101 Maple St.,* ☎ *530/889–6500.* *Free.* *Tues.–Sun. 10–4.*

The **Bernhard Museum Complex,** whose centerpiece is the former Traveler's Rest Hotel, was built in 1851. A residence and adjacent winery buildings reflect family life in the late Victorian era. The carriage house features period conveyances. ✉ *291 Auburn-Folsom Rd.,* ☎ *530/889–6500.* *$1 (includes entry to Gold Country Museum).* *Tues.–Fri. 10:30–3, weekends noon–4.*

The **Gold Country Museum** surveys life in the mines. Exhibits include a walk-through mine tunnel, a gold-panning stream, and a replica saloon. ✉ *1273 High St., off Auburn-Folsom Rd.,* ☎ *530/889–6500.* *$1 (includes entry to Bernhard Museum Complex).* ⏲ *Tues.–Fri. 10–3:30, weekends 11–4.*

Dining and Lodging

$–$$$ ✕ **Le Bilig French Café.** Simple and elegant cuisine is the goal of the chefs at this country-French café on the outskirts of Auburn. Escargots, coq au vin, and quiche are standard offerings; specials might include salmon in parchment paper. ✉ *11750 Atwood Rd., off Hwy. 49 near the Bel Air Mall,* ☎ *530/888–1491. MC, V. Closed Mon.–Tues. No lunch.*

$–$$$ ★ ✕ **Latitudes.** An 1870 Victorian is the setting for delicious multicultural cuisine. The menu (with monthly specials from diverse geographical regions) includes seafood, chicken, beef, and turkey entrées prepared with Mexican spices, curries, cheeses, or teriyaki sauce. Sunday brunch is deservedly popular, as are evenings at the bar downstairs, where mellow live music is performed Friday and Saturday. ✉ *130 Maple St.,* ☎ *530/885–9535. AE, D, MC, V. No lunch Sat., no dinner Mon.–Tues.*

$ ✕ **Awful Annie's.** Big patio umbrellas (and outdoor heaters when necessary) allow patrons to take in the view of the old town from this popular spot for breakfast—one specialty is an omelet with chili—or lunch. ✉ *160 Sacramento St.,* ☎ *530/888–9857. AE, MC, V. No dinner.*

$$–$$$ **Powers Mansion Inn.** This inn hints at the lavish lifestyle enjoyed by the gold-rush gentry. Two light-filled parlors have gleaming oak floors, Asian antiques, and ornate Victorian chairs and settees. A second-floor maze of narrow corridors leads to the guest rooms, which have brass and pencil-post beds with handmade quilts. The honeymoon suite has a fireplace and heart-shape tub. ✉ *164 Cleveland Ave., 95603,* ☎ *530/885–1166,* FAX *530/885–1386. 12 rooms, 1 suite. AE, MC, V. BP.*

$$ **Holiday Inn.** On a hill above the freeway across from Old Auburn, the hotel has an imposing columned entrance but a welcoming lobby. Rooms are chain-standard but attractively furnished. All have work areas and coffeemakers. Those nearest the parking lot can be noisy. ✉ *120 Grass Valley Hwy., 95603,* ☎ *530/887–8787 or 800/814–8787,* FAX *530/887–9824. 88 rooms, 8 suites. Restaurant, bar, in-room data ports, room service, pool, spa, exercise room, business services, convention center. AE, D, DC, MC, V.*

$ **Best Inns and Suites.** The decor at this well-maintained property is contemporary, softened with teal and pastel colors. Though a short distance from the freeway, the inn is fairly quiet. The expanded Continental breakfast includes many choices of baked goods, cereals, fruits and juices. ✉ *1875 Auburn Ravine Rd. (Forest Hill exit north from I–80), 95603,* ☎ *530/885–1800 or 800/626–1900,* FAX *530/888–6424. 77 rooms, 2 suites. No-smoking floor, pool, spa, coin laundry, meeting rooms. AE, D, DC, MC, V. CP.*

Coloma

18 mi south of Auburn on Hwy. 49.

The California gold rush started in Coloma. "My eye was caught with the glimpse of something shining in the bottom of the ditch," James Marshall recalled. Marshall himself never found any more "color," as gold came to be called.

★ 18 Most of Coloma lies within **Marshall Gold Discovery State Historic Park.** Though crowded with tourists in summer, Coloma hardly resembles the mob scene it was in 1849, when 2,000 prospectors staked out claims along the streambed. The town's population grew to 4,000, supporting seven hotels, three banks, and many stores and businesses. But when reserves of the precious metal dwindled, prospectors left as quickly as they had come. A working replica of John Sutter's mill lies near the spot where John Marshall first saw gold. A trail leads to a monument marking Marshall's discovery. The museum is not as interesting as the outdoor exhibits. ✉ *Hwy. 49,* ☎ *530/622–3470.* *$2 per vehicle (day use).* ⏲ *Park daily 8 AM–sunset. Memorial Day–Labor Day, daily 10–5; Labor Day–Memorial Day, daily 10–4:30.*

Lodging

$$ **Coloma Country Inn.** Five of the rooms at this B&B on 5 acres in the State Historic Park are inside a restored 1852 Victorian. Two suites, one with a kitchenette, are in the carriage house. Appointments include antique double and queen-size beds, handmade quilts, stenciled friezes, and fresh flowers. Ballooning and white-water-rafting packages are available. ✉ *345 High St., 95613,* ☎ *530/622–6919,* FAX *530/622–1795. 5 rooms, 2 with shared bath; 2 suites. No credit cards. BP.*

Placerville

10 mi south of Coloma on Hwy. 49; 44 mi east of Sacramento on U.S. 50.

It's hard to imagine now, but in 1849 about 4,000 miners staked out every gully and hillside in Placerville, turning the town into a rip-roaring camp of log cabins, tents, and clapboard houses. The area was then known as Hangtown, a graphic allusion to the nature of frontier justice. It took on the name Placerville in 1854 and became an important supply center for the miners. Mark Hopkins, Philip Armour, and John Studebaker were among the industrialists who got their starts here.

★ 19 **Hangtown's Gold Bug Mine,** owned by the city of Placerville, features a fully lighted mine shaft open for self-guided touring. A shaded stream runs through the park, and there are picnic facilities. ✉ *1 mi off U.S. 50, north on Bedford Ave.,* ☎ *530/642–5238.* *$3.* ⏲ *Mid-Apr.–mid-Oct., tours daily 10–4; mid-Oct.–mid-Apr., weekends only, tours 10–4. Gift shop closed Dec.–Feb.*

OFF THE BEATEN PATH

APPLE HILL – Roadside stands sell fresh produce from more than 50 family farms in this area. During the fall harvest season (from September through December) members of the Apple Hill Growers Association open their orchards and vineyards for apple and berry picking, picnicking, and wine and cider tasting. Many sell baked items and picnic food. ✉ *About 5 mi east of Hwy. 49; take Camino exit from U.S. 50,* ☎ *530/644–7692.*

Dining and Lodging

$$–$$$ ★ **Zachary Jacques.** It's not easy to locate, so call for directions. Finding this country-French restaurant is worth the effort. Appetizers on the seasonal menu might include escargots or mushrooms prepared in several ways, roasted garlic with olive oil served on toast, or spicy lamb sausage. Entrées such as roast rack of lamb, beef stew, and scallops and prawns in lime butter receive traditional preparation. The attached wine bar, open during the daytime, sells box lunches to go. ✉ *1821 Pleasant Valley Rd. (3 mi east of Diamond Springs),* ☎ *530/626–8045. AE, MC, V. Closed Mon.–Tues. No lunch.*

$–$$$ **Lil' Mama D. Carlo's Italian Kitchen.** This comfortable Italian restaurant with a pleasant staff serves large portions of homemade pasta, chicken, and some vegetarian dishes, heavy on the garlic. Local wines are available. ✉ *482 Main St.,* ☎ *530/626–1612. AE, MC, V. Closed Mon.–Tues. No lunch.*

$$ ✕ **Café Luna.** Tucked into the back of the Creekside Place shopping complex is a small restaurant with about 30 seats inside, plus outdoor tables overlooking a creek. The healthful entrées include grilled chicken breast with blueberry and pasilla salsa. ✉ *451 Main St.,* ☏ *530/642–8669. AE, D, MC, V. Closed Sun. No dinner Mon.–Tues.*

$$–$$$ **The Seasons Bed & Breakfast.** A 10-minute walk from downtown Placerville, one of the town's oldest historic homes has been transformed into a lovely and relaxing oasis. Decorated in an eclectic yet sophisticated manner, the main house, two cottages, and the wonderful gardens are filled with original artwork. Privacy is treasured here; each guest room has its own entrance. A spacious suite with a sitting room and stained glass windows takes up the entire top floor of the main house. One cottage has a little white picket fence around its own minigarden; the other has a two-person shower. ✉ *2934 Bedford Ave., 95667,* ☏ *530/626–4420. 3 rooms, 1 suite. No-smoking rooms. MC, V. BP.*

$$–$$$ **Shadowridge Ranch and Lodge.** In the wooded hills outside Placerville, you'll find a bit of rustic heaven in the form of a beautifully restored lodge complex. The immaculate hand-hewn log and stone cottages, most with wood-burning stoves, are filled with interesting artifacts of ranch and lodge life—including some dramatic taxidermy specimens—as well as many modern amenities. Each unit has its own patio. In the afternoon, guests are served complimentary local wines and a huge appetizer platter in the 19th-century stone wine cellar or on the patio off the main house. ✉ *3500 Fort Jim Rd., 95667,* ☏ *530/295–1000 or 800/644–3498,* FAX *530/626–5613. 4 suites. No-smoking rooms, minibars, refrigerators, hiking. AE, MC, V. Closed Jan.–Mar. BP.*

$$ **Best Western Placerville Inn.** This motel's serviceable rooms are done in the chain's trademark pastels. The pool comes in handy during the hot summer months. ✉ *6850 Greenleaf Dr., near U.S. 50's Missouri Flats exit, 95667,* ☏ *530/622–9100 or 800/854–9100,* FAX *530/622–9376. 105 rooms. Restaurant, pool, outdoor hot tub. AE, D, DC, MC, V.*

Shenandoah Valley

20 mi south of Placerville on Shenandoah Rd., east of Hwy. 49.

The most concentrated Gold Country wine-touring area lies in the rolling hills of the Shenandoah Valley, east of Plymouth. Robust zinfandel is the primary grape grown here, but vineyards also produce cabernet sauvignon, sauvignon blanc, and other varietals. Most wineries are open on weekend afternoons; several have shaded picnic areas, gift shops, and galleries or museums. Maps are available from the **Amador County Chamber of Commerce** (☞ Contacts and Resources *in* Sacramento and the Gold Country A to Z, *below*).

Sobon Estate (✉ 14430 Shenandoah Rd., ☏ 209/245–6554) operates the Shenandoah Valley Museum, illustrating pioneer life and wine making in the valley. It's open daily from 10 to 5. **Charles Spinetta Winery** (✉ 12557 Steiner Rd., ☏ 209/245–3384), which features a wildlife art gallery in addition to wine tasting, is open daily between 9 and 4. The gallery at **Shenandoah Vineyards** (✉ 12300 Steiner Rd., ☏ 209/245–4455), open daily from 10 to 5, displays contemporary art.

Lodging

$$–$$$ **Indian Creek Bed & Breakfast.** This log and stone lodge near Plymouth is a western movie buff's *and* a nature lover's dream. Built in 1932 by a Hollywood producer who hosted parties for stars such as John Wayne, the house emphasizes a Hollywood version of the West. The two-story great room features a 28-ft-high stone fireplace, while the dining room (where breakfast is served) is dominated by a 14-ft oak table. The 10-acre spread includes a creek and frog pond and is a haven

for birds of all kinds. ✉ *21950 Hwy. 49, 95669,* ☎ *209/245–4648,* FAX *209/245–3230. 4 rooms. Pool, outdoor hot tub. D, MC, V. BP.*

$$ **Amador Harvest Inn.** This B&B adjacent to Deaver Vineyards occupies a bucolic lakeside spot in the Shenandoah Valley. A contemporary Cape Cod–style structure has homey guest rooms with private baths. Public areas include a living room with fireplace and a music room with a view of the lake. ✉ *12455 Steiner Rd., 95669,* ☎ *209/245–5512 or 800/217–2304,* FAX *209/245–5250. 4 rooms. AE, MC, V. BP.*

Amador City

6 mi south of Plymouth on Hwy. 49.

The history of tiny Amador City mirrors the boom-to-bust-to-boom cycle of many Gold Country towns. With an output of $42 million in gold, its Keystone Mine was one of the most productive in the Mother Lode. After all the gold was extracted, the miners cleared out and the area suffered. Amador City now derives its wealth from tourists, who come to browse its antiques and specialty shops, many of them on or off Highway 49.

Dining and Lodging

$$ ★ ✕ **Imperial Hotel.** The whimsically decorated rooms at this 1879 hotel mock Victorian excesses in a modern way. Antique furnishings include iron and brass beds; gingerbread flourishes; and, in one room, Art Deco appointments. The two front rooms, which can be noisy, have balconies. The hotel's fine restaurant, whose menu changes quarterly, serves meals in a bright dining room and on the patio. The cuisine ranges from vegetarian to country-hearty to contemporary eclectic. ✉ *Hwy. 49, 95601,* ☎ *209/267–9172 or 800/242–5594,* FAX *209/267–9249. 6 rooms. Restaurant, bar. AE, D, DC, MC, V. 2-night minimum on weekends. Restaurant closed Mon.–Tues. No lunch. BP.*

Sutter Creek

★ 20 *2 mi south of Amador City on Hwy. 49.*

Sutter Creek is a charming conglomeration of balconied buildings, Victorian homes, and neo–New England structures. The stores along Highway 49 (called Main Street in the town proper) are worth visiting for works by the many local artists and craftspeople. Seek out the **J. Monteverde General Store** (✉ 3 Randolph St.), a typical turn-of-the-20th-century emporium with vintage goods on display (but not for sale), an elaborate antique scale and a chair-encircled potbellied stove in the corner. The museum is open weekends 10–3 or by asking at the **Sutter Creek Visitor's Center** next door (☎ 209/267–1344 or 800/400–0305).

OFF THE BEATEN PATH

DAFFODIL HILL – Each spring a 4-acre hillside east of Sutter Creek erupts in a riot of yellow and gold as 300,000 daffodils burst into bloom. The garden is the work of members of the McLaughlin family, which has owned this site since 1887. Daffodil plantings began in the 1930s. The display usually takes place between mid-March and mid-April. ✉ *From Main St. (Hwy. 49) in Sutter Creek take Shake Ridge Rd. east 13 mi,* ☎ *209/223–0350.* *Free.* *Daily in season 9–5.*

Dining and Lodging

$$–$$$ ✕ **Zinfandel's.** Black-bean chili in an edible bread tureen and smoked mussels and bay shrimp with roasted garlic cloves are among the appetizers at this casual restaurant with an adventurous menu. A favorite entrée is rack of lamb marinated in red wine, rosemary, and garlic on garlic smashed potatoes with mushroom port sauce. There's also a cozy

wine and espresso bar with a fireplace, open Friday and Saturday nights. ✉ *51 Hanford St.,* ☎ *209/267–5008. AE, D, MC, V. Closed Mon.–Wed. No lunch.*

$–$$ ✕ **Chatterbox Café.** This classic 1940s luncheonette has only five tables and 14 counter stools. Read a vintage newspaper or examine the jazz instruments and Disney memorabilia on the shelves while you wait for your chicken-fried steak, burger, homemade pie, or hot fudge sundae. The menu is as big as the Chatterbox is small. Beer and wine are available, and dinner on Tuesday night features a fancier, five-course *prix fixe* menu with such offerings as prime rib and shrimp scampi. ✉ *39 Main St.,* ☎ *209/267–5935. AE, D, MC, V. Closed Wed. and Thurs. No dinner.*

$ ✕ **Somewhere in Time.** Sip tea, sample a sinful dessert, or lunch on sandwiches and salads before or after browsing through the antiques shops in this complex that's part Victorian boutique, part dining room. The building, erected in 1860, was originally a miners' saloon run by Chinese immigrants. ✉ *34 Main St.,* ☎ *209/267–5789. D, MC, V. No dinner.*

$$$ ★ **The Foxes Bed & Breakfast.** The rooms in this white 1857 clapboard house are handsome, with high ceilings, antique beds, and lofty armoires. All have queen-size beds; five have wood-burning fireplaces or cable TV with VCRs. Breakfast is cooked to order and delivered on a silver service to your room or the gazebo in the garden. Innkeepers Min and Pete Fox have pampered guests here since 1980, and they are full of local wisdom. ✉ *77 Main St., 95685,* ☎ *209/267–5882 or 800/987–3344,* FAX *209/267–0712. 5 rooms, 2 suites. No-smoking rooms. D, MC, V. BP.*

$$–$$$ **Grey Gables Inn.** Charming yet modern, this inn brings a touch of the English countryside to the Gold Country. Each room, named after a British literary figure, has a gas-log fireplace. Afternoon tea and evening refreshments are served in the parlor. Birds flit about the wisteria in the terraced garden. ✉ *161 Hanford St., 95685,* ☎ *209/267–1039 or 800/473–9422,* FAX *209/267–0998. 8 rooms. MC, V. BP.*

$–$$ **Picture Rock Inn.** Original redwood paneling, wainscoting, beams, and cabinets lend the Picture Rock a cozy feel, as do leaded- and stained-glass windows. Eclectic furnishings span eras from Victorian to Art Deco; a 1920s carousel horse is suspended mid-leap in the front room. Most rooms have views and gas-log fireplaces. ✉ *55 Eureka St., 95685,* ☎ *209/267–5500 or 800/399–2389. 5 rooms. AE, D, MC, V. BP.*

$ **Aparicio's Hotel.** Budget-minded travelers will appreciate this clean hotel whose rooms contain two queen-size beds. Three rooms are wheelchair-friendly. ✉ *271 Hanford St., 95685,* ☎ *209/267–9177,* FAX *209/267–5303. 52 rooms. D, MC, V.*

Jackson

21 *8 mi south of Sutter Creek on Hwy. 49.*

Jackson once had the world's deepest and richest mines, the Kennedy and the Argonaut, which together produced $70 million in gold. These were deep-rock mines with tunnels extending as much as a mile underground. Most of the miners who worked the lode were of Serbian or Italian origin, and they gave the town a European character that persists to this day. Jackson has aboveground pioneer cemeteries whose headstones tell the stories of local Serbian and Italian families. The terraced cemetery on the grounds of the handsome **St. Sava Serbian Orthodox Church** (✉ 724 N. Main St.) is the most impressive.

Jackson wasn't the Gold Country's rowdiest town, but the party lasted longer here than most anywhere else: "Girls' dormitories" (brothels) and nickel slot machines flourished until the mid-1950s. The heart of Jackson's historic section is the **National Hotel** (✉ 2 Water St.), which operates an old-time saloon in the lobby. The hotel is especially active on weekends, when people come from miles around to participate in the Saturday-night sing-alongs.

The **Amador County Museum,** built in the late 1850s as a private home, provides a colorful take on gold-rush life. Displays include a kitchen with a woodstove, the Amador County bicentennial quilt, and a classroom. A time line recounts the county's checkered past. The museum conducts hourly tours of large-scale working models of the nearby Kennedy Mine. ✉ *225 Church St.,* ☎ *209/223–6386.* *Museum free, building with mine $1.* ⏲ *Wed.–Sun. 10–4.*

Dining and Lodging

$$–$$$ ✕ **Upstairs Restaurant.** Chef Layne McCollum takes a creative approach to contemporary American cuisine—fowl, fresh seafood, and meat—in his 12-table restaurant with a menu that changes weekly. The baked-Brie and roast-garlic appetizer and homemade soups are specialties. Local wines are reasonably priced. Downstairs there's a streetside bistro and wine bar. ✉ *164 Main St.,* ☎ *209/223–3342. AE, D, MC, V. Closed Mon.–Tues.*

$ ✕ **Rosebud's Classic Café.** Art Deco decor and music from the 1930s and 1940s set the mood at this homey café. Among the classic American dishes served are hot roast beef, turkey, and meat loaf with mashed potatoes smothered in gravy. Charbroiled burgers, freshly baked pies, and espresso or gourmet coffees round out the lunch menu. Omelets, hotcakes, and many other items are served for breakfast. ✉ *26 Main St.,* ☎ *209/223–1035. MC, V. No dinner.*

$$–$$$ **Court Street Inn.** This Victorian has tin ceilings and a redwood staircase. The cozy first-floor Angel Court room has a fireplace; the Crystal Court room has a large whirlpool and a Wedgwood stove. The Indian House, a two-bedroom cottage, has a large bathroom, a TV with VCR, and a stereo. A third building, Vintage Court, is decorated in wine colors and contains two guest rooms that share a parlor and deck. ✉ *215 Court St., 95642,* ☎ *209/223–0416 or 800/200–0416,* FAX *209/223–5429. 5 rooms, 2 suites. Outdoor hot tub. AE, D, MC, V. BP.*

$–$$ **Best Western Amador Inn.** Convenience and price are the main attractions of this two-story motel right on the highway. Rooms are nicely decorated; many have gas fireplaces. ✉ *200 S. Hwy. 49, 95642,* ☎ *209/223–0211 or 800/543–5221,* FAX *209/223–4836. 118 rooms. Restaurant, pool, laundry service. AE, D, DC, MC, V.*

Angels Camp

22 *20 mi south of Jackson on Hwy. 49.*

Angels Camp is famed chiefly for its May jumping-frog contest, based on Mark Twain's "The Jumping Frog of Calaveras County." The writer reputedly heard the story of the jumping frog from Ross Coon, proprietor of Angels Hotel, which has been operating since 1856.

Angels Camp Museum has gold-rush relics—photos, rocks, petrified wood, old mining equipment, and a horse-drawn hearse. The huge Pelton Water Wheel exhibit explains how the apparatus supplied water power to the mines. The carriage house out back holds 25 carriages and an impressive display of mineral specimens. ✉ *753 S. Main St.,* ☎ *209/736–2963.* *$1.* ⏲ *Jan.–Feb., weekends 10–3; Mar.–Nov., daily 10–3. Closed Dec.*

OFF THE BEATEN PATH

THE CALIFORNIA CAVERNS AND MOANING CAVERN – A ½-mi subterranean trail at the California Caverns winds through large chambers and past underground streams and lakes. There aren't many steps to climb but it's a hefty walk, with some narrow passageways and steep spots. The caverns, at a constant 53°F, contain crystalline formations not found elsewhere; the 80-minute guided tour includes fascinating history and geology. A 235-step spiral staircase leads into the vast Moaning Cavern. More adventurous sorts can rappel into the chamber—ropes and instruction are provided. Otherwise, the only way inside is via the 45-minute tour, during which you'll see giant (and still growing) stalactites and stalagmites and an archaeological site that holds some of the oldest human remains yet found in America (unlucky people have fallen into the cavern an average of once every 130 years starting 13,000 years ago). ✉ *California Caverns: 9 mi east of San Andreas on Mountain Ranch Rd., then about 3 mi on Cave City Rd. (follow the signs),* ☎ *209/736–2708.* 🎫 *$9.* ⏲ *Usually May–Dec., but call ahead.* ✉ *Moaning Cavern: Parrots Ferry Rd., 2 mi south of town of Vallecito, off Hwy. 4 east of Angels Camp,* ☎ *209/736–2708.* 🎫 *$8.75.* ⏲ *May–Oct., daily 9–6; Nov.–Apr., weekdays 10–5, weekends and holidays 9–5.*

Murphys

23 *10 mi east of Angels Camp on Hwy. 4.*

Murphys is a well-preserved town of white picket fences, Victorian houses, and interesting shops. Horatio Alger and Ulysses S. Grant are among the guests who have signed the register at **Murphys Historic Hotel and Lodge.** The men were among the 19th-century visitors to the giant sequoia groves in nearby Calaveras Big Trees State Park.

The **Kautz Ironstone Winery and Caverns** is worth a visit even if you don't drink wine. Tours take visitors into underground tunnels cooled by a waterfall from a natural spring; they include a performance of a huge automated pipe organ. The winery schedules concerts during spring and summer in its huge outdoor amphitheater, plus art shows and other events on weekends. On display is a 44-pound specimen of crystalline gold. A deli offers lunch items. ✉ *1894 Six Mile Rd.,* ☎ *209/728–1251.* ⏲ *Daily 11–5.*

Dining and Lodging

$–$$ ✕ **Grounds.** Light Italian entrées, grilled vegetables, chicken, seafood, and steak are the specialties at this bistro and coffee shop. Sandwiches, salads, and homemade soups are served for lunch. The atmosphere is friendly and the service attentive. ✉ *402 Main St.,* ☎ *209/728–8663. MC, V. Closed Tues. No dinner Mon.*

$–$$ ✕🏨 **Murphys Historic Hotel & Lodge.** This 1855 stone hotel figured in Bret Harte's short story "A Night at Wingdam," and Mark Twain and the bandit Black Bart signed the register. Accommodations are in the hotel and a modern motel-style addition. The older rooms are furnished with antiques, many of them large and hand-carved. The hotel has a convivial old-time saloon, which can be noisy into the wee hours. ✉ *457 Main St., 95247,* ☎ *209/728–3444 or 800/532–7684,* FAX *209/728–1590. 29 rooms (9 historic rooms share baths). Restaurant, bar, meeting rooms. AE, D, DC, MC, V.*

$$–$$$$ 🏨 **Redbud Inn.** Some rooms at this inn have double-sided fireplaces, cathedral ceilings, garden balconies, or claw-foot tubs. A room with brass beds and a tin ceiling replicates a miner's cabin. Wine and snacks are served in the parlor each evening. ✉ *402 Main St., 95247,* ☎ *209/728–8533 or 800/827–8533,* FAX *209/728–9123. 12 rooms, 1 suite. D, MC, V. BP.*

$$$ ★ **Dunbar House 1880.** The oversize rooms in this elaborate Italianate-style home have brass beds, down comforters, gas-burning stoves, and claw-foot tubs. Broad wraparound verandas encourage lounging, as do colorful gardens and shady elm trees. The Cedar Room's sunporch has a two-person whirlpool tub and a view of a white-flowering almond tree; in the Sequoia Room you can gaze at the garden while soaking in a bubble bath. Guests are served an appetizer and wine tray in their rooms in the afternoon, and breakfast is an extravagant, candlelit affair. ✉ *271 Jones St., 95247,* ☎ *209/728–2897 or 800/692–6006,* FAX *209/728–1451. 3 rooms, 2 suites. Refrigerators, in-room VCRs. AE, MC, V. BP.*

OFF THE BEATEN PATH

CALAVERAS BIG TREES STATE PARK – This state park is home to hundreds of the largest and rarest living things on the planet—magnificent giant sequoia redwood trees. Some are almost 3,000 years old, 90 ft around at the base, and about 250 ft tall. The park's self-guided trails range from a 200-yard trail to 1-mi and 5-mi loops through the groves. There are campgrounds and picnic areas; swimming, wading, fishing, and sunbathing on the Stanislaus River are popular in summer. ✉ *Off Hwy. 4, 15 mi northeast of Murphys (4 mi northeast of Arnold),* ☎ *209/795–2334.* *$2 per vehicle (day use); $12 for campsites. Disposal station, fire rings, flush toilets, hot showers, water.* ⏲ *Park sunrise–sunset (day use). Visitor center May–Oct., daily 10–4; Nov.–Apr., weekends 11–3.*

Columbia State Historic Park

★ 24 *14 mi south of Angels Camp, Hwy. 49 to Parrots Ferry Rd.*

Columbia State Historic Park, known as the Gem of the Southern Mines, comes as close to a gold-rush town in its heyday as any site in the Gold Country. You can ride a stagecoach, pan for gold, or watch a blacksmith working at an anvil. Street musicians perform in summer. Restored or reconstructed buildings include a Wells Fargo Express office, a Masonic temple, stores, saloons, two hotels, a firehouse, churches, a school, and a newspaper office. All are staffed to simulate a working 1850s town. ☎ *209/532–4301.* *Free.* ⏲ *Daily 9–5.*

Dining and Lodging

$–$$ ✕ **City Hotel.** The rooms in this restored 1856 hostelry are furnished with period antiques. Two have balconies overlooking Main Street, and six rooms open onto a second-floor parlor. All the accommodations have private half-baths with showers nearby; robes and slippers are provided. The restaurant ($$–$$$; closed Monday), one of the Gold Country's best, serves French-accented California cuisine complemented by a huge selection of wines from California. The What Cheer Saloon is right out of a western movie. ✉ *22768 Main St., Columbia 95310,* ☎ *209/532–1479 or 800/532–1479,* FAX *209/532–7027. 10 rooms. Restaurant, bar. AE, D, MC, V. CP.*

$–$$ **Fallon Hotel.** The state of California restored this 1857 hotel. All rooms have antiques and a private half-bath; there are separate men's and women's showers. If you occupy one of the five balcony rooms, you can sit outside with your morning coffee and watch the town wake up. ✉ *11175 Washington St., Columbia 95310,* ☎ *209/532–1470,* FAX *209/532–7027. 14 rooms. AE, D, MC, V. CP.*

Nightlife and the Arts

Sierra Repertory Theater Company (☎ 209/532–4644), a local professional company, presents a full season of plays, comedies, and musicals at the Historic Fallon House Theater and another venue in East Sonora. The City Hotel (☞ *above*) offers combined lodging, dinner, and theater packages.

Sonora

25 *4 mi south of Columbia, Parrots Ferry Rd. to Hwy. 49.*

Miners from Mexico founded Sonora and made it the biggest town in the Mother Lode. Following a period of racial and ethnic strife, the Mexican settlers moved on. Yankees built the commercial city that is visible today. Sonora's downtown historic section sits atop the Big Bonanza Mine, one of the richest in the state. Another mine, on the site of nearby Sonora High School, yielded 990 pounds of gold in a single week in 1879. Reminders of the gold rush are everywhere in Sonora, in prim Victorian houses, typical Sierra-stone storefronts, and awning-shaded sidewalks. Reality intrudes beyond the town's historic heart with strip malls, shopping centers, and modern motels. If the countryside surrounding Sonora seems familiar, that's because much of it has appeared in many movie over the years. Scenes from *High Noon, For Whom the Bell Tolls, The Virginian, Back to the Future III,* and *Unforgiven* were filmed here.

The **Tuolumne County Museum and History Center** occupies a building that served as a jail until 1951. Restored to an earlier period, it houses a jail museum, vintage firearms and paraphernalia, a case with gold nuggets, a cute exhibit on soapbox derby racing in hilly Sonora, and the libraries of an historical society and a genealogical society. ✉ *158 W. Bradford St.,* ☎ *209/532–1317.* 🎫 *Free.* ⏲ *Sun.–Mon. 10–4, Tues.–Fri. 10–4, Sat. 10–3:30.*

Dining and Lodging

$$–$$$ ✕ **Josephine's California Trattoria.** Seared ahi tuna, duckling with polenta, crayfish risotto, and angel-hair pasta with fresh seafood are among the dishes you might find on the seasonal menu. Single-portion pizzas are a staple. The reasonably priced wine list showcases Sierra foothill and Italian vintages. Musicians perform on some nights. ✉ *Gunn House Hotel, 286 S. Washington St.,* ☎ *209/533–4111. Restaurant, bar. AE, D, MC, V. Closed Mon. No lunch.*

$–$$ ✕ **Banny's Cafe.** Its pleasant environment and hearty yet refined dishes make Banny's a quiet alternative to Sonora's noisier eateries. Try the grilled salmon fillet with scallion rice and ginger wasabi soy aioli. ✉ *83 S. Stewart St.,* ☎ *209/533–4709. D, MC, V.*

$ ✕ **Garcia's Taqueria.** This casual, inexpensive eatery serves Mexican and southwestern fare with an emphasis on seafood dishes. Murals of Yosemite and other California landscapes adorn the walls. The spicy roasted-garlic soup is popular. ✉ *145 S. Washington St.,* ☎ *209/588–1915. No credit cards. Closed Sun.*

$$–$$$ 🏨 **Ryan House 1855 Bed & Breakfast Inn.** Attentive innkeepers make this 1850s farmhouse a fine place to stay, and there's more privacy than might be expected at such a small inn. A suite in the attic has a large sitting area set into the gables, a pink and burgundy bathroom with a double soaking tub, and a brass-and-iron bed. Everyone has access to the four parlors and the sunny kitchen, where complimentary snacks and beverages are always available. In springtime the garden blooms with colorful flowers of all kinds, including some antique roses as old as the house itself. Lodging-and-theater packages are available. ✉ *153 S. Shepherd St., 95370,* ☎ *209/533–3445 or 800/831–4897. 2 rooms, 1 suite. AE, MC, V. BP.*

$–$$ 🏨 **Best Western Sonora Oaks Motor Hotel.** The standard motel-issue rooms at this East Sonora establishment are clean and roomy. The larger ones have outside sitting areas. Suites have fireplaces, whirlpool tubs, and tranquil hillside views. Because the motel is right off Highway 108, the front rooms can sometimes be noisy. ✉ *19551 Hess Ave., 95370,* ☎ *209/533–4400 or 800/532–1944,* FAX *209/532–1964. 96 rooms, 4* *suites. Restaurant, lounge, pool, outdoor hot tub, meeting rooms. AE, D, DC, MC, V.*

Jamestown

26 *4 mi south of Sonora on Hwy. 49.*

Compact Jamestown supplies a touristy, superficial view of gold-rush-era life. Shops filling brightly colored buildings along Main Street sell antiques and gift items.

The California State Railroad Museum operates **Railtown 1897** at what were the headquarters and general shops of the Sierra Railway from 1897 to 1955. The railroad has appeared in more than 200 movies and television productions, including *Petticoat Junction, The Virginian, High Noon,* and *Unforgiven.* You can view the roundhouse, an air-operated 60-ft turntable, shop rooms, and old locomotives and coaches. Six-mile, 40-minute steam train rides through the countryside are operated on weekends during part of the year. ⊠ *5th Ave. and Reservoir Rd., off Hwy. 49,* ☎ *209/984–3953.* *$2 roundhouse tour; $6 train ride.* ⏲ *Daily 9:30–4:30. Train rides Apr.–Oct., weekends 11–3; Nov., Sat. 11–3.*

Dining and Lodging

$$–$$$ ✕ **National Hotel.** In business since 1859, the decor here is authentic—brass beds, patchwork quilts, and lace curtains—but not overly embellished. Some rooms have no phone. The saloon, which still has its original 19th-century redwood bar, is a great place to linger. The popular restaurant ($$–$$$) serves big lunches: hamburgers and fries, salads, and Italian entrées. More upscale Continental cuisine is prepared for dinner (reservations essential). ⊠ *77 Main St., 95327,* ☎ *209/984–3446; 800/894–3446 in CA;* FAX *209/984–5620. 9 rooms. Restaurant, bar. AE, D, DC, MC, V. CP.*

Mariposa

27 *50 mi south of Jamestown on Hwy. 49.*

Mariposa marks the southern end of the Mother Lode. Much of the land in this area was part of a 44,000-acre land grant Colonel John C. Fremont acquired from Mexico before gold was discovered and California became a state.

At the **California State Mining and Mineral Museum** a glittering, 13-pound chunk of crystallized gold makes it clear what the rush was about. Displays include a replica of a typical tunnel dug by hard-rock miners, a miniature stamp mill, and a panning and sluicing exhibit. ⊠ *Mariposa County Fairgrounds, Hwy. 49,* ☎ *209/742–7625.* *$2.* ⏲ *May–Sept., Wed.–Mon. 10–6; Oct.–Apr., Wed.–Sun. 10–4.*

Dining and Lodging

$$–$$$ ✕ **Ocean Sierra Restaurant.** Deep in the woods about 14 mi southeast of Mariposa is this comfortable spot for seafood, meat, pasta, and vegetarian dishes. The owner-chef grows many of her own fresh ingredients, including the delicate crystallized rose petals atop some of the desserts. ⊠ *3292 E. Westfall Rd. (from Hwy. 49 take Triangle Rd. 2 mi northeast),* ☎ *209/742–7050. D, MC, V. May–Sept., closed Mon.–Tues.; Oct.–Apr., closed Mon.–Thurs. No lunch.*

$ ✕ **Castillo's Mexican Food.** Tasty tacos, enchiladas, chili rellenos, and burrito combinations, plus chimichangas, fajitas, steak, and seafood, are served in a casual storefront setting. ⊠ *4995 5th St.,* ☎ *209/742–4413. MC, V.*

$$ **Little Valley Inn.** Pine paneling, historical photos, and old mining tools recall Mariposa's heritage at this modern B&B with three charming guest bungalows. A suite that sleeps five people includes a full kitchen. All rooms have private entrances and decks. The large grounds include a creek where guests can pan for gold (a helpful dog stirs the creek bed). The enthusiastic innkeepers will also take guests to their offsite claim for prospecting. ✉ *3483 Brooks Rd., off Hwy. 49, 95338,* ☎ *209/742–6204 or 800/889–5444,* FAX *209/742–5099. 4 rooms, 1 suite. Refrigerators, in-room VCRs, horseshoes. AE, MC, V. BP.*

$–$$ **Comfort Inn of Mariposa.** This white three-story building with a broad veranda sits on a hill above Mariposa. Some of the comfortable rooms have sitting areas and an expanded Continental breakfast is included in the room rate. ✉ *4994 Bouillon St., 95338,* ☎ *209/966–4344,* FAX *209/966–4655. 59 rooms, 2 suites. No-smoking rooms, pool, outdoor hot tub. AE, D, DC, MC, V. CP.*

SACRAMENTO AND THE GOLD COUNTRY A TO Z

Arriving and Departing

By Bus

Greyhound (☎ 800/231–2222) serves Sacramento, Auburn, and Placerville. It's a two-hour trip from San Francisco's Transbay Terminal at 1st and Mission streets to the Sacramento station at 7th and L streets.

By Car

Sacramento lies at the junction of I–5 and I–80, about 90 mi northeast of San Francisco. The 406-mi drive north on I–5 from Los Angeles takes seven–eight hours. Interstate 80 continues northeast through the Gold Country toward Reno, about 163 mi (three hours or so) from Sacramento.

By Plane

Sacramento International Airport (✉ 6900 Airport Blvd., 12 mi northwest of downtown off I–5, ☎ 916/874–0700) is served by Alaska, America West, American, Delta, Horizon Air, Northwest, Southwest, TWA, and United airlines. *See* Air Travel *in* Smart Travel Tips A to Z for airline phone numbers.

By Train

Several trains operated by **Amtrak** (☎ 800/872–7245) stop in Sacramento. Trains making the 2½-hour trip from **Jack London Square** (✉ 245 2nd St., Oakland) stop in Emeryville, Richmond, Martinez, and Davis; some stop in Berkeley and Suisun-Fairfield as well. Shuttle buses connect the **Emeryville station** (✉ 5885 Landregan St.), across the bay from San Francisco, and the city's **Ferry Building** (✉ 30 Embarcadero); other San Francisco pickup points are at the main entrance to Pier 39 and 835 Market Street at Powell Street, near Union Square.

Getting Around

By Bus

Sacramento Regional Transit (☎ 916/321–2877) buses and light-rail vehicles transport passengers in Sacramento. Most buses run from 6 AM to 10 PM, most trains from 5 AM to midnight. A DASH (Downtown Area Shuttle) bus and the number 30 city bus both link Old Sacramento, midtown, and Sutter's Fort in a loop that travels eastward on J Street and westward on L Street. The fare is 50 cents within this area.

By Car

Traveling by car is the most convenient way to see the Gold Country. From Sacramento three highways fan out toward the east, all intersecting with Highway 49: Interstate 80 heads 30 mi northeast to Auburn; U.S. 50 goes east 40 mi to Placerville; and Highway 16 angles southeast 45 mi to Plymouth. Highway 49 is an excellent two-lane road that winds and climbs through the foothills and valleys, linking the principal Gold Country towns.

By Taxi and Water Taxi

A water taxi run by **River Otter Taxi Co.** (☎ 916/446–7704) serves the Old Sacramento waterfront during spring and summer, stopping at points near restaurants and other sights. **Yellow Cab** (☎ 916/444–2208) serves all of Sacramento.

Contacts and Resources

Emergencies

Ambulance (☎ 911). **Fire** (☎ 911). **Police** (☎ 911).

Mercy Hospital of Sacramento (✉ 4001 J St., ☎ 916/453–4424). **Sutter General Hospital** (✉ 2801 L St., ☎ 916/733–8900). **Sutter Memorial Hospital** (✉ 52nd and F Sts., ☎ 916/733–1000).

Guided Tours

Channel Star Excursions (✉ 110 L St., Sacramento 95814, ☎ 916/552–2933 or 800/433–0263) operates the *Spirit of Sacramento,* a paddlewheel riverboat, which takes passengers on happy-hour, dinner, luncheon, and champagne brunch cruises in addition to one-hour narrated river tours. The **Coloma Country Inn** (☎ 530/622–6919) offers rafting excursions on the American River and balloon rides as part of B&B packages. **Gold Prospecting Adventures, LLC** (☎ 209/984–4653 or 800/596–0009), based in Jamestown, arranges gold-panning trips. **Gray Line/Frontier Tours** (✉ 2600 North Ave., Sacramento 95838, ☎ 916/927–2877 or 800/356–9838) operates city tours for groups of 10 or more.

Visitor Information

Amador County Chamber of Commerce (✉ 125 Peek St., Jackson 95642, ☎ 209/223–0350). **El Dorado County Chamber of Commerce** (✉ 542 Main St., Placerville 95667, ☎ 530/621–5885 or 800/457–6279). **Grass Valley/Nevada County Chamber of Commerce** (✉ 248 Mill St., Grass Valley 95945, ☎ 530/273–4667 or 800/655–4667). **Mariposa County Visitors Bureau** (✉ 5158 Hwy. 140, Mariposa 95338, ☎ 209/966–7081 or 800/208–2434). **Placer County Tourism Authority** (✉ 13464 Lincoln Way, Auburn 95603, ☎ 530/887–2111 or 800/427–6463). **Sacramento Convention and Visitors Bureau** (✉ 1303 K St., Sacramento 95814, ☎ 916/264–7777). **Tuolumne County Visitors Bureau** (✉ 542 Stockton St., Sonora 95370, ☎ 209/533–4420 or 800/446–1333).

6 LAKE TAHOE

THE CALIFORNIA AND NEVADA SHORES

The largest alpine lake in North America is famous for its clarity, deep blue water, and snowcapped peaks. Though Lake Tahoe possesses abundant natural beauty and accessible wilderness, nearby towns are highly developed and roads around the lake are often congested with traffic. Summertime is generally cooler here than in the Sierra Nevada foothills, and the clean mountain air is bracingly crisp. When it gets hot, the plentiful beaches and brisk water are only minutes away.

Updated by Deke Castleman

LAKE TAHOE lies 6,225 ft above sea level in the Sierra Nevada range, straddling the state line between California and Nevada. The border gives this popular resort region a split personality. About half the visitors here arrive intent on low-key sightseeing, hiking, fishing, camping, and boating. The rest head directly for the Nevada side, where bargain dining, big-name entertainment, and the lure of a jackpot draw them into the glittering casinos. Tahoe is also a popular wedding and honeymoon destination: couples can get married with no waiting period or blood tests at chapels all around the lake. On Valentine's Day the chapels become veritable assembly lines—four times as many ceremonies take place on that day than on any other. Incidentally, the legal marrying age in California and Nevada is 18 years, but one must be 21 to gamble or drink.

Summer's cool temperatures provide respite from the heat in the surrounding desert and valleys. Swimming in Lake Tahoe is always brisk—68°F is about as warm as the water gets—and the lake's beaches are generally crowded at this time of year. Those who prefer solitude can escape to the many state parks, national forests, and protected tracts of wilderness that ring the 22-mi-long, 12-mi-wide lake. From mid-autumn to late spring, multitudes of skiers and winter-sports enthusiasts are attracted to Tahoe's downhill resorts and cross-country centers, North America's largest concentration of skiing facilities. Ski resorts try to open by Thanksgiving, if only with machine-made snow, and can operate through May or later. Most accommodations, restaurants, and even a handful of parks are open year-round.

The first white explorer to gaze upon this spectacular region was Captain John C. Fremont in 1844, guided by famous scout Kit Carson. Not long afterward, silver was discovered in Nevada's Comstock Lode at Virginia City. As the mines grew larger and deeper, the Tahoe Basin's forests were leveled to provide lumber for subterranean support. By the early 1900s wealthy Californians were building lakeside estates here, some of which still stand. Improved roads brought the less affluent in the 1920s and 1930s, when modest bungalows began to appear. The first casinos opened in the 1940s. Ski resorts inspired another development boom in the 1950s and 1960s and turned the lake into a year-round destination.

During some summer weekends it seems that absolutely every tourist—100,000 at peak periods—is in a car on the main road that circles the 72-mi shoreline. The crowds and congestion increase as the day wears on. But at a vantage point overlooking Emerald Bay early in the morning, on a trail in the national forests that ring the basin, or on a sunset cruise on the lake itself, you can forget the hordes and commercial development and absorb the grandeur.

Pleasures and Pastimes

Camping

Campgrounds abound in the Tahoe area, operated by the state's park department, the U.S. Forest Service, city utility districts, and private operators. Sites range from primitive and rustic to upscale and luxurious. Make reservations far ahead in summer, when sites are in high demand (☞ Contacts and Resources *in* Lake Tahoe A to Z, *below*).

Dining

On weekends and in high season expect a long wait in the more popular restaurants. During slower periods some places may close temporarily or limit their hours, so call ahead to make sure your choice is open.

Casinos use their restaurants to attract gaming customers. Marquees often tout "$5.99 prime rib dinners" or "$1.49 breakfast specials." Some of these meal deals, usually found in the coffee shops and buffets, may not be top quality. But the finer restaurants in casinos generally deliver good food, service, and atmosphere.

Unless otherwise noted, even the most expensive Tahoe restaurants welcome customers in casual clothes—not surprising in this year-round vacation mecca—but don't expect to be served in most places if you're barefoot, shirtless, or wearing a skimpy bathing suit.

CATEGORY	COST*
$$$$	over $50
$$$	$30–$50
$$	$20–$30
$	under $20

**per person for a three-course meal, excluding drinks, service, and 7%–7¼% tax*

Gambling

Nevada's major casinos are also full-service hotels and resorts. They offer discounted lodging packages throughout the year. The casinos share an atmosphere of garish neon and noise, but air conditioning and no-smoking areas have eliminated the hazy pall of the past. Six casinos are clustered on a strip of U.S. 50 in Stateline—Caesars, Harrah's, Harvey's, Horizon, and Lakeside, plus Bill's, a lower-stakes "junior" casino (no lodging) that appeals to frugal gamblers. Five other casinos operate on the north shore: the Hyatt Regency, Cal-Neva, Tahoe Biltmore, Crystal Bay Club, and Jim Kelley's Nugget. Open 24 hours a day, 365 days a year, these gambling parlors have table games (craps, blackjack, roulette, baccarat, poker, keno, pai gow poker, bingo, and big six), race and sports books, and thousands of slot and video poker machines—1,575, for instance, at Harrah's. There is no charge to enter and there is no dress code.

Golf

The Tahoe area is nearly as popular with golfers as it is with skiers. A half-dozen superb courses dot the mountains around the lake, with magnificent views, thick pines, fresh cool air, and lush fairways and greens. Encountering wildlife is not uncommon if you have to search for your ball out-of-bounds.

Hiking

There are five national forests in the Tahoe Basin and a half-dozen state parks. The main areas for hiking include the Tahoe Rim Trail, a 150-mi path along the ridgelines above the lake; Desolation Wilderness, a vast 63,473-acre preserve of granite peaks, glacial valleys, subalpine forests, the Rubicon River, and more than 50 lakes; and the trail systems near Lake Tahoe Visitor Center and D. L. Bliss, Emerald Bay, Sugar Pine Point, and Lake Tahoe–Nevada state parks.

Lodging

Quiet inns on the water, motels near the casino area, rooms at the casinos themselves, lodges close to ski runs, and condos everywhere else are among the Tahoe options. During summer and ski season the lake is crowded; reserve space as far ahead as possible. Spring and fall give you a little more leeway and lower—sometimes significantly lower—rates. Price categories listed below reflect high-season rates.

CATEGORY	COST*
$$$$	over $175
$$$	$120–$175
$$	$80–$120
$	under $80

**All prices are for a standard double room, excluding 9%–10% tax.*

following the text of a review is your signal that the property has a Web site, where you will find details and, usually, images; for a link, visit www.fodors.com/urls.

Skiing

The Lake Tahoe area is a Nordic skier's paradise. You can even cross-country ski on fresh snow right on the lakeshore beaches. Skinny skiing (slang for cross-country) at the resorts can be costly, but you get the benefits of machine grooming and trail preparation. If it's bargain Nordic you're after, take advantage of thousands of acres of public forest and parkland trails.

The mountains around Lake Tahoe are bombarded by blizzards throughout most winters (during dry years skiers and resort operators pray for snowstorms) and sometimes the fall and spring; 10- to 12-ft bases are not uncommon. The profusion of downhill resorts guarantees a nearly infinite variety of terrains, conditions, and challenges. To save money, look for packages offered by lodges and resorts; some include interchangeable lift tickets that allow you to try different slopes. Midweek packages are usually cheaper, and most resorts offer family discounts. Free shuttle-bus service is available between most ski resorts and lodgings.

Exploring Lake Tahoe

The most common way to explore the Lake Tahoe area is to drive the 72-mi road that follows the shore through wooded flatlands and past beaches, climbing to vistas on the rugged west side of the lake and descending to the busiest commercial developments and casinos on its northeastern and southeastern edges. Undeveloped Lake Tahoe–Nevada State Park occupies more than half of the Nevada side of Lake Tahoe, stretching north a few miles from Spooner Lake to just south of the upscale community of Incline Village. The California side, particularly South Lake Tahoe, is more developed, though much wilderness remains.

Great Itineraries

Although, or perhaps because, the distance around Lake Tahoe is relatively short, the desire to experience the whole area can be overwhelming. It takes only one day "to see it"—drive around the lake, stretch your legs at a few overlooks, take a nature walk, and wander among the casinos at Stateline. If you have more time, you can laze on a beach and swim, venture onto the lake or into the mountains, and sample Tahoe's finer restaurants. If you have five days, you may become so attached to Tahoe that you begin visiting real-estate agents.

Numbers in the text correspond to numbers in the margin and on the Lake Tahoe map.

IF YOU HAVE 3 DAYS

On your first day, stop in **South Lake Tahoe** ① and pick up provisions for a picnic lunch. Start with some morning beach fun at the **Pope-Baldwin Recreation Area** ③ and check out the area's Tallac Historic Site. Head west on Highway 89, stopping at the **Lake Tahoe Visitor Center** ④ and the **Emerald Bay State Park** ⑤ lookout. Have lunch at the lookout, or hike down to Vikingsholm, a Viking castle replica. In the

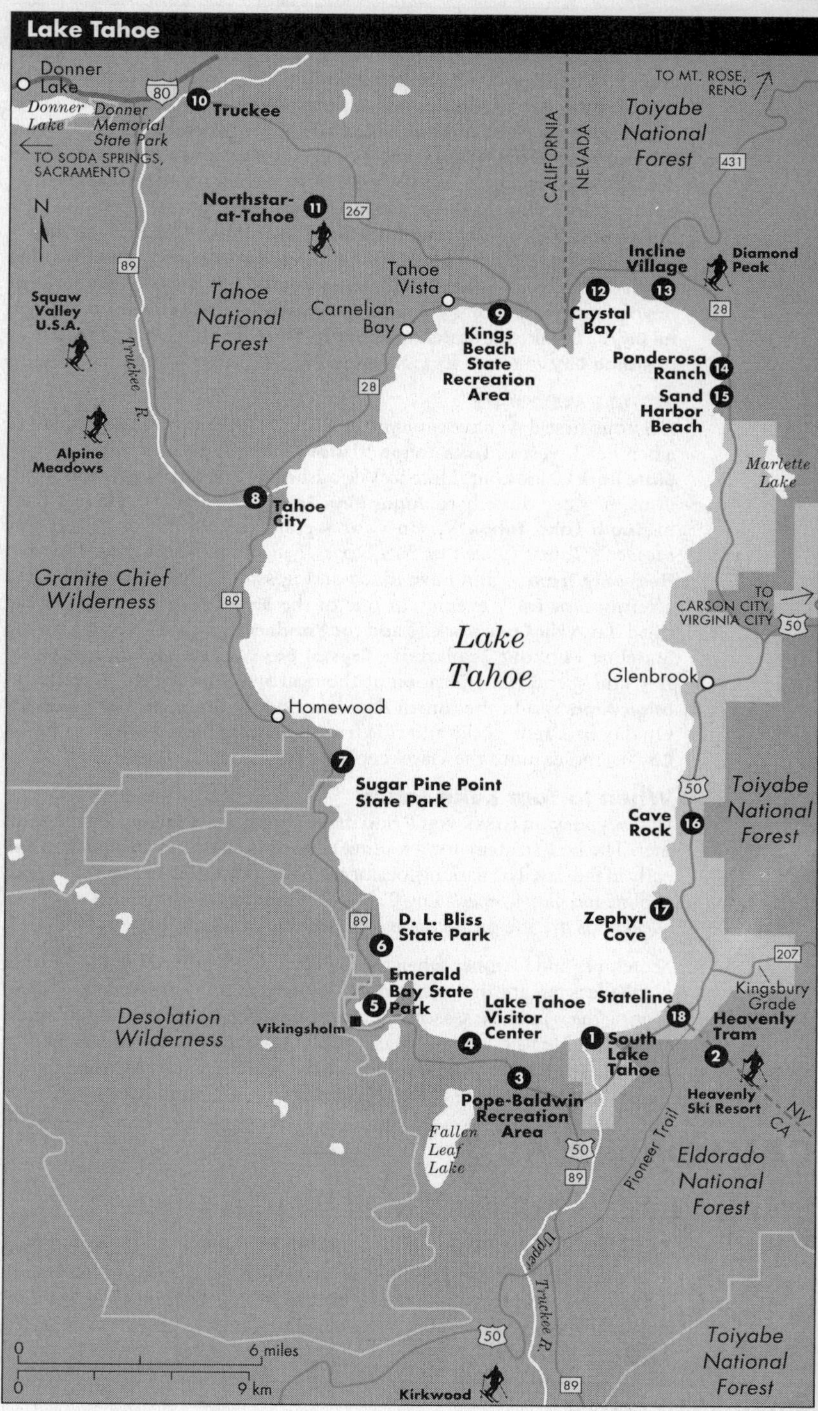
Lake Tahoe
Donner Lake
Donner Lake
Donner Memorial State Park
TO SODA SPRINGS, SACRAMENTO
80
10 Truckee
N
Northstar-at-Tahoe 11
267
89
Tahoe National Forest
Squaw Valley U.S.A.
Truckee R.
Alpine Meadows
Tahoe Vista
Carnelian Bay
9 Kings Beach State Recreation Area
28
CALIFORNIA
NEVADA
TO MT. ROSE, RENO
Toiyabe National Forest
431
Incline Village 13
Diamond Peak
12 Crystal Bay
28
Ponderosa Ranch 14
Sand Harbor Beach 15
Marlette Lake
8 Tahoe City
Granite Chief Wilderness
89
Lake Tahoe
TO CARSON CITY, VIRGINIA CITY
50
Glenbrook
Homewood
7 Sugar Pine Point State Park
50
Toiyabe National Forest
Cave Rock 16
Zephyr Cove 17
89
6 D. L. Bliss State Park
Emerald Bay State Park 5
Vikingsholm
Desolation Wilderness
4 Lake Tahoe Visitor Center
3 Pope-Baldwin Recreation Area
Stateline 18
1 South Lake Tahoe
207
Kingsbury Grade
Heavenly Tram 2
Heavenly Ski Resort
NV CA
Fallen Leaf Lake
50
89
Pioneer Trail
Eldorado National Forest
Upper Truckee R.
50
89
Toiyabe National Forest
Kirkwood
0 6 miles
0 9 km

late afternoon explore the trails and mansions at **Sugar Pine Point State Park** ⑦, then backtrack on Highway 89 and U.S. 50 for dinner in **Stateline** ⑱. On your second day, cruise on the *Hornblower's Tahoe Queen* glass-bottom stern-wheeler out of South Lake Tahoe or the MS *Dixie II* stern-wheeler out of **Zephyr Cove** ⑰ in the morning, and then ride the **Heavenly Tram** ② at Heavenly Ski Resort. Have lunch high above the lake and (except in snow season) take a walk on one of Heavenly's nature trails. You'll have an hour or two to try your luck at the Stateline casinos before it's time for dinner. Start your third day by heading north on U.S. 50, stopping at **Cave Rock** ⑯ and (after turning north on Highway 28) at **Sand Harbor Beach** ⑮. If *Bonanza* looms large in your memory, drop by **Ponderosa Ranch** ⑭, or continue on to **Crystal Bay** ⑫ to hike the Stateline Lookout Trail. If you have the time, drive to **Tahoe City** ⑧ to see its Gatekeeper's Log Cabin Museum.

IF YOU HAVE 5 DAYS

On your first day, have a picnic at **Pope-Baldwin Recreation Area** ③. Then head west to **Lake Tahoe Visitor Center** ④ and the **Emerald Bay State Park** ⑤ lookout. Hike to Vikingsholm or, if that seems too strenuous, proceed directly to **Sugar Pine Point State Park** ⑦. Have dinner in **South Lake Tahoe** ①. On your second day, cruise on the *Hornblower's Tahoe Queen* or MS *Dixie II* in the morning, then ride the **Heavenly Tram** ② and have lunch and possibly a hike. Spend the late afternoon or early evening at one of the **Stateline** ⑱ casinos. On the third day, visit **Cave Rock** ⑯ and the **Ponderosa Ranch** ⑭, and hike the Stateline Lookout Trail above **Crystal Bay** ⑫. Have lunch in Crystal Bay and spend the afternoon at the nearby **Kings Beach State Recreation Area** ⑨. On the fourth day, hang out at **Sand Harbor Beach** ⑮. On day five, rent a bike and ride from **D. L. Bliss State Park** ⑥ to **Tahoe City** ⑧ and explore the Gatekeeper's Log Cabin Museum.

When to Tour Lake Tahoe

Unless you want to ski, you'll find that Tahoe is most fun during the summer. The best strategy for avoiding crowds is to do as much as you can early in the day. The parking lots for the Lake Tahoe Visitor Center, Vikingsholm, and Gatekeeper's Log Cabin Museum can be jammed at any time. Weekends are the most congested, but weekdays are busy as well.

September and October, when the throngs have dispersed but the weather is still pleasant, are among the most satisfying months to visit Lake Tahoe. During the winter ski season Tahoe's population swells on the weekends. If you're able to come midweek, you'll have the resorts and neighboring towns almost to yourself. Most of the visitor centers, mansions, state parks, and beaches are closed between November and May.

CALIFORNIA SIDE

South Lake Tahoe to Kings Beach

Lake Tahoe lends itself to a geopolitical division between the two states that share it. The California side is the more developed, both with commercial enterprises—restaurants, motels, lodges, resorts, residential subdivisions—and public-access facilities, such as historic sites, parks, campgrounds, and beaches.

South Lake Tahoe

❶ *50 mi south of Reno on U.S. 395 and U.S. 50; 198 mi northeast of San Francisco on I–80 to U.S. 50.*

South Lake Tahoe's raison d'être is tourism. The lake region's largest community feeds the casinos at Stateline; the ski slopes at Heavenly Valley; the beaches, docks, bike trails, and campgrounds of the south shore; and the backcountry of Eldorado National Forest and Desolation Wilderness. Motels, lodges, and restaurants line U.S. 50 heading northeast into town, but if you head northwest on Highway 89, which follows the lakefront, commercial development gives way to national forests and state parks.

★ ❷ Whether you ski or not, you'll appreciate the impressive view of Lake Tahoe from the 50-passenger **Heavenly Tram,** which runs 2,000 ft up the slopes of Heavenly Ski Resort to 8,200 ft. When the weather's fine you can take one of three (successively more difficult) hikes around the mountaintop. Monument Peak Restaurant, open daily during tram hours, serves both cafeteria-style food and fancier fare for breakfast, lunch, dinner, and Sunday brunch in summer, breakfast and lunch in winter. ✉ *Head north on Ski Run Blvd. off U.S. 50 and follow signs to parking lot,* ☎ *775/586–7000.* *$12.* *Tram runs June–Oct., daily 9–9; Nov.–May, daily 9–4.*

The 500-passenger ***Hornblower's Tahoe Queen*** (✉ Ski Run Marina, off U.S. 50, ☎ 530/541–3364 or 800/238–2463), a glass-bottom paddle wheeler, makes 1½-hour happy-hour cruises, 2¼-hour sightseeing cruises, and 3-hour dinner-dance cruises year-round from South Lake Tahoe. Fares range from $18 to $45. In winter the boat becomes the only waterborne ski shuttle in the world: $85 covers hotel transfers, breakfast, transportation across the lake to Squaw Valley, and a lift ticket; $105 includes dinner.

Dining and Lodging

$$–$$$ ✕ **Nepheles.** A chalet on the road to Heavenly Ski Resort houses this cozy restaurant that serves creative contemporary cuisine. Entrées range from ahi tuna in a pineapple vinaigrette to grilled tenderloin of elk with a sauce made from black currants and merlot. Appetizers include escargots, swordfish egg rolls, and seafood cheesecake. ✉ *1169 Ski Run Blvd.,* ☎ *530/544–8130. AE, D, DC, MC, V. No lunch.*

$$–$$$ ✕ **Swiss Chalet.** Swiss decor is carried out with great consistency at this Tahoe institution. The steep sloping roof, wrought-iron grillwork, Swiss clocks, and cowbells may make you feel as if you've been transported to the Alps. The Continental menu includes schnitzel, sauerbraten, fondue, steaks, and homemade pastries. ✉ *2544 U.S. 50,* ☎ *530/544–3304. AE, MC, V. Closed late Nov.–early Dec. No lunch.*

$–$$ ✕ **Scusa!** This intimate Italian restaurant on the road to the Heavenly Ski Resort has a smart, modern decor. Capellini, linguine, fettuccine, and penne are on the menu, along with steak, chicken, and fresh fish. The panfried calamari with red peppers and capers shouldn't be missed. Don't pass up the rosemary-flavored flat bread, baked fresh daily. ✉ *1142 Ski Run Blvd.,* ☎ *530/542–0100. AE, MC, V. No lunch.*

$ ✕ **Red Hut Waffle Shop.** A vintage Tahoe diner, all chrome and red plastic, the Red Hut is a tiny place with a dozen counter stools and a dozen booths. It's a traditional breakfast spot for locals and visitors in the know, all of whom appreciate the huge omelets; the banana, pecan, and coconut waffles; and other tasty vittles. ✉ *2749 U.S. 50,* ☎ *530/541–9024. Reservations not accepted. No credit cards. No dinner.*

$$–$$$$ ✕ **Christiania Inn.** An antiques-filled bed & breakfast across the street from the base of the Heavenly Tram, the Christiania has been a local favorite for 35 years. The American-Continental menu emphasizes fresh seafood, prime beef, and veal. Upstairs at the inn, two rooms and four suites come with king- or queen-size beds and private baths. Three of the suites are two-story affairs with wood-burning fireplaces and wet bars; two have saunas and one has a whirlpool tub. ✉ *3819 Saddle Rd., 96151,* ☎ *530/544–7337,* FAX *530/544–5342. 6 rooms. Restaurant, bar. MC, V. CP.*

$$$–$$$$ ★ **Embassy Suites.** In this opulent all-suites hotel, decorated Sierra-lodge style, fountains and waterwheels splash in the nine-story atriums, where complimentary breakfasts and evening cocktails are served daily. Glass elevators rise to guest suites, each with a living room, dining area, and separate bedroom. ✉ *4130 Lake Tahoe Blvd., 96150,* ☎ *530/544–5400 or 800/362–2779,* FAX *530/544–4900. 400 suites. 4 restaurants, indoor pool, hot tub, sauna, exercise room, nightclub. AE, D, DC, MC, V. BP.*

$$$–$$$$ **Tahoe Seasons Resort.** Most rooms at this resort, which is set among pine trees on a mountain across from the Heavenly Ski Resort, are outfitted with fireplaces. Every room has a whirlpool and a small kitchen. The earth tones of the contemporary decor reflect the natural surroundings. ✉ *3901 Saddle Rd., 96157,* ☎ *530/541–6700 or 800/540–4874,* FAX *530/541–0653. 183 suites. Restaurant, refrigerators, pool, hot tub, 2 tennis courts, volleyball. AE, DC, MC, V.*

$$–$$$$ ★ **Inn by the Lake.** Across the road from a beach, this luxury motel has spacious rooms furnished in contemporary style. All have balconies; some have lake views, wet bars, and kitchens. You can summon the casino shuttles from a direct-dial phone in the lobby. ✉ *3300 Lake Tahoe Blvd., 96150,* ☎ *530/542–0330 or 800/877–1466,* FAX *530/541–6596. 87 rooms, 12 suites. Pool, hot tub, sauna, bicycles, coin laundry. AE, D, DC, MC, V. CP.*

$$–$$$$ **Lakeland Village Beach and Ski Resort.** This complex with 1,000 ft of private beach has a range of accommodations: studios, suites, and town houses, all with kitchens, fireplaces, and private decks or balconies. Ask about custom ski packages. ✉ *3535 Lake Tahoe Blvd., 96150,* ☎ *530/544–1685 or 800/822–5969,* FAX *530/544–0193. 210 units. 2 pools, wading pool, hot tub, sauna, 2 tennis courts, beach, boating, fishing, coin laundry. AE, MC, V.*

$$–$$$ ★ **Best Western Station House Inn.** This inn has won design awards for its exterior and interior. The rooms have king- and queen-size beds and double-vanity bathrooms. The location is good, one block from a private beach and two blocks to the casinos. ✉ *901 Park Ave., 96150,* ☎ *530/542–1101 or 800/822–5953,* FAX *530/542–1714. 100 rooms, 2 suites. Restaurant, pool, hot tub. AE, D, DC, MC, V.*

$$–$$$ **Forest Inn Suites.** The location is excellent—5½ acres bordering a forest, a half block from Harrah's and Harvey's, and adjacent to a supermarket, cinema, and shops. Rooms are modern and pleasant. Ski rentals are available, and free shuttles to Heavenly and Kirkwood ski areas stop here. ✉ *1101 Park Ave., 96150,* ☎ *530/541–6655 or 800/822–5950,* FAX *530/544–3135. 17 rooms, 101 suites. Kitchenettes, 2 pools, 2 hot tubs, sauna, 5 putting greens, health club, volleyball, bicycles, coin laundry. AE, D, DC, MC, V.*

$–$$$ **Royal Valhalla Motor Lodge.** Two- and three-bedroom suites with complete kitchens make this motel attractive to families. Some of the simple, modern rooms have private balconies with views of the mountains. ✉ *4104 Lakeshore Blvd., 96150,* ☎ *530/544–2233 or 800/999–4104,* FAX *530/544–1436. 80 suites. Pool, hot tub, coin laundry. AE, DC, MC, V. CP.*

$$ **Travelodge.** There are three members of the national chain in South Lake Tahoe. All are convenient to casinos, shopping, and recreation and have some no-smoking rooms. Free local calls, cable TV, and in-room coffee add to the budget appeal. ✉ *3489 U.S. 50, at Bijou Center, 96150,* ☎ *530/544–5266 or 800/982–1466,* FAX *530/544–6985. 59 rooms. Restaurant, pool.* ✉ *4011 U.S. 50, 96150,* ☎ *530/544–6000* *or 800/982–3466, FAX 530/544–6869. 50 rooms. Pool.* ✉ *4003 U.S. 50, 96150,* ☎ *530/541–5000 or 800/982–2466,* FAX *530/544–6910. 66 rooms. Pool. AE, D, DC, MC, V.*

$–$$ **Lake Tahoe Inn.** Near Harrah's and directly behind Heavenly Ski Resort, this large motel on 6 acres has modern rooms decorated in soothing colors. ✉ *4110 Lake Tahoe Blvd., 96150,* ☎ *530/541–2010 or 800/972–8557,* FAX *530/542–1428. 392 rooms, 8 suites. Restaurant, 2 pools, hot tub. AE, D, DC, MC, V. BP.*

$ **Best Tahoe West Inn.** The Tahoe West is three blocks from the beach and casinos. The exterior is rustic, rooms are neatly furnished, and beds are queen-size. Twelve rooms have kitchenettes. The inn offers every kind of discount there is; ask and ye might receive. ✉ *4107 Pine Blvd., 96150,* ☎ *530/544–6455 or 800/522–1021,* FAX *530/544–0508. 60 rooms. Pool, hot tub, sauna. AE, D, DC, MC, V.*

Outdoor Activities and Sports

CROSS-COUNTRY SKIING

For the ultimate in groomed conditions head to the nation's largest cross-country ski resort, **Royal Gorge** (✉ follow signs from Soda Springs–Norden exit off I–80, Box 1100, Soda Springs 95728, ☎ 530/426–3871), which has 197 mi of 18-ft-wide track for all abilities, 88 trails on 9,172 acres, two ski schools, and 10 warming huts. Four cafés, two hotels, and a hot tub and sauna are among the facilities. **Kirkwood Ski Resort** (☞ *below*) has 50 mi of groomed-track skiing, with skating lanes, instruction, and rentals.

DOWNHILL SKIING

Heavenly Ski Resort. When first seen from the California side, Heavenly's mogul-choked slopes look impossibly difficult. But this vast resort—composed of nine peaks, two valleys, and three base-lodge areas—has something for every skier. Beginners can choose wide, well-groomed trails accessed via the Heavenly Tram, or short and gentle runs in the Enchanted Forest area. The Sky Express high-speed quad chair whisks intermediate and advanced skiers to the summit for wide cruisers or steep tree skiing. Mott and Killebrew canyons draw expert skiers to the Nevada side for the steep chutes and thick-timbered slopes. For snowboarders there's the Airport Park near the Olympic lift. The ski school, like everything else at Heavenly, is large and offers everything from learn-to-ski packages for novices to canyon adventure tours for advanced skiers. Skiing lessons and day care are available for children age four and up. ✉ *Ski Run Blvd. off Hwy. 89/U.S. 50 (mailing address: Box 2180, Stateline, NV 89449),* ☎ *775/586–7000 or 800/243–2836; 530/541–7544 snow phone. 82 trails on 4,800 acres, rated 20% beginner, 45% intermediate, 35% expert. Longest run 5½ mi, base 6,540′, summit 10,040′. Lifts: 26, including 1 aerial tram, 1 high-speed 6-passenger lift, and 3 high-speed quads.*

Kirkwood Ski Resort. Thirty-six miles south of Lake Tahoe, Kirkwood is a destination resort with 120 condominiums and several shops and restaurants. Most of the runs off the top are rated expert-only, but intermediate and beginning skiers have their own vast bowl, where they can ski through trees or on wide, open trails. Snowboarding is permitted on all runs and in an exclusive terrain park. Skiing and snowboarding lessons and equipment rentals and sales are available. The children's ski school has programs for ages 4–12, and day care is available for children ages 2–6. Arrangements for younger children must be made in advance. For Nordic skiing, *see* Cross-Country Skiing, *above.* ✉ *Hwy. 88 off Hwy. 89 (mailing address: Box 1, Kirkwood, CA 95646),* ☎ *209/258–6000; 209/258–7000 lodging information; 209/258–3000 snow phone. 65 trails on 2,300 acres, rated 15% beginner, 50% in-*

termediate, 20% advanced, 15% expert. Longest run 2½ mi, base 7,800′, summit 9,800′. Lifts: 12.

Fishing

Tahoe Sports Fishing, in business for 46 years, is one of the largest and oldest fishing-charter services on the lake. It runs a variety of charters (morning, afternoon, or all-day). Trips include all necessary gear and bait, and the the crew cleans and packages your catch. ✉ *Ski Run Marina, South Lake Tahoe,* ☎ *530/541–5448 or 800/696–7797 (in California).*

Kayaking

For more than a decade **Kayak Tahoe** has been in the business of teaching people to kayak on Lake Tahoe and the Truckee River. A variety of lessons and excursions (Emerald Bay, Cave Rock, Zephyr Cove) are offered June through September. ✉ *Timber Cover Marina at Tahoe Paradise,* ☎ *530/544–2011.*

Shopping

There's some good shopping—Levi's, Van Heusen, Oneida—south of town at the **Factory Outlet Stores** (✉ *U.S. 50 at Hwy. 89).*

Pope-Baldwin Recreation Area

3 *5 mi west of South Lake Tahoe on Hwy. 89.*

George S. Pope, who made his money in shipping and lumber, hosted the business and cultural elite of 1920s America at his home, the **Pope House.** The magnificently restored 1894 mansion and two other estates—those of entrepreneur "Lucky" Baldwin (which holds a museum of Baldwin memorabilia and Washoe Indian artifacts) and Walter Heller (the Valhalla, used for community events)—form the heart of the Pope-Baldwin Recreation Area's **Tallic Historic Site.** The lakeside site, a pleasant place to take a stroll or have a picnic, hosts cultural activities (including a Renaissance festival) throughout the summer. Docents conduct tours of the Pope House during summer. ☎ *530/541–5227.* *Pope House tour $2.* ⏲ *Tallac Historic Site grounds dawn–sunset; house and museum hrs vary.*

4 The U.S. Forest Service operates the **Lake Tahoe Visitor Center** on Taylor Creek. You can visit the site of a Washoe Indian settlement; walk self-guided trails through meadow, marsh, and forest; and inspect the Stream Profile Chamber, an underground underwater display with windows that afford views right into Taylor Creek. (In the fall you may see spawning kokanee salmon digging their nests.) In summer Forest Service naturalists organize discovery walks and nighttime campfires, with singing and marshmallow roasts. ✉ *Hwy. 89,* ☎ *530/573–2674 (in season only).* ⏲ *June–Sept., daily 8–5:30; Oct., weekends 8–5:30.*

Emerald Bay State Park

★ 5 *4 mi west of Pope-Baldwin Recreation Area on Hwy. 9.*

Emerald Bay, a 3-mi-long and 1-mi-wide fjordlike bay, was carved by massive glaciers millions of years ago. Famed for its jewel-like shape and colors, it surrounds Fannette, Tahoe's only island. Highway 89 curves high above the lake through Emerald Bay State Park; from the Emerald Bay lookout, the centerpiece of the park, you can survey the whole scene.

A steep, 1-mi-long trail from the lookout leads down to **Vikingsholm,** a 38-room estate completed in 1929. The original owner, Lora Knight, had this precise replica of a 1,200-year-old Viking castle built out of materials native to the area. She furnished it with Scandinavian antiques and hired artisans to custom-build period reproductions. The sod roof sprouts wildflowers each spring. There are picnic tables nearby and a gray-sand beach for strolling. The hike back up is hard (especially if you're not yet acclimated to the elevation), but there are benches and stone culverts to rest on. At the 150-ft-high peak of Fannette Island are the remnants of a stone structure known as the Tea House, built in 1928 so that guests of Lora Knight could have a place to enjoy afternoon refreshments after a motorboat ride. The island is off-limits from February through June to protect nesting Canada geese. The rest of the year it's open for day use only. ☎ *530/525–7277.* 🎫 *$2.* ⏲ *Memorial Day–Labor Day, daily 10–4.*

D. L. Bliss State Park

❻ *3 mi north of Emerald Bay State Park on Hwy. 89.*

D. L. Bliss State Park takes its name from Duane LeRoy Bliss, a 19th-century lumber magnate. At one time Bliss owned nearly 75% of Tahoe's lakefront, along with local steamboats, railroads, and banks. The Bliss family donated these 1,200 acres to the state in the 1930s. The park now shares 6 mi of shoreline with Emerald Bay State Park. At the north end of Bliss is **Rubicon Point,** which overlooks one of the lake's deepest spots. Short trails lead to an old lighthouse and Balancing Rock, which weighs in at 250,000 pounds and balances on a fist of granite. Longer trails lead to remote beaches and all the way to Vikingsholm. ☎ *530/525–7277.* 🎫 *$2 per vehicle (day use).* ⏲ *Memorial Day–Sept., daily sunrise–sunset.*

Camping

⛺ **D. L. Bliss State Park Campground.** A wooded, hilly, quiet setting makes for blissful family camping near the lake. You're allowed to make reservations up to seven months in advance. ✉ *Off Hwy. 89,* ☎ *800/444–7275. 168 sites.* 🎫 *$12.* ⏲ *Memorial Day–Sept.*

Sugar Pine Point State Park

★ ❼ *8 mi north of D. L. Bliss State Park on Hwy. 89.*

The main attraction at Sugar Pine Point State Park is **Ehrman Mansion,** a stone-and-shingle 1903 summer home, furnished in period style. In its day it was the height of modernity, with a refrigerator, an elevator, and an electric stove. Also in the park are a trapper's log cabin from the mid-19th century, a nature preserve with wildlife exhibits, a lighthouse, the start of the 10-mi-long biking trail to Tahoe City, and an extensive system of hiking and cross-country trails. ☎ *530/525–7232 year-round; 530/525–7982 in season.* 🎫 *$2 per vehicle (day use).* ⏲ *Memorial Day–Labor Day, daily 11–4.*

Camping

⛺ **General Creek Campground.** This homey campground on the mountain side of Highway 89 is one of the few public ones to remain open in winter, primarily for cross-country skiers. ✉ *Hwy. 89,* ☎ *800/444–7275. 175 sites.* 🎫 *$12–$16.* ⏲ *Year-round; facilities available Memorial Day–Labor Day.*

Tahoe City

❽ *10 mi north of Sugar Pine Point State Park on Hwy. 89; 14 mi south of Truckee on Hwy. 89.*

Tahoe City is home to many stores and restaurants within a compact area, and to the Outlet Gates, where water is spilled into the Truckee

River to control the surface level of the lake. Giant trout, common before the severe drought of the late 1980s and early 1990s, have returned; look down and see them from Fanny Bridge, so called for the views of the backsides of visitors leaning over the railing. Here, Highway 89 turns north from the lake and leads to Squaw Valley, Donner Lake, and Truckee, and Highway 28 continues northeast around the lake toward Kings Beach and Nevada.

★ The **Gatekeeper's Cabin Museum** in Tahoe City preserves a little-known part of the region's history. Between 1910 and 1968 the gatekeeper who lived on this site was responsible for monitoring the level of the lake, using a hand-turned winch system to keep the water at the correct level. That winch system is still used today. ✉ *130 W. Lake Blvd.,* ☎ *530/583–1762.* 🎫 *Free.* ⏲ *May 15–Sept., daily 11–5.*

The **Watson Cabin Living Museum,** a 1909 log cabin built by Robert M. Watson and his son and filled with century-old furnishings, is in the middle of Tahoe City. Costumed docents act out the daily life of a typical pioneer family. ✉ *560 N. Lake Blvd.,* ☎ *530/583–8717 or 530/583–1762.* 🎫 *Free.* ⏲ *June 15–Labor Day, daily noon–4.*

Dining and Lodging

$$–$$$ ✕ **Christy Hill.** Panoramic lake views and fireside dining distinguish this restaurant, which serves California cuisine including fresh seafood (such as ahi with a ginger-pepper crust in a cabernet demi-glace) and game (including broiled New Zealand venison). ✉ *Lakehouse Mall, 115 Grove St.,* ☎ *530/583–8551. AE, MC, V. Closed Mon. (spring and fall); no lunch.*

$$–$$$ ★ ✕ **Wolfdale's.** An intimate restaurant inside a 100-year-old house, Wolfdale's food has Japanese and Californian overtones. The menu, which changes weekly, showcases several imaginative entrées, such as sole with shiitake wine sauce and butternut squash potatoes, and braised lamb shank with tomatoes, rosemary, and parsnip puree. ✉ *640 N. Lake Blvd.,* ☎ *530/583–5700. MC, V. No lunch.*

$–$$$ ✕ **Grazie! Ristorante & Bar.** The smell of garlic warms you as soon as you enter this northern Italian restaurant, as does the fire in the wide, double-side fireplace. Hearty pasta dishes and pizzas are on the menu, but the stars are the antipasti and pasta salads. Chicken is cooked on a wood-burning rotisserie; the lamb stew is a specialty. Most of the dishes are served with homemade sauces. ✉ *Roundhouse Mall, 700 N. Lake Blvd.,* ☎ *530/583–0233. AE, D, DC, MC, V.*

$–$$$ ★ ✕ **Jake's on the Lake.** Handsome rooms of oak and glass provide a suitably soothing waterfront setting for Continental food. The varied dinner menu includes meat and poultry but emphasizes fresh fish. The seafood bar here is extensive. ✉ *Boatworks Mall, 780 N. Lake Blvd.,* ☎ *530/583–0188. AE, MC, V.*

$$–$$$$ ★ ✕🏨 **Sunnyside Restaurant and Lodge.** This impressive lodge has a marina and an expansive lakefront deck with steps down to a narrow gravel beach. Rooms are decorated in a crisp nautical style. Prints of boats hang on the pinstripe wall coverings and sea chests act as coffee tables. Each room has its own deck with a lake or mountain view. Seafood is the specialty of the unique alpine-lodge dining room ($$–$$$). ✉ *1850 W. Lake Blvd., Box 5969, 96145,* ☎ *530/583–7200 or 800/822–2754,* FAX *530/583–2551. 18 rooms, 5 suites. Restaurant, room service, beach. AE, MC, V. CP.*

$$$$ ★ 🏨 **Chinquapin Resort.** A deluxe development on 95 acres of forested land and a mile of lakefront 3 mi northeast of Tahoe City contains roomy one- to four-bedroom town houses and condos with great views of the lake and the mountains. Each unit has a fireplace, a fully equipped kitchen, and a washer and dryer. A one-week minimum stay is required in July, August, and late December. In winter the minimum is two nights. ✉ *3600 N. Lake Blvd., 96145,* ☎ *530/583–6991 or 800/732–6721,* FAX *530/583–0937. 172 town houses and condos. Pool, saunas, 7 tennis courts, hiking, horseshoes, 2 beaches. AE, D, MC, V.*

$$$$ **Resort at Squaw Creek.** Nearly half the rooms are suites at this complex composed of a main lodge, an outdoor arcade of shops and boutiques, and a 404-room hotel. Some units have fireplaces and full kitchens, and all have original art, custom furnishings, and good views. Outside the hotel entrance is a triple chairlift to Squaw Valley's slopes. Dining options range from haute cuisine to pastries and coffee. ✉ *400 Squaw Creek Rd., Olympic Valley 96146,* ☎ *530/583–6300 or 800/327–3353,* FAX *530/581–5407. 204 rooms, 200 suites. 5 restaurants, bar, 3 pools, 4 hot tubs, sauna, spa, 18-hole golf course, 2 tennis courts, health club, ice-skating. AE, D, DC, MC, V.*

$–$$ **Peppertree Inn.** This skinny seven-story tower is within easy walking distance of the beaches, marina, shops, and restaurants of Tahoe City. Rooms are clean and comfortable, if not luxurious, and have great lake views. ✉ *645 N. Lake Blvd., 96145,* ☎ *530/583–3711 or 800/624–8590,* FAX *530/583–6938. 45 rooms, 5 suites. Pool, hot tub. AE, D, DC, MC, V.*

Outdoor Activities and Sports

DOWNHILL SKIING

Alpine Meadows Ski Area. The two peaks here are an intermediate skier's paradise. For snowboarders there's a terrain park with a half-pipe. The ski area has some of Tahoe's most reliable conditions; this is usually one of the first areas to open in November, and one of the last to close in May. There is a ski school for adults and children of all skill levels and for skiers with disabilities. There's also an area for overnight RV parking. ✉ *6 mi northwest of Tahoe City off Hwy. 89, 13 mi south of I–80 (mailing address: Box 5279, 96145),* ☎ *530/583–4232; 530/581–8374 snow phone; 800/441–4423 information. 100 trails on 2,000 acres, rated 25% easier, 40% more difficult, 35% most difficult. Longest run 2½ mi, base 6,835′, summit 8,637′. Lifts: 12, including 1 high-speed 6-passenger lift and 1 high-speed quad.*

Squaw Valley USA. Home to some of the toughest skiing in the Tahoe area, Squaw was the site of the 1960 Olympics. Although the immense resort has changed significantly since then, the skiing is still world-class, with steep chutes and cornices on six peaks. Expert skiers often head directly to the untamed terrain of the infamous KT-22 face, which has bumps, cliffs, and gulp-and-go chutes. Plenty of wide, groomed trails start near the beginner-designated High Camp lift and around the more challenging Snow King Peak. Snowboarders have the run of two terrain parks. You can ski until 9 PM, and lift tickets for skiers under 12 are only $5. Nonskiing recreational opportunities—bungee jumping, rock climbing, and ice skating—abound. The Village Mall has shops, eateries, and accommodations. ✉ *Hwy. 89, 5 mi northwest of Tahoe City (mailing address: Box 2007, Olympic Valley, 96146),* ☎ *530/583–6985; 800/545–4350 reservations; 530/583–6955 snow phone. 100 trails on 4,300 acres, rated 25% beginner, 45% intermediate, 30% advanced. Longest run 3 mi, base 6,200′, summit 9,050′. Lifts: 29, including a gondola, a cable car, and 5 high-speed quads.*

BIKING

Cyclepaths Mountain Bike Adventures (✉ 1785 W. Lake Blvd., Tahoe City, ☎ 530/581–1171), is a combination bike shop and bike-adventure outfitter. It offers instruction in mountain biking, guided tours (half-day to weekend excursions), tips for self-guided bike touring, bike repairs, and books and maps on the area.

GOLF

Resort at Squaw Creek Golf Course (✉ 400 Squaw Creek Rd., Olympic Valley, ☎ 530/583–6300), an 18-hole championship course, was designed by Robert Trent Jones Jr. The $90–$120 greens fee includes the use of a cart. Golfers use pull carts at the nine-hole **Tahoe City Golf Course** (✉ Hwy. 28, Tahoe City, ☎ 530/583–1516). The greens fees are $28–$32 for nine holes, $40–$50 for 18; a power cart is $8–$12 additional.

Carnelian Bay to Kings Beach

5–10 mi northeast of Tahoe City on Hwy. 28.

The small lakeside commercial districts of Carnelian Bay and Tahoe Vista service the thousand or so locals who live in the area year-round and the thousands more who have summer residences or launch their boats here. Kings Beach, the last town heading east on Highway 28 before the Nevada border, is to Crystal Bay what South Lake Tahoe is to Stateline: a bustling California village full of motels and rental condos, restaurants and shops, used by the hordes of hopefuls who pass through on their way to the casinos.

9 The 28-acre **Kings Beach State Recreation Area,** one of the largest such areas on the lake, is open year-round. The long beach becomes crowded with people swimming, sunbathing, jet skiing, riding in paddleboats, spiking volleyballs, and tossing Frisbees. There's a good playground here. ✉ *N. Lake Blvd., Kings Beach,* ☎ *530/546–7248.* *Free.*

Dining

$$–$$$ ✕ **Captain Jon's.** On chilly evenings a fireplace with a brick hearth warms diners at this cozy establishment. The lengthy dinner menu is country French with an emphasis on fish and hearty salads. There are also two dozen daily specials. The restaurant's lounge, which serves light meals, has a pier where hungry boaters can come ashore. ✉ *7220 N. Lake Blvd., Tahoe Vista,* ☎ *530/546–4819 or 775/831–4176. AE, DC, MC, V. No lunch during ski season.*

$–$$$ ✕ **Gar Woods Grill and Pier.** Boating photographs on the walls remind diners of the area's past at this stylish but casual restaurant. A river-rock fireplace keeps out the chill, and floor-to-ceiling picture windows overlook the lake. The menu includes dishes such as prime rib, filet mignon, free-range chicken, and fresh fish specials. There's an extensive wine list, and Sunday brunch is served. ✉ *5000 N. Lake Blvd., Carnelian Bay,* ☎ *530/546–3366. AE, MC, V.*

$ ✕ **Log Cabin Caffe.** Almost always hopping, this Kings Beach eatery specializes in healthful, hearty breakfast and lunch entrées—pancakes, waffles, freshly baked pastries, and sandwiches. It's a good place on the north shore for an espresso or cappuccino. Get here early on weekends for the popular brunch. ✉ *8692 N. Lake Blvd., Kings Beach,* ☎ *530/546–7109. MC, V.*

Outdoor Activities and Sports

SNOWMOBILING

Snowmobiling Unlimited (✉ Hwys. 267 and 28, Kings Beach, ☎ 530/583–5858) is the oldest snowmobiling concession on the lake. It conducts 1½-, 2-, and 3-hour guided cross-country tours, mostly along the trails in the nearby national forest. You can rent everything from snowmobiles to mittens.

SWIMMING

The **North Tahoe Beach Center** has a 26-ft hot tub and a beach with an enclosed swimming area and four sand volleyball courts. The complex includes a barbecue and picnic area, a fitness center, windsurfing and nonmotorized boat rentals, a snack bar, and a clubhouse with games. ✉ *7860 N. Lake Blvd., Kings Beach,* ☎ *530/546–2566.* 🎟 *$7.*

Truckee

⑩ *13 mi northwest of Kings Beach on Hwy. 267; 14 mi north of Tahoe City on Hwy. 89.*

Old West facades line the main street of Truckee, a favorite stopover for people traveling from the San Francisco Bay Area to the north shore of Lake Tahoe. Galleries and boutiques are plentiful, but you will also find low-key diners, discount skiwear, and an old-fashioned five-and-dime store. Stop by the **information booth** in the Amtrak depot (✉ Railroad St. at Commercial Rd.) for a walking-tour map of historic Truckee.

Donner Memorial State Park commemorates the Donner Party, a group of 89 westward-bound pioneers who were trapped in the Sierra in the winter of 1846–47 in snow 22 ft deep. Only 47 survived, some by cannibalism and others by eating animal hides. The Immigrant Museum's hourly slide show details the Donner Party's plight. Other displays relate the history of other settlers and of railroad development through the Sierra. ✉ *Off I–80, 2 mi west of Truckee,* ☎ *530/582–7892.* 🎟 *$2.* ⏲ *Daily 9–4.*

Northstar-at-Tahoe

⑪ *6 mi south of Truckee on Hwy. 267; 15 mi north of Tahoe City on Hwy. 28 to Hwy. 267.*

Dining and Lodging

$$$–$$$$ ✕🏨 **Northstar-at-Tahoe Resort.** This is the area's most complete destination resort. The center of action is the Village Mall, a concentration of restaurants, shops, recreation facilities, and accommodations—hotel rooms, condos, and private houses. The many sports activities make the resort especially popular with families. Summer rates are lower than winter rates. ✉ *Off Hwy. 267, Box 129, 96160,* ☎ *530/562–1010 or 800/466–6784,* FAX *530/562–2215. 230 units. 4 restaurants, deli, 18-hole golf course, 10 tennis courts, horseback riding, bicycles, downhill skiing, sleigh rides, snowmobiling, recreation room, baby-sitting. AE, D, MC, V.*

Outdoor Activities and Sports

CROSS-COUNTRY AND DOWNHILL SKIING

Northstar-at-Tahoe Resort. Two northeast-facing, wind-protected bowls provide some of the best powder skiing in the area, including steep chutes and long cruising runs. Top-to-bottom snowmaking and intense grooming assure good conditions on the 40 mi of trails. There's a wide skating lane for Nordic skiers and a terrain park and trails with such features as dragon tails and magic moguls for snowboarders. The school offers programs for skiers ages five and up, and day care is available for children older than two. ✉ *Hwy. 267 between Truckee and Kings Beach (mailing address: Box 129, Truckee 96160),* ☎ *530/562–1010; 530/562–1330 snow phone,* FAX *530/562–2215. 63 trails on 1,800 acres, rated 25% beginner, 50% intermediate, 25% advanced. Longest run 2.9 mi, base 6,400′, summit 8,600′. Lifts: 12 lifts, including a gondola and 4 high-speed quads.*

HORSEBACK RIDING

Northstar-at-Tahoe Resort is the place for horseback riding in summer. With stables for three dozen horses, Northstar offers guided 45-minute, half-day, and full-day (for experienced riders only) rides. Instruction is provided, ponies are available for tots, and you can even board your own horse here. ✉ *Mailing address: Box 129, Truckee 96160,* ☎ *530/562–2480.*

NEVADA SIDE

From Crystal Bay to Stateline

You don't need a roadside sign to know when you've crossed from California into Nevada. The lake's water and the pine trees may be identical, but the flashing lights and elaborate marquees of casinos announce legal gambling in garish hues.

Crystal Bay

12 *1 mi east of Kings Beach on Hwy. 28; 30 mi north of South Lake Tahoe on U.S. 50 to Hwy. 28.*

Right at the Nevada border, Crystal Bay holds a cluster of casinos. One, the **Cal-Neva Lodge** (☞ Dining and Lodging, *below*), is bisected by the state line. This joint opened in 1927 and has weathered nearly as many scandals—the largest involving former-owner Frank Sinatra (he lost his gaming license in the 1960s for alleged mob connections)—as it has blizzards. The **Tahoe Biltmore** serves its popular $1.99 breakfast special 24 hours a day. **Jim Kelley's Nugget** shuts down during the winter—the only casino in Nevada that ever closes.

Dining and Lodging

$$–$$$ ★ ✕ **Soule Domain.** A romantic 1927 pine-log cabin is the setting for some of Lake Tahoe's most creative and delicious dinners. Chef-owner Charles Edward Soule IV's specialties include curried cashew chicken, smoked rabbit ravioli, rock shrimp with sea scallops, and a vegan sauté. ✉ *Cove St. across from Tahoe Biltmore,* ☎ *530/546–7529. Reservations essential on weekends. AE, DC, MC, V. No lunch.*

$–$$$$ 🏨 **Cal-Neva Lodge.** All the rooms in this hotel-casino have views of Lake Tahoe and the mountains. The hotel also boasts seven two-bedroom chalets and 12 cabins with living rooms. There is an arcade with video games for children and cabaret entertainment for grown-ups. ✉ *2 Stateline Rd., Box 368, 89402,* ☎ *775/832–4000 or 800/225–6382,* FAX *775/831–9007. 261 rooms, 20 suites, 19 cabins. Restaurant, coffee shop, pool, hot tub, sauna, tennis court, casino, 3 chapels. AE, D, DC, MC, V.*

Incline Village

13 *3 mi east of Crystal Bay on Hwy. 28.*

Incline Village, one of Nevada's few privately owned towns, dates back to the early 1960s when an Oklahoma developer bought 10,000 acres north of Lake Tahoe and sketched out a plan that avoided a central commercial district in an effort to prevent congestion and to preserve a natural feel. One-acre lakeshore lots originally fetched $12,000–$15,000; today, you couldn't touch even the land for less than several million. To get a look at what progress has wrought over the past 40 years, check out **Lakeshore Drive** to see some of the most expensive real estate in Nevada. The town's **Recreation Center** (✉ 980 Incline Way, ☎ 775/832–1300) has an eight-lane swimming pool and a fitness area, basketball court, game room, and snack bar.

OFF THE BEATEN PATH

MOUNT ROSE – If you want to ski some of the highest slopes in the Lake Tahoe region, Highway 431 leads north out of Incline Village to Mount Rose. Reno is another 30 mi farther. On the way is Tahoe Meadows, the most popular area near north lake for non-commercial sledding, tubing, snowshoeing, cross-country skiing, and snowmobiling. ☎ *775/849–0704.*

14 The 1960s television western *Bonanza* inspired the **Ponderosa Ranch** theme park. Attractions include the Cartwrights' ranch house, a western town complete with museums, shops, snack bars, gunfight and stunt show, roping demonstrations, petting zoo, and a big saloon. There's a self-guided nature trail; free pony rides for children; and, if you're here from 8 to 9:30 in the morning, a breakfast hayride. ✉ *Hwy. 28, 2 mi south of Incline Village,* ☎ *775/831–0691.* *$9.50, breakfast $2 extra.* *Mid-Apr.–Oct., daily 9:30–5.*

Dining and Lodging

$–$$$ ✕ **Stanley's Restaurant and Lounge.** With its intimate bar and pleasant dining room, this local favorite is a good bet any time for American fare on the hearty side, such as barbecued pork ribs. Lighter bites, such as seafood Cobb salad, are also available. Ample breakfasts featuring eggs Benedict and chili-cheese omelets are served weekends. There's a deck for outdoor dining in summer. ✉ *941 Tahoe Blvd.,* ☎ *775/831–9944. AE, D, MC, V.*

$–$$ ✕ **Azzara's.** An Italian trattoria with light, inviting decor, Azzara's serves a dozen pasta dishes and many pizzas, as well as chicken, lamb, veal, shrimp, and beef. Dinners include soup or salad, a vegetable, a pasta, and garlic bread. ✉ *Incline Center Mall, 930 Tahoe Blvd.,* ☎ *775/831–0346. MC, V. Closed Mon.*

$$–$$$$ ✕ **Hyatt Lake Tahoe Resort Hotel/Casino.** All of the rooms in this luxurious hotel on the lake are top-notch, and many have fireplaces. The restaurants are the Lone Eagle Grille (fairly good Continental food—steak, seafood, pasta, and rotisserie dishes), Ciao Mein Trattoria (Asian-Italian), and the Sierra Café (open 24 hours). ✉ *Lakeshore and Country Club Drs., 89450,* ☎ *775/831–1111 or 800/233–1234,* FAX *775/831–7508. 432 rooms, 28 suites. 3 restaurants, coffee shop, lobby lounge, room service, pool, 2 saunas, spa, 2 tennis courts, health club, beach, bicycles, casino, children's programs, laundry service. AE, D, DC, MC, V.*

Outdoor Activities and Sports

BOAT CRUISE

The ***Sierra Cloud*** (☎ 775/831–1111), a trimaran with a big trampoline lounging surface, cruises the north-shore area mornings and afternoons May through October from the Hyatt Regency Hotel in Incline Village. Fares run between $45 and $60.

CROSS-COUNTRY AND DOWNHILL SKIING

Diamond Peak. A fun, family atmosphere prevails at Diamond Peak, which has many special programs and affordable rates. Snowmaking covers 80% of the mountain, and runs are groomed nightly. The ride up the 1-mi Crystal chair rewards you with the best views of the lake from any ski area. Diamond Peak is less crowded than some of the larger areas and provides free shuttles to nearby lodging. A first-timer's package, which includes rentals, a lesson, and a lift ticket, is $39. A parent-child ski package is $45, with each additional child's lift ticket $7. There is a half-pipe for snowboarders. **Diamond Peak Cross-Country** (✉ off Hwy. 431, ☎ 775/832–1177) has 22 mi of groomed track with skating lanes. The trail system rises from 7,400 ft to 9,100 ft with endless wilderness to explore. ✉ *1210 Ski Way, off Hwy. 28 to Country*

Club Dr., Incline Village, NV 89450, ☎ 775/832–1177 or 800/468–2463. 29 trails on 655 acres, rated 18% beginner, 46% intermediate, 36% advanced. Longest run 2½ mi, base 6,700′, summit 8,540′. Lifts: 6, including 2 high-speed quads.

GOLF

Incline Championship (✉ 955 Fairway Blvd., ☎ 775/832–1144) is an 18-hole, par-72 course with a driving range. The greens fee of $95–$115 includes an optional power cart. **Incline Mountain** (✉ 690 Wilson Way, ☎ 775/832–1150) is an easy 18-holer; par is 58. The greens fee—from $40 to $50—includes an optional power cart.

OFF THE BEATEN PATH

CARSON CITY AND VIRGINIA CITY – Nevada's capital, Carson City, is a 30-minute drive from Stateline. At Spooner Junction, south of San Harbor Beach, head east on U.S. 50. In 10 mi you reach U.S. 395, where you go 1 mi north to Carson City. Most of its historic buildings and other attractions, including the Nevada State Museum and the Nevada Railroad Museum are along U.S. 395, the main street through town. At the south end of town is the **Carson City Chamber of Commerce** (✉ 1900 S. Carson St., Carson City, ☎ 775/882–1565), which has visitor information. About a 30-minute drive up Highway 342 northeast of Carson City is the fabled mining town of Virginia City, one of the largest and most authentic historical mining towns in the west. It's chock full of mine tours; mansions; museums; saloons; and, of course, dozens of shops selling everything from amethysts to yucca.

Sand Harbor Beach

★ 15 *4 mi south of Incline Village on Hwy. 28; 22 mi north of South Lake Tahoe on U.S. 50 to Hwy. 28.*

Sand Harbor Beach, within the Lake Tahoe–Nevada State Park, has a popular beach that is sometimes filled to capacity by 11 AM on summer weekends. Stroll the boardwalk and read the information signs to get a good lesson in the local ecology. A **pop-music festival** (☎ 775/832–1606 or 800/468–2463) is held here in July and a **Shakespeare festival** (☎ 775/832–1616) every August.

U.S. 50 from Spooner Junction to Zephyr Cove

13 mi south of Sand Harbor Beach (to Cave Rock), Hwy. 28 to U.S. 50.

★ 16 **Cave Rock,** 25 yards of solid stone at the southern end of Lake Tahoe–Nevada State Park, is the throat of an extinct volcano. Tahoe Tessie, the lake's version of the Loch Ness monster, is reputed to live in a cavern below the impressive outcropping. For the Washoe Indians this area is a sacred burial site. Cave Rock towers over a parking lot, a lakefront picnic ground, and a boat launch. The rest area provides the best vantage point of this cliff. ✉ *U.S. 50, 3 mi south of Glenbrook.*

17 The largest settlement between Incline Village and Stateline is **Zephyr Cove,** which is still only a tiny resort. It has a beach, marina, campground, picnic area, coffee shop in an historic log lodge, rustic cabins, and nearby riding stables. The 550-passenger ***MS Dixie II*** (☎ 775/588–3508), a stern-wheeler, sails year-round from Zephyr Cove Marina to Emerald Bay on lunch and dinner cruises. Fares range from $18 to $42. The ***Woodwind*** (☎ 775/588–3000), a glass-bottom trimaran, sails on regular and champagne cruises from April through October from Zephyr Cove Resort. Fares range from $20 to $45.

OFF THE BEATEN PATH **KINGSBURY GRADE** – This road, also known as Route 207, is one of three roads that access Tahoe from the east. Originally a toll road used by wagon trains to get over the crest of the Sierra, it has sweeping views of the Carson Valley. Off Route 206, which intersects Route 207, is Genoa, the oldest settlement in Nevada. Along Main Street are a museum in Nevada's oldest courthouse, a small state park, and the state's longest-standing saloon.

Stateline

18 *5 mi south of Zephyr Cove on U.S. 50.*

Stateline is a great border town in the Nevada tradition. Its four high-rise casinos are as vertical and contained as the commercial district of South Lake Tahoe on the California side is horizontal and sprawling. And Stateline is as relentlessly indoors-oriented as the rest of the lake is focused on the outdoors. This strip is where you'll find the most concentrated action at Lake Tahoe: restaurants (including the typically Nevadan buffets), showrooms with famous headliners and razzle-dazzle revues, luxury rooms and suites, and 24-hour casino gambling.

Dining and Lodging

$$$–$$$$ ✕ **Chart House.** It's worth the drive up the steep grade to see the view from here. Try to arrive for sunset. The American menu of steak and seafood is complemented by an abundant salad bar. The restaurant has a children's menu. ✉ *329 Kingsbury Grade,* ☎ *775/588–6276. AE, D, DC, MC, V. No lunch.*

$$–$$$ ★ ✕ **Llewellyn's Restaurant.** Elegantly decorated in blond wood and pastels, the restaurant atop Harvey's casino merits special mention. Almost every table has superb views of Lake Tahoe. Dinner entrées—seafood, meat, and poultry—are served with unusual accompaniments, such as sturgeon in potato crust with saffron sauce or veal with polenta, herbs, and pancetta. Lunches are reasonably priced, with gourmet selections as well as hamburgers. ✉ *Harvey's Resort, U.S. 50,* ☎ *775/588–2411 or 800/553–1022. AE, D, DC, MC, V.*

$$$–$$$$ ✕🏨 **Harrah's Tahoe Hotel/Casino.** Luxurious guest rooms here have two full bathrooms, each with a television and telephone. All rooms have views of the lake and the mountains. Top-name entertainment is presented in the South Shore Room. Among the restaurants, the romantic 16th-floor Summit is a standout. The menu changes nightly and includes lamb, venison, and seafood entrées with delicate sauces and sensuous desserts. Other restaurants serve Italian, deli, and traditional meat-and-potatoes cuisine. There's also a 24-hour coffee shop, a buffet with a view, and a candy store. ✉ *U.S. 50, Box 8, 89449,* ☎ *775/588–6611 or 800/427–7247,* FAX *775/588–6607. 470 rooms, 62 suites. 6 restaurants, room service, indoor pool, barbershop, beauty salon, hot tubs, health club, casino, video games, laundry service, kennel. AE, D, DC, MC, V.*

$$$–$$$$ ★ ✕🏨 **Harvey's Resort Hotel/Casino.** Owner Harvey Gross played an important role in persuading the state to keep U.S. 50 open year-round, making Tahoe accessible in winter. His namesake hotel, which started as a cabin in 1944, is now the largest resort in Tahoe. Any description of the place runs to superlatives, from the 40-ft-tall crystal chandelier in the lobby to the 88,000-square-ft casino. Rooms have custom furnishings, oversize marble baths, and minibars. Use of the health club, spa, and pool is free to guests—a rarity for this area. ✉ *U.S. 50, Box 128, 89449,* ☎ *775/588–2411 or 800/648–3361,* FAX *775/782–4889. 705 rooms, 38 suites. 8 restaurants, pool, barbershop, beauty salon, hot tub, spa, health club, casino, chapel. AE, D, DC, MC, V.*

$$–$$$$ **Caesars Tahoe.** Most of the rooms and suites at this 16-story hotel-casino have oversize tubs, king-size beds, two telephones, and a view of Lake Tahoe or the encircling mountains. The opulent casino encompasses 40,000 square ft. Top-name entertainers perform in the 1,600-seat Circus Maximus. Planet Hollywood is here, plus Chinese, Italian, and American restaurants, a 24-hour coffee shop with a buffet, and a frozen-yogurt emporium. ✉ *55 U.S. 50, Box 5800, 89449,* ☎ *775/588–3515; 800/648–3353 reservations and show information,* FAX *775/586–2068. 328 rooms, 112 suites. 5 restaurants, indoor pool, hot tub, saunas, spa, 4 tennis courts, health club, showroom. AE, D, DC, MC, V.*

$–$$$$ **Horizon Casino Resort.** Many of the guest rooms at this hotel-casino have lake views. The casino has a beaux arts decor, brightened by pale molded wood and mirrors. The Grande Lake Theatre, Golden Cabaret, and Aspen Lounge present shows, as well as up-and-coming and name entertainers. Le Grande Buffet has a nightly prime-rib special. ✉ *U.S. 50, Box C, 89449,* ☎ *775/588–6211 or 800/322–7723,* FAX *775/588–1344. 516 rooms, 23 suites. 3 restaurants, pool, 3 hot tubs, exercise room, casino, meeting rooms. AE, D, DC, MC, V.*

$–$$$ **Lakeside Inn and Casino.** The smallest of the Stateline casinos, the Lakeside has a rustic look. Guest rooms are in two-story motel-style buildings away from the casino area. ✉ *U.S. 50 at Kingsbury Grade, Box 5640, 89449,* ☎ *775/588–7777 or 800/624–7980,* FAX *775/588–4092. 115 rooms, 9 suites. Restaurant, pool, casino. AE, D, DC, MC, V.*

Nightlife

The top entertainment venues are the Circus Maximus at Caesars Tahoe, the Emerald Theater at Harvey's, the South Shore Room at Harrah's, and Horizon's Grand Lake Theatre. Comedy fans might laugh with Jay Leno, while music lovers could catch Johnny Mathis. For Las Vegas–style production shows—fast-paced dancing, singing, and novelty acts—try Harrah's or the Horizon. The big showrooms occasionally present performances of musicals by touring Broadway companies. Reservations are almost always required for superstar shows. Depending on the act, cocktail shows usually cost from $12 to $40. Smaller casino cabarets sometimes have a cover charge or drink minimum.

Bars around the lake present pop and country-western singers and musicians, and in winter the ski resorts do the same. Summer alternatives are outdoor music events, from chamber quartets to rock performers, at Sand Harbor and the Lake Tahoe Visitors Center amphitheater.

Outdoor Activities and Sports

GOLF

Edgewood Tahoe (✉ U.S. 50 and Lake Pkwy., behind Horizon Casino, Stateline, ☎ 775/588–3566), located right on the lake, is an 18-hole, par-72 course with a driving range. The $150 greens fee includes a cart (though you can walk if you wish); the course is open from 7 AM to 4 PM between May and October. The 18-hole, par-70 **Lake Tahoe Golf Course** (✉ U.S. 50, between Lake Tahoe Airport and Meyers, ☎ 530/577–0788) has a driving range. The greens fee is $50; a cart (mandatory from Friday to Sunday) costs $22.

SCUBA DIVING

Sun Sports (✉ 1018 Herbert Ave., No. 4, South Lake Tahoe, ☎ 530/541–6000) is a full-service PADI dive center with rentals and instruction.

LAKE TAHOE A TO Z

Arriving and Departing

By Bus

Greyhound (☏ 800/231–2222) stops in Sacramento, Truckee, and Reno, Nevada.

By Car

Lake Tahoe is 198 mi northeast of San Francisco, a drive of less than four hours when traffic and the weather cooperate. Try to avoid the heavy traffic leaving the San Francisco area for Tahoe on Friday afternoon and returning on Sunday afternoon. The major route is I–80, which cuts through the Sierra Nevada about 14 mi north of the lake. From there Highway 89 and Highway 267 reach the west and north shores, respectively. U.S. 50 is the more direct route to the south shore, taking about 2½ hours from Sacramento. From Reno you can get to the north shore by heading west on Highway 431 (a total of 35 mi). For the south shore, head south on U.S. 395 through Carson City, and then turn west on U.S. 50 (50 mi total).

By Plane

Reno–Tahoe International Airport (✉ U.S. 395, Exit 65B, Reno, NV, ☏ 775/328–6400), 35 mi northeast of the closest point on the lake, is served by airlines that include Alaska, American, America West, Continental, Delta, Northwest, Skywest, Southwest, and United. *See* Air Travel *in* Smart Travel Tips A to Z for airline phone numbers. **Tahoe Casino Express** (☏ 775/785–2424 or 800/446–6128) has daily scheduled transportation from the airport in Reno to Stateline casinos from 6:15 AM to 12:30 AM, $17 one-way and $30 round-trip.

Lake Tahoe Airport (☏ 530/542–6180) on U.S. 50 is 3 mi south of the lake's shore. No commercial carriers operate scheduled service to this airport; for charters, contact **Alpine Lake Aviation** (☏ 775/588–4748).

Getting Around

By Bus

South Tahoe Area Ground Express (STAGE, ☏ 530/573–2080) runs along U.S. 50 and through the neighborhoods of South Lake Tahoe daily from 6 AM to 12:15 AM. **Tahoe Area Regional Transit** (TART, ☏ 530/581–6365 or 800/736–6365) operates buses along Lake Tahoe's northern and western shores between Tahoma (from Meeks Bay in summer) and Incline Village daily from 6:30 AM to 6:30 PM. Free shuttle buses run among the casinos, major ski resorts, and motels of South Lake Tahoe.

By Car

The scenic 72-mi highway around the lake is marked Highway 89 on the southwest and west, Highway 28 on the north and northeast shores, and U.S. 50 on the east and southeast. Sections of Highway 89 sometimes close during winter, making it impossible to complete the circular drive. Interstate 80, U.S. 50, and U.S. 395 are all-weather highways, but there may be delays as snow is cleared during major storms. Carry tire chains from October through May (car-rental agencies provide them with their vehicles). *See* Road Conditions, *below,* for hot line phone numbers.

By Taxi

Yellow Cab (☏ 530/544–5555 or 530/544–2900) serves all of Tahoe Basin. On the north shore try **Tahoe-Truckee Taxi** (☏ 530/582–8294).

Contacts and Resources

Emergencies

Ambulance (☎ 911). **Fire** (☎ 911). **California Highway Patrol** (☎ 530/587–3510). **Nevada Highway Patrol** (☎ 775/687–5300). **Police** (☎ 911).

Guided Tours

BY BOAT

Hornblower's Tahoe Queen (☞ South Lake Tahoe *in* California Side, *above*), the ***Sierra Cloud*** (☞ Incline Village *in* Nevada Side, *above*), and the **MS *Dixie II*** and the ***Woodwind*** (☞ U.S. 50 from Spooner Junction to Zephyr Cove *in* Nevada Side, *above*) all operate guided boat tours.

BY BUS OR CAR

Gray Line and Frontier Tours (☎ 775/331–1147 or 800/882–6009) runs daily tours to South Lake Tahoe, Carson City, and Virginia City. **Tahoe Lake Lapper** (☎ 530/542–5900) provides daily around-the-lake transportation in both directions: the Green Bus travels clockwise and the Blue Bus travels counterclockwise. Buses leave South Lake Tahoe at 7, 10, and 11 AM and 1, 2, 4, and 5 PM; a late Blue Bus leaves at 8 PM on Friday and Saturday. The fare is $5. **Lake Tahoe Adventures** (✉ 2286 Utah Ave., South Lake Tahoe 96150, ☎ 530/541–5875) operates a summer trek skirting the Desolation Wilderness on the Rubicon Trail in four-wheel-drive all-terrain vehicles; in winter, they head across Carson Valley to the Pine Nut Mountains for two-hour excursions on ATVs and snowmobiles.

BY HOT-AIR BALLOON

Lake Tahoe Balloons (☎ 530/544–1221) conducts excursions year-round over the lake or over the Carson Valley for $109 per person for half-hour flights and $175 for hour-long flights (champagne brunch included).

BY PLANE

CalVada Seaplanes Inc. (☎ 530/546–3984) provides rides over the lake for $60 to $100 per person, depending on the length of the trip. **High Country Soaring** (☎ 775/782–4944) glider rides over the lake and valley depart from the Douglas County Airport, Gardnerville.

Reservations Agencies

Park.net (☎ 800/444–7275 for campgrounds in California state parks). **Lake Tahoe Visitors Authority** (☎ 800/288–2463 for south-shore lodging). **North Lake Tahoe Resort Association** (☎ 800/824–6348 for north-shore lodging).

Road Conditions

California roads in Tahoe area (☎ 530/445–7623). **California roads approaching Tahoe** (☎ 800/427–7623). **Nevada roads** (☎ 775/793–1313).

Visitor Information

California State Department of Parks and Recreation (☎ 916/324–4442). **Lake Tahoe Hotline** (☎ 530/542–4636 for south-shore events; 530/546–5253 for north-shore events; 775/831–6677 for Nevada events). **Lake Tahoe Visitors Authority** (✉ 1156 Ski Run Blvd., South Lake Tahoe, CA 96150, ☎ 530/544–5050 or 800/288–2463). **North Lake Tahoe Resort Association** (✉ Box 5578, Tahoe City, CA 96145, ☎ 530/583–3494 or 800/824–6348, FAX 530/581–4081). **Ski Report Hotline** (☎ 415/864–6440). **U.S. Forest Service** backcountry recording (☎ 530/587–2158).

7 THE SIERRA NATIONAL PARKS

WITH MONO LAKE AND MAMMOTH LAKES

The highlight for many California travelers is a visit to one of the national parks in the Sierra Nevada range. Yosemite, the state's most famous park, is every bit as sublime as one expects. Its U-shape valleys were carved by glaciers during the Ice Age. Other glacial valleys are found about 150 mi southeast in Kings Canyon and Sequoia national parks, which are adjacent to each other and usually visited together. All the Sierra national parks contain groves of giant sequoia (*Sequoiadendron giganteum*) trees, nature's largest living things.

Updated by Herb Benham

YOSEMITE, KINGS CANYON, AND SEQUOIA national parks are famous throughout the world for their granite peaks, towering waterfalls, and giant sequoias, among other natural wonders. Yosemite, especially, should be on your "don't miss" list. Unfortunately, it's on everyone else's as well (the park receives about 4 million visitors annually), so lodging reservations are essential. The time to see Yosemite is in the winter or early spring when you're not tripping over throngs of tourists. During a week's stay you can exit and reenter the parks as often as you wish by showing your pass.

Pleasures and Pastimes

Camping

One highlight of camping in the Sierra national parks is awakening to the sights of nearby meadows and streams and, in the distance, the unforgettable landscape of giant granite. Another is gazing up at an awe-inspiring number of constellations and spying a shooting star in the night sky. For reservations and other information *see* Contacts and Resources *in* Yosemite National Park A to Z *and* Kings Canyon and Sequoia National Parks A to Z, *below.*

Dining

Snack bars, coffee shops, and cafeterias in the parks are not expensive, but you may not want to waste precious time finding food, especially during the day. Stop at a grocery store and fill your ice chest with picnic supplies to enjoy under giant trees.

The three fanciest lodgings within Yosemite National Park are also the prime dining spots. If the roads are clear of traffic or snow, you may also want to drive out of the park to dine at restaurants in the border towns (☞ Outside Yosemite National Park, *below*). With few exceptions, which are noted, dress is casual at the restaurants listed below.

CATEGORY	COST*
$$$$	over $50
$$$	$30–$50
$$	$20–$30
$	under $20

**per person for a three-course meal, excluding drinks, service, and 10% tax*

Hiking

Hiking is the primary outdoor activity in the Sierra national parks. Whether you walk the paved loops that pass by major attractions or head off the beaten path into the backcountry, a hike through groves, meadows, or alongside streams and waterfalls will allow you to see, smell, and feel nature up close. Some of the most popular trails are described briefly in this chapter; stop by the visitor centers for maps and advice from park rangers.

Lodging

Most accommodations inside Yosemite, Kings Canyon, and Sequoia national parks can best be described as "no frills." Some have no electricity or indoor plumbing. Other than the Ahwahnee and Wawona hotels in Yosemite, lodgings tend to be basic motels or rustic cabins. Except during the off-peak season, from November through March, rates in Yosemite are pricey given the general quality of the lodging. Reserve well ahead, especially during summer; you can reserve up to a year and a day in advance. *See* Contacts and Resources *in* Yosemite National Park A to Z, *below,* for the phone number of the park's reservations service.

Reservations are recommended for visits to Kings Canyon and Sequoia at any time of the year because it's a long way back to civilization if the lodgings there are full. All the park's lodges and cabins are open during the summer months, but in winter only some in Grant Grove remain open. Lodging rates are consistent throughout the year. The town of Three Rivers, on Highway 198 southwest of Sequoia, has some lodgings. *See* Contacts and Resources *in* Kings Canyon and Sequoia National Parks A to Z, *below,* for park lodging reservation numbers.

CATEGORY	COST*
$$$$	over $175
$$$	$120–$175
$$	$80–$120
$	under $80

**All prices are for a standard double room, excluding 10% tax.*

following the text of a review is your signal that the property has a Web site, where you will find details and, usually, images; for a link, visit www.fodors.com/urls.

Nature Lore

In Yosemite from early May to late September and during some holiday periods, actor Lee Stetson portrays naturalist John Muir, bringing to life Muir's wit, wisdom, and storytelling skill. You can also join park rangers on free 60- to 90-minute nature walks focusing on geology, wildlife, waterfalls, forest ecology, and other topics. Locations and times for both are listed in the *Yosemite Guide,* the newspaper visitors receive upon entering the park.

Exploring the Sierra National Parks

For the full Sierra experience, stay in the parks themselves instead of the "gateway cities" in the foothills or the Central Valley. Save your time and energy for exploring, not driving to and from the parks. Yosemite Valley is the primary destination for many visitors. Because the valley is only 7 mi long and averages less than 1 mi in width, you can visit its attractions in whatever order you choose and return to your favorites at different times of the day. Famous for hiking trails and giant sequoias, Kings Canyon and Sequoia provide a true wilderness experience, less interrupted by civilization and crowds.

Separate A to Z information listings follow the Yosemite National Park, Outside Yosemite National Park, Mammoth Lakes, and Kings Canyon and Sequoia National Parks sections, below.

Numbers in the text correspond to numbers in the margin and on the Yosemite and the Kings Canyon and Sequoia national parks maps.

Great Itineraries

IF YOU HAVE 3 DAYS

If your time is limited, choose Yosemite National Park to explore. Enter the park via the Big Oak Flat Entrance, and head east on Big Oak Flat Road. As you enter the valley, traffic is diverted onto a one-way road. Continue east, following the signs to the **Valley Visitor Center** ①. Loop back west for a short hike near **Yosemite Falls** ②, the highest waterfall in North America. Continue west for a valley view of famous **El Capitan** ⑦ peak. This area is a good place for a picnic. Backtrack onto Southside Drive, stopping at misty **Bridalveil Fall** ③, then follow Highway 41/Wawona Road south 14 mi to the Chinquapin junction and make a left turn onto Glacier Point Road. From **Glacier Point** ⑨ (road closed in winter) you'll get a phenomenal bird's-eye view of the entire valley, including **Half Dome** ⑧, **Vernal Fall** ⑤, and **Nevada Fall** ⑥. If you want to avoid the busloads of tourists at Glacier Point, stop at **Sentinel Dome** ⑩ instead. After a mildly strenuous 1-mi hike you get a view similar to the one from Glacier Point. Head south on Highway 41 to the Wawona Hotel (closed weekdays much of winter), where you can have a relaxing drink on the veranda or in the cozy lobby bar and listen to pianist Tom Bopp play folk songs.

On day two, visit the **Mariposa Grove of Big Trees** ⑫ and return to Wawona to tour the **Pioneer Yosemite History Center** ⑪. Head back to Yosemite Valley on Wawona Road for an early evening beverage at the Ahwahnee Hotel's bar (enjoy the patio in good weather), and view the paintings of Native American tribal leaders hanging the hotel's lobby. On the third day have breakfast near the Valley Visitor Center before hiking to **Vernal Fall** or **Nevada Fall.**

IF YOU HAVE 5 DAYS

Spend your first day exploring the **Yosemite Valley area** ①–⑩. On the second day, pack some food and drive to **Hetch Hetchy Reservoir** (closed in winter) via Big Oak Flat Road and Highway 120. Then continue east on Tioga Road to **Tuolumne Meadows,** the largest subalpine meadow in the Sierra. Time permitting, head east through 9,900-ft Tioga Pass to **Mono Lake** and, possibly, **Bodie Ghost Town** ⑬. (Tioga Road closes for several months after the first snow; if the road isn't open, on day two you can instead take a hike to **Vernal Fall** ⑤ or **Nevada Fall** ⑥.) Wake up early on day three and spend the morning visiting Wawona's **Pioneer Yosemite History Center** ⑪ and wandering beneath the giant sequoias at the nearby **Mariposa Grove of Big Trees** ⑫. Then head south to **Kings Canyon National Park** (about a three- to four-hour drive), entering on Highway 180 at the Big Stump Entrance. Stop to see the sequoias at **Grant Grove** ⑮. If you're camping, you'll need to get situated before sunset; if you're staying at one of the park's lodges, check in and have dinner. On the fifth day, pass briefly through **Lodgepole** ㉑ in **Sequoia National Park** and pick up tickets to **Crystal Cave** ㉔. Visit the **Giant Forest** ㉒ before stopping at the cave.

When to Tour the Sierra National Parks

Summer is the most crowded season for all the parks, though things never get as hectic at Kings Canyon and Sequoia as they do at Yosemite. During extremely busy periods—when snow closes high-country roads in late spring or on crowded summer weekends—Yosemite Valley may be closed to all vehicles unless their drivers have overnight reservations. Avoid these restrictions by visiting from mid-April through Memorial Day and from Labor Day to mid-October, when the parks are less busy and the weather is usually hospitable.

The falls at Yosemite are at their most spectacular in May and June. By the end of summer, some will have dried up. They begin flowing again in late fall with the first storms, and during winter they may be hung with ice, a dramatic sight. Snow on the floor of Yosemite Valley is never deep, so you can camp there even in winter (January highs are in the mid-40s, lows in the mid-20s). Tioga Road is usually closed from late October through May; unless you ski or snowshoe in, you can't see Tuolumne Meadows then. The road to Glacier Point beyond the turnoff for Badger Pass is not cleared in winter, but it is groomed for cross-country skiing.

YOSEMITE NATIONAL PARK

Yosemite Valley, Wawona, the High Country

Yosemite, with 1,169 square mi of parkland, is 94½% undeveloped wilderness, most of it accessible only to backpackers and horseback riders. The western boundary dips as low as 2,000 ft in the chaparral-covered foothills; the eastern boundary rises to 13,000 ft at points along the Sierra crest.

Yosemite is so large that it functions as five parks. **Yosemite Valley** and **Wawona** are open all year. **Hetch Hetchy** closes after the first big snow and reopens in May or June. The high country, **Tuolumne Meadows,** is open for summer hiking and camping; in winter, it's accessible only by cross-country ski or snowshoe. **Badger Pass Ski Area** is open in winter only. The fee to visit Yosemite National Park (good for seven days) is $20 per car, $10 per person if you don't arrive in a car.

Yosemite Valley Area

214 mi southeast of San Francisco, I–80 to I–580 to I–205 to Hwy. 120; 330 mi northeast of Los Angeles, I–5 to Hwy. 99 to Hwy. 41.

Yosemite Valley has been so extravagantly praised (John Muir described it as "a revelation in landscape affairs that enriches one's life forever") and so beautifully photographed (by Ansel Adams and others) that you may wonder if the reality can possibly measure up. For almost everyone it does. Yosemite is truly a reminder of what "breathtaking" really means. The Miwok people, the last of several Native American tribes who inhabited the Yosemite area, called the valley "Ahwahnee," which is said to mean "the place of the gaping mouth." Members of the tribe, who were forced out of the area by gold miners in 1851, called themselves the Ahwahneechee.

❶ You can get your bearings, pick up maps, and obtain information from park rangers at the **Valley Visitor Center.** The adjacent **Yosemite Museum** has an Indian Cultural Exhibit with displays about the Miwok and Pauite people who lived in the region; there's a re-created Ahwahneechee village behind it. The nearby **Ansel Adams Gallery** shows works of the master Yosemite photographer. They're all part of **Yosemite Village,** which contains restaurants, stores, a post office, the Ahwahnee Hotel, Yosemite Lodge, a medical clinic, and other facilities. **A Changing Yosemite,** a 1-mi paved loop from the visitor center, traces the park's natural evolution. ✉ *Off Northside Dr.,* ☎ *209/372–0200.* ⏲ *Daily 9–5; extended hrs in summer.*

The staff at the **Wilderness Center** provides trail-use reservations (recommended for popular trailheads from May through September and on weekends), permits ($3), maps, and advice to hikers heading into the backcountry. When the Wilderness Center is closed, you can make inquiries at the nearby Valley Visitor Center or other information stations. *See* Hiking *in* Outdoor Activities and Sports, *below,* for more information about backcountry permits. ✉ *Yosemite Village near Ansel Adams Gallery (Box 545, Yosemite 95389),* ☎ *209/372–0200 for information; 209/372–0740 for reservations.* ⏲ *Apr.–Oct., daily 8–5.*

★ ❷ **Yosemite Falls** is the highest waterfall in North America and the fifth-highest in the world. The upper fall (1,430 ft), the middle cascades (675 ft), and the lower fall (320 ft) combine for a total of 2,425 ft and, when viewed from the valley, appear as a single waterfall. A ¼-mi trail leads from the parking lot to the base of the falls. The Upper Yosemite Fall

Yosemite National Park

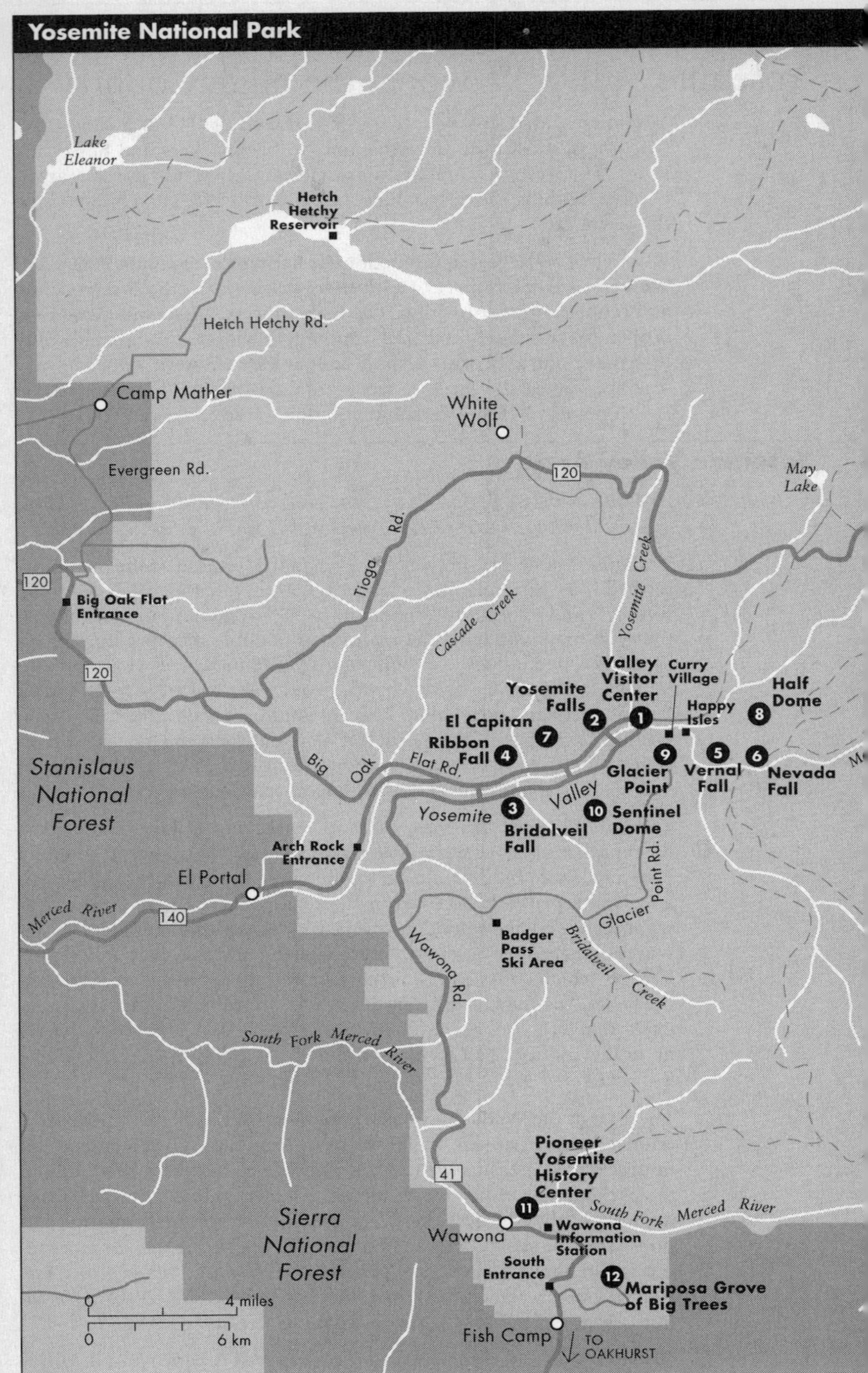

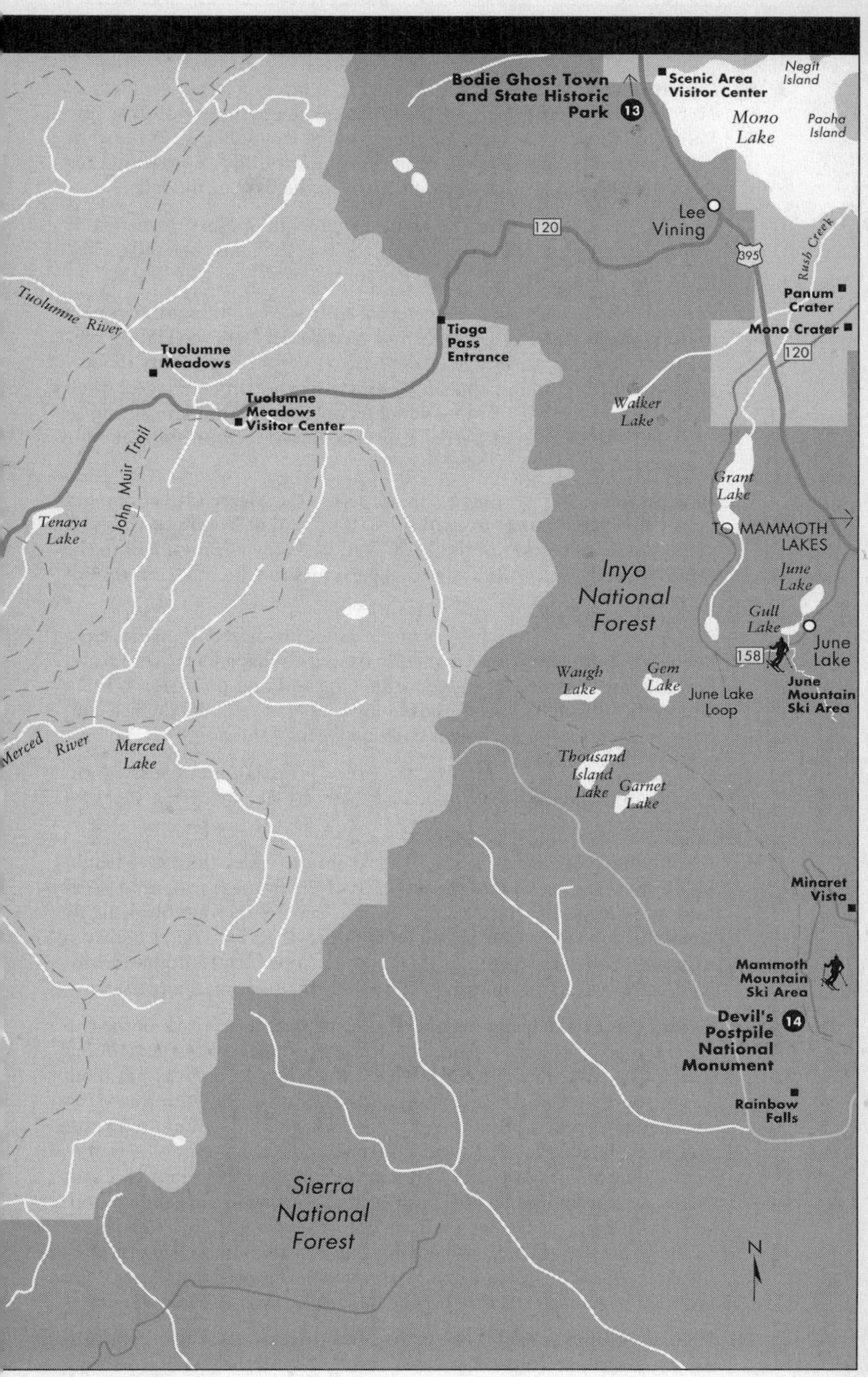

Bodie Ghost Town and State Historic Park
13
Scenic Area Visitor Center
Negit Island
Mono Lake
Paoha Island
Lee Vining
120
395
Rush Creek
Panum Crater
Mono Crater
120
Tuolumne River
Tuolumne Meadows
Tioga Pass Entrance
Tuolumne Meadows Visitor Center
Walker Lake
John Muir Trail
Grant Lake
TO MAMMOTH LAKES
Tenaya Lake
Inyo National Forest
June Lake
Gull Lake
June Lake
158
June Mountain Ski Area
Waugh Lake
Gem Lake
June Lake Loop
Merced River
Merced Lake
Thousand Island Lake
Garnet Lake
Minaret Vista
Mammoth Mountain Ski Area
Devil's Postpile National Monument
14
Rainbow Falls
Sierra National Forest
N

Trail, a strenuous 3½-mi climb rising 2,700 ft, takes you above the top of the falls. It starts at Sunnyside Campground.

★ 3 **Bridalveil Fall,** a filmy fall of 620 ft that is often diverted as much as 20 ft one way or the other by the breeze, is the first view of Yosemite Valley for those who arrive via the Wawona Road. Native Americans called the fall Pohono ("spirit of the puffing wind"). A ¼-mi trail leads from the parking lot off Wawona Road to the base of the falls.

4 At 1,612 ft, **Ribbon Fall** is the highest single fall in North America. It is also the first waterfall in the valley to dry up; the rainwater and melted snow that create the slender fall evaporate quickly at this height.

5 Fern-covered black rocks frame **Vernal Fall** (317 ft), and rainbows play in the spray at its base. The hike on a paved trail from the Happy Isles Nature Center to the bridge at the base of Vernal Fall is only moderately strenuous and less than 1 mi long. It's another steep (and often wet) ¾ mi up the Mist Trail—which is open only from late spring to early fall—to the top of Vernal Fall. Allow two to four hours for the 3-mi round-trip hike.

6 **Nevada Fall** (594 ft) is the first major fall as the Merced River plunges out of the high country toward the eastern end of Yosemite Valley. A strenuous 2-mi section of the Mist Trail leads from Vernal Fall to the top of Nevada Fall. Allow six to eight hours for the full 7-mi round-trip hike.

The roads at the eastern fringes of the valley are closed to private cars, but a free shuttle bus runs frequently from the village. Both Vernal and Nevada falls can also be viewed from Glacier Point (☞ *below*). From about May through October the Happy Isles Nature Center, which contains ecology exhibits, is open daily between 9 and 5.

★ 7 **El Capitan,** rising 3,593 ft above the valley, is the largest exposed granite monolith in the world, almost twice the height of the Rock of Gibraltar.

★ 8 Astounding **Half Dome** rises 4,733 ft from the valley floor to a height 8,842 ft above sea level. The west side of the dome is fractured vertically and cut away to form a 2,000-ft cliff. The 16¾-mi round-trip, highly strenuous **John Muir Trail** (which incorporates the Mist Trail) leads from Yosemite Valley to the top of Half Dome. Allow 10–12 hours for this hike; start early in the morning and beware of afternoon thunderstorms.

★ 9 **Glacier Point** yields what may be the most spectacular vistas of the valley and the High Sierra—especially at sunset—that you can get without hiking. The Glacier Point Road leaves Wawona Road (Highway 41) about 23 mi southwest of the valley; then it's a 16-mi drive, with fine views into higher country. From the parking area walk a few hundred yards and you'll be able to see Nevada, Vernal, and Yosemite falls as well as Half Dome and other peaks. You can hike to the valley floor (3,214 ft below) via the Panorama or Four-Mile trails. To avoid a grueling round-trip, catch a ride to Glacier Point on one of the three daily hikers' buses ($10.50 one way, $20.50 round trip) that run from late spring through October (☎ 209/372–1240 for reservations). The road to Glacier Point is closed beyond the turnoff for the Badger Pass Ski Area in winter.

10 The view from **Sentinel Dome** is similar to that from Glacier Point, except you can't see the valley floor. A 1.1-mi path begins at a parking lot on Glacier Point Road a few miles below Glacier Point. The trail is long and steep enough to keep the crowds and tour buses away, but not overly rugged.

OFF THE BEATEN PATH

HETCH HETCHY RESERVOIR AND TUOLUMNE MEADOWS – The Hetch Hetchy Reservoir, which supplies water and hydroelectric power to San Francisco, is about 40 mi from Yosemite Valley via Big Oak Flat Road to Highway 120 to Evergreen Road to Hetch Hetchy Road. Some say John Muir died of heartbreak when this valley was dammed and flooded beneath 300 ft of water in 1913. Tioga Road (Highway 120) stays open until the first big snow of the year, usually about mid-October. The road is the scenic route to Tuolumne Meadows, altitude 8,575 ft, which is 55 mi from Yosemite Valley. The largest subalpine meadow in the Sierra and the trailhead for many backpack trips into the High Sierra, the area contains campgrounds, a gas station, a store (with limited and expensive provisions), stables, a lodge, and a visitor center that is open from late June until Labor Day from 8 AM to 7:30 PM.

Dining, Lodging, and Camping

$$–$$$ ✕ **Mountain Room Restaurant.** The food becomes secondary when you see Yosemite Falls through this dining room's wall of windows. Almost every patron has a view of the falls. Gulf shrimp stuffed with crabmeat, grilled halibut, steak, pasta, and several children's dishes are on the menu. ✉ *Yosemite Lodge, off Northside Dr.,* ☎ *209/372–1281. D, DC, MC, V. No lunch; closed weekdays from Thanksgiving–Easter except for holiday periods.*

$$$$ ★ ✕🏨 **Ahwahnee Hotel & Dining Room.** This grand 1920s-era mountain lodge, designated a National Historical Landmark, is constructed of rocks and sugar-pine logs. The decorative style of the Great Lounge and Solarium is a tribute to the Miwok and Paiute tribes that inhabited the area; the Native American motifs continue in the room decor. The Ahwahnee Dining Room ($$–$$$), with its 34-ft-tall trestle-beam ceiling, full-length windows, and wrought-iron chandeliers, is by far the most impressive and romantic eating establishment in the park. Such classic American specialties as New York steak, broiled swordfish fillet, and prime rib are competently prepared. For dessert try the chocolate banana layer cake or the napoleon with espresso caramel sauce. ✉ *Ahwahnee Rd. north of Northside Dr.,* ☎ *559/252–4848 for lodging reservations; 209/372–1489 for restaurant. 99 rooms, 4 suites, 24 cottages. Restaurant, lounge, pool, tennis. AE, D, DC, MC, V.*

$$ ✕🏨 **Yosemite Lodge.** This lodge near Yosemite Falls, which dates from 1915, once housed the U. S. Army Calvary. Typical motel-style rooms have two double beds, while the larger "lodge rooms" also have dressing areas and balconies. None have TVs or air-conditioning. Of the lodge's three eating places, the Mountain Room Restaurant (☞ *above*) is the most formal. The Garden Terrace Restaurant, open seasonally, prepares an all-you-can-eat buffet of salads, soups, pastas, and hot meats. A cafeteria serves three meals a day. ✉ *Off Northside Dr.,* ☎ *559/252–4848. 245 rooms. 2 restaurants, cafeteria, bar, pool. AE, D, DC, MC, V.*

$–$$ 🏨 **Curry Village.** Opened in 1899 as a place where travelers could enjoy the beauty of Yosemite for a modest price, Curry Village offers plain accommodations: standard motel rooms, cabins, and "tent cabins" with rough wood frames and canvas walls and roofs. It's a step up from camping, as linens, blankets, and maid service are provided, although many cabins have shared shower and toilet facilities.✉ *South side of Southside Dr.,* ☎ *209/372–8333; 559/252–4848 for reservations. 19 rooms, 182 cabins, 80 without bath, 427 tent cabins. Cafeteria, pizzeria, pool. D, DC, MC, V.*

$ ⛺ **Housekeeping Camp.** These rustic three-wall cabins with canvas roofs, set on a beach along the Merced River, are difficult to come by; reserving a year in advance is advised. You can cook here on gas stoves rented from the front desk. ✉ *North side of Southside Dr. near Curry Village,* ☎ *209/372–8338; 559/252–4848 for reservations. 266 units without bath. Toilet and shower in central building. D, DC, MC, V. Closed early Oct.–late Apr.*

Outdoor Activities and Sports

BICYCLING

The eastern valley has 8 mi of bike paths, or you can ride on 196 mi of paved park roads. **Yosemite Lodge and Curry Village** both have bicycle rentals (☎ 209/372–1208 for Yosemite Lodge; 209/372–8319 for Curry Village). Rentals at the lodge are year-round; Curry Village rents from April through October. Bikes are $5.25 an hour or $20 per day. Baby-jogger strollers and bikes with child trailers are also available.

CAMPING

For information about campground reservations, *see* Yosemite National Park A to Z, *below.*

HIKING

Yosemite's 840 mi of hiking trails range from short strolls to rugged, multiday treks. The park's visitor centers have trail maps and information. Rangers will recommend easy trails to get you acclimated to the altitude. Overnight backpackers need wilderness permits, which can be obtained during the off-season at permit stations within the park. Reservations ($5 per person) are strongly advised during summer and can be made through the Yosemite Valley **Wilderness Center** (Box 545, Yosemite, 95389, ☎ 209/372–0740).

HORSEBACK RIDING

Yosemite Valley Stables (☎ 209/372–8348) offers two-hour guided trail rides.

ROCK CLIMBING

Yosemite Mountaineering (☎ 209/372–8344) conducts rock-climbing, backpacking, cross country skiing, and skate-skiing classes.

WINTER SPORTS

Badger Pass Ski Area, off Yosemite's Glacier Point Road, has nine downhill runs, 90 mi of groomed cross-country trails, and two excellent ski schools. Its gentle slopes make **Yosemite Ski School** (☎ 209/372–8430) an ideal spot for children and beginners. The highlight of the **cross-country skiing center** is a 21-mi loop from Badger Pass to Glacier Point. You can rent cross-country skis for $16 per day. The **outdoor ice-skating rink** (☎ 209/372–8341) at Curry Village in Yosemite Valley is open from Thanksgiving Day through April. The cost is $5.

Wawona

25 mi south of Yosemite Valley on Hwy. 41; 16 mi north of Fish Camp on Hwy. 41.

⓫ The historic buildings in **Pioneer Yosemite History Center** were moved to Wawona from their original sites in the park. From Wednesday through Sunday in summer costumed park employees re-create life in 19th-century Yosemite in a blacksmith's shop, a Wells Fargo office, a jail, and other structures. Ranger-led walks leave from the covered bridge on Saturday at 10 AM. Near the center are a post office, a general store, and a gas station. ✉ *On Hwy. 41.* ⏲ *Historic buildings open year-round (hrs vary).*

⓬ **Mariposa Grove of Big Trees,** Yosemite's largest grove of giant sequoias, can be visited on foot—trails all lead uphill—or, during the summer, on one-hour tram rides. The Grizzly Giant, the oldest tree here, is estimated to be 2,700 years old. If the road to the grove is closed (which happens when Yosemite is crowded) park in Wawona and take the free shuttle; passengers are picked up near the gas station. The access road to the grove may also be closed by snow for extended periods from November to mid-May. You can still usually walk, snowshoe, or ski in. ✉ *Off Hwy. 41 near the Fish Camp entrance to Yosemite National Park.* 💳 *Free; tram $8.50.* ⏲ *Grove, 24 hrs; tram, May–Oct., daily 9–4; shuttle, Memorial Day–Labor Day, daily 9–5.*

Dining and Lodging

$$–$$$ ✕🏨 **Wawona Hotel and Dining Room.** This 1879 National Historic Landmark sits at the southern end of Yosemite National Park, near the Mariposa Grove of Big Trees. It's an old-fashioned New England-style estate of whitewashed buildings with wraparound verandas. The hotel has small but pleasant rooms, none of which have TVs or phones. You can watch deer graze on the meadow while dining in the romantic, candlelit dining room ($$–$$$; reservations essential), which dates from the late 1800s. The smoky corn trout soup hits the spot on cold winter nights. After dinner, head for the great room to hear pianist Tom Bopp play folk songs. ✉ *Hwy. 41, 95389,* ☎ *559/252–4848 (reservations); 209/375–6556 (front desk); 209/375–1425 (dining room),* FAX *559/456–0542. 104 rooms, 52 without bath. Restaurant, lounge, pool, 9-hole golf course, tennis, horseback riding. D, DC, MC, V. Closed weekdays Nov.–Easter except holidays.*

Yosemite National Park A to Z

Arriving and Departing

BY BUS

Greyhound (☎ 800/231–2222) serves Fresno and Merced from many California cities. **Yosemite VIA** (✉ 710 W. 16th St., Merced, ☎ 209/384–1315 or 800/369–7275) runs three daily buses from Merced to Yosemite Valley; buses also depart daily from Mariposa. The 2½- to 4½-hour trip from Merced costs $38 per person round-trip, which includes admission to the park. For $68 you get the trip, lunch, park admission, and two-hour tour.

BY CAR

Yosemite is a four- to five-hour drive from San Francisco (take Interstate–80 to Interstate–580 to Interstate–205 to Highway 120) and a six-hour drive from Los Angeles (take Interstate–5 north to Highway 99 to Fresno, and Highway 41 north to Yosemite). Highways 41, 120, and 140 all intersect with Highway 99, which runs north–south through the Central Valley. Try to fill up your gas tank in one of the gateway towns near the park; there's no gas station in Yosemite Valley. Within the park, gas stations are in Crane Flat, Wawona, and, in summer only, Tuolumne Meadows.

Via Highway 41: If you're coming from the south, Highway 41—which passes through Fresno in the San Joaquin Valley and then climbs through hills to Oakhurst and past Bass Lake—is the most direct path to Yosemite. Called Wawona Road inside the park, it provides the most stunning entrance, via the Wawona Tunnel, into Yosemite Valley. The distance from Fresno is 105 mi, but the latter part of the trip can be quite slow; allow 2½ hours. If you're coming from Madera, 60 mi away, take Highway 145 to Highway 41, then go north.

Via Highway 140: Arch Rock Entrance is 75 mi northeast of Merced via Highway 140, the least mountainous route into the park. The highway is undergoing extensive widening and reconstruction that is slated to continue for several years. Construction if often halted, however, during busy summer months and holiday periods.

Via Highway 120: Highway 120 is the northernmost route—the one that travels farthest and slowest through the foothills. You'll arrive at the park's Big Oak Flat Entrance, 88 mi east of Manteca. If you are coming from the east, you could cross the Sierra from Lee Vining on Highway 120 (Tioga Road). This route, open in summer only, takes you over the Sierra crest and past Tuolumne Meadows. It's scenic, but the mountain driving may be stressful for some.

BY PLANE

Fresno Air Terminal (✉ 5175 E. Clinton Way, ☎ 559/498–4095), the nearest major airport, is served by Delta, American, United Express, Allegiance, Horizon, US Airways, and several regional carriers. *See* Air Travel *in* Smart Travel Tips A to Z for airline phone numbers.

Getting Around

BY BUS

A free shuttle runs around the eastern end of Yosemite Valley (between 7 AM and 10 PM in the summer and early fall, from 9 AM to 10 PM the rest of the year). A free shuttle connects Wawona to the Mariposa Grove of Big Trees in summer only from 9 AM to 4:30 PM. The last return shuttle from the grove departs at 5 PM. Free shuttle buses from Yosemite Valley to Badger Pass operate in ski season.

BY CAR

Auto traffic in Yosemite National Park is sometimes restricted during peak periods. Check conditions before driving in. Large RVs and trailers are not allowed on some roads. Carry tire chains from mid-October through April.

Contacts and Resources

CAMPING

Yosemite Campground Reservations (☎ 800/436–7275) handles bookings for the reservable campgrounds within the park (☞ *below*). Beginning on the 15th of each month you can reserve a site up to five months in advance. **Yosemite Concession Services Corporation** (☎ 559/252–4848) handles reservations for the tent-cabin and other sites in Yosemite Valley at Curry Village and at the camping shelters at Housekeeping Camp.

Most of Yosemite's 15 campgrounds are found in Yosemite Valley and along the Tioga Road. Glacier Point and Wawona have one each. None have water or electric hookups, but there are dump stations and shower facilities in Yosemite Valley year-round. The dump stations in Wawona and Tuolumne Meadows are open in summer only. Several campgrounds operate on a first-come, first-served basis. During summer, reservations are strongly recommended for the campgrounds at Tuolumne Meadows, Hodgdon Meadow, Lower Pines, North Pines, Upper Pines, Wawona, and Crane Flat; the rest of the year, some of these are first-come, first-served. With a total of 1,840 sites open in summer, it's sometimes possible to get a campsite upon arrival by stopping at the Campground Reservations Office in Yosemite Valley, but this is a risky strategy. Some 400 sites remain open year-round.

When you're at your site, use the metal food-storage boxes to prevent bears from pilfering your edibles. Move all food, coolers, and items with a scent (including toiletries and air fresheners) from your car to the metal storage box. (Canisters for backpackers can be rented for $3 a day in most park stores.) Keep an eye peeled for rattlesnakes, which live below 7,000 ft. Though rarely fatal, their bites require a doctor's attention. Marmots, small members of the squirrel family, enjoy getting under a vehicle and chewing on radiator hoses and car wiring. Always check under the hood before driving away. Don't drink water directly from streams and lakes, as intestinal disorders may result.

EMERGENCIES

Ambulance (☏ 911). **Fire** (☏ 911). **Police** (☏ 911).

GUIDED TOURS

California Parlor Car Tours (☏ 415/474–7500 or 800/227–4250) in San Francisco serves Yosemite. Lodging and some meals are included. **Yosemite Concession Services Corporation** (☏ 209/372–1240) operates daily guided bus tours of the Yosemite Valley floor year-round, plus seasonal tours of Glacier Point and the Mariposa Grove of Big Trees. The company's Grand Tour ($45.25), offered between Memorial Day and October 29, weather permitting, covers the park's highlights.

LODGING RESERVATIONS

Yosemite Concession Services Corporation (✉ Central Reservations, 5410 E. Home Ave., Fresno 93727, ☏ 559/252–4848).

ROAD CONDITIONS

Yosemite Area Road and Weather Conditions (☏ 209/372–0200).

VISITOR INFORMATION

Yosemite Concession Services Corporation (☏ 209/372–1000). **Yosemite National Park** (✉ Information Office, Box 577, Yosemite National Park 95389, ☏ 209/372–0200 or 209/372–0264).

OUTSIDE YOSEMITE NATIONAL PARK

Mono Lake, Bodie, and the Gateway Cities

The area to the north and east of Yosemite National Park includes some ruggedly handsome terrain, most notably around Mono Lake. Bodie Ghost Town is north of the lake. Several gateway towns to the south and west of Yosemite National Park, most within an hour's drive of Yosemite Valley, have food, lodging, and other services.

Mono Lake

20 mi east of Tuolumne Meadows, Hwy. 120 to U.S. 395; 30 mi north of Mammoth Lakes on U.S. 395.

★ Eerie tufa towers—calcium carbonate formations that often resemble castle turrets—rise from impressive **Mono Lake.** Since the 1940s the city of Los Angeles has diverted water from streams that feed the lake, lowering its water level and exposing the tufa. Court victories by environmentalists in the 1990s forced a reduction of the diversions, and the lake has since risen about 9 ft. Millions of migratory birds nest in and around Mono Lake.

The best place to view the tufa is at the south end of the lake along the mile-long **South Tufa Trail.** To reach it drive 5 mi south from Lee Vining on U.S. 395, then 5 mi east on Highway 120. Pay the $2 fee at the trail or at the **Scenic Area Visitor Center** (✉ U.S. 395, Lee Vining, ☏ 760/647–3044); the center is open daily from April through October, 9–5:30, and the rest of the year Thursday through Monday, 9–4. You can swim (or float) in the highly salty water at Navy Beach near the South Tufa Trail or take a kayak or canoe trip for close-up views of the tufa. Check with rangers for boating restrictions during bird-nesting season (April–August). Rangers and naturalists lead walking tours of the tufa daily in summer and on weekends only (sometimes on cross-country skis) in winter.

Bodie Ghost Town and State Historic Park

13 *23 mi from Lee Vining, north on U.S. 395, east on Hwy. 270 (last 3 mi are unpaved). Snow may close Hwy. 270 in winter and early spring, but park stays open.*

Old shacks and shops, abandoned mine shafts, a Methodist church, the mining village of Rattlesnake Gulch, and the remains of a small ★ Chinatown are among the sights at fascinating **Bodie Ghost Town.** The town, at an elevation of 8,200 ft, boomed from about 1878 to 1881 as gold prospectors, having worked the best of the western Sierra mines, headed to the high desert on the eastern slopes. Bodie was a mean place—the booze flowed freely, shootings were commonplace, and licentiousness reigned. The big strikes were made during the boom years, and though some mining continued into the 1930s, the town had long since begun its decline. By the late 1940s, all its residents had departed. A state park was established in 1962, with a mandate to preserve but not restore the town. Evidence of Bodie's wild past survives at an excellent museum, and you can tour an old stamp mill (where ore was stamped into fine powder to extract gold and silver) and a ridge that contains many mine sites. No food, drink, or lodging is available in Bodie, and the nearest picnic area is ½ mi away. ✉ *Museum: Main and Green Sts.,* ☎ *760/647–6445.* 🎫 *Park $2; museum free.* ⏲ *Park Memorial Day–mid-Sept., daily 8–7; rest of yr, daily 8–4; Museum May–Oct., daily 10–5; open sporadically rest of yr.*

Bass Lake

18 mi south of Yosemite National Park's South Entrance, Hwy. 41 to Bass Valley Rd.

Dining

$$–$$$ ✕ **Ducey's on the Lake.** With elaborate chandeliers sculpted from deer antlers, the lodge-style restaurant at Ducey's (part of the larger Pines Resort complex) attracts boaters, locals, and tourists with its lake views and standard lamb, beef, seafood, and pasta dishes. Burgers, salads, tacos, and sandwiches are served at the upstairs Ducey's Bar & Grill. Sunday brunch is served from 10 to 2. ✉ *54432 Rd. 432,* ☎ *559/642–3121. AE, D, DC, MC, V.*

Outdoor Activities and Sports

Pines Marina (✉ Bass Lake Reservoir, ☎ *559/642–3565*), open from April through October, rents ski boats, houseboats, and fishing boats.

El Portal

14 mi west of Yosemite Valley on Hwy. 140.

The gas station in this small community is a good place to fill up before entering the park. There's also a small convenience store and a post office.

Lodging

$$–$$$ 🏨 **Cedar Lodge.** The lobby of this rustic lodge in the pines is filled with teddy bears. Rooms range from suites with kitchenettes to family units to romantic accommodations with whirlpool tubs for two. ✉ *9966 Hwy. 140, 95318,* ☎ *209/379–2612,* FAX *209/379–2712. 188 rooms, 22 suites, 2 apartments, 1 house. Restaurant, 2 pools, hot tub. AE, MC, V.*

$$–$$$ **Yosemite View Lodge.** Many rooms with balconies overlook the boulder-strewn Merced River and majestic pines. Also in view is a picnic patio with hot tubs and heated pools. The pleasant facility is on the public bus route to Yosemite National Park and near fishing and river rafting. Many of the rooms have spa baths, fireplaces, and kitchenettes. ✉ *11136 Hwy. 140, 95318,* ☎ *209/379–2681,* FAX *209/379–2704. 276 rooms. Restaurant, bar, indoor pool, 2 pools, 4 hot tubs, coin laundry, meeting room. MC, V.*

Fish Camp

37 mi south of Yosemite Valley floor on Hwy. 41; 4 mi south of Yosemite National Park's South Entrance on Hwy. 41.

In the small town of Fish Camp are a service station, a post office, a general store, and the **Yosemite Mountain Sugar Pine Railroad,** featuring a narrow-gauge steam engine that chugs through the forest. It follows 4-mi of the route the Madera Sugar Pine Lumber Company cut through the forest in 1899 in order to harvest timber. Saturday evening's Moonlight Special excursion (reservations essential) includes dinner and music by the Sugar Pine Trio. ✉ *56001 Hwy. 41,* ☎ *559/683–7273.* *$11.50; $33.50 for Moonlight Special.* ⏲ *Mar.–Oct., daily.*

Dining and Lodging

$$$$ ✕ **Tenaya Lodge.** One of the region's largest hotels, the Tenaya Lodge is ideal for people who enjoy wilderness treks by day but prefer luxury at night. A Southwestern motif prevails in the ample regular rooms. The deluxe rooms have minibars and other extras, and the suites have balconies. The cozy Sierra Restaurant ($–$$$) offers Continental cuisine; the fare at the lodge's casual Jackalopes Bar and Grill includes burgers, salads, and sandwiches. ✉ *1122 Hwy. 41, Box 159, 93623,* ☎ *559/683–6555 or 888/514–2167;* FAX *559/683–0249. 244 rooms, 6 one-bedroom suites. 2 restaurants, bar, deli, in-room data ports, room service, pool, hot tubs, health club, hiking, mountain bikes, cross-country skiing, children's programs, playground, laundry service, meeting rooms. AE, D, DC, MC, V.*

$$–$$$ ✕ **Narrow Gauge Inn.** This motel-style property is comfortably furnished with old-fashioned decor and railroad memorabilia. The inn's restaurant ($$), which serves cuisine inspired by the California ranchero era of the late 1800s, is festooned with moose, bison, and other wildlife trophies. ✉ *48571 Hwy. 41, 93623,* ☎ *559/683–7720 or 888/644–9050,* FAX *559/683–2139. 24 rooms, 1 suite. Restaurant, bar, pool, hot tub. AE, D, MC, V. Closed Nov.–Mar.*

Oakhurst

50 mi south of Yosemite Valley on Hwy. 41; 23 mi south of Yosemite National Park's South Entrance on Hwy. 41.

Motels and restaurants line both sides of Highway 41 as it cuts through the town of Oakhurst. You can stock up on major provisions at the grocery and general stores.

Dining and Lodging

$$$$ ★ ✕ **Erna's Elderberry House.** The restaurant, operated by Vienna-born Erna Kubin, owner of Château du Sureau (☞ *below*), is another expression of her passion for beauty, charm, and impeccable service. Red walls and dark beams accent the dining room's high ceilings, and arched windows reflect the glow of many candles. A seasonal six-course prix-fixe dinner is elegantly paced and accompanied by superb wines. The moment the wait staff places all the plates on the table in perfect synchronicity, you know this will be a meal to remember. ✉ *48688*

Victoria La., ☎ 559/683–6800. AE, MC, V. Closed 1st 3 wks in Jan. No lunch Mon.–Tues.

$$$$ ★ **Château du Sureau.** This romantic inn, adjacent to Erna's Elderberry House (☞ *above*), is out of a children's book. From the moment you drive through the wrought-iron gates and up to the fairy-tale castle, you will be pampered. A winding staircase seems to carry you up to your room. You'll fall asleep in the glow of a crackling fire amid goose-down pillows and a fluffy comforter. When you raise the curtains the next morning, you'll breathe in the cool, fragrant air from the gardens and the mist-shrouded pines. After a hearty European breakfast in the dining room, relax in the piano room, which has an exquisite ceiling mural. ✉ *48688 Victoria La., Box 577, 93644, ☎ 559/683–6860, FAX 559/683–0800. 10 rooms, 1 villa. Restaurant, pool. AE, D, MC, V. BP.*

$$$–$$$$ **The Homestead Cottages.** Serenity is the order of the day at this secluded getaway in Ahwahnee, 6 mi west of Oakhurst. On 160 acres that once held a Miwok village, these cottages have fireplaces, living rooms, fully equipped kitchens, and queen-size beds. The cottages, built by hand by the owners, also feature soft green robes, oversized towels, and a good supply of paperback books. Smoking and pets are not allowed. ✉ *41110 Rd. 600, 2½ mi off Hwy. 49, Ahwahnee, 93601, ☎ 559/683–0495, FAX 559/683–8165. 4 cottages, 1 loft. AE, D, MC, V.*

$$ **Shilo Inn.** The Shilo's recently remodeled rooms are spacious and sunny and come with microwaves, refrigerators, and satellite TV. ✉ *40644 Hwy. 41, 93644, ☎ 559/683–3555, FAX 559/683–3386. 80 rooms, 1 suite. Pool, hot tub, sauna, steam room, exercise room, coin laundry. AE, D, DC, MC, V. CP.*

Outside Yosemite National Park A to Z

Arriving and Departing

See Yosemite National Park A to Z, *above.*

Getting Around

The area surrounding Yosemite National Park is best visited by car. U.S. 395, the main north–south road on the eastern side of the Sierra Nevada, passes by the west edge of Mono Lake and west of Bodie Ghost Town. Highway 140 heads east from the San Joaquin Valley to El Portal. Highway 41 heads north from Fresno to Oakhurst and Fish Camp; Bass Lake is off Highway 41.

Visitor Information

Bodie State Historic Park (✉ Box 515, Bridgeport 93517, ☎ 760/647–6445). **Mono Lake** (✉ Box 49, Lee Vining 93541, ☎ 760/647–3044). **Yosemite Sierra Visitors Bureau** (✉ 40637 Hwy. 41, Box 1998, Oakhurst 93644, ☎ 559/683–4636).

MAMMOTH LAKES

A jewel in the eastern Sierra Nevada, the town of Mammoth Lakes provides California's finest skiing and snowboarding south of Lake Tahoe. At 11,053-ft-high Mammoth Mountain, skiers hit the slopes as late as June or even July. As soon as snows melt, Mammoth transforms itself into a warm-weather playground—fishing, mountain biking, hiking, and horseback riding are among the options. Nine deep-blue lakes form the Mammoth Lakes Basin, and another 100 lakes dot the surrounding countryside. Crater-pocked Mammoth Mountain hasn't had a major eruption for 50,000 years, but the region is alive with hot springs, mud pots, fumaroles, and steam vents.

Mammoth Lakes

30 mi south of Mono Lake on U.S. 395.

Much of the architecture in the hub town of Mammoth Lakes, elevation 7,800 ft, is in the faux-alpine category. You'll find basic services here, plus plenty of dining and lodging options.

Even if you don't ski, it makes sense to start at the aptly named landmass in the middle of it all—Mammoth Mountain. **Gondolas** serve skiers in winter and mountain bikers and sightseers in summer. The high-speed 8-passenger Panorama Gondola whisks you from the chalet to the summit. The boarding area for the lower gondola is at the main lodge of the ski area. ☎ *760/934–2571 ext. 3850.* *$10.* *July 4–Oct., daily 9:30–5; Nov.–July 3, daily 8:30–4.*

The sawtooth, glacial-carved spires of the Minarets, the remains of an ancient lava flow, are best viewed from the **Minaret Vista,** off Highway 203 west of Mammoth Lakes.

The **lakes of the Mammoth Lakes Basin,** reached by Lake Mary Road southwest of town, are popular for fishing and boating in summer. First comes **Twin Lakes,** at the far end of which is Twin Falls, where water cascades 300 ft over a shelf of volcanic rock. Also popular are **Lake Mary,** is the largest lake in the basin, **Lake Mamie,** and **Lake George.** **Horseshoe Lake** is the only lake in which you can swim.

14 An easy 10-minute walk from the ranger station at **Devils Postpile National Monument** takes you to a geologic formation of smooth, vertical basalt columns sculpted by volcanic and glacial forces. A short but steep trail winds to the top of the 60-ft-high rocky cliff for a bird's-eye view of the columns. A 2-mi hike past the Postpile leads to the monument's second scenic wonder, **Rainbow Falls,** where a branch of the San Joaquin River plunges more than 100 ft over a lava ledge. When the water hits the pool below, sunlight turns the resulting mist into a spray of color. Walk down a bit from the top of the falls for the best viewing. During the summer the area is accessible only via a shuttle bus ($9) that begins operation as soon as the road is cleared of snow—usually in June, but sometimes as late as July. The shuttle departs from Mammoth Mountain Inn (☞ *below*) every 20 minutes from 7:30 to 5:30. The shuttle stops running after Labor Day, but you can drive to the falls until snows come again, usually around the beginning of November. Scenic picnic spots dot the bank of the San Joaquin River. ✉ *Box 501; follow Hwy. 203 13 mi west from Mammoth Lakes, 93546.* ☎ *760/934–2289; 760/934–0606 for shuttle bus information.* *Free.* *Late June–late Oct., daily, weather permitting.*

The **June Lake Loop** (Hwy. 158 west from U.S. 395), a wonderfully scenic 17-mi drive that follows an old glacial canyon past Grant, June, Gull, and other lakes, is especially colorful in fall.

OFF THE BEATEN PATH

HOT CREEK GEOLOGIC SITE/HOT CREEK FISH HATCHERY – Forged by an ancient volcanic eruption, the Hot Creek Geologic Site is a landscape of boiling hot springs, fumaroles, and occasional geysers about 10 mi southeast of the town of Mammoth Lakes. You can soak (at your own risk) in hot springs or walk along boardwalks through the canyon to view the steaming volcanic features. Fly-fishing for trout is popular upstream from the springs. En route to the geologic site is the Hot Creek Fish Hatchery, the breeding ponds for most of the 3 million–5 million fish the state stocks annually in eastern Sierra lakes and rivers. ✉ *Hot Creek Hatchery Rd., east off U.S. 395,* ☎ *760/924–5500 for site; 760/934–*

2664 for hatchery. Free. Site daily sunrise–sunset; hatchery daily 8–4, weather permitting.

Dining and Lodging

$$–$$$ **Nevados.** In a restaurant scene known mostly for meat, potatoes, and pizza, Nevados serves contemporary cuisine in a bistro setting. The menu changes frequently but always includes creative soups and salads, fresh seafood, and grilled meats. Eggplant lasagna, sesame-crusted ahi tuna, and orange-scented duckling are popular entrées. Ask about the three-course prix fixe menu. *Main St. and Minaret Rd., 760/934–4466. Reservations essential. AE, D, DC, MC, V. No lunch; closed 1 wk in early June and late Oct.–early Nov.*

$–$$$ **The Mogul.** This longtime steak house has a friendly, relaxed ambience. The charbroiled shrimp and the grilled beef or chicken come with a baked potato or rice pilaf and soup or salad. A children's menu is available. *Mammoth Tavern Rd. off Old Mammoth Rd., 760/934–3039. AE, D, MC, V. No lunch.*

$–$$ **Berger's.** Don't even think about coming to this bustling pine-panel restaurant unless you're hungry. Berger's is known, appropriately enough, for burgers and generously sized sandwiches. Everything comes in mountainous portions. For dinner try the beef ribs or the buffalo steak. *Minaret Rd. near Canyon Blvd., 760/934–6622. MC, V. Closed 4–6 wks in May and June and 4–6 wks in Oct. and Nov.*

$–$$ **Giovanni's Pizza.** Children enjoy this casual restaurant that serves standard Italian dinners (but your best bet is to stick to the pizza). Don't come here for quiet conversation—it's a high-decibel atmosphere. *Minaret Village Mall, Old Mammoth Rd. and Meridian St., 760/934–7563. AE, MC, V. No lunch Sun.*

$ **Blondie's Kitchen and Waffle Shop.** A good place to stoke up before a morning on the slopes or trails (it opens at 6 AM), this comic-strip-theme diner serves up waffles, pancakes, omelets, and Dagwood "pig-out" plates. *Main and Lupin Sts., 760/934–4048. AE, D, DC, MC, V. No dinner.*

$$–$$$$ **Mammoth Mountain Inn.** If you want to be within walking distance of the Mammoth Mountain ski area, this is the place to stay. You can check your skis with the concierge after a day on the slopes and pick them up in the morning and head directly to the lifts. The staff keeps you apprised of snow conditions. The accommodations, some of which are cramped, include standard hotel rooms and condo units; the latter have kitchenettes and many have lofts. The inn has licensed on-site child care. *Minaret Rd., Box 353, 4 mi west of Mammoth Lakes, 93546, 760/934–2581 or 800/228–4947, FAX 760/934–0701. 124 rooms, 91 condos. 2 restaurants, bar, hot tubs, video games, nursery, playground, meeting rooms. AE, MC, V.*

$$–$$$$ **Snowcreek Resort.** In a valley surrounded by mountain peaks, this 355-acre condominium community on the outskirts of Mammoth Lakes contains one- to four-bedroom units. All have kitchens, living and dining rooms, fireplaces, and TVs with VCRs; some have laundry facilities. Guests have free use of the well-supplied athletic club. *Old Mammoth Rd., Box 1647, 93546, 760/934–3333 or 800/544–6007, FAX 760/934–1619. 150 condos. 2 pools, hot tubs, sauna, 9-hole golf course, 9 tennis courts, health club, racquetball, nursery, meeting rooms. AE, MC, V.*

$–$$$$ **Tamarack Lodge Resort.** Nordic skiers (and, in summer, nature lovers) favor this lodge that overlooks Twin Lakes, about 3 mi west of town. The main building occupies a quiet, woodsy setting, and cross-country ski trails loop past the cabins. In warm months, fishing, canoeing, hiking, and mountain biking are close by. The cozy cabins are modern, neat, and clean, with knotty-pine kitchens and private baths; some have fireplaces or wood-burning stoves. Alert the children: there are no TVs. ✉ *Box 69; take Lake Mary Rd. off Hwy. 203, 93546,* ☎ *760/934–2442; 800/237–6879 in CA and NV,* FAX *760/934–2281. 11 rooms, 25 cabins. Restaurant, cross-country skiing, ski shop. D, MC, V.*

$$–$$$ **Sierra Lodge.** This motel on Main Street has spacious rooms. A covered parking garage with ski lockers is helpful in winter. Free shuttles take skiers to Mammoth Mountain. All rooms are no-smoking. ✉ *3540 Main St., 93546,* ☎ *760/934–8881; 800/356–5711 in southern CA,* FAX *760/934–7231. 35 rooms. Kitchenettes, hot tub, ski storage. MC, V. CP.*

$–$$ **Swiss Chalet.** One of the most reasonably priced motels in town, the Swiss Chalet has great views of the mountains. Among the amenities are an indoor sauna and hot tub, a fish-cleaning area, and a freezer to keep your summer catch fresh. ✉ *3776 Viewpoint Rd., Box 16, 93546,* ☎ *760/934–2403 or 800/937–9477,* FAX *760/934–2403. 21 rooms. Kitchenettes, hot tub, sauna. AE, D, MC, V.*

Nightlife and the Arts

The summertime jazz, folk, blues, country-western, and rock concerts of **Mammoth Mountain Music** (☎ 760/934–0606 or 800/228–4947) take place at Yodler Pavilion at the Mammoth Mountain ski area.

Goats Bar (✉ Mono and Main Sts., ☎ 760/934–4629), a popular watering hole, has a pool table and a dartboard. Rock, country, and blues acts perform at **La Sierra's** (✉ Main St. near Minaret Rd., ☎ 760/934–8083), which has Mammoth's largest dance floor. The bar at **Whiskey Creek** (✉ Main St. and Minaret Rd., ☎ 760/934–2555) hosts musicians on weekends year-round and on most nights in winter.

Outdoor Activities and Sports

BICYCLING

Mammoth Mountain Bike Park (☎ 760/934–0706), at the ski area, opens when the snows melt, usually by July, with 70-plus mi of single-track trails—from mellow to super-challenging. Chairlifts and shuttles provide trail access, and rentals are available.

DOGSLEDDING

Dog Sled Adventures (☎ 760/934–6270) operates 25-minute rides through the forest on dogsleds pulled by teams of 10 dogs.

FISHING

Crowley Lake is the top trout-fishing spot in the area; Convict Lake, June Lake, and the lakes of the Mammoth Basin are other prime spots. One of the best trout rivers is the San Joaquin near Devils Postpile (☞ *above*). Hot Creek (☞ *above*), a designated Wild Trout Stream, is renowned for fly-fishing (catch and release only). The fishing season runs from the last Saturday in April until the end of October. **Kittredge Sports** (✉ Main St. and Forest Trail, ☎ 760/934–7566) rents rods and reels and conducts guided trips.

HIKING

Trails wind around the Lakes Basin and through pristine alpine scenery. Stop at the U.S. Forest Service ranger station (☞ Visitor Information, *below*) for a trail map and permits for backpacking in wilderness areas.

HORSEBACK RIDING

Stables are typically open from June through September. Outfitters include **Mammoth Lakes Pack Outfit** (✉ Box 61, along Lake Mary Rd., 93546, ☎ 760/934–2434); **McGee Creek Pack Station** (Box 162, Rte. 1, 93546, ☎ 760/935–4324 or 800/854–7407); and **Sierra Meadows Ranch** (✉ Sherwin Creek Rd., ☎ 760/934–6161).

HOT-AIR BALLOONING

The balloons of **Mammoth Ballooning** (☎ 760/934–7188 or 800/484–6936 ext. 1122) glide over the countryside in the morning from spring until fall, weather permitting.

SKIING AND SNOWBOARDING

June Mountain Ski Area. This low-key resort 20 mi north of Mammoth Mountain is a favorite of snowboarders, who have a halfpipe all to themselves. Seven lifts service the area, which has a 2,590-ft vertical drop; the skiing ranges from beginner to expert. A rental and repair shop, a ski school, a sport shop, and a child-care area are all on the premises. ✉ *Box 146, off June Lake Loop (Hwy. 158), June Lake 93529,* ☎ *760/648–7733 or 888/586–3668.*

Mammoth Mountain Ski Area. With 30 lifts and more than 3,500 acres of skiable terrain, Mammoth is one of the West's largest ski areas. The base elevation is 7,953 ft. When it's not too windy, you can ski off the top of the mountain (11,053 ft), for a 3,100-ft vertical drop. The terrain includes beginning-to-expert runs. Snowboarders are welcome on all slopes; the Unbound Snowboard Arena has a halfpipe and two freestyle terrain parks. Mammoth's season begins in November and often lingers until June or beyond. Night skiing is available on Friday and Saturday, from Christmas to Easter. Lessons and rental equipment are available, and there's a children's ski and snowboard school. ✉ *Minaret Rd. west of Mammoth Lakes, Box 24, 93546,* ☎ *760/934–0745 or 888/462–6668.*

Trails at **Tamarack Cross Country Ski Center** (✉ Lake Mary Rd. off Hwy. 203, ☎ 760/934–2442), adjacent to Tamarack Lodge (☞ *above*) meander around several lakes. Rentals are available.

Sandy's Ski & Sport (✉ Main St., near Center St., ☎ 760/934–7518) rents and sells equipment.

SNOWMOBILING

Mammoth Snowmobile Adventures, at the Main Lodge at the Mammoth Mountain Ski Area (☎ 760/934–9645), conducts guided tours along wooded trails.

Mammoth Lakes A to Z

Arriving and Departing

BY CAR

In summer and early fall (or whenever snows aren't blocking Tioga Road) you can drive from San Francisco to Mammoth via Highway 120 (to U.S. 395 south) through the Yosemite high country, a distance of about 300 mi. The quickest route when Tioga Road is closed is I–80 to U.S. 50 in the Lake Tahoe area; from the lake's Nevada side take the Kingsbury Grade (Route 207) east to U.S. 395 south to Highway 203 west. This trip is a total of 320 mi. From the Los Angeles area, the route is the same all year: Highway 14 and U.S. 395 north to Highway 203 west, a distance of about 310 mi. If you're coming from San Diego or Orange County, take I–15 north to U.S. 395 and follow that north to 203; the trip from San Diego is about 375 mi.

Getting Around

BY CAR

Highway 203 heads west from U.S. 395, becoming Main Street as it passes through the town of Mammoth Lakes and later Minaret Road (which makes a right turn) as it continues west to the Mammoth Mountain ski area and Devils Postpile National Monument. To get to the Lakes Basin, take Highway 203 (Main St.) to Lake Mary Road, going straight at the Minaret Road intersection.

BY SHUTTLE BUS

Mammoth Mountain runs four free **shuttle bus** (☎ 760/934–0687) routes around town to and from the ski area. Buses run from 7 AM to 5:30 PM daily in snow season, with limited night service from Christmas to Easter.

BY TAXI

Mammoth Shuttle (☎ 760/934–3030) provides airport and ski-lift transport.

Contacts and Resources

EMERGENCIES

Ambulance (☎ 911). **Fire** (☎ 911). **Police** (☎ 911).

VISITOR INFORMATION

Mammoth Lakes Visitors Bureau (✉ Box 48; along Hwy. 203 [Main St.], near Sawmill Cutoff Rd., 93546, ☎ 760/934–2712 or 888/466–2666). **Snow Report** (☎ 760/934–7669 or 888/766–9778). **U.S. Forest Service ranger station** (✉ along Hwy. 203 [Main St.], near Sawmill Cutoff Rd., 93546, ☎ 760/924–5500).

KINGS CANYON AND SEQUOIA NATIONAL PARKS

Grant Grove, Cedar Grove, and Lodgepole

Though they're overshadowed by Yosemite, naturalist John Muir thought no less of Kings Canyon (then called General Grant) and Sequoia national parks. He declared that the beauty of Kings Canyon rivaled that of Yosemite and described the sequoia trees as "the most beautiful and majestic on Earth." *Sequoiadendron giganteum* trees are not as tall as the coast redwoods (*Sequoia sempervirens*), but on average they are older and more massive. Exhibits at the visitor centers explain the special relationship between these trees and fire (their thick, fibrous bark helps protect them from fire and insects) and their ability to live so long and grow so big.

A little more than 1.5 million people visit Kings Canyon and Sequoia annually, wandering trails through groves and meadows or tackling the rugged backcountry. The topography of the two parks runs the gamut from chaparral, at an elevation of 1,500 ft, to the giant sequoia belt, at 5,000–7,000 ft, to the towering peaks of the Great Western Divide and the Sierra Crest. Mount Whitney, the highest point in the contiguous United States at 14,494 ft, is the crown jewel of the less-crowded eastern side.

Kings Canyon and Sequoia national parks share their administration and a main highway, called the Generals Highway, which connects Highway 180 in Kings Canyon to Highway 198 in Sequoia. The entrance fee to Kings Canyon and Sequoia (good for admission to both on seven consecutive days) is $10 per vehicle, $5 for those who don't arrive by car. An information-packed quarterly newspaper and a map are handed out at the parks' entrances.

Grant Grove and Cedar Grove

100 mi southeast of Oakhurst, Hwy. 41 to Hwy. 180.

15 **Grant Grove** (✉ Kings Canyon Hwy./Hwy. 180, 1 mi from Big Stump Entrance), Kings Canyon's most highly developed area, is the original grove that was designated as General Grant National Park in 1890. A walk along the 1-mi **Big Stump Trail,** which starts near the park en-

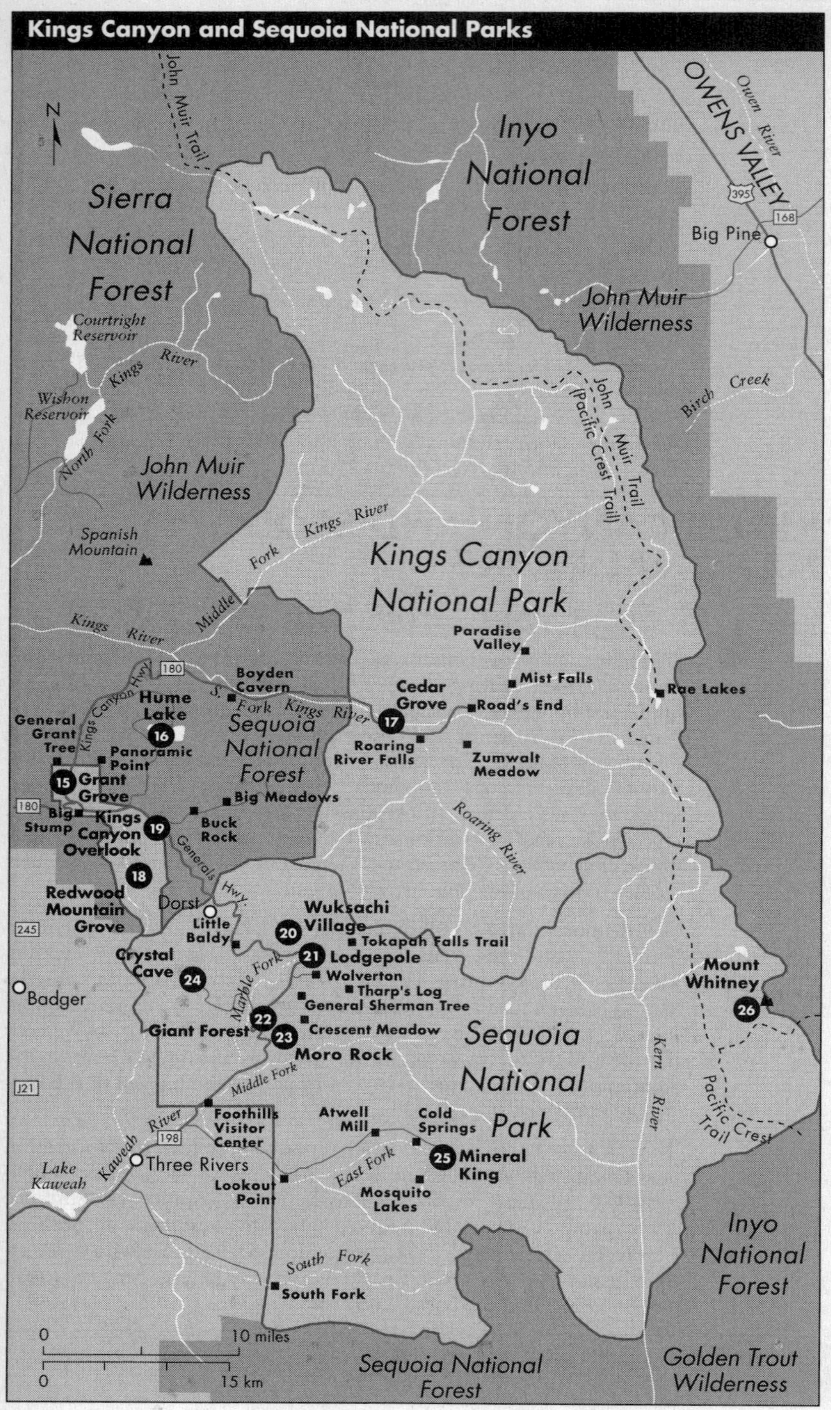
Kings Canyon and Sequoia National Parks
N
Sierra National Forest
Inyo National Forest
OWENS VALLEY
Owen River
395
168
Big Pine
John Muir Trail
Courtright Reservoir
Kings River
Wishon Reservoir
North Fork
John Muir Wilderness
John Muir Wilderness
Birch Creek
John Muir Trail (Pacific Crest Trail)
Spanish Mountain
Middle Fork Kings River
Kings Canyon National Park
Kings River
Paradise Valley
180
Boyden Cavern
Mist Falls
Rae Lakes
Kings Canyon Hwy.
Hume Lake
S. Fork Kings River
Cedar Grove
Road's End
General Grant Tree
16
Sequoia National Forest
17
Panoramic Point
Roaring River Falls
Zumwalt Meadow
15 Grant Grove
Big Meadows
180
Big Stump
Kings Canyon Overlook
19
Buck Rock
Roaring River
Generals Hwy.
18
Redwood Mountain Grove
Dorst
Wuksachi Village
245
Little Baldy
20
Tokopah Falls Trail
Crystal Cave
21 Lodgepole
24
Wolverton
Mount Whitney
Badger
Marble Fork
Tharp's Log
General Sherman Tree
26
22
Giant Forest
23
Crescent Meadow
Sequoia National Park
Moro Rock
Kern River
Pacific Crest Trail
J21
Middle Fork
Foothills Visitor Center
Atwell Mill
Cold Springs
Kaweah River
198
25 Mineral King
Lake Kaweah
Three Rivers
East Fork
Lookout Point
Mosquito Lakes
Inyo National Forest
South Fork
South Fork
0
10 miles
0
15 km
Sequoia National Forest
Golden Trout Wilderness

trance, graphically demonstrates the toll heavy logging takes on the wilderness. An alternative ⅓-mi trail is fairly accessible to travelers with disabilities; there are some rough spots and rain can muddy up the trail. The **General Grant Tree Trail,** a paved ⅜-mi path through Grant Grove, winds past the **General Grant,** an enormous, 2,000-year-old sequoia that's designated the nation's Christmas Tree. The **Gamlin Cabin,** an 1867 structure listed on the National Register of Historic Places, is a pioneer cabin. Also within Grant Grove is the **Centennial Stump,** the remains of a huge sequoia cut for display at the 1876 Philadelphia Centennial Exhibition.

Grant Grove Village has a visitor center (☎ *559/335–2856*), a grocery store, a gift shop, campgrounds, a restaurant that has family as well as fine dining, overnight lodging, a horse-rental concession, and a post office. The visitor center has exhibits on the sequoias and the area.

16 **Hume Lake** (✉ Hwy. 180 northeast 8 mi from Grant Grove off Hume Lake Rd.), a reservoir built in the early 1900s by loggers, is now the site of several church-affiliated camps, a gas station, and a public campground. This small lake outside Kings Canyon's borders has views of high mountains in the distance.

★ 17 The **Cedar Grove** area is a valley that snakes along the south fork of the Kings River. A spectacular 30-mi descent along Kings Canyon Highway takes about one hour from Grant Grove to the end of the road, where you can hike, camp, or turn right around for the drive back up. Built by convict labor in the 1930s, the road (usually closed from mid-October to April) clings to some dramatic cliffs along the way: watch out for falling rocks. The highway passes the scars where large groves of sequoias were felled at the beginning of the 20th century. It runs along the south fork and through dry foothills covered with yuccas that bloom in the summer. There are amazing views into the deepest gorge in the United States, at the confluence of the two forks, and up the canyons to the High Sierra.

Cedar Grove was named for the incense cedars that grow in the area. You can rent horses here, a good way to continue your explorations; campgrounds, lodgings, a small visitor center (☎ *559/565–3793*), a snack bar, a restaurant, a convenience market, a gift shop, and a gas station round out the facilities.

Short trails circle **Zumwalt Meadow.** The trails from the meadow lead to the base of **Roaring River Falls.** Hikers can self-register for wilderness permits at **Road's End,** 6 mi east of Cedar Grove Village. Permits are free and are given out on a first-come, first-served basis from mid-May to late September. You can also pay $10 for a 21-day-advance reservation (☎ *559/565–3766*).

Dining, Lodging, and Camping

$$ ✕🏨 **Cedar Grove Lodge.** Although accommodations are close to the road, Cedar Grove manages to retain a quiet atmosphere. Book far in advance—the lodge has only 18 rooms. Each room is air-conditioned and has two queen-size beds, and three have kitchenettes. You can order trout, hamburgers, hot dogs, and sandwiches at the snack bar and take it to one of the picnic tables along the river's edge. ✉ *Kings Canyon Hwy., 31 mi east of Grant Grove Village,* ☎ *559/335–5500. 18 rooms. Snack bar. AE, MC, V. Closed mid-Oct.–mid-May.*

$–$$ ✕🏨 **Grant Grove Cabins.** Some of the wood-panel cabins here have heaters, electric lights, and private baths, but most have woodstoves, battery lamps, and shared baths. Those who don't mind roughing it might opt for the tents. Meadowview Fine Dining ($$–$$$) is an upscale eatery; the Grant Grove Restaurant ($-$$), a family-style coffee shop, serves American standards for breakfast, lunch, and dinner. ✉ *Kings Canyon Hwy. in Grant Grove Village, ☎ 559/335–5500 or 559/335–2354, FAX 559/335–2498. 33 cabins, 24 with shared bath, 19 tents. Restaurant, coffee shop. AE, MC, V.*

$$$–$$$$ **John Muir Lodge.** This new lodge is nestled in a wooded area near Grant Grove Village. The 30 rooms and six suites all have queen beds and private baths. There's a comfortable lobby with a stone fireplace, but no restaurant. ✉ *Kings Canyon Hwy., ¼ mi north of Grant Grove Village, ☎ 559/335–5500. 32 rooms, 6 suites. Meeting rooms. MC, V.*

$–$$$ **Montecito-Sequoia Lodge.** Located in the Sequoia National Forest just south of Kings Canyon National Park, this family-oriented resort features all-inclusive holidays that include all meals and activities. It offers everything from skiing and snowboarding in the winter to sailing and horseback riding in the summer. ✉ *Generals Hwy., 11 mi south of Grant Grove, ☎ 559/565–3388 or 800/227–9900, FAX 650/967–0540. 32 rooms, 14 cabins. Dining room, snack bar, tennis courts, archery, hiking, horseback riding, boating, waterskiing, fishing, cross-country skiing, children's programs. AE, DC, MC, V.*

Azalea Campground. One of three campgrounds in the Grant Grove area (the other two are Sunset and Crystal Springs, both open May–September only), Azalea sits amid giant sequoias yet is close to restaurants, stores, and other facilities. Pay showers are available nearby. The 144 sites are allocated on a first-come, first-served basis. ✉ *Kings Canyon Hwy., ¼ mi north of Grant Grove Village, ☎ 559/565–3341 ext. 2. $12. Year-round.*

Outdoor Activities and Sports

WINTER SPORTS

Grant Grove Village (☎ 559/335–2665) has a cross-country ski concession with marked trails; rentals are available.

YEAR-ROUND SPORTS

Montecito-Sequoia Lodge (✉ Generals Hwy., 11 mi south of Grant Grove, ☎ 559/565–3388 or 800/227–9900), in the Sequoia National Forest, provides year-round family-oriented recreation. Winter activities include cross-country skiing and lessons, snowshoeing, and snowboarding. Among the summer activities offered are canoeing, sailing, horseback riding, tennis, archery, and water-skiing on the resort's private lake.

Along the Generals Highway

The **Generals Highway** begins south of Grant Grove, continuing through the lower portion of Kings Canyon National Park and through a grand section of the Sequoia National Forest before entering Sequoia National Park.

★ 18 The **Redwood Mountain Grove** is the largest grove of redwoods in the world. As you exit Kings Canyon on the Generals Highway, several paved turnouts allow you to look out over the grove (and into the smog of the Central Valley). The grove itself is accessible only on foot or horseback.

19 **Kings Canyon Overlook,** a large turnout on the north side of the Generals Highway less than 2 mi from Redwood Mountain Grove, has views across the canyon of mountain peaks and the backcountry. If you drive east on Highway 180 to Cedar Grove along the south fork, you will see these canyons at much closer range.

Wuksachi Village

20 *21 mi south of Grant Grove on the Generals Hwy.*

The new northern gateway to Sequoia National Park, **Wuksachi Village,** opened in 1999. New dining and lodging facilities (☞ *below*) have been built here to replace the antiquated facilities in the old Giant Forest Village. The onetime Giant Forest Market is being converted into a museum, scheduled to open in 2001.

Dining and Lodging

$$–$$$ ✕🏨 **Wuksachi Village.** Three wooden three-story lodges feature comfortable rooms with TVs, and phones with modem hookups, and room to store your skis. The Wuksachi Village Restaurant ($–$$$) serves standard American cuisine. ✉ *Generals Hwy., 21 mi south of Grant Grove,* ☎ *559/565–4070 or 888/252–5757. 102 rooms. Restaurant, bar, in-room data ports, hiking, cross-country skiing, meeting rooms. D, MC, V.*

Lodgepole

21 *5 mi south of Wuksachi Village on the Generals Hwy.*

Lodgepole sits in a canyon on the Marble Fork of the Kaweah River. Lodgepole pines, rather than sequoias, grow here because the U-shape canyon funnels in air from the high country that is too cold for the big trees. This area has a campground, a market and deli, a public laundry, a gift shop, and a post office. A pizza stand, an ice cream parlor, and showers are open in the summer only.

The **Lodgepole Visitor Center** has the best exhibits in Sequoia or Kings Canyon, a small theater that shows films about the parks, and a first aid center. You can buy tickets for the Crystal Cave (☞ *below*), get advice from park rangers, purchase maps and books, and pick up wilderness permits (except during summer, when they're available from 7 AM to 4 PM at the permit office next door). ✉ *Generals Highway, 5 mi south of Wuksachi Village,* ☎ *559/565–3782.* ⏲ *Mid-June–Labor Day, daily 8–6; rest of yr, daily 9–6.*

The **Tokopah Falls Trail** is an easy and rewarding 3½-mi round-trip hike from the Lodgepole Campground up the Marble Fork of the Kaweah River. The walk to the 1,200-ft falls, which flow down granite cliffs, is the closest you can get to the high country without putting substantial wear and tear on your hiking boots. Trail maps are available at the Lodgepole Visitor Center. Bring insect repellent during the summer; the mosquitoes can be ferocious.

Camping

⛺ **Lodgepole Campground.** The largest of the campgrounds in the Lodgepole area is also the noisiest, though things do quiet down at night. Restrooms are nearby. Lodgepole and Dorst (a mile or so to the west) are the two campgrounds within Sequoia where reservations are accepted (up to five months in advance for stays between mid-May and mid-October). ✉ *Off Generals Hwy.,* ☎ *559/565–3341 ext. 2 for information; 800/365–2267 for reservations.* 💳 *$12–$16.* ⏲ *Year-round.*

Outdoor Activities and Sports

Wolverton (☎ 559/565–3435), near Lodgepole, has a cross-country ski center (rentals available) and marked trails.

Giant Forest

22 *4 mi south of Lodgepole on the Generals Hwy.*

The Giant Forest is known for its trails through a series of sequoia groves. You can get the best views of the big trees from the park's meadows, where flowers are in full bloom by June or July. **Round Meadow,** which has a ⅓-mi, wheelchair-accessible "Trail for All People," is easiest to reach. John Muir called **Crescent Meadow** the "gem of the Sierra"—brilliant wildflowers bloom here by midsummer; a $1\frac{8}{10}$-mi trail loops around the meadow. A $1\frac{6}{10}$-mi round-trip trail that begins at Crescent Meadow leads to **Tharp's Log,** named for Hale Tharp, who built a pioneer cabin (still standing) out of a fire-hollowed sequoia.

★ The most famous sequoia in the area is the **General Sherman Tree,** off the Generals Highway 3 mi south of Lodgepole and about 1 mi north of the Giant Forest. Benches allow you to sit and contemplate the tree's immensity: weighing in at 2.7 million pounds, it has the greatest volume of any living thing in the world. The first major branch is 130 ft above the ground.

The paved **Congress Trail,** the area's most popular hike, starts at the General Sherman Tree and loops through the heart of the Giant Forest. Pick up a booklet (75¢) from one of the racks at the trailhead for detailed information about the ecology of the groves.

The **Moro Rock–Crescent Meadow Road** is a 3-mi spur road (closed in winter) that begins just south of the old Giant Forest Village and leads to Crescent and Log meadows, passing several landmarks along the way. The Auto Log is a wide fallen tree that you can drive onto to pose for photographs. The road also passes through the Tunnel Log, which is exactly that. If your vehicle is too tall—7 ft, 9 inches and more—a bypass is provided.

★ 23 **Moro Rock,** an immense, granite monolith, also lies along the road, rising 6,725 ft from the edge of the Giant Forest. Four hundred steps lead to the top; the trail often climbs along narrow ledges over steep drops. The view from the top is striking. To the southwest you look down the Kaweah River to Three Rivers, Lake Kaweah, and—on clear days—the Central Valley and the Coast Range. To the northeast are views of the High Sierra. Thousands of feet below lies the middle fork of the Kaweah River.

★ 24 **Crystal Cave** is the best known of Sequoia's many caves. Its interior, which was formed from limestone that metamorphosed into marble, is decorated with stalactites and stalagmites of various shapes, sizes, and colors. To visit the cave, you must first stop at the Lodgepole Visitor Center (☞ *above*) or the Foothills Visitor Center at Ash Mountain (on the Generals Highway, 1 mi inside Sequoia National Park) to buy tickets—they're not sold at the cave. Drive to the end of a narrow, twisting, 7-mi road off the Generals Highway, 2.2 mi south of the old Giant Forest Village. From the parking area it is a 15-minute hike down a steep path to the cave's entrance. It's cool inside—48°F—so bring a sweater. ✉ *Crystal Cave Rd., off Generals Hwy.,* ☎ *559/565–3759.* 🎫 *$6.* ⏲ *Guided tours (45 min) mid-June–Labor Day, daily 10–3 on the half hr; mid-May–mid-June and Labor Day–Sept., Fri.–Mon. 10–3 on the hr; closed rest of yr.*

Mineral King

㉕ *52 mi south of Lodgepole on the Generals Hwy. and Mineral King Rd.*

The Mineral King area was incorporated into Sequoia National Park in 1978. It is accessible from Memorial Day weekend through October (weather permitting) by a narrow, twisting, steep road (trailers and RVs are prohibited) off Highway 198 several miles outside the park entrance. This is a tough but exciting 25-mi drive (budget 90 minutes each way) to an alpine valley. There are two campgrounds and a ranger station here. Facilities are limited, but some supplies are available. Many backpackers use this as a trailhead. Fine day-hiking trails lead from here as well.

Mount Whitney

㉖ *13 mi west of Lone Pine on Whitney Portal Rd. Whitney Portal Rd. intersects Hwy. 395.*

A favorite game for travelers on Highway 395 is to try to guess which peak is Mount Whitney on their way through Lone Pine. Almost no one gets it right, because Mount Whitney is hidden behind other peaks.

At 14,496 ft, Mount Whitney is the highest mountain in the continental United States. The hiking trail is 11 beautiful but gut-wrenching miles to the top. If you're smart—and many aren't—you'll take two days to make your way to the top in order to get used to the altitude. If you don't, don't be surprised if you get altitude sickness, which might include terrible headaches.

The trail is free of snow from July to early October. But don't be fooled by warm weather at lower elevations, as temperatures at the top are cool during the day and quite cold at night. Warm clothing, in addition to good boots, sunscreen, and mosquito repellent, are a must all year.

Camping

⛺ **Whitney Portal** has 44 campsites spread out among the towering pines. These are popular with hikers, so it's best to call ahead. There are picnic tables, grills, and a fishing pond. Whitey Portal also has a store and café that are open during the summer months. ✉ *Whitney Portal Rd., 13 mi west of Lone Pine,* ☎ *800/280–2267. Fire rings, flush toilets, water.* 💳 *$10.* ⏲ *Year-round.*

Kings Canyon and Sequoia National Parks A to Z

Arriving and Departing

BY BUS

Greyhound (☎ 800/231–2222) serves nearby Fresno and Visalia.

BY CAR

Under average conditions, it takes about six hours to reach Kings Canyon and Sequoia national parks from San Francisco and about five hours from Los Angeles. Two major routes, Highways 180 and 198, intersect with Highway 99, which runs north–south through the San Joaquin Valley.

From the north, enter Kings Canyon via Highway 180, 53 mi east of Fresno. From the south, enter Sequoia via Highway 198, 36 mi from Visalia. If you are coming from Los Angeles, take Highway 65 north from Bakersfield to Highway 198 east of Visalia.

BY PLANE

Fresno Air Terminal (✉ 5175 E. Clinton Way, ☎ 559/498–4095) is the nearest airport to Kings Canyon and Sequoia national parks. *See* Arriving and Departing *in* Yosemite National Park, *above,* for more information.

Getting Around

BY CAR

Try to fill up your tank before you arrive. Buying gas in the parks is difficult, though there are stations 10 mi from Grant Grove at Hume Lake Christian Camp and 15 mi from the Grove at King's Canyon Lodge. Emergency gas is sold at the park markets.

Most people take Highway 180 to Kings Canyon–Sequoia, coming into Kings Canyon National Park at the Big Stump Entrance. Highways 180 and 198 are connected by the Generals Highway, a paved two-lane road that is open year-round, though portions between Lodgepole and Grant Grove may be closed for weeks at a time following heavy snowstorms (carry chains in winter). Drivers of RVs over 22 ft in length and those who are not comfortable negotiating mountain roads should avoid the twisting, narrow, 16-mi southern stretch between the Potwisha Campground and the old Giant Forest Village. The rest of the Generals Highway is a well-graded two-lane road and a pleasure to drive in good weather.

Highway 180 (called Kings Canyon Highway inside the park) beyond Grant Grove to Cedar Grove is open late spring through October—weather permitting—as is the road to Mineral King. Both roads can be challenging to inexperienced drivers. Large vehicles are discouraged, and trailers and RVs are not permitted on the Mineral King road.

Contacts and Resources

CAMPING

Campgrounds near each of the major tourist centers in Kings Canyon and Sequoia parks are equipped with tables, fire grills, garbage cans, and either flush or pit toilets. All the sites have drinking water, but you may want to bring your own water, especially during off-season when taps can freeze. Except for Lodgepole and Dorst in Sequoia, all sites in the two parks are assigned on a first-come, first-served basis; on weekends in July and August they are often filled by Friday afternoon. *See* Reservations, *below,* for contact numbers.

RVs and trailers are permitted in most of the campgrounds, though space is scarce at some. The length limit is 40 ft for RVs and 35 ft for trailers, but the park service recommends that trailers be no longer than 22 ft. Disposal stations are available in most of the main camping areas. Lodgepole, Potwisha, and Azalea campsites stay open all year, but Lodgepole is not plowed and camping is limited to snow tenting or recreational vehicles in plowed parking lots. Other campgrounds are open from whenever the snow melts until late September or early October. Use the bear-proof food-storage containers that are provided.

EMERGENCIES

Ambulance (☎ 911). **Fire** (☎ 911). **Police** (☎ 911).

GUIDED TOURS

From mid-May to mid-October **Sequoia–Kings Canyon Park Services Company** (☎ 559/335–5500)offers tour guides.

RESERVATIONS

Lodgepole/Dorst campgrounds (☎ 559/565–3774 or 800/365–2267). **Other campgrounds** (☎ 559/565–3341).

Kings Canyon Lodging (☎ 559/335–5500). **Sequoia Lodging** (☎ 559/561–3314 or 888/252–5757).

ROAD CONDITIONS

Sequoia–Kings Canyon Road and Weather Information (☎ 559/565–3341).

Northern California Road Conditions (☎ 800/427–7623).

VISITOR INFORMATION

National Park Service (✉ Fort Mason, Bldg. 201, San Francisco 94123, ☎ 415/556–0560). **Sequoia and Kings Canyon National Parks** (✉ Three Rivers 93271, ☎ 559/565–3341 or 559/565–3134).

8 THE SAN JOAQUIN VALLEY

FROM STOCKTON TO BAKERSFIELD

The San Joaquin Valley, one of the world's most fertile agricultural zones, is California's heartland. This sun-baked region contains a wealth of rivers, lakes, and waterways. The water, in turn, nurtures vineyards, dairy farms, orchards, fields, and pastures that stretch to the horizon. Cities, mountains, and national parks are just beyond the Valley, but you'll find that the area possesses attractions of its own, beginning with the warmth of its land and people.

Updated by Herb Benham

UNTIL THE MID-19TH CENTURY the San Joaquin Valley was a desert waiting to bloom. Millions of acres of flat, often parched land lay in wait for workers and water. When settlers and irrigation techniques did arrive, the region was transformed into a miracle of cultivation. Gold discoveries, starting in the 1850s, sparked the birth of some towns; the coming of the railroads in the next few decades spurred the development of others. During the past century and a half the Valley's open lands and untapped resources have attracted a polyglot of pioneers, adventurers, farmers, ranchers, developers, railroad tycoons, gold prospectors, oil riggers, dairymen, sheepherders, and war refugees—including immigrants from places as diverse as Portugal, China, Mexico, Armenia, and Laos.

The mix has produced sometimes volatile labor relations—most prominently in the United Farm Workers Union's grape boycotts beginning in the 1960s. There's also been much social strife, seen in early battles between railroad men and farmers, long-standing discrimination against Chinese and other people of Asian heritage. But the region's diversity has also created a vibrant social fabric that has been chronicled by some of the country's finest writers. Fresno native and Pulitzer Prize winner William Saroyan, Stockton native Maxine Hong Kingston, 19th-century novelist Frank Norris, and *Grapes of Wrath* author John Steinbeck have all contributed to the Valley's literary heritage.

Though the Valley's agricultural riches remain, potential changes whirl like dust devils in the fields. Modesto, Fresno, and Bakersfield are among the fastest growing cities in the country, as big-city dwellers arrive in search of cheaper real estate, safer neighborhoods, and more space. With development has come unsightly sprawl, traffic jams, air pollution, and pressure on crucial water supplies, all of which threatens to overwhelm the Valley's traditional charms.

For most travelers the Valley is primarily a place to pass through en route to Yosemite, Sequoia, and Kings Canyon national parks or while driving between San Francisco and Los Angeles. But if you spend a few hours or days here, you'll discover historic mansions, abundant outdoor recreation, and friendly people proud of their local treasures.

Pleasures and Pastimes

Dining

Fast-food places and chain restaurants dominate Valley highways and major intersections, but off the main drag the possibilities increase. Armenian, Basque, and Vietnamese restaurants—along with more common Mexican, Chinese, and Italian eateries—reflect the Valley's ethnic mix. A few cutting-edge bistros serve the type of California cuisine found in San Francisco and Los Angeles. And why not? The Valley produces many of the ingredients used by big-city chefs.

CATEGORY	COST*
$$$$	over $50
$$$	$30–$50
$$	$20–$30
$	under $20

**per person for a three-course meal, excluding drinks, service, and 7¼% tax*

Festivals, Tours, and Tastings

Anyone who likes to eat can enjoy an agricultural theme trip through the San Joaquin Valley. Apple ranches, almond and pistachio orchards, and cheese and chocolate factories are among the many options. Watch for seasonal farmers' markets. Some towns block off entire streets and turn the weekly markets into minifestivals. Official Valley festivals celebrate everything from the asparagus and raisin crops to residents' Chinese, Greek, Swedish, and Tahitian roots. Especially in the fall, call the local chamber of commerce (☞ Visitor Information *in* the San Joaquin Valley A to Z, *below*) for festival information.

Lodging

Chain motels and hotels are the norm in the San Joaquin Valley. Most are utilitarian but perfectly clean and comfortable, and prices tend to be considerably lower than those in more touristy destinations. A few Victorian-style bed-and-breakfasts, some of them great values, also operate here.

CATEGORY	COST*
$$$$	over $175
$$$	$120–$175
$$	$80–$120
$	under $80

**All prices are for a standard double room, excluding 8% tax.*

🖱 *following the text of a review is your signal that the property has a Web site, where you will find details and, usually, images; for a link, visit www.fodors.com/urls.*

Outdoor Activities and Sports

Several cities and towns serve as convenient starting points for whitewater rafting trips on the Stanislaus, Merced, Kings, and Kern rivers. Fishing is another favored activity in the rivers and lakes; the lakes are also prime spots for boating and windsurfing. Stockton is a popular rental area for houseboating on the Sacramento Delta, and Bakersfield is a center for NASCAR racing. Wildlife refuges provide opportunities for watching birds and other animals.

Exploring the San Joaquin Valley

The 225-mi San Joaquin Valley cuts through San Joaquin, Stanislaus, Merced, Madera, Fresno, Kings, Tulare, and Kern counties, and is bounded by the mighty Sierra Nevada to the east and the smaller coastal ranges to the west. Besides the San Joaquin, other rivers include the Stanislaus, Tuolumne, Fresno, and Kern; an elaborate system of sloughs and canals also provides water to the countryside. Interstate 5 runs north–south through the Valley, as does Highway 99.

Numbers in the text correspond to numbers in the margin and on the San Joaquin Valley and Fresno Area maps.

Great Itineraries

IF YOU HAVE 1 DAY

Touring the Fresno area is a good strategy if you only have a day to spend in the Valley. Within the **Chaffee Zoological Gardens** in **Roeding Park** ⑦ is a striking tropical rain forest; **Playland** and **Storyland** are great stops if you have children. Don't miss the **Forestiere Underground Gardens** ⑥ on Shaw Avenue if it's open. In springtime take the self-guided **Blossom Trail** driving tour through orchards, vineyards, and fields. Along the trail in **Reedley** is the **Mennonite Quilt Center.** Depending on your mood and the weather, you can spend part of the afternoon at **Wild Water Adventures** or visit the **Fresno Metropolitan Museum** ⑧, whose highlights include an exhibit about author William Saroyan.

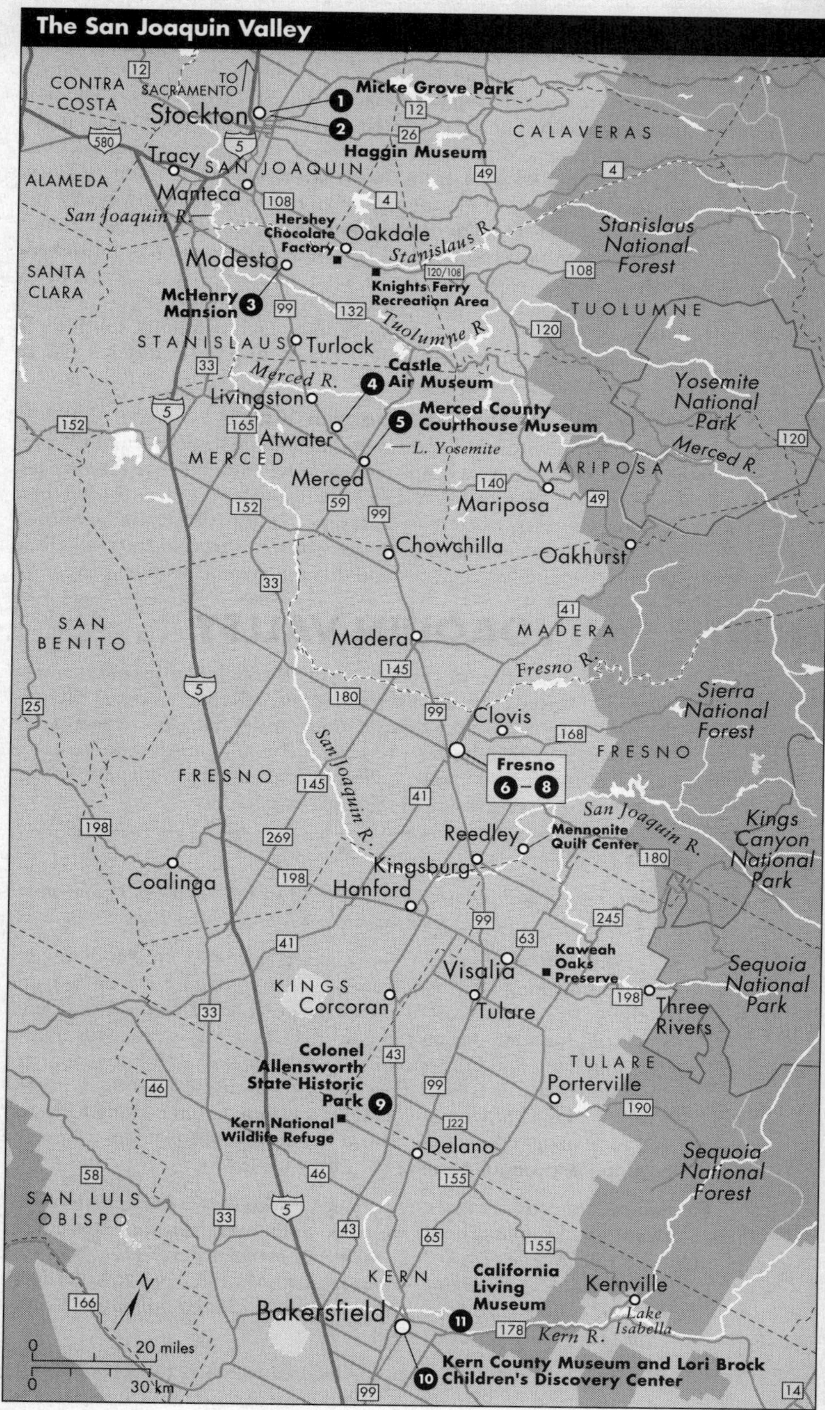
The San Joaquin Valley
Micke Grove Park
Stockton
Haggin Museum
Tracy
Manteca
Hershey Chocolate Factory
Oakdale
Modesto
Knights Ferry Recreation Area
McHenry Mansion
Turlock
Castle Air Museum
Livingston
Merced County Courthouse Museum
Atwater
Merced
L. Yosemite
Mariposa
Chowchilla
Oakhurst
Madera
Clovis
Fresno
Reedley
Mennonite Quilt Center
Kingsburg
Hanford
Coalinga
Visalia
Kaweah Oaks Preserve
Tulare
Corcoran
Three Rivers
Porterville
Colonel Allensworth State Historic Park
Kern National Wildlife Refuge
Delano
Bakersfield
California Living Museum
Kernville
Lake Isabella
Kern R.
Kern County Museum and Lori Brock Children's Discovery Center
CONTRA COSTA
ALAMEDA
SAN JOAQUIN
SANTA CLARA
STANISLAUS
MERCED
CALAVERAS
TUOLUMNE
MARIPOSA
MADERA
SAN BENITO
FRESNO
KINGS
TULARE
KERN
SAN LUIS OBISPO
Stanislaus National Forest
Yosemite National Park
Sierra National Forest
Kings Canyon National Park
Sequoia National Park
Sequoia National Forest
San Joaquin R.
Stanislaus R.
Tuolumne R.
Merced R.
Fresno R.
TO SACRAMENTO
0 20 miles
0 30 km
N

IF YOU HAVE 3 DAYS

On your first morning, visit the **Stockton** area. Start at the **Micke Grove Park** ①, 10 mi north of the city off Highway 99. That afternoon wander around the **Haggin Museum** ② in Stockton proper. The next morning, stop off at the **Castle Air Museum** ④ north of Merced in Atwater or proceed directly to **Fresno** ⑥–⑧. In the evening take in a show at **Roger Rocka's** or the **Tower Theatre,** both in Fresno's Tower District. On the third morning, drive to **Hanford** via Highways 99 and 43 and stroll around **Courthouse Square** and **China Alley.** After lunch continue south on Highway 43 to **Colonel Allensworth State Historic Park** ⑨, which is on the site of a now deserted town founded by African Americans in 1908. Head south on Highway 43 and east on Highway 46 to return to Highway 99, which continues south to **Bakersfield.** If you arrive before it closes, stop in for a quick visit to the **Kern County Museum** ⑩.

When to Visit the San Joaquin Valley

Spring, when wildflowers are in bloom and the scent of fruit blossoms is in the air, and fall, when leaves turn red and gold, are the prettiest times to visit. Many of the Valley's top festivals take place during these seasons. Summer, when temperatures often top 100°F, can be oppressive. Many attractions close in winter, which can get cold and raw. Thick, ground-hugging fog is a common driving hazard this time of year.

NORTH SAN JOAQUIN VALLEY

The northern section of the Valley cuts through San Joaquin, Stanislaus, and Merced counties, from the edges of the Sacramento Delta and the fringes of the Gold Country south to the flat, almost featureless terrain between Modesto and Merced. If you're heading to Yosemite National Park from northern California, chances are you'll pass through (or very near) at least one of these gateway cities.

Stockton Area

80 mi from San Francisco, east on I–80 to I–580 to I–205 and north on I–5; 45 mi south of Sacramento on I–5 or Hwy. 99.

California's first inland port—connected since 1933 to San Francisco via a 60-mi-long deepwater channel—is wedged between I–5 and Highway 99, on the eastern end of the great Sacramento River Delta. Stockton, founded during the gold rush as a way station for miners traveling from San Francisco to the Mother Lode, and now a city of 250,000, helps distribute the Valley's agricultural products to the world. Its best-known natives include author Maxine Hong Kingston and rock singer Chris Isaak. If you're here in late April, don't miss the **Stockton Asparagus Festival** (☎ 209/943–1987).

❶ Among the attractions at oak-shaded **Micke Grove Park,** halfway between Stockton and Lodi, are a zoo and an agricultural museum. ✉ *11793 N. Micke Grove Rd.; take Armstrong Rd. off Hwy. 99, 8 mi north of Stockton, then go ½ mi west to Micke Grove Rd., Lodi,* ☎ *209/331–7400.* *$2 weekdays, $4 weekends and holidays.* ⏲ *Feb.–Nov., 10–5; Dec.–Jan., 10–4.*

Ring-tailed lemurs and other endangered primates found only on the African island of Madagascar inhabit the An Island Lost in Time exhibit at the **Micke Grove Zoo.** Mountain lions have the run of Paseo Pantera, another highlight of this compact facility. ✉ *Micke Grove Park,* ☎ *209/331–7270.* *$1.50.* ⏲ *May–Aug., weekdays 10–5, weekends 10–7; Sept.–Apr., daily 10–5.*

The rides and other diversions at **Funderwoods,** a family-oriented amusement park, are geared to children under 10. Ride tickets cost $1 (10 for $8). ✉ *Micke Grove Park,* ☎ *209/369–5437.* ⏲ *Feb.–Easter, weekends 10:30–dusk; Easter–Nov., daily 10:30–dusk. Closed Dec.–Jan.*

★ ❷ The **Haggin Museum** in pretty Victory Park has one of the San Joaquin Valley's finest art collections. Late-19th-century American and French paintings—landscapes by Albert Bierstadt and Thomas Moran, a still life by Paul Gauguin, and a Native American gallery—are among the highlights. There's also an Egyptian mummy. ✉ *1201 N. Pershing Ave.,* ☎ *209/462–4116.* 🎫 *Free; suggested donation $2.* ⏲ *Tues.–Sun. 1:30–5.*

Dining and Lodging

$$$–$$$$ ✕ **Le Bistro.** The dishes at one of the Valley's most upscale restaurants are fairly standard Continental fare—lamb tenderloin, fillet of sole, sautéed prawns, soufflé Grand Marnier—but you can count on high-quality ingredients and presentation with a flourish. ✉ *Marina Center Mall, 3121 W. Benjamin Holt Dr. (off I–5, behind Lyon's),* ☎ *209/951–0885. AE, D, DC, MC, V.*

$–$$ ✕ **On Lock Sam.** Run by the same family since 1898, this Stockton landmark is in a modern pagoda-style building, with framed Chinese prints on the walls, a garden outside one window, and a sparkling bar area. One touch of old-time Chinatown remains: a few booths have curtains that can be drawn for complete privacy. The Cantonese food would be ho-hum in San Francisco, but it's among the Valley's best. ✉ *333 S. Sutter St.,* ☎ *209/466–4561. AE, D, MC, V.*

$–$$$ 🏨 **Best Western Stockton Inn.** Four miles from downtown, this good-size motel has a convenient location off Highway 99. The large central courtyard with a pool and lounge chairs is a big plus on hot days. Most rooms are spacious; free in-room movies are provided by satellite. ✉ *4219 Waterloo Rd., 95215,* ☎ *209/931–3131,* FAX *209/931–0423. 141 rooms. Restaurant, bar, no-smoking rooms, pool, wading pool, hot tub, laundry service, meeting rooms. AE, D, DC, MC, V. www.bestwesterncalifornia.com*

$–$$ 🏨 **La Quinta Inn.** Close to downtown and near many upscale restaurants, this is a good choice for business and pleasure travelers alike. The spacious and quiet rooms have large desks and televisions with access to first-run movies. Guests have workout privileges at a nearby health club. ✉ *2710 W. March La., 95219,* ☎ *209/952–7800,* FAX *209/472–0732. 158 rooms. In-room data ports, pool, no-smoking rooms, laundry service, meeting rooms. AE, D, DC, MC, V.* 🎁

Outdoor Activities and Sports

Several companies rent houseboats (of various sizes, usually for three, four, or seven days) on the Delta waterways near Stockton. Call the **Delta Rental Houseboat Hotline** (☎ 209/477–1840), or try **Herman & Helen's** (✉ Venice Island Ferry, ☎ 209/951–4634), **King Island Resort** (✉ 11530 W. Eight Mile Rd., ☎ 209/951–2188), or **Paradise Point Marina** (✉ 8095 Rio Blanco Rd., ☎ 209/952–1000).

En Route The top attraction in Manteca, the largest town between Stockton and Modesto, is **Manteca Waterslides.** Kids will head to the new Thunder Falls, which features three three-story slides. ✉ *874 E. Woodward Ave., between I–5 and Hwy. 99,* ☎ *209/239–2500.* 🎫 *Admission $21.* ⏲ *Memorial Day–Labor Day, weekdays 10-5, weekends 10-7.*

Modesto

29 mi south of Stockton on Hwy. 99.

Modesto, a gateway to Yosemite and the southern reaches of the Gold Country, was founded in 1870 to serve the Central Pacific Railroad. The frontier town was originally to be named Ralston, after a railroad baron, but as the story goes he modestly declined—thus "Modesto." The Stanislaus County seat, a tree-lined city of 190,000, is perhaps best known as the site of the annual Modesto Invitational Track Meet and Relays and birthplace of film producer-director George Lucas, creator of *Star Wars* and *American Graffiti*.

The **Modesto Arch** (✉ 9th and I Sts.) bears Modesto's motto: "Water, Wealth, Contentment, Health." Modesto holds a well-attended **International Festival** (☎ 209/521–3852) in early October that celebrates the cultures, crafts, and cuisines of many nationalities. The **Blue Diamond Growers Store** (✉ 4800 Sisk Rd., ☎ 209/545–3222) offers free samples, shows a film about almond-growing, and sells nuts in many flavors.

★ ❸ A wheat farmer and banker built the 1883 **McHenry Mansion,** the city's sole surviving original Victorian home. The Italianate-style mansion has been decorated to reflect Modesto life in the late 19th century. Oaks, elms, magnolias, redwoods, and palms shade the grounds. ✉ *15th and I Sts.,* ☎ *209/577–5341.* *Free.* *Sun.–Thurs. 1–4, Fri. noon–3. Closed last 2 wks of Nov.*

The **McHenry Museum** is a jumbled repository of early Modesto and Stanislaus County memorabilia, including re-creations of an old-time barbershop, a doctor's office, a blacksmith's shop, and a general store—the latter stocked with goods from hair crimpers to corsets. ✉ *1402 I St.,* ☎ *209/577–5366.* *Free.* *Tues.–Sun. noon–4.*

Dining and Lodging

$$–$$$ ✕ **Tresetti's.** One of the bright new restaurants in downtown Modesto, Tresetti's is part wine shop, part restaurant. For a small fee the staff will uncork any wine you select from the shop. The menu changes seasonally, but the smoked chicken quesadilla is outstanding, as are the Cajun-style crab cakes. ✉ *927 11th St.,* ☎ *209/572–2990. No reservations. AE, DC, MC, V. Sun.*

$–$$$ ✕ **Early Dawn Cattlemen's Steakhouse and Saloon.** The parking lots overflow at this local hangout, and so do the platters bearing barbecued steaks of 2 pounds and even heavier. The whiskey-marinated saloon steak, cooked over Santa Maria red oak, is a house specialty; chicken and seafood are among the lighter choices. ✉ *1000 Kansas Ave.,* ☎ *209/577–5833. AE, D, MC, V. No lunch Sat.*

$–$$ ✕ **Hazel's Elegant Dining.** Hazel's is *the* special-occasion restaurant in Modesto. The seven-course dinners include Continental entrées served with soup, salad, pasta, dessert, and beverage. Members of the Gallo family, who own much vineyard land in the San Joaquin Valley, eat here often, perhaps because the wine cellar is so comprehensive. ✉ *431 12th St.,* ☎ *209/578–3463. AE, D, DC, MC, V. Closed Sun.–Mon. No lunch Sat.*

$–$$ ✕ **St. Stan's.** This eatery is home to Modesto's most famous microbrewery, makers of St. Stan's beers. There are 14 on tap; try the Whistle Stop Pale Ale. The restaurant is casual and serves up good corned beef sandwiches loaded with sauerkraut and a tasty beer sausage nibbler. ✉ *821 L St.,* ☎ *209/524–4782. AE, D, MC, V.*

$$–$$$ **Best Western Mallard's Inn.** The duck decor is, thankfully, unobtrusive at this nicely landscaped motel off Highway 99. The comfortably furnished rooms are large and all have coffeemakers. Some rooms have microwaves and refrigerators stocked with milk and cookies. ✉ *1720 Sisk Rd., 95350,* ☎ *209/577–3825 or 800/294–4040,* FAX *209/577–1717. 126 rooms. Restaurant, no-smoking rooms, room service, pool, hot tub, exercise room, laundry service, business services, meeting rooms. AE, D, DC, MC, V.*

$$ **Doubletree Hotel.** Modesto's largest lodging towers 15 stories over downtown. The rooms have coffeemakers, irons, desks, and three phones. The convention center is adjacent, and a good brew pub, St. Stan's, is across the street. ✉ *1150 9th St., 95354,* ☎ *209/526–6000,* FAX *209/526–6096. 258 rooms. Restaurant, café, bar, no-smoking rooms, room service, pool, hot tub, sauna, exercise room, nightclub, laundry service, meeting rooms, airport shuttle. AE, D, DC, MC, V.*

Oakdale

15 mi east of Modesto on Hwy. 108.

Oakdale, a bit off the beaten path from Modesto, has two year-round attractions of great interest to children. If you're here in mid-May, check out the **Oakdale Chocolate Festival** (☎ 209/847–2244).

The **Hershey Chocolate Factory** in Oakdale is the only one in the country that allows the public to tour its production facilities. After the half-hour guided tours—which cover the chocolate-making process from cocoa bean to candy bar—everyone gets a sample. ✉ *120 S. Sierra Ave.,* ☎ *209/848–8126. Free. Tours weekdays 8:30–3, visitor center weekdays 8:30–5.*

★ The featured attraction at the **Knights Ferry Recreation Area** is the 355-ft-long Knights Ferry covered bridge. The beautiful and haunting structure, built in 1863, crosses the Stanislaus River near the ruins of an old grist mill. The park has picnic and barbecue areas along the riverbanks. Fishing, hiking, rafting, and canoeing are among the activities here. ✉ *Corps of Engineers Park, 18020 Sonora Rd., Knights Ferry; 12 mi east of Oakdale via Hwy. 108,* ☎ *209/881–3517. Free. Dawn–dusk.*

You can sample the wares at **Oakdale Cheese & Specialties** (✉ 10040 Hwy. 120, ☎ 209/848–3139), which has tastings (try the aged gouda) and cheese-making tours. There's a picnic area next to a pond and a petting zoo.

Merced and Atwater

38 mi south of Modesto (to Merced) on Hwy. 99; 53 mi from Oakdale, west and then south on Hwy. 108 and south on Hwy. 99.

Merced, population 56,000, is a common stopover en route to Yosemite National Park. The city will be the site of the newest branch of the University of California. The town of Atwater is 6 mi north of Merced on Highway 99.

❹ At the outdoor **Castle Air Museum,** adjacent to the former Castle Air Force Base (now Castle Aviation, an industrial park) you can stroll among fighter planes and other historic military aircraft. The 44 restored vintage war birds include the B-25 Mitchell medium-range bomber (best known for the "Jimmy Doolittle raid" on Tokyo following the attack on Pearl Harbor) and the speedy SR-71 Blackbird, used for reconnaissance over Vietnam and Libya. ✉ *Santa Fe Dr. and Buhach Rd. (take the Buhach Rd. exit off Hwy. 99 in Atwater and follow signs), Atwater,* ☎ *209/723–2178. $5. Memorial Day–Oct., daily 9–5; Nov.–Memorial Day, daily 10–4.*

5 Even if you don't go inside, be sure to swing by the **Merced County Courthouse Museum.** The three-story former courthouse, built in 1875, is a striking example of the Victorian Italianate style. The upper two floors are now a museum of early Merced history. Highlights include an ornate restored courtroom and an 1870 Chinese temple with carved redwood altars. ✉ *21st and N Sts., Merced,* ☎ *209/723–2401.* *Free.* *Wed.–Sun. 1–4.*

The **Merced Multicultural Arts Center** displays paintings, sculpture, and photography. Threads, a festival that celebrates the area's ethnic diversity, is held here on a mid-October weekend. ✉ *645 W. Main St., Merced,* ☎ *209/388–1090.* *Free.* *Weekdays 9–5, Sat. 10–2.*

Dining and Lodging

$$–$$$$ ★ ✕ **DeAngelo's.** Not only the best restaurant in Merced, it's one of the best in the entire San Joaquin Valley. Chef Vincent DeAngelo, a graduate of the Culinary Institute of America, brings his considerable skill to everything from mussels from the East Coast to clams from the Pacific Northwest. He relies heavily on locally grown produce. The delicious, crusty bread, from the Golden Sheath in Watsonville, is a meal in itself. ✉ *350 W. Main St., Merced,* ☎ *209/383–3020. AE, D, DC, MC, V. Closed Sun., except Dec.–Feb.*

$–$$$ ✕ **Vinnie D's Chop House.** The focus here is the wood-burning stove where the chefs prepare certified Angus steaks. Start with the coconut fried shrimp or the barbecued Pacific oysters, which are hot and incredibly fresh. For dessert, the crème brûlée is a must. ✉ *510 W. Main St.,* ☎ *209/725–9446. Reservations essential. AE, D, MC, V. Closed Mon.*

$ ✕ **Main Street Café.** This bright downtown café dishes up soups, pizza, salads, sandwiches, pastries, ice cream, and espresso. Sandwiches (try the chicken breast with pesto mayonnaise on Francesi bread) are served with tasty side salads. ✉ *460 W. Main St.,* ☎ *209/725–1702. AE, MC, V. Closed Sun. No dinner.*

$ **Days Inn.** The compact rooms at this very nice motel manage to pack in an impressive array of amenities: writing table, refrigerator, microwave, radio, coffeemaker, bathroom phone, safe, and a 27-inch TV with cable and a VCR (tapes are for rent in the lobby). ✉ *1199 Motel Dr., near the intersection of Hwys. 99 and 140, 95340,* ☎ *209/722–2726,* FAX *209/722–7083. 24 rooms. No-smoking rooms, refrigerators, in-room VCRs, pool. AE, D, DC, MC, V.*

Outdoor Activities and Sports

At **Lake Yosemite Regional Park** (✉ N. Lake Rd., off Yosemite Ave., 5 mi northeast of Merced, ☎ 209/385–7426), you can boat, swim, windsurf, waterski, and fish on a 387-acre reservoir. Boat rentals and picnic areas are available.

MID–SAN JOAQUIN VALLEY

Fresno, Hanford, and Visalia

The mid–San Joaquin Valley extends over three counties—Fresno, Kings, and Tulare. From Fresno, Highway 41 leads north 95 mi to Yosemite and Highway 180 snakes east 55 mi to Kings Canyon (Sequoia National Park is 30 mi farther). From Visalia, Highway 198 winds east 35 mi to the Generals Highway, which leads into Sequoia and Kings Canyon. Historic Hanford, about 16 mi west of Visalia along Highway 198, is a gem of a town.

Fresno

50 mi south of Merced on Hwy. 99; 110 mi north of Bakersfield on Hwy. 99.

Sprawling Fresno, with more than 400,000 people, is the center of the richest agricultural county in America; grapes, cotton, oranges, and turkeys are among the major products. The city's most famous native, Pulitzer Prize–winning playwright and novelist William Saroyan (*The Time of Your Life, The Human Comedy*), was born here in 1908. The seemingly endless parade of strip malls and fast-food joints can be depressing, but local character does lurk beneath the commercialization. The city is home to 75 ethnic communities (from Armenian to Vietnamese), a burgeoning arts scene, and several public parks. The Tower District, with its restaurants, theaters, and coffeehouses, offers a taste of San Francisco.

Woodward Park, 300 acres of jogging trails, picnic areas, and playgrounds in the northern reaches of the city, is especially pretty in the spring when plum and cherry trees, magnolias, and camellias bloom. Big-band concerts take place in summer. Well worth a look is the **Shin Zen Japanese Friendship Garden,** which has a teahouse, a koi pond, arched bridges, a waterfall, and lakes. ✉ *Audubon Dr. and Friant Rd.,* ☎ *559/498–1551.* 🎫 *Parking $2; admission $1.* ⏲ *Mar.–Oct., daily 7 AM–10 PM; Nov.–Dec., daily 7–5; Jan.–Feb., daily 7–7.*

Sicilian immigrant Baldasare Forestiere spent four decades (1906–1946)
★ 6 carving out the **Forestiere Underground Gardens,** a subterranean realm of rooms, tunnels, grottoes, alcoves, and arched passageways that extends for more than 10 acres beneath busy, mall-pocked Shaw Avenue. Only a fraction of Forestiere's prodigious output is on view, but you can tour his underground living quarters, including bedrooms (one with a fireplace), the kitchen, the living room, the bath, a fish pond, and an aquarium. Skylights allow exotic, full-grown fruit trees—including one that through grafting bears seven kinds of citrus—to flourish at more than 20 ft below ground. ✉ *5021 W. Shaw Ave., 2 blocks east of Hwy. 99,* ☎ *559/271–0734.* 🎫 *$6. Reservations essential.* ⏲ *Memorial Day–Labor Day, Wed.–Sun. 10–4 (tours at 10, noon, 2, and 4); Easter–Memorial Day and Labor Day–Thanksgiving (weather permitting; tour hrs vary), weekends noon–3. Closed Dec.–Mar.*

★ 7 Tree-shaded **Roeding Park,** Fresno's largest park, has picnic areas, playgrounds, tennis courts, and a zoo (☞ *below*). ✉ *Olive and Belmont Aves.,* ☎ *559/498–4239.* 🎫 *Parking $1.* ⏲ *Mar.–Oct., daily 7 AM–10 PM; Oct.–Mar., daily 7–7.*

The most striking exhibit at **Chaffee Zoological Gardens** is the tropical rain forest, where exotic birds often greet visitors along the paths and bridges. Elsewhere you'll find tigers, grizzly bears, sea lions, tule elk, camels, elephants, and hooting siamangs. Also here are a high-tech reptile house and a petting zoo. ✉ *Roeding Park,* ☎ *559/498–2671.* 🎫 *$4.95.* ⏲ *Mar.–Oct., daily 9–5; Nov.–Feb., daily 10–4.*

A miniature train, a Ferris wheel, a small roller-coaster, and a merry-go-round are among the amusements at **Playland** (✉ Roeding Park, ☎ 559/486–2124), which is open (days and hours vary) between February and November. Children can explore attractions with fairy-tale themes and attend puppet shows at **Storyland** (✉ Roeding Park, ☎ 559/264–2235), which is open between February and November. Admission is $3.

The drive along palm-lined Kearney Boulevard is one of the best reasons to visit the **Kearney Mansion Museum,** which stands in shaded

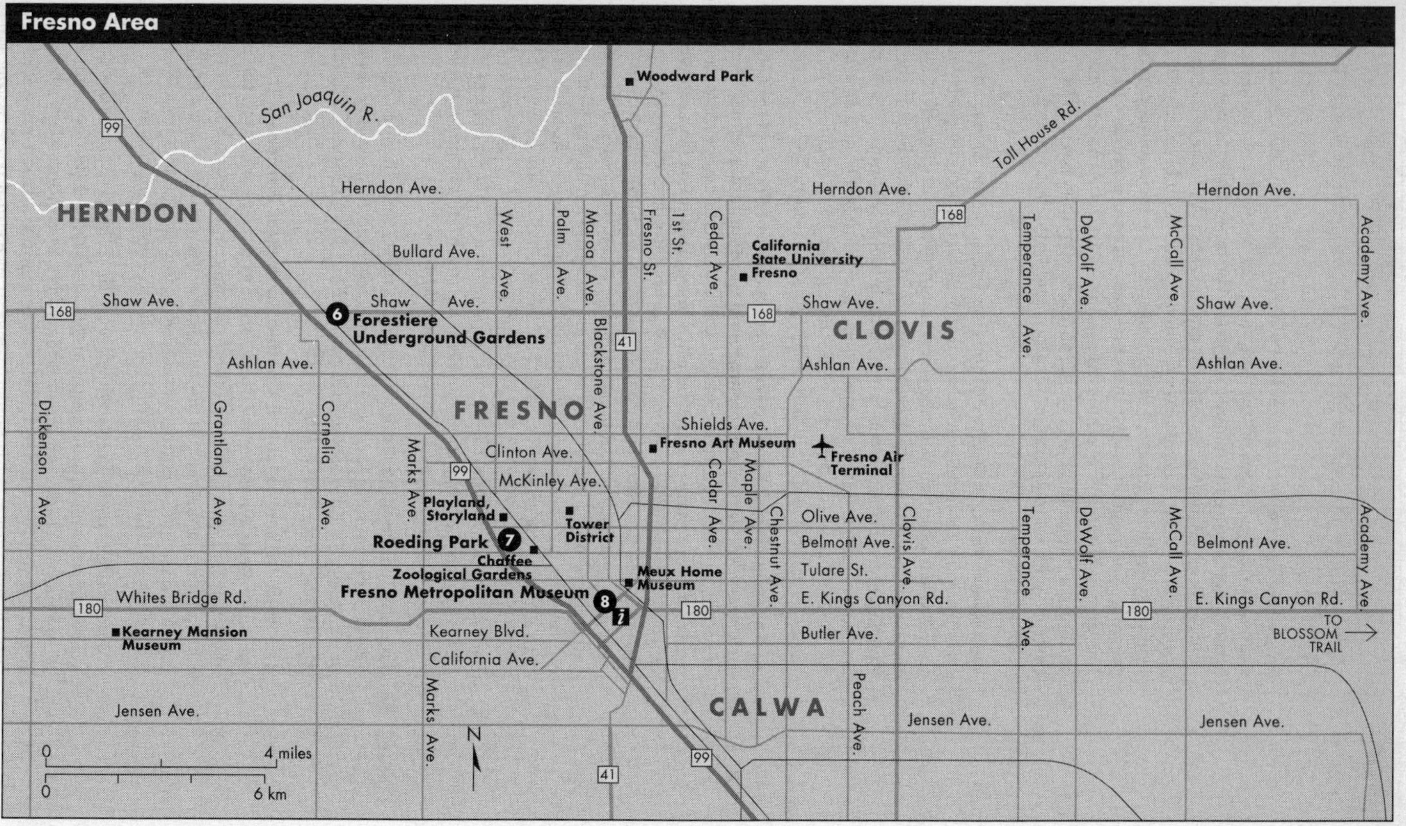
Fresno Area
Woodward Park
San Joaquin R.
99
Toll House Rd.
Herndon Ave.
Herndon Ave.
Herndon Ave.
HERNDON
168
West Ave.
Palm Ave.
Maroa Ave.
Fresno St.
1st St.
Cedar Ave.
California State University Fresno
Temperance Ave.
DeWolf Ave.
McCall Ave.
Academy Ave.
Bullard Ave.
168
Shaw Ave.
Shaw Ave.
Shaw Ave.
Shaw Ave.
168
6 Forestiere Underground Gardens
Blackstone Ave.
41
CLOVIS
Ashlan Ave.
Ashlan Ave.
Ashlan Ave.
FRESNO
Dickenson Ave.
Grantland Ave.
Cornelia Ave.
Shields Ave.
Fresno Art Museum
Fresno Air Terminal
Marks Ave.
Clinton Ave.
99
McKinley Ave.
Cedar Ave.
Maple Ave.
Chestnut Ave.
Playland, Storyland
Tower District
Olive Ave.
Clovis Ave.
Temperance Ave.
DeWolf Ave.
McCall Ave.
Academy Ave.
Roeding Park 7
Belmont Ave.
Belmont Ave.
Chaffee Zoological Gardens
Tulare St.
Meux Home Museum
Fresno Metropolitan Museum 8
E. Kings Canyon Rd.
E. Kings Canyon Rd.
Whites Bridge Rd.
180
180
180
Kearney Mansion Museum
Kearney Blvd.
Butler Ave.
TO BLOSSOM TRAIL
California Ave.
CALWA
Peach Ave.
Jensen Ave.
Jensen Ave.
Jensen Ave.
Marks Ave.
N
0
4 miles
0
6 km
41
99

225-acre Kearney Park, 7 mi west of town. Guided 45-minute tours take you through the century-old home of M. Theo Kearney, Fresno's onetime "Raisin King." ✉ *7160 W. Kearney Blvd.,* ☎ *559/441–0862.* *$4 (park entrance $3, waived for museum visitors).* *Museum Fri.–Sun., tours at 1, 2, and 3.*

The **Legion of Valor Museum,** is a real find for military history buffs of all ages. It has German bayonets and daggers, a Japanese Namby pistol, a full-size Gatlin gun, and an extensive collection of Japanese, German, and American uniforms. The staff is extremely enthusiastic. ✉ *2425 Fresno St.,* ☎ *559/498–0510.* *Free.* *Mon.–Sat. 10–3.*

8 The **Fresno Metropolitan Museum** mounts art, history, and hands-on science exhibits, many of them quite innovative. The William Saroyan History Gallery presents a riveting introduction in words and pictures to the author's life and times. ✉ *1555 Van Ness Ave.,* ☎ *559/441–1444.* *$6.* *Tues.–Sun. 11–5 (Thurs. until 8).*

The **Fresno Art Museum** exhibits American, Mexican, and French art; highlights of the permanent collection include pre-Columbian works and graphic art from the post-Impressionist period. The 152-seat Bonner Auditorium hosts lectures, films, and concerts. ✉ *Radio Park, 2233 N. 1st St.,* ☎ *559/441–4220.* *$2; free Tues.* *Tues.–Fri. 10–5, weekends noon–5. Closed last 2 wks of Aug.*

The **Meux Home Museum,** inside a restored 1888 Victorian, displays furnishings and decor typical of early Fresno. Guided tours lead from the front parlor to the backyard carriage house. ✉ *Tulare and R Sts.,* ☎ *559/233–8007.* *$4.* *Feb.–Dec., Fri.–Sun. noon–4.*

OFF THE BEATEN PATH

BLOSSOM TRAIL – This 62-mi self-guided driving tour takes in Fresno-area orchards, citrus groves, and vineyards during spring blossom season. Almond, plum, apple, orange, lemon, apricot, and peach blossoms shower the landscape with shades of white, pink, and red. (The most colorful and aromatic time to go is from late February to mid-March.) The route passes through several small towns and past rivers, lakes, and canals. The **Fresno Convention & Visitors Bureau** (✉ 848 M St., 3rd floor, ☎ 559/233–0836 or 800/788–0836) has route maps; directional and crop identification signs also mark the trail. Allow at least two to three hours for the tour.

Dining and Lodging

$$–$$$ ✕ **Giulia's Italian Trattoria.** The look here is light and airy, but the Abruzzi cuisine (from southern Italy's Adriatic coast) is hearty and intensely flavored. Bruschetta, steamed mussels, and polenta with grilled sausage are top choices. The adjoining b. b.'s Oyster Bar & Grill serves sandwiches and seafood appetizers; many patrons have cocktails there before dining at Giulia's. ✉ *Winepress Shopping Center, 3050 W. Shaw Ave.,* ☎ *559/276–3573. AE, D, DC, MC, V. Closed Sun. No lunch weekends.*

$ ✕ **Armenian Cuisine.** Local Armenians flock to this small restaurant for tasty lamb, beef, and chicken kebabs, which come with pita bread, eggplant salad, and stuffed grape leaves. ✉ *742 W. Bullard Ave.,* ☎ *559/435–4892. AE, DC, MC, V. Closed Sun.*

$ ✕ **Kim's Vietnamese Restaurant.** Specialties here include hot beef salad, sizzling chicken, and sautéed seafood with ginger. Complete lunches or dinners—from soup to dessert and tea, with salad, entrée, and rice in between—cost as little as $10. ✉ *5048 N. Maroa St.,* ☎ *559/225–0406. MC, V. Closed Sun.*

$–$$$$ **Piccadilly Inn Shaw.** This two-story property is attractively landscaped, with a big central swimming pool on 7½ acres. The sizable rooms have king- and queen-size beds, full-size robes, ironing boards, fresh cookies, and coffeemakers; some rooms have refrigerators, microwaves, and fireplaces. ✉ *2305 W. Shaw Ave., 93711,* ☎ *559/226–3850,* FAX *559/226–2448. 188 rooms, 6 suites. No-smoking rooms, pool, hot tub, exercise room, coin laundry, laundry service, business services, meeting rooms. AE, D, DC, MC, V.*

$ **La Quinta Inn.** Rooms are of good size at this basic but decent three-story motel near downtown. Some rooms have king-size beds, microwaves, and refrigerators. ✉ *2926 Tulare St., 93721,* ☎ *559/442–1110,* FAX *559/237–0415. 130 rooms. No-smoking rooms, pool. AE, D, DC, MC, V. CP.*

Nightlife and the Arts

The **Tower Theatre for the Performing Arts** (✉ 815 E. Olive Ave., ☎ 559/485–9050), a onetime movie house that has given its name to the trendy Tower District of theaters, clubs, restaurants, and cafés, presents theatrical, ballet, classical, jazz, and other cultural events from spring to fall. **Roger Rocka's Music Hall** (✉ 1226 N. Wishon Ave., ☎ 559/266–9494 or 800/371–4747), a dinner theater in the Tower District, stages six Broadway-style musicals or comedies a year. The **Fresno Philharmonic Orchestra** (☎ 559/261–0600) performs classical concerts (sometimes pops) on weekends, usually at the William Saroyan Theatre (✉ 700 M St.), from September through June.

Outdoor Activities and Sports

Wild Water Adventures (✉ 11413 E. Shaw Ave., Clovis, ☎ 559/299–9453 or 800/564–9453), a 50-acre water theme park about 10 mi east of Fresno, is open from late May to early September.

Shopping

Old Town Clovis (✉ 5th and Pollasky Sts., Clovis) is an area of restored brick buildings and brick sidewalks, with numerous antiques shops and art galleries (along with restaurants and saloons). Head east on Fresno's Shaw Avenue about 10 mi to get to Clovis.

OFF THE BEATEN PATH

MENNONITE QUILT CENTER – The colorful handiwork of local Mennonite quilters is on display here. Try to visit on Monday (except holidays), when two dozen or so quilters come in to stitch, patch, and chat over coffee. Prime viewing time—with the largest number of quilts—is in February and March, right before the center holds its early April auction. Ask a docent to take you to the locked upstairs room, where most of the quilts are hung; she'll explain the fine points of patterns such as the Log Cabin Romance, the Dahlia, and the Snowball-Star. ✉ *1012 G St. (take Manning Ave. exit off Hwy. 99 and head east 12 mi), Reedley,* ☎ *559/638–3560.* *Free.* *Weekdays 9:30–4:30, Sat. 10–2.*

Hanford

★ *35 mi from Fresno, south on Hwy. 99 and Hwy. 43.*

Founded in 1877 as a Southern Pacific Railroad stop, Hanford had one of California's largest Chinatowns—the Chinese came to help build the railroads and stayed to farm and open restaurants. You can take a self-guided walking tour or sign up in advance for guided tours ($2.50) arranged by the **Hanford Visitor Agency** (☎ *559/582–5024*). One tour explores the restored historic buildings of Courthouse Square. Another heads to narrow China Alley, with stops at the town's Taoist Temple and other sights.

The **Hanford Carnegie Museum,** inside the former Carnegie Library, a Romanesque building dating from 1905, displays fashions, furnishings, toys, and military artifacts. ✉ *109 E. 8th St.,* ☎ *559/584–1367.* 🎫 *$1.* ⏲ *Tues.–Fri. noon–3, Sat. noon–4.*

A first-floor museum in the 1893 **Taoist Temple** displays photos, furnishings, and kitchenware from Hanford's once-bustling Chinatown. The second-floor temple, largely unchanged for a century, contains altars, carvings, and ceremonial staves. You can visit as part of a guided walking tour (☞ *above*) or by calling the temple directly and making an appointment two weeks in advance. ✉ *12 China Alley,* ☎ *559/582–4508.* 🎫 *Free; donations welcome.* ⏲ *By appointment only.*

Dining and Lodging

$–$$$ ✕ **Imperial Dynasty.** Despite its name and elegant teak-and-porcelains Chinese decor, Imperial Dynasty serves primarily French cuisine. Its heyday was in the 1970s and '80s, but this spot is still one of the better restaurants in the Valley. For a memorable meal, start with the garlicky escargots and continue with the veal sweetbreads or rack of lamb. The extensive wine list contains many prized vintages. ✉ *China Alley (corner of 7th and Green Sts.),* ☎ *559/582–0196. AE, MC, V. Closed Mon. No lunch.*

$–$$ ✕ **La Fiesta.** Mexican-American families, farmworkers, and farmers all eat here. La Fiesta features traditional Mexican dishes such as enchiladas and tacos. The Fiesta Special—for two or more—includes nachos, garlic shrimp, deviled-style shrimp, clams, and two pieces of top sirloin. ✉ *106 N. Green St.,* ☎ *559/583–8775. AE, D, DC, MC, V.*

$–$$$ ★ 🏨 **Irwin Street Inn.** This inn is one of the few lodgings in the Valley that warrants a detour. Four tree-shaded, restored Victorian homes have been converted into spacious, comfortable rooms and suites. Most have antique armoires, dark wood detailing, leaded-glass windows, and four-poster beds; bathrooms have old-fashioned tubs, brass fixtures, and marble basins. ✉ *522 N. Irwin St., 93230,* ☎ *559/583–8000 or 888/583–8080,* FAX *559/583–8793. 27 rooms. Restaurant, pool. AE, D, DC, MC, V. CP.*

Nightlife and the Arts

The 1,000-seat, restored Moorish-Castillian–style **Hanford Fox Theater** (✉ 326 N. Irwin St., ☎ 559/584–7423), built as a movie palace in 1929, now periodically hosts country-western bands and other live performances.

Visalia

16 mi from Hanford, east on Hwy. 198; 40 mi from Fresno, south on Hwy. 99 and east on Hwy. 198.

A native of Visalia, Kentucky, founded Visalia, the Tulare County seat, in 1852. The center of one of the world's top milk-producing regions, the town, with a population of close to 100,000, is also a major exporter of oranges, grapes, plums, peaches, and cotton. On a clear day the views of the Sierra Nevada peaks to the east are stunning. Visalia contains a number of historic homes; ask at the **visitor center** (✉ 301 E. Acequia Ave., 93921, ☎ 559/738–3435 or 800/524–0303) for a free guide.

The **Chinese Cultural Center,** housed in a pagoda-style building, mounts exhibits about Asian art and culture. ✉ *500 Akers Rd., at Hwy. 198,* ☎ *559/625–4545.* 🎫 *Free.* ⏲ *Wed.–Sun. 11–6.*

In oak-shaded **Mooney Grove Park** you can picnic alongside duck ponds, rent a boat in a lagoon, and view a replica of the famous *End of the Trail* statue. The original, designed by James Earl Fraser for the

1915 Panama-Pacific International Exposition, is now in the Cowboy Hall of Fame in Oklahoma. ✉ *27000 S. Mooney Blvd., 5 mi south of downtown,* ☎ *559/733–6616.* *$4 per car.* ⏲ *Daily 8 AM–sunset.*

The indoor-outdoor **Tulare County Museum** contains several re-created environments from the pioneer era. On display are Yokuts tribal artifacts (basketry, arrowheads, clamshell-necklace currency) as well as saddles and guns, Victorian-era dolls, and quilts and gowns. ✉ *Mooney Grove Park, 27000 S. Mooney Blvd., 5 mi south of downtown,* ☎ *559/733–6616.* *Free.* ⏲ *June–Aug., Mon. and Wed.–Fri. 10–4, weekends noon–6; Sept.–Oct., Thurs.–Mon. 10–4; Nov.–Feb., Mon., Thurs., Fri. 10–4, weekends 1–4; Mar.–May, Thurs.–Mon. 10–4.*

Trails at the 300-acre **Kaweah Oaks Preserve,** a wildlife sanctuary off the main road to Sequoia National Park and accessible only to hikers, lead past oak, sycamore, cottonwood, and willow trees. Among the 125 bird species you might spot are hawks, hummingbirds, and great blue herons. Lizards, coyotes, and cottontails also live here. ✉ *Follow Hwy. 198 for 7 mi east of Visalia, turn north on Rd. 182, and proceed ½ mi to gate on left-hand side of road,* ☎ *559/738–0211.* *Free.* ⏲ *Daily sunrise–sunset.*

Dining and Lodging

$–$$$ ★ ✕ **The Vintage Press.** Built in 1966, the Vintage Press is the best restaurant in the San Joaquin Valley. Cut-glass doors and bar fixtures decorate the artfully designed rooms. The California-Continental cuisine includes dishes such as baby abalone in champagne butter sauce, wild mushrooms in puff pastry, and sturgeon in caviar butter. The chocolate Grand Marnier cake is a standout among the many wonderful homemade desserts and ice creams. The wine list has more than 900 selections. ✉ *216 N. Willis St.,* ☎ *559/733–3033. AE, DC, MC, V.*

$ ✕ **Café 225.** High ceilings and warm yellow and blue walls help make this downtown restaurant a standout. The oak-rotisserie chicken is excellent alone or in a sandwich. The butcher-paper table coverings and crayons are child-friendly. ✉ *225 W. Main St.,* ☎ *559/733–2967. AE, D, DC, MC, V. Closed Sun.*

$–$$ **The Lamp Liter Inn.** Rooms here are of a decent size, and some have refrigerators. A large, tree-shaded pool beckons on hot days. Large common areas make this a good choice for family reunions. ✉ *3300 W. Mineral King Ave., off Hwy. 198, 93291,* ☎ *559/732–4511,* FAX *559/732–1840. 100 rooms. Restaurant, coffee shop, lounge, pool, meeting rooms. AE, D, DC, MC, V.*

$–$$ **The Spalding House.** This restored colonial-revival B&B—decked out with antiques, Oriental rugs, handcrafted woodwork, and glass doors—is one of several historic homes in the vicinity. The house, built in 1901, has three guest suites that each have a separate sitting room and private bath, but no phone or TV. ✉ *631 N. Encina St., 93291,* ☎ *559/739–7877,* FAX *559/625–0902. 3 suites. No-smoking rooms. MC, V. BP.*

Colonel Allensworth State Historic Park

★ ❾ *40 mi from Visalia, south on Hwy. 99, west on J22 (at town of Earlimart) and south on Hwy. 43.*

A former slave who rose to become the country's highest-ranking black military officer of his time founded Allensworth—the only California town settled, governed, and financed by African-Americans—in 1908. After enjoying early prosperity, Allensworth was plagued by hardships and was eventually deserted. Its buildings have been rebuilt or restored to reflect the era when it thrived. Each October three days of festivities mark the town's rededication. ✉ *4129 Palmer Ave.,* ☎ *661/849–3433.* 🎫 *$3 per car.* ⏲ *Daily 10–4:30.*

OFF THE BEATEN PATH

KERN NATIONAL WILDLIFE REFUGE – Ducks, snowy egrets, peregrine falcons, warblers, and other birds inhabit the marshes and wetlands here from November through April. Follow the 3½-mi radius tour route (pick up maps at the entrance) to find good viewing spots. ✉ *10811 Corcoran Rd., 19 mi west of Delano on Hwy. 155 (Garces Hwy.); from Allensworth take Hwy. 43 south to Hwy. 155 west,* ☎ *661/725–2767.* 🎫 *Free.* ⏲ *Feb.–Sept., daily sunrise–sunset; Oct.–Jan., Wed. and Sat. sunrise–sunset.*

SOUTHERN SAN JOAQUIN VALLEY

Bakersfield and Kernville

When gold was discovered in Kern County in the 1860s, settlers flocked to the southern end of the San Joaquin Valley. Black gold—oil—is now the area's most valuable commodity, but Kern is also the country's third-largest agriculture-producing county. From the flat plains around Bakersfield, the landscape graduates to rolling hills and then mountains as it climbs east to Kernville, which lies in the Kern River Valley.

Bakersfield

80 mi from Visalia, west on Hwy. 198, south on Hwy. 99; 288 mi from San Francisco, east on I–80 and I–580, south on I–5; 112 mi north of Los Angeles, I–5 to Hwy. 99.

Bakersfield's founder, Colonel Thomas Baker, arrived with the discovery of gold in the nearby Kern River Valley in 1851. Now Kern County's biggest city (population 212,000, including the largest community of Basque people in this country), Bakersfield probably is best known as "Nashville West," a country-music haven and hometown of performers Buck Owens and Merle Haggard. It's also home to a symphony orchestra and two good museums.

★ ⓾ The **Kern County Museum and Lori Brock Children's Discovery Center** form one of the San Joaquin Valley's top museum complexes. The indoor-outdoor Kern County Museum—whose centerpiece is an open-air, walk-through historic village with more than 50 restored or re-created buildings—pays homage to the era of the 1860s to 1940s. The indoor part of the museum holds exhibits about Native Americans and the "Bakersfield Sound" in country music. The adjacent Children's Discovery Center has permanent and changing hands-on displays and activities. ✉ *3801 Chester Ave.,* ☎ *661/861–2132.* 🎫 *$5.* ⏲ *Weekdays 8–5, Sat. 10–5, Sun. noon–5.*

★ ⓫ At the **California Living Museum,** a combination zoo, botanical garden, and natural-history museum, the emphasis is on zoo. All animal and plant species displayed are native to the state. Within the reptile house lives every species of rattlesnake found in California. The landscaped grounds—nestled among the rolling hills about a 20-minute drive northeast of Bakersfield—also shelter bald eagles, tortoises, coyotes, mountain lions, black bears, and foxes. ✉ *14000 Alfred Harrell Hwy. (Hwy. 178 east, then 3½ mi northwest on Alfred Harrell Hwy.),* ☎ *661/872–2256.* 🎫 *$3.50.* ⏲ *Tues.–Sun. 9–5.*

Close-Up

BAKERSFIELD'S FAVORITE SON

EVERY FRIDAY AND SATURDAY night, Buck Owens and the Buckaroos hit the stage at Crystal Palace in Bakersfield. In between sets, the country music star sings "Happy Birthday" to elderly fans, recognizes couples celebrating anniversaries, and congratulates customers on retirements or new jobs.

Why would Owens, who has racked up more than 20 Number 1 singles and 12 Number 1 albums and earned a spot in the Country Music Hall of Fame, continue to play to a hometown crowd? It turns out that the 71-year-old Owens just loves performing. In that sense, he's not that far from the lanky 25-year-old who used to play on broiling summer nights at such Bakersfield honky-tonks as the Blackboard and the Lucky Spot.

"This is a different kind of show," Owens said. "Customers write the requests down on a napkin and send them up. It reminds me of the old days at the Blackboard when I could play everybody's music and not just my own."

When Owens arrived nearly five decades ago, a new kind of music was emerging from Bakersfield, a dusty farm town in the southern San Joaquin Valley that would soon be dubbed "Nashville West." The "Bakersfield Sound" was rough and rowdy, born of weeks spent in the cotton fields and weekends spent in the churches. In a sense, the Bakersfield Sound was gospel played country-style.

After moving from a small town on the Texas border to the San Joaquin Valley in 1951, Owens found a job playing guitar in a band called the Orange Blossom Playboys. One night when he and the boys were performing at the Blackboard, front man Bill Woods got laryngitis. He asked Owens to do the singing. The rest, along with Owens' secondhand Fender Telecaster guitar he bought for $30, is history.

Owens, along with Ferlin Husky, Red Simpson, Billy Mize, and Merle Haggard, played a big part in establishing the Bakersfield Sound. Owens dropped the drippy violins favored by Nashville musicians and added a snappy fiddle. He replaced unobtrusive percussion with rock-and-roll rhythms. And he always led with the hard-driving twang of his electric guitar. The result, Owens has often said, hit listeners "hard as a freight train." Between 1963 and 1974, Owens racked up more than 50 songs in *Billboard*'s Top Ten.

By the late '70s, Owens had grown tired of traveling for concerts and to tape *Hee-Haw,* the top-rated syndicated television show in history. Owens told people of his dream to build a concert hall in his adopted-hometown of Bakersfield so that he would have a place where he and his friends could perform. In 1996 Owens spent more than $8 million to build the Crystal Palace—part nightclub, part museum, and part restaurant—next to the town's oil companies and the busiest truck stop in town.

The Crystal Palace, with a façade designed to look like the street of an old western town, is a country music Disneyland. Inside is a 35-ft mural depicting Owens' rise from the cotton fields to entertaining at the White House. His prized Pontiac hangs on the wall behind the Buckmobile bar. The walls of the Buck Owens Museum display more than 1,000 oversized photos of Owens and other country stars.

If anyone doubted that the Crystal Palace would be a success, they were proven wrong from the first sold-out performance. Since then, the 550-seat concert hall has hosted standing-room-only concerts by performers such as George Jones, Merle Haggard, Don Williams, Willie Nelson, and the Dixie Chicks. But it's always jammed on Friday and Saturday nights when Owens, the town's favorite son, starts to play.

— Herb Benham

Dining and Lodging

$$ ✕ **Noriega Hotel.** Established in 1893, this Basque restaurant is part of the oldest boarding house in California, home to generations of sheepherders. The restaurant is known for its thick and tender lamb chops, oxtail stew, prime rib, soup, pink beans, hors d'oeuvres, vegetables, and potatoes—all served family-style. Lunch is served promptly at noon, and dinner at 7, so don't dawdle. ✉ *525 Sumner St.,* ☎ *661/322–8419. No credit cards. Closed Mon.*

$–$$ ✕ **Uricchio's Trattoria.** This downtown restaurant draws everyone from office workers to oil barons—all attracted by the tasty food, open kitchen, and indoor and outdoor seating. *Panini* (Italian sandwiches, served at lunch only), pasta, and Italian-style chicken dishes dominate the menu; the chicken piccata outsells all other offerings. ✉ *1400 17th St.,* ☎ *661/326–8870. AE, D, DC, MC, V. Closed Sun. No lunch Sat.*

$ ✕ **Jake's Original Tex-Mex Cafe.** Don't let the cafeteria-style service fool you; this is probably the best lunch place in Bakersfield. The chicken burritos and the chili fries (with meaty chili ladled on top) are worth a visit. For dessert try the Texas sheet cake or the homemade chocolate-chip cookies. Open for dinner, too. ✉ *1710 Oak St.,* ☎ *661/322–6380. No reservations. AE, DC, MC, V. Closed Sun.*

$–$$$ 🏨 **Four Points Hotel.** The grounds of this hotel, voted the best in the Sheraton chain in 1999, are lush and green. A mile west of Highway 99, this hotel features rooms with such amenities as coffeemakers, irons and ironing boards, and hair driers. There's also a free airport shuttle. ✉ *5101 California Ave., 93309,* ☎ *661/325–9700,* FAX *661/323–3508. 197 rooms, 8 suites. In-room data ports, no-smoking rooms, pool, hot tub, exercise room. AE, D, DC, MC, V.*

$–$$ 🏨 **Doubletree Hotel.** The location is convenient, off Highways 99, 58, and 178. The spacious rooms have coffeemakers, irons, ironing boards, hair dryers, and balconies or patios. ✉ *3100 Camino Del Rio Ct., 93308,* ☎ *661/323–7111,* FAX *661/323–0331. 248 rooms and 14 suites. Restaurant, bar, coffee shop, no-smoking rooms, room service, pool, hot tub, dry cleaning, business services, meeting rooms, free airport shuttle. AE, D, DC, MC, V.*

$ 🏨 **Quality Inn.** Near downtown in a relatively quiet location off Highway 99, this two-story motel offers good value. Most rooms have king- or queen-size beds, and all have free in-room movies. Some have refrigerators and a patio or a balcony looking out on the heated pool. Complimentary coffee and donuts are served. ✉ *1011 Oak St., 93304,* ☎ *661/325–0772,* FAX *661/325–4646. 90 rooms. Pool, indoor hot tub, exercise room, coin laundry. AE, D, DC, MC, V.*

Nightlife and the Arts

The **Bakersfield Symphony Orchestra** (☎ 661/323–7928) performs classical music concerts at the Convention Center (✉ 1001 Truxton Ave.) on Sunday from October through May.

Buck Owens' Crystal Palace (✉ 2800 Buck Owens Blvd., ☎ 661/328–7560) is a combination nightclub, restaurant, and showcase of country-music memorabilia. Country-western singers—owner Buck Owens among them—perform. Buck Owens and the Buckaroos perform Friday and Saturday. A dance floor beckons customers who can still twirl after sampling the menu of steaks, burgers, nachos, and gooey desserts. Entertainment is free on most weeknights; Friday and Saturday nights bring a $6 cover charge, and some big-name acts require tickets.

Outdoor Activities and Sports

CAR RACING

At **Bakersfield Speedway** (✉ 304 Egret Ct., ☎ 661/393–3373), stock and sprint cars race around a ⅓-mi clay oval track. **Mesa Marin Race-**

way (✉ 11000 Kern Canyon Rd., ☎ 661/366–5711) presents high-speed stock-car, super-truck, and NASCAR racing on a ½-mi paved oval course.

SKATING

If you have children who can't get enough of inline skating or skateboarding, Bakersfield has two great skate parks. The **Vans Skate Park** (✉ 3737 Rosedale Hwy., off Hwy. 99, ☎ 661/327–1794) is a 30,000-square-ft facility with ramps, rails, and half pipes. Two hour sessions are $9–$11. The free skate park at **Beach Park** (corner of Oak and 21st Sts.) has good street skating as well as a relaxing grassy area for parents.

Shopping

Many antiques shops are on 18th and 19th streets between H and R streets, and H Street between Brundage Lane and California Avenue. **Central Park Antique Mall** (✉ 701 19th St., ☎ 661/633–1143), and the **Great American Antique Mall** (✉ 625 19th St., ☎ 661/322–1776) all have huge selections.

Dewar's Candy Shop (✉ 1120 Eye St., ☎ 661/322–0933) was founded in 1909 and has been owned by the Dewar family ever since. Try the hand-dipped chocolate cherries and the Dewar's Chews, a mouthwatering taffy concoction available in peanut butter, peppermint, caramel, and almond. There's also an old-fashioned soda fountain.

Kernville

50 mi from Bakersfield, northeast on Hwy. 178 and north on Hwy. 155.

The wild and scenic Kern River, which flows through Kernville en route from Mount Whitney to Bakersfield, delivers some of the most exciting white-water rafting in the state. Kernville (population 1,200) rests in a mountain valley on both banks of the river, and also at the northern tip of Lake Isabella (a dammed portion of the river used as a reservoir and for recreation). A center for rafting outfitters, Kernville has lodgings, restaurants, and antiques shops. The main streets are lined with Old West–style buildings, reflecting Kernville's heritage as a rough-and-tumble gold-mining town known as Whiskey Flat. (Present-day Kernville dates from the 1950s, when it was moved upriver to make room for Lake Isabella). The scenic road from Bakersfield winds between the rushing river on one side and sheer granite cliffs on the other.

Dining and Lodging

$–$$ ✕ **Robin's River Restaurant.** This down-home restaurant serves up some of the best food in town. The hamburgers and fried chicken are the stars of the show—along with the colorful talk from the locals, who drop in for biscuits and gravy or meat loaf. Don't miss the freshly baked pastries, pies, and cobblers. *✉ 13423 Sierra Way, ☎ 760/376–4663. DC, MC, V.*

$ ✕ **That's Italian.** For Northern Italian cuisine in a typical trattoria atmosphere, this is the spot. Try the chicken marsala stuffed with prosciutto and mozzarella or the pasta with clams, mussels, calamari, and white fish in a red or white clam sauce. *✉ 9 Big Blue Rd., ☎ 760/376–6020. AE, D, MC, V. No lunch Nov.–Apr.*

$$–$$$ **Whispering Pines Lodge.** Located on the banks of the Kern River, this inn features rustic cottages and bungalows. Some accommodations have full kitchens, fireplaces, and whirlpool tubs; all have refrigerators, coffeemakers, and cable TV. *✉ 13745 Sierra Way, 93238, ☎ 760/376–3733, FAX 760/376–6513. 17 rooms. Pool. AE, D, MC, V. BP.*

$–$$ **River View Lodge.** This rustic motel has knotty-pine walls and compact but clean rooms, some with microwaves and VCRs. And yes, many units do have river views. Picnic and barbecue facilities are in the tree-shaded yard. ✉ *2 Sirretta St., off Kernville Rd., 93238,* ☎ *760/376–6019,* FAX *760/376–4147. 10 rooms. No-smoking rooms, refrigerators. AE, DC, MC, V. CP.*

Outdoor Activities and Sports

BOATING, FISHING, AND WINDSURFING

The Lower Kern River, which extends from Lake Isabella to Bakersfield and beyond, is open for fishing year-round. Catches include rainbow trout, catfish, smallmouth bass, crappie, and bluegill. Lake Isabella is popular with anglers, water skiers, sailors, and windsurfers. Its shoreline marinas—**French Gulch Marina** (☎ 760/379–8774), **Red's Kern Valley Marina** (☎ 760/379–1634 or 800/553–7337), and **Dean's North Fork Marina** (☎ 760/376–1812)—have boats for rent, bait and tackle, and moorings year-round.

WHITE-WATER RAFTING

The three sections of the **Kern River**—known as the Lower Kern, Upper Kern, and the Forks—add up to nearly 50 mi of white water, ranging from Class I to Class V (easy to expert). The Lower and Upper Kern are the most popular and accessible sections. Organized trips can last from one hour (for as little as $15) to two days and more. Rafting season generally runs from late spring until the end of summer. Outfitters include **Chuck Richards Whitewater** (☎ 760/379–4444), **Kern River Tours** (☎ 760/379–4616), **Mountain & River Adventures** (☎ 760/376–6553 or 800/861–6553), and **Sierra South** (☎ 760/376–3745 or 800/457–2082).

THE SAN JOAQUIN VALLEY A TO Z

Arriving and Departing

By Bus

Greyhound (☎ 800/231–2222) stops in Stockton, Modesto, Merced, Fresno, Visalia, and Bakersfield.

By Car

To drive to the San Joaquin Valley from San Francisco, take I–80 east to I–580, and I–580 east to I–5, which leads south into the Valley (several roads from I–5 head east to Highway 99); or continue east on I–580 to I–205, which leads to I–5 north to Stockton or (via Highway 120) east to Highway 99 at Manteca. To reach the Valley from Los Angeles, follow I–5 north; Highway 99 veers north about 15 mi after entering the Valley.

By Plane

Fresno Air Terminal (✉ 5175 E. Clinton Way, ☎ 559/498–4095) is serviced by America West Express, American and American Eagle, Skywest, United Express, and US Airways Express. **Kern County Airport at Meadows Field** (✉ 1401 Skyway Dr., Bakersfield, ☎ 661/393–7990) is serviced by American and American Eagle, America West Express, Skywest-Delta, and United Express. United Express flies from San Francisco to **Modesto City Airport** (✉ 617 Airport Way, ☎ 209/577–5318) and **Visalia Municipal Airport** (✉ 9500 Airport Dr., ☎ 559/738–3201). *See* Air Travel *in* Smart Travel Tips A to Z for airline phone numbers.

By Train

Amtrak's (☎ 800/872–7245) daily *San Joaquin* trains travel between San Jose, Oakland, and Bakersfield, stopping in Stockton, Riverbank (near Modesto), Merced, Fresno, and Hanford. Amtrak Thruway bus service connects Bakersfield with Los Angeles.

Getting Around

By Bus

Greyhound (☎ 800/231–2222) provides service between major Valley cities. **Orange Belt Stages** (☎ 800/266–7433) provides bus service, including Amtrak connections, to many Valley locations, including Stockton, Merced, Madera, Fresno, Hanford, and Bakersfield.

By Car

Highway 99 is the main route between the Valley's major cities and towns. Interstate 5 runs roughly parallel to it to the west, but misses the major population centers; its main use is for quick access from San Francisco or Los Angeles. Major roads that connect I–5 with Highway 99 are Highways 120 (to Manteca), 132 (to Modesto), 140 (to Merced), 152 (to Chowchilla, via Los Banos), 198 (to Hanford and Visalia), and 58 (to Bakersfield).

Contacts and Resources

Car Rentals

All the major car rental agencies except Alamo have outlets in the San Joaquin Valley. *See* Car Rental *in* Smart Travel Tips A to Z for company phone numbers.

Emergencies

Ambulance (☎ 911). **Fire** (☎ 911). **Police** (☎ 911).

Guided Tours

Central Valley Tours (✉ 1869 E. Everglade Ave., Fresno 93720, ☎ 559/323–5552) provides general and customized tours of the Fresno area and the Valley. **Kings River Expeditions** (✉ 211 N. Van Ness Ave., Fresno, ☎ 559/233–4881 or 800/846–3674) arranges white-water rafting trips on the Kings River. Contact **River Journey** (✉ 14842 Orange Blossom Rd., Oakdale, ☎ 209/847–4671 or 800/292–2938) and **Sunshine River Adventures** (✉ Box 1445, Oakdale 95361, ☎ 209/848–4800 or 800/829–7238) to raft the Stanislaus River.

Visitor Information

Fresno City & County Convention and Visitors Bureau (✉ 808 M St., 93721, ☎ 559/233–0836 or 800/788–0836). **Greater Bakersfield Convention & Visitors Bureau** (✉ 1325 P St., 93301, ☎ 661/325–5051 or 800/325–6001). **Hanford Visitor Agency** (✉ 200 Santa Fe Ave., Suite D, 93230, ☎ 559/582–5024). **Kern County Board of Trade** (✉ 2101 Oak St., Bakersfield 93302, ☎ 661/861–2367 or 800/500–5376). **Merced Conference and Visitors Bureau** (✉ 690 W. 16th St., 95340, ☎ 209/384–3333 or 800/446–5353). **Modesto Convention and Visitors Bureau** (✉ 1114 J St., 95353, ☎ 209/571–6480). **Stockton/San Joaquin Convention and Visitors Bureau** (✉ 46 W. Fremont St., Stockton 95202, ☎ 209/943–1987 or 800/350–1987). **Visalia Convention and Visitors Bureau** (✉ 301 E. Acequia, 93291, ☎ 559/738–3435 or 800/524–0303).

9 MONTEREY BAY

FROM SANTA CRUZ TO CARMEL VALLEY

The Monterey Peninsula is steeped in history. The town of Monterey was California's first capital, the Carmel Mission headquarters for California's mission system. The peninsula also has a rich literary past. John Steinbeck's novels immortalized the area in *Cannery Row,* and Robert Louis Stevenson strolled its streets, gathering inspiration for *Treasure Island.* The present is equally illustrious. Blessed with a natural splendor undiminished by time or commerce, the peninsula is home to high-tech marine habitats and luxurious resorts.

Updated by John Andrew Vlahides

THE OHLONE INDIANS SETTLED IN THE MONTEREY AREA about 2,500 years ago, the first Native American people to build a community that centered on the region's maritime bounty. In 1542, Monterey Bay's white-sand beaches, pine forests, and rugged coastline captivated explorer Juan Rodríguez Cabrillo, who claimed it for Spain. Spanish missionaries, Mexican rulers, and land developers would come and go, all of them, perhaps, instinctively knowing not to destroy the peninsula's natural assets or historical sites.

The region has never relied solely on its looks, however. You can't ignore its deep green forests of Monterey cypress—oddly gnarled trees that grow naturally nowhere else—its aquamarine waters, or the dance of cloud shadows upon its rolling emerald hills and winsome meadows. Yet there are industrial, and a bit messy, claims to fame—whaling and sardines. And the meticulously preserved adobe houses and missions, layers of a Spanish and Mexican past left remarkably undisturbed, create a terra-cotta skyline that testifies to the Monterey Peninsula's singular place in California history.

With the arrival of Father Junípero Serra and Commander Don Gaspar de Portola from Spain in 1770, Monterey became the military and ecclesiastical capital of Alta California (the Spanish-held territory north of present-day Baja California, in Mexico). Portola established the first of California's four Spanish presidios. Serra founded the second of 21 Franciscan missions, later moving it from Monterey to Carmel.

Century magazine, whose publisher was a major booster of California, printed in the 1890s the reflections of Brigida Briones, a Monterey resident during the days of Spanish and Mexican rule. "The ladies of Monterey in 1827," she wrote, "were rarely seen in the street, except very early in the morning on their way to church. . . . The *rebozo* (shawl) and the petticoat being black, always of cheap stuff. . . . All classes wore the same; the padres told us that we must never forget that all ranks of men and women were equal in the presence of the Creator." Briones writes elsewhere in the magazine about the participants at a carnival ball held in 1829, "all on horseback and full of gaiety and youthfulness such as only a race that lives outdoors in such a climate as California, and without cares or troubles, can show."

Modern historians might argue that equality for all was more theory than practice for many in Briones's class. The ladies may have led a carefree life at this time, but their husbands were caught up in the conflict between Mexico and the United States for control of California—with both nations casting a wary eye on England, which was thought to have designs on the region as well. Captain John Charles Fremont of the United States wrote later that "the men who understood the future of our country . . . regarded the California coast as the boundary fixed by nature to round off our national domain . . . it was naturally separated from Mexico, and events pointed to its sure and near political separation."

The Mexican government, which was formed in 1822 when Mexico revolted against Spain, disputed these notions about Alta California's natural and political separation from the rest of Mexico, but between the time of Mexican independence and the mid-1840s, Monterey had changed. It had grown into a lively seaport that drew many Yankee sea traders. By July 7, 1846, when Commodore John Sloat raised the American flag over the Custom House and claimed California for the United States, many Monterey-area residents supported the U.S. cause.

Economics was a major factor. The majority of Monterey's businessmen felt that being under the Yankee umbrella would be far more profitable than being aligned with Mexico. Their hunch proved correct, at least for them. For the Ohlone Indian population, the transition was disastrous: state and federal laws passed during the first half-century of U.S. rule divested them of rights and property granted under Spanish and Mexican rule.

California's constitution was framed in Monterey's Colton Hall, but the town was all but forgotten once gold was discovered at Sutter's Mill on the American River. After the gold rush, the state capital moved to Sacramento, while Monterey became a sleepy backwater—though the whaling industry boomed in the last half of the 19th century and thrived until the early 1900s.

As the 20th century dawned, the Monterey Peninsula had begun to draw tourists with the opening of the Del Monte Hotel, the most palatial resort the West Coast had ever seen. Writers and artists such as John Steinbeck (1902–1968), Henry Miller (1891–1980), Robinson Jeffers (1887–1962), and Ansel Adams (1902–1984) also discovered the peninsula, adding their legacy to the region while capturing its magic on canvas, paper, and film. In the 1920s and 1930s Cannery Row's sardine industry took off, but by the late 1940s and early 1950s the fish had disappeared. The causes are still in dispute, though overfishing, water contamination, and a change in ocean currents that lowered the area's water temperature were the likely culprits. Sardines were packed again in 1995 in nearby Salinas for the first time since the 1950s. Visitors can buy them on Cannery Row, where activity has returned in the form of renovated buildings that house shops, restaurants, hotels, and the Monterey Bay Aquarium.

All aspects of the peninsula's diverse cultural and maritime heritage can be felt today, from Monterey's 19th-century buildings to its busy harbor and wharf. Modern-day attractions include the Monterey Jazz Festival and the Monterey Bay National Marine Sanctuary—the nation's largest undersea canyon, bigger and deeper than the Grand Canyon. The sanctuary supports a rich brew of marine life, from fat, barking sea lions to tiny, plantlike anemones. Annual events and festivities such as Pacific Grove's Butterfly Parade, the Carmel Shakespeare Festival, and Monterey's Christmas in the Adobes pay tribute to old traditions and link the past with the present.

Pleasures and Pastimes

Dining

Monterey is the richest area for dining along the coast between San Francisco and Los Angeles. The surrounding waters abound with fish, wild game roams the foothills, and the inland valleys are the vegetable basket of California; nearby Castroville dubs itself the Artichoke Capital of the World. Except at beachside stands and the inexpensive eateries listed below, casual but attractive resort wear is the norm. The few places where more formal attire is required are noted.

CATEGORY	COST*
$$$$	over $50
$$$	$30–$50
$$	$20–$30
$	under $20

**per person for a three-course meal, excluding drinks, service, and 7¼%–8¼% tax*

Golf

Since the opening of the Del Monte Golf Course in 1897, golf has been an integral part of the Monterey Peninsula's social and recreational scene. Pebble Beach's championship courses host prestigious tournaments, and though the greens fees at these courses can run well over $200, elsewhere on the peninsula you'll find less expensive—but still challenging and scenic—options. Many hotels will help with golf reservations or have golf packages; inquire when you book your room.

Lodging

Monterey-area accommodations range from no-frills motels and historic hotels to upscale establishments that are a bit impersonal and clearly designed for conventions. Others pamper the individual traveler in grand style, especially some of the area's small inns and bed-and- breakfasts, many of which provide full breakfasts and afternoon or early evening wine and hors d'oeuvres. Pacific Grove has quietly turned itself into the region's B&B capital; Carmel also has fine B&Bs. More luxurious are the resorts in exclusive Pebble Beach and some of those in pastoral Carmel Valley. The rates below are for two people in the high season, from April through October. Rates during winter, especially at the larger hotels, may drop by 50% or more, and B&Bs often offer midweek specials in the off-season. Bear in mind that all categories of the area's lodging are expensive, and most properties require a two-night stay on weekends. If you book through Monterey's 800/555–9283 number, or through its Web site, www.gomonterey.org, request an informational brochure and discount coupons that are good at restaurants, attractions, and shops.

CATEGORY	COST*
$$$$	over $175
$$$	$120–$175
$$	$80–$120
$	under $80

**All prices are for a standard double room, excluding 10%–10½% tax.*

[web icon] following the text of a review is your signal that the property has a Web site, where you will find details and, usually, images; for a link, visit www.fodors.com/urls.

Whale-Watching

On their annual migration between the Bering Sea and Baja California, thousands of gray whales pass by not far off the Monterey coast. They are sometimes visible through binoculars from shore, but a whale-watching cruise is the best way to get a close look at these magnificent 45-ft mammals. The migration south takes place between December and March. January is prime viewing time. The migration north occurs between March and June. In addition, some 2,000 blue whales and 600 humpbacks pass the coast and are easily spotted in late summer and early fall. Smaller numbers of minke whales, orcas, sperm whales, and fin whales have been sighted in mid-August. Even if no whales surface, bay cruises almost always encounter some unforgettable marine life, including sea otters, sea lions, and porpoises.

Exploring Monterey Bay

The individual charms of the towns here complement Monterey Bay's natural beauty. Santa Cruz sits at the northern tip of the crescent formed by Monterey Bay; the Monterey Peninsula, including Monterey, Pacific Grove, and Carmel, occupies the southern end. In between, Highway 1 cruises along the coastline, passing windswept beaches piled high with sand dunes. Along the route are artichoke fields and the towns of Watsonville and Castroville.

Numbers in the text correspond to numbers in the margin and on the Monterey Bay, Monterey and Pacific Grove, and Carmel and 17-Mile Drive maps.

Great Itineraries

Despite its compact size, the Monterey Peninsula is packed with diversions. If you have an interest in California history and historic preservation, the place to start is Monterey, with its adobe buildings along the downtown Path of History. Fans of Victorian architecture will want to search out the many fine examples in Pacific Grove. In Carmel you can shop till you drop, and when summer and weekend hordes overwhelm the town's clothing boutiques, art galleries, housewares outlets, and gift shops, you can slip off to enjoy the coast.

IF YOU HAVE 3 DAYS

Start at the far end of Cannery Row in **Monterey** ②–⑲ with a visit to the **Monterey Bay Aquarium** ⑲. Have lunch there or at one of the restaurants on Cannery Row. As you walk Cannery Row, stop at **Steinbeck's Spirit of Monterey Wax Museum** ⑯ or the **Wing Chong Building** ⑱, then continue on foot via the oceanfront recreation trail to **Fisherman's Wharf** ⑬ to enjoy the sights and catch the sunset. If you're not up to the hubbub along the wharf, slip into the serene bar at the Monterey Plaza Hotel and Spa. On the following day, visit the **Larkin House** ⑥, **Cooper-Molera Adobe** ⑦, **Stevenson House** ⑧, and other historic Monterey buildings, stopping for lunch when the need hits. Then pick up some late-afternoon snacks and motor through **17-Mile Drive** ㉕–㉙. Linger for sunset views along 17-Mile Drive or at nearby **Point Lobos State Reserve** ㉞. On the third day, drive to **Carmel** ㉚–㉝. Visit the **Carmel Mission** ㉛ and have lunch while browsing through the Ocean Avenue shopping area before stopping (if open) at **Tor House** ㉜, the residence of the late poet Robinson Jeffers. No matter what time of year you visit Monterey Bay, stroll over to Scenic Road and spend time on Carmel Beach before leaving the area.

IF YOU HAVE 5 DAYS

On your first three days, visit **Monterey** ②–⑲, stopping at the **Custom House** ②, **Larkin House** ⑥, **Cooper-Molera Adobe** ⑦, **Stevenson House** ⑧, and **Colton Hall** ⑨ on day one. On your second morning, get a visceral feel for Monterey Bay marine life by boarding a whale-watching or other cruise vessel at **Fisherman's Wharf** ⑬. Have lunch at the wharf upon your return, and then visit Cannery Row for **Steinbeck's Spirit of Monterey Wax Museum** ⑯ and the **Wing Chong Building** ⑱. On day three, tour the **Monterey Bay Aquarium** ⑲, have lunch along Cannery Row, and then spend the rest of the afternoon either enjoying the Monterey waterfront or tasting wine at Ventana Vineyards on the Monterey–Salinas Highway. On your fourth day, visit **Carmel Mission** ㉛ and **Tor House** ㉜ and have lunch while exploring the shops along Ocean Avenue in Carmel. Pick up some late-afternoon snacks for a spin on **17-Mile Drive** ㉕–㉙. Catch the sunset along 17-Mile Drive or at nearby **Point Lobos State Reserve** ㉞. On day five, explore the shoreline and Victorian houses of **Pacific Grove** ⑳–㉔. If you have time, visit **San Juan Bautista** ㊲, a classic mission village 35 mi from Monterey (take Highway 1 to Highway 156).

When to Tour Monterey Bay

Summer is peak season, with crowds everywhere and generally mild weather. A sweater or windbreaker is nearly always necessary along the coast, where a cool breeze usually blows and fog is on the way in

Monterey Bay

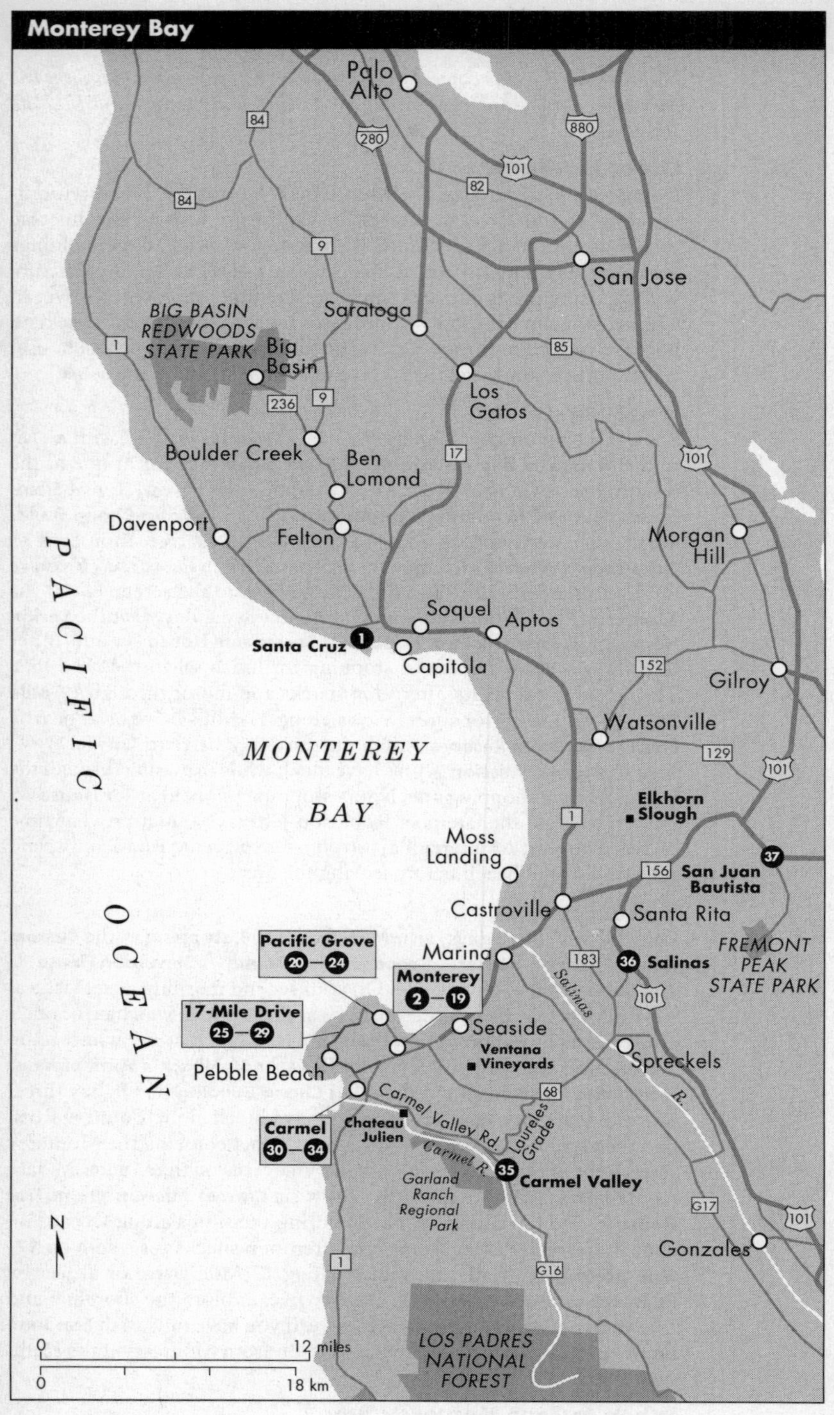

or out. Inland, temperatures in Salinas or Carmel Valley can be a good 15 or 20 degrees warmer than those in Carmel and Monterey. Off-season, from November through April, fewer people visit and the mood is more introspective. Rains fall heaviest in January and February. Most of the sights in Monterey are open daily.

MONTEREY BAY

Santa Cruz to Carmel Valley

Set along a 90-mi crescent of coastline like jewels in a tiara, the towns of Monterey Bay combine the somewhat funky, beachcomber aspects of California's culture with the state's more refined tendencies. Past and present merge gracefully here. As the city of Monterey's first mayor, Carmel Martin, described it early in the 20th century: "Monterey Bay is the one place where people can live without being disturbed by manufacturing and big factories. I am certain that the day is coming when this will be the most desirable place in the whole state of California."

Santa Cruz

❶ *74 mi south of San Francisco, I–280 to Hwy. 17 to Hwy. 1; 48 mi north of Monterey on Hwy. 1.*

The beach town of Santa Cruz is sheltered by the surrounding mountains to the north and south from the coastal fog and from the smoggy skies of the San Francisco Bay Area. The climate here is mild, and it is usually warmer and sunnier than elsewhere along the coast this far north. A haven for those opting out of the rat race and a bastion of 1960s-style counterculture values, Santa Cruz has been at the forefront of such very Californian trends as health food, recycling, and environmentalism. The heart of the downtown area is along Pacific Avenue, where you'll find shops, restaurants, and other establishments in the outdoor **Pacific Garden Mall.** Although it remains less manicured than its upmarket neighbors to the south, Santa Cruz is more urban than the agricultural towns between it and the Monterey Peninsula. Nearby Capitola, Soquel, and Aptos are home to some quality restaurants, small inns, resorts, and antiques shops.

The town gets some of its youthful spirit from the nearby **University of California at Santa Cruz.** The school's harmonious redwood buildings are perched on the forested hills above the town, and the campus is tailor-made for the contemplative life, with a juxtaposition of sylvan settings and sweeping vistas over open meadows onto the bay. ✉ *Bay and High Sts.,* ☏ *831/459–0111.*

Santa Cruz has been a seaside resort since the mid-19th century. The Looff carousel and classic wooden Giant Dipper roller-coaster at the ★ **Santa Cruz Beach Boardwalk** date from the early 1900s. Elsewhere along the boardwalk, the Casino Fun Center has its share of video-game technology. But this is still primarily a place for good old-fashioned fun for toddlers, teens, and adults. Take a break from the rides with boardwalk favorites such as corn dogs or chowder fries. ✉ *Along Beach St. west from San Lorenzo River,* ☏ *831/423–5590 or 831/426–7433.* *$21.95 (day pass for unlimited rides).* ⏲ *Memorial Day–Labor Day, 11–11; rest of yr, weekends only, weather permitting (call for hrs).*

The **Santa Cruz Municipal Wharf,** just up the beach from the Boardwalk, is lined with restaurants, shops, and seafood takeout windows. The barking and baying of sea lions that lounge in heaps under the wharf's pilings enliven the area. Down the West Cliff Drive promontory at **Seal Rock,** pinnipeds hang out, sunbathe, and occasionally frolic.

The **Mark Abbott Memorial Lighthouse,** southwest of the wharf, has a surfing museum with artifacts that include the remains of a board a shark munched on. ✉ *W. Cliff Dr.,* ☎ *831/420–6289.* *Free.* *Museum Thurs.–Mon. noon–4.*

West of the lighthouse is secluded **Natural Bridges State Beach,** a stretch of soft sand with tidal pools and a natural rock bridge nearby. From October to early March a colony of monarch butterflies resides here. ✉ *2531 W. Cliff Dr.,* ☎ *831/423–4609.* *$3 parking fee.* *Park 8 AM–sunset. Visitor center Oct.–Feb., daily 10–4; Mar.–Sept., weekends 10–4.*

Dining and Lodging

$$–$$$ ★ ✕ **Bittersweet Bistro.** An old tavern houses the popular bistro of chef-owner Thomas Vinolus. Start with a pizzetta or a mesclun salad, then move on to a grilled vegetable platter, a seafood puttanesca, or grilled lamb tenderloins. Finish with any of the chocolate desserts. ✉ *787 Rio Del Mar Blvd., off Hwy. 1, Aptos,* ☎ *831/662–9799. AE, MC, V. Closed Mon. No lunch Sat.–Tues.*

$$–$$$ ★ ✕ **Chez Renee.** The husband-and-wife team that owns this redwood-shaded retreat cooks and serves French-inspired cuisine. Specialties include sweetbreads with marsala sauce, duck with home-preserved brandied cherries, and sea scallops garnished with smoked salmon and dill. Save room for the excellent dessert soufflés. ✉ *9051 Soquel Dr., Aptos,* ☎ *831/688–5566. MC, V. Closed Sun.–Mon. No lunch Tues. and Sat.*

$$–$$$ ✕ **Oswald's.** Intimate and stylish, this tiny courtyard bistro serves a sophisticated yet unpretentious menu of Mediterranean-inspired dishes such as sherry-steamed mussels, and sautéed veal livers. ✉ *1547 Pacific Ave.,* ☎ *831/423–7427. Reservations essential on weekends. AE, DC, MC, V. Closed Mon. dinner.*

$$–$$$ ✕ **Pearl Alley Bistro.** Every local's top choice, this bustling bistro changes its menu monthly to focus on a particular country's cuisine. Book a table in advance, or sit at the marble-top bar, and meet the bon vivants of Santa Cruz. ✉ *110 Pearl Alley (off Walnut Ave.),* ☎ *831/429–8070. Reservations essential. AE, MC, V.*

$–$$$ ✕ **El Palomar.** The restaurant of the Palomar Hotel has well-preserved Spanish architecture with vaulted ceilings, wood beams, and an atrium that opens up in warm weather. Among the best Tex-Mex dishes are ceviche tostadas, chili verde, and fish tacos. The attractive taco bar, off to one side, is open all day. ✉ *1336 Pacific Ave.,* ☎ *831/425–7575. Reservations not accepted for Fri.–Sat. dinner. AE, D, DC, MC, V.*

$–$$$ ✕ **Gabriella Café.** In a small brown stucco building, this café is intimate without being stuffy. The seasonal Italian menu highlights local organic produce. Watch for such dishes as steamed mussels, braised lamb shank, and grilled Portobello mushrooms. ✉ *910 Cedar St.,* ☎ *831/457–1677. AE, DC, MC, V.*

$–$$ ✕ **Dolphin Restaurant.** Occupying a scenic site at the end of the Municipal Wharf, this small, weather-beaten restaurant serves filling breakfasts—hotcakes, French toast, omelets—plus seafood lunches and dinners. For a quick bowl of chowder or plate of fish and chips, visit the adjacent takeout window. ✉ *At the end of Santa Cruz Municipal Wharf,* ☎ *831/426–5830. MC, V.*

$–$$ ✕ **Positively Front Street.** Seafood chowder, steamed clams, and oysters on the half shell are among the seafood entrées at this lively bar and fish house near the wharf. It also serves pizza and burgers to the beach and boardwalk crowd. ✉ *44 Front St.,* ☎ *831/426–1944. AE, MC, V.*

$ ✕ **Zachary's.** With its mostly young clientele, this noisy café defines the funky essence of Santa Cruz. It also dishes up great breakfasts: omelettes, sourdough pancakes, artichoke frittatas, and Mike's Mess—eggs scrambled with bacon, mushrooms, and home fries, then topped with sour cream, melted cheese, and fresh tomatoes. ✉ *819 Pacific Ave.,* ☎ *831/427–0646. Reservations not accepted. MC, V. No dinner. Closed Mon.*

$$$$ **Inn at Depot Hill.** This inventively designed B&B in a former rail depot sees itself as a link to the era of luxury train travel. Each double room or suite, complete with fireplace and feather beds, is inspired by a different destination— Italy's Portofino, France's Côte d'Azur, Japan's Kyoto. One suite is decorated like a Pullman car for a railroad baron. Some accommodations have private patios with hot tubs. All are no-smoking. ✉ *250 Monterey Ave. (Box 1934), Capitola-by-the-Sea 95010,* ☎ *831/462–3376 or 800/572–2632,* FAX *831/462–3697. 6 rooms, 6 suites. In-room data ports, in-room VCRs, hot tub. AE, D, MC, V. BP.*

$$$$ **Seascape Resort.** On a bluff overlooking Monterey Bay, Seascape is a place to unwind. The spacious all-suite units sleep from two to six people, and each has a kitchenette, a fireplace, and an ocean-view patio with a barbecue grill. The resort is about 9 mi south of Santa Cruz. ✉ *1 Seascape Resort Dr., Aptos 95003,* ☎ *831/688–6800 or 800/929–7727,* FAX *831/685–2753. 285 suites. Restaurant, in-room data ports, room service, 3 pools, 3 hot tubs, spa, sauna, golf privileges, health club, beach, children's programs, laundry service, convention center, meeting rooms. AE, D, DC, MC, V.*

$$$$ **WestCoast Santa Cruz Hotel.** Within a short stroll of the boardwalk and wharf, this resort opens right onto Cowell Beach. Though the hotel is a monolithic concrete structure, all rooms have private balconies or patios overlooking the Pacific. If it's too cold to swim in the ocean, you can head for the heated swimming pool and tub. Children under 12 stay free in their parents' room. ✉ *175 W. Cliff Dr., Santa Cruz 95060,* ☎ *831/426–4330 or 800/426–0670,* FAX *831/427–2025. 147 rooms, 16 suites. Restaurant, 2 bars, refrigerators, room service, pool, 2 hot tubs, laundry service. AE, D, DC, MC, V.*

$$$–$$$$ **Babbling Brook Inn.** Though smack in the middle of Santa Cruz, the lush gardens, running stream, and tall trees of this B&B make you feel as though you are in a secluded wood. Most rooms have fireplaces (though a few are electric) and private patios; some have Jacuzzi tubs. Complimentary wine, cheese, and fresh-baked cookies are available in the afternoon. ✉ *1025 Laurel St., 95060,* ☎ *831/427–2456 or 800/866–1131,* FAX *831/427–2457. 13 rooms. AE, DC, MC, V. BP.*

$$$–$$$$ **Inn at Manresa Beach.** Ansel Adams once occupied the 1867 mansion that Brian Denny and Susan Van Horn moved to a country setting about 10 mi south of Santa Cruz. The rooms in their comfortable B&B, which are all no-smoking and have nature-theme decor, contain gas fireplaces; most have whirlpool baths. ✉ *1258 San Andreas Rd., La Selva Beach 95076,* ☎ *831/728–1000 or 888/523–2244,* FAX *831/728–8294. 9 rooms. In-room VCRs, 2 tennis courts, volleyball. AE, D, MC, V. No smoking indoors. BP.*

$$$–$$$$ **Ocean Pacific Lodge.** By staying a few blocks from the beach, you can save money at this modern multistory motel with a heated pool and two hot tubs. ✉ *120 Washington St., 95060,* ☎ *831/457–1234 or 800/995–0289,* FAX *831/457–0861. 44 rooms, 13 suites. In-room VCRs, refrigerators, pool, 2 hot tubs, exercise room. AE, D, DC, MC, V. CP.*

$$–$$$ **Apple Lane Inn.** This small B&B offers modest accommodations in a century-old farmhouse decorated with country furniture. There is a working barn on the property with horses, goats, and geese. ✉ *6265 Soquel Dr., Aptos 95003,* ☎ *831/475–6868 or 800/649–8980,* FAX *831/464–5790. 5 rooms. AE, D, MC, V. BP.*

Nightlife and the Arts

Shakespeare Santa Cruz (✉ Performing Arts Complex, University of California at Santa Cruz, ☎ 831/459–2121) stages a six-week Shakespeare festival in July and August that also may include one modern work. Most performances are outdoors in the striking Redwood Glen. There is also a program around the holidays in December.

Outdoor Activities and Sports

BICYCLING

Bicycle Rental and Tour Center (✉ 131 Center St., ☎ 831/426–8687).

BOATS AND CHARTERS

Chardonnay Sailing Charters (☎ 831/423–1213) accommodates 49 passengers for year-round cruises on Monterey Bay aboard the 70-ft *Chardonnay II,* leaving from the yacht harbor in Santa Cruz. Reservations are essential. **Original Stagnaro Fishing Trips** (✉ center of Santa Cruz Municipal Wharf, ☎ 831/423–2010) operates salmon and rockcod fishing expeditions; the fees ($36–$40) include bait. The company also runs whale-watching cruises ($20) between December and April.

SURFING

Manresa State Beach (✉ Manresa Dr., La Selva Beach, ☎ 831/761–1795), south of Santa Cruz, has premium surfing conditions, but the currents can be treacherous. The surf at **New Brighton State Beach** (✉ 1500 State Park Dr., Capitola) is challenging; campsites are available. Surfers gather for the spectacular waves and sunsets at **Pleasure Point** (✉ East Cliff and Pleasure Point Drs.). **Steamer's Lane,** near the lighthouse on West Cliff Drive, has a decent break. The area plays host to several competitions in the summer.

Cowell's Beach 'n' Bikini Surf Shop (✉ 109 Beach St., ☎ 831/427–2355) rents surfboards and wet suits.

Monterey

48 mi south of Santa Cruz on Hwy. 1; 122 mi south of San Francisco on I–280 to Hwy. 17 to Hwy. 1; 334 mi north of Los Angeles on U.S. 101 to Hwy. 68 west from Salinas.

★ Much of Monterey's early history can be gleaned from the well-preserved adobe buildings of **Monterey State Historic Park** (☎ 831/649–7118). Far from being a hermetic period museum, the park facilities are an integral part of the day-to-day business life of the town—within some of the buildings are a store, a theater, and government offices. The 2-mi Path of History, marked by round gold tiles set into the sidewalk, passes by several landmark buildings. A $5 all-day park ticket gains you entrance to Casa Soberanes, the Cooper-Molera Adobe, the Larkin House, the Pacific House, and the Stevenson House (☞ *below*) and includes a selection of guided walking tours.

❷ The **Custom House,** an adobe structure built by the Mexican government in 1827—now California's oldest standing public building—was the first stop for sea traders whose goods were subject to duties. An upper story was later added. At the beginning of the Mexican-American War in 1846, Commodore John Sloat raised the American flag over the building and claimed California for the United States. The house's lower floor displays typical cargo from a 19th-century trading ship. ✉ *1 Custom House Plaza, across from Fisherman's Wharf,* ☎ *831/649–2909.* 🎫 *Free.* ⏲ *Daily 10–5.*

❸ The **Maritime Museum of Monterey** includes the private collection of maritime artifacts of Allen Knight, who was Carmel's mayor from 1950–52. Among the exhibits of ship models, scrimshaw items, and nauti-

Monterey and Pacific Grove

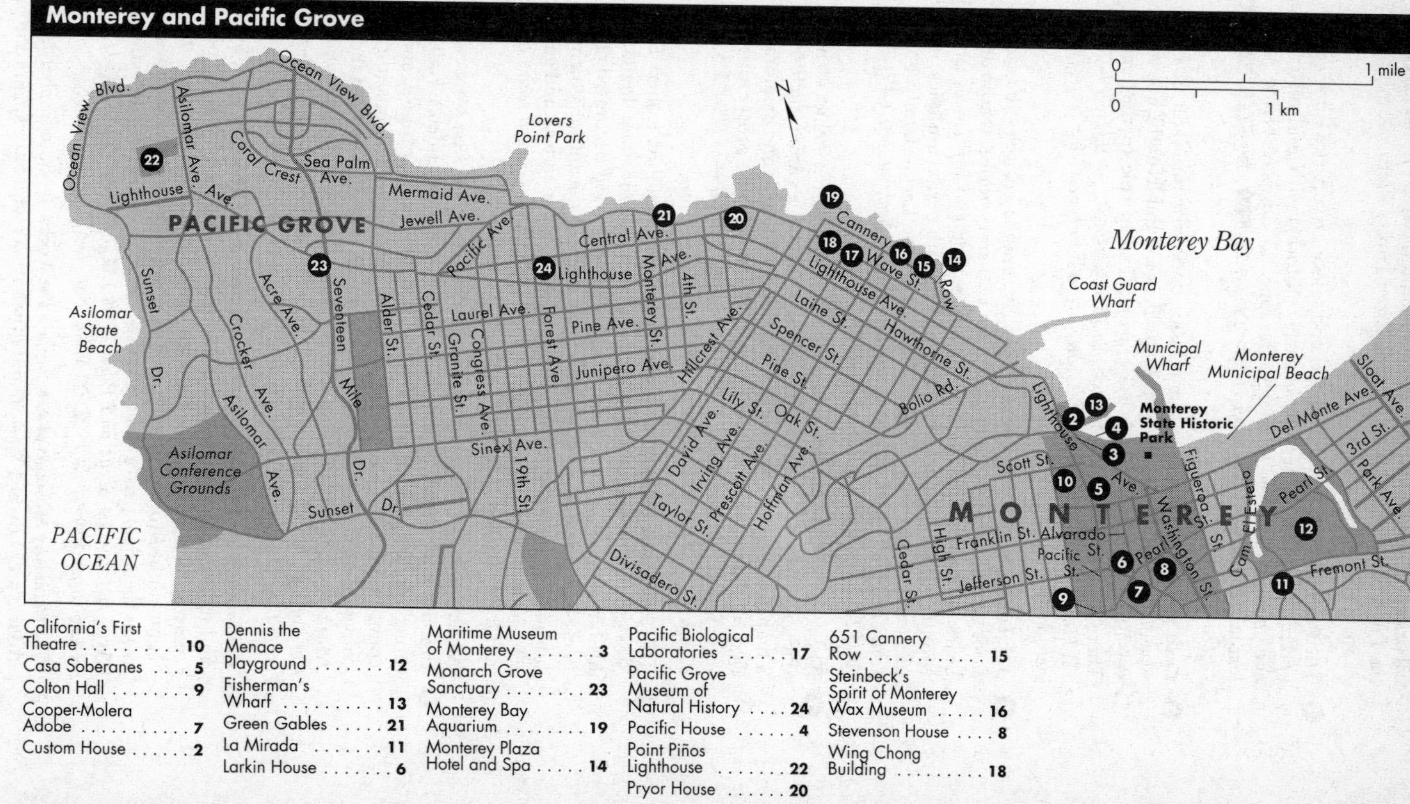

- California's First Theatre 10
- Casa Soberanes 5
- Colton Hall 9
- Cooper-Molera Adobe 7
- Custom House 2
- Dennis the Menace Playground 12
- Fisherman's Wharf 13
- Green Gables 21
- La Mirada 11
- Larkin House 6
- Maritime Museum of Monterey 3
- Monarch Grove Sanctuary 23
- Monterey Bay Aquarium 19
- Monterey Plaza Hotel and Spa 14
- Pacific Biological Laboratories 17
- Pacific Grove Museum of Natural History 24
- Pacific House 4
- Point Piños Lighthouse 22
- Pryor House 20
- 651 Cannery Row 15
- Steinbeck's Spirit of Monterey Wax Museum 16
- Stevenson House 8
- Wing Chong Building 18

cal prints, the highlight is the enormous multifaceted Fresnel lens from the Point Sur Light Station. ✉ *5 Custom House Plaza,* ☎ *831/375–2553.* 🎫 *$3.* ⏲ *Daily 10–5.*

4 The **Pacific House,** a former hotel and saloon, is a park visitor center and museum that surveys life in early California with gold-rush relics and photographs of old Monterey. The upper floor displays Native American artifacts. ✉ *10 Custom House Plaza,* ☎ *831/649–7118.* 🎫 *$2.* ⏲ *Daily 10–5.*

5 **Casa Soberanes,** a low-ceiling classic adobe structure built in 1842, was once a Custom House guard's residence. Exhibits at the house survey life in Monterey from the era of Mexican rule to the present. There's a peaceful garden in back. ✉ *336 Pacific St.,* ☎ *831/649–7118.* 🎫 *House $2, garden free.* ⏲ *Guided tours daily; call for times. Garden daily 8–5.*

6 The **Larkin House** was built in 1835. A veranda encircles the second floor of this architecturally significant two-story adobe, whose design bears witness to the Mexican and New England influences on the Monterey style. The rooms are furnished with period antiques, many of them brought from New Hampshire by the Larkin family. ✉ *510 Calle Principal, between Jefferson and Pacific Sts.,* ☎ *831/649–7118.* 🎫 *$2.* ⏲ *Guided tours daily; call for times.*

7 The restored **Cooper-Molera Adobe,** a 2-acre complex, includes a house dating from the 1820s, a visitor center, and a large garden enclosed by a high adobe wall. The mostly Victorian-era antiques and memorabilia that fill the house provide a glimpse into the life of a prosperous pioneer family. ✉ *Polk and Munras Sts.,* ☎ *831/649–7118.* 🎫 *$2.* ⏲ *Guided tours daily; call for times.*

8 The **Stevenson House** was named in honor of author Robert Louis Stevenson, who boarded here briefly in a tiny upstairs room. Items from his family's estate furnish Stevenson's room. Period-decorated chambers elsewhere in the house include a gallery of the author's memorabilia and a children's nursery stocked with Victorian toys and games. ✉ *530 Houston St.,* ☎ *831/649–7118.* 🎫 *$2.* ⏲ *Guided tours daily; call for times. Gardens daily 8–5.*

A convention of delegates met in 1849 to draft the first state constitution at **Colton Hall,** California's equivalent of Independence Hall. The
9 stone building, which has served as a school, a courthouse, and the county seat, is a museum furnished as it was during the constitutional convention. The extensive grounds outside the hall surround the Old Monterey Jail. ✉ *500 block of Pacific St., between Madison and Jefferson Sts.,* ☎ *831/646–5640.* 🎫 *Free.* ⏲ *Mar.–Oct., daily 10–noon and 1–5; Nov.–Feb., daily 10–noon and 1–4.*

10 **California's First Theatre** was constructed in the 1840s by Jack Swan, an English sailor who settled in Monterey, as a saloon with adjoining apartments. Soldiers from the New York Volunteers who were on assignment in Monterey put on plays in the building. Melodramas and other theatrical performances are still staged here (☞ Nightlife and the Arts, *below*). ✉ *Scott and Pacific Sts.,* ☎ *831/649–7118; 831/375–4916 (box office).* 🎫 *Free.* ⏲ *Wed.–Sat. 1–5.*

The **Monterey Museum of Art** displays the works of photographers Ansel Adams and Edward Weston and other artists who have spent time on the peninsula. Another focus is international folk art; the colorful collection ranges from Kentucky hearth brooms to Tibetan prayer wheels. ✉ *559 Pacific St., across from Colton Hall,* ☎ *831/372–7591.* 🎫 *$5.* ⏲ *Wed.–Sat. 11–5, Sun. 1–4.*

11 At **La Mirada,** Asian and European antiques fill a 19th-century adobe house. A newer 10,000-square-ft gallery space, designed by Charles Moore, houses Asian and Californian regional art and a large netsuke collection. Outdoors are magnificent rose and rhododendron gardens. ✉ *720 Via Mirada, at Fremont St.,* ☎ *831/372–3689.* *$5.* *Wed.–Sat. 11–5, Sun. 1–4.*

★ 12 El Estero Park's **Dennis the Menace Playground** (✉ Pearl St. and Camino El Estero) is an imaginative play area designed by local resident and cartoonist Hank Ketcham. The equipment is on a grand scale and made for daredevils; there's a roller slide, a clanking suspension bridge, and a real Southern Pacific steam locomotive. You can rent a rowboat or a paddleboat to cruise about U-shape Lake El Estero, home to a varied assortment of ducks, mud hens, and geese.

The mournful barking of sea lions draws visitors to Monterey's waterfront. The whiskered marine mammals are best enjoyed while walk-
13 ing along **Fisherman's Wharf,** an aging pier across from Custom House Plaza that's lined with souvenir shops, fish markets, seafood restaurants, and popcorn stands. Although most commercial fishermen have moved to Wharf No. 2, a five-minute walk away, Fisherman's Wharf, a lively and entertaining place to bring children, is still the departure point for fishing, diving, and whale-watching trips. The shallow waters of **Monterey Municipal Beach,** east of Wharf No. 2, are usually warm and calm enough for wading.

Cannery Row has undergone several transformations since it was immortalized in John Steinbeck's 1945 novel of the same name. The street that Steinbeck described was crowded with sardine canneries processing, at their peak, nearly 200,000 tons of the smelly silver fish a year. During the mid-1940s, however, the sardines disappeared from the bay, causing the canneries to close. Through the years the old tin-roof canneries have been converted into restaurants, art galleries, and malls with shops selling T-shirts, fudge, and plastic sea otters. Recent tourist development along the row has been more tasteful, however, and includes several stylish inns and hotels.

14 The **Monterey Plaza Hotel and Spa** (✉ 400 Cannery Row), on the site of a historic estate, is a good place to relax over a drink and watch for sea otters. Though John Steinbeck would have trouble recognizing Cannery Row today, wisps of its colorful past can still be detected. Check
15 out **651 Cannery Row.** Its tiled Chinese dragon roof dates from 1929.

16 Characters from the novel *Cannery Row* are depicted at **Steinbeck's Spirit of Monterey Wax Museum,** which presents an easy-to-digest 25-minute narration of 400 years of Monterey history, recorded by an actor playing John Steinbeck. ✉ *700 Cannery Row,* ☎ *831/375–3770.* *$6.95.* *Memorial Day–Labor Day, daily 10–9; Labor Day–Memorial Day, Mon.–Thurs. 11–5, Fri. and Sun. 10–8, Sat. 10–10.*

17 A weathered wooden building at 800 Cannery Row was the **Pacific Biological Laboratories** where Edward F. Ricketts, the inspiration for Doc
18 in *Cannery Row,* did much of his marine research. The **Wing Chong Building** (✉ 835 Cannery Row) is the former Wing Chong Market that Steinbeck called Lee Chong's Heavenly Flower Grocery in *Cannery Row.*

★ 19 The Outer Bay wing of the **Monterey Bay Aquarium** contains a million-gallon indoor ocean—observed through the largest window on Earth—that re-creates the sunlit blue water where Monterey Bay meets the open sea. In this habitat soupfin sharks, barracuda, pelagic stingrays, ocean sunfish (which can weigh several hundred pounds), green sea turtles, and schools of fast-moving tuna swim together. The Outer Bay wing also houses a mesmerizing collection (the largest in the nation) of jellyfish. Expect long lines and sizable crowds at the aquarium on weekends, especially during the summer, but it's worth it. Don't miss the original wing's three-story Kelp Forest exhibit, the only one of its kind in the world, or the display of the sea creatures and vegetation found in Monterey Bay. Among other standouts are a bat-ray petting pool where you can touch their velvetlike skin; a 55,000-gallon sea-otter tank; an enormous outdoor artificial tidal pool that supports anemones, crabs, sea stars, and other colorful creatures; and Splash Zone, a hands-on activity center geared especially to families with small children. ✉ *886 Cannery Row,* ☎ *831/648–4888; 800/756–3737 in CA for advance tickets.* *$15.95.* ⏲ *Daily 10–6 (9:30–6 in summer and major holiday periods).*

A short drive from downtown Monterey leads to **Ventana Vineyards,** known for chardonnays and Johannisberg rieslings. Ventana's knowledgeable and hospitable owners, Doug and LuAnn Meador, invite guests to bring lunch to eat while tasting wines on a patio. ✉ *2999 Monterey–Salinas Hwy. (Hwy. 68),* ☎ *831/372–7415.* ⏲ *Daily 11–5.*

OFF THE BEATEN PATH

ELKHORN SLOUGH – A few miles north of Monterey, east of the tiny harbor town of Moss Landing, is one of only two federal research reserves in California, the Elkhorn Slough at the National Estuarine Research Reserve. Its 1,400 acres of tidal flats and salt marshes form a complex environment that supports more than 200 species of birds. A walk along the meandering waterways and wetlands can reveal hawks, white-tailed kites, owls, herons, and egrets. Wander at your leisure, or take a guided walk (10 AM and 1 PM) to the heron rookery on weekends. ✉ *1700 Elkhorn Rd., Watsonville,* ☎ *831/728–2822.* *$2.50; free with any California hunting or fishing license.* ⏲ *Wed.–Sun. 9–5.*

Dining and Lodging

$$$–$$$$ ✕ **Fresh Cream.** The views of the bay are as superb as the imaginative French cuisine at this outstanding restaurant in Heritage Harbor. The menu, which changes weekly, might include rack of lamb Dijonnaise, roast boned duck in black-currant sauce, or blackened ahi tuna with pineapple rum-butter sauce. ✉ *99 Pacific St., Suite 100C,* ☎ *831/375–9798. Reservations essential. AE, D, DC, MC, V. No lunch.*

$$$–$$$$ ★ ✕ **Whaling Station Prime Steaks and Seafood.** A modern decor and lively atmosphere make this restaurant above Cannery Row a festive yet comfortable place to enjoy real USDA prime beef and fresh seafood. ✉ *763 Wave St.,* ☎ *831/373–3778. Reservations essential. AE, D, DC, MC, V. No lunch.*

$$$ ✕ **Duck Club.** The elegant and romantic dining room of the Monterey Plaza Hotel and Spa (☞ *below*) is built over the waterfront on Cannery Row. The dinner menu highlights inventive dishes such as pumpkin-seed-crusted halibut and air-dried, wood-roasted duck, and includes seafood, meat, and house-made pasta. It also serves breakfast. ✉ *400 Cannery Row,* ☎ *831/646–1706. AE, D, DC, MC, V. No lunch.*

$$–$$$ ✕ **Domenico's.** Italian seafood preparations, mesquite-grilled meats, and homemade pastas are the specialties at Domenico's. The nautical decor keeps the place comfortably casual; white drapery lends an air of elegance other wharf restaurants lack. ✉ *50 Fisherman's Wharf,* ☎ *831/372–3655. AE, D, DC, MC, V.*

$$–$$$ ✕ **Monterey's Fish House.** Casual yet stylish and away from the hubbub of the wharf, this always-packed seafood restaurant attracts locals and frequent travelers to the city. If the dining room is full, you can wait at the bar with deliciously plump oysters on the half shell. The bartenders and wait staff will gladly advise you on the perfect wine

to go with your poached, blackened, or oak-grilled seafood. ✉ *2114 Del Monte Ave.,* ☎ *831/373–4647. Reservations essential. AE, D, DC, MC, V. No lunch weekends.*

$$–$$$ ✕ **Montrio.** Style reigns at this trendy, eclectic downtown restaurant that was formerly Monterey's firehouse. Wrought-iron trellises, metal sculpture, and rawhide complement the artful presentations of California cuisine. Clean, strong flavors typify the cooking here. Grilled Portobello mushrooms with polenta and rotisserie chicken with garlic mashed potatoes are two of the menu highlights. ✉ *414 Calle Principal,* ☎ *831/648–8880. Reservations essential. AE, D, MC, V.*

$$–$$$ ★ ✕ **Stokes Adobe.** Chef Brandon Miller's restaurant, set inside an 1833 adobe, seamlessly balances innovative cooking and traditional design. Miller specializes in the cuisines of Provence, northern Italy, and Catalan Spain, turning out imaginative pasta, seafood, and vegetarian dishes that change with the seasons. His creations have included seared ahi tuna with lentil tomato salad, rustic pasta tubes with fennel sausage and Manila clams, and a vegetable napoleon of crêpes and house-made ricotta with smoked tomato sauce. ✉ *500 Hartnell St.,* ☎ *831/373–1110. Reservations essential. AE, DC, MC, V.*

$–$$$ ✕ **Abalonetti Seafood.** Squid is the specialty here: deep-fried, sautéed with wine and garlic, or baked with eggplant. Abalone is another highlight, and the fresh fish is broiled or blackened and served with beurre blanc or pesto. Next door, the Abalonetti Deli serves up antipasti and fried squid in casual surroundings. ✉ *57 Fisherman's Wharf,* ☎ *831/373–1851. AE, D, DC, MC, V.*

$–$$$ ✕ **Cafe Fina.** Mesquite-grilled fish dishes and linguine in clam sauce with baby shrimp and tomatoes are among the highlights at this understated Italian restaurant on the wharf. The wine list is extensive. ✉ *47 Fisherman's Wharf,* ☎ *831/372–5200. AE, D, DC, MC, V.*

$–$$$ ✕ **Paradiso Trattoria and Oyster Bar.** Follow the aroma of marinating olives, roasted garlic, and platters of focaccia to this bright Cannery Row establishment. Mediterranean specialties and pizzas from a wood-burning oven are the luncheon fare. Seafood is a good choice for dinner, served in a dining room overlooking a lighted beachfront or at a gleaming oyster bar. ✉ *654 Cannery Row,* ☎ *831/375–4155. AE, D, DC, MC, V.*

$–$$$ ✕ **Tarpy's Roadhouse.** Fun, dressed-down roadhouse lunch and dinner are served in this renovated farmhouse from the early 1900s. The kitchen cooks everything Mom used to make, only better. Eat indoors by a fireplace or outdoors in the courtyard. ✉ *2999 Monterey–Salinas Hwy. (Hwy. 68), at Canyon Del Rey Rd.,* ☎ *831/647–1444. Reservations essential. AE, D, MC, V.*

$ ✕ **India's Clay Oven** Serving Southern Indian fare, this second-floor restaurant features tandoori specialties and fiery curries, as well as an inexpensive lunchtime and weekend buffet. Family-owned and operated, the staff is gracious and attentive. ✉ *150 Del Monte Ave.,* ☎ *831/373–2529. AE, D, DC, MC, V.*

$ ✕ **Old Monterey Cafe.** Breakfast here, which is served until closing time (2:30 PM), might include fresh-baked muffins and eggs Benedict. Soups, salads, and sandwiches appear on the lunch menu. This is also a good place to relax with a cappuccino after touring Monterey's historic adobes. ✉ *489 Alvarado St.,* ☎ *831/646–1021. Reservations not accepted. D, MC, V. No dinner.*

$$$$ 🏨 **Embassy Suites.** As you drive into Monterey from the north on Highway 1, you can't miss the high-rise Embassy Suites, which towers over the town of Seaside just before the Monterey line. Two blocks from the beach, it has views of Laguna Grande Lake and Monterey Bay. All accommodations here are smallish two-room suites with microwaves, refrigerators, and coffeemakers. Complimentary cocktails are available each evening. ✉ *1441 Canyon Del Rey, Seaside 93955,* ☎ *831/393–1115,* FAX *831/393–1113. 225 suites. Restaurant, bar, kitchenettes, indoor pool, hot tub, sauna, exercise room, meeting room. AE, D, DC, MC, V. BP.*

$$$$ **Hotel Pacific.** All the rooms at this modern adobe-style hotel are junior suites, handsomely appointed with featherbeds, hardwood floors, fireplaces, and balconies or patios. The rates include breakfast and afternoon snacks. ✉ *300 Pacific St., 93940,* ☎ *831/373–5700 or 800/554–5542,* FAX *831/373–6921. 105 rooms. Minibars, refrigerators, 2 hot tubs, meeting rooms. AE, D, DC, MC, V. CP.*

$$$$ **Hyatt Regency Monterey.** Although its rooms and atmosphere are less glamorous than those at some other resorts in the region, the facilities here are very good. ✉ *1 Old Golf Course Rd., 93940,* ☎ *831/372–1234; 800/824–2196 in CA,* FAX *831/372–4277. 535 rooms, 40 suites. Restaurant, café, bar, 2 pools, 2 hot tubs, massage, 18-hole golf course, 6 tennis courts, exercise room, bicycles, children's programs, concierge, meeting rooms. AE, D, DC, MC, V.*

$$$$ **Monterey Bay Inn.** On Cannery Row, this hotel takes full advantage of its location on the water, even providing guests with binoculars for viewing marine life. Rooms have private balconies. ✉ *242 Cannery Row, 93940,* ☎ *831/373–6242 or 800/424–6242,* FAX *831/373–7603. 47 rooms. In-room VCRs, refrigerators, 2 hot tubs, sauna, exercise room, meeting rooms, free parking. AE, D, DC, MC, V. CP.*

$$$$ **Monterey Hotel.** Standard rooms in this restored Victorian are small but contain well-chosen reproduction antique furniture. The master suites have fireplaces and oval bathtubs. ✉ *406 Alvarado St., 93940,* ☎ *831/375–3184 or 800/727–0960,* FAX *831/373–2899. 39 rooms, 6 suites. AE, D, DC, MC, V. CP.*

$$$$ ★ **Monterey Plaza Hotel and Spa.** This sophisticated full-service hotel commands a waterfront location on Cannery Row, where frolicking sea otters can be observed from the wide outdoor patio and many room balconies. The architecture and decor blend early Californian and Mediterranean styles and retain elements of the old cannery design. The property is meticulously maintained and offers a variety of accommodations from simple to luxurious. Guests have use of a new full-service rooftop spa facility. ✉ *400 Cannery Row, 93940,* ☎ *831/646–1700 or 800/631–1339; 800/334–3999 in CA;* FAX *831/646–0285. 285 rooms, 3 suites. 2 restaurants, minibars, room service, spa, exercise room, laundry service, concierge, meeting rooms. AE, D, DC, MC, V.*

$$$$ ★ **Old Monterey Inn.** One of just two residential-area B&Bs in Monterey, this inn conjures up both the past history and the present beauty of the Monterey Peninsula. The three-story English Tudor country manor, completed in 1929, is replete with hand-carved window frames, balustrades, and Gothic archways. Loving restoration by proprietors Gene and Ann Swett included a rose garden surrounded by giant holly trees, gnarled oaks, and majestic redwoods. The inn is legendary for its 20 different bathroom amenities, featherbeds with down comforters, sumptuous breakfast, and solicitous service. ✉ *500 Martin St., 93940,* ☎ *831/375–8284 or 800/350–2344,* FAX *831/375–6730. 8 rooms, 2 suites. Concierge. MC, V. BP.*

$$$$ ★ **Spindrift Inn.** This small hotel on Cannery Row, under the same management as the Hotel Pacific and the Monterey Bay Inn, has beach access and a rooftop garden that overlooks the water. Spacious rooms with sitting areas, hardwood floors, fireplaces, and down comforters are among the indoor pleasures. ✉ *652 Cannery Row, 93940,* ☎ *831/646–8900 or 800/841–1879,* FAX *831/646–5342. 42 rooms. Refrigerators. AE, D, DC, MC, V. CP.*

$$$–$$$$ **Best Western Monterey Beach Hotel.** The rooms here may be nondescript, but this hotel has a great waterfront location about 2 mi north of town affording views of the bay and the city skyline. The grounds are pleasantly landscaped, and there's a large pool with a sunbathing area. ✉ *2600 Sand Dunes Dr., 93940,* ☎ *831/394–3321 or 800/242–8627,* FAX *831/393–1912. 196 rooms. Restaurant, lounge, pool, hot tub, exercise room. AE, D, DC, MC, V.*

$$–$$$$ **Merritt House.** Built around an historic adobe and its garden, this inn provides simple, yet attractive accommodations within walking distance of Fisherman's Wharf. All rooms have gas fireplaces and refrigerators, and upstairs rooms have vaulted ceilings. Suites are located in the adobe. ✉ *386 Pacific Ave., 93940,* ☎ *831/646–9686,* FAX *831/646–5392. 22 rooms, 3 suites. Room service and laundry services. AE, D, MC, V. CP.*

$$–$$$$ ★ **Monterey Bay Lodge.** Its location on the edge of Monterey's El Estero Park gives this motel an edge over those along the busy Munras Avenue motel row. Indoor plants and a secluded courtyard with a heated pool are other pluses. ✉ *55 Camino Aguajito Rd., 93940,* ☎ *831/372–8057 or 800/558–1900,* FAX *831/655–2933. 45 rooms. Restaurant, pool. AE, D, DC, MC, V.*

$$–$$$$ **Quality Inn Cannery Row.** Gas fireplaces are among the amenities at this small hotel on a street above Cannery Row. Some rooms have private balconies with bay views. ✉ *200 Foam St., 93940,* ☎ *831/649–8580 or 800/876–8580,* FAX *831/649–2566. 32 rooms. Refrigerators, hot tub. AE, D, MC, V. CP.*

$$–$$$ **Quality Inn Monterey.** This attractive motel has a friendly, country-inn atmosphere. Rooms are light and airy. All have refrigerators, microwaves, and VCRs; some have fireplaces. Breakfast is served in a blue-wallpaper lobby. ✉ *1058 Munras Ave., 93940,* ☎ *831/372–3381,* FAX *831/372–4687. 55 rooms. Indoor pool, hot tub. AE, D, DC, MC, V. CP.*

Nightlife and the Arts

BARS, CLUBS

Bluefin (✉ 685 Cannery Row, ☎ 831/375–7000) offers live music, dancing, and 19 pool tables. **Planet Gemini** (✉ 625 Cannery Row, ☎ 831/373–1449) presents comedy shows on weekends, and dancing to a DJ or live music. **Sly McFlys** (✉ 700-A Cannery Row, ☎ 831/649–8050) has live jazz and blues every night.

MUSIC FESTIVALS

Dixieland Monterey (✉ 177 Webster St., Suite A-206, ☎ 831/443–5260 or 888/349–6879), held on the first full weekend of March, presents Dixieland jazz bands in cabarets, restaurants, and hotel lounges on the Monterey waterfront. The **Monterey Bay Blues Festival** (☎ 831/394–2652 or 831/649–6544) draws blues fans to the Monterey Fairgrounds over a June weekend. The **Monterey Jazz Festival,** the world's oldest, (☎ 831/373–3366) attracts jazz and blues greats from around the world to the Monterey Fairgrounds on the third full weekend of September.

THEATER

California's First Theatre (✉ Scott and Pacific Sts., ☎ 831/375–4916) is home to the Troupers of the Gold Coast, who perform 19th-century melodramas year-round, mostly on weekends. **Monterey Bay Theatrefest** (☎ 831/622–0700) presents free outdoor performances at Custom House Plaza on weekend afternoons and evenings from late June to mid-July. The **Wharf Theater** (✉ Fisherman's Wharf, ☎ 831/649–2332) focuses on American musicals past and present.

Outdoor Activities and Sports

BICYCLING

For bicycle rentals try **Bay Bikes** (✉ 640 Wave St., ☎ 831/646–9090) or **Adventures by the Sea Inc.** (✉ 299 Cannery Row, ☎ 831/372–1807).

CAR RACING

Five major races take place each year on the 2.2-mi, 11-turn **Laguna Seca Raceway** (✉ 1021 Monterey–Salinas Hwy., ☎ 831/648–5100 or 800/327–7322).

FISHING

For half- and full-day fishing trips, contact **Monterey Sport Fishing** (✉ 96 Fisherman's Wharf, ☎ 831/372–2203 or 800/200–2203), **Randy's Fishing Trips** (✉ 66 Fisherman's Wharf, ☎ 831/372–7440 or 800/251–7440), or **Sam's Fishing Fleet** (✉ 84 Fisherman's Wharf, ☎ 831/372–0577 or 800/427–2675).

GOLF

The greens fee at the 18-hole **Del Monte Golf Course** (✉ 1300 Sylvan Rd., ☎ 831/373–2700) is $80, plus $18 per person for an optional cart. The $20 twilight special (plus cart rental) begins two hours before sunset.

KAYAKING

Monterey Bay Kayaks (✉ 693 Del Monte Ave., ☎ 831/373–5357; 800/649–5357 in CA) rents equipment and conducts classes and natural-history tours.

ROLLERSKATING AND IN-LINE SKATING

Adventures by the Sea Inc. (✉ 299 Cannery Row, ☎ 831/372–1807) rents skates. **Del Monte Gardens** (✉ 2020 Del Monte Ave., ☎ 831/375–3202) is an old-fashioned rink for rollerskating and in-line skating.

SCUBA DIVING

The staff at **Aquarius Dive Shops** (✉ 2040 Del Monte Ave., ☎ 831/375–1933; ✉ 32 Cannery Row, ☎ 831/375–6605) gives diving lessons and tours and rents equipment. The **scuba-diving conditions information line** (☎ 831/657–1020) is updated regularly.

WHALE-WATCHING

Monterey Sport Fishing (✉ 96 Fisherman's Wharf, ☎ 831/372–2203 or 800/200–2203), **Randy's Fishing Trips** (✉ 66 Fisherman's Wharf, ☎ 831/372–7440 or 800/251–7440), and **Sam's Fishing Fleet** (✉ 84 Fisherman's Wharf, ☎ 831/372–0577 or 800/427–2675) operate whale-watching expeditions.

Shopping

Alicia's Antiques (✉ 835 Cannery Row, ☎ 831/372–1423) occupies the back of the Wing Chong Building. Owner Alicia Harby-DeNoon, who knew John Steinbeck and Doc Ricketts, will tell you about the old Cannery Row. **Old Monterey Book Co.** (✉ 136 Bonifacio Pl., off Alvarado St., ☎ 831/372–3111) specializes in rare old books and prints.

Pacific Grove

3 mi from Monterey south on Hwy. 1 and west on Hwy. 68; from Cannery Row, Wave St. heading west becomes Ocean View Blvd. at Monterey–Pacific Grove border.

If not for the dramatic strip of coastline in its backyard, Pacific Grove could easily pass for a typical small town in the Heartland. The town, which began as a summer retreat for church groups more than a century ago, recalls its prim and proper Victorian heritage in its host of tiny board-and-batten cottages and stately mansions.

Even before the church groups flocked here, Pacific Grove had been receiving thousands of annual guests in the form of bright orange-and-black monarch butterflies. Known as Butterfly Town USA, Pacific Grove is the winter home of monarchs that migrate south from Canada and the Pacific Northwest to take residence in pine and eucalyptus groves from October through March. The sight of a mass of butterflies hanging from the branches like a long, fluttering veil is unforgettable.

A prime way to enjoy Pacific Grove is to walk or bicycle along its 3 mi of city-owned shoreline, a cliff-top area following Ocean View Boulevard that is landscaped with native plants and has benches on which to sit and gaze at the sea. You can spot many types of birds here, including colonies of web-footed cormorants drawn to the massive rocks rising out of the surf.

20 Among the Victorians of note is the **Pryor House** (✉ 429 Ocean View Blvd.), a massive shingled structure with a leaded- and beveled-glass
21 doorway. **Green Gables** (✉ 5th St. and Ocean View Blvd.), a romantic Swiss Gothic–style mansion with steeply peaked gables and stained-glass windows, is a B&B.

The view of the coast is gorgeous from **Lovers Point Park,** on Ocean View Boulevard midway along the waterfront. The park's sheltered beach has a children's pool and picnic area. Glass-bottom boat rides, which provide views of the plant and sea life below, are offered in summer.

★ 22 At the 1855-vintage **Point Piños Lighthouse,** the oldest continuously operating lighthouse on the West Coast, you can learn about the lighting and foghorn operations and wander through a small museum containing U.S. Coast Guard memorabilia. ✉ *Lighthouse Ave. off Asilomar Blvd.,* ☎ *831/648–3116.* *Free.* *Thurs.–Sun. 1–4.*

Monarchs sometimes vary their nesting sites from year to year, but the
23 **Monarch Grove Sanctuary** (✉ 1073 Lighthouse Ave., at Ridge Rd.) is a fairly reliable spot for viewing the butterflies.

If you are in Pacific Grove when the monarch butterflies aren't, you
24 can view the well-crafted butterfly tree exhibit at the **Pacific Grove Museum of Natural History.** The museum also displays 400 mounted birds and has a Touch Gallery for children. ✉ *165 Forest Ave.,* ☎ *831/648–3116.* *Free.* *Tues.–Sun. 10–5.*

★ **Asilomar State Beach,** a beautiful coastal area, is on Sunset Drive between Point Piños and the Del Monte Forest in Pacific Grove. The 100 acres of dunes, tidal pools, and pocket-size beaches form one of the region's richest areas for marine life.

Dining and Lodging

$$$–$$$$ ★ ✕ **Old Bath House.** A romantic, nostalgic atmosphere permeates this converted bathhouse overlooking the water at Lovers Point. The classic regional menu makes the most of local produce and seafood (such as Monterey Bay prawns). The restaurant has a less expensive menu for late-afternoon diners. ✉ *620 Ocean View Blvd.,* ☎ *831/375–5195. AE, D, DC, MC, V. No lunch.*

$$–$$$$ ✕ **Fandango.** With its stone walls and country furniture, Fandango has the earthy feel of a southern European farmhouse. Complementing the ambience are the robust flavors of the cuisine, which ranges from southern France, Italy, Spain, and Greece to North Africa, from paella and cannelloni to couscous. ✉ *223 17th St.,* ☎ *831/372–3456. AE, D, DC, MC, V.*

$$–$$$ ✕ **Crocodile Grill.** South American artwork and artifacts form the decor, and a Latin flavor permeates many of the adventurous concoctions, such as crispy squid with spicy orange-cilantro vinaigrette and

black bean–goat cheese ravioli. Fresh fish is paired with a variety of creative sauces. Wines are an exceptional value here. ✉ *701 Lighthouse Ave.,* ☎ *831/655–3311. AE, D, MC, V. Closed Tues. No lunch.*

$$–$$$ ✕ **Fishwife.** Fresh fish with a Latin accent makes this a favorite of locals for lunch or a casual dinner. ✉ *1996½ Sunset Dr., at Asilomar Blvd.,* ☎ *831/375–7107. AE, D, MC, V. Closed Sun.*

$$–$$$ ✕ **Gernot's.** The ornate Victorian-era Hart Mansion is a delightful setting in which to dine on seafood and game served with light sauces. Austrian/Continental specialties include wild-boar bourguignon, roast venison, and rack of lamb. ✉ *649 Lighthouse Ave.,* ☎ *831/646–1477. AE, MC, V. Closed Mon. No lunch.*

$$–$$$ ✕ **Joe Rombi's.** Pastas, fish, and veal are the specialties at this modern trattoria. The atmosphere is convivial and welcoming. Try the sautéed veal with red-wine reduction, mozzarella, and herbs. ✉ *208 17th St.,* ☎ *831/373–2416. AE, MC, V. Closed Mon. and Tues.*

$–$$ ✕ **Cypress Grove.** A favorite for local restaurateurs, this casual, inviting bistro serves a diverse variety of house-made specialties including pot-pies and jambalaya, as well as more traditional meats and seafood. Open all day and evening, this is a great bet for a snack or a full meal. Sit by the fireplace or at the bar with the locals. Brunch is served weekends. ✉ *663 Lighthouse Ave.,* ☎ *831/375–1743. AE, MC, V.*

$–$$ ✕ **Peppers Mexicali Cafe.** This cheerful white-walled restaurant serves fresh seafood and traditional dishes from Mexico and Latin America. The red and green salsas are excellent. ✉ *170 Forest Ave.,* ☎ *831/373–6892. AE, D, DC, MC, V. Closed Tues. No lunch Sun.*

$–$$ ✕ **Toasties Cafe.** Three-egg omelets, burritos, pancakes, waffles, French toast, and other breakfast items are served at this crowded café until 3 PM. The lunch selections include burgers and other sandwiches. Toasties also serves dinner—fish and chips, seafood pasta—but it's best to stick to daytime meals. ✉ *702 Lighthouse Ave.,* ☎ *831/373–7543. AE, D, MC, V.*

$$$–$$$$ ★ **Centrella Hotel.** A handsome century-old Victorian mansion two blocks from Lovers Point Beach, the Centrella fills its guest rooms and cottages with wicker and brass furnishings and claw-foot bathtubs. A buffet breakfast is served each morning, and a sideboard in the large parlor is laden with cookies and hors d'oeuvres in the afternoon. ✉ *612 Central Ave., 93950,* ☎ *831/372–3372 or 800/233–3372,* FAX *831/372–2036. 17 rooms, 4 suites, 5 cottages. Concierge. AE, D, MC, V. BP.*

$$$–$$$$ **The Inn at 213 Seventeen Mile Drive.** Set in a residential area just past town, this carefully restored 1920's Craftsman-style home and cottage has spacious, well-appointed rooms. The affable innkeepers offer complimentary wine and hors d'oeuvres in the evening and tea and snacks throughout the day. Redwood, cypress, and eucalyptus trees tower over the garden and outdoor spa. ✉ *213 Seventeen Mile Dr., 93950,* ☎ *831/642–9514 or 800/526–5666,* FAX *831/642–9546. 14 rooms. Spa. AE, MC, V. BP.*

$$$–$$$$ ★ **Martine Inn.** Most B&Bs in Pacific Grove are in Victorian houses; this one is in a pink-stucco, Mediterranean-style villa overlooking the water. The many antiques include a mahogany suite exhibited at the 1893 Chicago World's Fair, movie costume designer Edith Head's bedroom suite, and an 1860 Chippendale Revival four-poster bed. The glassed-in parlor and several rooms have stunning ocean views. Lavish breakfasts are served on lace-clad tables set with china, crystal, and silver. ✉ *255 Ocean View Blvd., 93950,* ☎ *831/373–3388 or 800/852–5588,* FAX *831/373–3896. 25 rooms, 1 suite. Refrigerators. AE, D, MC, V. BP.*

$$$–$$$$ **Seven Gables Inn.** An elegant Victorian mansion and four smaller buildings share a corner lot and a great view of the ocean. The main house was built in 1886, the others between 1910 and 1940. European antiques of various periods—gold-leaf mirrors, crystal chandeliers, and marble statues—create a formal atmosphere. The gracious innkeeper, Susan Flatley, grew up in the house and shares her knowledge about it and the area. ✉ *555 Ocean View Blvd., 93950,* ☎ *831/372–4341,* FAX *831/372–2544. 10 rooms, 4 cottages. MC, V. BP.*

$$–$$$$ ★ **Green Gables Inn.** Stained-glass windows framing an ornate fireplace and other interior detail work compete with the spectacular ocean views at this Queen Anne–style mansion built by a businessman for his mistress in 1888. Rooms in a carriage house perched on a hill out back are larger, have more modern amenities, and afford more privacy, but rooms in the main house have more charm. ✉ *104 5th St., 93950,* ☎ *831/375–2095 or 800/722–1774,* FAX *831/375–5437. 10 rooms, 4 with shared bath; 1 suite. Bicycles. AE, MC, V. BP.*

$$–$$$$ **Lighthouse Lodge and Suites.** Located on two sides of Lighthouse Avenue—the lodge is on one side, the all-suites facility on the other—this complex near the tip of the peninsula provides a woodsy alternative to downtown Pacific Grove's B&B scene. The suites have fireplaces, whirlpool tubs, and kitchenettes. The rooms are simple, but they're decent in size and much less expensive. ✉ *1150 and 1249 Lighthouse Ave., 93950,* ☎ *831/655–2111 or 800/858–1249,* FAX *831/655–4922. 64 rooms, 31 suites. Pool, hot tub. AE, D, DC, MC, V. BP.*

$$–$$$ **Gosby House Inn.** Though in the town center, this turreted yellow Queen Anne Victorian B&B has an informal, country air. The two most private rooms are in the rear carriage house; they have fireplaces, balconies, and whirlpool tubs. Buffet breakfast is served in the parlor or garden. *643 Lighthouse Ave., 93950,* ☎ *831/375–1287 or 800/527–8828,* FAX *831/655–9621. 22 rooms, 2 with shared bath. AE, DC, MC, V. BP.*

$–$$$ **Asilomar Conference Center.** A summer-camp atmosphere prevails at this assortment of 28 rustic but comfortable lodges in the middle of a woodsy 105-acre state park near the beach. Rooms are available when they're not booked for conferences. ✉ *800 Asilomar Blvd., Box 537, 93950,* ☎ *831/372–8016,* FAX *831/372–7227. 314 rooms. Cafeteria, pool. MC, V. BP.*

Outdoor Activities and Sports

GOLF

The greens fee at the 18-hole **Pacific Grove Municipal Golf Links** (✉ 77 Asilomar Blvd., ☎ 831/648–3177) runs between $31 and $36 (you can play nine holes for between $16 and $19), with an 18-hole twilight rate of $15. Optional carts cost $26. The course has spectacular ocean views on its back nine. Tee times may be reserved up to seven days in advance.

TENNIS

Pacific Grove Municipal Courts (✉ 515 Junipero St., ☎ 831/648–3129) are available for public play.

Shopping

American Tin Cannery Outlet Center (✉ 125 Ocean View Blvd., ☎ 831/372–3071) carries designer clothing, jewelry, accessories, and home decorating items at discounts between 25% and 65%. **Wooden Nickel** (✉ Central and Fountain Aves., ☎ 831/646–8050) sells accent pieces for the home.

17-Mile Drive and Pebble Beach

Off Sunset Dr. in Pacific Grove or N. San Antonio Rd. in Carmel.

Primordial nature resides in quiet harmony with palatial estates along ★ **17-Mile Drive,** which winds through an 8,400-acre microcosm of the Monterey coastal landscape. Dotting the drive are rare Monterey cypress, trees so gnarled and twisted that Robert Louis Stevenson once described them as "ghosts fleeing before the wind." Some sightseers balk at the $7.50-per-car fee collected at the gates—this is the only private toll road west of the Mississippi—but most find the drive well worth the price. An alternative is to grab a bike; cyclists tour for free, as do visitors with confirmed lunch or dinner reservations at one of the hotels.

25 **Bird Rock,** the largest of several islands at the southern end of the Monterey Country Club's golf course, teems with harbor seals, sea lions,
26 cormorants, and pelicans. Sea creatures and birds also make use of **Seal
Rock,** the larger of a group of islands south of Bird Rock. The most
27 photographed tree along 17-Mile Drive is the weather-sculpted **Lone
Cypress** that grows out of a precipitous outcropping above the waves.
You can stop for a view of the Lone Cypress at a parking area, but
you can't walk out to the tree.

Many of the stately homes along 17-Mile Drive reflect the classic Monterey or Spanish Mission style typical of the region. A standout
28 is the **Crocker Marble Palace,** a waterfront estate inspired by a Byzantine castle. This mansion is easily identifiable by its dozens of marble arches.

29 The ocean plays a major role in the 18th hole of the famed **Pebble Beach Golf Links** (☞ Outdoor Activities and Sports, *below*). Each winter the course is the main site of the AT&T Pebble Beach Pro-Am (formerly the Bing Crosby Pro-Am), where show-business celebrities and pros team up for one of the nation's most glamorous golf tournaments. Views of the impeccable greens at two tournament golf courses can be enjoyed over a drink or lunch at the Lodge at Pebble Beach or the Inn at Spanish Bay, the pair of resorts located along the drive.

Dining and Lodging

$$$$ ★ ✕▣ **Inn at Spanish Bay.** This 269-room resort sprawls across a breathtaking stretch of shoreline along 17-Mile Drive. Under the same management as the Lodge at Pebble Beach (☞ *below*), the inn has a slightly more casual feel, though its 600-square-ft rooms are no less luxurious. The inn has its own tennis courts and golf course, but guests also have privileges at both facilities. Peppoli's restaurant ($$$), which serves Tuscan cuisine, overlooks the coast and the golf links. Try Roy's Restaurant for more casual and innovative Euro-Asian fare. ✉ *2700 17-Mile Dr., Box 1418, Pebble Beach 93953,* ☎ *831/647–7500 or 800/654–9300,* FAX *831/644–7960. 252 rooms, 17 suites. 3 restaurants, bar, pool, massage, 8 tennis courts, health club, hiking, horseback riding, concierge. AE, D, DC, MC, V.*

$$$$ ★ ✕▣ **Lodge at Pebble Beach.** Luxurious rooms with fireplaces and wonderful views set the tone at this renowned resort that was built in 1919. The golf course, tennis club, and equestrian center are highly regarded. Guests of the lodge have privileges at the Inn at Spanish Bay. Overlooking the 18th green, the very fine Club XIX restaurant ($$$–$$$$; jackets recommended) is an intimate, clublike dining room serving expertly prepared French cuisine. ✉ *1700 17-Mile Dr., Box 1128, Pebble Beach 93953,* ☎ *831/624–3811 or 800/654–9300,* FAX *831/644–7960. 142 rooms, 19 suites. 3 restaurants, bar, coffee shop, pool, hot tub, massage, sauna, spa, 18-hole golf course, 12 tennis courts, exercise room, health club, horseback riding, beach, bicycles, concierge. AE, D, DC, MC, V.*

Carmel and 17-Mile Drive

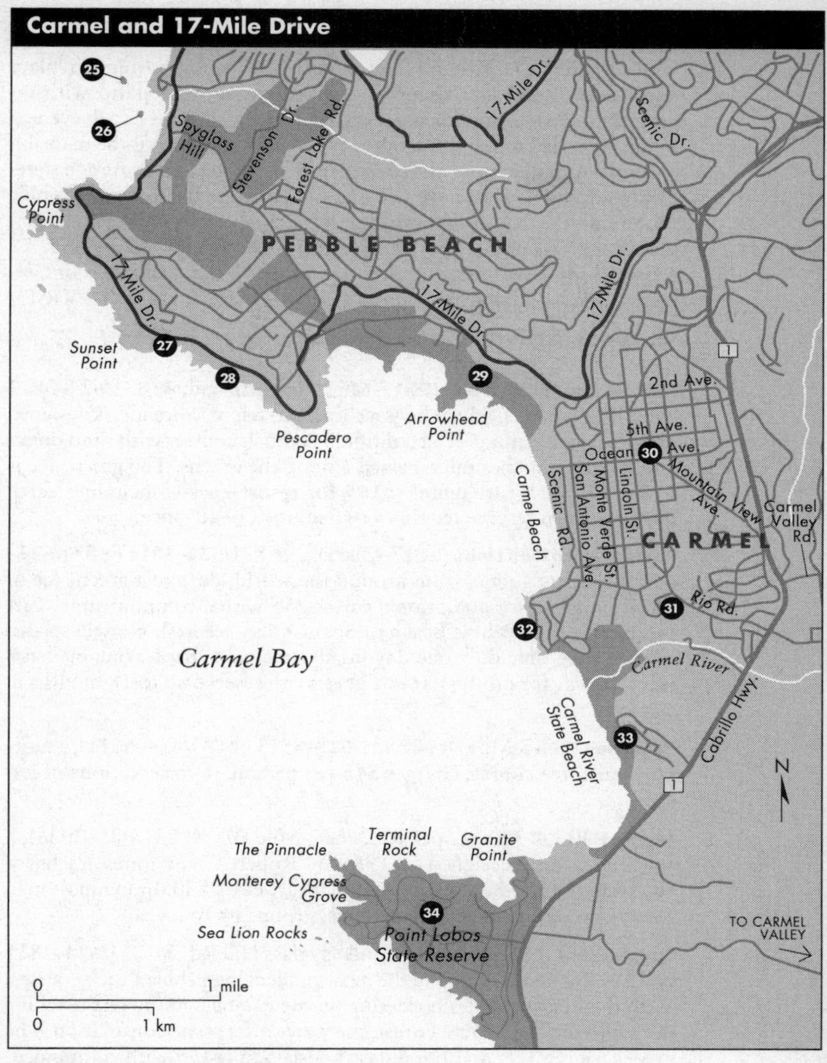

Bird Rock	25	Lone Cypress	27
Carmel Mission	31	Pebble Beach Golf Links	29
Carmel Plaza	30	Point Lobos State Reserve	34
Carmel River State Beach	33	Seal Rock	26
Crocker Marble Palace	28	Tor House	32

$$$$ ★ Casa Palmero. The pinnacle of luxury, this exclusive spa resort captures the essence of a Mediterranean villa. The rooms are decorated with sumptuous fabrics and fine art, each has a wood-burning fireplace and heated floor, and some have a private outdoor patio with in-ground Jacuzzi. Complimentary cocktail service is offered each evening in the main hall and library, the only remaining rooms of the mansion around which the resort was constructed. The hotel also features a state-of-the-art spa. Guests have use of all facilities at the Lodge at Pebble Beach and the Inn at Spanish Bay (☞ *above*). ✉ *1518 Cypress Dr., 93953,* ☎ *831/622–6650 or 800/654–9300,* FAX *831/622–6655. 21 rooms, 3 suites. Mini-bars, room service, pool, spa, exercise room, bicycles, billiards, concierge, laundry service. AE, D, DC, MC, V. CP.*

Outdoor Activities and Sports

GOLF

The Links at Spanish Bay (✉ 17-Mile Dr., north end, ☎ 831/624–3811 or 831/624–6611), which hugs a choice stretch of shoreline, is designed in the rugged manner of a traditional Scottish course, with sand dunes and coastal marshes interspersed among the greens. The greens fee is $185, plus $25 cart rental ($165 for resort guests, including cart); nonguests can reserve tee times two months in advance.

Pebble Beach Golf Links (✉ 17-Mile Dr., ☎ 831/624–3811 or 831/624–6611) attracts golfers from around the world, despite a greens fee of $305, plus $25 for an optional cart ($255 with a complimentary cart for guests of the Pebble Beach or Spanish Bay resorts). Nonguests can reserve a tee time only one day in advance on a space-available basis (up to a year for groups); resort guests can reserve up to 18 months in advance.

Peter Hay (✉ 17-Mile Dr., ☎ 831/625–8518 or 831/624–6611), a nine-hole par-three course, charges $15 per person, no reservations necessary.

Poppy Hills (✉ 3200 Lopez Rd., at 17-Mile Dr., ☎ 831/625–2035), a splendid course designed in 1986 by Robert Trent Jones Jr., has a greens fee of $115–$130; an optional cart costs $30. Individuals may reserve up to one month in advance, groups up to a year.

Spyglass Hill (✉ Stevenson Dr. and Spyglass Hill Rd., ☎ 831/624–3811 or 831/624–6611) is among the most challenging Pebble Beach courses. With the first five holes bordering on the Pacific and the rest reaching deep into the Del Monte Forest, the views offer some consolation. The greens fee is $225; an optional cart costs $25 ($195 with complimentary cart for resort guests). Reservations are essential and may be made up to one month in advance (18 months for guests).

HORSEBACK RIDING

The **Pebble Beach Equestrian Center** (✉ Portola Rd. and Alva La., ☎ 831/624–2756) offers guided trail rides along the beach and through 26 mi of bridle trails in the Del Monte Forest.

Carmel

5 mi south of Monterey on Hwy. 1 (or via 17-Mile Drive's Carmel Gate).

Although the community has grown quickly through the years and its population quadruples with tourists on weekends and during the summer, Carmel retains its identity as a quaint village. The town is populated by many former major and minor celebrities, and it has a lot of quirky ordinances. Women wearing high heels do not have the right to pursue legal action if they trip and fall on the cobblestone streets, and drivers who hit a tree and leave the scene will be charged with hit-

and-run. Live music is banned in local watering holes, and buildings still have no street numbers–and consequently, no mail delivery. (If you really want to see the locals, go to the post office.) Artists started this community, and their legacy is evident in the numerous galleries. Wander the side streets at your own pace, poking into hidden courtyards and stopping at cafés for tea and crumpets.

Downtown Carmel's chief lure is shopping. Its main street, **Ocean Avenue,** is a mishmash of ersatz Tudor, Mediterranean, and other styles.
30 **Carmel Plaza,** in the east end of the village proper at Ocean and Junipero avenues, holds more than 50 shops and restaurants.

Long before it became a shopping and browsing mecca, Carmel was an important religious center during the establishment of Spanish California. That heritage is preserved in the Mission San Carlos Borromeo
★ 31 del Rio Carmelo, more commonly known as the **Carmel Mission.** Founded in 1770, it served as headquarters for the mission system in California under Father Junípero Serra. Adjoining the stone church are a tranquil garden planted with California poppies. Museum rooms at the mission include an early kitchen, Serra's spartan sleeping quarters, and the oldest college library in California. ✉ *3080 Rio Rd. (at Lasuen Dr.),* ☎ *831/624–3600.* *$2.* *Sept.–May, Mon.–Sat. 9:30–4:30, Sun. 10:30–4:30; June–Aug., Mon.–Sat. 9:30–7:30, Sun. 10:30–7:30.*

Scattered throughout the pines in Carmel are the houses and cottages that were built for writers, artists, and photographers who discovered
32 the area decades ago. Among the most impressive dwellings is **Tor House,** a stone cottage built in 1919 by the poet Robinson Jeffers on a craggy knoll overlooking the sea. Portraits, books, and unusual art objects fill the low-ceiling rooms. The highlight of the small estate is Hawk Tower, a detached edifice set with stones from the Carmel coastline as well as one from the Great Wall of China. The docents who lead tours (six persons maximum) are well informed about the poet's work and life. ✉ *26304 Ocean View Ave.,* ☎ *831/624–1813 or 831/624–1840.* *$7. No children under 12.* *Tours Fri. and Sat. 10–3; reservations recommended.*

Carmel's greatest beauty is its rugged coastline, with pine and cypress forests and countless inlets. **Carmel Beach,** an easy walk from downtown shops, has sparkling white sands and magnificent sunsets. ✉ *End of Ocean Ave.*

33 **Carmel River State Beach** stretches for 106 acres along Carmel Bay. On sunny days the waters appear nearly as turquoise as those of the Caribbean. The sugar-white beach is adjacent to a bird sanctuary where you might spot pelicans, kingfishers, hawks, and sandpipers. ✉ *Off Scenic Rd., south of Carmel Beach,* ☎ *831/624–4909.* *Free.* *Daily 9 AM–sunset.*

★ 34 **Point Lobos State Reserve,** a 350-acre headland harboring a wealth of marine life, lies a few miles south of Carmel. The best way to explore the reserve is to walk along one of its many trails. The Cypress Grove Trail leads through a forest of Monterey cypress (one of only two natural groves remaining), clinging to the rocks above an emerald-green cove. Sea Lion Point Trail is a good place to view sea lions. From those and other trails you may also spot otters, harbor seals, and (during winter and spring) migrating whales. An additional 750 acres of the reserve is an undersea marine park open to qualified scuba divers. Arrive early (or in late afternoon) to avoid crowds; the parking lots fill up. No pets are allowed. ✉ *Hwy. 1,* ☎ *831/624–4909; 831/624–8413 for scuba-diving reservations.* *$3 per vehicle.* *May–Sept., daily 9–7; Oct.–Apr., daily 9–5.*

Dining and Lodging

$$$–$$$$ ✕ **Anton and Michel.** Expect superb European cuisine at this elegant restaurant in Carmel's shopping district. The tender lamb dishes are fantastic and well complemented by the wines. The ultimate treats, however, are the flaming desserts. You can dine in the outdoor courtyard in summer. ✉ *Mission St. and 7th Ave.,* ☎ *831/624–2406. Reservations essential. AE, D, DC, MC, V.*

$$–$$$$ ✕ **French Poodle.** Specialties on the traditional French menu at this intimate restaurant include the duck breast in port and the abalone. The floating island—a meringue and custard combo—for dessert is delicious. ✉ *Junipero and 5th Aves.,* ☎ *831/624–8643. Reservations essential. AE, DC, MC, V. Closed Sun. No lunch.*

$$$ ★ ✕ **Robert's Boulevard Bistro.** At chef-owner Robert Kincaid's French bistro, dried sage and lavender hanging from exposed ceiling beams, painted floors, and ochre-washed walls will make you feel as if you've stepped into an old farmhouse in Provence. The menu stresses seasonal ingredients, cassoulet made with white beans, duck confit, rabbit sausage, and garlic prawns is always on the stove. Leave room for dessert, particularly the soufflé with lemon and orange zest or the chocolate bag with chocolate shake, a masterful invention. ✉ *Crossroads Center, 217 Crossroads Blvd.,* ☎ *831/624–9626. Reservations essential. AE, D, DC, MC, V. No lunch.*

$$–$$$ ★ ✕ **Casanova.** Southern French and northern Italian cuisine come together at Casanova, one of the most romantic restaurants in Carmel. A heated outdoor garden and the more than 1,000 domestic and imported vintages from the hand-dug wine cellar enhance the dining experience. The menu, which changes monthly, includes such delights as *cotelette de veau aux morilles* (grilled veal chop with sautéed morel mushrooms). All entrées come with an antipasto plate and choice of appetizers. ✉ *5th Ave. between San Carlos and Mission Sts.,* ☎ *831/625–0501. Reservations essential. MC, V.*

$$–$$$ ✕ **Flying Fish.** This Japanese-California seafood restaurant is simple in its appearance, yet bold with its flavors. It has quickly established itself as one of Carmel's most inventive eateries. Among the best entrées is the almond-crusted sea bass with Chinese cabbage and rock shrimp stir-fry. ✉ *Mission St. between Ocean and 7th Aves.,* ☎ *831/625–1962. AE, D, DC, MC, V. Closed Tues. No lunch.*

$$–$$$ ✕ **Portabella.** Set in a cozy, thatch-roof house on Carmel's main shopping street, this romantic restaurant serves hearty Southern European-inspired cooking. Sit outside on the heated flagstone patio or inside by the fire. Roasted corn and crab bisque, and the braised veal with wild mushrooms are two of the house specialties. ✉ *Ocean Ave. between Lincoln and Monte Verde sts.,* ☎ *831/624–4395. Reservations essential. AE, D, DC, MC, V.*

$$–$$$ ✕ **Raffaello.** Sparkling Raffaello serves exceptional pasta, seafood, and meat dishes such as Monterey Bay prawns with garlic butter, local sole poached in champagne, and the specialty of the house, veal Piemontese. ✉ *Mission St. between Ocean and 7th Aves.,* ☎ *831/624–1541. Reservations essential. AE, DC, MC, V. Closed Tues. and first 2 wks in Jan. No lunch.*

$–$$$ ✕ **Flaherty's Oyster Bar & Seafood Grill.** These bright and inviting side-by-side fish houses crank out steaming bowls of mussels, clams, cioppino, and crab chowder. Seafood pastas and daily fresh fish selections are also available. The Oyster Bar, with counter seating and a few tables, is the more casual and less expensive of the two restaurants. ✉ *6th Ave. and San Carlos St.,* ☎ *831/624–0311 (Oyster Bar); 831/625–1500 (Seafood Grill). AE, D, DC, MC, V.*

$–$$$ ✕ **The General Store.** This former blacksmith's shop houses a lively bar and restaurant suited to all ages and tastes. Known for its USDA prime steaks, the menu also has a variety of excellent sandwiches and pizzas. ✉ *5th Ave. and Junipero Ave.,* ☎ *831/624–2233. AE, D, MC, V.*

$–$$$ ✕ **Lugano Swiss Bistro.** Fondue is the centerpiece here. The house specialty is an original version made with Gruyère, Emmental, and Appenzeller. Rosemary chicken, plum-basted duck, and fennel pork loin rotate on the rotisserie. Ask for a table in the back room, which contains a hand-painted street scene of Lugano. ✉ *The Barnyard, Hwy. 1 and Carmel Valley Rd.,* ☎ *831/626–3779. AE, MC, V.*

$–$$$ ✕ **Rio Grill.** Don't let its shopping-center location fool you. The Rio Grill is one of the Monterey Peninsula's most appealing restaurants. The best bets in this lively Santa Fe–style setting are the meat and seafood cooked over an oak-wood grill. The fire-roasted artichoke and the Monterey Bay squid are exceptional starters. ✉ *Crossroads Center, 101 Crossroads Blvd., Hwy. 1 and Rio Rd.,* ☎ *831/625–5436. Reservations essential. AE, D, MC, V.*

$$ ✕ **La Bohème.** The chefs at campy La Bohème prepare one entrée each night, accompanied by soup and salad. You may find yourself bumping elbows with your neighbor in the faux-European-village courtyard, but the predominantly French cuisine is delicious, and the atmosphere is convivial. ✉ *Dolores St. and 7th Ave.,* ☎ *831/624–7500. Reservations not accepted. MC, V. No lunch.*

$–$$ ✕ **Cafe Gringo.** The zesty variations on Mexican cuisine here include the fresh tamales with spinach, zucchini, and mushrooms and the quesadilla with Monterey Jack and manchego cheeses, bacon, and roasted *pasilla* chilies, topped with mango salsa. The bar serves margaritas, Mexican beers, and South American and local wines. Outdoor tables beckon in warm weather. ✉ *Paseo San Carlos Courtyard, San Carlos St. between Ocean and 7th Aves.,* ☎ *831/626–8226. AE, MC, V.*

$–$$ ✕ **Caffé Napoli.** Redolent of garlic and olive oil, this small, atmospheric Italian restaurant is a favorite of locals who come for the crisp-crusted pizzas, house-made pastas, and fresh seafood. Specialties include grilled artichokes, fresh salmon and grilled vegetable risotto, and fisherman's pasta. There's a good Italian wine list. ✉ *Ocean Ave. and Lincoln St.,* ☎ *831/625–4033. Reservations essential. MC, V.*

$–$$ ✕ **The Cottage Restaurant.** The best breakfast in Carmel is served here. This local favorite offers six different preparations of eggs Benedict, sweet and savory crepes, and a variety of sandwiches and homemade soups at lunch. Dinner is served on weekends, but the best meals here are in the daytime. ✉ *Lincoln St. between Ocean and 7th Aves.,* ☎ *831/625–6260. MC, V. No dinner Sun.–Wed.*

$–$$ ✕ **Jack London's.** Carmel's only restaurant to serve food until 1 AM, this is where the locals eat and drink in a relaxed, publike atmosphere. The menu features everything from snacks to steaks. ✉ *San Carlos between 5th and 6th Aves.,* ☎ *831/624–2336. AE, D, DC, MC, V.*

$$$$ ✕🏨 **Highlands Inn.** High on a hill overlooking the Pacific, the views here are superb. Accommodations are in spa suites (with a Jacuzzi) and condominium-style units, a number with full kitchens, fireplaces, and decks overlooking the ocean. Though some of them will be sold as time-shares starting in 2001, the majority of the property remains under the management of Hyatt Hotels. The excellent menu at the inn's Pacific's Edge restaurant ($$$–$$$$) blends French technique and California cooking. Menu stand-outs include rack of lamb with Japanese eggplant and potato gratin, and pink-peppercorn-crusted tuna. ✉ *Hwy. 1, Box 1700, 93921,* ☎ *831/624–3801 or 800/682–4811; 831/622–5445 restaurant;* FAX *831/626–1574. 105 suites, 37 rooms. 2 restaurants, lounge, refrigerators, pool, 3 hot tubs, bicycles, baby-sitting. AE, D, DC, MC, V.* 😎

$$$$ ▣ **Carriage House Inn.** This small inn with a wood-shingle exterior has spacious rooms with beam ceilings, fireplaces, down comforters, and, in most, whirlpool baths. Afternoon wine and hors d'oeuvres are included. ✉ *Junipero Ave. between 7th and 8th Aves., Box 1900, 93921,* ☎ *831/625–2585 or 800/422–4732,* FAX *831/624–0974. 11 rooms, 2 suites. In-room safes, minibars, refrigerators. AE, D, MC, V. CP.*

$$$$ ★ ▣ **Tickle Pink Inn.** Atop a towering cliff, this inn has views of the Big Sur coastline, which you can contemplate from your private balcony. Fall asleep to the sound of surf crashing below and wake up to Continental breakfast and the morning paper in bed. If you prefer the company of fellow travelers, breakfast is also served buffet-style in the lounge, as are complimentary wine and cheese in the afternoon. Many rooms have wood-burning fireplaces, and there are four luxurious spa suites. ✉ *155 Highlands Dr., 93923,* ☎ *831/624–1244 or 800/635–4774,* FAX *831/626–9516. 24 rooms, 11 suites. Refrigerators, outdoor hot tub. AE, MC, V. BP.*

$$$–$$$$ ▣ **Best Western Carmel Mission Inn.** This motel on the edge of Carmel Valley has a lushly landscaped pool and hot tub area and is close to the Barnyard and Crossroads shopping centers. Rooms are large, some with spacious decks. ✉ *3665 Rio Rd., at Hwy. 1, 93923,* ☎ *831/624–1841 or 800/348–9090,* FAX *831/624–8684. 163 rooms, 2 suites. Restaurant, bar, refrigerators, pool, 2 hot tubs. AE, D, DC, MC, V.*

$$$–$$$$ ▣ **The Briarwood.** This ivy-covered B&B offers comfortable accommodations within steps of Carmel's shops and galleries. Most rooms have fireplaces and flower-lined verandas. Continental breakfast is available in your room or in the common area. ✉ *San Carlos between 4th and 5th Aves., Box 5245, 93921,* ☎ *831/626–9056 or 800/999–8788,* FAX *831/626–8900. 11 rooms. AE, MC, V. CP.*

$$$–$$$$ ▣ **Carmel River Inn.** Besides attracting those looking for a relative bargain in pricey Carmel, this half-century-old inn appeals to travelers who enjoy a bit of distance from the madding crowd—downtown Carmel in July, for instance. Yet the area's beaches are only 1½ mi away. The blue and white motel at the front of the property contains units with cable TV, small refrigerators, and coffeemakers. Cabins out back sleep up to six; some have fireplaces and kitchens. ✉ *Hwy. 1 at Carmel River Bridge, Box 221609, 93922,* ☎ *831/624–1575 or 800/882–8142,* FAX *831/624–0290. 19 rooms, 24 cabins. Refrigerators, pool. MC, V.*

$$$–$$$$ ★ ▣ **Cypress Inn.** When Doris Day became part owner of this inn in 1988, she added her own touches, such as posters from her many movies and photo albums of her favorite canines. (Pets are welcome in most rooms here.) In nice weather, you can enjoy breakfast in a garden surrounded by bougainvillea. ✉ *Lincoln St. and 7th Ave., Box Y, 93921,* ☎ *831/624–3871 or 800/443–7443,* FAX *831/624–8216. 33 rooms, 1 suite. Bar, refrigerators. AE, D, MC, V. CP.*

$$$–$$$$ ▣ **La Playa Hotel.** Norwegian artist Christopher Jorgensen built the original structure in 1902 for his bride, a member of the Ghirardelli chocolate clan. The property has since undergone many additions and now resembles a Mediterranean estate. Though some of the rooms are small and could use a few modern amenities, the history and location more than compensate. The central garden, riotous with color, has vistas of Carmel's magnificent coastline. Some accommodations have ocean views as well. You can also opt for a cottage; most have full kitchens and wood-burning fireplaces, and all have a patio or a terrace. ✉ *Camino Real at 8th Ave., Box 900, 93921,* ☎ *831/624–6476 or 800/582–8900,* FAX *831/624–7966. 75 rooms, 5 cottages. Restaurant, bar, pool, laundry service. AE, DC, MC, V.*

$$–$$$$ ★ ▣ **Cobblestone Inn.** Thick quilts and country antiques, stone fireplaces in guest rooms and the sitting-room area, and a complimentary breakfast buffet and afternoon tea contribute to the homey feel at this English-style inn. ✉ *8th and Junipero Aves., Box 3185, 93921,* ☎ *831/625–5222 or 800/833–8836,* FAX *831/625–0478. 22 rooms, 2 suites. Refrigerators. AE, DC, MC, V. BP.*

$$–$$$$ **Mission Ranch.** Sheep graze in the ocean-side pasture near the main 19th-century farmhouse at Mission Ranch. The six rooms in the main house are set around a Victorian parlor; other options include cottages, a hayloft, and a bunkhouse. Handmade quilts and carved wooden beds lend a country ambience. ✉ *26270 Dolores St., 93923,* ☎ *831/624–6436 or 800/538–8221,* FAX *831/626–4163. 31 rooms. Restaurant, piano bar, 6 tennis courts, exercise room, pro shop. AE, MC, V.*

$$–$$$$ **Pine Inn.** A favorite of generations of Carmel visitors, the Pine Inn has a red and black Victorian-style decor, complete with grandfather clock, padded fabric wall panels, antique tapestries, and marble-top furnishings. Only four blocks from the beach, the complex includes a brick courtyard of specialty shops and a modern Italian restaurant, Il Fornaio. ✉ *Ocean Ave. and Lincoln St., Box 250, 93921,* ☎ *831/624–3851 or 800/228–3851,* FAX *831/624–3030. 43 rooms, 6 suites. Restaurant. AE, D, DC, MC, V.*

$$–$$$$ **Tally Ho Inn.** This inn with an English garden courtyard is one of the few in Carmel's center with good views of the ocean. The penthouse units have fireplaces. ✉ *Monte Verde St. and 6th Ave., Box 3726, 93921,* ☎ *831/624–2232 or 800/624–2290,* FAX *831/624–2661. 12 rooms, 2 suites. AE, D, DC, MC, V. CP.*

$$–$$$ **Lobos Lodge.** The white stucco motel units here are set amid cypress, oaks, and pines on the edge of the business district. All accommodations have fireplaces and some have private patios. ✉ *Monte Verde St. and Ocean Ave., Box L–1, 93921,* ☎ *831/624–3874,* FAX *831/624–0135. 28 rooms, 2 suites. Refrigerators. AE, MC, V. CP.*

$$–$$$ **Sea View Inn.** Located in a residential area a few hundred feet from the beach, this restored 1905 home features a double parlor with two fireplaces, Oriental rugs, canopy beds, and a spacious front porch. Afternoon tea and evening wine and cheese are offered daily. ✉ *Camino Real between 11th and 12th Aves., Box 4138, 93921,* ☎ *831/624–8778,* FAX *831/625–5901. 8 rooms. MC, V. CP.*

Nightlife and the Arts

MUSIC

Carmel Bach Festival (☎ 831/624–2046) has presented the works of Johann Sebastian Bach and his contemporaries in concerts and recitals since 1935. The festival runs for three weeks, starting in mid-July. **Monterey County Symphony** (☎ 831/624–8511) performs concerts—from classical to pop—from September through May in Salinas and Carmel.

THEATER

Pacific Repertory Theater (☎ 831/622–0700) specializes in contemporary comedy and drama. **Sunset Community Cultural Center** (✉ San Carlos St. between 8th and 10th Aves., ☎ 831/624–3996), which presents concerts, lectures, and headline performers, is the Monterey Bay area's top venue for the performing arts.

Shopping

ART GALLERIES

Carmel Art Association (✉ Dolores St. between 5th and 6th Aves., ☎ 831/624–6176) exhibits the paintings, sculpture, and prints of local artists. **Cottage Gallery** (✉ Mission St. and 6th Ave., ☎ 831/624–7888) focuses on representational art, sculpture, and heirloom-quality collectible furniture. **Highlands Sculpture Gallery** (✉ Dolores St. between 5th and 6th Aves., ☎ 831/624–0535) is devoted to indoor and outdoor sculpture, primarily works done in stone, bronze, wood, metal, and glass. **Masterpiece Gallery** (✉ Dolores St. and 6th Ave., ☎ 831/

624–2163) shows early California Impressionist art. **Photography West Gallery** (✉ Ocean Ave. and Dolores St., ☎ 831/625–1587) exhibits photography by Ansel Adams and other 20th-century artists.

CHILDREN

Mischievous Rabbit (✉ Lincoln Ave. between 7th and Ocean Aves., ☎ 831/624–6854) sells toys, nursery accessories, books, music boxes, china, and children's clothing, with a specialty in Beatrix Potter items.

CLOTHING AND ACCESSORIES

Madrigal (✉ Carmel Plaza and Mission St., ☎ 831/624–3477) carries sportswear, sweaters, and accessories for women. **Pat Areias Sterling** (✉ Lincoln Ave., between Ocean and 7th Aves., ☎ 831/626–8668) puts a respectfully modern spin on the Mexican tradition of silversmithing in its line of sterling silver belt buckles, jewelry, and accessories.

GARDEN

Shop in the Garden (✉ Lincoln Ave. between Ocean and 7th Aves., ☎ 831/624–6047) is an indoor-outdoor sculpture garden where you can buy fountains or garden accoutrements. You'll hear the tinkle of its wind chimes before you see the courtyard establishment.

Carmel Valley

35 *5–10 mi east of Carmel, Hwy. 1 to Carmel Valley Rd.*

Carmel Valley Road, which turns inland at Highway 1 south of Carmel, is the main thoroughfare through the town of Carmel Valley, a secluded enclave of horse ranchers and other well-heeled residents who prefer the area's sunny climate to the fog and wind on the coast. Tiny Carmel Valley village holds several crafts shops and art galleries. **Garland Ranch Regional Park** (✉ Carmel Valley Rd., 9 mi east of Carmel, ☎ 831/659–4488) has hiking trails and picnic tables.

The beautiful **Château Julien** winery, recognized internationally for its chardonnays and merlots, gives tours on weekdays at 10:30 and 2:30 and weekends at 12:30 and 2:30, all by appointment. The tasting room is open daily. ✉ *8940 Carmel Valley Rd.*, ☎ *831/624–2600.* ⏲ *Weekdays 8–5, weekends 11–5.*

Dining and Lodging

$ ✕ **Wagon Wheel Coffee Shop.** Grab a seat at the counter or wait for a table at this local hangout decorated with wood-beam ceilings, hanging wagon wheels, cowboy hats, and lassos. Then chow down on substantial breakfasts of huevos rancheros, Italian sausage and eggs, or trout and eggs; this is also the place to stoke up on biscuits and gravy. For lunch choose among a dozen types of burgers or other sandwiches. ✉ *Valley Hill Center, Carmel Valley Rd. next to Quail Lodge,* ☎ *831/624–8878. No credit cards. No dinner.*

$$$$ ★ ✕🏨 **Bernardus Lodge.** A first-rate spa and outstanding cuisine are the focus at this latest addition to Carmel Valley's luxury lodging scene. Built in 2000 by the owner of the nearby Bernardus Winery, services here are geared to oenophiles and gourmands, with a range of classes on wines and food. The spacious rooms feature vaulted ceilings, featherbeds, fireplaces, patios, and double-size bathtubs. Marinus, the intimate formal dining room ($$$$), emphasizes modern French technique. The menu changes daily to reflect the availability of local game and produce. Chef Cal Stamenov's signature dishes include Portobello mushroom soup with goat cheese, foie gras, and white truffle oil; and pancetta-wrapped venison with chanterelles and huckleberries. ✉ *415 Carmel Valley Rd., 93924,* ☎ *831/659–3131 or 888/648–9463,* FAX *831/*

659–3529. 57 rooms. 2 restaurants, bar, minibars, refrigerators, room service, pool, beauty salon, spa, hot tub, sauna, steam room, tennis courts, croquet, concierge, meeting rooms. AE, D, DC, MC, V.

$$$$ ★ **Quail Lodge.** Guests at this resort on the grounds of a private country club have access to golf, tennis, and an 850-acre wildlife preserve frequented by deer and migratory fowl. Modern rooms with European decor are clustered in several low-rise buildings. Each room has a private deck or patio overlooking the golf course, gardens, or a lake. The Covey at Quail Lodge ($$$–$$$$; jacket required) serves European cuisine in a romantic lakeside setting. The menu changes daily, but look for rack of lamb, mustard-crusted salmon, and mousseline of sole, all accompanied by fresh local produce. ✉ *8205 Valley Greens Dr., 93923,* ☎ *831/624–1581 or 800/538–9516,* FAX *831/624–3726. 86 rooms, 14 suites. 2 restaurants, 2 bars, room service, 2 pools, hot tub, sauna, 18-hole golf course, putting greens, 4 tennis courts, hiking, bicycles, concierge. AE, DC, MC, V.*

$$$$ ★ **Carmel Valley Ranch Resort.** This all-suites resort, well off Carmel Valley Road on a hill overlooking the valley, is typical of contemporary California architecture. Standard ammenities include wood-burning fireplaces and watercolors by local artists. Rooms have cathedral ceilings, fully stocked wet bars, and large decks. The greens fee for guests at the resort's 18-hole golf course is $145, including cart rental; special golf packages can reduce this rate considerably. ✉ *1 Old Ranch Rd., 93923,* ☎ *831/625–9500 or 800/422–7635,* FAX *831/624–2858. 144 suites. 2 restaurants, 2 pools, 2 hot tubs, 2 saunas, 18-hole golf course, 13 tennis courts. AE, D, DC, MC, V.*

$$$$ ★ **Stonepine Estate Resort.** The former estate of the Crocker banking family on 330 pastoral acres has been converted to an ultra-deluxe inn. The oak-paneled, antiques-laden main château holds eight elegantly furnished rooms and suites and a dining room for guests, though with advance reservations it is possible for others to dine here. The property's romantic cottages include one that is straight out of *Hansel and Gretel.* An equestrian center offers riding lessons. ✉ *150 E. Carmel Valley Rd., Box 1543, 93924,* ☎ *831/659–2245,* FAX *831/659–5160. 8 rooms, 4 suites, 3 cottages. Dining room, minibars, room service, in-room VCRs, 2 pools, 5-hole golf course, 2 tennis courts, archery, exercise room, hiking, horseback riding, mountain bikes, library. AE, MC, V. BP.*

$$$–$$$$ **Carmel Valley Lodge.** In this small inn there are rooms surrounding a garden patio and separate one- and two-bedroom cottages with fireplaces and full kitchens. ✉ *8 Ford Rd., at Carmel Valley Rd., Box 93, 93924,* ☎ *831/659–2261 or 800/641–4646,* FAX *831/659–4558. 19 rooms, 4 suites, 8 cottages. Pool, hot tub, sauna, exercise room. AE, MC, V. CP.*

Outdoor Activities and Sports

GOLF

Golf Club at Quail Lodge (✉ 8000 Valley Greens Dr., ☎ 831/624–2770) incorporates several lakes into its course. Depending on the season and day of the week, greens fees range from $105 to $125 for guests and $125 to $165 for nonguests, including cart rental. **Rancho Cañada Golf Club** (✉ 4860 Carmel Valley Rd., 1 mi east of Hwy. 1, ☎ 831/624–0111) is a public course with 36 holes, some of them overlooking the Carmel River. Fees range from $30 to $75, plus $32 cart rental, depending on course and tee time.

Salinas

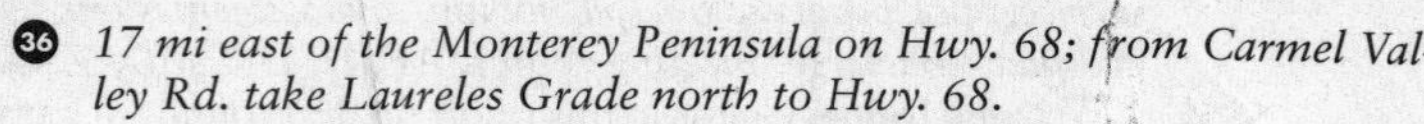

36 *17 mi east of the Monterey Peninsula on Hwy. 68; from Carmel Valley Rd. take Laureles Grade north to Hwy. 68.*

Salinas is the population center of a rich agricultural valley where fertile soil, an ideal climate, and a good water supply produce optimum growing conditions for crops such as lettuce, broccoli, tomatoes, strawberries, flowers, and wine grapes. This unpretentious town may lack the sophistication and scenic splendors of the coast, but it will interest literary and architectural buffs. Turn-of-the-20th-century buildings have been the focus of ongoing renovation, much of it centered on the original downtown area of South Main Street, with its handsome stone storefronts. The memory and literary legacy of Salinas native (and winner of the Pulitzer and Nobel prizes) John Steinbeck are well honored here.

The **National Steinbeck Center** is a museum and archive dedicated to the life and works of John Steinbeck. Many exhibits are interactive, bringing to life Steinbeck worlds such as Cannery Row, Hooverville (from *The Grapes of Wrath*), and the Mexican Plaza (from *The Pearl*). The library and archives contain Steinbeck first editions, notebooks, photographs, and audiotapes. Access to the archives is by appointment only. The center has information about Salinas' annual Steinbeck Festival in August and about tours of area landmarks mentioned in his novels. ✉ *1 Main St.,* ☎ *831/796–3833.* 🎫 *$8.* ⏲ *Daily 10–5.*

The **Jose Eusebio Boronda Adobe** contains furniture and artifacts depicting the lifestyle of Spanish California in the 1840s. Call for directions. ✉ *333 Boronda Rd.,* ☎ *831/757–8085.* 🎫 *Free (donation requested).* ⏲ *Weekdays 10–2, Sun. 1–4.*

Dining

$–$$ ✕ **Spado's.** One of several trendy new restaurants in Salinas, gleaming Spado's brings Monterey-style culinary sophistication to the valley. For lunch, visit the antipasto bar for fresh salads and Mediterranean morsels; the *panini* (Italian sandwiches) are also excellent. For dinner, try the pizza with chicken and sun-dried-tomato pesto, the angel-hair pasta and prawns, or the risotto of the day. ✉ *66 W. Alisal St.,* ☎ *831/424–4139. AE, D, DC, MC, V. No lunch weekends.*

$ ✕ **Steinbeck House.** John Steinbeck's birthplace, a Victorian frame house, has been converted into a lunch-only (11:30 AM–2 PM) eatery run by the volunteer Valley Guild. The restaurant displays some Steinbeck memorabilia. The set menu, which includes such dishes as zucchini lasagna and spinach crepes, incorporates locally grown produce. ✉ *132 Central Ave.,* ☎ *831/424–2735. MC, V. Closed Sun. and 3 wks in late Dec. and early Jan.*

Outdoor Activities and Sports

The **California Rodeo** (☎ 831/757–2951), one of the oldest and most famous rodeos in the West, takes place in mid-July.

San Juan Bautista

37 *18 mi north of Salinas on U.S. 101, then 2 mi east on Hwy. 156.*

Sleepy San Juan Bautista, protected from development since 1933, when ★ much of it became **San Juan Bautista State Historic Park,** is about as close to early 19th-century California as you can get. On Living History Day, which takes place on the first Saturday of each month, costumed volunteers engage in quilting bees, tortilla making, butter churning, and other period activities. ✉ *2nd and Franklin Sts., off Hwy. 156,* ☎ *831/623–4881.* 🎫 *$2.* ⏲ *Daily 10–4:30.*

The centerpiece of San Juan Bautista is a wide, green plaza ringed by historic buildings: a restored blacksmith shop, a stable, a pioneer cabin, and a jailhouse. Running along one side of the square is **Mission San Juan Bautista,** a long, low, colonnaded structure founded by Father Fermin Lasuen in 1797. Adjoining it is Mission Cemetery, where more than 4,300 Native Americans who converted to Christianity are buried in unmarked graves. ✉ *408 S. 2nd St.,* ☏ *831/623–2127.* 🎫 *$2.* ⏲ *Mon.–Sat. 9:30–5, Sun. 10–5.*

After the mission era, San Juan Bautista became an important crossroads for stagecoach travel. The principal stop in town was the **Plaza Hotel,** a collection of adobe buildings with furnishings from the 1860s. The **Castro-Breen Adobe,** furnished with Spanish colonial antiques, presents a view of domestic life in the village.

Shopping

Small antiques shops and art galleries line San Juan Bautista's side streets.

MONTEREY BAY A TO Z

Arriving and Departing

By Bus

Greyhound (☏ 800/231–2222) serves Monterey from San Francisco three times daily. The trip takes about 4½ hours.

By Car

The drive south from San Francisco to Monterey can be made comfortably in three hours or less. The most scenic way is to follow Highway 1 down the coast past flower, pumpkin, and artichoke fields and the seaside communities of Pacifica, Half Moon Bay, and Santa Cruz. Unless you drive on sunny weekends when locals are heading for the beach, the two-lane coast highway may take no longer than the freeway.

A sometimes faster route is I–280 south from San Francisco to Highway 17, south of San Jose. Highway 17 crosses the redwood-filled Santa Cruz mountains between San Jose and Santa Cruz, where it intersects with Highway 1. The traffic can crawl to a standstill, however, heading into Santa Cruz. Another option is to follow U.S. 101 south through San Jose to Prunedale, and then take Highway 156 west to Highway 1 south into Monterey; the latter part passes along the coast.

From Los Angeles, the drive to Monterey can be made in five to six hours by heading north on U.S. 101 to Salinas and then heading west on Highway 68. The spectacular but slow alternative is to take U.S. 101 to San Luis Obispo and then follow the hairpin turns of Highway 1 up the coast. Allow about three extra hours if you take this route.

By Plane

Monterey Peninsula Airport (✉ 200 Fred Kane Dr., ☏ 831/648–7000) is 3 mi east of downtown Monterey on Highway 68 to Olmsted Road. It is served by American Eagle, Skywest-Delta, United, United Express, and US Airways Express. *See* Air Travel *in* Smart Travel Tips A to Z for airline phone numbers.

By Train

The **Amtrak** (☏ 800/872–7245) *Coast Starlight,* which runs between Los Angeles, Oakland, and Seattle, stops in Salinas (✉ 11 Station Pl.). Connecting Amtrak Thruway buses serve Monterey and Carmel.

Getting Around

By Bus

Monterey–Salinas Transit (☎ 831/424–7695) provides frequent service between the peninsula's towns and many major sightseeing spots and shopping areas. The base fare is $1.50, with an additional $1.50 for each zone you travel into. A day pass costs from $3 to $6, depending on how many zones you'll be traveling through. The transit company runs the WAVE shuttle, which links major attractions on the Monterey waterfront. The shuttle operates daily between Memorial Day and Labor Day from 9 AM to 6:30 PM. The fare is $1 per day for unlimited rides.

By Car

Highway 1 runs north–south, linking the towns of Santa Cruz, Monterey, and Carmel. Highway 68 runs northeast from Pacific Grove toward Salinas, which U.S. 101 bisects. North of Salinas, U.S. 101 links up with Highway 156 to San Juan Bautista. Parking is especially difficult in Carmel and in heavily touristed areas of Monterey.

Contacts and Resources

B & B Reservations Services

Monterey Peninsula Reservations (☎ 888/655–3424). **Santa Cruz County Bed and Breakfast Referral Service** (☎ 831/425–8212). **Time to Coast Reservations** (☎ 800/555–9283).

Doctors

Community Hospital of Monterey Peninsula (✉ 23625 Holman Hwy., Monterey, ☎ 831/624–5311). **Monterey County Medical Society** (☎ 831/655–1019).

Emergencies

Ambulance (☎ 911). **Fire** (☎ 911). **Police** (☎ 911).

Guided Tours

California Parlor Car Tours (☎ 415/474–7500 or 800/227–4250) operates motor-coach tours from San Francisco to Los Angeles that include the Monterey Peninsula. **Rider's Guide** (✉ 484 Lake Park Ave., Suite 255, Oakland 94610, ☎ 510/653–2553) produces a self-guided audiotape tour detailing the history, landmarks, and attractions of the Monterey Peninsula and Big Sur for $12.95 plus $2.50 postage and, for California residents, sales tax.

Pharmacy

The pharmacy at **Surf 'n' Sand** (✉ 6th and Junipero Aves., Carmel, ☎ 831/624–1543) is open on weekdays from 9 to 6, Saturday from 9 to 1.

Visitor Information

Monterey Peninsula Visitors and Convention Bureau (✉ 380 Alvarado St., Monterey 93942, ☎ 831/649–1770). **Monterey County Vintners and Growers Association** (☎ 831/375–9400). **Salinas Valley Chamber of Commerce** (✉ 119 E. Alisal St., Salinas 93901, ☎ 831/424–7611). **Santa Cruz County Conference and Visitors Council** (✉ 1211 Ocean St., Santa Cruz 95060, ☎ 831/425–1234 or 800/833–3494). **Santa Cruz Mountain Winegrowers Association** (☎ 831/479–9463).

10 THE CENTRAL COAST

FROM BIG SUR TO SANTA BARBARA

Highway 1 between Big Sur and Santa Barbara is a spectacular stretch of terrain. The curving road demands an unhurried pace, but even if it didn't, you'd find yourself stopping often to take in the scenery. Don't expect much in the way of dining, lodging, or even history until you arrive at Hearst Castle, publisher William Randolph Hearst's testament to his own fabulousness. Sunny, well-scrubbed Santa Barbara's Spanish-Mexican heritage is reflected in the architectural style of its courthouse and mission.

Updated by Tim Lohnes

THE COASTLINE BETWEEN CARMEL and Santa Barbara, a distance of about 200 mi, is one of the most popular drives in California. Except for a few smallish cities—Ventura and Santa Barbara in the south and San Luis Obispo in the north—the area is sparsely populated. The countryside's few inhabitants relish their isolation at the sharp edge of land and sea. Around Big Sur the Santa Lucia mountains drop down to the Pacific with dizzying grandeur, but as you move south, the shoreline gradually flattens into rolling hills dotted with cattle and the long, sandy beaches of Santa Barbara and Ventura.

Artists create and sell their works in such towns as Cambria and Ojai. The wineries of the Santa Ynez Valley are steadily building reputations for quality vintages. The Danish town of Solvang is an amusing stopover for hearty Scandinavian fare and an architectural change of pace. Santa Barbara, only 95 mi north of Los Angeles, is your introduction to the unhurried hospitality and easy living of southern California.

Pleasures and Pastimes

Dining

The Central Coast from Big Sur to Solvang is far enough off the interstate to ensure that nearly every restaurant or café has its own personality—from chic to down-home and funky. There aren't many restaurants between Big Sur and Hearst Castle. Cambria's cooks, true to the town's British-Welsh origins, craft English dishes complete with peas and Yorkshire pudding but also serve Continental and contemporary fare.

The dishes of Santa Barbara's chefs rival those of their counterparts in the state's larger centers. Fresh seafood is plentiful, prepared old-style American in longtime wharf-side hangouts or with trendier accents at newer eateries. If you're after good, cheap food with an international flavor, follow the locals to Milpas Avenue on the eastern edge of Santa Barbara's downtown. Dining attire on the Central Coast is generally casual, though slightly dressy casual wear is the custom at pricier restaurants.

CATEGORY	COST*
$$$$	over $50
$$$	$30–$50
$$	$20–$30
$	under $20

**per person for a three-course meal, excluding drinks, service, and 7¼%–7¾% sales tax*

Lodging

Big Sur has only a few lodgings, but even its budget accommodations have character. Many moderately priced hotels and motels—some nicer than others, but most of them basic places to hang your hat—can be found between San Simeon and San Luis Obispo. Wherever you stay, make reservations for the summer well ahead of time.

CATEGORY	COST*
$$$$	over $175
$$$	$120–$175
$$	$80–$120
$	under $80

**All prices are for a standard double room, excluding 9%–10% tax.*

🕮 following the text of a review is your signal that the property has a Web site, where you will find details and, usually, images; for a link, visit www.fodors.com/urls.

Missions

Three important California missions established by Franciscan friars are within the Central Coast region. La Purisima is the most fully restored, Mission Santa Barbara is perhaps the most beautiful of the state's 21 missions, and Mission San Luis Obispo de Tolosa has a fine museum with many Chumash Indian artifacts.

Wineries

Centered in the Solvang area and spreading north toward San Luis Obispo and south toward Santa Barbara is a wine-making region with much of the variety but none of the glitz or crowds of northern California's Napa and Sonoma valleys. The many wineries in the rolling hills of the Santa Maria and Santa Ynez valleys tend to be small, but most have tasting rooms (some have tours), and you'll often meet the wine makers themselves. There are maps and brochures at the visitor centers in Solvang, San Luis Obispo, and Santa Barbara, or you can contact the wine associations of Paso Robles and Santa Barbara (☞ Contacts and Resources *in* The Central Coast A to Z, *below*).

Exploring the Central Coast

Numbers in the text correspond to numbers in the margin and on the Central Coast and Santa Barbara maps.

Great Itineraries

Driving is the easiest way to experience the Central Coast. The three-day itinerary below is arranged in two ways: as a loop from San Francisco or from Los Angeles. The seven-day trip is organized from north to south.

IF YOU HAVE 3 DAYS

Especially in the summertime, make reservations for a visit to Hearst Castle well before you depart for the coast. From Los Angeles maximize your time by taking U.S. 101 directly to **San Luis Obispo** ⑩. North of town, poke your head into the kitschy **Madonna Inn.** Continue on to **Mission San Luis Obispo de Tolosa** and the nearby **County Historical Museum.** Drive west on Highway 46 and north on Highway 1 and stay overnight in 🏨 **Cambria.** Take a morning tour of **Hearst Castle** ⑦, spend some time viewing the exhibits at the visitor center, and then drive up to **Nepenthe** ⑤ in **Big Sur,** for a late lunch. After lunch, head south on U.S. 101 to 🏨 **Santa Barbara** ⑮–㉚. Spend the late afternoon and early evening exploring **Stearns Wharf** ⑱ and other waterfront sights. The next morning, tour the **Santa Barbara County Courthouse** ㉕ and **Mission Santa Barbara** ㉙. In the afternoon, stroll **State Street** if you like to shop, or catch some rays at **East Beach** ⑳. From San Francisco, drive down the coast to **Big Sur.** Have lunch at **Nepenthe,** ⑤ and continue south to 🏨 **Cambria.** The next day, tour **Hearst Castle,** ⑦ drive through **Morro Bay** and **San Luis Obispo** ⑩ and on to **Santa Barbara** ⑮–㉚. Spend the night and explore town the next morning.

IF YOU HAVE 7 DAYS

Make 🏨 **Big Sur** your destination for the first day and most of the second. If you're in the area on a weekend, tour the **Point Sur State Historic Park** ②. Watch the waves break on **Pfeiffer Beach** ④, one of the few places where you can actually set foot on the shore. Observe the glories of **Los Padres National Forest** up close by hiking one of the many trails in the **Ventana Wilderness,** or stay along the shore and hunt for

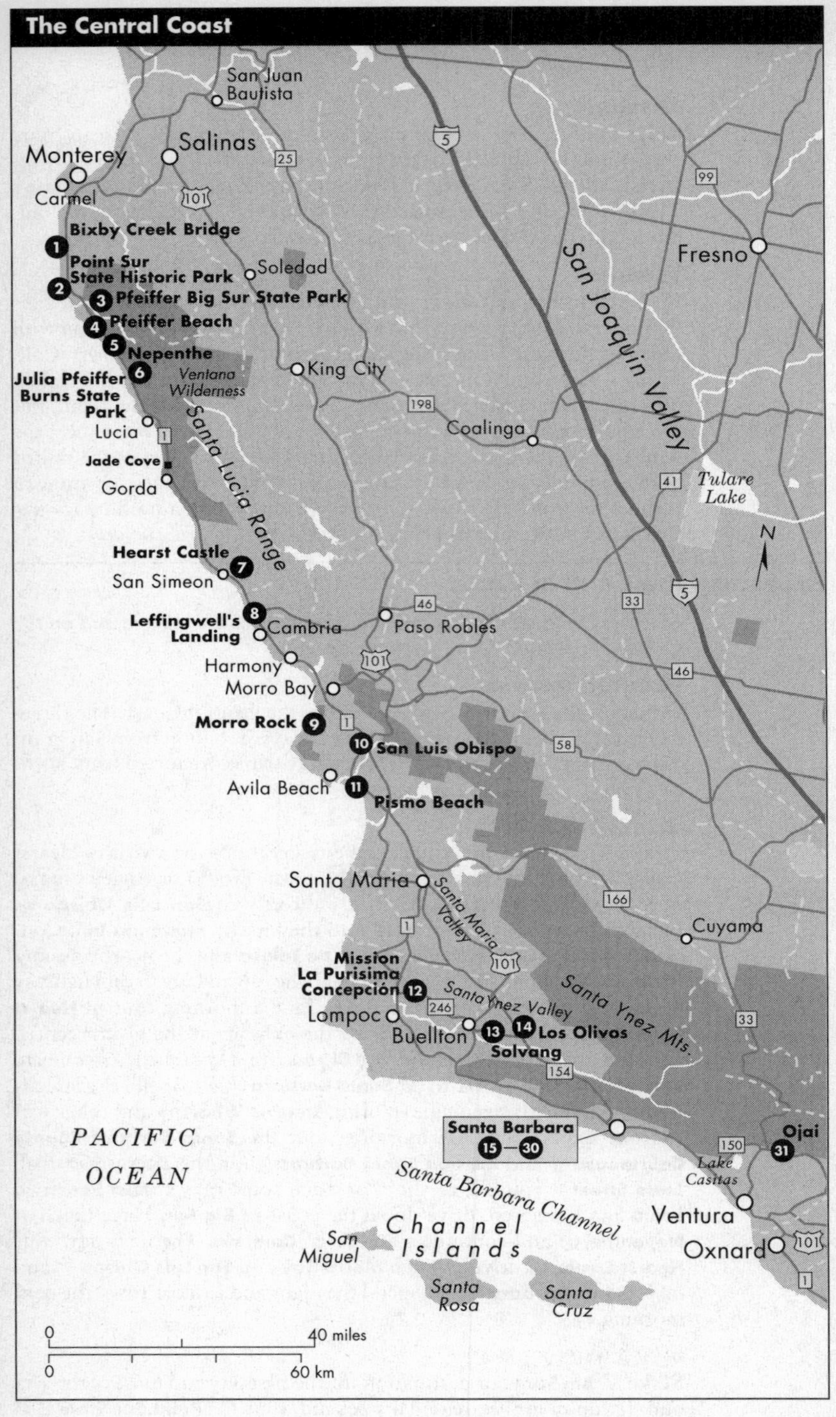
The Central Coast
San Juan Bautista
Salinas
Monterey
Carmel
Bixby Creek Bridge
Point Sur State Historic Park
Soledad
Pfeiffer Big Sur State Park
Pfeiffer Beach
Nepenthe
Julia Pfeiffer Burns State Park
Ventana Wilderness
King City
Lucia
Santa Lucia Range
Jade Cove
Gorda
Coalinga
San Joaquin Valley
Fresno
Tulare Lake
Hearst Castle
San Simeon
Leffingwell's Landing
Cambria
Paso Robles
Harmony
Morro Bay
Morro Rock
San Luis Obispo
Avila Beach
Pismo Beach
Santa Maria
Santa Maria Valley
Cuyama
Mission La Purisima Concepción
Santa Ynez Valley
Santa Ynez Mts.
Lompoc
Buellton
Los Olivos
Solvang
Santa Barbara
Ojai
Lake Casitas
Ventura
Oxnard
PACIFIC OCEAN
Santa Barbara Channel
Channel Islands
San Miguel
Santa Rosa
Santa Cruz
40 miles
60 km

jade at **Jade Cove.** Plan to reach **Cambria** by the evening of day two. Have dinner and explore the town's shops. On day three, have a beachfront breakfast at **Morro Bay,** tour **Hearst Castle** ⑦, have lunch, and take U.S. 101 south to Highway 246 west to get to **Mission La Purisima Concepción** ⑫. Loop back east on Highway 246 to U.S. 101 and head south to **Santa Barbara** ⑮–㉚. On day four, visit **Stearns Wharf** ⑱ and walk or bike to **East Beach** ⑳ and the **Andree Clark Bird Refuge** ㉑. Have dinner on **State Street** and check out the area's shops and clubs. On your fifth day, get a feel for the city's architecture, history, and vegetation at, respectively, the **Santa Barbara County Courthouse** ㉕, **Mission Santa Barbara** ㉙, and the **Santa Barbara Botanic Garden** ㉘. Have dinner in **Montecito** and explore the Coast Village Road shopping district. It's a short walk south from here to the shore to catch the sunset before or after you eat. On your sixth day, experience the area's marine life on a half-day cruise of the **Channel Islands.** On day seven, take U.S. 101 south to Highway 150 east to reach **Ojai** ㉛.

When to Tour the Central Coast

The Central Coast is hospitable most of the year. Fog often rolls in north of Pismo Beach during the summer; you'll need a jacket, especially after sunset, close to the shore. The rains usually come between December and March. Santa Barbara is pleasant year-round. Hotel rooms fill up in the summer, but from April to early June and in the early fall the weather is almost as fine and it's less hectic. Most hotels offer considerable discounts during the winter.

HIGHWAY 1 TO SOLVANG

Big Sur, San Simeon, and San Luis Obispo

Big Sur

152 mi from San Francisco, south on I–280 and U.S. 101, west on Hwy. 68 and south on Hwy. 1; 27 mi south of Monterey on Hwy. 1.

Long a retreat of artists and writers, Big Sur contains ancient forests and a rugged coastline that residents have protected from overdevelopment. Much of the area lies within several state parks and the more than 165,000-acre **Ventana Wilderness,** itself part of the Los Padres National Forest. The counterculture spirit of Big Sur is evident today in tie-dyed clothing some locals wear and the presence of the Esalen Institute, a mecca of the human growth-potential movement. Established in 1910 as a haven with curative baths, Esalen exploded in the 1960s as a place to explore consciousness, environmental issues, and nude bathing.

❶ The graceful arc of **Bixby Creek Bridge** (✉ Hwy. 1, 13 mi south of Carmel) is a photographer's dream. From the parking area on the north side you can admire the view or walk across the 550-ft span.

★ ❷ **Point Sur State Historic Park** a century-old beacon, still stands watch from atop a sandstone cliff. Four lighthouse keepers lived here with their families until 1974 when the light station was automated. Their homes and working spaces are open to the public on 2½- to 3-hour, ranger-led tours. Considerable walking, including two stairways, is involved. ✉ *Hwy. 1, 19 mi south of Carmel,* ☎ *831/625–4419.* *$2.* *Tours generally Sat. 10* AM *and 2* PM*, Sun. 10* AM*, plus Apr.–Oct., Wed. 10 and 2; call ahead to confirm.*

❸ A short hiking trail at **Pfeiffer Big Sur State Park** leads through a redwood-filled valley to a waterfall. You can double back or continue on the more difficult trail along the valley wall for views of the tops of the trees you were just walking among. Stop in at the **Big Sur Station,** west of the park entrance, for information about the entire area. ✉ *Hwy. 1, 8½ mi south of Point Sur State Historic Park,* ☎ *831/667–2315.* 🎫 *$3 per vehicle (day use).* ⏲ *Daily sunrise–sunset.*

4 Through a hole in one of the big rocks at secluded **Pfeiffer Beach** you can watch the waves break first on the sea side and then on the beach side. ✉ *Off Hwy. 1; the 2-mi road to beach is immediately past Big Sur Station.* 🎫 *$3 per vehicle (day use).*

5 **Nepenthe** (✉ Hwy. 1, 2½ mi south of Big Sur Station) overlooks lush meadows to the ocean below. The house was once owned by Orson Welles and Rita Hayworth, though they reportedly spent little time here. Downstairs from the on-site restaurant and café is a gift shop displaying, among other items, the work of the acclaimed fabric designer Kaffe Fassett, who grew up at Nepenthe.

6 **Julia Pfeiffer Burns State Park** offers some fine hiking, from an easy ½-mi stroll with marvelous coastal views to a strenuous 6-mi trek through the redwoods. Summer crowds lessen the appeal of the big attraction here, an 80-ft waterfall that drops into the ocean, but you'll still get an idea why the park's namesake, the daughter of one of the area's first white settlers, liked to sit here and contemplate nature. Migrating whales, not to mention harbor seals and sea lions, can sometimes be spotted not far from shore. ✉ *Hwy. 1, 12 mi south of Big Sur Station,* ☎ *831/667–2315.* 🎫 *$3.* ⏲ *Daily sunrise–sunset.*

Dining, Lodging, and Camping

$$–$$$ ✕ **Nepenthe.** You'll not find a grander coastal view between San Francisco and Los Angeles than the one from here. The American food—burgers, sandwiches, and salads at lunchtime—is overpriced. The superb location is the draw, so don't bother coming after dark. Nepenthe serves dinner, too; the outdoor Café Kevah serves breakfast and lunch. ✉ *Hwy. 1, south end of town,* ☎ *831/667–2345. AE, MC, V.*

$$–$$$ ✕ **Ragged Point Inn.** A good place to lunch on the way into or out of the area's parks, this restaurant perched over the southernmost end of Big Sur is not as fancy as the places farther north. But neither are the prices, and the food—sandwiches, salads, pastas, and fish and meat dishes—is tasty. ✉ *Hwy. 1, 16 mi north of San Simeon,* ☎ *805/927–5708. AE, D, MC, V.*

$$$$ ★ ✕🏨 **Post Ranch Inn.** This luxurious retreat is the ultimate in environmentally conscious architecture. The redwood guest houses, all with dizzyingly splendid views of the Pacific Ocean or the mountains, blend unobtrusively into a wooded cliff 1,200 ft above the ocean. Each unit, done in a spare style, has its own spa tub, fireplace, stereo, private deck, and massage table. A refrigerator holds free snacks. On-site activities include everything from guided hikes to tarot-card readings. The inn's restaurant, which serves a four-course prix fixe menu of cutting-edge American food, is the best in the area. ✉ *Hwy. 1, Box 219, 93920,* ☎ *831/667–2200 or 800/527–2200,* FAX *831/667–2512 or 831/687–2824. 30 units. Restaurant, bar, pool, wading pool, spa, exercise room, library. AE, MC, V. CP.*

$$$$ ★ ✕🏨 **Ventana Inn.** The activities at this quintessential California getaway are purposely limited to sunning at poolside—there is a clothing-optional deck—and walks in the nearby hills. Buildings that blend into the rugged surroundings are scattered in clusters on a wooded hillside above the Pacific. All rooms have natural-wood walls and cool tile floors, while some of the more expensive ones also have private hot tubs on their patios. For a real event, try brunching on the terrace while taking in the spectacular views. ✉ *Hwy. 1, 93920,* ☎ *831/667–*

2331 or 800/628–6500, FAX 831/667–2419. 59 rooms, 3 houses. Restaurant, 2 pools, 2 Japanese baths, sauna, exercise room, library. AE, D, DC, MC, V. 2-night minimum stay on weekends and holidays. CP.

$–$$$$ **Big Sur River Inn.** The Big Sur River flows past the forested grounds of this old wooden structure. Guests often sip afternoon drinks on the river's banks in the summer. Some rooms are merely functional, but others are quite nice. Ask for one of the upper-floor, gnarled-redwood–panel rooms. When there's a chill in the air, a fire roars in the stone fireplace in the inn's huge dining room ($–$$), which serves fresh fish and specials such as pasta Castroville (with artichokes and chicken in a pesto cream sauce). *Hwy 1. at Pheneger Creek, 93920, 831/667–2700, FAX 831/667–2743. 14 rooms, 6 suites. Restaurant, bar, pool, store. AE, D, DC, MC, V.*

$–$$$$ **Deetjen's Big Sur Inn.** This inn amid the redwoods has rustic charm, especially if you're not too attached to creature comforts. The room doors lock only from the inside, half the rooms have only wood-burning stoves to supply heat, and your neighbor can often be heard through the walls. Still, Deetjen's is a special place. The restaurant (reservations essential) in the main house serves stylish food that includes roasted half duck, steak, and lamb chops for dinner and wonderfully light and flavorful pancakes for breakfast. *Hwy. 1, south end of town, 93920, 831/667–2377 for inn; 831/667–2378 for restaurant, FAX 831/667–0466. 20 rooms. Restaurant. MC, V.*

$$–$$$$ **Big Sur Lodge.** The motel-style cottages of this property in Pfeiffer Big Sur State Park make it a good choice for families. The lodging area sits in a meadow surrounded by redwood and oak trees. Some accommodations have fireplaces, some have kitchens; none have TVs or phones. *Hwy. 1, Box 190, 93920, 831/667–3100 or 800/424–4787, FAX 831/667–3110. 61 rooms. Restaurant, grocery, pool, shop. AE, MC, V.*

$$–$$$ **Glen Oaks Motel.** At this simple lodging in the heart of Big Sur you can choose between bland motel-style rooms and log cabins in the woods that combine Laura Ashley flourishes with frontier style. *Hwy. 1, 93920, 831/667–2105. 15 rooms, 2 cottages. No credit cards.*

Pfeiffer Big Sur State Park. Redwood trees tower over this large campground. It's often crowded in summer, so reserve a site as far ahead as possible. *Hwy. 1, 8½ mi south of Point Sur State Historic Park, 831/667–2315 for information; 800/444–7275 to reserve a site. 218 sites. $12.*

En Route Highway 1 snakes south along the coast from Big Sur toward San Simeon. Ten miles south of the town of Lucia is **Jade Cove,** a well-known jade-hunting spot. Rock hunting is allowed on the beach, but you may not remove anything from the walls of the cliffs.

San Simeon

57 mi south of Big Sur on Hwy. 1.

Whalers founded San Simeon in the 1850s but had virtually abandoned the town by the time Senator George Hearst reestablished it 20 years later. Hearst bought up most of the surrounding ranch land, built a 1,000-ft wharf, and turned San Simeon into a bustling port. His son, William Randolph, further developed the area during the construction of Hearst Castle. Today the town, which is 3 mi east of the road leading to the castle, is basically a row of gift shops, restaurants, and motels along Highway 1.

★ 7 **Hearst Castle,** known officially as the Hearst San Simeon State Historical Monument, sits in solitary splendor atop La Cuesta Encantada (the Enchanted Hill). Its buildings and gardens are spread over the 127 acres that were the heart of newspaper magnate William Randolph Hearst's 250,000-acre ranch.

Hearst devoted nearly 30 years and about $10 million to building this elaborate estate. He commissioned renowned architect Julia Morgan—who was also responsible for buildings at the University of California at Berkeley—but was very much involved with the final product, a hodgepodge of Italian, Spanish, Moorish, and French styles. The 115-room main building and three huge "cottages" are connected by terraces and staircases and surrounded by pools, gardens, and statuary. In its heyday the castle was a playground for Hearst, Hollywood celebrities, and the rich and powerful from around the world.

Although construction began in 1919, the project was never officially completed. Work was halted in 1947 when Hearst had to leave San Simeon due to failing health. The Hearst family presented the property to the state of California in 1958.

Buses from the visitor center zigzag up the hillside to the neoclassical extravaganza above. Guides conduct four different daytime tours and (part of the year) one evening tour of various parts of the main house and grounds. Tour No. 1, the most basic, is recommended for newcomers. Daytime tours take about two hours. Docents in period costume portray Hearst's guests and staff for the slightly longer evening tour, which begins at sunset. All tours include a ½-mi walk and between 150 and 400 stairs. A 40-minute film shown at a giant-screen theater gives a sanitized version of Hearst's life and of the construction of the castle. Reservations for the tours, which can be made up to eight weeks in advance, are necessary. ✉ *San Simeon State Park, 750 Hearst Castle Rd.,* ☎ *805/927–2020 or 800/444–4445.* 🎟 *$10 for daytime tours, $20 for evening tours.* ⏲ *Tours daily 8:20–3:20 (later in summer); additional tours take place most Fri. and Sat. evenings Mar.–May and Sept.–Dec. MC, V.* ♿

Dining and Lodging

$$ ✕ **Europa.** The menu here includes dishes from Germany, Hungary, and Italy—goulash with späetzle, stuffed pork roast with kielbasa, and homemade pasta. Steaks and fresh fish are also served. Crisp linen tablecloths brighten the small dining room. ✉ *9240 Castillo Dr. (Hwy. 1),* ☎ *805/927–3087. MC, V. Closed Sun. No lunch.*

$$–$$$$ ★ 🏨 **Best Western Cavalier.** Reasonable rates, an oceanfront location, and well-equipped rooms—all with TVs with VCRs and some with wood-burning fireplaces and private patios—make this motel a good choice. ✉ *9415 Hearst Dr., 93452,* ☎ *805/927–4688 or 800/826–8168,* FAX *805/927–6472. 90 rooms. 2 restaurants, refrigerators, 2 pools, hot tub, exercise room, coin laundry. AE, D, DC, MC, V.* ♿

Cambria

9 mi south of San Simeon on Hwy. 1.

Cambria, an artists' colony with many late-Victorian homes, is divided into the newer West Village and the original East Village. Each section has B&Bs, restaurants, art galleries, and shops. You can still detect traces of the Welsh miners who settled in Cambria in the 1890s. Motels line Moonstone Beach Drive, which runs along the coast.

8 **Leffingwell's Landing,** a state picnic ground, is a good place for examining tidal pools and watching otters as they frolic in the surf. Footpaths wind along the beach side of the the drive. ✉ *Moonstone Beach Dr., northern end.*

Dining and Lodging

$$–$$$ ✕ **The Sea Chest.** By far the best seafood restaurant in town, this clifftop inn serves all kinds of fish, much of it locally caught. The oyster bar is highly recommended. Come early to catch the sunset. ✉ *6216 Moonstone Beach Dr.,* ☎ *805/927–4514. Reservations not accepted. No credit cards. No lunch.*

$–$$$ ★ ✕ **Hamlet at Moonstone Gardens.** In the middle of 3 acres of luxuriant gardens, this restaurant, open for lunch and dinner daily, has an enchanting patio that's perfect for relaxing. The views from the upstairs dining room aren't bad, either. Entrées range from hamburgers to rack of lamb. The output of more than 50 wineries is represented downstairs at the Pacific Wine Works. ✉ *Hwy. 1 at Moonstone Beach Dr.,* ☎ *805/927–3535. MC, V.*

$–$$ ✕ **The Greenwoods.** Ribs, filet mignon, and large New York steaks lure locals and tourists to the restaurant attached to the Cambria Pines Lodge. Bands in the lounge play light rock, jazz, and other music. ✉ *2905 Burton Dr.,* ☎ *805/927–4200. AE, D, DC, MC, V.*

$–$$ ✕ **Robin's.** Multiethnic only begins to describe the dining possibilities at this antiques-filled restaurant nestled amid Monterey pines. Tandoori prawns, quesadillas, a Thai red curry, an array of salads (more for lunch than dinner), numerous vegetarian entrées, hamburgers for the kids, and some truly fine desserts are all on Robin's menu. ✉ *4095 Burton Dr.,* ☎ *805/927–5007. MC, V.*

$$$–$$$$ **Pelican Suites.** This beachfront abode offers great views and extremely comfortable rooms. The storied king-size beds, complete with steps leading up to the mattress, the large fireplaces, and the low-key wallpapering along with the hot tubs in some of the rooms make this a good romantic getaway. Ask for an ocean view. ✉ *6316 Moonstone Beach Dr., 93428,* ☎ *805/927–1500,* FAX *805/927–0218. 24 rooms. Refrigerators, pool, hot tubs, exercise room. AE, D, MC, V.*

$$–$$$$ **Blue Dolphin.** The luxurious beachfront rooms here look like they've been transported straight out of a middle-class home in Surrey circa 1910. Heavy on frills and pinks and pastels, they have TVs with VCRs, fireplaces, and superb ocean views. Five rooms have whirlpool tubs. ✉ *6470 Moonstone Beach Dr., 93428,* ☎ *805/927–3300,* FAX *805/927–7311. 18 rooms. Refrigerators. AE, D, DC, MC, V. CP.*

$$–$$$$ **Cypress Cove Inn.** Like many hotels on the beach, this romantic getaway was designed in the Welsh style, with outside walls made of old stone and rooms on the upper floors crisscrossed by wood beams. Many rooms face the Pacific. ✉ *6348 Moonstone Beach Dr., 93428,* ☎ *805/927–2600 or 800/568–8517. 21 rooms, 1 suite. In-room VCRs, no-smoking rooms, refrigerators, hot tub. AE, D, DC, MC, V.*

$$–$$$ **Fog Catcher Inn.** Its landscaped gardens and 10 thatch-roof buildings resemble an English country village. Most rooms (among them 10 minisuites) have ocean views. All have fireplaces and are done in floral chintz with light-wood furniture. ✉ *6400 Moonstone Beach Dr., 93428,* ☎ *805/927–1400 or 800/425–4121,* FAX *805/927–0204. 50 rooms, 10 suites. Pool, hot tub. AE, D, DC, MC, V. CP.*

$$–$$$ **Squibb House.** Owner Bruce Black restored this 1877 Gothic Revival–Italianate structure, and his craftsmen built many of the pine furnishings. The rooms contain antiques but have modern conveniences such as reading lamps with ample light, and showers with sufficient water pressure. ✉ *4063 Burton Dr., 93428,* ☎ *805/927–9600,* FAX *805/927–9606. 5 rooms. No-smoking rooms. AE, MC, V. CP.*

$–$$$ **Best Western Fireside Inn.** This modern motel has spacious rooms with sofas, upholstered lounge chairs, refrigerators, and coffeemakers. Some rooms have whirlpools and all have toasty gas fireplaces. The inn is across from a particularly striking rocky outcrop of the beach. ✉ *6700*

Moonstone Beach Dr., 93428, ☎ 805/927–8661 or 888/910–7100, FAX 805/927–8584. 46 rooms. Pool, hot tub. AE, D, DC, MC, V. CP.

$–$$$ **Bluebird Motel.** Rooms at this garden motel near Cambria's East Village include simply furnished doubles and nicer creekside suites with patios, fireplaces, refrigerators, and TVs with VCRs. The Bluebird isn't the fanciest place, but if you don't require beachside accommodations it's a decent bargain. The wooded gardens are beautiful. ✉ *1880 Main St., 93428, ☎ 805/927–4634 or 800/552–5434, FAX 805/927–5215. 37 rooms. AE, D, DC, MC, V.*

$$ **San Simeon Pines Resort.** Amid 9 acres of pines and cypress, this motel-style resort has its own golf course and is directly across from Leffingwell's Landing. The accommodations include cottages with landscaped backyards. Some parts of the complex are for adults only; others are reserved for families. ✉ *7200 Moonstone Beach Dr. (mailing address: Box 117, San Simeon 93452), ☎ 805/927–4648. 58 rooms. Pool, 9-hole golf course, croquet, shuffleboard, playground. AE, MC, V.*

Nightlife

Cambria doesn't have much of a nightlife, but if you're looking for a bar with music, cruise up Main Street until you hear some sounds that suit your fancy. A crowd of all ages hangs out at **Camozzi's Saloon** (✉ 2262 Main St., ☎ 805/927–8941), where the atmosphere is old-time cowboy but the music is rock and R&B.

En Route Seven miles south of Cambria on Highway 1 is the town of **Harmony,** population 18. The **Harmony Pottery Studio Gallery** (✉ Hwy. 1, ☎ 805/927–4293) shows some fine work.

Morro Bay

20 mi south of Cambria on Hwy. 1.

Fishermen in the town of Morro Bay slog around the harbor in galoshes, and old-style ships teeter in its protected waters. Chumash Indians were the area's main inhabitants when Portuguese explorer Juan Rodríguez Cabrillo dropped anchor in 1542. The Spanish claimed the region in 1587, but Morro Bay remained a relatively quiet place until the second half of the 19th century, when an enterprising farmer built the town's wharf. Fishing was the main industry in the early 20th century, and it remains a vital part of the economy.

★ 9 Locals are proud of the 576-ft-high **Morro Rock,** one of nine such small volcanic peaks, or "morros," in the area. A short walk leads to a breakwater, with the harbor on one side and the crashing waves of the Pacific on the other. Morro Bay is a wildlife preserve where endangered falcons and other birds nest. You can't climb on Morro Rock, but even from its base you'll be able to divine that the peak is alive with birds.

The center of the action on land is the **Embarcadero,** which holds lodgings and the restaurants that make up the area's au courant dining scene. The town's well-designed aquarium is here, as is the outdoor Giant Chessboard, made up of nearly life-size hand-carved pieces.

Dining and Lodging

$$–$$$$ ✕ **Hoppe's Hip Pocket Bistro.** Morro Bay's most notable restaurant is the one place in town where you can get real caviar. Enjoy fresh fish prepared with style while taking in the great views of the harbor. ✉ *901 Embarcadero, ☎ 805/772–9012. AE, D, MC, V. No lunch Mon. and Tues.*

$$–$$$ ✕ **The Great American Fish Company.** Opposite Morro Rock, this is a great spot to come and watch the seagulls and look out for frolick-

ing otters. The only drawback is the power plant looming behind the restaurant. Shark steaks, filet mignon with scampi, squid burgers, and other entrées come in generous portions. ✉ *1185 Embarcadero,* ☎ *805/772–4707. MC, V.*

$–$$$ ✕ **Dorn's.** This seafood café that overlooks the harbor resembles a Cape Cod cottage. It's open for breakfast, lunch, and dinner. Excellent fish and calamari steaks are on the dinner menu. ✉ *801 Market Ave.,* ☎ *805/772–4415. AE, MC, V.*

$$–$$$$ **Ascot Suites.** A hop and a skip away from the Embarcadero, the rooms in this upscale hotel have all the modern conveniences. There are large hot tubs in most of the bathrooms, well-stocked wet bars, and gas fireplaces. ✉ *260 Morro May Blvd., 93442,* ☎ *805/772–4437 or 800/887–6454,* FAX *805/772–8860. 31 suites. Refrigerators, pool, hot tubs. AE, D, MC, V.*

$$–$$$$ **Embarcadero Inn.** A drab metallic-color wooden exterior hides a more welcoming interior with sparkling clean rooms, all of them with old maritime photographs on the walls and balconies that face the sea. ✉ *456 Embarcadero, 93442,* ☎ *805/772–2700 or 800/292–7625,* FAX *805/772–1060. 29 rooms, 3 suites. Refrigerators, 2 hot tubs. AE, D, DC, MC, V.*

$$–$$$$ **The Inn at Morro Bay.** This upscale hotel complex has romantic country French–style rooms. Some have fireplaces, whirlpool tubs, and bay views; others look out at extensive gardens. There's a golf course across the road, and a heron rookery nearby. (Even bird lovers shouldn't book a room near the nesting grounds, as the morning din can be overwhelming.) ✉ *60 State Park Rd., 93442,* ☎ *805/772–5651 or 800/321–9566,* FAX *805/772–4779. 98 rooms, 1 cottage. Restaurant, bar, room service, pool, massage, meeting rooms. AE, D, DC, MC, V.*

$$–$$$ **Grays Inn and Gallery.** With only three rooms, you may have trouble getting a reservation at this tiny beachfront property. But make an effort, because the place is a hidden treasure with cozy rooms facing the sea. ✉ *561 Embarcadero, 93442,* ☎ *805/772–3911. 3 rooms. Kitchenettes. AE, MC, V.*

$–$$$ **Adventure Inn.** Nautical murals decorate this small motel facing Morro Rock. Rooms are plain but comfortable. Amenities include coffeemakers and free HBO and local calls. ✉ *1150 Embarcadero, 93442,* ☎ *805/772–5607; 800/799–5607 in CA;* FAX *805/772–8377. 16 rooms. Restaurant, refrigerators, pool, hot tub. AE, MC, V. CP.*

Outdoor Activities and Sports

Kayaks of Morro Bay (✉ 699 Embarcadero, ☎ 805/772–1119) rents canoes and kayaks. **Sub-Sea Tours** (✉ 699 Embarcadero, ☎ 805/772–9463) operates rides in glass-bottom boats. **Virg's Sport Fishing** (✉ 1215 Embarcadero, ☎ 805/772–1222 or 800/762–5263) conducts deep-sea fishing trips.

San Luis Obispo

10 *14 mi south of Morro Bay on Hwy. 1; 230 mi south of San Francisco on I–280 to U.S. 101; 112 mi north of Santa Barbara on U.S. 101.*

About halfway between San Francisco and Los Angeles, San Luis Obispo is an appealing urban center set among rolling hills and extinct volcanos. It is home to two decidedly different institutions: California Polytechnic State University, known as Cal Poly, and the exuberantly garish Madonna Inn. The town has restored its old railroad depot as well as several Victorian-era homes. The Chamber of Commerce (☞ Contacts and Resources *in* the Central Coast A to Z, *below*) has a list of self-guided historic walks. On Thursday from 6 AM to 9 PM a four-block-long farmers market lines Higuera Street.

★ **Mission San Luis Obispo de Tolosa,** established in 1772, overlooks San Luis Obispo Creek. A museum exhibits artifacts of the Chumash Indians and early Spanish settlers. ✉ *751 Palm St.,* ☎ *805/543–6850.* 🎟 *$2 suggested donation.* ⏲ *Late May–Dec., daily 9–5; Jan.–late May, daily 9–4.*

Inside a recently renovated redbrick building across from the mission, ★ the **County Historical Museum** holds a captivating hodgepodge of exhibits—Native American arrows, tiles from the original mission roof, and an intriguing late-19th-century hand organ. ✉ *696 Monterey St.,* ☎ *805/543–0638.* 🎟 *$2.* ⏲ *Daily 9–5.*

Dining and Lodging

$–$$$ ✕ **Beau's Russian Tea Room.** As the name suggests, Russian food dominates this elegant restaurant. From caviar to borscht to chicken Kiev, it's all here. Desserts are excellent. Service can be slightly slow. ✉ *699 Higuera St.,* ☎ *805/784–0174. AE, MC, V.*

$–$$ ✕ **Buona Tavola.** Homemade *agnolotti* pasta with scampi in a creamy saffron sauce and braised lamb shank with grilled polenta are among the northern Italian dishes served at this local favorite. In good weather you can dine on the flower-filled patio. ✉ *1037 Monterey St.,* ☎ *805/545–8000. D, MC, V.*

$–$$ ✕ **Cafe Roma.** Authentic northern Italian cuisine is the specialty of this restaurant on Railroad Square. Under a large mural of sunny Tuscany, you can dine on squash-filled ravioli with sage and butter sauce or filet mignon glistening with port and Gorgonzola. ✉ *1010 Railroad Ave.,* ☎ *805/541–6800. AE, D, DC, MC, V. Closed Mon. No lunch weekends.*

$ ★ ✕ **Big Sky Café.** The menu here roams the world—the Mediterranean, North Africa, and the Southwest—but many of the ingredients are local: organic fruits and vegetables, hormone-free chicken, and pork and chicken sausages produced right in town. Big Sky is a hip gathering spot for breakfast, lunch, and dinner. ✉ *1121 Broad St.,* ☎ *805/545–5401. MC, V.*

$$$–$$$$ ★ 🏨 **Apple Farm.** Decorated to the hilt with floral bedspreads and watercolors by local artists, this is the most comfortable place to stay in town. Each room in the country-style hotel has a gas fireplace; some have canopy beds and cozy window seats. There's a working grist mill in the courtyard. An American restaurant and cluttered gift shop cater to guests. ✉ *2015 Monterey St., 93401,* ☎ *805/544–2040; 800/374–3705 in CA;* FAX *805/546–9495. 104 rooms. Restaurant, pool, hot tub. AE, D, MC, V.*

$$–$$$$ 🏨 **Madonna Inn.** From its rococo bathrooms to its pink-on-pink, froufrou dining areas, the Madonna Inn is the ultimate in kitsch. Each room is unique, to say the least: Rock Bottom is all stone; the Safari Room is decked out in animal skins. Humor value aside, the Madonna is pretty much a gussied-up motel, so don't expect much in the way of luxury. ✉ *100 Madonna Rd., 93405,* ☎ *805/543–3000 or 800/543–9666,* FAX *805/543–1800. 87 rooms, 22 suites. Restaurant, bar, café, dining room, shops. MC, V.*

$$ 🏨 **La Cuesta Inn.** The decor at this adobe-style motel on the northern edge of town is understated, almost to the point of being generic. If you can forgo elegance, this is a good bet. ✉ *2074 Monterey St., 93401,* ☎ *805/543–2777 or 800/543–2777,* FAX *805/544–0696. 72 rooms. Pool, hot tub. AE, D, DC, MC, V. CP.*

$–$$ 🏨 **Adobe Inn.** The friendly owners of this establishment of cheerful motel-style rooms serve excellent breakfasts. They'll also help you plan your stay in the area. ✉ *1473 Monterey St., 93401,* ☎ *805/549–0321 or 800/676–1588,* FAX *805/549–0383. 15 rooms. Kitchenettes. AE, D, DC, MC, V. BP.*

Nightlife and the Arts

The **San Luis Obispo Mozart Festival** (☎ 805/781–3008) takes place in late July and early August. Not all the music is Mozart; you'll hear Haydn and other composers. The **Festival Fringe** presents free concerts outdoors. The **Performing Arts Center** (✉ 1 Grand Ave., ☎ 805/756–7222) at Cal Poly hosts concerts and recitals.

The club scene in this college town is centered around Higuera Street off Monterey Street. The **Frog and Peach** (✉ 728 Higuera St., ☎ 805/595–3764) is a decent spot to nurse a beer and listen to music. **Linnaea's Cafe** (✉ 110 Garden St., ☎ 805/541–5888), a mellow java joint, sometimes hosts poetry readings, blues and alternative rock performances, and other diversions. The **San Luis Obispo Brewing Company** (✉ 1119 Garden St., ☎ 805/543–1843), popular with pool players, always serves several tasty ales and frequently hosts rock bands in the upstairs restaurant.

En Route From San Luis Opisbo, take Highway 101 south 10 mi to **Avila Beach** and the neighboring **Port San Louis.** Both are funky old fishing villages, facing southward onto a cove and thus escaping the fog that rolls in off the water. The port is still functioning, with a vibrant fish market lining the pier. Unfortunately, the Diablo Canyon nuclear power plant is situated right next to the port.

Pismo Beach

⓫ *15 mi south of San Luis Obispo.*

About 20 mi of sandy, southern California–style shoreline begins at the town of Pismo Beach, optimistically nicknamed the "Bakersfield Riviera." The southern end of town runs along sand dunes, some of which are open to cars and other vehicles. The northern section sits perched above chalky cliffs.

For a town with a population of less than 10,000, Pismo Beach has a slew of hotels and restaurants. Despite the neon signs announcing all accommodations and dining spots, the area doesn't feel inundated by tourists. Most of the best hotels and restaurants provide great views of the Pacific Ocean. Good beachfront walks, top-quality clam chowder, a growing Dixieland jazz festival in February, and a colony of Monarch butterflies in the town's eucalyptus grove are some of the attractions.

Dining and Lodging

$$–$$$ ✕ **F. McLintocks.** A cross between a truck stop and a cowboy saloon, this place prides itself on enormous portions of Western cuisine. Before you even order your meal, you'll find a large bowl of onion rings in front of you. Every cut of steak you can imagine is here, along with piles of ribs, lobsters, and much more. ✉ *750 Mattie Rd.,* ☎ *805/773–1892. AE, D, MC, V.*

$$–$$$ ✕ **Shore Cliff.** With probably the best seafood and clam chowder in town, this restaurant also has spectacular cliff-top views. The interior feels very airy, with glass windows drawing in oodles of light. ✉ *2555 Price St.,* ☎ *805/773–4671. AE, D, DC, MC, V.*

$$$$ 🏨 **The Cliffs at Shell Beach.** With a Spanish-modern exterior surrounded by manicured palm trees, this spot offers everything you would expect in a beachfront resort. Many of the modern rooms have fine ocean views (make sure your room faces the beach). Suites have huge marble bathrooms and hot tubs. ✉ *2757 Shell Beach Rd., 93449,* ☎ *805/773–5000 or 800/826–7827,* FAX *805/773–0764. 142 rooms, 23 suites. Restaurant, bar, pool, spa, meeting rooms. AE, D, DC, MC, V.*

$$–$$$$ 🏨 **Sea Venture Resort.** The rooms here aren't high on atmosphere, but those with an ocean view are perched over a beautiful stretch of sand.

The best amenity is the private hot tub on most balconies. ✉ *100 Ocean View Ave., 93449,* ☎ *805/773–4994 or 800/662–5545,* FAX *805/773–0924. 50 rooms. Restaurant, pool, hot tubs. AE, D, DC, MC, V. CP.*

La Purisima Mission State Historic Park

58 mi south of San Luis Obispo, Hwy. 1 to Hwy. 246 east or U.S. 101 to Hwy. 246 west.

★ ⓬ **Mission La Purisima Concepción,** the most fully restored mission in the state, was founded in 1787. Its stark and still-remote setting powerfully evokes the lives of California's Spanish settlers. Displays illustrate the secular and religious activities at the mission, and once a month from March through September costumed docents demonstrate crafts. A corral near the parking area holds farm animals, including sheep that are descendants of the original mission stock. ✉ *2295 Purisima Rd., off Mission Gate Rd.,* ☎ *805/733–3713; 805/733–1303 for tours.* *$2 per vehicle.* *Daily 9–5.*

Solvang

⓭ *On Hwy. 246, 23 mi east of Mission La Purisima Concepción; 3 mi east of U.S. 101.*

You'll know when you've reached the Danish town of Solvang: the architecture suddenly turns to half-timbered buildings and windmills. The town has a genuine Danish heritage—more than two-thirds of the residents are of Danish descent. A good way to get your bearings is to browse in a few of the 300 or so shops that sell Danish goods; many are along Copenhagen Drive and Alisal Road. As an alternative, take a guided tour on a horsedrawn streetcar that leaves from the visitors center, at 2nd and Copenhagen, every half hour. If Solvang seems too serene and orderly to be true, find a copy of William Castle's 1961 film *Homicidal,* which used the town as the backdrop for gender-bending murder and mayhem.

En Route Known as the Flower-Seed Capital of the World, **Lompoc** is home to vast fields of brightly colored flowers that bloom from May through August. Each June the Lompoc Valley Flower Festival features a parade, carnival, and a crafts show. You'll pass through the area as you take Highway 1 between Pismo Beach and Santa Barbara.

Dining and Lodging

$$–$$$ ✕ **The Hitching Post.** You'll find everything from grilled artichokes to ostrich at this casual eatery in Buellton, but most people come for what is said to be the best Santa Maria–style barbecue in the state. The oak used in the barbecue imparts a wonderfully smoky taste. ✉ *406 E. Hwy. 246, Buellton,* ☎ *805/688–0676. AE, MC, V. No lunch.*

$–$$$ ✕ **Restaurant Molle-Kroen.** Locals come to this cheerful upstairs dining room when they want a good Danish meal at a reasonable price. ✉ *435 Alisal Rd.,* ☎ *805/688–4555. AE, D, DC, MC, V.*

$–$$ ✕ **Bit O' Denmark.** Perhaps the most authentic Danish eatery in Solvang, this restaurant is in an old beamed building that was a church until 1929. The dishes have such names as *Frikadeller* (heavy meatballs with pickled red cabbage, potatoes, and thick brown gravy) and *Medisterpolse* (Danish beef and pork sausage with cabbage). ✉ *473 Alisal Rd.,* ☎ *805/688–5426. AE, D, MC, V.*

$$$$ ✕ **Alisal Guest Ranch and Resort.** About 1,600 head of cattle graze the 10,000-acre grounds of Alisal Ranch, which opened to guests in 1946 and soon attracted the likes of Clark Gable and Doris Day. More recent guests have included Barbra Streisand and Kevin Costner. Rooms are plain, with appealing Western touches; all have refrigerators and wood-burning fireplaces. The 90-acre lake is perfect for sailing, windsurfing, pedal boating, and fishing. Hearty meals are served home-style in the rustic yet elegant Ranch Room if the weather isn't warm enough for an outdoor barbecue. Breakfast and dinner are included in the room rates, but many activities cost extra. ✉ *1054 Alisal Rd., 93463,* ☎ *805/688–6411 or 800/425–4725,* FAX *805/688–2510. 36 rooms, 37 suites. Restaurant, bar, pool, 2 18-hole golf courses, 7 tennis courts, croquet, Ping-Pong, shuffleboard, volleyball, bike rentals, billiards, children's programs. AE, DC, MC, V.*

$$$–$$$$ **Story Book Inn.** Someone in Solvang had to do it: all the rooms at this B&B are named after Hans Christian Andersen stories. Some rooms are on the small side, but others are large and luxurious. All have a light, airy feel. The suites have four-poster beds and roomy whirlpool tubs. ✉ *409 1st St., 93463,* ☎ *805/688–1703 or 800/786–7925,* FAX *805/688–0953. 7 rooms, 2 suites. D, MC, V. BP.*

$$–$$$$ **Chimney Sweep Inn.** In a town of kitsch, this well maintained dwelling with a manicured garden gives a good impersonation of authenticity. Six cottages were inspired by the C. S. Lewis children's series, *The Chronicles of Narnia.* They have kitchens and fireplaces; five also have hot tubs. ✉ *1564 Copenhagen Dr., 93463,* ☎ *805/688–2111 or 800/824–6444,* FAX *805/688–8824. 50 rooms, 6 cottages. Refrigerators, spa. AE, D, MC, V. CP.*

$$–$$$$ ★ **Inn at Petersen Village.** As with most of the buildings in Solvang, this property is heavy on the wood. The overall effect is along the lines of a hunting lodge. The four-poster beds here are plush, the bathrooms small but sparkling. The inn welcomes children over age seven. ✉ *1576 Mission Dr., 93463,* ☎ *805/688–3121 or 800/321–8985,* FAX *805/688–5732. 39 rooms, 1 suite. Café, bar. AE, MC, V. BP.*

$–$$ **Best Western King Fredric.** Rooms at this comfortable and central motel are fairly spacious. If you're traveling with the children and don't want to spend a fortune, this is a good bet. ✉ *1617 Copenhagen Dr., 93463,* ☎ *805/688–5515,* FAX *805/688–1600. 39 rooms. Pool, hot tub. AE, D, DC, MC, V.*

OFF THE BEATEN PATH

SAN MARCOS PASS – Highway 154 winds its spectacular way south from Solvang (drive east on Highway 246 to Highway 154) through the Los Padres National Forest. This former stagecoach route rejoins U.S. 101 north of Santa Barbara. The lively Cold Spring Tavern (☞ Santa Barbara Dining and Lodging, *below*) has been serving travelers since the stagecoach days.

Nightlife and the Arts

Pacific Conservatory of the Performing Arts (☎ 805/922–8313; 800/549–7272 in CA) presents contemporary and classic plays, along with a few musicals, in different theaters in Solvang and Santa Maria. Summer events in Solvang are held in the open-air Festival Theatre, on 2nd Street off Copenhagen Drive.

Outdoor Activities and Sports

Cachuma Lake (✉ Hwy. 154, ☎ 805/688–4658), a jewel of an artificial lake 12 mi east of Solvang, has hiking, fishing, boating, and nature programs.

BICYCLING

Quadricycles, four-wheel carriages, and bicycles are available at **Surrey Cycle Rental** (✉ 475 1st St., ☎ 805/688–0091).

GLIDER RIDES

The scenic rides operated by **Windhaven Glider** (✉ Santa Ynez Airport, Hwy. 246 east of Solvang, ☎ 805/688–2517) cost between $75 and $150 and last up to 40 minutes.

Los Olivos

⓮ *5 mi north of Solvang on Alamo Pintado Rd.*

This pretty village in the Santa Ynez Valley was once on the Spanish-built El Camino Real and later on major stagecoach and rail routes. It's so sleepy today, though, that TV's *Return to Mayberry* was filmed here. A row of art galleries, antiques stores, and country markets lines Grand Avenue. At **Los Olivos Tasting Room & Wine Shop** (✉ 2905 Grand Ave., ☎ 805/688–7406) you can sample locally produced wines and pick up winery maps. There are also several other tasting rooms along the same block. **Sanone Gallery** (✉ 2948 Nojoqui Ave., ☎ 805/693–9769) boasts the best artwork in town.

Dining and Lodging

$$$–$$$$ ✕🏨 **Fess Parker's Wine Country Inn and Spa.** The rooms at this luxury inn—the only place you can spend the night in Los Olivos—are in a lawn-fronted house and an equally attractive residence across the street with a pool and a hot tub. The spacious accommodations have fireplaces, seating areas, and wet bars; six also have private hot tubs. At the Vintage Room ($$–$$$), well-selected local wines complement entrées such as oven-roasted salmon and grilled lamb T-bone. Unfortunately, the inn's service is not as special under its new ownership, and the restaurant's quality has slipped. ✉ *2860 Grand Ave., 93441,* ☎ *805/688–7788 or 800/446–2455,* FAX *805/688–1942. 20 rooms, 1 suite. Restaurant, pool, hot tub, spa. AE, MC, V.*

SANTA BARBARA

45 mi south of Solvang on U.S. 101.

Santa Barbara has long been an oasis for Los Angeles residents in need of rest and recuperation. The attractions in Santa Barbara begin with the ocean and end in the foothills of the Santa Ynez Mountains. In the few miles between the beaches and the hills are downtown; then the old mission; and, a little higher up, the botanic gardens. A few miles farther up the coast, but still very much a part of Santa Barbara, is the exclusive residential district of Hope Ranch. To the east is the district called Montecito, whose Coast Village Road has shops and restaurants.

Santa Barbara is on a jog in the coastline, so the ocean is actually to the south. Directions can be confusing. "Up" the coast toward San Francisco is west, "down" toward Los Angeles is east, and the mountains are north. A car is handy but not essential if you're planning to stay in town. The beaches and downtown are easily explored by bicycle or on foot, and the Santa Barbara Trolley (☞ Contacts and Resources in the Central Coast A to Z, *below*) takes visitors to most major hotels and sights, which can also be reached on the local buses.

The Waterfront

You'll hear locals refer to the waterfront as "the ocean," but by any name it's a beautiful area, with palm-studded promenades and plenty of sand.

A Good Tour

Start your tour at the **Santa Barbara Yacht Harbor** ⑮ and stop inside the new **Santa Barbara Maritime Museum** ⑯. Take Cabrillo Boulevard, the main harbor-front drag, to **Stearns Wharf** ⑱, where the **Sea Center** ⑲ is a major attraction. Unless you're an inveterate walker, drive east along Cabrillo Boulevard to **East Beach** ⑳ and the nearby **Andree Clark Bird Refuge** ㉑. More creatures await at the **Santa Barbara Zoo** ㉒, which is adjacent to the refuge.

TIMING

You could make this an all-day excursion or devote only two or three hours to it if you drive and only stop briefly at the various attractions. A spin through the zoo takes about an hour.

Sights to See

㉑ **Andree Clark Bird Refuge.** This peaceful lagoon and gardens sits north of East Beach. Bike trails and footpaths, punctuated by signs identifying native and migratory birds, skirt the lagoon. ✉ *1400 E. Cabrillo Blvd.* 🎟 *Free.*

OFF THE BEATEN PATH

CHANNEL ISLANDS NATIONAL PARK AND NATIONAL MARINE SANCTUARY– The five Channel Islands often appear in a haze on the Santa Barbara horizon. The most popular is Anacapa Island, 11 mi off the coast. The islands' remoteness and unpredictable seas protected them from development, making them a nature-enthusiast's paradise. On a good day you'll be able to view seals, sea lions, and much bird life. Migrating whales can be seen close up from December through March. Tidal pools are often accessible. Divers can view fish, giant squid, and coral. Frenchy's Cove, on the west end of the island, has a beach and fine snorkeling. The waters of the channel are often choppy and can make for a rough ride out to the islands (☞ Boats and Charters *in* Outdoor Activities and Sports, *below,* for information about group outings).

⑳ **East Beach.** The wide swath of sand at the east end of Cabrillo Boulevard is a great spot for people-watching. Sand volleyball courts, summertime lifeguard and sports competitions, and arts-and-crafts shows on Sunday and holidays make for an often lively experience. Showers (no towels), lockers, and beach rentals—also a weight room—are provided at the **Cabrillo Pavilion Bathhouse** (✉ 1118 Cabrillo Blvd., ☎ 805/965–0509). Next to the boathouse, there's an elaborate jungle-gym play area for children.

Moreton Bay Fig Tree. Planted in 1874 and transplanted to its present location in 1877, this tree is so huge it reputedly can provide shade for 1,000 people. ✉ *Chapala St. at U.S. 101.*

⑯ **Santa Barbara Maritime Museum** This recently opened museum focuses on all aspects of our seafaring history. High-tech, hands-on exhibits, such as a virtual submarine voyage, make this a fun stop for children and adults. ✉ *6 Harbor Way,* ☎ *805/962–8404.* 🎟 *$2.* ⏲ *Tues.–Thurs. 10–5, Fri.–Sun. 10–8. Closed Mon.*

⑮ **Santa Barbara Yacht Harbor.** You can take a ½-mi walk along the breakwater that protects the harbor. Check out the tackle and bait shops, grab some lunch, or hire a boat. ✉ *West end of Cabrillo Blvd.*

㉒ **Santa Barbara Zoo.** The natural settings of the zoo shelter elephants, gorillas, exotic birds, and big cats such as the rare amur leopard, a thick-furred, high-altitude dweller from Asia. For the children there's a scenic railroad and barnyard petting zoo. ✉ *500 Niños Dr.,* ☎ *805/962–5339.* 🎟 *$7.* ⏲ *Daily 10–5.*

⑲ **Sea Center.** A branch of the Santa Barbara Museum of Natural History, the Sea Center specializes in marine life. Aquariums, life-size models of whales and dolphins, undersea dioramas, interactive com-

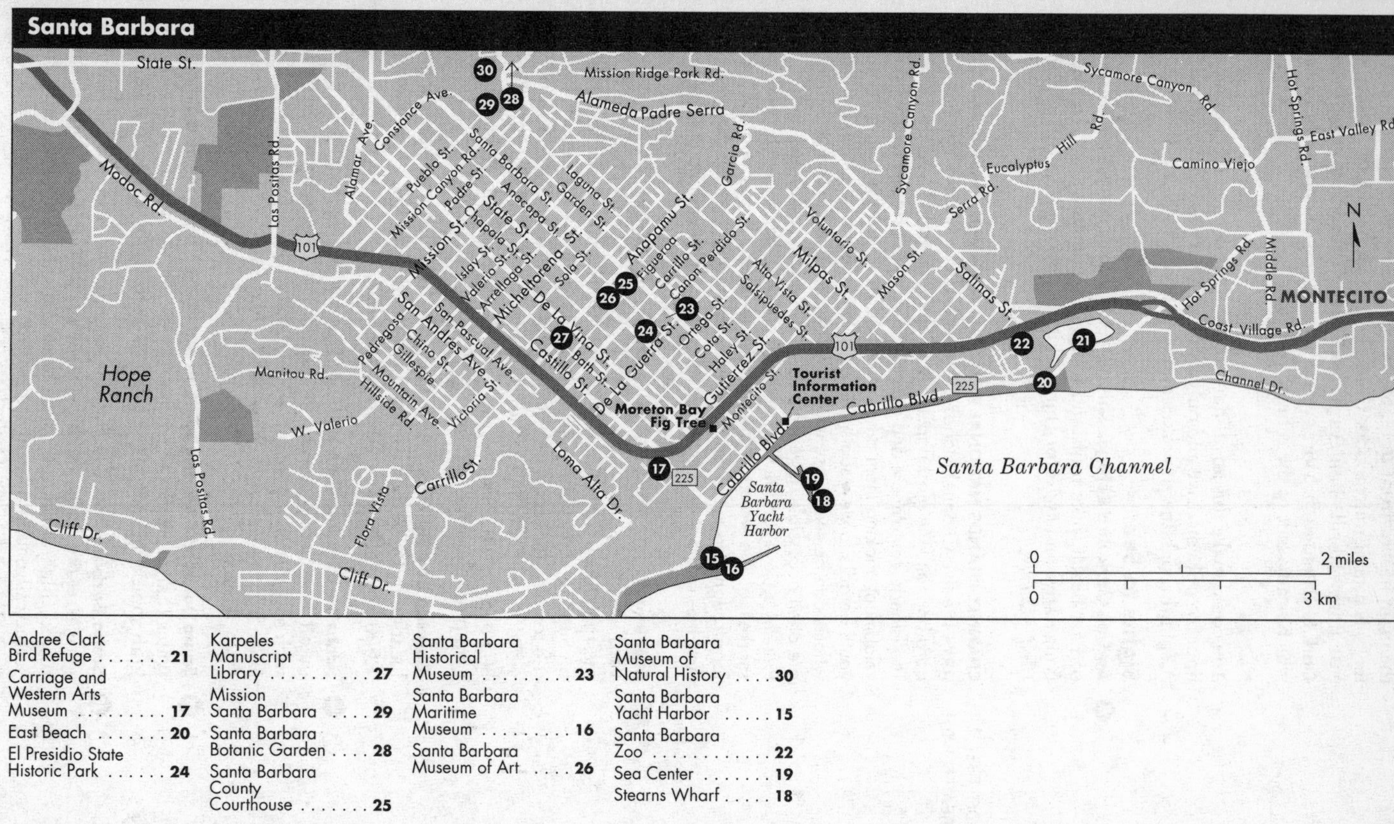
Santa Barbara
State St.
Mission Ridge Park Rd.
Alameda Padre Serra
Sycamore Canyon Rd.
Hot Springs Rd.
East Valley Rd.
Camino Viejo
Eucalyptus Hill Rd.
Serra Rd.
Sycamore Canyon Rd.
Garcia Rd.
Modoc Rd.
Las Positas Rd.
Alamar Ave.
Constance Ave.
Pueblo St.
Mission Canyon Rd.
Padre St.
Santa Barbara St.
Anacapa St.
Laguna St.
Garden St.
State St.
Chapala St.
Mission St.
Islay St.
Valerio St.
Arrellaga St.
Micheltorena St.
Sola St.
Anapamu St.
Figueroa
Carrillo St.
Canon Perdido St.
De La Vina St.
Bath St.
Castillo St.
De La Guerra St.
Ortega St.
Cota St.
Haley St.
Gutierrez St.
Alta Vista St.
Salsipuedes St.
Milpas St.
Voluntario St.
Mason St.
Salinas St.
Hot Springs Rd.
Middle Rd.
MONTECITO
Coast Village Rd.
Channel Dr.
San Pascual Ave.
San Andres Ave.
Pedregosa
Chino St.
Gillespie
Mountain Ave.
Victoria St.
Hillside Rd.
Manitou Rd.
W. Valerio
Hope Ranch
Las Positas Rd.
Carrillo St.
Flora Vista
Loma Alta Dr.
Cliff Dr.
Cliff Dr.
Montecito St.
Moreton Bay Fig Tree
Tourist Information Center
Cabrillo Blvd.
Cabrillo Blvd.
101
101
225
225
Santa Barbara Yacht Harbor
Santa Barbara Channel
N
0
2 miles
0
3 km
Andree Clark Bird Refuge 21
Carriage and Western Arts Museum 17
East Beach 20
El Presidio State Historic Park 24
Karpeles Manuscript Library 27
Mission Santa Barbara 29
Santa Barbara Botanic Garden 28
Santa Barbara County Courthouse 25
Santa Barbara Historical Museum 23
Santa Barbara Maritime Museum 16
Santa Barbara Museum of Art 26
Santa Barbara Museum of Natural History 30
Santa Barbara Yacht Harbor 15
Santa Barbara Zoo 22
Sea Center 19
Stearns Wharf 18

puter-video displays, and the remains of shipwrecks depict marine activity from the Santa Barbara coastline to the Channel Islands. At the Touch Tank children can handle invertebrates, fish, and plants collected from nearby waters. ✉ *211 Stearns Wharf,* ☎ *805/962–0885.* 🎫 *$3.* ⏲ *Sea Center Sept.–May, weekdays noon–5, weekends 10–5; June–Sept., daily 10–5. Touch Tank weekdays noon–4, weekends noon–5.*

18 **Stearns Wharf.** Extending the length of three city blocks into the Pacific, the wharf has a view of Santa Barbara that gives visitors a good sense of the city's size and general layout. Although it's a nice walk from the Cabrillo Boulevard parking areas, you can also drive out and park on the pier and then wander through the shops or stop for a meal at one of the wharf's restaurants or the snack bar. ✉ *Cabrillo Blvd. at the foot of State St.,* ☎ *805/564–5518.*

Downtown and the Foothills

A Good Tour

Begin at the **Karpeles Manuscript Library** ㉗ on Anapamu Street west of State Street. Walk across State to the **Santa Barbara Museum of Art** ㉖. Behind the museum, past the Spanish-style public library, the **Santa Barbara County Courthouse** ㉕ faces Anacapa. On Anacapa head toward the water past **El Paseo,** a handsome shopping arcade built around an old adobe home. Make a right at East Cañon Perdido Street to reach **El Presidio State Historic Park** ㉔. From here, walk toward the water one block, then take a left on De La Guerra Street to reach the entrance of the **Santa Barbara Historical Museum** ㉓.

Hop in your car and take State Street northwest (away from the water) to Los Olivos Street. Turn right and you'll soon see **Mission Santa Barbara** ㉙. From the mission you can walk the block north to the **Santa Barbara Museum of Natural History** ㉚. You'll probably want to drive the 1½ mi north to the **Santa Barbara Botanic Garden** ㉘.

TIMING

This tour takes at least a half day. Set aside an hour each for the art and natural-history museums and for the botanic gardens. Add plenty of time if you're a shopper. The stores and galleries around State Street may sidetrack you for hours.

Sights to See

17 **Carriage and Western Arts Museum.** The country's largest collection of old horse-drawn vehicles—painstakingly restored—is exhibited here. Everything from polished hearses to police transport buggies to old stagecoaches and circus vehicles are on display. In August the Old Spanish Days Fiesta borrows many of the vehicles for a jaunt about town. This is one of the city's true hidden gems, a wonderful place to help history come alive for the children. ✉ *129 Castillo St.,* ☎ *805/982–2353.* 🎫 *Free.* ⏲ *Daily 10–4.*

24 **El Presidio State Historic Park.** Founded in 1782, El Presidio was one of four military strongholds established by the Spanish along the coast of California. El Cuartel, the adobe guardhouse, is the oldest building in Santa Barbara and the second oldest in California. ✉ *123 E. Cañon Perdido St.,* ☎ *805/965–0093.* 🎫 *Free.* ⏲ *Daily 10:30–4:30.*

Kids' World public playground. Children and adults enjoy this complex maze of fantasy climbing structures, turrets, slides, and tunnels built by Santa Barbara parents. ✉ *Santa Barbara St. near Micheltorena St.*

27 **Karpeles Manuscript Library.** Ancient political tracts and old Disney cartoons are among the varied holdings of this facility, which also houses one of the world's largest privately owned collections of rare manuscripts.

Fifty cases contain a sampling of the archive's million-plus documents. ✉ *21 W. Anapamu St.,* ☎ *805/962–5322.* *Free.* *Daily 10–4.*

OFF THE BEATEN PATH

LOTUSLAND – Only a limited number of people are permitted to visit the 37-acre estate that once belonged to Polish opera singer Ganna Walska; the hours that Lotusland is open are limited, and one must take part in a 1½- to 2-hour guided group tour. It's worth trying to get a reservation to see the celebrated gardens. Many of the exotic trees and other subtropical flora were planted in 1882 by horticulturist R. Kinton Stevens. Among the highlights are an outdoor theater, a topiary garden, a huge collection of rare bromeliads, and a lotus pond. ✉ *Ganna Walska Lotusland, 695 Ashley Rd., Montecito,* ☎ *805/969–9990.* *$10.* *Tours mid-Feb.–mid-Nov., Wed.–Sun. 10:30 AM and 1:30 PM.*

★ 29 **Mission Santa Barbara.** The architecture and layout of this mission, which was established in 1786, evolved from adobe-brick buildings with thatch roofs to more permanent edifices as its population burgeoned. An earthquake in 1812 destroyed the third church built on the site. Its replacement, the present structure, is still a Catholic church, though during the post-Mission era it also served as a boys school and a seminary. Cacti, palms, and other succulents grow beside the mission. ✉ *2201 Laguna St.,* ☎ *805/682–4713.* *$4.* *Daily 9–5.*

★ 28 **Santa Barbara Botanic Garden.** Five-plus miles of trails meander through the garden's 65 acres of native plants. The Mission Dam, built in 1806, stands just beyond the redwood grove and above the partially uncovered aqueduct that once carried water to Mission Santa Barbara. An ethnobotanical display contains replicas of the plants used by the Chumash Indians. ✉ *1212 Mission Canyon Rd.,* ☎ *805/682–4726.* *$5.* *Mar.–Oct., weekdays 9–5, weekends 9–6; Nov.–Feb., weekdays 9–4, weekends 9–5. Guided tours Thurs.–Tues. at 2; additional tour at 10:30 AM Thurs., Sat., and Sun.*

★ 25 **Santa Barbara County Courthouse.** Hand-painted tiles and a spiral staircase infuse the courthouse with the grandeur of a Moorish palace. This magnificent building was completed in 1929, part of a rebuilding process after a 1925 earthquake destroyed many downtown structures. At the time Santa Barbara was also in the midst of a cultural awakening, and the trend was toward an architecture appropriate to the area's climate and history. The result is the harmonious Mediterranean-Spanish look of much of the downtown area, especially municipal buildings. An elevator rises to an arched observation area in the courthouse tower that provides a panoramic view of the city. The murals in the supervisors' ceremonial chambers on the courthouse's second floor were painted by an artist who did backdrops for some of Cecil B. DeMille's films. Stop by at night to see the courthouse lit by spotlights. ✉ *1100 block of Anacapa St.,* ☎ *805/962–6464.* *Daily 8:30–4:45. Free 1-hr guided tours Mon., Tues., and Fri. 10:30 AM, Mon.–Sat. 2 PM.*

23 **Santa Barbara Historical Museum.** The historical society's museum exhibits decorative and fine arts, furniture, costumes, and documents from the town's past. Adjacent is the Gledhill Library, a collection of books, photographs, maps, and manuscripts about the area. ✉ *136 E. De La Guerra St.,* ☎ *805/966–1601.* *Museum $3 suggested donation, library $2–$5 per hr for research.* *Museum Tues.–Sat. 10–5, Sun. noon–5; library Tues.–Fri. 10–4, 1st Sat. of month 10–1:30. Free guided tours Wed., Sat., and Sun. 1:30 PM.*

26 **Santa Barbara Museum of Art.** The highlights of this museum's fine permanent collection include ancient sculpture, Asian art, Impressionist paintings, and American works in several media. ✉ *1130 State*

St., ☎ 805/963–4364. $5; free Thurs. and 1st Sun. of month. ⏲ Tues.–Sat. 11–5 (until 9 Fri.), Sun. noon–5. Guided tours Tues.–Sun. 1 PM, special subject tours at noon.

30 **Santa Barbara Museum of Natural History.** The gigantic skeleton of a blue whale greets visitors at the entrance of this complex. The major draws include the planetarium and E. L. Wiegand Space Lab. A room of dioramas illustrates Chumash Indian history and culture. Startlingly lifelike stuffed specimens, complete with nests and eggs, roost in the bird diversity room. Many of the exhibits have interactive components. *✉ 2559 Puesta del Sol Rd., ☎ 805/682–4711. $6. ⏲ Mon.–Sat. 9–5, Sun. 10–5.*

Dining and Lodging

$$$–$$$$ ★ ✕ **Citronelle.** At this offspring of chef Michel Richard's Citrus in Los Angeles, intriguing flavors animate dishes such as the lamb loin with couscous and cumin sauce and the seared ahi tuna with an Anaheim-chili sauce. The desserts are stupendous. The dining room's picture windows yield splendid, sweeping views of the sunset. *✉ 901 E. Cabrillo Blvd., ☎ 805/963–0111. Reservations essential. AE, D, DC, MC, V.*

$$$–$$$$ ★ ✕ **Wine Cask.** Sautéed swordfish and potato wrapped whitefish, each prepared with a wine-based sauce, are among the most popular entrées at this slick restaurant with a beautiful wood interior. In fine weather couples seek out the romantic outdoor patio. *✉ 813 Anacapa St., ☎ 805/966–9463. AE, DC, MC, V.*

$$–$$$$ ✕ **Arigato Sushi.** Sushi fans will appreciate the fresh seafood served in this atmospheric Japanese restaurant and sushi bar. Innovation reigns, with creations such as sushi pizza on seaweed and Hawaiian sashimi salad. *✉ 11 W. Victoria St., ☎ 805/965–6074. Reservations not accepted. AE, MC, V. No lunch.*

$$–$$$$ ✕ **Bouchon.** This upscale restaurant exists as a showcase for fine local wines. Food runs to the meaty, such as braised rabbit and honey-soaked venison. The atmosphere is intimate and the wine selection huge. *✉ 11 W. Victoria St., ☎ 805/730–1160. AE, MC, V. No lunch.*

$$$ ✕ **Emilio's.** Starters on the seasonal northern Italian menu at this harborside restaurant might include crispy roast duck on a risotto cake. The main courses of ravioli stuffed with butternut squash or potato gnocchi with rock shrimp are standouts. During the week a vegetarian tasting menu is available, as are two prix-fixe wine-tasting menus. *✉ 324 W. Cabrillo Blvd., ☎ 805/966–4426. AE, D, MC, V. No lunch.*

$$$ ✕ **The Stonehouse.** This atmospheric restaurant in a century-old granite farmhouse is part of the San Ysidro Ranch resort. The contemporary southern fare includes dry-aged New York steak with smoked tomato-horseradish sauce and clam hash, seared ahi tuna in an herb crust with sun-dried-tomato couscous, and excellent vegetarian options. Even better than the generally wonderful food is the pastoral setting. Have lunch—salads, pastas, and sandwiches—on the tree-house-like outdoor patio. At night the candlelit interior is seriously romantic. *✉ 900 San Ysidro La., Montecito, ☎ 805/969–4100. Reservations essential. AE, DC, MC, V.*

$$–$$$ ✕ **Brophy Bros.** The outdoor tables at this casual restaurant have perfect views of the harbor. A fine place to lunch, Brophy Bros. serves enormous, exceptionally fresh fish dishes. Try the seafood salad. *✉ 119 Harbor Way, ☎ 805/966–4418. AE, MC, V.*

$$–$$$ ✕ **Harbor Restaurant.** This sparkling spot on the pier is where locals take out-of-town guests for great views and standard American food. The nautical-theme bar and grill upstairs serves sandwiches, large salads, and many appetizers; on a sunny day the outdoor terrace is a glorious spot for a sandwich or a beer. Downstairs you can dine on seafood, prime rib, and steaks. *✉ 210 Stearns Wharf, ☎ 805/963–3311. AE, MC, V.*

$$–$$$ ✕ **Palace Grill.** The Palace has won acclaim for Cajun and Creole dishes such as blackened redfish and jambalaya with dirty rice. Caribbean fare here includes delicious coconut shrimp. If the dishes aren't spicy enough for you, each table has a bottle of hot sauce. Be prepared to wait as long as 45 minutes on weekends. ✉ *8 E. Cota St.,* ☎ *805/963–5000. AE, MC, V.*

$$–$$$ ✕ **Trattoria Mollie's.** Ethiopian-born chef-owner Mollie Ahlstrand spent several years in Italy before ending up in California. Her seafood pasta and plate of seafood and vegetables are among the many subtly flavored entrées. Lush potted plants surround the tables at this chic, popular trattoria. ✉ *1250 Coast Village Rd.,* ☎ *805/565–9381. Reservations essential on weekends. AE, MC, V. Closed Mon.*

$–$$$ ✕ **Brigitte's.** This lively State Street café serves California cuisine and local wines at relatively low prices. The individual pizzas are always worth trying, as are the pastas, grilled fish, and roast lamb. ✉ *1325–1327 State St.,* ☎ *805/966–9676. AE, D, DC, MC, V. No lunch Sun.*

$–$$$ ✕ **Café Buenos Aires.** Salads, sandwiches, pastas, and traditional Argentine empanadas (small turnovers filled with chicken, beef, or vegetables) are on the lunch menu at this elegant Buenos café. Dinner can be fashioned from potato omelets, Spanish red sausage in beer sauce, octopus stewed with tomato and onion, and other tapas. Pastas, fish, larger empanadas, or grilled rib-eye steak (imported from Argentina) sautéed in sweet butter are among the entrées. ✉ *1316 State St.,* ☎ *805/963–0242. Reservations essential. AE, DC, MC, V.*

$$ ✕ **Pane & Vino.** This tiny trattoria with an equally small sidewalk terrace sits in a tree-shaded, flower-decked shopping center. The cold antipasto is very good, as are the salads, pastas, and grilled meats and fish. ✉ *1482 E. Valley Rd., Montecito,* ☎ *805/969–9274. Reservations essential. AE, MC, V. No lunch Sun.*

$–$$ ★ ✕ **Cold Spring Tavern.** Well worth the drive out of town, this old roadhouse, off Hwy. 154 near Cachuma Lake, is on the former stagecoach route through the San Marcos Pass. It's part Harley-biker hangout and part romantic country hideaway, a mix that works surprisingly well. Game dishes—rabbit, venison, quail—are the specialty, along with American standards such as ribs, steak, and a great chili. It's a one-of-a-kind spot. ✉ *5995 Stagecoach Rd., San Marcos Pass,* ☎ *805/967–0066. AE, MC, V.*

$–$$ ✕ **Montecito Café.** The ambience is upscale yet casual at this restaurant that serves contemporary cuisine—fresh fish, grilled chicken, steak, and pasta. The salads and lamb dishes are particularly inventive. ✉ *1295 Coast Village Rd.,* ☎ *805/969–3392. AE, MC, V.*

$–$$ ✕ **Palazzio.** The only reservations are for 5:30 and then the waiting list begins at this casual, spirited, Italian restaurant. The portions of tasty pasta dishes are family style, the staff is great, and the garlic rolls are legendary. ✉ *336 W. Cabrillo Blvd.,* ☎ *805/966–3000. AE, D, DC, MC, V.*

$ ✕ **D'Angelo.** The bread served by many of the town's best restaurants comes from the ovens of this bakery, which has a few indoor and outdoor tables. Come for breakfast—the brioches are awesome—or for a sandwich, slice of gourmet pizza, or a pastry. ✉ *25 W. Gutierrez St.,* ☎ *805/962–5466. MC, V. No dinner.*

$ ✕ **Roy.** Owner-chef Leroy Gandy serves a $15 fixed-price dinner—a real bargain—that includes a small salad, fresh soup, and a selection from a rotating roster of Cal-Mediterranean main courses. Expect a wait at this downtown storefront on weekends. ✉ *7 W. Carrillo St.,* ☎ *805/966–5636. AE, D, DC, MC, V.*

$ ★ ✕ **La Super-Rica.** Praised by Julia Child, this food stand with a patio serves some of the spiciest Mexican dishes between Los Angeles and San Francisco. Fans drive for miles to fill up on the soft tacos and incredible beans. ✉ *622 N. Milpas St., at Alphonse St.,* ☎ *805/963–4940. No credit cards.*

$ ✕ **Your Place.** Tasty seafood (try the sea scallops garnished with crispy basil), curries, and vegetarian dishes keep this small restaurant packed for lunch and dinner. Your Place has consistently been named as the best Thai restaurant by local periodicals. ✉ *22 N. Milpas St.,* ☎ *805/966–5151. AE, MC, V. Closed Mon.*

$$$$ ★ ✕ **Four Seasons Biltmore Hotel.** Surrounded by lush (but always perfectly manicured) gardens, Santa Barbara's grande dame has long been the favored spot for the town's high society and the visiting rich and famous to indulge in quiet California-style luxury. Muted pastels and bleached woods give the cabanas behind the main building an airy feel without sacrificing the hotel's reputation for understated elegance. Dining is indoors and formal at the hotel's La Marina Restaurant—the California-Continental menu changes monthly—and outdoors and more casual at The Patio. ✉ *1260 Channel Dr., Montecito 93108,* ☎ *805/969–2261 or 800/332–3442,* FAX *805/565–8329. 217 rooms, 13 suites. 2 restaurants, bar, pool, hot tub, spa, putting green, 3 tennis courts, health club, croquet, shuffleboard. AE, DC, MC, V.*

$$$$ **El Encanto Hotel.** Actress Hedy Lamarr and President Franklin D. Roosevelt are among the guests who have unwound at this woodsy property near Mission Santa Barbara. Mediterranean-style villas dot the lush 10-acre grounds, along with Craftsman cottages with pine beds and living rooms with old brick fireplaces. ✉ *1900 Lasuen Rd., 93103,* ☎ *805/687–5000 or 800/346–7039,* FAX *805/687–3903. 83 rooms. Restaurant, bar, minibars, room service, pool, tennis court. AE, D, MC, V.*

$$$$ **Montecito Inn.** Every room at this late-1920s marble palace is adorned with original posters from the films of Charlie Chaplin. The glass doors to the conference room are etched with the great man's image, and the video library contains his entire oeuvre. The rooms on the second floor lead onto a cloisterlike arched colonnade. The bathrooms are fairly basic, although some suites have large marble whirlpool tubs. The suites also have vast Romanesque-style marble fireplaces. ✉ *1295 Coast Village Rd., 93108,* ☎ *805/969–7854 or 800/843–2017,* FAX *805/969–0623. 53 rooms, 7 suites. Restaurant, bar, refrigerators, in-room VCRs, pool, exercise room, hot tub, bicycles. AE, D, DC, MC, V. CP.*

$$$$ ★ **San Ysidro Ranch.** At this luxury "ranch" you can feel at home in jeans and cowboy boots, but be prepared to dress for dinner. A hangout for the Hollywood set, this romantic hideaway hosted John and Jackie Kennedy on their honeymoon. Guest cottages, all with down comforters and wood-burning stoves or fireplaces, are scattered among 14 acres of orange trees and flower beds. The Eucalyptus Cottage comes with a private butler. Hiking trails crisscross 500 acres of open space surrounding the property. The Stonehouse Restaurant (☞ *above*) is a Santa Barbara institution. The hotel, which welcomes children and pets, provides personal beauty services and 24-hour room service. ✉ *900 San Ysidro La., Montecito 93108,* ☎ *805/969–5046 or 800/368–6788,* FAX *805/565–1995. 21 cottages with total of 38 rooms. Restaurant, room service, pool, massage, spa, 2 tennis courts, boccie, exercise room, horseshoes, playground. AE, DC, MC, V. 2-day minimum stay on weekends, 3 days on holidays.*

$$$$ ★ **Simpson House Inn.** Traditional B&B fans will enjoy the beautifully appointed Victorian main house of this inn on a quiet acre in the heart of town. Those seeking total privacy and sybaritic comfort should choose one of the exceptional cottages or century-old barn suites, each with a wood-burning fireplace, luxurious bedding, and state-of-the-art electronics, and several with a whirlpool bath. In-room spa services such as massage and body wraps are available. ✉ *121 E. Arrellaga St., 93101,* ☎

805/963–7067 or 800/676–1280, FAX 805/564–4811. 7 rooms, 4 suites, 3 cottages. AE, D, MC, V. 2-night minimum stay on weekends. BP.

$$$–$$$$ **Cheshire Cat Inn.** A five-minute walk from downtown, this B&B with an *Alice in Wonderland* motif is accessible yet quiet. The largest rooms hold king-size beds and sunken whirlpool tubs. The smaller rooms come with low-lying armchairs and have a twee, Edwardian look. *36 W. Valerio St., 93101, 805/569–1610, FAX 805/682–1876. 14 rooms, 4 cottages. AE, D, MC, V. 2-night minimum stay on weekends. BP.*

$$$–$$$$ **The Upham.** This restored Victorian hotel set in an acre of gardens in the historic downtown area was established in 1871. Period furnishings and antiques adorn the rooms and cottages, some of which have fireplaces and private patios. The rooms vary from small to quite spacious. *1404 De La Vina St., 93101, 805/962–0058 or 800/727–0876, FAX 805/963–2825. 46 rooms, 4 suites. Restaurant, meeting rooms. AE, D, DC, MC, V. 2-night minimum stay on weekends. CP.*

$$–$$$$ ★ **Glenborough Inn.** One of the best B&Bs in Santa Barbara County, this inn is composed of four buildings constructed around 1900. Several of the very private, theme rooms retain an old, dark-wood feel. If you stay in the Craftsman Room, you'll nearly be swallowed up by the vast bed. As with several of the accommodations in this romantic abode, a private hot tub perches on the patio outside the room. *1327 Bath St., 93101, 805/966–0589 or 800/962–0589, FAX 805/564–8610. 7 rooms, 7 suites. AE, D, DC, MC, V. BP.*

$$–$$$$ **Hotel Santa Barbara.** The central location of this hotel makes it one of the better bargains in town. You won't experience all the luxuries of Santa Barbara's pricier accommodations, but the rooms are clean and modern, if a tad charmless. The top-floor rooms have ocean views. Ask for a room in back, away from the noise of State Street. *533 State St., 93101, 888/259–7700. 72 rooms, 3 suites. Concierge. AE, D, DC, MC, V.*

$$–$$$$ **Old Yacht Club Inn.** Built in 1912 as a private home in the California Craftsman style, this inn near the beach was one of Santa Barbara's first B&Bs. The rooms have century-old furnishings and Oriental rugs. The adjacent Hitchcock House holds five rooms with private entrances. *431 Corona del Mar Dr., 93103, 805/962–1277 or 800/676–1676; 800/549–1676 in CA; FAX 805/962–3989. 10 rooms, 2 suites. No smoking. AE, MC, V. BP.*

$$–$$$$ **Villa Rosa.** The rooms and intimate lobby of this Spanish-style stucco-and-wood hotel one block from the beach are decorated in an informal Southwestern style. *15 Chapala St., 93101, 805/966–0851, FAX 805/962–7159. 18 rooms. Pool, hot tub. AE, MC, V. 2-night minimum stay on weekends, 3-night minimum during holidays. CP.*

Nightlife and the Arts

Most major hotels present entertainment nightly during the summer season and on weekends all year. State Street has a good jazz scene. Santa Barbara supports a professional symphony and a chamber orchestra. The proximity to the University of California at Santa Barbara assures an endless stream of visiting artists and performers. To see what's scheduled around town pick up a copy of the free weekly *Santa Barbara Independent* newspaper.

BARS AND CLUBS

Rich leather couches, a crackling fire in chilly weather, a cigar balcony, and pool tables draw a fancy Gen-X crowd to **Blue Agave** (20 E. Cota St., 805/899–4694) for good food and designer martinis. **The James Joyce** (513 State St., 805/962–2688), which sometimes hosts folk and rock performers, is a good place to while away an evening, beer in hand.

Old jazz photos and low lighting lend **Jazz Hall** (✉ 29 E. Victoria. St.) an ambience that's about as close to Greenwich Village as you're likely to get in these parts. Musicians perform on weekends. **Joe's Cafe** (✉ 536 State St., ☎ 805/966–4638), where steins of beer accompany hearty bar food, is a fun, if occasionally rowdy, collegiate scene.

The bartenders at **Left at Albuquerque** (✉ 803 State St., ☎ 805/564–5040) pour 141 tequilas, making the Southwestern-style bar one of your less sedate nightspots. The determinedly pretentious **Madhouse** (✉ 434 State St., ☎ 805/962–5516) hosts a chic crowd that sits on high stools and basks in fluorescent lighting (if you're not in the prime of youth, you'll look awful). The **Plow & Angel** (✉ San Ysidro Ranch, 900 San Ysidro La., Montecito, ☎ 805/969–5046) books mellow jazz performers. The bar is perfect for those seeking quiet conversation, even romance. **Soho** (✉ 1221 State St., ☎ 805/962–7776), a hip restaurant and bar, presents weeknight jazz music; on weekends the mood livens with good blues and rock.

PERFORMING ARTS

Arlington Theater (✉ 1317 State St., ☎ 805/963–4408), a Moorish-style auditorium, is home to the Santa Barbara Symphony. **Center Stage Theatre** (✉ 700 block of State St., 2nd floor, ☎ 805/963–0408) presents plays and readings. **Ensemble Theatre Company** (✉ 914 Santa Barbara St., ☎ 805/962–8606) stages plays by authors ranging from Priestley to Mamet.

The **Granada Theatre** (✉ 1216 State St., ☎ 805/966–2324), a restored movie palace, is the headquarters of the Santa Barbara Civic Light Opera. The **Lobero Theatre** (✉ 33 E. Cañon Perdido St., ☎ 805/963–0761), a state landmark, hosts community theater groups and touring professionals. The **Music Academy of the West** (✉ 1070 Fairway Rd., Montecito, ☎ 805/687–7820) showcases orchestral and operatic works.

Outdoor Activities and Sports

BEACHES

Santa Barbara's beaches don't have the big surf of the shoreline farther south, but they also don't have the crowds. You'll usually find a solitary spot. Fog often hugs the coast until about noon in June and July.

The usually gentle surf at **Arroyo Burro County Beach** (✉ Cliff Dr. at Las Positas Rd.) makes it ideal for families with young children. **Goleta Beach Park** (✉ Ward Memorial Hwy.) is a favorite with college students from the nearby University of California campus. Successively west of Santa Barbara off U.S. 101 are **El Capitan, Refugio, and Gaviota state beaches,** each with campsites, picnic tables, and fire rings. East of the city is sheltered, sunny, often crowded **Carpinteria State Beach.**

BICYCLING

The level, two-lane, 3-mi Cabrillo Bike Lane passes the Santa Barbara Zoo, the Andree Clark Bird Refuge, beaches, and the harbor. There are restaurants along the way, or you can stop for a picnic along the palm-lined path looking out on the Pacific. **Beach Rentals** (✉ 22 State St., ☎ 805/966–6733) has bikes, quadricycles, and skates. **Cycles 4 Rent** (✉ Fess Parker's Doubletree Resort, 633 E. Cabrillo Blvd., ☎ 805/564–4333 ext. 444; ✉ 101 State St., ☎ 805/652–0462) has bikes and quadricycles.

BOATS AND CHARTERS

Adventure Outdoor Excursions (☎ 805/963–2248) arranges everything from kayak to mountain bike excursions. **Island Packers** (☎ 805/642–1393) conducts day trips and camping excursions (reservations essential in summer) to the five Channel Islands. **Santa Barbara Sail-**

ing Association (✉ Santa Barbara Yacht Harbor launching ramp, ☏ 805/962–2826 or 800/350–9090) provides sailing instruction, rents and charters sailboats, and organizes dinner and sunset champagne cruises, island excursions, and whale-watching expeditions. **Sea Landing Aquatic Center** (✉ Cabrillo Blvd. at Bath St. and the breakwater, ☏ 805/963–3564) operates surface and deep-sea fishing charters year-round, plus dinner cruises and island and whale-watching excursions.

GOLF

Sandpiper Golf Course (✉ 7925 Hollister Ave., Goleta, ☏ 805/968–1541) is a challenging 18-hole, par-72 course. The greens fee ranges from $70 to $110; an optional cart costs $24. **Santa Barbara Golf Club** (✉ Las Positas Rd. and McCaw Ave., ☏ 805/687–7087) has an 18-hole, par-70 course. The greens fee is $25–$35; an optional cart costs $10.

HORSEBACK RIDING

The Circle Bar B Guest Ranch (✉ 1800 Refugio Rd., Goleta, ☏ 805/968–1113) operates trail rides.

TENNIS

Many hotels in Santa Barbara have courts. Day permits ($3) can be purchased for excellent public courts: **Las Positas Municipal Courts** (✉ 1002 Las Positas Rd.), **Municipal Courts** (✉ near Salinas St. and U.S. 101). For permits, call ☏ 805/564–5418. For **Pershing Park** (✉ Castillo St. and Cabrillo Blvd.), call ☏ 805/564–5517.

Shopping

State Street, the commercial hub of Santa Barbara, is a joy to shop. Chic malls, quirky storefronts, antiques emporiums, elegant boutiques, and funky thrift shops are on or near the street, and they're all accessible on foot or by taking the battery-powered trolley (25¢) that runs between the waterfront and the 1300 block. Swank boutiques line Montecito's **Coast Village Road,** where members of the landed gentry pick up truffle oil, picture frames, and designer sweats.

SHOPPING AREAS

Shops, art galleries, and studios share the courtyard and gardens of **El Paseo** (✉ Cañon Perdido St. between State and Anacapa Sts.), an arcade rich in history. Lunch on the outdoor patio is a nice break during a downtown tour. Open-air **Paseo Nuevo** (✉ 700 and 800 blocks of State St.), home to chains such as the Eddie Bauer Home Collection and Macy's, also contains cherished local institutions such as the children's clothier This Little Piggy.

Antiques and gift shops are clustered in restored Victorian buildings on **Brinkerhoff Avenue** (✉ 2 blocks west of State St. at West Cota St.). Serious antiques hunters head a few miles south of Santa Barbara to the beach town of **Summerland,** which is rife with shops and markets. For a map and guide to Santa Barbara antiques dealers, drop by the Tourist Information Center.

BOOKS

Barnes & Noble (✉ 829 State St., ☏ 805/962–8509) and **Borders** (✉ 900 State St., ☏ 805/899–3668) hold court on State Street. **Chaucer's Bookstore** (✉ Loreta Plaza, 3321 State St., ☏ 805/682–6787) is a well-stocked independent. **Sullivan Goss** (✉ 7 E. Anapamu St., ☏ 805/730–1460) stocks books on California history and art. **The Book Den** (✉ 11 E. Anapamu St., ☏ 805/962–3321) has the town's largest selection of used books.

CLOTHING

The complete line of **Big Dog Sportswear** (✉ 6 E. Yanonali St., ☏ 805/963–8728) is sold at the Santa Barbara–based company's flagship store. **Pacific Leisure** (✉ 929 State St., ☎ 805/962–8828) stocks the latest in casual wear, shoes, and beach towels. **Territory Ahead** (✉ 515 State St., ☎ 805/962–5558), a high-quality outdoorsy catalog company, sells fashionably rugged clothing for men and women. **Tienda Ho** (✉ 1105 State St., ☎ 805/564–7030) is a bohemian bazaar combining Indian, Moroccan, and Indonesian influences.

Wendy Foster–Pierre LaFond (✉ 833 State St., ☎ 805/966–2276), an upscale local clothier, captures the fluid California style of women's wear. There are two even tonier branches in Montecito (✉ 516 San Ysidro Rd., ☎ 805/565–1502; ✉ 1121 Coast Village Rd., ☎ 805/565–1599). The store on Coast Village Road goes by the name Angel.

OJAI

31 *40 mi southeast of Santa Barbara, U.S. 101 to Hwy. 150 to Hwy. 33.*

The acres of orange and avocado groves in and around rural Ojai look like the postcard images of agricultural southern California from decades ago. Recent years have seen an influx of artists, showbiz types, and others who have opted for a life out of the fast lane. The Ojai Valley, which director Frank Capra used as a backdrop for his 1936 film *Lost Horizon,* sizzles in the summer, when temperatures routinely reach 90°F.

Compact Ojai can be easily explored on foot, or you can hop on **The Ojai Valley Trolley,** (25 ¢) which takes riders on a one-hour loop (between 7:40 and 5:40 on weekdays, 9 and 5 on weekends). Tell the driver you're a visitor, and you'll get an informal guided tour.

The works of local artists can be seen in the Spanish-style shopping arcade along the main street. **The Art Center** (✉ 113 S. Montgomery, ☎ 805/646–0117) exhibits artwork and presents theater and dance. **The Ojai Valley Museum** (✉ 130 W. Ojai Ave., ☎ 805/640–1390) documents the valley's history and displays Native American artifacts.

Native oaks shelter the used titles at **Bart's Books** (✉ 302 W. Matilija, ☎ 805/646–3755), an outdoor store. **Local Hero** (✉ 254 E. Ojai Ave., ☎ 805/646–3165) sells books and hosts music, readings, and book signings on weekend evenings. There's also a café here.

Organic and specialty growers sell their produce on Sunday from 10 to 2 (9 to 1 in summer) at the **Farmers Market** behind the arcade. On Wednesday evening in summer the free all-American music played by the Ojai Band draws crowds to **Libbey Park** (✉ Ojai Ave. in downtown Ojai).

The 9-mi **Ojai Valley Trail** is one of several paths in the hills surrounding town. **Ojai Valley Chamber of Commerce** (✉ 150 W. Ojai Ave., ☎ 805/646–8126) publishes a regional trail map and runs a visitor center.

For more than five decades the **Ojai Music Festival** (☎ 805/646–2094) has attracted internationally known progressive and traditional musicians for outdoor concerts in Libbey Park on the weekend after Memorial Day.

Dining and Lodging

$$$ ✕ **The Ranch House.** The town's best eatery serves rich paté appetizers and main dishes such as chicken soaked in vermouth and salmon poached in white wine. The verdant patio is a delight. ✉ *S. Lomita Ave.,* ☎ *805/646–2360. AE, D, DC, MC, V.*

$$–$$$ ✕ **Go Fish California Sushi & Grill.** Sushi mingles with American and Mexican seafood dishes on the menu of this fun place. Entertainers perform on the patio on weekend nights. ✉ *469 E. Ojai Ave.,* ☎ *805/640–1057. MC, V.*

$$–$$$ ✕ **L'Auberge.** Tasty French–Belgian food is paired with a terrific country setting here. When the weather's fine, those in the know reserve an early table on the patio so they can accompany their rack of lamb with a glorious sunset. ✉ *314 El Paseo Rd.,* ☎ *805/646–2288. AE, MC, V. No lunch weekdays.*

$$–$$$ ✕ **Suzanne's Cuisine.** Peppered filet mignon, linguine with steamed clams, and salmon with sauerkraut in a dill beurre blanc are among the offerings at this European-style restaurant. Pastas and meat dishes dominate the dinner menu and salads and soups star at lunchtime. Most of the bread and all the desserts are made on the premises. ✉ *502 W. Ojai Ave.,* ☎ *805/640–1961. MC, V. Closed Tues. and 1st 2 wks in Jan.*

$$$$ ✕🏨 **Oaks at Ojai.** Comfortable but not luxurious, this spa has a fitness package that includes lodging, use of the spa facilities, 18 fitness classes, and three nutritionally balanced low-calorie meals. ✉ *122 E. Ojai Ave., 93023,* ☎ *805/646–5573 or 800/753–6257,* FAX *805/640–1504. 46 rooms. Dining room, pool, beauty salon, hot tub, massage, sauna, spa, exercise room. D, MC, V. 2-day minimum stay.*

$$$$ ★ 🏨 **Ojai Valley Inn & Spa.** This outdoorsy golf-oriented resort is set on beautifully landscaped grounds. The peaceful setting comes with hillside views in nearly all directions. Nearby is the inn's 800-acre ranch, where you can hike, mountain bike, and ride horses. Some of the nicest rooms are in the original adobe building. Families can make use of Camp Ojai, held in summer and on holidays for children from age 3 to 12, and the remarkable collection of miniature animals in the petting farm. The spa has massage and treatment rooms, a cardiovascular floor, a beauty salon, and quiet rooms. The two restaurants tout "Ojai regional cuisine" that incorporates locally grown produce and locally made foods. ✉ *905 Country Club Rd., 93023,* ☎ *805/646–5511 or 800/422–6524,* FAX *805/646–7969. 207 units. 2 restaurants, bar, 2 pools, spa, 18-hole golf course, 8 tennis courts, hiking, horseback riding, mountain bikes, meeting rooms. AE, D, DC, MC, V.*

$$–$$$$ 🏨 **The Blue Iguana Inn.** Local artists run this Southwestern-style hotel west of downtown. Small and cozy, the inn is designed around a courtyard. The work of the artist-owners decorate the rooms. If you like a particular work, you can purchase it. The suites have kitchenettes. ✉ *11794 N. Ventura Ave. (Hwy. 33), 93023,* ☎ *805/646–5277. 4 rooms, 7 suites. Refrigerators, pool, hot tub. AE, D, DC, MC, V.*

$$ 🏨 **Best Western Casa Ojai.** This modern hotel sits on Ojai's main drag, across from Soule Park Golf Course. Rooms are simple and clean. ✉ *1302 E. Ojai Ave., 93023,* ☎ *805/646–8175 or 800/255–8175,* FAX *805/640–8247. 43 rooms, 2 suites. Pool, hot tub. AE, D, DC, MC, V. CP.*

THE CENTRAL COAST A TO Z

Arriving and Departing

By Bus

Greyhound (☎ 800/231–2222) provides service from San Francisco and Los Angeles to San Luis Obispo and Santa Barbara.

By Car

U.S. 101 and Highway 1 are the main routes into the Central Coast from Los Angeles and San Francisco. Interstate 280 to U.S. 101 to San Luis Obispo is the quickest route from San Francisco to the southern portion of the Central Coast, but it's not the scenic route. Highway 46 heads west from the Central Valley to Paso Robles, where it becomes narrower as it continues to the coast, intersecting Highway 1 a few miles south of Cambria. Highway 33 heads south from the Central Valley to Ojai; about 60 mi north of Ojai, Highway 166 leaves Highway 33, traveling due west through the Sierra Madre Mountains. Highway 166 intersects with U.S. 101 north of Santa Maria, and then continues west to Highway 1.

By Plane

Alaska Commuter Airlines, America West Express, American/American Eagle, Skywest/Delta, United/United Express, and US Airways Express fly into **Santa Barbara Municipal Airport** (✉ 500 Fowler Rd., ☎ 805/683–4011), 8 mi from downtown. *See* Air Travel *in* Smart Travel Tips A to Z for airline phone numbers.

Santa Barbara Airbus (☎ 805/964–7759 or 800/733–6354) shuttles travelers between Santa Barbara and Los Angeles for $35 one-way and $65 round-trip (slight discount with 24-hour notice, larger discount for groups of two or more). The **Santa Barbara Metropolitan Transit District** (☎ 805/683–3702) Bus 11 runs every 30 minutes from the airport to the downtown transit center.

By Train

The **Amtrak** (☎ 800/872–7245) *Coast Starlight,* which runs between Los Angeles, Oakland, and Seattle, stops in Santa Barbara and San Luis Obispo. Several *San Diegan* trains operate daily between Santa Barbara, Los Angeles, and San Diego. Local numbers: ☎ 805/963–1015 in Santa Barbara; 805/541–0505 in San Luis Obispo.

Getting Around

By Bus

From Monterey and Carmel, **Monterey–Salinas Transit** (☎ 831/899–2555) operates buses to Big Sur between May and September. From San Luis Obispo, **Central Coast Transit** (☎ 805/541–2228) runs buses around Santa Maria and out to the coast. **Santa Barbara Metropolitan Transit District** (☎ 805/683–3702 or 805/963–3364) provides local service. The **State Street and Waterfront shuttles** cover their respective sections of Santa Barbara during the day.

By Car

The best way to see the most dramatic section of the Central Coast, the 70 mi between Big Sur and San Simeon, is by car. Heading south on Highway 1, you'll be on the ocean side of the road and will get the best views. Don't expect to make good time along here. The road is narrow and twisting with a single lane in each direction, making it difficult to pass the many lumbering RVs. In fog or rain the drive can be downright nerve-racking. Once you start south from Carmel, there is no route east from Highway 1 until Highway 46 heads inland from Cambria to connect with U.S. 101.

Highway 1 and U.S. 101 run north–south and more or less parallel, with Highway 1 hugging the coast and U.S. 101 remaining a few to a few dozen miles inland. Along some stretches the two roads join and run together for a while. At Morro Bay, Highway 1 moves inland for 13 mi and connects with U.S. 101 at San Luis Obispo. From here south to Pismo Beach the two highways run concurrently. U.S. 101 is the quicker route to Santa Barbara; Highway 1 rejoins it north of town at Las Cruces.

Contacts and Resources

B&B Reservations Service

Bed & Breakfast Santa Barbara (☎ 805/898–1905 or 800/557–7898).

Doctors

Cottage Hospital (✉ Pueblo St. at Bath St., Santa Barbara, ☎ 805/682–7111; 805/569–7210 for emergency).

Emergencies

Ambulance (☎ 911). **Fire** (☎ 911). **Police** (☎ 911).

Guided Tours

Eagle- and wildlife-watching excursions take place on the *Osprey,* a 48-ft cruiser that plies Cachuma Lake, a 20-minute drive from Solvang and a 40-minute one from Santa Barbara. For additional information, contact the **Cachuma Lake Recreation Area,** Santa Barbara County Park Department (✉ Star Route, Santa Barbara 93105, ☎ 805/688–4658).

A motorized San Francisco–style cable car operated by **Santa Barbara Trolley Co.** (☎ 805/965–0353) makes 90-minute runs from 10 AM to 4 PM past major hotels, shopping areas, and attractions. Get off when you wish to, and pick up another trolley when you're ready to move on. The trolley departs from and returns to Stearns Wharf. The fare is $9.

Road Conditions

Caltrans (☎ 800/427–7623).

Visitor Information

Central Coast Tourism Council (✉ Box 14011, San Luis Obispo, 93406, ☎ 805/544–0241). **Ojai Chamber of Commerce** (✉ Box 1134, 150 W. Ojai Ave., 93024, ☎ 805/646–8126). **Paso Robles Chamber of Commerce** (✉ 1225 Paso Robles, 93446, ☎ 805/238–0506). **Paso Robles Vintners and Growers Association** (✉ 1940 Spring St., Paso Robles 93446, ☎ 805/239–8463). **San Luis Opisbo Chamber of Commerce** (✉ 1039 Chorro St., San Luis Opisbo, 93401, ☎ 805/781–2777). **Santa Barbara Conference and Visitors Bureau** (✉ 12 E. Carrillo St., 93101, ☎ 805/966–9222 or 800/927–4688). **Santa Barbara County Vintners' Association** (✉ Box 1558, Santa Ynez 93460, ☎ 805/688–0881 or 800/218–0881). **Solvang Conference & Visitors Bureau** (✉ 1511 Mission Dr., 93434, ☎ 805/688–6144).

11 LOS ANGELES

In certain lights Los Angeles displays its Spanish heritage, but even more evident is its vibrancy as a Pacific Rim cultural and economic center. Hollywood, the beaches, and the valleys are all within an hour's drive. There are also important examples of 20th-century domestic architecture, miles of freeways, and glamorous enclaves such as Beverly Hills. Everything about Los Angeles is grand—even overdone—which is part of the city's charm. It's all for show, but the show's usually a good one.

DON'T BELIEVE EVERYTHING YOU'VE HEARD about Los Angeles. Chances are it's an exaggeration, good or bad, and the truth is probably somewhere in between. Few places on this planet are as hard to categorize as L.A. It's too large and diverse. The city of 3.5 million sprawls across 476 square mi of desert basin, mountain canyons, and coastal beaches. Outside the city limits, another 6 million people live in 80 incorporated cities within Los Angeles County. Another 5 million reside in the four surrounding counties.

The largest population of Pacific Islanders in the nation lives here, as well as the world's third-largest Hispanic population (after Mexico City and Guadalajara). People from more than 100 countries call Los Angeles home. Signs in Spanish, Korean, Thai, Chinese, Japanese, Armenian, and Russian are as common in some areas of the city as English signs. What isn't so well known is that this diversity dates back to the city's beginnings: Indians, blacks, mestizos, and Spaniards were among the 44 settlers who first arrived from the Mexican provinces of Sonora and Sinaloa in September 1781.

Though its myriad cultures lend the city variety, life is not uniformly harmonious. There's ceaseless rankling about bilingual education in the schools, and bloody rioting has divided the city along racial lines more than once, most recently in 1992 when the acquittal of police officers accused of beating motorist Rodney King provoked the nation's worst civil unrest ever. That experience left a scar of misunderstanding and mistrust that has yet to heal completely.

But communities throughout the region pulled together after the devastating 1994 Northridge earthquake and two years later, when wildfires raged in Malibu. The cooperation of Angelenos in these times of crisis contradicts the stereotype of a self-indulgent populace concerned only about going to the gym and buying expensive gadgets.

If there's a universal symbol of Los Angeles, it's the automobile. As for the freeways—well, they're really not so bad. They're well-signed and for travel at times other than rush hour, they're the best route from one end of the city to the other. Here are a couple tips: most freeways are known by both a name and a number; for example, the Hollywood Freeway is also U.S. 101. Depending on the time of day you're traveling, distance in miles doesn't mean much. The 10 mi between the San Fernando Valley and downtown Los Angeles, for instance, might take an hour to travel during rush hour but only 20 minutes at other times.

EXPLORING LOS ANGELES

Revised and updated by Stephen Dolainski

Looking at a map of sprawling Los Angeles, first-time visitors are sometimes overwhelmed. Where to begin? What to see first? And what about all those freeways? Here's some advice: relax. Begin by setting your priorities—movie and television fans should first head to Hollywood, Universal Studios, and a taping of a television show. Beach lovers and outdoorsy types might start out in Santa Monica or Venice or Malibu, or spend an afternoon in Griffith Park, one of the largest city parks in the country. Those with a cultural bent will probably make a beeline for the Getty Center in Brentwood (make parking reservations in advance) or the reorganized Los Angeles County Museum of Art. Urban explorers might begin with downtown Los Angeles.

Downtown Los Angeles

Most visitors to Los Angeles who aren't staying at one of the big convention hotels downtown never make it to this part of the city. But downtown is the heart of this great city, its financial core, as well as its historical and cultural soul and the site of the sleek new Staples Center (☞ Spectator Sports *in* Outdoor Activities and Sports).

A Good Tour

Numbers in the text correspond to numbers in the margin and on the Downtown Los Angeles map.

A convenient and inexpensive minibus service—DASH, or Downtown Area Short Hop—has several routes that travel past most of the sights on this tour, stopping every two blocks or so. Each ride costs 25¢, so you can hop on and off without spending a fortune. Special routes operate on weekends. Call **DASH** (☎ from all Los Angeles area codes, 808–2273) for routes and hours of operation.

Begin a downtown tour by heading north on **Broadway** ① from 8th or 9th Street. At the southeast corner of Broadway and 3rd Street is the **Bradbury Building** ②. Across the street is the **Grand Central Market** ③. Once you've made your way through its tantalizing stalls you'll come out the opposite side onto Hill Street. Cross Hill Street and climb aboard **Angels Flight Railway** ④, a funicular that sweeps you up a steep incline to a courtyard called Watercourt (it's surrounded by bubbling, cascading fountains). From here, walk toward the glass pyramidal skylight topping the **Museum of Contemporary Art** ⑤, visible a half block north on Grand Avenue.

You can now either retrace your steps to Watercourt for the Angels Flight descent to Hill Street, Grand Central Market, and your car; or walk two blocks south on Grand Avenue to 5th Street. There you'll find two of downtown's historical and architectural treasures: the **Regal Biltmore Hotel** ⑥ and the **Central Library** ⑦. Behind the library are the tranquil MacGuire Gardens. Across 5th Street are the **Bunker Hill Steps** ⑧.

Back in your car, continue north on Broadway to 1st Street. A right turn here will take you into **Little Tokyo** ⑨ and the expanded **Japanese American National Museum** ⑩. The **Geffen Contemporary** ⑪ art museum, an arm of MOCA, is just one block north on Central Avenue. For a tranquil respite, backtrack on Central Avenue to 2nd Street and head two blocks north to Los Angeles Street to get to the rooftop **Japanese Garden** ⑫ at the New Otani Hotel.

From Little Tokyo, turn left (north) from 1st Street onto Alameda Street. As you pass over the freeway, you'll come to the next stop, **Union Station** ⑬, on the right. Street parking is limited, so your best bet is to park in the pay lot at Union Station (about $5). After a look inside this grand railway terminal, cross Alameda Street to **Olvera Street** ⑭.

From Union Station, turn right on Alameda Street and then immediately left on Cesar Chavez Avenue for three blocks. At Broadway, turn right to **Chinatown** ⑮. If you have children in tow, reverse your route on Broadway from Chinatown; cross back over the freeway, and at Temple Street make a left for the three-block drive to the **Los Angeles Children's Museum** ⑯ at the Los Angeles Mall. Look to the right as you drive down Temple Street to see the back of **Los Angeles City Hall** ⑰. A few blocks farther west at Grand Avenue is the **Performing Arts Center of Los Angeles County** ⑱.

Exploring Los Angeles *(Boxes Refer to Detail Maps)*

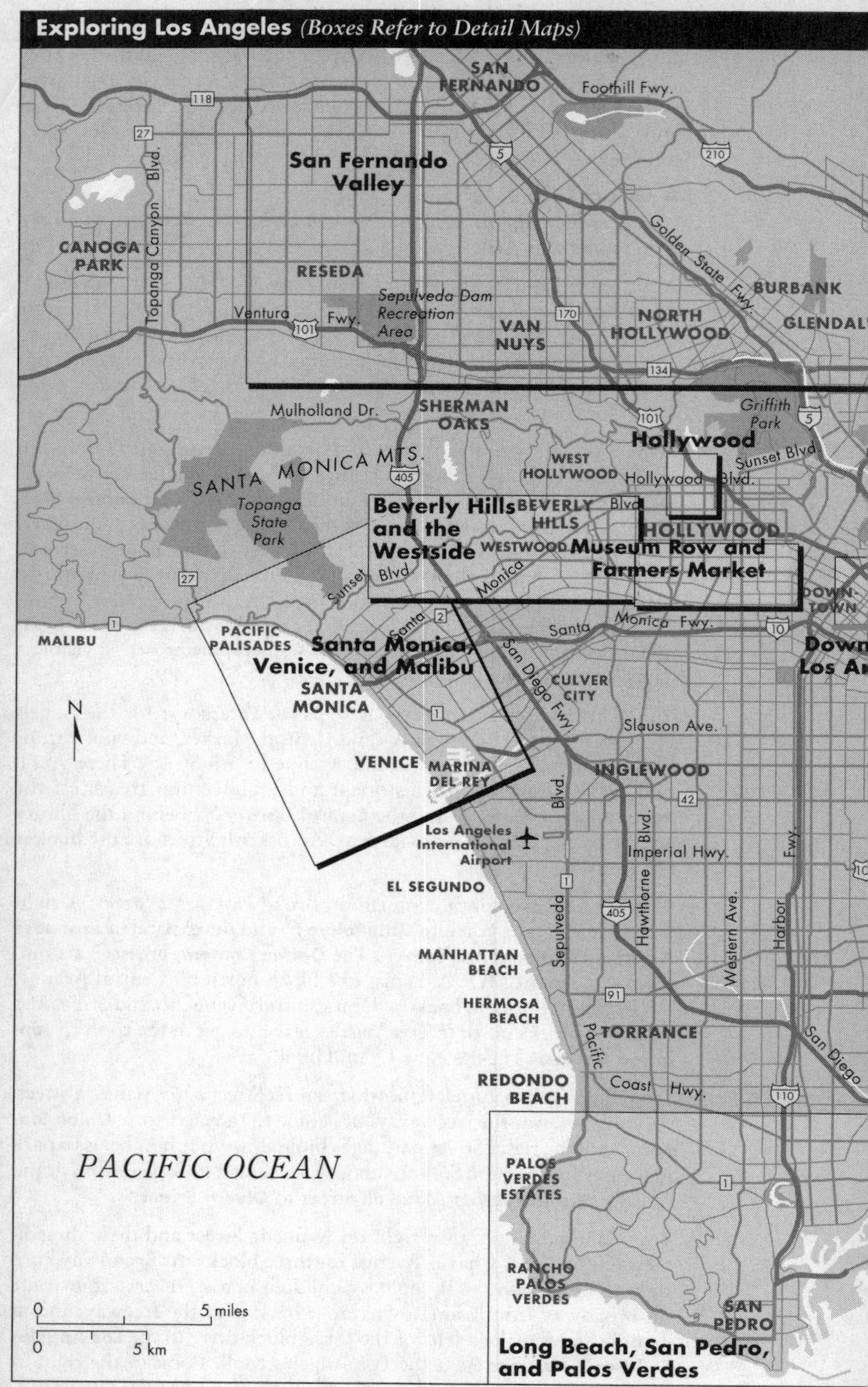

SAN FERNANDO
Foothill Fwy.
San Fernando Valley
CANOGA PARK
Topanga Canyon Blvd.
RESEDA
Sepulveda Dam Recreation Area
Ventura Fwy.
VAN NUYS
Golden State Fwy.
BURBANK
NORTH HOLLYWOOD
GLENDAL
Mulholland Dr.
SHERMAN OAKS
Griffith Park
Hollywood
SANTA MONICA MTS.
WEST HOLLYWOOD
Sunset Blvd
Hollywood Blvd.
Topanga State Park
Beverly Hills and the Westside
BEVERLY HILLS
HOLLYWOOD
WESTWOOD
Museum Row and Farmers Market
Sunset Blvd
Monica
DOWNTOWN
Santa Monica Fwy.
MALIBU
PACIFIC PALISADES
Santa Monica, Venice, and Malibu
San Diego Fwy.
CULVER CITY
SANTA MONICA
Slauson Ave.
VENICE
MARINA DEL REY
INGLEWOOD
Los Angeles International Airport
Imperial Hwy.
EL SEGUNDO
Sepulveda Blvd.
Hawthorne Blvd.
Western Ave.
Harbor Fwy.
MANHATTAN BEACH
HERMOSA BEACH
TORRANCE
Pacific Coast Hwy.
San Diego
REDONDO BEACH
PACIFIC OCEAN
PALOS VERDES ESTATES
RANCHO PALOS VERDES
SAN PEDRO
Long Beach, San Pedro, and Palos Verdes
0 5 miles
0 5 km

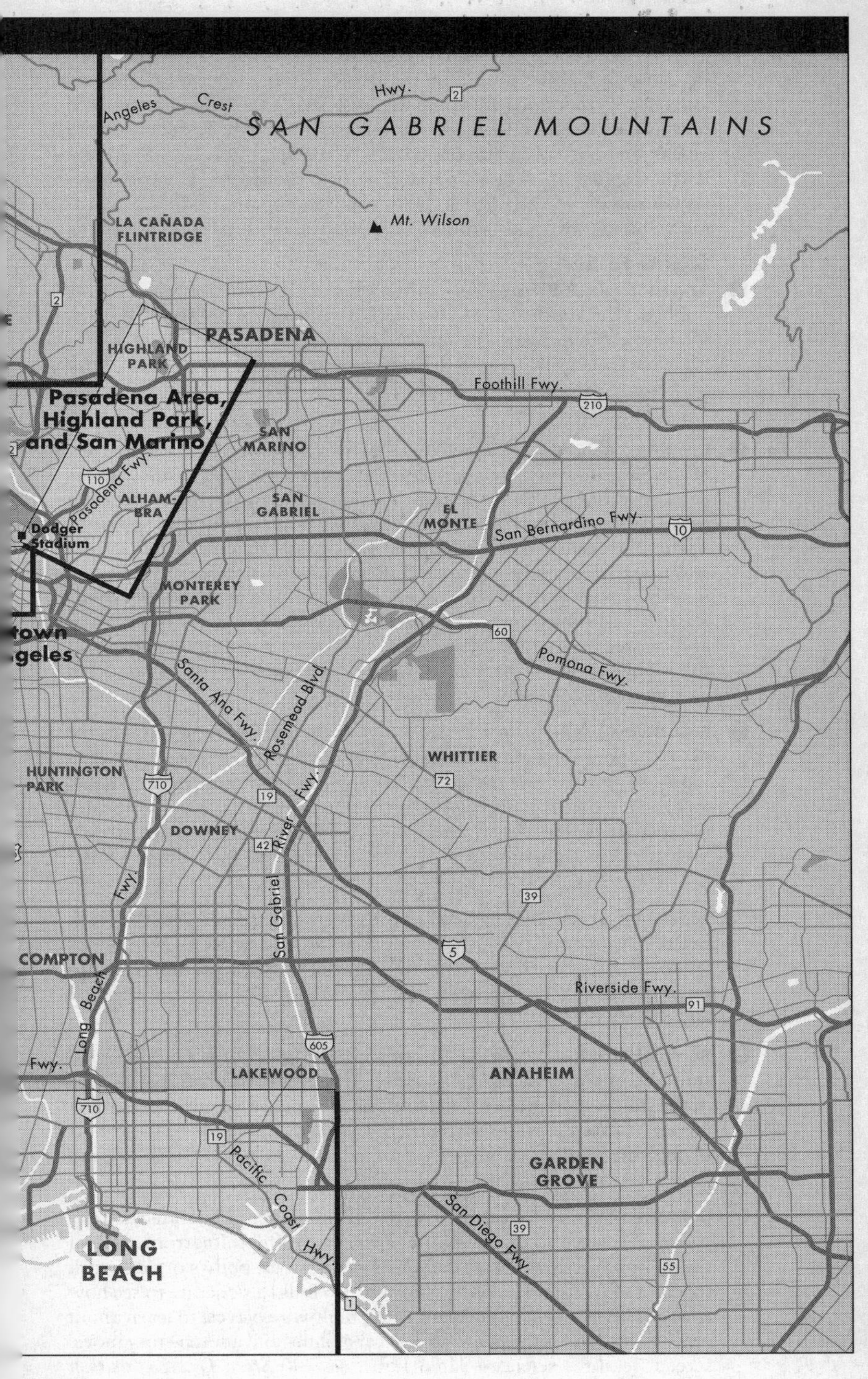

SAN GABRIEL MOUNTAINS
Angeles Crest Hwy.
Mt. Wilson
LA CAÑADA FLINTRIDGE
PASADENA
HIGHLAND PARK
Pasadena Area, Highland Park, and San Marino
SAN MARINO
Pasadena Fwy.
ALHAMBRA
SAN GABRIEL
EL MONTE
Foothill Fwy.
San Bernardino Fwy.
Dodger Stadium
MONTEREY PARK
Pomona Fwy.
Santa Ana Fwy.
Rosemead Blvd.
WHITTIER
HUNTINGTON PARK
DOWNEY
San Gabriel River Fwy.
COMPTON
Long Beach Fwy.
Riverside Fwy.
LAKEWOOD
ANAHEIM
GARDEN GROVE
Pacific Coast Hwy.
San Diego Fwy.
LONG BEACH

TIMING

The weekend is the best time to explore downtown. There's less traffic, parking is easier to find on the streets (bring quarters for meters), and cheaper day rates prevail in the lots. Seeing everything mentioned on this tour would take at least a full day, if not two. Expect to spend at least an hour in Chinatown, Olvera Street, and Little Tokyo—longer if you stop to eat, watch a parade, or visit a museum. The **Los Angeles Conservancy** (☎ 213/623–2489) regularly conducts Saturday morning walking tours of downtown architectural landmarks and districts.

Sights to See

4 **Angels Flight Railway.** This turn-of-the-20th-century funicular was dubbed "the shortest in the world." Two original orange-and-black wooden cable railway cars take riders on a 70-second ride up a 298-ft incline from Hill Street to the Watercourt at California Plaza. ✉ *Hill St. between 3rd and 4th Sts.,* ☎ *213/626–1901.* 🎫 *25¢ one-way.* ⏲ *Daily 6:30 AM–10 PM.*

★ 2 **Bradbury Building.** Designed in 1893 by a novice architect who drew his inspiration from a science-fiction story and a conversation with his dead brother via a Ouija board, this building is a marvelous specimen of Victorian-era commercial architecture. Originally the site of turn-of-the-20th-century sweatshops, it now houses somewhat more genteel firms. The interior atrium courtyard, with its glass skylight and open balconies and elevator, is frequently used as a movie locale (*Blade Runner* was filmed here). The building is open weekdays from 9 to 6 and on weekends until 5 for a peek, as long as you don't wander past the lobby. ✉ *304 S. Broadway (southeast corner Broadway and 3rd St.),* ☎ *213/626–1893.*

1 **Broadway.** From the late 19th century to the 1950s Broadway was the main shopping and entertainment street downtown. Photos taken during those glory days show sidewalks crowded with shoppers and lights ablaze on movie marquees. About the only evidence of that period are the few movie palaces still in operation between 8th and 5th streets: look for the **Orpheum** (✉ 842 S. Broadway) and the **Million Dollar** (✉ 307 S. Broadway).

Much of the historical character of Broadway has suffered over the years, but the avenue today is as colorful, vibrant, and noisy as ever. Shops and businesses catering to a mostly Mexican and Central American immigrant clientele have moved into the old movie palaces between 1st and 9th streets.

8 **Bunker Hill Steps.** A "stream" flows down the center of this monumental staircase into a small pool at its base. The stream originates at the top of the stairs where Robert Graham's nude female sculpture *Source Figure* stands atop a cylindrical base that mimics the shape of the trunks of the surrounding palm trees. ✉ *5th St., between Grand Ave. and Figueroa St.*

★ **California Science Center.** Interactive exhibits here illustrate the relevance of science to everyday life. Tess, the 50-ft Animatronic star of the exhibit "Body Works," demonstrates how the body's organs work together to maintain balance. You can also build a structure to see how it stands up to an earthquake, or ride a high-wire bicycle to learn about gravity. The IMAX theater, with 3-D capabilities and a seven-story movie screen, features science-related films. ✉ *700 State Dr., Exposition Park,* ☎ *323/724–3623; IMAX 213/744–2019.* 🎫 *Free, except for IMAX (prices vary); parking $5.* ⏲ *Daily 10–5.*

Downtown Los Angeles

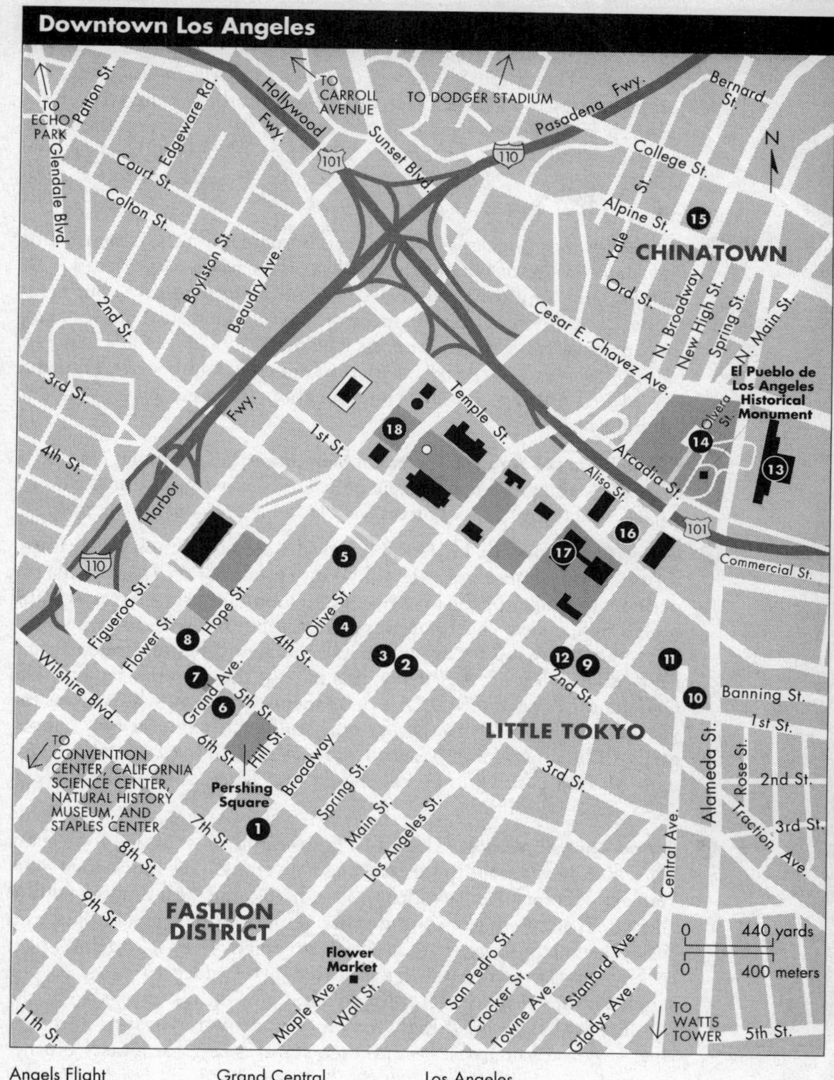

- Angels Flight Railway 4
- Bradbury Building 2
- Broadway 1
- Bunker Hill Steps 8
- Central Library 7
- Chinatown 15
- Geffen Contemporary 11
- Grand Central Market 3
- Japanese American National Museum 10
- Japanese Garden 12
- Little Tokyo 9
- Los Angeles Children's Museum 16
- Los Angeles City Hall 17
- Museum of Contemporary Art 5
- Olvera Street 14
- Performing Arts Center of Los Angeles County 18
- Regal Biltmore Hotel 6
- Union Station 13

★ 7 **Central Library.** Major fires in the 1980s closed the library for six years. Today, at twice its former size, it's the third-largest public library in the nation. The original building, designed by Bertram Goodhue, was completely restored to its 1926 condition, with the pyramid tower and its torch symbolizing the Light of Learning still crowning the building. ✉ *630 W. 5th St. (at Flower St.),* ☎ *213/228–7000.* 🎫 *Free.* ⏲ *Mon.–Thurs. 10–5:30, Fri.–Sat. 10–6, Sun. 1–5; docent tours weekdays at 12:30, Sat. at 11 and 2, Sun. at 2.*

15 **Chinatown.** Los Angeles's Chinatown is bordered by Yale, Bernard, Ord, and Alameda streets, but North Broadway is the heart. More than 15,000 Chinese and Southeast Asians live in the Chinatown area, but many thousands more regularly frequent the savory markets. Dim sum parlors are another big draw; **Empress Pavilion** (✉ 988 N. Hill St., ☎ 213/617–9898) is one of the best. Call the **Chinese Chamber of Commerce** (☎ 213/617–0396) for information about Chinese New Year and other events.

El Pueblo de Los Angeles Historical Monument. This site that commemorates Los Angeles's heritage encompasses many significant buildings, a park, and festive **Olvera Street** (☞ *below*). ✉ *Olvera and Temple Sts.*

11 **Geffen Contemporary.** In 1982, Los Angeles architect Frank Gehry transformed a warehouse in Little Tokyo into a temporary space while the permanent home for the ☞ **Museum of Contemporary Art** was being built a mile away. The Temporary Contemporary, with its large, flexible space allowing for wacky installations and big multimedia projects, was such a hit that it remains part of the museum facility. The Geffen houses part of MOCA's permanent collection, which spans the years from the 1940s to the present, and usually one or two temporary exhibits. ✉ *152 N. Central Ave.,* ☎ *213/626–6222.* 🎫 *$6, free with MOCA admission on same day; free Thurs. 5–8.* ⏲ *Tues.–Sun. 11–5, Thurs. until 8.*

★ 3 **Grand Central Market.** The city's largest and most active food market is also a testament to Los Angeles's diversity. This block-long marketplace of colorful and exotic produce, herbs, and meat draws a faithful clientele from the Latino community, senior citizens on a budget, and Westside matrons for whom money is no object. Even if you don't plan to buy anything, the market is a delightful place to browse. The butcher shops display everything from lambs' heads to pigs' tails; the produce stalls are piled high with locally grown avocados and very ripe, very red tomatoes. Several taco stands make for a tasty on-the-go meal. ✉ *317 S. Broadway,* ☎ *213/624–2378.* 🎫 *Free.* ⏲ *Mon.–Sat. 9–6; Sun. 10–6.*

★ 10 **Japanese American National Museum.** What was it like to grow up on a coffee plantation in Hawaii? How was life for Japanese Americans interned in concentration camps during World War II? These questions are addressed by changing exhibits at this museum in Little Tokyo. Volunteer docents are on hand to share their own stories and experiences. ✉ *369 E. 1st St., at Central Ave.,* ☎ *213/625–0414.* 🎫 *$6.* ⏲ *Tues.–Thurs. and weekends 10–5, Fri. 11–8.*

12 **Japanese Garden.** Landscape architect Sentaru Iwaki modeled this rooftop oasis at the New Otani Hotel and Garden after a 400-year-old garden in Tokyo. ✉ *New Otani Hotel and Garden, 120 S. Los Angeles St.,* ☎ *213/629–1200.* 🎫 *Free.*

9 **Little Tokyo.** The original neighborhood of Los Angeles's Japanese community, this downtown area has been deserted by most of those immigrants, who have moved to suburban areas such as Gardena and

West Los Angeles. Still, Little Tokyo remains a cultural focal point. Nisei Week ("nisei" is the name for second-generation Japanese) is celebrated here every August with traditional drums, dancing, a carnival, and a huge parade. Bounded by 1st, San Pedro, 3rd, and Central streets, Little Tokyo has dozens of sushi bars, tempura restaurants, and trinket shops. **The Japanese American Cultural and Community Center** (✉ 244 S. San Pedro St., ☎ 213/628–2725) presents traditional and contemporary cultural events.

16 **Los Angeles Children's Museum.** Hands-on exhibits allow children to record a song, make a TV show, learn about recycling, create arts and crafts, build a city out of pillows, and practice being a firefighter. ✉ *310 N. Main St.,* ☎ *213/687–8800.* *$5.* ⏲ *Late June–Labor Day, daily 10–5; Labor Day–late June, weekends 10–5.*

17 **Los Angeles City Hall.** This often-photographed, very recognizable building has made numerous appearances on *Superman, Dragnet,* and other popular television shows. Erected in the late 1920s with a pointy spire at the top, the 28-story Art Deco treasure is closed for seismic renovations, and is expected to reopen in mid 2001. ✉ *200 N. Spring St.*

★ 5 **Museum of Contemporary Art (MOCA).** The 5,000-piece permanent collection of MOCA is split between the ☞ **Geffen Contemporary** and the galleries at California Plaza, in a red sandstone building designed by Japanese architect Arata Isozaki. The collection represents art from 1940 to the present, including works by Mark Rothko, Franz Kline, Susan Rothenberg, Diane Arbus, and Robert Frank. MOCA also sponsors at least 20 exhibitions a year by both established and new artists in all visual media. ✉ *250 S. Grand Ave.,* ☎ *213/626–6222.* *$6; free on same day with Geffen Contemporary admission, and also Thurs. 5–8.* ⏲ *Tues., Wed., Fri.–Sun. 11–5; Thurs. 11–8.*

★ **Natural History Museum of Los Angeles County.** The museum has a rich collection of prehistoric fossils and extensive bird, insect, and marine-life exhibits. A brilliant display of stones can be seen in the Gem and Mineral Hall. Exhibits typifying various cultural groups include pre-Columbian artifacts and a display of crafts from the South Pacific. The Times Mirror Hall of Native American Cultures delves into the history of Los Angeles's earliest inhabitants. The Ralph M. Parsons Discovery Center for children has hands-on exhibits. ✉ *900 Exposition Blvd.,* ☎ *213/763–3466.* *$8; free 1st Tues. of month.* ⏲ *Weekdays 9:30–5, weekends and holidays 10–5.*

★ 14 **Olvera Street.** Lively, one-block Olvera Street tantalizes with tile walkways, piñatas, mariachis, and authentic Mexican food. Restored as an open-air Mexican market in 1930, the street is the symbol of the city's beginnings when the original settlers built earthen and willow huts near the river. Vendors sell puppets, tooled leather goods, sandals, and other items from little stalls that line the center of the narrow street. On weekends the restaurants are packed, and there is usually music in the plaza and along the street. Two Mexican holidays, Cinco de Mayo (May 5) and Independence Day (September 16), draw huge crowds. To see Olvera Street at its quietest, visit late on a weekday afternoon. For information, stop by the **Olvera Street Visitors Center,** housed in the Sepulveda House (✉ 622 N. Main St., ☎ 213/628–1274), a Victorian built in 1887 as a hotel and boardinghouse. The center is open from Monday through Saturday between 10 and 3.

Pelanconi House (✉ W-17 Olvera St.), built in 1855, was the first brick building in Los Angeles and has been home to La Golondrina restaurant for 60 years.

Avila Adobe (✉ E-10 Olvera St.), built in 1818, is considered the oldest building still standing in Los Angeles. This graceful, simple adobe with a traditional interior courtyard is furnished in the style of the 1840s. It is open daily from 9 to 5 (until 4 in winter).

The south wall of the **Italian Hall building** (✉ 650 N. Main St.) bears a controversial mural. Mexican muralist David Alfaro Siqueiros shocked his patrons when, in the 1930s, he depicted the oppressed workers of Latin America held in check by a menacing American eagle. The anti-imperialist mural was promptly whitewashed into oblivion. The whitewash has since been removed and work is underway to shelter the mural and allow public viewing of it.

At the beginning of Olvera Street is **The Plaza,** a wonderful Mexican-style park shaded by a huge Moreton Bay fig tree. On weekends, mariachis and folkloric dance groups often perform. Two annual events particularly worth seeing are the Blessing of the Animals and Las Posadas. The blessing takes place on the Saturday before Easter. Residents bring their pets to be blessed by a priest. For Las Posadas (every night between December 16 and 24), merchants and visitors parade up and down the street, led by children dressed as angels, to commemorate Mary and Joseph's search for shelter on Christmas Eve.

The Old Firehouse, an 1884 building on the south side of the Plaza, contains early fire-fighting equipment and old photographs. Free 50-minute walking tours start from the docent office next door and take in the Merced Theater, Masonic Hall, Pico House, and Garnier Block—all ornate examples of the late-19th-century style. On request, the docent will show you the tunnel passageways under the buildings that were once used by Chinese immigrants. Tours leave on the hour, from 10 to 1, every day but Monday.

NEED A BREAK?

Dining choices on Olvera Street range from fast-food stands to comfortable, sit-down restaurants. The most authentic Mexican food is at **La Luz del Dia** (✉ 107 Paseo de la Plaza, ☎ 213/628–7495). The handmade tortillas are patted out in a practiced rhythm by the women behind the counter.

18 **Performing Arts Center of Los Angeles County.** Until recently known as the Music Center and L.A.'s major performing arts venue since its opening in 1964, the Performing Arts Center is home to the Los Angeles Philharmonic, the Los Angeles Opera, and the Center Theater Group—and has also been the site of the Academy Awards. The largest and grandest of the three theaters is the **Dorothy Chandler Pavilion,** named after the wife of former *Los Angeles Times* publisher Norman Chandler (she was instrumental in raising the money to build the complex). The round building in the middle, the **Mark Taper Forum,** is a smaller theater showing mainly experimental works, many on a pre-Broadway run. The **Ahmanson,** at the north end, is the venue for big musicals. The Walt Disney Concert Hall, will be the fourth venue at the center when it opens for the 2002–2003 season. The vast complex's cement plaza has a fountain and a Jacques Lipchitz sculpture. ✉ *135 N. Grand Ave., at 1st St.,* ☎ *213/972–7211; 213/972–7483 tour information.* *Free.* *60-min tour year-round, but call for days and times.*

6 **Regal Biltmore Hotel.** The beaux-arts Biltmore opened in 1923. The lobby has the feel of a Spanish palace, the indoor pool looks like a Roman bath, and the ornate Rendezvous Court is a civilized retreat for an afternoon cocktail. The Academy Awards were held here in the 1930s, and the hotel has also been used in many films, such as *The Fabulous Baker Boys* and *Independence Day.* ✉ *506 S. Grand Ave.,* ☎ *213/624–1011.*

★ 13 **Union Station.** This building is familiar
It was built in 1939 in a Spanish Mission
Streamline Moderne and Moorish design elem
alone is worth a look, its majestic scale evocative
800 N. Alameda St.

OFF THE BEATEN PATH

WATTS TOWERS – The jewel of rough South Central L.A. is the leg Simon Rodia, a tile setter who emigrated from Italy to California an erected one of the world's greatest folk-art structures. From 1921 until 1954, without any help, this eccentric man built the three main cement towers, using pipes, bed frames, and anything else he could find. He embellished them with bits of colored glass, broken pottery, and more than 70,000 seashells. The towers still stand preserved, now the centerpiece of a state historic park and cultural center. ✉ *Watts Towers Arts Center, 1727 E. 107th St. (take I–110 to I–105 east; exit north at S. Central Ave., turn right onto 108th St., left onto Willowbrook Ave.),* ☎ *323/847–4646.* *Free; weekend tours (scheduled to resume summer 2001) $1.* ⏲ *Tues.–Sat. 10–4, Sun. noon–4.*

Hollywood

For nine decades Hollywood has lured us with its carefully manufactured images promising glitz and glamour. As visitors, we just want a chance to come close enough to be able to say, "I was there!" Reality check: the magic of Hollywood takes place, for the most part, on sound stages that are not even in Hollywood anymore, and in nondescript film-processing labs and editing bays. Go to Beverly Hills and look at jewelry store windows if you want glitz. As for glamour, well, Hollywood is really a working town. Granted, many of the people who work in Hollywood—actors, directors, writers, composers—are among the highest paid and most celebrated workers in the world. But most of them face the same workaday grind as the rest of us, commuting daily and working long hours every day. So much for glamour. But Hollywood is still the entertainment capital of the world. Here's a tour that will get you as close to some of that magic as possible.

A Good Tour

Numbers in the text correspond to numbers in the margin and on the Hollywood map.

Drive up into the Hollywood Hills on Beachwood Drive (off Franklin Avenue, just east of Gower Street) for an up-close look at one of the world's most familiar icons: the **HOLLYWOOD sign** ①. Follow the small sign pointing the way to the LAFD Helispot. Turn left onto Rodgerton Drive, which twists and turns higher into the hills. At Deronda Drive, turn right and drive to the end. The Hollywood sign looms off to the left. Turn around and retrace your route down the hill, back to Beachwood Drive for the drive into Hollywood.

Make a right (west) at Franklin Avenue, and prepare to turn left at the next light at Gower Street. Stay on Gower Street, driving through the section of Sunset Boulevard known as **Gower Gulch.** At Gower Street and Santa Monica Boulevard, look for the entrance to **Hollywood Forever Cemetery** ② (formerly Hollywood Memorial Park), a half-block east on Santa Monica. If you visit the park, retrace your route back to Gower Street and turn left to drive along the western edge of the cemetery flanking Gower Street. Abutting the cemetery's southern edge is **Paramount Pictures** ③. The famous gate Norma Desmond (Gloria Swanson in *Sunset Boulevard*) was driven through is no longer acces-

plica marks the new entrance on Melrose
wer Street to reach the gate.

f Gower Street) on Melrose Avenue for three
urn right, and continue to **Hollywood and**
n whose fame is worldwide. Across the street,
tack" **Capitol Records Tower** ⑤ resembles a pile
on **Ivar Street** ⑥ are the former homes of literary
ner and Nathanael West.

ollywood Boulevard for a look at the bronze stars
ollywood Walk of Fame ⑦. If you want to stop along
e Lingerie Museum at the purple **Frederick's of Hol-
lyw**... **Hollywood Wax Museum** ⑨—both shrines to Hollywood camp—...etered parking is fairly easy to find.

At Hollywood Boulevard and Las Palmas Avenue is the **Egyptian Theatre** ⑩. Restored to its 1922 splendor, it now houses American Cinematheque, which screens classic and independent films. Continue west on Hollywood Boulevard. At the northwest corner of Hollywood Boulevard and Highland Avenue the new $385 million **Hollywood & Highland** hotel–retail–entertainment complex is going up. Plans are to stage the annual Academy Awards broadcast from the 3,300-seat theater here starting in 2001.

West of Highland Avenue, on the north side of Hollywood Boulevard is **Mann's Chinese Theatre** ⑪, a genuine, if kitschy, monument to Hollywood history. The elaborate pagoda-style movie palace is still the biggest draw along the boulevard. Also on the north side of the boulevard and west of the Chinese Theatre is the **Hollywood Entertainment Museum** ⑫. From the museum, cross Hollywood Boulevard and loop back east along the boulevard past the historic **Hollywood Roosevelt Hotel** ⑬.

Several blocks north of the boulevard on Highland Avenue is the **Hollywood Bowl** ⑭, where you can visit its interesting museum in the daytime or enjoy the outdoor concerts summer evenings.

From Hollywood Boulevard, travel south on Highland Avenue or La Brea Avenue and drive to the next major intersection, at Sunset Boulevard. Turn west on Sunset Boulevard toward West Hollywood, for a swing along the fabled **Sunset Strip** nightclub district.

TIMING

Plan to spend the better part of a morning or afternoon taking in Hollywood. A walking tour of Paramount Studios will add at least 2½ hours to your itinerary. Hollywood Boulevard attracts a sometimes-bizarre group of folks; if you've got children in tow, your best bet for a safe walk down the boulevard is during the day. Later in the evening, you can return to Hollywood for a cabaret performance at the Cinegrill, a movie at the Chinese or Egyptian, or a summertime concert at the Hollywood Bowl.

Sights to See

★ ❺ **Capitol Records Tower.** The romantic story about the origin of this symbol of '50s chic is that singer Nat King Cole and songwriter Johnny Mercer suggested that the record company's headquarters be shaped to look like a stack of 45s. Architect Welton Beckett claimed he just wanted to design a structure that economized space. On its south wall, artist Richard Wyatt's mural *Hollywood Jazz, 1945–1972,* immortalizes musical greats Duke Ellington, Billie Holiday, Ella Fitzgerald, and Miles Davis. ⊠ *1750 N. Vine St.*

❿ **Egyptian Theatre.** Hollywood's first movie palace, complete with hieroglyphics, was built by impresario Sid Grauman in 1922. That year

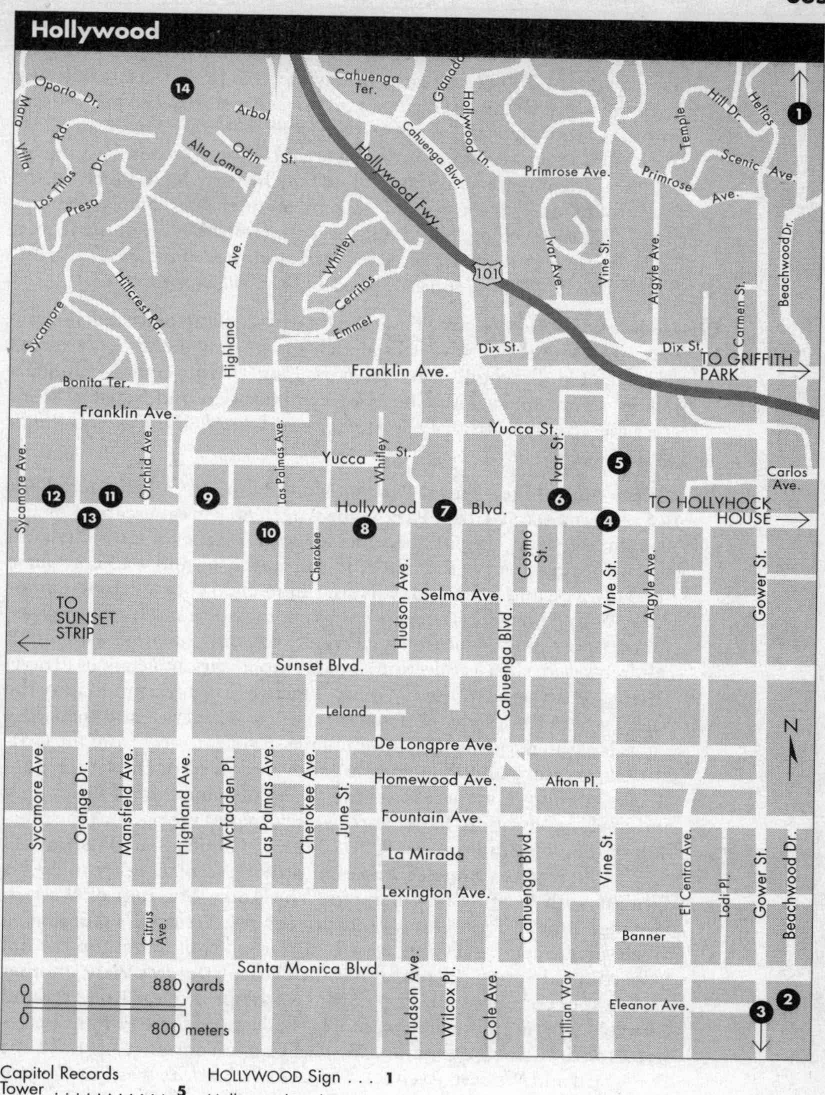

Capitol Records Tower 5

Egyptian Theatre . . . 10

Frederick's of Hollywood 8

Hollywood Bowl 14

Hollywood Entertainment Museum 12

Hollywood Forever Cemetery 2

Hollywood Roosevelt Hotel 13

HOLLYWOOD Sign . . . 1

Hollywood and Vine 4

Hollywood Walk of Fame 7

Hollywood Wax Museum 9

Ivar Street. 6

Mann's Chinese Theatre 11

Paramount Pictures 3

Robin Hood, starring Douglas Fairbanks, premiered. Over the years films such as *The Ten Commandments* (1923) and *Funny Girl* (1968) premiered at the 1,200-seat theater. But, with a cast of various owners, the Egyptian slumped toward disrepair and closed in 1992. The historic theater was renovated and reopened in 1999 to house American Cinematheque, a nonprofit film-screening organization. Daytime visitors can watch a documentary about Hollywood history, have lunch in the restaurant, and visit the grand forecourt of the theater. Film screenings are held in the evening. Silent films, accompanied by live music from a 1922 Wurlitzer organ, are screened on Tuesday evening. ✉ *6712 Hollywood Blvd.,* ☎ *323/466–3456.* *Free. Film screenings $7.*

8 **Frederick's of Hollywood.** Though you can stock up on risqué lingerie here, the real reason to visit Frederick's is to view the undergarments of some of Hollywood's legends: in the **Lingerie Museum**, Madonna's bustier shares space with Cher's kinky underwear and Marilyn Monroe's merry widow from *Let's Make Love.* ✉ *6608 Hollywood Blvd.,* ☎ *323/466–8506.*

Griffith Park. Like Central Park in Manhattan, or Golden Gate Park in San Francisco, Griffith Park is the Angeleno's great escape. On any pleasant weekend, the park becomes a bucolic escape for inner-city families who spread out in the shade. Joggers, cyclists, and walkers course its roadways, and golfers play its four municipal courses come rain or shine. Within the park, there are tennis courts; horse stables; pony rides; a merry-go-round (evocatively decrepit, but only open occasionally); children's railroads; a collection of old railroad cars and engines (**Travel Town**); and the 6,100-seat **Greek Theatre** (take Vermont into the park), where Rod Stewart, Tina Turner, Jose Carreras, and the Gipsy Kings have all performed. The mountains-to-ocean view from the **Griffith Observatory and Planetarium** (above Ferndell or the Greek Theatre) is fabulous and there is an interesting free museum of astronomy and space exploration. In the northwest corner of the park, at the junction of the Ventura Freeway (U.S. 134) and Golden State Freeway (I–5), the 80-acre **Los Angeles Zoo** is improving, replacing worn 1970s exhibits with exciting new habitats. The **Autry Museum of Western Heritage** is next door. Other points of interest are **Amir's Gardens,** a lovely picnic spot accessible only by fire-road trail (climb up the hill from Mineral Springs Picnic, off Griffith Drive); **Dante's View,** another garden spot en route to the top of Mt. Washington (elev. 1,652 ft); and **Ferndell,** where California sycamores shade more than 50 fern species (look for the dell off the park's Western Canyon entrance off Los Feliz Boulevard and Western Avenue). ✉ *Los Feliz Blvd. at Western Canyon Rd., Vermont Ave., Crystal Springs Dr., and Riverside Dr.,* ☎ *323/664–1191 observatory and planetarium; 818/901–9405 laserium; 323/644–6400 zoo; 323/667–2000 Autry museum; 323/665–1927 Greek Theater; 323/662–5874 Travel Town; 323/664–6903 railroad; 323/664–3266 pony rides; 323/665–3051 carousel.* *Observatory and Hall of Science free; planetarium $4; laserium $7–$9; zoo $8.25 (Safari Shuttle Tour $3.50); Autry Museum $7.50; Travel Town free; railroad $2; pony rides $1.50; carousel $1.* ⏲ *Observatory and planetarium, mid-June–Labor Day, daily 12:30 PM–10 PM; early Sept.–mid-June, Tues.–Fri. 2 PM–10 PM, weekends 12:30 PM–10 PM; zoo, daily, 10–5, July–Labor Day 10–6 (animals removed from view starting at 4:30); Autry Museum, Tues.–Sun. 10–5; theater performances Apr.–Oct.; Travel Town weekdays 10–4, weekends and holidays 10–5; railroad daily 10–4:30 (later late June–Labor Day); carousel, weekends only (daily late June–Labor Day); pony rides, Tues.–Sun. 10–4 (later in late June–Labor Day), weather permitting.*

OFF THE BEATEN PATH **HOLLYHOCK HOUSE** – The first of several houses Frank Lloyd Wright designed in Los Angeles, this 1921 manse is a perfect example of the pre-Columbian style that Wright was so fond of at that time. It contains original, Wright-designed furniture. Barnsdall Art Park, site of Hollyhock House and city-offered art classes and events, closed in summer 2000 for renovation and is not due to open for a year. ✉ *Barnsdall Art Park, 4800 Hollywood Blvd.,* ☎ *323/913–4157.* 🎫 *$2.* ⏲ *Tours Wed.–Sun., noon, 1, 2, and 3.*

⓮ **Hollywood Bowl.** Summer evening concerts have been a tradition since 1922 at this amphitheater cradled in the Hollywood Hills. The Bowl is the summer home of the Los Angeles Philharmonic, but musical fare also includes pop and jazz. The 17,000-plus seating capacity ranges from boxes to concrete bleachers in the rear. Come early for a picnic in the surrounding grounds. Before the concert, or during the day, visit the **Hollywood Bowl Museum** (☎ 323/850–2058) for a capsule version of the Bowl's long history. ✉ *2301 N. Highland Ave.,* ☎ *323/850–2000.* ⏲ *Museum: Tues.–Sat. 10–4:30; July–mid-Sept. concert nights, 10 AM–8:30 PM; grounds daily sunrise–sunset (call for performance schedule).*

⓬ **Hollywood Entertainment Museum.** A multimedia presentation in the main rotunda and interactive exhibits track the evolution of Hollywood, from the low-tech silent era to today's hyper-tech world of special effects. Highlights are the marvelously detailed miniature model of 1936 Hollywood, and sets from television shows such as the bar from TV's *Cheers.* ✉ *7021 Hollywood Blvd.,* ☎ *323/465–7900.* 🎫 *$7.50.* ⏲ *June–Sept., daily 10–6; Sept.–June, Mon., Tues., Thurs.–Sun. 11–6.*

❷ **Hollywood Forever Cemetery.** Rudolph Valentino, Tyrone Power, and Jayne Mansfield are among the celebrities buried here. Sadly, the cemetery has fallen into a state of neglect. You can pick up a map of the grounds in the office at the entrance. ✉ *6000 Santa Monica Blvd.,* ☎ *323/469–1181.* ⏲ *Daily 8–5.*

⓭ **Hollywood Roosevelt Hotel.** The first Academy Awards banquet was held here in 1927. A display of vintage Hollywood photographs and other historical memorabilia occupies the hotel's mezzanine level. In the hotel is Cinegrill, a cabaret steeped in Hollywood history. Have a look at the pool out back: David Hockney was commissioned to paint the "mural" at the bottom (actually nothing more than a series of blue blotches). ✉ *7000 Hollywood Blvd.,* ☎ *323/466–7000.*

★ ❶ **HOLLYWOOD Sign.** With letters 50 ft tall, Hollywood's trademark sign can be spotted from miles away. The sign, which originally spelled out "Hollywoodland," was erected in the Hollywood Hills in 1923 to promote a real-estate development. In 1949 the "land" portion of the sign was taken down. Over the years pranksters have altered it, albeit temporarily, to spell out "Hollyweed" (in the 1970s, to commemorate lenient marijuana laws) and "Go Navy" (before a Rose Bowl game). In 1994, a fence and surveillance equipment were installed to deter intruders.

❹ **Hollywood and Vine.** In the old days this was the hub of the radio and movie industry, and there was nothing unusual about film stars such as Gable and Garbo hurrying in or out of office buildings at the intersection on their way to or from their agents' offices. These days, Hollywood and Vine is far from the action. The **Brown Derby** restaurant once stood a half-block south of the intersection (✉ 1628 N. Vine St.). Nearby is the **Palace Theater** (✉ 1735 N. Vine St.), where the 1950s TV show *This Is Your Life* was recorded; it's now a rental venue for rock shows. Within a block or two of the intersection, however, you can still see the **Capitol Records** building (☞ *above*) and the **Pantages Theater** (✉ 6233 Hollywood Blvd.), a former opulent movie palace now used to house large-scale Broadway musicals on tour. Even the Metro Rail Red Line subway station, which opened here in 1999, keeps up the Hollywood theme, with film reels, the Yellow Brick Road, and giant movie projectors decorating the station.

★ 7 **Hollywood Walk of Fame.** All along this mile-long stretch of Hollywood Boulevard sidewalk, entertainment legends' names are embossed in brass, each at the center of a pink star embedded in dark-gray terrazzo. The first eight stars were unveiled in 1960 at the northwest corner of Highland Avenue and Hollywood Boulevard. Since then, more than 2,000 others have been immortalized. The honor doesn't come cheaply. Upon selection by a special committee, the personality in question (or more likely his or her movie studio or record company) pays about $7,500 for the privilege. Here's a miniguide to a few of the more famous celebs' stars: Marlon Brando at 1765 Vine, Charlie Chaplin at 6751 Hollywood, W. C. Fields at 7004 Hollywood, Clark Gable at 1608 Vine, Marilyn Monroe at 6774 Hollywood (in front of McDonald's), Rudolph Valentino at 6164 Hollywood, Michael Jackson at 6927 Hollywood, and John Wayne at 1541 Vine. Call the **Hollywood Chamber of Commerce** (✉ 7018 Hollywood Blvd., ☎ 213/469–8311) or the **Hollywood Visitor Information Center** (✉ 6541 Hollywood Blvd., ☎ 213/236–2331 or 213/689–8822) to find out where your favorite celebrity's star can be found. Ask when the next sidewalk star installation ceremony is scheduled to take place. The honoree usually shows up for the event.

9 **Hollywood Wax Museum.** Here you'll spot celebrities that real life can no longer provide (Mary Pickford, Elvis Presley, and Clark Gable) and a few that even real life never did (such as the *Star Trek* cast). A short film on Academy Award winners screens daily. ✉ *6767 Hollywood Blvd.,* ☎ *323/462–8860.* 💵 *$8.95.* ⏲ *Sun.–Thurs. 10 AM–midnight, Fri.–Sat. 10 AM–1 AM.*

NEED A BREAK?

Musso & Frank Grill (✉ 6667 Hollywood Blvd., ☎ 323/467–5123), open since 1919, is the last remaining Old Hollywood watering hole. Wash down a plate of lamb chops, spinach, and sourdough bread with a martini, or just stop in for a soda and soak up some atmosphere. Expect high prices and some attitude.

6 **Ivar Street.** William Faulkner wrote *Absalom, Absalom!* while he lived at the old **Knickerbocker Hotel** (✉ 1714 N. Ivar St.), and Nathanael West wrote *The Day of the Locust* in his apartment at the **Parva Sed-Apta** (✉ 1817 N. Ivar St.).

★ 11 **Mann's Chinese Theatre.** The former "Grauman's Chinese," a fantasy of Chinese pagodas and temples, is a place only Hollywood could turn out. You have to buy a movie ticket to appreciate the interior trappings, but the courtyard is open to the public. Here you'll see those famous cement hand- and footprints. This tradition is said to have begun at the theater's opening in 1927, with the premiere of Cecil B. DeMille's *King of Kings,* when actress Norma Talmadge accidentally stepped into the wet cement. Now more than 160 celebrities have contributed imprints of their appendages for posterity, along with a few other oddball imprints, like the one of Jimmy Durante's nose. ✉ *6925 Hollywood Blvd.,* ☎ *323/464–8111.*

3 **Paramount Pictures.** The last major studio still located in Hollywood is the best place to see what a real Hollywood movie studio looks like.

Two-hour guided walking tours of the 86-year-old studio include historical narrative about Rudolph Valentino, Mae West, Mary Pickford, Lucille Ball, and other stars who worked on the lot. Movies and TV shows are still filmed here. If you're lucky, you might see a show being produced. Tours are first-come, first-served and leave from the pedestrian walk-up gate on Melrose Street; park in the lot at Bronson and Melrose avenues. Children under 10 are not admitted. ✉ *5555 Melrose Ave.,* ☎ *323/956–5575.* 🎫 *$15.* 🕒 *2-hr walking tour weekdays on the half hr, 9–2.*

Museum Row and Farmers Market

East of Fairfax Avenue in the Miracle Mile district is the three-block stretch of Wilshire Boulevard known as Museum Row. A few blocks away is the historic Farmers Market.

A Good Tour

Numbers in the text correspond to numbers in the margin and on the Museum Row and Farmers Market map.

Start the day with coffee and fresh-baked pastries at **Farmers Market** ①, a few blocks north of Wilshire Boulevard at 3rd Street and Fairfax Avenue. Drive south on Fairfax Avenue to the **Miracle Mile** ② district of Wilshire Boulevard. The black-and-gold Art Deco building on the northeast corner is a former department store that's now called LACMA West and houses satellite exhibition galleries of the Los Angeles County Museum of Art (LACMA) and the **Southwest Museum at LACMA West.** Turn left onto Wilshire Boulevard and proceed to Ogden Drive or a block farther to Spaulding Avenue, where you can park the car and explore the museums on foot.

The large complex of contemporary buildings surrounded by a park (on the corner of Wilshire Boulevard and Ogden Drive) is the **Los Angeles County Museum of Art** ③. It's the largest museum west of Chicago and houses works spanning the history of art from ancient times to the present. Also occupying the park are the prehistoric **La Brea Tar Pits** ④, where many of the fossils displayed at the adjacent **Page Museum at the La Brea Tar Pits** ⑤ were found. Across Wilshire Boulevard are the **Craft and Folk Art Museum (CAFAM)** ⑥; the **Carole & Barry Kaye Museum of Miniatures** ⑦; and, back at the corner of Wilshire Boulevard and Fairfax Avenue, the **Petersen Automotive Museum** ⑧, which surveys the history of the car in Los Angeles.

TIMING

The museums open between 10 and noon, so plan your tour around the opening time of the museum you wish to visit first. LACMA is closed Wednesday, and has extended hours into the evening, closing at 8 (9 on Friday). The other museums are closed on Monday (except the Page, which is open Mondays in the summer). Weekends bring the largest crowds to the Farmers Market and the museums. On the second Tuesday of the month, admission to all but ticketed exhibits at LACMA is free. Set aside a good portion of the day to do this tour: an hour for the Farmers Market and four–five hours for the museums.

Sights to See

7 **Carole & Barry Kaye Museum of Miniatures.** Besides scaled-down models of the Hollywood Bowl, the Vatican, and several famous European châteaux, the George Stuart Gallery of miniature historical figures is one of the highlights of this pint-size world. There's also a tribute to America's First Ladies (as far back as Martha Washington), dolled up in their inaugural ball gowns. ✉ *5900 Wilshire Blvd.,* ☎ *323/937–6464.* 🎫 *$7.50.* 🕒 *Tues.–Sat. 10–5, Sun. 11–5.*

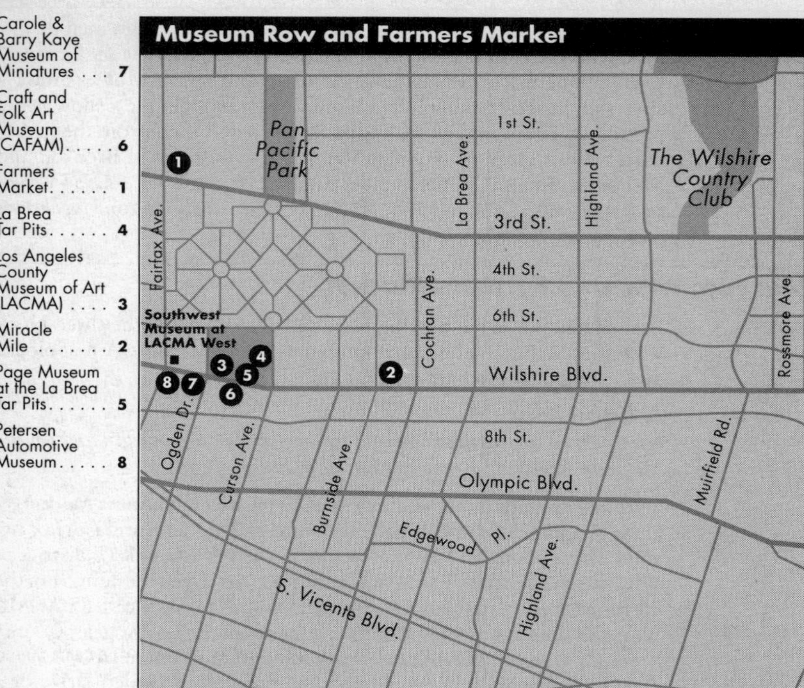

❻ **Craft and Folk Art Museum.** A small, but important, cultural landmark in the city, CAFAM early on pioneered support in Los Angeles of traditional folk arts. Now, reorganized in a partnership with the city's Cultural Affairs division, CAFAM is charged with the mission of providing programming that reflects the diverse culture groups and crafts artists in Southern California. Rotating exhibitions are presented in the museum's single gallery space, where you might see photographs and costumes of carnival celebrations around the world; lace, embroidery, and needlepoint from the Victorian era; Turkish textiles; or contemporary crafts from Asia. In October, 2000, CAFAM reinstituted its beloved Festival of Masks as a biennial event. ✉ *5814 Wilshire Blvd.,* ☎ *323/937–4230.* 🎫 *$3.50, free 1st Wed. of month.* ⏲ *Wed.–Sun. 11–5.*

★ ❶ **Farmers Market.** In July 1934, two entrepreneurs envisioned a European-style open-air market, to be built near the corner of 3rd Street and Fairfax Avenue, where farmers would sell their produce to local housewives. The idea was an instant success. Soon after the marketplace opened, Blanche Magee, a local restaurateur, drove by and saw a crowd of customers buying produce and flowers from the backs of the trucks. The next day she returned with a hamper full of sandwiches and soft drinks, which she sold to the farmers and customers. Soon afterward, **Magee's Kitchen and Deli** became the Farmers Market's first restaurant. Today the market has more than 110 stalls and more than 20 restaurants. Close to CBS Television Studios, the market is a major hub for stars and stargazers, tourists and locals. It's one of the few community gathering points in the sprawling city. Parking is free. ✉ *6333 W. 3rd St.,* ☎ *323/933–9211.* ⏲ *May–Oct., daily 10–6; Nov.–Apr., daily 10–5.*

NEED A BREAK? At Farmers Market, stop for a BLT on sourdough, a chicken chopped salad chock-full of veggies, or a slice of apple-ginger-buttermilk coffee cake and a mocha–French-roast malt at **Kokomo Café** (☏ 213/933–0773), a favorite fueling station among celebs, black-clad hipsters, and people who like good food. At **Bob's Coffee & Donuts** (☏ 213/933–8929), Bob Tusquellas, a.k.a. "the Donut Man," churns out nearly 2,000 fresh-made jelly-filled, cinnamon-rolled, and glazed creations every day.

★ ❹ **La Brea Tar Pits.** About 40,000 years ago, deposits of oil rose to the earth's surface, collected in shallow pools, and coagulated into sticky asphalt. In the early 20th century, geologists discovered that the sticky goo contained the largest collection of Pleistocene, or Ice Age, fossils ever found at one location: more than 600 species of birds, mammals, plants, reptiles, and insects. More than 100 tons of fossil bones have been removed in excavations over the last seven decades. Statues of a family of mammoths in the big pit near the corner of Wilshire Boulevard and Curson Avenue suggest how many of them were entombed: edging down to a pond of water to drink, animals were caught in the tar. The ☞ **Page Museum at the La Brea Tar Pits** displays fossils from the tar pits. ✉ *Hancock Park.*

❸ **Los Angeles County Museum of Art (LACMA).** Still a young museum (it opened in 1966), LACMA has assembled an encyclopedic collection of more than 150,000 works from around the world. Its collection is widely considered the most comprehensive in the western United States. Islamic, South and Southeast Asian, Far Eastern, and American works are especially well represented. The museum's five buildings also house fine collections of modern and contemporary art, costumes and textiles, decorative arts, European paintings and sculpture, photography, drawings, and prints.

Galleries of Islamic art are arranged chronologically, emphasizing visual connections and recurrent themes. South and Southeast Asian galleries, with one of the finest collections outside Asia, contain several new acquisitions, including the *Hindu Saint Manikkavacakar,* an elegant 12th-century South Indian bronze statue, and *Buddha Calling the Earth to Witness,* a bronze image from 11th-century Tibet.

LACMA's collection of American art from the Colonial era to the early 20th century is one of the finest in the nation. A core of galleries presents these works together. In addition to furniture, silver, glass, ceramics, paintings, and sculpture of the same periods, there are landscape and genre paintings from the Federal period, frontier art, works from the Ash Can School, and regional developments such as California impressionism and surrealism. Masterworks such as George Bellows's *Cliff Dwellers,* Mary Cassatt's *Mother About to Wash Her Sleepy Child,* and Winslow Homer's *The Cotton Pickers* have been cleaned and restored. ✉ *5905 Wilshire Blvd.,* ☏ *323/857–6000; 323/857–0098 TDD.* *$7, free 2nd Tues. of month.* ⏲ *Mon., Tues., and Fri. noon–9; Thurs. noon–8; weekends 11–8.*

❷ **Miracle Mile.** The strip of Wilshire Boulevard between La Brea and Fairfax avenues was vacant land in the 1920s, when a developer bought the parcel to develop into a shopping and business district. The auto age was just emerging and nobody thought the venture could be successful, so the strip became known as Miracle Mile. It was the world's first linear downtown, with building designs incorporating wide store windows to attract attention from passing automobiles. The area went into a decline in the '50s and '60s, but it's now enjoying a comeback, as Los Angeles's Art Deco architecture has come to be appreciated, preserved, and restored.

5 **Page Museum at the La Brea Tar Pits.** At the La Brea Tar Pits, this member of the Natural History Museum family is set, bunkerlike, half underground. A bas-relief around four sides depicts life in the Pleistocene era, and the museum has more than 3 million Ice Age fossils. Exhibits include reconstructed, life-size skeletons of mammoths, wolves, sloths, eagles, and condors. A permanent installation shows a robotic saber-toothed cat attacking a huge ground sloth. A hologram magically puts flesh on 9,000-year-old "La Brea Woman," and an interactive tar mechanism shows just how hard it would be to free oneself from the sticky mess. ✉ *5801 Wilshire Blvd.,* ☎ *323/934–7243.* *$6, free 1st Tues. of month.* ⏲ *Tues.–Sun. 10–5, summer daily 10–5.*

★ 8 **Petersen Automotive Museum.** More than just a building full of antique or unique cars, the Petersen is highly entertaining and informative. Rotating exhibits may include Hollywood-celebrity and movie cars (for example, Fred's rockmobile from *The Flintstones*), "muscle" cars (such as a 1969 Dodge Daytona 440 Magnum), motorcycles, and commemorative displays of the Ferrari. ✉ *6060 Wilshire Blvd.,* ☎ *323/930–2277.* *$7.* ⏲ *Tues.–Sun. 10–6.*

Southwest Museum at LACMA West. L.A.'s oldest museum expanded in 1998 from its main Mt. Washington facility in Highland Park into this 8,000-square-ft satellite location. The additional space gives the museum a chance to present even more of its fine collection of Native American art and culture dating from 1800 to the present. Contrasting with the Art Deco exterior of the LACMA West structure, the design of the museum's galleries suggests an adobe structure awash in hues of cactus and red earth. A museum store sells contemporary Native American weavings, jewelry, toys, and books. ✉ *Northeast corner of Fairfax Ave. and Wilshire Blvd.,* ☎ *323/933–4510.* *$5.* ⏲ *Daily 9–8.*

Beverly Hills and Century City

If you've got money to spend—lots of it—come to Beverly Hills. Rodeo Drive is the platinum vein of its commercial district (a.k.a. the Golden Triangle) and has been likened to Rome's Via Condotti and London's Bond Street. Beverly Hills means expensive retailers such as Tiffany, Gucci, and Cartier; sky-high real estate prices; legendary hotels; high-powered restaurants; and—most of all—movie stars. Fable-making Hollywood and fabled Beverly Hills are inseparably linked in the popular imagination. Mary Pickford and Douglas Fairbanks Sr. led the way 80 years ago by setting up house in an old hunting lodge in Benedict Canyon, renovating it into what became known as Pickfair. Hollywood royalty followed suit, and pretty soon Beverly Hills, once a tract of bean patches known as Morocco Junction, was on its way to becoming hometown to the movie industry's elite. The allure of Beverly Hills continues to draw armies of visitors on the lookout for a famous face and a glimpse of an opulent lifestyle.

A Good Tour

Numbers in the text correspond to numbers in the margin and on the Beverly Hills and the Westside map.

Begin a tour of Beverly Hills with a drive into the hills above Sunset Boulevard for a look at **Greystone Mansion** ① on Loma Vista Drive. Less than a mile west on Sunset Boulevard is the landmark **Beverly Hills Hotel** ②. Behind the hotel, on Elden Way, is the **Virginia Robinson Gardens** ③, the oldest estate in Beverly Hills.

Across the street from the hotel is the little triangular park named for the cowboy-philosopher Will Rogers, who was once honorary mayor

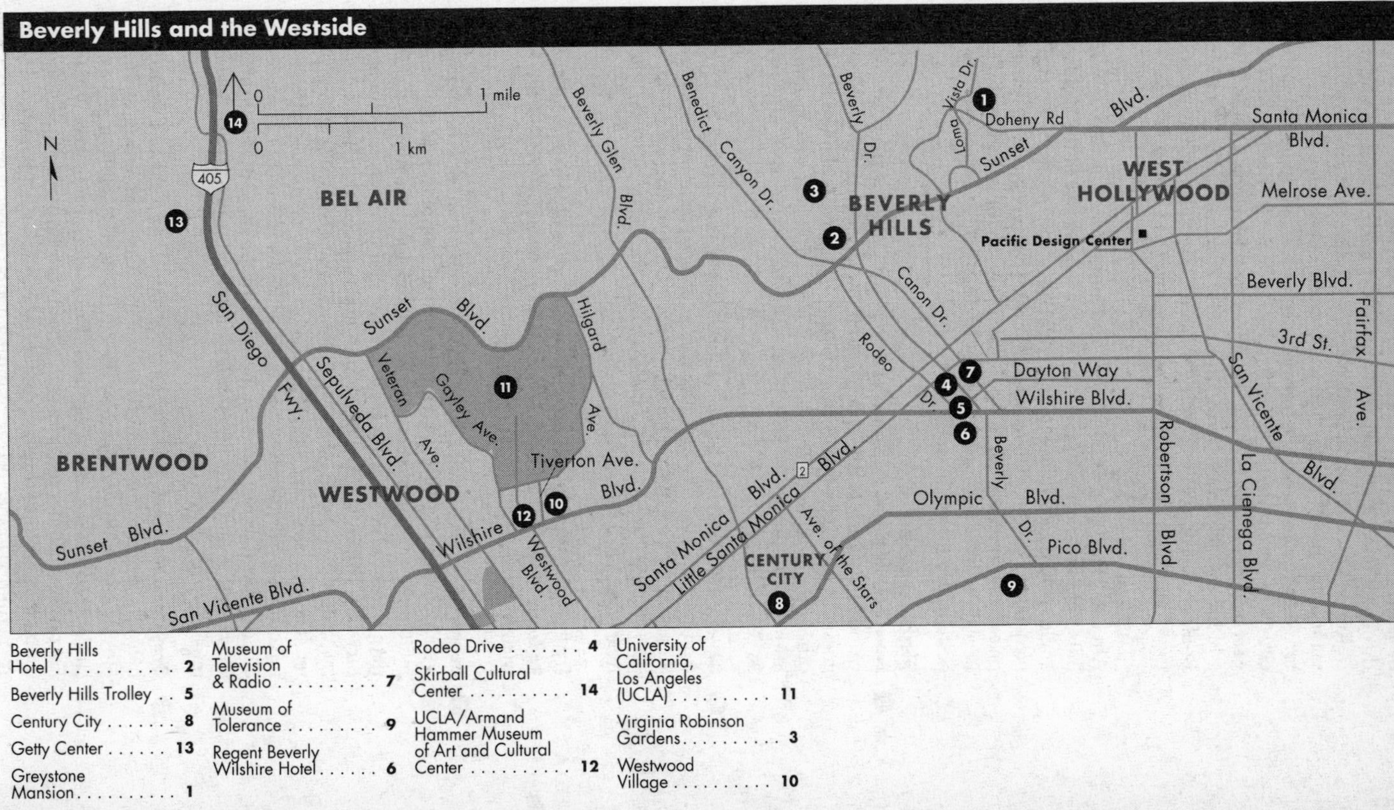
Beverly Hills and the Westside
N
0
1 mile
0
1 km
405
BEL AIR
BRENTWOOD
WESTWOOD
BEVERLY HILLS
WEST HOLLYWOOD
CENTURY CITY
Pacific Design Center
San Diego Fwy.
Sepulveda Blvd.
Veteran Ave.
Gayley Ave.
Hilgard Ave.
Tiverton Ave.
Sunset Blvd.
Beverly Glen Blvd.
Benedict Canyon Dr.
Beverly Dr.
Loma Vista Dr.
Doheny Rd
Santa Monica Blvd.
Melrose Ave.
Beverly Blvd.
3rd St.
Fairfax Ave.
San Vicente Blvd.
La Cienega Blvd.
Robertson Blvd.
Canon Dr.
Rodeo Dr.
Dayton Way
Wilshire Blvd.
Olympic Blvd.
Pico Blvd.
Ave. of the Stars
Little Santa Monica Blvd.
Westwood Blvd.
San Vicente Blvd.
2
Beverly Hills Hotel 2
Beverly Hills Trolley . . 5
Century City 8
Getty Center 13
Greystone Mansion 1
Museum of Television & Radio 7
Museum of Tolerance 9
Regent Beverly Wilshire Hotel 6
Rodeo Drive 4
Skirball Cultural Center 14
UCLA/Armand Hammer Museum of Art and Cultural Center 12
University of California, Los Angeles (UCLA) 11
Virginia Robinson Gardens 3
Westwood Village 10

of Beverly Hills. Turn south here onto **Rodeo Drive** ④. You'll pass through a residential neighborhood before hitting the shopping stretch of Rodeo Drive south of Santa Monica Boulevard. This is where you'll want to get out of the car and walk around. At Rodeo Drive and Dayton Way, the **Beverly Hills Trolley** ⑤ departs for 40-minute tours of the city (between May and December). Across Wilshire Boulevard is the **Regent Beverly Wilshire Hotel** ⑥. The **Museum of Television & Radio** ⑦ stands a block east of Rodeo Drive, on Beverly Drive at Little Santa Monica Boulevard. Adjacent to Beverly Hills on the west is the high-rise office-tower and shopping-center complex known as **Century City** ⑧.

TIMING

After a drive along Sunset Boulevard and a foray or two up into the hills for a look at the opulent homes, plan to arrive in the Golden Triangle of Beverly Hills at midday. Park the car in one of several municipal lots, and stroll along Rodeo Drive. There are plenty of reasonably priced cafés and restaurants for lunch. The major routes in and out of Beverly Hills—Wilshire and Santa Monica boulevards—get very congested during rush hours.

Sights to See

★ ❷ **Beverly Hills Hotel.** Built in 1912, the Pink Palace is steeped in Hollywood lore. Greta Garbo, Howard Hughes, and other movie-industry guests kept low profiles when staying at this pastel landmark, while other film luminaries, notably Cecil B. DeMille, cut very visible deals in the **Polo Lounge.** ✉ *9641 Sunset Blvd., 1 mi west of Doheny Dr.,* ☎ *310/276–2251.*

❺ **Beverly Hills Trolley.** The 40-minute "Sights and Scenes" or "Art and Architecture" tour swings into the residential area for a look at former homes of Hollywood celebrities. ✉ *Dayton Way and Rodeo Dr.,* ☎ *310/285–2438.* *$5.* ⏲ *May–Dec., Sat. only on the hr noon–4; Nov.–Dec., call for additional tours.*

NEED A BREAK?

Try the courtyard of the unpretentious and not terribly expensive **Café Rodeo** (✉ Summit Hotel, 360 N. Rodeo Dr., ☎ 310/273–0300). Sandwiches, salads, and pizzas are big enough to split.

❽ **Century City.** This 280-acre mixed-use development of office buildings, a shopping center, hotels, an entertainment complex, and housing was built in the '60s on what used to be the back lot of the film studio Twentieth Century Fox. The focal point is the pair of silvery triangular **Century City Towers** (✉ Ave. of the Stars and Constellation Blvd.), designed by Minoru Yamasaki, who also designed New York's World Trade Center. The **Century City Shopping Center** is one of the last open-air retail centers, with a festive, marketplacelike arrangement of eateries and cinemas. At the cavernous **Shubert Theater** in the ABC Entertainment Center (✉ Ave. of the Stars and Constellation Blvd.), big Broadway musicals are performed.

❶ **Greystone Mansion.** Doheny Drive is named for oilman Edward Doheny, the original owner of this 1927 neo-Gothic mansion of 46,000-plus square ft. Now owned by the city of Beverly Hills, it sits on 18½ landscaped acres and has been used in such films as *The Witches of Eastwick* and *Indecent Proposal*. The gardens are open for self-guided tours, and peeking (only) through the windows is permitted. Picnics are permitted in specified areas during hours of operation. ✉ *905 Loma Vista Dr.,* ☎ *310/550–4796.* *Free.* ⏲ *May–Oct., daily 10–6; Nov.–Apr., daily 10–5.*

7 **Museum of Television & Radio.** Search for your favorite commercials and television and radio shows on easy-to-use computers, and then watch or listen to them in an adjacent room. The museum also presents special exhibits of television- and radio-related art and costumes, and schedules daily screenings and listening series, as well as frequent seminars with television and radio cast members. ✉ *465 N. Beverly Dr.,* ☎ *310/786–1000.* 🎟 *$6.* ⊙ *Wed. and Fri.–Sun. noon–5, Thurs. noon–9.*

6 **Regent Beverly Wilshire Hotel.** Anchoring the south end of Rodeo Drive at Wilshire Boulevard since opening in 1928, the hotel often hosts visiting royalty and celebrities. ✉ *9500 Wilshire Blvd.,* ☎ *310/275–5200.*

★ 4 **Rodeo Drive.** Rodeo Drive is one of southern California's bona fide tourist attractions. Just as if they were at Disneyland or in Hollywood, tourists wander along this tony stretch of avenue, window-shopping at Tiffany & Co., Gucci, Armani, Harry Winston, and Lladro. Fortunately the browsing is free, and strolling the section of Rodeo between Santa Monica and Wilshire boulevards is a fun way to spend the afternoon. At the southern end of Rodeo Drive (at Wilshire Boulevard) is Via Rodeo, a curvy cobblestone street designed to resemble a European shopping *via.*

3 **Virginia Robinson Gardens.** The estate, the oldest in Beverly Hills, was owned by department store heir Harry Robinson and his wife, Virginia, who bequeathed it to the County of Los Angeles. The classic Mediterranean-style villa is surrounded by nearly 6 acres of lush planted grounds. Call in advance to schedule a tour. *Address available when advance reservations are made,* ☎ *310/276–5367.* 🎟 *$7.* ⊙ *Tours by appointment.*

The Westside

An informal and unscientific survey of Westside districts such as West Los Angeles, Westwood, Bel-Air, Brentwood, and Pacific Palisades would probably reveal high concentrations of plastic surgeons and Land Rovers. The Westside, however, is also rich cultural territory, and the rewards of visiting UCLA's Westwood campus, the Museum of Tolerance, and the Getty Center in Brentwood are great.

A Good Tour

Numbers in the text correspond to numbers in the margin and on the Beverly Hills and the Westside map.

The major sights on the Westside are spread out, so the best strategy is to select one of the major attractions as a destination and plan your visit accordingly. A visit to the **Museum of Tolerance** ⑨ in the morning, for example, can be easily followed with lunch and shopping in Beverly Hills or Century City. Afterward, you might drive through **Westwood Village** ⑩, home of the **UCLA** ⑪ campus and the **Fowler Museum of Cultural History,** stopping at the **UCLA/Armand Hammer Museum of Art and Cultural Center** ⑫. The vast **Getty Center** ⑬, fortresslike atop a hill in Brentwood, is currently L.A.'s most high-profile attraction. About 2 mi north on Sepulveda Boulevard is the **Skirball Cultural Center** ⑭ and its gallery exhibition of Jewish life.

For a less destination-oriented tour of the posh Westside, simply follow Wilshire Boulevard west out of low-rise Beverly Hills as it turns into a canyon of million-dollar condos. Once past the San Diego Freeway (I–405), detour to the right onto San Vicente Boulevard and the upscale urban-village center of **Brentwood.** At the Santa Monica city line, turn right on 26th Street and follow it as it turns into Allenford Avenue. The route will loop you around to Sunset Boulevard. A left turn here will take you to Pacific Palisades and the ocean. A right leads back toward Beverly Hills and West Hollywood.

TIMING

Advance reservations are required for visits to the Museum of Tolerance, closed Saturday, and the Getty Center, closed Monday. Each museum merits at least a half day. In the evening and on weekends, Westwood Village and Brentwood's commercial district on San Vicente Boulevard comes alive with a busy restaurant, café, and street scene. The afternoon rush hour is congested along Wilshire and Sunset boulevards.

Sights to See

Brentwood. From the looks of it, Brentwood seems more like a posh urban village than the scene of such mysteries as the death of Marilyn Monroe and the murder of Nicole Brown Simpson. San Vicente Boulevard, the main drag, sports chic restaurants, cafés, and shops.

★ 13 **Getty Center.** Architect Richard Meier designed the white city on a hill to house the world's richest museum and its affiliated research, conservation, and philanthropic institutes. The crunch of visitors has subsided somewhat, and those essential parking reservations are available, though limited.

J. Paul Getty, the billionaire oil magnate and art collector, began collecting Greek and Roman antiquities and French decorative arts in the 1930s. He opened the J. Paul Getty Museum at his Malibu estate in 1954. In the 1970s, he built a re-creation of an ancient Roman villa to house his initial collection. When Getty died in 1976, the museum received an endowment of $700 million that has grown to a reported $4.2 billion. The Malibu villa closed in 1997, but it will reopen in 2001, to house only the antiquities.

All visitors arrive at the entrance pavilion at the bottom of the hill. Those with parking reservations are guaranteed entrance. Those who arrive by public bus (MTA #561 or Santa Monica Big Blue #14), cab, or private shuttle may encounter long lines before gaining entrance, or, depending on attendance, may be turned away. A tram transports visitors to the top of the hill. There, the principal destination for most visitors is the museum, a series of five pavilions built around a central courtyard and bridged by walkways. Outside, the structures are clad primarily in cleft-cut Italian travertine stone. In a ravine separating the museum and the Getty Research Institute, artist Robert Irwin created the **Central Garden,** whose focal point is an azalea maze in a pool. Inside the pavilions are the galleries featuring the permanent collections of European paintings, drawings, sculpture, illuminated manuscripts, and decorative arts, as well as American and European photographs. The Getty's renowned collection of French furniture and decorative arts is on view, including a paneled Régence salon from 1710 and a neoclassical salon from 1788. Notable among the paintings are Rembrandt's *Portrait of Marten Looten* and *The Abduction of Europa,* van Gogh's *Irises,* Monet's *Wheatstack, Snow Effects, Morning,* and James Ensor's *Christ's Entry Into Brussels.* Joining three other works of Paul Cezanne that the Getty owns is *Young Italian Woman Leaning on Her Elbow,* a recent Getty purchase (estimated at $25 to $30 million).

Interconnected pavilions around the courtyard allow you to choose various paths through the museum, so you may head straight for the pavilion that interests you most. The curators have also organized a quick tour that takes in 15 highlights of the collection. It's outlined in a brochure available in the entrance hall. There's an instructive audio tour ($2) with commentaries by art historians. The complex includes a restaurant (reservations required), a cafeteria, and an outdoor coffee bar. ✉

1200 Getty Center Dr., ☎ *310/440–7300; TTY 310/440–7305.* *Free, $5 parking.* *Tues.–Wed. 11–7, Thurs.–Fri. 11–9, weekends 10–6; call several months ahead for parking reservations.*

★ 9 **Museum of Tolerance.** Using state-of-the-art interactive technology, this important museum adjacent to the Simon Wiesenthal Center challenges visitors to confront bigotry and racism. One of the most affecting sections covers the Holocaust, with actual film footage of deportation scenes and simulated sets of concentration camps. Each visitor is issued a "passport" bearing the name of a child whose life was dramatically changed by the German Nazi rule and by World War II. Later, you learn the fate of that child. Anne Frank artifacts are part of the museum's permanent collection. To ensure a visit to the museum, make reservations in advance and plan to spend at least three hours there. ✉ *9786 W. Pico Blvd.,* ☎ *310/553–8403.* *$8.* *Sun. 10:30–5, Mon.–Thurs. 10–4, Fri. 10–1.*

14 **Skirball Cultural Center.** The core exhibition here is "Visions and Values: Jewish Life from Antiquity to America," the story of the Jewish immigration experience. Highlights include a large collection of Judaica and a ⅔-size replica of the torch of the Statue of Liberty. Children can participate in an outdoor simulated archaeological dig at the interactive Discovery Center. ✉ *2701 N. Sepulveda Blvd.,* ☎ *310/440–4500.* *$8.* *Tues.–Sat. noon–5, Sun. 11–5.*

12 **UCLA/Armand Hammer Museum of Art and Cultural Center.** The eclectic permanent collection here contains thousands of works, including some by Daumier, van Gogh, Gauguin, Degas, and Cassatt. In addition to paintings by Old Masters, French Impressionists, and Postimpressionists, there's an important collection of drawings by Michelangelo, Raphael, and Rembrandt. ✉ *10899 Wilshire Blvd.,* ☎ *310/443–7000.* *$4.50, free Thurs. 6–9; parking $2.75 with validation.* *Tues.–Wed. and Fri.–Sat. 11–7, Thurs. 11–9, Sun. 11–5. Tours Sun. at 1.*

11 **University of California, Los Angeles.** The parklike UCLA campus makes for a fine stroll. In the heart of the north campus, the **Franklin Murphy Sculpture Garden** contains more than 70 works of artists such as Henry Moore and Gaston Lachaise. The **Mildred Mathias Botanic Garden** is in the southeast section of the campus and is accessible from Tiverton Avenue. West of the main campus bookstore, the **Morgan Center Hall of Fame** displays the sports memorabilia and trophies of the university's athletic departments. Many visitors head straight to the **UCLA Fowler Museum of Cultural History** (☎ 310/825–4361), which presents changing exhibits on the art and culture of past and present peoples of Latin America, Oceania, Africa, and Asia.

Campus maps and information are available at drive-by kiosks at major entrances seven days a week, and free 90-minute walking tours of the campus are given on weekdays at 10:15 and 2:15, and Sat day at 10:15. Call 310/825–8764 for reservations several days vance. The campus has indoor and outdoor cafés, plus booksto UCLA Bruins paraphernalia. The main entrance gate is o Boulevard. Campus parking costs $5. ✉ *Main entranc Plaza; Le Conte, Hilgard, and Gayley Aves. and S the campus.* *Campus free; Fowler Museum f*

10 **Westwood Village.** Next to the Los Angeles of California, Westwood Village is one of on weekend evenings. The lures are a c theaters, eateries, and a lively youth busy during the summer that ma visitors must park at the **Fede**

eran Ave.) and shuttle over. Behind one of the behemoth office buildings on Wilshire Boulevard is **Westwood Village Memorial Park** (⊠ 1218 Glendon Ave.). Marilyn Monroe is buried in a simply marked crypt on the north wall. Also buried here are Truman Capote and Natalie Wood.

Santa Monica, Venice, and Malibu

In Los Angeles all roads lead, eventually, to the beach and Santa Monica, Venice, and Malibu. These coastal communities hug the Santa Monica Bay, in an arc of diversity, from the rich-as-can-be Malibu to the bohemian-seedy mix of Venice. What they have in common, however, is cleaner coastal air and an emphasis on being out in the sunshine.

A Good Drive

Numbers in the text correspond to numbers in the margin and on the Santa Monica, Venice, and Malibu map.

Look for the arched neon sign at the foot of Colorado Avenue marking the entrance to the **Santa Monica Pier** ①, the city's number-one landmark, built in 1906. Park on the pier and take a turn through **Pacific Park** ②, a 2-acre amusement park. The wide swath of sand on the north side of the pier is Santa Monica Beach, on hot summer weekends one of the most crowded beaches in southern California. From the pier, walk to Ocean Avenue, where **Palisades Park** ③, a strip of lawn and palms above the cliffs, provides panoramic ocean views. Three blocks inland is **Third Street Promenade** ④, an active outdoor mall with shopping, dining, and entertainment.

Retrieve the car and drive two blocks inland on Colorado Avenue to Main Street. Turn right and continue to Ocean Park Boulevard. Look for a colorful mural on the side of the building on the southeast corner. On the southwest corner you'll find the **California Heritage Museum** ⑤. The next several blocks south along Main Street are great for browsing.

Next stop: **Venice Boardwalk** ⑥. Walk up Main Street through the trendy shopping district until you hit Rose Avenue. Ahead on the left you'll spot an enormous pair of binoculars, the front of the Frank Gehry–designed Chiat-Day Mojo building. Turn right toward the sea. The main attraction of this dead end is the boardwalk, where the classic California beach scene is in progress.

For the drive to **Malibu,** retrace your route along Main Street. At Pico Boulevard, turn west, toward the ocean, and then right on Ocean Avenue. When you pass the pier, prepare to turn left down the California Incline (the incline is at the end of Palisades Park at Wilshire Boulevard) to Pacific Coast Highway (Highway 1), also known as PCH.
ter Malibu. Unfortunately, Malibu Pier
torm damage and a lack of funds to re-
and take a walk on **Malibu Lagoon State**
rider Beach. On the highway side of the
Adamson House and Malibu Lagoon Mu-
great Pacific view. From here, you can
h that fronts the famed Malibu Colony,
e of film, television, and recording stars.

your coastal visit into two excursions:
e, and Malibu in another. The best way
ities is to park the car, and walk, cycle,
side bike path. Late morning is a good
as Santa Monica Pier, Main Street, and

Santa Monica, Venice, and Malibu

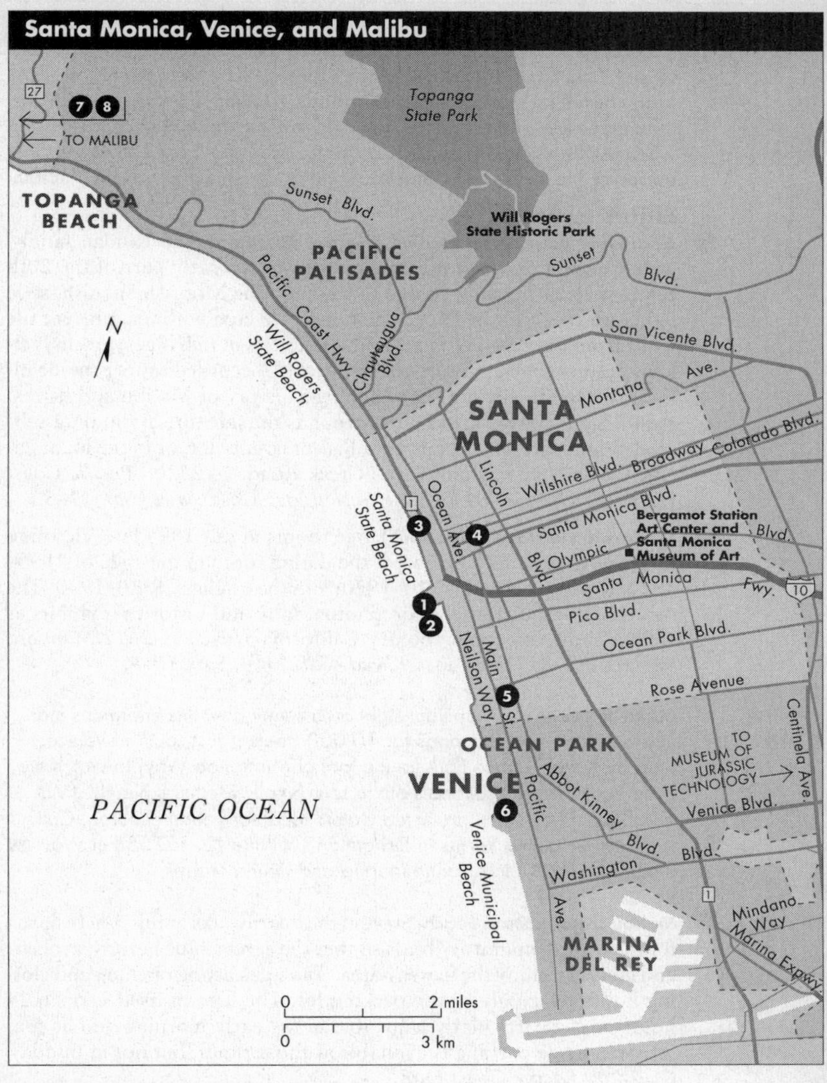

Adamson House and Malibu Lagoon Museum 8
California Heritage Museum 5
Malibu Lagoon State Beach 7
Pacific Park. 2
Palisades Park. 3
Santa Monica Pier . . . 1
Third Street Promenade 4
Venice Boardwalk . . . 6

the Venice Boardwalk are more interesting to observe as the day progresses. Avoid the boardwalk at night, when the crowd becomes unsavory. You can park on the Santa Monica Pier and in small lots close to the beach in Venice (the smart thing to do, since break-ins are common in the area) and Malibu. Avoid driving to Malibu during rush hour, when traffic along the Pacific Coast Highway moves at a snail's pace—but do try to be there at sunset to watch the sun dip into the Pacific.

Sights to See

8 **Adamson House and Malibu Lagoon Museum.** The Rindge family, which owned much of the Malibu area in the early part of the 20th century, also originally owned this home. The Moorish Spanish–style structure was built in 1929. The house, covered with magnificent tile work from the now-defunct Malibu Potteries in rich blues, greens, yellows, and oranges, is right on the beach. Docent-led tours provide insights on family life here as well as the history of Malibu and its real estate. Signs posted around the grounds outside direct you on a self-guided tour as well. Park in the adjacent county lot, or in the lot at Pacific Coast Highway and Cross Creek Road. ⊠ *23200 Pacific Coast Hwy.,* ☎ *310/456–8432.* 🎟 *House tours, $2.* ⏲ *Wed.–Sat. 11–3.*

5 **California Heritage Museum.** Three rooms in this 1894 late-Victorian house have been fully restored: the dining room in the style of 1890–1910; the living room, 1910–1920; and the kitchen, 1920–1930. The second-floor galleries contain photography and historical exhibits as well as shows by contemporary California artists. ⊠ *2612 Main St.,* ☎ *310/392–8537.* 🎟 *$3.* ⏲ *Wed.–Sat. 11–4, Sun. 10–4.*

OFF THE BEATEN PATH

MARINA DEL REY – A brilliant sight on a sunny day, this enormous man-made marina with moorings for 10,000 boats is just south of Venice. Stop by Burton Chace Park (at the foot of Mindanao Way) to watch the wind carry colorful sailboats out to sea. Small "Mother's Beach" (Marina Beach) has calm, protected waters ideal for young children. Call **Hornblower Dining Yachts** in Fisherman's Village (⊠ 13755 Fiji Way, ☎ 310/301–9900) to arrange marina and dining cruises.

7 **Malibu Lagoon State Beach.** Stay on the boardwalks at this 5-acre haven for native and migratory birds so that the egrets, blue herons, avocets, and gulls can enjoy the marshy area. The signs listing opening and closing hours refer only to the parking lot. The lagoon itself is open 24 hours and is particularly enjoyable in the early morning and at sunset. Street-side parking is available at those times, but not at midday. ⊠ *23200 Pacific Coast Hwy.*

2 **Pacific Park.** The 12 rides at Santa Monica Pier's 2-acre amusement facility include a giant Ferris wheel, a flying submarine, and a motion-simulated action ride. ⊠ *380 Santa Monica Pier, Santa Monica,* ☎ *310/260–8747.* 🎟 *Rides $1–$4, all-day pass $15.* ⏲ *Entire park open daily May–Sept.; winter, selected rides and games Mon.–Thurs., entire park Fri. evening–Sun. evening; call for hrs.*

3 **Palisades Park.** The ribbon of green that runs along the top of the cliffs from Colorado Avenue to just north of San Vicente Boulevard has flat walkways where casual strollers and joggers come to enjoy spectacular views of the Pacific. Sunsets here are hard to beat.

NEED A BREAK?

For a beach picnic you can buy food at one of the many fast-food stands that line the boardwalk. For a more relaxing meal, stand in line for a table at **Sidewalk Café** (⊠ 1401 Ocean Front Walk, ☎ 310/399–5547). It's worth the wait for a patio table.

★ ❶ **Santa Monica Pier.** Eateries, souvenir shops, a psychic adviser, arcades, ☞ **Pacific Park**, and the new **UCLA Discovery Center** (a small interactive aquarium) are all part of this truncated pier at the foot of Colorado Boulevard below Palisades Park. The pier's trademark 46-horse carousel, built in 1922, has appeared in many films, including *The Sting*. ✉ *Colorado Ave. and the ocean,* ☎ *310/458–8900; carousel 310/458–8867.* *Rides 25¢ and 50¢.* ⏲ *Carousel: May–Sept., Tues.–Fri. 11–9, weekends 10–9; Oct.–Apr., Sat. 11–6, Sun. 11–5; Discovery Center: July–Labor Day, Tues.–Fri. 3–6, weekends 11-5; Labor Day–June, weekends 11–5.*

❹ **Third Street Promenade.** Only foot traffic is allowed along a three-block stretch of 3rd Street, just a whiff away from the Pacific. Outdoor cafés, street vendors, several movie theaters, and a rich nightlife make this one of Santa Monica's main gathering spots. The mix of folks down here is great, from elderly couples out for a bite to skateboarders and street musicians. ✉ *3rd St. between Wilshire Blvd. and Broadway.*

★ ❻ **Venice Boardwalk.** "Boardwalk" may be something of a misnomer—it's really a paved walkway—but this L.A. must-see delivers year-round action: bicyclists zip along and bikini-clad roller and in-line skaters attract crowds as they put on impromptu demonstrations, vying for attention with magicians, fortune tellers, a chain-saw juggler, and street artists. A local bodybuilding club works out on the adjacent "Muscle Beach." It's nearly impossible not to stop and ogle the strongmen's pecs. You can rent in-line skates, roller skates, and bicycles (some with baby seats) at the south end of the boardwalk (also known as Ocean Front Walk), along Washington Street, near the Venice Pier.

OFF THE BEATEN PATH

WILL ROGERS STATE HISTORIC PARK – The late cowboy-humorist Will Rogers lived on this site in the 1920s and 1930s. The ranch-house museum features Rogers memorabilia. Rogers was a polo enthusiast, and in the 1930s, his front-yard polo field attracted such friends as Douglas Fairbanks, Sr., for weekend games. The tradition continues, with free weekend games scheduled April–October, weather permitting. The park is excellent for picnicking, and there's hiking on miles of trails. From Pacific Coast Highway, turn inland at Sunset Boulevard. Follow Sunset for about 5 mi to the park entrance. ✉ *1501 Will Rogers State Park Rd., Pacific Palisades,* ☎ *310/454–8212.* *Free, parking $6.* ⏲ *Park, daily 8–sunset daily; house tours, daily 10:30–4:30.*

The San Fernando Valley

There are other valleys in the Los Angeles area, but this is the one that people refer to simply as the Valley. Large portions of the Valley are bedroom communities of neat bungalows and shopping centers, but most of the major film and television studios, such as Warner Bros., NBC, and ABC, are also here. Universal City is a one-industry town, and that industry is Universal Studios. The studio has been at this site since 1915.

A Good Drive

Numbers in the text correspond to points of interest on the San Fernando Valley map.

On a clear day or evening, a drive along **Mulholland Drive** gives you a spectacular view of the sprawling San Fernando Valley below. Just over the hill from Hollywood via the Hollywood Freeway (U.S. 101, north) is Universal City, which has its own freeway off-ramp (Universal Center Drive). **Universal Studios Hollywood** ① is on a large hill overlooking the San Fernando Valley, a city-within-a-city. As you exit Universal, follow signs to Barham Boulevard, where you turn left toward Burbank. After driving about a mile, the street curves around **Warner Bros. Studios** ②, whose outside wall is covered with billboards of current films and television shows. After the curve, you will be on West Olive Avenue. Keep to the right and look for the entrance to Gate No. 4 at Hollywood Way.

Just a minute away at the second big intersection, West Olive and Alameda avenues, is the main entrance to **NBC Television Studios** ③. Continue east on Alameda; on the next block to your right is **Disney Studios** ④, a very colorful bit of architecture. Drive south on Buena Vista and then turn left on Riverside to get a good look at the whimsical architecture.

To reach **Mission San Fernando Rey de España** ⑤, drive north on either the San Diego (I–405) or Golden State (I–5) freeway; Alameda Avenue will lead you to I–5, as will the Hollywood Freeway (Hwy. 170, north). Drive about 12 mi and exit at San Fernando Mission Boulevard. From I–405, drive east; from I–5, drive west. The mission is about ½ mi from either freeway on the north side of the street. (A scenic, but lengthy, route back to L.A. is via Mulholland Drive, whose exit is about 15 mi, or 20 minutes, from the mission off I–405.)

TIMING

The Valley is surrounded by mountains, and the major routes to and from it go through mountain passes. During rush hour, traffic jams on the Hollywood Freeway (U.S. 101/Hwy. 170), San Diego Freeway (I–405), and Ventura Freeway (U.S. 101/Hwy. 134) can be brutal. Expect to spend a full day at Universal Studios Hollywood and CityWalk. Studio tours at NBC and Warner Bros. last about two hours. A visit to the mission will eat up more time driving to and from it than touring the grounds.

Sights to See

❹ **Disney Studios.** Although tours of this animation and film studio are not available, a peek from Riverside Drive shows you that Disney's innovations go beyond the big and small screens to fanciful touches of architecture as well (note the little Mickey Mouse heads mounted on the surrounding fence). Disney's animation operation is housed in a Michael Graves–designed building, erected in 1995, that's made almost entirely of glass. It's clearly visible from the Ventura (Hwy. 134) Freeway. ✉ *500 S. Buena Vista, Burbank.*

❺ **Mission San Fernando Rey de España.** An important member of a chain of 21 California missions established by Franciscan friars, Mission San Fernando was founded in 1797 and named in honor of King Ferdinand III of Spain. Fifty-six Native Americans joined the mission and made it a self-supporting community. In 1834, after Mexico extended its rule over California, a civil administrator was appointed for the mission and the priests were restricted to religious duties. The Native Americans began leaving, and what had been flourishing one year before became unproductive. Twelve years later the mission, along with its properties (those being the entire San Fernando Valley), was sold for $14,000. During the next 40 years, the mission buildings were neglected; settlers stripped roof tiles, and the adobe walls were ravaged by the weather. In 1923 a restoration program was initiated. Inside the mission, Native American designs and artifacts of Spanish craftsmanship depict the mission's 18th-century culture. Look for the small museum and gift shop. ✉ *15151 San Fernando Mission Blvd., Mission Hills,* ☎ *818/361–0186.* 💵 *$4.* ⏲ *Daily 9–4:30.*

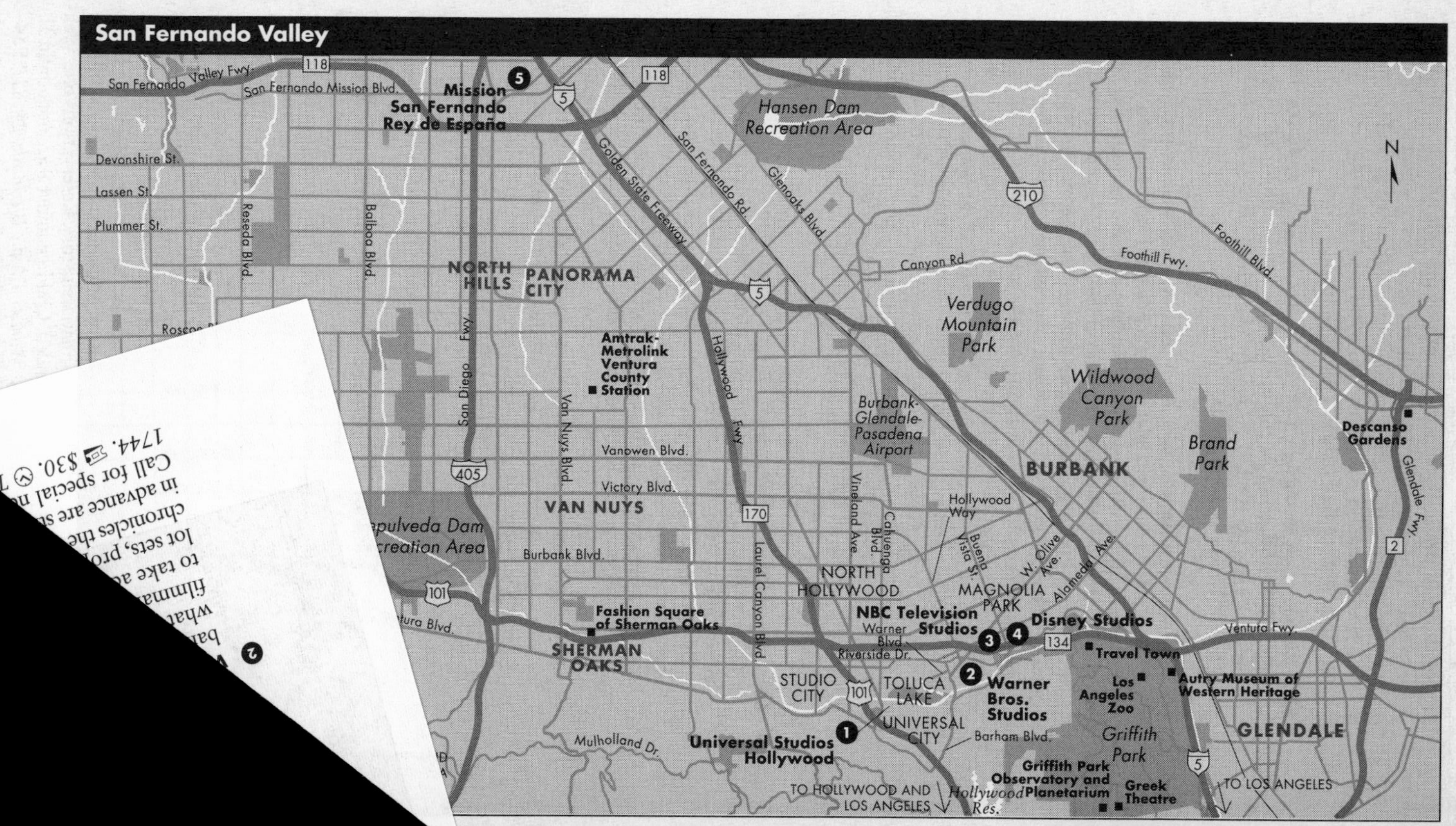
San Fernando Valley
118
San Fernando Valley Fwy.
San Fernando Mission Blvd.
Mission San Fernando Rey de España
5
Hansen Dam Recreation Area
Devonshire St.
Lassen St.
Plummer St.
Reseda Blvd.
Balboa Blvd.
Golden State Freeway
San Fernando Rd.
Glenoaks Blvd.
210
Foothill Blvd.
Foothill Fwy.
Canyon Rd.
N
NORTH HILLS
PANORAMA CITY
Verdugo Mountain Park
Wildwood Canyon Park
Amtrak-Metrolink Ventura County Station
San Diego Fwy.
Van Nuys Blvd.
Hollywood Fwy.
Burbank-Glendale-Pasadena Airport
Descanso Gardens
Brand Park
Glendale Fwy.
2
Vanowen Blvd.
405
Victory Blvd.
BURBANK
VAN NUYS
170
Vineland Ave.
Cahuenga Blvd.
Hollywood Way
Buena Vista St.
W. Olive Ave.
Alameda Ave.
Sepulveda Dam Recreation Area
Burbank Blvd.
Laurel Canyon Blvd.
NORTH HOLLYWOOD
MAGNOLIA PARK
101
Ventura Blvd.
Fashion Square of Sherman Oaks
NBC Television Studios
Disney Studios
Warner Blvd.
134
Ventura Fwy.
Travel Town
SHERMAN OAKS
Riverside Dr.
STUDIO CITY
TOLUCA LAKE
Warner Bros. Studios
Los Angeles Zoo
Autry Museum of Western Heritage
UNIVERSAL CITY
Barham Blvd.
Griffith Park
GLENDALE
Mulholland Dr.
Universal Studios Hollywood
Griffith Park Observatory and Planetarium
Greek Theatre
TO HOLLYWOOD AND LOS ANGELES
Hollywood Res.
TO LOS ANGELES

Mulholland Drive. Driving the length of the hilltop road is slow and can be treacherous, but the rewards are sensational views of valley and city on each side and expensive homes along the way. From Hollywood reach Mulholland via Outpost Drive off Franklin Avenue or Cahuenga Boulevard West via Highland Avenue north.

3 **NBC Television Studios.** Free tickets are available for tapings of the various NBC shows, and 70-minute walking tours of the studio are given on weekdays. ✉ *3000 W. Alameda Ave., Burbank,* ☎ *818/840–3537.* 🎟 *$7.* ⏲ *Tour weekdays 9–3.*

OFF THE BEATEN PATH

PARAMOUNT RANCH–Tucked in the Santa Monica Mountains between Malibu and Agoura, this 2,400-acre ranch has long been used as a location setting for Western movies and television shows, including *Dr. Quinn, Medicine Woman.* Now part of the Santa Monica National Recreation Area, the ranch is open to the public. Besides taking a stroll along the main street of the Western town set used on *Dr. Quinn* (her medical office and the little library are still intact), visitors can spread out on the grassy meadow for a picnic (there are no picnic tables, however). Getting to the ranch can be a bit tricky: Exit the Ventura Freeway (U.S. 101) at Kanan Road. Travel south—toward the mountains—about ¾ mi to Cornell Road and turn left. Bear right on Cornell Road and continue for about 2½ mi, when you should see a large sign for the ranch on the right. Don't forget to bring plenty of bottled drinking water. ✉ *Paramount Ranch Rd., off Cornell Rd.,* ☎ *805/370–2301.* 🎟 *Free.* ⏲*. Open daily dawn–dusk.*

★ 1 **Universal Studios Hollywood.** Though you probably won't see anything that actually has to do with making a real film, visiting the theme park is an enlightening (if somewhat sensational) introduction to the principles of special effects. Seated aboard a comfortable tram (narrated, hour-long tours traverse the 420-acre complex all day), you can experience the parting of the Red Sea, an avalanche, and a flood; meet a 30-ft-tall version of King Kong; live through an encounter with a runaway train; be attacked by the ravenous killer shark of *Jaws* fame; endure a confrontation by aliens armed with death rays; and survive an all-too-real simulation of an earthquake that measured 8.3 on the Richter scale—complete with collapsing earth. The park's latest attraction is *Terminator 2–3D.* Based on the Arnold Schwarzenegger movies, it mixes 3-D with virtual reality and live action. *Jurassic Park—The Ride* is a tour through a jungle full of dinosaurs with an 84-ft water drop. Long lines form at *Back to the Future,* a flight simulator disguised as a DeLorean car that shows off state-of-the-art special effects. Within the slew of shops and restaurants known as **CityWalk**, the Wolfgang Puck Café is a poor man's version of Spago, Puck's star-studded Sunset Strip restaurant. ✉ *100 Universal City Plaza, Universal City,* ☎ *818/508–9600.* 🎟 *$41.* ⏲ *Mid-June–Labor Day, daily 8AM–10PM; Labor Day–early June, daily 9–7.*

Warner Bros. Studios. Two-hour tours at this major studio center in Bur[illegible]nk involve a lot of walking, so dress comfortably and casually. Some[illegible] technically oriented and centered more on the actual workings of [illegible]king than the ones at Universal, tours here vary from day to day [illegible]dvantage of goings-on at the lot. Most tours take in the back[illegible]p construction department, and sound complex. A museum [illegible] studio's film and animation history. Reservations one week [illegible]rongly recommended. Children under 8 are not admitted. [illegible]eeds. ✉ *4000 Warner Blvd., Burbank,* ☎ *818/954–* [illegible]*ours weekdays 9–3 on the hr.*

Pasadena Area

Although now fully absorbed into the general Los Angeles sprawl, Pasadena is a separate and distinctly defined city. Its varied residential architecture, augmented by lush landscaping, is among the most spectacular in southern California. Nearby Highland Park has three excellent museums and San Marino is home to the famous Huntington Library, Art Collections, and Botanical Gardens.

To reach Pasadena from downtown Los Angeles, drive north on the Pasadena Freeway (I–110). From Hollywood use the Glendale Freeway (Hwy. 2, north), and from the San Fernando Valley use the Ventura Freeway (Hwy. 134, east), which cuts through Glendale before arriving in Pasadena.

A Good Tour

Numbers in the text correspond to numbers in the margin and on the Pasadena Area, Highland Park, and San Marino map.

A good place to start a short driving tour of Pasadena is on Orange Grove Boulevard, a.k.a. Millionaire's Row, where wealthy Easterners built grand mansions. One example is the **Wrigley Mansion** ①. To get there, take the Orange Grove exit off the Ventura Freeway (Hwy. 134); turn right at Orange Grove and travel five blocks. From the Pasadena Freeway (Hwy. 110), stay on the freeway until it ends at Arroyo Parkway. From Arroyo Parkway turn left at California Boulevard and then right at Orange Grove.

From the Wrigley Mansion, travel north on Orange Grove to Walnut Street and the **Fenyes Mansion** ②, now headquarters of the Pasadena Historical Society. Continue on Orange Grove to Arroyo Terrace, where a left turn will take you into an architectural wonderland. Greene and Greene, the renowned Pasadena architects, designed all of the houses on Arroyo Terrace, as well as others in the area. To view their Craftsman masterpiece, the three-story, shingle **Gamble House** ③, turn right on Westmoreland Place. Also in this section is the Frank Lloyd Wright–designed Millard House ("La Miniatura") on Prospect Crescent (from Westmoreland Place, turn left onto Rosemont Avenue, right on Prospect Terrace, and right onto Prospect Crescent to No. 645). The famous **Rose Bowl** ④ is nestled in a gulley just to the west off Arroyo Boulevard. Leave this area via Rosemont Avenue, driving away from the hills to the south. From Rosemont Avenue, turn right onto Orange Grove Boulevard. Then, at Colorado Boulevard, turn left. Immediately on the left is the contemporary, austere **Norton Simon Museum** ⑤. Continue east on Colorado Boulevard and, after a few blocks, you'll cross the historic concrete-arched Colorado Street Bridge, built in 1913, rising 160 ft above the Arroyo Seco gorge.

After leaving the block-long overpass, you'll enter **Old Town Pasadena** ⑥. You'll want to walk around this section of Pasadena, heading east. For a look at domed Pasadena City Hall, turn left on Fair Oaks Avenue, then right on Holly Street. Garfield Avenue will bring you back to Colorado Boulevard. The next intersection is Los Robles Avenue. One-half block north on Los Robles Avenue is the **Pacific Asia Museum** ⑦. Back on Colorado Boulevard, head three blocks east to El Molino Avenue. Turn right past the **Pasadena Playhouse** (✉ 39 S. El Molino Ave., ☎ 626/356–7529) and, if you have youngsters, continue along four blocks to **Kidspace** ⑧.

From this point it's a short drive south on El Molino Avenue to California Boulevard, where a left turn will take you into San Marino and

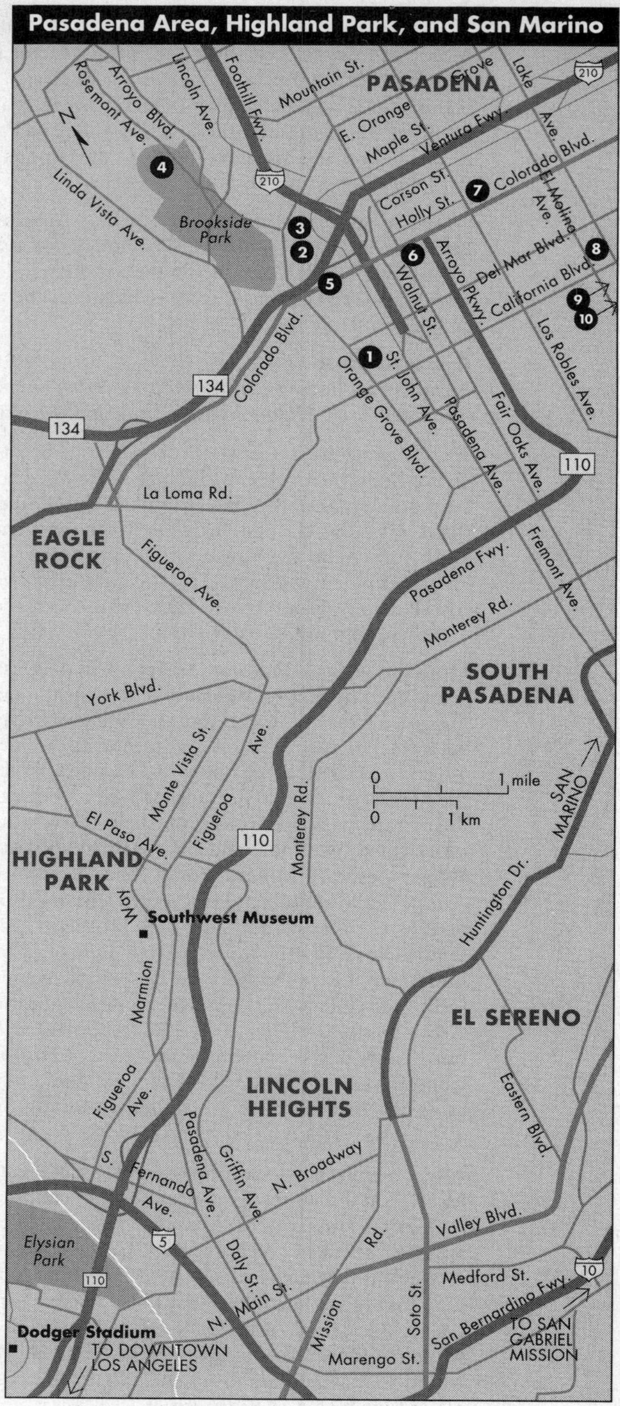

Pasadena Area, Highland Park, and San Marino
PASADENA
Mountain St.
Foothill Fwy.
Lincoln Ave.
Arroyo Blvd.
Rosemont Ave.
Linda Vista Ave.
Brookside Park
E. Orange Grove
Maple St.
Ventura Fwy.
Lake Ave.
Corson St.
Holly St.
Colorado Blvd.
El Molino Ave.
Del Mar Blvd.
California Blvd.
Arroyo Pkwy.
Walnut St.
Los Robles Ave.
St. John Ave.
Orange Grove Blvd.
Pasadena Ave.
Fair Oaks Ave.
Colorado Blvd.
La Loma Rd.
EAGLE ROCK
Figueroa Ave.
Fremont Ave.
Pasadena Fwy.
Monterey Rd.
SOUTH PASADENA
York Blvd.
Monte Vista St.
Ave.
Figueroa
El Paso Ave.
Monterey Rd.
0 1 mile
0 1 km
SAN MARINO
HIGHLAND PARK
Way
Southwest Museum
Huntington Dr.
Marmion
EL SERENO
LINCOLN HEIGHTS
Figueroa Ave.
Eastern Blvd.
Pasadena Ave.
Griffin Ave.
N. Broadway
S. Fernando Ave.
Elysian Park
Daly St.
Rd.
Valley Blvd.
N. Main St.
Medford St.
Mission
Soto St.
San Bernardino Fwy.
TO SAN GABRIEL MISSION
Dodger Stadium
TO DOWNTOWN LOS ANGELES
Marengo St.

the **Huntington Library, Art Collections, and Botanical Gardens** ⑨ (follow the signs). Also in this area is the historic **El Molino Viejo** ⑩.

TIMING

Get a late-morning or early afternoon start to see the important architectural sights on this tour, saving Old Pasadena for last. It has one of the best evening street scenes in southern California. You'll want to allow a half day for the entire driving tour. A stop at the Gamble House may take an hour, leaving plenty of time for an afternoon visit to the Norton Simon Museum. Set aside an entire day for the Huntington Library, Art Collections, and Botanical Gardens.

Sights to See

❿ **El Molino Viejo.** Built in 1816 as a grist mill for the San Gabriel Mission, El Molino Viejo is one of the last remaining examples of Spanish Mission architecture in southern California. ✉ *1120 Old Mill Rd., San Marino,* ☎ *626/449–5458.* 🎟 *Free.* ⏲ *Tues.–Sun. 1–4.*

❷ **Fenyes Mansion.** The 1905 mansion, one of the Pasadena Historical Museums, still has its original furniture and paintings on the main and second floors. Basement exhibits trace Pasadena's history. ✉ *470 W. Walnut St., Pasadena,* ☎ *626/577–1660.* 🎟 *$4.* ⏲ *Thurs.–Sun. 1–4, 1-hr docent-led tour.*

★ ❸ **Gamble House.** Built by Charles and Henry Greene in 1908, this is a spectacular example of Craftsman-style bungalow architecture. To wealthy Easterners such as the Gambles (as in Procter & Gamble), this type of vacation home seemed informal compared with their mansions back home. Check out the hand craftsmanship, including a teak staircase and cabinetry, Greene-designed furniture, and an Emil Lange glass door. To see more Greene and Greene homes in the neighborhood, buy a self-guided tour map in the Gamble House's bookstore. ✉ *4 Westmoreland Pl., Pasadena,* ☎ *626/793–3334.* 🎟 *$5.* ⏲ *Thurs.–Sun. noon–3, 1-hr tour every 15–20 min..*

★ ❾ **Huntington Library, Art Collections, and Botanical Gardens.** If you have time for only one stop in the Pasadena area, it should be San Marino, where railroad tycoon Henry E. Huntington built his hilltop home in the early 1900s. Since then, this institution has established a reputation as one of the most extraordinary cultural complexes in the world. The library contains more than 600,000 books and some 300 manuscripts, including such treasures as a Gutenberg Bible, the Ellesmere manuscript of Chaucer's *Canterbury Tales,* George Washington's genealogy in his own handwriting, and first editions by Ben Franklin and Shakespeare. The Huntington Gallery, housed in the original Georgian mansion built by Henry Huntington in 1911, holds a world-famous collection of British paintings, including the original *Blue Boy* by Gainsborough; *Pinkie,* a companion piece by Thomas Lawrence; and the monumental *Sarah Siddons as the Tragic Muse* by Joshua Reynolds. American paintings and decorative arts are housed in the Virginia Steele Scott Gallery of American Art.

An awesome 150-acre garden, formerly the grounds of the estate, the Huntington Gardens now include a 12-acre Desert Garden featuring the world's largest group of mature cacti and other succulents, arranged by continent. The Japanese Garden holds traditional Japanese plants, stone ornaments, a drum bridge, a Japanese house, a bonsai court, and a Zen rock garden. Besides these gardens, there are collections of azaleas and 1,500 varieties of camellias, the world's largest public collection. The 3-acre rose garden is displayed chronologically, so the development leading to today's strains of roses can be observed. On the grounds is the charming **Rose Tea Garden Room,** where traditional high tea is served. A 1¼-hour guided tour of the gardens is led by docents at posted times, and inexpensive, self-guided tour leaflets are available in the entrance pavilion. ✉ *1151 Oxford Rd., San Marino,* ☎ *626/405–2100; recorded information 626/405–2141.* 🎫 *$8.50, free 1st Thurs. of month.* ⏲ *Sept.–May, Tues.–Fri. noon–4:30; weekends 10:30–4:30; June–Aug., Tues.–Sun. 10:30–4:30.*

8 **Kidspace.** At this children's museum housed in the gymnasium of an elementary school, kids can direct a television or radio station; dress up in the real uniforms of a firefighter, astronaut, or football player; or play in the sand of an indoor beach. "Critter Caverns" beckons with its large tree house and secret tunnels for exploring insect life firsthand. ✉ *390 S. El Molino Ave., Pasadena,* ☎ *626/449–9143.* 🎫 *$5.* ⏲ *Sept.–July 1, Tues. 1:30–5, Wed.–Fri. 1–5, Sat. 10–5, Sun. 1–5; hrs vary during school vacations.*

OFF THE BEATEN PATH

MISSION SAN GABRIEL ARCHANGEL – In 1771 Father Junípero Serra dedicated this mission to the great archangel and messenger from God, St. Gabriel. As the founders approached the mission site, they were confronted by Native Americans. In the heat of battle, one of the padres revealed the canvas painting *Our Lady of Sorrows,* which so impressed members of the tribe that they laid down their bows and arrows. Within the next 50 years, the San Gabriel Archangel grew to become the wealthiest of all California missions. In 1833 the Mexican government confiscated the mission and it began to decline. In 1855 the U.S. government returned the mission to the church, but by this time the Franciscans had departed. In 1908 the Claretian Missionaries took charge, and much care and respect has since been poured into the mission. Today, Mission San Gabriel Archangel's adobe walls preserve an era of history, and the magnificent cemetery stands witness to the many people who lived here. ✉ *428 S. Mission Dr., San Gabriel,* ☎ *626/457–3048.* 🎫 *$4.* ⏲ *Daily 9–4:30.*

★ 5 **Norton Simon Museum.** Familiar to television viewers of the Rose Parade, this sleek, modern building makes a stunning background for the passing floats. In 1974 Simon reorganized the failing Pasadena Art Institute and assembled one of the world's finest collections, richest in works by Rembrandt, Goya, Picasso, and, most of all, Degas. This is one of the only two U.S. institutions to hold the complete set of the artist's model bronzes (the other is the Metropolitan Museum of Art, in New York). There are also several Rodin sculptures throughout the museum. Rembrandt's development can be traced in three oils—*The Bearded Man in the Wide Brimmed Hat, Self Portrait,* and *Titus.* The most dramatic Goyas are two oils—*St. Jerome in Penitence* and the *Portrait of Dona Francisca Vicenta Chollet y Caballero.* Picasso's renowned *Woman with a Book* highlights a comprehensive collection of his paintings, drawings, and sculptures. The museum's collections of Impressionist and Cubist work is extensive, and the Asia collection is one of the country's best. Early Renaissance, Baroque, and Rococo artwork are additional specialties. A magical Tiepolo ceiling highlights the Rococo period. The museum's recent and extensive remodeling was designed by architect Frank O. Gehry. Noted California landscape designer Nancy Goslee Power transformed the outdoor space into a new 79,000-square-ft sculpture garden inspired by Claude Monet's Giverny, with a natural pond at its center. ✉ *411 W. Colorado Blvd., Pasadena,* ☎ *626/449–6840.* 🎫 *$6.* ⏲ *Thurs.–Sun. noon–6.*

6 **Old Town Pasadena.** Once the victim of decay, the area was revitalized in the 1990s as a blend of restored 19th-century brick buildings with a yuppie overlay. Cafés and restaurants are now plentiful and var-

ied. Old Town's shopping-mall mix of retailers includes Pottery Barn, Banana Republic, and Z Galerie, as well as specialty bookstores and boutiques. In the evenings and on weekends, streets are packed with people. The 12-block historic district is anchored along Colorado Boulevard, between Pasadena Avenue and Arroyo Parkway. West of Old Town, Colorado Boulevard rises onto the **Colorado Street Bridge,** a raised section of roadway on graceful arches. On New Year's Day throngs of people line Colorado Boulevard to watch the Rose Parade.

NEED A BREAK? Walk down to Fair Oaks Avenue to the **Market City Cafe** (✉ 33 S. Fair Oaks Ave., ☎ 626/568–0203), which you'll recognize by the life-size black-and-white cow in the window. Imaginative Italian fare is served both indoors and alfresco.

7 **Pacific Asia Museum.** Designed in the style of a Chinese imperial palace with a central garden, this building is devoted entirely to the arts and culture of Asia and the Pacific Islands. *✉ 46 N. Los Robles Ave., ☎ 626/449–2742. 🎫 $5, free 3rd Sat. of month. ⏲ Wed.–Sun. 10–5.*

4 **Rose Bowl.** With an enormous rose, the city of Pasadena's logo, tattooed onto its exterior, it's hard to miss this 100,000-seat stadium, host of many Super Bowls and home to the UCLA Bruins. The facility is closed except during games and special events such as the monthly Rose Bowl Swap Meet. Held the second Sunday of the month, it is considered the granddaddy of West Coast flea markets. *✉ Rosemont Ave., Pasadena, ☎ 626/577–3100. ⏲ Flea market, 2nd Sun. of month, 9–5.*

OFF THE BEATEN PATH **SOUTHWEST MUSEUM** – Readily spotted from the Pasadena Freeway (Highway 110), this huge Mission Revival building stands halfway up Mt. Washington. Inside is an extensive collection of Native American art and artifacts, with special emphasis on the people of the Plains, Northwest coast, Southwest coast, and California. The basket collection is outstanding. *✉ 234 Museum Dr., off Ave. 43 exit, Highland Park, ☎ 323/221–2163. 🎫 $5. ⏲ Tues.–Sun. 10–5.*

1 **Wrigley Mansion.** The chewing gum magnate, William Wrigley, purchased this white Italian Renaissance–style house in 1914. The mansion is now the headquarters for the Tournament of Roses Association. The gardens, with some 1,500 varieties of roses, are open daily. *✉ 391 S. Orange Grove Blvd., Pasadena, ☎ 626/449–4100. ⏲ House tours Feb.–Aug., Thurs. 2–4; gardens, daily sunrise–sunset.*

Long Beach, San Pedro, and Palos Verdes

Long Beach, wholly separate from the city of Los Angeles, began as a seaside resort in the 19th century. During the early part of the 20th century, an oil boom brought Midwesterners and Dust Bowlers in search of a better life. Bust followed boom and the city eventually took on a somewhat raw, neglected tone. A long-term redevelopment program begun in the '70s has done much to brighten the city's image. Across the Vincent Thomas Bridge from Long Beach is San Pedro, L.A's working harbor, and the hilly Palos Verdes Peninsula, a gentrified community of expensive estates.

A Good Tour

Numbers in the text correspond to numbers in the margin and on the Long Beach map.

A single drive around these three South Bay towns would cover more than 100 mi, so it's best to approach the area on two separate tours.

Begin a tour of Long Beach at what is still the city's most famous attraction, the Art Deco ship the ***Queen Mary*** ①. Take the Queens Way Bridge back across the bay to the **Long Beach Aquarium of the Pacific** ②. From here, stops along Shoreline Drive at **Shoreline Aquatic Park** ③ or the waterfront shopping center **Shoreline Village** ④ afford the best views of the harbor and the Long Beach skyline. At Ocean Boulevard, Shoreline Drive turns into Alamitos Avenue. Continue on Alamitos Avenue to the corner of 7th Street to the **Museum of Latin American Art** ⑤. Return to Ocean Boulevard, and turn east. Just past the commercial district lie the **Long Beach Museum of Art** ⑥ and grand old homes dating from the early 20th century. From Ocean Boulevard, turn onto Livingston Drive and then 2nd Street to drive through Belmont Shores before arriving at Alamitos Bay and **Naples** ⑦, a picturesque enclave of canals and marinas, and the place to take a gondola ride.

For an overview of Palos Verdes and San Pedro, begin at the **South Coast Botanic Garden** ⑧, on Crenshaw Boulevard 1 mi south of the Pacific Coast Highway (exit from I–405 at Crenshaw Boulevard and head west). Continue west on Crenshaw Boulevard to Crest Road. Turn right on Crest Road and follow it to Hawthorne Boulevard. Turn left at Hawthorne Boulevard, and left again at Palos Verdes Drive. Less than a mile farther on your right you'll see Point Vicente Lighthouse, a good spot to watch for whales, and, another 2 mi away, on your left, you'll see the all-glass **Wayfarers Chapel** ⑨. Continue south and you'll hit San Pedro and Los Angeles Harbor. Follow the signs to Cabrillo Beach, where you'll find the stark-white building that houses the **Cabrillo Marine Aquarium** ⑩.

TIMING

Guided tours of the *Queen Mary* last an hour; the Long Beach Aquarium of the Pacific could occupy most of a morning or an afternoon. Set aside about 45 minutes for a visit to the Museum of Latin American Art and 90 minutes for a stop at the Long Beach Museum of Art. If you've planned in advance, you could end the day with a sunset gondola cruise on the canals in Naples. In Palos Verdes, the South Coast Botanic Garden could occupy you for a couple of hours. The Wayfarers Chapel, less than 20 minutes from the garden, is a half-hour stopover. If you have children in tow, expect to stay a couple of hours at San Pedro's Cabrillo Marine Aquarium, longer if you join one of the tide-pool walks. Factor in 10 or 15 minutes of driving time between attractions.

Sights to See

⑩ **Cabrillo Marine Aquarium.** This gem of a small museum is dedicated to the marine life that flourishes off the southern California coast. A modern Frank Gehry–designed building right on the beach houses 35 saltwater tanks. Don't miss the shark tank, the whale and dolphin room, and the see-through tidal tank that enables you to see the long view of a wave. Exhibits are intimate, instructive, and fun—on the back patio, you can reach into a shallow tidepool tank to touch starfish and sea anemones. After visiting the museum, go play on the gentle beach (with playground equipment) right across the parking lot. ✉ *3720 Stephen White Dr., San Pedro,* ☎ *310/548–7562.* *Suggested donation $2, parking $6.50.* ⏲ *Tues.–Fri. noon–5, weekends 10–5.*

★ ② **Long Beach Aquarium of the Pacific.** A full-scale model of a blue whale, the largest living creature in the Pacific and on the planet, is suspended above the Great Hall, the entrance to this new aquarium. Seventeen major exhibit tanks and 30 smaller focus tanks contain some 10,000 live marine animals—including sea lions and otters—that inhabit the Pacific Ocean and its environment. Large tanks full of shimmering, mov-

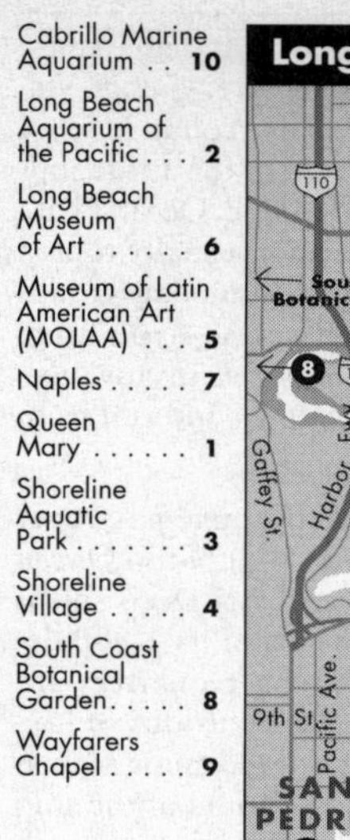

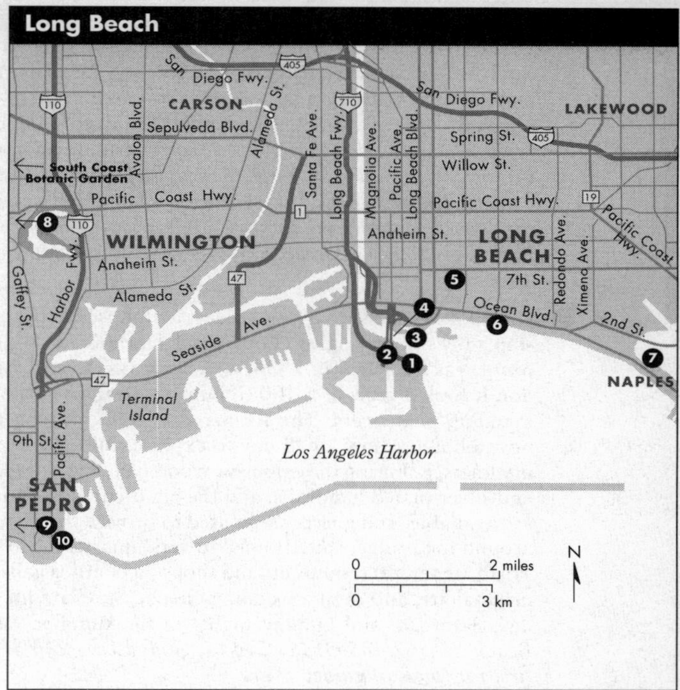

ing fish are a visual wonder; well-informed docents make this a truly educational experience. The living coral and leafy sea-dragon exhibits are revelatory of a world so different from our own terrestrial one. The exhibits focus on three regions of the Pacific Ocean: southern California and Baja, the northern Pacific, and the tropical Pacific. You'll also learn about conservation problems such as pollution, endangered coral reefs, and overharvesting. ✉ *100 Aquarium Way, Long Beach,* ☎ *562/590–3100.* 🎫 *$13.95.* ⏲ *Daily 10–6.*

6 **Long Beach Museum of Art.** The museum celebrated its 50th anniversary in 2000 by expanding into a new pavilion next door to its present home, a 1912 historic oceanfront mansion. That means more room for its permanent collection, which focuses on European and American art. The museum is renowned for its video art collection, one of the largest in the world. ✉ *2300 E. Ocean Blvd., Long Beach,* ☎ *562/439–2119.* 🎫 *$2.* ⏲ *Wed.–Sun. 10–5, Fri. 10–8.*

5 **Museum of Latin American Art.** The only museum in the country dedicated to contemporary art of Mexico and Central and South America moved into a converted skating rink in 1996, with just two small galleries. Two years later, MOLAA practically exploded onto the art scene when it debuted its renovation of 10,000 square ft of additional gallery space with a spectacular show of Oaxacan artist Laura Hernandez. ✉ *628 Alamitos Ave., Long Beach,* ☎ *562/437–1689.* 🎫 *$5.* ⏲ *Tues.–Sat. 11:30–7:30, Sun. noon–6.*

7 **Naples.** Arthur Parsons, the developer who came up with the Naples canal idea, learned from the mistakes and bad luck that did in those in Venice, just up the coast, and built the canals to take full advantage of the tidal flow that would keep them clean. Actually three small islands in man-made Alamitos Bay, Naples is best experienced on foot. Park near Bay Shore Avenue and 2nd Street and walk across the bridge,

where you can meander around the quaint streets with Italian names. This well-restored neighborhood has eclectic architecture: vintage Victorians, Craftsman bungalows, and Mission Revivals. You may spy a real gondola or two on the canals. You can hire them for a ride, but not on the spur of the moment. **Gondola Getaway** (5437 E. Ocean Blvd., Long Beach, ☎ 562/433–9595) offers one-hour rides, usually touted for romantic couples, although their gondolas can accommodate groups of up to 14 people, and serve bread, salami, and cheese—you bring the wine. Reservations are essential at least one week in advance. Rides cost $55 per couple, $10 each additional person, and run from 11 AM to 11 PM.

★ ❶ ***Queen Mary.*** Be sure to get at least a glimpse of this huge passenger ship, now sitting snugly in Long Beach Harbor. The 80,000-ton *Queen Mary* was launched in 1934, a floating treasure of Art Deco splendor. It took a crew of 1,100 to minister to the needs of its 1,900 demanding passengers. The former first-class passenger quarters are now a hotel. Allow a half day to explore this most luxurious of luxury liners, admiring the extensive wood paneling, the gleaming nickel- and silver-plated handrails, and the hand-cut glass. Tours of the ship are available, and guests are invited to browse the 12 decks and walk around the bridge, staterooms, officers' quarters, and engine rooms. There are several restaurants and shops on board, a gallery of the ship's original art, and even a wedding chapel. Stay late for fireworks Friday, Saturday, and Sunday nights in the summer. ✉ *Pier J, Long Beach,* ☎ *562/435–3511.* *$15, guided 1-hr tour $7 extra.* ⏲ *Call first for times of guided tours.*

❸ **Shoreline Aquatic Park.** Set literally in the middle of Long Beach Harbor is this much-sought-after resting place for RVers. Kite flyers love the winds here, and casual passersby can enjoy a short walk, where the modern skyline, quaint Shoreline Village, the *Queen Mary,* and the ocean all vie for attention. ✉ *E. Shoreline Dr.*

❹ **Shoreline Village.** This stretch of 24 gift shops and four restaurants between downtown Long Beach and the *Queen Mary* is a good place for a stroll, day or evening. This is also the place to hop aboard the "AquaBus" water taxi ($1), which travels between major harbor attractions, including the aquarium and the *Queen Mary.* ✉ *Shoreline Dr. and Shoreline Village Rd., Long Beach,* ☎ *562/435–2668.* ⏲ *May–Sept., daily 10–10; Oct.–Apr., daily 10–9.*

★ ❽ **South Coast Botanic Garden.** This Rancho Palos Verdes botanical garden began life ignominiously—as a garbage dump-cum-landfill. With the intensive ministerings of the experts from the L.A. County Arboreta Department, the dump soon sprouted lush gardens, with all the plants eventually organized into color groups. Self-guided walking tours take visitors past flower and herb gardens, rare cacti, and a lake with ducks. The Water-Wise Garden showcases alternatives to grass lawns in the parched southern California climate. Picnicking is limited to a lawn area outside the gates. ✉ *26300 S. Crenshaw Blvd., Rancho Palos Verdes,* ☎ *310/544–6815.* *$5.* ⏲ *Daily 9–5.*

❾ **Wayfarers Chapel.** Architect Lloyd Wright, son of Frank Lloyd Wright, designed this modern glass church in 1949 to blend in with an encircling redwood forest. The redwoods are gone, but another forest has taken their place, lush with ferns and azaleas, adding up to a breathtaking combination of ocean, vegetation, and an architectural wonder. This "natural church" is a popular wedding site, so avoid visiting on weekends. ✉ *5755 Palos Verdes Dr. S, Rancho Palos Verdes,* ☎ *310/377–1650.* ⏲ *Daily 7–5.*

DINING

By Bill Stern

L.A.'s restaurants reflect both the city's well-deserved reputation for culinary innovation and its rich ethnic cornucopia. Los Angeles is home not only to many of the country's best-known chefs—Wolfgang Puck, Joachim Splichal, Michel Richard—but also to many unheralded chefs who delight Angelenos daily with the cuisines of Shanghai, Oaxaca, Tuscany, and elsewhere.

CATEGORY	COST*
$$$$	over $50
$$$	$30–$50
$$	$20–$30
$	under $20

**per person for a three-course meal, excluding drinks, service, and 8¼% tax*

following the text of a review is your signal that the property has a Web site, where you will find details and, usually, images; for a link, visit www.fodors.com/urls.

Beverly Hills, Century City, Hollywood, and West Hollywood

Beverly Hills

AMERICAN

$$–$$$$ ✕ **Grill on the Alley.** This fashionable place for power lunching features tasty, simple American fare, including chicken potpies, crab cakes, creamy Cobb salad, and homemade rice pudding, as well as high-quality steaks and seafood. ✉ *9560 Dayton Way,* ☎ *310/276–0615. Reservations essential. AE, DC, MC, V. No lunch Sun.*

CHINESE

$$ ✕ **The Mandarin.** The Mandarin serves Szechuan and Chinese country dishes in a serene, traditional Chinese setting, with roomy bamboo armchairs, soft Chinese music, and linens and crystal. Specialties include minced chicken wrapped in lettuce leaves, scallion pancakes, Singapore noodles, and Beijing duck (order ahead of time). ✉ *430 N. Camden Dr.,* ☎ *310/859–0926. Reservations essential. AE, DC, MC, V. No lunch weekends.*

CONTEMPORARY

$$–$$$$ ★ ✕ **The Dining Room at the Regent Beverly Wilshire.** Businesspeople and area residents use this formal but comfortable room for elegant break[illegible] fasts, lunches, and dinners. Grilled swordfish with barbecued shri[illegible] sometimes appears on the prix-fixe lunch menu, which generally [illegible] about $28. The dinner menu may include warm fig-and-wild-[illegible] room salad and Maine lobster with mascarpone-and-potato g[illegible] A la carte choices are also available. ✉ *9500 Wilshire Blvd.,* [illegible] *275–5200. Jacket required. AE, D, DC, MC, V. No lunch* [illegible] *Sun.*

$$–$$$ ★ ✕ **Nouveau Café Blanc.** Chef-owner Tommy Harase h[illegible] modern yet warm and unpretentious restaurant one of [illegible] unexpected treats—especially when lunchtime entrées [illegible] salmon with basil vinaigrette or poached Maine lobst[illegible] Equally good-value is the five-course prix-fixe dinne[illegible] feature exquisite sautéed foie gras with corn cho[illegible] scallops stuffed with black bean sauce, and roas[illegible] vice is both gracious and unobtrusive. ✉ *9777 Li*[illegible] ☎ *310/888–0108. Reservations essential. AE* [illegible] *and Mon.*

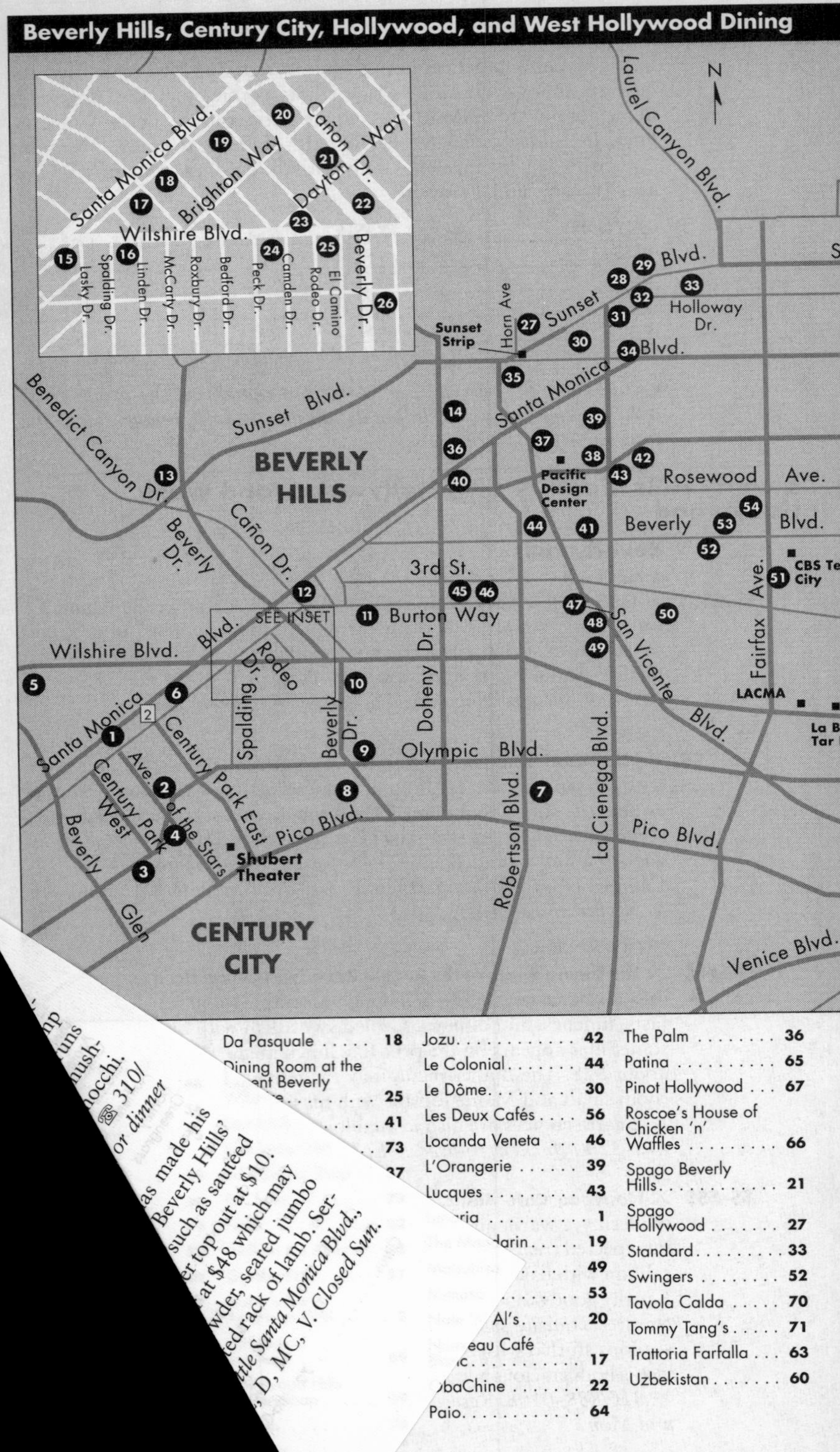
Beverly Hills, Century City, Hollywood, and West Hollywood Dining
Santa Monica Blvd.
Brighton Way
Cañon Dr.
Dayton Way
Wilshire Blvd.
Lasky Dr.
Spalding Dr.
Linden Dr.
McCarty Dr.
Roxbury Dr.
Bedford Dr.
Peck Dr.
Camden Dr.
Rodeo Dr.
El Camino
Beverly Dr.
Laurel Canyon Blvd.
Sunset Blvd.
Holloway Dr.
Sunset Strip
Horn Ave
Santa Monica Blvd.
Benedict Canyon Dr.
BEVERLY HILLS
Pacific Design Center
Rosewood Ave.
Beverly Blvd.
CBS Television City
3rd St.
SEE INSET
Burton Way
Doheny Dr.
San Vicente Blvd.
Fairfax Ave.
LACMA
Olympic Blvd.
Robertson Blvd.
La Cienega Blvd.
Century Park East
Ave. of the Stars
Century Park West
Beverly Glen
Shubert Theater
Pico Blvd.
CENTURY CITY
Venice Blvd.
Da Pasquale 18
Jozu 42
Le Colonial 44
Le Dôme 30
Les Deux Cafés 56
Locanda Veneta . . . 46
L'Orangerie 39
Lucques 43
Paio 64
The Palm 36
Patina 65
Pinot Hollywood . . . 67
Roscoe's House of Chicken 'n' Waffles 66
Spago Beverly Hills 21
Spago Hollywood 27
Standard 33
Swingers 52
Tavola Calda 70
Tommy Tang's 71
Trattoria Farfalla . . . 63
Uzbekistan 60

and Lodging

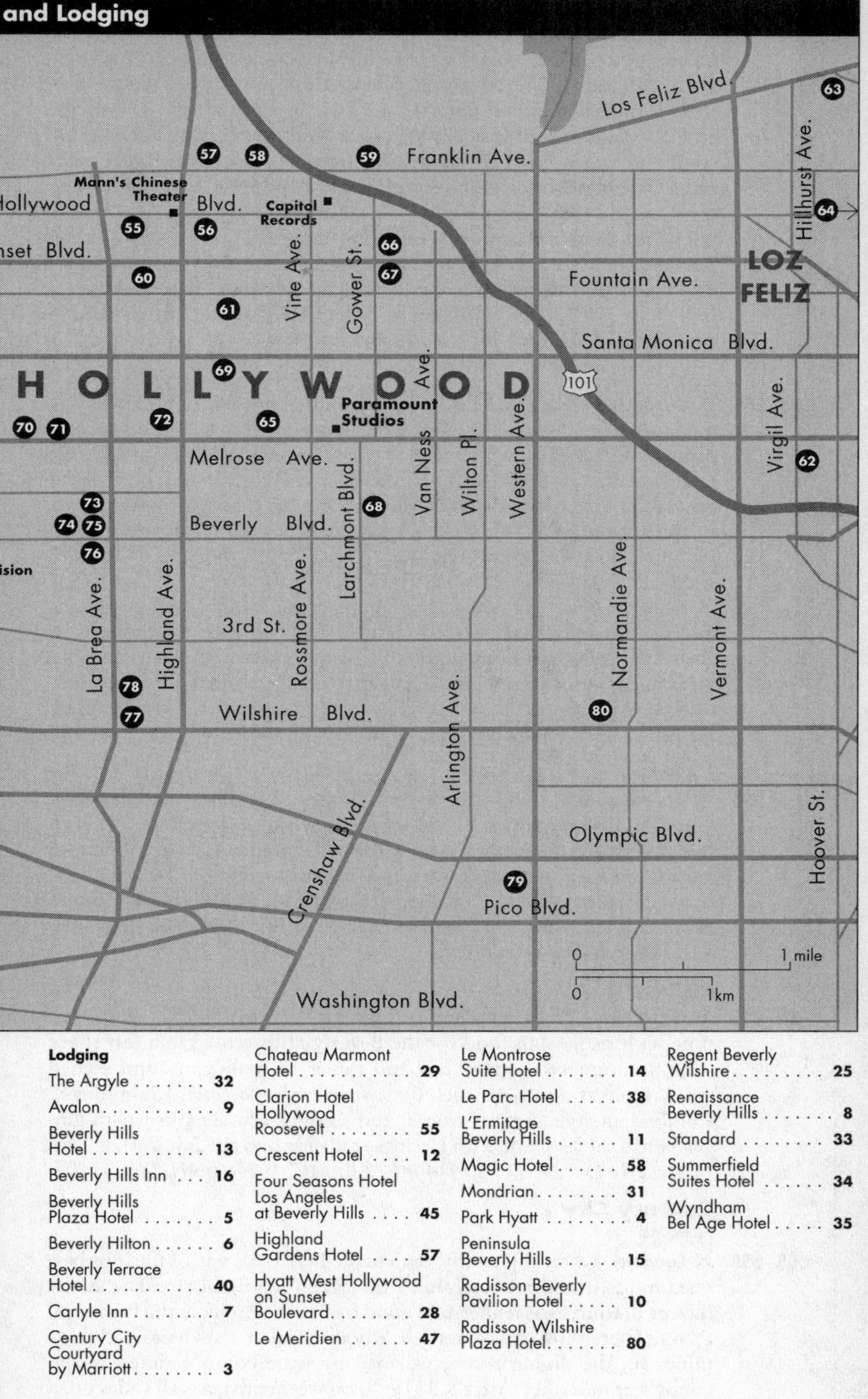

Lodging

The Argyle **32**

Avalon **9**

Beverly Hills Hotel **13**

Beverly Hills Inn . . . **16**

Beverly Hills Plaza Hotel **5**

Beverly Hilton **6**

Beverly Terrace Hotel **40**

Carlyle Inn **7**

Century City Courtyard by Marriott **3**

Chateau Marmont Hotel **29**

Clarion Hotel Hollywood Roosevelt **55**

Crescent Hotel **12**

Four Seasons Hotel Los Angeles at Beverly Hills **45**

Highland Gardens Hotel **57**

Hyatt West Hollywood on Sunset Boulevard **28**

Le Meridien **47**

Le Montrose Suite Hotel **14**

Le Parc Hotel **38**

L'Ermitage Beverly Hills **11**

Magic Hotel **58**

Mondrian **31**

Park Hyatt **4**

Peninsula Beverly Hills **15**

Radisson Beverly Pavilion Hotel **10**

Radisson Wilshire Plaza Hotel **80**

Regent Beverly Wilshire **25**

Renaissance Beverly Hills **8**

Standard **33**

Summerfield Suites Hotel **34**

Wyndham Bel Age Hotel **35**

$$–$$$ ✕ **Spago Beverly Hills.** Wolfgang Puck, the chef who helped define California cuisine at his original Sunset Strip venue wows celebrity and business circles in a smart Beverly Hills location designed by his wife, Barbara Lazaroff. The restaurant centers around an outdoor courtyard, from which diners can glimpse the large open kitchen. The menu changes daily offering such starters as white-bean and duck-confit soup and warm crayfish salad with mustard potatoes. Entrées have ranged from wild striped bass with celery-root puree to roasted Cantonese duck with persimmons, pomegranate, and ginger. Also worth trying are Puck's Austrian "childhood favorites," such as *Kärntner Käsenudeln* (cheese ravioli) with hazelnut butter and his renowned pizzas. This Spago attracts as many of Hollywood's who's who as the original does. ✉ *176 N. Cañon Dr.,* ☎ *310/385–0880. Reservations essential. AE, D, DC, MC, V. No lunch Sun.*

DELI

$$–$$$ ★ ✕ **Barney Greengrass.** This *haute* deli on the fifth floor of Barneys has an appropriately high-class aesthetic: limestone floors, mahogany furniture, and a wall of windows. You can savor everything from $99 beluga caviar to a $6.75 peanut butter–and–jelly sandwich. But the specialties are flawless smoked salmon, sturgeon, and whitefish flown in fresh from New York. This deli keeps store hours, closing Thursday at 8, Sunday at 6, and every other day at 7. ✉ *Barneys, 9570 Wilshire Blvd., Beverly Hills,* ☎ *310/777–5877. AE, MC, V.*

$ ✕ **Nate 'n' Al's.** A famous gathering place for Hollywood comedians and Beverly Hills shoppers, Nate 'n' Al's has regulars bantering with their favorite waitresses who serve first-rate matzo-ball soup, lox and scrambled eggs, cheese blintzes, potato pancakes, and deli sandwiches. ✉ *414 N. Beverly Dr.,* ☎ *310/274–0101. Reservations not accepted. AE, MC, V. Free parking.*

ITALIAN

$$ ✕ **Da Pasquale.** An affordable meal is hard to find here in the land of Gucci and Bijan, which is one reason to visit Da Pasquale. An even better reason is the pizza topped with such ingredients as fresh tomato, garlic, and basil or three cheeses and prosciutto. Standards such as antipasti, pastas, and roast chicken are also good. ✉ *9749 Little Santa Monica Blvd.,* ☎ *310/859–3884. AE, MC, V. Closed Sun. No lunch Sat. Free parking after 6 PM.*

PAN-ASIAN

$$–$$$ ✕ **ObaChine.** Wolfgang Puck and Barbara Lazaroff strike again: this time with pan-Asian food for the Beverly Hills crowd in a loft space with a hammered-copper bar and tables of mahogany and etched glass. Interesting dishes include savory crab *shui mai* (dumplings), Cambodian-style shrimp crepes, and sizzling whole catfish with ginger-ponzu sauce (made with Japanese radishes and citrus juices). ✉ *242 N. Beverly Dr.,* ☎ *310/274–4440. AE, MC, V. No lunch Sun.*

Century City

FRENCH

$$–$$$ ✕ **Lunaria.** Bernard Jacoupy, who made Bernard's one of the '80s best restaurants, has done it again at this jazz-friendly bistro. The sunny flavors of tomatoes, fennel, and good fresh fish dominate the Provençal menu. There's also an oyster bar. Roomy wicker armchairs and large tables fill the dining room, warmed by watercolors painted by Jacoupy's grandfather. After 8:30 (9:30 on weekends), a wall slides open to reveal the stage and the evening's featured jazz group. ✉ *10351 Santa Monica Blvd.,* ☎ *310/282–8870. AE, DC, MC, V. Closed Sun. No lunch Sat., no dinner Mon.*

ITALIAN

$$–$$$ ✕ **Harry's Bar & American Grill.** The dark wood–paneled maritime decor and the selection of dishes—paper-thin carpaccio, *grigliata mista di pesce* (mixed seafood grill), and tagliatellini con *luganega* (sausage)—are intended to evoke Harry's Bar in Venice, but the check will be far lower than in Italy. ✉ *2020 Ave. of the Stars,* ☏ *310/277–2333. Reservations essential. AE, DC, MC. No lunch weekends.*

Hollywood

AMERICAN/CASUAL

$$ ✕ **Hollywood Hills Coffee Shop.** Despite the modest name, this little café often has surprisingly good food. Breakfast promises classics such as huevos rancheros, cheese blintzes, and even a whole grilled salmon trout, its reddish flesh set off by eggs and salsa. For dinner, there are vegetarian choices as well as fish and meat. ✉ *6145 Franklin Ave.,* ☏ *323/467–7678. Reservations not accepted. MC, V.*

$–$$ ✕ **Hollywood Canteen.** In the heart of working Hollywood, near soundstages, recording studios, and lighting companies, this handsome "diner" with a secluded back patio functions as a canteen for executives, actors, and technicians, who come here for simple but upscale grub: organic field-green salads, swordfish sandwiches, burgers, risotto with asparagus and shrimp, and various soups. ✉ *1006 Seward St.,* ☏ *323/465–0961. AE, MC, V. Closed Sun. No lunch Sat.*

CAJUN/CREOLE

$ ✕ **Gumbo Pot.** This outdoor Cajun/Creole café in the Farmers Market serves a mean smoky and spicy gumbo rich with shrimp and chicken. It's also the place for *muffulettas* (hero sandwiches), jambalaya, and beignets dusted with powdered sugar. ✉ *Farmers Market, 6333 W. 3rd St.,* ☏ *323/933–0358. Reservations not accepted. MC, V.*

CONTEMPORARY

$$$$ ★ ✕ **Patina.** The exterior of Joachim Splichal's flagship restaurant is so understated that it's easy to miss, and the interior is a study in spare elegance. Generally considered one of the best restaurants in Los Angeles, this is the wellspring from which the various Pinot bistros have sprung. Among the mainstays are a corn blini filled with fennel-marinated salmon and crème fraîche, and scallops wrapped in potato slices with brown-butter vinaigrette. ✉ *5955 Melrose Ave.,* ☏ *323/467–1108. Reservations essential. AE, D, DC, MC, V. No lunch Wed.–Mon.*

$$$–$$$$ ★ ✕ **Citrus.** Chef Michel Richard has opened restaurants elsewhere, but Citrus has remained his hottest ticket, especially within the entertainment industry. Lunch begins on the light side, with starters such as artichoke terrine or ahi tuna carpaccio, followed by sautéed Chilean sea bass with black chanterelle crust or chicken ravioli with Parmesan sauce. The dinner menu features crab cakes with tomato-mustard sauce. ✉ *6703 Melrose Ave.,* ☏ *323/857–0034. Reservations essential. AE, MC, V. No lunch weekends.*

$$–$$$ ✕ **Pinot Hollywood.** This link in the chain of glamorous bistros Joachim "Patina" Splichal has laid out across the city occupies a walled compound almost next door to Paramount Studios. Lunch entrées, which range from $13 to $18, include poached-salmon salad with tomato vinaigrette, papardelle with braised lamb, and grilled albacore tuna with shrimp pot stickers. For dinner you might find fresh grilled sardines à la Provençal or parsnip gnocchi with lobster and veal shank and caramelized root vegetables. ✉ *1448 N. Gower St.,* ☏ *323/461–8800. Reservations essential. AE, D, DC, MC, V. No lunch Sat. Closed Sun.*

FRENCH

$$–$$$ ★ ✕ **Café des Artistes.** At its best, as here, new Hollywood is tasting a lot like old Paris. Behind tall hedge, in the midst of film production

companies, a California bungalow has been turned into cozy bistro where smart film and music folk flock. They can start off with mussels Provençal, asparagus and fennel salad, or even a major seafood platter (oysters, clams, crab, shrimp, periwinkles). Then go on to monkfish with olives, fennel and lemon confit followed by a cheese plate or brioche pudding, chocolate mousse or lemon sorbet with vodka. All abetted by a modest but well-selected wine list. ✉ *1534 McCadden Pl.,* ☎ *323/469–7300. AE, MC, V. Closed Sun.*

$–$$$ ✕ **Les Deux Cafés.** This handsomely refitted 1904 house with a hidden dining terrace and an even more intimate herb garden is unexpectedly set in a parking lot behind a barbed-wire-topped wall. Chef David Winn appeals to easily bored tastes with inventions such as lobster-and-tabbouleh salad, and a salad of beets, spinach, and horseradish. He also turns out a splendid skate sautéed in brown butter. ✉ *1683 Las Palmas Ave.,* ☎ *323/465–0509. Reservations essential. AE, MC, V. Closed Sun. No lunch Sat.*

INDIAN

$ ✕ **East India Grill.** With its combination of high-tech sheet metal decor and low-tech tandoori oven this popular café serves traditional, zesty Indian food with a California edge. Traditional dishes such as green-coconut curries, *makhani tikka masalas* (tomato-based curries), and *sagwalas* (spinach dishes) are just as well prepared as the more imaginative, California-influenced novelties such as mango ribs and garlic-basil nan. ✉ *345 N. La Brea Ave.,* ☎ *323/936–8844. AE, MC, V. Free garage parking.*

JAPANESE

$$ ✕ **Ita-Cho.** Now more than ever, in its larger, smarter more minimalist location, Ita-Cho is a chic destination for those in the know. Specializing in *koryori-ya,* the Japanese pub cuisine that features delicately cooked dishes, the small dining room also serves flawless sashimi (but no sushi). Also try the tender pork simmered in sake and soy for two days. ✉ *7311 Beverly Blvd.,* ☎ *323/938–9009. Reservations essential. AE, MC, V. Closed Sun.*

MEXICAN

$–$$ ★ ✕ **El Cholo.** The progenitor of a chain, this landmark south of Hollywood has been packing them in since the '20s. L.A.-Mex standards are served—chicken enchiladas; *carnitas* (shredded fried pork); and, from July through October, green-corn tamales. Portions are large and prices reasonable. ✉ *1121 S. Western Ave.,* ☎ *323/734–2773. AE, DC, MC, V.*

RUSSIAN

$–$$ ✕ **Uzbekistan.** Brightly colored murals lend a fittingly folksy air to this restaurant, which serves a mix of Russian and Central Asian cuisine. Start with any of the meat dumplings and go on to eggplant sautéed with tomatoes and garlic or a fragrant stir fry of beef, noodles, and vegetables perfumed with cumin. ✉ *7077 Sunset Blvd.,* ☎ *323/464–3663. MC, V.*

SOUL

$ ✕ **Roscoe's House of Chicken 'n' Waffles.** The name of this casual eatery doesn't sound all that appetizing, considering the strange combination of foods mentioned, but don't be fooled: this is *the* place for real down-home Southern cooking. ✉ *1514 N. Gower St.,* ☎ *323/466–9329. Reservations not accepted. AE, D, DC, MC, V.*

THAI

$–$$ ✕ **Chan Dara.** A rock 'n' roll and showbiz crowd frequents this casual eatery, which occupies an old Spanish house in a block of doctors' offices near Paramount Pictures. Try any of the noodle dishes, especially those with crab and shrimp. ✉ *310 N. Larchmont Blvd.,* ☎ *323/467–1052. AE, D, DC, MC, V. No lunch weekends.*

Los Feliz/Silver Lake

CARIBBEAN

$–$$$ ✕ **Cha Cha Cha.** Because it's off the beaten path, Cha Cha Cha attracts a discerning, eclectic crowd. It's hip yet not pretentious or overly trendy. The giant map pinpoints the restaurant's Caribbean influences. Standard options are Jamaican jerk chicken, fried plantain chips, pork chops with apricot salsa, and assorted flans. Cha Cha Cha is open daily for breakfast, lunch, and dinner. ✉ *656 N. Virgil Ave.,* ☎ *323/664–7723. AE, D, DC, MC, V.*

ECLECTIC

$$ ✕ **Paio.** This little restaurant has put Silver Lake, a mixed gay and straight, upwardly mobile neighborhood, on the culinary map. Chef Alisa Reynolds combines traditional appetizers such as white bean soup with Asian-influenced inventions such as deep-fried salmon wontons. Her entrées include roasted quail and fried barbecued chicken. Bringing your own wine helps keep the tab down. ✉ *2520 Hyperion Ave.,* ☎ *323/953–1973. AE, MC, V. Closed Sun. and Mon. No lunch. Free parking.*

ITALIAN

$$ ✕ **Trattoria Farfalla.** This reliable, brick-walled trattoria brought Los Feliz out of the spaghetti-and-meatballs mode in the '80s and has remained a favorite ever since. Regulars tend to order the Caesar salad on a pizza-crust bed; roasted herbed free-range chicken; and pasta *alla Norma* (studded with rich, smoky eggplant). ✉ *1978 N. Hillhurst Ave.,* ☎ *323/661–7365. AE, DC, MC, V. No lunch weekends. Street parking.*

West Hollywood

AMERICAN/CASUAL

$$ ✕ **Dominick's.** This re-do of a long-time Hollywood-star-studded watering hole is still strong on high quality meat and potatoes, including Black Angus filet mignon and grilled lamb chops. But now they're balanced by fish with vegetables including grilled ahi tuna with baby bok choy and sautéed Chilean sea bass with vegetable couscous. The largely show biz clientele tends towards the young agent and d-boy and -girl (for story development) crowd. ✉ *8715 Beverly Blvd.,* ☎ *310/652–7272. AE, MC, V. Closed Sun.*

$ ✕ **Ed's Coffee Shop.** The coffee shop of choice for decorators and clients from the nearby Pacific Design Center, Ed's serves delicious omelets, huevos rancheros, egg salad, stuffed peppers, meat loaf, and homemade pies. ✉ *460 N. Robertson Blvd.,* ☎ *310/659–8625. Reservations not accepted. No credit cards. No lunch Sat. No dinner.*

$ ✕ **Swingers.** Everyone from powerlunchers to Doc Marten–clad posers takes to this all-day, late-night coffee shop, so be prepared for a wait. Eat at sidewalk tables or inside the pseudo-diner on the ground floor of the no-frills Beverly-Laurel Hotel. Loud alternative music plays to the Gen-X crowd, and a casual menu—breakfast burritos, hamburgers, and chicken breast sandwiches on fresh French bread—goes easy on your pocketbook. ✉ *8020 Beverly Blvd.,* ☎ *323/653–5858. AE, D, MC, V.*

CONTEMPORARY

$$$–$$$$ ✕ **Fenix.** You'll find abundant Art Deco splendor at the Argyle Hotel's culinary outpost on the Sunset Strip. The bi-level dining room–bar, accented in dark purple and brushed gold, has plush banquettes, a grand piano, and a romantic city view. Chef Gaetan Crosier starts you off with the likes of lobster tortellini or ahi tuna in rice paper and then moves on to tandoori-spiced Chilean sea bass or braised lamb shank with polenta. ✉ *8358 Sunset Blvd.,* ☎ *323/848–6677. Reservations essential. AE, D, DC, MC, V.*

$$$ ✕ **Asia de Cuba.** Can't get into the Sky Bar? Well, you can watch those who can from this hot spot which shares the Mondrian Hotel's city-view patio. Prices are high but portions are definitely large enough to share. Some, such as the carpaccio, are mostly lettuce, but the tuna tartare and the roast pork pancakes are more substantial. "Hacked" lime chicken and yucca-crusted mahi mahi are a lot less peculiar than they sound. You'll also find here what are arguably the most beautiful people in town, and that's saying a lot for L.A. ✉ *8440 W. Sunset Blvd.,* ☎ *323/848–6000. Reservations essential. AE, MC, V.*

$$–$$$ ✕ **Boxer.** This small, chic restaurant continues to satisfy its faithful following under its young new chef, Brooke Williamson, who presents seasonal menus. Because there is no wine license, you can buy your own bottle from the owner's well-stocked wine shop next door or bring your own for a modest $6 corkage fee. ✉ *7615 Beverly Blvd.,* ☎ *323/932–6178. AE, MC, V. Closed Mon.*

$$–$$$ ★ ✕ **Campanile.** Mark Peel and Nancy Silverton (also the force behind the adjacent La Brea Bakery) blend robust Mediterranean flavors with those of homey Americana. Among the entrées are bourride of snapper and Manila clams, and loin of venison with quince purée. Here is also where you'll find some of the best desserts anywhere—try the light-as-a-feather bitter-almond *panna cotta* (an Italian variation on caramel custard), or a garden fresh strawberry crisp. Don't miss weekend brunch on the enclosed patio with a vintage fountain. ✉ *624 S. La Brea Ave.,* ☎ *323/938–1447. Reservations essential. AE, D, DC, MC, V. No dinner Sun.*

$$–$$$ ✕ **Jozu.** The Japanese name, which means *excellent,* and Japanese-theme decor hint at the bias of executive chef Preech Narkthong's Cal-Asian menu. Start with crisp Sonoma quail with tangerine glaze or deep-fried Ipswich clams. As an entrée, you might try roasted Chilean sea bass with ponzu sauce and cabbage salad. ✉ *8360 Melrose Ave.,* ☎ *323/655–5600. AE, DC, MC, V. No lunch.*

$$–$$$ ★ ✕ **Lucques.** This historic brick building, once silent-film star Harold Lloyd's carriage house, has been attractively transformed into a restaurant that's been an instant hit with the younger well-heeled set. And the cooking—by Suzanne Goin, formerly of Campanile—is smart, too: consider Moroccan squash soup with crème fraîche followed by seared scallops with fennel and saffron. ✉ *8474 Melrose Ave.,* ☎ *323/655–6277. Reservations essential. AE, D, DC, MC, V. Closed Mon. No lunch.*

$$–$$$ ✕ **Spago Hollywood.** This is the restaurant that propelled chef-owner Wolfgang Puck into the international culinary spotlight in the 1980s. Make reservations far in advance to sample tempura Maryland soft-shell crabs, venison with black cherry–port wine sauce, and grilled Alaskan salmon with lemongrass. ✉ *1114 Horn Ave.,* ☎ *310/652–4025. Reservations essential. D, DC, MC, V. Closed Mon. No lunch.*

$$ ✕ **The Standard.** With its 90's take on 50's design the Standard Hotel helped prepare the revitalized Sunset Strip to soar into the new millennium. And its restaurant, a former coffee shop, flies right too: it's also a place of pilgrimage for younger, hipper, cost-conscious local entertainment and design industry trend-setters, and it's open 24 hours a day. The food's really good, too. Locals love roasted butternut squash

soup or shrimp summer rolls followed by roast pork with apple compote or miso-glazed black cod and, naturally, burgers and steaks with A-one fries. ✉ *8300 Sunset Blvd.,* ☎ *323/650–9090. Reservations required. AE, MC, V.*

DELI

$ ✕ **Canter's.** This granddaddy of Los Angeles delicatessens (it opened in 1928) pickles its own corned-beef pastrami and has its own in-house bakery. Next door is the Kibitz Room, where there's live music every night. ✉ *419 N. Fairfax Ave.,* ☎ *323/651–2030. Reservations not accepted. MC, V. Parking in lot.*

FRENCH

$$$$ ★ ✕ **L'Orangerie.** Elegant French Mediterranean cuisine is served in this rococo dining room, complete with white flower arrangements and oils depicting European castles. Specialties include coddled eggs served in the shell and topped with caviar, duck with foie gras, rack of lamb for two, and a rich apple tart accompanied by a jug of double cream. ✉ *903 N. La Cienega Blvd.,* ☎ *310/652–9770. Reservations essential. AE, D, DC, MC, V. Closed Mon. No lunch.*

$$$–$$$$ ✕ **Le Dôme.** This fancy show- and music-biz bistro mixes French country dishes and hearty American fare: escargots Burgundy-style (served with garlic, shallots, and parsley) and coq au vin appeal to Francophiles, while center-cut pork chops and grilled Sonoma lamb chops satisfy patriots. The look is art deco and the crowd—men in ponytails and pressed jeans—looks as if it favors the music business. ✉ *8720 Sunset Blvd.,* ☎ *310/659–6919. Reservations essential. AE, MC, V. Closed Sun. No lunch Sat..*

$$–$$$ ✕ **Mimosa.** Chef Jean-Pierre Bosc's menu is country French with a Provençal bent. There's Lyonnaise salad, a *tarte flambée alsacienne* (a pizzalike wood-fired onion tart), and hearty chicken terrine with onion marmalade. Standout entrées are bouillabaisse and fillet of sole *au pistou* (with basil-garlic paste). ✉ *8009 Beverly Blvd.,* ☎ *323/655–8895. AE, MC, V. Closed Sun. No lunch Sat.*

ITALIAN

$$ ★ ✕ **Ca'Brea.** Chef Antonio Tommasi turns out lamb chops with black-truffle and mustard sauce, whole boneless chicken marinated and grilled with herbs, and a very popular osso buco. Starters make the meal—try baked goat cheese wrapped in pancetta and served atop a Popeye-size mound of spinach. ✉ *346 S. La Brea Ave.,* ☎ *323/938–2863. AE, D, DC, MC, V. Closed Sun. No lunch weekends.*

$$ ✕ **Locanda Veneta.** This upmarket Italian trattoria has an open kitchen that cooks up specialties such as flattened grilled chicken, veal chops, lobster ravioli with saffron sauce, and an unusual apple tart with polenta crust and caramel sauce. ✉ *8638 W. 3rd St.,* ☎ *310/274–1893. Reservations essential. AE, D, DC, MC, V. Closed Sun. No lunch Sat.*

$ ✕ **Tavola Calda.** This low-tech Italian favorite draws a budget-watching crowd, with many entrées priced under $10. Best bets on the limited menu are unusual pizzas, such as the cheeseless vegetarian pie, and the seafood and porcini risottos. ✉ *7371 Melrose Ave.,* ☎ *323/658–6340. AE, DC, MC, V.*

JAPANESE

$$$–$$$$ ★ ✕ **Matsuhisa.** Cutting-edge Pacific Rim cuisine is pushed to new limits at this modest-looking yet high-profile Japanese bistro. Chef Nobu Matsuhisa creatively infuses his dishes with flavors encountered during his sojourn in Peru. Consider his caviar-capped tuna stuffed with black truffles, and the sea urchin wrapped in a *shiso* leaf. Tempuras are lighter than usual, and the sushi is fresh and authentic. ✉ *129 N. La Cienega Blvd.,* ☎ *310/659–9639. Reservations essential. AE, DC, MC, V.*

SOUTHWESTERN

$–$$ ✕ **Authentic Cafe.** The Gen-X crowd can't get enough of the Santa Fe salad, wood-grilled chicken with mole, chicken casserole with cornbread crust, and excellent vegetarian dishes. You'll have to wait at peak hours. Breakfast is served on weekends. ✉ *7605 Beverly Blvd.,* ☎ *323/939–4626. Reservations not accepted. MC, V.*

SPANISH

$$–$$$ ✕ **Cava.** This two-level tapas bar and restaurant is in the Beverly Plaza Hotel. The artsy dining room is a bit noisy but lots of fun. You can graze on tapas—baked artichoke topped with bread crumbs and tomato, or a fluffy potato omelet served with crème fraîche. Those with bigger appetites can try a paella or aged New York steak with a traditional Argentine steak sauce. Wash it all down with a glass or three of sangria. ✉ *8384 W. 3rd St.,* ☎ *323/658–8898. AE, D, DC, MC, V.*

STEAK

$$$–$$$$ ✕ **Arnie Morton's of Chicago.** In addition to a 24-ounce porterhouse, a New York strip, and a double-cut filet mignon, there are giant veal and lamb chops, thick cuts of prime rib, swordfish steaks, and Maine lobsters at market prices. ✉ *435 S. La Cienega Blvd.,* ☎ *310/246–1501. AE, DC, MC, V. No lunch.*

$$$–$$$$ ✕ **The Palm.** All the New York elements are present at this West Coast replay of the famous Manhattan steak house—mahogany booths, tin ceilings, boisterous atmosphere, and New York–style waiters rushing you through your cheesecake (flown in from the Bronx). This is where you'll find the biggest and best lobster, good steaks, prime rib, chops, great French-fried onion rings, and paper-thin potato slices. ✉ *9001 Santa Monica Blvd.,* ☎ *310/550–8811. Reservations essential. AE, DC, MC, V. No lunch weekends.*

THAI

$–$$ ✕ **Tommy Tang's.** A lot of people-watching goes on at this Melrose Avenue grazing ground. Portions are on the small side but decidedly innovative. Try crisp duck marinated in honey-ginger sauce, pan-seared sea scallops, or the spinach salad tossed with grilled chicken. ✉ *7313 Melrose Ave.,* ☎ *323/937–5733. AE, DC, MC, V.*

VIETNAMESE

$$–$$$ ✕ **Le Colonial.** Like the original Le Colonial in Manhattan, this is a bi-level restaurant with an opulent bar upstairs, and below, a seductive dining room serving dishes such as roasted chicken with lemongrass; fried spring rolls packed with pork, mushrooms, and shrimp; and shredded chicken and cabbage doused in lime juice. ✉ *8783 Beverly Blvd.,* ☎ *310/289–0660. AE, DC, MC, V. No lunch weekends.*

Coastal and Western Los Angeles

Bel-Air

CONTEMPORARY

$$$–$$$$ ★ ✕ **Hotel Bel-Air.** Nestled in the midst of a luxuriant canyon, the restaurant in the Hotel Bel-Air spills out into a romantic country garden with gurgling fountains and a swan lake. Chef Gary Clauson charms diners with such seasonal appetizers as pan-seared foie gras with rhubarb–star anise compote and a roasted beet–and–goat cheese gâteau, which may be followed by Angus beef with Stilton or pan-roasted sea bass with fennel. The Hotel Bel-Air hosts one of the best high teas in town. ✉ *701 Stone Canyon Rd.,* ☎ *310/472–1211. Reservations essential. Jacket and tie. AE, DC, MC, V.*

Coastal Los Angeles Dining and Lodging

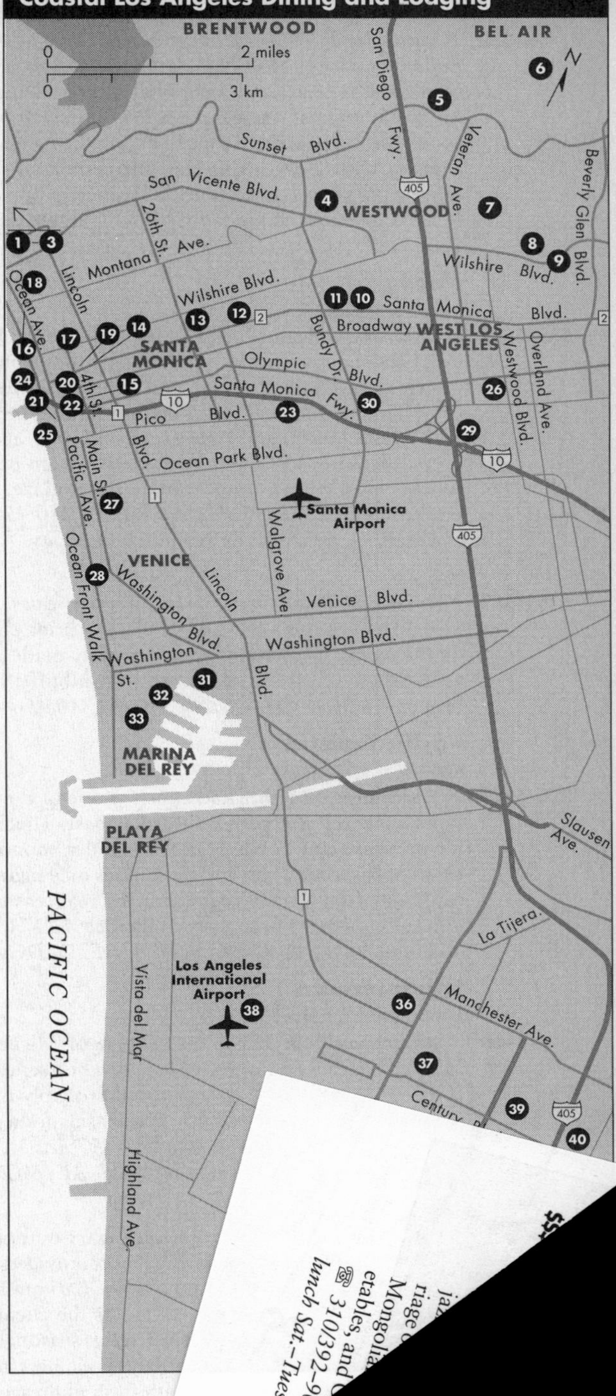

Dining

Bombay Cafe	30
Border Grill	15
Broadway Deli	19
Chinois on Main	27
Drago	13
Encounter	38
Gladstone's 4 Fish	2
Granita	1
Hotel Bel-Air	6
JiRaffe	14
JR Seafood	10
La Serenata Gourmet	26
Lavande	21
Monte Alban	12
Ocean Avenue Seafood	22
Tra di Noi	3
U-Zen	11
Valentino	23
Vincenti	4

Lodging

Barnabey's Hotel	34
Best Western Royal Palace Inn & Suites	29
Cal Mar Hotel	18
Century Wilshire Hotel	8
Fairmont Miramar	17
Furama Hotel Los Angeles	36
Holiday Inn LAX	39
Hotel Bel-Air	6
Hotel California	24
Hotel Carmel	20
Hotel Del Capri	9
Hotel Oceana	16
Loews Santa Monica Beach Hotel	21
Marina Beach Marriott	33
Marina International Hotel and Bungalows	32
Marina Pacific Hotel & Suites	28
Ritz-Carlton, Marina del Rey	31
Shutters on the Beach	25
Summerfield Suites	35
Summit Hotel Bel-Air	5
Westin Los Angeles Airport	40
W Los Angeles	7
Wyndham Hotel at Los Angeles Airport	37

LAX

ECLECTIC

$$–$$$ ✕ **Encounter.** In 1961 one of Los Angeles' first modern icons—the Theme Building with its 135-ft-high parabolic steel arches—opened in the very center of Los Angeles International Airport. With vistas from the ocean to the mountains, it now houses Encounter, whose intergalactic atmosphere includes a crater-shape bar. On the menu are a grilled breast of chicken with Gorgonzola and prosciutto, and horseradish-crusted salmon. Be sure to book ahead if you want one of the window tables. Locals come for the food, not for a flight. ✉ *209 World Way,* ☎ *310/215–5151. AE, MC, V.*

Malibu

CONTEMPORARY

$$$–$$$$ ★ ✕ **Granita.** Wolfgang Puck's famed Granita is a glamourous—some call it garish—fantasy world of handmade tiles embedded with seashells, blown-glass lighting fixtures, and etched-glass panels with wavy edges. Chef Jennifer Naylor's menu favors seafood, including polenta crepes with Maine lobster and bigeye tuna with spicy miso glaze. She has also prepared sautéed foie gras with spiced Asian pears and roasted Cantonese duck with a pomegranate-plum glaze. Brunch is served on weekends. ✉ *23725 W. Malibu Rd.,* ☎ *310/456–0488. Reservations essential. D, DC, MC, V. No lunch weekdays.*

ITALIAN

$$–$$$ ✕ **Tra di Noi.** Regular customers, film celebrities, and non-showbiz folk turn up here, but it's also a great place to bring children. Nothing fancy on the menu, just hearty lasagna, freshly made pasta, mushroom and veal dishes, and fresh salads. An Italian buffet is laid out for Sunday brunch. ✉ *3835 Cross Creek Rd.,* ☎ *310/456–0169. AE, MC, V.*

Pacific Palisades

AMERICAN/CASUAL

$$$–$$$$ ✕ **Gladstone's 4 Fish.** Gladstone's is one of the most popular restaurants along the southern California coast. The food is notable mostly for its size: giant bowls of crab chowder, mounds of steamed clams, heaps of barbecued ribs, and the famous mile-high chocolate cake, which can easily feed a small regiment. The real reason to visit Gladstone's is the glorious vista of sea, sky, and beach. ✉ *17300 Pacific Coast Hwy., at Sunset Blvd.,* ☎ *310/454–3474. AE, D, DC, MC, V.*

Santa Monica

AMERICAN/CASUAL

$–$$ ★ ✕ **Broadway Deli.** This joint venture of Michel Richard and Bruce Marder is a cross between a European brasserie and an upscale diner. Whatever you feel like eating, you'll probably find it on the menu—a platter of assorted smoked fish, Caesar salad, shepherd's pie, or broiled salmon with creamed spinach. ✉ *1457 3rd St. Promenade,* ☎ *310/451–0616. Reservations not accepted. AE, MC, V.*

CONTEMPORARY

$–$$$$ ★ ✕ **Chinois on Main.** A once-revolutionary outpost in Wolfgang Puck's repertoire, this is still one of L.A.'s most crowded restaurants—and one of the noisiest. Puck's wife and partner, Barbara Lazaroff, designed the
zzy interior, which is just as loud as the clientele. The happy mar-
f Asian and French cuisines yields seasonal dishes such as grilled
n lamb chops with cilantro vinaigrette and wok-fried veg-
Cantonese duck with fresh plum sauce. ✉ *2709 Main St.,*
5. Reservations essential. AE, D, DC, MC, V. No

$$$–$$$$ ✕ **Lavande.** Chef Alain Giraud, who was previously at Citrus, conjures up robust Provençal cuisine: crayfish tartlets, classic fish soup Provençal with garlic croutons and rouille, and roasted Chilean sea bass with artichokes. For dessert, the vacherin cheese with lavender ice cream and strawberries is a must. ✉ *Loews Santa Monica Beach Hotel, 1700 Ocean Ave.,* ☎ *310/576–3181. AE, D, DC, MC, V. No dinner Sun.*

$$–$$$ ✕ **JiRaffe.** The menu at this wood-panel restaurant is as tasteful as the decor. Seasonal appetizers, such as goat cheese, leek, and roast tomato ravioli or a roast beet salad with caramelized walnuts and dried bing cherries, are excellent before roast Chilean sea bass with a ragout of sweet corn, spring peas, and pearl onions or roast rack of lamb with eggplant caviar. ✉ *502 Santa Monica Blvd.,* ☎ *310/917–6671. Reservations essential. AE, DC, MC, V. Closed Mon. No lunch weekends.*

ITALIAN

$$–$$$$ ★ ✕ **Valentino.** Rated among the nation's best Italian restaurants, Valentino is also generally considered to have the best wine list outside Western Europe. Try the carpaccio with arugula and shaved Parmesan, spaghetti with garlic and *bottarga* (tuna roe), and lamb shank with saffron risotto. Don't miss the daily specials. ✉ *3115 Pico Blvd.,* ☎ *310/829–4313. Reservations essential. AE, DC, MC, V. Closed Sun. No lunch Sat.–Thurs.*

$$$ ★ ✕ **Drago.** Celestino Drago's home-style fare, though pricey, is carefully prepared and attentively served in stark designer surroundings. Sample pappardelle with pheasant ragout, squid-ink risotto, or ostrich breast with red-cherry sauce. ✉ *2628 Wilshire Blvd.,* ☎ *310/828–1585. AE, DC, MC, V. No lunch weekends.*

MEXICAN

$$ ★ ✕ **Border Grill.** Hipsters love this loud, trendy eating hall designed by minimalist architect Josh Schweitzer and owned by the talented team of Mary Sue Milliken and Susan Feniger. It's perhaps the most eclectic Mexican restaurant in L.A., with a menu ranging from Yucatán grilled-fish tacos to vinegar-and-pepper-grilled turkey to daily seviche specials. ✉ *1445 4th St.,* ☎ *310/451–1655. AE, D, DC, MC, V. No lunch Mon.*

SEAFOOD

$$–$$$$ ✕ **Ocean Avenue Seafood.** This cavernous restaurant isn't right on the water, but the Pacific is just across the street—ask for a table by the window for an ocean view. Popular dishes include cioppino, a fish stew made with Dungeness crab, clams, mussels, and prawns; and Chilean sea bass marinated in a sake *kasu* sauce (a mixture of sake, soy sauce, white wine, and rice wine vinegar). The oyster-bar offers a dizzying selection. ✉ *1401 Ocean Ave.,* ☎ *310/394–5669. AE, DC, MC, V.*

West Los Angeles

CHINESE

$–$$ ✕ **JR Seafood.** Westsiders who once had to drive to Monterey Beach to get a good plate of shrimp in spicy salt have made this place a huge hit. The Hong Kong–style restaurant serves all the Chinese seafood-house standards—seafood soup, rock cod in garlic sauce, kung-pao scallops—that are so plentiful in the San Gabriel Valley but so scarce in these parts. The service can be slow, but as long as the shrimp keeps coming, no one seems to mind. ✉ *11901 Santa Monica Blvd.,* ☎ *310/268–2463. MC, V. Free parking.*

INDIAN

$–$$ ✕ **Bombay Cafe.** It's many devoted fans have followed this popular Indian to its new, smarter location. Regulars swear by the chili-laden lamb frankies (sausages), *sev puri* (little wafers topped with onions, potatoes, and chutneys), and other vibrant small dishes. ✉ *12021 Pico Blvd.,* ☎ *310/473–3388. MC, V. Closed Mon. No lunch weekends.*

ITALIAN

$$$ ★ **Vincenti.** This spot has quickly become one of the Westside's hottest culinary destinations. A big, open kitchen is the heart of this handsome, white-tile restaurant, and revolving on its mammoth rotisserie are the savory meats for which chef Gino Angelini is known. This is authentic Northern Italian cooking as seen through an adept modern sensibility. ✉ *11930 San Vicente Blvd.,* ☎ *310/207–0127. Reservations essential. AE, MC, V. Closed Sun. and Mon. No lunch Sat. or Tues.–Thurs.*

JAPANESE

$–$$ ✕ **U-Zen.** This highly regarded Japanese café serves fresh sushi and sashimi, a good selection of sakes, and pub food such as fried spicy tofu and salmon-skin salad. ✉ *11951 Santa Monica Blvd.,* ☎ *310/477–1390. Reservations not accepted. MC, V. No lunch weekends. Self parking.*

MEXICAN

$–$$ ★ ✕ **La Serenata Gourmet.** Crowding in this handsome Westside branch of the East Los Angeles original can be uncomfortable, but the restaurant scores points for its flavorful Mexican cuisine. Moles and pork dishes are delicious, but seafood is the real star. ✉ *10924 W. Pico Blvd.,* ☎ *310/441–9667. Reservations not accepted. AE, D, MC, V.*

$–$$ ★ ✕ **Monte Alban.** This family-owned café serves the subtle cooking of one of Mexico's most respected culinary regions, Oaxaca. Flavors here are intense without being spicy: try the bright green chile peppers stuffed with chicken, raisins, and ground nuts; any of the superb moles—dense, complex green, red, yellow, or black sauces made from dozens of spices and seeds—with chicken pork or salmon; or extra-tender stewed goat with toasted avocado leaves. ✉ *11927 Santa Monica Blvd.,* ☎ *310/444–7736. DC, MC, V.*

Downtown

AMERICAN/CASUAL

$$–$$$ ✕ **Water Grill.** This somewhat noisy brasserie is always packed with well-dressed attorneys, brokers, and other downtown business folk who are joined in the evenings by theater and concert goers. The oyster bar alone is worth a trip. Avoid the pastas and complicated dishes and stick with fresh seafood. ✉ *544 S. Grand Ave.,* ☎ *213/891–0900. Reservations essential. AE, DC, MC, V. No lunch weekends.*

$ ★ ✕ **Philippe the Original.** This downtown landmark near Union Station and Chinatown has been serving its famous French dip sandwich (four kinds of meat on a freshly baked roll) since 1908. The home cooking includes hearty breakfasts, potato salad, sandwiches, salads, and an enormous pie selection brought in fresh daily from a nearby bakery. The best bargain: a cup of java for only 10¢. ✉ *1001 N. Alameda St.,* ☎ *213/628–3781. Reservations not accepted. No credit cards.*

CHINESE

$–$$$ ✕ **Yang Chow.** This longtime Chinatown favorite is known for its slippery shrimp (crisp, juicy, sweet, hot, and sour all at once), fiery Szechuan dumplings, dried-fried string beans, and panfried dumplings. ✉ *379 N. Broadway,* ☎ *213/625–0811. Reservations essential. AE, MC, V.*

Downtown Los Angeles Dining and Lodging

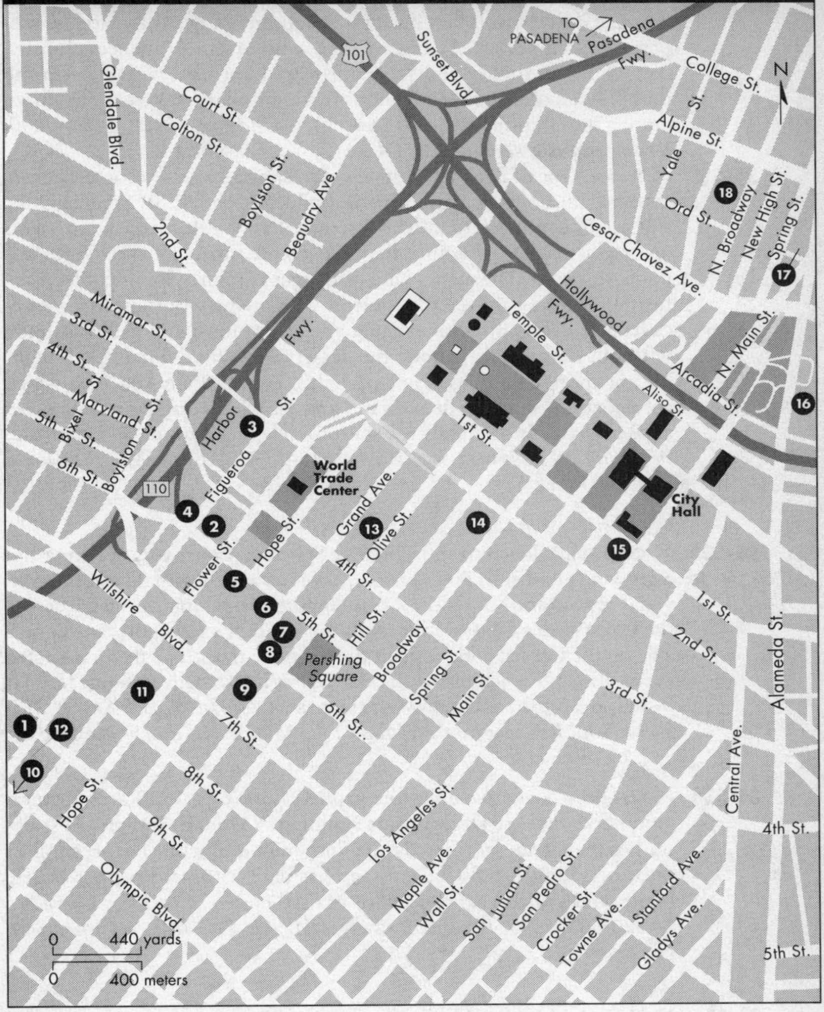

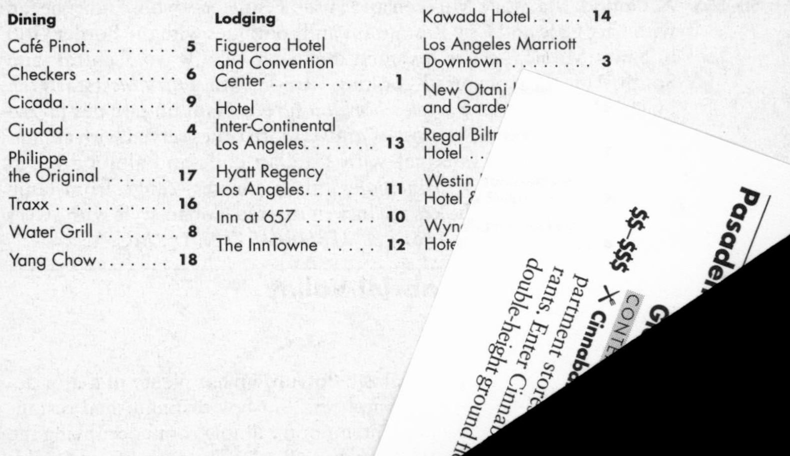

Dining

Café Pinot. 5
Checkers 6
Cicada. 9
Ciudad. 4
Philippe the Original 17
Traxx 16
Water Grill 8
Yang Chow. 18

Lodging

Figueroa Hotel and Convention Center 1
Hotel Inter-Continental Los Angeles. 13
Hyatt Regency Los Angeles. 11
Inn at 657 10
The InnTowne 12
Kawada Hotel. 14
Los Angeles Marriott Downtown 3
New Otani
and Garde
Regal Biltr
Hotel . .
Westin
Hotel &
Wyn
Hote

CONTEMPORARY

$$$–$$$$ ✕ **Checkers.** In the rear of the elegant Wyndham Checkers Hotel, this is one of downtown's best business restaurants. Chef Tony Hodges prepares contemporary American food with Asian influences: lobster, dandelion, and curly endive salad; seared sea bass with rice-shrimp dumpling; and grilled lamb chops in a pumpkin-seed crust have been among the tempting options. ✉ *535 S. Grand Ave.,* ☎ *213/624–0000. Reservations essential. AE, DC, MC, V.*

$$–$$$ ✕ **Traxx.** One of Downtown's newest restaurants serves contemporary cooking in a spectacular historic building—the 1939 Spanish Mission–style Union Station. The Asian-Italian-Californian menu seems just right inside a structure that was created to unite three railroads under one roof. The menu, which changes regularly, has included such fusion dishes as ahi tuna Napoleon with crispy wontons and wasabi caviar; grilled lamb with arugula and red onions; and grilled salmon with olive tapenade. Among the desserts, rosemary bread pudding is an unexpected, but welcome, delight. The well-stocked bar, which specializes in single-malt Scotches and 100% blue agave tequilas, occupies what was originally the station's telephone room. ✉ *Union Station, 800 N. Alameda St.,* ☎ *213/625–1999. AE, D, MC, V. Closed Sun. No lunch Sat.*

FRENCH

$$–$$$ ★ ✕ **Café Pinot.** Joachim and Christine Splichal, proprietors of Patina and a growing number of Pinot bistros, have succeeded with this warm, convivial restaurant housed in a contemporary pavilion in the garden of the Los Angeles Central Library. If the weather's fine, you can eat outside on the terrace under one of the old olive trees. The menu is rooted in traditional French bistro standards, but it also delivers some low-fat dishes, fresh fish, and a few worthy pastas. ✉ *700 W. 5th St.,* ☎ *213/239–6500. Reservations essential. DC, MC, V. No lunch weekends.*

ITALIAN

$$–$$$ ✕ **Cicada.** Cicada occupies the ground floor of a 1928 architectural landmark, the Art Deco Oviatt Building. "Modern Italian" best describes the menu: marinated tuna with mint and white beans; smoked duck ravioli; sautéed Chilean sea bass with a roasted pepper beurre blanc, and grilled veal chop with braised endive. ✉ *617 S. Olive St.,* ☎ *323/655–5559. Reservations essential. AE, DC, MC, V. Closed Sun. No lunch Sat.*

LATIN

$$–$$$ ✕ **Ciudad.** Mary Sue Milliken and Susan Fenniger—whose fame began with City Cafe and City Restaurant and continues with the Border Grill in Santa Monica—have invented their own new wave, Central- and South American–inspired cooking. Among the *entradas* (starters), imagine the tastes of *pasteles boriqua* (green plantain tamales jazzed with pork, olives, and raisins) or *arepas* (corn cakes served with cumin-perfumed merguez sausage) with Catalan chile-and-almond-based romesco sauce. *Platos principales* (main courses) range from lamb shank with baby artichokes to chicken roasted Cuban-style with sweet garlic. ✉ *445 S. Figueroa St.,* ☎ *213/486–5171. AE, MC, V.*

…a, Glendale, San Gabriel Valley

…lendale

…MPORARY

…r. Glendale's revitalized downtown has plenty of major de… and movie complexes, but few distinguished restau… …bar, a hip, contemporary dining room occupying the …floor of an early 1930s Art Deco commercial building. Try the charbroiled ostrich tenderloin, spicy lemongrass bouillabaisse, and roasted halibut with kale and asparagus. ✉ *933 S. Brand Blvd.,* ☎ *818/551–1155. D, DC, MC, V. Closed Mon. No lunch weekends.*

MEXICAN

$–$$ ★ ✕ **La Cabañita.** This is as far from the rice and beans routine as you can get. Savor the thick handmade tortillas wrapped around *picadillo* (ground beef with raisins, almonds, and cinnamon) or on top of a ramekin of roasted mild poblano chilis with sour cream and black beans, then go on to *chuletas* (tender pork) in a delicate pasilla chili sauce. ✉ *3447 N. Verdugo Rd.,* ☎ *818/957–2711. AE, MC, V.*

Pasadena

CHINESE

$$–$$$ ★ ✕ **Yujean Kang's Gourmet Chinese Cuisine.** Forget any and all preconceived notions of what Chinese food should look and taste like. Kang's cuisine is nouvelle-Chinese. Start with tender slices of veal on a bed of enoki mushrooms, topped with a tangle of quick-fried shoestring yams; or sea bass with kumquats and passion-fruit sauce. Finish with poached plums or watermelon ice under a mantle of white chocolate. ✉ *67 N. Raymond Ave.,* ☎ *626/585–0855. AE, D, DC, MC, V.*

CONTEMPORARY

$$$ ✕ **Derek's Bistro.** This casually elegant restaurant brought Pasadena into the '90s with its smart Asian-tinged cuisine. Dinner might start with seared foie gras with caramelized mango followed by osso buco with braised vegetables. The mostly dressy crowd dines inside or on the patio. ✉ *181–185 E. Glenarm St.,* ☎ *626/799–5252. AE, D, MC, V. Closed Sun. and Mon. No lunch Sat.*

$$ ★ ✕ **Shiro.** Hideo Yamashiro made quite a splash when he first began serving sizzling whole catfish with a tangy soy-citrus-ponzu sauce. The dish has shown up on other menus, but Yamashiro's is still the best. For a sweet conclusion, try the warm souffléed lemon pudding. ✉ *1505 Mission St.,* ☎ *626/799–4774. Reservations essential. AE, DC, MC, V. Closed Mon. No lunch.*

ECLECTIC

$$–$$$ ✕ **Parkway Grill.** The setting of this well-respected restaurant is all-American—brick walls, wood floors, a carved-wood bar, lots of greenery, and a khaki-clad wait staff. The always-interesting dishes incorporate all kinds of influences, from Italian to Mexican to Chinese. ✉ *510 S. Arroyo Pkwy.,* ☎ *626/795–1001. Reservations essential. AE, DC, MC, V. No lunch weekends.*

FRENCH

$$$ ✕ **Bistro 45.** As stylish and sophisticated as any Westside hot spot, Bistro 45 blends rustic French cooking—cassoulet, bouillabaisse, caramelized apple tarts—with more modern and fanciful California hybrids, such as seared ahi tuna with black and white sesame crust. ✉ *45 S. Me[illegible] tor Ave.,* ☎ *626/795–2478. Reservations essential. AE, MC, V. Cl[illegible] Mon., except for wine-maker dinner 4th Mon. of month. No lunch [illegible] ends.*

INDIAN

$–$$ ✕ **All India Cafe.** In addition to meat curries and tikkas, th[illegible] vegetarian selections at this authentic Indian restaurant[illegible] as palatable as the meals: a full lunch costs less than [illegible] bination dinners are also a good value. ✉ *39 Fair O[illegible] 440–0309. Reservations recommended on weeker[illegible] parking garage across the street.*

Dining

All India Cafe **7**
Bistro 45 . . . . **9**
Cinnabar . . **10**
Derek's Bistro **8**
La Cabañita . . . **5**
Parkway Grill **3**
Saladang . . . **4**
Shiro **2**
Yujean Kang's Gourmet Chinese Cuisine **6**

Lodging

Ritz-Carlton Huntington Hotel **1**

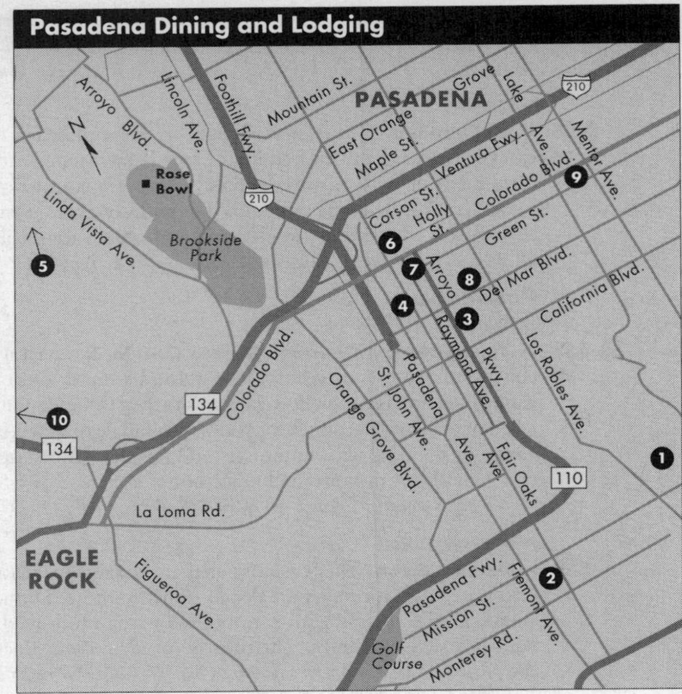

THAI

\$–\$\$ ✕ **Saladang.** Although it's a bit off the beaten track—several blocks south of Old Pasadena—its reasonably priced spinach and duck salad, seafood soup, rice noodles with basil and bean sprouts, and beef *panang* (spicy curry) have ensured Saladang a lively following. ✉ *363 S. Fair Oaks Blvd.,* ☎ *626/793–8123. Reservations essential. AE, DC, MC, V. Free parking in lot.*

San Fernando Valley

Calabasas

AMERICAN

\$\$\$–\$\$\$\$ ★ ✕ **Saddle Peak Lodge.** When you've had enough big-city attitude, head for this paradisical retreat in the Santa Monica Mountains. What was once allegedly a bordello is now a restaurant oozing with Ralph Lauren–style rugged romance and hunting trophies. The food is a perfect match for the upscale lodge setting: updated American classics with an emphasis on game. ✉ *419 Cold Canyon Rd.,* ☎ *818/222–3888. Reservations essential on weekends. AE, MC, V. Closed Mon.–Tues. ...h except Sun. brunch.*

...ood

...ea establishment draws showbiz and non- ... such classics as sautéed fresh rock shrimp ...ce; citrus-marinated chicken wings braised ...ary, and sage; and linguine with scallops and ... *Cahuenga Blvd.,* ☎ *818/985–4669. Reserva- ...ends. AE, DC, MC, V. No lunch Sat.*

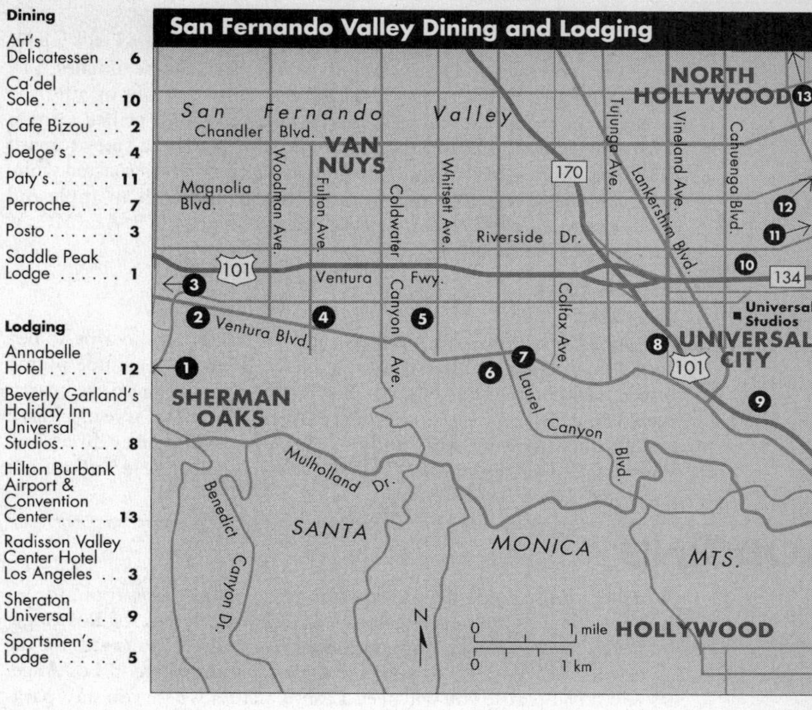

Sherman Oaks

CONTEMPORARY

$$–$$$ ✕ **JoeJoe's.** This is American cooking for the next century. Try grilled shiitakes with smoked mozzarella, seared scallops with apple wood–smoked bacon, and pistachio-crusted halibut. End with the zippy lemon tart. ✉ *13355 Ventura Blvd.,* ☎ *818/990–8280. Reservations essential. AE, MC, V. Closed Mon.*

$$ ★ ✕ **Cafe Bizou.** This is *the* place for fine California-French bistro fare at bargain prices. Entrée sauces are classic, soups are rich, and combinations are creative. If it's on the menu, order the homemade ravioli appetizer, stuffed with lobster and salmon purée. Those who bring their own bottle pay a mere $2 corkage fee. ✉ *14016 Ventura Blvd.,* ☎ *818/788–3536. Reservations essential. AE, MC, V.*

ITALIAN

$$$–$$$$ ✕ **Posto.** Owner Piero Selvaggio—of Santa Monica's Valentino—has brought his modern Italian cuisine to the Valley and made this one of the most prestigious restaurants in the area. Start with fried crab and potato chips or roasted rabbit and beets, then continue with pumpkin risotto with a roasted quail, or chicken and asparagus in marsala sauce. ✉ *14928 Ventura Blvd.,* ☎ *818/784–4400. AE, D, DC, MC, V. Closed Sun. No lunch Sat.*

Studio City

DELI

$ ★ ✕ **Art's Delicatessen.** One of the best Jewish-style delicatessens in the city, this mecca serves mammoth corned beef and pastrami sandwiches. Matzo-ball soup and sweet-and-sour cabbage soup are specialties, and there is good chopped chicken liver. ✉ *12224 Ventura Blvd.,* ☎ *818/762–1221. Reservations not accepted. AE, D, DC, MC, V.*

FRENCH

$$$ ✕ **Perroche.** It's worth going out of your way to eat at this still-young neighborhood favorite. Refreshing two- and three-course lunches, $14 and $17 respectively, can begin with house-smoked trout or a terrine of zucchini, tomatoes, and mozzarella. Entrées include grilled salmon with roasted parsnips and spaghetti with chorizo and a spicy tomato and caper sauce. On the dinner menu you might also find roasted white sea bass with a vegetable ragout or a roasted pork with an apple and shallot sauce. ✉ *1929 Ventura Blvd.,* ☎ *818/766–1179. AE, MC, V. Closed Sun. No lunch Sat.*

Toluca Lake

AMERICAN

$ ✕ **Paty's.** Near NBC, Warner Bros., and the Disney Studio, this homey coffee shop is a reliable, affordable place. Breakfasts include plump omelets and homemade biscuits. For lunch or dinner there are hearty, comforting dishes such as roast turkey and beef stew. If you're in a hurry, call ahead with your order and the restaurant will deliver directly to your car. ✉ *10001 Riverside Dr.,* ☎ *818/761–9126. Reservations not accepted. AE, DC, MC, V.*

LODGING

Whether you're going high-style or budget, select a hotel room for location as well as ambience, amenities, and price. Prices for Los Angeles hotels run the gamut from reasonable to sky high. Tax rates for the area will add 9%–14% to your bill depending on where in Los Angeles you stay. Because you will need a car no matter where you stay, parking is another expense to consider. A few hotels have free parking, but most charge for the privilege. Some resorts have valet parking only.

Hotels listed below are organized according to their location, then by price category.

CATEGORY	COST*
$$$$	over $300
$$$	$210–$300
$$	$120–$210
$	under $120

**All prices are for a standard double room, excluding 14% occupancy tax.*

Downtown

$$$–$$$$ **Regal Biltmore Hotel.** The Spanish–Italian Renaissance building (☞ Exploring, *above*) has rooms you can sink into (flowing draperies, French-style armoires, and overstuffed chairs), making even one night feel like a great escape. Afternoons and evenings, soak up some atmosphere in the beautifully restored Rendezvous Court. ✉ *506 S. Grand Ave., 90071,* ☎ *213/624–1011 or 800/245–8673,* FAX *213/612–1545. 683 rooms, 86 suites. 3 restaurants, 3 bars, 2 cafés, in-room data ports, in-room safes, minibars, no-smoking floors, room service, indoor pool, hot tub, spa, health club, dry cleaning, laundry service, concierge, concierge floor, business services, meeting rooms, car rental, parking (fee). AE, D, DC, MC, V.*

$$$ **Hotel Inter-Continental Los Angeles.** Service here is top-notch. Rooms in the residential-style building are your basic business contemporary, although floor-to-ceiling windows add a dash of excitement. Little extras include separate bath and shower stalls (in most rooms) and TV sound in the bathrooms. ✉ *251 S. Olive St., 90012,* ☎ *213/617–3300*

or 800/442–5251, FAX 213/617–3399. 439 rooms, 18 suites. Restaurant, bar, in-room data ports, minibars, no-smoking floors, room service, pool, exercise room, dry cleaning, laundry service, concierge, concierge floor, business services, meeting rooms, parking (fee). AE, D, DC, MC, V.

$$–$$$ **Los Angeles Marriott Downtown.** The 14-story building near the First Interstate World Trade Center and the Pacific Stock Exchange provides a convenient location for the business traveler. Guest rooms are oversize, with marble baths and wall-to-wall windows with city views. The extensive business center provides secretarial services. A brand new fitness center is located on the second floor. Complimentary limo service is provided within a 5-mi radius. ✉ *333 S. Figueroa St., 90071,* ☎ *213/617–1133 or 800/228–9290, FAX 213/613–0291. 469 rooms. 3 restaurants, 2 bars, in-room data ports, in-room safes, minibars, no-smoking floors, room service, pool, 4 cinemas, piano, dry cleaning, laundry service, concierge, business services, meeting rooms, parking (fee). AE, D, DC, MC, V.*

$$–$$$ ★ **New Otani Hotel and Garden.** "Japanese Experience" rooms at the New Otani have tatami mats and futon beds, extra-deep bathtubs, and shoji screens on windows. You can also have tea and shiatsu massage in the comfort of your own otherwise somewhat plain American-style room. The cuisine in all three of the hotel's restaurants is authentically Japanese, although American fare is also served. ✉ *120 S. Los Angeles St., 90012,* ☎ *213/629–1200, 800/273–2294 in CA, 800/421–8795 elsewhere in the U.S. and Canada, FAX 213/622–0980. 434 rooms, 18 suites. 3 restaurants, 3 bars, in-room safes, minibars, no-smoking rooms, refrigerators, room service, sauna, health club, dry cleaning, laundry service, concierge, business services, meeting rooms, car rental, parking (fee). AE, D, DC, MC, V.*

$$–$$$ **Westin Bonaventure Hotel & Suites.** You can't miss this hotel's image on the downtown L.A. skyline: Its five cylindrical towers are tall (35 stories) and mirrored. Inside is a futuristic lobby with fountains, an indoor lake, and lots of activity. Accommodations, with new furniture and updated decor, are on the small side, but floor-to-ceiling glass windows provide terrific views of the city to the south and east, the mountains to the north, and the ocean to the west. ✉ *404 S. Figueroa St., 90071,* ☎ *213/624–1000 or 800/937–8461, FAX 213/612–4800. 1,354 rooms, 135 suites. 17 restaurants, 5 bars, minibars, no-smoking floors, room service, pool, beauty salon, health club, spa, indoor track, dry cleaning, laundry service, concierge, business services, meeting rooms, travel services, car rental, parking (fee). AE, D, DC, MC, V.*

$$ **Hyatt Regency Los Angeles.** Windows with dramatic city views jazz up the mahogany- and cherry-wood–filled rooms at this hotel near the Music Center. If you're here to work, ask for the Business Plan, available on floors above the 18th—you'll have access to laptop computers and fax machines. ✉ *711 S. Hope St., 90017,* ☎ *213/683–1234 or 800/233–1234, FAX 213/629–3230. 485 rooms, 41 suites. 2 restaurants, 2 bars, in-room data ports, no-smoking floors, room service, exercise room, dry cleaning, laundry service, concierge, concierge floor, business services, meeting rooms, parking (fee). AE, D, DC, MC, V.*

$$ **Inn at 657.** Apartment-size suites at this small bed-and-breakfast–style inn near the University of Southern California have down comforters on the beds, Oriental silks on the walls, and huge dining tables. Homey touches include kitchens with microwave, and private room entrances off the garden. ✉ *657 W. 23rd St., 90007,* ☎ *213/741–2200 or 800/347–7512. 5 suites. In-room data ports, kitchenettes, no-smoking suites, refrigerators, in-room VCRs, hot tub, laundry service, business services, free parking. MC, V. BP.*

$$ ★ **Wyndham Checkers Hotel.** Opened as the Mayflower Hotel in 1927, Checkers has more character than most downtown hotels, with a lobby full of fine antique furniture, and rooms with oversize beds and upholstered easy chairs. Enjoy afternoon tea in the wood-paneled library. The hotel's highly regarded restaurant, Checkers, is one of downtown's best business restaurants. There's complimentary car service mornings within a 2-mi radius, but the financial district is within walking distance. ✉ *535 S. Grand Ave., 90071,* ☎ *213/624–0000 or 800/996–3426,* FAX *213/626–9906. 188 rooms, 9 suites. Restaurant, bar, in-room data ports, minibars, no-smoking floors, room service, pool, hot tub, spa, exercise room, library, dry cleaning, laundry service, concierge, business services, meeting rooms, parking (fee). AE, D, DC, MC, V.*

$ **Figueroa Hotel and Convention Center.** The Spanish feel of this 12-story hotel built in 1926 is accented by terra-cotta–color rooms; hand-painted furniture; wrought-iron beds; and, in many rooms, ceiling fans. The hotel's Music Room serves steak dinners and the Lobby Café is open for breakfast and pasta lunches and dinners. ✉ *939 S. Figueroa St., 90015,* ☎ *213/627–8971 or 800/421–9092,* FAX *213/689–0305. 285 rooms, 2 suites. 2 restaurants, 2 bars, café, in-room data ports, pool, hot tub, coin laundry, dry cleaning, concierge, car rental, free parking. AE, DC, MC, V.*

$ **The Inn Towne.** This modern three-story hotel just 1½ blocks from the convention center has large rooms with beige-and-white or gray-and-white color schemes. Palm trees and a small garden surround the swimming pool. ✉ *913 S. Figueroa St., 90015,* ☎ *213/628–2222 or 800/457–8520,* FAX *213/687–0566. 168 rooms, 2 suites. Bar, coffee shop, pool, coin laundry, dry cleaning, meeting room, car rental, free parking. AE, D, DC, MC, V.*

$ **Kawada Hotel.** This eclectic three-story redbrick hotel near the Music Center and local government buildings has European flair. Immaculate guest rooms are on the small side, but come with two phones and a wet bar. A complimentary shuttle traverses the downtown area. ✉ *200 S. Hill St., 90012,* ☎ *213/621–4455 or 800/752–9232,* FAX *213/687–4455. 115 rooms, 1 suite. Restaurant, bar, deli, in-room VCRs, kitchenettes, no-smoking rooms, refrigerators, room service, coin laundry, dry cleaning, laundry service, concierge, business services, meeting rooms, parking (fee). AE, D, DC, MC, V.*

Beverly Hills, Century City, Hollywood, and West Hollywood

Beverly Hills and Vicinity

$$$$ ★ **Beverly Hills Hotel.** Celebrities favor the bungalows that have all of life's little necessities: wood-burning fireplaces, period furniture, and even (in some cases) grand pianos. Standard rooms are characteristically decadent, with original artwork, butler-service buttons, walk-in closets, and huge marble bathrooms. All rooms are soundproofed and have stereos with CD players and personal fax machines. Some have kitchenettes. Twelve acres of landscaped (and carpeted) walkways make for prime strolling grounds if you can bear to leave your room. The fabled Polo Lounge remains a Hollywood meeting place. ✉ *9641 Sunset Blvd., 90210,* ☎ *310/276–2251 or 800/283–8885,* FAX *310/887–2887. 203 rooms, 21 bungalows. 4 restaurants, bar, in-room data ports, in-room safes, no-smoking rooms, room service, pool, barbershop, beauty salon, hot tub, massage, 2 tennis courts, exercise room, jogging, piano, dry cleaning, laundry service, concierge, parking (fee). AE, DC, MC, V.*

$$$$ ★ **Four Seasons Hotel Los Angeles at Beverly Hills.** With an employee-to-guest ratio greater than one to one, the Four Seasons takes exemplary care of its guests. Extra touches include everything from complimentary cellular phones to limo service every 15 minutes to Rodeo Drive shops. Impeccable guest rooms are eclectic and bright with VCRs, CD players, and bathroom TVs. Suites have French doors and balconies. ✉ *300 S. Doheny Dr., 90048,* ☎ *310/273–2222 or 800/332–3442,* FAX *310/859–3824. 179 rooms, 106 suites. Restaurant, café, bar, in-room data ports, minibars, no-smoking floors, room service, pool, hot tub, exercise room, laundry service and dry cleaning, concierge, business services, meeting rooms, car rental, free parking and parking (fee). AE, DC, MC, V.*

$$$$ **L'Ermitage Beverly Hills.** There's a sophisticated city feel to this Beverly Hills charmer. The smallish hotel just off Rodeo Drive has spacious, uncluttered rooms with lavish baths, silk bedding, walk-in closets, and French doors that open to either the city or the mountains. The rooftop pool has drop-dead views and poolside cabanas. ✉ *9291 Burton Way, 90210,* ☎ *310/278–3344 or 800/800–2113,* FAX *310/278–8247. 111 rooms, 13 suites. 2 restaurants, 2 bars, in-room data ports, minibars, no-smoking floors, room service, pool, massage, steam room, exercise room, dry cleaning, laundry service, concierge, business services, meeting rooms, parking (fee). AE, D, DC, MC, V.*

$$$$ ★ **Peninsula Beverly Hills.** The interior of this grand, French Renaissance–style hotel feels a world removed from the bustle on Little Santa Monica Boulevard. Rooms resemble luxury apartments, with antiques and marble floors. Some suites in the two-story villas have whirlpool tubs, terraces, fireplaces, and CD players. The fifth-floor pool, looking out at the Hollywood Hills, is a gem of a place to relax. Other frivolities include an on-site Bijan store and a courtesy Rolls-Royce for Beverly Hills shopping. ✉ *9882 Little Santa Monica Blvd., 90212,* ☎ *310/551–2888 or 800/462–7899,* FAX *310/788–2319. 196 rooms, 32 suites. 2 restaurants, bar, in-room data ports, in-room safes, in-room VCRs, minibars, no-smoking floors, room service, lap pool, spa, health club, shops, concierge, business services, parking (fee). AE, D, DC, MC, V.*

$$$$ ★ **Regent Beverly Wilshire.** A Four Seasons Hotel since 1993, the Regent offers the franchise's plush accommodations as well as its exemplary service. A refurbishment fluffed up rooms in the older (1928) Wilshire wing of this landmark Italian Renaissance–style hotel, as well as overhauled and upgraded the contemporary accommodations in the hotel's Beverly wing. Throughout the hotel, beds are so comfortable that guests have been known to ask where they can buy the mattresses. Personal services include fresh strawberries and cream and bottled water delivered to your room upon arrival. Guests can enjoy leisure time at the expanded pool area that includes open-air cabanas. ✉ *9500 Wilshire Blvd., 90212,* ☎ *310/275–5200, 800/427–4354 in CA, 800/421–4354 elsewhere in the U.S.,* FAX *310/274–2851. 393 rooms, 118 suites. 2 restaurants, bar, lobby lounge, in-room data ports, in-room safes, minibars, no-smoking floors, room service, pool, beauty salon, spa, health club, piano, dry cleaning, laundry service, concierge, business services, meeting rooms, parking (fee). AE, DC, MC, V.*

$$$–$$$$ **Beverly Hilton.** With an imposing white exterior, and glass- and marble-filled public areas, the Beverly Hilton is owner Merv Griffin's mix of glitz and luxury. Guest rooms are spacious and tasteful. Service here is extra-helpful. The hotel provides complimentary transportation within a 3-mi radius for exploring Beverly Hills and nearby Century City. ✉ *9876 Wilshire Blvd., 90210,* ☎ *310/274–7777 or 800/445–8667,* FAX *310/285–1313. 581 rooms, 42 suites. 2 restaurants, coffee shop, lobby lounge, in-room data ports, minibars, no-smoking floors, refrigerators, room service, pool, massage, exercise room, shops, dry*

cleaning, laundry service, concierge, business services, meeting rooms, travel services, car rental, parking (fee). AE, D, DC, MC, V.

$$$–$$$$ **Le Meridien.** Rooms and suites at this high-tech hotel have fax machines and bedside gizmos that control in-room lighting and temperature as well as the TV, VCR, and CD player. Management thoughtfully tends to even the smallest needs: weary travelers get to sit, rather than stand, through the check-in process, and parking is free. ✉ *465 S. La Cienega Blvd., 90048,* ☎ *310/247–0400 or 800/645–5687,* FAX *310/247–0315. 297 rooms, 10 suites. Restaurant, bar, in-room data ports, in-room VCRs, minibars, no-smoking floors, room service, pool, massage, sauna, exercise room, dry cleaning, laundry service, concierge, business services, meeting rooms, free parking, parking (free). AE, D, DC, MC, V.*

$$–$$$$ **Beverly Hills Plaza Hotel.** Suites have an airy feel, decorated in warm tones of beige, gold, and cream, and each features a convenient kitchen. Accommodations come equipped with bathrobes, hair dryers, in-room movies, and Nintendo; VCRs can be rented. ✉ *10300 Wilshire Blvd., 90024,* ☎ *310/275–5575 or 800/800–1234,* FAX *310/278–3325. 116 suites. Restaurant, bar, in-room safes, kitchenettes, minibars, pool, exercise room, dry cleaning, laundry service, concierge, business services, parking (fee). AE, D, DC, MC, V.*

$$$ **Radisson Beverly Pavilion Hotel.** This eight-floor boutique hotel is in prime shopping territory, within blocks of Rodeo Drive. Guest rooms and executive suites have private balconies. The Radisson's frequent rate specials make it an economical alternative to some of the neighborhood's pricier establishments. ✉ *9360 Wilshire Blvd., 90212,* ☎ *310/273–1400 or 800/441–5050,* FAX *310/859–8551. 100 rooms, 10 suites. Restaurant, bar, in-room data ports, no-smoking floors, room service, pool, dry cleaning, laundry service, concierge, business services, meeting rooms, parking (fee). AE, D, DC, MC, V.*

$$$ **Renaissance Beverly Hills.** This chic, Beverly Hills–adjacent, European-style boutique hotel offers an extremely good value for this excellent location. The lobby, with wood burning fireplace, and adjoining terrace, has a sophisticated, residential air. Spacious guest rooms and suites feature comfortable oversize furniture, writing desks, and private balconies. Six suites are equipped with whirlpool tubs. There is a complimentary sedan service to local business centers and shopping districts. ✉ *1224 S. Beverwil Dr., 90035,* ☎ *310/277–2800 or 800/421–3212,* FAX *310/203–9537. 129 rooms, 8 suites. Restaurant, bar, in-room data ports, pool, exercise room, laundry service, concierge, business service, meeting rooms, parking (fee). AE, D, DC, MC, V.*

$–$$$ **Carlyle Inn.** Wine and cheese on weekday afternoons and in-room extras such as bathrobes and hair dryers make this four-story inn a good choice. In a safe neighborhood close to Restaurant Row, Century City, and Beverly Hills, a complimentary shuttle runs within a 5-mi radius. A sundeck and hot tub are added bonuses. ✉ *1119 S. Robertson Blvd., 90035,* ☎ *310/275–4445 or 800/322–7595,* FAX *310/859–0496. 32 rooms. In-room data ports, in-room VCRs, minibars, no-smoking rooms, hot tub, exercise room, dry cleaning, laundry service, business services, parking (fee). AE, D, DC, MC, V. BP.*

$$ **Avalon.** From the remains of the old Beverly Carlton hotel (once the preferred living quarters of Marilyn Monroe) comes Avalon, a reinvented Beverly Hills boutique hotel mercifully priced for the nonfamous crowd. Rooms at the three-building property are decorated with a bit of '50s retro and some classic pieces from Nelson, Eames, and Thonet; little luxuries such as bathrobes, fax machines, and high-tech CD players are added. The downside may be the lack of a view, as many rooms face the backs of other buildings (although some look out over the pool). ✉ *9400 W. Olympic Blvd., 90212,* ☎ *310/277–5221 or 800/535–4715,*

FAX 310/277–4928. 78 rooms, 10 suites. Restaurant, bar, in-room VCRs, no-smoking rooms, refrigerators, room service, pool, exercise room, coin laundry, dry cleaning, laundry service, concierge, business services, meeting rooms, parking (fee). AE, DC, MC, V.

$$ ★ **Beverly Hills Inn.** The 50-room Inn has gotten raves for supplying Beverly Hills luxury at a more palatable cost than some of the more mammoth hotels. Rooms at this gem surround a courtyard with a pool. Each has a refrigerator, and some have French doors leading to an outdoor sitting area. In addition to complimentary breakfast delivered to your door each morning, cheese and fresh fruit are served every evening, and dried fruits are left instead of mints at nightly turndown. Reserve well in advance. ✉ *125 S. Spalding Dr., 90212,* ☎ *310/278–0303 or 800/463–4466,* FAX *310/278–1728. 46 rooms, 4 suites. Bar, in-room data ports, no-smoking floor, refrigerators, pool, sauna, exercise room, dry cleaning, laundry service, concierge, business services, meeting room, free parking. AE, DC, MC, V. CP.*

$–$$ **Beverly Terrace Hotel.** Rooms are basic (except for the leopard-print bedspreads), and bathrooms have shower stalls, not tubs, but the price is right. On the corner of Santa Monica Boulevard, the hotel is on the fringes of Beverly Hills and West Hollywood, close to the Sunset Strip. Complimentary breakfast is served outside by the pool. Trattoria Amici, the on-site Italian restaurant, is known to attract some of the neighborhood's high-profile clientele. ✉ *469 N. Doheny Dr., 90210,* ☎ *310/274–8141,* FAX *310/385–1998. 39 rooms. Restaurant, pool, free parking. AE, D, DC, MC, V. CP.*

$–$$ **Crescent Hotel.** The small, European-style Crescent Hotel serves a Continental breakfast, afternoon tea, and complimentary snacks and fresh fruit all day long. Standard rooms are on the spartan side, but unexpected touches such as original paintings on the walls and clothes hangers that double as art spice up the mood. Junior suites are a bit expensive considering that the only features that distinguish them from the standard rooms are large-screen TVs and tubs. ✉ *403 N. Crescent Dr., 90210,* ☎ *310/247–0505 or 800/451–1566,* FAX *310/247–9053. 39 rooms, 2 suites. No-smoking rooms, free parking. AE, D, DC, MC, V. CP.*

Century City

$$$$ **Park Hyatt.** Rooms at this elegant luxury hotel are big and comfortable. Nice touches include high tea in the lobby and complimentary limousine service within Century City and Beverly Hills. ✉ *2151 Ave. of the Stars, 90067,* ☎ *310/277–1234 or 800/233–1234,* FAX *310/785–9240. 367 rooms, 189 suites. Restaurant, 2 bars, in-room data ports, minibars, no-smoking rooms, room service, 2 pools, hot tub, massage, sauna, spa, steam room, health club, piano, dry cleaning, laundry service, concierge, business services, meeting rooms, parking (fee). AE, D, DC, MC, V.*

$$ **Century City Courtyard by Marriott.** Near the Century City business complex, this Marriott is well situated and nicely priced. Room amenities include hair dryers, coffeemakers, irons and boards, and Nintendo. A complimentary shuttle zips guests to businesses, shopping, dining, and entertainment options within a 3-mi radius. ✉ *10320 W. Olympic Blvd., 90064,* ☎ *310/556–2777 or 800/321–2211,* FAX *310/203–0563. 134 rooms. Restaurant, bar, in-room data ports, minibars, room service, no-smoking floors, no-smoking rooms, exercise room, dry cleaning, laundry service, concierge, business services, car rental, parking (fee). AE, D, DC, MC, V.*

West Hollywood

$$$$ **Le Parc Hotel.** Suites in this modern low rise have sunken living rooms with fireplaces and private balconies; other little extras include

microwaves, coffeemakers, stereos with CD players, Nintendo, bathrobes, and slippers. The hotel is on a tree-lined residential street close to CBS Television City and the Pacific Design Center. ✉ *733 N.W. Knoll Dr., 90069,* ☎ *310/855–8888 or 800/578–4837,* FAX *310/659–8508. 154 suites. Restaurant, in-room data ports, in-room VCRs, kitchenettes, minibars, no-smoking floors, pool, hot tub, sauna, tennis court, basketball, health club, coin laundry, dry cleaning, laundry service, concierge, business services, meeting rooms, parking (fee). AE, D, DC, MC, V.*

$$$$ ★ **Wyndham Bel Age Hotel.** There's a residential feel to this all-suites hotel near the Sunset Strip. All rooms have private terraces. South-facing rooms look out over the Los Angeles skyline, and on a clear day you can see as far as the Pacific Ocean. The hotel caters to the entertainment industry, so keep an eye out for celebs. ✉ *1020 N. San Vicente Blvd., 90069,* ☎ *310/854–1111 or 800/996–3426,* FAX *310/854–0926. 200 suites. 2 restaurants, bar, in-room data ports, no-smoking floors, room service, pool, beauty salon, exercise room, dry cleaning, laundry service, concierge, meeting rooms, parking (fee). AE, D, DC, MC, V.*

$$$–$$$$ ★ **The Argyle.** You can't miss the gunmetal-gray, pink, and burgundy Art Deco facade. Rooms are also deco; marble bathrooms have black-and-white fixtures. Though small, each accommodation has a separate living room with fax machine, two-line speakerphones, and plenty of plants. ✉ *8358 Sunset Blvd., 90069,* ☎ *323/654–7100 or 800/225–2637,* FAX *323/654–9287. 20 rooms, 44 suites. Restaurant, bar, in-room data ports, in-room safes, in-room VCRs, minibars, no-smoking floors, room service, pool, sauna, exercise room, dry cleaning, laundry service, concierge, business services, meeting rooms, parking (fee). AE, D, DC, MC, V.*

$$$–$$$$ **Le Montrose Suite Hotel.** Don't judge this hotel's clientele by its facade. What once was an apartment complex, now plays host to many Hollywood celebs who value their privacy and anonymity. Once inside, guests are welcomed into a space with finely carved furniture, elaborate floral bouquets and impeccable service. Each suite features a sunken living room, fireplace, platform bed, private balconies and kitchenettes. ✉ *900 Hammond St., 90069,* ☎ *310/855–1115 or 800/776–0666,* FAX *310/657–9192. 132 suites. Restaurant, room service, in-room data ports, pool, tennis court, health club, bicycles, coin laundry, dry cleaning, laundry service, concierge, meeting rooms, parking (fee). AE, D, DC, MC, V.*

$$$–$$$$ **Summerfield Suites Hotel.** Suites here are basic, almost dormlike, but frequent specials make them a good value. Each suite has a private balcony, sleeper sofa (in addition to beds), a gas fireplace, separate vanities, and microwave; most have kitchens as well. The hotel is steps from Santa Monica Boulevard, close to the Sunset Strip and La Cienega Boulevard's Restaurant Row. ✉ *1000 Westmount Dr., 90069,* ☎ *310/657–7400 or 800/833–4353,* FAX *310/854–6744. 109 suites. Breakfast room, in-room data ports, in-room VCRs, no-smoking suites, refrigerators, pool, exercise room, coin laundry, dry cleaning, laundry service, meeting room, parking (fee). AE, D, DC, MC, V. CP.*

$$$ **Hyatt West Hollywood on Sunset Boulevard.** Its proximity to L.A.'s clubs of the moment makes this Hyatt popular with music-industry types. Rooms that face the boulevard have balconies; those facing the hills do not. Some rooms have aquariums, and all have a deco feel. The view from the rooftop pool is extraordinary—you can practically see inside some of the Hollywood Hills dwellings. ✉ *8401 Sunset Blvd., 90069,* ☎ *323/656–1234 or 800/233–1234,* FAX *323/650–7024. 262 rooms, 21 suites. Restaurant, bar, in-room data ports, no-smoking floors,*

room service, pool, dry cleaning, laundry service, business services, meeting rooms, parking (fee). AE, D, DC, MC, V.

$$$ ★ **Mondrian.** Mod apartment-size accommodations at this hip Ian Schrager property have floor-to-ceiling windows, slipcovered sofas, and marble coffee tables; many have kitchens. Suave touches include scented candles, flowers, wool lap blankets, and vintage movie magazines in each room. At 5 PM the lobby lights are dimmed, candles are lit, and a carpet of light creates visual magic. Meander over to the Sky Bar, where patrons (many celebrities) pay exorbitant prices for the right to drink cocktails out of plastic cups by a pool. ✉ *8440 Sunset Blvd., 90069,* ☎ *323/650–8999 or 800/525–8029,* FAX *323/650–5215. 53 rooms, 185 suites. Restaurant, 2 bars, outdoor café, in-room data ports, kitchenettes, no-smoking rooms, refrigerators, room service, pool, massage, sauna, spa, steam room, health club, dry cleaning, laundry service, concierge, business services, meeting rooms, parking (fee). AE, D, DC, MC, V.*

$–$$$ **The Standard.** This smart, new kid on the Sunset Strip looks almost as good as many of its expensive, stylish neighbors. Hotelier Andre Balazs has created an affordable, hip hotel in a chic neighborhood. The unusual, modern decor, which some might consider tacky, includes ultrasuede sectionals, Warhol poppy print curtains and blue AstroTurf poolside. Guest rooms feature silver beanbag chairs, inflatable sofas and surfboard tables. The basics, such as the mattresses on the king-size platform beds, are also excellent. ✉ *8300 Sunset Blvd., 90069,* ☎ *323/650–9090,* FAX *323/650–2820. 138 rooms, 8 suites. Bar, coffee shop, in-room VCRs, minibars, room service, pool, barber shop, dry cleaning, laundry service, concierge, meeting room, parking (fee). AE, D, DC, MC, V.*

Hollywood and Vicinity

$$$–$$$$ ★ **Chateau Marmont Hotel.** The exterior is every bit the French castle the name suggests. Entertainment-industry moguls have been known to love the hotel's opulent suites, cottages, bungalows, and penthouses (notwithstanding John Belushi's ill-fated stay here in the 1980s). The 1920s feel is authentic, if perhaps more dated than antique. Rooms in the cottages have Frank Lloyd Wright-inspired fabrics; the 1956 bungalows are more contemporary. A recent renovation provides air-conditioning in all rooms. An on-call beauty therapist, masseur, private trainers, and airport meet-and-greeters are all at your beck and call. The trendy Bar Marmont, adjacent to the hotel, has its own kitchen and serves food until 1:30 AM—unusual in L.A. ✉ *8221 Sunset Blvd., 90046,* ☎ *323/656–1010 or 800/242–8328,* FAX *323/655–5311. 10 rooms, 53 suites. Restaurant, bar, in-room data ports, in-room safes, in-room VCRs, minibars, no-smoking rooms, room service, pool, massage, exercise room, dry cleaning, laundry service, concierge, business services, parking (fee). AE, DC, MC, V.*

$$ **Clarion Hotel Hollywood Roosevelt.** The hotel was the site of the original Academy Awards. The Hollywood legacy lives on in the little museum on the second floor and in the 40 suites, named for such stars as Shirley Temple. The Hollywood Walk of Fame, Mann's Chinese Theatre, and the Hollywood Entertainment Museum are all within walking distance, but the neighborhood isn't the best. A multimillion dollar entertainment and shopping complex is in progress just across from the hotel which, when completed, will bring the Academy Awards venue back to Hollywood. If you'd rather stay in at night, you can dance to live jazz music at the Cinegrill. ✉ *7000 Hollywood Blvd., 90028,* ☎ *323/466–7000 or 800/950–7667,* FAX *323/462–8056. 320 rooms, 39 suites. Restaurant, bar, lobby lounge, no-smoking floors, room service, pool, hot tub, exercise room, dry clean-*

ing, laundry service, concierge, business services, meeting rooms, parking (fee). AE, D, DC, MC, V.

$$ **Radisson Wilshire Plaza Hotel.** Guests here will find oak desks, upholstered furniture, and floor-to-ceiling windows offering magnificent views of Hollywood or downtown. The hotel has a small exercise room, but guests also have use of a nearby health club. ✉ *3515 Wilshire Blvd., 90010,* ☎ *213/381–7411 or 800/333–3333,* FAX *213/386–7379. 380 rooms, 13 suites. 2 restaurants, bar, café, in-room data ports, minibars, no-smoking floor, room service, pool, barbershop, exercise room, dry cleaning, laundry service, concierge, business services, meeting rooms, parking (fee). AE, D, DC, MC, V.*

$–$$ **Magic Hotel.** This is a great place for college kids and young people on vacation. There's a nice pool, which some rooms overlook. Larger rooms have kitchens with eating areas. The hotel is close to the Hollywood Walk of Fame. ✉ *7025 Franklin Ave., 90028,* ☎ *323/851–0800 or 800/741–4915,* FAX *323/851–4926. 10 rooms, 30 suites. No-smoking rooms, refrigerators, pool, coin laundry, free parking. AE, D, DC, MC, V.*

$ **Highland Gardens Hotel.** Most studios and standard rooms here have kitchens with vinyl chairs and Formica tables. Basic but spacious sleeping areas have either two queen-size beds, or a king bed with a queen-size sleeper sofa. The hotel is just blocks from the Walk of Fame and a few minutes' drive to the Sunset Strip. ✉ *7047 Franklin Ave., 90028,* ☎ *323/850–0536 or 800/404–5472,* FAX *323/850–1712. 70 rooms, 48 suites. Kitchenettes, no-smoking rooms, refrigerators, pool, free parking. AE, MC, V. CP.*

Coastal and Western Los Angeles

Bel-Air

$$$$ ★ **Hotel Bel-Air.** Locals swear by this luxury treasure tucked in a wooded canyon. Bungalow-style country French rooms feel like fine homes with extras such as a stereo with CD player, thick terry bathrobes, and slippers. Six of the suites have private outdoor Jacuzzis; most rooms have wood-burning fireplaces. For the quietest accommodations, ask for a room in either the far north or far south sections. ✉ *701 Stone Canyon Rd., 90077,* ☎ *310/472–1211 or 800/648–4097,* FAX *310/476–5890. 52 rooms, 40 suites. Restaurant, bar, in-room data ports, in-room safes, in-room VCRs, minibars, no-smoking rooms, room service, pool, health club, dry cleaning, laundry service, concierge, business services, meeting rooms, parking (fee). AE, DC, MC, V.*

$$$ **Summit Hotel Bel-Air.** Although the Summit Hotel caters primarily to business travelers, its proximity to the Getty Center has also made it popular with museum visitors. Transportation to the Getty Center can be secured upon demand and will run $5 for the round trip. The low-rise building has sleek, modern guest rooms, with patios and terraces overlooking 8 acres of gardens. ✉ *11461 Sunset Blvd., 90049,* ☎ *310/476–6571 or 800/468–3541,* FAX *310/476–1371. 161 rooms, 8 suites. Restaurant, bar, in-room data ports, minibars, no-smoking floors, room service, pool, massage, spa, tennis court, exercise room, dry cleaning, laundry service, concierge, business services, meeting rooms, parking (fee). AE, D, DC, MC, V.*

LAX

$$$ ★ **Summerfield Suites.** This all-suite hotel is ideal for guests who want to spread out and for families. One- and two-bedroom suites are extra large, with bedrooms as well as sleeper sofas in the living room. Guests can either cook in their kitchens (standard in all suites), or make use of one of the gas grills outside. There are plenty of restaurants within

walking distance. ✉ *810 S. Douglas Ave., El Segundo 90245, ☎ 310/725–0100 or 800/833–4353, FAX 310/725–0900. 122 suites. Breakfast room, in-room data ports, no-smoking rooms, pool, hot tub, basketball, exercise room, coin laundry, dry cleaning, laundry service, business services, meeting rooms, free parking. AE, D, DC, MC, V. CP.*

$$ **Holiday Inn LAX.** This 12-story international-style hotel appeals to families as well as businesspeople. Refrigerators can be rented. ✉ *9901 La Cienega Blvd., Los Angeles 90045, ☎ 310/649–5151 or 800/624–0025, FAX 310/670–3619. 401 rooms, 1 suite. Restaurant, bar, in-room data ports, pool, exercise room, video games, coin laundry, airport shuttle, parking (fee). AE, D, DC, MC, V.*

$$ ★ **Westin Los Angeles Airport.** This is a great place to stay if you want to be pampered but also need to be close to the airport. Rooms and suites are spacious; many suites have private outdoor hot tubs. ✉ *5400 W. Century Blvd., Los Angeles 90045, ☎ 310/216–5858 or 800/937–8461, FAX 310/670–1948. 723 rooms, 42 suites. Restaurant, bar, in-room data ports, minibars, no-smoking floors, refrigerators, pool, hot tub, sauna, exercise room, dry cleaning, laundry service, business services, meeting rooms, airport shuttle, car rental, parking (fee). AE, D, DC, MC, V.*

$$ **Wyndham Hotel at Los Angeles Airport.** You'll get to your plane in a hurry from this hotel that bills itself as the closest to LAX. Guest rooms are on the small side but have plenty of perks, such as fax machines, voice mail, direct-dial phones, and movies. ✉ *6225 W. Century Blvd., Los Angeles 90045, ☎ 310/670–9000 or 800/996–3426, FAX 310/670–8110. 591 rooms, 12 suites. 2 restaurants, bar, in-room data ports, minibars, no-smoking floors, refrigerators, pool, hot tub, sauna, exercise room, dry cleaning, laundry service, concierge, business services, meeting rooms, parking (fee). AE, D, DC, MC, V.*

$ **Furama Hotel Los Angeles.** In a quiet residential area, the Furama is convenient to jogging paths, tennis, and golf. Rooms all have views of either the pool, the airport, or, if you're high enough up in the tower, the ocean. A shuttle service goes to LAX (about a mile away), Marina del Rey, Venice Beach, and the Santa Monica Mall. ✉ *8601 Lincoln Blvd., Los Angeles 90045, ☎ 310/670–8111 or 800/225–8126, FAX 310/337–1883. 760 rooms, 6 suites. Restaurant, bar, no-smoking floors, room service, pool, hot tub, exercise room, dry cleaning, laundry service, concierge, business services, meeting rooms, airport shuttle, parking (fee). AE, D, DC, MC, V.*

Manhattan Beach

$$ ★ **Barnabey's Hotel.** Modeled after a 19th-century English inn, Barnabey's has tidy rooms with lace curtains, antique furniture, flowered wallpaper, and vintage books. Added luxuries such as a heated towel rack in the bathrooms, down comforters on the beds, and video games are all set to make you relax. Doggie and kitty snacks are available for the hotel's four-legged guests. ✉ *3501 Sepulveda Blvd., at Rosecrans Ave., 90266, ☎ 310/545–8466 or 800/552–5285, FAX 310/545–8621. 120 rooms. Restaurant, pub, in-room data ports, no-smoking rooms, pool, hot tub, bicycles, nightclub, dry cleaning, laundry service, business services, meeting rooms, airport shuttle, car rental, parking (fee). AE, D, DC, MC, V. BP.*

Marina del Rey

$$$$ ★ **Ritz-Carlton, Marina del Rey.** This European-style hotel occupies a patch of prime real estate right on the docks of the marina, affording panoramic views of the Pacific. Traditionally styled rooms have French doors, marble baths, and honor bars; there's also twice-daily maid service and 24-hour room service. ✉ *4375 Admiralty Way, 90292, ☎ 310/823–1700 or 800/241–3333, FAX 310/823–2403. 306*

rooms, 12 suites. 2 restaurants, lobby lounge, in-room safes, minibars, no-smoking floors, room service, pool, hot tub, massage, spa, tennis court, basketball, health club, bicycles, dry cleaning, laundry service, concierge, business services, meeting rooms, parking (fee). AE, D, DC, MC, V. 🙈

$$$ ★ 🏨 **Marina Beach Marriott.** This Mediterranean-style, nine-story high-rise has a high-tech design softened by pastel tones and accents of brass and marble. There's a gazebo on the patio, and some rooms have water views—ask for upper-floor rooms that face the marina. ✉ *4100 Admiralty Way, 90292,* ☎ *310/301–3000 or 800/228–9290,* FAX *310/448–4870. 371 rooms, 18 suites. Restaurant, bar, in-room data ports, no-smoking floors, room service, pool, exercise room, dry cleaning, laundry service, concierge, business services, meeting rooms, car rental, parking (fee). AE, D, DC, MC, V.* 🙈

$$ 🏨 **Marina International Hotel & Bungalows.** White shutters on each window and private balconies overlooking the flower-filled courtyard evoke a European village–like feel. Large rooms have contemporary decor and French doors; some rooms have partial views of the water. The split-level bungalows are huge. Across from a sandy beach within the marina, the hotel is a good choice for families with children. ✉ *4200 Admiralty Way, 90292,* ☎ *310/301–2000 or 800/529–2525,* FAX *310/301–6687. 110 rooms, 25 bungalows. Restaurant, bar, in-room data ports, minibars, room service, pool, hot tub, health club, dry cleaning, laundry service, concierge, business services, meeting rooms, airport shuttle, free parking. AE, DC, MC, V.* 🙈

Santa Monica

$$$$ ★ 🏨 **Shutters On The Beach.** You might forget you're only minutes from the city if you stay at Los Angeles's only hotel sitting directly on the sand. Spacious rooms have sliding shutter doors that open onto tiny balconies, and deep whirlpool tubs from which, in some rooms, you can gaze at the ocean. Suites have fireplaces, and all accommodations have beds with luxurious Frette linens. ✉ *1 Pico Blvd., 90405,* ☎ *310/458–0030 or 800/334–9000,* FAX *310/458–4589. 186 rooms, 12 suites. 2 restaurants, bar, lobby lounge, in-room data ports, in-room safes, in-room VCRs, minibars, no-smoking floors, room service, pool, hot tub, sauna, spa, health club, beach, mountain bikes, dry cleaning, laundry service, concierge, business services, meeting rooms, parking (fee). AE, D, DC, MC, V.* 🙈

$$$–$$$$ 🏨 **Fairmont Miramar.** Central for shopping and sunning, the Fairmont nevertheless feels like a secluded island resort. There's a bit of Old Hollywood to this 1889 mansion, particularly in the lavish bungalows stocked with huge whirlpool tubs, stereos with CD, and bathroom speakers. Rooms in the 10-story tower have spectacular ocean views. There are also residential-style rooms in the historic wing. ✉ *101 Wilshire Blvd., 90401,* ☎ *310/576–7777 or 800/325–3535,* FAX *310/458–7912. 213 rooms, 55 suites, 32 bungalows. 2 restaurants, bar, in-room data ports, in-room safes, minibars, no-smoking floors, pool, beauty salon, spa, health club, piano, dry cleaning, laundry service, concierge, business services, meeting rooms, travel services, car rental, parking (fee). AE, D, DC, MC, V.* 🙈

$$$–$$$$ 🏨 **Hotel Oceana.** Thoughtful touches at this all-suite hotel across the street from the ocean include desks large enough for a computer (which the concierge will bring upon request) and refrigerators stocked with goodies such as Wolfgang Puck frozen dinners. For those who prefer the real thing, the hotel provides room service via the nearby Wolfgang Puck Café. Some suites have ocean-view patios. ✉ *849 Ocean Ave., 90403,* ☎ *310/393–0486 or 800/777–0758,* FAX *310/458–1182. 63 suites. Bar, in-room data ports, kitchenettes, no-smoking rooms,*

refrigerators, room service, pool, spa, exercise room, coin laundry, dry cleaning, laundry service, concierge, business services, parking (fee). AE, D, DC, MC, V. CP.

$$$–$$$$ **Loews Santa Monica Beach Hotel.** Proximity to the beach is the selling point of the Loews: the sand's just outside the door. Most of the airy, attractive rooms have spectacular views of the Pacific Ocean; some have balconies. ✉ *1700 Ocean Ave., 90401,* ☎ *310/458–6700 or 800/235–6397,* FAX *310/458–6761. 350 rooms, 24 suites. 2 restaurants, café, bar, in-room data ports, minibars, no-smoking floors, room service, indoor-outdoor pool, beauty salon, hot tub, massage, sauna, spa, steam room, health club, beach, windsurfing, baby-sitting, children's programs (ages 5–12), dry cleaning, laundry service, concierge, business services, meeting rooms, travel services, car rental, parking (fee). AE, D, DC, MC, V.*

$$–$$$ ★ **Hotel California.** This gem of a hotel can easily be missed in its prime location, where several of Santa Monica's biggest and best hotels dwarf it. The intimate Spanish style two-story beachfront inn (with private and gated beach access) surrounds a quiet central courtyard enhanced by lush greenery. Rooms and suites have blond hardwood floors, skylights, hand-carved headboards, and crisp white fabrics; some have ocean views, some VCRs. ✉ *1670 Ocean Ave., 90401,* ☎ *310/393–2363 or 800/537–8483,* FAX *310/393–1063. 18 rooms, 8 suites with kitchens. Refrigerators, no-smoking rooms, free parking. AE, DC, MC, V.*

$–$$ **Cal Mar Hotel.** Situated in a residential section, one block from the Third Street Promenade and within walking distance to the beach, this low profile, two story all suite hotel offers a real bargain. Rates begin at $99 and all units include fully equipped kitchens. Standard and master one bedroom suites feature king or twin beds and a full-size sofa bed. Furnishings are contemporary and comfortable without much thought given to decor, but the atmosphere is friendly and informal, reminiscent of a European pension, and units front an inviting heated swimming pool. ✉ *220 California Ave., 90403,* ☎ *310/395–5555,* FAX *310/451–1111. 36 suites. Kitchenettes, coin laundry, free parking. AE, MC, V.*

$–$$ **Hotel Carmel.** Price and location are the calling cards of this hotel. Basic rooms are spacious, and some have ocean views. You can stroll to the Third Street Promenade or to the beach. Make reservations months ahead. ✉ *201 Broadway, 90401,* ☎ *310/451–2469 or 800/445–8695,* FAX *310/393–4180. 96 rooms, 8 suites. In-room data ports, dry cleaning, laundry service, parking (fee). AE, D, DC, MC, V. CP.*

Venice

$$ **Marina Pacific Hotel & Suites.** The price is right at this hotel that faces the Pacific and one of the world's most vibrant boardwalks. It's nestled among Venice's art galleries, shops, and offbeat restaurants. The marina is nearby, giving guests easy access to ocean swimming and roller skating along the strand. ✉ *1697 Pacific Ave., 90291,* ☎ *310/399–7770 or 800/421–8151,* FAX *310/452–5479. 57 rooms, 35 suites. Restaurant, laundry service, meeting rooms, free parking. AE, D, DC, MC, V.*

Westwood

$$–$$$$ **W Los Angeles.** This hotel combines style (contemporary decor) and substance and offers sophisticated, luxurious surroundings enhanced by the latest in cutting edge technology. The exteriors are as highly cultivated as the interiors: a beautiful garden terrace overlooks a welcoming swimming pool. The hotel is located adjacent to UCLA and Westwood Village. ✉ *930 Hilgard Ave., 90024,* ☎ *310/208–8765 or 800/421–2317,* FAX *310/824–0355. 258 suites. 2 restaurants, bar, café, in-room*

data ports, minibars, no-smoking floors, refrigerators, room service, 2 pools, dry cleaning, laundry service, concierge, business services, meeting rooms, parking (fee). AE, D, DC, MC, V.

$–$$ **Hotel Del Capri.** Despite the modest motel sign, you're just as likely to see Jaguars in the parking lot here as Jettas. Midway between Beverly Hills and Westwood, the small hotel has traditional rooms, many with kitchenettes. Most rooms have whirlpool tubs, and VCRs can be rented for a small fee. Ask about discounts for those in the arts. ✉ *10587 Wilshire Blvd., 90024,* ☎ *310/474–3511 or 800/444–6835,* FAX *310/470–9999. 34 rooms, 45 suites. No-smoking rooms, pool, coin laundry, dry cleaning, laundry service, business services, meeting rooms, free parking. AE, DC, MC, V. CP.*

West Los Angeles

$ **Century Wilshire Hotel.** This homey, English-style hotel, within walking distance of UCLA and Westwood Village, is a favorite among the European crowd. Quaint reminders of the hotel's former life as an apartment building abound. There are milk-delivery traps at the bottom of the room doors, and many of the small, well-kept rooms have kitchens. ✉ *10776 Wilshire Blvd., 90024,* ☎ *310/474–4506 or 800/421–7223,* FAX *310/474–2535. 41 rooms, 58 suites. Breakfast room, no-smoking rooms, pool, baby-sitting, dry cleaning, laundry service, travel services, car rental, free parking. AE, D, DC, MC, V. CP.*

$ **Best Western Royal Palace Inn & Suites.** Low prices and convenient facilities make this Best Western a good deal. Contemporary rooms have microwaves and coffeemakers and Continental breakfast is provided daily. ✉ *2528 S. Sepulveda Blvd. 90064,* ☎ *310/477–9066 or 800/251–3888,* FAX *310/478–4133. 23 rooms, 32 suites. Refrigerators, pool, hot tub, sauna, exercise room, billiards, coin laundry, meeting room, free parking. AE, D, DC, MC, V. CP.*

San Fernando Valley

Burbank

$$ **Anabelle Hotel.** The Anabelle recently reinvented herself right down to the foundation. The hotel offers traditionally furnished rooms and amenities such as bathrobes and room service. Guests find the hotel ultra-friendly. Those doing studio business will like the convenient location: just a straight-shot mile from NBC and 3 mi from Warner Bros. ✉ *2011 W. Olive Ave., 91506,* ☎ *818/845–7800 or 800/782–4373,* FAX *818/845–0054. 47 rooms, 6 suites. Restaurant, lobby lounge, in-room data ports, no-smoking rooms, refrigerators, room service, pool, exercise room, coin laundry, dry cleaning, laundry service, airport shuttle, free parking. AE, DC, MC, V.*

$$ **Hilton Burbank Airport & Convention Center.** Across the street from the Burbank Airport, this contemporary Hilton is geared toward business travelers. Guest rooms have coffeemakers, irons and boards, hair dryers, and in-room movies. Ask for a room with a mountain view. ✉ *2500 Hollywood Way, 91505,* ☎ *818/843–6000 or 800/468–3576,* FAX *818/842–9720. 486 rooms, 77 suites. Restaurant, bar, in-room data ports, no-smoking floors, room service, 2 pools, outdoor hot tub, sauna, exercise room, coin laundry, dry cleaning, laundry service, concierge, convention center, airport shuttle, parking (fee). AE, D, DC, MC, V.*

North Hollywood

$$ **Beverly Garland's Holiday Inn Universal Studios.** There's a country-club atmosphere to this lodgelike hotel in two separate buildings near Universal Studios. Rooms have distressed furniture and muted color schemes. Private balconies and patios overlook the Sierra Madre and Santa Monica mountains. The hotel is next to the Hollywood Free-

way, which can be noisy. Ask for a room facing Vineland Avenue. ✉ *4222 Vineland Ave., 91602, ☎ 818/980–8000 or 800/238–3759, FAX 818/766–5230. 246 rooms, 12 suites. Restaurant, bar, no-smoking rooms, room service, pool, sauna, tennis, dry cleaning, laundry service, meeting rooms, airport shuttle, free parking. AE, D, DC, MC, V.*

Sherman Oaks

$$ **Radisson Valley Center Hotel Los Angeles.** Standard accommodations here are bolstered by the hotel's excellent service. The hotel is conveniently located at the intersection of I–405 and Highway 101, in the Sherman Oaks business district, close to the Fashion Square Mall and excellent restaurants. ✉ *15433 Ventura Blvd., 91403, ☎ 818/981–5400 or 800/333–3333, FAX 818/981–3175. 188 rooms, 12 suites. Restaurant, bar, in-room data ports, no-smoking floors, room service, pool, beauty salon, hot tub, exercise room, dry cleaning, laundry service, concierge, business services, meeting rooms, car rental, parking (fee). AE, D, DC, MC, V. CP.*

Studio City

$$ **Sportsmen's Lodge.** A low-slung, English country–style structure, this hotel is surrounded by waterfalls, a swan-filled lagoon, and a gazebo. The pool area and lush garden make you forget you're near a city. Although service may not be everything you've dreamed of, the accommodations are comfortable and convenient. ✉ *12825 Ventura Blvd., 91604, ☎ 818/769–4700 or 800/821–8511, FAX 213/877–3898. 191 rooms. 3 restaurants, bar, no-smoking floors, room service, pool, barbershop, beauty salon, hot tub, exercise room, coin laundry, dry cleaning, laundry service, travel services, airport shuttle, car rental, free parking. AE, D, DC, MC, V.*

Universal City

$$$ **Sheraton Universal.** With a bit of glitz and lots of comforts, the Sheraton Universal has become a favorite among those visiting Universal Studios. Literally on the back lot of the famed movie studio and theme park, the hotel has warm, stylish rooms with floor-to-ceiling windows from which to gaze at some remarkable Hollywood views. Complimentary transportation takes you to Universal Studios, but you could just as easily walk. ✉ *333 Universal Terrace Pkwy., 91608, ☎ 818/980–1212 or 800/325–3535, FAX 818/509–4980. 442 rooms, 25 suites. 2 restaurants, bar, in-room data ports, in-room safes, minibars, no-smoking floors, room service, pool, hot tub, exercise room, laundry service and dry cleaning, concierge, business services, meeting rooms, car rental, parking (fee). AE, D, DC, MC, V.*

San Gabriel Valley

Pasadena

$$$ ★ **Ritz-Carlton Huntington Hotel.** The main building of this 1906 landmark hotel is a Mediterranean-style structure that blends in seamlessly with the lavish houses of the surrounding San Marino neighborhood. Past the intimate lobby and the central courtyard, a wood-paneled grand lounge has a sweeping view of Los Angeles in the distance. Traditionally styled guest rooms are handsome, if a bit small for the high price. The formal Grill features excellent renditions of classic and contemporary grill cuisine. ✉ *1401 S. Oak Knoll Ave., 91106, ☎ 626/568–3900 or 800/241–3333, FAX 626/585–1842. 387 rooms, 31 suites. 2 restaurants, bar, in-room data ports, in-room safes, in-room VCRs, minibars, room service, pool, beauty salon, hot tub, mineral baths, spa, tennis court, health club, baby-sitting, dry cleaning, laundry service, concierge, business services, meeting rooms, travel services, car rental, parking (fee). AE, D, DC, MC, V.*

NIGHTLIFE AND THE ARTS

Revised and updated by Kate Sullivan and Anne E. Wells

Most bars, clubs, and bistros in this fast-paced city have a shelf life shorter than the miniskirts on Melrose. Hollywood, the locus of L.A. nightlife, is without question the place to start your search. You can't help but stumble into a happening joint if you cruise the streets long enough. L.A. is one of the best cities in the country in which to catch soon-to-be-famous rock bands or check out jazz, blues, and classical acts. Culture vultures will find plenty going on in this hustling, bustling city, from ballet to film to theater.

For the most complete listing of weekly events, consult the current issue of *Los Angeles* magazine. The Calendar section of the *Los Angeles Times* also lists a wide survey of arts events, as do the more alternative publications, the *L.A. Weekly* and the *New Times Los Angeles* (both free). Most tickets can be purchased by phone (with a credit card) from **Ticketmaster** (☎ 213/365–3500), **TeleCharge** (☎ 800/762–7666), **Good Time Tickets** (☎ 323/464–7383), **Tickets L.A.** (☎ 323/660–8587), or **Murray's Tickets** (☎ 323/234–0123).

The Arts

Concerts

MAJOR CONCERT HALLS

Part of the Performing Arts Center of Los Angeles County (formerly the Music Center) and—with the Hollywood Bowl—the center of L.A.'s classical music scene, the 3,200-seat **Dorothy Chandler Pavilion** (✉ 135 N. Grand Ave., ☎ 213/972–7211) is the home of the Los Angeles Philharmonic and the Los Angeles Master Chorale. The L.A. Opera presents classics from September through June.

In Griffith Park, the open-air auditorium known as the **Greek Theater** (✉ 2700 N. Vermont Ave., ☎ 323/665–1927), presents big-name performers in its mainly pop-rock-jazz schedule from June through October.

Ever since it opened in 1920 in a park surrounded by mountains, trees, and gardens, the **Hollywood Bowl** (✉ 2301 Highland Ave., ☎ 323/850–2000 or 323/851–3588) has been one of the world's largest and most atmospheric outdoor amphitheaters. Its season runs from early July through mid-September. The L.A. Philharmonic spends its summer season here. There are performances daily except Monday (and some Sundays); the program ranges from jazz to pop to classical. Concert goers usually arrive early, bringing or buying picnic suppers. There are plenty of picnic tables, and box-seat subscribers can reserve a table right in their own box. Restaurant dining is available on the grounds (☎ 323/850–2000 or 323/851–3588); reserve ahead. Be sure to bring a sweater—it gets chilly here in the evening. You might also bring or rent a cushion, as the seats are made of wood. A convenient way to enjoy the Hollywood Bowl experience without the hassle of parking is to take one of the Park-and-Ride buses, which leave from various locations around town; call the Bowl for information.

The one-of-a-kind 6,300-seat ersatz Arabic **Shrine Auditorium** (✉ 665 W. Jefferson Blvd., ☎ 213/749–5123) hosts touring companies from all over the world, assorted gospel and choral groups and other musical acts, as well as high-profile televised awards shows such as the Academy Awards, the American Music Awards, and the Grammys. Adjacent to Universal Studios, the 6,250 seat **Universal Amphitheater,** ✉ 100 Universal City Plaza, ☎ 818/622–4440, hosts over 100 performances a year, including the Radio City Christmas Spectacular, star-studded benefit concerts, and the full range of rock and pop performers. The **Wiltern Theater** (✉ 3790 Wilshire Blvd., ☎ 213/380–5005 or 213/388–1400), a green terra-cotta, Art Deco masterpiece, schedules pop, rock, jazz, and dance performances.

Dance

High-caliber companies dance at various performance spaces around town. Check the *L.A. Weekly* free newspaper under "Dance" to see who is dancing where. **Bella Lewitsky Dance Co.** (☎ 213/580–6338), one of L.A.'s major resident companies, schedules modern dance performances at various locations.

Film

ART HOUSES

The 14-screen **Loews Cineplex** (✉ Beverly Center, 8522 Beverly Blvd., 8th floor, West Hollywood, ☎ 310/652–7760) shows foreign films as well as first-run features. **Laemmle Theater** (see newspaper ads for listings) chain hosts the best of the latest foreign releases at its theaters in Beverly Hills, West Hollywood, Santa Monica, West Los Angeles, and Encino. The Encino location is the only art house in the San Fernando Valley. The multiscreen **Los Feliz Theater** (✉ 1822 N. Vermont Ave., Los Feliz, ☎ 323/664–2169) features hip, indie flicks of the moment. **Melnitz Hall** (✉ 405 Hilgard Ave., Westwood, ☎ 310/825–2345) is UCLA's main film theater; here you'll find the old, the avant-garde, and the neglected. Film festivals, Hollywood classics, documentaries, and notable foreign films are the fare at the **New Beverly Cinema** (✉ 7165 Beverly Blvd., ☎ 323/938–4038). **Nuart** (✉ 11272 Santa Monica Blvd., West L.A., ☎ 310/478–6379) is the best-kept of L.A.'s revival houses. The **American Cinematèque Independent Film Series** (✉ 6712 Hollywood Blvd., Hollywood, ☎ 323/466–3456) screens rare vintage and current independent films in its outlandish Egyptian Theater. New films by independent filmmakers and foreign films are the usual fare at the **Royal Theatre** (✉ 11523 Santa Monica Blvd., Santa Monica, ☎ 310/478–1041).

MOVIE PALACES

Mann's Chinese Theater (✉ 6925 Hollywood Blvd., Hollywood, ☎ 323/464–8111) is perhaps the world's best-known theater, with gala premieres and three movie screens. Across the street from Mann's Chinese Theater is the recently restored **Pacific's El Capitan** (✉ 6838 Hollywood Blvd., Hollywood, ☎ 323/467–7674), another classic Art Deco masterpiece. First-run movies are on the bill, and the theater often features live stage shows in conjunction with Disney animation debuts. At the intersection of Hollywood and Sunset boulevards, the 70-year-old **Vista Theater** (✉ 4473 Sunset Dr., Los Feliz, ☎ 323/660–6639) was once Bard's Hollywood Theater, where both moving pictures and vaudeville played.

Television

Audiences Unlimited (✉ 100 Universal City Plaza, Bldg. 153, Universal City, 91608, ☎ 818/506–0043) helps fill seats for television programs (and sometimes theater events). There's no charge, but tickets are distributed on a first-come, first-served basis. Shows that may be taping or filming include *Will and Grace, Everybody Loves Raymond, Third Rock from the Sun,* and *The Drew Carey Show.* Tickets can be picked up at Fox Television Center (✉ 5746 Sunset Blvd., Van Ness Ave. entrance), open weekdays from 8:30 to 6. You must be 16 or older to attend a taping. For a schedule, send a self-addressed, stamped envelope to Audiences Unlimited a few weeks prior to your visit.

Theater

MAJOR THEATERS

Geffen Playhouse (✉ 10886 Le Conte Ave., Westwood, ☎ 310/208–6500 or 310/208–5454), an acoustically superior, 498-seat theater showcases new plays in the summer—primarily musicals and comedies. The city of Los Angeles bought the 1,021-seat **James A. Doolittle Theatre** (✉ 1615 N. Vine St., Hollywood, ☎ 323/462–6666) in December, 1999, with plans to lease it to the Ricardo Montalban–Nosotros Foundation for conversion into a Latino-oriented entertainment center. In addition to theater performances, lectures, and children's programs, free summer concerts and performances take place at the **John Anson Ford Amphitheater** (✉ 2580 Cahuenga Blvd. E, Hollywood, ☎ 323/461–3673), an outdoor venue in the Hollywood Hills.

There are three theaters in the big downtown complex known as **Performing Arts Center of Los Angeles County** (✉ 135 N. Grand Ave., ☎ 213/972–7211). The 2,140-seat **Ahmanson Theatre** (☎ 213/628–2772), presents both classics and new plays. The 3,200-seat **Dorothy Chandler Pavilion** (☞ *above*) shows a smattering of plays in between performances of the L.A. Philharmonic, L.A. Master Chorale, and L.A. Opera. The 760-seat **Mark Taper Forum** (☎ 213/972–7211), under the direction of Gordon Davidson, presents new works that often go on to Broadway, such as *Angels in America* and *Master Class*.

Pantages (✉ 6233 Hollywood Blvd., Hollywood, ☎ 323/468–1700) is a splendid example of high-style Hollywood Art Deco, offering large-scale Broadway musicals such as *Phantom of the Opera*. The **Shubert Theater** (✉ 2020 Ave. of the Stars, Century City, ☎ 310/201–1500) hosts major theatrical productions such as *Rent* and *Ragtime*. The 1,900-seat, Art Deco **Wilshire Theater** (✉ 8440 Wilshire Blvd., Beverly Hills, ☎ 323/468–1716 or 323/468–1799) presents Broadway musicals and occasional concerts.

SMALLER THEATERS

The founders of **Actor's Gang Theater** (✉ 6209 Santa Monica Blvd., Hollywood, ☎ 323/465–0566) include film star Tim Robbins. Located in the heart of Beverly Hills, **Canon Theater** (✉ 205 Canon Dr., Beverly Hills, ☎ 310/859–2830), presents original plays, often featuring favorite stars from television and movies. Musicals, revivals, and avant-garde improv pieces are performed at the **Cast Theater** (✉ 804 N. El Centro, Hollywood, ☎ 323/462–0265). Excellent original musicals and new dramas are the specialties at the **Coast Playhouse** (✉ 8325 Santa Monica Blvd., West Hollywood, ☎ 323/650–8507).

East West Players (✉ 120 Judge John Aliso St., Little Tokyo, ☎ 213/625–7000) is a well-respected small theater company dedicated to the Asian-American voice. The **Fountain Theater** (✉ 5060 Fountain Ave., Hollywood, ☎ 323/663–1525) is a venue for original American dramas and flamenco dance concerts. Not far from the famous corner of Hollywood and Vine, the **Henry Ford Theater** (✉ 6126 Hollywood Blvd., Hollywood, ☎ 310/859–2830), specializes in new dramatic productions. With seating for 110, **Highways Performance Space** (✉ 1651 18th St., Santa Monica, ☎ 310/453–1755), is one of the primary venues for avant-garde, off-beat, and alternative performance art, theater, dance, and comedy programs. The community-oriented **Japan America Theater** (✉ 244 S. San Pedro St., Downtown, ☎ 213/680–3700) hosts local theater groups, dance troupes, and the L.A. Chamber Orchestra, plus numerous children's theater groups.

The **Morgan-Wixon Theatre** (✉ 2627 Pico Blvd., Santa Monica, ☎ 310/828–7519) presents varied children's fare. The **Santa Monica**

Playhouse (✉ 1211 4th St., Santa Monica, ☎ 310/394–9779) is worth visiting for its cozy atmosphere, as well as its high-quality comedies, dramas, and children's programs. Many highly inventive productions have been hosted in the 99-seat **Skylight Theater** (✉ 1816½ N. Vermont Ave., Los Feliz, ☎ 323/666–2202). Angelenos crowd into the **Theatre/Theater** (✉ 1715 Cahuenga Blvd., Hollywood, ☎ 323/871–0210) to view original works by local authors and international playwrights.

Nightlife

Despite the high energy level of the L.A. nightlife crowd, don't expect to be partying until dawn—this is still an early-to-bed city. Liquor laws require that bars stop serving alcohol at 2 AM. By this time, with the exception of a few after-hours venues and coffeehouses, most clubs have closed for the night. Due to the new smoking ban, most bars and clubs with a cover charge now allow "in and outs," in which patrons may leave the premises and return (usually with a hand stamp or paper bracelet).

Nighttime diversions on the Sunset Strip run the gamut from comedy clubs and hard-rock spots to cocktail lounges and restaurants with piano bars. There's a good mix of nightlife in the Mid-Wilshire area, which encompasses the area west of the Harbor Freeway (I–110), east of La Cienega Boulevard, south of Beverly Boulevard, and north of the Santa Monica (I–10) Freeway. Local beer bars abound in Westwood. Downtown Los Angeles has a small contingent of artsy performance spaces and galleries, and a handful of clubs and movie palaces. Some of Los Angeles's best jazz clubs, discos, and comedy clubs are scattered throughout the San Fernando and San Gabriel valleys. In West Hollywood, Santa Monica Boulevard is the heart of the gay-and-lesbian club and coffeehouse scene.

Bars

BEL-AIR AND BEVERLY HILLS

There's serene musical entertainment every night (either a pianist or a vocalist) at the romantically secluded **Hotel Bel-Air** (✉ 701 Stone Canyon Rd., Bel-Air, ☎ 310/472–1211). A quaint bar with an immense wine selection, **La Scala** (✉ 410 N. Canon Dr., Beverly Hills, ☎ 310/275–0579) fills with celebrities nightly. Behind the oak bar and brass rail at **R. J.'s** (✉ 252 N. Beverly Dr., Beverly Hills, ☎ 310/274–3474 or 310/274–7427) are 800 bottles stacked to the ceiling. Plush sofas, high tables and live piano music set the atmosphere at the elegant Lobby Lounge of the **Regent Beverly Wilshire** (✉ 9500 Wilshire Blvd., Beverly Hills, ☎ 310/275–5200).

CENTURY CITY

Harper's Bar and Grill (✉ 2040 Ave. of the Stars, ☎ 310/553–1855) is a central place to meet friends for cocktails before a show at the Shubert Theater.

DOWNTOWN

Downtown's loft-dwelling elite frequent **Boyd Street** (✉ 410 Boyd St., ☎ 213/617–2491), a downtown bar-restaurant with a streamlined '80s motif. In the Biltmore Hotel, the sleek **Grand Avenue Sports Bar** (✉ 506 S. Grand Ave., ☎ 213/612–1532) serves pricey drinks late into the night. Atop the 32-story Transamerica Building, **Windows, Steaks, and Martinis** (✉ 1150 S. Olive St., ☎ 213/746–1554) is an elegant cocktail bar and restaurant with an unbeatable view.

HOLLYWOOD

For a pick-me-up margarita (but not food), stop by the kitschy landmark **El Coyote** (✉ 7312 Beverly Blvd., ☎ 323/939–7766). The old Hollywood restaurant and watering hole **Formosa Cafe** (✉ 7156 Santa Monica Blvd., West Hollywood, ☎ 323/850–9050) was featured in *L.A. Confidential;* it's long been a favorite of both hipsters and old-timers.

Film-studio moguls and movie extras flock to **Musso and Frank Grill** (✉ 6667 Hollywood Blvd., ☎ 323/467–5123). Meet at **Yamashiro's** (✉ 1999 N. Sycamore Ave., ☎ 323/466–5125) for cocktails at sunset on the terrace.

LOS FELIZ AND SILVER LAKE

An unassuming '40s-style bar, **Dresden Room** (✉ 1760 N. Vermont Ave., Los Feliz, ☎ 323/665–4294) was rediscovered during the mid-'90s lounge craze and immortalized in the film *Swingers*. The tastefully rendered Chinese motif and dim lighting make the trendy **Good Luck Bar** (✉ 1514 Hillhurst Ave., Los Feliz, ☎ 323/666–3524) an ideal spot for a romantic cocktail. **Tiki Ti** (✉ 4427 W. Sunset Blvd., Silver Lake, ☎ 323/669–9381) serves some of the city's best tropical rum drinks in an intimately cozy simulated Tahitian hut.

MARINA DEL REY

Ex-cinematographer Burt Hixon collected tropical-drink recipes on his South Seas forays. Here, at **The Warehouse** (✉ 4499 Admiralty Way, ☎ 310/823–5451), he whips up a sinfully rich mai tai.

MID-WILSHIRE AREA

Both après-work business types and Gen-Xers frequent **HMS Bounty** (✉ 3357 Wilshire Blvd., ☎ 213/385–7275), an elegant old watering hole in the historic Gaylord apartment building. One of L.A.'s most frequented Irish pubs, **Tom Bergin's** (✉ 840 S. Fairfax Ave., ☎ 323/936–7151) is plastered with Day-Glo shamrocks bearing the names of the masses of regular patrons who have passed through its door.

PASADENA

Beckham Place (✉ 77 W. Walnut St., ☎ 626/796–3399), a fancy "Olde English" pub, is known for its huge drinks and free roast-beef sandwiches at Happy Hour. With two pool tables, a nautical motif, and very reasonable prices, **The Colorado Bar** (✉ 2640 E. Colorado Blvd., ☎ 626/449–3485) is a divey refuge for art students, Gen-Xers, and aging barflies. In Pasadena's Old Town, **Market City Cafe** (✉ 33 S. Fair Oaks Ave., ☎ 626/568–0203) draws a crowd at lunchtime and in the early evening. A young collegiate crowd frequents **Q's** (✉ 99 E. Colorado Blvd., ☎ 626/405–9777), an Old Town haunt featuring three bars, 20 pool tables, and a restaurant. With brass fixtures, an oversize fireplace, and a marble-top bar, the **Ritz-Carlton Huntington Hotel** (✉ 1401 S. Oak Knoll Ave., ☎ 626/568–3900) is a genteel setting for nighttime drinks.

SAN FERNANDO VALLEY

Residuals (✉ 11042 Ventura Blvd., Studio City, ☎ 818/761–8301) is a *Cheers*-style bar attracting industry types—writers, makeup artists, actors, and the like—for easygoing shop talk. The lounge at **Sportsmen's Lodge** (✉ 12833 Ventura Blvd., Sherman Oaks, ☎ 818/984–0202) has a tranquil setting with brooks and swan-filled ponds. **Sagebrush Cantina** (✉ 23527 Calabasas Rd., Calabasas, ☎ 818/222–6062), an indoor-outdoor saloon next to a Mexican restaurant, is the Valley's version of the Via Veneto café scene. Motorcycle hippies mix comfortably with computer moguls and showbiz folk, including a platoon of stunt people.

SANTA MONICA

Chez Jay (✉ 1657 Ocean Ave., ☎ 310/395–1741) is a charmingly "shabby-chic" setting for inventive seafood fare and regular celebrity sightings. **Gotham Hall** (✉ 1431 3rd St. Promenade, ☎ 310/394–8865) is designed like something off the set of *Batman*. From motorcycles to carriages, something old has been glued or nailed to every square inch of **Oar House** (✉ 2941 Main St., ☎ 310/396–4725). **The Room S.M.** (✉ 1323 Santa Monica Blvd., ☎ 310/458–0707), is a dark and friendly everyman's hangout with stiff drinks and relaxing sounds ranging from Aretha Franklin to Frank Sinatra.

VENICE

Abstract art decorates the walls of **Hal's Bar & Grill** (✉ 1349 Abbott Kinney Blvd., ☎ 310/396–3105), a regular haunt of local well-to-do professionals.

WEST HOLLYWOOD

A mahogany bar and art nouveau mirrors make **Barefoot** (✉ 8722 W. 3rd St., ☎ 310/276–6223) a swanky place to drink expertly mixed martinis. At the hetero hangout in an ultragay neighborhood **J. Sloane's** (✉ 8623 Melrose Ave., ☎ 310/659–0250) fun includes Wednesday night turtle-racing, games on eight TVs, and live music on weekends. The circular bar at **Le Dôme** (✉ 8720 W. Sunset Blvd., ☎ 310/659–6919) draws the likes of Rod Stewart and Richard Gere. Patrons (many celebrities) must either have a Mondrian room key, screen credit, or a model's body to enter **Skybar** (✉ 8440 Sunset Blvd., ☎ 323/650–8999), the poolside bar at the Hotel Mondrian. The **Whiskey Bar** at the Sunset Marquis (✉ 1200 N. Alta Loma Rd., ☎ 310/657–1333) is a convenient watering hole for many visiting celebs.

WESTSIDE

There's a good assortment of Mexican beers at **Acapulco** (✉ 1109 Glendon Ave., Westwood, ☎ 310/208–3884), a convivial Mexican restaurant and bar that's big with the college crowd. The Westside's contribution to the Cocktail Nation, **Liquid Kitty** (✉ 11780 W. Pico Blvd., West L.A., ☎ 310/473–3707) sports hip clientele, DJs (with live jazz Sunday night), and no cover.

Cabaret, Performance, and Variety

The Cinegrill (✉ Clarion Hollywood Roosevelt Hotel, 7000 Hollywood Blvd., Hollywood, ☎ 323/466–7000) is well worth a visit, not only to hear top-tier jazz performers, but also to admire all the Hollywood artifacts lining the lobby of the landmark hotel. **Glaxa Studios** (✉ 3707 Sunset Blvd., Silver Lake, ☎ 323/663–5295) is a bohemian café-arts venue presenting music, poetry, and performance with an emphasis on the literate, the avant-garde, and the offbeat. Hours and cover (for shows only) vary. Westside Bohemians come to **Highways** (✉ 1651 18th St., Santa Monica, ☎ 310/453–1755) to hear and see avant-garde spoken-word and performance artists. Reservations are recommended. Musician/producer Jon Brion (Fiona Apple, Rufus Wainwright, et al.) hosts a popular evening of disc-and-tale-spinning Friday at **Largo** (✉ 432 N. Fairfax Ave., Hollywood, ☎ 323/852–1073). Other nights cabaret and singer-songwriter fare is on offer at this cozy supper club/bar. Bar stools are open but reservations are required for tables. Drag queens strut their stuff at **Luna Park** (✉ 665 Robertson Blvd., West Hollywood, ☎ 310/652–0611), an eclectic venue serving fine American cuisine and showcasing an international mix of music. At **Queen Mary** (✉ 12449 Ventura Blvd., Studio City, ☎ 818/506–5619), female impersonators vamp it up as Diana Ross and Barbra Streisand Friday–Sunday. The **Silent Movie Theatre** (✉ 611 N. Fairfax Ave., Hollywood, ☎ 323/655–2520), puts on varied shows around silent-movie double features.

Coffeehouses

Amid the murals and neon of Downtown's artsy loft district, **Bloom's General Store** (✉ 714 3rd St., Downtown, ☎ 213/687–6571) sells cigars, candy, and videos, and is also connected to a soul-food restaurant and art gallery.

Half tiki, half sci-fi, with hand-painted tabletops, tiny **Cacao** (✉ 11609 Santa Monica Blvd., West L.A., ☎ 310/473–7283) is an aesthetic gem. Valley poets, artists, and hipsters hang out at **Eagle's** (✉ 5231 Lankershim Blvd., North Hollywood, ☎ 818/760–4212), a laid-back café with occasional live music and spoken-word readings. **Highland Grounds** (✉ 742 Highland Ave., Hollywood, ☎ 323/466–1507) is one of L.A.'s oldest coffeehouses and features tasty breakfast, lunch, and dinner, nightly live entertainment, and one of the best cups of coffee in the city.

Comedy

Los Angeles's premier comedy showcase, **Comedy Store** (✉ 8433 Sunset Blvd., West Hollywood, ☎ 323/656–6225) has been going strong for more than a decade. **Groundlings Theatre** (✉ 7307 Melrose Ave., Hollywood, ☎ 323/934–9700) is considered a breeding ground for *Saturday Night Live* performers, with original skits, music, and improv.

Dance Clubs

A dressed-to-impress crowd frequents **The Century Club** (✉ 10131 Constellation Blvd., Century City, ☎ 310/553–6000), where dance grooves range from Latin to hip hop to electronic. The **Coconut Club** (✉ 9876 Wilshire Blvd., Beverly Hills, ☎ 310/285–1358) has big-band music, DJs, and a classic supper-club menu. The club takes over the Grand Ballroom of the Beverly Hilton Hotel on Friday and Saturday nights. If you're nostalgic for the 1960s, stop by the tourist-friendly **Crush Bar** (✉ 1743 Cahuenga Ave., Hollywood, ☎ 323/461–9017), open Friday through Sunday.

Garden of Eden (✉ 7080 Hollywood Blvd., Hollywood, ☎ 323/465–3336) is an exotically decorated space hosting four nights of dancing for a trendy, youngish crowd. Music leans toward house and trip-hop. Wednesday–Sunday, a different promoter each night takes over **The Ruby** (✉ 7070 Hollywood Blvd., Hollywood, ☎ 323/467–7070), a popular three-room dance venue on the ground floor of a Hollywood office building. You might find anything from house and hip-hop to trance and techno, plus occasional live music.

Gay and Lesbian Clubs

An ethnically mixed gay and straight crowd flocks to **Circus Disco and Arena** (✉ 6655 Santa Monica Blvd., Hollywood, ☎ 323/462–1291), two huge side-by-side discos with techno and rock music, as well as a full bar and patio. With live music and drag shows, **Club 7969** (✉ 7969 Santa Monica Blvd., West Hollywood, ☎ 323/654–0280) caters to gay, lesbian, and mixed crowds depending on the night. There's a large dance floor and a super sound system. L.A.'s more glamorous lesbians show up for parties sponsored by **Girl Bar** (☎ 323/460–2531). Call the information line for locations. **Jewel's Catch One** (✉ 4067 W. Pico Blvd., Mid-Wilshire, ☎ 323/734–8849) attracts gays and straights, blacks and whites, and everyone in between. Its late hours—2 AM weeknights, 3 AM Sunday and 4 AM Friday and Saturday—and its underground vibe make it a prime destination for the serious dance fanatic.

A friendly, publike lesbian bar with pool tables and a patio, **The Palms** (✉ 8572 Santa Monica Blvd., West Hollywood, ☎ 310/652–6188) has DJ dancing most nights and live shows on others. **Rage** (✉ 8911 Santa Monica Blvd., West Hollywood, ☎ 310/652–7055) is a longtime favorite of the "gym boy" set.

Jazz

The eclectic entertainment at the **Atlas Bar &Grill** (✉ 3760 Wilshire Blvd., Mid-Wilshire, ☎ 213/380–8400) includes torch singers as well as Latin and jazz bands. The snazzy supper club is inside the historic Wiltern building. Crowds squeeze in like sardines to hear powerhouse jazz and blues at the tiny **Baked Potato** (✉ 3787 Cahuenga Blvd. W, North Hollywood, ☎ 818/980–1615). Or visit the larger, snazzier **Baked Potato Hollywood** (✉ 6266½ Sunset Blvd., Hollywood, ☎ 323/461–6400) for your fix of jazz-n-spuds. Big-name acts and innovators play at **Catalina Bar and Grill** (✉ 1640 N. Cahuenga Blvd., Hollywood, ☎ 323/466–2210), a top Hollywood jazz spot. Continental cuisine is served.

You can hear exceptional jazz performers at **Club Brasserie** (✉ Bel Age Hotel, 1020 N. San Vicente Blvd., West Hollywood, ☎ 310/358–7776) Thursday–Saturday. Impressionist paintings on the wall compete with the expansive city view. Best of all, there's no cover. In the Crenshaw District's Leimert Park arts enclave, **Fifth Street Dick's Coffee Company** (✉ 3335 W. 43rd Pl., Crenshaw District, ☎ 323/296–3970) is a great spot for coffee and traditional jazz. Come to **Jazz Bakery** (✉ 3233 Helms Ave., Culver City, ☎ 310/271–9039), inside the former Helms Bakery, for coffee, beer and wine, snacks and desserts, and world-class jazz concerts (usually at 8 and 9:30).

Live Music

One of L.A.'s oldest rock dives, **Al's Bar** (✉ 305 S. Hewitt St., downtown, ☎ 213/625–9703) is still going strong. **B.B. King's Blues Bar** (✉ 1000 Universal Center Dr., Universal City, ☎ 818/622–5464) is a large venue located at Universal CityWalk, with music nightly, Southern cooking, and gospel brunch every Sunday. **Blue Saloon** (✉ 4657 Lankershim Blvd., North Hollywood, ☎ 818/766–4644) is a friendly club with rock and roll, blues, country, and rockabilly.

At **Coconut Teaszer** (✉ 8117 Sunset Blvd., West Hollywood, ☎ 323/654–4773) you can dance to live music—raw rock at its best—for lively fun. **The Conga Room** (✉ 5364 Sunset Blvd., Mid-Wilshire, ☎ 323/938–1696) is one of L.A.'s hippest Latin venues, with plenty of live music from salsa to Afro-Peruvian and points between; dance lessons; a kitchen; and, of course, libations aplenty. Put on the ritz at **The Derby** (✉ 4500 Los Feliz Blvd., Los Feliz, ☎ 323/663–8979), a spacious, elegant club. There's live music nightly—swing, jazz, surf, and rock. Dark, grungy, mysterious—everything a rock-and-roll dive should be—**Dragonfly** (✉ 6510 Santa Monica Blvd., Hollywood, ☎ 323/466–6111) plays an edgy mix of live and dance music.

The gloriously restored Art Deco **El Rey Theater** (✉ 5515 Wilshire Blvd., Mid-Wilshire, ☎ 323/936–6400) showcases top-name bands, and the city's premier goth club, known as Coven 13. Chandeliers and hubcaps decorate **The Garage** (✉ 4519 Santa Monica Blvd., Silver Lake, ☎ 323/662–6166), a rock dive with some of the best in local and alternative bands. At the longtime music industry hangout known as **Ghenghis Cohen Cantina** (✉ 740 N. Fairfax Ave., Hollywood, ☎ 323/653–0640), you can hear up-and-coming talent in a refreshingly mellow format. A plus is the restaurant's updated Chinese cuisine. The **House of Blues** (✉ 8430 Sunset Blvd., West Hollywood, ☎ 323/848–5100) is home to popular jazz, rock, and blues performers, including Etta James, Lou Rawls, Billy Bragg, Cheap Trick, and Lucinda Williams. Some shows are presented cabaret style, including dinner. Every Sunday there's a gospel brunch. **Jack's Sugar Shack** (✉ 1707 N. Vine St., Hollywood, ☎ 323/466–7005) features big-name alternative rock, surf, blues, rockabilly, Cajun, and country performers in cartoony, Polynesian-style surroundings.

The Key Club (☒ 9039 Sunset Blvd., West Hollywood, ☎ 310/786–1712) is a flashy, multitiered Sunset Strip rock club featuring current bands of varying genres and dancing with guest DJs afterward. A restaurant serving till 1 AM makes it easy to stay for a while. Vintage LPs hang from the ceiling at **The Mint** (☒ 6010 W. Pico Blvd., Mid-Wilshire, ☎ 323/954–9630), which features some of the best in blues, jazz, rockabilly, and bluegrass. **McCabe's Guitar Shop** (☒ 3101 Pico Blvd., Santa Monica, ☎ 310/828–4497; 310/828–4403 concert information) is rootsy-retro-central, where all things earnest and (preferably) acoustic are welcome–including live folk, rock, bluegrass, jazz and soul. Coffee, herbal tea, apple juice, and homemade sweets are served during intermission. Make reservations well in advance.

One of the best concert venues in town, **The Palace** (☒ 1735 N. Vine St., Hollywood, ☎ 323/462–3000) is a multilevel Art Deco building with lively entertainment, a fabulous sound system, laser lights, two dance floors, four bars, and a full bar and dining room on the top-level patio. Patrons dress to kill. Friday nights are packed. **The Roxy** (☒ 9009 Sunset Blvd., West Hollywood, ☎ 310/276–2222) is a Sunset Strip fixture, featuring local and touring alternative, country, blues, and rockabilly bands. The hottest bands of tomorrow perform at the cozy **Spaceland** (☒ 1717 Silver Lake Blvd., Silver Lake, ☎ 213/833–2843), a former disco that's ground zero for the burgeoning "Silver Lake scene" (and offers an unusually large smoking room, complete with bar and jukebox). Monday is usually free.

The Troubadour (☒ 9081 Santa Monica Blvd., West Hollywood, ☎ 310/276–6168) has weathered the test of time since the '60s, when it first opened as a folk-music club. Once a focal point for the '80s heavy metal scene, this all-ages venue is again popular, now that it books hot alternative rock acts. At the **Viper Room** (☒ 8852 Sunset Blvd., West Hollywood, ☎ 310/358–1880), a notorious hangout for musicians and movie stars, the decor is tastefully deco but the live music is loud and purely contemporary, with an alternative bent. **Whisky A Go Go** (☒ 8901 Sunset Blvd., West Hollywood, ☎ 310/652–4202) is the most famous rock-and-roll club on the Sunset Strip, with up-and-coming alternative, hard rock, and punk bands. Mondays launch L.A.'s cutting-edge acts.

OUTDOOR ACTIVITIES AND SPORTS

Updated by Lina Lecaro

Transplants to Los Angeles know they've become acclimated when they go to a movie on a beautiful, sunny day. For those who can't stay inside on a beautiful day—of which there are many—Los Angeles supports a range of activities for every level of athlete.

Beaches

From downtown, the easiest way to hit the coast is by taking the Santa Monica Freeway (I–10) due west. Once you reach the end of the freeway, I–10 runs into the famous Highway 1, better known as the Pacific Coast Highway, or PCH. Other routes from the downtown area include Pico, Olympic, Santa Monica, Sunset, and Wilshire boulevards. The MTA bus line runs every 20 minutes to and from the beaches along each of these streets.

Los Angeles County beaches (and state beaches operated by the county) have lifeguards on duty year-round with more watching the water in the summer season. Public parking is usually available, though fees can often be as much as $8; in some areas, it's possible to find free street and highway parking. Generally, the northernmost beaches are best for surfing, hiking, and fishing, and the wider and sandier southern beaches are better for tanning and relaxing. Almost all are great for swimming, but beware: pollution in Santa Monica Bay sometimes approaches dangerous levels, particularly after storms (**beach conditions,** ☏ 310/457–9701 Malibu, 310/578–0478 Santa Monica, and 310/379–8471 Manhattan and Redondo).

The following beaches are listed in north–south order:

Leo Carrillo State Beach. On the very edge of Ventura County, this narrow beach is better for exploring than swimming or sunning. On your own or with a ranger, venture down at low tide to examine the tide pools among the rocks. Sequit Point creates secret coves, sea tunnels, and boulders on which you can perch and fish. The crowd is a mix of hippie canyon residents, semiprofessional surfers, and families. Picturesque campgrounds are set back from the beach. ✉ *35000 Pacific Coast Highway, Malibu,* ☏ *818/880–0350; 800/444–7275 (camping reservations).*

Robert H. Meyer Memorial State Beach. Perhaps Malibu's most beautiful coastal area, this state beach is made up of three separate minibeaches: El Pescador, La Piedra, and El Matador—all with the same spectacular view. Scramble down the steps to the rocky coves where nude sunbathers like to gather. The huge, craggy boulders that make this beach private and lovely also make it somewhat dangerous. Watch the tide and don't get trapped between the boulders when it comes in. ✉ *32350, 32700, and 32900 PCH, Malibu,* ☏ *310/457–1324.*

Zuma Beach Park. Two miles of white sand usually littered with tanning teenagers, this is a great beach for swimming and socializing. It's also a favorite of families with small children. The surf is rough but inconsistent. ✉ *30050 PCH, Malibu,* ☏ *310/457–9891.*

Malibu Lagoon State Beach/Surfrider Beach. Steady, 3- to 5-ft waves make this beach, just north of the dilapidated and currently closed Malibu Pier, a popular surfing location. Water runoff from Malibu Canyon forms a natural lagoon that's a sanctuary for 250 species of birds. Unfortunately, the lagoon is often polluted and algae-filled, and the debris tends to spill over into the surf. Take a walk on one of the nature trails. ✉ *23200 block of PCH, Malibu,* ☏ *818/880–0350.*

Topanga State Beach. The beginning of miles of solid public beach, Topanga has good surfing at the western end. Close to a busy section of the PCH and rather narrow, Topanga is not as serene as other beaches, with hordes of teenagers zipping over Topanga Canyon Boulevard from the Valley. ✉ *18700 block of PCH, Malibu,* ☏ *310/394–3266.*

Will Rogers State Beach. A dozen volleyball nets, gymnastics equipment, and playground equipment for children make this clean, sandy, 3-mi beach a favorite of families and young singles. It also has a sizable gay and lesbian following. Surf is even and gentle, but the beach has the dubious distinction of being one of the area's most polluted—beware after a storm. ✉ *15100 PCH, 2 mi north of Santa Monica pier, Pacific Palisades,* ☏ *310/394–3266.*

Santa Monica State Beach. The first beach you'll hit after the Santa Monica Freeway (I–10) runs into the PCH, this is one of L.A.'s best-known beaches. Be prepared for a mob scene on summer weekends, when parking becomes an expensive ordeal. The pier has an amusement park with a roller coaster, Ferris wheel, antique carousel, arcade, and food. For a memorable view, climb up the stairway over the PCH to Palisades Park. ⊠ *1642 Promenade, PCH at California Incline, Santa Monica,* ☏ *310/394–3266.*

Venice City Beach. The surf and sands of Venice are fine, but the main attraction here is the boardwalk scene: a mile and a half of T-shirt shops, pizza stands, and tattoo parlors. Wander along the path and watch as musicians, magicians, fortune tellers, and dancers compete for your spare change. Around 18th Avenue, look for "Muscle Beach," a big cage where bodybuilders pump iron. For bike rentals try **Venice Pier Bike Shop** (⊠ 21 Washington Blvd., ☏ 310/301–4011); **Skatey's** (⊠ 102 Washington Blvd., ☏ 310/823–7971) is a good bet for skates. Whatever you do, hold on to your wallet. ⊠ *West of Pacific Ave., Venice,* ☏ *310/394–3266.*

Manhattan Beach. Rows of volleyball courts on a wide, sandy strip make this the preferred destination of muscled, tanned young professionals. ⊠ *West of Strand, Manhattan Beach,* ☏ *310/372–2166.*

Redondo Beach. The Redondo Beach Pier marks the starting point of this wide, sandy, busy beach, which continues south for about 2 mi along a heavily developed shoreline community. There are plenty of activities here. Restaurants and shops flourish along the pier; excursion boats and privately owned craft depart from launching ramps; and a reef formed by a sunken ship creates prime fishing and snorkeling conditions. Rock and jazz concerts take place at the pier every summer. ⊠ *Foot of Torrance Blvd., Redondo Beach,* ☏ *310/372–2166.*

Parks and Playgrounds

Parks

In the **Angeles National Forest,** above Pasadena, you can drive to the top of Mt. Wilson for spectacular views of Los Angeles. The **Chilao Visitors Center,** 13 mi north of Mt. Wilson, has exhibits about the forest, and trails for nature walks. The main park in the city of Los Angeles is the 4,000-acre **Griffith Park. Hancock Park** is most notable for the La Brea Tar Pits. Outdoorspeople cherish the canyons, waterfalls, lake, and more than 30 mi of trails at **Malibu Creek State Park,** at the summit of Malibu Canyon Road. **Will Rogers State Historic Park** in Pacific Palisades is ideal for children, with broad lawns, walking trails, and even polo games on weekends in summer (☏ 310/454–8212 for polo information).

Playgrounds

Santa Monica's **Douglas Park** (⊠ 1155 Chelsea Ave.) has a busy playground at the quiet end of the park, with street parking only a few feet away. **Griffith Park** has several small playgrounds amid a large area of lawn, hills, and trees. A free map of the park is available at the rangers station (⊠ 4730 Crystal Springs Dr.).

Participant Sports

For information about tennis courts, hiking and biking trails, and anything else sports-related, call the **City of Los Angeles Department of Recreation and Parks** (☏ 213/738–2961) or the **Los Angeles County Department of Parks and Recreation** (☏ 213/738–2961).

Bicycling

The most famous bike path in the city, and definitely the most beautiful, can be found on the **Pacific Ocean beach,** a 22-mi route from Temescal Canyon down to Redondo Beach. You can park at one of the many lots along the Pacific Coast Highway (be prepared to pay a high fee). Rent bikes at one of many rental shops along the bike path, including **Rental on the Beach** (✉ 2100 Ocean Front Walk, ☎ 310/821–9338), which has several additional locations on the path in Venice. Rates are $5 per hour or $18 a day.

Griffith Park (✉ entrance at Crystal Springs Dr. and Los Feliz Blvd.) has a tree-lined bike route with several options ranging from easy to hard. Stay on Crystal Springs Drive for an easier ride; turn left up Griffith Park Drive for a tougher ride that rewards with great views. For rentals, try **The Annex** (✉ 3157 Los Feliz Blvd., ☎ 323/661–6665), which charges $15 per day. Call the **M.T.A.** (☎ 213/626–4455) for a map of more bike trails.

Many of the areas mentioned in Hiking (☞ *below*) have mountain-biking paths.

Fishing

Shore fishing and surf casting are excellent on many of the beaches, and pier fishing is popular because no license is necessary to fish off public piers. The **Santa Monica** and **Redondo Beach piers** all have nearby bait-and-tackle shops.

Marina del Rey Sport Fishing (✉ Dock 52, Fiji Way, ☎ 310/822–3625) runs excursions for $22 per half day. **Redondo Sport Fishing Company** (✉ 233 N. Harbor Dr., ☎ 310/372–2111) has half-day charters starting at $23 per person. Both companies run whale-watching excursions in winter.

Golf

The Parks and Recreation Department lists seven public 18-hole courses in Los Angeles. **Rancho Park Golf Course** (✉ 10460 W. Pico Blvd., ☎ 310/838–7373) is one of the most heavily played links in the country. It's a beautifully designed course, but the towering pines present an obstacle for those who slice or hook.

Several good public courses are in the San Fernando Valley. The **Balboa and Encino Golf courses** (✉ 16821 Burbank Blvd., Encino, ☎ 818/995–1170) are next to each other. The **Woodley Lakes Golf Course** (✉ 6331 Woodley Ave., Van Nuys, ☎ 818/780–6886) is flat as a board and has hardly any trees.

Griffith Park has two splendid 18-hole courses along with a challenging nine-hole course. **Harding Municipal Golf Course** and **Wilson Municipal Golf Course** (✉ 4730 Crystal Springs Dr. for both, ☎ 323/663–2555) are about 1½ mi inside the park entrance at Riverside Drive and Los Feliz Boulevard. Bridle paths surround the outer fairways, and the San Gabriel Mountains make a scenic background. The nine-hole **Roosevelt Municipal Golf Course** (✉ 2650 N. Vermont Ave., ☎ 323/665–2011) can be reached through the park's Vermont Avenue entrance.

Health Clubs

There are dozens of health-club chains in the city; some sell daily or weekly memberships. Two that do are **Bodies in Motion** (✉ 1950 Century Park E, Century City, ☎ 310/836–8000), with a full range of aerobics classes including aerobic boxing and kickboxing classes, and **24 Hour Fitness** (☎ 800/204–2400), with eight locations in the Los Angeles area. These clubs charge $15–$20 per day.

Hiking

One of the best places to begin is **Griffith Park**; pick up a map from the ranger station (✉ 4730 Crystal Springs Dr.). Many of the paths in the park are not shaded and can be quite steep. A short hike from Canyon Drive, at the southwest end of the park, takes you to **Bronson Caves.**

Begin at the Observatory for a 3-mi round-trip hike to the top of **Mt. Hollywood.**

Head west for ocean views. At **Topanga State Park,** miles of trails wind high in the Santa Monica Mountains. **Will Rogers Historic State Park,** off Sunset Boulevard in Pacific Palisades, abuts Topanga and has a splendid nature trail. A 2-mi hike from Rogers' historic home takes you to a stunning ocean-to-downtown view atop Inspiration Point.

For further information on hiking locations and scheduled outings in Los Angeles, contact the **Sierra Club Los Angeles Chapter** (✉ 3345 Wilshire Blvd., Suite 508, Los Angeles, 90010, ☎ 213/387–4287) or **Treepeople** (☎ 818/753–4631).

Horseback Riding

More than 50 mi of beautiful bridle trails are open to the public in the Griffith Park area. **Griffith Park Horse Rentals** (✉ 480 Riverside Dr., Burbank, ☎ 818/840–8401) has a going rate of $15 per hour plus a $15 deposit. **Sunset Ranch** (✉ 3400 Beachwood Dr., Hollywood, ☎ 323/469–5450) rents horses for $15 an hour, plus a $10 deposit. A Friday-evening package includes a trail ride over the hill into Burbank, where riders tie up their horses and dine at a Mexican restaurant. The package costs $35, not including the cost of dinner.

In-Line and Roller-Skating

For Rollerblades, **Boardwalk Skates** (✉ 201½ Ocean Front Walk, Venice, ☎ 310/450–6634) charges $4 an hour or $12 for the day. **Skatey's** (✉ 102 Washington St., Venice, ☎ 310/823–7971) charges $5 per hour or $10 per day.

For indoor skating, head to **Moonlight Rollerway** (✉ 5110 San Fernando Rd., Glendale, ☎ 818/241–3630) or **Skateland** (✉ 18140 Parthenia St., Northridge, ☎ 818/885–1491).

Jogging

San Vicente Boulevard in Santa Monica has a wide grassy median that splits the street for several picturesque miles. The reservoir at **Lake Hollywood,** just east of Cahuenga Boulevard in the Hollywood Hills, is encircled by a 3.3-mi asphalt path with a view of the Hollywood sign. Within hilly **Griffith Park** are thousands of acres' worth of hilly paths and challenging terrain. **Circle Drive,** around the perimeter of UCLA in Westwood, provides a 2½-mi run through academia.

Tennis

Many public parks have courts that require an hourly fee. **Lincoln Park** (✉ Lincoln and Wilshire Blvds., Santa Monica), **Westwood Park** (✉ 1375 Veteran Ave., West L.A.), and **Barrington Recreational Center** (✉ Barrington Ave., south of Sunset Blvd., West L.A.) all have well-maintained courts with lights. **Griffith Park** has lighted courts on Riverside Drive just south of Los Feliz Boulevard and just north of the Vermont Avenue entrance. For a complete list of public courts, contact the **L.A. Department of Recreation and Parks** (☎ 213/473–7070).

Water Sports

BOATING AND KAYAKING

Action Water Sports (✉ 4144 Lincoln Blvd., Marina del Rey, ☎ 310/306–9539) rents single kayaks for $40 and doubles for $45 per day.

SCUBA DIVING AND SNORKELING

Diving and snorkeling off Leo Carrillo State Beach, Catalina, and the Channel Islands is considered some of the best on the Pacific coast. Dive shops, such as **New England Divers** (✉ 2936 Clark Ave., Long Beach,

☎ 562/421–8939) and **Dive 'n Surf** (✉ 504 N. Broadway, Redondo Beach, ☎ 310/372–8423), will provide you with everything you need for your voyage beneath the waves.

SURFING

The surfing culture began here, and the area remains a destination for pros from afar. Novices should beware of rocks and undertows. **Malibu Ocean Sports** (✉ 22935 PCH, Malibu, ☎ 310/456–6302) gives lessons and rents boards.

Spectator Sports

The best source for tickets to all sporting events is **Ticketmaster** (☎ 213/480–3232). Some of the major sports venues in the area are **Edison Field** (✉ 2000 Gene Autry Way, ☎ 714/940–2000), the **Great Western Forum** (✉ 3900 W. Manchester Blvd., Inglewood, ☎ 310/419–3100), **L.A. Sports Arena** (☎ 213/748–6136), **L.A. Memorial Coliseum** (✉ 3939 S. Figueroa St., Downtown, ☎ 213/748–6131), and **Arrowhead Pond** (✉ 2695 E. Katella Ave., Anaheim, ☎ 714/704–2500).

The newest addition to the sports scene is the 20,000-seat **STAPLES Center** (✉ corner of 11th St. and S. Figueroa St., Downtown, ☎ 877/305–1111), home of basketball's Los Angeles Lakers and Clippers and hockey's L.A. Kings.

Baseball

The **Dodgers** take on their National League rivals at the ever-popular Dodger Stadium (✉ 1000 Elysian Park Ave., exit off I–110, Pasadena Fwy., ☎ 323/224–1400 for ticket information). The **Anaheim Angels** continue their quest for the pennant in the American League West. For Angels ticket information, contact Anaheim Stadium (☎ 714/663–9000).

Basketball

COLLEGE

The **University of Southern California** (☎ 213/740–8480) plays at the L.A. Sports Arena, and the Bruins of the **University of California at Los Angeles** (☎ 310/825–8699 athletic department; 310/825–2101 tickets) play at Pauley Pavilion on the UCLA campus.

PROFESSIONAL

The **Los Angeles Lakers** (☎ 310/419–3182) have enjoyed great seasons since the arrivals of superstar center Shaquille O'Neal and young star Kobe Bryant in 1996. Their home court is the Forum. L.A.'s "other" team, the much-maligned **Clippers** (☎ 213/748–8000) make their home at the L.A. Sports Arena; tickets are generally cheaper and easier to get than those for Lakers games. Relatively new to the pro basketball scene in L.A. is the all-female **Los Angeles Sparks** (☎ 310/419–3193). Though Sparks stars such as Lisa Leslie have drawn unexpectedly large crowds to the Forum, tickets are almost always available (the team plays in summer) and quite inexpensive.

Football

The **Anaheim Piranhas** (☎ 714/475–0838) play arena football at the Arrowhead Pond in Anaheim. The **USC Trojans'** (☎ 213/740–8480) home turf is the Coliseum. The **UCLA Bruins** (☎ 310/825–2101) pack 'em in at the Rose Bowl. Each season, the two teams face off in one of college football's oldest and most exciting rivalries.

Golf

The hot golf ticket in town each February is the PGA **Nissan Open** (☎ 800/752–6736), played in Pacific Palisades at the Riviera Country Club.

Hockey

The National Hockey League's **L.A. Kings** (☎ 310/673–6003) put their show on ice at the Forum. Disney's **Mighty Ducks** (☎ 714/704–2701) push the puck at the Pond in Anaheim.

Horse Racing

Santa Anita Race Track (✉ Huntington Dr. and Colorado Pl., Arcadia, ☎ 626/574–7223) is the dominant site for exciting Thoroughbred racing. Expect the best racing in the world, from October to mid-November and late December to late April.

The track next to the Forum in Inglewood in **Hollywood Park** (✉ Century Blvd. and Prairie Ave., ☎ 310/419–1500) is another favorite racing venue. It's open from early November to late December and from late April to mid-July.

Soccer

The **Los Angeles Galaxy** (☎ 626/432–1540) professional soccer team plays from March through September at the Rose Bowl in Pasadena.

Tennis

The **Infiniti Open** (☎ 310/824–1010), held in summer at UCLA, attracts top-seeded pro players.

SHOPPING

Updated by Anne E. Wells

Most stores in Los Angeles are open from 10 to 6, although many stay open until 9 or later, particularly those on Melrose Avenue and in Santa Monica. Melrose shops, on the whole, don't get moving until 11 AM. In most areas, shops are open for at least a few hours on Sunday. Most stores accept credit cards; traveler's checks are also often allowed with proper identification. Check the *Los Angeles Times* or *L.A. Weekly* for sales.

Beverly Hills Vicinity

Shopping in Beverly Hills centers mainly around the three-block stretch of **Rodeo Drive,** between Santa Monica and Wilshire boulevards, and the streets surrounding it.

SHOPPING CENTERS AND MALLS

The **Beverly Center** (✉ 8500 Beverly Blvd., ☎ 310/854–0070), bound by Beverly, La Cienega, and San Vicente boulevards and 3rd Street, covers more than 7 acres and contains some 200 stores. The **Rodeo Collection** (✉ 421 N. Rodeo Dr., ☎ 310/276–9600), between Brighton Way and Santa Monica Boulevard, is one of several European-style shopping enclaves in Beverly Hills. **Two Rodeo Drive** (✉ 2 Rodeo Dr., at Wilshire Blvd., ☎ 310/247–7040), a.k.a. Via Rodeo, is a collection of glossy retail shops housed on a private cobblestone street.

DEPARTMENT STORES

Barneys New York (✉ 9570 Wilshire Blvd., ☎ 310/276–4400) is a favorite among young hipsters who come to look at cutting-edge (and pricey) designer clothing. **Neiman-Marcus** (✉ 9700 Wilshire Blvd., ☎ 310/550–5900) has a spectacular selection of women's fashions and accessories. **Robinsons-May** (✉ 9900 Wilshire Blvd., ☎ 310/275–5464) has seen better days but is still a reliable source for simple necessities such as panty hose or lipstick. **Saks Fifth Avenue** (✉ 9600 Wilshire Blvd., ☎ 310/275–4211) is one of the best accessory, shoe, and fragrance resources in town.

CHILDREN'S CLOTHING

Oilily (✉ 9520 Brighton Way, ☎ 310/859–9145) is filled with wonderfully whimsical clothing and gifts for children, infants, and even their moms. **Tartine et Chocolat** (✉ 316 N. Beverly Dr., ☎ 310/786–7882) features au courant French wearables and accessories for newborns up to children's size 16.

HOME ACCESSORIES AND GIFTS

Del Mano Gallery (✉ 11981 San Vicente Blvd., Brentwood, ☎ 310/476–8508) houses the work of some of the country's best contemporary artists in a variety of mediums. **Pratesi** (✉ 9024 Burton Way, ☎ 310/274–7661) is a luxurious linen emporium. **Tesoro** (✉ 401 N. Canon Dr., ☎ 310/273–9890) features unusual dishware and art objects.

JEWELRY

Cartier (✉ 370 N. Rodeo Dr., ☎ 310/275–4272; 220 N. Rodeo Dr., ☎ 310/275–5155) carries all manner of luxury gifts and jewelry. **Harry Winston** (✉ 371 N. Rodeo Dr., ☎ 310/271–8554) is the preferred destination for many celebrities looking for Oscar-night jewels. **Tiffany & Co.** (✉ 210 N. Rodeo Dr., ☎ 310/273–8880), the famous name in fine jewelry, silver, and more, packages each purchase in a signature blue Tiffany box. **Van Cleef & Arpels** (✉ 300 N. Rodeo Dr., ☎ 310/276–1161) sells extravagant baubles and fine jewelry.

MEN'S FASHIONS

Battaglia (✉ 306 N. Rodeo Dr., ☎ 310/276–7184) features accessories, shoes, and elegant Italian fashions for men who aren't afraid to dress up. **Bernini** (✉ 326 N. Rodeo Dr., ☎ 310/246–1121) specializes in contemporary Italian designer fashions. **Bijan** (✉ 420 N. Rodeo Dr., ☎ 310/273–6544) is a store shrouded in exclusivity and some say pretention; shopping is by appointment only.

WOMEN'S FASHIONS

BCBG Max Azria (✉ 201C N. Rodeo Dr., ☎ 310/278–3263) is the designer line of the moment on the West Coast. The tiny boutique carries hip, affordable sportswear. **Chanel** (✉ 400 N. Rodeo Dr., ☎ 310/278–5500) houses two floors of ultra-elegant fashions and cosmetics. **Harari** (✉ 9646 Brighton Way, ☎ 310/859–1131) is a favorite haunt of shoppers looking for distinctive, forward-looking fashions and accessories that are less about labels than looks. **Prada** (✉ 9521 Brighton Way, ☎ 310/276–8889) is a must for ladies who crave the signature bags, as well as the sleek, postmodern sportswear.

WOMEN'S AND MEN'S FASHIONS

Emporio Armani Boutique (✉ 9533 Brighton Way, ☎ 310/271–7790) houses three levels of this famous Italian designer's architecturally inspired sportswear, as well as elegant home and fashion accessories, and perfumes. **Gianfranco Ferre** (✉ 2 Rodeo Dr., ☎ 310/273–6311) carries high-quality sportswear and dress apparel for men and women. **Gianni Versace** (✉ 421 N. Rodeo Dr., ☎ 310/205–3921), part of the Rodeo Collection, is the resource for the trendsetting Italian designs. **Gucci** (✉ 347 N. Rodeo Dr., ☎ 310/278–3451), is a starkly beautiful store featuring shoes, bags, and accessories. **Shauna Stein** (✉ Beverly Center, 8500 Beverly Blvd., ☎ 310/652–5511) is a distinctive destination for female fans of Eurochic. Labels such as Dolce & Gabanna, Moschino, and Jean-Paul Gaultier beckon shoppers more concerned with panache than price. **Traffic** (✉ Beverly Center, 8500 Beverly Blvd., ☎ 310/659–4313), for men, and **Traffic Studio** (✉ Beverly Center, 8500 Beverly Blvd. ☎ 310/659–3438), for women, are adjoining boutiques featuring men's and women's sportswear and dress apparel by such names as Hugo Boss, Donna Karan, and Alexander McQueen.

Century City Area

Century City is L.A.'s errand central, where entertainment executives and industry types do their serious shopping.

SHOPPING MALLS

Century City Shopping Center & Marketplace (✉ 10250 Santa Monica Blvd., ☎ 310/277–3898), set among gleaming, tall office buildings on what used to be Twentieth Century Fox film studios' back lot, is an open-air mall with an excellent roster of shops, including Macy's and Bloomingdale's.

BOOKSTORES

Brentano's (✉ Century City Shopping Center, 10250 Santa Monica Blvd., ☎ 310/785–0204) is the champagne of bookstores. Well-known authors often do book signings here.

TOYS

Allied Model Trains (✉ 4411 S. Sepulveda Blvd., ☎ 310/313–9353) feels like a huge train museum, with dozens of working train sets toot-tooting around the store.

Downtown

SHOPPING CENTERS

The **Citadel Factory Stores** (✉ 5675 E. Telegraph Rd., off I–5, Commerce, ☎ 323/888–1220), on the historic landmark site of the former Uniroyal Tire factory, carry the latest in off-price fashions from famous names such as Joan & David, Ann Taylor, and Betsey Johnson.

The Fashion District (✉ roughly between I–10 and Main, San Julian, and 8th Sts.) is the center of California's apparel industry. Although largely devoted to wholesale, there is an extensive, well-defined retail corridor, including open air marketplaces along Santee Street, where shoppers can get bargains on all types of clothing. A map can be obtained by calling ☎ 213/488–1153.

GIFTS

Gonzales Candle Shop (✉ W-14 Olvera St., ☎ 213/625–8771), inside the historic Sepulveda House, lets you soak up the colorful atmosphere of Olvera Street. Since 1929 the artisans here have supplied shoppers with everything from novelty candles to gothic and religious candles, both large and small. **Museum of Contemporary Art Store** (✉ MOCA, 250 S. Grand Ave., ☎ 213/621–1710) sells art posters, books, tableware, children's toys, and jewelry by local and international artists.

Melrose Avenue Vicinity

This bohemian shopping street is a great place to pick up everything from inexpensive trinkets and used clothing to pricey Americana antiques. It's had its ups and downs as a retail area, but with the recent opening of the Miu Miu, Liza Bruce, and Betsey Johnson stores, it looks like Melrose is headed for another turnaround.

ANTIQUES

J. F. Chen Antiques (✉ 8414 Melrose Ave., ☎ 323/655–6310) specializes in ancient Asian pieces. **Licorne** (✉ 8432 Melrose Pl., ☎ 323/852–4765) sells fine 17th-century furnishings.

BOOKSTORES AND MUSIC STORES

A Different Light, ✉ 8853 Santa Monica Blvd., West Hollywood, ☎ 310/854–6601, is dedicated to books by and about gays, lesbians, and bisexuals. **Aron's Records** (✉ 1150 N. Highland Ave., ☎ 323/469–4700) has an excellent selection of vinyl as well as the latest CD releases. **Bodhi Tree Bookstore,** ✉ 8585 Melrose Ave., West Hollywood, ☎ 310/659–1733, is the place to go for books about the New Age, philosophy, astrology, Eastern religions, and modern spirituality. **Book Soup** (✉

8818 Sunset Blvd., ☎ 310/659–3110), one of L.A.'s most prominent literary bookstores, is a frequent book-signing venue for authors.

FURNITURE AND HOME ACCESSORIES

Freehand (✉ 8413 W. 3rd St., ☎ 323/655–2607) is an aesthetically pleasing gallery showcasing contemporary American crafts, clothing, and jewelry, mostly by California artists. **Golyester** (✉ 136 S. La Brea Ave., ☎ 323/931–1339) sells funky used clothes and home furnishings. **Zipper** (✉ 8316 W. 3rd St., ☎ 323/951–0620) focuses on design trends from the 1930s to the 1990s.

TOYS AND GAMES

Hollywood Magic Shop (✉ 6614 Hollywood Blvd., ☎ 323/464–5610), a Tinseltown institution, sells costumes year-round and has a wide selection of tricks for beginners and experts.

VINTAGE CLOTHING

Wasteland (✉ 7428 Melrose Ave., ☎ 323/653–3028) carries the kind of retro clothing you might see on Winona Ryder and her celeb contemporaries. The store sells new clothing as well, at reasonable prices.

WOMEN'S FASHIONS AND ACCESSORIES

shu uemura (✉ 8606 Melrose Ave., West Hollywood, ☎ 310/652–6230) is the makeup emporium choice for celebrity artists and their clients. The store is especially known for their sable Japanese makeup brushes. **Tyler Trafficante** (✉ 7290 Beverly Blvd., ☎ 323/931–9678) carries designer Richard Tyler's exquisitely tailored, albeit pricey, women's sportswear and evening wear.

WOMEN'S AND MEN'S FASHIONS

Maxfield (✉ 8825 Melrose Ave., ☎ 310/274–8800) is the supplier of choice for celebs and costumers responsible for dressing some of the more fashionable shows on television. **Miu Miu** (✉ 8025 Melrose Ave., ☎ 323/651–0073) could change the face of Melrose shopping. Expect nothing less from the most whimsical extension of the Prada line. **Nicole Miller,** ✉ 8633 Sunset Blvd., West Hollywood, ☎ 310/652–1629, carries everything from neckties to boxers to dresses in the designer's witty and whimsical silk prints. **Swell Store** (✉ 126 N. La Brea Ave., ☎ 323/937–2096) is a vogue place for shoes, plus men's and women's clothing and accessories.

Santa Monica

Less frenetic and status-conscious than Beverly Hills, Santa Monica is an ideal place for a leisurely shopping stroll. On Wednesday, some of the streets in Santa Monica are blocked off for the weekly farmers market, where parking is next to impossible.

SHOPPING CENTERS AND STREETS

3rd Street Promenade is a pedestrian-only street lined with boutiques, movie theaters, clubs, pubs, and restaurants. Mainstream and funky boutiques line **Main Street,** which leads from southern Santa Monica to Venice. **Montana Avenue** is a pedestrian street surrounded by quaint residential cottages and bungalows. Many of the best shops are between 9th and 17th streets. **Santa Monica Place** (✉ Colorado Ave. and 2nd St.) is a three-story enclosed mall with department stores and chains and a few unusual L.A. stores.

HOME ACCESSORIES AND FURNITURE

Brenda Cain (✉ 1211-A Montana Ave., ☎ 310/395–1559) sells antique jewelry and home accessories, but the hot ticket here is the amazing array of Arts and Crafts pottery. **Imagine** (✉ 927 Montana Ave., ☎ 310/395–9553) carries custom-designed furniture and bedding as well as a large assortment of European wooden toys and gifts.

WOMEN'S FASHIONS AND ACCESSORIES

Moondance Jewelry Gallery (✉ 1530 Montana Ave., ☎ 310/395–5516) carries the unique jewelry of 70-odd artists. **Weathervane** (✉ 1209 Montana Ave., ☎ 310/393–5344) has a friendly staff and fine European women's designer collections.

WOMEN'S AND MEN'S FASHIONS

ABS Clothing (✉ 1533 Montana Ave., ☎ 310/393–8770) sells contemporary sportswear designed in L.A. **A/X Armani Exchange** (✉ 2940 Main St., ☎ 310/396–8799) markets the coveted Giorgio Armani label to the masses via T-shirts as well as other sportswear for women and men.

San Fernando and San Gabriel Valleys

Ventura Boulevard is the lifeblood of Valley shopping, which is more renowned for shopping malls than any other neighborhood in L.A.

SHOPPING MALLS

Glendale Galleria (✉ 2148 Central Blvd., Glendale, ☎ 818/240–9481) has a Nordstrom, Macy's, and assorted specialty stores. **Media City Center** (✉ 201 E. Magnolia Blvd., Burbank, ☎ 818/566–8617) houses a beautiful Macy's as well as Mervyn's and Sears. **The Promenade** (✉ 6100 Topanga Canyon Blvd., Woodland Hills, ☎ 818/884–7090), at the northern edge of the Valley, has a 24-hour hot line announcing daily bargains. Within the mall are Macy's and a separate Macy's Men's Store.

ANTIQUES, HOME ACCESSORIES, AND GIFTS

Cranberry House (✉ 12318 Ventura Blvd., Studio City, ☎ 818/506–8945) is an expansive shopping cooperative covering half a city block with 140 kiosks run by L.A.'s leading antiques dealers. **Imagine That!** (✉ 13335 Ventura Blvd., Sherman Oaks, ☎ 818/784–8215) is a fun-filled emporium of toys, gifts, decorative accessories, and aromatherapy products for adults and children of all ages.

SIDE TRIPS FROM LOS ANGELES

Big Bear and Lake Arrowhead, both two or three hours away in the San Bernardino mountains, are rustic resorts with beautiful lakes, crisp air, and snowy winters. Catalina Island, an hour's boat ride off the coast, is the Greek isle of the West Coast, with crystal blue waters, a gentle climate, and a friendly, small-town feeling. For approximate costs of dining and lodging establishments, *see* the price charts, *above.*

Lake Arrowhead and Big Bear Lake

Big Bear comes alive in winter with downhill ski and snowboard resorts, cross-country trails, lodges, and an active village. Summer draws crowds to Lake Arrowhead, known for its cool mountain air, trail-threaded woods, and brilliant lake. The Rim of the World Scenic Byway, which connects with Lake Arrowhead and Big Bear Lake, is a magnificent drive.

Numbers in the margin correspond to points of interest on the Lake Arrowhead and Big Bear Lake map.

Lake Arrowhead

90 mi from Los Angeles, I–10 east to I–215 north to Hwy. 30 east (mountain resorts turnoff) to Hwy. 18 (Waterman Ave.), then Hwy. 138 north to Hwy. 173 (Lake Arrowhead turnoff); follow signs from there.

1 **Lake Arrowhead Village** is an alpine community with offices, shops, outlet stores, and eateries that descend the hill to the lake. You can take a scenic 45-minute cruise on the ***Arrowhead Queen,*** operated daily by LeRoy Sports (☎ 909/336–6992) from the waterfront marina. Tickets are first-come, first-serve and cost $10. Call ahead for departure times. The **Lake Arrowhead Children's Museum** (✉ lower level of village, ☎ 909/336–1332) has plenty to entertain pint-size explorers, including hands-on exhibits, a climbing maze, and a puppet stage.

2 Past the town of Rim Forest, follow Bear Springs Road 2 mi north to the fire lookout tower at **Strawberry Peak.** Brave the steep stairway to the tower, and you'll be treated to a magnificent view and a lesson on fire-spotting by the lookout staff. Call the Ranger Station (☎ FAX 909/337–2444) to find out when staff is on hand.

3 If you're up for a barbecue in a wooded setting, visit **Baylis Park Picnic Ground,** on Highway 18.

4 **Lake Gregory,** at the ridge of Crestline, was formed by a dam constructed in 1938. Because the water temperature in summer is seldom very cold, this is the best swimming lake in the mountains. It's open in summer only, and there's a nominal charge to swim. Fishing is permitted, there are water slides, and you can rent rowboats at Lake Gregory Village.

Dining and Lodging

$$–$$$ ✕ **Casual Elegance.** The menu changes weekly at this intimate house with a fireplace. The steaks and seafood are first-rate. ✉ *26848 Hwy. 189, Agua Fria,* ☎ *909/337–8932. AE, D, DC, MC, V.*

$$–$$$ **Lake Arrowhead Resort.** This lakeside lodge has an Old World feeling reminiscent of the Alps. Guests have free access to the attached Village Bay Club and Spa. ✉ *27984 Hwy. 189, Lake Arrowhead Village, 92352,* ☎ *909/336–1511 or 800/800–6792,* FAX *909/336–1378. 177 rooms, 4 suites, 5 condos. Restaurant, coffee shop, lobby lounge, pool, health club, beach. AE, D, DC, MC, V.*

$–$$ **Carriage House Bed & Breakfast.** Down comforters and lake views add to the charm of this New England–style bed-and-breakfast. ✉ *472 Emerald Dr., Lake Arrowhead 92352,* ☎ *909/336–1400 or 800/526–5070,* FAX *909/336–6092. 3 rooms. AE, D, MC, V. BP.*

Big Bear Lake

110 mi from Los Angeles, I–10 east to I–215 north to Hwy. 30 east; Hwy. 330 north to Hwy. 18 east; chains are sometimes needed in winter.

5 You'll spot an occasional chaletlike building in **Big Bear Lake,** an alpine- and Western-mountain-style town on the lake's south shore. The paddle-wheeler ***Big Bear Queen*** (☎ 909/866–3218) departs daily from Big Bear Marina, from May through October, for 90-minute scenic tours of the lake; the cost is $9.50. Fishing-boat and equipment rentals are available from several lakeside marinas, including Pine Knot Landing (☎ 909/866–2628). **Big Bear City,** at the east end of the lake, has more restaurants, motels, and a small airport.

6 Southeast of Big Bear Village is **Snow Summit,** one of the area's top ski resorts. It has an 8,200-ft peak and 31 trails, along with two high-speed quads and nine other lifts. Summit has more advanced runs than nearby ski resorts and usually has the best snow. Trails are open to mountain bikers in summer. ✉ *880 Summit Blvd., off Big Bear Blvd.,* ☎ *909/866–5766; 888/786–6481 for snow reports.*

7 **Bear Mountain Ski Resort,** also southeast of Big Bear Lake Village, has 12 chairlifts and 33 trails. Bear Mountain is best for intermediate skiers. On busy winter weekends and holidays, reserve tickets before

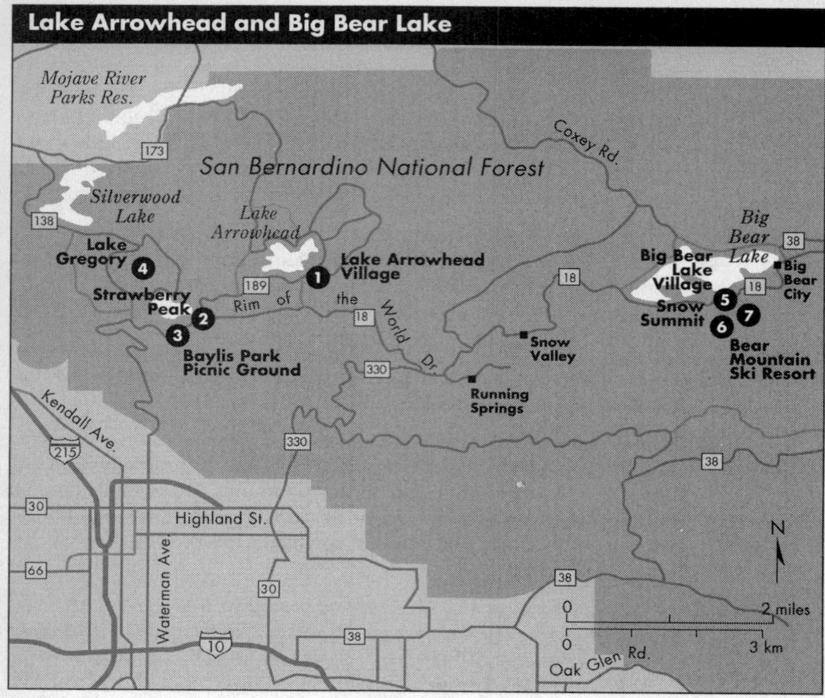

heading to the mountain. ✉ *43101 Goldmine Dr., off Moonridge Rd.,* ☎ *909/585–2519.*

Dining and Lodging

$$–$$$$ ✕ **Madlon's.** Inside this gingerbread-style cottage you'll be treated to sophisticated home cooking: lamb chops with Gorgonzola butter, cream of jalapeño soup, or perhaps Asian black peppercorn filet mignon. Reservations are essential on weekends. ✉ *829 W. Big Bear Blvd., Big Bear City,* ☎ *909/585–3762. D, MC, V.*

$$–$$$ ✕ **The Iron Squirrel.** Hearty French fare such as veal Normandie (veal scallopini sautéed with apples, calvados, and cream) and duck à l'orange (roasted duckling with a Grand Marnier sauce) are two specialties at this country French–style restaurant, but you'll also find a big selection of fresh fish and grilled meats on the menu. ✉ *646 Pine Knot Blvd.,* ☎ *909/866–9121. AE, MC, V.*

$–$$$$ **Holiday Inn Big Bear Chateau.** Two minutes from the lake, Big Bear's grandest hotel resembles a mountain château in the European tradition. ✉ *42200 Moonridge Rd., 92315,* ☎ *909/866–6666 or 800/232–7466,* FAX *909/866–8988. 77 rooms, 3 suites. Restaurant, lobby lounge, pool, exercise room. AE, D, DC, MC, V.*

$$ ★ **Apples Bed & Breakfast Inn.** Despite its location on a busy road to the ski lifts, the Apples Inn feels remote and peaceful, thanks to the surrounding pine trees. The colorful rooms have working gas fireplaces, and four have hot tubs. ✉ *42430 Moonridge Rd., 92315,* ☎ *909/866–0903. 12 rooms. AE, D, MC, V. BP.*

$–$$ **Northwoods Resort.** Northwoods is a giant log cabin with all the amenities of a resort. The lobby resembles a 1930s hunting lodge, with canoes, antlers, fishing poles, and a grand stone fireplace. Rooms are large but cozy; some have fireplaces and whirlpool tubs. Ski packages are available. ✉ *40650 Village Dr., 92315,* ☎ *909/866–3121 or 800/*

866–3121, FAX *909/878–2122. 140 rooms, 8 suites. Restaurant, pool, outdoor hot tub, sauna, exercise room. AE, D, DC, MC, V.*

$–$$ **Robinhood Inn.** Across the street from the Pine Knot Marina, this family-oriented motel has affordable rooms, most with fireplaces and some with whirlpool tubs or minikitchens. All accommodations face a courtyard with an outdoor whirlpool. ✉ *40797 Lakeview Dr., 92315,* ☎ *909/866–4643 or 800/990–9956,* FAX *909/866–4645. 17 rooms, 4 suites. Restaurant, outdoor hot tub. AE, MC, V.*

Lake Arrowhead and Big Bear Lake Essentials

LODGING RESERVATIONS

Most lodgings require a two-night stay on weekends. **Lake Arrowhead Communities Chamber of Commerce** (☞ *below*) has information on camping and lodging. **Big Bear Lake Resort Association** (✉ Box 1936, Big Bear Lake 92315, ☎ 909/866–7000) will help with lodging arrangements.

VISITOR INFORMATION

Big Bear Chamber of Commerce (✉ Box 2860, 630 Bartlett Rd., Big Bear Lake 92315, ☎ 909/866–4607). **Lake Arrowhead Communities Chamber of Commerce** (✉ Box 219, 28200 Hwy. 189, Bldg. F, Suite 290, Lake Arrowhead 92352, ☎ 909/337–3715).

Catalina Island

Just 22 mi across the sea from the L.A. coastline, Catalina has virtually unspoiled mountains, canyons, coves, and beaches. Best of all, it gives you a glimpse of what undeveloped southern California once looked like.

Summer, weekends, and holidays, Catalina crawls with thousands of L.A.-area boaters. Although Catalina is not known for wide, sandy beaches, sunbathing and water sports are big draws. Divers and snorkelers come for the exceptionally clear water surrounding the island. The main town of Avalon is a charming, old-fashioned beach community.

Cruise ships sail into Avalon twice a week and smaller boats shuttle between Avalon and Two Harbors, a small isthmus cove on the island's western end. You can also take bus excursions beyond Avalon. Roads are limited and nonresident vehicles prohibited, so hiking (by permit only) is the only other means of exploring.

In 1975 the Santa Catalina Island Conservancy, a nonprofit foundation, acquired about 86% of the island to help preserve the area's natural resources. These days the conservancy is restoring the rugged interior country with plantings of native grasses and trees. Bus or van tours take you to this interior.

Catalina can be seen in a day, but several inviting hotels make it worth extending your stay for one or more nights. A short itinerary might include breakfast along the boardwalk, a tour of the interior, a snorkeling excursion at Casino Point, and dinner in Avalon.

Avalon

1- to 2-hr ferry ride from Long Beach; 15-min helicopter ride from Long Beach or San Pedro.

Avalon, Catalina's only real town, extends from the shore of its natural harbor to the surrounding hillsides. Most activity is centered along the pedestrian mall of Crescent Avenue, and most sights are easily reached on foot. Private cars are restricted and rental cars aren't allowed, but taxis, trams, and shuttles can take you anywhere you need to go. Bicycles and golf carts can also be rented. Permits for hiking the interior

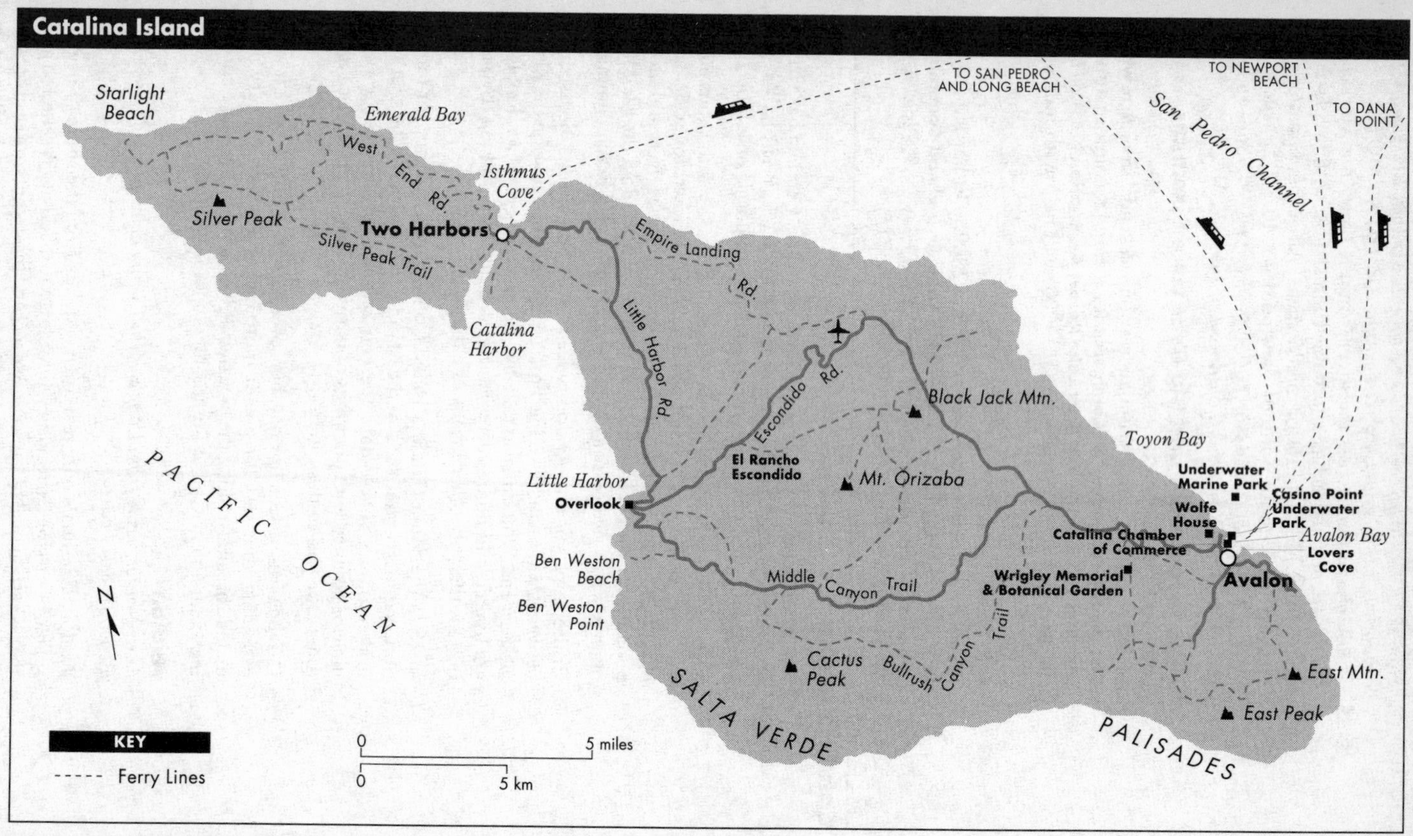

Catalina Island
Starlight Beach
Emerald Bay
West End Rd.
Isthmus Cove
Silver Peak
Two Harbors
Silver Peak Trail
Empire Landing Rd.
Catalina Harbor
Little Harbor Rd.
Escondido Rd.
TO SAN PEDRO AND LONG BEACH
TO NEWPORT BEACH
TO DANA POINT
San Pedro Channel
Black Jack Mtn.
Toyon Bay
El Rancho Escondido
Mt. Orizaba
Little Harbor
Overlook
Underwater Marine Park
Casino Point Underwater Park
Wolfe House
Avalon Bay
Catalina Chamber of Commerce
Lovers Cove
Avalon
PACIFIC OCEAN
Ben Weston Beach
Middle Canyon Trail
Wrigley Memorial & Botanical Garden
Ben Weston Point
N
Canyon Trail
Cactus Peak
Bullrush Canyon
East Mtn.
East Peak
SALTA VERDE
PALISADES
KEY
Ferry Lines
0
5 miles
0
5 km

of the island are available free from the Santa Catalina Island Conservancy.

A walk along **Crescent Avenue** is a nice way to begin a tour of the town. Vivid art deco tiles adorn the avenue's fountains and planters. Head to the **Green Pleasure Pier,** at the center of Crescent Avenue. Stand with your back to the harbor and you'll be in a good position to survey the sights. At the top of the hill on your left you'll spot the Inn at Mt. Ada, now a top-of-the-line B&B but once a getaway estate built by William Wrigley, Jr., for his wife. On the pier you'll find the Catalina Island Visitor's Bureau, snack stands, the Harbor Patrol, and scads of squawking seagulls.

On the northwest point of Avalon Bay (looking to your right from Green Pleasure Pier), is the majestic landmark **Casino.** This circular white structure is considered one of the finest examples of Art Deco architecture anywhere. Its Spanish-inspired floors and murals show off brilliant blue and green Catalina tiles. "Casino" is the Italian word for "gathering place" and in this case has nothing to do with gambling. Casino life revolves around the magnificent ballroom: the same big-band dances that made the Casino famous in the 1930s and '40s still take place on holiday weekends. Call 310/510–1520 for tickets to the New Year's Eve dance, a hugely popular event that sells out well in advance. Daytime tours (☎ 310/510–8687) of the establishment, lasting about 55 minutes, cost $8.50. You can also visit the **Catalina Island Museum,** in the lower level of the Casino, which investigates 7,000 years of island history; or stop at the **Casino Art Gallery,** which displays works of local artists. First-run movies are screened at the **Avalon Theatre,** noteworthy for its 1929 theater pipe organ. ✉ *1 Casino Way,* ☎ *310/510–2414 for museum; 310/510–0808 for art gallery; 310/510–0179 for Avalon Theatre.* 🎫 *Museum $2, art gallery free.* ⏲ *Museum: Easter–Dec., daily 10–4; Jan.–Easter, Fri.–Wed. 10–4; art gallery: June–Sept., daily 10:30–4; Oct.–May, Fri.–Sun. and Wed. 10:30–4.*

In front of the Casino, snorkelers and divers explore the crystal-clear waters of the **Casino Point Underwater Park,** where moray eels, bat rays, spiny lobsters, and other sea animals cruise around kelp forests and along the sandy bottom. The area is protected from boats and other watercraft. Snorkeling equipment can be rented on and near the pier. **Lover's Cove,** east of the boat landing, is also good for snorkeling.

Two miles south of the bay via Avalon Canyon Road is the **Wrigley Memorial and Botanical Garden,** where you'll find plants native to southern California, including several that grow only on Catalina Island. The Wrigley family commissioned the garden as well as the monument, which has a grand staircase and a Spanish mausoleum inlaid with colorful Catalina tile. Tram service between the memorial and Avalon is available daily between 8 AM and 5 PM during summer, and less regularly in winter. ✉ *Avalon Canyon Rd.,* ☎ *310/510–2288.* 🎫 *$3.* ⏲ *Daily 8–5.*

Walk through the residential hills of Avalon and you'll see such interesting architecture as the modern **Wolfe House,** on Chimes Tower Road, built in 1928 by noted architect Rudolf Schindler. Its terraced frame is carefully set into a steep site, affording extraordinary views. The house is a private residence, but you can get a good view of it from the path below and from the street. Across the street the **Zane Grey Pueblo** (✉ 199 Chimes Tower Rd., ☎ 310/510–0966 or 800/378–3256) has been transformed into a rustic hotel.

Dining and Lodging

$$–$$$ ✕ **Cafe Prego.** This Italian waterfront restaurant specializes in pasta, seafood, and steak. Reserve ahead, or be prepared for a long wait. ✉ *603 Crescent Ave.,* ☎ *310/510–1218. AE, D, DC, MC, V.*

$$–$$$ ★ ✕ **Channel House.** A longtime Avalon family owns this restaurant, serving dishes such as Catalina swordfish, coq au vin, and pepper steak with a Continental flair. ✉ *205 Crescent Ave.,* ☎ *310/510–1617. AE, D, MC, V.*

$$–$$$ ✕ **Rick's Cafe.** On the second floor of the Hotel Vista del Mar, Rick's has a bird's-eye view of the bay. Specialties are local seafood, top sirloin, and pasta. ✉ *417 Crescent Ave.,* ☎ *310/510–0333. AE, MC, V.*

$$$$ **Inn on Mt. Ada.** Occupying the onetime Wrigley mansion, the island's most exclusive hotel has all the comforts of a millionaire's home at millionaire's prices. All meals, beverages, snacks, and use of a golf cart are complimentary. The six bedrooms are traditional and elegant. The hilltop view of the Pacific is spectacular. ✉ *398 Wrigley Rd., 90704,* ☎ *310/510–2030 or 800/608–7669. 6 rooms. MC, V. FAP.*

$–$$$$ **Hotel Metropole and Market Place.** This romantic hotel could easily be in the heart of New Orleans' French Quarter. Some guest rooms have balconies overlooking a flower-filled courtyard of restaurants and shops; others have ocean views. ✉ *205 Crescent Ave., 90704,* ☎ *310/510–1884 or 800/541–8528. 44 rooms, 4 suites. AE, MC, V. CP.*

$$ **Pavilion Lodge.** Across the street from the beach, this popular motel has simple, spacious rooms. There's a large, grassy courtyard in the center of the complex. ✉ *513 Crescent Ave., 90704,* ☎ *800/851–0217. 73 rooms. AE, D, DC, MC, V. CP.*

$–$$ **Hotel Vista del Mar.** Contemporary rooms full of rattan furniture and greenery open onto a skylighted atrium. Some rooms have fireplaces, whirlpool tubs, and wet bars. Two larger rooms have ocean views. ✉ *417 Crescent Ave., 90704,* ☎ *310/510–1452 or 800/601–3836,* FAX *310/510–2917. 15 rooms. AE, D, MC, V. CP.*

Nightlife

Warm summer afternoons bring loads of party goers to Catalina's many happy-hour bars, where festivities continue late into the night. **El Galleon** (✉ 411 Crescent Ave., ☎ 310/510–1188) has microbrews and karaoke. At **Luau Larry's** (✉ 509 Crescent Ave., ☎ 310/510–1919), you can drink your cocktail with an oyster shooter while wearing a calypso hat.

Two Harbors

45- to 60-min ferry ride (summer only) or 90-min bus ride from Avalon; 3-hr ferry ride (summer only) from Los Angeles.

This fairly primitive resort toward the western end of the island has long been a summer boating destination. The area is named for its two harbors, which are separated by a ½-mi-wide isthmus. Two Harbors recalls the days before tourism became the island's major industry. This side of the island is less tame, with abundant wildlife. Activities here include swimming, diving, boating, hiking, mountain biking, beachcombing, kayaking, and sportfishing.

Lodging

Tiny Two Harbors has limited overnight accommodations, including a few campgrounds. All reservations are made through the **visitor services** office (✉ Box 5086, Two Harbors 90704, ☎ 310/510–0303), which you'll see when you arrive.

Catalina Island Essentials

ARRIVING AND DEPARTING

By Boat: Catalina Cruises (☎ 800/228–2546) jet boats or slower classic ferries depart Long Beach several times daily, taking 55 minutes or

an hour and 45 minutes to reach Avalo
bors. There is no service to Two Harbor
destination is $35 (jet boats) or $25 (slowe
Express (☏ 310/519–1212 or 800/995–43
run from Long Beach or San Pedro to Avalon an
San Pedro to Two Harbors; round-trip fare from
Pedro is $38. Reservations are advised in summer

Service from Newport Beach is available through **Cat**
Service (☏ 949/673–5245). Boats leave from Balboa Pa
take 75 minutes to reach the island, and cost $36 (reservatio
Return boats leave Catalina at 4:30 PM.

By Bus: Catalina Safari Shuttle Bus (☏ 310/510–0303 or 800/322–
has regular bus service (limited in winter) between Avalon and
Harbors; the trip takes two hours and costs $18 one-way.

By Helicopter: Island Express (☏ 310/510–2525) flies hourly from San Pedro and Long Beach (8 AM–sunset). The trip takes about 15 minutes and costs $67 one-way, $123 round-trip.

GETTING AROUND

By Bicycle: Bike rentals are widely available in Avalon for about $6 per hour. Look for rental stands on Crescent Avenue and Pebbly Beach Road.

On Foot: The requisite free permits for hikes into the island's interior are available daily from 9 to 5 at the **Santa Catalina Island Conservancy** (✉ 3rd and Claressa Sts., ☏ 310/510–2595) and at **visitor services** (✉ Box 5086, 90704, ☏ 310/510–0303) in Two Harbors. No permit is required for shorter hikes, such as the one from Avalon to the Botanical Garden. The Conservancy has maps of the island's east-end hikes, such as Hermit's Gulch trail. If you plan to backpack overnight, you'll need a camping reservation. The interior is dry and desertlike; bring plenty of water.

By Golf Cart: Golf carts constitute the island's main form of transportation. You can rent them along Avalon's Crescent Avenue and Pebbly Beach Road for about $30 per hour (although you generally pay for two hours up front). Try **Island Rentals** (✉ 125 Pebbly Beach Rd., ☏ 310/510–1456).

GUIDED TOURS

Santa Catalina Island Company (☏ 310/510–8687 or 800/322–3434) and **Catalina Adventure Tours** (☏ 310/510–2888) conduct tours of the region.

VISITOR INFORMATION

The **Catalina Island Visitor's Bureau** (✉ Green Pleasure Pier, Box 217, Avalon 90704, ☏ 310/510–1520, FAX 310/510–7606).

LOS ANGELES A TO Z

Arriving and Departing

By Bus

Greyhound Lines (☏ 800/231–2222) serves Los Angeles from many U.S. cities. The terminal is at 1716 East 7th Street, at the corner of Alameda Street.

By Car

Los Angeles is at the western terminus of I–10, a major interstate highway that runs all the way east to Florida. I–15, angling southwest from Las Vegas, swings through the eastern communities around San

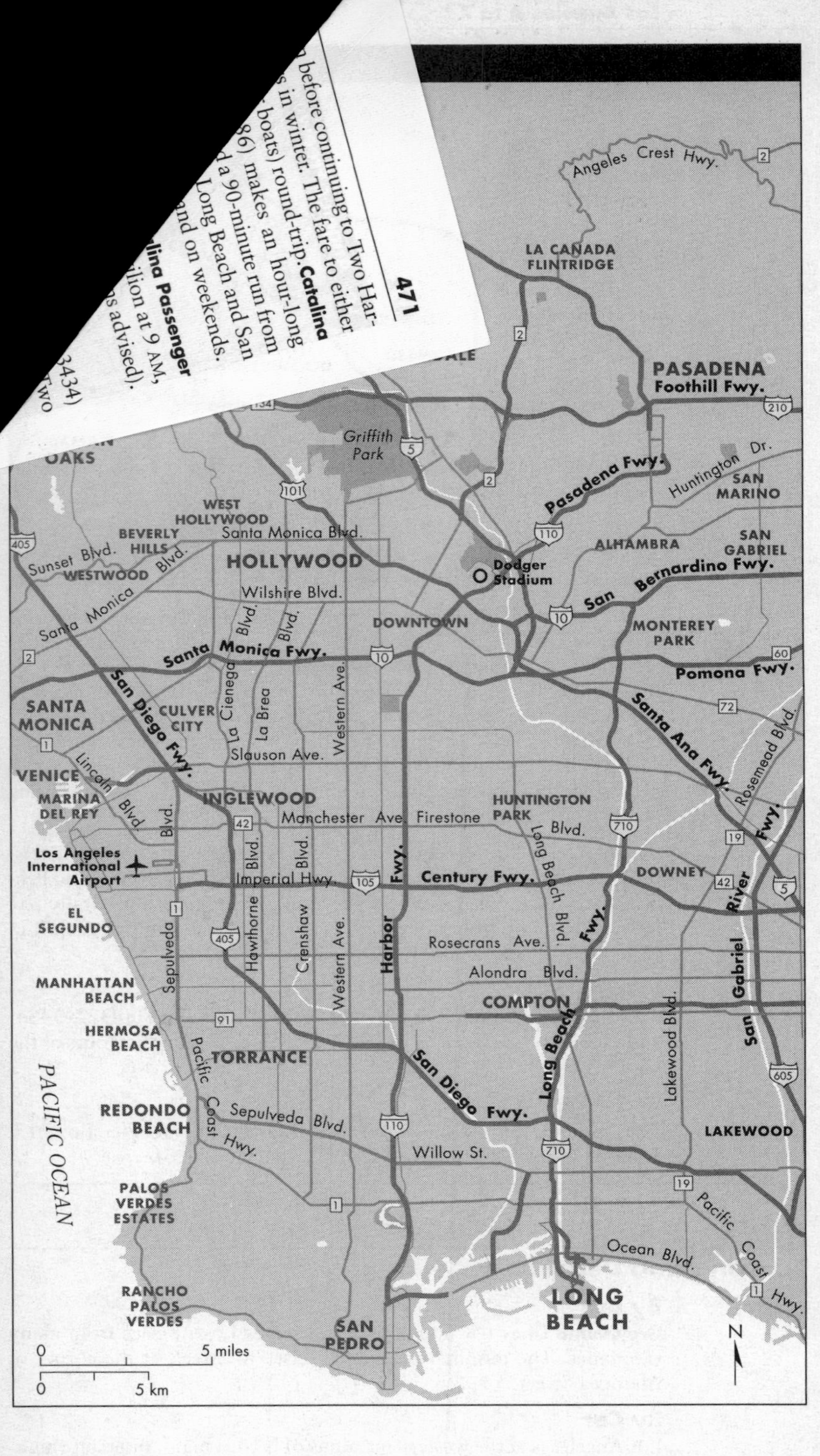

Angeles Crest Hwy.
LA CANADA FLINTRIDGE
PASADENA
Foothill Fwy.
Griffith Park
OAKS
Pasadena Fwy.
Huntington Dr.
SAN MARINO
WEST HOLLYWOOD
BEVERLY HILLS
Santa Monica Blvd.
Sunset Blvd.
WESTWOOD
HOLLYWOOD
Dodger Stadium
ALHAMBRA
SAN GABRIEL
San Bernardino Fwy.
Wilshire Blvd.
Santa Monica Blvd.
DOWNTOWN
MONTEREY PARK
Santa Monica Fwy.
Pomona Fwy.
San Diego Fwy.
SANTA MONICA
CULVER CITY
La Cienega Blvd.
La Brea Blvd.
Western Ave.
Santa Ana Fwy.
Rosemead Blvd.
Slauson Ave.
VENICE
Lincoln Blvd.
MARINA DEL REY
INGLEWOOD
HUNTINGTON PARK
Manchester Ave.
Firestone Blvd.
Long Beach Blvd.
Los Angeles International Airport
Imperial Hwy.
Century Fwy.
Harbor Fwy.
DOWNEY
River Fwy.
EL SEGUNDO
Sepulveda Blvd.
Hawthorne Blvd.
Crenshaw Blvd.
Western Ave.
Rosecrans Ave.
Alondra Blvd.
MANHATTAN BEACH
COMPTON
Long Beach Fwy.
San Gabriel
Lakewood Blvd.
HERMOSA BEACH
TORRANCE
Pacific Coast Hwy.
San Diego Fwy.
PACIFIC OCEAN
REDONDO BEACH
Sepulveda Blvd.
LAKEWOOD
Willow St.
PALOS VERDES ESTATES
Pacific Coast Hwy.
Ocean Blvd.
RANCHO PALOS VERDES
LONG BEACH
SAN PEDRO
0 5 miles
0 5 km
N
2 134 5 101 2 110 210 405 10 10 60 2 72 1 710 42 19 105 42 5 1 405 91 605 110 710 19 1 1

Bernardino before heading on to San Diego. Interstate 5, which runs north–south through California, leads up to San Francisco and down to San Diego.

By Plane

The major gateway to Los Angeles is **Los Angeles International Airport** (☏ 310/670–3413), commonly called LAX; it is serviced by more than 85 major airlines, including Alaska, America West, American, Continental, Delta, Northwest, Skywest, Southwest, TWA, United, and US Airways. *See* Air Travel *in* Smart Travel Tips for phone numbers.

Long Beach Airport (☏ 562/570–2600), at the southern tip of Los Angeles County, is served by America West, American, and Sunjet International.

Burbank/Glendale/Pasadena Airport (☏ 818/840–8847) serves the San Fernando Valley. Alaska, America West, American, Skywest, Southwest, and United are among the airlines that fly here.

Ontario International Airport (✉ Airport Dr., south from Vineyard Ave. exit of I–10, ☏ 909/937–2700), about 35 mi east of Los Angeles, serves the San Bernardino–Riverside area and is served by Alaska, America West, American, Continental, Delta, Northwest, Skywest, Southwest, TWA, United, and US Air Express.

John Wayne Airport Orange County (☏ 949/252–5006) (☞ Orange County A to Z *in* Chapter 12).

BETWEEN THE AIRPORT AND DOWNTOWN

A taxi ride to downtown from LAX can take as little as 30 minutes, but substantially longer in traffic. Visitors should request the flat fee (about $30) to downtown or choose from the several ground transportation companies that offer set rates.

If you're **driving from LAX to downtown L.A.,** take the San Diego Freeway (I–405) north to the Santa Monica Freeway (I–10) east to the Harbor Freeway (I–110) north until you hit downtown. **To get to Beverly Hills,** take the San Diego Freeway north, exit at Santa Monica Boulevard, and turn right.

From Ontario Airport to downtown L.A., take the Harbor Freeway west to the San Diego Freeway north to the Harbor Freeway south; **to Beverly Hills,** take the Santa Monica Freeway west to the San Diego Freeway north, exit at Santa Monica Boulevard, and turn right.

From Long Beach Airport to downtown L.A., take the San Diego Freeway north to Highway 710 north to the Golden State Freeway (I–5) north. **To Beverly Hills,** take the San Diego Freeway north to the Santa Monica Freeway east, and exit at Century Park. **From the Burbank/Glendale/Pasadena Airport to downtown L.A.,** take the Golden State Freeway to the Harbor Freeway south. From the Burbank airport **to Beverly Hills,** take the Golden State Freeway south to the Ventura Freeway (Highway 134) west to the Hollywood Freeway (U.S. 101) north to the San Diego Freeway south, and exit at Santa Monica Boulevard.

For directions to downtown and Beverly Hills from **John Wayne Airport,** *see* Orange County A to Z *in* Chapter 12.

SuperShuttle (☏ 310/782–6600 or 323/775–6600) offers direct service between the airport and hotels. You can use the SuperShuttle courtesy phone in the luggage area; the van should arrive within 15 minutes. **Shuttle One** (☏ 310/670–6666) provides door-to-door service from LAX to hotels in the Disneyland/Anaheim area. **Airport Bus** (☏ 714/938–8900 or 800/772–5299) provides regular service between LAX and the

Pasadena and Anaheim areas. **Van Nuys Flyaway Service** (☎ 818/994–5554) offers transportation between LAX and a terminal in the central San Fernando Valley for $3.50.

From Ontario International, ground transportation possibilities include SuperShuttle as well as **Inland Express** (☎ 909/626–6599) and **Southern California Coach** (☎ 714/978–6415). At John Wayne, **Airport Bus** (☎ 800/772–5299) provides ground transportation.

MTA (☎ 213/626–4455) has limited airport service to all areas of greater L.A.; bus lines depart from bus docks at the Transit Center attached to parking lot C. Prices vary from $1.35 to $3.10; some routes require transfers. The best line to take to downtown is Bus 42 ($1.35) or the express Bus 439 ($1.85). Both take about 70 minutes.

By Train

Los Angeles can be reached by **Amtrak** (☎ 800/872–7245). Trains terminate at **Union Station** (✉ 800 N. Alameda St.) in downtown Los Angeles.

Getting Around

By Bus

A ride on the **Metropolitan Transit Authority (MTA)** (☎ 213/626–4455) costs $1.35, with 25¢ for each transfer.

DASH (Downtown Area Short Hop) minibuses travel around the downtown area, stopping every two blocks or so. There are six different routes with pickups at five-minute intervals. You pay 25¢ every time you get on. Buses generally run on weekdays between 6 AM and 7 PM and on Saturday between 10 AM and 5 PM; a few downtown weekend routes run on Sunday as well.

By Car

A car is a necessity in Los Angeles. If you plan to drive extensively, consider buying a *Thomas Guide,* which contains detailed maps of the entire county. Despite what you've heard, traffic is not always a major problem, especially if you avoid rush hour (between 7 and 9 AM and 3 and 7 PM). Seat belts must be worn by all passengers at all times. A right turn on red after stopping is permitted unless a sign indicating otherwise is posted. Pedestrians have the right of way.

If your car breaks down on an interstate highway, try to pull over onto the shoulder of the road and either wait for the state police to find you or, if you have other passengers who can wait in the car, walk to the nearest emergency roadside phone and call the state police. If you carry a cellular or car telephone, *55 is the emergency number. When calling for help, note your location according to the small green mileage markers posted along the highway. Other highways are also patrolled but may not have emergency phones or mileage markers.

More than 35 major companies and dozens of local rental companies serve a steady demand for cars at Los Angeles International Airport and various city locations. For a list of the major car-rental companies, *see* Car Rentals *in* Smart Travel Tips.

Parking rules are strictly enforced in Los Angeles; illegally parked cars are ticketed and towed very quickly. Parking is generally available in garages or parking lots; prices vary from 25¢ to $2 per half hour, or a few dollars to $25 per day. In the most heavily trafficked areas, garage rates may be as high as $20 an hour, though prices tend to drop on weekends. Metered parking is also widely available; meter rates vary from 25¢ for 15 minutes in the most heavily trafficked areas to 25¢

for one hour. In some areas, metered parking is free on weekends or on Sunday.

By Limousine

Reputable companies include **Dav-El Livery** (☎ 310/550–0070 or 800/922–0343), **First Class** (☎ 310/676–9771 or 800/400–9771), and **Spectrum Limousine Service** (☎ 800/901–4546).

By Subway

The long-awaited Metro Rail's Red Line (☎ 800/266–6883, 🎫 $1.35) follows a westward route from Union Station downtown and has been completed in segments; it now extends from Union Station to Hollywood and Vine. Additional segments reaching to Hollywood Boulevard and Highland Avenue in Hollywood and to Universal City and North Hollywood in the San Fernando Valley were, at press time, expected to come on line in 2000.

By Taxi

You probably won't be able to hail a cab on the street. Instead, you should phone one of the many taxi companies. The rate is $1.90 to start and $1.60 per mile. Two reputable companies are **Independent Cab Co.** (☎ 213/385–8294) and **United Independent Taxi** (☎ 323/653–5050).

By Train

The Metro Rail Blue Line (☎ 213/626–4455) runs daily between 5 AM and 10 PM from downtown Los Angeles (corner of Flower and 7th Sts.) to Long Beach (corner of 1st St. and Long Beach Ave.), with 18 stops en route, most of them in Long Beach. The fare is $1.35 one-way.

Contacts and Resources

Emergencies

Ambulance (☎ 911). **Fire** (☎ 911). **Police** (☎ 911).

Most large hospitals in Los Angeles have 24-hour emergency rooms. Two are **Cedar-Sinai Medical Center** (✉ 8700 Beverly Blvd., ☎ 310/855–5000) and **Queen of Angels Hollywood Presbyterian Medical Center** (✉ 1300 N. Vermont Ave., ☎ 213/413–3000).

Guided Tours

Los Angeles is so spread out and has such a wealth of sightseeing possibilities that a tour may prove useful. Reservations must be made in advance. Many hotels can book them for you.

ORIENTATION TOURS

L.A. Tours and Sightseeing (☎ 323/937–3361 or 800/286–8752) has a $42 tour covering various parts of the city, including downtown, Hollywood, and Beverly Hills. The company also operates tours to Disneyland, Universal Studios, Magic Mountain, beaches, and stars' homes. **Starline Tours of Hollywood** (☎ 800/959–3131 or 323/463–3333) picks up passengers from area hotels as well as around the corner from Mann's Chinese Theater (✉ 6925 Hollywood Blvd.). Universal Studios, Sea World, Knott's Berry Farm, stars' homes, Disneyland, and other attractions are on this company's agenda. Prices range from $29 to $75. **Casablanca Tours** (☎ 323/461–0156 or 800/498–6871) conducts a four-hour insider's look at Hollywood and Beverly Hills. Tours are in minibuses with a maximum of 14 people, and the prices are equivalent to the large bus tours—from $35 to $68.

WALKING TOURS

The **Los Angeles Conservancy** (☎ 213/623–2489) offers low-cost walking tours of the downtown area. Each Saturday at 10 AM one of several tours leaves from the Olive Street entrance of the Regal Biltmore

Hotel. The cost is $5 per person. Make a reservation, because group size is limited.

Late-Night Pharmacies

Most area towns have a Thrifty, Sav-On, or Rite-Aid pharmacy that stays open late; check local listings.

Visitor Information

Hollywood Visitor Information Center (✉ 6541 Hollywood Blvd., ☎ 213/689–8822). **Los Angeles Convention and Visitors Bureau** (✉ 633 W. 5th St., Suite 6000, 90071, ☎ 213/624–7300 or 800/228–2452).

12 ORANGE COUNTY

No place in southern California evokes the stereotype of California's good life quite the way Orange County does: million-dollar mansions dot the coastline, lush golf courses line beaches and meander through inland hills, and tony convertibles glide down Pacific Coast Highway. But, while visitors and residents are adept at relaxing under swaying palm trees while lounging beachfront, the inland cities are alive with amusement parks, professional sporting events, and dozens of hotels and restaurants, all within minutes of one another.

Updated by Cindy LaFavre Yorks

FEW OF THE CITRUS GROVES that gave Orange County its name remain. This region south and east of Los Angeles is now a high-tech business hub where tourism is the number-one industry. Anaheim's theme parks lure hordes of visitors; numerous festivals celebrate the county's culture and relatively brief history; and the area supports fine dining, upscale shopping, and several standout visual and performing arts facilities. With its tropical flowers and palm trees, the stretch of coast between Seal Beach and San Clemente is often called the "American Riviera." Exclusive Newport Beach, artsy Laguna, and the up-and-coming surf town of Huntington Beach are the stars, but lesser-known gems such as Corona del Mar are also worth visiting.

Pleasures and Pastimes

Dining

Italian restaurants and burger joints abound, but you'll also find French, Thai, Scandinavian, Cuban, and other types of cuisine, in every type of setting.

CATEGORY	COST*
$$$$	over $50
$$$	$30–$50
$$	$20–$30
$	under $20

**per person for a three-course meal, excluding drinks, service, and 8¼% tax*

Lodging

The prices listed in this chapter are based on summer rates. Prices are often lower in winter, especially near Disneyland, unless there's a convention in Anaheim. Weekend rates are frequently rock-bottom at business hotels. It's worth calling around to search for bargains.

CATEGORY	COST*
$$$$	over $175
$$$	$120–$175
$$	$80–$120
$	under $80

**All prices are for a standard double room, excluding 14% occupancy tax.*

following the text of a review is your signal that the property has a Web site, where you will find details and, usually, images; for a link, visit www.fodors.com/urls.

Outdoor Activities and Sports

Water sports rule the coast of Orange County, but other sports don't lag far behind. The sight of people jogging, walking, biking, and blading is nearly inescapable. Wave action along Orange County's coastline ranges from beginner to expert. Surfing is permitted at most beaches year-round (check local newspapers or talk to lifeguards for conditions). The best waves are usually at San Clemente, Newport Beach, and Huntington Beach. Keep a lookout for signs warning of dangerous conditions: undertow, strong currents, and big waves can all be hazardous. Never go in the water when flags with a black circle are flying, and avoid swimming near surfers. Many beaches close just after sunset.

Golf and tennis are two more reasons to visit Orange County. A few public golf courses are listed in this chapter. For more information contact the Southern California Golf Association or the Southern California Public Links Golf Association (☞ Visitor Information *in* Orange

County A to Z, *below*). Many hotels have tennis courts, and there are public tennis facilities throughout the county.

For those who wish to enjoy the coastline by bike or on foot, the Santa Ana Riverbed Trail hugs the Santa Ana River for 20½ mi between Pacific Coast Highway (PCH) at Huntington State Beach and Imperial Highway in Yorba Linda. There are entrances, rest rooms, and drinking fountains at all crossings.

Exploring Orange County

Like Los Angeles, Orange County stretches over a large area, lacks a singular focal point, and has limited public transportation. You'll need a car and a sensible game plan to make the most of your visit. If you're headed to Disneyland, you'll probably want to stay in or near Anaheim, organize your activities around the inland-county attractions, and take excursions to the coast.

Numbers in the text correspond to numbers in the margin and on the Orange County map.

Great Itineraries

IF YOU HAVE 1 DAY

You're going to **Disneyland** ①.

IF YOU HAVE 3 DAYS

You're still going to **Disneyland** ① (stay overnight in **Anaheim**), but get up early on day two and head to **Laguna Beach,** before the crowds arrive. On day three, visit **Dana Point** or **Huntington Beach,** then either hang out on the sand with a surfboard or head inland to **Costa Mesa,** where you can browse through **South Coast Plaza** ⑬, one of the world's largest retail, entertainment, and dining complexes.

When to Tour Orange County

The sun shines year-round in Orange County, but you can beat the crowds and the heat by visiting during spring and fall. If you're traveling with children, you could easily devote several days to the theme parks—a day or two at the Magic Kingdom, a day at Knott's Berry Farm, and perhaps a day for some of the area's lesser-known diversions.

INLAND ORANGE COUNTY

About a 35-minute drive from downtown Los Angeles on I–5 (also known as the Golden State Freeway) is Anaheim, Orange County's tourist hub, which centers around the big D.

Anaheim

26 mi southeast of Los Angeles, I–5.

The snowcapped Matterhorn, the centerpiece of the Magic Kingdom, dominates Anaheim's skyline and is an enduring reminder of the role Disneyland has played in the growth of Orange County. Disneyland has attracted millions of visitors and thousands of workers, and Anaheim has been their host, becoming Orange County's most populous city and accounting for more than half the county's 40,000 hotel rooms. Anaheim's vast tourism complex also includes Edison International Field, home of the Anaheim Angels baseball team; the Arrowhead Pond, where the Mighty Ducks hockey team plays; and the enormous Anaheim Convention Center.

★ ❶ **Disneyland** occupies a unique place in the Disney legend, the only one of the four parks overseen by Walt himself. Mr. Disney's personal stamp

Balboa Pavilion 19
Bolsa Chica Ecological Reserve 17
Bowers Museum of Cultural Art 8
Children's Museum at La Habra 5
Crystal Cathedral . . . 7
Disneyland 1
Entertainment Center at Irvine Spectrum 11
Huntington Pier 15
International Surfing Museum 16
Irvine Museum 9
Knott's Berry Farm . . . 2
Laguna Art Museum 22
Mission San Juan Capistrano 24
Movieland Wax Museum 3
Newport Harbor . . . 18
Ocean Institute 23
Old Towne Orange 6
Orange County Museum of Art 20
Orange County Performing Arts Center 14
Richard Nixon Presidential Library and Birthplace 4
San Juan Capistrano Library 25
Sherman Library and Gardens 21
South Coast Plaza 13
University of California at Irvine 10
Wild Rivers Water Park 12

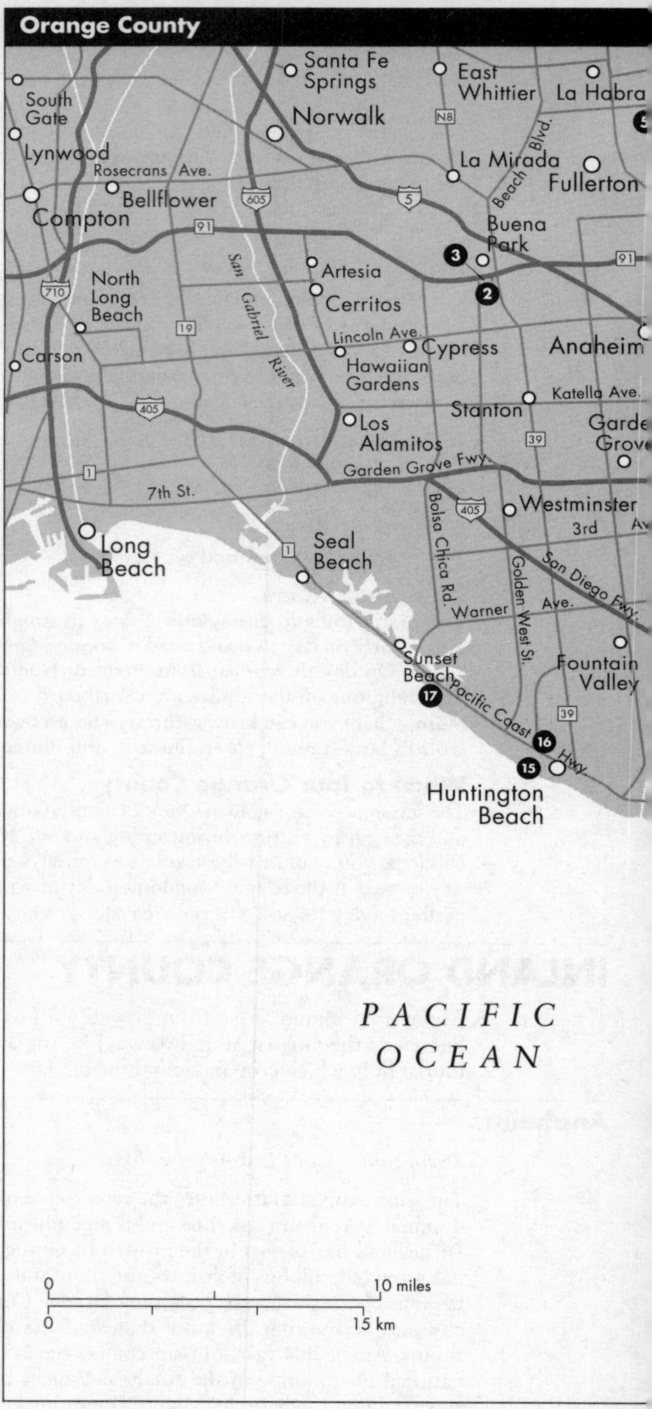

Orange County

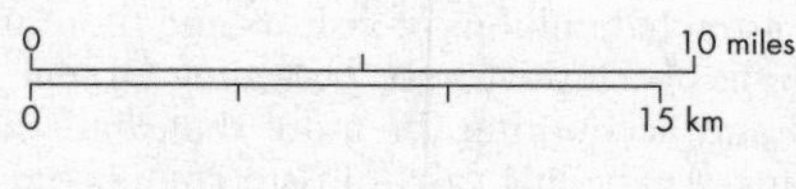

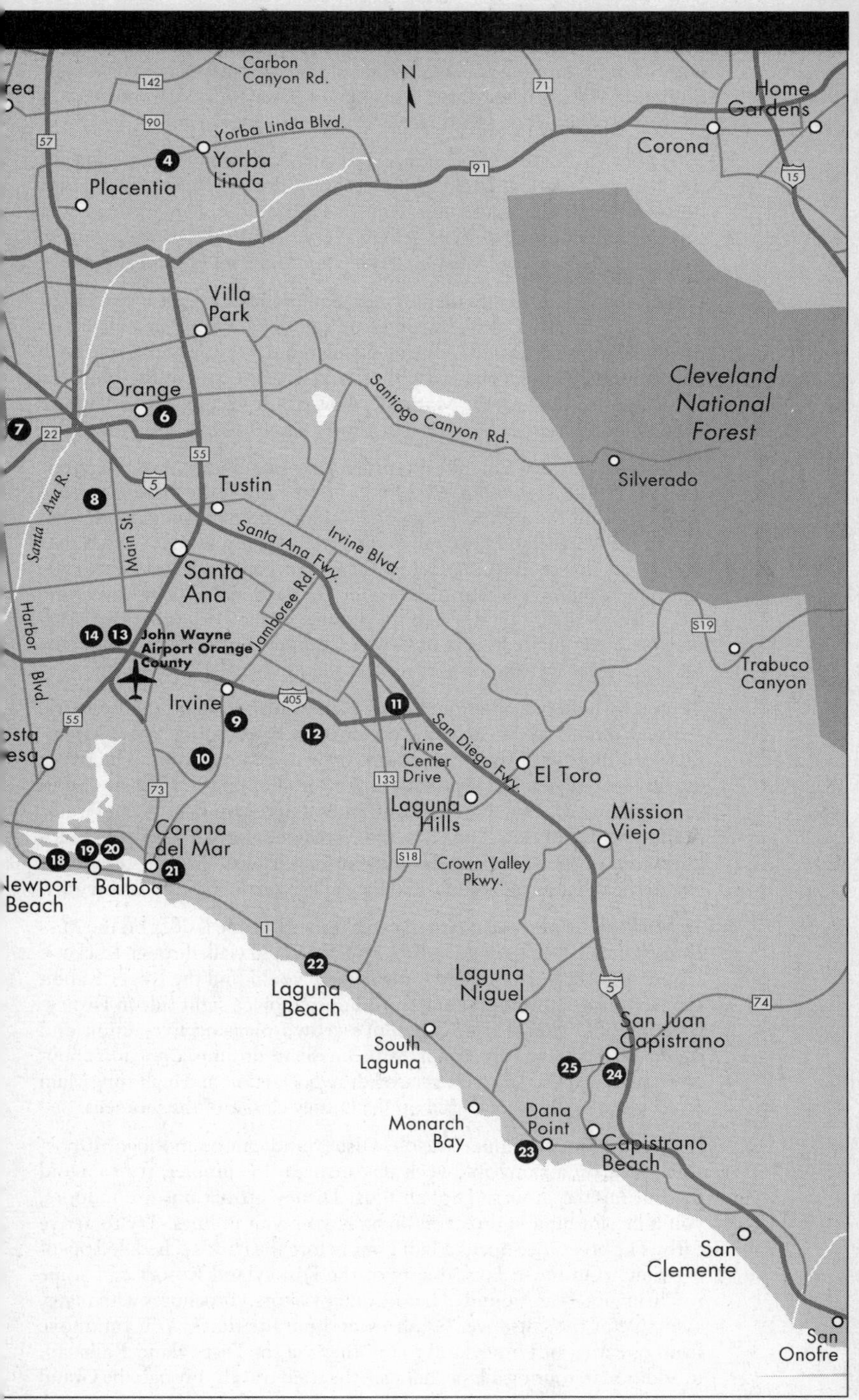
Carbon
Canyon Rd.
N
142
71
Home
Gardens
Corona
90
Yorba Linda Blvd.
57
Yorba
Linda
Placentia
91
15
Villa
Park
Cleveland
National
Forest
Orange
Santiago Canyon Rd.
22
55
Silverado
5
Tustin
Santa Ana R.
Main St.
Santa Ana Fwy.
Irvine Blvd.
Santa
Ana
Jamboree Rd.
Harbor Blvd.
John Wayne
Airport Orange
County
S19
Trabuco
Canyon
Irvine
405
55
San Diego Fwy.
Irvine
Center
Drive
133
El Toro
73
Laguna
Hills
Mission
Viejo
Corona
del Mar
S18
Crown Valley
Pkwy.
Newport
Beach
Balboa
1
Laguna
Beach
Laguna
Niguel
5
74
San Juan
Capistrano
South
Laguna
Monarch
Bay
Dana
Point
Capistrano
Beach
San
Clemente
San
Onofre

has made an imprint that can be felt in the park's genuinely historic feel. There's plenty here that you won't find anywhere else. Storybook Land, with its miniature replicas of classic animated Disney scenes, is a Fantasyland favorite. The Matterhorn, the Indiana Jones Adventure, and the new Rocket Rods speed ride are unique to Disneyland.

Start your visit with a stroll along **Main Street,** a romanticized image of small-town America, circa 1900. Trolleys, double-decker buses, and horse-drawn wagons travel up and down a quaint thoroughfare lined with rows of interconnected shops selling everything from Disney products to magic tricks, crystal ware, sports memorabilia, and photo supplies.

Disneyland is divided into theme lands. **Fantasyland,** its entrance marked by Sleeping Beauty Castle, is where you can fly on Peter Pan's Flight, go down the rabbit hole with Alice in Wonderland, take an aerial spin with Dumbo the Flying Elephant, twirl around in giant cups at the Mad Tea Party, bobsled through the Matterhorn, or visit It's a Small World, where robot children representing 100 countries sing the well-known song.

In **Frontierland** you can take a cruise on the steamboat *Mark Twain* or the sailing ship *Columbia.* Children of every age enjoy rafting to Tom Sawyer Island for an hour or so of climbing and exploring. Some visitors to **Adventureland** have taken the Jungle Cruise so many times that they know the operators' patter by heart. Special effects and decipherable hieroglyphics entertain guests on line for the Indiana Jones Adventure, a don't-miss thrill ride through the Temple of the Forbidden Eye. Also here are the animated bears of **Critter Country; Splash Mountain,** Disney's steepest, wettest adventure; and the Enchanted Tiki Room.

Tomorrowland has a fictional *Buck Rogers* feel. Ride on the futuristic Astro Orbitor rockets, zip along on the Rocket Rods, ride Space Mountain, or tinker with the toys of tomorrow at Innoventions. The twisting streets of **New Orleans Square** are for shopping and browsing in the company of strolling Dixieland musicians. Also here is the Pirates of the Caribbean ride. The Haunted Mansion, populated by 999 holographic ghosts, is nearby. Theme shops sell hats, Mardi Gras merchandise, and gourmet foods, and the gallery carries original Disney art.

At **Mickey's Toontown** children can climb up a rope ladder on the *Miss Daisy* (Donald Duck's boat), talk to a mailbox, and walk through Mickey's House to meet Mickey. Here is also where you'll find the Roger Rabbit Car Toon Spin, the largest and most unusual black-light ride in Disneyland history. The Magic Kingdom's crowd-pleasing live-action and special-effects show Fantasmic! features exhilarating music and just about every animated Disney character ever drawn. Daytime and nighttime Main Street parades are often based on the Disney classic of the moment.

During the busy summer season, Disneyland can be mobbed. If possible, visit on a rainy midweek day instead. In summer, try to avoid the hot midday hours. Though most Disney attractions are indoors, you'll be standing in direct sunlight as you wait in lines. Try to arrive early. The box office opens a half hour before the park's scheduled opening time. (On most days, guests of the Disneyland Resort and some Anaheim hotels are admitted before other visitors.) Brochures with maps, available at the entrance, list show and parade times. You can move from one area of Disneyland to another via the Disneyland Railroad. In addition to touring all the "lands," the train travels through the Grand Canyon and a prehistoric jungle.

Characters appear for autographs and photos throughout the day, but you'll probably have to wait in line. Check with a Disneyland employee for information about character stops. You can also meet some of the

Close-Up

DISNEY'S NEWEST ADVENTURE

THE 55-ACRE DISNEY'S California Adventure is slated to open in February, 2001. Adjacent to Disneyland, it's a microcosm of the Golden State, with 22 rides and attractions, a variety of restaurants, a 2,000-seat theater, and a dozen shops. Disneyland is rooted in fantasy, but Disney's California Adventure is, according to the company's designers, very much "a showcase for pop-culture," celebrating the richness, diversity, and pioneering spirit of California through theme areas and rides. As visitors enter, they walk under a mock Golden Gate Bridge (actually the monorail track), and see a giant sun icon, Disney's emblem for the Golden State.

Condor Flats represents the high desert and has an aviation theme. Excitement is supplied by the Soarin' Over California hang-glider ride (actually an 87-person suspended theater that floats above an IMAX-style screen to simulate hang gliding). In a hangarlike building, the magic of computer graphics and an advanced sound system make an air show seem real, as if such famous aircraft as the space shuttle and Howard Hughes's *Spruce Goose* are flying overhead.

At **Grizzly Peak,** which depicts the Sierra Nevada mountain wilderness, the Redwood Creek Challenge Trail play area, a campfire spot for storytelling, and the Grizzly River Run rapids ride are the main draws. With a 45-ft climb and two 30° drops (the biggest is 22 ft, the longest of any rapids ride), Grizzly River Run offers some of this park's best thrills as riders spin 360°.

The **San Francisco** district features an artisans' workshop and the Circle of Hands California-history film and presentation, highlighting the many peoples who have contributed to the state's success and cultural diversity. Among others, there are scenes of Chinese immigrants working on the railroad and Cesar Chavez organizing farmworkers.

At **Paradise Pier** the theme is a seaside amusement park, with roller coasters, a Ferris wheel, the Orange Stinger swings, a Jumpin' Jellyfish drop ride, a carousel, a children's play area, midway games, and street entertainers. California Screamin' is a looping steel coaster that resembles an old-time wooden one, but with a 107-ft drop, a 360° loop in the shape of Mickey Mouse's head, and with an acceleration from 0 to 55 mph in about four seconds in a catapultlike launch, it's the fastest ride at either of Disney's Anaheim parks.

Pacific Wharf is reminiscent of Monterey's Cannery Row. Exhibits include sourdough bread making and a tortilla factory.The Bountiful Valley Farm area has a tractor play section as well as a California Aqueduct water-play region. There is a demonstration farm here that shows off basic food crops, an important part of the Golden State, whose Central Valley is the "Produce Basket to the World." A mission-style winery complex includes tasting rooms and a demonstration vineyard. A 3-D film gives visitors a bug's-eye perspective on agriculture à la Disney's computer-animated movie *A Bug's Life.*

At the Hollywood-theme area elaborate buildings turn out to be, in true moviemaking fashion, false fronts. Highlights here are a Muppet Vision 3-D film and the Broadway-style Hyperion Theater. This area's big attraction for the ride-minded is Superstar Limo, which simulates a limousine dash through freeway traffic to the beach and other L.A. locations before reaching a replica Chinese Theatre.

Like its sister park, California Adventure has a daily parade. Entry fees are similar to those for Disneyland.

animated icons at one of the character meals served at the Disneyland or Disneyland Pacific hotels (both open to the public).

Plan meals to avoid peak meal times. If you want to eat at the Blue Bayou restaurant in New Orleans Square, it's best to make reservations as soon as you get to the park. Fast-food spots abound, and healthy snacks such as fruit, pasta, and frozen yogurt are sold at various locations. For a quick lunch on the go, try the Blue Ribbon Bakery's gourmet sandwiches.

You can store belongings and purchases in lockers just off Main Street. Purchases can also be sent to the Package Pickup desk at the front of the park. If you're planning on staying for more than a day or two, ask about the Flex Pass, which gives you five-day admission to Disneyland for roughly the same price as a two-day passport (about $68 at press time). The passes are not sold at the park itself, but you can buy them through travel agents and at most area hotels. Disneyland will expand considerably with the opening of its second theme park, the California Adventure. Because of construction detours, your best bet for getting to the park will be to use transportation provided by your hotel. ✉ *1313 Harbor Blvd.,* ☎ *714/781–4565.* *$39.* *June–mid-Sept., Sun.–Fri. 9 AM–midnight, Sat. 9 AM–1 AM; mid-Sept.–May, weekdays 10–6, Sat. 9–midnight, Sun. 9–10.*

Dining and Lodging

Most Anaheim hotels have complimentary shuttle service to Disneyland, though many are within walking distance.

$$–$$$$ ✕ **Yamabuki.** Part of the Disneyland Pacific Hotel complex, this stylish Japanese restaurant serves traditional dishes and has a full sushi bar. The plum-wine ice cream is a treat. ✉ *Disneyland Pacific Hotel, 1717 S. West St.,* ☎ *714/956–6755. AE, DC, MC, V. No lunch weekends.*

$$–$$$ ✕ **Anaheim White House.** Several small dining rooms are set with crisp linens and candles in this flower-filled 1909 mansion. The northern Italian menu includes pasta, rack of lamb, and a large selection of fresh seafood. A three-course prix-fixe lunch, served weekdays only, costs $16. ✉ *887 S. Anaheim Blvd.,* ☎ *714/772–1381. AE, MC, V. No lunch weekends.*

$$–$$$ ✕ **The Catch Seafood Grill.** Across from Anaheim Stadium, this restaurant and sports bar draws a crowd at night. The Catch serves hearty portions of steak, "Certified Angus" prime rib, fresh seafood, pasta, and salads. ✉ *1929 S. State College Blvd.,* ☎ *714/634–1829. AE, D, DC, MC, V.*

$$–$$$ ✕ **Mr. Stox.** Oriental rugs, intimate booths, and linen tablecloths create an elegant setting at this family-owned restaurant. Prime rib, mesquite-grilled rack of lamb, and fresh fish specials are excellent; the pasta, bread, and pastries are homemade; and the wine list wins awards. The valet parking is an added bonus. ✉ *1105 E. Katella Ave.,* ☎ *714/634–2994. AE, D, DC, MC, V. No lunch weekends.*

$–$$$ ✕ **Luigi's D'Italia.** Despite the simple surroundings—red vinyl booths and plastic checkered tablecloths—Luigi's serves outstanding Italian cuisine: spaghetti marinara, cioppino, and all the classics. Children will feel at home here. ✉ *801 S. State College Blvd.,* ☎ *714/490–0990. AE, MC, V.*

$$$$ **Anaheim Marriott.** Rooms at this busy convention hotel are well equipped for business travelers, with desks, two phones, and data ports. Some rooms have balconies, and accommodations on the north side have good views of Disneyland's summer fireworks shows. Discounted weekend and Disneyland packages are available. Two restaurants are on site: JW's Steak House and Cafe del Sol. ✉ *700 W. Convention Way, 92802,* ☎ *714/750–8000 or 800/228–9290,* FAX *714/*

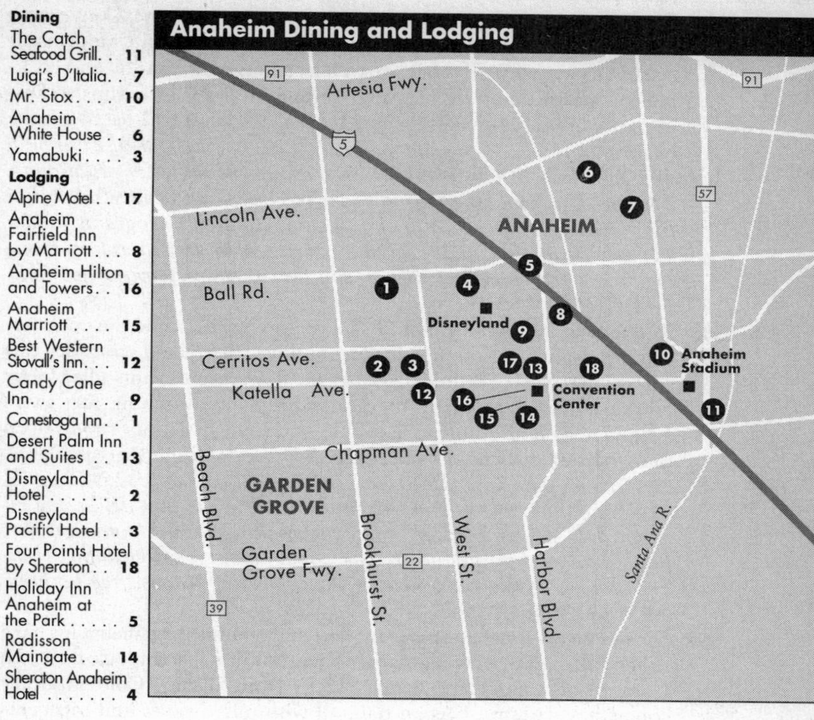

750–9100. 1,033 rooms, 52 suites. 2 restaurants, lounge, in-room data ports, in-room safes, no-smoking floors, room service, 2 pools, 2 hot tubs, health club, piano, coin laundry, dry cleaning, laundry service, concierge, concierge floor, meeting rooms, car rental, parking (fee). AE, D, DC, MC, V.

$$$$ ★ **Disneyland Hotel.** Disney products are for sale everywhere at this resort with a kitschy, 1950s charm. At Goofy's Kitchen, children can dine with their favorite Disney characters. The cove pools have a sandy area for volleyball and sunning. The Peter Pan theme pool has a wooden bridge, a water slide, and a whirlpool. Rooms in the Bonita tower overlook the Fantasy Waters, a fountain that's illuminated at night. On most days, guests staying at the hotel are admitted to the park before the gates open to the general public. Room-and-ticket packages are available. ✉ *1150 W. Cerritos Ave., 92802,* ☎ *714/778–6600,* FAX *714/956–6582. 990 rooms, 62 suites. 5 restaurants, 2 bars, in-room data ports, in-room safes, minibars, refrigerators, room service, 3 pools, hot tub, exercise room, beach, dry cleaning, laundry service, concierge, concierge floor, business services, travel services, airport shuttle, car rental, parking (fee). AE, D, DC, MC, V.*

$$$$ **Disneyland Pacific Hotel.** As part of the Disneyland hotel empire, this has many of the same Disney touches as the Disneyland Hotel, but the atmosphere is a bit quieter and more ordinary. From here you can walk to Disneyland (a feat that will become easier once construction slows down) or pick up a shuttle or monorail. Start the day with the Minnie and Friends character breakfast, or visit with Mary Poppins in her parlor at the Practically Perfect Tea. ✉ *1717 S. West St., 92802,* ☎ *714/999–0990,* FAX *714/956–6582. 488 rooms, 14 suites. 2 restaurants, 2 lounges, no-smoking rooms, room service, pool, hot tub, exercise room, dry cleaning, laundry service, concierge, concierge floor, parking (fee). AE, D, DC, MC, V.*

$$$–$$$$ **Anaheim Hilton and Towers.** Next to the Anaheim Convention Center, this busy Hilton is the largest hotel in southern California: It even has its own post office, as well as shops, restaurants, and cocktail lounges. Rooms are pleasingly bright, and a shuttle runs to Disneyland, or you can walk the few blocks. There's a $12 fee to use the health club. ✉ *777 Convention Way, 92802,* ☎ *714/750–4321 or 800/445–8667,* FAX *714/740–4460. 1,576 rooms, 95 suites. 4 restaurants, 2 lounges, no-smoking floors, room service, pool, beauty salon, hot tub, massage, sauna, health club, piano, children's programs (under 12), dry cleaning, laundry service, concierge, business services, meeting rooms, travel services, airport shuttle, car rental, parking (fee). AE, D, DC, MC, V.*

$$$–$$$$ ★ **Sheraton Anaheim Hotel.** If you're hoping to escape the commercial atmosphere of the hotels surrounding Disneyland, consider this sprawling replica of a Tudor castle. In the flowers-and-plants-filled lobby you're welcome to sit by the grand fireplace, watching fish swim around in a pond. Rooms are sizable, and some first-floor rooms open onto interior gardens and pool area. A Disneyland shuttle is available. ✉ *1015 W. Ball Rd., 92802,* ☎ *714/778–1700 or 800/325–3535,* FAX *714/535–3889. 447 rooms, 42 suites. Restaurant, bar, deli, some in-room data ports, in-room safes, no-smoking rooms, room service, pool, outdoor hot tub, health club, coin laundry, dry cleaning, laundry service, concierge, concierge floor, meeting rooms, free parking. AE, D, DC, MC, V.*

$$$ **Four Points Hotel by Sheraton.** Even in hotel-filled Anaheim, it's hard to miss the shiny, new, upmarket Sheraton. It's just a block from the Convention Center and a few blocks from Disney. Contemporary rooms have a hint of Asian flair, all with microwaves and refrigerators. This is an entirely smoke-free establishment. ✉ *515 W. Katella Ave., 92802,* ☎ *714/991–6868 or 888/543–7878,* FAX *714/991–6565. 104 rooms, 1 suite. Restaurant, bar, in-room data ports, in-room safes, in-room VCRs, no-smoking floors, refrigerators, room service, pool, hot tub, exercise room, video games, coin laundry, dry cleaning, laundry service, business services, meeting rooms, free parking. AE, D, DC, MC, V.*

$$$ **Radisson Maingate.** Some rooms at this friendly hotel have pull-out sofas as well as beds. Regular shuttles zip you to Disneyland or Knott's Berry Farm. ✉ *1850 S. Harbor Blvd., 92802,* ☎ *714/750–2801 or 800/624–6855,* FAX *714/971–4754. 314 rooms. Restaurant, bar, in-room data ports, no-smoking floors, room service, pool, exercise room, coin laundry, dry cleaning, laundry service, concierge, meeting rooms, free parking. AE, D, DC, MC, V.*

$$–$$$ **Holiday Inn Anaheim at the Park.** Families frequent this Mediterranean-style hotel. Complimentary shuttle service takes guests to popular nearby attractions, including Disneyland, Knott's Berry Farm, the Movieland Wax Museum, Medieval Times, and the Main Place and Anaheim Plaza shopping areas. ✉ *1221 S. Harbor Blvd., 92805,* ☎ *714/758–0900 or 800/545–7275,* FAX *714/533–1804. 252 rooms, 2 suites. Restaurant, bar, in-room data ports, no-smoking floors, room service, pool, outdoor hot tub, meeting rooms, free parking. AE, D, DC, MC, V.*

$–$$$ ★ **Candy Cane Inn.** One of the Disneyland area's first hotels (deeds were executed Christmas Eve, hence the name) the Candy Cane has spacious, basic rooms. Deluxe rooms have refrigerators and coffeemakers. A free Disneyland shuttle runs every half hour. ✉ *1747 S. Harbor Blvd., 92802,* ☎ *714/774–5284 or 800/345–7057,* FAX *714/772–5462 or 714/772–1305. 172 rooms. No-smoking rooms, some refrigerators, pool, wading pool, outdoor hot tub, coin laundry, dry cleaning, laundry service, free parking. AE, D, DC, MC, V. CP.*

$–$$$ **Desert Palm Inn and Suites.** This hotel midway between Disneyland and the convention center is a great value, with $80 one-bedroom suites that can accommodate the whole family. All rooms, including the standard variety, have microwaves and refrigerators. A light Continental breakfast (coffee, juice, and Danish) is included daily. ✉ *631 W. Katella Ave., 92802,* ☎ *714/535–1133 or 800/635–5423,* FAX *714/491–7409. 50 rooms, 50 suites. In-room data ports, no-smoking rooms, refrigerators, pool, outdoor hot tub, sauna, coin laundry, dry cleaning, laundry service, free parking. AE, D, DC, MC, V. CP.*

$$ **Conestoga Inn.** Pint-size cowboys will love this Old West–style hotel with swinging saloon doors and a *Bonanza*-style lobby. The restaurants look like saloons, and there's a nice pool area for relaxing. A complimentary shuttle heads to Disneyland every hour. ✉ *1240 S. Walnut Ave., 92802,* ☎ *714/535–0300 or 800/824–5459,* FAX *714/491–8953. 229 rooms, 23 suites. Restaurant, bar, no-smoking rooms, room service, pool, outdoor hot tub, dry cleaning, laundry service, meeting rooms, free parking. AE, D, DC, MC, V.*

$–$$ **Anaheim Fairfield Inn by Marriott.** This hotel provides friendly, detail-oriented service and spacious rooms, most with sleeper sofas as well as beds. Across the street from Disneyland, the hotel runs a free shuttle service to the park. ✉ *1460 S. Harbor Blvd., 92802,* ☎ *714/772–6777 or 800/228–2800,* FAX *714/999–1727. 467 rooms. Restaurant, snack bar, no-smoking floors, refrigerators, room service, pool, outdoor hot tub, travel services, free parking. AE, D, DC, MC, V.*

$–$$ **Best Western Stovall's Inn.** Nice touches at this well-kept motel include a small topiary garden, a free shuttle to Disneyland, and Nintendo and movie rentals. Ask about discounts if you're staying several nights. ✉ *1110 W. Katella Ave., 92802,* ☎ *714/778–1880 or 800/854–8175,* FAX *714/778–3805. 290 rooms. Bar, no-smoking rooms, 2 pools, outdoor hot tub, coin laundry, dry cleaning, laundry service, meeting room free parking. AE, D, DC, MC, V.*

$ **Alpine Motel.** With a lobby that looks like a snow-covered lodge, this convenient hotel is just steps from Disneyland and the convention center. Two-room suites are a great value, even during the busy summer season. ✉ *715 W. Katella Ave., 92802,* ☎ *714/535–2186 or 800/772–4422,* FAX *714/535–3714. 41 rooms, 8 suites. No-smoking rooms, pool, coin laundry, dry cleaning, laundry service, free parking. AE, D, DC, MC, V. CP.*

Outdoor Activities and Sports

Pro baseball's **Anaheim Angels** play at Edison International Field (✉ 2000 Gene Autry Way, ☎ 714/634–2000). The National Hockey League's **Mighty Ducks of Anaheim** play at Arrowhead Pond (✉ 2695 E. Katella Ave., ☎ 714/740–2000). There are six public tennis courts at **Pearson Park** (✉ 400 N. Harbor Blvd.); call the **Parks and Recreation Department** (☎ 714/765–5191) for details. **Dad Miller Golf Course** (✉ 430 N. Gilbert St., ☎ 714/765–4653), an 18-hole par-71 course, requires reservations seven days in advance. Greens fees range from $19 to $25; optional cart rental is $24.

Buena Park

25 mi south of Los Angeles, I–5.

A humble farmer in Buena Park created the boysenberry by mixing red raspberries, blackberries, and loganberries. Now on his land is Knott's Berry Farm, a major amusement park.

★ 2 **Knott's Berry Farm** got its start in 1934, when Cordelia Knott began serving chicken dinners on her wedding china to supplement her family's income. Or so the story goes. The dinners and her boysenberry pies proved more profitable than husband Walter's berry farm, so the two moved first into the restaurant business and then into the entertainment business. Their park is now a 150-acre complex with 100-plus rides and attractions, 60 food concessions and restaurants, and 60 shops.

GhostRider was Orange County's first wooden roller coaster. Traveling 56 mph at its fastest and reaching 118 ft at its highest, the coaster is riddled with sudden dips and curves. Your next stop might be **Ghost Town,** whose authentic old buildings have been relocated from their original mining-town sites. You can stroll down the street, stop and chat with the blacksmith, pan for gold, crack open a geode, ride in an authentic 1880s passenger train, or take the Gold Mine ride and descend into a replica of a working gold mine. A real treasure here is the antique Dentzel carousel.

Camp Snoopy is a miniature High Sierra wonderland where Snoopy and his friends from the "Peanuts" comic strip hang out. Nearby is **Big Foot Rapids,** where you can ride white water in an inner tube and commune with the native peoples of the Northwest coast in the spooky Mystery Lodge. For more water thrills, check out the dolphin and sea lion shows in the Pacific Pavilion at **The Boardwalk,** which houses several attractions including rides such as the **Boomerang** roller coaster and the new **Perilous Plunge,** billed as the world's tallest, steepest and — thanks to its big splash — wettest thrill ride; **Kingdom of the Dinosaurs,** a *Jurassic Park*–like thrill ride; and **Montezooma's Revenge,** a roller coaster that goes from 0 to 55 mph in less than five seconds. **Jaguar!** simulates the motions of a cat stalking its prey, twisting, spiraling, and speeding up and slowing down as it takes guests on its stomach-dropping course. **Wind Jammer** is the country's first outdoor dual-action roller coaster, with two cars racing simultaneously through twists and turns at top speed. Shows are scheduled in the Good Time Theater throughout the day. ✉ *8039 Beach Blvd., between La Palma Ave. and Crescent St.,* ☎ *714/220–5200.* 🎟 *$38.* ⏲ *June–mid-Sept., daily 9 AM–midnight; mid-Sept.–May, weekdays 10–6, Sat. 10–10, Sun. 10–7; closed during inclement weather.*

3 More than 75 years of movie magic are immortalized at the **Movieland Wax Museum,** which holds several hundred wax sculptures of Hollywood's stars and American political figures, including Michael Jackson, John Wayne, Marilyn Monroe, and George Burns. You can buy a combination ticket for $16.90 that also allows you admission to the so-so Ripley's Believe It or Not, across the street. ✉ *7711 Beach Blvd., between La Palma and Orangethorpe Aves.,* ☎ *714/522–1155.* 🎟 *$12.95.* ⏲ *Weekdays 10–6; weekends 9–7.*

Dining and Lodging

$ ✕ **Mrs. Knott's Chicken Dinner Restaurant.** The restaurant, at the park's entrance, still serves all-American crispy fried chicken, along with tangy cole slaw and Mrs. Knott's signature chilled cherry-rhubarb compote. Long lines on weekends may not be worth your valuable time. It's open for breakfast, lunch, and dinner and, on Sunday afternoon, for brunch. ✉ *Knott's Berry Farm, 8039 Beach Blvd.,* ☎ *714/220–5080. AE, D, DC, MC, V.*

$$ **The Radisson Resort at Knott's Berry Farm.** The hotel, on Knott's Berry Farm grounds, has recently been given a total face lift, with new paint and wallpaper, carpets, furniture, even light fixtures. New, too, are enhanced guest services and resort amenities, such as a second swimming pool and tennis courts. There's shuttle service to Disneyland, packages that include entry to Knott's Berry Farm, and family-oriented "camp rooms" that are decorated in the amusement park's Camp Snoopy motif. ✉ *7675 Crescent Ave., 90620,* ☎ *714/995–1111,* FAX *714/828–8590. 313*

rooms, 20 suites. 2 restaurants, bar, room service, 2 pools, hot tub, health club coin laundry, laundry service, concierge. AE, D, DC, MC, V.

Yorba Linda, La Habra, and Brea

7–12 mi north of Anaheim, Hwy. 57.

Clustered together just north of Anaheim, Yorba Linda, La Habra, and Brea are quiet suburban towns characterized by lush parks and family-oriented shopping centers. Yorba Linda's main claim to fame is the

4 **Richard Nixon Presidential Library and Birthplace,** final resting place of the 37th president and his wife, Pat. Exhibits illustrate the checkered career of Nixon, from heralded leader of the free world to beleaguered resignee. Visitors can listen to the so-called smoking-gun tape from the Watergate days, among other recorded material. Life-size sculptures of foreign world leaders, gifts Nixon received from international heads of state, and a large graffiti-covered section of the Berlin Wall are on display. In contrast to some of the high-tech displays here are Pat Nixon's tranquil rose garden and the small farmhouse where Richard Nixon was born in 1913. Don't miss the bookstore, selling everything from commemorative birdhouses to photos of Nixon with Elvis. ✉ *18001 Yorba Linda Blvd., at Imperial Hwy., Yorba Linda,* ☎ *714/993–3393.* *$5.95.* ⊙ *Mon.–Sat. 10–5, Sun. 11–5.*

5 The **Children's Museum at La Habra** is housed in a 1923-vintage Union Pacific railroad depot, with old railroad cars resting nearby. Children can climb behind the wheel of Buster the Bus, a retired transit bus; "dig up" bones in the huge Dinosaur Dig sandbox; or pretend they're early settlers fishing, camping, and exploring caves. ✉ *301 S. Euclid St., La Habra,* ☎ *562/905–9793.* *$4.* ⊙ *Mon.–Sat. 10–5, Sun. 1–5.*

Dining

$$$–$$$$ ★ ✕ **La Vie en Rose.** It's worth the detour to Brea to sample the stylishly presented traditional French cuisine served in this reproduction Norman farmhouse, complete with a large turret. There's seafood; lamb; veal; and for dessert, a silky crème brûlée and a Grand Marnier soufflé. ✉ *240 S. State College Blvd. (across from Brea mall),* ☎ *714/529–8333. AE, MC, V. Closed Sun.*

Garden Grove and Orange

South of Anaheim, I–5 to Hwy. 22.

Orange, like any well-rounded city, is a mix of old and new. New is **The Block at Orange,** a dining, shopping, and 30-screen AMC movie theater complex, near the 5 and 22 freeways. The complex also features a Van's skate park for skateboarders. Around the intersection of Glassell Street and Chapman Avenue is Orange Plaza (or Orange Cir-

6 cle, as locals call it), the heart of **Old Towne Orange.** One of the few historic towns in Orange County, this area is a must-stop for antiques browsers and architecture aficionados. Locals take great pride in their many California Craftsman–style cottages; Christmas is a particularly lovely time to visit, when many of the area's charming homes are festooned with tasteful yet elaborate decorations. If the town looks familiar to you, perhaps it's because many a film crew has popped in for shooting, including Tom Hanks and clan for *That Thing You Do.*

7 In Garden Grove the main attraction is the **Crystal Cathedral,** the domain of television evangelist Robert Schuller. Designed by Philip Johnson, the sparkling glass structure resembles a four-pointed star, with more than 10,000 panes of glass covering a weblike steel truss to form transparent walls. ✉ *12141 Lewis St. (take I–5 to Chapman Ave. W),*

Garden Grove, ☎ *714/971–4013.* 🎫 *Donation requested for tours. Tickets for pageants are $20–$30.* ⏲ *Guided tours Mon.–Sat. 9–3:30; call for schedule. Sunday services at 9:30, 11, 1 (in Spanish), and 6.*

Dining

$$–$$$$ ✕ **Citrus City Grill.** Innovative cuisine and striking decor combining history and modernity characterize one of the best restaurants in the county. The citrus theme plays out in everything, including the art on the walls. Don't miss the *ahi poke* salad (tuna on wonton strips). The inviting, elegantly lit half-moon bar is a surefire lively gathering place for martini aficionados. ✉ *122 N. Glassell St., Orange,* ☎ *714/639–9600. AE, DC, MC, V. Closed Sun. and Mon.*

Santa Ana

12 mi south of Anaheim, I–5 to Hwy. 55.

8 The main attraction in Santa Ana, the county seat, is the **Bowers Museum of Cultural Art.** Permanent exhibits include Pacific Northwest wood carvings, dazzling beadwork of the Plains cultures, and still-life paintings. The interactive exhibits at the **Bowers Kidseum** (✉ 1802 N. Main St.) are geared toward children ages 6–12. ✉ *2002 N. Main St., off I–5,* ☎ *714/567–3600.* 🎫 *$8.* ⏲ *Tues.–Sun. 10–4, Thurs. 10–9.*

Dining

$$$–$$$$ ★ ✕ **Gustaf Anders/Back Pocket.** At this cool, Scandinavian restaurant, you'll find top-notch grilled gravlax, and a wonderful fillet of beef prepared with Stilton cheese, a red-wine sauce, and creamed morel mushrooms. Next door is the more casual, less expensive Gustaf Anders' Back Pocket, with equally excellent food. ✉ *South Coast Plaza Village, 3851 Bear St.,* ☎ *714/668–1737. AE, DC, MC, V. No lunch Sun. at Back Pocket; both restaurants closed Mon.*

$–$$ ✕ **Topaz.** Inside the Bowers Museum, this unique ethnic eatery touts a Zuni Native American influence in its regular menu as well as specials. Dine alfresco or inside the funky main dining room and watch the "chef theater" where the spicy, imaginative dishes are prepared. ✉ *2002 N. Main St.,* ☎ *714/835–2002. AE, DC, MC, V. Lunch daily 11–3; dinner Thurs., Fri. 5–9.*

Irvine

6 mi south of Santa Ana, Hwy. 55 to I–405; 12 mi south of Anaheim, I–5.

Irvine, with its tree-lined streets, uniformly manicured lawns, and pristine parks, may feel surreal to urban visitors. It's ranked in several national surveys as America's safest city. The master-planned community has top-notch schools, a university and a community college, plus dozens of shopping centers as well as a network of well-lit walking and biking paths.

9 Some of the Californian impressionist paintings on display at the small yet intriguing **Irvine Museum** depict the state's rural landscape in the years before freeways and housing developments. The paintings, which are displayed on the 12th floor of the cylindrical marble-and-glass Tower 17 building, were assembled by Joan Irvine Smith, granddaughter of James Irvine, who once owned one-quarter of what is now Orange County. ✉ *18881 Von Karman Ave., at Martin St.,* ☎ *949/476–2565.* 🎫 *Free.* ⏲ *Tues.–Sat. 11–5.*

10 The **University of California at Irvine** was established on 1,000 acres of rolling ranch land donated by the Irvine family in the mid-1950s. The campus contains more than 11,000 trees from all over the world and features a stellar biological science department and creative writ-

ing program. The **Art Gallery at UC Irvine** (☎ 949/824–6610) sponsors exhibitions of student and professional art. It's free and open from mid-September through mid-June, Monday through Saturday from noon to 5. ✉ *I–405 to Jamboree Rd., west to Campus Dr. S,* ☎ *949/824–5011.*

11 The mind-boggling 32-acre **Entertainment Center at Irvine Spectrum** contains a huge, 21-theater cinema complex (with a six-story IMAX 3-D theater), several lively restaurants (including Crazy Horse Steakhouse and Saloon, a local bastion of country music that moved here last year) and cafés, 150 shops, as well as a virtual-reality experience set inside the NASCAR Silicon Motor Speedway. Other highlights: Gameworks, a high-tech arcade for children and the newly-moved-to-these-premises Improvisation comedy club. ✉ *Exit Irvine Center Dr. at intersection of I–405, I–5, and Hwy. 133,* ☎ *949/450–4900 for film listings.*

12 **Wild Rivers Water Park** has more than 40 rides and attractions, including a wave pool, a few daring slides, a river inner-tube ride, and several cafés and shops. ✉ *8770 Irvine Center Dr., off I–405,* ☎ *949/768–9453.* *$23.* ⏲ *Mid-May–Sept.; call for hrs.*

Dining and Lodging

$$$ ✕ **Bistango.** A sleek, postmodern, art-filled bistro serves first-rate American cuisine with a European flair: salads, seafood, pasta, Mediterranean pizzas, and grilled ahi tuna. An attractive group comes to savor the food, listen to live jazz, and mingle with their well-dressed peers. ✉ *19100 Von Karman Ave.,* ☎ *949/752–5222. AE, D, DC, MC, V.*

$$–$$$ ★ ✕ **Prego.** Reminiscent of a Tuscan villa, this is a much larger version of the Beverly Hills Prego, with soft lighting, golden walls, and an outdoor patio. Try the spit-roasted meats and chicken, charcoal-grilled fresh fish, or pizzas from the oak-burning oven. ✉ *18420 Von Karman Ave.,* ☎ *949/553–1333. AE, DC, MC, V. No lunch weekends.*

$–$$$ ✕ **Sam Woo.** From fresh- and saltwater tanks comes seafood cooked to order at this formal Chinese restaurant. Whole fish is presented tableside. Service is gracious and the setting peaceful. Next door is Sam Woo Express for BBQ. ✉ *15333 Culver Dr., Suite 720,* ☎ *949/262–0688. AE, D, MC, V.*

$–$$ ✕ **Kitima Thai Cuisine.** Orange County's best Thai restaurant is a favorite with the business-lunch crowd. The names may be gimmicky—Rock-and-Roll Shrimp Salad, Rambo Chicken (sautéed with green chilis and sweet basil)—but fresh ingredients are used in every dish. ✉ *2010 Main St., Suite 170,* ☎ *949/261–2929. AE, MC, V. Closed Sun.*

$$$–$$$$ 🏨 **Atrium Hotel.** Across the street from John Wayne Airport and near most area offices, this garden-style hotel caters to business travelers. Rooms have large work areas, coffeemakers, and two phones, and most offer private balconies overlooking either the pool or gardens. ✉ *18700 MacArthur Blvd., 92612,* ☎ *949/833–2770 or 800/854–3012,* FAX *949/757–1228. 214 rooms. Restaurant, bar, pool, health club, car rental. AE, D, DC, MC, V.*

$$$–$$$$ 🏨 **Hyatt Regency Irvine.** The sleek, ultramodern rooms here offer practical amenities such as coffeemakers, irons, and hair dryers. Special golf packages at nearby Tustin Ranch and Pelican Hills are available, and a complimentary shuttle runs to the airport. Rates are lower on weekends. ✉ *17900 Jamboree Rd., 92614,* ☎ *949/975–1234 or 800/233–1234,* FAX *949/852–1574. 536 rooms, 20 suites. 2 restaurants, 2 bars, pool, 4 tennis courts, health club, bicycles, concierge, business services. AE, D, DC, MC, V.*

$$$–$$$$ **Irvine Marriott.** Towering over Koll Business Center, the Marriott offers a convenient location and amenities designed to appeal to business travelers. The hotel has an intimate feel, owing in part to the convivial lobby with love seats and evening entertainment (usually a jazz pianist). Weekend discounts and packages are usually available, and there's a courtesy van to South Coast Plaza and the airport. ✉ *18000 Von Karman Ave., 92612,* ☎ *949/553–0100 or 800/228–9290,* FAX *949/261–7059. 484 rooms, 8 suites. 2 restaurants, coffee bar, sushi bar, indoor-outdoor pool, hot tub, 4 tennis courts, health club, concierge floors, business services, airport shuttle. AE, D, DC, MC, V.*

Costa Mesa

6 mi northeast of Irvine, I–405 to Bristol St.

Though it's probably best known for its top-notch shopping mall, Costa Mesa is also the performing-arts hub of Orange County, and a formidable local business center. Patrons of the domestic and international theater, opera, and dance productions fill area restaurants and nightspots. Cinema buffs have several theaters to choose from, too.

★ 13 Costa Mesa's most famous landmark, **South Coast Plaza** is an immense retail, entertainment, and dining complex consisting of two enclosed shopping areas—Jewel Court and the new Crate and Barrel Wing—and an open-air collection of boutiques at South Coast Village. The Plaza rivals Rodeo Drive in its number of top international designers' shops—Gucci, Armani, Christian Dior, Versace, and Prada, to name just a few—along with standard upscale shops such as J. Crew, Ralph Lauren, Liz Claiborne, and F.A.O. Schwarz. A free shuttle transports the Plaza's 33 million annual visitors between sections. ✉ *3333 S. Bristol St., off I–405,* ☎ *714/435–2000.* ⏲ *Weekdays 10–9, Sat. 10–7, Sun. 11–6:30.*

14 The **Orange County Performing Arts Center** (✉ 600 Town Center Dr., east of Bristol St., ☎ 714/556–2787) contains a 3,000-seat facility for opera, ballet, symphony, and musicals. Richard Lippold's enormous *Firebird,* a triangular-shape sculpture of polished metal surfaces that resembles a bird taking flight, extends outward from the glass-enclosed lobby. Within walking distance of the center is the **California Scenario** (✉ 611 Anton Blvd.), a 1½-acre sculpture garden designed by Isamu Noguchi.

Dining and Lodging

$$$ ★ ✕ **Diva.** Ideal for patrons of the South Coast Repertory Theater and the Performing Arts Center, Diva offers unexpected combinations of ingredients presented in ways almost too pretty to eat. Entrées such as jumbo potato-wrapped scallops and 16-oz. rib-eye steaks are heartwarmingly good, and the dessert soufflés are renowned. ✉ *600 Anton Blvd.,* ☎ *714/754–0600. AE, DC, MC, V. No lunch weekends; no dinner Mon.; no dinner Sun. unless there is a show.*

$$–$$$ ✕ **Habana Restaurant and Bar.** With rustic candelabras and murals in a candlelit former industrial space, Habana blends an Old World flavor with a hip '90s flair. The Cuban and Caribbean specialties are as flavorful as the setting is cool: Try the *ropa vieja* (shredded beef) or the plantain-crusted chicken. Chocolate lovers can't miss the Café Cubano—chocolate mousse topped with chocolate whipped cream and rum sauce. With entertainment three nights a week (including flamenco on Saturday) this restaurant is fast becoming a popular Orange County nightspot. ✉ *2930 Bristol St.,* ☎ *714/556–0176. AE, D, DC, MC, V.*

$$–$$$ ✕ **Pinot Provence.** The county's hottest new French dining spot showcases the innovative cuisine of chef Joachim Splichal (of L.A.'s Patina). Discover the wildly imaginative mix of fresh California ingredients and traditional Provençal cooking, which results in such innovative fare as pistou of milk-fed lamb ragout. The well-heeled meet in the main dining room amid 18th-century antiques to be seen (and unfortunately heard), so many prefer the more intimate patio dining. ✉ *686 Anton Blvd.,* ☎ *714/444–5900. Reservations essential. AE, D, DC, MC, V.*

$–$$$ ★ ✕ **Bangkok IV.** Despite its shopping-mall location, this restaurant's stark white-and-black interior, with striking flower arrangements on every table, defies conventional mall dining. The deep-fried catfish with a chile-garlic-lemongrass sauce, is exceptional. Or try the *kai pudd keng,* succulent ginger chicken with mushrooms and garlic. ✉ *South Coast Plaza, 3333 Bear St., in the Crate and Barrel Wing,* ☎ *714/540–7661. AE, D, DC, MC, V.*

$–$$ ★ ✕ **Memphis Soul Café and Bar.** The gumbo here is the best in the county, and the pork chops are a work of art. ✉ *2920 Bristol St.,* ☎ *714/432–7685. AE, DC, MC, V.*

$$$–$$$$ 🏨 **Westin South Coast Plaza.** This downtown high-rise adjoins the South Coast Plaza complex, making it convenient for shoppers and businesspeople. ✉ *686 Anton Blvd., 92626,* ☎ *714/540–2500 or 800/228–3000,* FAX *714/662–6695. 373 rooms, 17 suites. Restaurant, pool, 2 tennis courts. AE, D, DC, MC, V.*

$–$$$$ 🏨 **Country Inn and Suites.** Here you'll get close to the bed-and-breakfast experience with rooms and common areas that look more like Mom's house than a hotel. The Queen Anne–style rooms, with a vaguely European feel, are homey and inviting. ✉ *325 Bristol St., 92626,* ☎ *714/549–0300 or 800/322–9992,* FAX *714/662–0828. 150 rooms, 150 suites. Restaurant, bar, 2 pools, 2 hot tubs, exercise room, business center. AE, D, DC, MC, V. BP.*

$$–$$$ 🏨 **Doubletree Hotel.** Near John Wayne Airport, this modern, spacious hotel has a glittering atrium lobby with glass elevators. ✉ *3050 Bristol St., 92626,* ☎ *714/540–7000,* FAX *714/438–4949. 484 rooms, 10 suites. Restaurant, lobby lounge, pool, beauty salon, hot tub, health club. AE, D, DC, MC, V.*

THE COAST

Running along the Orange County coastline is the scenic Pacific Coast Highway (Highway 1, known locally as PCH). It's well worth the effort to take this route instead of the freeways. Pull over on PCH and a public beach is often just steps away.

Huntington Beach

25 mi west of Anaheim, Hwy. 57 south to Hwy. 22 West to I–405.

Once a sleepy residential town with little more than a string of rugged surf shops, Huntington Beach is slowly transforming into a resort destination. The town's appeal is its broad white-sand beaches with often-towering waves. A lively pier, a large shopping pavilion on Main Street, and the luxurious Waterfront Hilton beckon various locals and visitors.

15 **Huntington Pier** stretches 1,800 ft out to sea, well past the powerful waves that made Huntington Beach America's "Surf City." At the end of the pier sits Ruby's (☎ 714/969–7829), part of a California chain of '40s-style burger-centered eateries. The **Pierside Pavilion,** across Pacific Coast Highway from the pier, contains shops, restaurants, bars with live
16 music, and a theater complex. Just up Main Street, the **International Surf-**

ing Museum (✉ 411 Olive Ave., ☎ 714/960–3483), open from Wednesday through Sunday between noon and 5 (🎫 $2), pays tribute to the sport's greats with the Surfing Hall of Fame.

Huntington City Beach stretches for 3 mi from the pier area. The beach is most crowded around the pier. Amateur and professional surfers brave the waves daily on its north side. Continuing north, **Huntington State Beach** (☎ 714/536–1454) parallels Pacific Coast Highway. On the state and city beaches there are changing rooms, concessions, lifeguards (except in winter), and ample parking. The state beach also has barbecue pits. At the northern section of the city, **Bolsa Chica State Beach** (☎ 714/846–3460) has barbecue pits and RV campsites and is usually less crowded than its southern neighbors.

★ 17 **Bolsa Chica Ecological Reserve** beckons wildlife lovers and bird-watchers with an 1,180-acre salt marsh that is home to 315 species of birds, including great blue herons, snowy and great egrets, and common loons. Throughout the reserve are trails for bird-watching. Free guided tours depart from the walking bridge the first Saturday of each month at 9 AM. ✉ *Entrance at Warner Ave. and PCH, opposite Bolsa Chica State Beach,* ☎ *714/840–1575.* 🎫 *Free.* ⏲ *Daily dawn–sunset.*

Dining and Lodging

$–$$$ ✕ **Baci.** Romantic or kitschy, depending on your style, Baci nevertheless serves dependable Italian food. Among the best dishes are carpaccio with shrimp, tortellini soup, and cannoli for dessert. ✉ *18748 Beach Blvd.,* ☎ *714/965–1194. AE, D, DC, MC, V.*

$$ ✕ **Louise's Trattoria.** The local branch of this Italian chain is across the street from the Huntington Beach pier. The chicken marsala and fettuccine with sun-dried tomatoes in a chardonnay-cream sauce hit the spot, and the pizzas are stellar. ✉ *300 PCH,* ☎ *714/960–0996. AE, D, DC, MC, V.*

$ ✕ **Alice's Breakfast in the Park.** Tranquillity is the buzzword at this wooden brunch house nestled among Huntington Park's eucalyptus trees near Huntington Lake. There's seating on the outdoor patio, from which children can feed the ducks, and a small, indoor dining room with flowers and antiques. Be sure to try Alice's "outrageous cinnamon roll." ✉ *6622 Lakeview Dr., off Edwards St.,* ☎ *714/848–0690. No credit cards. No dinner.*

$ ✕ **Wahoo's Fish Taco.** Mahimahi- and wahoo-filled tacos are the specialty of this casual, incredibly popular restaurant. ✉ *120 Main St.,* ☎ *714/536–2050. MC, V.*

$$$$ 🏨 **Waterfront Hilton.** Rising 12 stories above the surf, this Mediterranean-style resort occupies a spot on 8½ mi of white-sand beach. All rooms have private lanais, many with panoramic ocean views. ✉ *21100 PCH, 92648,* ☎ *714/960–7873 or 800/822–7873,* FAX *714/845–8424. 258 rooms, 32 suites. 2 restaurants, bar, pool, hot tub, 2 tennis courts, exercise room, children's programs (ages 5–12; summer only), concierge floor. AE, DC, MC, V.*

Newport Beach

6 mi south of Huntington Beach, Hwy. 1.

Newport Beach has two distinct personalities. It's best known for its island-dotted yacht harbor and wealthy residents. And then there's inland Newport Beach, southwest of John Wayne Airport, a business and commercial hub lined with shopping centers and a clutch of high-rise office buildings and hotels.

★ 18 **Newport Harbor,** which shelters nearly 10,000 small boats, may seduce even those who don't own a yacht. Exploring the charming avenues and surrounding alleys can be great fun. To see Newport Harbor from the water, take a one-hour gondola cruise operated by the Gondola Company of Newport (✉ 3400 Via Oporto, Suite 102B, ☎ 949/675–1212). It costs $75 for two.

Within Newport Harbor are eight small islands, including Balboa and Lido. The houses lining the shore may seem modest, but this is some of the most expensive real estate in the world.

Newport Pier, which juts out into the ocean near 20th Street, is the heart of Newport's beach community. On the pier you can go fishing or grab a burger and shake at **Ruby's** (☎ 949/675–7829). Street parking is difficult at the pier, so grab the first space you find and be prepared to walk. A stroll along West Ocean Front reveals much of the town's character. On weekday mornings, head for the beach near the pier, where fishermen hawk their predawn catches. On weekends the walk is alive with children of all ages on in-line skates, skateboards, and bikes dodging pedestrians and whizzing past fast-food joints, swimsuit shops, and bars.

19 Newport's best beaches are on **Balboa Peninsula,** whose many jetties pave the way to ideal swimming areas. The **Balboa Pavilion,** on the bay side of the Balboa Peninsula, was built in 1905 as a bath- and boathouse. Today it houses a restaurant and shops and is a departure point for harbor and whale-watching cruises. Look for it on Main Street, off Balboa Boulevard. Adjacent to the pavilion is the three-car ferry that connects the peninsula to Balboa Island.

20 The **Orange County Museum of Art** has gathered an esteemed collection of Abstract Expressionist paintings and cutting-edge contemporary works by California artists. The museum displays some of its collection at a gallery at South Coast Plaza (☞ Costa Mesa, *above*), as well; it's open the same hours as the mall. ✉ *850 San Clemente Dr.,* ☎ *949/759–1122.* *$5.* ⏲ *Tues.–Sun. 11–5.*

Dining and Lodging

$$$–$$$$ ✕ **The Ritz.** Indeed, this is one of the ritziest restaurants in southern California, complete with black-leather booths, polished-brass trim, and the requisite attitude. Don't pass up the "carousel" appetizer—cured gravlax, prawns, Dungeness crab legs, Maine lobster tails, goose liver pâté, fillet of smoked trout, Parma prosciutto, filet mignon tartare, and marinated herring, all served on a lazy Susan. ✉ *880 Newport Center Dr.,* ☎ *949/720–1800. Reservations essential. AE, DC, MC, V. No lunch weekends.*

$$–$$$$ ★ ✕ **Aubergine.** The husband-and-wife team who run this restaurant (he mans the kitchen and she handles the dining room) have set new standards for fine cuisine in Orange County. The three-, five-, and nine-course prix-fixe menus (and an exceptional wine list) are unforgettable. You can also order à la carte. Classic French dishes are prepared with a modern flair. ✉ *508 29th St.,* ☎ *949/723–4150. Reservations essential. AE, MC, V. Closed Sun.–Mon. No lunch.*

$$–$$$$ ✕ **Twin Palms.** The area's most beautiful people congregate under the tentlike atmosphere at this haute eatery. Pasta, chicken, pizza, fish specials, and salads are all on the creative menu in this sister property to the original Twin Palms in Pasadena. There's live music three nights a week, plus dance music Saturday after 10. ✉ *630 Newport Center Dr.,* ☎ *949/721–8288. AE, DC, MC, V.*

$–$$ ★ ✕ **El Torito Grill.** The tortilla soup is to die for, as is the carne asada. Just-baked tortillas with fresh salsa replace the usual chip basket. The bar serves hand-shaken margaritas and 80 brands of tequila. ✉ *Fash-*

ion Island, 951 Newport Center Dr., ☎ 949/640–2875. AE, D, DC, MC, V.

$–$$ ✕ **P. F. Chang's China Bistro.** The tasty Cal-Chinese food at this trendy chain restaurant includes Mongolian spicy beef and Chang's chicken, stir-fried in a sweet-and-spicy Szechuan sauce. Almost every table has an ocean view. ✉ *Fashion Island, 1145 Newport Center Dr., ☎ 949/759–9007. Reservations not accepted. AE, MC, V.*

$$$$ ★ **Four Seasons Hotel.** A stylish hotel in an ultrachic neighborhood, the Four Seasons caters to luxury seekers by offering weekend golf packages (in conjunction with the nearby Pelican Hill golf course), and the use of extensive fitness facilities. Guest rooms have outstanding views, private bars, and original artwork on the walls. Children are given special treatment: balloons, cookies and milk, game books, and more. ✉ *690 Newport Center Dr., 92660, ☎ 949/759–0808 or 800/332–3442, FAX 949/759–0568. 285 rooms, 93 suites. 3 restaurants, bar, pool, beauty salon, massage, sauna, 2 tennis courts, health club, mountain bikes, concierge, business services. AE, D, DC, MC, V.*

$$$$ **Sutton Place Hotel.** An eye-catching ziggurat design is the trademark of this ultramodern hotel in Koll Center. Despite its futuristic exterior, the inside reflects a traditional elegance with tasteful beige and burgundy accents. ✉ *4500 MacArthur Blvd., 92660, ☎ 949/476–2001 or 800/243–4141, FAX 949/476–0153. 435 rooms, 28 suites. 2 restaurants, 2 bars, in-room data ports, minibars, refrigerators, pool, spa, 2 tennis courts, health club, bicycles, concierge, business services, airport shuttle. AE, D, DC, MC, V.*

$$–$$$$ **Newport Beach Marriott Hotel and Tennis Club.** Popular with the international set, this hotel overlooking Newport Harbor features a distinctive fountain surrounded by a plant-filled atrium. Rooms are in one of two towers; all have balconies or patios that look out onto lush gardens or the Pacific. ✉ *900 Newport Center Dr., 92660, ☎ 949/640–4000 or 800/228–9290, FAX 949/640–5055. 577 rooms, 6 suites. Restaurant, bar, 2 pools, sauna, 8 tennis courts, health club, concierge, business services. AE, D, DC, MC, V.*

$$–$$$ **Sheraton Newport Beach.** Bamboo trees and palms in the lobby add to the tropical feel of this hotel 5 mi from the beach. Vibrant teals, mauves, and peaches make up the guest-room color scheme. The hotel is convenient to John Wayne Airport. ✉ *4545 MacArthur Blvd., 92660, ☎ 949/833–0570 or 800/325–3535, FAX 949/833–3927. 335 rooms, 4 suites. Restaurant, bar, pool, tennis court, basketball, exercise room. AE, D, DC, MC, V.*

Laguna Beach

★ *10 mi south of Newport Beach on Hwy. 1; 60 mi south of Los Angeles, I–5 south to Hwy. 133, which turns into Laguna Canyon Rd.*

Traditionally a haven of conservative wealth, Laguna Beach attracted the beat, hip, and far-out during the 1950s and '60s (along with what has grown to be Orange County's most visible gay community). Art galleries dot the village streets, which can be unbearably congested in the summer. The surrounding canyons and hills provide a beautiful backdrop to the beachfront village. A 1993 fire, which destroyed more than 300 homes in the hillsides surrounding Laguna Beach, miraculously left the village untouched.

The town's main street, Pacific Coast Highway, is referred to as either South Coast or North Coast Highway, depending on the address. All along the highway and side streets such as Forest or Ocean avenues, you'll find dozens of eclectic fine-art and crafts galleries, clothing boutiques, and jewelry shops.

At the **Pageant of the Masters** (☎ 949/494–1145 or 800/487–3378), Laguna's most impressive event and part of the city's annual Festival of Arts, live models and carefully orchestrated backgrounds are arranged in striking mimicry of classical and contemporary paintings. The festival usually takes place in July and August.

22 The **Laguna Art Museum** displays American art, with an emphasis on California artists and works. ✉ *307 Cliff Dr.,* ☎ *949/494–6531.* *$5.* ⏲ *Tues.–Sun. 11–5.*

Dining and Lodging

$$$–$$$$ ★ ✕ **Five Feet.** Others have attempted to mimic this restaurant's innovative blend of Chinese and French cooking styles, but Five Feet remains the leader. Among the standout dishes is the house catfish. The setting is pure Laguna: exposed ceiling, open kitchen, high noise level, and brick walls hung with works by local artists. ✉ *328 Glenneyre St.,* ☎ *949/497–4955. AE, D, DC, MC, V. No lunch.*

$$$ ✕ **Sorrento Grille.** High ceilings and two walls of floor-to-ceiling windows create an illusion of space at this narrow restaurant on a quiet side street downtown. Mesquite steaks, seafood, and pastas predominate on the contemporary menu. ✉ *370 Glenneyre St.,* ☎ *949/494–8686. AE, DC, MC, V. No lunch.*

$$–$$$ ✕ **Odessa.** Fans of this hip spot favor the Chilean sea bass and the sesame-crusted ahi, just two of the eclectic dishes with a Southern accent. In the romantic, dimly lit space, you may not notice the celebrities at the next table—or the stylish crowd heading upstairs to the nightclub. ✉ *680 S. Coast Hwy.,* ☎ *949/376–8792. Reservations essential. AE, D, DC, MC, V. No lunch. Valet parking.*

$$–$$$ ✕ **Ti Amo.** A romantic setting and creative Mediterranean cuisine have earned this place acclaim. Try the seared ahi with a sesame-seed crust or farfalle with smoked chicken and tomato brandy cream sauce. All the nooks and crannies are charming, candlelit, and private, but to maximize romance, request a table in the enclosed garden in back. ✉ *31727 S. Coast Hwy.,* ☎ *949/499–5350. AE, D, DC, MC, V. No lunch.*

$–$$ ✕ **Tortilla Flats.** This hacienda-style restaurant with a fireplace has a wide selection of Mexican tequilas and beers, and a quiet upstairs bar. Sunday brunch is a lively affair. ✉ *1740 S. Coast Hwy.,* ☎ *949/494–6588. AE, MC, V.*

$ ✕ **Café Zinc.** Laguna Beach cognoscenti gather at the tiny counter and plant-filled patio of this vegetarian breakfast-and-lunch café. Oatmeal is sprinkled with berries, poached eggs are dusted with herbs, and the orange juice is fresh-squeezed. For lunch, try a sampler plate, with various salads like spicy Thai pasta, and asparagus salad with orange peel and capers, or one of the gourmet pizzettes. ✉ *350 Ocean Ave.,* ☎ *949/494–6302. No credit cards. No dinner.*

$$$$ ★ 🏨 **Surf and Sand Hotel.** Laguna's largest hotel is right on the beach, a rarity in environmentally conscious California. Tastefully decorated rooms have an appropriately beachlike feel, with soft sand colors, bleached-wood shutters, and private balconies. ✉ *1555 S. Coast Hwy., 92651,* ☎ *949/497–4477 or 800/524–8621,* FAX *949/497–1092. 164 rooms, 15 suites. Restaurant, bar, pool, health club, beach, concierge. AE, D, DC, MC, V.*

$$–$$$$ 🏨 **Coast Inn.** Gay men and some lesbians have been staying at the Coast Inn for more than three decades. Some rooms are standard motel-style; others are larger, with private decks and fireplaces. ✉ *1401 S. Coast Hwy.,* ☎ *949/494–7588 or 800/653–2697,* FAX *949/494–1735. 24 rooms. Restaurant, bar. AE, D, DC, MC, V.*

$$–$$$$ ★ 🏨 **Eiler's Inn.** A light-filled courtyard with a fountain is the focal point of this quaint bed-and-breakfast. Every room is unique, full of antiques and travelers' journals for you to fill in. Afternoon wine and cheese is served in the courtyard or in the cozy reading room, where you'll find the inn's only TV and phone. The Continental breakfast usually includes scrumptious homemade breads. A sundeck in back has an ocean view. ✉ *741 S. Coast Hwy., 92651,* ☎ *949/494–3004,* FAX *949/497–2215. 12 rooms. AE, D, MC, V. CP.*

$$–$$$$ **Hotel Laguna.** The oldest hotel in Laguna (opened in 1890) has manicured gardens, a private beach, and an ideal location downtown. Some rooms have canopy beds and reproduction Victorian furnishings. Others have whitewashed furniture and pastel bedspreads and curtains (none has air-conditioning). Complimentary wine and cheese are served weekday afternoon. ✉ *425 S. Coast Hwy., 92651,* ☎ *949/494–1151 or 800/524–2927,* FAX *949/497–2163. 65 rooms. 2 restaurants, bar, beach. AE, D, DC, MC, V. CP.*

$$–$$$$ **Inn at Laguna Beach.** On a bluff overlooking the ocean, the inn has a Mediterranean feel, with terra-cotta tiles and exotic flowers all over the grounds. Most guest rooms have views; those on the coastal level border Laguna's oceanfront cliffs. ✉ *211 N. Coast Hwy., 92651,* ☎ *949/497–9722 or 800/544–4479,* FAX *949/497–9972. 70 rooms. In-room VCRs, minibars, refrigerators, pool. AE, D, DC, MC, V.*

Dana Point

10 mi south of Laguna Beach, Hwy. 1.

Dana Point's claim to fame is its small-boat marina tucked into a dramatic natural harbor and surrounded by high bluffs. In late February, a whale festival features concerts, films, sports competitions, and a weekend street fair. **Dana Point Harbor** was first described more than 100 years ago by its namesake Richard Henry Dana in his book *Two Years Before the Mast.*

Inside Dana Point Harbor, **Swim Beach** has a fishing pier, barbecues, food stands, parking, rest rooms, and showers. At the south end of Dana Point, **Doheny State Park** (☎ 949/496–6171) is one of southern California's top surfing destinations. Here you'll also find five indoor tanks and an interpretive center devoted to the wildlife of the Doheny Marine Refuge. There are also food stands and shops, picnic facilities, volleyball courts, and a pier for fishing. Camping is permitted, though there are no RV hookups.

23 Two indoor tanks at the **Ocean Institute** contain touchable sea creatures, as well as the complete skeleton of a gray whale. Anchored near the institute is *The Pilgrim,* a full-size replica of the square-rigged vessel on which Richard Henry Dana sailed. You can tour the boat Sunday from 10 to 2:30. Weekend cruises are also available. You can arrange to go on marine-mammal exploration cruises from January through March, or to explore regional tide pools year-round. ✉ *24200 Dana Point Harbor Dr.,* ☎ *949/496–2274. Donation requested. Weekends 10–4:30.*

Dining and Lodging

$–$$$ ✕ **Luciana's.** This intimate Italian restaurant is a real find, especially for couples seeking a romantic evening. Dining rooms are small, dressed with crisp white linens and warmed by two fireplaces inside and yet another fireplace on the patio. Try the linguine with clams, prawns, calamari, and green-lip mussels in a light tomato sauce, or veal medallions with haricot verts and oven-dried tomatoes. ✉ *24312 Del Prado Ave.,* ☎ *949/661–6500. AE, DC, MC, V. No lunch.*

$ ✕ **Proud Mary's.** On a terrace overlooking the fishing boats and pleasure craft in Dana Point Harbor, Proud Mary's serves the best burgers and sandwiches in southern Orange County. Steaks, chicken, and other American standards are served at lunchtime, and you can order breakfast all day. ✉ *34689 Golden Lantern St., ☎ 949/493–5853. AE, D, MC, V. No dinner.*

$$$$ ★ ✕🏨 **Ritz-Carlton, Laguna Niguel.** An unrivaled setting on the edge of the Pacific combined with the hallmark Ritz-Carlton service have earned this grand hotel worldwide recognition. An imposing marble-column entryway is surrounded by landscaped grounds; the overall impression is that of a Mediterranean country villa. Rooms have marble bathrooms and private balconies with ocean or pool views. Tea is served afternoons in the library. In the formal Dining Room (men must wear jackets) chef Christian Rassinoux' French-Mediterranean prix-fixe menu includes items such as veal tournedos with chipollini onions, walnut emulsion, port wine and thyme cream. Subdued lighting, crystal chandeliers, and original paintings on the walls add to the dining experience. The Dining Room is open for dinner only; reservations are essential. ✉ *1 Ritz-Carlton Dr., 92629, ☎ 949/240–2000 or 800/241–3333, FAX 949/240–1061. 332 rooms, 31 suites. 3 restaurants, lobby lounge, 2 pools, beauty salon, massage, 2 tennis courts, health club, concierge. AE, D, DC, MC, V.*

$$$–$$$$ ★ 🏨 **Blue Lantern Inn.** Combining New England–style architecture with a southern California setting, this white clapboard inn rests on a bluff, overlooking the harbor and ocean. A fire warms the intimate, inviting living area. The French country–style guest rooms also have fireplaces, as well as soda-filled refrigerators and whirlpool tubs. The top-floor tower suite has a 180° ocean view. ✉ *34343 St. of the Blue Lantern, 92629, ☎ 949/661–1304, FAX 949/496–1483. 29 rooms. Exercise room, concierge. AE, DC, MC, V. BP.*

$$$–$$$$ 🏨 **Marriott's Laguna Cliffs Resort.** Formerly known as the Dana Point Resort, this whitewashed hillside hotel looks straight out of Cape Cod, except that its views are of the Pacific, not the Atlantic. ✉ *25135 Park Lantern, 92629, ☎ 949/661–5000 or 800/533–9748, FAX 949/661–5358. 332 rooms, 18 suites. Restaurant, bar, lobby lounge, 2 pools, 2 outdoor hot tubs, basketball, croquet, health club, volleyball. AE, D, DC, MC, V.*

San Juan Capistrano

5 mi north of Dana Point, Hwy. 74; 60 mi north of San Diego, I–5.

Quaint San Juan Capistrano, one of the few noteworthy historical districts in southern California, is best known for its Mission. It is to the mission that the swallows are supposed traditionally to return, migrating each year from their winter haven in Argentina, but these days they are more likely to choose other local sites. St. Joseph's Day, March 19, launches a week of festivities. After summering in the arches of the old stone church, the swallows head home on St. John's Day, October 23.

★ 24 **Mission San Juan Capistrano,** founded in 1776 by Father Junípero Serra, was the major Roman Catholic outpost between Los Angeles and San Diego. Though the original Great Stone Church is permanently supported by scaffolding, many of the mission's adobe buildings have been preserved to illustrate mission life, with exhibits of an olive millstone, tallow ovens, tanning vats, metalworking furnaces, and padres' living quarters. The bougainvillea-covered Serra Chapel is believed to be the oldest building standing in California. Mass takes place daily at 7 AM in the chapel and 8:30 in the new church. ✉ *Camino Capistrano and Ortega Hwy., ☎ 949/248–2049. $5. Daily 8:30–5.*

25 Near Mission San Juan Capistrano is the **San Juan Capistrano Library,** a postmodern structure erected in 1983. Michael Graves combined a classical design with the style of the mission to striking effect. ✉ *31495*

El Camino Real, ☎ *949/493–1752.* ⏲ *Mon.–Wed. 10–8, Thurs. 10–6, Sat. 10–5, Sun. noon–5.*

Dining

$$–$$$ ★ ✕ **Cedar Creek Inn.** Equally suitable for family meals and romantic getaway dinners, the inn has a children's menu as well as a secluded outdoor patio with a roaring fireplace for couples dining alone. The contemporary American menu features such crowd-pleasers as ahi burgers, rack of lamb, and herb-crusted halibut. ✉ *26860 Ortega Hwy.,* ☎ *949/240–2229. AE, MC, V.*

$$–$$$ ★ ✕ **L'Hirondelle.** Roast duck, rabbit, and a couple of Belgian dishes are on the menu at this French and Belgian restaurant. Try brunch on the patio filled with flowers. ✉ *31631 Camino Capistrano,* ☎ *949/661–0425. AE, MC, V. Closed Mon. No lunch Tues.*

$–$$ ✕ **The Ramos House Cafe.** This quaint outdoor café serves beautifully presented breakfasts in an intimate cobblestone patio setting. Don't miss the mountainous wild mushroom omelet. ✉ *31752 Los Rios St.,* ☎ *949/443–1342. AE, D, DC, MC, V. Closed Mon.*

OFF THE BEATEN PATH

SAN CLEMENTE – Travelers who shun the throngs in favor of a low-key beach experience where pure sea air and steamed mussels are more appealing than celebrity sightings and goat cheese appetizers should drive 10 mi south of Dana Point on Pacific Coast Highway to San Clemente. There, 20 square mi of prime bicycling terrain await. Camp Pendleton, the country's largest Marine Corps base, welcomes cyclists to use some of its roads—just don't be surprised to see a troop helicopter taking off right beside you. Surfers favor **San Clemente State Beach** (☎ 949/492–3156), which has camping facilities, RV hookups, and fire rings. San Onofre State Beach, just south of San Clemente, is another surfing destination. Below the bluffs are 3½ mi of sandy beach, where you can swim, fish, and watch wildlife.

ORANGE COUNTY A TO Z

Arriving and Departing

By Bus

The **Los Angeles MTA** (☎ 213/626–4455) has limited service to Orange County. From downtown, Bus 460 goes to Knott's Berry Farm and Disneyland. **Greyhound** (☎ 714/999–1256) serves Anaheim and Santa Ana.

By Car

The San Diego Freeway (I–405) and the Santa Ana Freeway (I–5) run north–south through Orange County. South of Laguna I–405 merges into I–5 (called the San Diego Freeway south from this point). Do your best to avoid freeways during rush hours (6 AM–9 AM and 3:30 PM–6 PM), when they can back up for miles.

By Plane

The county's main facility is **John Wayne Airport Orange County** (✉ MacArthur Blvd. at I–405, ☎ 949/252–5252), in Santa Ana. It is served by Alaska, America West, American, Continental, Delta, Northwest, Southwest, TWA, United, and US Airways, as well as other commuter airlines. *See* Air Travel *in* Smart Travel Tips A to Z for airline phone numbers.

Los Angeles International Airport, known as LAX, is only 35 mi west of Anaheim. **Ontario International Airport** is just northwest of Riverside, 30 mi north of Anaheim. **Long Beach Airport** is about 20 minutes by bus from Anaheim.

BETWEEN THE AIRPORTS AND HOTELS

Airport Bus (☎ 800/772–5299), a shuttle service, carries passengers from John Wayne and LAX to Anaheim and Buena Park. The fare from John Wayne to Anaheim is $10, from LAX to Anaheim $14.

Prime Time Airport Shuttle (☎ 800/262–7433) provides door-to-door service from Orange County hotels to LAX and the San Pedro cruise terminal. The fare is $12 per person and up, depending on your point of pickup and point of delivery. It's $9 a pop for each additional passenger, from area Anaheim hotels to LAX.

SuperShuttle (☎ 714/517–6600) provides 24-hour door-to-door service from all the airports to all points in Orange County. The fare to the Disneyland area is $10 per person from John Wayne, $34 from Ontario, $13 from LAX, and $34 from Long Beach Airport. There's a $9 charge for each additional passenger.

By Train

Amtrak (☎ 800/872–7245) makes several daily stops in Orange County: at Fullerton, Anaheim, Santa Ana, Irvine, San Juan Capistrano, and San Clemente.

Metrolink (☎ 800/371–5465) is a weekday commuter train that runs to and from Los Angeles and Orange County, starting as far south as Oceanside and stopping in San Juan Capistrano, San Clemente, Irvine, Santa Ana, Orange, Anaheim, and Fullerton.

Getting Around

By Bus

The **Orange County Transportation Authority** (OCTA, ☎ 714/636–7433) will take you virtually anywhere in the county, but it will take time. OCTA buses go from Knott's Berry Farm and Disneyland to Huntington Beach and Newport Beach. Bus 1 travels along the coast. There is also an express bus to Los Angeles.

By Car

Highways 55 and 91 head west to the ocean and east into the mountains: take Highway 91 to Garden Grove and inland points (Buena Park, Anaheim). Highway 55 leads to Newport Beach. Pacific Coast Highway (Highway 1) allows easy access to beach communities and is the most scenic route.

Contacts and Resources

Emergencies

Ambulance (☎ 911). **Fire** (☎ 911). **Police** (☎ 911).

Anaheim Memorial Medical Center (⊠ 1111 W. La Palma Ave., Anaheim, ☎ 714/774–1450). **Western Medical Center** (⊠ 1025 S. Anaheim Blvd., Anaheim, ☎ 714/533–6220). **Hoag Memorial Presbyterian Hospital** (⊠ 1 Hoag Dr., Newport Beach, ☎ 949/645–8600). **South Coast Medical Center** (⊠ 31872 PCH, Laguna Beach, ☎ 949/499–1311). **Children's Hospital of Orange County** (⊠ 455 S. Main St., Orange, ☎ 714/997–3000).

Guided Tours

Pacific Coast Gray Line Tours (☎ 714/978–8855) provides guided tours from Orange County hotels to Universal Studios Hollywood, Los Angeles/Hollywood, Six Flags Magic Mountain, the San Diego Zoo, Seaworld, Catalina Island, and the Long Beach Aquarium. They also offer a Los Angeles by Night tour.

Visitor Information

Anaheim-Orange County Visitor and Convention Bureau (✉ Anaheim Convention Center, 800 W. Katella Ave., 92802, ☎ 714/765–8888, 🌐). **Huntington Beach Conference and Visitors Bureau** (✉ 417 Main St., 92648, ☎ 714/969–3492, 🌐). **Laguna Beach Visitors Bureau and Chamber of Commerce** (✉ 252 Broadway, 92651, ☎ 949/494–1018, 🌐). **Newport Beach Conference and Visitors Bureau** (✉ 3300 W. Coast Hwy., 92663, ☎ 800/942–6278, 🌐). **San Juan Capistrano Chamber of Commerce and Visitors Center** (✉ 31781 Camino Capistrano, Suite 306, 92675, ☎ 949/493–4700, 🌐). **Southern California Golf Association** (☎ 818/980–3630). **Southern California Public Links Golf Association** (☎ 714/994–4747).

13 SAN DIEGO

Exploring San Diego is an endless adventure. To visitors, the city and county may seem like a conglomeration of theme parks: Old Town and the Gaslamp Quarter, historically oriented; the wharf area, a maritime playground; La Jolla, a throwback to southern California elegance; Balboa Park, a convergence of the town's cerebral and action-oriented personae. There are, of course, real theme parks—SeaWorld and the San Diego Zoo—but the great outdoors is the biggest of them all.

SAN DIEGO IS A BIG CITY with a small-town feel. San Diego County covers a vast area, extending from the coast to mile-high mountains to a point near sea level in the desert, but central San Diego is delightfully urban and accessible.

San Diego is strongly defined by its relationship to the ocean—to some degree by default. During the latter half of the 19th century the town was banking on a rail link to the east. A building boom in the 1880s was largely based on the assumption that San Diego would become the western terminus of the Santa Fe Railway. The link was completed in 1885, but it proved unsuccessful for a variety of reasons, including the placement of the line through Temecula Canyon, where 30 mi of track were washed out repeatedly in winter rainstorms.

Instead, San Diego's future was sealed in 1908, when President Theodore Roosevelt's Great White Fleet stopped here on a world tour to demonstrate U.S. naval strength. The U.S. Navy, impressed during that visit by the city's excellent harbor and temperate climate, decided to build a destroyer base on San Diego Bay in the 1920s. The newly developing aircraft industry soon followed (Charles Lindbergh's plane *Spirit of St. Louis* was built here). Through the years San Diego's economy became largely dependent on the military and its attendant enterprises, which provided jobs as well as a demand for local goods and services by those stationed here.

The city conducts most of its financial business in a single neighborhood, the downtown district fronting San Diego Bay, in this way resembling New York more than Los Angeles. San Diego has set some of its most prestigious scientific facilities on the water—Scripps Institution of Oceanography, as well as the Salk Institute.

San Diego also has the ocean to thank for its near-perfect weather. An almost perpetual high-pressure system from the North Pacific is responsible for the city's sunshine and dry air. Moderating breezes off the sea (caused by the water warming and cooling more slowly than the land) keep the summers relatively cool and the winters warm and help clear the air of pollution. In the late spring and early summer the difference between the earth and water temperatures generates coastal fogs.

EXPLORING SAN DIEGO

By Edie Jarolim

San Diego is more a chain of separate communities than a cohesive city. Many of the major attractions are separated by some distance from one another and freeways crisscross the county in a sensible fashion. If you are going to drive around San Diego, study your maps before you hit the road. If you stick with public transportation, plan on taking your time. The San Diego Trolley has expanded into Mission Valley; the Coaster commuter line runs from Oceanside into downtown; and the bus system covers almost all the county—but making the connections necessary to see the various sights is time-consuming.

Great Itineraries

IF YOU HAVE 3 DAYS

Head over to the San Diego Zoo in Balboa Park on the morning of your first day. It would be easy to spend your entire visit to the park here, but it would be a shame to miss the nearby El Prado and its rows of architecturally interesting museums. Start your second day downtown at Seaport Village. After browsing the shops catch a ferry from the Broadway Pier to Coronado. From Coronado's Ferry Landing Marketplace board a bus going down Orange Avenue to tour the town's Victorian extravaganza, the Hotel Del Coronado. Back in San Diego after lunch, stroll north on the Embarcadero to Ash Street. If you've returned from Coronado early enough, you can view the Maritime Museum. On the third morning, visit La Jolla. Have lunch before heading to the Gaslamp Quarter.

IF YOU HAVE 5 DAYS

Follow the three-day itinerary above, and begin your fourth day with a morning visit to Cabrillo National Monument. Have lunch at one of the seafood restaurants on Scott Street, and then head over to Old Town (take Rosecrans Street north to San Diego Avenue) to see portions of San Diego's earliest history brought to life. If the daily schedule lists low tide for the afternoon, reverse the order to catch the tide pools at Cabrillo. En route to North County stop off at Torrey Pines State Park. If you're not going to Legoland, take Interstate 5 north to Del Mar for lunch, shopping, and sea views. A visit to Mission San Luis Rey, slightly inland from Oceanside on Highway 76, will infuse some history and culture into the tour.

Balboa Park

Overlooking downtown and the Pacific Ocean, 1,200-acre Balboa Park is home to most of San Diego's museums and the world-famous San Diego Zoo. Many of the park's Spanish Colonial Revival buildings were intended to be temporary structures, housing exhibits for the Panama–California International Exposition of 1915, which celebrated the opening of the Panama Canal. Fortunately, city leaders realized the buildings' value and incorporated them in their plans for Balboa Park's acreage, which had been set aside by the city founders in 1868.

Parking near Balboa Park's museums is no small accomplishment, especially on sunny summer days, when lots fill up quickly. If you're driving in via the Laurel Street Bridge, the first parking area you'll come to is off the Prado to the right, going toward Pan American Plaza. Free trams that depart from the large lot on the east side of the park at Presidents Way provide an alternative way to get back to your car or bus. Trams run about every 8–10 minutes from 9:30 to 4 daily.

Two Good Walks

Numbers in the text correspond to numbers in the margin and on the Balboa Park map. *sends you to www.fodors.com/urls for Web links.*

It's impossible to cover all the park's museums in one day, so choose your focus before you head out. Enter via Cabrillo Bridge through the West Gate, which depicts the Panama Canal's linkage of the Atlantic and Pacific oceans. Park south of the **Alcazar Garden** ①. It's a short stretch north across El Prado to the landmark California Building, modeled on a cathedral in Mexico and now home to the **San Diego Museum of Man** ②. Look up to see busts and statues of heroes of the early days of the state. Next door is the Simon Edison Centre for the Performing Arts, which adjoins the sculpture garden of the **San Diego Museum of Art** ③, an ornate Plateresque-style structure built to resemble the 17th-century University of Salamanca in Spain.

Continuing east you'll come to the **Timken Museum of Art** ④, the **Botanical Building** ⑤, and the Spanish Colonial Revival–style Casa del Prado, where the San Diego Floral Association has its offices and a gift shop. At the end of the row is the **San Diego Natural History Museum** ⑥; you'll have to detour a block north to visit the **Spanish Village Art Center** ⑦. If you were to continue north, you would come to the **carousel** ⑧, the **miniature railroad** ⑨, and, finally, the entrance to the **San Diego Zoo** ⑩.

Exploring San Diego

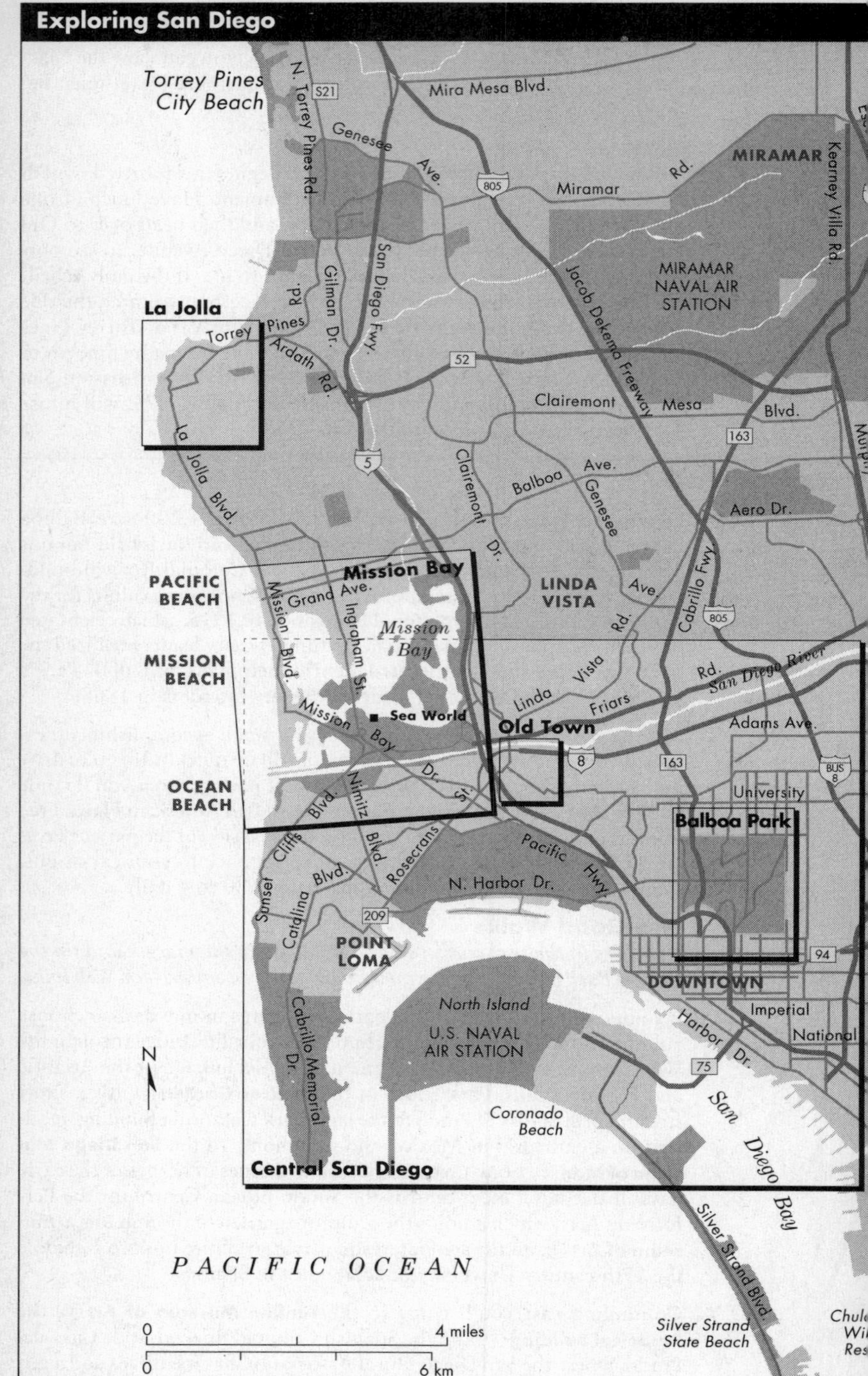

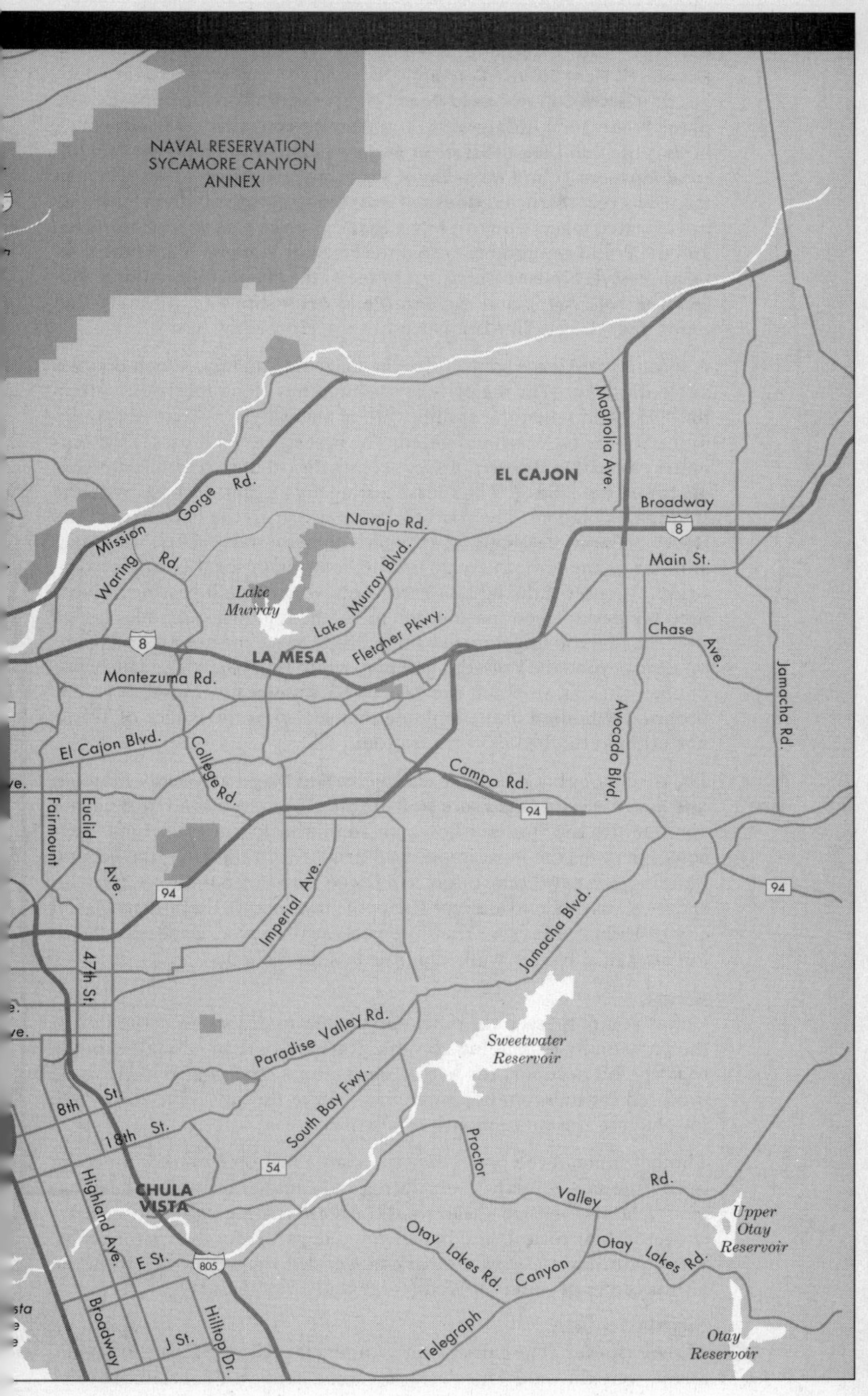
NAVAL RESERVATION
SYCAMORE CANYON
ANNEX
EL CAJON
LA MESA
CHULA VISTA
Magnolia Ave.
Broadway
Main St.
Chase Ave.
Jamacha Rd.
Avocado Blvd.
Mission Gorge Rd.
Waring Rd.
Navajo Rd.
Lake Murray
Lake Murray Blvd.
Fletcher Pkwy.
Montezuma Rd.
El Cajon Blvd.
College Rd.
Campo Rd.
Fairmount
Euclid Ave.
Imperial Ave.
Jamacha Blvd.
47th St.
Paradise Valley Rd.
Sweetwater Reservoir
South Bay Fwy.
8th St.
18th St.
Highland Ave.
E St.
Broadway
J St.
Hilltop Dr.
Proctor Valley Rd.
Otay Lakes Rd.
Canyon
Telegraph
Otay Lakes Rd.
Upper Otay Reservoir
Otay Reservoir
8
94
54
805

Return to the Natural History Museum and cross the Plaza de Balboa—its large central fountain is a popular meeting spot—to reach the **Reuben H. Fleet Science Center** ⑪. (Beyond the parking lot to the south lies the **Centro Cultural de la Raza** ⑫.) You're now on the opposite side of the Prado and heading west. You'll next pass Casa de Balboa, which houses the **San Diego Historical Society** ⑬ and **San Diego Model Railroad Museum** ⑬ and **Museum of Photographic Arts** ⑬. Next door in the newly reconstructed **House of Hospitality** ⑭ is the Balboa Park Visitors Center, where you can buy a reduced-price pass to the museums, and the Prado restaurant. Across the Plaza de Panama, the Franciscan mission–style House of Charm is home to the **Mingei International Museum of Folk Art** ⑮ and the **San Diego Art Institute** ⑮. Your starting point, the Alcazar Garden, is west of the House of Charm.

A second walk leads south from the Plaza de Panama, which doubles as a parking lot. The majority of the buildings along this route date to the 1935 fair, when the architecture of the Maya and native peoples of the Southwest was highlighted. The first sight you'll pass is the **Japanese Friendship Garden** ⑯. Next comes the ornate, crownlike **Spreckels Organ Pavilion** ⑰. The round seating area forms the base, with the stage as its diadem. The road forks here; veer to the left to reach the **House of Pacific Relations** ⑱, a Spanish mission–style cluster of cottages and one of the few structures on this route built for the earlier exposition. Another is the Balboa Park Club, which you'll pass next. Now used for park receptions and banquets, the building resembles a mission church; you might want to step inside to see the huge mural. Continue on beyond the Palisades Building, which hosts the Marie Hitchcock Puppet Theater, to reach the **San Diego Automotive Museum** ⑲, appropriately housed in the building that served as the Palace of Transportation in the 1935–36 exposition.

The road loops back at the spaceshiplike **San Diego Aerospace Museum and International Aerospace Hall of Fame** ⑳. As you head north again you'll notice the Starlight Bowl, an amphitheater on your right. Next comes perhaps the most impressive structure on this tour, the Federal Building, the new home of the San Diego Hall of Champions. Its main entrance was modeled after the Palace of Governors in the ancient Mayan city of Uxmal, Mexico. You'll be back at the Spreckels Organ Pavilion after this, having walked a little less than a mile.

TIMING

Unless you're pressed for time, you'll want to devote an entire day to the perpetually expanding zoo; there are more than enough exhibits to keep you occupied for five or more hours, and you're likely to be too tired for museum-hopping when you're through. The zoo is free for children the entire month of October.

Though some of the park's museums are open on Monday, most are open Tuesday–Sunday 10–4; during the summer a number have extended hours—phone ahead to ask. An alternating variety of free architectural, historical, and nature tours depart from the visitor center every Saturday at 10, while park ranger–led tours start out from the visitor center at noon on Wednesday and 11 on Sunday.

Sights to See

❶ **Alcazar Garden.** The gardens surrounding the Alcazar Castle in Seville, Spain, were the model for the landscaping here; you'll feel like royalty resting on the benches by the tile fountains. It's off El Prado, next to the House of Charm and across from the Museum of Man.

❺ **Botanical Building.** The graceful redwood-lathed structure built for the 1915 exposition houses more than 2,000 types of tropical and subtropical

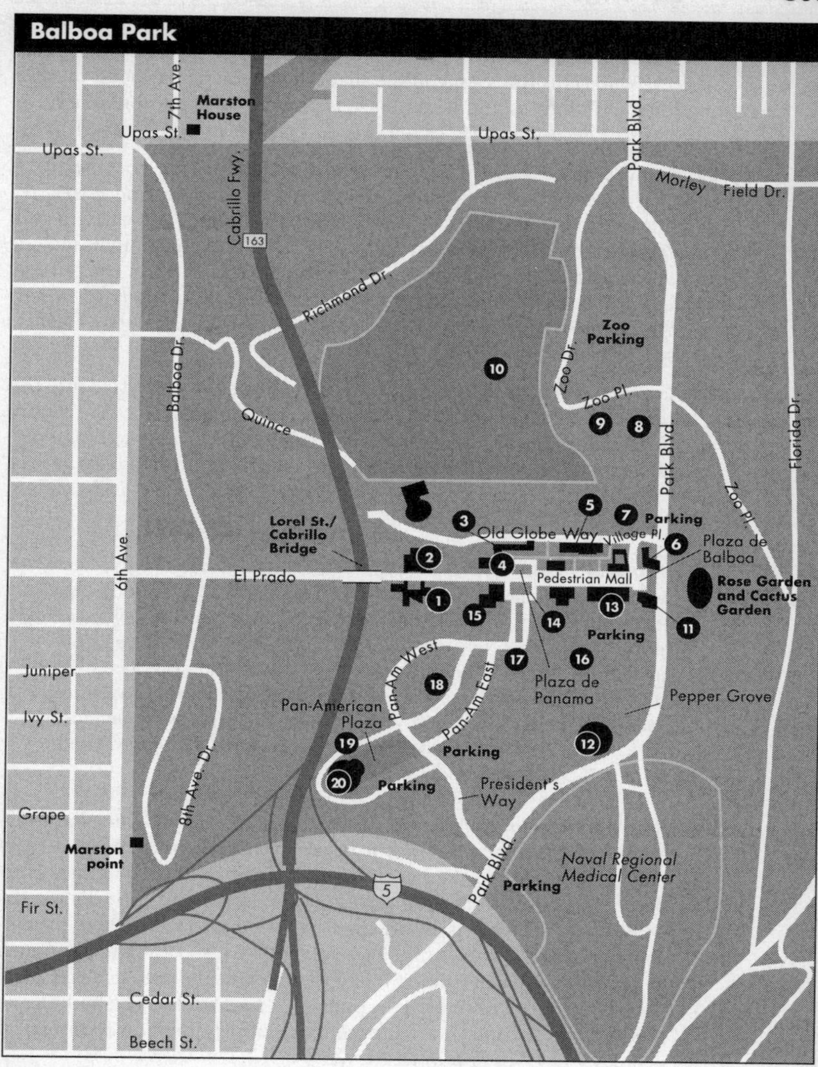

Alcazar Garden 1
Botanical Building . . . 5
Carousel 8
Centro Cultural de la Raza 12
House of Hospitality. 14
House of Pacific Relations 18
Japanese Friendship Garden. 16
Mingei International Museum of Folk Art. 15
Miniature Railroad 9
Museum of Photographic Arts. 13
Reuben H. Fleet Science Center 11
San Diego Aerospace Museum and International Aerospace Hall of Fame 20
San Diego Art Institute 15
San Diego Automotive Museum 19
San Diego Historical Society 13
San Diego Model Railroad Museum 13
San Diego Museum of Art 3
San Diego Museum of Man. 2
San Diego Natural History Museum 6
San Diego Zoo 10
Spanish Village Art Center. 7
Spreckels Organ Pavilion. 17
Timken Museum of Art 4

plants and changing seasonal displays. Ceiling-high tree ferns shade fragile orchids and feathery bamboo. There are benches beside miniature waterfalls for resting in the shade. The rectangular pond outside, filled with lotuses and water lilies, is popular with photographers. ✉ *1550 El Prado,* ☎ *619/239–0512.* *Free.* *Fri.–Wed. 10–4.*

8 **Carousel.** Riders on this antique merry-go-round stretch from their seats to grab the brass rings suspended an arm's-length away and earn a free ride (it's one of the few carousels in the world where you can still grab yourself a bonus). Hand-carved in 1910, the bobbing animals include zebras, giraffes, and dragons; real horsehair was used for the tails. ✉ *1889 Zoo Pl. (behind zoo parking lot).* *$1.25.* *Daily 11–6 during extended summer vacation; during school yr, only school holidays and weekends 11–5:30.*

12 **Centro Cultural de la Raza.** An old water tower was converted into this center for Mexican, Native American, and Chicano arts. Attractions include a gallery with rotating exhibits and a theater, as well as a permanent collection of mural art, a fine example of which may be seen on the tower's exterior. ✉ *2004 Park Blvd.,* ☎ *619/235–6135.* *Free.* *Thurs.–Sun. noon–5.*

OFF THE BEATEN PATH

HILLCREST – Northwest of Balboa Park, Hillcrest is San Diego's center for the gay community and artists of all types. University, 4th, and 5th avenues are filled with cafés and interesting boutiques. The self-contained residential-commercial Uptown District, on University Avenue at 8th Avenue, has shops and restaurants within easy walking distance of high-price town houses. To the northeast, Adams Avenue, reached via Park Boulevard heading north off Washington Street, has many antiques stores. Adams Avenue leads east into Kensington, a handsome old neighborhood that overlooks Mission Valley.

14 **House of Hospitality.** At the reconstructed home of the **Balboa Park Visitors Center** you can pick up schedules and route maps for the free trams that operate around the park. You can also purchase the Passport to Balboa Park, which affords entry to 12 museums for $21; it's worthwhile if you want to visit more than a few and aren't entitled to the discounts that most give to children, senior citizens, and military personnel. In addition, you can pick up a flyer that details the excellent free park tours that depart from here (or phone for a schedule). The building itself has won myriad awards for its painstaking attention to historical detail. ✉ *1549 El Prado,* ☎ *619/239–0512.* *Daily 9–4.*

18 **House of Pacific Relations.** This is not really a house but a cluster of red tile–roof, stucco cottages representing some 30 foreign countries. And the word "pacific" refers not to the ocean—most of the nations represented are European, not Asian—but to the goal of maintaining peace. The cottages, decorated with crafts and pictures, hold open houses each Sunday afternoon, during which you can chat with transplanted natives and try out different ethnic foods. Across the road from the cottages but not affiliated with them, the Spanish colonial–style **United Nations Building** is home to the United Nations Association's International Gift Shop, open daily, which has reasonably priced crafts, cards, and books. ✉ *2160 Pan American Rd. W,* ☎ *619/234–0739.* *Free.* *Sun. noon–5; hrs may vary with season.*

16 **Japanese Friendship Garden.** A koi pond with a water wall, a 60-ft-long wisteria arbor, a large activity center, and a sushi bar are highlights of the park's authentic Japanese garden, designed to inspire contemplation. You can wander the various peaceful paths, meditate in the traditional stone-and-sand garden, or, at times, learn such arts

as origami and flower arranging at the exhibit hall. ✉ *2215 Pan American Rd.,* ☎ *619/232–2780.* 🎟 *$3.* ⏲ *Tues.–Sun. 10–4.*

The Marston House. George W. Marston (1850–1946), a San Diego pioneer and philanthropist who financed the architectural landscaping of Balboa Park was visited by such prominent people as President Teddy Roosevelt and Booker T. Washington. His 16-room home at the northwest edge of the park was built in 1905. It's a classic example of the American Arts and Crafts style, as are the furnishings. Hour-long docent tours—the only way to see the house—illuminate many aspects of San Diego history. ✉ *3525 7th Ave.,* ☎ *619/298–3142.* 🎟 *$5.* ⏲ *Fri.–Sun. 10–4:30 (last tour at 3:45).*

★ 15 **Mingei International Museum of Folk Art.** All ages will enjoy the colorful and creative exhibits of toys, pottery, textiles, costumes, and gadgets from around the globe at the Mingei. Traveling and permanent exhibits in the high-ceiling, light-filled museum include everything from antique American carousel horses to the latest in Japanese ceramics. ✉ *House of Charm, 1439 El Prado,* ☎ *619/239–0003.* 🎟 *$5.* ⏲ *Tues.–Sun. 10–4.*

9 **Miniature railroad.** Adjacent to the zoo parking lot, a pint-size, 48-passenger train runs a ½-mi loop through eucalyptus groves. ✉ *2885 Zoo Pl.,* ☎ *619/239–4748.* 🎟 *$1.25.* ⏲ *Weekends and school holidays 11–5; during school summer break, daily 11–5.*

★ 13 **Museum of Photographic Arts.** World-renowned photographers such as Ansel Adams, Imogen Cunningham, Henri Cartier-Bresson, and Edward Weston are represented in the permanent collection, which includes everything from 19th-century daguerreotypes to contemporary images. Reopened in spring 2000 after quadrupling in size, the 32,000-square-ft facility now has a state-of-the-art theater for screening cinema classics as well as a learning center with a print-viewing room. ✉ *Casa de Balboa, 1649 El Prado,* ☎ *619/239–5262.* 🎟 *$6.* ⏲ *Mon.–Sat. 10–5, Sun. noon–5.*

★ 11 **Reuben H. Fleet Science Center.** Children and adults alike enjoy the Fleet Center's clever interactive exhibits that are sneakily educational. You can reconfigure your face to have two left sides, or, by replaying an instant video clip, watch yourself coming and going at different speeds. The IMAX Dome Theater screens exhilarating nature and science films. The SciTours simulator is designed to take visitors on virtual voyages—stomach lurches and all. The latest major addition, Meteor Storm, lets up to six players at a time have an interactive virtual reality experience. ✉ *1875 El Prado,* ☎ *619/238–1233.* 🎟 *Science Center and SciTours, $6.50; Science Center and IMAX Theater, $9; Science Center, IMAX Theater, and SciTours, $11.* ⏲ *Sun.–Thurs. 9:30–5, weekends 9:30–9 (hrs change seasonally; call ahead).*

20 **San Diego Aerospace Museum and International Aerospace Hall of Fame.** The streamlined edifice commissioned by the Ford Motor Company for the 1935–36 exposition looks unlike any other structure in the park; at night, with a line of blue neon outlining it, the round building appears—appropriately enough—to be a landlocked UFO. Every available inch of space in the rotunda is filled with exhibits about aviation and aerospace pioneers, including examples of enemy planes during the world wars. A collection of real and replicated aircraft fills the central courtyard. ✉ *2001 Pan American Plaza,* ☎ *619/234–8291.* 🎟 *$8.* ⏲ *Daily 10–4:30.*

15 **San Diego Art Institute.** Outside juries decide which works created by members of the Art Institute will be displayed in rotating shows. Painting, sculpture, watercolor—everything except crafts, reserved for the

excellent small gift shop—are represented. ✉ *House of Charm, 1439 El Prado,* ☎ *619/236–0011.* 🎫 *$3.* 🕒 *Tues.–Sat. 10–4, Sun. noon–4.*

19 **San Diego Automotive Museum.** The museum maintains a core collection of vintage motorcycles and cars, ranging from an 1886 Benz to a De Lorean. There's an ongoing automobile restoration program, and the museum sponsors many outdoor automotive events. ✉ *2080 Pan American Plaza,* ☎ *619/231–2886.* 🎫 *$7.* 🕒 *Daily 10–4.*

13 **San Diego Historical Society.** The San Diego Historical Society maintains its research library in the Casa de Balboa's basement and organizes shows on the first floor. Permanent and rotating exhibits, which are often more lively than you might expect, survey local urban history after 1850, when California became part of the United States. A 100-seat theater hosts public lectures, workshops, and educational programs, and a gift shop carries a good selection of books on local history as well as reproductions of old posters and other collectibles. ✉ *Casa de Balboa, 1649 El Prado,* ☎ *619/232–6203.* 🎫 *$6.* 🕒 *Tues.–Sun. 10–4:30.*

13 **San Diego Model Railroad Museum.** When the impressive, giant-scale exhibits of model trains of the Southwest are in operation, you'll hear the sounds of chugging engines, screeching brakes, and shrill whistles. And if you come in through the back door on Tuesday and Friday evenings, 7:30–11, there's no charge to watch the model-train layouts being created. ✉ *Casa de Balboa, 1649 El Prado,* ☎ *619/696–0199.* 🎫 *$4.* 🕒 *Tues.–Fri. 11–4, weekends 11–5.*

★ 3 **San Diego Museum of Art.** Known primarily for its Spanish Baroque and Renaissance paintings, including works by El Greco, Goya, Rubens, and van Ruisdael, San Diego's most comprehensive art museum also has strong holdings of South Asian art and contemporary California paintings. The Baldwin M. Baldwin collection includes more than 100 pieces by Toulouse-Lautrec. If traveling shows from other cities come to San Diego, you can expect to see them here. The IMAGE (Interactive Multimedia Art Gallery Explorer) system allows visitors to call up historical information on the works and artists, and print color reproductions. ✉ *Casa de Balboa, 1450 El Prado,* ☎ *619/232–7931.* 🎫 *$8.* 🕒 *Tues.–Sun. 10–4:30.*

2 **San Diego Museum of Man.** Exhibits at this highly respected anthropological museum focus on Southwestern, Mexican, and South American cultures. Carved monuments from the Mayan city of Quirigua in Guatemala, cast from the originals in 1914, are particularly impressive. Demonstrations of such skills as weaving are regularly held. For children there's a hands-on Children's Discovery Center. ✉ *California Bldg., 1350 El Prado,* ☎ *619/239–2001.* 🎫 *$5.* 🕒 *Daily 10–4:30.*

6 **San Diego Natural History Museum.** The flora and fauna of southern California and Baja California are the focus of the permanent exhibits, which also include a 185-pound brass Foucault pendulum, suspended on a 43-ft cable and designed to demonstrate the Earth's rotation; the Hall of Mineralogy, with its impressive collection of gems; and—the biggest kid pleasers—the dinosaur bones and the small live insect zoo. Additions in 2001 will include a grand exhibition atrium as well as a large-screen theater. ✉ *1788 El Prado,* ☎ *619/232–3821.* 🎫 *$6.* 🕒 *Daily 9:30–4:30.*

★ 10 **San Diego Zoo.** Balboa Park's—and perhaps the city's—most famous attraction is its 100-acre zoo, and it deserves all the press it gets. Nearly 4,000 animals of some 800 diverse species roam in hospitable, expertly crafted habitats that replicate natural environments as closely as possible. The flora in the zoo, including many rare species, is even more costly than the fauna. Walkways wind over bridges and past waterfalls ringed with tropical ferns; elephants in a sandy plateau roam so close you're tempted to pet them.

Exploring the zoo fully requires the stamina of a healthy hiker, but open-air trams that run throughout the day allow visitors to zip through 80% of the exhibits on a 35-minute, 3-mi tour. The Kangaroo bus tours include the same informed and amusing narrations as the others, but for a few dollars more you can get on and off as you like at eight stops. The Skyfari ride, which soars 170 ft above the ground, gives a good overview of the zoo's layout. Unless you come early, however, expect to wait to be moved around. If you come at midday on a weekend or school holiday, you'll be doing the in-line shuffle for a while.

In any case, the zoo is at its best when you wander the paths, such as the one that climbs through the huge, enclosed **Scripps Aviary,** where brightly colored tropical birds swoop between branches just inches from your face, and into the neighboring **Gorilla Tropics,** among the zoo's latest ventures into bioclimatic zone exhibits.

The zoo's simulated Asian rain forest, **Tiger River,** has 10 exhibits with more than 35 species of animals. In **Sun Bear Forest** playful beasts constantly claw apart the trees and shrubs. At the popular **Polar Bear Plunge,** where you can watch the featured animals take a chilly dive, Siberian reindeer, white foxes, and other Arctic creatures are separated from their predatory neighbors by a series of camouflaged moats. **Ituri Forest**—an African rain forest—lets you glimpse hippos frolicking underwater, and buffalo cavorting with monkeys. ✉ *2920 Zoo Dr.,* ☎ *619/234–3153 or 619/231–1515; giant panda hot line 888/697–2632.* 🎫 *$18 includes zoo, Children's Zoo, and animal shows; $26 includes above, plus 35-min guided bus tour and round-trip Skyfari ride; Kangaroo bus tour $8 additional ($3 additional for purchasers of $26 deluxe package); zoo free for children under 12 in Oct. and for all on Founder's Day (1st Mon. in Oct.); $38.35 pass good for admission to zoo and San Diego Wild Animal Park within 5 days. AE, D, MC, V.* ⏲ *Fall–spring, daily 9–4 (visitors may remain until 5); summer, daily 7:30 AM–9 PM (visitors may remain until 10); Children's Zoo and Skyfari ride close earlier.*

7 **Spanish Village Art Center.** Glassblowers, wood-carvers, sculptors, painters, and other artists rent space in the 35 red tile–roof studio-galleries that were set up for the 1935–36 exposition in the style of an ancient Spanish village. The artists give demonstrations of their work on a rotating basis. ✉ *1770 Village Pl.,* ☎ *619/233–9050.* 🎫 *Free.* ⏲ *Daily 11–4.*

17 **Spreckels Organ Pavilion.** The 2,000-seat pavilion, dedicated in 1915 by sugar magnates John D. and Adolph B. Spreckels, holds the 4,445-pipe Spreckels Organ, the largest outdoor pipe organ in the world. You can hear this impressive instrument at one of the year-round, 2 PM Sunday concerts. At Christmastime the park's Christmas tree and life-size Nativity display turn the pavilion into a seasonal wonderland. ✉ *2211 Pan American Rd. E,* ☎ *619/702–8138.*

4 **Timken Museum of Art.** Somewhat out of place in the architectural scheme of the park, the small museum houses a selection of works by major European and American artists as well as a superb collection of Russian icons. ✉ *1500 El Prado,* ☎ *619/239–5548.* 🎫 *Free.* ⏲ *Oct.–Aug., Tues.–Sat. 10–4:30, Sun. 1:30–4:30.*

Downtown

Downtown is San Diego's Lazarus. Written off as moribund by the 1970s, downtown is now one of the city's prime draws for tourists and real-estate agents. Massive redevelopment started in the late 1970s, giving rise to the Gaslamp Quarter Historic District, Horton Plaza shopping center, and a new convention center, which have spurred an upsurge of elegant hotels, upscale condominium complexes, and swank, trendy cafés and restaurants that have people lingering downtown well into the night—if not also waking up there the next morning.

The Martin Luther King Jr. Promenade project put 14 acres of greenery, a pedestrian walkway, and lots of artwork along Harbor Drive from Seaport Village to the convention center, and landscaped the railroad right-of-way from the Santa Fe depot to 8th Avenue. The San Diego Convention Center proved so successful with such events as the 1996 Republican National Convention that it will double in size to about 1.5 million square ft by fall 2001.

There are reasonably priced ($3–$6 per day) parking lots along Harbor Drive, Pacific Highway, and lower Broadway and Market Street. The price of many downtown parking meters is $1 per hour, with a maximum stay of two hours.

Numbers in the text correspond to numbers in the margin and on the Central San Diego map. sends you to www.fodors.com/urls for Web links.

Two Good Walks

To stay near the water, start a walk of the **Embarcadero** ① at the foot of Ash Street on Harbor Drive, where the *Berkeley,* headquarters of the **Maritime Museum** ②, is moored. A cement pathway runs south from the *Star of India* along the waterfront to the pastel B Street Pier. If you're traveling with firehouse fans, detour inland six blocks and north two blocks to the **Firehouse Museum** ③, at the corner of Cedar and Columbia in Little Italy. Otherwise, another two blocks south on Harbor Drive brings you to the foot of Broadway and the Broadway Pier, where you can catch harbor excursion boats and the ferry to Coronado. Take Broadway inland two long blocks to Kettner Boulevard to reach the **Transit Center** ④—you'll see the mosaic-dome Santa Fe Depot and the tracks for the trolley to Tijuana out front—and, right next door, the downtown branch of the **Museum of Contemporary Art, San Diego** ⑤. (If you've detoured to the Firehouse Museum, take Kettner Boulevard south to the Transit Center). Return to Harbor Drive and continue south past Tuna Harbor to **Seaport Village** ⑥.

A tour of the working heart of downtown can begin at the corner of 1st Avenue and Broadway, near Spreckels Theater, a grand old stage that presents pop concerts and touring plays. Two blocks east and across the street sits the historic **U. S. Grant Hotel** ⑦. If you cross Broadway, you'll be able to enter **Horton Plaza** ⑧, San Diego's favorite retail playland. Fourth Avenue, the eastern boundary of Horton Plaza, doubles as the western boundary of the 16-block **Gaslamp Quarter** ⑨. Head south to Island Avenue and Fourth Avenue to the **William Heath Davis House,** where you can get a touring map of the district. If you continue west on Island Avenue, you'll arrive at the **Children's Museum/Museo de los Niños** ⑩, which younger children might prefer over a historical excursion.

TIMING

The above walks take about an hour each, though there's enough to do in downtown San Diego to keep you busy for at least two days—or three if you really like to shop or if you decide to take a side trip to

Coronado or Tijuana. For a guided tour of the Gaslamp Quarter, plan to visit the area on Saturday.

Sights to See

10 **Children's Museum/Museo de los Niños.** This bilingual museum is a fun learning zone for children with interactive, experiential environments. Installations change annually. Art workshops may include bookmaking, T-shirt silk-screening, and calligraphy. ✉ *200 W. Island Ave.,* ☎ *619/233–8792.* *$6.* *Tues.–Fri. 10–3, weekends 10–4.*

1 **Embarcadero.** The bustle along Harbor Drive's waterfront walkway comes less these days from the activities of tuna and other fishing folk than from tourists eager for ocean views, but it remains the nautical soul of San Diego. Seafood restaurants line the piers, as do sea vessels of every variety—ferries, houseboats, and naval destroyers.

On the north end of the Embarcadero, at Ash Street, you'll find the Maritime Museum (☞ *below*). South of it, the **B Street Pier** is used by cruise lines as both a port of call and a departure point. The cavernous pier building has a cruise-information center.

Day-trippers getting ready to set sail gather at the **Broadway Pier,** also known as the excursion pier. Tickets for the harbor tours and whale-watching trips are sold here. The terminal for the Coronado Ferry (☞ *see* Coronado, *below*) lies just beyond the Broadway pier.

The U.S. Navy has control of the next few waterfront blocks to the south—**destroyers, submarines, and carriers** cruise in and out, some staying for weeks at a time. Unless the Navy is engaged in military maneuvers or activities, on weekends you can tour these floating cities (☎ 619/532–3130 for information on hours and types of ships; 619/545–2427 for the USS *Constellation*).The next bit of seafront greenery is a few blocks south along the paved promenade at **Embarcadero Marina Park North,** an 8-acre extension into the harbor from the center of Seaport Village (☞ *below*). The expanding **San Diego Convention Center,** on Harbor Drive between 1st and 5th avenues, was designed by Arthur Erickson. The center often holds trade shows that are open to the public, and tours of the building are available.

3 **Firehouse Museum.** Fire-fighting artifacts fill this converted fire station. Three large rooms contain everything from 19th-century horse- and hand-drawn fire engines to 20th-century motorized trucks, the latest dating to 1942. Ages 12 and under are free. ✉ *1572 Columbia St.,* ☎ *619/232–3473.* *$2.* *Thurs.–Fri. 10–2, weekends 10–4.*

9 **Gaslamp Quarter.** The 16-block national historic district centered between 4th and 5th avenues from Broadway to Market Street contains most of San Diego's Victorian-style commercial buildings from the late 1800s, when Market Street was the center of early downtown. Businesses thrived in this area in the latter part of the 19th century, but at the turn of the 20th century downtown's commercial district moved west toward Broadway, and many of San Diego's first buildings fell into disrepair. During the early 1900s the quarter became known as the Stingaree district. Prostitutes picked up sailors in lively area taverns, and dance halls and crime flourished.

As the move for downtown redevelopment emerged, there was talk of bulldozing the buildings in the quarter and starting from scratch. History buffs, developers, architects, and artists formed the Gaslamp Quarter Council in 1974. Bent on preserving the district, they gathered funds from the government and private benefactors and began restoring the finest old buildings, and attracting businesses and the public back to the heart of New Town.

Coronado

Coronado Museum of History and Art . . . **13**
Ferry Landing Marketplace **11**
Glorietta Bay Inn **15**
Hotel Del Coronado **14**
Orange Avenue **12**
Silver Strand State Beach **16**

Downtown

Children's Museum/Museo de los Niños **10**
Embarcadero **1**
Firehouse Museum . . . **3**
Gaslamp Quarter **9**
Horton Plaza **8**
Maritime Museum **2**
Museum of Contemporary Art, San Diego **5**
Seaport Village **6**
Transit Center **4**
U.S. Grant Hotel **7**

Harbor Island, Point Loma, and Shelter Island

Cabrillo National Monument **17**
Fort Rosecrans National Cemetery **18**
Harbor Island **22**
Scott Street **20**
Shelter Island **21**
Sunset Cliffs **19**

Mission Bay

Bahia Belle **28**
Belmont Park **29**
Fiesta Island **24**
Hospitality Point **27**
San Diego Visitor Information Center . . . **23**
SeaWorld of California **25**
Vacation Isle **26**

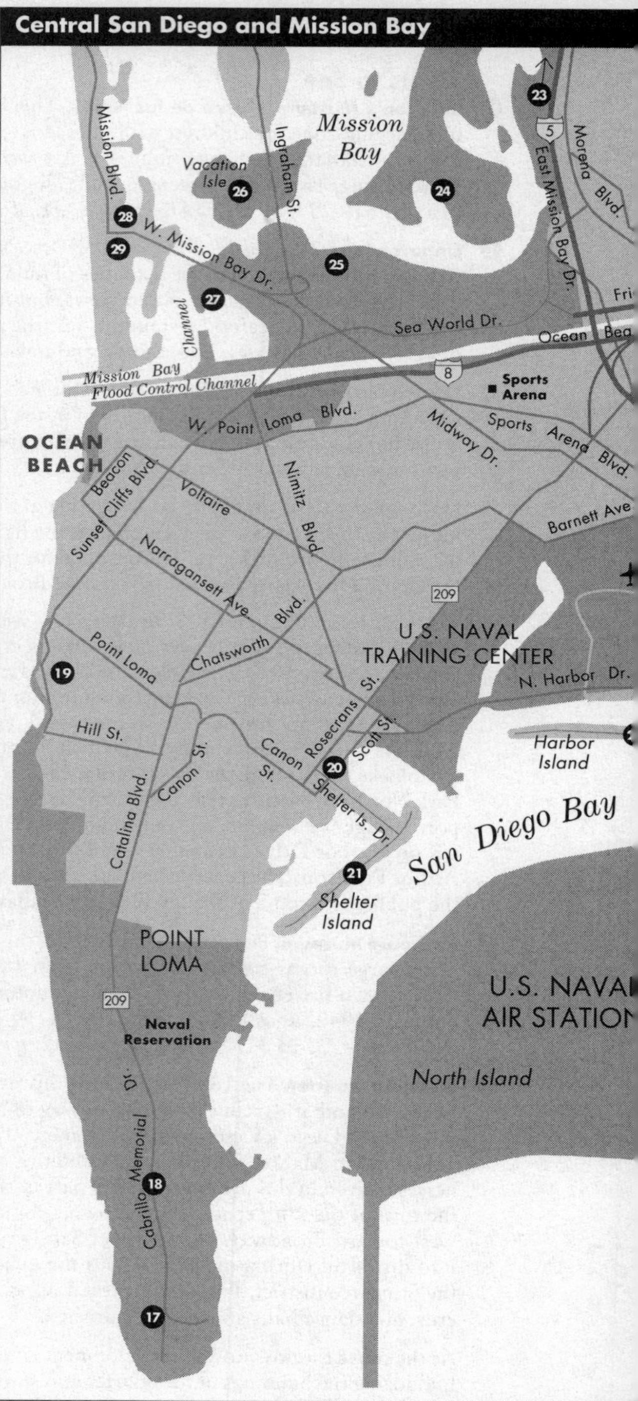

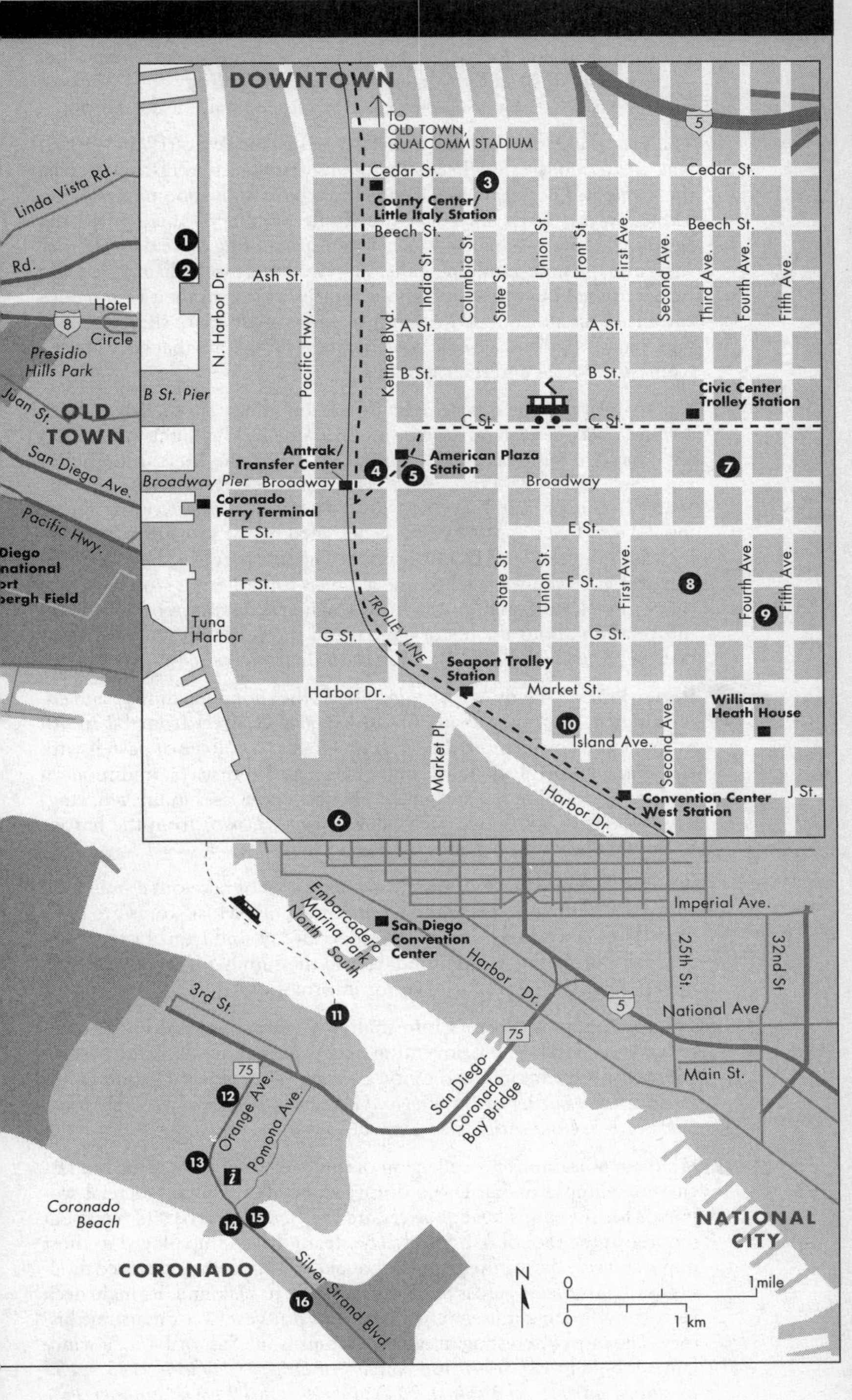

DOWNTOWN
TO OLD TOWN, QUALCOMM STADIUM
Cedar St.
County Center/ Little Italy Station
Beech St.
Ash St.
Linda Vista Rd.
Rd.
Hotel Circle
8
Presidio Hills Park
OLD TOWN
Juan St.
San Diego Ave.
Pacific Hwy.
B St. Pier
Broadway Pier
Broadway
Coronado Ferry Terminal
Amtrak/ Transfer Center
American Plaza Station
Civic Center Trolley Station
N. Harbor Dr.
Pacific Hwy.
Kettner Blvd.
India St.
Columbia St.
State St.
Union St.
Front St.
First Ave.
Second Ave.
Third Ave.
Fourth Ave.
Fifth Ave.
A St.
B St.
C St.
E St.
F St.
G St.
5
Tuna Harbor
TROLLEY LINE
Seaport Trolley Station
Harbor Dr.
Market St.
Market Pl.
Island Ave.
William Heath House
Convention Center West Station
J St.
Harbor Dr.
Imperial Ave.
Embarcadero Marina Park North South
San Diego Convention Center
Harbor Dr.
25th St.
32nd St.
National Ave.
Main St.
75
3rd St.
Orange Ave.
Pomona Ave.
San Diego-Coronado Bay Bridge
Coronado Beach
CORONADO
Silver Strand Blvd.
NATIONAL CITY
N
0
1 mile
0
1 km

The **William Heath Davis House** (✉ 410 Island Ave., at 4th Ave., ☎ 619/233–4692), one of the first residences in town, now serves as the information center for the Gaslamp Quarter. Two-hour walking tours of the historic district leave from the house on Saturday at 11; the cost for these is $5. The museum also has a detailed map of the district.

The Victorian **Horton Grand Hotel** (✉ 311 Island Ave., 619/544–1886) was created in the mid-1980s by joining together two historic hotels, the Kahle Saddlery and the Grand Hotel, built in the boom days of the 1880s; Wyatt Earp stayed at the Kahle Saddlery—then called the Brooklyn Hotel—while he was in town speculating on real estate ventures and opening gambling halls. The two hotels were dismantled and reconstructed on a new site, about four blocks from their original locations. A small Chinese Museum serves as a tribute to the surrounding Chinatown district, a collection of modest structures that once housed Chinese laborers and their families.

The majority of the quarter's landmark buildings are on 4th and 5th avenues, between Island Avenue and Broadway. Highlights on 5th Avenue include the Backesto Building (No. 614), the Mercantile Building (No. 822), the Louis Bank of Commerce (No. 835), and the Watts-Robinson Building (No. 903). The Tudor-style Keating Building (✉ 432 F St., at 5th Ave.) was designed by the same firm that created the famous Hotel Del Coronado. The section of G Street between 6th and 9th avenues has become a haven for galleries; stop in one of them to pick up a map of the downtown arts district. For additional information about the historic area, call the **Gaslamp Quarter Association** (☎ 619/233–5227) or log onto their Web site (🌐).

★ ❽ **Horton Plaza.** Downtown's centerpiece is the shopping, dining, and entertainment mall that fronts Broadway and G Street from 1st to 4th avenues and covers more than six city blocks. A collage of pastels with elaborate, colorful tile work on benches and stairways, and modern sculptures marking the entrances, Horton Plaza rises in uneven, staggered levels to six floors; great views of downtown from the harbor to Balboa Park and beyond can be had here.

A movie complex, restaurants, and a long row of take-out ethnic food shops and dining patios line the uppermost tier. Most stores are open from 10 to 9 weekdays, from 10 to 6 Saturday, and from 11 to 7 Sunday, but during the winter holidays and the summer many places stay open longer (☎ 619/238–1596 for information).

The **International Visitors Information Center,** operated in the complex by the San Diego Convention and Visitors Bureau, is the best resource for information on the city. ✉ *Visitors center: 11 Horton Plaza, street level at corner of 1st Ave. and F St.,* ☎ *619/236–1212.* ⏲ *Mon.–Sat. 8:30–5; June–Aug., also Sun. 11–5.* 🌐

★ ❷ **Maritime Museum.** This collection of three restored ships affords a fascinating glimpse of San Diego during its heyday as a commercial seaport. The museum's headquarters are the *Berkeley,* an 1898 ferryboat moored at the foot of Ash Street. The steam-driven ship played its most important role during the great earthquake of 1906, when it carried thousands of passengers across San Francisco Bay to Oakland. Its main deck serves as a floating museum, with exhibits on West Coast maritime history. The most interesting of the three ships is the *Star of India,* a windjammer built in 1863. ✉ *1306 N. Harbor Dr.,* ☎ *619/234–9153.* 🎟 *$5 (includes entry to all 3 ships).* ⏲ *Daily 9–8 (until 9* PM *in summer).* 🌐

❺ **Museum of Contemporary Art, San Diego.** The cutting-edge exhibitions here are perfectly complemented by the steel-and-glass transportation complex of which it's a part. Four small galleries in the two-story building host rotating shows, some from the permanent collection in the La Jolla branch, others loaned from far-flung international museums. Look for Wendy Jacob's "breathing" wall on the second floor's far gallery. ✉ *1001 Kettner Blvd.,* ☎ *619/234–1001.* 🎟 *Free.* ⏲ *Tues.–Sat. 10–5, Sun. noon–5.*

★ ❻ **Seaport Village.** On a prime stretch of waterfront that spreads out across 14 acres connecting the harbor with hotel towers and the convention center, the village's three bustling shopping plazas are designed to reflect the architectural styles of early California, especially New England clapboard and Spanish mission. A ¼-mi wooden boardwalk that runs along the bay and 4 mi of paths lead to shops as well as snack bars and restaurants, many with harbor views; there are about 75 in all. Seaport Village's shops are open daily 10–9 (until 10 in summer).

I. D. Looff crafted the hand-carved, hand-painted steeds on the **Broadway Flying Horses Carousel,** for the Coney Island amusement park in 1890. The ride was moved from its next home, Salisbury Beach in Massachusetts, and faithfully restored for Seaport Village's West Plaza; tickets are $1. Strolling clowns, balloon sculptors, mimes, musicians, and magicians are also on hand throughout the village to entertain children. ☎ *619/235–4014; 619/235–4013 for events hot line.*

❹ **Transit Center.** The Mission Revival–style **Santa Fe Depot,** which replaced the original 1887 station on this site, serves Amtrak and Coaster passengers. A booth at the graceful, tile-dome depot has bus schedules, maps, and tourist brochures. The landmark is overshadowed by **1 America Plaza** across the street. At the base of this 34-story office tower, designed by architect Helmut Jahn, is a center that links the train, trolley, and city bus systems. ✉ *Broadway and Kettner Blvd.*

❼ **U. S. Grant Hotel.** Far more formal than most other hotels in San Diego, the doyenne of downtown lodgings has a marble lobby, gleaming chandeliers, attentive doormen, and other touches that hark back to the more gracious era when it was built (1910). Funded in part by the son of the president for whom it was named, the hotel was extremely opulent. ✉ *326 Broadway,* ☎ *619/232–3121.*

OFF THE BEATEN PATH

VILLA MONTEZUMA – The former residence of Jesse Shepard, a pianist, spiritualist, and novelist, adapts the elements of high Queen Anne style to Shepard's unique aesthetic interests. The 1887 house is filled with fascinating period and personal details: stained-glass windows depicting Shakespeare, Beethoven, Mozart, Sappho, and Goethe; redwood panels; tile fireplaces; and tributes from Shepard's famous admirers. Architecture buffs will enjoy combining a visit here with one to the Marston House (☞ *above)* in Balboa Park, 10 minutes to the north. A dual admission ticket will save you $2.50. ✉ *1925 K St.,* ☎ *619/239–2211.* 🎟 *$5.* ⏲ *Fri.–Sun. 10–4:30 (last tour at 3:45); Dec., also open Thurs. 10–4:30.*

Coronado

Although it's actually an isthmus, easily reached from the mainland if you head north from Imperial Beach, Coronado has always seemed like an island—and is often referred to as such. The streets of Coronado are wide, quiet, and friendly, with lots of neighborhood parks. North Island Naval Air Station was established in 1911 on Coronado's north end, across from Point Loma, and was the site of Charles Lindbergh's departure on the transcontinental flight that preceded his famous transatlantic voyage.

Coronado is visible from downtown and Point Loma and accessible via the San Diego–Coronado Bridge. There is a $1 toll for crossing the bridge into Coronado, but cars carrying two or more passengers may enter through the free carpool lane. Until the bridge was completed in 1969, visitors and residents relied solely on the Coronado Ferry.

San Diego's Metropolitan Transit System runs a shuttle bus, No. 904, around the island; you can pick it up where you disembark the ferry and ride it out as far as the Silver Strand State Beach. Buses start leaving from the ferry landing at 10:30 AM and run once an hour on the half hour until 6:30 PM.

You can board the ferry, operated by **San Diego Harbor Excursion** (tel. 619/234–4111; 800/442–7847 in CA), at downtown San Diego's Embarcadero from the excursion dock at Harbor Drive and Broadway; you'll arrive at the Ferry Landing Marketplace. Boats depart every hour on the hour from the Embarcadero and every hour on the half hour from Coronado, Sunday through Thursday from 9 AM to 9:30 PM, Friday and Saturday until 10:30 PM; the fare is $2 each way, 50¢ extra for bicycles. San Diego Harbor Excursion also offers water taxi service from 10 AM to 10 PM between any two points in San Diego Bay. The fare is $5 per person for the North Bay, more for the South Bay. Call 619/235–8294 to book.

Numbers in the text correspond to numbers in the margin and on the Central San Diego map. *sends you to www.fodors.com/urls for Web links.*

A Good Tour

Coronado is easy to navigate without a car. When you depart the ferry, you can explore the shops at the **Ferry Landing Marketplace** ⑪ and from there rent a bicycle or catch the shuttle bus that runs down **Orange Avenue** ⑫, Coronado's main tourist drag. You might disembark the bus near the tourist information office, just off Orange Avenue, and pick up a map, return to Orange Avenue to visit the nearby **Coronado Museum of History and Art** ⑬, and then keep strolling along the boutiques-filled promenade until you reach the **Hotel Del Coronado** ⑭ at the end of Orange Avenue. Right across the street from the Del is the **Glorietta Bay Inn** ⑮, another of the island's outstanding early structures. If you've brought your swimsuit, you might continue on to **Silver Strand State Beach** ⑯.

TIMING

A leisurely stroll through Coronado takes an hour or so, more if you shop or walk along the beach. If you visit on Thursday or Saturday, you can combine the tour of Coronado's historic homes that departs from the Glorietta Bay Inn at 11 AM with a visit to the Coronado Museum of History and Art, open Tuesday through Saturday.

Sights to See

13 **Coronado Museum of History and Art.** The neoclassical-style Historic First Bank building, constructed in 1910, is the headquarters and archives of the Coronado Historical Society and a museum. Three galleries house permanent displays while a fourth hosts traveling exhibits. If you'd like to check out the town's historic houses, pick up a copy of the inexpensive *Coronado California Centennial History & Tour Guide* at the museum's gift shop. ✉ *1100 Orange Ave.,* ☎ *619/435–7242.* *Free; donations accepted.* *Tues.–Sat. 10–4.*

11 **Ferry Landing Marketplace.** This collection of shops at the point of disembarkation for the ferry is on a smaller—and generally less interesting—scale than downtown's Seaport Village, but you do get a great view of downtown's skyline from here. ✉ *1201 1st St. at B Ave.,* ☎ *619/435–8895.*

15 **Glorietta Bay Inn.** The former residence of John Spreckels, the original owner of North Island and the property on which the Hotel Del Coronado stands, is now a popular hotel. On Tuesday, Thursday, and Saturday mornings at 11 it's the departure point for a fun and informative 1½-hour walking tour of a few of the area's 86 officially designated historical homes. Sponsored by the Coronado Historical Association, the tour focuses on the Glorietta Bay Inn and the Hotel Del Coronado across the street. ✉ *1630 Glorietta Blvd.,* ☎ *619/435–5892; 619/435–5993 for tour information.* *$6 for historical tour.*

★ 14 **Hotel Del Coronado.** Selected as a national historic landmark in 1977, the "Del" has a colorful history, integrally connected with that of Coronado itself. The hotel opened in 1888 as the brainchild of financiers Elisha Spurr Babcock Jr. and H. L. Story, who saw the potential of Coronado's virgin beaches and its view of San Diego's emerging harbor. The Del's distinctive red-tile peaks and Victorian gingerbread architecture has served as a setting for many movies, political meetings, and extravagant social happenings. *Some Like It Hot,* starring Marilyn Monroe, was filmed here. Docent-led tours elaborate on the background of the hotel and point out the haunts of its resident ghost. ✉ *1500 Orange Ave.,* ☎ *619/435–6611.* *$15 for guided tour.* ⏲ *1-hr guided tours (from lobby) daily; call for times.*

12 **Orange Avenue.** This thoroughfare's clapboard houses, small restaurants, and boutiques are in some ways more characteristic of New England than they are of California. Just off Orange Avenue, the **Coronado Visitors Bureau** (✉ 1047 B Ave., ☎ 619/437–8788,) is open weekdays 8–5, Saturday 10–5, and Sunday 11–4 year-round.

16 **Silver Strand State Beach.** The stretch of sand that runs along Silver Strand Boulevard from the Hotel Del Coronado to Imperial Beach is a perfect family gathering spot, with rest rooms and lifeguards. Don't be surprised if you see groups exercising in military style along the beach; this is a training area for the U.S. Navy's underwater SEALS.

Harbor Island, Point Loma, and Shelter Island

Point Loma protects the center city from the Pacific's tides and waves. It's shared by military installations, funky motels and fast-food shacks, stately family homes, huge estates, and private marinas packed with sailboats and yachts. Newer to the scene, Harbor and Shelter islands are poster children for landfill. Created out of sand dredged from the San Diego Bay in the second half of the past century, they've become tourist hubs, their high-rise hotels, seafood restaurants, and boat-rental centers looking as solid as those anywhere else in the city.

Numbers in the text correspond to numbers in the margin and on the Central San Diego map. sends you to www.fodors.com/urls for Web links.

A Good Tour

Take Catalina Boulevard all the way south to the tip of Point Loma to reach **Cabrillo National Monument** ⑰; you'll be retracing the steps of the earliest European explorers if you use this as a jumping-off point for a tour. North of the monument, as you head back into the neighborhoods of Point Loma, you'll see the white headstones of **Fort Rosecrans National Cemetery** ⑱. Continue north on Catalina Boulevard to Hill Street and turn left to reach the dramatic **Sunset Cliffs** ⑲, at the western side of Point Loma near Ocean Beach. Return to Catalina Boulevard and backtrack south for a few blocks to find Canon Street, which leads toward the peninsula's eastern (bay) side. Almost at the shore you'll see **Scott Street** ⑳, Point Loma's main commercial drag. Scott Street is bisected by Shelter Island Drive, which leads to **Shelter Island** ㉑. For another example of what can be done with tons of material dredged from a bay, go back up Shelter Island Drive, turn right on Rosecrans Street, and make another right on North Harbor Drive to reach **Harbor Island** ㉒.

TIMING

If you're interested in seeing the tide pools at Cabrillo National Monument, call ahead (☞ *below*) to find out when low tide will occur. Scott Street is a good place to find yourself at lunchtime, and Sunset Cliffs Park is where you might want to be when the daylight starts to wane. This drive takes about an hour if you stop briefly at each sight, but you'll want to devote at least an hour to Cabrillo National Monument.

Sights to See

★ ⑰ **Cabrillo National Monument.** This 144-acre preserve marks the site of the first European visit to San Diego, made by 16th-century explorer Juan Rodríguez Cabrillo (circa 1498–1543). Cabrillo, who had earlier gone on voyages with Hernán Cortés, came to this spot, which he called San Miguel, in 1542. Government grounds were set aside to commemorate his discovery in 1913, and today the site, with its rugged cliffs and shores and outstanding overlooks, is one of the most frequently visited of all the national monuments.

The **visitor center** presents films and lectures about Cabrillo's voyage, the sea-level tide pools, and the gray whales migrating offshore. **Interpretive stations** with recorded information have been installed along the walkways that edge the cliffs. Directly south across the bay from the visitor center is the North Island Naval Air Station at the west end of Coronado. To the left on the shores of Point Loma is the Space and Naval Warfare Systems Center; nuclear-powered submarines are now docked where Cabrillo's small ships anchored in 1542.

The moderately steep 2-mi **Bayside Trail** (⏲ 9–4) winds through coastal sage scrub, curving under the cliff-top lookouts and bringing you ever closer to the bay-front scenery. You cannot reach the beach from this trail and must stick to the path. You'll see prickly pear cactus and yucca, black-eyed Susans, fragrant sage, and maybe a lizard or a hummingbird. The climb back is long but gradual, leading up to the **Old Point Loma Lighthouse** (⏲ 9–5).

Sea creatures can be seen in the **tide pools** (⏲ 9–4:30) at the foot of the monument's western cliffs. Drive north from the visitor center to the first road on the left, which winds down to the coast guard station and the shore. When the tide is low you can walk on the rocks around saltwater pools filled with starfish, crabs, anemones, octopuses, and hundreds of other sea creatures and plants. ✉ *1800 Cabrillo Memorial Dr.,* ☎ *619/557–5450 or 619/222–8211 (TTY).* 🎟 *$5 per car, $2 per person entering on foot or by bicycle; free for Golden Age, Golden Access, and Golden Eagle passport holders, and children under 17.* ⏲ *Park daily 9–5:15 (call for later summer hrs, which vary).*

⑱ **Fort Rosecrans National Cemetery.** It's impressive to see the rows upon rows of white headstones that overlook both sides of Point Loma just north of the Cabrillo National Monument. Some of those laid to rest at this place were killed in battles that predate California's statehood. The Bennington Monument, a 75-ft granite obelisk, commemorates the 66 crew members who died in a boiler explosion on board the USS *Bennington* in 1905. ☎ *619/553–2084.* ⏲ *Daily 9–5:30.*

㉒ **Harbor Island.** In 1961 this 1½-mi-long peninsula was created adjacent to San Diego International Airport out of sand and mud dredged from San Diego Bay. Restaurants and high-rise hotels now line its inner shores. The bay shore has pathways, gardens, and picnic spots. On the west point, Tom Ham's Lighthouse restaurant has a U.S. Coast Guard–approved beacon shining from its tower.

20 **Scott Street.** Running along Point Loma's waterfront from Shelter Island to the Marine Corps Recruiting Center on Harbor Drive, this thoroughfare is lined with deep-sea fishing charters and whale-watching boats. It's a good spot from which to watch fishermen (and women) haul marlin, tuna, and mackerel off their boats.

21 **Shelter Island.** Shelter Island—actually a peninsula—is the center of San Diego's yacht-building industry, and boats in every stage of construction are visible in the yacht yards. A long sidewalk runs from the landscaped lawns of the **San Diego Yacht Club** (tucked down Anchorage Street off Shelter Island Drive), past boat brokerages to the hotels and marinas, which line the inner shore, facing Point Loma. Families relax at picnic tables along the grass, where there are fire rings and permanent barbecue grills.

19 **Sunset Cliffs.** The 60-ft-high bluffs on the western side of Point Loma south of Ocean Beach are a perfect place to watch the sun descend over the sea. To view the tide pools along the shore, you can descend a staircase off Sunset Cliffs Boulevard at the foot of Ladera Street.

Mission Bay and SeaWorld

The 4,600-acre Mission Bay aquatic park is San Diego's monument to sports and fitness. Admission to its 27 mi of bay-shore beaches and 17 mi of ocean frontage is free.

Numbers in the text correspond to numbers in the margin and on the Central San Diego map. sends you to www.fodors.com/urls for Web links.

A Good Tour

If you're coming from Interstate 5, the **San Diego Visitor Information Center** ㉓ is just about at the end of the Clairemont Drive–East Mission Bay Drive exit (you'll see the prominent sign). At the point where East Mission Bay Drive turns into Sea World Drive you can detour left to **Fiesta Island** ㉔, popular with jet skiers and speedboat racers. Continue around the curve to the west to reach **SeaWorld of California** ㉕, the area's best-known attraction.

You'll next come to Ingraham Street, the central north–south drag through the bay. If you take it north, you'll shortly spot Vacation Road, which leads to the waterskiing mecca of **Vacation Isle** ㉖. At Ingraham, Sea World Drive turns into Sunset Cliffs Boulevard and intersects with West Mission Bay Drive. Past this intersection, Quivira Way leads west toward **Hospitality Point** ㉗, where there are nice, quiet places to have a picnic.

If you continue west on West Mission Bay Drive, just before it meets Mission Boulevard, you'll come to the Bahia Resort Hotel, where you can catch the ***Bahia Belle*** ㉘ for a cruise around the bay. Ventura Cove, opposite the Bahia Hotel, is another good spot to unpack your cooler. Almost immediately south of where West Mission Bay Drive turns into Mission Boulevard is the resurrected **Belmont Park** ㉙.

TIMING

It would take less than an hour to drive this tour. You may not find a visit to SeaWorld fulfilling unless you spend at least a half day; a full day is recommended. The park is open daily, but not all its attractions are open year-round.

Sights to See

28 ***Bahia Belle.*** At the dock of the Bahia Resort Hotel, on the eastern shores of West Mission Bay Drive, you can board a restored stern-wheeler for a sunset cruise of the bay and party on until the wee hours. The Belle's full bar opens at 9:30, but many revelers like to disembark at the Bahia's sister hotel, the Catamaran, and have a few rounds at the Cannibal Bar before reboarding (the boat cruises between the two hotels, which co-own it, stopping to pick up passengers every half hour). The first cruise on Sunday is devoted to children, but most cruises get a mixed crowd. ✉ *998 W. Mission Bay Dr.,* ☎ *858/488–0551.* 🎫 *$6 for unlimited cruising (9:30 PM or later, cruisers must be at least 21); free for guests of the Bahia and Catamaran hotels.* ⏲ *Oct.–Nov. and Jan.–June, Fri.–Sat. 7:30 PM–1:30 AM, departures every hr on the ½ hr; July–Sept., Wed.–Sun. on same schedule.*

29 **Belmont Park.** Between the bay and Mission Beach boardwalk is a shopping, dining, and recreation mecca. Twinkling lights outline the **roller coaster** on which screaming thrill-seekers ride more than 2,600 ft of track and 13 hills. Created as the Giant Dipper in 1925, this is one of the few old-time roller coasters left in the United States. **The Plunge,** an indoor swimming pool, also opened in 1925 as the largest—60 ft by 125 ft—saltwater pool in the world. It's had fresh water since 1951. Other attractions include **Pirate's Cove,** a fantastic maze of brightly colored tunnels, slides, an obstacle course, and more, all with a pirate theme; a video arcade; a submarine ride; bumper cars; and an antique carousel. ✉ *3146 Mission Blvd.,* ☎ *858/488–1549; 858/488–3110 for pool.* 🎫 *Prices vary.* ⏲ *Park opens at 11 daily, ride hrs vary seasonally; pool open weekdays 5:30–8 AM, noon–1 PM, and 2:30–8 PM.*

24 **Fiesta Island.** The most undeveloped area of Mission Bay Park is popular with bird-watchers (there's a large protected nesting site for the California tern at the northern tip of the island) as well as with dog owners—it's the only place in the park where their pets can run free.

27 **Hospitality Point.** This pretty, secluded spot has a view of sailboats and yachts entering the open sea. At the entrance to Hospitality Point, the Mission Bay Park Headquarters supplies area maps and other recreational information. ✉ *2581 Quivira Ct.,* ☎ *619/221–8901.* ⏲ *Weekdays 9–5; closed city holidays.*

23 **San Diego Visitor Information Center.** In addition to being an excellent resource for San Diego tourists—it makes hotel and motel reservations, sells discount tickets to local attractions, and offers various maps and guides—the center is also a gathering spot for runners, walkers, and exercisers. ✉ *2688 E. Mission Bay Dr.,* ☎ *619/276–8200.* ⏲ *Mon.–Sat. 9–5 (until 6 in summer), Sun. 9:30–4:30 (until 5:30 in summer).*

25 **SeaWorld of California.** One of the world's largest marine-life amusement parks, SeaWorld is spread over 100 tropically landscaped bayfront acres—and it seems to be expanding into every square inch of available space with new exhibits, shows, and activities.

The majority of the exhibits are walk-through marine environments. In a perpetual favorite, the **Penguin Encounter,** a moving sidewalk passes through a glass-enclosed Arctic area where hundreds of emperor penguins slide over glaciers into icy waters. (Consider bringing a light sweater along for this one). Children get a particular kick out of the **Shark Encounter,** where they come face-to-face with a variety of the scary-toothed predators. The hands-on **California Tide Pool** exhibit gives visitors a chance to get to know San Diego's indigenous marine life. At **Forbidden Reef** you can feed bat rays and go nose-to-nose with creepy moray eels. Visitors to **Rocky Point Preserve** can view bottlenose dolphins, as well as

Alaskan sea otters. At **Wild Arctic,** which starts out with a simulated helicopter ride to a research post at the North Pole, beluga whales, walruses, and polar bears can be viewed in areas decked out like the wrecked hulls of two 19th-century sailing ships. **Manatee Rescue** lets you watch the gentle-giant marine mammals cavorting in a 215,000-gallon tank. **Shamu's Happy Harbor** is a hands-on fun zone that features, among other attractions, a two-story ship, where pretend pirates aim water cannons at one another (be prepared with a change of dry clothes).

SeaWorld's highlights are its four large-arena entertainments. You can arrive 10 or 15 minutes in advance to get front row seats, and the stadiums are large enough for everyone to get a seat even at the busiest times. The traditional favorite is the **Shamu show,** with synchronized killer whales bringing down the house, but the less publicized **Marooned with Clyde and Seamore,** starring a sea lion and an otter, is more intimate and equally amusing.

Shipwreck Rapids is SeaWorld of California's first adventure ride. For five minutes nine "shipwrecked" passengers careen down a river in a raftlike inner tube, encountering a series of obstacles, including several waterfalls. There's no extra charge, making this one of SeaWorld's great bargains—which means that you should expect long lines.

It's hard to come away from here without spending a lot of money on top of the hefty entrance fee and parking tab. It's smart to take advantage of the two-day entry option, only $4 more than a single-day admission: If you try to get your money's worth by fitting everything in on a single day, you're all likely to end up tired and cranky. ✉ *1720 South Shores Rd., near the west end of I–8,* ☎ *619/226–3815; 619/226–3901 for recorded information.* 🎫 *$39, 2-day package $43; parking $7 cars, $4 motorcycles, $9 RVs and campers; 90-min behind-the-scenes walking tours $8 additional. AE, D, MC, V.* ⏲ *Daily 10–dusk; extended hrs during summer; call ahead for park hrs.*

26 **Vacation Isle.** Ingraham Street bisects this Mission Bay island. The west side is taken up by the San Diego Paradise Point Resort, but you don't have to be a guest to enjoy the hotel's lushly landscaped grounds and bay-front restaurants. The water-ski clubs congregate at **Ski Beach** on the east side of the island, where there's a parking lot as well as picnic areas and rest rooms.

La Jolla

La Jollans have long considered their village to be the Monte Carlo of California, and with good cause. Its coastline curves into natural coves backed by verdant hillsides covered with homes worth millions. Though La Jolla is considered part of San Diego, it has its own postal zone and a coveted sense of class; it's gotten far more plebeian these days, but old-monied residents still mingle here with visiting film stars.

To reach La Jolla from Interstate 5, if you're traveling north, take the Ardath Road exit, which veers into Torrey Pines Road, and turn right onto Prospect Street. If you're heading south, get off at the La Jolla Village Drive exit, which will also lead into Torrey Pines Road. Traffic is virtually always congested in this popular area. For those who enjoy meandering, the best way to approach La Jolla from the south is to drive through Mission and Pacific beaches on Mission Boulevard, past the crowds of rollerbladers, bicyclists, and sunbathers. The clutter and congestion ease up as the street becomes La Jolla Boulevard. Road signs along La Jolla Boulevard and Camino de la Costa direct drivers and bicyclists past homes designed by such respected architects as Frank Lloyd Wright and Irving Gill. As you approach the village,

La Jolla Boulevard turns into Prospect Street. Prospect Street and Girard Avenue, the village's main drags, are lined with expensive shops and office buildings.

Numbers in the text correspond to numbers in the margin and on the La Jolla map. *sends you to www.fodors.com/urls for Web links.*

A Good Tour

At the intersection of La Jolla Boulevard and Nautilus Street, turn toward the sea to reach Windansea Beach, one of the best surfing spots in town. **Mount Soledad** ①, about 1½-mi east on Nautilus Street, is La Jolla's highest spot. In the village itself you'll find the town's cultural center, the **Museum of Contemporary Art, San Diego** ②, on the less trafficked southern end of Prospect. Farther north, at the intersection of Prospect and Girard Avenue, sits the pretty-in-pink **La Valencia** ③. The hotel looks out onto the village's great natural attraction, **La Jolla Cove** ④, which can be accessed from Coast Boulevard, one block to the west. Past the far northern point of the cove, a trail leads to **La Jolla Caves** ⑤. The beaches along La Jolla Shores Drive north of the caves are some of the finest in the San Diego area. Nearby is the campus of the Scripps Institution of Oceanography. The institution's **Birch Aquarium at Scripps** ⑥ is inland a bit.

La Jolla Shores Drive eventually curves onto Torrey Pines Road, off which you'll soon glimpse the world-famous **Salk Institute** ⑦, designed by Louis I. Kahn. The same road that leads to the institute ends at the cliffs used as the Torrey Pines Gilder Port. The hard-to-reach stretch of sand at the foot of the cliffs is officially named **Torrey Pines City Park Beach** ⑧, but locals call it Black's Beach. At the intersection of Torrey Pines Road and Genesee Avenue you'll come to the northern entrance of the huge campus of the **University of California at San Diego** ⑨ and, a bit farther north, to the stretch of wilderness that marks the end of what most locals consider San Diego proper, **Torrey Pines State Beach and Reserve** ⑩.

TIMING

This tour makes for a leisurely day, though it can be driven in a couple of hours, including stops to take in the views and explore the village (though not to hit any of the beaches—or even a fraction of the pricey boutiques). The Museum of Contemporary Art is closed Monday, and guided tours of the Salk Institute are given on weekdays only.

Sights to See

6 **Birch Aquarium at Scripps.** The largest oceanographic exhibit in the United States, a program of the Scripps Institution of Oceanography, sits at the end of a signed drive leading off North Torrey Pines Road just south of La Jolla Village Drive. More than 30 tanks are filled with colorful saltwater fish, and a 70,000-gallon tank simulates a La Jolla kelp forest. ✉ *2300 Expedition Way,* ☎ *858/534–3474.* *$8.50, parking $3.* *Daily 9–5.*

5 **La Jolla Caves.** It's a walk down 145 sometimes slippery steps to Sunny Jim Cave, the largest of the grottoes in La Jolla Cove. The cave entrance is through the Cave Store, a throwback to a 1902 shop that served as the underground portal. ✉ *1325 Cave St.,* ☎ *858/459–0746.* *$2.* *Daily 9 until dark.*

★ 4 **La Jolla Cove.** The wooded spread that looks out over a shimmering blue inlet is what first attracted everyone to La Jolla, from Native Americans to the glitterati. You'll find the cove beyond where Girard Avenue dead-ends into Coast Boulevard, marked by towering palms that line a promenade. An underwater preserve at the north end of La Jolla Cove makes the adjoining beach the most popular one in the area. On summer days, when the water visibility reaches 20 ft deep or so, the

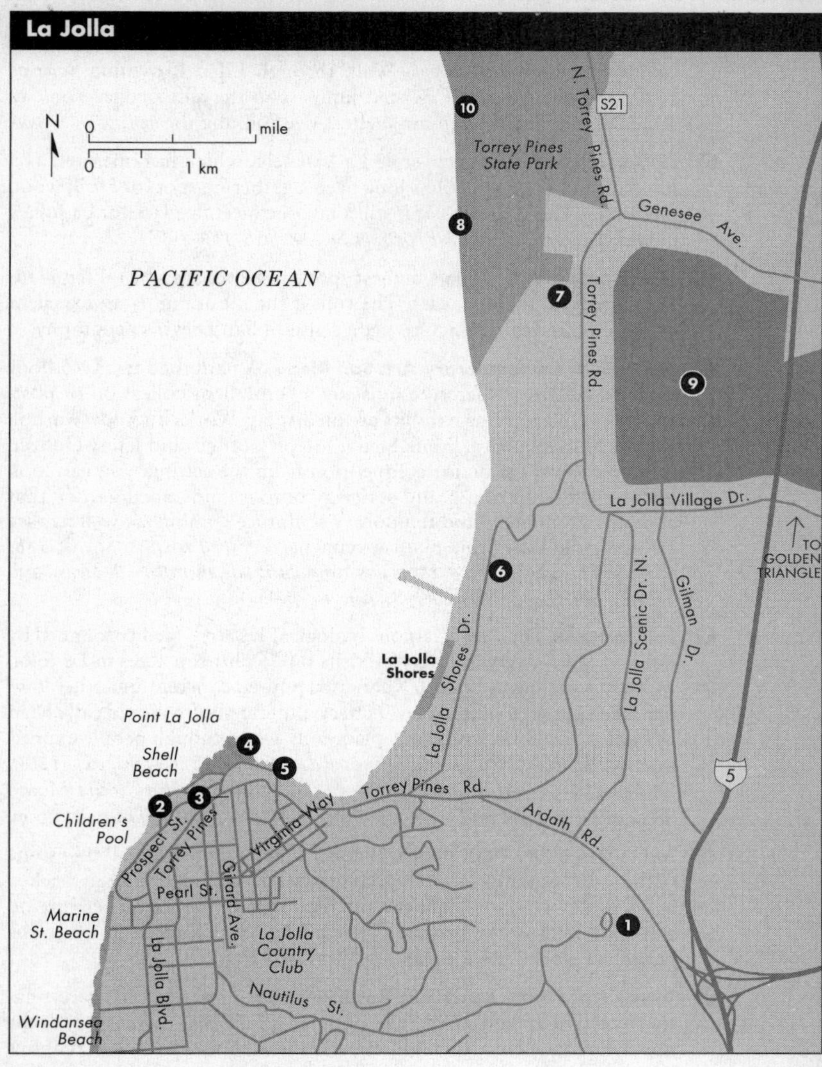

Birch Aquarium at Scripps 6

La Jolla Caves 5

La Jolla Cove 4

La Valencia Hotel . . . 3

Mount Soledad. 1

Museum of Contemporary Art, San Diego 2

Salk Institute 7

Torrey Pines City Park Beach 8

Torrey Pines State Beach and Reserve 10

University of California at San Diego 9

sea seems to disappear under the mass of bodies snorkeling. The **Children's Pool,** at the south end of the park, is protected by a seawall from strong currents and waves. Walk through **Ellen Browning Scripps Park,** past the groves of twisted junipers to the cliff's edge. You can picnic at one of the open-air shelters overlooking the sea.

3 **La Valencia.** The art deco–style La Valencia, which has operated as a luxury hotel since 1928, has long been a gathering spot for Hollywood celebrities. The Whaling Bar is still a favorite meeting place for La Jolla's power brokers. ✉ *1132 Prospect St.,* ☎ *858/454–0771.*

1 **Mount Soledad.** La Jolla's highest spot can be reached by taking Nautilus Street all the way east. The top of the mountain is an excellent vantage point from which to get a sense of San Diego's geography.

★ 2 **Museum of Contemporary Art, San Diego.** A patterned terrazzo floor leads to galleries where the museum's permanent collection of post-1950s art and rotating exhibits are on display. Works by Andy Warhol, Robert Rauschenberg, Frank Stella, Joseph Cornell, and Jenny Holtzer, to name a few, get major competition from the setting: you can look out from the top of a grand stairway onto a landscaped garden that contains permanent and temporary sculpture exhibits as well as rare 100-year-old California plant specimens. ✉ *700 Prospect St.,* ☎ *858/454–3541.* 🎟 *$4; free 1st Tues. and Sun. of month.* ⏲ *Tues. and Thurs.–Sat. 10–5, Wed. 10–8, Sun. noon–5.*

7 **Salk Institute.** The world-famous biological-research facility founded by polio vaccine inventor Jonas Salk sits on 26 cliff-top acres in La Jolla. Modernist architect Louis I. Kahn used poured concrete and other low-maintenance materials to clever effect. Building buffs should call ahead to book a free tour; tours take place only when enough people express interest. ✉ *10010 N. Torrey Pines Rd.,* ☎ *858/453–4100, ext. 1200.* 🎟 *Free.* ⏲ *Grounds weekdays 7–6; guided architecture tours Mon.–Wed. and Fri. at 11 and noon (every third Mon. 11 only), Thurs. at noon.*

8 **Torrey Pines City Park Beach.** Black's Beach—as locals call it—is one of the most beautiful and secluded stretches of sand in San Diego, backed by cliffs whose colors change with the angle of the sun. There are no rest rooms, showers, or snack shops. The paths leading down to the beach are steep—stick to the well-traveled trails.

10 **Torrey Pines State Beach and Reserve.** *Pinus torreyana,* the rarest native pine tree in the United States, enjoys a 1,750-acre sanctuary at the northern edge of La Jolla. Hiking trails lead to the cliffs, 300 ft above the ocean; trail maps are available at the park station. Wildflowers grow profusely in the spring, and the ocean panoramas are always spectacular. When the tide is out at the beach, it's possible to walk south all the way past the lifeguard towers to Black's Beach over rocky promontories. **Los Penasquitos Lagoon** at the north end of the reserve is a good place to watch shorebirds. Volunteers lead guided nature walks at 11:30 and 1:30 on most weekends. ✉ *N. Torrey Pines Rd. (also known as Old Hwy. 101). Exit I–5 onto Carmel Valley Rd. going west, then turn left (south) on Old Hwy. 101,* ☎ *858/755–2063.* 🎟 *Parking $4 (2 large parking lots on both sides of Los Penasquitos Lagoon; another up the hill by park visitor center).* ⏲ *Daily 8–sunset.*

9 **University of California at San Diego.** The campus of San Diego's most prestigious research university spreads over 1,200 acres of coastal canyons and eucalyptus groves. If you're interested in contemporary art, ask at one of the two information booths for a campus map that shows the location of the Stuart Collection, 14 thought-provoking sculptures arrayed around campus; Nam June Paik, William Wegman, Niki

de St. Phalle, and Jenny Holtzer are among the artists whose works are displayed. *Exit I–5 onto La Jolla Village Dr. going west; take the Gilman Dr. off-ramp to the right and continue on to the information kiosk at the campus entrance,* ☎ *858/534–4414 for campus tour information.* ⏲ *Campus tours Sun. at 2 from the South Gilman Information Pavilion; reserve before 3 Fri.*

Old Town

San Diego's Spanish and Mexican history and heritage are most evident in Old Town, north of downtown at Juan Street, near the intersection of Interstates 5 and 8. Old Town is the first European settlement in southern California, but the pueblo's true beginnings took place overlooking Old Town from atop Presidio Park, where Father Junípero Serra established the first of California's missions, San Diego de Alcalá, in 1769. On San Diego Avenue, the district's main drag, art galleries and expensive gift shops are interspersed with tacky curios shops, restaurants, and open-air stands selling inexpensive Mexican pottery, jewelry, and blankets. The Old Town Esplanade on San Diego Avenue between Harney and Conde streets is the best of several mall-like affairs constructed in mock Mexican-plaza style. Shops and restaurants also line Juan and Congress streets.

Two large parking lots linked to the park by an underground pedestrian walkway have helped ease some of the parking congestion, and signage leading from I–8 to the Transit Center is easy to follow. If you're not familiar with the area, however, don't try to reach Old Town from I–5; the exit on that freeway marked "Old Town" leaves you floundering near Mission Bay without further directions.

Numbers in the text correspond to numbers in the margin and on the Old Town San Diego map. *sends you to www.fodors.com/urls for Web links.*

A Good Tour

It's possible to trek around Old Town and see all its sights in one day, but we recommend making this a walking-driving combination.

Visit the information center at Seeley Stable, just off Old Town Plaza, to orient yourself to the various sights in **Old Town San Diego State Historic Park** ①. When you've had enough history, cross north on the west side of the plaza to **Bazaar del Mundo** ②, where you can shop or enjoy some nachos on the terrace of a Mexican restaurant. Walk down San Diego Avenue, which flanks the south side of Old Town's historic plaza, east to Harney Street and the **Thomas Whaley Museum** ③. Then continue east 2½ blocks on San Diego Avenue beyond Arista Street to the **El Campo Santo** ④ cemetery. **Heritage Park** ⑤ is perched on a hill above Juan Street, north of the museum and cemetery. Drive west on Juan Street and north on Taylor Street to Presidio Drive, which will lead you up the hill on which **Presidio Park** ⑥ and the **Junípero Serra Museum** ⑦ sit.

TIMING

Try to time your visit to coincide with the free daily tours of Old Town given at 11 AM and 2 PM by costumed park service employees at Seeley Stable. It takes about two hours to walk through Old Town. If you drive to Presidio Park, allot another hour to explore.

Sights to See

❷ **Bazaar del Mundo.** North of Old Town Plaza lies the area's unofficial center, built to represent a colonial Mexican square. The central courtyard is always in blossom, with magenta bougainvillea; scarlet hibiscus; and irises, poppies, and petunias in season. Ballet Folklorico and

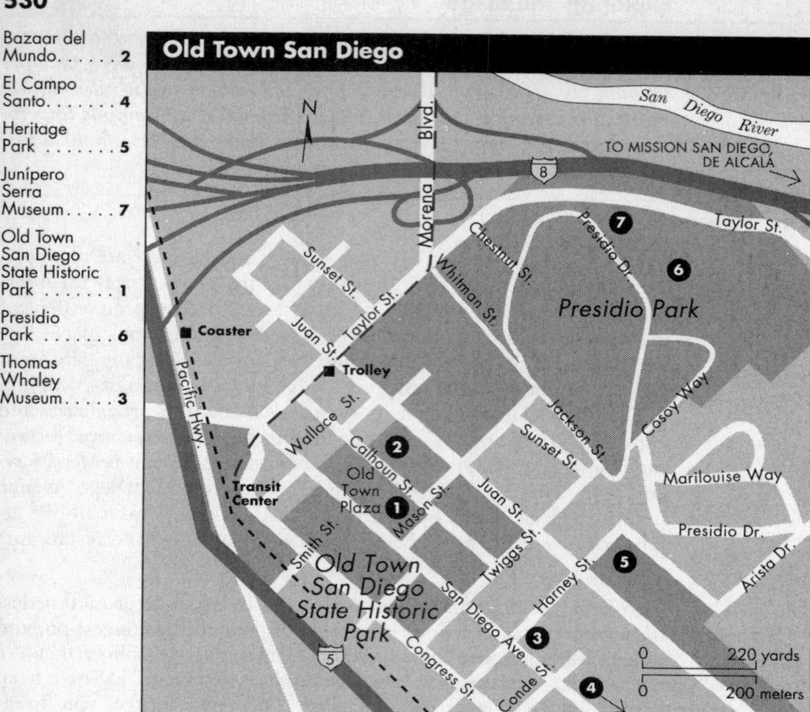

flamenco dancers perform on weekend afternoons. Prices here can be considerably higher than those at shops on the other side of Old Town Plaza. ✉ *2754 Calhoun St.*, ☎ *619/296–3161*. ⏲ *Shops daily 10–9.*

4 **El Campo Santo.** The old adobe-walled cemetery established in 1849 was the burial place for many members of Old Town's founding families, as well as for some gamblers and bandits who passed through town until 1880. ✉ *North side of San Diego Ave. S, between Arista and Ampudia Sts.*

5 **Heritage Park.** A number of San Diego's important Victorian buildings are the focus of this 7.8-acre park, up the Juan Street hill near Harney Street. The buildings were moved here and restored by Save Our Heritage Organization, and include southern California's first synagogue, a one-room Classic Revival–style structure built in 1889 for Congregation Beth Israel. The climb up to the park is a little steep, but the view of the harbor is great. ✉ *2455 Heritage Park Row (county parks office)*, ☎ *858/694–3049*.

7 **Junípero Serra Museum.** This Spanish mission–style museum is devoted to the history of the Presidio hill from the time it was occupied by the Kumeyaay Indians until 1929, when the museum was established, along with Presidio Park. Artifacts include Kumeyaay baskets, Spanish riding gear, and a painting that Father Serra would have viewed in Mission San Diego de Alcalá (☞ *below*). A new education room features hands-on investigation stations for children. ✉ *2727 Presidio Dr.*, ☎ *619/297–3258*. *$5*. ⏲ *Fri.–Sun. 10–4:30.*

OFF THE BEATEN PATH

MISSION SAN DIEGO DE ALCALÁ – Mission San Diego de Alcalá, the first of a chain of 21 missions stretching northward along the California coast, was established by Father Junípero Serra in 1769 on Presidio Hill, and moved to its present location in 1774. The present church is the fifth to be built on the site; it was reconstructed in 1931 following the outlines of the 1813 church. It's 150 ft long but only 35 ft wide because, without easy means of joining beams, the mission buildings were only as wide as the trees that served as their ceiling supports. From the peaceful palm-bedecked gardens out back you can gaze at the 46-ft-high *campanario,* the mission's most distinctive feature; one of its five bells was cast in 1822. ✉ *10818 San Diego Mission Rd. (from I–15, take Friars Rd. east and Rancho Mission Rd. south),* ☎ *619/281–8449.* *$3.* *Daily 9–5.*

★ ❶ **Old Town San Diego State Historic Park.** The six square blocks on the site of San Diego's original pueblo are the heart of Old Town. Most of the 20 historic buildings preserved or re-created by the park cluster around **Old Town Plaza.** You can see the presidio from behind the cannon by the flagpole. San Diego Avenue is closed to vehicle traffic here.

The **Robinson-Rose House** (☎ 619/220–5422) was the original commercial center of old San Diego, housing railroad offices, law offices, and the first newspaper press. In addition to serving as the park's visitor center and administrative center, it now hosts a model of Old Town as it looked in 1872, as well as various historic exhibits.

On Mason Street, at the corner of Calhoun Street, **La Casa de Bandini** is one of the prettiest haciendas in San Diego. Built in 1829 by a Peruvian, Juan Bandini, the house served as Old Town's social center during Mexican rule. Today the hacienda's colorful gardens and main-floor dining rooms house a popular Mexican restaurant.

Seeley Stable (✉ 2630 Calhoun St., ☎ 619/220–5427), next door to La Casa de Bandini, became San Diego's stagecoach stop in 1867 and was the transportation hub of Old Town until trains became the favored mode of travel. The stable houses an exhibit on the California *vaquero,* the original American cowboy, and an array of Native American artifacts. An excellent free walking tour of the park leaves from here daily at 11 and 2, weather permitting.

A tour pamphlet available here gives details about all of the historic buildings on the plaza and in its vicinity. Racine & Laramie, a painstakingly reproduced version of San Diego's first (1868) cigar store, is especially interesting. The noncommercial houses are open to visitors daily 10–5; none charge admission, though donations are appreciated.

La Casa de Estudillo was built on Mason Street in 1827 by the commander of the San Diego Presidio, Jose Maria Estudillo. The adobe home was occupied by members of the Estudillo family until 1887. It was purchased and restored in 1910 by sugar magnate and developer John D. Spreckels.

❻ **Presidio Park.** The rolling hillsides of the 40-acre green space overlooking Old Town from the north end of Taylor Street are popular with picnickers. It's a nice walk to the summit from Old Town if you're in good shape and wearing the right shoes—it should take about half an hour. You can also drive to the top of the park via Presidio Drive, off Taylor Street. Presidio Park has a private canyon surrounded by palms at the bottom of the hill, off Taylor Street before it intersects with Interstate 8.

If you do decide to walk, look in at the Presidio Hills Golf Course on Mason Street, which has an unusual clubhouse: it incorporates the ruins of Casa de Carrillo, the town's oldest adobe, constructed in 1820. At the end of Mason Street, veer left on Jackson Street to reach the **Presidio Ruins,** where adobe walls and a bastion have been built above the foundations of the original fortress and chapel. Archaeology students from San Diego State University have marked off the early chapel outlines. Also on the site are the 28-ft-high Serra Cross, built in 1913 out of brick tiles found in the ruins, and a bronze statue of Father Serra. Before you do much poking around here, however, it's a good idea to get some historical perspective at the Junípero Serra Museum (☞ *above*), just to the east. Take Presidio Drive southeast of the museum and you'll come to the site of Fort Stockton, built to protect Old Town and abandoned by the United States in 1848. Plaques and statues also commemorate the Mormon Battalion, which enlisted here to fight in the battle against Mexico.

❸ **Thomas Whaley Museum.** In 1856 Thomas Whaley built southern California's first two-story brick structure. The house, which served as the county courthouse and government seat during the 1870s has period furnishings and one of the six life masks that exist of Abraham Lincoln. The place is perhaps most famed, however, for the ghosts that are said to inhabit it. ✉ *2482 San Diego Ave.,* ☎ *619/298–2482.* 🎫 *$4.* ⏲ *Oct.–May, Wed.–Mon. 10–4:30; June–Sept., daily 10–4:30.*

DINING

By Kathryn Shevelow and David Nelson

A stroll down 5th Avenue will provide ample evidence of San Diego's love affair with Italian cuisine, echoed in other parts of the city. But the cooking of Spain and France, as well as the various cuisines of Latin America, Asia, the Middle East—and even the United States—are also well represented. San Diego is an informal city. The advised attire at most of the restaurants listed below is casual.

CATEGORY	COST*
$$$$	over $50
$$$	$30–$50
$$	$20–$30
$	under $20

*per person for a three-course meal, excluding drinks, service, and 7¾% sales tax

🖱 following the text of a review is your signal that the property has a Web site, where you will find details and, usually, images; for a link, visit www.fodors.com/urls.

Coronado

Contemporary

$–$$ ✕ **Rhinoceros Cafe & Grill.** Rhinoceros offers good value for the money with a really well-made Caesar salad; penne pasta in an eye-opening sauce with crumbled Italian sausage; a marinated, charbroiled jumbo pork chop; and spicy, Southwestern-style meat loaf. In addition to the charbroiled fish of the day, the kitchen brews a first-rate, San Francisco–style fish stew. ✉ *1166 Orange Ave.,* ☎ *619/435–2121. MC, V.*

Italian

$–$$$ ✕ **Il Fornaio.** This handsome restaurant occupies an amazing waterfront location, framing stellar views of downtown San Diego with windows that stretch from floor to ceiling. The menu is creative rather than traditional. The house antipasto, served for a minimum of two guests, makes a very nice way to start, no matter whether the main course will be lobster-stuffed ravioli or mesquite-grilled lamb chops. ✉ *1333 1st St.,* ☎ *619/437–4911. AE, D, MC, V.*

Seafood

$$$–$$$$ ★ ✕ **Azzura Point.** Decorated in a romantic, 1930s style, Azzura Point makes an ideal setting for a leisurely and memorable meal. Arrive be-

fore sunset and you'll get an amazing view that shoots straight up San Diego Bay to the Coronado Bridge and the downtown skyline. Seafood dishes include an appetizer of scallops with greens and horseradish dressing, roasted Pacific salmon with black truffle sauce and, perhaps best of all, mesquite-grilled swordfish crowned with a medallion of seared duck foie gras. ✉ *Loews Coronado Bay Resort, 4000 Coronado Bay Rd.,* ☎ *619/424–4000. AE, DC, MC, V. Closed Mon. No lunch.*

Downtown

Chinese

$–$$$ ✕ **Panda Inn.** One of the better Chinese restaurants in town, this dining room at the top of Horton Plaza serves subtly seasoned Mandarin and Szechuan dishes in an elegant setting. Try the honey walnut shrimp, the Peking duck, the spicy bean curd, and the Panda beef. ✉ *506 Horton Plaza,* ☎ *619/233–7800. AE, D, DC, MC, V.*

Contemporary

$$–$$$ ✕ **CHIVE.** The menu of daring CHIVE pleases with such inventive offerings as the pulled pork spring roll, the crisp potato "nest" stuffed with artichoke hearts and foie gras, and rack of lamb doused with lime and coconut-infused natural juices. ✉ *558 4th Ave.,* ☎ *619/232–4483. AE, D, MC, V. No lunch weekends.*

$$–$$$ ★ ✕ **Dobson's.** At lunchtime local politicos and media types rub elbows at the long polished bar of this well-regarded restaurant; evening patrons include many theatergoers. Dobson's signature dish, a superb mussel bisque, comes topped with a crown of puff pastry. The predominantly California wine list is excellent. ✉ *956 Broadway Circle,* ☎ *619/231–6771,* FAX *619/696–0861. AE, DC, MC, V. Closed Sun. No lunch Sat.*

French

$$–$$$ ★ ✕ **Vignola.** This excellent establishment just may serve the best food in the Gaslamp Quarter. As a point of interest, the elegant mahogany bar originally supported elbows in Joan Crawford's Beverly Hills mansion. The cooking of Provence inspires a menu that features such classics as duck confit and fish in light, aromatic sauces. On Thursday special three-course, fixed-priced menus provide culinary tours of different French provinces. ✉ *828 6th Ave.,* ☎ *619/231–1111. AE, D, MC, V. Closed Sun. No lunch.*

Irish

$–$$ ✕ **The Field.** The small sidewalk terrace is suitable for sipping a Guinness, but diners prefer the indoors for solid lunches and dinners. Start with potato leek soup or a cheese-rich Irish farmhouse salad, and continue with Irish stew, corned beef and cabbage, or, best of all, a boxty (a potato pancake with such fillings as sage-flavored chicken or Irish bacon and cheese). As the evening wears on, the crowd grows younger, livelier, louder, and sometimes rowdier. ✉ *544 5th Ave.,* ☎ *619/232–9840. MC, V.*

Italian

$$–$$$ ✕ **Bella Luna.** This small restaurant whose owner hails from the island of Capri has developed a loyal following among diners who prefer good cuisine to being seen. The service is gracious and attentive. The menu includes dishes from all over Italy. ✉ *748 5th Ave.,* ☎ *619/239–3222,* FAX *619/239–1202. AE, MC, V. No lunch weekends.*

$–$$ ✕ **Sammy's California Woodfired Pizza.** This small homegrown chain was the first local outfit to serve imaginative gourmet pizzas like those invented by Los Angeles celebrity chef Wolfgang Puck. The menu offers pastas and entrées as well. The casual setting features deep, comfortable booths as well as a narrow sidewalk terrace that surveys the lively Gaslamp Quarter scene. ✉ *720 4th Ave.,* ☎ *619/230–8888;* ✉

702 Pearl St., La Jolla, ☎ *858/456–5222;* ✉ 12925 El Camino Real, Del Mar, ☎ 858/259–6600; ✉ 1620 Camino de la Reina, Mission Valley, ☎ 619/298–8222. AE, MC, V.

Japanese

$–$$$ ✕ **Taka.** In this attractive 5th Avenue alternative, you could make a meal by starting with sushi and then ordering from the large selection of cold and hot appetizers: try the soft-shell crabs or the spicy Orient pancake. The entrée menu mixes Japanese standards such as salmon teriyaki with an occasional European selection, such as the good seafood linguine. ✉ *555 5th Ave.,* ☎ *619/338–0555. AE, D, DC, MC, V. No lunch.*

Mexican

$$–$$$ ✕ **Candelas.** Mexican nouvelle cuisine permeates the menu at this romantic hideaway. Candles glow everywhere around the small room, which often is populated primarily by well-dressed patrons from nearby Mexico. There isn't a burrito or taco in sight at this haven of stylish, imaginative cooking. ✉ *416 3rd Ave.,* ☎ *619/702–4455. MC, V. Closed Sun. No lunch.*

$$–$$$ ✕ **Las Fajitas.** Las Fajitas serves eight varieties of sizzling platters of highly seasoned meat, seafood, and vegetables, from basic steak and chicken models to versions based on plump shrimp, local lobster, and swordfish. The rest of the menu largely devotes itself to seafood. Desserts include bananas flamed in rum and a smooth coconut flan. The sidewalk terrace is cramped, but the intimate dining room is among the more attractive in this part of the Gaslamp Quarter. ✉ *628 5th Ave.,* ☎ *619/232–4242. AE, D, MC, V.*

Seafood

$$$–$$$$ ★ ✕ **Star of the Sea.** The flagship of Anthony's local fleet of seafood restaurants ensconces its patrons in its most formal dining room, making it an all-around favorite for location, cuisine, and decor. The menu changes seasonally, but expect to find contemporary preparations of fresh seafood. The outdoor patio takes full advantage of the choice waterfront location. ✉ *1360 N. Harbor Dr.,* ☎ *619/232–7408. AE, D, DC, MC, V. No lunch.*

$$–$$$$ ✕ **Blue Point Coastal Cuisine.** High ceilings, gleaming woodwork, and expansive windows give this seafood establishment an urbane air. Blue Point situates its cuisine firmly on the Pacific Rim, incorporating Asian accents and south-of-the-border flavors. Go for the appetizers and seafood entrées here—the pasta dishes are disappointing. The wine list is serious, and the service is efficient and friendly. ✉ *565 5th Ave.,* ☎ *619/233–6623. AE, D, DC, MC, V. No lunch.*

$$–$$$$ ✕ **Sally's.** The dining room is très chic postmodern, and similarly stylish is the cuisine: pan-Mediterranean with a light French accent. Seafood is the star here, although the menu has something for carnivores and vegetarians, as well. The light, greaseless crab cakes are the best in town. Jazz accompanies the Sunday brunch (11–3). ✉ *Hyatt Regency San Diego, 1 Market Pl.,* ☎ *619/687–6080,* FAX *619/687–6078. AE, D, DC, MC, V.*

$–$$$$ ✕ **The Fish Market.** A large variety of fresh mesquite-grilled fish is the specialty at this informal restaurant, where parents can dine with young children without sacrificing their own taste buds. The view is stunning: enormous plate-glass windows look directly out onto the harbor. Reservations are not accepted, but if you're lucky enough to get a window table, you can practically taste the salt spray. A more formal restaurant upstairs, the Top of the Market ($$–$$$$), is expensive but worth the splurge. The Solana Beach branch, which does not include a pricey Top of the Market component, is across the street from the Del Mar Racetrack. ✉ *750 N. Harbor Dr.,* ☎ *619/232–3474 for the Fish Market; 619/234–4867 for the Top of the Market;* ✉ *640 Via de la Valle, Solana Beach,* ☎ *858/755–2277. AE, D, DC, MC, V.*

Spanish

$$–$$$ ✕ **Sevilla.** Lines form on weekend nights, when largely youthful throngs wait to crowd both the ground-floor bar, where they enjoy drinks, tapas, and professional Flamenco dancing, and the downstairs club, where they dance to live music and dine on classics of the Spanish kitchen such as saffron-flavored shrimp and Basque-style red snapper. The kitchen does a respectable job with the seafood casseroles known as paella, the herb-flavored baked rabbit, and the roasted pork tenderloin. ✉ *555 4th Ave.,* ☎ *619/233–5979. AE, MC, V. No lunch.*

Steak Houses

$$$–$$$$ ★ ✕ **Morton's of Chicago.** This Chicago-based, international luxury steak-house chain chose a prime location in the soaring Harbor Club towers for its San Diego outpost. Morton's often can be crowded with conventioneers. Servers present the menu by wheeling up a cart laden with crimson prime steaks, behemoth veal and lamb chops, thick cuts of swordfish, and huge Maine lobsters that wave their claws in alarm when they hear the prices (based on the market, but always astronomical) quoted. ✉ *The Harbor Club, 285 J St.,* ☎ *619/696–3369. AE, D, MC, V. No lunch.*

$$$ ✕ **Jared's.** On the lower deck of a Mississippi River–style stern-wheeler moored on San Diego Bay, this stylish but laid-back steak house is a fun destination for expensive, high-quality steak and seafood dinners. The decor includes a display kitchen lined in burnished copper, and the view of the downtown towers twinkling across the water. Steaks range from a 12-ounce fillet to a 22-ounce porterhouse, and seafood cuts similarly are oversized. ✉ *880 E. Harbor Island Dr.,* ☎ *619/291–1028. AE, D, MC, V. No lunch.*

$$–$$$ ★ ✕ **Rainwater's on Kettner.** Downtown San Diego's premier home-grown steak house also ranks as the longest running of the pack, not least because this spacious, second-floor establishment has the luxurious look and mood of an old-fashioned Eastern men's club, with exceptionally deep banquettes. Order a starter of Rainwater's signature black bean soup with Rainwater Madeira, and let the tender, expertly roasted prime rib compete with a profusion of steaks for your favor. ✉ *1202 Kettner Blvd.,* ☎ *619/233–5757. AE, D, MC, V. No lunch weekends.*

Uptown

American

$–$$$ ✕ **Montanas American Grill.** One of Hillcrest's most popular restaurants serves hearty California-American food in a sleek, trendy setting. Stick with the least complicated dishes, such as the barbecued meats, chicken, and salmon. The appetizer duck cakes are tasty and rich. Microbrews are on tap. ✉ *1421 University Ave.,* ☎ *619/297–0722. AE, DC, MC, V. No lunch weekend*

$ ✕ **Hob Nob Hill.** With its dark wood booths and patterned carpets, Hob Nob Hill seems suspended in the 1950s, but you don't need to be a nostalgia buff to appreciate the bargain-priced American home cooking. Open all day seven days; reservations are suggested for Sunday breakfast. ✉ *2271 1st Ave.,* ☎ *619/239–8176. AE, D, MC, V.*

Contemporary

$$–$$$ ★ ✕ **California Cuisine.** The menu in this minimalist-chic dining room is consistently innovative. Daily selections might include grilled ostrich fillet and Atlantic salmon with grapefruit butter sauce; the popular en-

San Diego Dining

Azul La Jolla 5
Azzura Point 34
Belgian Lion 16
Bella Luna 44
Berta's Latin American Restaurant 18
Blue Point Coastal Cuisine 50
Bombay Exotic Cuisine of India 25
Brockton Villa Restaurant 8
Cafe Japengo 1
Cafe Pacifica 17
California Cuisine . . . 27
Candelas 49
The Cheesecake Factory 20
CHIVE 46
Dobson's 39
Dumpling Inn 21
El Tecolote 19
Emerald Chinese Seafood Restaurant . . 23
The Field 51
The Fish Market 37
George's at the Cove 6
Hob Nob Hill 30
Il Fornaio 32
Jared's 31
Jin Sang 11
La Bruschetta 3
Las Fajitas 45
Laurel 29
The Marine Room 4
The Mission Cafe and Coffeehouse . . . 15
Montanas American Grill 26
Morton's of Chicago 48
Nick's at the Beach . . 14
Palenque 12
Panda Inn 42
Phuong Trang 22
The Prado 28
Rainwater's on Kettner 36
Rhinoceros 33
Roppongi 9
Sally's 38
Sammy's 43
SamSon's 2
Sevilla 47
Star of the Sea 35
Sushi Ota 13
Taka 40
Tapenade 10
Taste of Thai 24
Top O' the Cove 7
Vignola 41

LA JOLLA
PACIFIC BEACH
MISSION BEACH
OCEAN BEACH
POINT LOMA
PACIFIC OCEAN
Mission Bay
Fiesta Island
SeaWorld
San Diego International Airport Lindbergh Field
Harbor Island
Shelter Island
North Island
U.S. NAVAL AIR STATION
Coronado
Cabrillo National Monument
Torrey Pines Rd.
Prospect St.
Ardath Rd.
Gilman Dr.
Genesee Ave.
Soledad Fwy.
Regents Rd.
La Jolla Blvd.
San Diego Fwy.
Clairemont Dr.
Balboa
Mission Blvd.
Garnet Ave.
Grand Ave.
Ingraham St.
W. Mission Bay Dr.
Linda
Juan St.
Nimitz Blvd.
Sunset Cliffs Blvd.
Rosecrans St.
Pacific
N. Harbor Dr.
Hill St.
Catalina Blvd.
Canon St.
Scott St.
Memorial Dr.
Cabrillo
N
0 1 mile
0 1 km

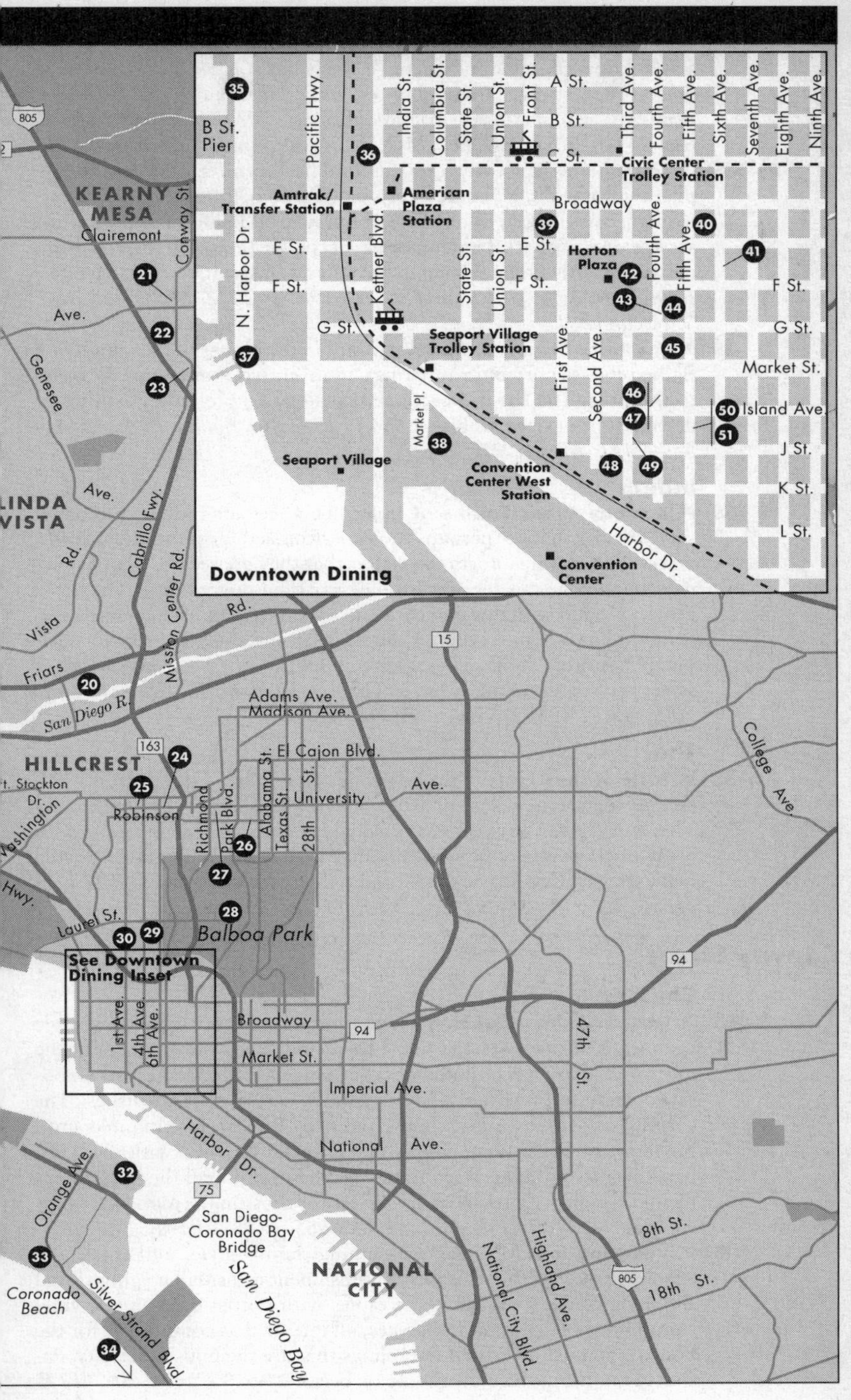
Downtown Dining
A St.
B St.
C St.
B St. Pier
Pacific Hwy.
India St.
Columbia St.
State St.
Union St.
Front St.
Third Ave.
Fourth Ave.
Fifth Ave.
Sixth Ave.
Seventh Ave.
Eighth Ave.
Ninth Ave.
Civic Center Trolley Station
Amtrak/ Transfer Station
American Plaza Station
Broadway
N. Harbor Dr.
E St.
F St.
G St.
Kettner Blvd.
Horton Plaza
Seaport Village Trolley Station
Market St.
First Ave.
Second Ave.
Island Ave.
J St.
K St.
L St.
Market Pl.
Seaport Village
Convention Center West Station
Harbor Dr.
Convention Center
KEARNY MESA
Clairemont
Conway St.
Ave.
Genesee
Ave.
LINDA VISTA
Rd.
Cabrillo Fwy.
Mission Center Rd.
Vista
Rd.
Friars
San Diego R.
Adams Ave.
Madison Ave.
El Cajon Blvd.
University
Ave.
College Ave.
HILLCREST
Ft. Stockton Dr.
Washington
Robinson
Richmond
Park Blvd.
Alabama St.
Texas St.
28th St.
Hwy.
Laurel St.
Balboa Park
See Downtown Dining Inset
1st Ave.
4th Ave.
6th Ave.
Broadway
Market St.
Imperial Ave.
47th St.
Harbor Dr.
National Ave.
Orange Ave.
San Diego-Coronado Bay Bridge
Coronado Beach
Silver Strand Blvd.
San Diego Bay
NATIONAL CITY
National City Blvd.
Highland Ave.
8th St.
18th St.
805
15
163
94
75
21
22
23
20
24
25
26
27
28
29
30
32
33
34
35
36
37
38
39
40
41
42
43
44
45
46
47
48
49
50
51

trée-size warm chicken salad is a regular feature. You can count on whatever you order to be carefully prepared and elegantly presented. The staff is knowledgeable and attentive, the wine list is good, and the baked desserts and sorbets are mighty tempting. Heat lamps make the garden patio a romantic year-round option. ✉ *1027 University Ave.,* ☏ *619/543–0790. AE, D, DC, MC, V. Closed Mon. No lunch weekends.*

$$–$$$ ✕ **Laurel.** Since the early 1990s Laurel has been regarded as the premier midtown dinner address, especially among those attending a performance at the Old Globe Theatre in nearby Balboa Park. Polished service and a smart, contemporary decor set the stage for an imaginative, expertly prepared menu that takes its inspiration from Mediterranean cuisine. ✉ *505 Laurel St.,* ☏ *619/239–2222. AE, D, DC, MC, V. No lunch.*

$$ ✕ **The Prado.** This beautiful restaurant in the House of Hospitality on Balboa Park's museum row brings an inventive, contemporary menu to this area. The bar has become a fashionable pre- and post-theater destination for light nibbles. ✉ *1549 El Prado, Balboa Park,* ☏ *619/557–9441. AE, D, MC, V.*

Indian

$–$$$ ✕ **Bombay Exotic Cuisine of India.** This elegant Indian restaurant serves dishes that are perhaps too Americanized for some aficionados, who should firmly inform the waiter that they are serious about spiciness, but no one can deny the loveliness of their presentation. The chef's generous hand with raw and cooked vegetables gives each course a colorful freshness reminiscent of California cuisine, though the flavors definitely hail from India. The curious should try the *dizzy noo shakk,* a sweet and spicy banana curry. ✉ *Hillcrest Center, 3975 5th Ave., Suite 100,* ☏ *619/298–3155. AE, D, DC, MC, V.*

Thai

$–$$ ✕ **Taste of Thai.** Usually packed with value-minded diners, this modest café seats you at close quarters but compensates by serving yummy Thai and vegetarian cuisine at reasonable prices. The menu's enormous array of choices include spicy noodles with chicken, whole or filleted fish with garlic or ginger sauce, and red or yellow curries. ✉ *527 University Ave.,* ☏ *619/291–7525. AE, D, DC, MC, V.*

Convoy Street

Chinese

$–$$$ ★ ✕ **Emerald Chinese Seafood Restaurant.** As the first Hong Kong–style restaurant to open in San Diego, this handsome establishment at the foot of Convoy Street holds pride of place among fanciers of elaborate, carefully prepared, and sometimes costly seafood dishes. The shrimp, prawns, lobsters, clams, and fish all reside live in tanks until the moment of cooking. Simple preparations flavored with scallions, black beans, and ginger are among the best, although the kitchen has plenty of high-style tricks up its sleeves for those in the mood for fancy cooking. ✉ *3709 Convoy St.,* ☏ *858/565–6888. AE, MC, V.*

$ ✕ **Dumpling Inn.** Modest, unassuming, family-style, authentic, and absolutely wonderful, this tiny establishment in a small neighborhood shopping center loads down its tables with bottles of aromatic vinegar and jars of chili oils and pastes, all intended as condiments for the boiled, steamed, and fried dumplings that are the house specialty. Patrons may bring their own wine or beer. ✉ *4619 Convoy St., #F,* ☏ *858/268–9638. Reservations not accepted. No credit cards. Closed Mon.*

Vietnamese

$ ✕ **Phuong Trang.** This large, relatively spare dining room gets packed to the rafters. The menu lists no fewer than 248 appetizers, soups, noodle dishes, and main courses. Waiters tend to steer guests to such tasty offerings as the Vietnamese-style fried egg rolls, the char-grilled shrimp paste wrapped around lengths of sugarcane, the beef in grape leaves, and the fresh spring rolls. ✉ *4170 Convoy St.,* ☏ *858/565–6750. MC, V.*

Beaches

American/Casual

$–$$ ✕ **The Mission Cafe and Coffeehouse.** This comfy, laid-back Mission Beach café opens early in the morning and remains open as a coffeehouse until the wee hours. The cuisine is dubbed "Chino-Latino." All menu items can be made vegetarian. The café serves good beer on tap, specialty coffee drinks, and shakes and smoothies. The North Park branch has a friendly neighborhood ambience and a more elaborate dinner menu. ✉ *3795 Mission Blvd., Mission Beach,* ☏ *619/488–9060;* ✉ *2801 University Ave., North Park,* ☏ *619/220–8992. AE, MC, V.*

$–$$ ✕ **Nick's at the Beach.** While beach-area eateries do their best to avoid the appearance of sophistication, Nick's interesting menu outdoes the competition. The casual setting, easy-going service, and virtually nonexistent dress code does conform to beach standards, but the menu plunges boldly into California cuisine with seared ahi salad in Thai ginger dressing, horseradish-crusted halibut, and apple-brandy pork chops. ✉ *809 Thomas Ave., Pacific Beach,* ☏ *858/270–1730. AE, D, MC, V.*

Belgian

$$–$$$ ★ ✕ **Belgian Lion.** The signature dish here is the cassoulet, a rich stew of white beans, sausage, and duck. Wonderful fresh fish dishes include oven-seared scallops and the sea bass *au vert,* braised in white wine with spinach and sorrel. Or try the *confit de canard* (slowly simmered duck). An impressive selection of wines complements the food. ✉ *2265 Bacon St., Ocean Beach,* ☏ *619/223–2700. Reservations essential. AE, D, DC, MC, V. Closed Sun.–Wed. No lunch.*

Japanese

$–$$ ★ ✕ **Sushi Ota.** Wedged into a mini-mall between a convenience store and a looming medical building, Sushi Ota seems less than prepossessing, but it prepares San Diego's best sushi. Besides the usual California roll and tuna and shrimp sushi, sample the sea urchin or surf clam sushi, and the soft-shell crab roll. ✉ *4529 Mission Bay Dr.,* ☏ *619/270–5670. Reservations essential. AE, D, MC, V. No lunch Sat.–Mon.*

Mexican

$–$$ ✕ **Palenque.** This family-run restaurant in Pacific Beach serves regional Mexican dishes. Piñatas and paper birds dangle from the thatch ceiling, and seating is in comfortable round-back leather chairs; in warm weather you can dine on a small deck in front. Palenque is a bit hard to spot from the street and service is often slow, but the food is worth your vigilance and patience. ✉ *1653 Garnet Ave., Pacific Beach,* ☏ *619/272–7816. AE, D, DC, MC, V. No lunch Mon.*

La Jolla

Contemporary

$$$–$$$$ ✕ **The Marine Room.** Diners can gaze at the ocean from this venerable La Jolla Shores mainstay with dining-and-dancing. Appetizers include baked oysters in potato jackets, and pyramid of salmon tartare and Maine sea scallops. A representative entrée would be Alaskan halibut in a potato net, served with artichokes, crawfish tails, chanterelle mushrooms, and candied *cipollini* (onions), in a mustard-seed Riesling essence. Sunday brunch is lavish; in winter call for information about the high-tide breakfasts. ✉ *2000 Spindrift Dr.,* ☏ *619/459–7222. AE, D, DC, MC, V.*

$$$–$$$$ ✕ **Top O' the Cove.** The elegant but comfortable Top O' the Cove receives high marks for the romantic ocean view from its cottage windows and its fine contemporary European-American cuisine. Inquire about the day's fresh salmon or swordfish creations. The adventuresome might select the roasted medallions of North American elk. The service is attentive but not overbearing, and the wine list is enormous. ✉ *1216 Prospect St.,* ☎ *619/454–7779. AE, DC, MC, V.*

$$$ ✕ **Azul La Jolla.** Blessed with what may be the most glamorous view of La Jolla Cove, this sizable restaurant also has dining on a broad, sheltered terrace. The view fades with the sunset, and once darkness falls, the deep banquettes are preferable to the window-side tables. The "artisan's" appetizer plate offers as many as a dozen clever bites and should be shared by two diners. The entrée list pays attention to seafood, but really shines with olive-crusted rack of lamb and a bone-in New York steak in a musky Spanish blue-cheese sauce. ✉ *1250 Prospect St.,* ☎ *858/454–9616. AE, D, MC, V. No lunch Mon.*

$$–$$$ ✕ **Cafe Japengo.** In one of the most stylish dining rooms in town, framed by elegant marbled walls accented with leafy bamboo trees and unusual black-iron sculptures, this Pacific Rim restaurant serves Asian-inspired cuisine with many North and South American touches. Service can be slow. ✉ *Aventine Center, 8960 University Center La.,* ☎ *619/450–3355,* FAX *619/552–6064. AE, D, DC, MC, V. No lunch weekends.*

$$–$$$ ★ ✕ **Roppongi.** The contemporary dining room, with a row of comfortable booths lining a wall, is lovely, done in wood tones and accented with Asian statuary. It can get noisy when crowded (which is almost always); tables near the bar are generally quieter. The menu invites you to choose among a range of imaginative Euro-Asian tapas that you may order as appetizers or combine to make a full meal. Recommended entrées include wok-fried garlic shrimp with lo mein noodles, grilled Chilean sea bass with vegetables, and Chinese duck confit. ✉ *875 Prospect St.,* ☎ *619/551–5252. AE, D, DC, MC, V.*

$–$$$ ✕ **Brockton Villa Restaurant.** This informal restaurant in a restored historic beach cottage overlooks La Jolla Cove and the ocean. You'll have to fight the crowds on sunny weekends. ✉ *1235 Coast Blvd.,* ☎ *619/454–7393. AE, D, MC, V. No dinner Mon.*

Deli

$–$$$ ✕ **SamSon's.** This large, sometimes noisy eatery has a vast menu and enormous portions. Good options include a lox plate for breakfast, and an overstuffed corned beef and slaw sandwich or one of the soup-and-sandwich specials (especially the whitefish when it's available) for lunch. Dinners are less interesting. ✉ *8861 Villa La Jolla Dr.,* ☎ *619/455–1462. AE, D, DC, MC, V.*

French

$$$–$$$$ ★ ✕ **Tapenade.** The celebrated restaurant Tapenade (named after the delicious Provençal black-olive and anchovy paste that accompanies the bread) takes its inspiration from the South of France. In an unpretentious, light, and airy room it serves cuisine to match. Very fresh ingredients, a delicate touch with sauces, and an emphasis on seafood make this a winner. Desserts are excellent. The tables can be cramped, however, and the service does not rise to the level of the cooking. ✉ *7612 Fay Ave., between Kline and Pearl,* ☎ *619/551–7500. AE, D, DC, MC, V. Closed Mon.*

Italian

$$–$$$ ✕ **La Bruschetta.** Chef/proprietor Nino Zizzo will, when asked, whip up a mean antipasto plate that most likely will include a variety of cured meats; surprisingly seasoned seafood nibbles; and, usually, the best sweet-sour eggplant salad to be found in San Diego County. Book ahead if

you want to try the tender veal osso buco that is offered Friday and Saturday only. ✉ *2151 Avenida de la Playa,* ☎ *858/551–1221. AE, DC, MC, V.*

Japanese

$$–$$$ ✕ **Jin Sang.** Jin Sang specializes in shabu shabu, a Japanese dish in which arrangements of seafood, chicken, or beef are cooked tableside in boiling broth, along with separate courses of vegetables and noodles. Because the cooking process is so simple, the restaurant emphasizes very high-quality ingredients, and the basic U.S. prime beef dinner is a treat. The server gets the party going, but guests learn to use chopsticks and cook the items themselves. ✉ *7614 Fay Ave.,* ☎ *858/456–4545. AE, D, MC, V. No lunch.*

Seafood

$$$ ★ ✕ **George's at the Cove.** The elegant main dining room, with a wall-length window overlooking La Jolla Cove, is renowned for its daily fresh seafood specials and its fine preparations of beef and lamb. For starters, try the signature smoked chicken, broccoli, and black-bean soup, or the wonderful baked fresh mussels. The helpfully arranged wine list offers an extensive selection. For more informal dining and a sweeping view of the coast try the rooftop Ocean Terrace (or order from its menu in the second-story bar). Wonderful for breakfast, lunch, or brunch on a fine day (but also serving dinner), the Terrace does not take reservations. ✉ *1250 Prospect St.,* ☎ *619/454–4244. Reservations essential. AE, D, DC, MC, V.*

Mission Valley

American

$$ ✕ **The Cheesecake Factory.** The Cheesecake Factory opened with a bang in the city's hottest shopping mall, Fashion Valley, and has retained its immense popularity ever since. Everyone seems to like the multipage menu, which opens with such appetizers as barbecued duck-filled spring rolls and sweet corn tamale cakes, and meanders leisurely through classic and innovative pizzas, gigantic salads, pastas, and more. The cheesecake is huge and creamy. When the crowd is in full cry the noise can be deafening. ✉ *Fashion Valley Center, 6067 Friars Rd.,* ☎ *619/683–2800. AE, D, MC, V.*

Mexican

$–$$ ✕ **El Tecolote.** One pretty good watering hole in the culinary desert of Mission Valley is the long-established El Tecolote (The Owl). The restaurant does a fine job with the usual taco-burrito fare, but also with the enchiladas in mole, the chicken breast with poblana or ancho chili sauce, and the rich Aztec layered cake (tortillas stacked with cheese, chilies, enchilada sauce, guacamole, and sour cream). ✉ *6110 Friars Rd. W,* ☎ *619/295–2087. AE, D, DC, MC, V. No lunch Sun.*

Old Town

Latin American

$–$$ ✕ **Berta's Latin American Restaurant.** A San Diego rarity, Berta's serves wonderful Latin American dishes. The food manages to be tasty and health conscious at the same time. Try the Brazilian seafood *vatapa* (shrimp, scallops, and fish served in a sauce flavored with ginger, coconut, and chilies) or the Peruvian *pollo a la huancaina* (chicken with chilies and a feta-cheese sauce). ✉ *3928 Twiggs St.,* ☎ *619/295–2343. AE, MC, V.*

Seafood

$$–$$$ ✕ **Cafe Pacifica.** The airy Cafe Pacifica serves eclectic contemporary cuisine with an emphasis on seafood. Fresh fish is grilled with your

choice of savory sauces. Other good bets include the griddle-fried mustard catfish, the seared ahi tuna, and the grilled lamb chops. The crème brûlée is worth blowing any diet for. Cafe Pacifica's wine list has received kudos from *Wine Spectator* magazine. ✉ *2414 San Diego Ave.,* ☎ *619/291–6666. AE, D, DC, MC, V. No lunch.*

LODGING

By Sharon K. Gillenwater and Edie Jarolim

Updated by Arian E. Collins

San Diego is spread out, so the first thing to consider when selecting lodging is location. If you choose one of the many hotels with a waterfront location and extensive outdoor sports facilities, you need never leave the premises. But if you plan to sightsee, take into account a hotel's proximity to the attractions you most want to visit. In general, price need not be a major factor in your decision. Even the most expensive areas have some reasonably priced rooms.

If you are planning an extended stay or need lodgings for four or more people, consider an apartment rental. **Oakwood Apartments** (☎ 800/888–0808, 🌐) rents comfortable furnished apartments in the Mission Valley and La Jolla Colony areas; there's a three-night minimum stay. Several hotels also offer special weekly rates, especially in the beach communities. The **Bed and Breakfast Guild of San Diego** (☎ 619/523–1300) lists high-quality member inns. The **Bed & Breakfast Directory for San Diego** (✉ Box 3292, 92163, ☎ 619/297–3130 or 800/619–7666) covers San Diego County.

Most hostels require an international passport to check in. Rooms are usually dorm style with four to six bunks; however, some hostels have a few private or double rooms. Some hostels have limitations on accepting American travelers so it is best to call before arriving.

CATEGORY	COST*
$$$$	over $175
$$$	$120–$175
$$	$80–$120
$	under $80

**Prices are for a double room in high (summer) season, excluding 10½% San Diego room tax.*

Coronado

Quiet, out-of-the-way Coronado feels like something out of an earlier, more gracious era. With boutiques and restaurants lining Orange Avenue and its fine beaches, Coronado is great for a getaway. But if you plan to see many of San Diego's attractions, you'll probably spend a lot of time commuting.

$$$$ ★ 🏨 **Coronado Island Marriott Resort.** Flamingos greet you at the entrance to this 16-acre landscaped resort, formerly Le Meridien. Large rooms and suites in low-slung buildings are done in a cheerful California-country French fashion, with colorful Impressionist prints; all rooms have separate showers and tubs and come with plush robes. The spa facilities are top-notch. ✉ *2000 2nd St., 92118,* ☎ *619/435–3000; 800/543–4300 for central reservations,* FAX *619/435–3032. 265 rooms, 35 suites. 2 restaurants, bar, in-room data ports, room service, 3 pools, barbershop, beauty salon, 2 outdoor hot tubs, massage, sauna, spa, 6 tennis courts, aerobics, health club, beach, snorkeling, windsurfing, boating, jet skiing, waterskiing, bicycles, pro shop, shops, children's programs, laundry service, concierge, business services, convention center, meeting rooms, parking (fee). AE, D, DC, MC, V.* 🌐

$$$$ **Loews Coronado Bay Resort.** You can park your boat at the 80-slip marina of this elegant resort set on a secluded 15-acre peninsula on the Silver Strand. Rooms are tastefully decorated, and all have furnished balconies with views of water—either bay, ocean, or marina. The hotel lounge has nightly entertainment. The Azzura Point restaurant (☞ Dining, *above*) has won numerous awards. ✉ *4000 Coronado Bay Rd., 92118,* ☎ *619/424–4000 or 800/815–6397,* FAX *619/424–4400. 403 rooms, 37 suites. 3 restaurants, 3 bars, deli, in-room data ports, minibars, room service, 3 pools, barbershop, beauty salon, 3 hot tubs, 5 tennis courts, health club, beach, windsurfing, boating, jet skiing, waterskiing, bicycles, pro shop, children's programs, laundry service, concierge, business services, convention center, meeting rooms, parking (fee). AE, D, DC, MC, V.*

$$$–$$$$ ★ **Hotel Del Coronado.** Preserving the memory of seaside vacations long gone by, "The Del" is a social and historic Victorian landmark (☞ Exploring, *above*). Whimsical red turrets, white siding, and balconied walkways on each floor give a casual impression, but past guests have included U.S. presidents and European royalty. Rooms and suites of the 1888 gingerbread building now have air-conditioning and Victorian-theme decor. There's a lot of bustle in the public areas of the older hotel; for quieter quarters, consider the modern rooms of the seven-story Ocean Towers. ✉ *1500 Orange Ave., 92118,* ☎ *619/435–6611 for hotel; 619/522–8000; 800/468–3533 for reservations,* FAX *619/522–8262. 676 rooms. 2 restaurants, 4 bars, piano bar, coffee shop, deli, in-room data ports, room service, 2 pools, barbershop, beauty salon, outdoor hot tub, massage, sauna, spa, steam room, 3 tennis courts, exercise room, beach, bicycles, shops, video games, children's programs, laundry service, concierge, business services, convention center, meeting rooms, parking (fee). AE, D, DC, MC, V.*

$$–$$$$ **Glorietta Bay Inn.** Across the street from the Hotel Del Coronado and adjacent to the Coronado harbor, the main building of this property was built in 1908 for sugar baron John D. Spreckels, who once owned much of downtown San Diego. Rooms in this Edwardian-style mansion and in the newer motel-style buildings are attractively furnished. The well-appointed inn is much smaller than the Hotel Del; its clients experience a quieter and less expensive stay. Tours ($6) of the island's historical buildings depart from the inn three mornings a week. Some rooms have kitchenettes, patios, and balconies. ✉ *1630 Glorietta Blvd., 92118,* ☎ *619/435–3101 or 800/283–9383,* FAX *619/435–6182. 100 rooms. In-room data ports, refrigerators, pool, outdoor hot tub, bicycles, coin laundry, laundry service, library, concierge, business services, free parking. AE, MC, V. CP.*

Downtown

Much to see is within walking distance of downtown accommodations—Seaport Village, the Embarcadero, the Gaslamp Quarter, theaters and nightspots, galleries and coffeehouses, and Horton Plaza.

$$$$ ★ **Hyatt Regency San Diego.** This high-rise adjacent to Seaport Village successfully combines Old-World opulence with California airiness. Palm trees pose next to ornate tapestry couches in the light-filled lobby, and all of the British Regency–style guest rooms have views of the water. The hotel's proximity to the convention center attracts a large business trade. The Business Plan includes access to an area with desks and office supplies; each room on the special business floor has a fax machine. A trolley station is one block away. Sally's (☞ Dining, *above*) serves inventive cuisine, and the 40th-floor lounge has 360-degree views. ✉ *1 Market Pl., 92101,* ☎ *619/232–1234; 800/233–1234 for central reservations,* FAX *619/233–6464. 820 rooms, 55 suites and Regency Club rooms.*

3 restaurants, 2 bars, in-room data ports, minibars, room service, pool, outdoor hot tub, sauna, steam room, 4 tennis courts, health club, boating, bicycles, shops, laundry service, dry cleaning, business services, meeting rooms, car rental, parking (fee). AE, D, DC, MC, V.

$$$$ ★ **Westgate Hotel.** A nondescript, modern high-rise across from Horton Plaza hides what must be the most opulent hotel in San Diego. The lobby, modeled after the anteroom at Versailles, has hand-cut Baccarat chandeliers; rooms are individually furnished with antiques, Italian marble counters, and bath fixtures with 24-karat-gold overlays. From the ninth floor up the views of the harbor and city are breathtaking. Afternoon high tea is served in the lobby to the accompaniment of piano music. The San Diego Trolley stops right outside the door. ✉ *1055 2nd Ave., 92101,* ☎ *619/238–1818 or 800/221–3802; 800/522–1564 in* CA, FAX *619/557–3737. 223 rooms. 2 restaurants, bar, deli, in-room data ports, room service, barbershop, exercise room, bicycles, concierge, business services, meeting rooms, airport shuttle, parking (fee). AE, D, DC, MC, V.*

$$$–$$$$ **Embassy Suites San Diego Bay.** It's a short walk to the convention center, the Embarcadero, and Seaport Village from one of downtown's most popular hotels. The front door of each spacious suite opens out onto the 12-story atrium. The contemporary decor is pleasant, and the views from rooms facing the harbor are spectacular. Families can make good use of the in-room refrigerators, microwaves, and separate sleeping areas. A cooked-to-order breakfast and afternoon cocktails are complimentary, as are airport transfers and daily newspaper. A trolley station is nearby. ✉ *601 Pacific Hwy., 92101,* ☎ *619/239–2400; 800/362–2779 for central reservations,* FAX *619/239–1520. 337 suites. Restaurant, bar, in-room data ports, room service, pool, outdoor hot tub, barbershop, beauty salon, sauna, tennis court, health club, bicycles, shops, coin laundry, laundry service, concierge, business services, meeting rooms, airport shuttle, car rental, parking (fee). AE, D, DC, MC, V.*

$$$–$$$$ **Westin Hotel San Diego–Horton Plaza.** Although it is fronted by a startling lighted blue obelisk, this high-rise is all understated marble and brass. The spacious rooms are in pastels of coral blue and pale orange. With its prime downtown location, the hotel attracts many business travelers. The lobby lounge is packed every night with local financiers and weary shoppers from the adjacent Horton Plaza. ✉ *910 Broadway Circle, 92101.* ☎ *619/239–2200,* ☎ FAX *619/557–3737. 450 rooms, 14 suites. 2 restaurants, sports bar, lounge, in-room data ports, room service, pool, hot tub, 2 tennis courts, health club, basketball, shops, dry cleaning, laundry service, business services, meeting rooms, airport shuttle, parking (fee). AE, D, DC, MC, V.*

$$$ **U. S. Grant Hotel.** Across the street from the Horton Plaza shopping center, this San Diego classic was built in 1910 by the grandson of President Ulysses S. Grant. Crystal chandeliers and polished marble floors in the lobby and Queen Anne–style mahogany furnishings in the stately rooms recall a more gracious era when such dignitaries as President Franklin D. Roosevelt and Charles Lindbergh stayed here. High-power business types still gather at the hotel's clubby Grant Grill, and English high tea is served in the lobby from 2 to 6. ✉ *326 Broadway, 92101,* ☎ *619/232–3121 or 800/237–5029,* FAX *619/232–3626. 220 rooms, 60 suites. 3 restaurants, 2 bars, café, room service, exercise room, shops, concierge, business services, meeting rooms, airport shuttle, parking (fee). AE, D, DC, MC, V.*

$$$ **Wyndham Emerald Plaza Hotel.** This property's office and conference facilities draw many business travelers. Still, the Wyndham is also fine for vacationers who want to be near downtown shopping and restaurants. Many of the upper-floor accommodations have panoramic views. The bland, beige-dominated standard rooms are not overly large. The health club is quite good. ✉ *400 W. Broadway, 92101,* ☎ *619/239–*

4500 or 800/996–3426, FAX 619/239–4527. 416 rooms, 20 suites. Restaurant, bar, in-room data ports, room service, pool, outdoor hot tub, sauna, spa, steam room, health club, exercise room, shops, laundry service, concierge, business services, meeting rooms, airport shuttle, parking (fee). AE, D, DC, MC, V.

$$–$$$ ★ **Clarion Hotel Bay View.** Two blocks from the Gaslamp Quarter and close to the San Diego Convention Center, this is a good hotel for budget conventioneers who want to be close to shopping, nightlife, and restaurants. Surrounded to the north and east by the warehouse district, the area around the hotel can seem a little seedy, but it is safe. The two-room suites have wet bars, and you can request microwaves, mini-refrigerators, and video players for added fees. A San Diego Trolley station is two blocks away. ✉ *660 K St., 92101,* ☎ *619/696–0234 or 800/766–0234, FAX 619/231–8199. 264 rooms, 48 suites. Restaurant, bar, minibars, in-room data ports, room service, pool, hot tub, sauna, spa, exercise room, video games, shops, coin laundry, laundry service, concierge, meeting rooms, airport shuttle, car rental, parking (fee). AE, D, DC, MC, V.*

$$–$$$ **Horton Grand Hotel.** A Victorian confection in the heart of the historic Gaslamp Quarter, the Horton Grand comprises two 1880s hotels moved brick by brick from nearby locations and fit together. Its delightfully retro rooms are furnished with period antiques, ceiling fans, and gas-burning fireplaces. The choicest rooms overlook a garden courtyard that twinkles with miniature lights each night. Service can be erratic. ✉ *311 Island Ave., 92101,* ☎ *619/544–1886 or 800/542–1886, FAX 619/239–3823. 108 rooms, 24 suites. Restaurant, piano bar, kitchenettes (some), theater, business services, meeting rooms, airport shuttle, parking (fee). AE, D, DC, MC, V.*

$$ **Holiday Inn San Diego–Bayside.** On the Embarcadero and overlooking San Diego Bay, this twin high-rise hotel is convenient for vacationers and business travelers. Rooms are unsurprising but spacious and comfortable, and views from the balconies are hard to beat. While the hotel grounds are nice if fairly sterile, San Diego Bay is just across the street and offers boat rides, restaurants, and picturesque walking areas. The English-style Elephant and Castle Pub is a great place for food, drink, and meeting people. ✉ *1355 N. Harbor Dr., 92101,* ☎ *619/232–3861; 800/877–8920 for central reservations, FAX 619/232–4924. 600 rooms, 17 suites. Restaurant, bar, in-room data ports, 2 pools, outdoor hot tub, sauna, exercise room, shops, coin laundry, meeting rooms, airport shuttle, parking (fee). AE, D, DC, MC, V.*

$$ **Radisson Hotel–Harbor View.** This 22-story hotel dwarfs most buildings in the area (many are two-story Victorian homes), providing many rooms with great views of San Diego Bay and the downtown skyline. The art-deco rooms are standard, but clean, and most have balconies. The hotel is practically adjacent to a freeway offramp, but you would have to open the sliding glass door to get much noise. There are two restaurants in the building, but the eateries and coffeehouses of nearby Little Italy are more enjoyable. The hotel is also close to the airport. ✉ *1648 Front St., 92101,* ☎ *619/239–6800 or 800/333–3333, FAX 619/238–9543. 313 rooms, 20 suites. 2 restaurants, bar, pool, hot tub, sauna, exercise room, shops, laundry service, business services, meeting rooms, airport shuttle, parking (fee). AE, D, DC, MC, V.*

$–$$ **Gaslamp Plaza Suites.** Listed on the National Registry of Historic Places, this 11-story structure a block from Horton Plaza was built in 1913 as San Diego's first "skyscraper." Appealing public areas have old marble, brass, and mosaics. Although most rooms are rather small, they are well decorated with dark wood furnishings. Guests can enjoy the view and a complimentary Continental breakfast on the rooftop terrace. Book ahead if you're visiting in the summer. ✉ *520 E St., 92101,* ☎ *619/232–9500* *or 800/874–8770, FAX 619/238–9945. 52 suites. Restaurant, bar, refrigerators, nightclub, parking (fee). AE, D, DC, MC, V. CP.*

$–$$ **Rodeway Inn.** On one of downtown's quieter streets, this chain property in Cortez Hill is clean, comfortable, and nicely decorated. The hotel is near Balboa Park, the zoo, and freeways. ✉ *833 Ash St., 92101,* ☎ *619/239–2285; 800/228–2000 for central reservations; 800/522–1528 in CA, FAX 619/235–6951. 45 rooms. In-room data ports, refrigerators, hot tub, sauna, coin laundry, business services, meeting rooms, free parking. AE, D, DC, MC, V. CP.*

$ **HI–San Diego Downtown.** This Gaslamp Quarter two-story hostel has new and modern furnishings and facilities. A special event is scheduled every evening. There are 150 beds, a large common kitchen, and a TV room. Most rooms are dorm style with four bunks each. There are a few doubles, coed dorms, and group rooms (with 10 beds). ✉ *521 Market St., 92101,* ☎ *619/525–1531 or 800/909–4776 code 43, FAX 619/338–0129. Bicycles, billiards, coin laundry. MC, V.*

$ **Ramada Inn & Suites – Downtown.** Formerly the St. James Hotel, this historic 1913 building's 12 stories made it the tallest building in the city when it was built. The hotel is one of several boutique hotels sprouting up in renovated buildings. At the north end of the Gaslamp Quarter, the hotel is close to the area's many restaurants, nightclubs, and shops, but away from the hustle and bustle on 4th and 5th avenues. A complimentary daily newspaper is provided. ✉ *830 6th Ave., 92101,* ☎ *619/431–8877 or 800/272–6232, FAX 619/231–8307. 82 rooms, 17 suites. Restaurant, in-room data ports, minibars, room service. AE, D, DC, MC, V. CP.*

$ **Super 8 Bayview.** This motel's location is less noisy than those of other low-cost establishments. The accommodations are nondescript but clean, and some have refrigerators. ✉ *1835 Columbia St., 92101,* ☎ *619/544–0164 or 800/800–8000, FAX 619/237–9940. 101 rooms. Pool, spa, exercise room, coin laundry, laundry service, airport shuttle, car rental, free parking. AE, D, DC, MC, V. CP.*

Harbor Island, Shelter Island, and Point Loma

Harbor Island and Shelter Island both have grassy parks, lavish hotels, and good restaurants. Harbor Island is closest to the downtown area and less than five minutes from the airport. Narrower Shelter Island is nearer to Point Loma. Both locations command views of the bay and the downtown skyline. Not all the lodgings listed here are on the islands themselves, but all are in the vicinity.

$$$$ **Sheraton Harbor Island San Diego.** Of this property's two high-rises, the smaller, more intimate West Tower has larger rooms with separate areas suitable for business entertaining. The East Tower has better sports facilities. Rooms throughout are California style. Views from the upper floors of both sections are superb, but because the West Tower is closer to the water it has fine outlooks from the lower floors, too. ✉ *1380 Harbor Island Dr., 92101,* ☎ *619/291–2900; 800/325–3535 for central reservations, FAX 619/692–2337. 1,045 rooms, 50 suites. 3 restaurants, 2 bars, deli, patisserie, in-room data ports, minibars, room service, 3 pools, wading pool, 2 outdoor hot tubs, sauna, massage, 4 tennis courts, health club, jogging, beach, boating, bicycles, pro shop, dry cleaning, business services, meeting rooms, airport shuttle, free parking. AE, D, DC, MC, V. CP.*

$$$–$$$$ **Humphrey's Half Moon Inn & Suites.** This sprawling South Seas–style resort has grassy open areas with palms and tiki torches. Rooms, some with kitchens and some with harbor or marine views, have modern furnishings. Locals throng to Humphrey's, the on-premises seafood restaurant, and to the jazz lounge; the hotel also hosts outdoor jazz

and pop concerts from June to October. ✉ *2303 Shelter Island Dr., 92106,* ☎ *619/224–3411; 800/345–9995 for reservations,* FAX *619/224–3478. 128 rooms, 54 suites. Restaurant, bar, in-room data ports, kitchenettes (some), minibars, room service, pond, pool, hot tub, putting green, croquet, Ping-Pong, boating, bicycles, concert hall, coin laundry, business services, meeting rooms, airport shuttle, free parking. AE, D, DC, MC, V.*

$$–$$$$ **Best Western Island Palms Hotel & Marina.** This waterfront inn, with an airy skylighted lobby, is a good choice if you have a boat to dock; the adjacent marina has guest slips. Both harbor- and marina-view rooms are available. Standard accommodations are fairly small; if you're traveling with family or more than one friend, the two-bedroom suites with kitchens are a good deal. ✉ *2051 Shelter Island Dr., 92106,* ☎ *619/222–0561 or 800/922–2336,* FAX *619/222–9760. 48 rooms, 29 suites. Restaurant, bar, fans, in-room data ports, kitchenettes (some), pool, outdoor hot tub, spa, exercise room, jogging, boating, coin laundry, laundry service, business services, meeting rooms, free parking. AE, D, DC, MC, V.*

$$–$$$ **Bay Club Hotel & Marina.** Rooms in this appealing low-rise Shelter Island property are large, light, and furnished with rattan tables and chairs and Polynesian tapestries; all have refrigerators and views of either the bay or the marina from outside terraces. A buffet breakfast and limo service to and from the airport or Amtrak station are included. ✉ *2131 Shelter Island Dr., 92106,* ☎ *619/224–8888 or 800/672–0800,* FAX *619/225–1604. 95 rooms, 10 suites. Restaurant, bar, room service, refrigerators, pool, outdoor hot tub, exercise room, shops, video games, concierge, business services, meeting rooms, airport shuttle, free parking. AE, D, DC, MC, V.*

$$–$$$ **Shelter Pointe Hotel & Marina.** This 11-acre property has been refurbished in a mixture of Mexican and Mediterranean styles. The spacious and light-filled lobby, with its Maya sculptures and terra-cotta tiles, opens onto a lush esplanade that overlooks the hotel's marina. The rooms are well appointed, if a bit small, and most look out onto either the marina or San Diego Bay. ✉ *1551 Shelter Island Dr., 92106,* ☎ *619/221–8000 or 800/566–2524,* FAX *619/221–5953. 206 rooms, 26 suites. Restaurant, bar, room service, kitchenettes (some), 2 pools, 2 hot tubs, 2 saunas, 2 tennis courts, jogging, health club, volleyball, beach, boating, bicycles, meeting rooms, airport shuttle, free parking. AE, D, DC, MC, V.*

$$–$$$ **Travelodge Hotel–Harbor Island.** Lodgers here get the views and amenities of more expensive hotels for less, with such perks as in-room coffeemakers and free local phone calls. Every room has a balcony. Those staying on the two executive floors also get a free buffet breakfast. The public areas and guest rooms are bright and airy. The Waterfront Cafe & Club overlooks the marina. ✉ *1960 Harbor Island Dr., 92101,* ☎ *619/291–6700; 800/578–7878 for central reservations,* FAX *619/293–0694. 201 rooms, 6 suites. Restaurant, bar, in-room data ports, room service, pool, outdoor hot tub, exercise room, shops, laundry service, meeting rooms, airport shuttle, free parking. AE, D, DC, MC, V.*

$$ **Best Western Posada Inn.** Many of the rooms at this comfortable if plain inn have harbor views. Some rooms have microwaves, mini-refrigerators, and video players. Point Loma's seafood restaurants are within walking distance. ✉ *5005 N. Harbor Dr., 92106,* ☎ *619/224–3254 or 800/231–3811,* FAX *619/224–2186. 112 rooms. Restaurant, bar, in-room data ports, pool, outdoor hot tub, exercise room, laundry service, meeting rooms, airport shuttle, free parking. AE, D, DC, MC, V. CP.*

$ **HI–Elliott International Hostel–Point Loma.** This hostel is different in that it's in a large converted house, in a quiet area. It isn't very close to any of San Diego's attractions or nightlife, but there's a bus stop

- Bahia Resort Hotel 22
- Balboa Park Inn 45
- Banana Bungalow San Diego 16
- Bay Club Hotel & Marina 30
- Best Western Blue Sea Lodge 19
- Best Western Hacienda Suites–Old Town 38
- Best Western Island Palms Hotel & Marina 29
- Best Western Posada Inn 33
- Catamaran Resort Hotel 17
- Clarion Hotel Bay View 62
- Coronado Island Marriott Resort 45
- Crystal Pier Hotel . . .15
- Dana Inn & Marina 23
- Days Inn-Hotel Circle 44
- Diamond Head Hotel 12
- Doubletree Hotel San Diego Mission Valley 41
- Embassy Suites San Diego Bay 54
- Gaslamp Plaza Suites 59
- Glorietta Bay Inn 47
- Grande Colonial La Jolla 4
- Hanalei Hotel 40
- Heritage Park Inn 39
- HI–Elliott International Hostel–Point Loma . . .26
- HI–San Diego Downtown 61
- Hilton La Jolla Torrey Pines 8
- Hilton San Diego Mission Valley 43
- Hilton San Diego Resort 20
- Holiday Inn Express-La Jolla 9
- Holiday Inn Hotel & Suites Old Town 37
- Holiday Inn San Diego-Bayside 53
- Horton Grand Hotel 63
- Hotel Del Coronado 48
- Humphrey's Half Moon Inn & Suites 31
- Hyatt Islandia 24

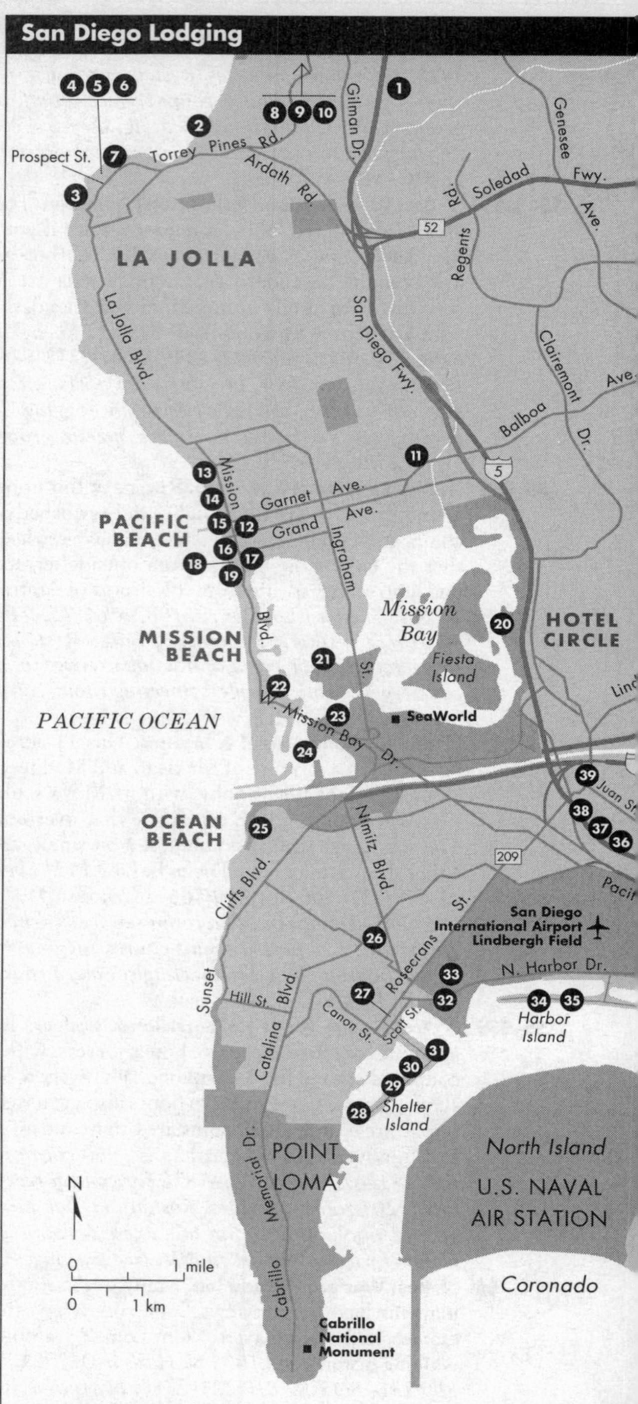

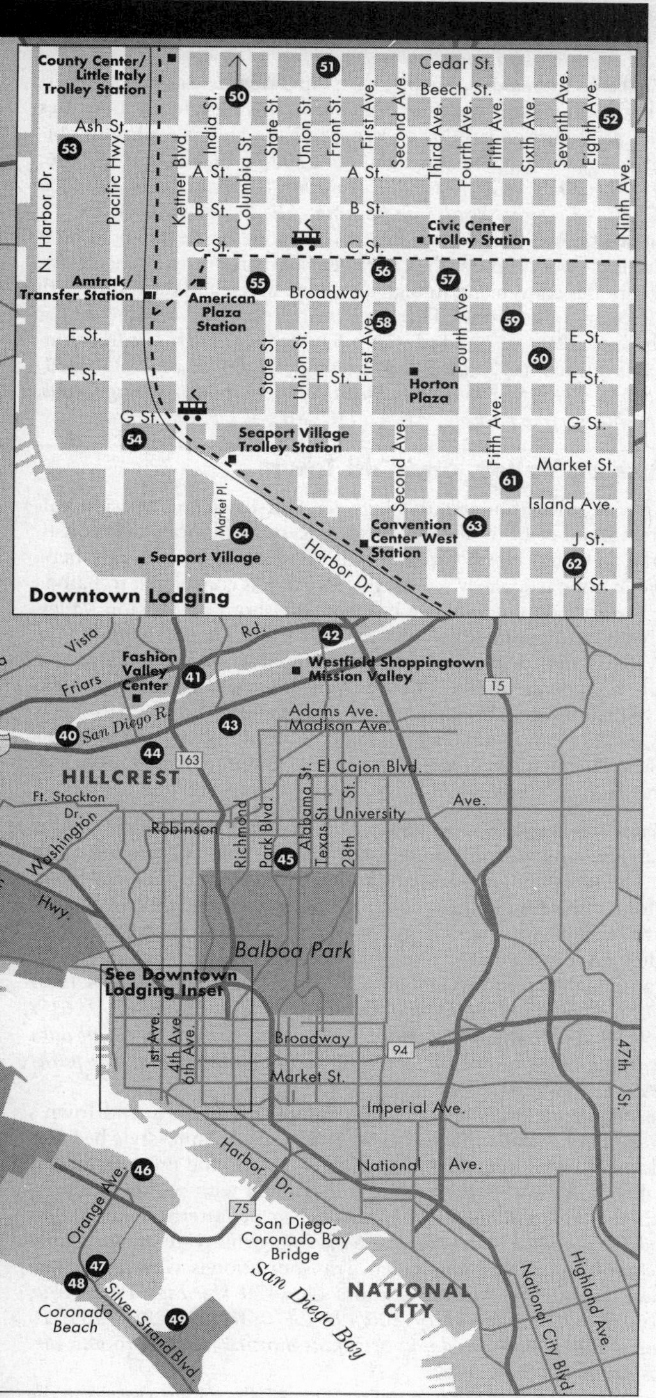

Hyatt Regency La Jolla 1
Hyatt Regency San Diego 64
La Jolla Cove Suites 7
La Valencia 6
Lodge at Torrey Pines 10
Loews Coronado Bay Resort 49
Ocean Beach International Backpackers Hostel 25
Pacific Shores Inn . . . 14
Pacific Terrace Hotel 13
Point Loma Travelodge 32
Prospect Park Inn 5
Radisson Hotel–Harbor View 51
Ramada Inn & Suites–Downtown 60
Ramada Limited – Harborview 27
Ramada Limited – Old Town 36
Rodeway Inn 52
San Diego Marriott Mission Valley 42
San Diego Paradise Point Resort 21
Scripps Inn 3
Sea Lodge 2
Shelter Pointe Hotel & Marina 28
Sheraton Harbor Island San Diego 35
Super 8 Bayview 50
Surfer Motor Lodge 18
Travelodge Hotel-Harbor Island 34
U.S. Grant Hotel 57
Vagabond Inn San Diego Mission Bay 11
Westgate Hotel 56
Westin Hotel San Diego–Horton Plaza 58
Wyndham Emerald Plaza Hotel 55

nearby. Special events are scheduled weekly. The hostel has a large kitchen and patio and a TV room. ✉ *3790 Udall St., 92107,* ☎ *619/223–4778. 61 beds. Bicycles, coin laundry, free parking. MC, V.*

$ **Point Loma Travelodge.** You'll get the same view here as at the higher-price hotels—for far less money. Of course, there are fewer amenities and the neighborhood isn't as serene, but the rooms—all with coffeemakers—are adequate and clean. ✉ *5102 N. Harbor Dr., 92106,* ☎ *619/223–8171; 800/578–7878 for central reservations,* FAX *619/222–7330. 45 rooms. Pool, free parking. AE, D, DC, MC, V.*

$ **Ramada Limited–Harborview.** Recent renovations make this motel nicer than its next-door neighbor the Outrigger, but there are no kitchen units. The location is convenient, though on a busy street, and the rooms with bay views are quite a deal. There is a heated pool and a bay-view bar with billiards. Pets are allowed with a $20 deposit. There is a free shuttle to area attractions. ✉ *1403 Rosecrans St., 92106,* ☎ *619/225–9461,* FAX *619/225–1163. 86 rooms. Bar, breakfast room, pool, meeting rooms, airport shuttle, free parking. AE, D, DC, MC, V. CP.*

Hotel Circle, Mission Valley, and Old Town

Lining both sides of Interstate 8 between Old Town and Mission Valley are a number of moderately priced accommodations that constitute the so-called Hotel Circle. A car is an absolute necessity here. Although not particularly scenic, this location is convenient to Balboa Park, the zoo, downtown, the beaches, the shops of Mission Valley, Old Town, and public transit (including the San Diego Trolley). Mission Valley hotels, near movie theaters, restaurants, and shops, are more upscale than those of Hotel Circle to the west and generally less expensive than comparable properties at the beaches. Old Town itself has a few picturesque lodgings and some modestly priced chain hotels near Interstate 5; when you're making reservations, request a room that doesn't face the freeway.

$$–$$$$ **Hilton San Diego Mission Valley.** Directly fronting Interstate 8, this property has soundproof rooms decorated in a colorful contemporary style. The stylish public areas and lush greenery in the back will make you forget the hotel's proximity to the freeway. Although geared toward business travelers—the hotel has a business center and guests are allowed complimentary use of a personal computer—children stay free, and small pets are accepted ($25 deposit). ✉ *901 Camino del Rio S, 92108,* ☎ *619/543–9000, 800/733–2332, or 800/445–8667,* FAX *619/543–9358. 342 rooms, 8 suites. 2 restaurants, 2 bars, in-room data ports, pool, outdoor hot tub, exercise room, video games, free parking. AE, D, DC, MC, V.*

$–$$$$ ★ **Heritage Park Inn.** The beautifully restored mansions in Old Town's Heritage Park include this romantic 1889 Queen Anne–style bed and breakfast. Rooms range from smallish to ample, and most are bright and cheery. A two-bedroom suite is decorated with period antiques, and there is also a minisuite. A full breakfast and afternoon tea are included. Some rooms share a bath. Classic vintage films are shown nightly in the parlor on a small film screen. Transportation is available to area attractions and the Amtrak station. ✉ *2470 Heritage Park Row, 92110,* ☎ *619/299–6832 or 800/995–2470,* FAX *619/299–9465. 10 rooms, 2 suites. In-room data ports, fans, library, meeting rooms, airport shuttle. AE, MC, V.*

$$$ ★ **San Diego Marriott Mission Valley.** This 17-floor high-rise sits in the middle of the San Diego River valley near Qualcomm Stadium and the Rio Vista Plaza shopping center, minutes from the Mission Valley and Fashion Valley malls. The San Diego Trolley stops across the street. The hotel is well equipped for business travelers—the front desk provides 24-hour fax and photocopy services—but the Marriott also caters to vacationers by providing comfortable rooms (with individual balconies), a friendly staff, and free transportation to the malls. ✉ *8757 Rio San Diego Dr., 92108,* ☎ *619/692–3800; 800/228–9290 for central reservations,* FAX *619/692–0769. 350 rooms, 5 suites. Restaurant, sports bar, in-room data ports, minibars, room service, pool, outdoor hot tub, sauna, tennis court, exercise room, health club, shops, nightclub, coin laundry, concierge, business services, airport shuttle, free parking. AE, D, DC, MC, V.*

$$–$$$ **Best Western Hacienda Suites–Old Town.** Pretty and white, with balconies and Spanish-tile roofs, the Hacienda is in a quiet part of Old Town, away from the freeway and the main retail bustle. The layout is somewhat confusing, and accommodations are not large enough to earn the "suite" label the hotel gives them, but they're decorated in tasteful Southwestern style and equipped with microwaves, coffeemakers, mini-refrigerators, and video players. ✉ *4041 Harney St., 92110,* ☎ *619/298–4707 or 800/888–1991,* FAX *619/298–4771. 169 rooms. Restaurant, bar, pool, outdoor hot tub, spa, exercise room, coin laundry, laundry service, concierge, meeting rooms, travel services, airport shuttle, free parking. AE, D, DC, MC, V.*

$$–$$$ **Hanalei Hotel.** As its name suggests, the theme of this friendly Hotel Circle property is Hawaiian: palms, waterfalls, koi ponds, and tiki torches abound. Rooms are decorated in tropical prints. What used to be a golf course next door has been restored as a bird sanctuary. Free transportation is provided to local malls and Old Town. The hotel is virtually surrounded by heavy traffic, which can make for a noisy stay. ✉ *2270 Hotel Circle N, 92108,* ☎ *619/297–1101 or 800/882–0858,* FAX *619/297–6049. 402 rooms, 14 suites. 2 restaurants, bar, room service, in-room data ports, pool, hot tub, exercise room, laundry service, meeting rooms, travel services, car rental. AE, D, DC, MC, V.*

$$ **Doubletree Hotel San Diego Mission Valley.** Near Fashion Valley Center and adjacent to the Hazard Center—which has a seven-screen movie theater, four major restaurants, a food pavilion, and more than 20 shops—the Doubletree is also convenient to Highway 163 and Interstate 8. A San Diego Trolley station is within walking distance. Public areas are light filled and comfortable, well suited to this hotel's large business clientele. ✉ *7450 Hazard Center Dr., 92108,* ☎ *619/297–5466; 800/547–8010 for central reservations,* FAX *619/297–5499. 294 rooms, 6 suites. Restaurant, 2 bars, in-room data ports, minibars, room service, 2 pools, outdoor hot tub, sauna, exercise room, 2 tennis courts, shops, nightclub, business services, meeting rooms, airport shuttle, free parking. AE, D, DC, MC, V.*

$$ **Holiday Inn Hotel & Suites Old Town.** The hacienda-style hotel has Spanish colonial–style fountains and courtyards, and painted tiles and Southwestern decor in the rooms. Breakfast, cocktail reception, and transfers to the airport, bus, and Amtrak stations are complimentary. Business-class rooms have modem lines and other amenities. ✉ *2435 Jefferson St., 92110,* ☎ *619/260–8500 or 800/255–3544,* FAX *619/297–2078. 174 rooms, 19 suites. Restaurant, bar, pool, outdoor hot tub, exercise room, laundry service, meeting rooms, airport shuttle, free parking. AE, D, DC, MC, V.*

$$ ★ **Ramada Limited–Old Town.** Already an excellent value for Old Town, this cheerful property throws in such perks as garage parking and afternoon snacks. The rooms have a European look, and you'll find modern conveniences such as coffeemakers, microwave ovens, and refrigerators. The pool off the shaded courtyard is heated. ✉ *3900 Old Town Ave., 92110,* ☎ *619/299–7400 or 800/272–6232,* FAX *619/299–1619. 125 rooms. Restaurant, in-room data ports, refrigerators, room service, pool, outdoor hot tub, shops, coin laundry, laundry service,*

concierge, business services, meeting rooms, airport shuttle, free parking. AE, D, DC, MC, V. CP.

$–$$ **Days Inn–Hotel Circle.** Rooms in this large complex are par for a chain motel but have the bonus of Nintendo for the children and irons and ironing boards; some units have kitchenettes. Airport, Amtrak, zoo, and SeaWorld shuttles are provided. ✉ *543 Hotel Circle S, 92108,* ☎ *619/297–8800 or 800/329–7466,* FAX *619/298–6029. 280 rooms. Restaurant, refrigerators, pool, barbershop, beauty salon, outdoor hot tub, shops, coin laundry, laundry service, meeting rooms, airport shuttle, free parking. AE, D, DC, MC, V.*

La Jolla

Million-dollar homes line the beaches and hillsides of La Jolla, a beautiful and prestigious community. The village—the heart of La Jolla—is chockablock with expensive boutiques, galleries, and restaurants.

$$$$ ★ **Hilton La Jolla Torrey Pines.** The low-rise, high-class hotel blends discreetly into the Torrey Pines cliff top, looking almost insignificant until you step inside the luxurious lobby and gaze through native and subtropical foliage at the Pacific Ocean and the 18th hole of the Torrey Pines Municipal Golf Course. Amenities include complimentary butler service and free town-car service to La Jolla and Del Mar. The oversize accommodations are simple but elegant; most have balconies or terraces. In addition to easy access to the golf course, guests also have privileges ($7.50) next door at the fine health club–sports center at the Scripps Clinic. The fare at the hotel's chic Torreyana Grille changes with the seasons. ✉ *10950 N. Torrey Pines Rd., 92037,* ☎ *858/558–1500; 800/325–3535 for central reservations,* FAX *858/450–4584. 392 rooms, 17 suites. 3 restaurants, 3 bars, in-room data ports, in-room safes, minibars, room service, pool, outdoor hot tub, sauna, putting green, 2 tennis courts, aerobics, exercise room, bicycles, video games, concierge, business services, meeting rooms, airport shuttle, car rental, parking (fee). AE, D, DC, MC, V.*

$$$$ ★ **Hyatt Regency La Jolla.** The Hyatt is in the Golden Triangle area, about 10 minutes from the beach and the village of La Jolla. The postmodern design elements of architect Michael Graves' striking lobby continue in the spacious rooms, where warm cherry-wood furnishings contrast with austere gray closets. Down comforters and cushy chairs and couches make you feel right at home, though, and business travelers will appreciate the endless array of office and in-room services. The hotel's four restaurants include Cafe Japengo (☞ Dining, *above*). Rates are lower here on weekends. ✉ *Aventine Center, 3777 La Jolla Village Dr., 92122,* ☎ *858/552–1234; 800/233–1234 for central reservations,* FAX *858/552–6066. 419 rooms, 20 suites. 4 restaurants, bar, room service, pool, beauty salon, outdoor hot tub, massage, 2 tennis courts, aerobics, basketball, health club, dry cleaning, laundry service, business services, meeting rooms, parking (fee). AE, D, DC, MC, V.*

$$$$ ★ **La Valencia.** This pink Spanish-Mediterranean confection drew film stars down from Hollywood in the 1930s and '40s for its setting and views of La Jolla Cove. Many rooms have a genteel European look, with antique pieces and rich-color rugs. The personal attention provided by the staff, as well as in-room features such as plush robes and grand bathrooms, make the stay even more pleasurable. The hotel is near the shops and restaurants of La Jolla Village and what is arguably the prettiest beach in San Diego. ✉ *1132 Prospect St., 92037,* ☎ *858/454–0771 or 800/451–0772,* FAX *858/456–3921. 88 rooms, 12 suites. 3 restaurants, bar, lounge, minibars, room service, pool, outdoor hot tub, sauna, health club, massage, shuffleboard, Ping-Pong, bicycles, concierge, business services, meeting rooms, airport shuttle, parking (fee). AE, D, DC, MC, V.*

$$$–$$$$ **Sea Lodge.** Palms, fountains, red-tile roofs, and Mexican tile work lend a Spanish flavor to this low-lying compound on La Jolla Shores beach. Rooms, a few with kitchenettes, have rattan furniture and floral-print bedspreads; all have wood balconies that overlook lush landscaping and the sea. Tennis lessons are offered by an on-site professional instructor. ✉ *8110 Camino del Oro, 92037,* ☎ *858/459–8271 or 800/237–5211,* FAX *858/456–9346. 128 rooms. Restaurant, bar, in-room data ports, refrigerators, kitchenettes (some), room service, pool, outdoor hot tub, massage, sauna, spa, 2 tennis courts, exercise room, jogging, Ping-Pong, beach, coin laundry, business services, meeting rooms, free parking. AE, D, DC, MC, V.*

$$–$$$$ **Grande Colonial La Jolla.** This is the oldest hotel in La Jolla, with buildings dating to 1913 and 1926. In keeping with the period, the decor of the rooms is formal. Ocean views cost more than village views. The inn is on one of La Jolla's main thoroughfares, near boutiques, restaurants, and La Jolla Cove. Mini-refrigerators are provided in some rooms. ✉ *910 Prospect St., 92037,* ☎ *619/454–2181; 800/832–5525; 800/826–1278 in CA,* FAX *619/454–5679. 58 rooms, 17 suites. Restaurant, bar, in-room data ports, room service, pool, business services, meeting rooms, parking (fee). AE, DC, MC, V. CP.*

$$–$$$$ **Scripps Inn.** You'd be wise to make reservations well in advance for this small, quiet inn tucked away on Coast Boulevard; its popularity with repeat visitors ensures that it is booked year-round. Lower weekly and monthly rates (not available in summer) make it attractive to long-term guests. Rooms are done with Mexican and Spanish decor, white plaster walls, and wood floors, and all have ocean views and in-room safes. Some have fireplaces, coffeemakers, microwaves, and refrigerators. ✉ *555 S. Coast Blvd., 92037,* ☎ *858/454–3391 or 800/439–7529,* FAX *858/456–0389. 13 rooms. Refrigerators (some), free parking. AE, D, MC, V. CP.*

$$–$$$ **La Jolla Cove Suites.** It may lack the charm of some of the older properties of this exclusive area, but this motel with studios and suites (some with spacious oceanfront balconies) gives its guests the same first-class views of La Jolla Cove at much lower rates. The beach is across the street and down a short cliff, and snorkelers and divers can take advantage of lockers and outdoor showers. The free underground lot is also a bonus in a section of town where a parking spot is a prime commodity. ✉ *1155 S. Coast Blvd., 92037,* ☎ *858/459–2621 or 800/248–2683,* FAX *858/454–3522. 96 rooms. Kitchenettes, pool, hot tub, putting green, bicycles, coin laundry, business services, meeting rooms, airport shuttle, free parking. AE, D, DC, MC, V. CP.*

$$–$$$ **Lodge at Torrey Pines.** On a bluff between La Jolla and Del Mar, the lodge commands a view of miles and miles of coastline. The Torrey Pines Municipal Golf Course is adjacent, and scenic Torrey Pines State Beach and Reserve are close by; the village of La Jolla is a 10-minute drive away. Most rooms have dark-wood furnishings and colorful fabrics. One drawback—the building is old; walls between units are thin, and the plumbing can be noisy. Still, the service is excellent and the lodge is a good value, especially for golfers. ✉ *11480 N. Torrey Pines Rd., 92037,* ☎ *858/453–4420 or 800/995–4507,* FAX *858/453–0691. 75 rooms. 2 restaurants, 2 bars, pool, golf privileges, free parking. AE, D, DC, MC, V.*

$$–$$$ **Prospect Park Inn.** One block from the beach and near some of the best shops and restaurants, this European-style inn with a delightful staff sits in a prime spot in La Jolla Village. Many rooms (some with kitchenettes) have sweeping ocean views from their balconies; one spectacular penthouse suite faces the ocean, another the village. An upstairs sundeck with fantastic views is a great spot to enjoy the complimentary Continental breakfast. ✉ *1110 Prospect St., 92037,* ☎ *858/*

454–0133 or 800/433–1609, FAX 858/454–2056. 20 rooms, 2 suites. In-room data ports, kitchenettes (some), library, business services, free parking. AE, D, DC, MC, V. CP.

$–$$ **Holiday Inn Express–La Jolla.** Many rooms at this modest property in the southern section of La Jolla are remarkably large, with huge closets; some have kitchenettes, and three suites have separate eat-in kitchens. The decor is nothing to write home about, but this is a good value for La Jolla. ✉ *6705 La Jolla Blvd., 92037,* ☎ *858/454–7101 or 800/451–0358, FAX 858/454–6957. 51 rooms, 10 suites. Kitchenettes (some), pool, outdoor hot tub, sauna, spa, exercise room, coin laundry, meeting rooms, airport shuttle, free parking. AE, D, DC, MC, V. CP.*

Mission Bay and the Beaches

Mission Bay Park, with its beaches, bike trails, boat-launching ramps, golf course, and grassy parks—not to mention SeaWorld—is a hotel haven. Mission Beach and Pacific Beach have many small hotels, motels, and hostels. You can't go wrong with any of these locations, as long as the frenzy of crowds at play doesn't bother you.

$$$$ **Crystal Pier Hotel.** A landmark since 1927, the cottages of the Crystal Pier Hotel are rustic little oases that have a charm all their own. True, they lack some of the amenities of comparably priced hotels, but you're paying for character and proximity to the ocean—the blue-and-white cottages here are literally on the pier. The units sleep four but cost the same no matter what the occupancy. Call four to six weeks in advance for reservations. The minimum stay permitted is three nights from mid-June through mid-September, two nights the rest of the year. ✉ *4500 Ocean Blvd., 92109,* ☎ *858/483–6983 or 800/748–5894, FAX 858/483–6811. 29 cottages. Kitchenettes, fishing, free parking. D, MC, V.*

$$$$ **Pacific Terrace Hotel.** This terrific hotel, overlooking the beach, offers great ocean views from most rooms. It's a perfect place for those who love to watch sunsets. Private balconies (or patios) and mini-refrigerators come with every room. Half the rooms have kitchenettes and all have pay-movies available. Eight of the suites have indoor Jacuzzis. Continental breakfast is complimentary, as is the daily delivery of the *San Diego Union-Tribune*. Even the smallest room is fairly large. ✉ *610 Diamond St., 92109,* ☎ *858/581–3500 or 800/344–3370, FAX 858/274–3341. 73 rooms, 12 suites. Kitchenettes (some), pool, outdoor hot tub, coin laundry, meeting rooms, parking (fee). AE, D, DC, MC, V.*

$$$–$$$$ **Hilton San Diego Resort.** Trees, Japanese bridges, and ponds surround the bungalow accommodations at this deluxe resort; rooms and suites in the high-rise building have views of Mission Bay Park. Most of the well-appointed rooms have wet bars, mini-refrigerators, coffeemakers, spacious bathrooms, and patios or terraces. Children stay free, and there's complimentary day care for children over age five (daily during the summer, on weekends the rest of the year). ✉ *1775 E. Mission Bay Dr., 92109,* ☎ *619/276–4010; 800/445–8667 for central reservations, FAX 619/275–7991. 337 rooms, 20 suites. 2 restaurants, 2 bars, in-room data ports, refrigerators, minibars, pool, wading pool, 2 hot tubs, spa, 4 putting greens, 5 tennis courts, basketball, exercise room, Ping-Pong, beach, boating, waterskiing, bicycles, video games, playground, concierge, business services, meeting rooms, travel services, car rental, free parking. AE, D, DC, MC, V.*

$$$–$$$$ **San Diego Paradise Point Resort.** The landscape at this 44-acre resort on Vacation Isle is so beautiful that it's been the setting for a number of movies, and it provides a wide range of recreational activities as well as access to a marina. Bright fabrics and plush carpets make for a cheery ambience; unfortunately, the walls here are motel-thin. The botanical gardens with their ponds, waterfalls, footbridges, and waterfowl, have more than 600 varieties of tropical plants. ✉ *1404 W. Vacation Rd., 92109,* ☎ *858/274–4630 or 800/344–2626,* FAX *858/581–5929. 462 cottages. 3 restaurants, 2 bars, room service, refrigerators, pond, 6 pools, outdoor hot tub, massage, sauna, 18-hole putting green, 6 tennis courts, aerobics, croquet, exercise room, shuffleboard, volleyball, beach, boating, jet skiing, bicycles, concierge, business services, meeting rooms, airport shuttle, free parking. AE, D, DC, MC, V.*

$$–$$$$ ★ **Catamaran Resort Hotel.** Exotic birds often perch in the lush lobby of this appealing hotel, set on Mission Bay in Pacific Beach. Tiki torches light the way through grounds thick with tropical foliage for guests staying at one of the six two-story buildings or the 14-story high-rise. The room decor—dark wicker furniture and tropical prints—echoes the historical Hawaiian theme. The popular Cannibal Bar hosts rock bands. The resort's many water-oriented activities include complimentary cruises on Mission Bay aboard a stern-wheeler. ✉ *3999 Mission Blvd., 92109,* ☎ *858/488–1081 or 800/422–8386,* FAX *858/488–1387 for reservations; 858/488–1619 for front desk. 313 rooms. Restaurant, 2 bars, refrigerators, kitchenettes (some), in-room data ports, room service, pool, outdoor hot tub, exercise room, volleyball, boating, jet skiing, bicycles, shops, video games, nightclub, business services, meeting rooms, parking (fee). AE, D, DC, MC, V.*

$$–$$$$ **Hyatt Islandia.** Its location in appealing Mission Bay Park is one of the many pluses of this property, which has rooms in several low-level, lanai-style units, as well as marina suites and rooms in a high-rise building. Many of the modern rooms overlook the hotel's gardens and koi fish pond; others have dramatic views of the bay area. Whale-watching expeditions depart from the Islandia's marina in winter. ✉ *1441 Quivira Rd., 92109,* ☎ *858/224–1234; 800/233–1234 for central reservations,* FAX *858/224–0348. 346 rooms, 76 suites. 2 restaurants, bar, in-room data ports, room service, pool, outdoor hot tub, exercise room, boating, fishing, shops, dry cleaning, laundry service, concierge, meeting rooms, car rental, free parking. AE, D, DC, MC, V.*

$$$ **Best Western Blue Sea Lodge.** All rooms at this Pacific Beach low-rise have patios or balconies, and many have ocean views. A shopping center with restaurants and boutiques is nearby. ✉ *707 Pacific Beach Dr., 92109,* ☎ *858/488–4700 or 800/258–3732,* FAX *858/488–7276. 52 rooms, 48 suites. Kitchenettes (some), in-room safes, pool, outdoor hot tub, fishing, laundry service, concierge, travel services, parking (fee). AE, D, DC, MC, V.*

$$–$$$ **Bahia Resort Hotel.** This huge complex on a 14-acre peninsula in Mission Bay Park has furnished studios and suites with kitchens; many have wood-beam ceilings and tropical decor. The hotel's *Bahia Belle* offers complimentary cruises on Mission Bay at sunset and also has a Blues Cruise on Saturday night and live entertainment on Friday night. Rates are reasonable for a place within walking distance of the ocean. ✉ *998 W. Mission Bay Dr., 92109,* ☎ *858/488–0551; 800/288–0770; 800/233–8172 in Canada,* FAX *858/488–1387. 321 rooms. Restaurant, 2 bars, refrigerators, kitchenettes (some), in-room data ports, room service, pool, outdoor hot tub, 2 tennis courts, exercise room, boating, bicycles, shops, video games, business services, meeting rooms, free parking. AE, D, DC, MC, V.*

$$ **Dana Inn & Marina.** This hotel with an adjoining marina is a bargain. Rooms are in bright pastels, and the lobby includes a fun aquarium. High ceilings in the second-floor rooms give a welcome sense of space, and some even have a view of the inn's marina. SeaWorld and the beach are within walking distance. Children under 18 stay free. ✉ *1710 W. Mission Bay Dr., 92109,* ☎ *619/222–6440 or 800/445–3339,* FAX *619/222–5916. 196 rooms. Restaurant, bar, room service, pool, outdoor hot tub, spa, 2 tennis courts, Ping-Pong, shuffleboard,* *boating, waterskiing, fishing, bicycles, coin laundry, business services, meeting rooms, airport shuttle, free parking. AE, D, DC, MC, V.*

$–$$ **Pacific Shores Inn.** One of the better motels in the Mission Bay area, this property is less than a half block from the beach. Rooms, some of them spacious, are decorated in a simple contemporary style. Kitchen units with multiple beds are available at reasonable rates; your pet (under 20 pounds) can stay for an extra $25. Continental breakfast is included, and all rooms have mini-refrigerators. ✉ *4802 Mission Blvd., 92109,* ☎ *858/483–6300 or 800/826–0715,* FAX *858/483–9276. 55 rooms. Refrigerators, kitchenettes (some), pool, coin laundry, free parking. AE, D, DC, MC, V.*

$ **Banana Bungalow San Diego.** Literally a few feet from the beach, this hostel's location is its greatest asset. However, dampness and sand take their toll, and some parts of the hostel need repair. A 1999 renovation repaired rooms and added kitchen facilities. All dorm rooms at this Pacific Beach hostel are coed and there are a total of 70 beds. There are lockers and a small TV room. ✉ *707 Reed Ave., 92109,* ☎ *858/273–3060 or 800/546–7835.* FAX *858/273–1440. Volleyball, beach, surfing, bicycles, airport shuttle. MC, V. CP.*

$ **Diamond Head Hotel.** Many rooms of this hotel overlook the beach, but it's not a noisy place because it's far enough away from Pacific Beach's main drag—Garnet Avenue. Restaurants and nightspots are within walking distance. Pets are allowed for a $25 additional charge. ✉ *605 Diamond St., 92109,* ☎ *858/273–1900,* FAX *858/274–3341. 21 rooms. Kitchenettes (some), beach, free parking. AE, D, DC, MC, V. CP.*

$ **Ocean Beach International Backpackers Hostel.** This converted 1920s hotel is two blocks from the beach and offers free use of surfboards and boogie boards. There are 100 beds. Private rooms with private baths are available. Continental breakfast is complimentary, and dinner is free on Tuesday and Friday. The hostel, which is close to many Ocean Beach restaurants and nightspots, has kitchen facilities, a storage area, a TV room, a patio, and Internet access. ✉ *4961 Newport Ave., 92107,* ☎ *619/223–7873 or 800/339–7263,* FAX *619/223–7881. Bicycles, recreation room, coin laundry, airport shuttle. MC, V.*

$ **Surfer Motor Lodge.** This four-story building is on the beach and directly behind a shopping center with restaurants and boutiques. Rooms are plain, but those on the upper floors have good views. ✉ *711 Pacific Beach Dr., 92109,* ☎ *858/483–7070 or 800/787–3373,* FAX *858/274–1670. 52 rooms. Restaurant, pool, bicycles, free parking. AE, DC, MC, V.*

$ **Vagabond Inn San Diego Mission Bay.** This modest hotel is near freeways and Mission Bay and the price is right for its simple but clean rooms. Pets are allowed for a $10 charge per pet, per night. The three-story building has no elevator. ✉ *4540 Mission Bay Dr., 92109,* ☎ *858/274–7888 or 800/522–1555. 117 rooms. In-room safes, pool, coin laundry, airport shuttle, free parking. AE, D, DC, MC, V. CP.*

Uptown

$–$$$ **Balboa Park Inn.** Directly across the street from Balboa Park, this all-suites B&B is housed in four Spanish colonial–style 1915 residences connected by courtyards. Prices are reasonable for the romantic one- and two-bedroom suites. Some have fireplaces, wet bars, whirlpool tubs, patios, and kitchens with microwaves. The lack of off-street parking is a bit inconvenient, but the location is great. The San Diego Zoo is a 10-minute stroll from here. ✉ *3402 Park Blvd., 92103,* ☎ *619/298–0823 or 800/938–8181,* FAX *619/294–8070. 26 suites. AE, D, DC, MC, V. CP.*

NIGHTLIFE AND THE ARTS

Updated by Rob Aikens

Check the *Reader,* a free weekly, for band information or *San Diego* magazine's "Restaurant & Nightlife Guide" for the full slate of after-dark possibilities. Call the **SRH Info Hotline** (☎ 619/973–9269) to locate hip to downright bizarre one-night events.

Nightlife

California law prohibits the sale of alcoholic beverages after 2 AM. Last call is usually at about 1:40. Bars, nightclubs, and restaurants are smoke-free by law.

Bars and Nightclubs

Bitter End (✉ 770 5th Ave., Gaslamp Quarter, ☎ 619/338–9300) is a sophisticated martini bar and a hip dance club. **Blind Melons** (✉ 710 Garnet Ave., Pacific Beach, ☎ 858/483–7844) is great during the day but even better at night when well-known local and national bands play rock and blues tunes. **Blue Tattoo** (✉ 835 5th Ave., Gaslamp Quarter, ☎ 619/238–7191) is popular with young professionals, who often wait in long lines to get in. The club is open Wednesday through Sunday with an enforced dress code (no jeans, T-shirts, hats, sweatshirts, or tennis shoes) on Friday and Saturday nights. **'Canes Bar and Grill** (✉ 3105 Ocean Front Walk, Mission Beach, ☎ 858/488–1780) is closer to the ocean than any other music venue in town. National rock, reggae, and hip-hop acts grace the stage. **Cannibal Bar** (✉ 3999 Mission Blvd., Pacific Beach, ☎ 858/488–1081) hosts local bands playing oldies, contemporary jazz, blues, and swing for an all-ages crowd.

Club 66 (✉ 901 5th Ave., Gaslamp Quarter, ☎ 619/234–4166), under the Dakota Grill restaurant, spins disco, funk, and high-energy house Friday and Saturday. **E Street Alley** (✉ 919 4th Ave., Gaslamp Quarter, ☎ 619/231–9200), one of the most popular clubs in the Gaslamp Quarter, is a smartly designed, spacious dance club with a DJ spinning Top 40 and club tunes Thursday through Saturday. **Jimmy Love's** (✉ 672 5th Ave., Gaslamp Quarter, ☎ 619/595–0123) combines a dance club, a sports bar, and a restaurant all into one venue. Rock and jazz bands alternate nightly. Expect lines. **Karl Strauss' Old Columbia Brewery & Grill** (✉ 1157 Columbia St., downtown, ☎ 619/234–2739) was the first microbrewery in San Diego. **Martini Ranch** (✉ 528 F St., Gaslamp Quarter, ☎ 619/235–6100) mixes more than 30 varieties of its namesake. Jazz groups often perform on weekdays, and a DJ spins an eclectic mix of contemporary favorites on Friday and Saturday.

Moose McGillycuddy's (✉ 1165 Garnet Ave., Pacific Beach, ☎ 858/274–2323; ✉ 535 5th Ave., Gaslamp Quarter, ☎ 619/702–5595), a major pick-up palace, is also a great place to hang out. Fun music powers the dance floor, and the staff serves up drinks and Mexican food. **O'Hungrys** (✉ 2547 San Diego Ave., Old Town, ☎ 619/298–0133) is famous for its yard-long beers and sing-alongs. This landmark saloon closes at midnight. **Pacific Beach Bar & Grill** (✉ 860 Garnet Ave., Pacific Beach, ☎ 858/272–4745) has a huge outdoor patio. The lines here on the weekends are generally very long. There is plenty to see and do, from billiards and satellite TV sports to an interactive trivia game.

Coffeehouses

Brockton Villa Restaurant (✉ 1235 Coast Blvd., La Jolla, ☎ 858/454–7393), a palatial café overlooking La Jolla Cove, has indoor and outdoor seating. It closes at 9. **Café Crema** (✉ 1001 Garnet Ave., Pacific Beach, ☎ 858/273–3558) is a meeting spot for the pre- and post-bar crowd. **Claire de Lune** (✉ 2906 University Ave., North Park, ☎ 619/688–9845), on a corner in artsy North Park, hosts local musicians and poets and San Diego's largest open-mike poetry night every Tuesday. **Extraordinary Desserts** (✉ 2929 5th Ave., Hillcrest, ☎ 619/294–7001) is a trendy spot with unique, award-winning desserts and a Japanese-theme patio. **Javanican** (✉ 4338 Cass St., Pacific Beach, ☎ 858/483–8035; ✉ 3710 Mission Blvd., Pacific Beach, ☎ 858/488–8065) has two locations serving a good cup of joe and live acoustic entertainment. **Pannikin** (✉ 7467 Girard Ave., La Jolla, ☎ 858/454–5453) is a bright coffeehouse, with indoor and outdoor seating. Other locations are scattered throughout the county. **Zanzibar Coffee Bar and Gallery** (✉ 976 Garnet Ave., Pacific Beach, ☎ 858/272–4762), a cozy, dimly lit spot, is a great place to mellow out.

Comedy and Cabaret

Comedy Store La Jolla (✉ 916 Pearl St., La Jolla, ☎ 858/454–9176), like its sister establishment in Hollywood, hosts top touring and local talent. **Lips** (✉ 2770 5th Ave., Hillcrest, ☎ 619/295–7900) serves you dinner while saucy female impersonators entertain.

Country-Western

In Cahoots (✉ 5373 Mission Center Rd., Mission Valley, ☎ 619/291–8635), with its great sound system, large dance floor, and occasional big-name performers, is the destination of choice for cowgirls, cowboys, and city slickers alike. Free dance lessons are given every day except Wednesday. Happy hour seven days a week is one of this bar's many lures. **Tio Leo's** (✉ 5302 Napa St., Bay Park, ☎ 619/542–1462) is a throwback to the days when lounges were dark and vinyl filled. The crowd is retro-attired as well. The lounge is within a Mexican restaurant, and an incredible variety of country, rockabilly, and swing acts perform.

Dance Clubs

Buffalo Joe's (✉ 600 5th Ave., Gaslamp Quarter, ☎ 619/236–1616) has a rocking dance floor. Retro disco and 1980s cover bands are the norm. **Club Montage** (✉ 2028 Hancock St., Middletown, ☎ 619/294–9590) is one of the largest and best clubs in town. This three-level club was originally oriented to the gay crowd, but now all types come for the high-tech lighting system and world-class DJs. **Plan B** (✉ 945 Garnet Ave., Pacific Beach, ☎ 858/483–9920) has a stainless-steel dance floor and numerous places from which to view it, making the interior of this club a standout among the other beach clubs. National bands play on Friday. The crowd is more upscale than one usually finds at the beach. **Sevilla** (✉ 555 4th Ave., Gaslamp Quarter, ☎ 619/233–5979) has a Latin flavor with its mix of contemporary and traditional music. This is the best place in San Diego to take lessons in salsa and lambada.

Gay and Lesbian

Bourbon Street (✉ 4612 Park Blvd., University Heights, ☎ 619/291–0173) is a piano bar with live entertainment nightly. **Brass Rail** (✉ 3796 5th Ave., Hillcrest, ☎ 619/298–2233), a fixture since the early 1960s, hosts dancing nightly. **Club Bom Bay** (✉ 3175 India St., Middletown, ☎ 619/296–6789) occasionally has live entertainment and always attracts a lesbian dancing crowd. It also hosts Sunday barbecues. **The Flame** (✉ 3780 Park Blvd., Hillcrest, ☎ 619/295–4163) is a friendly dance club that caters to lesbians most of the week. On Tuesday the DJ spins for the popular Boys' Night. **Flicks** (✉ 1017 University Ave., Hillcrest, ☎ 619/297–2056) plays music and comedy videos on four big screens. **Kickers** (✉ 308 University Ave., Hillcrest, ☎ 619/491–0400) rounds up country-music cowboys to do the latest line dance. Free lessons are given weeknights from 7 to 8:30.

Jazz

Crescent Shores Grill (✉ 7955 La Jolla Shores Dr., La Jolla, ☎ 619/459–0541), on the top floor of the Hotel La Jolla, delivers an ocean view and a lineup of nationally and internationally acclaimed jazz musicians. **Croce's** (✉ 802 5th Ave., Gaslamp Quarter, ☎ 619/233–4355), the intimate jazz cave of restaurateur Ingrid Croce (singer-songwriter Jim Croce's widow), books superb acoustic-jazz musicians. Next door, Croce's Top Hat puts on live R&B nightly from 9 to 2. **Humphrey's by the Bay** (✉ 2241 Shelter Island Dr., Shelter Island, ☎ 619/523–1010 for concert information) hosts the city's best outdoor jazz, folk, and light-rock concert series from June to September. The rest of the year the music moves indoors for some first-rate jazz most Sunday, Monday, and Tuesday nights, with piano-bar music on other nights.

Juke Joint Café (✉ 327 4th Ave., Gaslamp Quarter ☎ 619/232–7685) sports a bistro up front and a supper club in the back. It offers up authentic jazz jams Thursday through Saturday, with a little bit of soul and R&B mixed in on Saturday nights. **Old Venice** (✉ 2910 Canon St., Point Loma, ☎ 619/222–1404) could well be the Italian restaurant Billy Joel was singing about. This coastal neighborhood restaurant/bar stays true to the 'hood, highlighting the sounds of local bands.

Piano Bars/Mellow

Hotel Del Coronado (✉ 1500 Orange Ave., Coronado, ☎ 619/435–6611) has piano music in its Crown Room and Palm Court. **Inn at the Park** (✉ 3167 5th Ave., Hillcrest, ☎ 619/296–0057) makes for a nice stop after a day in Balboa Park. **Palace Bar** (✉ 311 Island Ave., Gaslamp Quarter, ☎ 619/544–1886), in the Horton Grand Hotel, is one of the most mellow lounges in the Gaslamp Quarter. Rest up in an overstuffed chair. **Top O' the Cove** (✉ 1216 Prospect St., La Jolla, ☎ 858/454–7779) pianists play show tunes and standards from the 1940s to the '80s at this restaurant. **U. S. Grant Hotel** (✉ 326 Broadway, downtown, ☎ 619/232–3121) is the classiest spot in town for meeting fellow travelers while relaxing with a Scotch or a martini at the mahogany bar. **Westgate Hotel** (✉ 1055 2nd Ave., downtown, ☎ 619/238–1818), one of the most elegant settings in San Diego, has piano music in the Plaza Bar.

Rock, Pop, Folk, Reggae, and Blues

Belly Up Tavern (✉ 143 S. Cedros Ave., Solana Beach, ☎ 858/481–9022) attracts people of all ages. Within converted Quonset huts, critically acclaimed artists play everything from reggae and folk to—well, you name it. **Casbah** (✉ 2501 Kettner Blvd., Middletown, near the airport, ☎ 619/232–4355) is a small club with a national reputation. Nirvana, Smashing Pumpkins, and Alanis Morissette all played the Casbah on their way to stardom. **Patrick's II** (✉ 428 F St., Gaslamp Quarter, ☎ 619/233–3077) serves up live New Orleans–style jazz, blues, and rock in an Irish setting. **Winston's Beach Club** (✉ 1921 Bacon St., Ocean Beach, ☎ 619/222–6822), a bowling alley–turned–rock club, is a sure bet for quality music in Ocean Beach. Local bands, reggae groups, and occasionally 1960s-type bands play.

The Arts

Half-price tickets to most theater, music, and dance events can be bought on the day of performance at **Times Arts Tix** (✉ Horton Plaza, ☎ 619/497–5000). Only cash is accepted. Advance full-price tickets are also sold. **Ticketmaster** (☎ 619/220–8497) sells tickets to many performances. Service charges vary according to the event, and most tickets are nonrefundable.

Dance

California Ballet Company (☎ 619/560–5676 or 619/560–6741) performs contemporary and traditional works from September to May.

Music

La Jolla Chamber Music Society (☎ 858/459–3724) presents internationally acclaimed chamber ensembles, orchestras, and soloists at Sherwood Auditorium and the Civic Theatre. **Open-Air Theatre** (✉ San Diego State University, ☎ 619/594–6947) presents top-name rock, reggae, and popular artists in summer concerts under the stars. **San Diego Chamber Orchestra** (☎ 760/753–6402), a 35-member ensemble, performs once a month, October to April. **San Diego Opera** (✉ Civic Theatre, Third Ave. and B St., downtown, ☎ 619/232–7636) draws international artists. Its season runs January–May and in 2001 includes a concert by Luciano Pavarotti.

Spreckels Organ Pavilion (✉ Balboa Park, ☎ 619/702–8138) holds a giant outdoor pipe organ. Concerts are given on most Sunday afternoons and on most Monday evenings in summer. **Spreckels Theatre** (✉ 121 Broadway, ☎ 619/235–0494), a designated-landmark theater, hosts musical events—everything from mostly Mozart to small rock concerts. Ballets and theatrical productions are also held here. Its good acoustics make this a special venue.

Theater

Coronado Playhouse (✉ 1775 Strand Way, Coronado, ☎ 619/435–4856), a cabaret-type theater, stages regular dramatic and musical performances. Friday and Saturday dinner packages are available. **Horton Grand Theatre** (✉ Hahn Cosmopolitan Theatre, 444 4th Ave., downtown, ☎ 619/234–9583) stages comedies, dramas, mysteries, and musicals at a 250-seat venue. **La Jolla Playhouse** (✉ Mandell Weiss Center for the Performing Arts, University of California at San Diego, 2910 La Jolla Village Dr., ☎ 858/550–1010) crafts innovative productions from May to November. Many Broadway shows have previewed here.

La Jolla Stage Company (✉ Parker Auditorium, 750 Nautilus St., La Jolla, ☎ 858/459–7773) presents lavish productions of Broadway favorites and popular comedies year-round on the La Jolla High School campus. **Lamb's Players Theatre** (✉ 1142 Orange Ave., Coronado, ☎ 619/437–0600) has a regular season of five productions from February through November and stages a musical, "Festival of Christmas", in December. **Marie Hitchcock Puppet Theatre** (✉ 2130 Pan American Rd. W, Balboa Park, ☎ 619/685–5045) presents amateur and professional puppeteers and ventriloquists five days a week. The cost is just a few dollars. **Old Globe Theatre** (✉ Simon Edison Centre for the Performing Arts, Balboa Park, 1363 Old Globe Way, ☎ 619/239–2255) is the oldest professional theater in California, performing classics, contemporary dramas, and experimental works.

San Diego Comic Opera Company (✉ Casa del Prado Theatre, Balboa Park, ☎ 619/231–5714) presents four Gilbert and Sullivan productions and similar works from October through July. **San Diego Repertory Theatre** (✉ Lyceum, 79 Horton Plaza, ☎ 619/235–8025), San Diego's first resident acting company, performs contemporary works year-round. **Sledgehammer Theatre** (✉ 1620 6th Ave., ☎ 619/544–1484), one of San Diego's cutting-edge theaters, stages avant-garde pieces in St. Cecilia's church. **Starlight Musical Theatre** (✉ Starlight Bowl, Balboa Park, ☎ 619/544–7827 during season), a summertime favorite, is a series of musicals performed in an outdoor amphitheater from mid-June through early September. **The Theatre in Old Town** (✉ 4040

Twiggs St., Old Town, ☎ 619/688–2494) presents punchy revues and occasional classics.

OUTDOOR ACTIVITIES AND SPORTS

Updated by Rob Aikens

People in this outdoors-oriented community recreate more than spectate. It's hard not to, with the variety of choices available, plus the constant sunshine.

Beaches

San Diego's beaches are among its greatest natural attractions. In some places the shorefront is wide and sandy; in others it's narrow and rocky or backed by impressive sandstone cliffs. The beaches below are listed from south to north.

Coronado

Silver Strand State Beach. The water is relatively calm, lifeguards and rangers are on duty year-round, and there are places to rollerblade or ride bikes. Four parking lots provide room for more than 1,500 cars. Sites at a campground ($12–$16 per night) for self-contained RVs are available on a first-come, first-served basis; stays are limited to seven nights. *From San Diego–Coronado Bay Bridge, turn left onto Orange Ave., which becomes Hwy. 75, and follow signs,* ☎ *619/435–5184.* *Parking $4, but not always collected Labor Day–Feb.*

Coronado Beach. With the famous Hotel Del Coronado as a backdrop, this stretch of sandy beach is one of San Diego County's largest and most picturesque. Parking can be difficult on the busiest days. There are plenty of rest rooms and service facilities, as well as fire rings. *From the bridge, turn left on Orange Ave. and follow signs.*

Point Loma

Sunset Cliffs. Beneath the jagged cliffs of Point Loma is one of the more secluded beaches in the area. At the south end of the peninsula, near Cabrillo Point, tidal pools teeming with small sea creatures are revealed at low tide. Farther north the waves lure surfers and the lonely coves attract sunbathers. Stairs at the foot of Bermuda and Santa Cruz avenues provide beach access, as do some (treacherous at points) cliff trails. There are no facilities. A visit here is more enjoyable at low tide. *Take I–8 west to Sunset Cliffs Blvd. and head west.*

San Diego

Ocean Beach. This mile-long beach is a haven for volleyball players, sunbathers, and swimmers. The area around the municipal pier at the south end is a hangout for surfers and transients; people fish from the pier, which has a restaurant at the middle. The beach is south of the channel entrance to Mission Bay. You'll find food vendors and fire rings; limited parking is available. Swimmers should beware of unusually vicious rip currents here. *Take I–8 west to Sunset Cliffs Blvd. and head west. Turn right on Santa Monica Ave.*

Mission Beach. San Diego's most popular beach draws huge crowds on hot summer days. The 2-mi-long continuous stretch extends from the north entrance of Mission Bay to Pacific Beach. A narrow boardwalk is popular with runners, roller skaters, bladers, and bicyclists. Surfers, swimmers, and volleyball players congregate at the south end. Toward the north end, near the Belmont Park roller coaster, the beach narrows and the water becomes rougher. The crowds grow thicker and somewhat rougher as well. Parking can be a challenge, but there are plenty of rest rooms and restaurants. *Exit I–5 at Garnet Ave. and head west to Mission Blvd. Turn south and look for parking.*

Pacific Beach/North Pacific Beach. The boardwalk turns into a sidewalk here, but there are still bike paths and picnic tables along the beachfront. Pacific Beach runs from the north end of Mission Beach to Crystal Pier. North Pacific Beach extends from the pier north. There are designated surfing areas, and fire rings are available. On-street parking is your best bet, or you can try the big lot at Belmont Park near the south end. *Exit I–5 at Garnet Ave. and head west to Mission Blvd. Turn north and look for parking.*

La Jolla

Tourmaline Surfing Park. This is one of the area's most popular beaches for surfing and sailboarding year-round. There is a 175-space parking lot at the foot of Tourmaline Street. *Take Mission Blvd. north (it turns into La Jolla Blvd.) and turn west on Tourmaline St.*

Windansea Beach. The beach's sometimes towering waves (caused by an underwater reef) are truly world class for surfing. With its incredible views and secluded sunbathing spots set among sandstone rocks, Windansea is very romantic. *Take Mission Blvd. north (it turns into La Jolla Blvd.) and turn west on Nautilus St.*

Marine Street Beach. Wide and sandy, this strand of beach often teems with sunbathers, swimmers, walkers, and joggers. The water is good for surfing and bodysurfing, though you'll need to watch out for riptides. *Accessible from Marine St., off La Jolla Blvd.*

Children's Pool. This shallow lagoon protected by a seawall has small waves and panoramic views. It's a good place to watch marine mammals—so many seals and sea lions frequent the cove that it is now closed to swimmers. *Follow La Jolla Blvd. north. When it forks, take the left, then turn right onto Coast Blvd.*

Shell Beach. This small cove is accessible by stairs. The exposed rocks off the coast have been designated a protected habitat for sea lions; you can watch them sun themselves and frolic in the water. *Continue along Coast Blvd. north from Children's Pool.*

La Jolla Cove. This is one of the prettiest spots in the world. A palm-lined park sits on top of cliffs formed by the incessant pounding of the waves. You can explore the tidal pools, cliff caves, and the underwater delights of the San Diego–La Jolla Underwater Ecological Reserve. The cove is also a favorite of rough-water swimmers for whom buoys mark distances. *Follow Coast Blvd. north to signs, or take the La Jolla Village Dr. exit from I–5, head west to Torrey Pines Rd., turn left, and drive down hill to Girard Ave. Turn right and follow signs.*

La Jolla Shores. On summer holidays all access routes are usually closed to one of San Diego's most popular beaches. The lures here are a wide sandy beach and the most gentle waves in San Diego. A concrete boardwalk parallels the beach. Arrive early to get a parking spot in the lot at the foot of Calle Frescota. *From I–5 take La Jolla Village Dr. west and turn left onto La Jolla Shores Dr. Head west to Camino del Oro or Vallecitos St. Turn right.*

Black's Beach. The powerful waves at this beach, officially known as Torrey Pines City Park Beach, attract surfers, and its relative isolation appeals to nudists (though by law nudity is prohibited). There are no lifeguards on duty, and strong ebb tides are common—only experienced swimmers should take the plunge. The cliffs are dangerous to climb. *Take Genesee Ave. west from I–5 and follow signs to Glider Port; easier access, via a paved path, available on La Jolla Farms Rd., but parking is limited to 2 hrs.*

Del Mar

Del Mar Beach. The numbered streets of Del Mar, from 15th to 29th, end at a wide beach popular with volleyball players, surfers, and sunbathers. Parking can be a problem on nice summer days. The portions of Del Mar south of 15th Street are lined with cliffs and are rarely crowded. *Take the Via de la Valle exit from I–5 west to S21 (also known as Camino del Mar in Del Mar) and turn left.*

Torrey Pines State Beach/Reserve. One of San Diego's best beaches contains 1,700 acres of bluffs, bird-filled marshes, and sandy shoreline. A network of trails leads through rare pine trees to the coast below. Lifeguards are on duty weekends (weather permitting) from Easter until Memorial Day, daily from then until Labor Day, and again on weekends through September. Torrey Pines tends to get crowded during the summer, but more isolated spots under the cliffs are a short walk in either direction. *Take the Carmel Valley Rd. exit west from I–5, turn left on S21, ☎ 858/755–2063. Parking $4.*

Cardiff-by-the-Sea

San Elijo State Beach. There are **campsites** (☎ 800/444–7275 for reservations) atop a scenic bluff at this park, which also has a store and shower facilities plus beach access for swimmers and surfers. Sites run $17–$23. *From I–5 turn west on Lomas Santa Fe Dr. to S21 (Old Hwy. 101) and turn right, ☎ 760/753–5091. Parking $4.*

Encinitas

Swami's. Extreme low tides expose tidal pools that harbor anemones, starfish, and other sea life. Remember to look but don't touch; all sea life here is protected here. The beach is also a top surfing spot; the only access is by a long stairway leading down from the cliff-top park. *Follow S21 north from Cardiff, or exit I–5 at Encinitas Blvd., go west to S21, and turn left.*

Moonlight Beach. Large parking areas and a wide range of facilities make this beach, tucked into a break in the cliffs, a pleasant stop. Sand is trucked in every year, making it a popular beach with sunbathers. The volleyball courts on the north end attract a few professionals who live in the area. *Take the Encinitas Blvd. exit from I–5 and head west until you hit the Moonlight parking lot.*

Participant Sports

Ballooning

Ballooning companies include **A Balloon Adventure by California Dreamin'** (✉ 162 S. Rancho Santa Fe Rd., Suite F35, Encinitas, ☎ 800/373–3359), and **Skysurfer Balloon Company** (✉ 1221 Camino del Mar, Del Mar, ☎ 858/481–6800 or 800/660–6809).

Bicycling

On any given summer day Highway S21 from La Jolla to Oceanside looks like a freeway for cyclists. Never straying more than ¼-mi from the beach, it is easily the most popular and scenic bike route around. A free comprehensive map of all county bike paths is available from the local office of the **California Department of Transportation** (✉ 2829 Juan St., San Diego 92110, ☎ 619/688–6699).

Bicycle Barn (✉ 746 Emerald St., ☎ 858/581–3665), in Pacific Beach, will rent you a bike to get you cruising the boardwalk. Once you're off the ferry in Coronado, you can rent a bike from **Bikes and Beyond** (✉ 1201 First Ave., Coronado, ☎ 619/435–7180). **Hamel's Action Sports Center** (✉ 704 Ventura Pl., ☎ 858/488–5050), in Mission Beach, rents bikes, skates, and beach gear.

Diving

Enthusiasts the world over come to San Diego to snorkel and scuba-dive off La Jolla and Point Loma. At La Jolla Cove you'll find the **San Diego–La Jolla Underwater Ecological Park.** Because all sea life is protected here, it's the best place to see large lobster, sea bass, and sculpin, as well as numerous golden Garibaldi, the state fish. It's not uncommon to see hundreds of beautiful leopard sharks schooling on the north end of the cove, near La Jolla shores. Farther north, off the south end of Black's Beach, the rim of **Scripps Canyon** lies in about 60 ft of water. The canyon plummets to more than 900 ft in some sections. Another popular diving spot is **Sunset Cliffs** in Point Loma, where the sea life and flora are relatively close to shore. Strong rip currents make it an area best enjoyed by experienced divers.

Diving equipment and boat trips can be arranged by **San Diego Divers Supply** (✉ 4004 Sports Arena Blvd., ☎ 619/224–3439; ✉ 1084 Broadway, Chula Vista, ☎ 619/420–5441); **Ocean Enterprises Scuba Diving** (✉ 7710 Balboa Ave., ☎ 619/565–6054); **Del Mar Oceansports** (✉ 2148 Jimmy Durante Blvd., ☎ 858/792–1903); and the **Diving Locker** (✉ 1020 Grand Ave., ☎ 858/272–1120; ✉ 405 N. Hwy. 101, Solana Beach, ☎ 858/755–6822). For recorded diving information, contact the **San Diego City Lifeguards Office** (☎ 619/221–8884).

Fishing

The Pacific Ocean is full of corbina, croaker, and halibut. No license is required to fish from a public pier, such as the Ocean Beach pier. A fishing license from the state **Department of Fish and Game** (✉ 4949 Viewridge Ave., San Diego 92123, ☎ 619/467–4201), available at most bait-and-tackle stores, is required for fishing from the shoreline.

Several companies conduct half-day, full-day, or multiday fishing expeditions in search of marlin, tuna, and other deep-water fish. **Fisherman's Landing** (✉ 2838 Garrison St., ☎ 619/221–8500) in Point Loma; **H&M Landing** (✉ 2803 Emerson St., ☎ 619/222–1144) in Point Loma; and **Seaforth Boat Rentals** (✉ 1641 Quivira Rd., ☎ 619/223–1681) in West Mission Bay are among the companies operating from San Diego. **Helgren's Sportfishing** (✉ 315 Harbor Dr. S, Oceanside, ☎ 760/722–2133) has trips from Oceanside Harbor.

Golf

The **Southern California Golf Association** (☎ 818/980–3630) publishes an annual directory with detailed and valuable information on all clubs. Another good resource for golfers is the **Southern California Public Links Golf Association** (☎ 714/994–4747). Most public courses in the area provide a list of fees for all San Diego courses. The greens fee is included for each course. Carts (in some cases mandatory), instruction, and other costs are additional.

COURSES

Coronado Municipal Golf Course (✉ 2000 Visalia Row, Coronado, ☎ 619/435–3121) has 18 holes, a driving range, equipment rentals, and a snack bar. Views of San Diego Bay and the Coronado Bridge from the back nine holes on this good walking course make it popular—but rather difficult to get on. Greens fee: $20–$32.

Mission Bay Golf Resort (✉ 2702 N. Mission Bay Dr., ☎ 619/490–3370) has 18 holes, a driving range, equipment rentals, and a restaurant. A not-very-challenging executive (par 3 and 4) course, Mission Bay is lit for night play with final tee time at 8 PM. Greens fee: $16–$18.

Torrey Pines Municipal Golf Course (✉ 11480 N. Torrey Pines Rd., La Jolla, ☎ 800/985–4653) has 36 holes, a driving range, and equipment rentals. One of the best public golf courses in the United States, Torrey Pines has views of the Pacific from every hole and is sufficiently challenging to host the Buick Invitational in February. Greens fee: $47–$52.

RESORTS

Carmel Highland Doubletree Golf and Tennis Resort (✉ 14455 Penasquitos Dr., ☎ 858/672–9100), a fairly hilly, well-maintained course south of Rancho Bernardo, has 18 holes, a driving range, equipment rentals, and a clubhouse with restaurant. Greens fee: $50–$65.

La Costa Resort and Spa (✉ 2100 Costa del Mar Rd., Carlsbad, ☎ 760/438–9111 or 800/854–5000) has two 18-hole PGA-rated courses, a driving range, a clubhouse, equipment rentals, an excellent golf school, and a pro shop. La Costa is one of the premier golf resorts in southern California. Greens fee: $145–$185.

Morgan Run Resort and Club (✉ 5690 Cancha de Golf, Rancho Santa Fe, ☎ 858/756–2471), a very popular walking course near polo grounds and stables, has 27 holes that can be played in three combinations of 18, a driving range, equipment rentals, and a pro shop. Greens fee: $80–$100.

Rancho Bernardo Inn and Country Club (✉ 17550 Bernardo Oaks Dr., Rancho Bernardo, ☎ 858/675–8470, ext. 1) has 45 holes on site, a driving range, equipment rentals, and a restaurant. Guests can play three other golf courses at company-operated resorts: Mount Woodson, Temecula Creek, and Twin Oaks. Ken Blanchard's Golf University of San Diego, based here, is world famous. Greens fee: $85–$105.

Redhawk (✉ 45100 Redhawk Pkwy., Temecula, ☎ 909/302–3850 or 800/451–4295) has 18 holes in an arboretumlike setting, a driving range, a putting green, and a snack bar. The par-72 course offers enough challenges to have earned a Top 10 ranking from *California Golf Magazine*. Greens fee: $50–$75.

Hiking and Nature Trails

Guided hikes are conducted regularly through Los Penasquitos Canyon Preserve and the Torrey Pines State Beach and Reserve (☞ La Jolla *above*). The **San Dieguito River Valley Regional Open Space** (✉ 21 mi north of San Diego on I–5 to Lomas Santa Fe Dr., east 1 mi to Sun Valley Rd., north into park, ☎ 619/235–5440) is a 55-mi corridor that begins at the mouth of the San Dieguito River in Del Mar, heading from the riparian lagoon area through coastal sage scrub and mountain terrain to end in the desert just east of Volcan Mountain near Julian. The **Tijuana Estuary** (✉ Borden Field State Park, Exit I–5 at Dairy Mart Rd., ☎ 619/575–3613) offers a look at one of the last extant riparian environments in southern California. The freshwater and saltwater marshes give refuge to migrant and resident waterfowl.

Mission Trails Regional Parks (✉ 1 Father Junípero Serra Trail, 92119, ☎ 619/668–3275), which encompasses nearly 6,000 acres of mountains, wooded hillsides, lakes, and riparian streams, is 8 mi northeast of downtown. Trails include one with a superb city view from Cowles Mountain and another along a historic missionary path.

Jet Skiing

Waveless Mission Bay and the small **Snug Harbor Marina** (☎ 760/434–3089), east of the intersection of Tamarack Avenue and Interstate 5 in Carlsbad, are favorite spots. **California Water Sports** (☎ 760/434–3089) has information about equipment rentals. **Seaforth Boat Rentals** (☎ 619/223–1681) rents jet skis for use in the South Bay Marina in Coronado, and they are also available at Snug Harbor in Carlsbad.

Skating

The sidewalks at Mission Bay are perfect for blading and skating. **Bicycle Barn, Bikes and Beyond,** and **Hamel's Action Sports Center** (☞ Bicycling, *above*), rent rollerblades and skates as well as bikes.

Surfing

If you're a beginner, consider paddling in the waves off Mission Beach, Pacific Beach, Tourmaline, La Jolla Shores, Del Mar, or Oceanside. More experienced surfers usually head for Sunset Cliffs, the La Jolla reef breaks, Black's Beach, or Swami's in Encinitas. *See* Beaches, *above,* for descriptions. **Kahuna Bob's Surf School** (☎ 760/721–7700) conducts two-hour lessons seven days a week. **Surf Diva Surf School** (✉ 2160–A Avenida de la Playa, La Jolla, ☎ 858/454–8273) offers seminars, surf trips, and private lessons especially formulated for women.

You can rent surf and bodyboards at **Hamel's Action Sports Center** (☞ Bicycling, *above*) in Mission Beach, **Star Surfing Company** (☎ 858/273–7827) in Pacific Beach, and **La Jolla Surf Systems** (☎ 858/456–2777) and **Hansen's** (☎ 760/753–6595) in Encinitas.

Volleyball

Ocean Beach, South Mission Beach, Del Mar Beach, Moonlight Beach, and the western edge of Balboa Park are major congregating points for volleyball enthusiasts. Contact the **San Diego Volleyball Club** (☎ 858/486–6885) to find out about organized games and tournaments.

Waterskiing

Mission Bay is one of the most popular waterskiing areas in southern California. It's best to get out early, when the water is smooth and the crowds are thin. Boats and equipment can be rented from **Seaforth Boat Rentals** (✉ 1641 Quivira Rd., near Mission Bay, ☎ 619/223–1681). The private **San Diego and Mission Bay Boat and Ski Club** (✉ 2606 N. Mission Bay Dr., ☎ 858/270–0840) operates a slalom course and ski jump in Mission Bay's Hidden Anchorage. Permission from the club or the Mission Bay Harbor Patrol (☎ 619/221–8985) is required.

Windsurfing

Also known as sailboarding, windsurfing is a sport best practiced on smooth waters, such as Mission Bay or the Snug Harbor Marina at the intersection of Interstate 5 and Tamarack Avenue in Carlsbad. Rentals and instruction are available at the **Bahia Resort Hotel** (✉ 998 W. Mission Bay Dr., ☎ 858/488–0551); the **Catamaran Resort Hotel** (✉ 3999 Mission Blvd., ☎ 858/488–1081); **Mission Bay Sports Center** (✉ 1010 Santa Clara Pl., ☎ 858/488–1004); and **Windsport** (✉ 844 W. Mission Bay Dr., ☎ 858/488–4642), all in the Mission Bay area. The **Snug Harbor Marina** (✉ 4215 Harrison St., Carlsbad, ☎ 760/434–3089) has rentals and instruction. Wave jumping is especially popular at the Tourmaline Surfing Park in La Jolla and in the Del Mar area.

SHOPPING

By Bobbi Zane

Coronado

Orange Avenue, in the center of town, has six blocks of ritzy boutiques and galleries. The **Hotel Del Coronado** (✉ 1500 Orange Ave., ☎ 619/435–6611, ext. 7274) houses specialty shops. **Ferry Landing Marketplace** (✉ 1201 1st St., at B Ave.), with a great view of the San Diego skyline, has many trinket and gift stores.

Downtown

Horton Plaza, bordered by Broadway, 1st Avenue, G Street, and 4th Avenue is an open-air visual delight accented by pastel-painted walls, original neon signs, and flag-draped facades. The multilevel shopping, dining, and entertainment complex has department stores, including Macy's, Nordstrom, and Mervyn's. There are fast-food counters, upscale restaurants, the Lyceum Theater, cinemas, and about other 140 stores. There's a parking garage under the plaza. Any Horton Plaza shop, restaurant, or theater will validate your parking ticket after a purchase, which is good for three hours of free parking.

Victorian buildings and renovated warehouses in the historic **Gaslamp Quarter** along 4th and 5th avenues house art galleries, antiques, and specialty shops. Northwest of the convention center, **Seaport Village** (✉ West Harbor Dr., at Kettner Blvd.) is a waterfront complex of shops and restaurants.

Hillcrest, North Park, Uptown

Though their boundaries blur, each of these three established neighborhoods north and northeast of downtown contains a distinct urban village with shops, many ethnic restaurants and cafés, and entertainment venues. Most of the activity is on University Avenue and Washington Street, and along the side streets connecting the two.

Gay and funky **Hillcrest,** north of Balboa Park, is home to many gift, book, and music stores. Retro rules in **North Park.** Nostalgia shops along Park Boulevard and University Avenue at 30th Street carry clothing, accessories, furnishings, wigs, and bric-a-brac of the 1920s–1960s. The **Uptown District,** an open-air shopping center on University Avenue, includes several furniture, gift, and specialty stores.

La Jolla

Familiar mall shops such as Victoria's Secret and Ann Taylor have found their way into spots along once-exclusive Prospect Street, but you'll find plenty of chic boutiques along side streets such as Girard and Drury. Shopping hours vary widely in La Jolla, so it's wise to call specific stores in advance. The **Green Dragon Colony** (✉ Prospect St., near Ivanhoe St.) is La Jolla's historic shopping area.

University Towne Centre (✉ La Jolla Village Dr. between I–5 and I–805, ☎ 858/546–8858), an outdoor mall several miles east of La Jolla, has 160 shops, department stores, cinemas, and restaurants, plus a skating rink. Department stores include Nordstrom, Robinson's-May, Macy's, and Sears.

Mission Valley/Hotel Circle

The Mission Valley/Hotel Circle area, northeast of downtown near Interstate 8 and Highway 163, has major shopping centers. **Fashion Valley Center** (✉ 452 Fashion Valley Dr.) has more than 100 shops and restaurants. The upscale mall, which has a San Diego Trolley station, operates shuttles to and from major hotels. The major department stores are Macy's, Nordstrom, Saks Fifth Avenue, Neiman Marcus, Robinsons-May, and JCPenney.

Park Valley (✉ 1750 Camino de la Reina), across from Westfield Shoppingtown Mission Valley, is a strip mall anchored by OFF 5th (☎ 619/296–4896), which offers fashions by Ralph Lauren, Armani, and Burberry once seen in Saks Fifth Avenue but at Costco prices.

Westfield Shoppingtown Mission Valley (✉ 1640 Camino del Rio N) is San Diego's largest outdoor shopping mall. It appeals to the budget minded with discount stores carrying merchandise that might be found in the mall up the road at higher prices. Shops include Montgomery Ward, Macy's Home Store, and Nordstrom Rack.

Old Town

The colorful Old Town historic district recalls a Mexican marketplace. Adobe architecture, flower-filled plazas, fountains, and courtyards decorate the shopping areas of Bazaar del Mundo and Old Town Esplanade, where you'll find international goods, toys, souvenirs, and arts and crafts. The boutiques at **Bazaar del Mundo** (✉ 2754 Calhoun St., ☎ 619/296–3161) sell designer items, crafts, fine arts, and fashions from around the world. March brings the annual Santa Fe Market, when you can browse wares crafted by Southwestern artists.

SIDE TRIP TO THE SAN DIEGO NORTH COAST

By Bobbi Zane

North County attractions continue to multiply following the 1999 opening of the Legoland California theme park. There's been a significant increase in the number of visitors to the entire area, where major stops already include the San Diego Wild Animal Park, the mountain town of Julian, and miles of lovely shoreline.

Numbers in the margin correspond to points of interest on the San Diego North County map.

Del Mar

23 mi north of downtown San Diego on I–5, 9 mi north of La Jolla on S21.

Del Mar is best known for its racetrack, chic shopping strip, celebrity visitors, and wide beaches. Along with its collection of shops, **Del Mar Plaza** (✉ 15th St., at S21—a.k.a. Camino del Mar) also contains outstanding restaurants. Del Mar has become headquarters for hot-air-balloon excursions. The late afternoon is the best time to spot the colorful balloons as they float over the hills and coastline.

Access to Del Mar's beaches is from the streets that run east–west off Coast Boulevard. Summer evening concerts take place at **Seagrove Park** (✉ 15th St., west end), a small stretch of grass overlooking the ocean.

❶ The **Del Mar Fairgrounds** is home to the Del Mar Thoroughbred Club (✉ 2260 Jimmy Durante Blvd., ☎ 858/755–1141). The racing season here (usually July–September, Wednesday–Monday, post time 2 PM) is one of the most fashionable in California. Del Mar Fairgrounds hosts more than 100 different events each year, including the San Diego County Fair. *Head west at I–5's Via de la Valle Rd. exit, ☎ 858/793–5555.*

Dining and Lodging

$$–$$$ ✕ **Barone's Trattoria del Mare.** This Italian seafood restaurant with an outdoor terrace is on the southern rim of town. The old-world hosts specialize in good service and a sizable menu of sizable dishes, which include crab-stuffed mushrooms, linguine with assorted shellfish, and grilled beef fillet bedded on a creamy Gorgonzola cheese sauce. *✉ 2234 Carmel Valley Rd., #A, ☎ 858/259–9063. MC, V. No lunch Sun.*

$$–$$$ ✕ **Cilantros.** Seafood enchiladas, shark fajitas, and spit-roasted chicken with a mild chili sauce are among the subtly spiced Southwestern-style dishes served at this Del Mar favorite. *✉ 3702 Via de la Valle, ☎ 858/259–8777. AE, DC, MC, V.*

$$–$$$ ✕ **Pacifica Del Mar.** Pacifica Del Mar overlooks the nearby sea from the plush precincts of Del Mar Plaza. Highly innovative, the restaurant takes its own road by offering a Japanese-style clam chowder; marinated salmon sushi with a Vietnamese dipping sauce; pot-roasted short ribs with horseradish-flavored gravy; and barbecued, sugar-spiced king salmon. The entrée list does lean to seafood. *✉ Del Mar Plaza, 1515 Camino del Mar, ☎ 858/792–0476. AE, D, MC, V.*

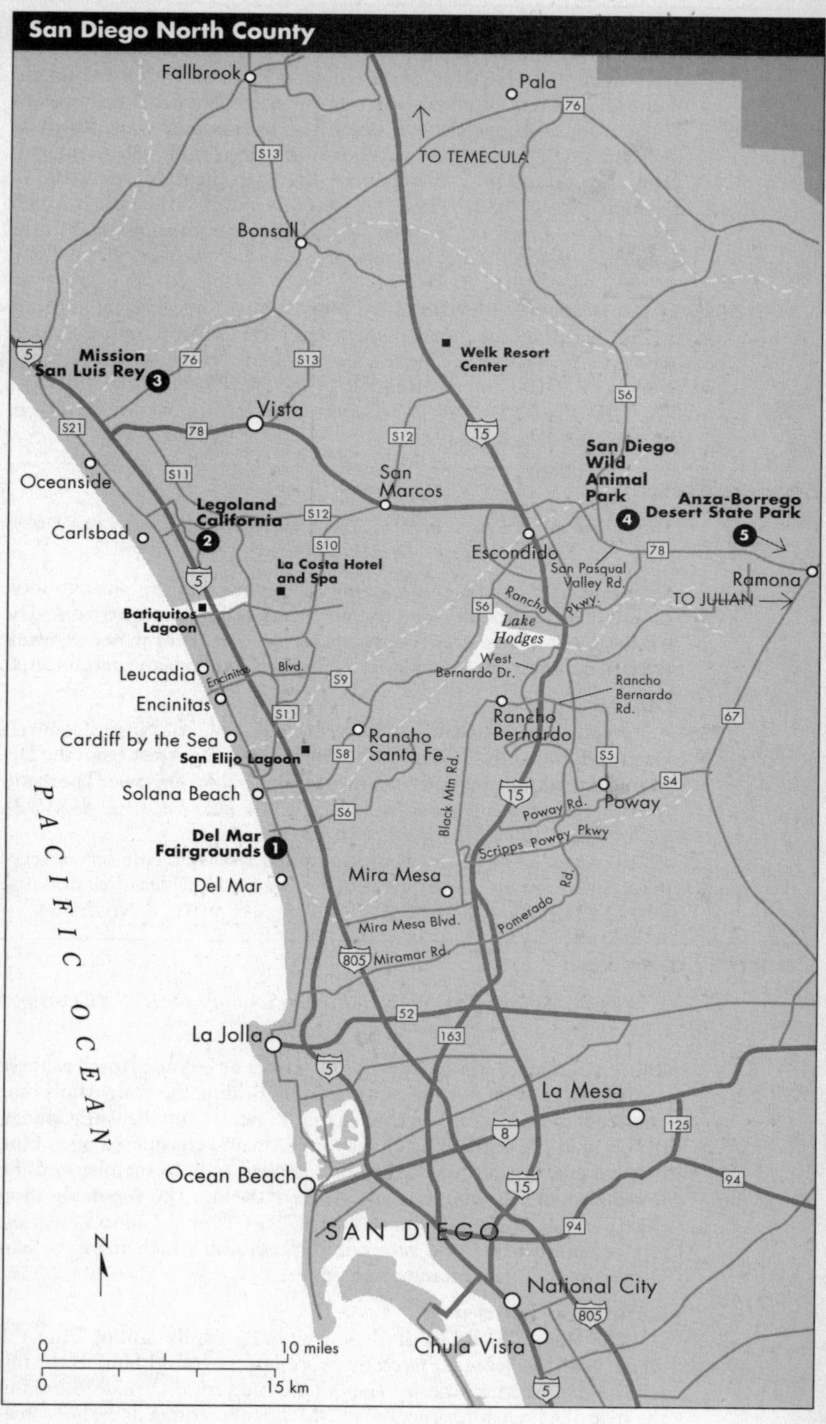
San Diego North County
Fallbrook
Pala
76
S13
TO TEMECULA
Bonsall
5
Mission San Luis Rey 3
76
S13
Welk Resort Center
S6
Vista
S21
78
S12
15
San Diego Wild Animal Park
Oceanside
S11
San Marcos
Legoland California
S12
Anza-Borrego Desert State Park
Carlsbad
2
4
5
S10
Escondido
78
La Costa Hotel and Spa
San Pasqual Valley Rd.
Ramona
5
Rancho Pkwy.
TO JULIAN
Batiquitos Lagoon
S6
Lake Hodges
West Bernardo Dr.
Leucadia
Encinitas Blvd.
S9
Rancho Bernardo Rd.
Encinitas
S11
Rancho Bernardo
67
Cardiff by the Sea
Rancho Santa Fe
S8
San Elijo Lagoon
S5
Solana Beach
Black Mtn Rd.
15
Poway Rd.
Poway
S4
S6
PACIFIC OCEAN
Del Mar Fairgrounds 1
Scripps Poway Pkwy
Del Mar
Mira Mesa
Pomerado Rd.
Mira Mesa Blvd.
805
Miramar Rd.
52
163
La Jolla
5
La Mesa
8
125
Ocean Beach
15
94
SAN DIEGO
94
N
National City
805
Chula Vista
0
10 miles
0
15 km
5

$$$$ 🏨 **L'Auberge Del Mar Resort and Spa.** L'Auberge is modeled on the Tudor-style hotel that once stood here, a playground for the early Hollywood elite. Today's inn has a relaxed elegance. All but two of the rooms have small balconies and most have gas fireplaces with timers. If you want some exercise, the beach is a three-minute walk downhill, there's a small lap pool, an outdoor cardio area, and even an on-staff tennis pro. Massages and facials are offered at the small spa. ✉ *1540 Camino del Mar, 92014,* ☎ *858/259–1515 or 800/553–1336,* FAX *858/755–4940. 112 rooms, 8 suites. Restaurant, bar, in-room data ports, 2 pools, outdoor hot tub, massage, spa, 2 tennis courts, exercise room, meeting rooms. AE, D, DC, MC, V.*

$$–$$$$ 🏨 **Best Western Stratford Inn of Del Mar.** During racing season this equestrian-theme inn hosts horse owners and jockeys. Ample rooms, many with ocean views or kitchenettes, are surrounded by 6 lushly landscaped acres. ✉ *710 Camino del Mar, 92014,* ☎ *858/755–1501 or 888/478–7829,* FAX *858/755–4704. 67 rooms, 33 suites. 2 pools, outdoor hot tub. AE, D, DC, MC, V. CP.*

Solana Beach

1 mi north of Del Mar on S21, 25 mi north of downtown San Diego on I–5 to Lomas Santa Fe Dr. west.

Solana Beach is quickly developing a reputation as *the* place to look for antiques, collectibles, and contemporary fashions and artwork. The Cedros Design District, occupying a long block near the new Amtrak station, contains shops, galleries, designers' studios, and restaurants.

Dining

$$$ ★ ✕ **Pamplemousse Grille.** Justly celebrated as one of North County's best restaurants, the "Grapefruit Grill" across the street from the Del Mar racetrack offers French country dining California style. The menu focuses on grand presentations. ✉ *514 Via de la Valle,* ☎ *858/792–9090. AE, D, DC, MC, V. No lunch Sat.–Tues.*

$ ✕ **Zinc Cafe.** Solana Beach's most popular sidewalk café serves vegetarian breakfast and lunch selections and some truly decadent desserts. ✉ *132 S. Cedros Ave.,* ☎ *858/793–5436. AE, MC, V. No dinner.*

Rancho Santa Fe

4 mi east of Solana Beach on S8 (Lomas Santa Fe Dr.), 29 mi north of downtown San Diego on I–5 to S8 east.

Rancho Santa Fe, east of Interstate 5 on Via de la Valle Road, is horse country. It's common to see entire families riding the many trails that crisscross the hillsides. The challenging Rancho Santa Fe Golf Course, the original site of the Bing Crosby Pro-Am and considered one of the best courses in southern California, is open only to members of the Rancho Santa Fe community and guests of the inn. The **Vegetable Shop** (✉ 6123 Calzada del Bosque, ☎ 858/756–3184) at Chino's farm offers premium fruits and rare baby vegetables, which many of San Diego's upscale restaurants snap up.

Dining and Lodging

$$$$ ★ ✕ **Mille Fleurs.** Mille Fleurs has a winning combination, from the warm Gallic welcome offered by proprietor Bertrand Hug to the talents of chef Martin Woesle. The quiet dining rooms are decorated in the style of a French-Moroccan villa. Menus are written daily, but sometimes feature lobster bisque with trout dumplings, Maine sea scallops poised on vegetable ravioli, grilled mahi mahi with pineapple-based curry sauce, and venison medallions with juniper-berry sauce. ✉ *Coun-*

try Squire Courtyard, 6009 Paseo Delicias, ☎ 858/756–3085. Reservations essential. AE, D, MC, V. No lunch weekends.

$$$$ ★ ✕🏨 **Rancho Valencia Resort.** One of southern California's hidden treasures has luxurious accommodations in Spanish-style casitas scattered among landscaped grounds. Spacious suites have corner fireplaces that can be seen from the bed, luxurious Berber carpeting, wet bars, and plantation-shuttered French doors leading to private patios shaded by market umbrellas. Rancho Valencia is adjacent to three well-designed golf courses and is one of the top tennis resorts in the nation. The inn's first-rate restaurant has earned raves for its California-Pacific cuisine. ✉ *5921 Valencia Circle, 92067, ☎ 858/756–1123 or 800/548–3664, FAX 858/756–0165. 43 suites. Restaurant, bar, minibars, refrigerators, room service, 2 pools, 3 outdoor hot tubs, spa, 18 tennis courts, croquet, health club, hiking, bicycles. AE, DC, MC, V.*

$$$–$$$$ 🏨 **Inn at Rancho Santa Fe.** Understated elegance is the theme of this genteel old resort in the heart of the village. This is the sort of place where people don their "whites" and play croquet on the lawn. Most accommodations are in red-tile-roof cottages scattered about the property's parklike 20 acres. The inn also maintains a beach house at Del Mar for guest use and has membership at the exclusive Rancho Santa Fe Golf Club. ✉ *5951 Linea del Cielo, 92067, ☎ 858/756–1131 or 800/843–4661, FAX 858/759–1604. 73 rooms, 19 suites. Dining room, bar, room service, pool, golf privileges, 3 tennis courts, croquet, exercise room, library, meeting rooms. AE, DC, MC, V.*

Carlsbad

6 mi from Encinitas on S21, 36 mi north of downtown San Diego on I–5.

The millennium marked a turning point for once laid-back Carlsbad, a Bavarian-inspired coastal community that is popular with beachgoers and sun seekers. The 1999 opening of the Legoland California theme park moved much of the visitor appeal inland east of Interstate 5. The park is at the center of a tourist complex that includes resort hotels, a discount shopping mall with winery, colorful spring-blooming flower fields, and golf courses.

Carlsbad owes its name and Bavarian look to John Frazier, who lured people to the area a century ago with talk of the healing powers of mineral water bubbling from a coastal well. The **Alt Karlsbad Haus** (✉ 2802A Carlsbad Blvd., ☎ 442/434–1887), a stone building that houses a small day-spa and the Carlsbad Famous Water Co., is a 21st century version of Frazier's waterworks.

★ ❷ **Legoland California** offers a full day of entertainment for pint-size visitors. The experience is best appreciated by children ages 2–10. Highlights include a castle, miniature Lego block cities, and Aquazone Wave Racers, the first power ski water ride in North America. Children can climb on and over, operate, manipulate, and explore displays and attractions constructed out of plastic blocks. Stage shows are also part of the mix. ✉ *1 Lego Dr. (exit I–5 at Cannon Rd. and follow signs east ¼ mi), ☎ 442/918–5346. $34. ⏲ Mid-Sept.–mid-June, daily 10–5; mid-June–Labor Day, daily 9–9.*

In spring the hillsides are abloom at **Flower Fields at Carlsbad Ranch,** the largest bulb production farm in southern California, where you can walk through fields planted with thousands of ranunculuses displayed against a backdrop of the blue Pacific Ocean. ✉ *Paseo del Norte, east of I–5, ☎ 442/431–0352. $4. ⏲ Mar. 1–Apr. 30, daily 10–6.*

❸ **Mission San Luis Rey.** Built by Franciscan friars in 1798 under the direction of Father Fermin Lasuen to help educate and convert local Native Americans, the well-preserved Mission San Luis Rey was the 18th and largest of the California missions. The *sala* (parlor), a friar's bedroom, a weaving room, the kitchen, and a collection of religious art convey much about early mission life. Retreats are still held here, but a picnic area, a gift shop, and a museum (which has the most extensive collection of old Spanish vestments in the United States) are also on the grounds. The mission is on Highway 76, which becomes Mission Avenue inland from S21 (from the ocean, continue east on Highway 76 about 4 mi, past the Mission Avenue business district and Interstate 5). ✉ *4050 Mission Ave.,* ☎ *442/757–3651.* *$4.* *Daily 10–4:30.*

Dining and Lodging

$$$ ✕ **Bellefleur Winery & Restaurant.** At the north end of Carlsbad Company Stores, this winery/restaurant offers lunch and dinner in the main dining room and late-afternoon small-portion snacks in the casual Vintner's Bar. ✉ *5610 Paseo del Norte,* ☎ *442/603–1919. AE, D, DC, MC, V.*

$$–$$$ ✕ **Vivace.** This stylish dining room in the Four Seasons Aviara Resort generates rave reviews for its innovative Italian cuisine, attractive ambience, and attentive service. The well-chosen wine list features selections from Italy and California, some quite reasonably priced. There's a kind of minimalist ambience about the dining room, with soft salmon-color wall coverings contrasted with gleaming wood paneling. ✉ *7100 Four Seasons Point,* ☎ *442/603–6800. AE, D, DC, MC, V. No lunch.*

$$$$ ★ ✕ **Four Seasons Resort Aviara.** This hilltop resort sitting on 30 acres overlooking Batiquitos Lagoon features typical Four Seasons amenities: acres of gleaming marble corridors, original artwork on the walls, crystal chandeliers, and enormous flower arrangements in public areas. Rooms, somewhat smaller than those in nearby luxury resorts, have comfortable seating areas, private balconies or garden patios, and marble bathrooms with double vanities and deep soaking tubs. The resort is home to the Arnold Palmer–designed Aviara Golf Club. Vivace (☞ *above*) is the hotel's signature restaurant. ✉ *7100 Four Seasons Point, 92009,* ☎ *442/603–6800 or 800/332–3442,* FAX *442/603–6878. 287 rooms, 44 suites. 4 restaurants, bar, 2 pools, beauty salon, spa, 18-hole golf course, 6 tennis courts, health club, hiking, bicycles, children's programs, meeting rooms, car rental. AE, D, DC, MC, V.*

$$$$ ✕ **La Costa Resort and Spa.** This famous resort is surprisingly low-key, with low-slung buildings and vaguely Southwestern–style rooms. Rooms are large with opulent marble bathrooms; many have garden patios. The resort has one of the most comprehensive sports programs in the area. There are two PGA championship golf courses and a golf school, plus a large tennis center. The spa services range from massages to nutritional counseling in separate men's and women's facilities; spa cuisine is available in three restaurants. The complex includes Pisces restaurant, long one of San Diego's top seafood venues. ✉ *2100 Costa del Mar Rd., 92009,* ☎ *442/438–9111 or 800/854–5000,* FAX *442/931–7569. 397 rooms, 82 suites. 4 restaurants, 2 bars, in-room data ports, room service, 5 pools, beauty salon, spa, 2 18-hole golf courses, 21 tennis courts, croquet, health club, hiking, jogging, bicycles, meeting rooms, car rental. AE, D, DC, MC, V.*

$$$–$$$$ **Carlsbad Inn.** Gabled roofs, half-timbered walls, and stone supports distinguish this sprawling European-style inn and time-share condominium complex in the heart of Carlsbad, steps from the beach. Rooms, which range from cramped to large, are furnished in old-world fashion, with pencil-post beds. The inn has a full schedule of activities including parties and excursions to Los Angeles and Mexico. ✉ *3075*

Carlsbad Blvd., 92008, ☎ 442/434–7020 or 800/235–3939, FAX 442/729–4853. 61 rooms, 1 suite. Pool, outdoor hot tub, sauna, exercise room, bicycles, children's programs, playground, coin laundry, meeting rooms. AE, D, DC, MC, V.

San Diego North Coast Essentials

Arriving and Departing

BY BUS

The San Diego Transit District (☎ 619/233–3004) covers the city of San Diego up to Del Mar. The **North County Transit District** (☎ 800/266–6883) serves San Diego County from Del Mar north.

BY CAR

Interstate 5 is the main freeway artery connecting San Diego to Los Angeles. To the west, running parallel to it, is S21 (known locally, but signed only in some places as Old Highway 101, and at other points as Highway 101 or Coast Highway 101), which never strays too far from the ocean. Watch the signs, because the road has a different name as it passes through each community.

BY PLANE

McClellan Palomar Airport (✉ 2198 Palomar Airport Rd., Carlsbad, ☎ 442/431–4646) is a general-aviation airport run by the county of San Diego and open to the public. America West Express and United Express operate flights between here and Los Angeles International Airport and Phoenix Sky Harbor International Airport.

Visitor Information

Carlsbad Convention and Visitors Bureau (✉ Box 1246, Carlsbad, 92018, ☎ 442/434–6093 or 800/227–5722, 🌐). **Greater Del Mar Chamber of Commerce** (✉ 1101 Camino del Mar, 92014, ☎ 858/793–5292, 🌐). **Oceanside** Chamber of Commerce (✉ 928 North Coast Hwy., 92054, ☎ 442/722–1534, 🌐). **San Diego North Convention and Visitors Bureau** (✉ 360 N. Escondido Blvd., Escondido 92025, ☎ 442/745–4741, 🌐).

SIDE TRIPS INLAND

Numbers in the margin correspond to points of interest on the San Diego North County map.

Escondido

8 mi north of Rancho Bernardo on I–15, 31 mi northeast of downtown San Diego on I–15.

Escondido is a thriving, rapidly expanding residential and commercial city of more than 80,000 people and the center of a variety of attractions. Home to San Diego Wild Animal Park, the Welk Resort Center, and innumerable three-generation California families, the inland area of North County is the quiet rural sister to the rest of San Diego County.

The **California Center for the Arts** includes two theaters and an art museum. The museum, which focuses on 20th-century art, occasionally presents blockbuster exhibits such as the glass art of Dale Chilhuly and photos by Ansel Adams, making a side trip worthwhile. *✉ 340 N. Escondido Blvd., ☎ 442/738–4100 box office; 442/839–4120 museum. 🎟 Museum $5. ⏲ Museum Tues.–Sat. 10–5, Sun. noon–5.*

Deer Park Winery and Auto Museum is a branch of the award-winning Napa Valley Deer Park Winery. Tastings are available. The museum contains a collection of vintage convertibles and other automobile memorabilia. ✉ *29013 Champagne Blvd., 15 mi north of Escondido,* ☎ *442/749–1666.* 🎫 *Museum $6.* ⏲ *Daily 10–5.*

Orfila Vineyards offers tours and tastings. The Rose Arbor has a picnic area. ✉ *13455 San Pasqual Valley Rd.,* ☎ *442/738–6500.* ⏲ *Daily 10–6.*

★ ❹ **San Diego Wild Animal Park** is an extension of the San Diego Zoo. The 2,200-acre preserve in the San Pasqual Valley is designed to protect endangered species of animals. Exhibit areas have been carved out of the dry, dusty canyons, and mesas to represent the animals' natural habitats—North Africa, South Africa, East Africa, Heart of Africa, Australian Rain Forest, Asian Swamps, and Asian Plains.

The best way to see these preserves is on the 50-minute, 5-mi Wgasa Bushline Monorail ride (included in the price of admission). The 1¼-mi-long **Kilimanjaro Safari Walk** winds through some of the park's hilliest terrain in the East Africa section, with observation decks overlooking the elephants and lions. A 70-ft suspension bridge spans a steep ravine, leading to the final observation point and a panorama of the entire park and the San Pasqual Valley. Along the trails of 32-acre **Heart of Africa** you can travel through forests and lowlands, across a floating bridge to a research station where an expert is on hand; finally you arrive at Panorama Point where you capture an up-close view of cheetahs, a chance to feed the giraffes, and a distant glimpse of the expansive savanna where rhinos, impalas, wildebeest, oryx, and beautiful migrating birds hang out. You can also camp overnight in the park in summer on a Roar and Snore Campover ($95). ✉ *Take I–15 north to Via Rancho Pkwy. and follow signs (6 mi),* ☎ *442/480–0100.* 🎫 *$21.95, includes all shows and monorail tour; a combination pass ($38.35) grants entry, within 5 days of purchase, to both the San Diego Zoo and the San Diego Wild Animal Park; parking $5. D, MC, V.* ⏲ *Mid-June–Labor Day, 9–8, Sept.–mid-June, 9–4.*

Dining and Lodging

$$–$$$ ✕ **150 Grand Cafe.** The seasonal menu of this pretty restaurant showcases contemporary California-style dishes prepared with a European flair. It's within walking distance of the California Center for the Arts. ✉ *150 W. Grand Ave.,* ☎ *442/738–6868. AE, DC, MC, V. Closed Sun.*

$$–$$$ ✕ **Sirino's.** Here's an excellent choice for dining before attending an event at the nearby California Center for the Arts. The simpler dishes are particularly recommended. Try the steamed mussels followed by the grilled salmon with roasted garlic, the duck breast confit, or the rack of lamb. ✉ *113 W. Grand Ave.,* ☎ *760/745–3835. AE, D, MC, V. Closed Sun.–Mon. No lunch Sat.*

$$–$$$$ 🏨 **Welk Resort Center.** This resort sprawls over 600 acres of rugged, oak-studded hillside. Built by band leader Lawrence Welk in the 1960s, the resort includes a hotel, time-share condominiums, and a recreation and entertainment complex. A museum displays Welk memorabilia, a theater presents Broadway-style musicals year-round, and there are many shops on the premises. ✉ *8860 Lawrence Welk Dr., 92026,* ☎ *442/749–3000 or 800/932–9355,* FAX *442/749–6182. 137 rooms, 10 suites. Restaurant, deli, 3 pools, 3 outdoor hot tubs, 2 18-hole golf courses, theater, children's programs, meeting rooms. AE, D, DC, MC, V.*

Inland North County Essentials

Arriving and Departing

BY BUS

North County Transit District (☎ 800/266–6883) routes connect North County coastal communities with inland destinations such as Escondido, Rancho Bernardo, Ramona, and Fallbrook primarily via the Interstate 15 corridor.

BY CAR

Escondido sits at the intersection of Highway 78, which heads east from Oceanside, and Interstate 15, the inland freeway connecting San Diego to Riverside, which is 30 minutes north of Escondido. Del Dios Highway winds from Rancho Santa Fe through the hills past Lake Hodges to Escondido. Highway 76, which connects with Interstate 15 north of Escondido, veers east to Palomar Mountain. Interstate 15 continues north to Fallbrook and Temecula.

Visitor Information

Escondido Chamber of Commerce (✉ 720 N. Broadway, 92025, ☎ 442/745–2125, 🌐). **Rancho Bernardo Chamber of Commerce** (✉ 11650 Iberia Pl., Suite 220, 92128, ☎ 858/487–1767, 🌐). **San Diego North Convention and Visitors Bureau** (✉ 360 N. Escondido Blvd., Escondido, 92025, ☎ 442/745–4741, 🌐).

Anza-Borrego Desert State Park

5 *88 mi from downtown San Diego (to park border due west of Borrego Springs), east on I–8, north on Hwy. 67, east on S4 and Hwy. 78, north on Hwy. 79, and east on S2 and S22.*

Every spring the stark desert landscape east of the Cuyamaca Mountains explodes with colorful wildflowers. The beauty of this spectacle, as well as the natural quiet and blazing climate, lures many people each year to Anza-Borrego Desert State Park, less than a two-hour drive from central San Diego. The desert is best visited from October through May to avoid the extreme summer temperatures. Winter temperatures are comfortable, but nights are cold, so bring a warm jacket.

More than 600,000 acres are included in one of the few parks in the country where people can camp anywhere. Follow the trails and pitch a tent wherever you like. Rangers and displays at an excellent underground **Visitors Information Center** (✉ Palm Canyon Dr., Borrego Springs, ☎ 442/767–5311; 442/767–4684 wildflower hot line, 🌐; ⏲ Oct.–May, daily 9–5; June–Sept., weekends and holidays 9–5) can point you in the right direction.

Five hundred miles of paved and dirt roads traverse the park, and visitors are required to stay on them so as not to disturb the ecological balance. Many of the park's sites can be seen from paved roads, but some require driving on dirt roads. Rangers recommend using four-wheel-drive vehicles when traversing dirt roads. Carry the appropriate supplies: shovel and other tools, flares, blankets, and plenty of water. Canyons are susceptible to flash flooding; inquire about weather conditions before entering.

Narrows Earth Trail is a short walk off Highway 78, east of Tamarisk Grove, that reveals the many geologic processes involved in forming the canyons of the desert. Water, wind, and faulting created the commanding vistas along **Erosion Road,** a self-guided, 18-mi auto tour along county road S22. The **Southern Emigrant Trail** follows the route of the Butterfield Stage Overland Mail through the desert.

At **Borrego Palm Canyon,** a few minutes west of the Anza-Borrego Visitors Information Center, a 1½-mi trail leads to a small oasis with a waterfall and palms. The Borrego Palm Canyon campground is one of only two developed campgrounds with flush toilets and showers in the park. (The other is Tamarisk Grove Campground, at the intersection of Highway 78 and Yaqui Pass Road; sites at both are $15–$22, depending on the season.) ✉ *Park headquarters: 200 Palm Canyon Dr., Borrego Springs 92004,* ☎ *442/767–5311.* 🎫 *$5 for a permit to use unpaved roads.* ⏲ *Park, year-round 24 hrs.*

SAN DIEGO A TO Z

Arriving and Departing

By Bus

Greyhound (✉ 120 W. Broadway, ☎ 619/239–8082 or 800/231–2222) operates 26 buses a day between San Diego and Los Angeles. One-way fare to Los Angeles is $13, round-trip is $22. Many buses are express or nonstop; others make stops at coastal towns en route.

By Car

Interstate 5 stretches from Canada to the Mexican border and bisects San Diego. Interstate 8 provides access from Yuma, Arizona, and points east. Drivers coming from Nevada and the mountain regions beyond can reach San Diego on I–15.

By Plane

San Diego International Airport (☎ 619/231–2100), about a five-minute drive from downtown, is San Diego's main airport. The airport's three-letter code is SAN. Carriers serving the city include America West, American, American Eagle, British Airways, Continental, Delta, Northwest, Southwest, TWA, United, and US Airways. *See* Air Travel *in* Smart Travel Tips for airline phone numbers.

BETWEEN THE AIRPORT AND DOWNTOWN

San Diego Transit (☎ 619/233–3004) Flyers, red- and blue-striped express buses, cruise the airport's terminals at 10- to 15-minute intervals between 5 AM and 1 AM. These buses will drop you at most downtown businesses and hotels. The fare is $2, including transfer to local transit buses and the San Diego Trolley. **Cloud 9 Shuttle** (☎ 858/278–8877) and **San Diego Xpress Airport Shuttle** (☎ 619/220–8454) operate van shuttles that take you directly to your destination, often for less than a cab would cost.

If you have rented a car at the airport, take Harbor Drive, at the perimeter of the airport, to downtown, which is 3 mi east. Take Harbor Drive west to reach Shelter Island and Point Loma. Harbor Island is adjacent to the airport. To reach Interstates 5 and 8, take Harbor Drive west to Nimitz Boulevard, then right on Rosecrans Street. You can reach La Jolla and North County via I–5 North. I–8 East leads to Hotel Circle, Fashion Valley, Mission Valley, and Qualcomm Stadium. To reach Mission Bay continue on Nimitz Boulevard, which intersects with Sunset Cliffs Boulevard. To reach Coronado take Harbor Drive east and turn left on Grape Street to reach I–5 South. Take the CA–75 exit to cross the San Diego–Coronado Bay Bridge.

By Train

Amtrak (☎ 800/872–7245) services downtown San Diego's **Santa Fe Depot** (✉ 1050 Kettner Blvd., ☎ 619/239–9021) with daily trains to and from Los Angeles and Santa Barbara. Amtrak stops in San Diego North County at Solana Beach and Oceanside.

Coaster (☎ 800/262–7837) commuter trains, which run between Oceanside and San Diego, stop at stations in Del Mar, Solana Beach, Encinitas, and Carlsbad.

Getting Around

By Bus and Rail

San Diego Transit buses connect with the San Diego Trolley light rail system and serve San Diego Zoo, Balboa Park, the airport, Mission Beach, Pacific Beach, La Jolla, and shopping centers. Buses to these destinations typically run every 15 minutes. The bright orange San Diego Trolley provides service on Blue and Orange lines, which includes downtown San Diego, Mission Valley, Old Town, South Bay, the U.S. Border, and East County. The trolleys operate seven days a week, early morning to late night, at intervals of about 15 minutes. Bus connections are posted at each station The **San Diego Transit Information Line** (☎ 619/233–3004; 619/234–5005 TTY/TDD; in operation from 5:30 AM to 8:30 PM) has details about all routes.

By Car

A car is essential for San Diego's sprawling freeway system. Avoid the freeways during rush hour when possible. All the major car-rental companies are represented in San Diego. For a list, *see* Car Rentals *in* Smart Travel Tips.

By Ferry

The **San Diego–Coronado Ferry** (☎ 619/234–4111) leaves from the Broadway Pier daily, every hour on the hour, Sunday–Thursday 9–9, until 10 PM Friday and Saturday. The fare is $2 each way and 50¢ for each bicycle.

By Taxi

Taxis departing from the airport are subject to regulated fares—all companies charge the same rate (generally $1.80 for the first mile, $1.20 for each additional mile). Fares vary among companies on other routes, however, including the ride back to the airport. If you call ahead and ask for the flat rate ($7) you'll get it, otherwise you'll be charged by the mile (which works out to $9 or so). Taxi stands are located at shopping centers and hotels, otherwise you must call and reserve one. The companies listed below do not serve all areas of San Diego County. Cab companies that serve most areas of the city are **Silver Cabs** (☎ 619/280–5555), **Coronado Cab** (☎ 619/435–6211), **Orange Cab** (☎ 619/291–3333), and **Yellow Cab** (☎ 619/234–6161).

Contacts and Resources

Emergencies

Ambulance, Fire, Police (☎ 911).

Hotel Doctors (☎ 619/275–2663 or 800/468–3537) provides 24-hour medical service to guests at San Diego hotels.

For late-night or 24-hour pharmacies, try **Longs Drug Store** (✉ 5685 Balboa Ave., at the intersection of Genesee Ave., ☎ 858/279–2860) or **Rite Aid** (✉ 535 Robinson Ave., ☎ 619/291–3705).

Guided Tours

ORIENTATION TOURS

Gray Line Tours (✉ 1775 Hancock St., #130, ☎ 619/491–0011; 800/331–5077 outside CA) operates city sightseeing excursions. The **Old Town Trolley** (✉ 2115 Kurtz St., ☎ 619/298–8687) travels to almost every attraction and shopping area on open-air trackless trolleys. Drivers double as tour guides. You can take the full two-hour, narrated city tour or get on and off as you please at any of the nine stops. An all-day pass costs $24 for adults, $12 for children 4–12; under 4, free. The trolley, which leaves every 30 minutes, operates daily 9–4 in winter. It takes the trolley two hours to make a full loop.

Free two-hour trolley tours (35 passengers) of the downtown redevelopment area, including the Gaslamp Quarter, are hosted by **Centre City Development Corporation Downtown Information Center** (✉ 225 Broadway, Suite 160, ☎ 619/235–2222) the first and third Saturday of each month at 10 AM. Reservations are necessary.

Three companies operate one- and two-hour harbor cruises. **San Diego Harbor Excursions** (✉ 1050 N. Harbor Dr., ☎ 619/234–4111) and **Hornblower Invader Cruises** (✉ 1066 N. Harbor Dr., ☎ 619/234–8687) boats depart from the Broadway Pier. No reservations are necessary for the $12–$17 voyages, and both vessels have snack bars. **Classic Sailing Adventures** (✉ 1220 Rosecrans St., #137, ☎ 619/224–0800) has morning and afternoon tours of the harbor and San Diego Bay and evening cruises in summer for $45 per person. These companies also operate during whale-watching season from mid-December to mid-March.

Visitor Information

Balboa Park Visitors Center (✉ 1549 El Prado, ☎ 619/239–0512). **Coronado Visitor Center** (✉ 1047 B Ave., 92118, ☎ 619/437–8788 or 800/622–8300). **International Visitor Information Center** (✉ 11 Horton Plaza, at 1st Ave. and F St., ☎ 619/236–1212). **La Jolla Town Council** (✉ 7734 Herschel Ave., 92038, ☎ 858/454–1444). **San Diego Convention & Visitors Bureau** (✉ 401 B St., Suite 1400, San Diego, 92101, ☎ 619/236–1212, 🌐). **San Diego Visitor Information Center** (✉ 2688 E. Mission Bay Dr., off I–5 at the Clairemont Dr. exit, ☎ 619/276–8200).

14 PALM SPRINGS

THE DESERT RESORTS AND JOSHUA TREE

Palm Springs and its neighbors—Palm Desert, Rancho Mirage, Indian Wells—are among the fastest-growing and wealthiest communities in the nation. The desert lures visitors and residents for the same reasons: striking scenery and the therapeutic benefits of a warm, arid climate. Resort hotel complexes contain championship golf courses, tennis stadiums, and sparkling swimming pools. Lushly landscaped oases, towering palms, natural waterfalls, and hot mineral springs round out the picture.

By Bobbi Zane

THE DESERT AROUND PALM SPRINGS hasn't always been filled with luxury resorts, but various settlers through the years have recognized the region's rich natural attributes. The Agua Caliente Band of Indians discovered the hot springs in the Coachella Valley—the area in which the resorts are situated—and made use of their healing properties. In the last half of the 19th century, farmers established a date-growing industry at the southern end of the valley. By 1900, word had spread about the manifold health benefits of the area's dry climate, inspiring the gentry of the northern United States to winter under the warm desert sun.

By the time of the Great Depression, Palm Springs had caught Hollywood's eye. It was an ideal hideaway: celebrities could slip into town, play a few sets of tennis, lounge around the pool, attend a party or two, and, unless things got out of hand, remain safely beyond the reach of gossip columnists.

Growth hit the desert in the 1970s. Developers began to construct the world-class golf courses, country clubs, and residential communities that drew celebrities, tycoons, and politicians. Privacy is still the watchword here. Many communities are walled and guarded.

The downside to the region's growth has included urban sprawl and overbuilding (of sometimes less than stellar structures). The city of Palm Springs lost some of its luster as the wealthy moved on to newer, more glamorous communities such as Palm Desert, Rancho Mirage, and Indian Wells. But Palm Springs has reinvented itself. Formerly exclusive Palm Canyon Drive is now a lively avenue with coffeehouses, outdoor cafés and bars, and frequent special events.

You'll still find celebrities in the desert. Hollywood stars, sports personalities, politicians, and other high-profile folks can be spotted at charity events, in restaurants, or on the golf course. The prospect of a brush with glamour, along with the desert's natural beauty, heightens the area's appeal for tourists.

Pleasures and Pastimes

Desert Wildlife

Visitors who want to learn about the natural history of the desert and see some spectacular scenery can explore the terrain at ground level at the Living Desert Wildlife and Botanical Park and Joshua Tree National Park or take in the full panorama at the top of the Palm Springs Aerial Tramway. Exhibits in the Palm Springs Desert Museum (☞ Exploring Palm Springs, *below*) explain it all.

Dining

Long a culinary wasteland, the desert now supports many trendy if not overly adventurous restaurants. Although Italian cuisine remains popular, a new collection of ethnic and contemporary eateries has sprung up in recent years. Many menus include heart-healthy items for those who are careful about fat and cholesterol. Dining is casual. Many restaurants that were traditionally closed in summer are now opening on a limited basis; hours vary, so call in advance.

CATEGORY	COST*
$$$$	over $50
$$$	$30–$50
$$	$20–$30
$	under $20

**per person for a three-course meal, excluding drinks, service, and 7¾% tax*

Golf

The Palm Springs area has more than 95 golf courses, many of which are familiar to golfing fans as the sites of championship tournaments regularly seen on television. You can tee off where the pros play at PGA West, Mission Hills North, and La Quinta, all of which have instructors ready to help you finesse your swing.

Lodging

You can stay in Palm Springs for as little as $40 per night or for more than $1,000. Rates vary widely from summer (low) to winter (high) season. Budget lodgings are most easily found in Palm Springs proper. The city-operated **visitor center** (☎ 800/347–7746) represents 85 properties. Discounts are sometimes given for extended stays. **Palm Springs Desert Resorts** (☎ 800/417–3529) can also make accommodation reservations throughout the area. Condos, apartments, and individual houses may be rented by the day, week, month, or for longer periods. Some hotels, including Marriott's Desert Springs Resort and Spa, have villas for rent.

CATEGORY	COST*
$$$$	over $175
$$$	$120–$175
$$	$80–$120
$	under $80

**All prices are for a standard double room, excluding 9%–11% tax.*

following the text of a review is your signal that the property has a Web site, where you will find details and, usually, images; for a link, visit www.fodors.com/urls.

Nightlife and the Arts

The Fabulous Palm Springs Follies—a vaudeville-style revue starring retired professional performers—is a must-see for most visitors. Arts festivals occur on a regular basis, especially during the winter and spring. Nightlife options include a good jazz bar (Peabody's), a clutch of new "retro" shows and glamour clubs, several dance clubs, and hotel entertainment. The "Desert Guide" from *Palm Springs Life* magazine, available at most hotels and visitor information centers, has nightlife listings, as does the "Weekender" pullout in the Friday edition of the daily *Palm Desert Sun* newspaper. The gay scene is covered in the *Bottom Line* and in the *Gay Guide to Palm Springs,* published by the Desert Gay Tourism Guild.

Outdoor Sports and Activities

With almost 30,000 pools in the desert region, swimming (or at least hanging out poolside) is a daily ritual. Several hundred courts make playing or watching tennis a serious pursuit. More than 35 mi of bike trails crisscross the Palm Springs area; the terrain here is mostly flat. Indian Canyons, Mount San Jacinto State Park and Wilderness, Living Desert Wildlife and Botanical Park, Joshua Tree National Park, and Big Morongo Canyon Preserve have hiking trails. Avoid outdoor activities midday during the hot season. Take precautions against the sun, and wear a hat any time of the year. Always drink plenty of water to prevent dehydration.

Shopping

More than half the respondents to a recent visitor survey ranked shopping as the "recreation" they enjoyed most, which may be the reason the Palm Springs area has begun to look like one big mall. Boutiques, art galleries, and an ever-growing collection of consignment, estate-sale, and antiques shops make for diverse browsing. El Paseo in Palm Desert has galleries and shops, and Cabazon holds many factory outlets.

Exploring Palm Springs

Some visitors' idea of "exploring" Palm Springs is to navigate the distance from their hotel room to the pool or spa. This has, after all, always been a place for indulging oneself. Most social, sports, shopping, and entertainment scenes revolve around Palm Springs and Palm Desert. Cathedral City and Rancho Mirage are west of Palm Desert (and east of Palm Springs) on Highway 111. Indian Wells, La Quinta, and Indio are all east of Palm Desert on the highway. North of Palm Springs is Desert Hot Springs. As for the region's natural wonders, Joshua Tree National Park and other outdoor attractions are easily visited as day trips from any of the resort towns.

Numbers in the text correspond to numbers in the margin and on the Palm Springs Desert Resorts map.

Great Itineraries

IF YOU HAVE 1 DAY

If you've just slipped into town for the day, focus your activities around Palm Springs. Get an early morning scenic overview by taking the **Palm Springs Aerial Tramway** ① to the top of Mount San Jacinto. In the afternoon, head for **Palm Canyon Drive** ② in Palm Springs, have lunch alfresco at the Blue Coyote Grill, and drop by the **Showbiz Museum** at the Plaza Theater, where you can pick up tickets for an evening performance of the **Fabulous Palm Springs Follies** (better still, make reservations before your visit). In the afternoon, visit **Palm Desert,** the trendiest of the desert cities, for a walk through the canyons and hillsides of the **Living Desert Wildlife and Botanical Park** ⑨ and a pre-show dinner on **El Paseo** ⑧.

IF YOU HAVE 3 DAYS

On your first day head to the **Palm Springs Aerial Tramway** ① in the morning and have lunch on **Palm Canyon Drive** ②. Spend the afternoon browsing the Palm Canyon shops, or (unless it's the height of the summer) hiking through the **Indian Canyons** ⑥. On day two take an early morning drive to **Joshua Tree National Park** ⑪, where you can explore the terrain, crawl through the entrance to Hidden Valley, and stop by the Oasis of Mara visitor center. Have a picnic lunch in the park or head back to **El Paseo** ⑧ in Palm Desert for a midafternoon bite before exploring the chic shopping area. On the third morning take in the **Palm Springs Desert Museum** ④. In the afternoon pamper yourself at either Merv Griffin's Resort Hotel and Givenchy Spa or the Spa Hotel and Casino (☞ Lodging, *below,* for both). Then, appropriately relaxed, take in a performance of the **Fabulous Palm Springs Follies.**

When to Tour Palm Springs

With an average of 350 sunny days a year, a chance to lounge around the pool is almost assured whenever you visit. During the "season" (from January through April) the desert weather is at its best, with daytime temperatures ranging between 70° and 90°F. This is the time when you're most likely to see a colorful display of wildflowers and when most of the golf and tennis tournaments take place. Prices soar and accommodations can be difficult to secure at this time, so reserve ahead. The fall months are nearly as lovely, less crowded, and less expensive. During the summer months daytime temperatures rise to 110°F or higher, though evenings cool to the mid-70s. Some attractions and restaurants close during this period. Hotel prices are frequently 50% less in summer than in winter and early spring.

FROM PALM SPRINGS TO PALM DESERT

The Agua Caliente Band of Cahuilla Indians settled in and around the Coachella Valley about 1,000 years ago. They considered the mineral springs to be sacred, with great curative and restorative powers. The springs became a tourist attraction in 1871 when the tribe built a bathhouse on the site to serve passengers on a pioneer stage route. The Agua Caliente still own about 32,000 acres of desert, 6,700 of which lie within the city limits of Palm Springs. The Agua Caliente, longtime operators of the Spa Hotel and Casino in downtown Palm Springs, announced in early 2000 plans to open a second casino and resort alongside I–10 in Rancho Mirage. The casino is due to open early in 2001.

The desert became a Hollywood hideout in the 1920s, when La Quinta Hotel opened the Coachella Valley's first golf course. But it took a pair of tennis-playing celebrities to put Palm Springs on the map in the 1930s. Actors Charlie Farrell and Ralph Bellamy bought 200 acres of land for $30 an acre and opened the Palm Springs Racquet Club, which soon listed Ginger Rogers, Humphrey Bogart, and Clark Gable among its members. Farrell served as the town's mayor in the '50s.

Joshua Tree, upgraded from "monument" status in the mid-1990s, is beginning to blossom as a national park. Major projects and facilities within the park are still in the future, but it will only be a matter of time before development in the surrounding communities takes off. In the meantime, nature, particularly in the form of spring wildflowers, continues to bloom with spectacular regularity. The Cottonwood Springs area is one of the desert's best for wildflower viewing. Carpets of white, yellow, purple, and red flowers stretch as far as the eye can see on the hillsides east of the freeway.

Exploring the Desert

★ ❶ A trip on the **Palm Springs Aerial Tramway** provides a stunning overview of the desert through the picture windows of rotating gondolas. The 2½-mi ascent brings you to an elevation of 8,516 ft in less than 20 minutes. On clear days, which are common, the view stretches 75 mi from the peak of Mount San Gorgonio to the north to the Salton Sea in the southeast. At the top you'll find several diversions. The Mountain Station has a restaurant, cocktail lounge, apparel and gift shops, a theater that screens a 22-minute film on the history of the tramway, and picnic facilities. Ride-and-dine packages are available in late afternoon. The tram is a popular attraction, so lines can be long. ✉ *1 Tramway Rd.,* ☎ *760/325–1391 or 888/515–8726.* *$19.65; ride-and-dine package $24.* ⏲ *Tram cars depart at least every 30 min from 10 AM weekdays and 8 AM weekends; last car up leaves at 8 PM, last one down 9:45 PM.*

Mount San Jacinto Wilderness State Park, accessible only by hiking or taking the Palm Springs Aerial Tramway, has camping and picnic areas and 54 mi of hiking trails. Guided wilderness mule rides are available here during snow-free months. During winter the Nordic Ski Center rents cross-country ski equipment. ☎ *909/659–2607 for park information.* *Free; free permits required for day or overnight wilderness hiking.*

OFF THE BEATEN PATH

WINDMILLS – Four thousand windmills flutter mightily on the slopes surrounding Palm Springs, generating electricity used by southern California residents. Each windmill stands more than 150 ft high. EV Adventures conducts 1½-hour tours among the turbines. ✉ *20th Ave. north of I–10,* ☎ *760/251–1997.* *$23.* ⏲ *Tours daily 9–3.*

Palm Springs Desert Resorts

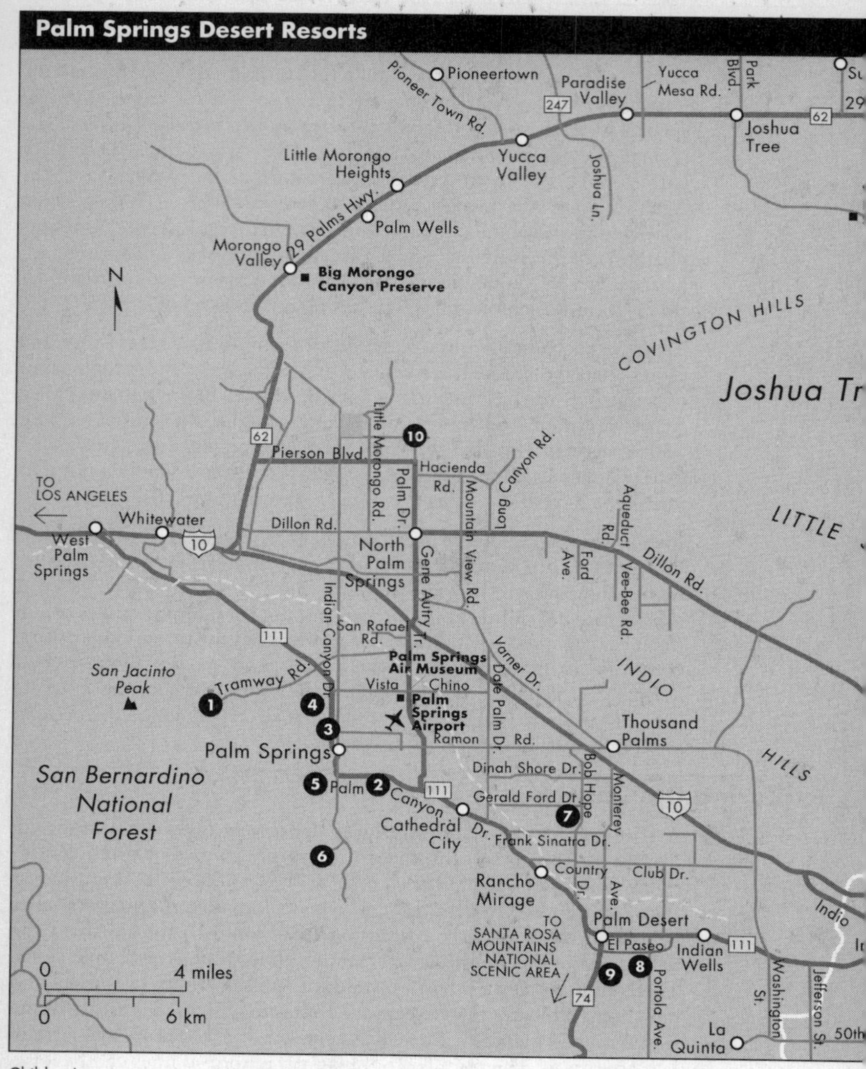

Children's Discovery Museum of the Desert 7
Desert Hot Springs 10
El Paseo 8
Indian Canyons 6
Joshua Tree National Park 11
Living Desert Wildlife and Botanical Park 9
Moorten Botanical Garden 5
Palm Canyon Drive 2
Palm Springs Aerial Tramway 1
Palm Springs Desert Museum 4
Village Green Heritage Center 3

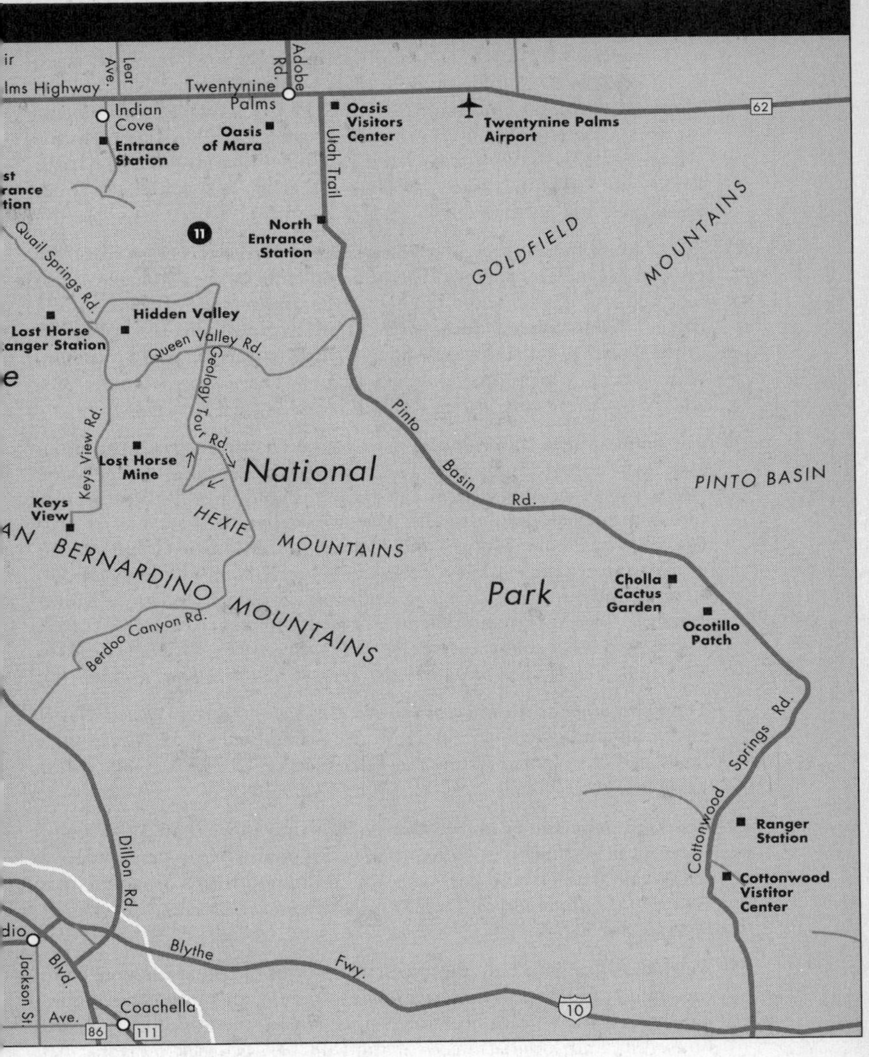

Twentynine Palms
Adobe Rd.
Lear Ave.
lms Highway
Indian Cove
Entrance Station
Oasis of Mara
Oasis Visitors Center
Utah Trail
Twentynine Palms Airport
62
North Entrance Station
GOLDFIELD MOUNTAINS
Quail Springs Rd.
Hidden Valley
Lost Horse Ranger Station
Queen Valley Rd.
Geology Tour Rd.
Pinto Basin Rd.
Keys View Rd.
Lost Horse Mine
National Park
PINTO BASIN
Keys View
HEXIE MOUNTAINS
SAN BERNARDINO MOUNTAINS
Cholla Cactus Garden
Ocotillo Patch
Berdoo Canyon Rd.
Cottonwood Springs Rd.
Ranger Station
Cottonwood Vistitor Center
Dillon Rd.
Blythe Fwy.
10
Jackson St.
Blvd.
Ave.
Coachella
86
111

❷ A stroll down **Palm Canyon Drive,** which is lined with shops, includes the **Palm Springs Starwalk,** with stars embedded in the sidewalk (à la the Hollywood Walk of Fame). Some of the names you'll recognize (such as Lauren Bacall and Liberace); others are local celebs. The tiny but illuminating **Showbiz Museum** (✉ 132 S. Palm Canyon Dr.) documents the area's roots in the entertainment industry. On Thursday night the ★ **Village Fest** fills the section between Tahquitz Canyon Way and Baristo Road with street musicians, a farmers' market, and stalls with food, crafts, art, and antiques.

❸ Three small museums at the **Village Green Heritage Center** illustrate pioneer life in Palm Springs. The **Agua Caliente Cultural Museum,** with free admission, is devoted to the culture and history of the Cahuilla tribe. The **McCallum Adobe,** with $1 admission, holds the collection of the Palm Springs Historical Society. **Rudy's General Store Museum,** with 50 cents admission, is a recreation of a general store from the '30s. *✉ 221 S. Palm Canyon Dr., ☎ 760/323–8297. ⏲ Hrs. vary.*

★ ❹ The **Palm Springs Desert Museum** focuses on natural science, the visual arts, and the performing arts. The display on the natural history of the desert is itself worth a visit, and the grounds hold several striking sculpture courts. A modern-art gallery has works by artists such as Alberto Giacometti, Henry Moore, and Helen Frankenthaler. Of interest to movie fans are the exhibits of the late actor William Holden's art collection, and furniture designed and crafted by actor George Montgomery. The Annenberg Theater presents plays, concerts, lectures, operas, and other cultural events. *✉ 101 Museum Dr., ☎ 760/325–7186. 🎟 $7.50; free 1st Fri. of month. ⏲ Tues.–Sat. 10–5, Sun. noon–5.*

The **Palm Springs Air Museum** showcases several dozen World War II aircraft including a B-17 Flying Fortress bomber, a P-51 Mustang, a Lockheed P-38, and a Grumman TBF Avenger. *✉ 745 N. Gene Autry Trail, ☎ 760/778–6262. 🎟 $7.50. ⏲ Daily 10–5.*

❺ Four-acre **Moorten Botanical Garden** nurtures more than 3,000 plant varieties in settings that simulate their original environments. Native American artifacts and rock, crystal, and wood forms are exhibited. *✉ 1701 S. Palm Canyon Dr., ☎ 760/327–6555. 🎟 $2. ⏲ Mon.–Sat. 9–4:30, Sun. 10–4.*

❻ The **Indian Canyons** hold the ancestral home of the Agua Caliente Band of Cahuilla Indians, who were drawn to the region's lush oases, abundant water, and wildlife. Visitors can see remnants of this life: rock art, house pits and foundations, irrigation ditches, bedrock mortars, pictographs, and stone houses and shelters built atop high cliff walls. Three areas are open: Palm Canyon, noted for its stand of Washingtonia palms; Murray Canyon, home of Peninsula bighorn sheep and a herd of wild ponies; and Andreas Canyon, where a stand of fan palms contrasts with sharp rock formations. The trading post in Palm Canyon has hiking maps, refreshments, Indian art, jewelry, and weavings. *✉ 38-500 S. Palm Canyon Dr., ☎ 760/325–5673. 🎟 $6. ⏲ Daily 8–5, summer 8–6.*

Much of the scenery in exclusive **Rancho Mirage** is behind the walls of gated communities and country clubs. The rich and famous live in estates or patronize the elegant resorts and fine-dining establishments, and the city's golf courses are the sight of world-class tournaments. The Betty Ford Center, for those recovering from alcohol or drug addiction, is also here.

❼ The **Children's Discovery Museum of the Desert** contains instructive hands-on exhibits for children—a miniature rock-climbing area, a magnetic sculpture wall, make-it-and-take-it-apart projects, a rope maze, and an area for toddlers. ✉ *71-701 Gerald Ford Dr., Rancho Mirage,* ☎ *760/321–0602,* *$5.* ⏲ *Tues.–Sat. 10–5, Sun. noon–5.*

8 Some of the best desert people-watching, shopping, and dining can be found along trendy **El Paseo,** west of Highway 111 in Palm Desert (☞ Shopping, *below*).

★ 9 Come eyeball to eyeball with coyotes, mountain lions, cheetahs, bighorn sheep, golden eagles, warthogs, and owls at the **Living Desert Wildlife and Botanical Park.** Easy to challenging trails traverse desert gardens populated with plants of the Mojave, Colorado, and Sonoran deserts. One exhibit highlights the path of the San Andreas earthquake fault across the valley. During the holidays the park presents Wildlights, an evening illumination show. Wildlife shows take place daily in Tennity Amphitheater. Shuttle service, strollers, and wheelchairs are available. The park is embarking on an expansion that will ultimately include re-creations of desert life on four continents. The three-acre African Wa TuTu village centers around a traditional marketplace. Animals on exhibit include camels, leopards, and hyenas. Children can touch African domestic animals, including goats and guinea fowl, in a petting kraal. ✉ *47-900 Portola Ave. (follow signs south from Hwy. 111), Palm Desert,* ☎ *760/346–5694.* *$8.50.* ⏲ *Sept.–mid-June, daily 9–5, mid-June–Aug., daily 8–1:30.*

The **Santa Rosa Mountains National Scenic Area Visitor Center,** operated by the Bureau of Land Management, contains exhibits illustrating the natural history of the desert and is staffed by knowledgeable volunteers. A landscaped garden displays native plants and frames a sweeping view. ✉ *51-500 Hwy. 74, Palm Desert,* ☎ *760/862–9984.* ⏲ *9–4.*

Most major hotels in the desert that have spas and fitness facilities—Merv Griffin's Resort Hotel and Givenchy Spa in Palm Springs and the Marriott Desert Springs resort in Palm Desert among them—offer day programs for nonguests as well as guests. **Spa du Jour** (✉ 555 S. Sunrise Way, Suite 305, Palm Springs, ☎ 760/864–4150) offers spa regimens ranging from two to six hours and including essential oil and aromatherapy wraps, massages, botanical and enzyme facials, beauty services, and healthy lunches. The **Palms at Palm Springs** (✉ 572 N. Indian Canyon Dr., Palm Springs, ☎ 760/325–1111, FAX 760/327–0867) has a one-day spa program that begins with a 6 AM walk. The package includes a choice of 16 classes, the use of exercise equipment, lectures, and individually designed low-calorie meals and snacks. Massage, facials, and wraps are among the options.

Dining

CATHEDRAL CITY

$$–$$$$ ✕ **The Wilde Goose.** Its name notwithstanding, the specialty of the house at the Wilde Goose is duck, served a number of ways. You'll also find steaks, poultry, fish, and extravagant desserts at this romantic restaurant. ✉ *67-938 E. Palm Canyon Dr.,* ☎ *760/328–5775. AE, D, DC, MC, V. No lunch.*

$$ ✕ **Oceans.** The many repeat customers at this small seafood restaurant tucked in the back of a shopping center testify to the creativity of its chefs and the hospitality of the staff. Bouillabaisse and other Continental-style dishes are so fresh you might forget you're dining in the desert. ✉ *Canyon Plaza South, 67-555 E. Palm Canyon Dr.,* ☎ *760/324–1554. Reservations essential on weekends. AE, D, DC, MC, V. No lunch weekends.*

INDIAN WELLS

$$$–$$$$ ✕ **Hamiltons.** Actor/entrepreneur George Hamilton selected celebrity-rich Indian Wells as the home of the second of his new group of showbiz-style restaurants. Part of the Hyatt Grand Champions complex, Hamiltons offers a glamorous atmosphere with Moroccan-inspired decor, tented ceilings, and a private pool. Local critics have raved about the food. The menu changes frequently but often includes such popular dishes as pancetta-wrapped pork loin, braised duck in orange and almonds with couscous, and tri-color linguine with lobster. ✉ *44-600 Indian Wells Lane,* ☎ *760/340–4499. AE, MC, V. No lunch Sun.–Thurs.*

LA QUINTA

$$–$$$$ ★ ✕ **La Quinta Cliffhouse.** Sweeping mountain views at sunset and the early California ambience of a western movie set draw patrons to this restaurant perched halfway up a hillside. The eclectic menu roams the globe: Caesar salad with grilled chicken; Szechuan-style ahi tuna; and, for dessert, Kimo's Hula Pie with house-made macadamia-nut ice cream. ✉ *78-250 Hwy. 111,* ☎ *760/360–5991. Reservations essential. AE, D, MC, V. No lunch.*

$$–$$$ ✕ **Cunard's Sandbar.** Sturdy steaks, hearty fish and pasta specials, and reasonable prices lure locals and celebrities to this quiet La Quinta eatery. ✉ *78-120 Calle Tampico,* ☎ *760/564–3660. AE, DC, MC, V. No lunch.*

PALM DESERT

$$$–$$$$ ✕ **Augusta.** Artwork fills this showplace, one of the region's most talked-about eateries. Two popular items on the eclectic menu are spit-roasted duck with a cilantro sauce and Chilean sea bass marinated in sake. ✉ *73-951 El Paseo,* ☎ *760/779–9200. Reservations essential. AE, DC, MC, V. Closed Aug. No lunch Sun.*

$$$–$$$$ ★ ✕ **Cuistot.** Chef-owner Bernard Dervieux trained with French culinary star Paul Bocuse, but he's taken a more eclectic approach at his own restaurant, tucked into the back of an El Paseo courtyard. Signature dishes include grilled shrimp with spinach linguine, Chinese-style duck in a mango-Madeira-ginger sauce, and rack of lamb with rosemary. ✉ *73-111 El Paseo,* ☎ *760/340–1000. Reservations essential. AE, DC, MC, V. Closed Mon. No lunch Sun.*

$$$–$$$$ ✕ **Mayo's.** Bob Mayo presides over a snazzy, retro supper club. There's even a private room dedicated to Hollywood's famed Rat Pack, decorated with larger-than-life-size photos of Frank Sinatra, Sammy Davis, and Dean Martin. The menu offers an updated version of Continental cuisine: pasta, Lake Superior whitefish, and New York steak. ✉ *73-990 El Paseo,* ☎ *760/346–2284. Reservations essential. AE, D, DC, MC, V.*

$$$–$$$$ ✕ **Morton's of Chicago.** Palm Springs residents like their steaks served with style as well as sizzle. Posh, clublike Morton's delivers. A regular slab will cost you about $32 (à la carte), but if only a 48-ounce porterhouse will satisfy, the charge is $62. Ask for a smaller portion and the price will go down slightly. The bar is always busy. Sinatra (and only Sinatra) plays softly in the background. ✉ *74-880 Country Club Dr.,* ☎ *760/340–6865. AE, DC, MC, V. No lunch.*

$$$ ✕ **Doug Arango's.** Even the dish of liver and onions receives star treatment at this bistro with colorful sidewalk umbrellas and tomato-red walls. The entrées include such inventive Euro-tinged creations as seared foie gras. ✉ *73-520 El Paseo,* ☎ *760/341–4120. Reservations essential. AE, D, DC, MC, V. Closed Mon. year-round. Closed Sun., no lunch June–mid-Sept.*

$$$ ✕ **Jillian's.** Husband-and-wife team Jay and June Trubee are the stars behind this fancy yet casual restaurant. He tends to the kitchen; she runs the business. Antiques and art decorate the three dining rooms, and the nighttime sky provides the ambience in the center courtyard. Try the monumental appetizer called tower of crab (layers of crab, tomatoes, avocados, and brioche), and main dishes such as salmon baked in parchment and fettuccine with lobster. Save room for the popular Hawaiian cheesecake with macadamia nut crust. Men will feel more comfortable wearing jackets. ✉ *74-155 El Paseo,* ☎ *760/776–8242. Reservations essential. AE, DC, MC, V. Closed 2nd week of June–Sept. No lunch.*

$$–$$$ ✕ **Café des Beaux Arts.** The café brings a little bit of Paris to the desert, with sidewalk dining, colorful flower boxes, and a bistro menu of French and Californian favorites such as a hefty bouillabaisse, and the broiled Portobello mushroom with grilled chicken and an artichoke heart, served with a sherry sauce. (Try to stop munching on those flavorful breads.) Leisurely dining is encouraged, which allows more time to savor the well-chosen French and domestic wines. ✉ *73-640 El Paseo,* ☎ *760/346–0669. AE, D, DC, MC, V. Closed July–mid-Sept.*

$$–$$$ ✕ **Gila Steaks and Seafood.** Talented chef Fernando Valenzuela (no, not the pitcher) whips up fresh fish, Cajun shrimp, garlic-roasted chicken, certified Angus beef, and other fine dishes at this Palm Springs favorite. The ambience is casual sleek, whether inside or on the patio. ✉ *74-950 Country Club Dr.,* ☎ *760/346–4452. Reservations essential. AE, D, DC, MC, V.*

$$–$$$ ✕ **Locanda Toscana.** Celebrities and celebrity-watchers patronize this Tuscan-style restaurant known for excellent service, many antipasti choices, and fine soups. Veal, chicken, and fish all receive snazzy preparation. ✉ *72-695 Hwy. 111,* ☎ *760/776–7500. Reservations essential. AE, D, DC, MC, V. No lunch.*

$$–$$$ ✕ **Omri and Boni.** Chef Omri Siklai showed the same flair decorating this establishment that he displays nightly in the kitchen preparing an eclectic menu of contemporary Mediterranean dishes. Caesar salads, homemade pastas, chicken and veal dishes—and even ostrich and kangaroo—are prepared with skill and imagination. Pastas and breads made on the premises are egg-free. ✉ *73-675 Hwy. 111,* ☎ *760/773–1735. Reservations essential. MC, V. Closed Mon. and July–Sept. No lunch.*

$$–$$$ ✕ **Palomino Euro Bistro.** One of the desert's longtime favorites specializes in grilled and roasted entrées: spit-roasted garlic chicken, oak-fired thin-crust pizza, paella, and oven-roasted prawns. Huge reproductions of famous French Impressionist paintings cover the walls of this active bistro. ✉ *73-101 Hwy. 111,* ☎ *760/773–9091. AE, D, DC, MC, V. No lunch.*

$$–$$$ ✕ **Ristorante Mamma Gina.** The greatest hits of Florence and Tuscany appear on the menu at this festive, upscale restaurant. The appetizers and salads are superb, but save room for pasta dishes or smartly crafted chicken, veal, and fish dishes. The wine selection favors Italian and Californian vintages. ✉ *73-705 El Paseo,* ☎ *760/568–9898. Reservations essential. AE, DC, MC, V. No lunch Sun.*

$–$$$ ✕ **Bananaz Grill and Bar.** The atmosphere at this large, boisterous eatery is exceedingly convivial. The food is cheap (for the area) and bountiful—husky sandwiches, roast chicken, and a dozen other options. The many TVs and frequent live entertainment will keep you amused while you dine. Bananaz becomes a nightclub after 10 with live music and dancing. ✉ *72–291 Hwy. 111,* ☎ *760/776–4333. AE, D, DC, MC, V.*

$–$$ ✕ **Daily Grill.** A combination upscale coffee shop and bar, the Daily Grill serves good salads (the Niçoise is particularly scrumptious), a fine gazpacho, zesty pasta dishes, and various blue-plate specials. The sidewalk terrace invites people-watching. Sunday brunch is a weekly party. ✉ *73-061 El Paseo,* ☎ *760/779–9911. AE, D, DC, MC, V.*

$ ✕ **McGowan's Irish Inn.** Home-style comfort foods—meat loaf, chicken and dumplings, corned beef and cabbage, and beef stew—get the full Irish treatment at this family-owned restaurant with a full bar and sidewalk dining. The portions are beyond generous, and the service is good-natured. ✉ *73-340 Hwy. 111,* ☎ *760/346–6032. MC, V. Closed Sun. June–Sept.*

PALM SPRINGS

$$$–$$$$ ✕ **Le Vallauris.** In a tasteful old home with a beautiful garden, Le Vallauris serves Californian-accented French cuisine—dishes such as grilled veal chop with porcini ravioli and grilled halibut with sun-dried-tomato crust and a lemon sauce. A pianist plays nightly. Sunday brunch is a hit with locals. ✉ *385 W. Tahquitz Canyon Way,* ☎ *760/325–5059. Reservations essential. AE, D, DC, MC, V. No lunch Wed.–Sat. July–Aug.*

$$–$$$ ✕ **Blue Coyote Grill.** Diners under blue umbrellas munch on burritos, tacos, fajitas (or more unusual items, such as Yucatán lamb or orange chicken) at this casual restaurant. Choose between several flower-decked patios and inside dining rooms. Two busy cantinas serve up tasty margaritas to a youngish crowd. ✉ *445 N. Palm Canyon Dr.,* ☎ *760/327–1196. AE, MC, V.*

$$–$$$ ✕ **Otani Garden Restaurant.** Sushi, tempura, and *teppan* (grilled) specialties are served in a serene garden setting at Otani. A fresh Sunday brunch buffet includes tempura, stir-fried entrées, salads, sushi, and desserts. ✉ *266 Avenida Caballeros,* ☎ *760/327–6700. AE, D, DC, MC, V. No lunch Sat.*

$$–$$$ ★ ✕ **Palmie.** The humble location in the back of a shopping arcade and the simple decor of Toulouse-Lautrec and other Gallic posters give nary a hint of the subtle creations prepared at this gem of a French restaurant. The two-cheese soufflé is one of several mouthwatering appetizers. Equally impressive are the duck confit and duck fillets entrée served with pear slices in red wine, and Palmie's signature dish, a perfectly crafted fish stew in a thin-yet-rich butter-cream broth. ✉ *Galeria Henry Frank, 276 N. Palm Canyon Dr.,* ☎ *760/320–3375. AE, DC, MC, V. Closed Aug.–mid-Sept. No lunch.*

$$–$$$ ✕ **St. James at the Vineyard.** A multihue interior, an outdoor terrace with street views, and a bubbling modern fountain set a playful mood at this hot spot for dining and sipping smart cocktails. Pastas, chicken dishes, and curries are the menu mainstays. The service can be mildly chaotic on weekend nights in high season. ✉ *265 S. Palm Canyon Dr.,* ☎ *760/320–8041. Reservations essential. AE, D, DC, MC, V. No lunch.*

$$ ✕ **Edgardo's Cafe Veracruz.** For a sampling of Mayan and Aztec flavors try some of the unique items on Edgardo's menu, such as soup made with *nopales* (cactus) and roast pork wrapped in banana leaves. The menu also features more popular items such as tamales and enchiladas. ✉ *494 N. Palm Canyon Dr.,* ☎ *760/320–3558. Reservations essential. AE, D, DC, MC, V.*

✕ **Capra's.** Even if you're not hungry, this is the place to see a real Oscar; it's one presented to famed director Frank Capra, who made films such as *It's a Wonderful Life* and *You Can't Take it With You.* Capra's son runs this cafe, which displays images of Hollywood's past including original movie posters and lobby cards as well as awards. The menu lists sandwiches, soups and salads, chicken, pasta, veal, and a Capra original called Spaghetti pie. ✉ *204 N. Palm Canyon Dr.,* ☎ *760/325–7030. MC, V. Closed Tues.*

RANCHO MIRAGE

$$–$$$ ✕ **Bangkok V.** Fresh flowers always adorn the tables at this attractively decorated Thai restaurant, where the food is prepared with sizzle (literally) and flair. Start with one of the spicy soups, followed by delicate wok-cooked catfish with garlic-cilantro sauce, or any of the curries. Make your level of comfort with spices known, or you may find your mouth on fire. ✉ *69-930 Hwy. 111,* ☎ *760/770–9508. AE, D, DC, MC, V.*

$$–$$$ ✕ **Shame on the Moon.** Superior service and high-quality food at reasonable prices have made this restaurant a perennial desert favorite. The kitchen turns out consistently delicious Continental fare such as roasted salmon with horseradish crust and calf's liver and onions with a bourbon glaze. The desserts are alluringly decadent. ✉ *69-950 Frank Sinatra Dr., ☎ 760/324–5515. Reservations essential. AE, MC, V. No lunch.*

$$ ✕ **Las Casuelas Nuevas.** Hundreds of artifacts from Guadalajara lend a festive charm to this casual Mexican-style restaurant with a 100-seat garden patio. Tamales and shellfish dishes are among the specialties of the house. The margaritas will make you wish you'd brought your cha-cha heels. ✉ *70-050 Hwy. 111, ☎ 760/328–8844. AE, D, DC, MC, V.*

Lodging

INDIAN WELLS

$$$$ **Hyatt Grand Champions Resort.** This stark white resort on 34 acres of natural desert specializes in pampering, with lavish accommodations and service provided by a multilingual staff. Suite-style rooms have balconies or terraces, sunken sitting areas, and minibars. The villas here may be the most luxurious accommodations in the desert. Resembling private residences, each has a secluded garden courtyard with outdoor whirlpool tub, a living room with fireplace, a dining room, and a bedroom. A private butler awaits your commands. The pool area has been transformed into a garden water park surrounded by palms and private cabanas. ✉ *44-600 Indian Wells La., 92210, ☎ 760/341–1000 or 800/233–1234, FAX 760/568–2236. 312 suites, 26 villas. 2 restaurants, bar, 4 pools, beauty salon, 3 outdoor hot tubs, massage, sauna, spa, steam room, driving range, 2 golf courses, putting green, 12 tennis courts, aerobics, health club, bicycles, pro shop, shops, children's programs, dry cleaning, laundry service, business services, convention center, meeting rooms, car rental. AE, D, DC, MC, V.*

$$$$ **Renaissance Esmeralda Resort.** The centerpiece of this luxurious Mediterranean-style resort is an eight-story atrium lobby with a fountain whose water flows through a rivulet in the floor, into cascading pools, and outside to lakes surrounding the property. Given its size, the hotel has a surprisingly intimate ambience. Spacious guest rooms are decorated in light wood with desert-color accents. Rooms have sitting areas, balconies, refreshment centers, two TV sets, and travertine vanities in the bathrooms. One pool has a sandy beach. Golf and tennis instruction are available. ✉ *44-400 Indian Wells La., 92210, ☎ 760/773–4444 or 800/408–3571, FAX 760/773–9250. 538 rooms, 22 suites. 3 restaurants, bar, snack bar, minibars, 3 pools, wading pool, 2 outdoor hot tubs, massage, sauna, spa, steam room, 2 golf courses, putting green, 4 tennis courts, basketball, health club, volleyball, bicycles, pro shop, shops, children's programs, laundry service, concierge, meeting rooms, car rental. AE, DC, MC, V.*

LA QUINTA

$$$$ ★ **La Quinta Resort and Club.** The desert's oldest resort, opened in 1926, is a lush green oasis. Rooms are in adobe casitas separated by broad expanses of lawn and in newer two-story units surrounding individual swimming pools and brilliant gardens. Fireplaces, stocked refrigerators, and fruit-laden orange trees contribute to a discreet and sparely luxurious atmosphere. A premium is placed on privacy, which accounts for La Quinta's continuing popularity with Hollywood celebrities. La Quinta arranges access to some of the desert's most celebrated golf courses. ✉ *49-499 Eisenhower Dr., 92253, ☎ 760/564–4111 or 800/598–3828, FAX 760/564–5768. 618 rooms, 27 suites, 110 vacation residences. 6 restaurants, 25 pools, spa, beauty salon, 38 outdoor hot tubs, 5 golf courses, 23 tennis courts, health club, shops, children's programs, concierge, business services, meeting rooms. AE, D, DC, MC, V.*

$$$$ **Two Angels Inn.** This bed-and-breakfast occupies a somewhat startling faux French château perched on the banks of a small lake. Innkeepers

Hap and Holly Harris offer luxurious accommodations. All rooms have fireplaces, patios or balconies, and carefully selected antique or contemporary furnishings. Two have private outdoor hot tubs. ✉ *78-120 Caleo Bay, 92253,* ☎ *760/564–7332 or 888/226–4546,* FAX *760/564–6356. 11 rooms. Pool, outdoor hot tub. AE, D, MC, V. BP.*

PALM DESERT

$$$$ **Marriott's Desert Springs Resort and Spa.** This sprawling convention-oriented hotel has a dramatic U-shape design. The building wraps around the desert's largest private lake, into which an indoor, stair-stepped waterfall flows. Rooms have lake or mountain views, balconies, and oversize bathrooms. There are long walks from the lobby to rooms; if driving, request one close to the parking lot. ✉ *74-855 Country Club Dr., 92260,* ☎ *760/341–2211 or 800/331–3112,* FAX *760/341–1872. 833 rooms, 51 suites. 5 restaurants, 2 bars, snack bar, minibars, 5 pools, 4 outdoor hot tubs, beauty salon, spa, driving range, 2 golf courses, putting green, 20 tennis courts, basketball, croquet, health club, jogging, volleyball, shops, children's programs, laundry service, business services, convention center, car rental. AE, D, DC, MC, V.*

$$$–$$$$ **Tres Palmas Bed & Breakfast.** Enormous windows, high open-beam ceilings, light wood, and textured peach tile floors lend this contemporary inn near El Paseo a bright and spacious feel. The Southwestern decor in common areas and guest rooms (more functional than luxurious) incorporates old Navajo rugs from the innkeepers' collection. ✉ *73-135 Tumbleweed La.,* ☎ *760/773–9858 or 800/770–9858,* FAX *760/776–9159. 4 rooms. Pool, outdoor hot tub. AE, MC, V. C.*

PALM SPRINGS

$$$$ **Hyatt Regency Suites.** This hotel's six-story asymmetrical atrium lobby holds an enormous metal sculpture suspended from the ceiling. One- and two-bedroom suites have private balconies and two TVs. The suites in the back have pool and mountain views. There's free underground parking, and guests have golf privileges at Rancho Mirage Country Club and four other area courses. ✉ *285 N. Palm Canyon Dr., 92262,* ☎ *760/322–9000 or 800/554–9277,* FAX *760/416–6588. 192 suites. 2 restaurants, bar, snack bar, pool, beauty salon, outdoor hot tub, spa, golf privileges, exercise room, concierge, business services, meeting rooms, airport shuttle. AE, D, DC, MC, V.*

$$$$ ★ **Merv Griffin's Resort Hotel and Givenchy Spa.** Indulgence is the word for this resort modeled after the Givenchy spa in Versailles. The ambience is totally French, from the Empire-style decor to the perfectly manicured rose gardens. Many rooms are one- or two-bedroom suites with separate salons, some with private patios and mountain or garden views. Personalized spa services include everything from facials to mud wraps to aromatherapy. Restaurants offer typical French fare as well as more heart-healthy options. ✉ *4200 E. Palm Canyon Dr., 92264,* ☎ *760/770–5000 or 800/276–5000,* FAX *760/324–6104. 63 rooms, 41 suites. 2 restaurants, 4 pools, beauty salon, spa, golf privileges, 6 tennis courts, croquet, health club, jogging, shops, concierge, business services, meeting rooms. AE, D, DC, MC, V.*

$$$$ **Palm Springs Hilton Resort and Racquet Club.** This venerable hotel, located across the street from the tented Spa Casino, has aged gracefully. Rooms, decorated in soft desert colors, are fairly spacious, but rather spare. All have private balconies or patios, some overlooking the hotel's lushly landscaped pool area. ✉ *400 E. Tahquitz Canyon Way, 92262,* ☎ *760/320–6868 or 800/522–6900,* FAX *760/320–2126. 200 rooms, 60 suites. Restaurant, 2 bars, pool, 2 outdoor hot tubs, golf privileges, 6 tennis courts, health club, video games, children's programs, concierge, business services. AE, D, DC, MC, V.*

$$$$ **Sundance Villas.** The two- and three-bedroom duplex homes in this complex have full kitchens, bathrooms with huge sunken tubs, outdoor pools and hot tubs, and laundry facilities. The villas are away from most desert attractions in a secluded residential area at the north end of Palm Springs. Rates, though high, are for up to six people. ✉ *303 W. Cabrillo Rd., 92262,* ☎ *760/325–3888 or 800/455–3888,* FAX *760/323–3029. 19 villas. In-room VCRs, pools, golf privileges, tennis court, concierge. AE, D, DC, MC, V.*

$$$$ ★ **Willows Historic Palm Springs Inn.** This luxurious hillside B&B is within walking distance of many village attractions. An opulent mansion built in the 1920s, it features natural hardwood and slate floors, stone fireplaces, fresco ceilings, hand-painted tiles, iron balconies, and a 50-ft waterfall that splashes into a pool outside the dining room. Guest rooms are decorated to recall the movies of Hollywood's golden era of the 1930s. ✉ *412 W. Tahquitz Canyon Way 92262,* ☎ *760/320–0771 or 800/966–9597,* FAX *760/320–0780. 8 rooms. Pool, outdoor hot tub. AE, D, DC, MC, V. BP.*

$$$–$$$$ **Ballantine's Hotel.** Known as the Mira Loma Hotel for 50 years, this small hotel hosted Marilyn Monroe and Gloria Swanson in the late '40s, when Monroe was still a teenager and Swanson was a big star. Both reportedly met lovers here out of sight of gossip columnists. A renovation completed in 1999 captures the essence of the '40s and 50s with furnishings by Eames, Biller, Bertoia, and Knoll. It's all quite retro . . . and a bit plastic . . . with rotary dial phones, period appliances in kitchenettes, and a collection of classic films to show on the VCR. Amenities include private sunbathing patios and complimentary in-room breakfast. ✉ *1420 N. Indian Canyon Dr., 92262,* ☎ *760/320–1178,* FAX *760/320–5308. 14 rooms. Bar, kitchenettes, pool, outdoor whirlpool, laundry service, dry cleaning, concierge. AE, MC, V.*

$$$–$$$$ **Harlow Club Hotel.** A resort that caters to a gay clientele, this is ideal for those seeking secluded accommodations in a lush garden setting. Rooms are in hacienda-style buildings surrounding a pool; many have fireplaces, private patios, and unusually large bathrooms. Crimson bougainvillea cascades from the rooftops. Date palms grow on the property, as do orange, tangerine, and grapefruit trees. There's a secluded clothing-optional sunbathing area. The room rates include breakfast and lunch. ✉ *175 E. El Alameda, 92262,* ☎ *760/323–3977 or 800/547–7881,* FAX *760/320–1218. 15 rooms, 1 suite. Pool, outdoor hot tub, exercise room. AE, D, DC, MC, V.*

$$$–$$$$ **Spa Hotel and Casino.** Rooms at this hotel built over the original Agua Caliente springs are decorated in soft pinks and blues and feature light wood furniture. The hotel, owned by the Agua Caliente tribe, appeals to an older crowd that appreciates its soothing waters and downtown location. The hotel's Spa Experience is a sampling of services—sink into a tub filled with naturally hot mineral water, rest in the cool white relaxation room, swim in the outdoor mineral pool, or let the sauna warm your spirits. ✉ *100 N. Indian Canyon Dr., 92262,* ☎ *760/325–1461 or 800/854–1279,* FAX *760/325–3344. 220 rooms, 10 suites. 2 restaurants, 2 bars, pool, beauty salon, 2 outdoor hot tubs, spa, steam room, 18-hole golf course, shops, casino, concierge, meeting rooms. AE, D, MC, V.*

$$$–$$$$ **Wyndham Palm Springs.** The main appeal of this hotel is its location near the Palm Springs Convention Center. The terra-cotta Spanish-colonial building surrounds the largest swimming pool in Palm Springs. Because most of the Wyndham's customers are here on business, the atmosphere is more serious than at most desert establishments. ✉ *888 Tahquitz Canyon Way, 92262,* ☎ *760/322–6000 or 800/822–4200,* FAX *760/416–29001. 252 rooms, 158 suites. Restaurant, 2 bars, pool, wad-*

ing pool, beauty salon, 2 outdoor hot tubs, sauna, golf privileges, exercise room, shops, business services, meeting rooms. AE, D, MC, V.

$$–$$$$ **Ingleside Inn.** This hacienda-style inn attracts its share of Hollywood personalities who appreciate the attentive service and relative seclusion. Many rooms have antiques, fireplaces, whirlpool tubs, stocked refrigerators, and private patios. The accommodations in the main building are dark and cool, even in summer. ✉ *200 W. Ramon Rd., 92264,* ☎ *760/325–0046 or 800/772–6655,* FAX *760/325–0710. 30 rooms. Restaurant, bar, pool, outdoor hot tub, concierge. AE, D, DC, MC, V. CP.*

$$–$$$$ **Korakia Pensione.** This Moorish-style villa, built in the 1920s by Scottish artist Gordon Coutts, has long been a haven for the creative set. Winston Churchill came here to paint. More recently photographer Annie Leibovitz has enjoyed the villa's scenic mountain view. Inside, rooms are furnished with antiques, handmade furniture, and Oriental rugs; some have fireplaces, and many have kitchens. ✉ *257 S. Patencio Rd., 92262,* ☎ *760/864–6411,* FAX *760/864–4147. 5 rooms, 17 suites. 2 pools. No credit cards. Closed mid-July–Labor Day. BP.*

$$–$$$$ **Santiago Resort.** This classy clothing-optional resort caters to a gay-male clientele. Spacious rooms are stylishly decorated and come appointed with refrigerators and microwaves. An expansive pool area is surrounded by colorful tropical gardens. Rates include breakfast and lunch. ✉ *650 San Lorenzo Rd., 92264,* ☎ *760/322–1300 or 800/710–7729,* FAX *760/416–0347. 23 rooms. Pool, outdoor hot tub, sauna. AE, D, MC, V.*

$–$$$$ **Casa Cody.** The service is personal and gracious at this Western-style B&B a few steps from the Palm Springs Desert Museum. Spacious studios and one- and two-bedroom suites are furnished simply. Some have fireplaces, and most have kitchens. In 1998, the owners opened an historic adobe on the property dating to 1910. ✉ *175 S. Cahuilla Rd., 92262,* ☎ *760/320–9346 or 800/231–2639,* FAX *760/325–8610. 14 rooms, 9 suites. 2 pools, outdoor hot tub. AE, D, DC, MC, V. CP.*

$$–$$$ **Bee Charmer Inn.** This Southwestern-style inn with a red-tile roof and terra-cotta tile floors caters exclusively to women. Spacious rooms, which surround a pool and tropical courtyard, come with refrigerators and microwaves. Most have wet bars, and one has a whirlpool bath. ✉ *1600 E. Palm Canyon Dr., 92264,* ☎ *760/778–5883 or 888/321–5699,* FAX *760/416–2200. 13 rooms. Pool. AE, D, DC, MC, V. CP.*

$$–$$$ **Hampton Inn.** This chain motel at the north end of Palm Springs offers views of Mount San Jacinto. Appointments are basic, but there are barbecues for guest use. ✉ *200 N. Palm Canyon Dr., 92262,* ☎ *760/320–0555 or 800/732–7755,* FAX *760/320–2261. 93 rooms. Pool, outdoor hot tub, meeting rooms. AE, D, DC, MC, V. CP.*

$$ **Inn Exile.** One of a cluster of a dozen or so motel-style accommodations near Warm Sands Drive that cater to gay men, the Inn Exile features attractive rooms decorated in Southwestern motifs. The entire complex is clothing-optional. Ask for a room facing the main pool. ✉ *545 Warm Sands Dr., 92264,* ☎ *760/327–6413 or 800/962–0182,* FAX *760/320–5745. 31 rooms. In-room VCRs, 4 pools, 2 hot tubs, steam room, health club, billiards. AE, D, DC, MC, V.*

$–$$ **Vagabond Inn.** Rooms are smallish at this centrally located motel but they're clean, comfortable, and a good value. ✉ *1699 S. Palm Canyon Dr., 92264,* ☎ *760/325–7211 or 800/522–1555,* FAX *760/322–9269. 117 rooms, 3 suites. Coffee shop, pool, outdoor hot tub, 2 saunas. AE, D, DC, MC, V.*

$ **Howard Johnson Lodge.** This typical motel-style property is popular with tour groups. Ask about special discounts. ✉ *701 E. Palm Canyon Dr., 92264,* ☎ *760/320–2700 or 800/854–4345,* FAX *760/320–1591. 202 rooms, 1 suite. Pool, 3 outdoor hot tubs, coin laundry, business services. AE, D, DC, MC, V.*

RANCHO MIRAGE

$$$$ ★ **Rancho Las Palmas Marriott Resort & Spa.** The atmosphere is luxuriously laid-back at this family-oriented resort on 240 landscaped acres. A Spanish theme prevails throughout the public areas and guest accommodations. Rooms in a series of two-story buildings are unusually large; all have sitting areas, private balconies or patios, and views of colorful gardens or well-manicured fairways and greens. A luxury spa with 26 treatment rooms and a salon opened in early 1999. ✉ *41-000 Bob Hope Dr., 92270,* ☎ *760/568–2727 or 800/458–8786,* FAX *760/568–5845. 450 rooms, 22 suites. 4 restaurants, bar, 2 snack bars, 3 pools, barbershop, beauty salon, 3 outdoor hot tubs, 27-hole golf course, putting green, 25 tennis courts, health club, jogging, pro shop, children's programs, playground, concierge, business services, convention center, car rental. AE, D, DC, MC, V.*

$$$$ ★ **Ritz-Carlton Rancho Mirage.** This hotel is tucked into a hillside in the Santa Rosa Mountains with sweeping views of the valley below. The surroundings are elegant, with gleaming marble and brass, original artwork, plush carpeting, and remarkable comfort. All rooms are spacious and meticulously appointed with antiques, fabric wall coverings, marble bathrooms, and often two phones and two TVs. The service is impeccable. ✉ *68-900 Frank Sinatra Dr., 92270,* ☎ *760/321–8282 or 800/241–3333,* FAX *760/321–6928. 219 rooms, 21 suites. 3 restaurants, 2 bars, pool, beauty salon, outdoor hot tub, spa, golf privileges, putting green, 10 tennis courts, basketball, croquet, health club, hiking, volleyball, shops, children's programs, concierge, concierge floor, business services, meeting rooms. AE, D, DC, MC, V.*

$$$$ **Westin Mission Hills Resort.** A sprawling Moroccan-style resort on 360 acres, the Westin is surrounded by fairways and putting greens. Rooms, in two-story buildings surrounded by patios and fountains, are decorated with soft desert colors. Paths and creeks meander through the complex, encircling a lagoon-style swimming pool with a several-story water slide. ✉ *71-333 Dinah Shore Dr., 92270,* ☎ *760/328–5955 or 800/335–3545,* FAX *760/321–2607. 472 rooms, 40 suites. 2 restaurants, bar, 3 snack bars, 3 pools, beauty salon, 4 outdoor hot tubs, steam room, 2 18-hole golf courses, 7 tennis courts, croquet, health club, shuffleboard, volleyball, recreation room, children's programs, meeting rooms. AE, D, DC, MC, V.*

Nightlife and the Arts

BARS AND CLUBS

Bananaz Grill & Bar (✉ 72–291 Hwy. 111, Palm Desert, ☎ 760/776–4333) has dancing nightly, live music on Sunday, a billiards room, and a big-screen TV. **Blue Guitar,** (✉ 120 S. Palm Canyon Dr., Palm Springs, ☎ 760/327–1549) owned by jazz artists Kal David and Lauri Bono, presents world-class jazz and blues. There are two shows nightly Thursday through Sunday. **Hair of the Dog English Pub** (✉ 238 N. Palm Canyon Dr., Palm Springs, ☎ 760/323–9890), is a friendly bar popular with a young crowd that likes to tip back English ales and ciders. **Peabody's Jazz Studio and Coffee Bar** (✉ 134 S. Palm Canyon Dr., Palm Springs, ☎ 760/322–1877) attracts everyone from grannies to grungers for live jazz. **Zelda's** (✉ 169 N. Indian Canyon Dr., Palm Springs, ☎ 760/325–2375) has two rooms, one featuring techno jazz and another with Top-40 dance music and a male dance revue.

CASINOS

The casino picture in the desert is undergoing a radical change since California voters legalized Las Vegas-style gambling in 2000. Native American tribes that operate casinos in the desert are expanding their facilities and adding new ones. The Agua Caliente expect to open a huge casino and resort hotel near I–10 at the intersection of Ramon

Road and Bob Hope Drive. The casino, set to open in 2001, will house 750 slot machines, 44 gaming tables, off-track betting, and four restaurants. For those who can't wait, several casinos are already up and running. **Casino Morongo** (✉ Cabazon off-ramp, I–10, ☎ 909/849–3080) is about 20 minutes west of Palm Springs. **Fantasy Springs Casino** (✉ Golf Club Parkway off I–10, ☎ 760/342–5000) is east of Palm Springs in Indio. **Spa Hotel and Casino** (✉ 140 N. Indian Canyon Dr., ☎ 760/323–5865) is in the middle of downtown. **Spotlight 29 Casino** (✉ 46-200 Harrison Pl., ☎ 760/775–5566) is east of Palm Springs in Coachella.

FESTIVALS

The mid-January **Nortel Palm Springs International Film Festival** (☎ 760/322–2930) brings stars and more than 150 feature films from 25 countries, plus panel discussions, short films, and documentaries, to Palm Desert's McCallum Theatre and other venues. The **La Quinta Arts Festival** (☎ 760/564–1244), normally held the third weekend in March, includes some fine work, entertainment, and food. The **White Party** (☎ 888/777–8886), held on Easter weekend, draws tens of thousands of gays from around the country.

THEATER

Annenberg Theater (✉ Palm Springs Desert Museum, 101 Museum Dr., ☎ 760/325–4490) hosts Broadway shows, opera, lectures, Sunday-afternoon chamber concerts, and other events. **Fabulous Palm Springs Follies** (✉ Plaza Theater, 128 S. Palm Canyon Dr., ☎ 760/327–0225), the hottest ticket in the desert, presents 10 sellout performances each week from November through May. The vaudeville-style revue stars extravagantly costumed, retired (but very much in shape) showgirls, singers, and dancers. Tickets are priced from $30 to $65. **McCallum Theatre** (✉ 73-000 Fred Waring Dr., Palm Desert, ☎ 760/340–2787), the principal cultural venue in the desert, presents film, classical and popular music, opera, ballet, and theater.

Outdoor Activities and Sports

BICYCLING

Big Horn Bicycles (✉ 302 N. Palm Canyon, Palm Springs, ☎ 760/325–3367) operates tours to celebrity homes and Indian Canyons and rents bikes. **Big Wheel Bike Tours** (✉ Box 4185, Palm Desert, ☎ 760/779–1837) will deliver mountain, three-speed, and tandem bikes to area hotels. **Palm Springs Recreation Department** (✉ 401 S. Pavilion Way, ☎ 760/323–8272) has maps of some city trails.

FAMILY FUN

Camelot Park (✉ 67-700 E. Palm Canyon Dr., Cathedral City, ☎ 760/770–7522) features miniature golf, bumper boats, batting cages, an arcade, and video games. **Oasis Waterpark** (✉ 1500 Gene Autry Trail, Palm Springs, ☎ 760/327–0499), open from mid-March through October (weekends only after Labor Day), has 13 water slides, a huge wave pool, an arcade, and other attractions.

FITNESS

Gold's Gym (✉ 4070 Airport Center Dr., Palm Springs, ☎ 760/322–4653; ✉ 39-605 Entrepreneur La., Palm Desert, ☎ 760/360–0565).

GOLF

Palm Springs hosts more than 100 golf tournaments annually. The Palm Springs Desert Resorts Convention and Visitors Bureau **Events Hotline** (☎ 760/770–1992) lists dates and locations. The **Bob Hope Desert Classic** takes place in late January and early February. The **Nabisco Championship** is a March or April event. **Golf a la Cart** (☎ 760/324–5012) can arrange tee-times on 32 courses.

Golf Resort at Indian Wells (✉ 44-500 Indian Wells La., Indian Wells, ☎ 760/346–4653), located next to the Hyatt Grand Champions Resort, has two 18-hole Ted Robinson–designed championship courses. Named one of the country's top 10 resorts by *Golf Magazine*, it features a 6,500–yard West Course and a 6,700–yard East Course. Greens fees Monday through Thursday are $130 and $140 on weekends; they may be discounted in summer. The resort also offers golf instruction through the Indian Wells Golf School. **Tahquitz Creek Palm Springs Golf Resort** (✉ 1885 Golf Club Dr., Palm Springs, ☎ 760/328–1005) has two 18-hole, par-72 courses and a 50-space driving range. The greens fees, including cart, range from $65–$90, depending on the course and day of the week. **Tommy Jacobs' Bel-Aire Greens Country Club** (✉ 1001 S. El Cielo Rd., Palm Springs, ☎ 760/322–6062) is a nine-hole executive course. The greens fee is $19 ($12 for replay). **PGA West** (✉ 49-499 Eisenhower Dr., La Quinta, ☎ 760/564–7170) operates two 18-hole, par-72 championship courses and provides instruction and golf clinics. The greens fee ranges from $85 on weekdays in summer to $260 in February and March. The fee includes a mandatory cart. **Westin Mission Hills Resort Golf Club** (✉ 71-501 Dinah Shore Dr., Rancho Mirage, ☎ 760/328–3198), an 18-hole, par-70 course designed by Pete Dye, hosts major tournaments and well-known politicians and movie stars. The greens fee is $175 during peak season, including a mandatory cart; off-season promotional packages during the summer are sometimes as low as $50. Gary Player designed the Westin's other links, an 18-hole, par-72 course where the greens fee ranges from $50 to $175, depending on when you play.

POLO

The **Eldorado Polo Club** (✉ 50-950 Madison St., Indio, ☎ 760/342–2223), known as the Winter Polo Capital of the West, is home to world-class polo events. You can pack a picnic and watch practice matches free during the week; there's a $6 per person charge on Sunday.

TENNIS

The **Tennis Masters Series** world-class professional tennis tournament (☎ 760/360–3346) is held at the Indian Wells Tennis Garden for 10 days in March. The stadium, opened in 2000, is the second largest in the nation with more than 16,000 seats.

Demuth Park (✉ 4375 Mesquite Ave., ☎ no phone) has four lighted courts. **Ruth Hardy Park** (✉ Tamarisk and Caballeros, ☎ no phone) has eight lighted courts.

Shopping

SHOPPING DISTRICTS

Palm Desert's **El Paseo,** a long, Mediterranean-style avenue with fountains and courtyards, contains French and Italian fashion boutiques, shoe salons, jewelry stores, children's shops, restaurants, and nearly 30 galleries. Stores here are generally open from 10 to 6 Monday through Saturday; some close in summer. **Gardens of El Paseo,** opened in 1999 and anchored by Saks Fifth Avenue, holds such stores as Eddie Bauer, Brooks Brothers, Ann Taylor, Banana Republic, and Williams–Sonoma. **Westfield Shoppingtown** (formerly Desert Town Center) is the largest enclosed mall in the desert, with an ice-skating rink and more than 140 specialty shops, department stores, movie theaters, and restaurants.

Palm Canyon Drive is the main shopping destination in the city of Palm Springs. Its commercial core extends from Alejo Road south to Ramon Road. Anchoring the center of the drive is the Desert Walk, with Saks Fifth Avenue and about 35 boutiques. The popular Village Fest, along Palm Canyon here on Thursday night, brings out craftspeople, antiques sellers, a farmers market, and entertainment.

ANTIQUES AND COLLECTIBLES

Some of the items for sale in the **Heritage Gallery and Antique District,** a collection of consignment and secondhand shops centered in the 700 and 800 blocks of North Palm Canyon Drive in Palm Springs, come from the homes of celebrities and other wealthy residents. **Celebrity Seconds** (✉ 333 N. Palm Canyon Dr., Palm Springs, ☎ 760/416–2072) sells hot items such as Ginger Rogers' private collection of gowns and jewelry and dresses once worn by Julie Andrews and Elizabeth Taylor. **Cheryl Rhodes Coleman for Angel & Archer Estate Jewelers** (✉ 73-833 El Paseo, Palm Desert, ☎ 760/341–1122) specializes in diamonds, antique engagement rings, and watches. **Classic Consignment Co.** (✉ 73-847 El Paseo, Palm Desert, ☎ 760/568–4948) shows Baccarat crystal, barely used contemporary glass and Lucite furnishings, accessories, fine art, and jewelry. Prices match the shop's trendy location. **Estate Sale Co.** (✉ 4185 E. Palm Canyon Dr., Palm Springs, ☎ 760/321–7628) is the biggest consignment store in the desert, with a warehouse of furniture, fine art, china and crystal, accessories, jewelry, movie memorabilia, and exercise equipment. Prices are set to keep merchandise moving. **The Village Emporium** (✉ 849 N. Palm Canyon Dr., Palm Springs, ☎ 760/320–6165) specializes in Oriental arts and furnishings.

CLOTHING

Caroldean El Paseo/Caroldean Body & Sole (✉ 73-130 El Paseo, Palm Desert, ☎ 760/341–8982) features designer fashions and shoes by Vera Wang, Natalie M, and Brighton. **Nicole Miller Palm Desert** (✉ 73-061 El Paseo, Palm Desert, ☎ 760/862–9242) carries a line of signature golf togs, plus funky ties, shirts, dresses, and accessories. **St. John Boutique** (✉ 73-061 El Paseo, Palm Desert, ☎ 760/568–5900) offers the latest knit fashions from the famed designer.

DRIED FRUIT

Hadley's Fruit Orchards (✉ 50130 Main St., Cabazon, ☎ 909/849–5255) sells dried fruit, nuts, date shakes, and wines. **Oasis Date Gardens** (✉ 59-111 Hwy. 111, Thermal, ☎ 760/399–5665) sells shakes and conducts twice-a-day tours that show how dates are pollinated, grown, sorted, stored, and packed for shipping. **Shields Date Gardens** (✉ 80-225 Hwy. 111, Indio, ☎ 760/347–0996) presents a continuous slide program on the history of the date and sells shakes.

FACTORY OUTLETS

Desert Hills Factory Stores (✉ 48-650 Seminole Rd., Cabazon, ☎ 909/849–6641) is an outlet center with more than 150 brand-name discount fashion shops, among them Polo, Giorgio Armani, Nike, and Spa Gear.

VINTAGE CLOTHING

Patsy's Clothes Closet (✉ 4121 E. Palm Canyon Dr., Palm Springs, ☎ 760/324–8825) specializes in high-fashion and designer clothing for women and men.

Side Trip to Joshua Tree National Park via Desert Hot Springs

Joshua Tree National Park in the Little San Bernardino Mountains preserves some of the desert's most interesting and beautiful scenery. For visitors it also provides a living example of the rigors of desert life. Highlights of rock formations, historic sites, and unusual plants can be seen in half a day. A more thorough expedition into the backcountry takes a day or more. There are campgrounds within the park, but no other accommodations (a few quaint lodgings can be found in the towns along the northern edge of the park). Desert Hot Springs, Joshua Tree, and Twentynine Palms are among the towns on the northern route to the park—Gene Autry Trail north from Palm Springs to Pierson Boulevard west in Desert Hot Springs to Highway 62. If you aren't going to visit Desert Hot Springs, you can take Interstate 10 northwest from Palm Springs to connect with Highway 62.

Desert Hot Springs

9 mi north of Palm Springs on Gene Autry Trail.

10 Known for its hot mineral springs, Desert Hot Springs is home to more than 40 spa resorts, ranging from tiny to large and offering a variety of exotic treatments.

LODGING

$$$$ **Two Bunch Palms Resort and Spa.** This gate-guarded resort (you must call for advance reservations) is the most exclusive and romantic resort in the desert. According to legend, gangster Al Capone built the stone-fortress watchtower. The resort is the spa of choice for celebrities who savor the 148° mineral waters, the laid-back atmosphere, and the privacy. Massage styles include Swedish, Japanese, and Native American. The landscaped grounds contain two rock-grotto mineral pools surrounded by palms, secluded picnic areas, meditation benches, and outdoor mud baths. Accommodations range from hotel-style rooms to luxury villas with living rooms, kitchens, private whirlpool tubs, and private patios. ✉ *67–425 Two Bunch Palms Trail, 92240,* ☎ *760/329–8791 or 800/472–4334,* FAX *760/329–1874. 19 rooms, 26 suites. Restaurant, bar, 2 pools, spa, 2 tennis courts, health club, hiking. AE, MC, V. CP.*

OFF THE BEATEN PATH **BIG MORONGO CANYON PRESERVE** – Once a Native American village and later a cattle ranch, this serene natural oasis contains a year-round stream and waterfalls that support a variety of birds and animals. Cottonwoods and willows line a stream favored by great horned owls and many songbirds. A shaded meadow is a fine place for a picnic, and hiking options include several choice trails. No pets are permitted. ✉ *East Dr., Morongo Valley,* ☎ *760/363–7190.* *Free.* *Daily 7:30 am–sunset.*

Joshua Tree

17 mi from Desert Hot Springs, north and east on Hwy. 62.

Primarily a gateway to the national park, the town of Joshua Tree has basic services, a few fast-food outlets, and one lodging of note.

LODGING

$$$–$$$$ **Joshua Tree Inn.** If these walls could talk: this 1950s-style B&B was a motel popular with rock stars in the 1970s and early 1980s. The building's cinder-block construction is still visible, but there's a nice garden and a pool. ✉ *61259 29 Palms Hwy., 92252,* ☎ *760/366–1188 or 800/366–1444,* FAX *760/366–3805. 8 rooms, 2 suites. In-room data ports, pool. AE, D, DC, MC, V. BP.*

Twentynine Palms

11 mi east of Joshua Tree on Hwy. 62, 56 mi from Palm Springs, northwest on I–10 and north and east on Hwy. 62.

Colorful outdoor murals depicting local history are among the ways this onetime liberty town for U.S. Marines is trying to lure visitors headed to Joshua Tree National Park.

LODGING

$–$$$$ **29 Palms Inn.** The funky 29 Palms, on the Oasis of Mara (☞ Joshua Tree National Park, *below*), comprises a collection of adobe and wood-frame cottages scattered about 70 acres. The contemporary fare at the inn's popular restaurant is more sophisticated than its Western ambience. ✉ *73950 Inn Ave., 92277,* ☎ *760/367–3505,* FAX *760/367–4425. 15 rooms, 4 suites. Restaurant, pool, hot tub. AE, D, DC, MC, V. CP.*

$$–$$$ **Homestead Inn.** An authentic throwback to the old days in the desert, the Homestead is run by a salt-of-the-earth innkeeper who keeps a flock of roadrunners as pets. The rooms are comfortable, but not particularly stylish; a couple have their original tiles and fixtures. Three have refrigerators, phones, TV/VCRs, microwaves, and private patios; two have fireplaces and whirlpool tubs. ✉ *74153 Two Mile Rd., 92277,* ☎ *760/367–0030 or 877/367–0030,* FAX *760/367–1108. 7 rooms. AE, D, MC, V. Closed early July–Aug. BP.*

$–$$$ **Roughley Manor.** No expense was spared by the wealthy pioneer who erected the stone mansion now occupied by this B&B. A 50-ft-long planked maple floor is the centerpiece of the great room, the carpentry on the walls throughout is intricate, and huge stone fireplaces warm the house on the rare cold night. Original fixtures still gleam in the bathrooms, and the elegant bedrooms are furnished with pencil and canopy beds. An acre or so of gardens shaded by Washingtonia palms surrounds the house. ✉ *74744 Joe Davis Dr., 92277,* ☎ *760/367–3238,* FAX *760/367–4483. 7 rooms, 5 with shared baths, 2 suites. Hot tub. AE, MC, V. BP.*

$–$$ **Best Western Gardens Motel.** This bright complex has smartly furnished rooms, some of which have coffeemakers, refrigerators, and microwaves. Hot tubs are available in three rooms. ✉ *71-487 Twentynine Palms Hwy., 92277,* ☎ *760/367–9141,* FAX *760/367–2584. 72 rooms, 12 suites. Pool, outdoor hot tub, coin laundry, business services. AE, D, DC, MC, V. CP.*

Joshua Tree National Park

★ ⓫ *61 mi from Palm Springs, northwest on I–10, north and east on Hwy. 62 to the town of Joshua Tree; from here head southeast on Park Blvd. to the park's west entrance or continue east on Hwy. 62 to Twentynine Palms and follow signs to Utah Trail and the north entrance.*

The 794,000-acre Joshua Tree National Park contains complex, ruggedly beautiful scenery. Its mountains of jagged rock, natural cactus gardens, and lush oases shaded by tall fan palms mark the meeting place of the Mojave (high) and Colorado (low) deserts. This is prime hiking, rock climbing, and exploring country, where coyotes, desert pack rats, and such exotic plants as the white yucca, red-tipped ocotillo, and cholla cactus reside. Extensive stands of Joshua trees give the park its name. The trees were named by early white settlers who felt their thick, stubby branches resembled the biblical Joshua raising his arms toward heaven.

Portions of the park can be seen in a half-day excursion from desert-resort cities. A full day's driving tour would allow time for a nature walk or two and stops at many of the 50 wayside exhibits, which provide insight into Joshua Tree's geology and rich vegetation. Some of the park is above 4,000 ft so it can be chilly in winter. There are no services within the park and little water. Visitors are advised to carry a gallon of water per person per day.

Those planning a half-day visit to Joshua Tree National Park should enter through the West Entrance Station off Highway 62 at Joshua Tree and follow the Park Boulevard loop road to the North Entrance Station near Twentynine Palms. The stands of Joshua trees along this route are particularly alluring in spring, when the upraised branches support creamy blossoms. The many piles of rocks in this section are fun to explore and climb.

Those planning to spend a full day in the park can proceed through the west entrance, explore the northern loop, stop at the Oasis Visitor Center, and then take the stunning but winding desert drive southward toward the Cottonwood Springs area, which in spring has one of the desert's best displays of wildflowers. The Cottonwood Visitor Center has a small museum, picnic tables, water, and a 1-mi interpretive trail to the **Cottonwood Spring Oasis,** which gets very crowded in spring.

The **Oasis Visitor Center** (✉ Utah Trail, ½ mi south of Hwy. 62) has many free and inexpensive brochures, books, posters, and maps as well as several educational exhibits. Rangers are on hand to answer questions. **Oasis of Mara** (a ½-mi walk from the visitor center), inhabited first by Native Americans and later by prospectors and homesteaders, now provides a home for birds, small mammals, and other wildlife.

A crawl through the big boulders that block **Hidden Valley,** once a cattle rustlers' hideout, reveals a bit of the wild and woolly human history of Joshua Tree. The 1⅒-mi loop trail from Hidden Valley to **Barker Dam** goes past petroglyphs (painted over by a film crew) on the way to a dam built by early ranchers and miners; today the dam collects rainwater and is used by wildlife.

Keys View is the most dramatic overlook in Joshua Tree National Park. At elevation 5,185 ft, the view extends across the desert to Mount San Jacinto and on clear days as far south as the Salton Sea. Sunrise and sunset are magical times, when the light throws rocks and trees into high relief before (or after) bathing the hills in brilliant shades of red, orange, and gold.

Geology Tour Road, recommended for four-wheel-drive vehicles, is a self-guided 18-mi dirt road that winds through some of the park's most fascinating landscapes.

At the **Cholla Cactus Gardens,** a huge stand of the legendary "jumping cactus," trail markers tell of the wildlife and plants typical of the Colorado Desert.

The ranger-led **Desert Queen Ranch Walking Tour** reveals details of the lives of early settlers Bill and Frances Keys, who spent 60 years eking out a living in this harsh climate. Recently restored to resemble the site in 1969 when Bill died, the ranch contains mining equipment, the ranch house, school, store, and workshop. Rangers lead tours daily; reservations are required (☎ 760/367–5555).

If you're entering the park from the south, you'll pass the Cottonwood Visitor Center a few miles after you exit Interstate 10 (head north) east of the town of Mecca. The center has a small museum, picnic tables, water, rest rooms, and a 1-mi trail to the **Cottonwood Spring Oasis.**

✉ *Joshua Tree National Park, 74-485 National Park Dr., Twentynine Palms 92277,* ☎ *760/367–5500.* *$10 per car; $5 for those who arrive by other means.* *Visitor centers daily 8–4:30, park 24 hrs.*

PALM SPRINGS A TO Z

Arriving and Departing

By Bus

Greyhound (☎ 800/231–2222) provides service to the Palm Springs Depot (✉ 311 N. Indian Canyon Dr., ☎ 760/325–2053).

By Car

Palm Springs is about a two-hour drive east of Los Angeles and a three-hour drive northeast of San Diego. Highway 111 brings you right onto Palm Canyon Drive, the main thoroughfare in Palm Springs and the connecting route to other desert communities. From Los Angeles take the San Bernardino Freeway (I–10) east to Highway 111. From San Diego, I–15 heading north connects with the Pomona Freeway (Highway 60), leading to the San Bernardino Freeway (I–10) east. An alternative, more scenic, good-weather route from San Diego begins east on I–8. Then take Highways 67, 78, and 79 north to Aguanga, where Highway 371 heads east to Highway 74 (Palms to Pines Highway), which joins Highway 111 between Palm Desert and Indian Wells. Desert exits are clearly marked: Highway 111 for Palm Springs, Monterey for Palm Desert, Washington for La Quinta. If you're coming from the Riverside area, you can also take Highway 74 east.

By Plane

Major airlines serving **Palm Springs International Airport** (☎ 760/323–8161) include Alaska, American/American Eagle, America West Express, Continental, Delta Connection/Skywest, Northwest, United/United Express, and United Shuttle. *See* Air Travel *in* Smart Travel Tips A to Z for airline phone numbers. Most hotels provide service to and from the airport, which is about 2 mi from downtown Palm Springs.

By Train

The **Amtrak** (☎ 800/872–7245) *Sunset Limited,* which runs between Florida and Los Angeles, stops in Palm Springs and Indio.

Getting Around

By Bus

SunBus, operated by the Sunline Transit Agency (☎ 760/343–3451), serves the entire Coachella Valley from Desert Hot Springs to Mecca.

By Car

The desert-resort communities occupy a stretch of about 20 mi between Interstate 10 in the east and Palm Canyon Drive in the west. Although some areas such as Palm Canyon Drive in Palm Springs and El Paseo are walkable, having a car is the best way to get around.

By Taxi

California Cab (☎ 760/772–1793) serves the Coachella Valley and Los Angeles and Ontario International airports. **A Valley Cabousine** (☎ 760/340–5845) serves the Coachella Valley.

Contacts and Resources

Car Rental

Most major car-rental companies are represented in the Palm Springs area (☞ Car Rental *in* Smart Travel Tips A to Z).

Emergencies

Ambulance (☎ 911). **Police** (☎ 911).

Desert Regional Medical Center (☎ 760/323–6500).

Guided Tours

AERIAL TOURS

Fantasy Balloon Flights (☎ 760/398–6322) organizes trips in the Coachella Valley. **Sunrise Balloons** (☎ 800/548–9912) offers private balloon excursions in the desert from April through October.

CELEBRITY TOURS

Palm Springs Celebrity Tours (✉ 4751 E. Palm Canyon Dr., Palm Springs, ☎ 760/770–2700) has hour-long and 2½-hour tours that cover Palm Springs area history, points of interest, and celebrity homes. Prices range from $17 to $20.

DESERT TOURS

Covered Wagon Tours (☎ 760/347–2161) takes visitors on an old-time, two-hour exploration of the desert with a cookout at the end of the journey. **Desert Adventures** (☎ 760/324–5337) takes to the wilds with Jeep tours of Indian canyons, off-road in the Santa Rosa Mountains, and into a mystery canyon. **Desert Safari Guides** (✉ Box 194, Rancho Mirage, ☎ 760/770–9191 or 888/867–2327) leads tours of various lengths through Indian Canyons and conducts nighttime full-moon desert excursions.

Vacation Rentals

McLean Company Rentals (✉ 477 S. Palm Canyon Dr., Palm Springs 92262, ☎ 760/322–7878). **Rental Connection** (✉ 170 E. Palm Canyon Dr., Palm Springs 92263, ☎ 760/320–7336 or 800/462–7256). **Sunrise Co.** (✉ 76-300 Country Club Dr., Palm Desert 92211, ☎ 800/869–1130).

Visitor Information

Palm Springs Desert Resorts (✉ 69-930 Hwy. 111, Suite 201, Rancho Mirage 92270, ☎ 760/770–9000; 800/417–3529; 760/770–1992 Activities Hotline). **Palm Springs Visitor Information Center** (✉ 2781 N. Palm Canyon Dr., Palm Springs 92262, ☎ 800/347–7746).

15 THE MOJAVE DESERT AND DEATH VALLEY

When most people assemble their "must-see" list of California attractions, the desert isn't often among the top contenders. With its heat and vast, sparsely populated tracts of land, the desert is no Disneyland. But that's precisely why it deserves a closer look. The natural riches here are overwhelming: rolling waves of sand dunes, black cinder cones thrusting up hundreds of feet from a blistered desert floor, riotous sheets of wildflowers, bizarrely shaped Joshua trees basking in the orange glow of a sunset, and an abundant silence that is both dramatic and startling. A single car speeding down an empty road can sound as loud as a low-flying airplane.

Updated by Sasha Abramsky

THE MOJAVE DESERT begins at the base of the San Bernardino Mountains, northeast of Los Angeles, and extends north 150 mi into the Eureka Valley and east 200 mi to the Colorado River. Death Valley lies north and east of the Mojave, jutting into Nevada near Beatty. The Mojave, with elevations ranging from 3,000 ft to 5,000 ft above sea level, is known as the High Desert. Death Valley, the Low Desert, drops to almost 300 ft below sea level and contains the lowest spot on land in the Western Hemisphere.

Because of the vast size of California's deserts, an area about as big as Ohio, and the frequently extreme weather, careful planning is essential. Conveniences, facilities, gas stations, and supermarkets do not lurk around the corner from many desert sights. Be sure to fill your tank before entering Death Valley. Fuel is cheaper on the interstates. Also, check your vehicle's fluids and tire pressure. Shut off your air-conditioning on steep grades to avoid engine overheating.

Believe everything you've ever heard about desert heat. It can be brutal. But during mornings and evenings, particularly in the spring and fall, the temperature ranges from cool and crisp to pleasantly warm and dry. If you don't mind freezing temperatures in the early mornings, winter is actually the best time to visit Death Valley. Bring sunglasses, a hat, and sufficient clothing to block the sun's rays or the wind. Reliable maps are a must, as signage is often limited or, in some places, nonexistent. Other important accessories include a compass, a cellular phone (though these don't always work in remote areas), extra food and water (three gallons per person per day is recommended, plus additional radiator water). If you have access to a four wheel drive, bring it: many of Death Valley's most spectacular canyons are only reachable in a 4 by 4. A pair of binoculars can come in handy, and don't forget your camera. You're likely to see things you've never seen before.

Pleasures and Pastimes

Camping

Because vegetation in the desert is sparse, campers are truly one with the elements, including the hot sun. Bring equipment that can handle extreme temperatures. Campgrounds are inexpensive or free. Most sites are primitive.

Dining

The restaurants in Death Valley range from a coffee shop to an upscale Continental restaurant. There are fast-food and chain establishments in Ridgecrest, Victorville, and Barstow, as well as some ethnic eateries. Experienced desert travelers carry an ice chest stocked with food and beverages. Replenish your food stash in the larger towns of Ridgecrest and Barstow, where you'll find a better selection and non-tourist prices.

CATEGORY	COST*
$$$$	over $50
$$$	$30–$50
$$	$20–$30
$	under $20

**per person for a three-course meal, excluding drinks, service, and tax*

Hiking

Hiking trails are abundant throughout the desert and meander toward sights that would be missed from the road. Plan your walks for before or after the noonday sun, bring protective clothing, and be wary of tarantulas, snakes, and other potentially hazardous creatures. (If you wear closed shoes and watch where you're walking, these shouldn't be a problem). Paths through canyons are sometimes partially shielded from the sun and not as hot, so if your time is limited, save these for midday. Some of the best trails are unmarked. Ask locals for directions.

Lodging

Larger towns such as Barstow seem to have a motel on every corner, but there are only three places to sleep indoors in all of Death Valley; the cheapest is in Stovepipe Wells Village. Those preferring quiet nights and an unfettered view of the desert sky and Mosaic Canyon will enjoy Stovepipe. Families with children may prefer the Furnace Creek end of Death Valley, where there's easy access to the visitor center and various sights.

CATEGORY	COST*
$$$$	over $175
$$$	$120–$175
$$	$80–$120
$	under $80

**All prices are for a standard double room, excluding tax.*

following the text of a review is your signal that the property has a Web site, where you will find details and, usually, images; for a link, visit www.fodors.com/urls.

Exploring the Desert

The Mojave Desert is a sprawling space, but many of its visitable attractions are conveniently situated on a north–south axis along U.S. 395 and Highway 178. The western Mojave region has Ridgecrest (on U.S. 395) as its major northern hub and Victorville (on I–15) as its southern one. If you plan to stop overnight en route to Death Valley, both Ridgecrest and Lone Pine have tourist services and accommodations, as do Barstow and Baker on I–15. The bulk of the eastern Mojave lies between the parallel routes of I–15 and I–40. Barstow, at the junction of the two interstates, is the region's western hub. Needles, just inside the Nevada border at the intersection of I–40 and U.S. 95, has the most services on the eastern side. You may spot fossils at some of the archaeological sites in the desert. Leave any fossils you find where they are; it's against the law to remove them.

Numbers in the text correspond to numbers in the margin and on the Mojave Desert and Death Valley maps.

Great Itineraries

IF YOU HAVE 3 DAYS

Well-preserved Randsburg, part of the **Rand Mining District** ②, is a good starting point from either San Francisco or Los Angeles. Pack a picnic lunch and drive through colorful **Red Rock Canyon State Park** ③. Drive north an hour and take a walk among the volcanic rock formations of **Fossil Falls** ④ before moving on to **Ridgecrest** ⑤ for a stop at the Maturango Museum. Have dinner and spend the night in Ridgecrest. The following day, see the surreal **Trona Pinnacles Natural National Landmark** ⑥, and then continue on to the **Furnace Creek** ⑬ visitor center before catching awe-inspiring perspectives of the Death Valley region from **Artists Palette** ⑯, **Zabriskie Point** ⑰, and **Dante's View** ⑱. Return home on the third day after stopping at the **Harmony**

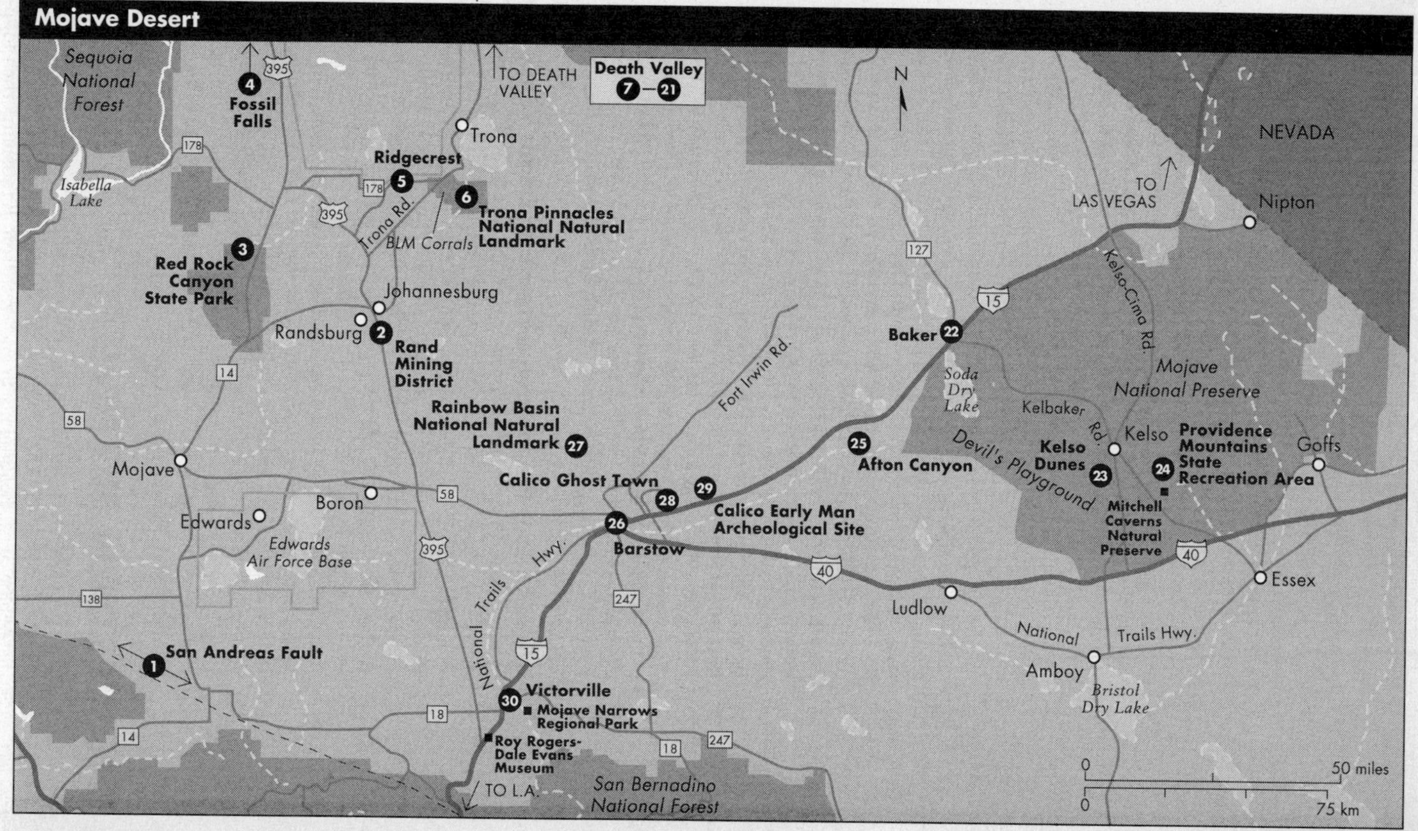
Mojave Desert
Sequoia National Forest
Isabella Lake
395
4
Fossil Falls
178
TO DEATH VALLEY
Death Valley
7—21
Trona
Ridgecrest
5
178
395
Trona Rd.
6
BLM Corrals
Trona Pinnacles National Natural Landmark
3
Red Rock Canyon State Park
Johannesburg
Randsburg
2
Rand Mining District
14
58
Rainbow Basin National Natural Landmark
27
Mojave
Boron
58
Edwards
Edwards Air Force Base
395
138
Calico Ghost Town
28
29
Calico Early Man Archeological Site
26
Barstow
Fort Irwin Rd.
National Trails Hwy.
247
15
1
San Andreas Fault
30
Victorville
Mojave Narrows Regional Park
18
Roy Rogers-Dale Evans Museum
18
247
TO L.A.
San Bernadino National Forest
N
127
15
Baker
22
Soda Dry Lake
25
Afton Canyon
40
Ludlow
TO LAS VEGAS
NEVADA
Nipton
Kelso-Cima Rd.
Mojave National Preserve
Kelbaker Rd.
Devil's Playground
Kelso
Kelso Dunes
23
24
Providence Mountains State Recreation Area
Mitchell Caverns Natural Preserve
Goffs
40
Essex
National Trails Hwy.
Amboy
Bristol Dry Lake
0
50 miles
0
75 km

Borax Works ⑫, where the famed 20-mule teams once toiled, and hiking through **Golden Canyon** ⑭.

IF YOU HAVE 6 OR 7 DAYS

If you're already in southern California, head to the **Western Mojave Desert,** touring the **Rand Mining District** ②, **Red Rock Canyon** ③, and **Fossil Falls** ④ before stopping in **Ridgecrest** ⑤ to dine and lodge. (If you're coming from northern California, visit Fossil Falls first and stop briefly at the Maturango Museum in Ridgecrest before driving to Red Rock Canyon and the Rand Mining District, where you can stay the night at the picturesque Cottage Hotel.) On your second day, visit the **Bureau of Land Management Regional Wild Horse and Burro Corrals** on the way to the **Trona Pinnacles Natural National Landmark** ⑥ and Death Valley's **Stovepipe Wells Village** ⑨. (If you're visiting on a spring or fall weekend, make advance arrangements at the Maturango Museum to tour the **Petroglyph Canyons.**) On the third morning, drive up to the old Charcoal Kilns, and then head to **Mosaic Canyon** for a brisk hike before driving north to spend an afternoon at **Scotty's Castle** ⑩ and **Ubehebe Crater** ⑪. Loop back toward **Furnace Creek** ⑬ and stop in at the visitor center in the late afternoon. If you're in the area on a performance day, zip down to Death Valley Junction to see the 7:45 PM show at **Marta Becket's Amargosa Opera House** ⑳. On day four, hike through **Golden Canyon** ⑭ and drive to **Badwater** ⑮ before returning via **Artists Palette** ⑯. Visit the lookout at **Zabriskie Point** ⑰ and walk along **Dante's View** ⑱ before driving south to **Baker** ㉒ to spend the night. Drive along Kelbaker Road to the **Kelso Dunes** ㉓ and visit the **Mitchell Caverns** in **Providence Mountains State Recreation Area** ㉔. If time and road conditions permit, drive through **Afton Canyon** ㉕ before staying overnight in **Barstow** ㉖. On day six, hike around the **Rainbow Basin National Natural Landmark** ㉗ and tour the **Calico Early Man Archeological Site** ㉙ (open from Wednesday through Sunday; the last tour starts at 3:30). On day seven, especially if you have children, visit **Calico Ghost Town** ㉘ before leaving the desert.

When to Tour the Mojave Desert and Death Valley

Spring and fall are the best seasons to tour the desert. Winters are generally mild, but summers can be brutal. If you're on a budget, keep in mind that room rates drop as the temperatures rise. Early morning is the best time to visit sights and avoid crowds, but some museums and visitor centers don't open until 10. If you schedule your town arrivals for late afternoon, you can drop by the visitor centers just before closing hours to line up an itinerary for the next day. It's best to visit the Rand Mining District on the weekend or, if you must come during the week, in the afternoon, when some of the antiques shops open up. Plan indoor activities for midday during hotter months. Because relatively few people visit the desert, many attractions have limited hours of access: Petroglyph Canyon tours are given on weekends only during fall and spring, the Calico Early Man Archeological Site does not offer tours Monday and Tuesday, and so on.

THE WESTERN MOJAVE

The prime western Mojave attractions are along or near U.S. 395 or Highways 14 and 178. After the San Andreas Fault the key sites are listed clockwise, heading north and west from Randsburg, then looping around eastward to the Trona Pinnacles.

❶ The infamous **San Andreas Fault** traverses the desert near Cajon Pass, a few miles south of I–15's U.S. 395 exit. If you're driving from Los Angeles, it's an apocalyptic way to start a desert trip.

Rand Mining District

❷ *137 mi northeast of Los Angeles, I–10 to I–15 to U.S. 395; 360 mi southeast of San Francisco, I–80 to I–580 to I–5 to Hwy. 178 to Hwy. 14 to U.S. 395.*

The towns of Randsburg, Red Mountain, and Johannesburg make up the Rand Mining District. **Randsburg** first boomed with the discovery of gold in the Rand Mountains in 1895 and, along with the neighboring settlements, grew to support the successful Yellow Aster Mine. Rich tungsten ore, used in World War I to make steel alloy, was discovered in 1907, and silver was found in 1919. Randsburg is one of the few gold-rush-era communities not to have become a ghost town; the tiny city jail is among the original buildings still standing. The small **Desert Museum** (✉ 161 Butte Ave., ☎ no phone) exhibits old mining paraphernalia and historic photos. Staffed by volunteers, it's open only on weekends and holidays, usually from late morning until mid-afternoon. **The Randsburg General Store** (✉ 35 Butte Ave., ☎ 760/374–2418) serves as the town's informal visitor center, selling maps, rockhounding guides, and a terrific selection of books on the gold rush and the Californian desert. With a century-old soda fountain, it's also a good place to stop to quench your thirst. It's open daily, unlike most of the town's dozen antiques shops, which tend to be shuttered during the week (though sometimes they open in the afternoon). **The White House Saloon,** open weekends, is one of the wild west's few surviving saloons, swinging wooden doors and all.

Johannesburg was founded as a slightly upmarket suburb of the rough gold-mining town of Randsburg. These days it's very ghostly, with spirits dwelling in the stunning Old West cemetery in the hills above town. It's one of the region's great hidden treasures.

Dining and Lodging

$ ✕ **Randsburg Opera House Café.** A very small diner in a very small town, this old wooden café is the meeting place for locals. Standard breakfast fare and a skimpy selection of burgers and sandwiches are about it here, but the staff is friendly. The only other options in town are the saloon and the general store. ✉ *26741 Butte Ave., Randsburg,* ☎ *760/374–1037. No credit cards.* ⏲ *Weekends only. No dinner.*

$ 🏨 **The Cottage Hotel.** An unexpectedly civilized lodging in rough-and-tumble Randsburg, this B&B resulted from a painstaking makeover of the boom-era hotel. You enter through an antiques shop to find wallpapered rooms done in Victorian style. All rooms have TVs and modern bathrooms, and two have private balconies. A back garden and a cedar-lined room with a hot tub are bonuses. The cottage next door has a kitchen, but its occupants don't get the breakfast guests of the hotel enjoy. ✉ *130 Butte Ave., Randsburg, 93554,* ☎ *760/374–2285 or 888/268–4622,* FAX *760/374–2132. 4 rooms, 1 cottage. Hot tub, meeting room. AE, D, MC, V. BP.*

$ 🏨 **HI-Death Valley Hostel.** You don't need a reservation at this basic ranch-style hostel. There are separate dorm-style quarters for men and women, a kitchen (fresh food is available for purchase), a dining area, and a common room with many books on the desert. Manager Michelle Mowey is a great desert character who loves to take the young people who stay with her on tours of the surrounding wilderness. ✉ *316 Hwy.*

395, Box 277, Johannesburg, 93528, ☎ FAX 760/374–2323. 2 dorm rooms, 1 private room, shared baths. No credit cards.

$ **Old Owl Inn.** This onetime whorehouse off Highway 395 still has a "Girl Wanted" sign on one wall and the original keys to the cubicles on another. In these tamer times, Lynn and Jeannie Walker run it as an antique shop and bed & breakfast. The larger cabin, constructed from the wood brought here by the old owner, can hold up to seven people. The smaller is slightly optimistically dubbed the Honeymoon Cottage. Both have small, functional bathrooms. Jeannie's grandfather came to the area in 1910 to dig for gold, and today she's a terrific source of information on the area. Ask her to point out the nearby mines and unmarked trails into the hills. ✉ *701 Hwy. 395, Red Mountain 93558,* ☎ *760/374–2235 or 888/653–6954,* FAX *760/374–2354. 2 cabins. D, MC, V.*

Red Rock Canyon State Park

❸ *17 mi west of U.S. 395 via Red Rock–Randsburg Rd., or you can enter from U.S. 14.*

A feast for the eyes with its layers of pink, white, red, and brown rocks, **Red Rock Canyon State Park** is a region of fascinating biological diversity—the ecosystems of the Sierra Nevada, the Mojave Desert, and the Basin Range all converge here. Entering the park from the south, you'll pass through a steep-walled gorge and come to a wide bowl tinted pink by what was once hot volcanic ash. Some anthropologists believe that the human history of this area goes back 20,000 years or more to the canyon dwellers known as the Old People; Mojave Indians roamed the land for centuries. Gold-rush fever hit the region in the mid-1800s, and you can still see remains of mining operations in the countryside. In the 20th century, Hollywood invaded the canyon, which has served as scenery for westerns, TV shows, commercials, and music videos. Its greatest claim to fame is as a backdrop in Steven Spielberg's *Jurassic Park*. If you are on Highway 14, check out the Red Cliffs Preserve, across the highway from the entrance to the Red Rock camping site. ✉ *Ranger station: Abbott Dr. off Hwy. 14,* ☎ *805/942–0662.* *$2 (day use).* *Visitor center weekends only.*

Camping

Red Rock Canyon State Park. The park's campground is in the colorful cliff region of the southern El Paso Mountains, which offer many hiking options. ✉ *Off Hwy. 14, 30 mi southwest of Ridgecrest,* ☎ *805/942–0662 for reservations. 50 sites.* *$10, $1 additional for dogs.* *Year-round.*

Fossil Falls

❹ *Off U.S. 395, 20 mi north of U.S. 395/Hwy. 14 junction.*

The stark, roughly hewn, mostly black basalt rocks at **Fossil Falls** (✉ Cinder Cone Rd., ½ mi east of U.S. 395) are the result of volcanic eruptions in the western Mojave region about 20,000 years ago. The fossils at Fossil Falls are the falls themselves—their source dried up centuries ago. The only time you'll see water here is when it's raining. A study in shape and texture, the falls drop off an impressive distance along a channel cut through hardened lava flows. A brief hike to the bottom of the formation leads to a spot where Native Americans once camped. South of the falls, the Owens River cut the huge valley between the Sierra Nevadas to the west and the Coso range to the east. There's a very primitive campsite amid the boulders.

Ridgecrest

5 *35 mi north of Randsburg, U.S. 395 to Hwy. 178.*

Ridgecrest, with dozens of stores, restaurants, and hotels, is a good base for exploring the northwestern Mojave.

The **Maturango Museum,** which also serves as a visitor information center, has pamphlets and books about the region. Small but informative exhibits detail the natural and cultural history of the northern Mojave. The museum runs wildflower tours in March and April. ✉ *100 E. Las Flores Ave., at China Lake Blvd., 93555,* ☎ *760/375–6900,* FAX *760/375–0479.* *$2; $5 for wildflower tour.* ⏲ *Daily 10–5.*

★ Guided tours offered by the Maturango Museum (☞ *above*) are the only way to the **Petroglyph Canyons,** among the desert's most amazing spectacles. (Call several months ahead, as space is limited on these full-day excursions.) The two canyons, commonly called Big and Little Petroglyph, are in the Coso mountain range on the million-acre U.S. Naval Weapons Center at China Lake. Each of the canyons holds a superlative concentration of rock art, the largest of its kind in the Northern Hemisphere. Thousands of images of animals and humans are scratched or pecked into the shiny desert varnish—oxidized minerals—that coats the canyon's dark basaltic rocks. The age of these well-preserved glyphs remains a matter of debate. Children under 10 are not allowed. ☎ *760/375–6900.* *$25; $45 for special extended trips for photographers and others who want to see sunrise and sunset in the Little Petroglyph Canyon.* ⏲ *Tours Mar.–June and Sept. or Oct.–1st weekend in Dec.*

OFF THE BEATEN PATH

WILD HORSE AND BURRO CORRALS – Animals gathered by the Bureau of Land Management from public lands throughout the Southwest are fed and prepared for adoption here. It's OK to bring along an apple or carrot to share with the horses (the burros are usually too wild to approach). ✉ *3 mi east of Ridgecrest via Hwy. 178 (make a right as the road reaches the top of the rise),* ☎ *760/446–6064; 800/446–6743 to arrange tours.* *Free.* ⏲ *Weekdays 7:30–4.*

6 **Trona Pinnacles National Natural Landmark** is not easy to reach, as the best road to the area can be impassable after a rainstorm. But it's worth the effort, especially to sci-fi buffs, who will recognize the landscape from the film *Star Trek V.* These fantastic looking formations of calcium carbonate, known as tufa, were formed underwater along fault lines in the bed of what is now Searles Dry Lake. A ½-mi trail winds around this surreal landscape of more than 500 spires, some of them rising as high as 140 ft. Wear sturdy shoes—tufa cuts like coral. ✉ *From the Trona–Red Mountain Rd., take Hwy. 178 east for 8 mi. Alternately, from U.S. 395 take Hwy. 178 for 29 mi to dirt intersection; turn southeast and go ½ mi to a fork. Continue south via right fork, cross railroad tracks, and drive onward 5 mi.*

The tiny town of Inyokern boasts the small outdoor **United States Aerospace Museum.** Old military fighters and transport planes are on display behind fencing. The locale, surrounded by mountains, is glorious in daylight. ✉ *Hwy. 178, just west of Inyokern.* *Free.*

Dining and Lodging

$–$$$ ★ ✕ **Santa Fe Grill.** Locals says this is the best of Ridgecrest's numerous restaurants. The many Hollywood crews that film in the Ridgecrest area might explain the presence of this unexpectedly hip and health-conscious New Mexican–style eatery in what is by and large a conservative military town. Hot tortillas, made on the premises, come to the table with a wonderful salsa, its distinctive smoky taste derived from fire-grilled chilies. Beans (not refried) and a sweet corn cake accompany most of the entrées. Specialties include seafood enchiladas and chicken fajitas. ✉ *901 N. Heritage Dr.,* ☎ *760/446–5404. AE, D, MC, V.*

$–$$ ✗🏨 **Heritage Inn.** All the rooms here have refrigerators and microwaves. The well-appointed, though somewhat bland, facility is geared toward commercial travelers, but the staff is equally attentive to tourists' concerns. A sister property nearby is an all-suites hotel. The Farris Restaurant, with a Continental menu, is a favorite fine-dining spot of locals. ✉ *1050 N. Norma St.,* ☎ *760/446–6543 or 800/843–0693,* FAX *760/446–2884. 125 rooms. Restaurant, bar, refrigerators, pool, hot tub, coin laundry, business services, meeting rooms. AE, D, DC, MC, V.*

$–$$ 🏨 **Carriage Inn.** This large, well-kept hotel caters both to visitors to the nearby military base and to travelers, with the Café Potpourri serving up an eclectic mix of California cuisine. Rooms are large and tastefully decorated. The poolside cabanas have a homier feel. A mister sprays water to cool off sunbathers during the hot summer months. ✉ *901 N. China Lake Blvd., 93555,* ☎ *760/446–7910 or 800/772–8527,* FAX *760/446–6408. 158 rooms, 2 suites, 2 cabanas. 2 restaurants, bar, pool, hot tubs, sauna, exercise room, meeting rooms. AE, D, DC, MC, V.*

$ 🏨 **The BevLen Bed & Breakfast.** A central location, country-cute rooms, and outgoing hosts—the retired couple Bev and Len de Geus—make this mustard-color, chalet-style B&B an appealing stop. The place is especially good for single guests, as the rates are low and only one of the three rooms is really large enough for two people. Atmospheric touches include antique log-burning stoves in the living rooms and a new wooden gazebo in the garden. ✉ *809 N. Sanders St., 93555,* ☎ *760/375–1988 or 800/375–1989,* FAX *760/375–6871. 3 rooms. Hot tub. AE, D, MC, V. BP.*

DEATH VALLEY

The topography of Death Valley is a lesson in geology. Two hundred million years ago seas covered the area, depositing layers of sediment and fossils. Between 35 million and 5 million years ago faults in the Earth's crust and volcanic activity pushed and folded the ground, causing mountain ranges to rise and the valley floor to drop. The valley was then filled periodically by lakes, which eroded the surrounding rocks into fantastic formations and deposited the salts that now cover the floor of the basin. The area has 14 square mi of sand dunes; 200 square mi of crusty salt flats; and hills, mountains, and canyons of many colors. There are more than 1,000 species of plants and trees—21 of which are unique to the valley, such as the yellow Panamint daisy and the blue-flowered Death Valley sage.

With more than 3.3 million acres, **Death Valley National Park** is the largest national park outside Alaska—and certainly the most uncomfortable at times. But seeing nature at its most extreme is precisely what attracts many people, especially Europeans. There are more visitors to Death Valley in July and August than in December and January. Distances can be deceiving: some sights appear in clusters, but others require extensive travel. The trip from Death Valley Junction to Scotty's Castle, for example, can take three hours or more. The entrance fee ($10 per vehicle), collected at the park's entrance stations and at the Visitor Center at Furnace Creek (☞ *below*), is valid for seven consecutive days.

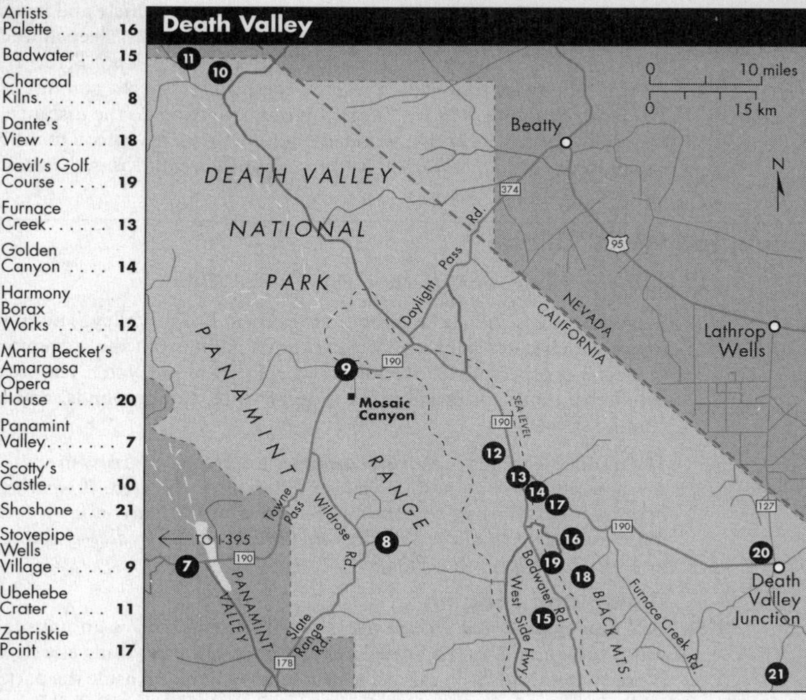

Panamint Valley

7 *75 mi north of Ridgecrest. Hwy. 178 to Hwy. 190 and 2 mi west on 190.*

This valley, located just before you reach the forbidding Panamint Range, is a great place to stop if you are arriving late in the day and don't want to drive over the windy mountain roads leading to Death Valley after dark. The views here are spectacular.

From Highway 178, turn north on Wildrose Canyon Road and east
8 onto the dirt track leading to the **Charcoal Kilns.** The drive will take about half an hour, but it's worth it. Ten stone kilns, 30-ft high and 25-ft wide stand, as if on parade, in a line up a mountain. The kilns, built by Chinese laborers in 1879, were employed to burn woods from pinyon pines into charcoal. The charcoal was then transported over the mountains and into Death Valley where it was used to extract lead and silver from the ore mined in the area. If you hike up the mountain, you will be rewarded with terrific views of the kilns, with Death Valley's phenomenal colors as a backdrop.

Dining, Lodging, and Camping

$–$$ ✕🏨 **Panamint Springs Resort.** This simple but comfortable establishment located just inside Death Valley National Park is the only place to stay for miles. The restaurant attached to the hotel looks like a diner but actually serves up a broad range of rather good Continental cuisine ($–$$). In the morning, if it's not too chilly, having breakfast on the veranda while watching the sunlight sweep over the barren mountains is a perfect introduction to Death Valley. ✉ *Hwy. 190, Death Valley National Park, Box 395, Ridgecrest, 93556,* ☎ *775/482–7680,* FAX *775/482–7682. 15 rooms. Restaurant, camping, shops. AE, D, MC, V.* ♻

Mahogany Flat. If you've got a four-wheel-drive vehicle and want to scale the park's highest mountain, you might want to sleep at one of the few shaded spots in Death Valley, located at a cool 8,133 ft. A 7-mi (one-way) trail leads from the campground to the summit of Telescope Peak (11,049 ft), but if you don't want to go the distance, many shorter strolls in this wooded high-country area afford terrific valley views. ✉ *Off Wildrose Rd., south of Charcoal Kilns. 10 sites.* *Free.* ⏲ *Mar.–Nov.*

Stovepipe Wells Village

9 *102 mi northeast of Ridgecrest, Hwy. 178 to Hwy. 190.*

Stovepipe Wells Village was the first resort in Death Valley. The tiny town, which dates back to 1926, takes its name from the stovepipe that early prospectors left to indicate where they found water. The area contains a motel, a restaurant, a grocery store, campgrounds, and a landing strip.

The multicolor walls of **Mosaic Canyon** are extremely narrow in spots. A reasonably easy ¾-mi hike yields the flavor of the area. If weather permits it's rewarding to continue farther into the canyon for a few more miles. ✉ *Off Hwy. 190, on 3 mi gravel road immediately southwest of Stovepipe Wells Village.*

Dining and Lodging

$–$$ **Stovepipe Wells Village.** An aircraft landing strip is an unusual touch for a motel, as is a heated mineral pool, but everything else here is pretty standard. Still, this is the best lodging bargain inside the park, with pleasant rooms at a reasonable rate. The Old West–style Toll Road restaurant ($–$$) serves up American cuisine—burgers, steaks, and the like. The adjoining Badwater Saloon provides the park's only nightlife outside Furnace Creek. ✉ *Hwy. 190, Death Valley National Park 92328,* ☎ *760/786–2387,* FAX *760/786–2389. 83 rooms. Restaurant, bar, pool. AE, D, MC, V.*

En Route Visible from Highway 190 heading east past Stovepipe Wells are **sand dunes** that cover a 14-square-mi field. The sand that forms the hills is actually minute pieces of quartz and other rock. Walking on the dunes offers some great views of the mountains.

Scotty's Castle Area

44 mi north of Stovepipe Wells Village; head east on Hwy. 190, then north at signs for castle.

10 **Scotty's Castle** is an odd apparition rising out of a canyon. This Moorish mansion, begun in 1924 and never completed, takes its name from Walter Scott, better known as Death Valley Scotty. An ex-cowboy, prospector, and performer in Buffalo Bill's Wild West Show, Scotty always told people the castle was his, financed by gold from a secret mine. In reality, there was no mine. The house belonged to a Chicago millionaire named Albert Johnson (advised by doctors to spend time in a warm, dry climate) whom Scott had finagled into investing in the fictitious mine. The house functioned for a while as a hotel—guests included Bette Davis and Norman Rockwell—and contains works of art, imported carpets, handmade European furniture, and a tremendous pipe organ. Costumed rangers re-create life at the castle circa 1939. Try to arrive for the first tour of the day to avoid having to wait. ☎ *760/786–2392.* *$8.* ⏲ *Daily 8–6; tours until 5.*

11 The impressive **Ubehebe Crater,** 500 ft deep and ½ mi across, is the result of violent underground steam and gas explosions about 3,000 years ago; its volcanic ash spreads out over most of the area, and the cinders are as thick as 150 ft near the crater's rim. You'll get some superb views of the valley from here, and you can take a fairly easy hike around the west side of the rim to Little Hebe Crater, one of a smaller cluster of craters to the south and west. It's always windy here, so hold on to your hat. *8 mi northwest of Scotty's Castle on North Death Valley Highway.* 🎫 *Free.*

Camping

⛺ **Mesquite Springs.** There are tent and RV spaces here, some of them shaded. ⊠ *2 mi south of Scotty's Castle. 30 sites.* 🎫 *$10.* ⏲ *Year-round.*

En Route On Highway 190, south of its junction with Scotty's Castle Road and 14 mi north of the town of Furnace Creek, is a 1-mi gravel road that leads to the ½-mi **Salt Creek Nature Trail.** The trail, a boardwalk circuit, loops through a spring-fed wash. The nearby hills are brown and gray, but the floor of the wash is alive with aquatic plants such as pickerelweed and salt grass. The trail is the best place for bird-watching in Death Valley. You might see ravens, common snipes, killdeer, or great blue herons.

Furnace Creek Area

54 mi south of Scotty's Castle, 25 mi southeast of Stovepipe Wells Village on Hwy. 190.

12 The renowned mule teams hauled borax from the **Harmony Borax Works** to the railroad town of Mojave, 165 mi away. Those teams were a sight to behold: 20 mules hitched up to two massive wagons, each carrying a load of 10 tons of borax through the burning desert. The teams plied the route between 1884 and 1907, when the railroad finally arrived in Zabriskie. The Borax Museum, 2 mi south of the borax works, houses original mining machinery and historical displays in a building that once served as a boardinghouse for miners. The adjacent structure is the original mule-team barn. ⊠ *Harmony Borax Works Rd., west off Hwy. 190.*

13 **Furnace Creek** is a center of activity amid the sprawling quiet of Death Valley. Covered with tropical landscaping, it has jogging and bicycle paths, golf, tennis, horseback riding, a general store, and, rare for these parts, dining options. The Furnace Creek Ranch (☞ Dining and Lodging, *below*) operates most of the above, plus guided carriage rides and hay rides. The rides traverse trails with views of the surrounding mountains, where multicolor volcanic rock and alluvial fans form a background for date palms and other vegetation.

Trail maps, brochures, and books and exhibits on the desert can be found at the **Visitor Center at Furnace Creek.** ⊠ *Hwy. 190,* ☎ *760/786–2331.* ⏲ *Daily 8–6.*

★ 14 **Golden Canyon** is named for the glowing color of its walls. An easy hike into this spacious landform affords some spectacular views of yellow and orange rock. Farther into the canyon you'll encounter a colorful formation called Red Cathedral. ⊠ *Badwater Rd., 3 mi south from Furnace Creek; turn left into parking lot.*

15 Reaching **Badwater,** you'll see a shallow pool containing mostly sodium chloride—saltier than the sea—lying almost lifeless against an expanse of desolate salt flats. It's a sharp contrast to the expansive canyons and elevation not too far away. Here's the legend: one of the early surveyors saw that his mule wouldn't drink from the pool and noted "bad-

water" on his map. At 282 ft below sea level, Badwater is the lowest spot on land in the Western Hemisphere, and also one of the hottest. ✉ *Badwater Rd., 19 mi south of Visitor Center at Furnace Creek.*

★ 16 The **Artists Palette,** named for the brilliant array of pigments created by volcanic deposits, is one of the most magnificent sights in Death Valley. Artists Drive, the approach to the area, is one-way heading north off Badwater Road, so if you're visiting Badwater it saves time to come here on the way back. The drive winds through foothills composed of colorful sedimentary and volcanic rocks. ✉ *8 mi north of Badwater, Badwater Rd. to Artists Dr.; 10 mi south of Furnace Creek, Hwy. 190 to Badwater Rd. to Artists Dr.*

17 **Zabriskie Point** is one of Death Valley National Park's most scenic spots. Not particularly high—only about 710 ft—it overlooks a striking badlands panorama with wrinkled, multicolor hills. Film buffs of a certain vintage may recognize it from the film *Zabriskie Point* by Italian director Michelangelo Antonioni. ✉ *Hwy. 190, 5 mi south of Furnace Creek.*

OFF THE BEATEN PATH

TWENTY MULE TEAM CANYON – The thrills in this colorful canyon are more than just natural. At times along the loop road off Highway 190 the soft rock walls reach high on both sides, making it seem like you're on an amusement-park ride. Remains of prospectors' tunnels are visible here, along with some brilliant rock formations. ✉ *Twenty Mule Team Rd. off Hwy. 190, 1½ mi south of Zabriskie Point. Trailers not permitted.*

★ 18 **Dante's View** is more than 5,000 ft up in the Black Mountains. In the dry desert air you can see across most of the 110 mi valley. The view up and down is equally astounding, as you can spot the highest and lowest points in the contiguous United States. The tiny blackish patch far below is Badwater, at 282 ft below sea level; on the western horizon is Mt. Whitney, which rises to 14,494 ft. ✉ *Dante's View Rd. off Hwy. 190, 21 mi south of Zabriskie Point.*

19 At **Devil's Golf Course** thousands of miniature salt pinnacles carved into surreal shapes by the desert wind dot the landscape. The salt was pushed up to the surface by pressure created as underground salt and water-bearing gravel crystallized. Nothing grows on this barren landscape. ✉ *Badwater Rd., 13 mi south of Visitor Center at Furnace Creek. Turn right onto dirt road and drive 1 mi.*

Dining, Lodging, and Camping

$$$–$$$$ ✕ **Inn Dining Room.** White stucco walls, lace tablecloths, two fireplaces, and windows with views of the Panamint Mountains make this restaurant a visual and culinary feast. The upscale menu may include seared ahi tuna and fire-roasted corn chowder as starters. Seasonally changing main courses might include chilled lobster salad or medallions of veal. A few vegetarian entrées are usually offered as well. ✉ *Furnace Creek Inn Resort, Hwy. 190, ☏ 760/786–2345 ext. 150. No jeans, shorts, or T shirts. AE, D, DC, MC, V.*

$$$–$$$$ **Furnace Creek Inn Resort.** This historic stone structure is something of a desert oasis. The creek meanders through beautifully landscaped gardens, and the pool here is spring-fed. All the rooms have views; about half have balconies. Rates drop considerably during the summer. ✉ *Hwy. 190, Box 1, Death Valley National Park 92328, ☏ 760/786–2361, FAX 760/786–2423. 66 rooms. Restaurant, bar, pool, sauna, massage, 4 tennis courts, meeting rooms. AE, D, DC, MC, V.*

$$–$$$ **Furnace Creek Ranch.** The ranch was originally crew headquarters for a borax company, which the on-site Borax Museum details. Four two-story buildings adjacent to the golf course have motel-type rooms that are good for families. The best rooms overlook the green lawns of the resort, with the mountains soaring in the background. The general store sells supplies and gifts. ✉ *Hwy. 190, Box 1, Death Valley National Park 92328,* ☎ *760/786–2345,* FAX *760/786–9945. 224 rooms. Restaurant, bar, coffee shop, pool, 18-hole golf course, 2 tennis courts, horseback riding. AE, D, DC, MC, V.*

Furnace Creek. This campground, 196 ft below sea level, has RV and tent sites (some shaded) and tables. Pay showers, a laundry, and a swimming pool are at nearby Furnace Creek Ranch (☞ *above*). Reservations are accepted for stays between mid-October and mid-April; at other times sites are available on a first-come, first-served basis. ✉ *Adjacent to Visitor Center at Furnace Creek,* ☎ *760/786–2331; 800/365–2267 for reservations. 136 sites.* *$16.* ⏲ *Year-round.*

Texas Spring. Open only from October through May, this campsite south of the Visitor Center at Furnace Creek has good facilities and is a few dollars cheaper than the main campground. ✉ *Just off Badwater Rd., south of the Visitor Center,* ☎ *800/365–2267. 92 sites.* *$12.* ⏲ *Open Oct.–May.*

Death Valley Junction

30 mi south of Furnace Creek, 25 mi south of Zabriskie Point on Hwy. 190.

20 **Marta Becket's Amargosa Opera House** is an unexpected novelty in the desert. Marta Becket, an artist and dancer from New York, first visited the former railway town of Amargosa while on tour in 1964. Three years later she returned and bought a boarded-up theater sitting amid a group of run-down mock-Spanish colonial buildings. To compensate for the sparse crowds in the early days, Becket painted a Renaissance-era Spanish audience on the walls and ceiling, turning the theater into a trompe l'oeil masterpiece. Becket, in her mid-seventies, now performs her blend of ballet, mime, and 19th-century melodrama to sell-out crowds (call ahead to reserve a seat). After the show you can meet her in the adjacent gallery, where she sells her paintings and autographs her books. ✉ *Hwy. 127,* ☎ *760/852–4441.* *$10. Call ahead for reservations.* ⏲ *Performances Nov., Feb., Mar., and Apr., Sat. and Mon. 7:45 PM; Oct., Dec., Jan., and May (through Mother's Day weekend), Sat. only.*

$ **Opera House Hotel.** Adjoining the theater is a quaint, 1920s-style adobe bungalow. A long row of rooms—with murals of antique furniture and clothes and lamps topped with frilly velvet shades—is available for opera guests. ✉ *Hwy. 127,* ☎ *760/852–4441,* FAX *760/852–4138. 14 rooms. MC, V.*

Shoshone

21 *30 mi south of Death Valley Junction on Hwy. 127.*

The unincorporated town of Shoshone started out as a mining town. Miners used to live nearby in small caves dynamited out of the rock. One miner who struck it rich was so attached to his hillside dwelling that he even hollowed out another cave for a garage to store his newly bought automobile. The history of the region goes back much further, as a small museum in Shoshone makes clear. Here you'll find a complete woolly mammoth skeleton recently excavated from the surrounding silt. Paleontologists also recently discovered saber-tooth tiger and camel footprints, preserved deep in the earth that had been excavated by miners in decades past.

$ ✕ **Crowbar Café & Saloon.** Housed in an old wooden building with antique photos adorning the walls and mining equipment standing in the corners, this establishment serves surprisingly good food in enormous helpings. Fare ranges from steaks to fajitas. Home-cooked fruit pies make fine desserts in the desert, and super-chilled beers are surefire thirst-quenchers. ✉ *Hwy. 127,* ☏ *760/852–4224. AE, D, MC, V.*

$–$$ **Shoshone Motel.** If you're looking for a place to stay while exploring the edge of Death Valley, this is a fine choice. Rooms are simple but cozy and the staff is friendly. The big draw here is the hot spring–fed swimming pool, built into the foothills of the craggy mountains. ✉ *State Hwy. 127, 92384,* ☏ *760/852–4224,* FAX *760/852–4250. 16 rooms. Restaurant, pool. AE, D, MC, V.*

THE EASTERN MOJAVE

The eastern Mojave, with more vegetation and cooler temperatures, is a sharp contrast to Death Valley. Much of this area is uninhabited, so be cautious when driving the many back roads where towns and services are few and far between.

Baker

22 *84 mi south of Death Valley Junction on Hwy. 127.*

The small town of Baker, unappealing except as a rest stop, lies between the eastern and western Mojave and Death Valley National Park. You can't miss the city's 134-ft thermometer, the height of which commemorates the corresponding U.S. temperature record in degrees Fahrenheit, which was set in Death Valley on July 10, 1913.

The thermometer is also a landmark for the National Park Service's **Mojave Desert Information Center** (☏ 760/733–4040). Baker offers only minimal provisions. There are a few restaurants, most of them fast-food outlets, one general store—as the seller of the most winning Lotto tickets in the state of California it tends to be popular—three motels, and several gas stations.

Dining and Lodging

$ ✕ **The Mad Greek.** Oozing with over-the-top ambience, this place has somehow fused Athens, Los Angeles, and the Mojave Desert. Deep blue ceramic tiles adorn the walls, and neo-classical statues pose amidst the tables. The food ranges from traditional Greek (gyros, kebabs, strong Greek coffees) through to classic American (hot dogs and ice cream sundaes). ✉ *I–15 at Baker Blvd.,* ☏ *760/733–4354. AE, D, DC, MC, V.*

$–$$ **Wills Fargo Motel.** Two of Baker's three motels have the same owner and they're just down the road from each other, so there's no little difference in rates or amenities. This one, however, has rooms with marginally more character, as well as a pool and a grassy lawn out front. ✉ *72252 Baker Blvd., 92309,* ☏ *760/733–4477,* FAX *760/733–4680. 30 rooms. Pool. AE, D, DC, MC, V.*

Mojave National Preserve

The 1.4 million acres set aside in 1994 as the Mojave National Preserve don't conform to the standard image of the desert, as they hold a surprising variety of plant and animal life at elevations up to nearly 8,000 ft. There's a good deal of evidence of human habitation as well, including abandoned army posts and the vestiges of towns that grew up around the area's mines and ranches. The town of Cima still has a small functioning store. But as you enter the preserve from the north, passing beautiful red-black cinder cones, you'll encounter stereotypical desert terrain in the **Kelso Dunes** (✉ Kelbaker Rd.; 42 mi south of Baker, 7 mi north of Kelso), perfect, pristine slopes of gold-white sand. The dunes cover 70 square mi, often at heights of 500 ft–600 ft, and can be reached in an easy ½-mi walk from where you park. When you reach the top of one of the dunes, kick a little bit of sand down the lee side and find out why they say the sand "sings." In the town of Kelso a Mission Revival–style train depot dating from 1925 is one of the few of its kind still standing.

★ 23 (margin marker beside "cal desert terrain in the Kelso Dunes")

24 The National Park Service administers most of the preserve, but **Providence Mountains State Recreation Area** is under the jurisdiction of the California Department of Parks. The visitor center, elevation 4,300 ft, has views of mountain peaks, dunes, buttes, crags, and desert valleys. The nearby **Mitchell Caverns Natural Preserve** provides the rare opportunity to see all three types of cave formations—dripstone, flowstone, and erratics—in one place. The year-round 65°F temperature provides a break from the heat. ✉ *Essex Rd., 16 mi north of I–40,* ☎ *760/928–2586.* 🎟 *$3.* ⏲ *Guided tours of caves Sept.–June, weekdays 1:30, weekends 10, 1:30, and 3; July–Aug., weekends only.*

Camping

⛺ **Hole-in-the-Wall Campground.** At a cool 4,500 ft above sea level and backed by sculptured volcanic rock formations, this is a fine place to spend a quiet night and use as a base for hiking. The area was named by Bob Hollimon, a member of the Butch Cassidy gang, because it reminded him of his former hideout in Wyoming. There's a visitor center nearby. ✉ *Black Canyon Rd. south of Kelso (for reservations write Mojave National Preserve, 222 E. Main St., Suite 202, Barstow 92311),* ☎ *760/733–4040. 35 campsites for motor homes and trailers, 2 walk-in tent sites.* 🎟 *$10. No credit cards. Reservations not taken.*

Afton Canyon

25 *27 mi southwest of Baker, I–15 to Afton Canyon Rd.*

Because of its colorful, steep walls, **Afton Canyon** is often called the Grand Canyon of the Mojave. Afton was carved over many thousands of years by the rushing waters of the Mojave River, which makes one of its few aboveground appearances here. Where you find water in the desert you'll also find trees, grasses, and wildlife. The canyon has been popular for a long time; Native Americans and later white settlers following the Mojave Trail from the Colorado River to the Pacific Ocean set up camp here. The dirt road that leads here is ungraded in spots, so the canyon is best visited via all-terrain vehicle. Check with the Mojave Desert Information Center in Baker (☞ *above*) regarding road conditions before you head in. ✉ *Take Afton turnoff and follow dirt road about 3 mi southwest.*

Camping

⛺ **Afton Canyon Campground.** The camping here, at elevation 1,408 ft, is in a wildlife area where the Mojave River surfaces. High-desert scenic cliffs and a mesquite thicket surround the campground. ✉ *Afton Canyon Rd. off I–15. 22 sites.* 🎟 *$6 (reservations not accepted).* ⏲ *Year-round.*

Barstow Area

26 *63 mi southwest of Baker on I–15.*

Barstow was established in 1886 when a subsidiary of the Atchison, Topeka, and Santa Fe Railway began construction of a depot and hotel here. Outlet stores and modern chain restaurants and motels are more common today, though old-time neon signs light up Barstow's main street. The town is most famous today, by the way, for being mentioned in the song "Route 66." The **California Welcome Center** (⊠ 2796 Tanger Way, ☏ 760/253–4813 or 760/253–4782) has exhibits about desert ecology, wildflowers, wildlife, and other features of the desert environment.

★ 27 **Rainbow Basin National Natural Landmark** looks like a martian landscape, perhaps because so many science-fiction movies depicting the red planet have been filmed here. The sense of upheaval is palpable; huge slabs of red, orange, white, and green stone tilt at crazy angles like ships about to capsize. Hike the many washes and you'll probably see the fossilized remains of creatures that roamed the basin from 16 million to 12 million years ago: mastodons, camels, rhinos, dogbears, birds, and insects. ⊠ *8 mi north of Barstow (take Fort Irwin Rd. 5 mi north to Fossil Bed Rd., a graded dirt road, and head west 3 mi),* ☏ *760/252–6000.*

28 What's now **Calico Ghost Town** was a wild and wealthy mining town after a rich deposit of silver was found around 1881. In 1886, after more than $85 million worth of silver, gold, and other precious metals were harvested from the multicolor hills, the price of silver fell and the town slipped into decline. Frank "Borax" Smith helped revive Calico in 1889 when he started mining the unglamorous but profitable mineral borax, but that boom had gone bust by the dawn of the 20th century. Many of the buildings here are authentic, but it's a theme-park version of the 1880s you get strolling the wooden sidewalks of Main Street, browsing through western shops, roaming the tunnels of Maggie's Mine, and taking a ride on the Calico–Odessa Railroad. Festivals in March, May, October, and November promote Calico's Wild West theme. ⊠ *Ghost Town Rd., 3 mi north of I–15,* ☏ *760/254–2122 or 800/862–2542.* *$6.* *Daily 8:30–sunset, shops 9–5.*

★ 29 If you're at all curious about life 200,000 years ago, the **Calico Early Man Archeological Site** is a must-see. Although many archeologists are wary of this site because it conflicts with the dominant theory that humans only populated America 13,000 years ago, nearly 12,000 toollike stones—scrapers, cutting tools, choppers, hand picks, stone saws, and the like—that are believed to be much older have been excavated from the site. Louis Leakey, the noted archaeologist, was so impressed with the findings that he became the Calico Project director in 1963, serving until his death in 1972; his old camp is now a visitor center and museum. The earliest known Americans fashioned the artifacts buried in the walls and floors of the excavated pits. The only way in is by guided tour (call ahead, as scheduled tours sometimes don't take place). ⊠ *15 mi northeast of Barstow, I–15 to Minneola Rd. north for 3 mi,* ☏ *760/252–6000.* *Small donation suggested.* *Guided tours of dig Wed.–Thurs. 1:30 and 3:30, Fri.–Sun. 9–3:30.*

Dining, Lodging, and Camping

$–$$ ✕ **Carlos & Toto's.** If you've tired of chain restaurants and food from your cooler, head for this touch of Mexico. Locally famous for its fajitas, the restaurant is open daily and lays out a Sunday buffet brunch from 9:30 to 2. ⊠ *901 W. Main St.,* ☏ *760/256–7513. AE, D, MC, V.*

$$ **Holiday Inn.** This large property has more facilities than the many other hotels that line Main Street, so it tends to attract business travelers. It's slightly more expensive than the others, but worth it if you want the highest level of comfort Barstow has to offer. ⊠

1511 E. Main St., ☎ 760/256–5673, FAX 760/256–5917. 148 rooms. Restaurant, pool, hot tub, laundry service, meeting rooms. AE, D, DC, MC, V.

Calico Ghost Town Regional Park. In addition to the campsites here there are six cabins ($28) and bunkhouse accommodations ($5 per person, with a 12-person minimum). ✉ *Ghost Town Rd., 3 mi north of I–15, east from Barstow, ☎ 760/254–2122; 800/862–2542 for reservations. 250 sites. $18 per night for tent camping, $22 for full RV hook-ups; 2-night minimum during festival weekends. ⏲ Year-round.*

Victorville

30 *34 mi southwest of Barstow on I–15.*

At the southwest corner of the Mojave is the sprawling town of Victorville, home of the Roy Rogers–Dale Evans Museum.

Mojave Narrows Regional Park makes use of one of the few spots where the Mojave River flows aboveground. The park has 87 camping units, hot showers, secluded picnic areas, and two lakes surrounded by cottonwoods and cattails. You'll find fishing, rowboat rentals, a bait shop, equestrian paths, and a trail for visitors with disabilities. ✉ *18000 Yates Rd., ☎ 760/245–2226. $5 per vehicle; camping $10, camping with utilities $15. ⏲ Daily 7:30–sunset.*

The **Roy Rogers–Dale Evans Museum** draws old-timers and cowboy kitsch fans who come to see the personal and professional memorabilia. Everything from glittering costumes and custom cars to cereal box promotions testifies to just how famous the museum's namesakes and their friends on the Western film circuit once were. Animal-rights activists will probably want to stay away; exhibits include safari trophies—stuffed exotic cats and other animals shot by Roy and sometimes Dale. Even Trigger and Buttermilk have been preserved, though they died of natural causes. ✉ *15650 Seneca Rd. (take Roy Rogers Dr. exit off I–15, then left on Civic Dr.), ☎ 760/243–4547. $7. ⏲ Daily 9–5.*

Lodging

$–$$ **Best Western Green Tree Inn.** This member of the chain sits off I–15 a few blocks from the Roy Rogers–Dale Evans Museum. Many of the rooms are suite-size and have refrigerators and microwaves, making the inn a good choice for families. The decor is no-nonsense but clean. ✉ *14173 Green Tree Blvd., 92392, ☎ 760/245–3461 or 800/528–1234, FAX 760/245–7745. 168 rooms. Restaurant, bar, coffee shop, pool, hot tub, shuffleboard, meeting rooms. AE, D, DC, MC, V.*

THE MOJAVE DESERT AND DEATH VALLEY A TO Z

Arriving and Departing

By Bus

Greyhound (☎ 800/231–2222) serves Baker, Barstow, Ridgecrest, and Victorville, but traveling by bus to the Mojave Desert is neither convenient nor cheap. There is no scheduled bus service to Death Valley National Park.

By Car

Much of the desert can be seen from the comfort of an air-conditioned car. Don't despair if you are without air-conditioning—just avoid the middle of the day and the middle of the summer.

The Mojave is shaped like a giant *L,* with one leg north and the other east. To travel north through the Mojave, take I–10 east out of Los Angeles to I–15 north and (just past Cajon Pass), pick up U.S. 395, which runs north through Victor Valley, Boron, the Rand Mining District, and China Lake. To travel east, continue on I–15 to Barstow. From Barstow you can take I–40, which passes through the mountainous areas of San Bernardino County, whisks by the Providence mountains, and enters Arizona at Needles. The more northerly option is I–15, which passes near the Kelso Sand Dunes and then veers northeast toward Las Vegas.

To avoid Cajon Pass, elevation 4,250 ft, take I–210 north of Los Angeles and continue north on Highway 14. Head east 67 mi on Highway 58 to the town of Barstow and pick up I–15 there. Continue east on I–15 to Highway 127, a very scenic route north through the Mojave to Death Valley.

Death Valley can be entered from the southeast or the west. From the southeast, take Highway 127 north from I–15 and then link up with Highway 178, which travels west into the valley and then cuts north toward Badwater before meeting up with Highway 190 at Furnace Creek. To enter from the west, exit U.S. 395 at either Highway 190 or 178.

By Plane

Inyokern Airport (✉ Inyokern Rd./Hwy. 178, 9 mi west of Ridgecrest, ☎ 760/377–5844) is served by **United Express** (☎ 800/241–6522) from Los Angeles. It takes about the same amount of time to drive from **McCarran International Airport** (☎ 702/261–5733) in Las Vegas (which is served by many more airlines) to Furnace Creek in Death Valley National Park as it does from Inyokern.

Getting Around

See Arriving and Departing, *above.*

Contacts and Resources

Camping

The Mojave Desert and Death Valley have about two dozen campgrounds in various desert settings. For further information the following booklets are useful: *High Desert Recreation Resource Guide,* from the Mojave Chamber of Commerce; *San Bernardino County Regional Parks,* from the Regional Parks Department; and *California Desert Camping,* from the Bureau of Land Management. *See* Visitor Information, *below,* for addresses and phone numbers.

Emergencies

Ambulance (☎ 911). **Fire** (☎ 911). **Police** (☎ 911).

BLM Rangers (☎ 760/255–8700). **Community Hospital** (✉ Barstow, ☎ 760/256–1761). **San Bernardino County Sheriff** (☎ 760/256–1796 for Barstow; 760/733–4448 for Baker).

Guided Tours

Gadabout Tours (✉ 700 E. Tahquitz Canyon Way, Palm Springs, ☎ 760/325–5556). **Nature Conservancy** (✉ Box 188, Thousand Palms, 92276, ☎ 760/343–1234). **Sierra Club** (✉ 3345 Wilshire Blvd., Suite 508, Los Angeles 90010, ☎ 213/387–4287).

Visitor Information

Bureau of Land Management (✉ California Desert District Office, 6 Box Springs Blvd., Riverside 92507, ☏ 909/697–5200). **California vision of Tourism** (☏ 800/862–2543). **Desert Discovery Center** (✉ 8 Barstow Rd., Barstow 92311, ☏ 760/252–6060). **Mojave Chamber Commerce** (✉ 15836 Sierra Hwy., Mojave 93591, ☏ 661/824–2481). **National Park Service** (✉ Visitor Center at Furnace Creek, 92328, ☏ 760/786–2331). **Ridgecrest Area Convention and Visitors Bureau** (✉ 100 W. California Ave., Ridgecrest 93555, ☏ 760/375–8202 or 800/847–4830). **San Bernardino County Regional Parks Department** (✉ 777 E. Rialto Ave., San Bernardino 92415, ☏ 909/387–2594).

BACKGROUND AND ESSENTIALS

Books and Videos

Maps of California

Smart Travel Tips A to Z

WHAT TO READ AND WATCH BEFORE YOU GO

San Francisco

BOOKS

Many novels are set in San Francisco, but none are better than *The Maltese Falcon,* by Dashiell Hammett, the founder of the hard-boiled school of detective fiction. *The Barbary Coast: An Informal History of the San Francisco Underworld,* published in 1933 and still in print, is Herbert Asbury's searing look at life in what really was a wicked city before the turn of the last century. Other standouts include Vikram Seth's *Golden Gate,* a novel in verse about life in San Francisco and Marin County in the early '80s, John Gregory Dunne's *The Red White and Blue,* and Alice Adams's *Rich Rewards. The Joy Luck Club* by Bay Area writer Amy Tan is a novel about four generations of Chinese American women in San Francisco.

For anecdotes, gossip, and the kind of detail that will make you feel almost like a native San Franciscan, get hold of any of the books by the late and much-loved San Francisco *Chronicle* columnist Herb Caen: *Baghdad-by-the-Bay, Only in San Francisco, One Man's San Francisco,* and *San Francisco: City on Golden Hills.* Armistead Maupin's gay-theme soap opera–style *Tales of the City* stories are set in San Francisco; you can read them or watch them on video.

VIDEOS

San Francisco (1936), starring Clark Gable and Jeanette MacDonald, recreates the 1906 earthquake with outstanding special effects. In *Escape from Alcatraz* (1979), Clint Eastwood plays the prisoner who allegedly escaped from the famous jail on a rock in the San Francisco Bay. *The Times of Harvey Milk,* about San Francisco's first openly gay elected official, won the Academy Award for best documentary feature in 1984. Alfred Hitchcock immortalized Mission Dolores and the Golden Gate Bridge in *Vertigo* (1958), the eerie story of a detective with a fear of heights, starring Jimmy Stewart and Kim Novak. A few other noteworthy films shot in San Francisco are *Dark Passage* (1947), with Humphrey Bogart; the 1978 remake of *Invasion of the Body Snatchers; Play It Again Sam* (1972) with Woody Allen; and the 1993 comedy *Mrs. Doubtfire,* starring Robin Williams.

Los Angeles

BOOKS

Los Angeles: The Enormous Village, 1781–1981, by John D. Weaver, and *Los Angeles: Biography of a City,* by John and LaRee Caughey, will give you a fine background in how Los Angeles came to be the city it is today. The unique social and cultural life of the whole southern California area is explored in *Southern California: An Island on the Land,* by Carey McWilliams.

One of the most outstanding features of Los Angeles is its architecture. *Los Angeles: The Architecture of Four Ecologies,* by Reyner Banham, relates the city's physical environment to its buildings. *Architecture in Los Angeles: A Complete Guide,* by David Gebhard and Robert Winter, is also very useful.

Two controversial books by Mike Davis, *Ecology of Fear: Los Angeles and the Imagination of Disaster* and *City of Quartz: Excavating the Future in Los Angeles,* offer historical analyses of the City of Angels.

Many novels have been written with Los Angeles as the setting. One of the very best, Nathanael West's *Day of the Locust,* was first published in 1939 but still rings true. Budd Schulberg's *What Makes Sammy Run?,* Evelyn Waugh's *The Loved One,* and Joan Didion's *Play It As It Lays* and

...*Album* are unforgettable. ...vels that give a sense of con-...rary life in Los Angeles are *Sex ... Rage,* by Eve Babitz, and *Less Than Zero,* by Bret Easton Ellis. Raymond Chandler and Ross Macdonald have written many suspense novels with a Los Angeles background.

VIDEOS AND TV

Billy Wilder's *Sunset Boulevard* (1950) is a classic portrait of a faded star and her attempt to recapture past glory. Roman Polanski's *Chinatown* (1974), arguably one of the best American films ever made, is a fictional account of the wheeling and dealing that helped make Los Angeles what it is today. Southern California's varied urban and rural landscapes are used to great effect (as is an all-star cast that includes Ethel Merman and Spencer Tracy) in Stanley Kramer's manic *It's a Mad, Mad, Mad, Mad World* (1963). *Rebel Without a Cause* (1955) offers a view from Griffith Observatory in the days before smog. *L.A. Story* (1991), written by and starring Steve Martin, gives a glimpse of modern-day Los Angeles, while *L.A. Confidential* (1997) provides a look at its seedy and salacious past.

San Diego

BOOKS

There is no better way to establish the mood for your visit to Old Town San Diego than by reading Helen Hunt Jackson's 19th-century romantic novel, *Ramona,* a steady seller for decades and still in print. The Casa de Estudillo in Old Town has been known for many years as Ramona's Marriage Place because of its close resemblance to the house described in the novel. Richard Henry Dana Jr.'s *Two Years Before the Mast* (1869), based on the author's experiences as a merchant sailor, provides a masculine perspective on early San Diego history.

Other novels with a San Diego setting include Raymond Chandler's mystery about the waterfront, *Playback*; Wade Miller's mystery, *On Easy Street;* Eric Higgs's thriller, *A Happy Man;* Tom Wolfe's satire of the La Jolla surfing scene, *The Pump House Gang;* and David Zielinski's modern-day story, *A Genuine Monster.*

VIDEOS AND TV

Filmmakers have taken advantage of San Diego's diverse and amiable climate since the dawn of cinema. Westerns, comedy-westerns, and tales of the sea were early staples: *Cupid in Chaps, The Sagebrush Phrenologist,* the 1914 version of *The Virginian,* and Lon Chaney's *Tell It to the Marines* were among the silent films shot in the area. Easy-to-capture outdoor locales have lured many productions south from Hollywood over the years, including the following military-oriented talkies, all or part of which were shot in San Diego: James Cagney's *Here Comes the Navy* (1934), Errol Flynn's *Dive Bomber* (1941), John Wayne's *The Sands of Iwo Jima* (1949), Ronald Reagan's *Hellcats of the Navy* (1956, co-starring Nancy Davis, the future First Lady), Rock Hudson's *Ice Station Zebra* (1967), Tom Cruise's *Top Gun* (1986), Sean Connery's *Hunt for Red October,* Charlie Sheen's *Navy Seals* (1990), and Danny Glover's *Flight of the Intruder* (1991).

In a lighter military vein, the famous talking mule hit the high seas in *Francis Joins the Navy* (1955), in which a very young Clint Eastwood has a bit part. The Tom Hanks–Darryl Hannah hit *Splash* (1984), *Spaceballs* (1987), *Wayne's World II* (1993), and *Mr. Wrong* (1996) are more recent comedies with scenes filmed here. Billy Wilder's *Some Like It Hot* (1959)—starring Marilyn Monroe, Jack Lemmon, and Tony Curtis—takes place at the Hotel Del Coronado (standing in for a Miami resort).

The amusing low-budget *Attack of the Killer Tomatoes* (1976) makes good use of local scenery. The producers must have liked what they found in town as they returned for three sequels: *Return of the Killer Tomatoes* (1988), *Killer Tomatoes Strike Back* (1990), and—proving just how versatile the region is as a film location—*Killer Tomatoes Go to France* (1991).

Television producers zip south for series and made-for-TV movies all the time. The alteration of San Diego's skyline in the 1980s was partially documented on the hit show *Simon & Simon.* San Diego is virtually awash in syndicated productions: *Silk Stalkings, Baywatch, High Tide,* and *Renegade* are among the shows that have been shot here. Reality and cop shows love the area, too: *Unsolved Mysteries, Rescue 911, America's Missing Children, Totally Hidden Video, America's Most Wanted,* and *America's Funniest People* have all taped in San Diego, making it one of the most-seen—yet often uncredited—locales in movie and video land.

Around the State

BOOKS

John Steinbeck immortalized the Monterey-Salinas area in numerous books, including *Cannery Row* and *East of Eden.* Joan Didion captured the heat—solar, political, and otherwise—of the Sacramento Delta area in *Run River.* Mark Twain's *Roughing It* and Bret Harte's *The Luck of Roaring Camp* evoke life during the Gold Rush. For a window on the past and present of the Central Valley, see *Highway 99: A Literary Journey Through California's Great Central Valley,* edited by Stan Yogi. Marc Reiser's *Cadillac Desert* explores the history and significance of the state's water rights. In her 1903 classic, *Land of Little Rain,* Mary Austin offers a detailed account of the terrain between Death Valley and the High Sierra. For a telling of what befell the Donner Party, see George Stewart's *Ordeal by Hunger,* and for a source on pioneer California, William Brewer's *Up and Down California in 1860-1864* is outstanding.

VIDEOS AND TV

John Steinbeck's *East of Eden* was a hit film starring James Dean and later a television movie. Buster Keaton's masterpiece *Steamboat Bill, Jr.* (1928) was shot in Sacramento. The exteriors in Alfred Hitchcock's *Shadow of a Doubt* (1943) were shot in Santa Rosa, and his creepy *The Birds* (1963) was shot in Bodega Bay, along the North Coast. *Shack Out on 101* is a loopy 1950s beware-the-Commies caper also set on the California coast. *Bagdad Café* (1988) captures the tedium of the Mojave Desert.

Erich von Stroheim used a number of northern California locations for his films: *Greed* takes place in San Francisco but includes excursions to Oakland and other points in the East Bay. Carmel is one of the locations for his *Foolish Wives.* The various Star Trek movies and Michelangelo Antonioni's *Zabriskie Point* are among the features that have made use of the eastern desert region. Initial footage of Sam Peckinpah's western *Ride the High Country* was shot in the Sierra Nevada mountains before his studio yanked him back to southern California, where he blended the original shots with ones of the Santa Monica Mountains and the Hollywood Hills.

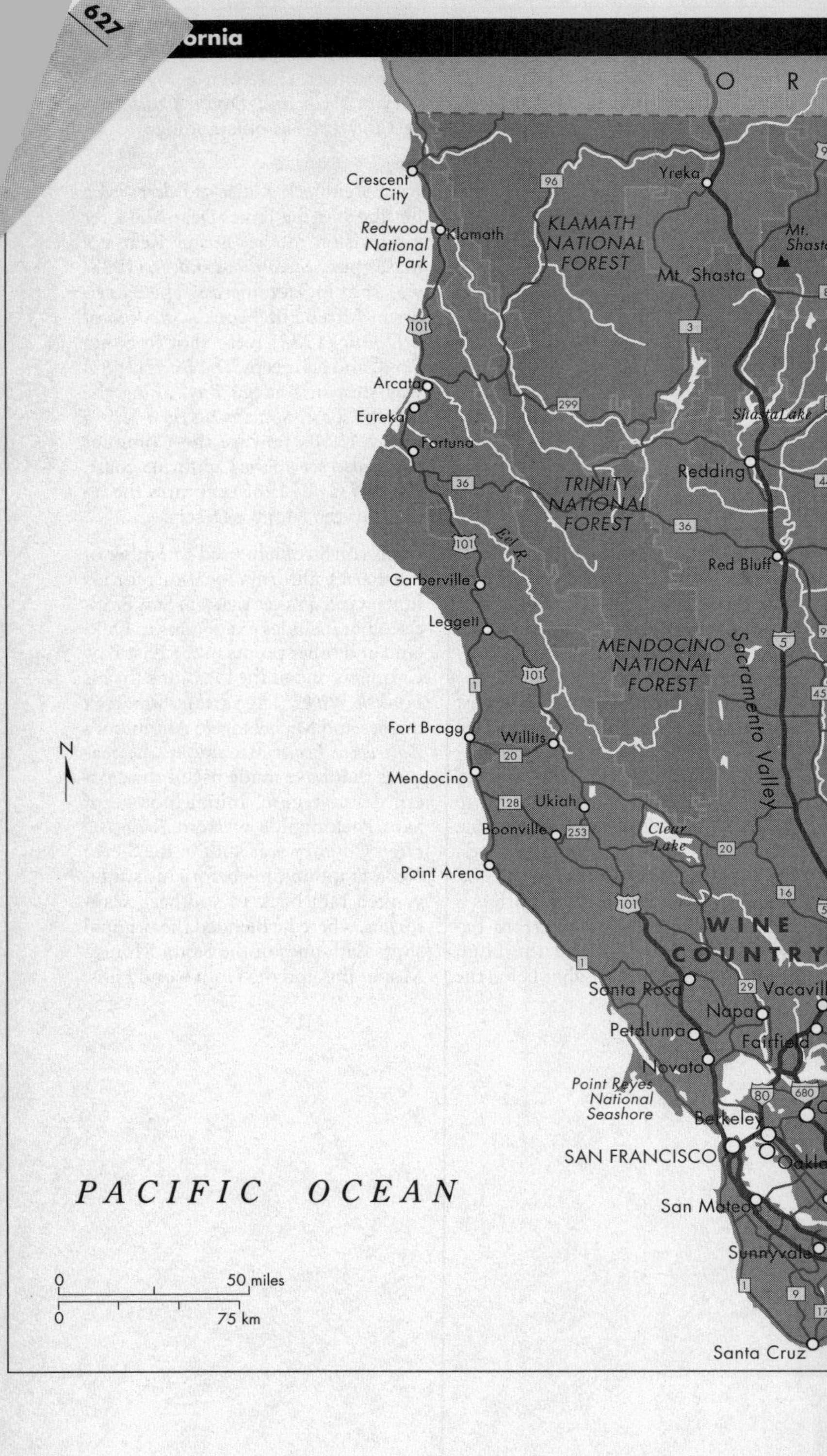
O R
Crescent City
Redwood National Park
Klamath
Yreka
KLAMATH NATIONAL FOREST
Mt. Shasta
Mt. Shasta
Arcata
Eureka
Fortuna
Shasta Lake
Redding
TRINITY NATIONAL FOREST
Eel R.
Red Bluff
Garberville
Leggett
MENDOCINO NATIONAL FOREST
Sacramento Valley
Fort Bragg
Willits
Mendocino
Ukiah
Boonville
Clear Lake
Point Arena
WINE COUNTRY
Santa Rosa
Vacaville
Napa
Petaluma
Fairfield
Novato
Point Reyes National Seashore
Berkeley
SAN FRANCISCO
Oakland
San Mateo
Sunnyvale
Santa Cruz
PACIFIC OCEAN
N
0 50 miles
0 75 km

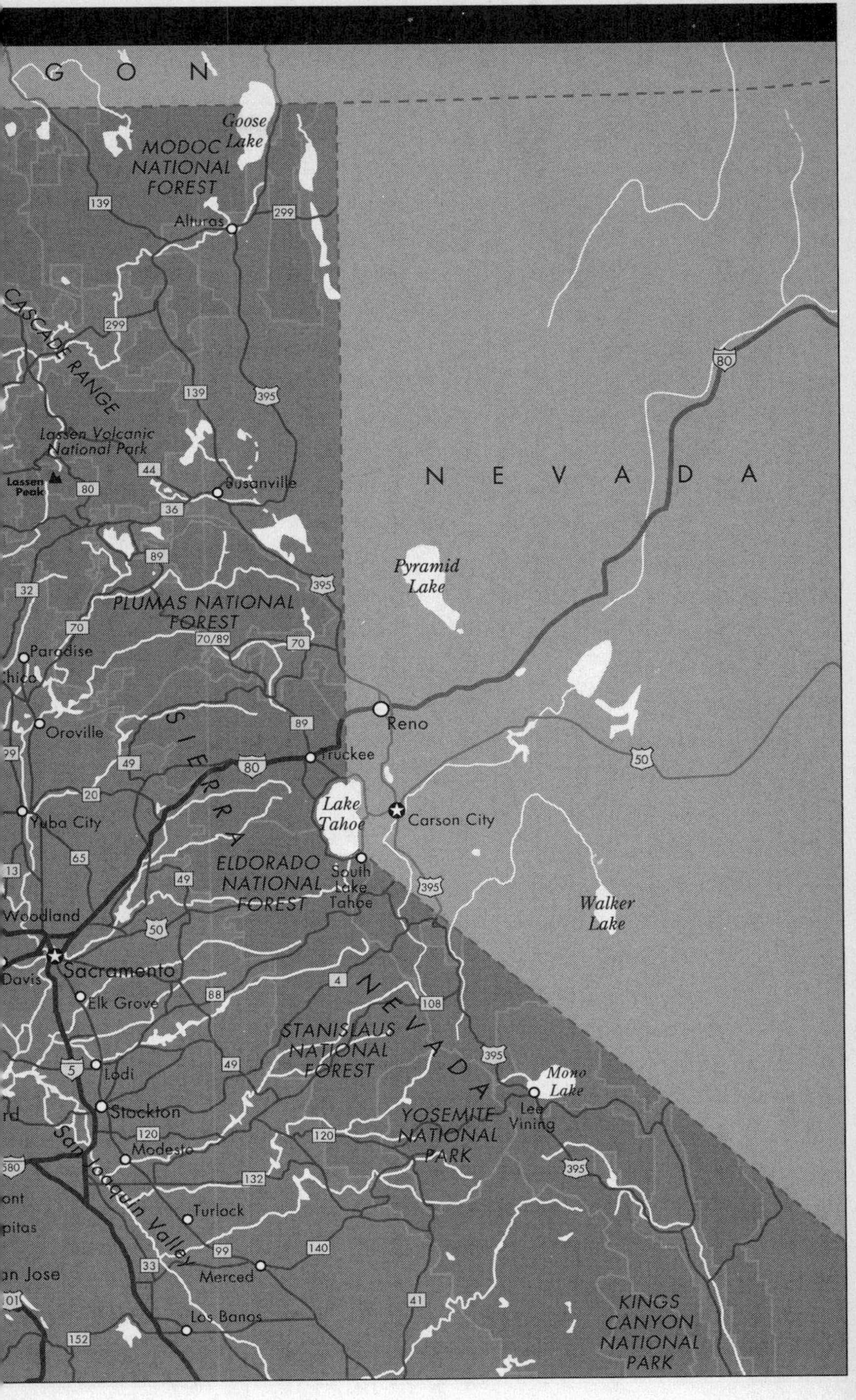

G O N
Goose Lake
MODOC NATIONAL FOREST
139
299
Alturas
CASCADE RANGE
299
139
395
Lassen Volcanic National Park
44
Lassen Peak
80
Susanville
36
89
32
395
PLUMAS NATIONAL FOREST
70
70/89
70
Paradise
Chico
Oroville
SIERRA
89
Truckee
49
80
20
Yuba City
65
13
ELDORADO NATIONAL FOREST
49
Woodland
50
Sacramento
Davis
Elk Grove
88
4
NEVADA
STANISLAUS NATIONAL FOREST
5
Lodi
49
Stockton
120
Modesto
San Joaquin Valley
580
132
Turlock
99
140
33
Merced
an Jose
Los Banos
152
41
108
395
Mono Lake
Lee Vining
YOSEMITE NATIONAL PARK
120
395
KINGS CANYON NATIONAL PARK
N E V A D A
80
Pyramid Lake
Reno
Lake Tahoe
Carson City
South Lake Tahoe
395
50
Walker Lake

Southern California

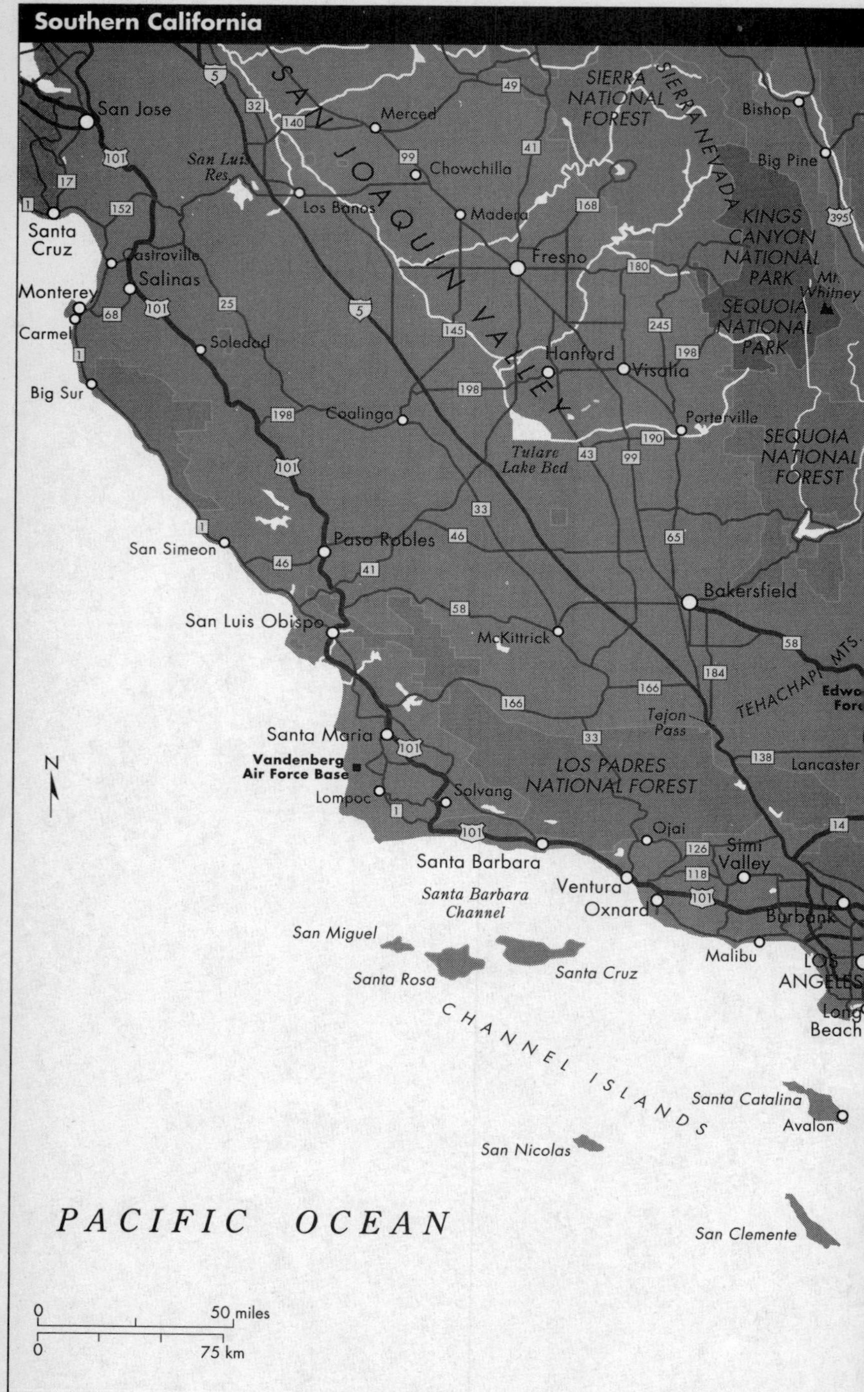

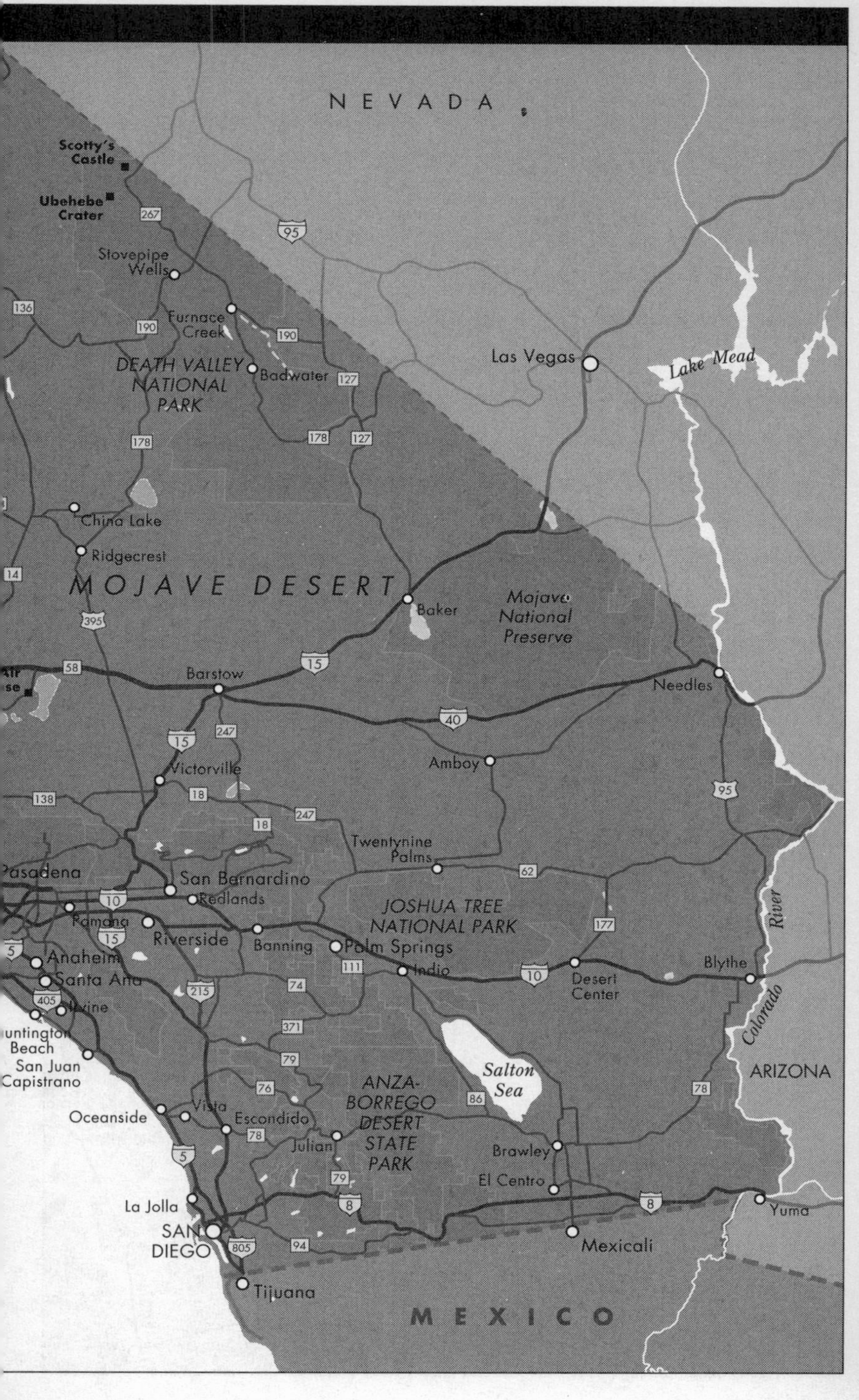
NEVADA
Scotty's Castle
Ubehebe Crater
Stovepipe Wells
Furnace Creek
DEATH VALLEY NATIONAL PARK
Badwater
Las Vegas
Lake Mead
China Lake
Ridgecrest
MOJAVE DESERT
Baker
Mojave National Preserve
Barstow
Needles
Victorville
Amboy
Twentynine Palms
Pasadena
San Bernardino
Redlands
JOSHUA TREE NATIONAL PARK
Pomona
Riverside
Banning
Palm Springs
Indio
Desert Center
Blythe
Anaheim
Santa Ana
Irvine
Huntington Beach
San Juan Capistrano
Colorado River
ARIZONA
Salton Sea
ANZA-BORREGO DESERT STATE PARK
Oceanside
Vista
Escondido
Julian
Brawley
El Centro
La Jolla
SAN DIEGO
Mexicali
Yuma
Tijuana
MEXICO

California Mileage and Driving Times

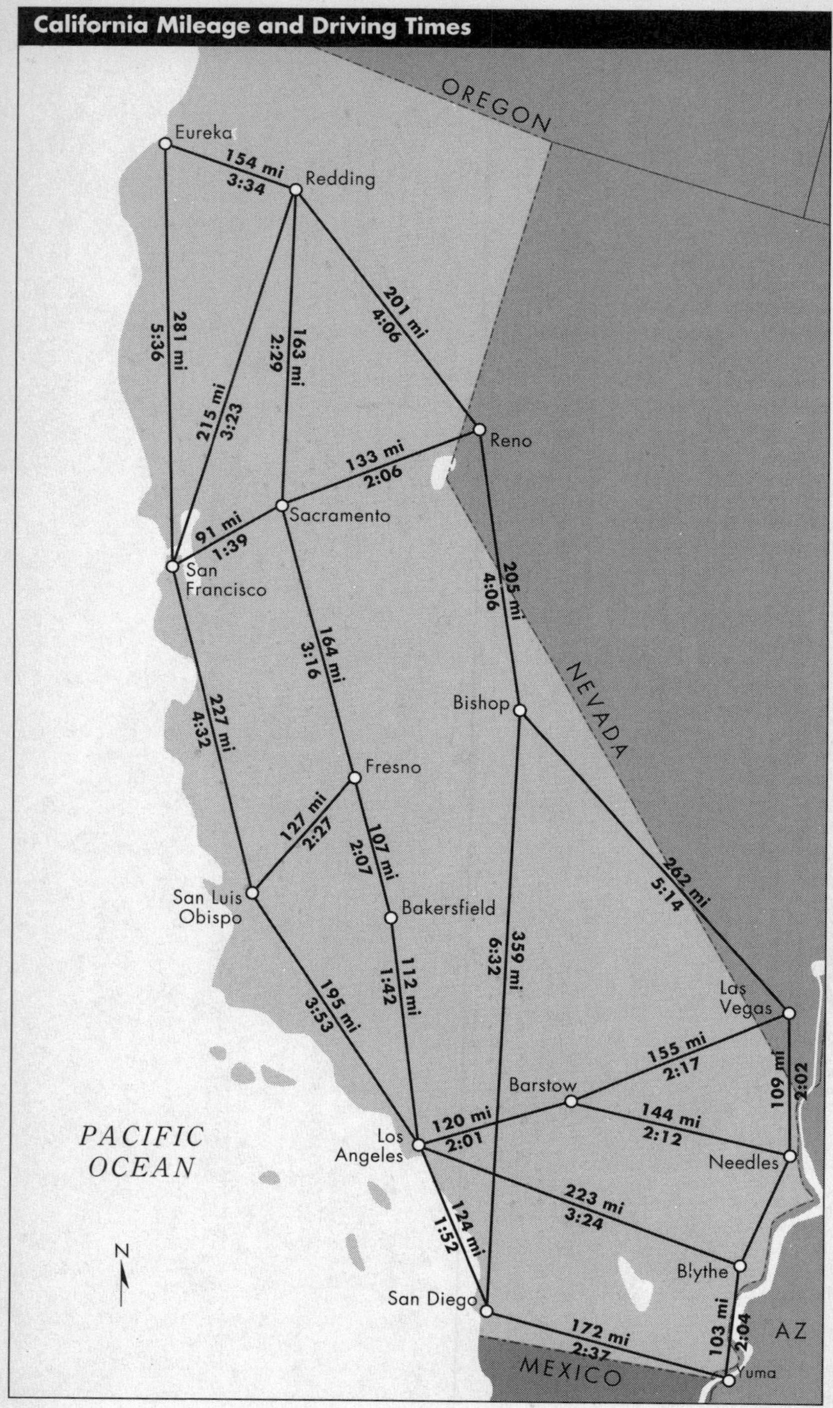

ESSENTIAL INFORMATION

AIR TRAVEL

BOOKING

When you book **look for nonstop flights** and **remember that "direct" flights stop at least once.** Try to avoid connecting flights, which require a change of plane. Because of frequent fog and weather delays there, **avoid booking tight connections in San Francisco.**

CARRIERS

United, with hubs in San Francisco and Los Angeles, has the greatest number of flights into and within California. But most national and many international airlines fly here.

➤ MAJOR AIRLINES: **Air Canada** (☎ 800/776–3000). **Alaska** (☎ 800/426–0333). **America West** (☎ 800/235–9292). **American** (☎ 800/433–7300). **British Airways** (☎ 800/247–9297). **Cathay Pacific** (☎ 800/233–2742). **Continental** (☎ 800/231–0856). **Delta** (☎ 800/221–1212). **Japan Air Lines** (☎ 800/525–3663). **Northwest/KLM** (☎ 800/225–2525). **Qantas** (☎ 800/227–4500). **Southwest** (☎ 800/435–9792). **TWA** (☎ 800/892–4141). **United** (☎ 800/241–6522). **US Airways** (☎ 800/428–4322).

➤ SMALLER AIRLINES: **American Trans Air** (☎ 800/435–9282). **Midwest Express** (☎ 800/452–2022). **Mountain Air** (☎ 562/595–1011 or 800/788–4247). **Reno Air** (☎ 800/736–6247). **Skywest** (☎ 800/453–9417).

➤ FROM THE U.K.: **American** (☎ 0345/789–789). **British Airways** (☎ 0345/222–111). **Delta** (☎ 0800/414–767). **United** (☎ 0800/888–555). **Virgin Atlantic** (☎ 01293/747–747).

CHECK-IN & BOARDING

Assuming that not everyone with a ticket will show up, airlines routinely overbook planes. When everyone does, airlines ask for volunteers to give up their seats. In return, these volunteers usually get a certificate for a free flight and are rebooked on the next flight out. If there are not enough volunteers, the airline must choose who will be denied boarding. The first to get bumped are passengers who checked in late and those flying on discounted tickets, so **get to the gate and check in as early as possible,** especially during peak periods.

Always **bring a government-issued photo I.D. to the airport.** You may be asked to show it before you are allowed to check in.

CUTTING COSTS

The least expensive airfares to California must usually be purchased in advance and are non-refundable. It's smart to **call a number of airlines, and when you are quoted a good price, book it on the spot**—the same fare may not be available the next day. Always **check different routings** and look into using different airports. Travel agents, especially low-fare specialists (☞ Discounts & Deals, *below*), are helpful.

Consolidators are another good source. They buy tickets for scheduled international flights at reduced rates from the airlines, then sell them at prices that beat the best fare available directly from the airlines, usually without restrictions. Sometimes you can even get your money back if you need to return the ticket. Carefully read the fine print detailing penalties for changes and cancellations, and **confirm your consolidator reservation with the airline.**

When you **fly as a courier,** you trade your checked-luggage space for a ticket deeply subsidized by a courier service. There are restrictions on when you can book and how long you can stay.

➤ CONSOLIDATORS: **Cheap Tickets** (☎ 800/377–1000). **Discount Airline Ticket Service** (☎ 800/576–1600). **Unitravel** (☎ 800/325–2222). **Up & Away Travel** (☎ 212/889–2345). **World Travel Network** (☎ 800/409–6753).

ENJOYING THE FLIGHT

For more legroom **request an emergency-aisle seat at check-in;** these seats are usually only assigned at the airport. Don't sit in the row in front of the emergency aisle or in front of a bulkhead, where seats may not recline. If you have dietary concerns, **ask for special meals when booking.** These can be vegetarian, low-cholesterol, or kosher, for example. On long flights, try to maintain a normal routine, to help fight jet lag. Reset your watch at the beginning of the flight. At night, **get some sleep.** By day, **eat light meals, drink water** (not alcohol), and **move around the cabin** to stretch your legs.

FLYING TIMES

Flying time is roughly six hours from New York and four hours from Chicago. Travel from London to Los Angeles or San Francisco takes about 10 hours, and from Sydney approximately 14. Flying between San Francisco and Los Angeles takes one hour.

HOW TO COMPLAIN

If your baggage goes astray or your flight goes awry, complain right away. Most carriers require that you **file a claim immediately.**

➤ AIRLINE COMPLAINTS: U.S. Department of Transportation **Aviation Consumer Protection Division** (✉ C-75, Room 4107, Washington, DC 20590, ☎ 202/366–2220, airconsumer@ost.dot.gov, www.dot.gov/airconsumer). **Federal Aviation Administration Consumer Hotline** (☎ 800/322–7873).

SAFETY

Those flying with a laptop computer should **be on the lookout for scam artists at the airport.** The ruse typically involves a pair who wait until your computer case is on the X-ray belt, then step through the portal and set off an alarm. While security checks that person for contraband—forcing you to wait—their partner walks off with your computer.

Be wary of solicitations at the airport. Recently, airline travelers have complained of harassment by solicitors, including some who pose as airport officials asking unsuspecting foreign passengers for "airport taxes," which don't exist. Officials have begun cracking down on all charities—some of which are legitimate—by allowing them to accept only checks or credit cards.

AIRPORTS

Major gateways to California are **Los Angeles International Airport (LAX), San Francisco International Airport (SFO),** and **San Diego International Airport (SAN).**

➤ AIRPORT INFORMATION: **Los Angeles International Airport** (☎ 310/646–5252). **San Diego International Airport** (☎ 619/231–2100). **San Francisco International Airport** (☎ 650/761–0800).

BIKE TRAVEL

There are beautiful places to bike throughout California. For each part of the state, please see the specific chapter.

BIKES IN FLIGHT

Most airlines accommodate bikes as luggage, provided they are dismantled and boxed. For bike boxes, often free at bike shops, you'll pay about $5 from airlines (at least $100 for bike bags). International travelers can sometimes substitute a bike for a piece of checked luggage at no charge; otherwise, the cost is about $100. Domestic and Canadian airlines charge $25–$50.

BUS TRAVEL

Because of the state's size, traveling by bus in California can be slow. But if you don't want to rent a car and wish to go where the train does not, a bus may be your only option. Greyhound is the major carrier for intermediate and long distances, though smaller, regional bus service is available in metropolitan areas. Check the specific chapters for the regions you plan to visit. Smoking is prohibited on all buses in California.

CUTTING COSTS

You can purchase an Ameripass through Greyhound up to 45 minutes prior to departure. Depending on which type you buy, an Ameripass offers unlimited travel on all routes for between one week and three months. Inquire also about seasonal advance-purchase fares. Reserving by phone with a credit card requires you have a U.S. billing address. Otherwise, you may purchase tickets only at a terminal.

➤ Bus Information: **Greyhound** (☎ 800/231–2222).

BUSINESS HOURS

Banks in California are typically open from 9 to 4 and are closed most holidays (☞ Holidays *below*). Smaller shops usually operate from 10 to 6, with larger stores remaining open until 8 or later. Hours vary for museums and historical sites, and many are closed one or more days a week. It's a good idea to **check before you visit a tourist site.** Many gas stations are open 24 hours, especially on interstate highways. In rural areas many close early, so fill up before nightfall.

CAMERAS & PHOTOGRAPHY

The pounding surf, glorious mountains, sprawling deserts, towering trees, and sparkling beaches—not to mention the cities and towns in between—make California a photographer's dream destination. Bring lots of film to capture the special moments of your trip.

➤ Photo Help: **Kodak Information Center** (☎ 800/242–2424). ***Kodak Guide to Shooting Great Travel Pictures,*** available in bookstores or from Fodor's Travel Publications (☎ 800/533–6478; $16.50 plus $5.50 shipping).

EQUIPMENT PRECAUTIONS

Always **keep your film and tape out of the sun.** Carry an extra supply of batteries, and **be prepared to turn on your camera or camcorder** to prove to security personnel that the device is real. Always **ask for hand inspection of film,** which becomes clouded after repeated exposure to airport X-ray machines, and **keep videotapes away from metal detectors.**

CAR RENTAL

A car is essential in most parts of California. In compact San Francisco, it's better to use public transportation to avoid parking headaches. In sprawling cities such as Los Angeles and San Diego, however, getting just about anywhere requires making use of the freeways.

Rates in Los Angeles begin at around $29 a day and $125 a week. This does not include tax on car rentals, which is 8¼%. In San Diego, rates for an economy car with unlimited mileage begin around $23 a day and $137 a week. The tax is an additional 7¾%. In San Francisco, rates begin around $30 a day and $150 a week. The tax is 8½%.

➤ Major Agencies: **Alamo** (☎ 800/327–9633; 020/8759–6200 in the U.K.). **Avis** (☎ 800/331–1212; 800/879–2847 in Canada; 02/9353–9000 in Australia; 09/525–1982 in New Zealand). **Budget** (☎ 800/527–0700; 0144/227–6266 in the U.K.). **Dollar** (☎ 800/800–4000; 020/8897–0811 in the U.K., where it is known as Eurodollar; 02/9223–1444 in Australia). **Hertz** (☎ 800/654–3131; 800/263–0600 in Canada; 020/8897–2072 in the U.K.; 02/9669–2444 in Australia; 03/358–6777 in New Zealand). **National InterRent** (☎ 800/227–7368; 0345/222525 in the U.K., where it is known as Europcar InterRent).

CONVERTIBLES AND SUVS

If you dream of driving down the coast with the top down, or you want to explore the desert landscape not visible from the road, consider renting a specialty vehicle. Agencies that specialize in convertibles and sport-utility vehicles will often arrange airport delivery in larger cities.

➤ Specialty Car Agencies: In San Francisco, **Specialty Rentals.com** (☎ 800/400–8412); in Los Angeles, **Budget of Beverly Hills** (☎ 800/729–7350); in San Diego, **Rent-a-Vette** (☎ 800/627–0808).

CUTTING COSTS

When pricing cars, **ask about the location of the rental lot.** Some off-airport locations offer lower rates, and their lots are only minutes from the terminal via complimentary shuttle. To get the best deal, **book through a travel agent who will shop around.** Also **price local car-rental companies,** although the service and maintenance may not be as good as those of a major player. Remember to ask about required deposits, cancellation penalties, and drop-off charges if you're planning to pick up the car in one city and leave it in another. If you're traveling during a holiday period, also make sure that a confirmed reservation guarantees you a car.

Do **look into wholesalers,** companies that do not own fleets but rent in bulk from those that do and often offer better rates than traditional car-rental operations.

➤ WHOLESALERS: **Auto Europe** (☎ 207/842–2000 or 800/223–5555, FAX 800/235–6321, www.autoeurope.com). **Kemwel Holiday Autos** (☎ 800/678–0678, FAX 914/825–3160, www.kemwel.com).

INSURANCE

When driving a rented car you are generally responsible for any damage to or loss of the vehicle as well as for any property damage or personal injury that you may cause. Before you rent see what coverage your personal auto-insurance policy and credit cards already provide.

For about $15 to $20 per day, rental companies sell protection, known as a collision- or loss-damage waiver (CDW or LDW), that eliminates your liability for damage to the car. Some states, including California, have capped the price of the CDW and LDW. In most states you don't need a CDW if you have personal auto insurance or other liability insurance. However, **make sure you have enough coverage to pay for the car.** If you do not have auto insurance or an umbrella policy that covers damage to third parties, purchasing liability insurance and a CDW or LDW is highly recommended. If you plan to take the car out of California, **ask if the policy is valid in other states or countries.** Most car rental companies will not insure a loss or damage that occurs outside of their coverage area—particularly in Mexico.

REQUIREMENTS & RESTRICTIONS

In California you must be 21 to rent a car, and rates may be higher if you're under 25. You'll pay extra for child seats (about $3 per day), which are compulsory for children under five, and for additional drivers (about $2 per day). Non-U.S. residents will need a reservation voucher, a passport, a driver's license, and a travel policy that covers each driver, when picking up a car.

SURCHARGES

Before you pick up a car in one city and leave it in another, **ask about drop-off charges or one-way service fees,** which can be substantial. Note, too, that some rental agencies charge extra if you return the car before the time specified in your contract. To avoid a hefty refueling fee, **fill the tank just before you turn in the car,** but be aware that gas stations near the rental outlet may overcharge.

CAR TRAVEL

Three major highways—Interstate 5 (I–5), U.S. 101, and Highway 1—run north-south through the state. The main routes into the state from the east are I–15 and I–10 in southern California and I–80 in northern California.

AUTO CLUBS

➤ IN AUSTRALIA: **Australian Automobile Association** (☎ 02/6247–7311).

➤ IN CANADA: **Canadian Automobile Association** (CAA, ☎ 613/247–0117).

➤ IN NEW ZEALAND: **New Zealand Automobile Association** (☎ 09/377–4660).

➤ IN THE U.K.: **Automobile Association** (AA, ☎ 0990/500–600). **Royal Automobile Club** (RAC, ☎ 0990/722–722 for membership; 0345/121–345 for insurance).

➤ IN THE U.S.: **American Automobile Association** (☎ 800/564–6222).

EMERGENCIES

Dial 911 to report accidents on the road and to reach police, the California Highway Patrol, or fire department. On some rural highways, look for emergency phones on the side of the road.

GASOLINE

Prices vary widely depending on location, oil company, and whether you buy full-serve or self-serve gasoline. Prices on the West Coast are significantly higher than in the Midwest, and it is less expensive to buy fuel in southern part of the state than in the north. If you are planning travel around the Nevada border, you can save a lot by purchasing it there. At press time, regular unleaded gasoline at self-serve stations averaged about $1.70 a gallon.

ROAD CONDITIONS

Rainly weather can make driving along the coast or in the mountains treacherous. Some of the smaller routes over the mountain ranges are prone to flash flooding. When the rains are severe, coastal Highway 1 can quickly become a slippery nightmare, buffeted by strong winds and obstructed by falling debris from the cliffs above. When the weather is particularly bad, Highway 1 may be closed. Drivers should **check road conditions before heading into stormy weather.**

Snow is an even bigger concern for drivers. If it is raining at the coast, it is usually snowing at higher elevations. Many smaller roads are closed in winter, and tire chains may be required on routes that are open. You should **purchase tire chains before you get to the mountains,** where the cost may double. Garages and gas stations on I–80 and US 50 will install chains for $20 or remove them for $10. On smaller roads, you are on your own. Always carry extra clothing, blankets, and food when driving to the mountains in the winter, and keep your gas tank full to prevent the fuel line from freezing.

In larger cities, the biggest driving hazards are traffic jams. **Avoid major urban highways, especially at rush hour.**

➤ ROAD CONDITIONS: Statewide hotline (☎ 800/427–7623). Northern California updates (☎ 916/445–7623). Southern California updates (☎ 213/628–7623).

ROAD MAPS

You can buy detailed maps in bookstores and gas stations and at some grocery and drug stores. The various California branches of the American Automobile Association (☞ *above*) have state and local maps that are free to members.

RULES OF THE ROAD

The speed limit on many rural highways is 70 mph. In the cities, freeway speed limits are between 55 mph and 65 mph. Many city routes have commuter lanes, but the operating rules vary from city to city: in San Francisco, for example, you need three people in a car to use these lanes, in Los Angeles only two.

Seat belts are required at all times. Tickets can be given for failing to comply. Small children must be in child safety seats. Unless otherwise indicated, right turns are allowed on red lights after you've come to a full stop, and left turns onto adjoining one-way streets are allowed at red lights after you've come to a full stop. Drivers with a blood-alcohol level higher than 0.08 who are stopped by police are subject to arrest, and police can detain those with a level of 0.05 if they appear impaired. The state's drunk-driving laws are extremely tough. The licenses of violators are immediately be suspended, and they may have to spend the night in jail and pay hefty fines.

CHILDREN IN CALIFORNIA

California is made to order for traveling with children: youngsters love Disneyland, the San Diego Zoo, the Monterey Aquarium, the San Francisco cable cars, the gold mine in Placerville, Forestiere Underground Gardens in Fresno, and the caverns near Lake Shasta.

If you are renting a car, don't forget to **arrange for a car seat** when you reserve.

➤ LOCAL INFORMATION: Consult Fodor's lively by-parents, for-parents ***Where Should We Take the Kids? California*** (available in bookstores, or ☎ 800/533–6478; $17).

FLYING

If your children are two or older, **ask about children's airfares.** As a general rule, infants under two not occupying a seat fly at greatly reduced fares or even for free. Experts agree that it's a good idea to use safety seats aloft for children weighing less than 40 pounds. Airlines set their own policies: U.S. carriers usually require that the child be ticketed, even if he or she is young enough to ride free, since the seats must be strapped into regular seats. Do **check your airline's policy about using safety seats during takeoff and landing.** And since safety seats are not allowed just everywhere in the plane, get your seat assignments early.

When reserving, **request children's meals or a freestanding bassinet** if you need them. But note that bulkhead seats, where you must sit to use the bassinet, may lack an overhead bin or storage space on the floor.

LODGING

Most hotels in California allow children under a certain age to stay in their parents' room at no extra charge, but others charge for them as extra adults; be sure to **find out the cutoff age for children's discounts.**

SIGHTS & ATTRACTIONS

Places that are especially appealing to children are indicated by a rubber duckie icon in the margin.

CONCIERGES

Concierges, found in many hotels, can help you with theater tickets and dinner reservations: a good one with connections may be able to get you seats for a hot show or prime-time dinner reservations at the restaurant of the moment. You can also turn to your hotel's concierge for help with travel arrangements, sightseeing plans, services ranging from aromatherapy to zipper repair, and emergencies. You should **always tip** a concierge who has been of assistance (☞ Tipping, *below*).

CONSUMER PROTECTION

Whenever shopping or buying travel services in California, **pay with a major credit card** so you can cancel payment or get reimbursed if there's a problem. If you're doing business with a particular company for the first time, **contact your local Better Business Bureau and the attorney general's offices** in your own state and the company's home state, as well. Have any complaints been filed? Finally, if you're buying a package or tour, always **consider travel insurance** that includes default coverage (☞ Insurance, *below*).

➤ BBBs: **Council of Better Business Bureaus** (✉ 4200 Wilson Blvd., Suite 800, Arlington, VA 22203, ☎ 703/276–0100, FAX 703/525–8277, www.bbb.org).

CUSTOMS & DUTIES

When shopping, **keep receipts** for all purchases. Upon reentering the country, **be ready to show customs officials what you've bought.** If you feel a duty is incorrect or object to the way your clearance was handled, note the inspector's badge number and ask to see a supervisor. If the problem isn't resolved, write to the appropriate authorities, beginning with the port director at your point of entry.

IN AUSTRALIA

Australian residents who are 18 or older may bring home $A400 worth of souvenirs and gifts (including jewelry), 250 cigarettes or 250 grams of tobacco, and 1,125 ml of alcohol (including wine, beer, and spirits). Residents under 18 may bring back $A200 worth of goods. Prohibited items include meat products. Seeds, plants, and fruits need to be declared upon arrival.

➤ INFORMATION: **Australian Customs Service** (Regional Director, ✉ Box 8, Sydney, NSW 2001, ☎ 02/9213–2000, FAX 02/9213–4000).

IN CANADA

Canadian residents who have been out of Canada for at least 7 days may bring home C$500 worth of goods duty-free. If you've been away less than 7 days but more than 48 hours, the duty-free allowance drops to C$200; if your trip lasts 24–48 hours, the allowance is C$50. You may not pool allowances with family members. Goods claimed under the C$500 exemption may follow you by mail; those claimed under the lesser exemptions must accompany you. Alcohol and tobacco products may be included in the 7-day and 48-hour exemptions but not in the 24-hour exemption. If you meet the age requirements of the province or territory through which you reenter Canada, you may bring in, duty-free, 1.14 liters (40 imperial ounces) of wine or liquor *or* 24 12-ounce cans or bottles of beer or ale. If you are 16 or older you may bring in, duty-free, 200 cigarettes and 50 cigars. Check ahead of time with Revenue Canada or the Department of Agriculture for policies regarding meat products, seeds, plants, and fruits.

You may send an unlimited number of gifts worth up to C$60 each duty-free to Canada. Label the package UNSOLICITED GIFT—VALUE UNDER $60. Alcohol and tobacco are excluded.

➤ INFORMATION: **Revenue Canada** (✉ 2265 St. Laurent Blvd. S, Ottawa, Ontario K1G 4K3, ☎ 613/993–0534; 800/461–9999 in Canada, FAX 613/957–8911, www.ccra-adrc.gc.ca).

IN NEW ZEALAND

Homeward-bound residents 17 or older may bring back $700 worth of souvenirs and gifts. Your duty-free allowance also includes 4.5 liters of wine or beer; one 1,125-ml bottle of spirits; and either 200 cigarettes, 250 grams of tobacco, 50 cigars, or a combination of the three up to 250 grams. Prohibited items include meat products, seeds, plants, and fruits.

➤ INFORMATION: **New Zealand Customs** (Custom House, ✉ 50 Anzac Ave., Box 29, Auckland, New Zealand, ☎ 09/359–6655, FAX 09/359–6732).

IN THE U.K.

From countries outside the EU, including the United States, you may bring home, duty-free, 200 cigarettes or 50 cigars; 1 liter of spirits or 2 liters of fortified or sparkling wine or liqueurs; 2 liters of still table wine; 60 ml of perfume; 250 ml of toilet water; plus £136 worth of other goods, including gifts and souvenirs. If returning from outside the EU, prohibited items include meat products, seeds, plants, and fruits.

➤ INFORMATION: **HM Customs and Excise** (✉ Dorset House, Stamford St., Bromley, Kent BR1 1XX, ☎ 020/7202–4227).

IN THE U.S.

➤ INFORMATION: **U.S. Customs Service** (✉ 1300 Pennsylvania Ave. NW, Washington, DC 20229, www.customs.gov; inquiries ☎ 202/354–1000; complaints c/o ✉ Office of Regulations and Rulings; registration of equipment c/o ✉ Resource Management, ☎ 202/927–0540).

DINING

California has led the pack in bringing natural and organic foods to the forefront of American cooking. The Asian and Latin influence in California cooking is also strong. Wherever you go, you're likely to find fresh local ingredients and produce being used.

The restaurants we list are the cream of the crop in each price category. Properties indicated by an ✕🏨 are lodging establishments whose restaurant warrants a special trip. Lunch hours are typically 11:30–2:30, and dinner service in most restaurants begins at 5:30 and ends at 10. Many restaurants in larger cities stay open until midnight or later.

RESERVATIONS & DRESS

Reservations are always a good idea: we mention them only when they're essential or not accepted. Book as far ahead as you can, and reconfirm as soon as you arrive. We mention dress only when men are required to wear a jacket or a jacket and tie.

WINE, BEER & SPIRITS

If you like wine, no trip to California can be complete without trying a few of the local vintages. Throughout the state, but especially in the famed regions of Napa and Sonoma valleys, you'll find wineries to visit with tours and tasting rooms available (☞ Chapter 3). In the Far North, beer lovers will want to stop at the Sierra Nevada Brewing Company (☞ Chapter 2). The legal drinking age is 21.

DISABILITIES & ACCESSIBILITY

California is a national leader in making attractions and facilities accessible to people with disabilities. The Americans with Disabilities Act (ADA) requires that all businesses make accommodations for individuals with any physical handicap, and state laws provide special privileges, such as license plates allowing special parking spaces, unlimited parking in time-limited spaces, and free parking in metered spaces. Insignia from other states are honored.

LODGING

When discussing accessibility with an operator or reservations agent, **ask hard questions.** Are there any stairs, inside *or* out? Are there grab bars next to the toilet *and* in the shower/tub? How wide is the doorway to the room? To the bathroom? For the most extensive facilities meeting the latest legal specifications, **opt for newer accommodations.**

PARKS

The National Park Service provides a Golden Access Passport for all national parks free of charge to those who are medically blind or have a permanent disability; the passport covers the entry fee for the holder and anyone accompanying the holder in the same private vehicle as well as a 50% discount on camping and various other user fees. Apply for the passport in person at a national recreation facility that charges an entrance fee; proof of disability is required.

TRANSPORTATION

Hertz and Avis (☞ Car Rental *above*) are able to supply cars modified for those with disabilities, but they require one- to two-days' advance notice. Discounts are available for travelers with disabilities on Amtrak (☞ Train Travel *below*). On Greyhound (☞ Bus Travel *above*), your companion can ride free.

➤ COMPLAINTS: **Disability Rights Section** (✉ U.S. Department of Justice, Civil Rights Division, Box 66738, Washington, DC 20035-6738, ☎ 202/514–0301 or 800/514–0301; TTY 202/514–0301 or 800/514–0301, FAX 202/307–1198) for general complaints. **Aviation Consumer Protection Division** (☞ Air Travel, *above*) for airline-related problems. **Civil Rights Office** (✉ U.S. Department of Transportation, Departmental Office of Civil Rights, S-30, 400 7th St. SW, Room 10215, Washington, DC 20590, ☎ 202/366–4648, FAX 202/366–9371) for problems with surface transportation.

TRAVEL AGENCIES

In the United States, the Americans with Disabilities Act requires that travel firms serve the needs of all travelers. Some agencies specialize in working with people with disabilities.

➤ TRAVELERS WITH MOBILITY PROBLEMS: **Access Adventures** (✉ 206 Chestnut Ridge Rd., Rochester, NY 14624, ☎ 716/889–9096, dltravel@prodigy.net), run by a former physical-rehabilitation counselor. **Accessible Vans of the Rockies** (✉ 2040 W. Hamilton Pl., Sheridan, CO 80110, ☎ 303/806–5047 or 888/837–0065, FAX 303/781–2329, www.access-able.com/avr/avrockies.htm). **CareVacations** (✉ 5-5110 50th Ave., Leduc, Alberta T9E 6V4, ☎ 780/986–6404 or 877/478–7827, FAX 780/986–8332, www.carevacations.com), for group tours and cruise vacations. **Flying Wheels Travel** (✉ 143 W. Bridge St., Box 382, Owatonna, MN 55060, ☎ 507/451–5005 or 800/535–6790, FAX 507/451–1685, thq@ll.net, www.flyingwheels.com). **Hinsdale Travel Service** (✉ 201 E. Ogden Ave., Suite 100, Hinsdale, IL 60521, ☎ 630/325–1335, FAX 630/325–1342, hinstrvl@interaccess.com). **Wilderness Inquiry, Inc.** (✉ 1313 5th St. SE, Box 84, Minneapolis, MN 55414-1546, ☎ 541/343–1284 or 800/728–0719) is a non-profit organization that plans outdoor adventures for all ages, backgrounds, and abilities.

➤ TRAVELERS WITH DEVELOPMENTAL DISABILITIES: **New Directions** (✉ 5276 Hollister Ave., Suite 207, Santa Barbara, CA 93111, ☎ 805/967–2841 or 888/967–2841, FAX 805/964–7344, newdirec@silcom.com, www.silcom.com/ánewdirec/). **Sprout** (✉ 893 Amsterdam Ave., New York, NY 10025, ☎ 212/222–9575 or 888/222–9575, FAX 212/222–9768, sprout@interport.net, www.gosprout.org).

DISCOUNTS & DEALS

Be a smart shopper and **compare all your options** before making decisions. A plane ticket bought with a promotional coupon from travel clubs, coupon books, and direct-mail offers may not be cheaper than the least expensive fare from a discount ticket agency. And always keep in mind that what you get is just as important as what you save.

DISCOUNT RESERVATIONS

To save money, **look into discount reservations services** with toll-free numbers, which use their buying power to get a better price on hotels, airline tickets, even car rentals. When booking a room, always **call the hotel's local toll-free number** (if one is available) rather than the central reservations number—you'll often get a better price. Always ask about special packages or corporate rates.

➤ AIRLINE TICKETS: ☎ **800/FLY-4-LESS.** ☎ **800/FLY-ASAP.**

➤ HOTEL ROOMS: **Accommodations Express** (☎ 800/444–7666, www.accommodationsexpress.com). **Central Reservation Service (CRS)** (☎ 800/548–3311). **Hotel Reservations Network** (☎ 800/964–6835, www.hoteldiscounts.com). **Quickbook** (☎ 800/789–9887, www.quickbook.com). **RMC Travel** (☎ 800/245–5738, www.rmcwebtravel.com). **Steigenberger Reservation Service** (☎ 800/223–5652, www.srs-worldhotels.com). **Turbotrip.com** (☎ 800/473–7829, www.turbotrip.com).

PACKAGE DEALS

Don't confuse packages and guided tours. When you buy a package, you travel on your own, just as though you had planned the trip yourself. Fly/drive packages, which combine airfare and car rental, are often a good deal.

DIVERS' ALERT

Do not fly within 24 hours of scuba diving.

ECOTOURISM

When travelling in wilderness areas and parks, remember to **pack-out what you pack-in.** Many remote camping areas do not provide waste disposal. It's a good idea to bring plastic bags to store refuse until you can dispose of it properly. Recycling programs are abundant in California, and trash at many state and national parks is sorted. Look for appropriately labeled garbage containers. Numerous ecotours are available in California (☞ Tours & Packages, *below*).

GAY & LESBIAN TRAVEL

San Francisco, Los Angeles, West Hollywood, San Diego, and Palm Springs are among the California cities with visible lesbian and gay communities. Though it is usually safe to be visibly "out" in many areas, you should always use common sense when in unfamiliar places. Gays bashings still occur in both urban and rural areas.

LOCAL INFORMATION

Many California cities large and small have lesbian and gay publications available in sidewalk racks and at bars and other social spaces; most have extensive events and information listings.

➤ COMMUNITY CENTERS: **Billy DeFrank Lesbian & Gay Community Center** (✉ 175 Stockton Ave., San Jose 95126, ☎ 408/293–2429). **Gay and Lesbian Community Services Center** (✉ 1625 N. Schrader Blvd., Los Angeles 90028, ☎ 323/993–7400). **Lambda Community Center** (✉ 920 20th St., Sacramento 95814, ☎ 916/442–0185). **The Lavender Youth Recreation & Information Center** (✉ 127 Collingwood St., San Francisco 94114, ☎ 415/703–6150; 415/863–3636 for HIV hotline). **Lesbian and Gay Men's Community Center** (✉ 3916 Normal St., San Diego 92103, ☎ 619/692–4297). **Pacific Center Lesbian, Gay and Bisexual Switchboard** (✉ 2712 Telegraph Ave., Berkeley 94705, ☎ 510/548–8283).

➤ LOCAL PUBLICATIONS: ***Bay Area Reporter*** (✉ 395 9th St., San Francisco 94103, ☎ 415/861–5019). ***Bottom Line*** (✉ 1243 N. Gene Autry Trail, Suite 121, Palm Springs 92262, ☎ 760/323–0552). ***Edge*** (✉ 6434 Santa Monica Blvd., Los Angeles

90038, ☎ 323/962–6994). *Update* (✉ 2801 4th Ave., San Diego, 92103, ☎ 619/299–0500). *Mom Guess What* (✉ 1725 L St., Sacramento 95814, ☎ 916/441–6397).

➤ GAY- & LESBIAN-FRIENDLY TRAVEL AGENCIES: **Different Roads Travel** (✉ 8383 Wilshire Blvd., Suite 902, Beverly Hills, CA 90211, ☎ 323/651–5557 or 800/429–8747, FAX 323/651–3678, leigh@west.tzell.com). **Kennedy Travel** (✉ 314 Jericho Turnpike, Floral Park, NY 11001, ☎ 516/352–4888 or 800/237–7433, FAX 516/354–8849, main@kennedytravel.com, www.kennedytravel.com). **Now Voyager** (✉ 4406 18th St., San Francisco, CA 94114, ☎ 415/626–1169 or 800/255–6951, FAX 415/626–8626, www.nowvoyager.com). **Skylink Travel and Tour** (✉ 1006 Mendocino Ave., Santa Rosa, CA 95401, ☎ 707/546–9888 or 800/225–5759, FAX 707/546–9891, skylinktvl@aol.com, www.skylinktravel.com), serving lesbian travelers.

HOLIDAYS

Major national holidays include New Year's Day (Jan. 1); Martin Luther King, Jr., Day (3rd Mon. in Jan.); President's Day (3rd Mon. in Feb.); Memorial Day (last Mon. in May); Independence Day (July 4); Labor Day (1st Mon. in Sept.); Thanksgiving Day (4th Thurs. in Nov.); Christmas Eve and Christmas Day (Dec. 24 and 25); and New Year's Eve (Dec. 31).

Most traditional businesses are closed these days, but tourist attractions and some restaurants are usually open except on Thanksgiving, Christmas, and New Year's Day.

INSURANCE

The most useful travel insurance plan is a comprehensive policy that includes coverage for trip cancellation and interruption, default, trip delay, and medical expenses (with a waiver for preexisting conditions).

Without insurance you will lose all or most of your money if you cancel your trip, regardless of the reason. Default insurance covers you if your tour operator, airline, or cruise line goes out of business. Trip-delay covers expenses that arise because of bad weather or mechanical delays. Study the fine print when comparing policies.

Always **buy travel policies directly from the insurance company**; if you buy them from a cruise line, airline, or tour operator that goes out of business you probably will not be covered for the agency or operator's default, a major risk. Before making any purchase, **review your existing health and home-owner's policies** to find what they cover away from home.

➤ TRAVEL INSURERS: In the U.S.: **Access America** (✉ 6600 W. Broad St., Richmond, VA 23230, ☎ 804/285–3300 or 800/284–8300, FAX 804/673–1583, www.previewtravel.com), **Travel Guard International** (✉ 1145 Clark St., Stevens Point, WI 54481, ☎ 715/345–0505 or 800/826–1300, FAX 800/955–8785, www.noelgroup.com).

➤ INSURANCE INFORMATION: In the U.K.: **Association of British Insurers** (✉ 51–55 Gresham St., London EC2V 7HQ, ☎ 020/7600–3333, FAX 020/7696–8999, info@abi.org.uk, www.abi.org.uk). In Australia: **Insurance Council of Australia** (☎ 03/9614–1077, FAX 03/9614–7924).

FOR INTERNATIONAL TRAVELERS

➤ CONSULATES: **Australia** (✉ Century Plaza Towers; 19th floor; 2049 Century Park E, Los Angeles 90067, ☎ 310/229–4800) or (✉ 1 Bush St., San Francisco, 94104, ☎ 415/362–6160). **Canada** (✉ 300 S. Grand Ave., Suite 1000, Los Angeles 90071, ☎ 213/346–2701). **New Zealand** (✉ 12400 Wilshire Blvd., Suite 1150, Los Angeles 90025, ☎ 310/207–1605) or (✉ One Maritime Plaza, Suite 700, San Francisco 94111, ☎ 415/399–1255). **United Kingdom** (✉ 11766 Wilshire Blvd., Suite 400, Los Angeles 90025, ☎ 310/477–3322) or (✉ One Sansome St., Suite 850, San Francisco, ☎ 415/981–3030).

CURRENCY

The dollar is the basic unit of U.S. currency. It has 100 cents. Coins include the copper penny (1¢); the silvery nickel (5¢), dime (10¢), quarter (25¢), and half-dollar (50¢); and the golden $1 coin, replacing a now-rare silver dollar. Bills are denominated $1, $5, $10, $20, $50, and $100, all green and identical in size; designs vary. The exchange rate at press time was $1.50 per British pound, 67¢ per Canadian dollar, 58¢ per Australian dollar, and 46¢ per New Zealand dollar.

CAR TRAVEL

Interstate highways—limited-access, multilane highways whose numbers are prefixed by "I–"—are the fastest routes. Interstates with three-digit numbers encircle urban areas, which may have other limited-access expressways, freeways, and parkways as well. Tolls may be levied on limited-access highways. So-called U.S. highways and state highways are not necessarily limited-access but may have several lanes.

Along larger highways, roadside stops with rest rooms, fast-food restaurants, and sundries stores are well spaced. State police and tow trucks patrol major highways and lend assistance. If your car breaks down on an interstate, pull onto the shoulder and wait for help, or have your passengers wait while you walk to an emergency phone. If you carry a cell phone, dial *55, noting your location on the small green roadside markers.

Driving in the United States is on the right. Do **obey speed limits.** Watch for lower limits in small towns and on back roads. California requires passengers to wear seat belts. Always **strap children under 40 pounds or four years into approved child-safety seats.**

In California you may turn right at a red light after stopping if there is no oncoming traffic unless a sign forbids you to do so. When in doubt, wait for the green. Be alert for one-way streets, "no left turn" intersections, and blocks closed to car traffic. On weekdays between 6 and 10 AM and again between 4 and 7 PM **expect heavy traffic.** To encourage carpooling, some freeways have special lanes for so-called high-occupancy vehicles (HOV)—cars carrying more than one passenger.

ELECTRICITY

The U.S. standard is AC, 110 volts/60 cycles. Plugs have two flat pins set parallel to each other.

EMERGENCIES

For police, fire, or ambulance, **dial 911** (0 in rural areas).

INSURANCE

Britons and Australians need extra medical coverage when traveling overseas.

➤ INSURANCE INFORMATION: **Association of British Insurers** (✉ 51–55 Gresham St., London EC2V 7HQ, ☎ 020/7600–3333, FAX 020/7696–8999). **Insurance Council of Australia** (☎ 03/9614–1077, FAX 03/9614–7924).

MAIL & SHIPPING

You can buy stamps and aerograms and send letters and parcels in post offices. Stamp-dispensing machines can occasionally be found in airports, bus and train stations, office buildings, drugstores, and the like. You can also deposit mail in the stout, dark blue, steel bins at strategic locations everywhere and in the mail chutes of large buildings; pickup schedules are posted.

For mail sent within the United States, you need a 33¢ stamp for first-class letters weighing up to 1 ounce (22¢ for each additional ounce) and 20¢ for domestic postcards. For overseas mail, you pay 60¢ for ½-ounce airmail letters, 50¢ for airmail postcards, and 35¢ for surface-rate postcards. For Canada you need a 52¢ stamp for a 1-ounce letter and 40¢ for a postcard. For 50¢ you can buy an aerogram—a single sheet of lightweight blue paper that folds into its own envelope, stamped for overseas airmail.

To receive mail on the road, have it sent c/o General Delivery at your destination's main post office (use the correct five-digit zip code). You must pick up mail in person within 30 days and show a driver's license or passport.

PASSPORTS & VISAS

Visitor visas are not necessary for Canadian citizens or for citizens of Australia, New Zealand, and the

United Kingdom staying fewer than 90 days.

➤ AUSTRALIAN CITIZENS: **Australian Passport Office** (☎ 131–232). The **U.S. Office of Australia Affairs** (✉ MLC Centre, 19-29 Martin Pl., 59th floor, Sydney NSW 2000).

➤ CANADIAN CITIZENS: **Passport Office** (☎ 819/994–3500 or 800/ 567–6868).

➤ NEW ZEALAND CITIZENS: **New Zealand Passport Office** (☎ 04/494–0700 for application procedures; 0800/225–050 in New Zealand for application-status updates). **U.S. Office of New Zealand Affairs** (✉ 29 Fitzherbert Terr., Thorndon, Wellington).

➤ U.K. CITIZENS: **London Passport Office** (☎ 0990/210–410) for application procedures and emergency passports. **U.S. Embassy Visa Information Line** (☎ 01891/200–290). **U.S. Embassy Visa Branch** (✉ 5 Upper Grosvenor Sq., London W1A 1AE); send a self-addressed, stamped envelope. **U.S. Consulate General** (✉ Queen's House, Queen St., Belfast BTI 6EO).

TELEPHONES

All U.S. telephone numbers consist of a three-digit area code and a seven-digit local number. Within most local calling areas, dial only the seven-digit number. Within the same area code, dial "1" first. To call between area-code regions, dial "1" then all 10 digits; the same goes for calls to numbers prefixed by "800," "888," and "877"—all toll-free. For calls to numbers preceded by "900" you must pay—usually dearly.

For international calls, dial "011" followed by the country code and the local number. For help, dial "0" and ask for an overseas operator. The country code is 61 for Australia, 64 for New Zealand, 44 for the United Kingdom. Calling Canada is the same as calling within the United States. Most local phone books list country codes and U.S. area codes. The country code for the United States is 1.

For operator assistance, dial "0". To obtain someone's phone number, call directory assistance, 555–1212 or occasionally 411 (free at public phones). To have the person you're calling foot the bill, phone collect; dial "0" instead of "1" before the 10-digit number.

At pay phones, instructions are usually posted. Usually you insert coins in a slot (10¢–35¢ for local calls) and wait for a steady tone before dialing. When you call long-distance, the operator will tell you how much to insert; prepaid phone cards, widely available in various denominations, are easier. Call the number on the back, punch in the card's personal identification number when prompted, then dial your number.

LODGING

The lodgings we list are the cream of the crop in each price category. We always list the facilities that are available, but we don't specify whether they cost extra. When pricing accommodations, always ask what's included and what costs extra. Properties indicated by an ✕🏨 are lodging establishments whose restaurant warrants a special trip.

Assume that hotels operate on the **European Plan** (EP, with no meals) unless we specify that they use the **Continental Plan** (CP, with a Continental breakfast), **Modified American Plan** (MAP, with breakfast and dinner), or the **Full American Plan** (FAP, with all meals).

Hotel taxes vary from city to city, but the average is around 10%, with higher rates in major urban areas.

APARTMENT & HOUSE RENTALS

If you want a home base that's roomy enough for a family and comes with cooking facilities, **consider a furnished rental.** These can save you money, especially if you're traveling with a group. Home-exchange directories sometimes list rentals as well as exchanges.

➤ INTERNATIONAL AGENTS: **Hideaways International** (✉ 767 Islington St., Portsmouth, NH 03801, ☎ 603/430–4433 or 800/843–4433, FAX 603/430–4444 info@hideaways.com www.hideaways.com; membership $99). **Vacation Home Rentals Worldwide** (✉

235 Kensington Ave., Norwood, NJ 07648, ☎ 201/767–9393 or 800/633–3284, FAX 201/767–5510, vhrww@juno.com, www.vhrww.com).

CAMPING

California offers numerous camping options from family campgrounds with all the amenities to secluded hike-in campsites with no facilities. Some are operated by the state, others are on federal land, and still others are private. Rules vary for each. You can camp anywhere in a National Forest, but in a National Park, you must use only specific sites. Whenever possible, **book well in advance**, especially when your trip will be in the summer or on a weekend.

➤ INFORMATION: **California Travel Parks Association** (✉ Box 5648, Auburn, CA 95604, ☎ 530/823–1076, FAX 530/823–6331).

➤ RESERVATIONS: **National Parks** (☎ 800/365–2267). **State Parks** (☎ 800/444–7275).

HOME EXCHANGES

If you would like to exchange your home for someone else's, **join a home-exchange organization,** which will send you its updated listings of available exchanges for a year and will include your own listing in at least one of them. It's up to you to make specific arrangements.

➤ EXCHANGE CLUBS: **HomeLink International** (✉ Box 650, Key West, FL 33041, ☎ 305/294–7766 or 800/638–3841, FAX 305/294–1448, usa@homelink.org, www.homelink.org; $98 per year). **Intervac U.S.** (✉ Box 590504, San Francisco, CA 94159, ☎ 800/756–4663, FAX 415/435–7440, www.intervac.com; $89 per year includes two catalogues).

HOSTELS

No matter what your age, you can **save on lodging costs by staying at hostels.** In some 5,000 locations in more than 70 countries around the world, Hostelling International (HI), the umbrella group for a number of national youth-hostel associations, offers single-sex, dorm-style beds and, at many hostels, rooms for couples and family accommodations. Membership in any HI national hostel association, open to travelers of all ages, allows you to stay in HI-affiliated hostels at member rates; one-year membership is about $25 for adults (C$26.75 in Canada, £9.30 in the U.K., $30 in Australia, and $30 in New Zealand); hostels run about $10–$25 per night. Members have priority if the hostel is full; they're also eligible for discounts around the world, even on rail and bus travel in some countries.

➤ ORGANIZATIONS: **Hostelling International—American Youth Hostels** (✉ 733 15th St. NW, Suite 840, Washington, DC 20005, ☎ 202/783–6161, FAX 202/783–6171, www.hiayh.org). **Hostelling International—Canada** (✉ 400–205 Catherine St., Ottawa, Ontario K2P 1C3, ☎ 613/237–7884, FAX 613/237–7868, www.hostellingintl.ca). **Youth Hostel Association of England and Wales** (✉ Trevelyan House, 8 St. Stephen's Hill, St. Albans, Hertfordshire AL1 2DY, ☎ 01727/855215 or 01727/845047, FAX 01727/844126, www.yha.uk). **Australian Youth Hostel Association** (✉ 10 Mallett St., Camperdown, NSW 2050, ☎ 02/9565–1699, FAX 02/9565–1325, www.yha.com.au). **Youth Hostels Association of New Zealand** (✉ Box 436, Christchurch, New Zealand, ☎ 03/379–9970, FAX 03/365–4476, www.yha.org.nz).

HOTELS

Most major hotel chains are represented in California. All hotels listed have private bath unless otherwise noted. Make any special needs known when you book your reservation. Guarantee your room with a credit card, or many hotels will automatically cancel your reservations if you don't show up by 4 PM. Many hotels, like airlines, overbook. It is best to **re-confirm your reservation with the hotel on the morning of your arrival date.**

➤ TOLL-FREE NUMBERS: **Best Western** (☎ 800/528–1234, www.bestwestern.com).**Choice** (☎ 800/221–2222, www.hotelchoice.com). **Clarion** (☎ 800/252–7466, www.choicehotels.com). **Colony** (☎ 800/777–1700. www.colony.com), **Comfort** (☎ 800/228–5150, www.comfortinn.com). **Days Inn** (☎ 800/325–2525. www.

daysinn.com). **Doubletree and Red Lion Hotels** (☎ 800/222–8733, www.doubletreehotels.com). **Embassy Suites** (☎ 800/362–2779, www.embassysuites.com). **Fairfield Inn** (☎ 800/228–2800, www.marriott.com). **Four Seasons** (☎ 800/332–3442, www.fourseasons.com). **Hilton** (☎ 800/445–8667, www.hiltons.com). **Holiday Inn** (☎ 800/465–4329, www.holiday-inn.com). **Howard Johnson** (☎ 800/654–4656, www.hojo.com). **Hyatt Hotels & Resorts** (☎ 800/233–1234, www.hyatt.com). **Inter-Continental** (☎ 800/327–0200, www.interconti.com). **La Quinta** (☎ 800/531–5900, www.laquinta.com). **Marriott** (☎ 800/228–9290, www.marriott.com). **Nikko Hotels International** (☎ 800/645–5687, www.nikko.com). **Quality Inn** (☎ 800/228–5151, www.qualityinn.com). **Radisson** (☎ 800/333–3333, www.radisson.com). **Ramada** (☎ 800/228–2828. www.ramada.com), **Renaissance Hotels & Resorts** (☎ 800/468–3571, www.hotels.com). **Ritz-Carlton** (☎ 800/241–3333, www.ritzcarlton.com). **Sheraton** (☎ 800/325–3535, www.sheraton.com). **Sleep Inn** (☎ 800/753–3746, www.sleepinn.com). **Westin Hotels & Resorts** (☎ 800/228–3000, www.starwood.com). **Wyndham Hotels & Resorts** (☎ 800/822–4200, www.wyndham.com).

MONEY MATTERS

Los Angeles and San Francisco tend to be expensive cities to visit, and rates at coastal and desert resorts are nearly comparable. Hotel rates average from $150 to $250 a night (though you can find cheaper places), and three-course meals at even moderately expensive restaurants often cost from $30 to $50 per person. Costs in the Gold Country, the Far North, and the Mojave Desert/Death Valley region are considerably less—many fine Gold Country B&Bs charge around $100 a night, and some motels in the Far North and the Mojave charge from $50 to $70.

Prices throughout this guide are given for adults. Reduced fees are almost always available for children, students, and senior citizens. For information on taxes, *see* Taxes, *below.*

ATMS

ATMs are readily available throughout California. If you withdraw cash from a bank other than your own, expect to pay a fee of up to $2.50. If you're going to very remote areas of the mountains or deserts, take some extra cash with you or find out ahead of time if you can pay with credit cards.

CREDIT CARDS

Throughout this guide, the following abbreviations are used: **AE,** American Express; **D,** Discover; **DC,** Diner's Club; **MC,** MasterCard; and **V,** Visa.

➤ REPORTING LOST CARDS: To report lost or stolen credit cards: **American Express** (☎ 800/327–2177); **Discover** (☎ 800/347–2683); **Diners Club** (☎ 800/234–6377); **MasterCard** (☎ 800/307–7309); and **Visa** (☎ 800/847–2911).

NATIONAL PARKS

Look into discount passes to save money on park entrance fees. The Golden Eagle Pass ($50) gets you and your companions free admission to all parks for one year. (Camping and parking are extra). Both the Golden Age Passport ($10), for those 62 and older, and the Golden Access Passport (free), for travelers with disabilities, entitle holders to free entry to all national parks, plus 50% off fees for the use of many park facilities and services. You must show proof of age and of U.S. citizenship or permanent residency (such as a U.S. passport, driver's license, or birth certificate) and, if requesting Golden Access, proof of disability. All three passes are available at all national parks wherever entrance fees are charged. Golden Eagle and Golden Access passes are also available by mail.

➤ PASSES BY MAIL: **National Park Service** (✉ National Park Service National Office, 1849 C St. NW, Washington, DC 20240-0001, ☎ 202/208–4747).

STATE PARKS

➤ INFORMATION: **California State Park System** (✉ Dept. of Parks and Recreation, Box 942896, Sacramento 94296, ☎ 916/653–6995).

OUTDOORS & SPORTS

California is an outdoors-lover's paradise—scale high peaks, hike through sequoia groves, fish, bike, sail, dive, ski, or golf. Whatever sport you love, you can do it in California. See the individual regional chapters for more information.

FISHING

You'll need a license to fish in California. State residents pay $28.10 ($4.25 for senior citizens and those on limited income), but nonresidents are charged $75.85 for a one-year license or $28.10 for a 10-day license. Both residents and nonresidents can purchase a one-day license for $6.55.

➤ INFORMATION: **Department of Fish and Game** (✉ 3211 S St., Sacramento 95816, ☎ 916/227–2244 or 916/227–2242).

PACKING

When packing for a California vacation, **prepare for changes in temperature.** Take along sweaters, jackets, and clothes for layering as your best insurance for coping with variations in temperature. **Know that San Francisco and other coastal towns can be chilly** at any time of the year, especially in summer when the fog descends in the afternoon. Always tuck in a bathing suit; many lodgings have pools, spas, and saunas. Casual dressing is a hallmark of the California lifestyle, but in the evening men will need a jacket and tie at some pricier restaurants, and women will be more comfortable in something dressier than sightseeing garb.

In your carry-on luggage, **pack an extra pair of eyeglasses or contact lenses and enough of any medication you take** to last the entire trip and a bathing suit if you are going to a warm destination. This way, if your luggage gets lost, you will have the essentials. You may also ask your doctor to write a spare prescription using the drug's generic name, since brand names may vary from country to country. In luggage to be checked, **never pack prescription drugs or valuables.** To avoid customs delays, carry medications in their original packaging. And don't forget to carry with you the addresses of offices that handle refunds of lost traveler's checks.

CHECKING LUGGAGE

How many carry-on bags you can bring with you is up to the airline. Most allow two, but not always, so make sure that everything you carry aboard will fit under your seat or in the overhead bin, and get to the gate early. Note that if you have a seat at the back of the plane, you'll probably board first, while the overhead bins are still empty.

If you are flying internationally, note that baggage allowances may be determined not by piece but by weight—generally 88 pounds (40 kilograms) in first class, 66 pounds (30 kilograms) in business class, and 44 pounds (20 kilograms) in economy.

Airline liability for baggage is limited to $1,250 per person on flights within the United States. On international flights it amounts to $9.07 per pound or $20 per kilogram for checked baggage (roughly $640 per 70-pound bag) and $400 per passenger for unchecked baggage. You can buy additional coverage at check-in for about $10 per $1,000 of coverage, but it excludes a rather extensive list of items, shown on your airline ticket.

Before departure, **itemize your bags' contents** and their worth, and label the bags with your name, address, and phone number. (If you use your home address, cover it so potential thieves can't see it readily.) Inside each bag, **pack a copy of your itinerary.** At check-in, **make sure that each bag is correctly tagged** with the destination airport's three-letter code. If your bags arrive damaged or fail to arrive at all, file a written report with the airline before leaving the airport.

SAFETY

California is generally a safe place, but travelers should observe all normal precautions. First, **avoid looking like a tourist.** Dress inconspicuously, remove badges when leaving convention areas, know the routes to your destination before you set out. Use common sense and **steer clear of unfamiliar neighborhoods** after dark. Like anywhere, women should use caution when walking in the evening and may do best by taking a taxi when possible.

SENIOR-CITIZEN TRAVEL

To qualify for age-related discounts, **mention your senior-citizen status up front** when booking hotel reservations (not when checking out) and before you're seated in restaurants (not when paying the bill). When renting a car, ask about promotional car-rental discounts, which can be cheaper than senior-citizen rates.

➤ EDUCATIONAL PROGRAMS: **Elderhostel** (✉ 75 Federal St., 3rd floor, Boston, MA 02110, ☎ 877/426–8056, FAX 877/426–2166, www.elderhostel.org). **Interhostel** (✉ University of New Hampshire, 6 Garrison Ave., Durham, NH 03824, ☎ 603/862–1147 or 800/733–9753, FAX 603/862–1113, www.learn.unh.edu).

SMOKING

In 1998 smoking became illegal in all the state's bars and restaurants. Though some bar owners have built outdoor patios or smoking rooms, others have refused to comply. There is typically not a lot of enforcement of this law, so take your cues from the locals. Hotels and motels are also decreasing their inventory of smoking rooms; inquire at the time you book your reservation if any are available. Additionally, there is a selective tax on cigarettes sold in California, and the prices can be as high as $4.50 per pack. You might want to bring a carton from home.

STUDENTS IN CALIFORNIA

To save money, **look into deals available through student-oriented travel agencies.** To qualify you'll need a bona fide student ID card. Members of international student groups are also eligible.

➤ I.D.S & SERVICES: **Council Travel** (CIEE; ✉ 205 E. 42nd St., 14th floor, New York, NY 10017, ☎ 212/822–2700 or 888/268–6245, FAX 212/822–2699, info@councilexchanges.org, www.councilexchanges.org) for mail orders only, in the U.S. **Travel Cuts** (✉ 187 College St., Toronto, Ontario M5T 1P7, ☎ 416/979–2406 or 800/667–2887, www.travelcuts.com) in Canada.

TAXES

Sales tax in California varies from about 5% to 8½% and applies to all purchases except for pre-packaged food; restaurant food is taxed. Hotel tax ranges from 10% to 16%. Airlines include departure taxes in the price of the ticket.

TELEPHONES

INTERNATIONAL CALLS

Dial 011 + country code + city code + number. The country code for Australia is 61; New Zealand, 64; and the United Kingdom, 44. The country code for Mexico is 52. To reach Canada, dial 1 + area code + number.

LONG-DISTANCE CALLS

Competitive long-distance carriers make calling within the United States relatively convenient and let you avoid hotel surcharges. By dialing an 800 number, you can get connected to the long-distance company of your choice.

➤ LONG-DISTANCE CARRIERS: **AT&T** (☎ 800/225–5288). **MCI** (☎ 800/888–8000). **Sprint** (☎ 800/366–2255).

PUBLIC PHONES

Pay phones cost 35¢ in California.

TIME

California is in the Pacific time zone. Pacific Daylight Time is in effect from early April through late October; Pacific Standard Time, the rest of the year. Clocks are set ahead one hour when Daylight Time begins, back one hour when it ends.

TIPPING

At restaurants, a 15% tip is standard for waiters; up to 20% may be expected at more expensive establishments. The same goes for taxi drivers, bartenders, and hairdressers. Coat-check operators usually expect $1; bellhops and porters should get $1–$2 per bag; hotel maids in upscale hotels should get about $1 per day of your stay. A concierge typically receives a tip of $5–$10, with an additional gratuity for special services or favors.

On package tours, conductors and drivers usually get $10 per day from the group as a whole; check whether this has already been figured into your cost. For local sightseeing tours, you may individually tip the driver-guide $1 if he or she has been helpful or informative. Ushers in theaters do not expect tips.

TOURS & PACKAGES

Because everything is prearranged on a prepackaged tour or independent vacation, you'll spend less time planning—and often get it all at a good price.

BOOKING WITH AN AGENT

Travel agents are excellent resources. But it's a good idea to collect brochures from several agencies as some agents' suggestions may be influenced by relationships with tour and package firms that reward them for volume sales. If you have a special interest, **find an agent with expertise in that area**; ASTA (☞ Travel Agencies, *below*) has a database of specialists worldwide.

Make sure your travel agent knows the accommodations and other services of the place they're recommending. Ask about the hotel's location, room size, beds, and whether it has a pool, room service, or programs for children, if you care about these. Has your agent been there in person or sent others whom you can contact?

Do some homework on your own, too: local tourism boards can provide information about lesser-known and small-niche operators, some of which may sell only direct.

BUYER BEWARE

Each year consumers are stranded or lose their money when tour operators—even large ones with excellent reputations—go out of business. So **check out the operator.** Ask several travel agents about its reputation, and try to **book with a company that has a consumer-protection program.** (Look for information in the company's brochure.) In the United States, members of the National Tour Association and the United States Tour Operators Association are required to set aside funds to cover your payments and travel arrangements in the event that the company defaults. It's also a good idea to choose a company that participates in the American Society of Travel Agents' Tour Operator Program (TOP); ASTA will act as mediator in any disputes between you and your tour operator.

Remember that the more your package or tour includes the better you can predict the ultimate cost of your vacation. Make sure you know exactly what is covered, and **beware of hidden costs.** Are taxes, tips, and transfers included? Entertainment and excursions? These can add up.

➤ TOUR-OPERATOR RECOMMENDATIONS: **American Society of Travel Agents** (☞ Travel Agencies, *below*). **National Tour Association** (NTA; ✉ 546 E. Main St., Lexington, KY 40508, ☎ 606/226–4444 or 800/682–8886, www.ntaonline.com). **United States Tour Operators Association** (USTOA; ✉ 342 Madison Ave., Suite 1522, New York, NY 10173, ☎ 212/599–6599 or 800/468–7862, FAX 212/599–6744, ustoa@aol.com, www.ustoa.com).

GROUP TOURS

Among companies that sell tours to California, the following are nationally known, have a proven reputation, and offer plenty of options. The classifications used below represent different price categories, and you'll probably encounter these terms when talking to a travel agent or tour operator. The key difference is usually in accommodations, which run from budget to better, and better-yet to best.

➤ TOUR-OPERATOR RECOMMENDATIONS: **American Society of Travel Agents** (☞ Travel Agencies, *below*). **National Tour Association** (NTA, ✉ 546 E. Main St., Lexington, KY 40508, ☎ 606/226–4444 or 800/682–8886). **United States Tour Operators Association** (USTOA, ✉ 342 Madison Ave., Suite 1522, New York, NY 10173, ☎ 212/599–6599 or 800/468–7862, FAX 212/599–6744).

➤ DELUXE: **Globus** (☎ 303/797–2800 or 800/221–0090). **Maupintour** (☎ 913/843–1211 or 800/255–4266). **Tauck Tours** (☎ 203/226–6911 or 800/468–2825).

➤ FIRST CLASS: **Brendan Tours** (☎ 818/785–9696 or 800/421–8446). **Caravan Tours** (☎ 312/321–9800 or

800/227–2826). **Collette Tours** (☎ 401/728–3805 or 800/340–5158). **Gadabout Tours** (☎ 760/325–5556 or 800/952–5068). **Mayflower Tours** (☎ 708/960–3430 or 800/323–7064). **Trafalgar Tours** (☎ 212/689–8977 or 800/854–0103).

➤ BUDGET: **Cosmos** (☎ 303/797–2800 or 800/221–0090).

PACKAGES

Like group tours, independent vacation packages are available from major tour operators and airlines. The companies listed below offer vacation packages in a broad price range.

➤ AIR/HOTEL: **American Airlines Vacations** (☎ 800/321–2121). **Continental Vacations** (☎ 800/634–5555). **Delta Vacations** (☎ 800/872–7786, FAX 954/357–4687). **United Vacations** (☎ 800/328–6877). **US Airways Vacations** (☎ 800/455–0123).

➤ CUSTOM PACKAGES: **Amtrak Vacations** (☎ 800/321–8684).

➤ FLY/DRIVE: **American Airlines Vacations** (☎ 800/321–2121). **Continental Vacations** (☎ 800/634–5555). **United Vacations** (☎ 800/328–6877).

➤ HOTEL ONLY: **Globetrotters** (☎ 800/333–1234).

THEME TRIPS

➤ ADVENTURE: **Access to Adventure** (☎ 530/469–3322 or 800/552–6284). **American Wilderness Experience** (☎ 303/444–2622 or 800/444–0099). **Mountain Travel-Sobek** (☎ 510/527–8100 or 888/687–6235). **Tahoe Trips & Trails** (☎ 530/583–4506 or 800/581–4453).

➤ BICYCLING: **Backroads** (☎ 510/527–1555 or 800/462–2848). **Imagine Tours** (☎ 530/758–8782 or 888/592–8687).

➤ ECOTOURS: **Coastwalk** (☎ 707/829–6689 or 800/550–6854). **Earthwatch** (☎ 800/776–0188). **Outward Bound** (☎ 800/547–3312). **Desert Survivors** (☎ 510/769–1706).

➤ FISHING: **Fishing International** (☎ 707/539–3366 or 800/950–4242). **Rod & Reel Adventures** (☎ 209/785–0444).

➤ LEARNING: **Naturequest** (☎ 949/499–9561 or 800/369–3033). **Oceanic Society Expeditions** (☎ 415/441–1106 or 800/326–7491). **Smithsonian Study Tours and Seminars** (☎ 202/357–4700).

➤ RIVER RAFTING: **Access to Adventure** (☞ Adventure, *above*). **James Henry River Tours** (☎ 415/868–1836 or 800/786–1830). **OARS** (☎ 209/736–4677 or 800/346–6277). **Whitewater Voyages** (☎ 510/222–5994 or 800/488–7238).

➤ TENNIS: **Championship Tennis Tours** (☎ 602/990–8760 or 800/468–3664).

➤ TRAIL RUNNING: **Backroads** (☞ Bicycling, *above*).

➤ WALKING/HIKING: **American Wilderness Experience** (☞ Adventure, *above*). **Backroads** (☞ Bicycling, *above*).

➤ YACHT CHARTERS: **Five Star Charters** (☎ 415/332–7187 or 800/762–6287).

TRAIN TRAVEL

Amtrak's *California Zephyr* train from Chicago via Denver terminates in Oakland. The *Coast Starlight* train travels between southern California and the state of Washington. The *Sunset Limited* heads west from Florida through New Orleans and Texas to Los Angeles.

➤ TRAIN INFORMATION: **Amtrak** (☎ 800/872–7245).

TRAVEL AGENCIES

A good travel agent puts your needs first. Look for an agency that has been in business at least five years, emphasizes customer service, and has someone on staff who specializes in your destination. In addition, **make sure the agency belongs to a professional trade organization.** The American Society of Travel Agents (ASTA), with 27,000 agents in some 170 countries, is the largest and most influential in the field. Operating under the motto "Integrity in Travel," it maintains and enforces a strict code of ethics and will step in to help mediate any agent-client disputes if necessary. ASTA also maintains a Web site that includes a directory of agents. (If a travel agency is also acting as your tour operator, *see*

Buyer Beware *in* Tours & Packages, *above.*)

➤ Local Agent Referrals: **American Society of Travel Agents** (ASTA; ☎ 800/965–2782 24-hr hot line, FAX 703/684–8319, www.astanet.com). **Association of British Travel Agents** (✉ 68–71 Newman St., London W1P 4AH, ☎ 020/7637–2444, FAX 020/7637–0713, information@abta.co.uk, www.abtanet.com). **Association of Canadian Travel Agents** (✉ 1729 Bank St., Suite 201, Ottawa, Ontario K1V 7Z5, ☎ 613/521–0474, FAX 613/521–0805, acta.ntl@sympatico.ca). **Australian Federation of Travel Agents** (✉ Level 3, 309 Pitt St., Sydney 2000, ☎ 02/9264–3299, FAX 02/9264–1085, www.afta.com.au). **Travel Agents' Association of New Zealand** (✉ Box 1888, Wellington 10033, ☎ 04/499–0104, FAX 04/499–0827, taanz@tiasnet.co.nz).

VISITOR INFORMATION

For general information about California, contact the California Division of Tourism; for the numbers of regional and city visitors bureaus and chambers of commerce, see the A to Z sections at the end of Chapters 2 to 16.

➤ Tourist Information: **California Division of Tourism** (✉ 801 K St., Suite 1600, Sacramento, CA 95814, ☎ 916/322–2881 or 800/862–2543, FAX 916/322–3402 or 916/322–0501).

➤ In the U.K.: **California Tourist Office** (✉ ABC California, Box 35, Abingdon, Oxfordshire OX14 4TB, ☎ 0891/200–278, FAX 020/7242–2838).

WEB SITES

Do check out the World Wide Web when you're planning. You'll find everything from current weather forecasts to virtual tours of famous cities. Fodor's Web site, www.fodors.com, is a great place to start your online travels. When you see a 🔗 in this book, go to www.fodors.com/urls for an up-to-date link to that destination's site.

GENERAL INFORMATION

The **California Division of Tourism** web site has travel tips, events calendars, and other resources, and the site will link you—via the Regions icon—to the web sites of city and regional tourism offices and attractions. www.gocalif.ca.gov

THE GREAT OUTDOORS

The no-frills site of the **California Department of Fish and Game** provides information on fishing and hunting zones, licenses, and schedules. www.dfg.ca.gov

The **California Parks Department** site has the lowdown on state-run parks and other recreational areas. www.cal-parks.ca.gov

A must-visit for outdoors and adventure travel enthusiasts, the **Great Outdoor Recreation Page** is arranged into three easily navigated categories: attractions, activities, and locations. www.gorp.com

DAILIES

The ***Los Angeles Times*** is the state's largest newspaper. www.latimes.com

The ***San Diego Union–Tribune***'s site covers news as well as local shopping and dining. www.signonsandiego.com The ***San Francisco Examiner*** covers the Bay area. www.examiner.com

WEEKLIES

The state's weekly newspapers are a great source of up-to-the-minute arts and entertainment information, from what shows are on the boards to who's playing the clubs.

L.A. Weekly maintains a hip site with lively features and and insiders' guides to dining, the arts, and nightlife in the L.A. metro area. www.laweekly.com

The smart features on **MetroActive,** the online version of *San Jose Metro,* include guides to nightlife, the arts, dining, and entertainment in the San Francisco Bay Area, including Silicon Valley and Santa Cruz. www.sanjosemetro.com

The site of the ***San Diego Reader*** isn't visually impressive, but it provides a thorough guide to what's happening in San Diego. www.sdreader.com

For current politics, or for thorough entertainment information, check out the ***San Francisco Bay Guardian.*** www.sfbayguardian.com

The colorful and easy-to-navigate web site of *SF Weekly* has the low-down on the San Francisco Bay Area. www.sfweekly.com

WINERIES

The site of the **Wine Institute,** which is based in San Francisco, provides events listings and detailed information about the California wine industry and has links to the home pages of regional wine associations. www.wineinstitute.org

WHEN TO GO

Any time of the year is the right time to go to California. The trick is that it's such a large state that when it's too hot in the southern parts, just head north. There won't be skiable snow in the mountains between Easter and Thanksgiving. It will be much too hot to enjoy Palm Springs or Death Valley in the summer. But San Francisco, Los Angeles, and San Diego are pleasant year-round.

CLIMATE

The climate varies amazingly in California, not only over distances of several hundred miles but occasionally within an hour's drive. A foggy, cool August day in San Francisco makes you grateful for a sweater, tweed jacket, or light wool coat. Head north 50 mi to the Napa Valley to check out the Wine Country and you'll probably wear short sleeves and thin cottons.

Daytime and nighttime temperatures may also swing widely apart. Take Sacramento, a city that is at sea level but in California's Central Valley. In the summer, afternoons can be very warm, in the 90s and occasionally over 100°. But the nights cool down, often dropping 40°.

It's hard to generalize much about the weather in this varied state. Rain comes in the winter, with snow at higher elevations. Summers are dry everywhere. As a rule, compared to the coastal areas, which are cool year-round, inland regions are warmer in summer and cooler in winter. As you climb into the mountains, there are more distinct variations with the seasons: Winter brings snow, autumn is crisp, spring is variable, and summer is clear and warm.

➤ FORECASTS: **Weather Channel Connection** (☎ 900/932–8437), 95¢ per minute from a Touch-Tone phone.

The following are average daily maximum and minimum temperatures for the major California cities.

Climate in California

LOS ANGELES

Jan.	64F	18C	May	72F	22C	Sept.	81F	27C
	44	7		53	12		60	16
Feb.	64F	18C	June	76F	24C	Oct.	76F	24C
	46	8		57	14		55	13
Mar.	66F	19C	July	81F	27C	Nov.	71F	22C
	48	9		60	16		48	9
Apr.	70F	21C	Aug.	82F	28C	Dec.	66F	19C
	51	11		62	17		46	8

SAN DIEGO

Jan.	62F	17C	May	66F	19C	Sept.	73F	23C
	46	8		55	13		62	17
Feb.	62F	17C	June	69F	21C	Oct.	71F	22C
	48	9		59	15		57	14
Mar.	64F	18C	July	73F	23C	Nov.	69F	21C
	50	10		62	17		51	11
Apr.	66F	19C	Aug.	73F	23C	Dec.	64F	18C
	53	12		64	18		48	9

SAN FRANCISCO

Jan.	55F	13C	May	66F	19C	Sept.	73F	23C
	41	5		48	9		51	11
Feb.	59F	15C	June	69F	21C	Oct.	69F	21C
	42	6		51	11		50	10
Mar.	60F	16C	July	69F	21C	Nov.	64F	18C
	44	7		51	11		44	7
Apr.	62F	17C	Aug.	69F	21C	Dec.	57F	14C
	46	8		53	12		42	6

FESTIVALS AND SEASONAL EVENTS

➤ JANUARY: Palo Alto's annual **East-West Shrine All-Star Football Classic** (☎ 800/232–8225) is America's oldest all-star sports event. In Pasadena, the annual **Tournament of Roses Parade and Football Game** (☎ 626/449–7673) takes place on New Year's Day, with lavish flower-decked floats, marching bands, and equestrian teams, followed by the Rose Bowl game.

➤ FEBRUARY: The legendary **AT&T Pebble Beach National Pro-Am** (formerly the Bing Crosby Pro-Am) golf tournament (☎ 831/649–1533) begins in late January and ends in early February. San Francisco's Chinatown is the scene of parades and noisy fireworks, all part of a several-day **Chinese New Year Celebration** (☎ 415/982–3000). Los Angeles also has a **Chinese New Year Parade** (☎ 213/617–0396). Indio's **Riverside County Fair and National Date Festival** (☎ 760/863–8247) is an exotic event with an Arabian Nights theme; camel and ostrich races, date exhibits, and tastings are among the draws.

➤ MARCH: **Snowfest** in North Lake Tahoe (☎ 775/832–7625) is the largest winter carnival in the West, with skiing, food, fireworks, parades, and live music. The finest female golfers in the world compete for the richest purse on the LPGA circuit at the **Nabisco Championship** (☎ 760/324–4546) in Rancho Mirage. The **Mendocino/Fort Bragg Whale Festival** (☎ 800/726–2780) includes whale-watching excursions, marine art exhibits, wine and beer tastings, crafts displays, and a chowder contest.

➤ APRIL: The **Cherry Blossom Festival** (☎ 415/563–2313), an elaborate presentation of Japanese culture and customs, winds up with a colorful parade through San Francisco's Japantown. The **Toyota Grand Prix** (☎ 562/436–9953) in Long Beach, the largest street race in North America, draws top competitors from all over the world.

➤ MAY: Thousands sign up to run the ***San Francisco Examiner* Bay to Breakers Race** (☎ 415/777–7770), a 7½-mi route from bay side to ocean side that's a hallowed San Francisco tradition. Inspired by Mark Twain's story "The Notorious Jumping Frog of Calaveras County," the **Jumping Frog Jubilee** (☎ 209/736–2561) in Angels Camp is for frogs and trainers who take their competition seriously. Sacramento hosts the four-day **Sacramento Jazz Jubilee** (☎ 916/372–5277); the late-May event is the world's largest Dixieland festival, with 125 bands from around the world. In Monterey, the squirmy squid is the main attraction for the Memorial Day weekend **Great Monterey Squid Festival** (☎ 831/649–6544). You'll see squid-cleaning and -cooking demonstrations, taste treats, and enjoy the usual festival fare: entertainment, arts and crafts, and educational exhibits.

➤ JUNE: Starting in late May and running into early June is a national ceramics competition and exhibition called **Feats of Clay** in the Gold Country (☎ 916/645–9713). The **Summer Solstice Ride & Arts Celebration** (☎ 209/296–5600) boosts spirits with bicycle rides, walks, and hands-on arts-and-crafts workshops for adults and children in Plymouth. During the first weekend in June, Pasadena City Hall Plaza hosts the

Chalk It Up Festival. Artists use the pavement as their canvas to create masterpieces that wash away when festivities have come to a close. There are also musical performances and exotic dining kiosks. The proceeds benefit arts and homeless organizations of the Light-Bringer Project (☎ 626/440–7379). The **Napa Valley Wine Auction** in St. Helena features open houses, a wine tasting, and an auction. Preregistration by fax in early March is required (☎ 707/942–9775, FAX 707/942–0171). During the latter part of June, Ojai hosts a noted outdoor **classical music festival** (☎ 805/646–2094).

➤ JULY: During the **Carmel Bach Festival** (☎ 831/624–1521), the works of Johann Sebastian Bach and 18th-century contemporaries are performed for three weeks; events include concerts, recitals, and seminars. During the last full weekend in July, Gilroy, the self-styled Garlic Capital of the World, celebrates its smelly but delicious product with the **Gilroy Garlic Festival** (☎ 408/842–1625), featuring such unusual concoctions as garlic ice cream.

➤ AUGUST: The **Cabrillo Music Festival** (☎ 831/426–6966) in Santa Cruz, one of the longest-running contemporary orchestral festivals, brings in American and other composers for two weeks in early August. The **California State Fair** (☎ 916/263–3000) showcases the state's agricultural side, with a rodeo, horse racing, a carnival, and big-name entertainment. It runs 18 days from August to Labor Day in Sacramento. Santa Barbara's **Old Spanish Days' Fiesta** (☎ 805/962–8101) is the nation's largest all-equestrian parade, featuring riders on horses and 19th-century carriages. The citywide celebration includes two parades, two Mexican marketplaces, costumed dancers and singers, a carnival, and a rodeo.

➤ SEPTEMBER: In Guerneville, jazz fans and musicians jam at Johnson's Beach for the **Russian River Jazz Festival** (☎ 707/869–3940). The **San Francisco Blues Festival** (☎ 415/826–6837) is held at Fort Mason in late September. The **Los Angeles County Fair** (☎ 909/623–3111) in Pomona is the largest county fair in the world. It hosts entertainment, exhibits, livestock, horse racing, food, and more.

➤ OCTOBER: The **Grand National Rodeo, Horse, and Stock Show** (☎ 415/469–6057) at San Francisco's Cow Palace is a 10-day, world-class competition straddling the end of October and the beginning of November. In Carmel, speakers and poets gather for readings on the beach, seminars, a banquet, and a book signing at the **Pismo Beach Clam Festival** on the Central Coast. Restaurants along Pomeroy Avenue engage in a competition for the best clam chowder. The **Tor House Fall Festival** (☎ 831/624–1813) honors the late poet Robinson Jeffers, an area resident for many years.

➤ NOVEMBER: The **Death Valley '49er Encampment,** at Furnace Creek commemorates the historic crossing of Death Valley in 1849, with a fiddlers' contest and an art show (☎ 760/786–2331). Pasadena's **Doo Dah Parade** (☎ 626/440–7379), a fun-filled spoof of the annual Rose Parade, features the Lounge Lizards, who dress as reptiles and lip-synch to Frank Sinatra favorites, and West Hollywood men in cheerleader drag.

➤ DECEMBER: For the **Newport Harbor Christmas Boat Parade** in Newport Beach (☎ 949/729–4400), more than 200 festooned boats glide through the harbor nightly December 17–23. In early December, the **Miner's Christmas Celebration** in Columbia (☎ 209/536–1672) features costumed carolers and children's piñatas. Related events include a Victorian Christmas feast at the City Hotel, lamplight tours, and Las Posados Nativity Procession. The internationally acclaimed **El Teatro Campesino** (☎ 831/623–2444) annually stages its nativity play *La Virgen Del Tepeyac* in the Mission San Juan Bautista.

INDEX

Icons and Symbols

★ Our special recommendations
✕ Restaurant
▦ Lodging establishment
✕▦ Lodging establishment whose restaurant warrants a special trip
Good for kids (rubber duck)
☞ Sends you to another section of the guide for more information
✉ Address
☎ Telephone number
Opening and closing times
Admission prices
Sends you to www.fodors.com/urls for up-to-date links to the property's Web site

Numbers in white and black circles ③ ❸ that appear on the maps, in the margins, and within the tours correspond to one another.

T

NOTES

FODOR'S CALIFORNIA 2001

EDITOR: Mark Sullivan

Editorial Contributors: Sasha Abramsky, Rob Aikens, Herb Benham, Deke Castleman, Arian Collins, Stephen Dolainski, Edie Jarolim, Lina Lecaro, Tim Lohnes, Andy Moore, David Nelson, Marty Olmstead, Bill Stern, Kate Sullivan, Valerie Summers, Daniel Taras, John Vlahides, Anne E. Wells, Cindy LaFavre Yorks, Gordon Young, Bobbi Zane

Editorial Production: Brian Vitunic

Maps: David Lindroth, *cartographer*; Robert Blake, Steven K. Amsterdam, *map editors*

Design: Fabrizio La Rocca, *creative director*; Guido Caroti, *art director*; Jolie Novak, *photo editor*; Melanie Marin, *photo researcher*

Cover Design: Pentagram

Production/Manufacturing: Robert B. Shields

COPYRIGHT

ISBN 0-679-00566-8

ISSN 0192-9925

SPECIAL SALES

Fodor's Travel Publications are available at special discounts for bulk purchases for sales promotions or premiums. Special editions, including personalized covers, excerpts of existing guides, and corporate imprints, can be created in large quantities for special needs. For more information, contact your local bookseller or write to Special Markets, Fodor's Travel Publications, 280 Park Avenue, New York, NY 10017. Inquiries from Canada should be directed to your local Canadian bookseller or sent to Random House of Canada, Ltd., Marketing Department, 2775 Matheson Boulevard East, Mississauga, Ontario L4W 4P7. Inquiries from the United Kingdom should be sent to Fodor's Travel Publications, 20 Vauxhall Bridge Road, London SW1V 2SA, England.

PRINTED IN THE UNITED STATES OF AMERICA

10 9 8 7 6 5 4 3 2 1

IMPORTANT TIP

Although all prices, opening times, and other details in this book are based on information supplied to us at press time, changes occur all the time in the travel world, and Fodor's cannot accept responsibility for facts that become outdated or for inadvertent errors or omissions. So always confirm information when it matters, especially if you're making a detour to visit a specific place.

PHOTOGRAPHY

Corbis: *Darrell Gulin, cover (Yosemite).*

Amargosa Opera House, Inc.: *Tony Scodwell, 24B.*

CalTour: *Robert Holmes, 2 top left, 2 top right, 2 bottom right, 3 top right 3 bottom left, 6C, 7A, 7C, 8B, 10A, 14A, 14B, 21B, 21C, 27B, 30C, 30F, 30H. John Poimiroo, 12C.*

Château du Sureau, *30E.*

© Disney Enterprises, *20B.*

Hearst San Simeon State Historical Monument: *Ellis-Sawyer, 17B.*

Robert Holmes, *7B, 8C, 9D, 13A, 15A, 15B, 23D.*

Clarissa Horowitz, *30B.*

Hotel Bel-Air, *30G.*

The Image Bank: *Alan Becker, 24A. Luis Castañeda, 28C. Gary Cralle, 9F. MacDuff Everton, 17A. Grant V. Faint, 19E, 26A, 32. Tracy Frankel, 1. Larry Dale Gordon, 19D. GK & Vikki Hart, 10B. Eddie Hironaka, 18–19A. Jeff Hunter, 30I. R. Johnson, 25F. Tom Mareschal, 16A. Michael Melford, 8 bottom. Piecework Productions, 6A, 9E, 11C, 12B, 16C, 25E. Andrea Pistolesi, 11E, 29D. Charles C. Place, 19F, 23B. Steve Proehl, 16D. Harald Sund, 6B, 25D. Joseph Van Os, 16B. Ulf E. Wallin, 24C. Stephen Wilkes, 8A, 18B, 20A.*

Kimpton Group: *Fred Licht, 3 bottom right, 30J.*

Lake Tahoe Visitors Authority, *13B.*

La Quinta Resort & Club, *23C.*

James Lemass, *11D, 21A.*

Northstar-at-Tahoe, *2 bottom center.*

The Ritz-Carlton, *Laguna Niguel, 30D.*

Robert Ordway, *13C.*

Palm Springs Tourism, *3 top left, 22A.*

San Diego Convention & Visitors Bureau: *James Blank, 29E. Bob Yarbrough, 2 bottom left.*

Santa Barbara Mission, *30A.*

Universal Studios, *18C.*

Nik Wheeler, *4–5, 12A, 15 bottom, 20C.*

ABOUT OUR WRITERS

Every trip is a significant trip. Acutely aware of that fact, we've pulled out all stops in preparing *California 2001*. To help you zero in on what to see in California, we've gathered some great color photos of the key sights in every region. To show you how to put it all together, we've created great itineraries and neighborhood walks. And to direct you to the places that are truly worth your time and money, we've rallied the team of endearingly picky know-it-alls we're pleased to call our writers. Having seen all corners of the regions they cover for us, they're real experts. If you knew them, you'd poll them for tips yourself.

Sasha Abramsky, a freelance journalist for numerous publications, took on the haunting Mojave Desert and Death Valley. A frequent visitor to California whose relatives live in the southern part of the state, he enjoyed the chance to explore one of the state's most fascinating regions. He is currently working on a book about the growth of the American prison system.

His father was a cotton and almond farmer in the area, so **Herb Benham** knows the San Joachin Valley and the neighboring Sierra National Parks well. He has published *Sitting on My Fat Wallet,* and *First Kisses and Other Miracles,* collections of columns he has written over the past 13 years for from the *Bakersfield Californian.* He is married and has four kids.

Deke Castleman, who updated the Lake Tahoe chapter, grew up in New York and Boston but fled the East Coast for the wide-open spaces of the American West. He discovered the region's many wonders while engaged in a variety of occupations—door-to-door vacuum-cleaner salesman in northern California, tour guide at Alaska's Denali National Park, and travel writer from Reno.

Tim Lohnes generally spends time working on maps for guide books, but donned the travel writer cap to update the Central Coast chapter. He enjoyed the excuse to spend time in the mountains and by the sea in this wonderful part of California. His number one recommendation: eat as much clam chowder as you can get your hands on!

Andy Moore was born across the street from Disney Studios near downtown Burbank. His childhood included many family vacations throughout the Golden State, including gold-panning expeditions with his grandfather, memories he relived while updating the Sacramento and the Gold Country chapter. Andy, a San Francisco resident for more than 20 years, is a frequent Fodor's contributor and also an independent filmmaker.

Marty Olmstead moved to the Sonoma Valley from San Francisco in 1989. She updated &n;the North Coast and Wine Country chapters for this book. She covers the wine-country≠ region for her weekly column in the *Marin Independent Journal* and other publications.

Monterey Bay and Smart Travel Tips updater **John Andrew Vlahides** spends his free time touring California on his motorcycle. A former concierge and member of Les Clefs d'Or, he now works as a freelance writer in San Francisco. His credits include *Fodor's UpClose California 2000.* He is a frequent contributor to *The Cubby Missalette,* an underground publication.

Gordon Young, our updater for the North Country, is a journalism professor at Santa Clara University. A former staff writer at *SF Weekly,* he won an Investigative Reporters and Editors award for magazine writing. Young was raised in scenic Flint, Michigan, where his accomplishments included learning to parallel park the family's Buick Electra 225 and never being laid off by the General Motors Corporation.

Frequent Fodor's contributor **Bobbi Zane,** who updated the Palm Springs chapter, has been visiting the region since her grandfather, a Hollywood producer, took her on weekend getaways to La Quinta Resort. Her articles on Palm Springs have appeared in the *Orange County Register* and *Westways* magazine. With her husband, Gregg, she publishes *Yellow Brick Road,* a newsletter about bed-and-breakfast inns.

We would also like to thank the many writers involved with the San Francisco, Los Angeles, Orange County, and San Diego chapters.

Don't Forget to Write

We love feedback—positive and negative—and follow up on all suggestions. So contact the California editor at editors@fodors.com or c/o Fodor's, 280 Park Avenue, New York, New York 10017. Have a wonderful trip!

Karen Cure
Editorial Director